Greece

a travel survival kit

Rosemary Hall

Greece – a travel survival kit

1st edition

Published by
    Lonely Planet Publications
    Head Office: PO Box 617, Hawthorn, Vic 3122, Australia
    Branches: 155 Filbert St, Suite 251, Oakland, CA 94607, USA
                 10 Barley Mow Passage, Chiswick, London W4 4PH, UK
                 71 bis rue du Cardinal Lemoine, 75005 Paris, France

Printed by
    Colorcraft Ltd, Hong Kong

Photographs by
    Rosemary Hall (RH)   David Hall (DH)   Bertold Daum (BD)
    Vicki Beale (VB)   Greg Alford (GA)   Jahan Byrne (JB)
    Front cover: Bell Tower, Thira (Santorini), Tadao Kimura, The Image Bank
    Back cover: The Parthenon, Athens, David Hall

Published
    February 1994

Although the authors and publisher have tried to make the information as accurate as possible, they accept no responsibility for any loss, injury or inconvenience sustained by any person using this book.

National Library of Australia Cataloguing in Publication Data

Hall, Rosemary
    Greece – a travel survival kit. ·

    1st ed.
    Includes index.
    ISBN 0 86442 193 1.

    1. Greece - Guidebooks. I. Title. (Series: Lonely Planet travel survial kit).

914.950476

text & maps © Lonely Planet 1994
photos © photographers as indicated 1994
climate charts compiled from information supplied by Patrick J Tyson, © Patrick J Tyson, 1994

Rosemary Hall

Rosemary was born in Sunderland, England. She graduated in fine art, but fame and fortune as an artist eluded her, so she spent a few months bumming around Europe and India. After teaching in northern England, she decided to find work somewhere more exotic, finally landing a job in Basra, Iraq. After two years the Iraqi government refused to renew her work permit, so she settled in London, tried to make it again as a painter, did supply teaching and travelled in India and South-East Asia. After the Iraq Gulf War ended, she went back to research the country for Lonely Planet's *West Asia on a shoestring*. Rosemary wrote the Greece chapter for LP's *Mediterranean Europe on a shoestring*, and, a glutton for punishment, returned to Greece to research and write this first edition of *Greece – a travel survival kit*.

From the Author

A big thank you to the following Lonely Planet staff: Rob van Driesum for his patient help and support; Michelle Coxall, the editor, for her constant advice, patience, support and good humour, far beyond the call of duty; and Tamsin Wilson for drawing the maps, which, considering the transliteration problems, must have been a tremendous undertaking.

I wish to thank my cousin David Hall for many things. Firstly, because he went where I could not go, Mt Athos, and wrote that section of the book. Thanks to him also for the use of his slides in this book, for loaning me his notebooks from his Greek trips, for his invaluable information, and for patiently putting up with my many telephone calls to him at all hours of the day and night. David himself would like to thank the staff of Room 222, the Ministry of Macedonia & Thrace; the British Consulate, Thessaloniki; Father Alexander of Athos; Sam; Jacob and his father; and Thasi and Eleni Papadimitriou.

A special thanks to my parents for their constant encouragement and support, despite my putting them off visiting me for so long. Apologies and thanks to all my friends who have remained my friends despite my long disappearance, and lack of communication, while I was travelling in Greece and chained to my word processor in London; especially Brenda Cameracanna, Pat Buckley, Doreen Jenkinson, Bridget Johnson, Phil Playfer and Ann Turner who kept me in touch with the outside world with their telephone calls, although these were never reciprocated.

I would like to thank the staff of the Greek National Tourist Office (GNTO) in London. Thanks also to Jennifer Cox, Charlotte Hindle and Andrea Webster at Lonely Planet's UK office, and to Paul Hellander, at the University of Adelaide, Australia, for assistance with transliteration and the Greek script.

So many people helped me while I was travelling in Greece that it would be impossible to name them all. Thanks to the staff of the many EOT offices, especially in Volos, Kavala, Alexandroupolis, Corfu and Iraklion; and the tourist police, especially in Patras and Agios Nikolaos. In Athens, I wish to thank George Scapettis for his help, Tassos for hospitality, and Monique for taking care of my excess baggage.

I would like to thank the following for help when I was on the road (and sea): David & Susan Perkins for assistance when I was roomless in Stoupa; Sue & Mick, from Greenwich, for transporting me around the Mani; the Greek yacht owner (whose name, regrettably, I cannot remember) who rescued me when I was marooned on Agathonisi; and Maeve Barry and Christos Mantourides, on Ios, and Frank Didcock and Kath Gambol on Leros, for warm hospitality. I am grateful to the following people for the information and advice they gave me: Greg Dallas of Didimotikho; Magda Tuvarelou of Volos; Nick Morgan-Mavrouenneas of Kardamili; Giannis Spiriounis, Director of the Dirou Caves; Kostos Irandos of Litohoro; and Val Kyne and Nora Lutja Schipholt on Thassos. Last, but not least, I wish to thank Dimitrios Gatzouras of Photo Profile, Karpathos, and Nikos Georgiadis, of Sparta.

The Dionysiaca XLVII by Nonnos (translated by Roger Lancelyn Green) at the beginning of the Naxos section appears with the kind permission of Penguin Books Ltd.

From the Publisher

Mapping, design, illustration and layout of this first edition of Greece – a travel survival kit were coordinated by Tamsin Wilson. Louise Keppie and Emma McNicol helped with additional illustrations, and Paul Clifton helped out with some last minute bromiding. Michelle Coxall edited this book, with assistance from Greg Alford, Vyvyan Cayley, Frith Pike and Tom Smallman. Peter Morris drew the cartoons for the cycling in Greece sections. Special thanks from Michelle to Lonely Planet's Rob van Driesum for his invaluable advice and assistance with the history sections and for his patient and supportive supervision; to Sally Steward for her help with the language section; to Dan Levin for computer advice and expertise; and to Rowan McKinnon for editing the index. Grateful thanks to Paul Hellander, Lecturer in Modern Greek at the University of Adelaide, for his invaluable assistance with the Greek script and transliteration, and for his notes on the perils and pleasures of cycling in Greece (Paul is happy to field enquiries from other actual or would-be intrepid cyclists; he can be contacted electronically on INTERNET: phelland@adam.adelaide.edu.au). Thanks also to Achilles Paparsenos, from the Consulate General of Greece, for those gorgeous glossy brochures; and to the Lonely Planet UK team – Charlotte Hindle, Andrea Webster and Jennifer Cox for despatching speedy missives to Rosemary.

Warning & Request

Things change – prices go up, schedules change, good places go bad and bad places go bankrupt – nothing stays the same. So if you find things better or worse, recently opened or long since closed, please write and tell us and help make the next edition better.

Your letters will be used to help update future editions and, where possible, important changes will be included in a Stop Press section in reprints.

We greatly appreciate all information that is sent to us by travellers. Back at Lonely Planet we employ a hard-working readers' letters team to sort through the many letters we receive. The best ones will be rewarded with a free copy of the next edition or another Lonely Planet guide if you prefer. We give away lots of books, but, unfortunately, not every letter or postcard receives one.

Contents

Map Legend

BOUNDARIES

—··—··—··—··	International Boundary
—··—··—··	Internal Boundary
++++++++++	National Park or Reserve
— — — — —	The Equator
·············	The Tropics

SYMBOLS

◉	NATIONAL	National Capital
●	PROVINCIAL	Provincial or State Capital
●	Major	Major Town
●	Minor	Minor Town
■		Places to Stay
▼		Places to Eat
⊠		Post Office
✈		Airport
i		Tourist Information
⊖		Bus Station or Terminal
66		Highway Route Number
☪ ✝ ⛪		Mosque, Church
✝		Cathedral or Monastery
∴		Temple or Ruin
✚		Hospital
☀		Lookout
⚑		Camping Area
⌇		Picnic Area
⌂		Hut or Chalet
▲		Mountain or Hill
⊢⊣		Railway Station
═		Road Bridge
╪		Railway Bridge
⇒ ⇐		Road Tunnel
→) (←		Railway Tunnel
⌢⌢⌢		Escarpment or Cliff
⌣		Pass
⊓⊓⊓		Ancient or Historic Wall

ROUTES

———	Major Road or Highway
- - - - -	Unsealed Major Road
———	Sealed Road
- - - - -	Unsealed Road or Track
═══	City Street
++++++++	Railway
●━━●━	Subway
··············	Walking Track
- - - - -	Ferry Route
++++++++	Cable Car or Chair Lift

HYDROGRAPHIC FEATURES

⌢⌣	River or Creek
- - -	Intermittent Stream
⬯ ⬭	Lake, Intermittent Lake
⌣	Coast Line
⌐	Spring
≈	Waterfall
⊥⊥⊥	Swamp
▦	Salt Lake or Reef
▨	Glacier

OTHER FEATURES

▦	Park, Garden or National Park
⊠	Built Up Area
▦	Market or Pedestrian Mall
▦	Plaza or Town Square
++++	Cemetery

Note: not all symbols displayed above appear in this book

Transliteration & Variant Spellings: an Explanation

The number of variant spellings and multiple place names which travellers encounter during their Greek sojourns can be a cause of some confusion. If you catch a ferry to Thira and arrive at Santorini, should you disembark or stay on board? Read on and all will be revealed!

The Library of Congress system for transliterating Greek into Latin script is sometimes not intuitive and very often bears no resemblance to actual transliteration in Greece itself, where frequently there is a great deal of inconsistency. For example, Piraeus is also spelt Pireos, Piraevs, Piraievs, or (believe it or not) Pireefs; and no doubt there are one or two other variants lurking somewhere.

The problem was compounded by the colonels who seized power in 1967. They reimposed *katharevousa* (an artificial language loosely based on Ancient Greek); this system was employed in conjunction with *demotiki* (the language of the people), which gave rise to a situation where there were instances of two words with one meaning, some totally different, and others differing in form. For example, the word *artopoieion* in katharevousa means 'baker's shop', but *fournos* in demotiki means the same thing. In the same vein, you have 'Athinai' for Athens in katharevousa, and 'Athina' in demotiki. Whilst this is not actually a problem of transliteration, it does occasionally cause confusion when town names appear in katharevousa and demotiki – even on adjacent road signs!

As if all that was not enough, there is also the issue of 'anglicised' vs 'hellenised' forms of place names; for example, Athina vs Athens; Korinthos vs Corinth; Thiva vs Thebes; Evia vs Euboia – the list goes on and on! Toponymic diglossy (the existence of both an official and everyday name for a place) is responsible for Kerkyra – Corfu, Zante – Zakynthos, and Santorini – Thira.

A further aberration is evident in the use of Mytilini for the island of Lesbos. This is due to a reluctance to use the word Lesbos and its derivative, Lesbian. In this book Lesbos has been used, followed in some instances by Mytilini in parentheses, to help eliminate confusion. The convention whereby well-known Greek names in English are retained has also been employed; for example, Athens, Corinth, etc.

Further problems arise because the Venetian and Turkish occupiers of Greece changed many place names, which are gradually either being changed back to their ancient names, or being given new names; however, many of the names given by the occupiers have stuck. Also, a street may have an official name and a colloquial name deriving from its character, or because it is the site of an important building. For example, Odos Panepistimiou ('university' in Greek) is so called because Athens' university is located there.

To top off the confusion, it seems that names (particularly of thoroughfares and squares) should change every few years. Greece spent the first 150 years of independence vacillating between republican and monarchal rule. During monarchal times streets and squares were often given the names of kings and queens, then during republican times, these names were changed, usually to the name of a mythological character, a saint, a hero, a benefactor or a contemporary politician. However, the name-changing persists, as heroes and politicians fall in and out of favour. Perhaps this is why the main square of a town is usually referred to simply as 'the square' by locals.

On more than one occasion during my research I asked the name of the street where a particular establishment was located and the proprietor looked perplexed, then proceeded into the street to look for its sign!

In villages with a maze of snaking alleyways, streets are often not given names – houses are identified by number only. *Odos* (street), *plateia* (square) and *leoforos* (avenue) are words which are often omitted from maps and other references, so the same has been done in this book, except when to do so would result in ambiguity.

Problems in transliteration have particular implications for vowels, especially given that there are six ways of rendering the vowel sound 'ee' in Greek, two ways of rendering the 'o' sound and two ways of rendering the 'e' sound. In most instances in this book, 'y' has been used for the 'ee' sound when a Greek *upsilon* (υ, Y) has been used, and 'i' for Greek *ita* (η, H) and *iota* (ι, I). In the case of the Greek vowel combinations that make the 'ee' sound, that is οι, ει and υι, an 'i' has been used. For the two 'e' Greek sounds, αι and ε, an 'e' has been employed.

As far as consonants are concerned, the Greek letter *gamma* (γ, Γ) appears as g rather than y throughout this book. This means that *agios* (Greek for male saint) is used rather than *ayios*, and *agia* (Greek for female saint) rather than *ayia*. However, because their words tend to be polysyllabic in the extreme, Greeks resort to abbreviations. This is understandable, except that this is often applied to short words also. Thus, agios or agia often appears as ag, which tells you that a saint is being referred to, but not its gender. The letter *delta* (δ, Δ) appears as d, rather than dh, throughout this book, so *domatia* (Greek for rooms), rather than *dhomatia*, is used, and *odos* (Greek for street) appears, rather than *odhos*. In the latter case the Greeks prefer od, or, more usually, omit the word completely. The letter *fi* (φ, Φ) can be transliterated as either f or ph. Here, a general rule of thumb is that classical names are spelt with a ph and modern names with an f. So Phaistos is used rather than Festos, and Folegandros is used rather than Pholegandros. The letter *kapa* (κ, K) should strictly speaking be k as there is no c in Greek, but I have not been consistent here, simply because the Greeks are not. I have used Kefallonia because it is more commonly used than Cefallonia, but Corinth because Korinth is rarely seen.

One final note: many guidebooks tend to retain accents in English transliterations of Greek; although accents are included in the Greek script in this book, accents have been omitted on English transliterations following the directive of the *Chicago Manual of Style* (13th ed).

In an endeavour to impose something approximating a consistent transliteration system on this book, the author and publisher are indebted to Paul Hellander, Lecturer in Modern Greek at the University of Adelaide, Australia. Any remaining transliteration aberrations should be attributed to editorial idiosyncrasies, as opposed to imprecision in Paul's excellent and informed advice. ∎

Introduction

Greece has always attracted visitors. Throughout its long history, inhabitants from all over Europe and beyond have landed on its shores. Conquerors (because of its strategic position) came to fight for possession of it, archaeologists to excavate (and often loot) its ancient sites, anthropologists to study its traditions, and artists and writers for the beauty of its landscape. In the 19th century, wealthy young aristocrats made it part of their Grand Tour; in this century it has become a favourite place of pilgrimage for sun and sea worshippers.

Philosophers muse that to journey to Greece is to return home, for the legacy of Ancient Greece pervades the consciousness of all Westerners, and there are allusions to it all around us. Greek Doric, Ionic and Corinthian columns adorn many of our buildings, our greatest literature is frequently inspired by the Greek myths, and many of our most eloquent words are Greek: chaos, drama, paradox, democracy and tragedy are just a few. However, a visit to Greece is also a journey into the unfamiliar, for during the long Ottoman rule it was severed from European culture. Many legacies of this time linger today, in its food, music and some traditions, giving Greece a culture which is a unique blend of East and West.

The most enduring attraction of Greece is its ancient sites. You can wander around the site of the capital of one of Europe's oldest civilisations (the Minoan) at Knossos, and see the ruins of the most venerated age of ancient times (the Classical), on the Acropolis. The remarkable Minoan, Mycenaean, and Classical Greek sites and elaborate Byzantine churches are part of Greece's heritage, but there are also legacies left by foreign occupiers: towering Venetian, Frankish and Turkish castles, and crumbling, forgotten mosques.

The sunshine and seductive landscape intensify the evocative atmosphere of these ruins, enabling the visitor to travel in their imagination to far-off times.

However, it is not only the renowned ancient sites which transport us to another age; conditions conducive to this are evident everywhere. For the Greek landscape is littered with broken columns and crumbling fragments of ancient walls. Moreover, there is hardly a meadow, river or mountain top which is not sacred because of its association with some deity, and the spectres of the past linger still.

It is not only Greece's ruins which evoke the past, but also the many centuries-old inhabited Greek towns and villages. There are medieval villages of grey stone houses; towns of grand, 19th-century neoclassical mansions; villages of labyrinthine alleyways and white cubic houses from the times of pirate raids; and in northern Greece, towns with picturesque Turkish-style wattle-and-daub houses.

Greece has clung to its traditions more

13

than most European countries. The hundreds of years of foreign occupation, traditions and religion were the unifying factors of the Greek people. Greeks today remain too conscious of the hardships their forebears endured, and of their tenacious preservation of these traditions, to allow them to die. Even hip young Greeks defend these traditions and enthusiastically participate in many.

The traditions manifest themselves in a variety of ways, including regional costumes, such as the baggy pantaloons and high boots worn by elderly Cretan men, and in the embroidered dresses and floral headscarves worn by the women of Olymbos, on Karpathos. Many traditions take the form of festivals, where Greeks express their *joie de vivre* through dancing, singing and feasting.

Festival time or not, the Greek capacity for enjoyment of life is immediately evident, for life is lived more out of doors, and communally, than elsewhere in Europe. If you arrive in a Greek town in the early evening in summer, you may quite plausibly think you've arrived on a festival day, for this is the time of the *volta*, when everyone takes to the streets, refreshed from their siesta, well turned out and raring to go. All this adds up to Greece being one of Europe's most relaxed and friendliest countries. But Greece is no European backwater locked in a time warp. In towns and cities you will find discos as lively as any in Italy, France or Britain, and boutiques as trendy.

If you're a beach lover, Greece, with its 1400 islands, has more coastline than any other country in Europe. You can choose between rocky outcrops, pebbled coves, or long swathes of golden sand.

Greece's scenery is as varied as her beaches. There is the semitropical lushness of the Ionian and North-Eastern Aegean islands and southern Crete; the bare sun-baked rocks of the Cyclades; and the forested mountains, icy lakes and tumbling rivers of northern Greece. Much of this breathtaking landscape is mantled with vibrant wild flowers.

Opportunities for exploration and adventure abound in Greece. You can climb Mt Olympus, abode of the gods and second highest mountain in the Balkans (Bulgaria's Musala peak tops it by just seven metres); gape at the amazing caldera of what was possibly the world's biggest volcanic eruption, on Thira (Santorini); trek through the Samaria Gorge, on Crete, Europe's longest; see Europe's only palm forest at Vai (Crete); take a ferry to Gavdos island, Europe's most southerly point, or to Kastellorizo, its most easterly, and take Europe's most spectacular train journey, on the rack and pinion line from Diakofto to Kalavryta, in the Peloponnese.

The magnetism of Greece is also due to less tangible attributes – the dazzling clarity of the light and the floral scents which permeate the air.

There is yet another phenomenon which even people cynical about anything hinting of the esoteric comment upon. It takes the form of inexplicable happenings, coincidences, or fortuitous occurrences. It could be meeting up with a long-lost friend, or bumping into the same person again and again on your travels, or missing the ferry and being offered a lift on a private yacht, or hot, hungry and thirsty, and miles from anywhere, stumbling upon a house whose occupants offer hospitality.

Perhaps these serendipitous occurrences can be explained as the work of the gods of Ancient Greece, who, some claim, have not entirely relinquished their power, and to prove it, occasionally come down to earth to intervene in the lives of mortals.

Facts about the Country

HISTORY
The geographical position of Greece at the crossroads of three continents has resulted in a long, complicated and turbulent history.

Stone Age
At least 700,000 years ago, Neanderthals were roaming northern Greece, hunting animals, collecting fruit and lighting fires. The most substantial evidence of this is the 700,000-year-old Neanderthal skull found in a cave on the Halkidiki peninsula of Macedonia. Bones and tools from Palaeolithic times have been found in the Pindos mountains of Greece.

During Neolithic times (7000-3000 BC) an evolutionary 'leap' took place when people settled down to agriculture and community life in the fertile area that is now Thessaly. They grew barley and wheat, and bred sheep and goats. Pots, vases and simple statuettes of the Great Mother (the Earth Goddess), who was worshipped at the time, were moulded from clay.

Around 3000 BC, people lived in settlements complete with streets, squares and mud-brick houses centred around a large palace-like structure which belonged to the tribal leader. The most complete Neolithic settlements in Greece are Dimini (inhabited from 4000 to 1200 BC) and Sesklo, both near the city of Volos.

Bronze Age
Around 3000 BC, Indo-European migrants introduced the processing of bronze (an alloy of copper and tin) into Greece – the beginning of three remarkable civilisations: the Cycladic, Minoan and Mycenaean.

Cycladic Civilisation The Cycladic civilisation is divided into three periods: Early (3000-2000 BC), Middle (2000-1500 BC), and Late (1500-1100 BC). The most impressive legacies of this civilisation are the statuettes carved from Parian marble – the famous Cycladic figurines. Like statuettes of Neolithic times they depicted images of the Great Mother. Other remains include bronze and obsidian tools and weapons, gold jewellery, and stone and clay vases and pots.

The peoples of the Cycladic civilisation were accomplished sailors who developed a prosperous maritime trade. They exported their wares to Asia Minor (the west of present-day Turkey), Europe and north Africa, as well as to Crete and continental Greece. The Cyclades islands were influenced by both the Minoan and Mycenaean civilisations.

Minoan Civilisation The glorious Minoan civilisation of Crete was influenced by two great civilisations of the east: the Mesopotamian and Egyptian. It was more advanced than anything which had appeared up till then in Europe. Archaeologists divide the Minoan civilisation, like the Cycladic, into three phases: Early (3000-2100 BC), Middle (2100-1500 BC) and Late (1500-1100 BC).

In the Early period many aspects of Neolithic life endured, but by 2500 BC most people on the island had been assimilated into a new and distinct culture which we now call the Minoan, after the mythical King Minos. In the Middle period the Minoan civilisation reached its peak, producing pottery and metalwork of remarkable beauty and a high degree of imagination and skill. The Late period saw the civilisation decline both commercially and militarily against Mycenaean competition from the mainland, until its abrupt end around 1100 BC, when Dorian invaders and natural disasters ravaged the island.

Like the Cycladic civilisation, the Minoan was a great maritime power which exported goods throughout the Mediterranean. The polychrome Kamares Ware pottery which flourished during the Middle period was highly prized by the Egyptians.

Around 1700 BC the palaces at Knossos,

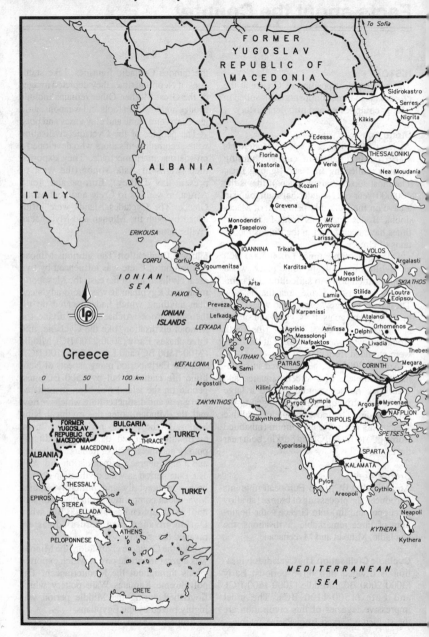

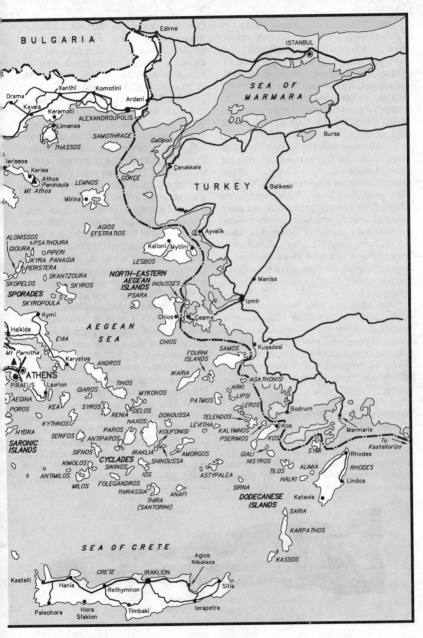

Phaestos, Malia and Zakros were wrecked by a violent earthquake. The Minoans rebuilt them to a more complex, almost 'labyrinthine' design with multiple storeys, sumptuous royal apartments, reception halls, storerooms, workshops, living quarters for staff and an advanced drainage system. The interiors were decorated with the celebrated Minoan frescoes, now on display in the Archaeological Museum at Iraklion.

The Minoans were also literate. Their first script resembled Egyptian hieroglyphs, the most famous example of which is the inscription on the Phaestos disc (1700 BC). They progressed to a syllable-based script which 20th-century archaeologists have dubbed Linear A, because it consists of linear symbols. Like the earlier hieroglyphs, it has not yet been deciphered, but archaeologists believe that it was used to document trade transactions and the contents of royal storerooms, rather than to express abstract concepts.

Some historians have suggested that the civilisation's decline after 1500 BC was brought about not just by Mycenaean invaders but by seismic waves caused by the volcanic explosion on the Cycladic island of Thira, an eruption which vulcanologists believe was more cataclysmic than any on record.

Mycenaean Civilisation The decline of the Minoan civilisation in the Late Minoan period coincided with the rise of the first great civilisation of the Greek mainland, the Mycenaean (1900-1100 BC), which reached its peak between 1500 and 1200 BC. Named after the ancient city of Mycenae, where the German archaeologist Heinrich Schliemann made his great finds in 1876, it is also known as the Achaean civilisation after the Indo-European branch of migrants who had settled on mainland Greece and absorbed many aspects of Minoan culture.

Unlike Minoan society, where the lack of city walls seems to indicate relative peace under some form of central authority, Mycenaean civilisation was characterised by independent city-states such as Corinth, Pylos, Tiryns and, the most powerful of them all, Mycenae. These were ruled by kings who inhabited palaces enclosed within massive walls on easily defensible hilltops.

The Mycenaeans' most impressive legacy is magnificent gold jewellery and ornaments, most of which can be seen in the National Archaeological Museum in Athens. The Mycenaeans wrote in what is called Linear B (unrelated to the Linear A of Crete), which has been deciphered as an early form of Greek. They also worshipped gods who were precursors of the later Greek gods.

Examples of Linear B have also been found on Crete, suggesting that Mycenaean invaders may have conquered the island, perhaps around 1500 BC, when many Minoan palaces were destroyed. Mycenaean influence stretched further than Crete: the Mycenaean city-states banded together to defeat Troy and thus to protect their trade routes to the Black Sea, and archaeological research has unearthed Mycenaean artefacts as far away as Egypt, Mesopotamia and Italy.

The Mycenaean civilisation came to an end during the 12th century BC, when Dorian tribes invaded Greece and swept all before them.

Bronze dagger found at Mycenae

Geometric Age (1200-800 BC)

The warrior-like Dorians fanned out over much of the mainland, razing the city-states and enslaving the inhabitants, and later conquered Crete and the south-west coast of Asia Minor. Other Indo-European tribes known as the Thessalians settled in what is now Thessaly. Of the original Greek tribal groups, the Aeolians fled to the north-west coast of Asia Minor; the Ionians sought refuge on the central coast and the islands of Lesbos, Samos and Chios, although they also held out in mainland Greece – in Attica and the well-fortified city of Athens.

The Dorians brought a traumatic break with the past, and the next 400 years are often referred to as Greece's Dark Age. But it would be unfair to dismiss the Dorians completely, as they brought with them iron and developed a new style of pottery, decorated with striking geometrical designs – although the art historians are still out to lunch as to whether the Dorians merely copied the designs perfected by Ionians in Attica. The Dorians worshipped male gods instead of fertility goddesses and adopted the Mycenaean gods of Poseidon, Zeus and Apollo, paving the way for the later Greek religious pantheon.

Perhaps most importantly, the Dorian warriors developed into a class of landholding aristocrats. This worsened the lot of the average farmer but also brought about the demise of the monarchy as a system of government by about 800 BC, along with a resurgence of the Mycenaean pattern of independent city-states, this time led by wealthy aristocrats instead of absolute monarchs – the beginnings of 'democratic' government.

Archaic Age (800-480 BC)

By this time, local agriculture and animal husbandry had become productive enough to trigger a resumption of maritime trading. New Greek colonies were established in north Africa, Italy, Sicily, southern France and southern Spain to fill the vacuum left by the decline of those other great Mediterranean traders, the Phoenicians.

The people of the various city-states were

Geometric detail from urn, 750 BC

unified by the invention of a Greek alphabet (of Phoenician origin, though the Greeks introduced vowels), the verses of Homer (which created a sense of a shared Mycenaean past), the establishment of the Olympic Games (which brought all the city-states together), and the setting up of central sanctuaries such as Delphi (a neutral meeting ground for lively negotiations), giving Greeks, for the first time, a sense of national identity. This period is known as the Archaic, or Middle, Age.

The city-states were built to a similar plan, with a fortified acropolis ('high city') at the highest point. The acropolis contained the cities' temples and treasury and also served as a refuge during invasions. Outside the acropolis was the agora ('market'), a bustling commercial quarter, and beyond it the residential areas.

The city-state was autonomous, free to pursue its own interests as it saw fit, which inevitably caused bickering and wars between them. As we have already seen, most city-states abolished monarchic rule in favour of an aristocratic form of government, usually headed by an archon (chief magistrate). Aristocrats were often disliked by the population because of their inherited privileges, and some city-states fell to rule by tyrants after Kypselos started the practice in Corinth around 650 BC. Tyrants seized their position rather than inheriting it, and were often perceived as having the welfare of ordinary citizens at heart by instituting improvements for the benefit of the majority.

Athens & Solon The seafaring city-state of Athens, meanwhile, was still in the hands of aristocrats, and a failed coup attempt by a would-be tyrant led the legislator Draco to draw up his infamous laws in 620 BC. These were so punitive that even the theft of a cabbage was punishable by death (hence the word 'draconian').

In 594 BC a remarkable man, Solon, was appointed archon of Athens with a far-reaching mandate to defuse the mounting tensions between the haves and the have-nots. He cancelled all debts and freed those who had become enslaved because of their debts. Declaring all free Athenians equal by law, he abolished inherited privileges and restructured political power along four classes based on wealth. Although only the first two classes were eligible for office, all four were allowed to elect magistrates and vote on legislation in the general assembly, the *ecclesia*. His reforms have led to him being regarded as the harbinger of democracy.

Sparta In the Peloponnese a very different kind of city-state existed in the form of Sparta, which was not really a city but a group of five villages. One of the few states to remain a monarchy, Sparta was ruled by two kings. The Spartans were descended from the Dorian invaders who used the Helots, the original inhabitants of Lakonia, as their slaves, and they ran their society along strict military rules laid down by the 9th century legislator Lycurgus.

Newborn babies were inspected, and if found wanting, were left to die on a mountain top. At the age of seven boys were taken from their homes to undergo rigorous training to make them into ace soldiers. Girls were spared military training but were forced to exercise vigorously to attain prime health in order to generate healthy sons. Spartan indoctrination was so effective that dissension was unknown and a degree of stability was achieved that other city-states could only dream of.

While Athens became powerful through trade, Sparta was the ultimate military machine. Both towered above the other city-states.

The Persian Wars In 519 BC Darius I ascended the throne of the expanding empire of Persia. The Ionians along the coast of Asia Minor were under Persian rule, having been conquered by Emperor Cyrus (ruled 550-530 BC), and were unhappy about their conditions.

In 499 BC Aristagoras, the tyrant of Miletus, organised a revolt of all the city-states along the coast. Darius managed to subdue things in a five-year campaign, and became hellbent on revenge against Athens, one of the few states outside the area that had helped the insurgents. He appealed to Sparta to attack Athens from behind, but the wily Spartans saw straight through his planned conquest of Greece and threw his envoy in a well.

The Persian army landed at Marathon in 490 BC. The 10,000 Athenian infantry were supported only by a small group of soldiers from Plataea (Sparta procrastinated because it was in the middle of a festival), but nevertheless they defeated the Persian archers and cavalry through a series of ingenious manoeuvres.

Darius died in 485 BC before his plans for

Spartan pottery design

another attempt reached fruition, so it was left to his son Xerxes to fulfil his father's ambition of conquering Greece. In 480 BC Xerxes gathered men from every nation of his far-flung empire and launched a coordinated invasion by army and navy, the size of which the world had never seen. The historian Herodotus gave five million as the number of Persian soldiers. No doubt this was a gross exaggeration, but it was obvious Xerxes intended to give the Greeks more than a bloody nose.

The Persians dug a canal near present-day Ierissos so that their navy could bypass the rough seas around the base of the Mt Athos peninsula (where they had been caught out before), and spanned the Hellespont with pontoon bridges for their army to march over.

Some 30 city-states of central and southern Greece met in Corinth to devise a common defence (others, including the oracle at Delphi, sided with the Persians). They agreed on a combined army and navy under Spartan command, with the Athenian leader Themistokles providing the strategy. The Spartan king Leonidas led the army to the pass at Thermopylae, near present-day Lamia, the main passage from northern into central Greece. This bottleneck was easy to defend, and although the Greeks were greatly outnumbered they held the pass until a traitor showed the Persians a way over the mountains. The Greeks were forced to retreat, but Leonidas, along with 300 of his Spartan elite troops, fought to the death. The fleet, which held off the Persian navy north of Euboea (Evia), had no choice but to retreat as well.

The Spartans and their Peloponnesian allies fell back on their second line of defence (an earthen wall across the Isthmus of Corinth), while the Persians advanced upon Athens. Themistokles ordered his people to flee the city: the women and children to Salamis, the men to sea on the Athenian fleet. The Persians razed Attica and burned Athens to the ground.

But by skilful manoeuvring the Greek navy then ensnared the large Persian ships in the narrow waters off Salamis, where they

became easy pickings for the agile Greek vessels. Xerxes, who watched the defeat of his mighty fleet from the shore, returned to Persia in disgust, leaving his general Mardonius to subdue Greece with the army. A year later, the Greeks under the Spartan general Pausanias obliterated the Persian army at the Battle of Plataea. The Athenian navy sailed to Asia Minor and destroyed what was left of the Persian fleet at Mykale, freeing the Ionian city-states there from Persian rule.

Classical Age (480-338 BC)

After the defeat of the Persians, the disciplined Spartans once again retreated to their 'fortress Peloponnese', while Athens basked in its role as liberator and embarked on a policy of blatant imperialism. In 477 BC it founded the Delian League, so called because the treasury was kept on the sacred island of Delos. The league consisted of almost every state with a navy, no matter how small, including many of the Aegean islands and some of the Ionian city-states in Asia Minor.

Ostensibly its purpose was twofold: to build and maintain a large navy to retrieve the Greek city-states that were still occupied by Persia, and to establish an effective defence against another Persian attack. The swearing of allegiance to Athens and an annual contribution of ships (later just money) were mandatory. Thus Athens achieved what had been its scheme all along: the transformation of the league into an Athenian empire.

Indeed, when Pericles became leader of Athens in 461 BC, he moved the treasury from Delos to the Acropolis and used its contents to begin a 'no-expenses-spared' building programme. His first objectives were to rebuild the temple complex of the Acropolis which had been destroyed by the Persians, and to link Athens to its lifeline, the port of Piraeus, with fortified walls designed to withstand any future siege.

Under Pericles' leadership (461-429 BC), Athens experienced a golden age with unprecedented cultural, artistic and scientific achievements, which had germinated in the Ionian cities in Asia Minor almost two centuries earlier. The city was riding the crest of a wave with rapidly expanding overseas trade.

Now that the Aegean Sea was safely under its wing, Athens began to look westwards for further expansion and came up against the city-states on the mainland. It also encroached on the trade area of Corinth, which belonged to the Peloponnesian League dominated by Sparta. A number of fickle alliances, skirmishes and provocations precipitated the Peloponnesian Wars.

First Peloponnesian War One of the major triggers was the Corcyra incident, in which Athens supported Corcyra (present-day Kerkyra or Corfu) in a controversy with its mother city, Corinth. Corinth, now under serious threat, called on Sparta to help. Sparta's power depended to a large extent on Corinth's wealth, so it rallied to the cause. The First Peloponnesian War (431-421) had begun.

Athens knew it couldn't defeat Sparta on land, so it abandoned Attica to the Spartan invaders, withdrew behind its mighty walls and blockaded the Peloponnese with its navy. Plague broke out in the overcrowded city, killing a third of the population including Pericles. Nevertheless, Sparta couldn't capture Athens-Piraeus and the blockade of the Peloponnese began to hurt, and the two adversaries eventually reached an uneasy truce.

The Sicilian Adventure Throughout the war Athens had maintained an interest in Sicily and its grain, which the soil in Attica was too poor to produce. The Greek colonies there mirrored the city-states in Greece, the most powerful being Syracuse, which had remained neutral during the war.

In 416 BC the Sicilian city of Segesta asked Athens to intervene in a squabble it was having with Selinus, an ally of Syracuse. A hot-headed second cousin of Pericles, Alkibiades, convinced the Athenian assembly to send a flotilla to Sicily; it could go on the pretext of helping Segesta, and then attack Syracuse.

The flotilla, under the joint leadership of Alkibiades, Nikias and Lamachos, was ill-fated from the outset. Alkibiades was called back to Athens on blasphemy charges arising from a drinking binge in which he knocked the heads off a few holy statues. Enraged, he travelled not to Athens but to Sparta and persuaded the surprised Spartans to go to the aid of Syracuse, which had been under siege from the Athenians for over three years. Nikias' health suffered and Lamachos, the most adept of the three, was killed. Sparta followed Alkibiades' advice and broke the siege in 413 BC, destroying the Athenian fleet and army.

Second Peloponnesian War Athens was depleted of troops, money and ships; its subject states were ripe for revolt and Sparta was there to lend them a hand. In 413 BC the Spartans occupied Decelea in Attica, from where they harassed farmers and slowly starved Athens which had begun to feel the loss of its Sicilian grain supplies. Darius II of Persia, who had been closely watching events in Sicily and Greece, offered Sparta money to build a navy, so long as Sparta promised to return the Ionian cities in Asia Minor to Persia.

Barefooted Greek Warriors

Athens put in one last effort and in the ensuing war even gained the upper hand for a while under the leadership of the reinstated Alkibiades. But when Persia entered the fray in Asia Minor and Sparta regained its composure under the outstanding general Lysander, Athens' days were numbered. In 404 BC it surrendered to Sparta.

Corinth urged the total destruction of Athens but Lysander felt honour-bound to spare the city that had saved Greece from the Persians. Instead he crippled it by confiscating its fleet, abolishing the Delian League and tearing down the walls between the city and Piraeus.

Greece Under Sparta The Peloponnesian Wars had exhausted the city-states. None were to return to their former glory and only Sparta had retained a semblance of power, which it now exerted over the rest. During the wars, Sparta had promised to restore liberty to the city-states who turned against Athens, but Lysander now installed oligarchies (governments run by the super-rich) supervised by Spartan garrisons. Soon there was widespread dissatisfaction.

Sparta further weakened its position when it began a campaign to reclaim the cities in Asia Minor from Persian rule. This brought the Persians and Persian money back into Greek affairs where they found willing clients in Athens and increasingly powerful Thebes. Thebes, which had freed itself from Spartan control and had revived the Boeotian League, soon became the main threat to Sparta, while Athens regained some of its former power at the head of a new league of Aegean states known as the Second Confederacy – this time aimed against Sparta rather than Persia.

The rivalry culminated in the decisive Battle of Leuktra in 371 BC, where Thebes, under the leadership of the remarkable statesman and general Epaminondas, was victorious. Sparta had never lost a pitched battle before, and consequently its influence over Greece collapsed while Thebes filled the vacuum.

In a surprise about-turn Athens now allied itself with Sparta, and their combined forces met the Theban army at Mantinea in the Peloponnese in 362 BC. The battle was won by Thebes, but the victory was hollow since Epaminondas was killed, and without his talents Theban power crumbled. Athens was unable to take advantage of the situation as the Second Confederacy became embroiled in infighting fomented by the Persians, and when the Confederacy collapsed, Athens lost its final chance of regaining its former glory.

The city-states were now spent forces and a new power was rising in the north: Macedon. This had not gone unnoticed by the inspirational orator Demosthenes in Athens, who, anticipating a Macedonian invasion, argued fervently for consolidation amongst the city-states. Only Thebes took heed of his warnings and the two cities formed an alliance.

The Rise of Macedon
While the Greeks engineered their own decline through the Peloponnesian Wars, Macedon (geographically the modern *nome*, or province, of Macedonia) was gathering strength in the north. Macedon had long been detached from developments in Greece. It had a monarchy, and in comparison with the Greeks of the city-states the inhabitants were a backward lot. Many belonged to primitive hill tribes who were only nominally overseen by the king. The Greeks considered them barbarians (those whose speech sounded like 'bar-bar', which meant anyone who didn't speak Greek).

However, with increasing land and sea communications, the culture of the city-states had begun to penetrate. King Archelaos (ruled 413-399 BC) made his court at Pella into a cultural centre, inviting artists and poets from the city-states to work there. But the first king of Macedon actively to meddle in Greek affairs was Philip II (ruled 382-336 BC).

As a boy, Philip had been held hostage in Thebes where Epaminondas had taught him a thing or two about military strategy. After organising his rebellious hill tribes into an efficient army of cavalry and long-lanced infantry, Philip made several forays south, and manipulated his way into membership of the Amphyctionic Council (a group of states whose job it was to protect the oracle at Delphi).

In 339 BC, on the pretext of helping the Amphyctionic Council sort out a sacred war with Amfissa, he marched his army into Greece. The result was the Battle of Khaironeia in Boeotia (338 BC), in which the Macedonias defeated a combined army of Athenians and Thebans. The following year Philip called together all the city-states (except Sparta, which remained aloof) at Corinth and persuaded them to form the League of Corinth and swear allegiance to Macedonia by promising he would lead them in a campaign against Persia. The barbarian upstart had become leader of all the Greeks.

Philip's ambition to tackle Persia never materialised, for in 336 BC he was assassinated by a Macedonian noble. His son, the 20-year-old Alexander, who had led the decisive cavalry charge at Khaironea, now became king.

Alexander the Great Alexander, highly educated (he had been tutored by the great Aristotle), an astute politician, fearless and ambitious, was intent upon fulfilling what his father had begun. Philip II's death had been the signal for rebellions throughout the budding empire, but Alexander wasted no time in crushing them, making an example of Thebes which he razed to the ground. After restoring order, he turned his attention to the Persian Empire and marched his army of 40,000 men into Asia Minor in 334 BC.

After a few bloody battles with the Persians, most notably at Issus (333 BC), Alexander succeeded in conquering Syria, Palestine and Egypt – where he was proclaimed pharaoh and founded the city of Alexandria. Hellbent on sitting on the Persian throne, he then began hunting down the Persian king, Darius III, defeating his army in Mesopotamia in 331 BC. Darius III fled eastward while Alexander mopped up his empire behind him, destroying the Persian palace at Persepolis in revenge for the sacking of the Acropolis 150 years earlier, and confiscating the well-endowed royal treasury. The following year Darius' body was found: he had been stabbed to death by a Bactrian (Afghan) dissident.

Alexander continued eastwards into what is now Uzbekistan, Bactria (where he married a local princess, Roxane) and northern India. His ambition was now to conquer the world, which he believed ended at the sea beyond India. But his soldiers grew weary and in 324 BC forced him to return to Mesopotamia, where he settled in Babylon and drew up plans for an expedition south into Arabia. The following year, however, he suddenly fell ill and died. At the young age of 33, Alexander hadn't yet organised an heir, and after his untimely death his generals swooped like vultures onto his extensive empire.

When the dust settled by 301 BC, Alexander's empire had fallen apart into three large kingdoms and several smaller states. The three generals with the richest pickings were Ptolemy, founder of the Ptolemaic dynasty in Egypt (capital: Alexandria), which died out when the last of the

Alexander the Great

dynasty, Cleopatra, committed suicide in 30 BC; Seleucus, founder of the Seleucid dynasty which ruled over Persia and Syria (capital: Antiochia); and Antigonus, who ruled over Asia Minor and whose Antigonid successors would win control over Macedonia proper.

Macedonia lost control of the Greek city-states to the south, who banded together into the Aetolian League centred around Delphi and the Achaean League based on the Peloponnese; Athens and Sparta joined neither. One of Alexander's officers established the mini-kingdom of Pergamum in Asia Minor, which reached its height under Attalos I (ruled 241-196 BC) when it rivalled Alexandria as the centre of culture and learning. The island of Rhodes developed into a powerful mini-state by taxing passing ships.

Still, Alexander's formidable achievements during his 13 years on the world stage earned him the epithet 'the Great'. He spread Greek culture throughout a large part of the 'civilised' world, encouraged intermarriage and dismissed the anti-barbarian snobbery of the Classical Greeks. In doing so, he ushered in the Hellenistic period of world history, in which Hellenic ('Greek') culture broke out of the narrow confines of the ancient Greek world and merged with the other proud cultures of antiquity to create a new cosmopolitan tradition.

Roman Rule

While Alexander the Great was forging his vast empire in the east, the Romans had been expanding in the west and now began making inroads into Greece. They found willing allies in Pergamum and Rhodes, who feared Syrian and Macedonian expansionism. The Romans defeated the Seleucid king, Antiochus III, in a three-year campaign and in 189 BC gave all of Asia Minor to Pergamum. Several wars were needed to subjugate Macedon, but in 168 BC Macedon lost the decisive Battle of Pydnaa and was turned into a Roman province 20 years later.

The Achaean League was defeated in 146 BC; the Roman consul Mummius made an example of the rebellious Corinthians by completely destroying their beautiful city, massacring the men and selling the women and children into slavery. Attalos III of Pergamum died without an heir in 133 BC, donating Asia Minor to Rome in his will. In 86 BC Athens joined in a rebellion against the Romans in Asia Minor, staged by the king of the Black Sea region, Mithridates VI; the Roman statesman Sulla invaded Athens, destroyed its walls and took off with its most valuable sculptures.

Soon most of Greece was under Roman rule and the area became a battleground as Roman generals fought for supremacy. In a decisive naval battle off Cape Actium (31 BC) Octavian was victorious over Antony and Cleopatra and consequently became Rome's first emperor, assuming the title Augustus, the Grand One.

For the next 300 years Greece, as the Roman province of Achaea, experienced an unprecedented period of peace, the Pax Romana. The Romans had always venerated Greek art, literature and philosophy, and aristocratic Romans sent their offspring to the many schools in Athens. Indeed, the Romans adopted most aspects of Hellenistic culture, spreading its unifying traditions throughout their empire.

Christianity & the Byzantine Empire

The Pax Romana began to crumble in 250 AD when the Goths invaded Greece, the first of a succession of invaders spurred on by the Great Migrations, which included the Visigoths in 395, the Vandals in 465, the Ostrogoths in 480, the Bulgars in 500, the Huns in 540, and the Slavs after 600.

But the new religion of Christianity had a much more lasting impact. St Paul had made several visits to Greece in the 1st century AD and made converts in many places. The definitive boost to the spread of Christianity in this part of the world came with the conversion of the Roman emperors and the rise of the Byzantine Empire, which blended Hellenistic culture with Christianity.

In 324 Emperor Constantine I, a Christian convert, transferred the capital of the empire from Rome to Byzantium, a city on the western shore of the Bosporus, which was renamed Constantinople (present-day Istanbul). This was as much due to insecurity in Italy itself as to the growing importance of the wealthy eastern regions of the empire. By the end of the 4th century the Roman Empire was formally divided into a western and eastern half. While Rome went into terminal decline, the eastern capital grew in wealth and strength, long outliving its western counterpart (the Byzantine Empire lasted until the capture of Constantinople by the Turks in 1453).

In 394 Emperor Theodosius I made Christianity the official religion in Greece and outlawed the worship of Greek/Roman gods, now branded as paganism. Athens remained an important cultural centre until 529, when Emperor Justinian forbade the teaching of Classical philosophy in favour of Christian theology, now seen as the supreme form of intellectual endeavour. The Hagia Sophia (Church of the Divine Wisdom) was built in Constantinople and many magnificent churches were also built in Greece, especially in Thessaloniki, a Christian stronghold much favoured by the Byzantine emperors.

The Crusades

It is one of the ironies of history that the demise of the Byzantine Empire was accelerated not by invasions of infidels from the east, or barbarians from the north, but by fellow Christians from the west. The First Crusade set out from France in 1095 – the first of several crusades over the next two centuries – to liberate the Holy Land from the Muslims, the adherents of Islam who had burst out of the Arabian peninsula in the 7th century. The crusaders were a rough lot, driven by greed as much as religious fervour. Not content with merely liberating Palestine, where they had to keep fighting off the Muslims, they set about conquering the now weak Byzantine Empire.

When the Fourth Crusade arrived in Constantinople in 1204, the crusaders sacked the city and created the so-called Latin Empire of Constantinople, partitioning much of the Byzantine Empire into feudal states ruled by self-styled 'Latin' princes. Greece now entered one of the most tumultuous periods of its history. The Byzantines fought to regain their lost capital and to keep the areas they had managed to hold on to (the so-called Empire of Nicaea, south of Constantinople in Asia Minor), while the 'Latin' (mostly Frankish) princes fought amongst themselves to expand their territories.

Meanwhile, Venice had secured a foothold in Greece. The Byzantine emperor Alexius had asked Venice to help when the Normans invaded Greece in 1196. The commercially ambitious Venetians acquiesced on condition that they could use Byzantine trade routes and be exempt from taxes. Over the next few centuries they acquired all of the most strategic Greek ports, including the island of Crete, and became the wealthiest and most powerful traders in the Mediterranean.

Despite this disorderly state of affairs Byzantium was not yet dead. In 1259, the Byzantine emperor Michael VIII Palaeologus recaptured the Peloponnese from the Frankish de Villehardouin family, and made the city of Mystra his headquarters. Many of the most eminent Byzantine artists, architects, intellectuals and philosophers converged on the city for a final burst of Byzantine creativity. Michael VIII managed to wrest Constantinople back from the Frankish conquerors in 1261, but by this time Byzantium was a shadow of its former self.

The Ottoman Empire

Soon a new power was threatening in the east: the Turkish Ottoman Empire, founded in central Asia in the late 13th century. The Muslim Turks rapidly expanded the areas under their control and by the mid-14th century were harassing the Byzantine Empire on all sides. Western Europe was too embroiled in the Hundred Years' War to come to the rescue, and in 1453 Constantinople fell to the Turks under Mohammed II the Conqueror. Once more Greece became a battleground, this time fought over by the Turks and Venetians. Eventually, with the exception of the Ionian islands, Greece became part of the Ottoman Empire.

Much has been made of the horrors of the Turkish occupation in Greece. However, in the early years of Ottoman rule Greeks probably marginally preferred Ottoman to Venetian or Frankish rule. Also, the Roman and Byzantine churches had been growing ever more apart since the pope in Rome and the patriarch in Constantinople excommunicated one another in 1054, and Mohammed II was careful to respect the patriarch's authority.

But life was not easy under the Turks, not least because of the high taxation they imposed. One of their most callous practices was the taking of one out of every five male children in a Greek family to become janissaries, personal bodyguards of the sultan. Many janissaries became infantrymen in the Ottoman army, but the cleverest rose to high office including grand vizier. Sometimes young Greek girls were taken from their families to become women of the sultan's harem. As time went on and the Ottoman Empire fell into decline, atrocities did take place, but generally the occupation was typified more by neglect than arrant brutality.

The Ottoman Empire reached its zenith under Sultan Süleyman the Magnificent (ruled 1520-66), who expanded it throughout the Balkans and Hungary to the gates of Vienna. In 1570, his successor, Selim the Sot, also intent upon expansion, invaded Cyprus, which was under Venetian jurisdiction but inhabited by Greeks. The Ottomans sacked the capital, Nicosia, and massacred 30,000 of its inhabitants.

This atrocity shocked and frightened Europe, and strengthened the burgeoning notion that Ottoman expansionism had to be checked. This was easier to achieve on sea than on land for the time being, and in the Battle of Lepanto (1571) off the northern Peloponnese coast the Ottoman navy was defeated by a combined Venetian and Spanish fleet, breaking Ottoman naval power in the eastern Mediterranean.

Russian Involvement

The ineffectual sultans of the 16th and 17th centuries hastened the Ottoman Empire's decline, and anarchy and rebellion became endemic. Corsairs terrorised coastal dwellers, gangs of klephts (anti-Ottoman fugitives and brigands) roamed the mountains, and there was an upsurge of opposition to Turkish rule by freedom fighters who fought one another more than the Turks.

In various enclaves of the Ottoman Empire, however, where intellectual Greeks had tenaciously preserved Greek culture, there were the first stirrings of what was to blossom into a more organised national rebellion. One such enclave was Odessa in Russia.

Russia's link with Greece went back to Byzantine times, when the Russians had been converted to Christianity by Byzantine missionaries. The Church hierarchies in Constantinople and Kiev (later Moscow) soon went separate ways, but when Constantinople fell to the Turks, the metropolitan (head) of the Russian Church declared Moscow the 'third Rome', the true heir of Christianity, and campaigned for the liberation of the fellow Christians in the south. This fitted in nicely with Russia's efforts to expand southwards and south-westwards into Ottoman territory – perhaps even to turn the Ottoman Empire back into a Byzantine Empire dependent on Russia.

When Catherine the Great became Empress of Russia in 1762, both the Republic of Venice and the Ottoman Empire were weak. She sent Russian agents to foment rebellion, first in the Peloponnese in 1770 and then in Epiros in 1786. Both were crushed ruthlessly – the latter by Ali Pasha, the governor of Ioannina, who proceeded to set up his own power base in Greece in defiance of the sultan.

Independence Parties

In the 1770s and 1780s Catherine booted the Turks from the Black Sea coast, created a number of towns in the region, including Odessa, and gave them Ancient Greek or Byzantine names. She offered Greeks financial incentives and free land to settle the region, and many took up her offer.

In Odessa in 1814, three businessmen – Athanasios Tsakalof, Emmanuel Xanthos and Nikolaos Skoufas – founded a Greek independence party, the Philiki Etairia (Friendly Society). The message of the society spread quickly and branches opened throughout Greece. Members met in secret and came from all walks of life. The leaders in Odessa held the firm belief that armed force was the only effective means of liberation, and made generous monetary contributions to the freedom fighters.

Meanwhile there were also stirrings of dissent amongst Greeks living in Constantinople. The Ottomans regarded it as beneath them to participate in commerce, and this had left the door open for Greeks in the city to become a powerful economic force. These wealthy Greek families were called Phanariots. Unlike the Philiki Etairia, who strove for liberation through rebellion, the Phanariots believed that by virtue of their positions they could effect a takeover from within. Influential Phanariots included Alexander Mavrokordatos and Alexander and Demitrios Ypsilantis.

The War of Independence

Ali Pasha's private rebellion against the sultan in 1820 gave the Greeks the opportunity they had been waiting for. On 25 March 1821 Bishop Germanos of Patras hoisted the Greek flag at the monastery of Agias Lavras in the Peloponnese, an act of defiance that marked the beginning of the War of Independence. Fighting broke out throughout the Peloponnese, with fearless Maniot freedom fighters, led by Petrobey Mavromichaelis, governor of the Mani, laying siege to the most strategic Turkish garrisons and razing the homes of thousands of Turks. The worst atrocity occurred in the city of Tripolitsa (present-day Tripolis) where 12,000 Turkish inhabitants were massacred.

The fighting escalated throughout the mainland and many islands. Within a year the Greeks had captured Monemvassia, Navarino (modern Pylos), Nafplion and Tripolitsa in the Peloponnese, and Messolongi, Athens and Thebes. Greek independence was proclaimed at Epidaurus on 13 January 1822. The Turks retaliated with massacres in Asia Minor, most notoriously on the island of Chios, where 25,000 civilians were killed.

The Western powers were reluctant to intervene, fearing the consequences of creating a power vacuum in south-eastern Europe, where the Turks still controlled much territory. But help did come from the philhellenes – aristocratic young men, recipients of a classical education, who saw themselves as the inheritors of a glorious civilisation and were willing to fight to liberate its oppressed descendants. Philhellenes included Shelley, Goethe, Schiller, Victor Hugo, Alfred de Musset and Lord Byron. Byron arrived in Messolongi – an important centre of resistance – in January 1824 and died three months later of pneumonia.

The prime movers in the revolution were the klephts Theodoros Kolokotronis (who led the siege on Nafplion) and Marko Botsaris; Georgios Koundouriotis (a ship owner) and Admiral Andreas Miaoulis, both from Hydra; and the Phanariots Alexander Mavrokordatos and Demitrios Ypsilantis. If you familiarise yourself with these names, walking along streets in Greece will take on a whole new meaning as a disproportionate number are named after these heroes.

The long list makes it clear that the cause was not lacking in leaders; what was lacking was unity of objectives and strategy. Internal disagreements twice escalated into civil war, the worst in the Peloponnese in 1824. The sultan took advantage of this, called in Egyptian reinforcements, and by 1827 captured Modon (Methoni) and Corinth, and recaptured Navarino, Messolongi and Athens.

At last the Western powers intervened, and a combined Russian, French and British fleet destroyed the Turkish-Egyptian fleet in the Bay of Navarino in October 1827. Sultan Mahmud II defied the odds and proclaimed a holy war. Russia sent troops into the Balkans and engaged the Ottoman army in yet another Russo-Turkish war. Fighting continued until 1829 when, with Russian troops at the gates of Constantinople, the sultan accepted Greek independence by the Treaty of Adrianople.

Birth of the Greek Nation

Meanwhile, the Greeks had begun organising the independent state they proclaimed several years earlier. In April 1827 they elected as their first president a Corfiot who had been the foreign minister of Tsar Alexander I, Ioannis Kapodistrias. Nafplion, in the Peloponnese, was selected as the capital.

With his Russian past, Kapodistrias believed in a strong centralised government. Although he was good at enlisting foreign support, his autocratic manner at home was unacceptable to many of the leaders of the War of Independence, particularly the Maniot chieftains who had always been a law unto themselves, and in 1831 he was assassinated.

In the ensuing anarchy, Britain, France and Russia once again intervened and declared that Greece should become a monarchy and that the throne should be given to a non-Greek in order to frustrate Greek power struggles. A fledgeling kingdom was now up for grabs amongst the offspring of the crowned heads of Europe, but no-one exactly ran to fill the empty throne. Eventually the 17-year-old Prince Otto of Bavaria became king, arriving in Nafplion in January 1833. The new kingdom (established by the London Convention of 1832) consisted of the Peloponnese, Sterea Ellada, the Cyclades and the Sporades.

King Otho (as his name became) got up the nose of the Greek people from the moment he set foot on their land – firstly, because he arrived with a bunch of upperclass Bavarian cronies, to whom he gave the most prestigious official posts; and secondly, because he was as autocratic as Kapodistrias had been. In 1834 Otho moved the capital to Athens.

Patience with his rule ran out in 1843 when demonstrations in the capital, led by the War of Independence leaders, called for a constitution. Otho mustered a National Assembly which drafted a constitution calling for parliamentary government consisting of a lower house and a senate. Otho's cronies were whisked out of power and replaced by War of Independence freedom fighters, who bullied and bribed the populace into voting in a way which suited them.

The Great Idea

By the middle of the 19th century the people of the new Greek nation were no better off materially than they had been under the Ottomans, and it was in this climate of despondency that the Megali Idea (Great Idea) of a new Greek Empire was born. This empire was to include all the lands that had once been under Greek influence, with Constantinople as the capital. Otho enthusiastically embraced the idea, which increased his popularity no end.

Not with the Greek politicians, however, who still sought ways to increase their own power in the face of his autocratic rule. By the end of the 1850s, most of the stalwarts from the War of Independence had been replaced by a new breed of university graduates (Athens University had been founded in 1837). In 1862 they staged a bloodless revolution and deposed the king. But they weren't quite able to set their own agenda, because in the same year Britain returned the Ionian islands (a British protectorate since 1815) to Greece, and in the general euphoria the British were able to push forward young Prince William of Denmark, who became King George I (the Greek monarchy retained its Danish links from that time).

His 50-year reign brought stability to the troubled country, beginning with a new constitution in 1864 which established the power of democratically elected representatives and pushed the king further towards a largely ceremonial role. In 1866-68, an uprising in Crete against Turkish rule was suppressed by the sultan, but in 1881 Greece did acquire Thessaly and part of Epiros as a result of another Russo-Turkish war.

Kharilaos Trikoupis became prime minister in 1882 and prudently concentrated his efforts on domestic issues, rather than pursuing the Great Idea. The 1880s showed the first signs of economic growth, the country's first railway lines and paved roads had been constructed, the Corinth Canal (begun in 62 AD!) was completed enabling Piraeus to become a major Mediterranean port, and the merchant navy was growing rapidly.

However, the Great Idea had not been buried, and reared its head again after Trikoupis' death in 1896. In 1897 there was another uprising in Crete, and the hot-headed prime minister Diliyiannis sent a Greek army which resulted in open war with Turkey. It was only through the intervention of the great powers that the Turkish army was prevented from taking Athens, and Crete came under international administration.

The day-to-day government of the island was gradually handed over to Greeks, and in 1905, the president of the Cretan assembly, Eleutherios Venizelos, announced Crete's union *(enosis)* with Greece, although this was not recognised by international law until 1913. Venizelos went on to become prime minister of Greece in 1910 and was the country's leading politician until his republican sympathies brought about his downfall in 1935.

The Balkan Wars At the beginning of the 20th century, the Ottoman Empire was in its death throes but was still clinging on to Macedonia. The newly formed Balkan countries of Serbia and Bulgaria, as well as Greece, were hoping to add Macedonia to their territory. These territorial ambitions led to two Balkan wars; in the first (1912) Serbia, Bulgaria and Greece fought Turkey, and in the second (1913) Serbia and Greece fought Bulgaria. The outcome of these wars was the Treaty of Bucharest (August 1913), which greatly expanded Greek territory by adding the southern part of Macedonia, part of Thrace, another chunk of Epiros, and the North-East Aegean Islands, as well as recognising the union with Crete.

In March 1913, King George was assassinated by a lunatic and his son Constantine became king.

WW I & Smyrna
King Constantine, who was married to the sister of the German emperor, insisted that Greece remain neutral when WW I broke out in August 1914. However, the Allies (Britain, France and Russia) put pressure on Venizelos to join forces with them against Germany and Turkey. As the war dragged on, the Allies made heedless promises which they couldn't hope to fulfil, including land in Asia Minor. Venizelos set up a rebel government, first in Crete and then in Thessaloniki, and joined the war on the Allied side. The landing of Allied troops in Greece forced the king's abdication in June 1917, and he was replaced by his more amenable second son Alexander.

Greek troops served with distinction on the Allied side, but when the war ended in 1918, the promised land in Asia Minor was not forthcoming. Venizelos took matters into his own hands and, with Allied acquiescence, landed troops in Smyrna (present-day Izmir) in May 1919 under the guise of protecting the half a million Greeks living in that city (just under half the population there). With a firm foothold in Asia Minor Venizelos now organised an invasion inland.

The war-depleted Ottoman Empire must have appeared as a pushover to Venizelos, but this was not to be the case. In 1908 the Young Turks movement had been formed and was pressing for Western-style reforms to bring Turkey into the 20th century. One of its members was a remarkable young general, Mustafa Kemal (later to become Atatürk), who believed that Turkey needed a modern government in place of the absolute sultanate. The Greek invasion was just the cause he needed to win public support.

By September 1921 the Greeks were close to Ankara, but the Turkish troops drove them back to Smyrna and massacred many of the Greek inhabitants. Mustafa Kemal was now a national hero, the sultanate was abolished and Turkey became a republic. The outcome of the failed Greek invasion and the revolution in Turkey was the Treaty of Lausanne of July 1923. This gave eastern Thrace and the islands of Imbros and Tenedos to Turkey, and the Italians kept the Dodecanese (which they had temporarily acquired in 1912 and would hold until 1947).

The treaty also called for a population exchange between Greece and Turkey to prevent any future disputes. The Great Idea, which had been such an enormous drain on the country's finances over the decades, was at last laid to rest. Almost 1.5 million Greeks left Turkey and almost 400,000 Turks left Greece. Many Greeks abandoned a privileged life in Asia Minor for one of penury in shantytowns in Greece. But although the exchange put a tremendous strain on the Greek economy and caused great hardship for the individuals concerned, in the long term it was advantageous. The refugees introduced new agricultural and industrial techniques, and many eventually became prominent in the arts and business.

The Republic of 1924-35

The arrival of the refugees coincided with, and compounded, a period of political instability which was unprecedented even by Greek standards. In October 1920, King Alexander had died from a monkey bite, and a plebiscite in December restored his father, King Constantine. In 1922 a military coup deposed Constantine and replaced him with his first son, George II, who became a mere puppet of the military dictators. More coups and counter-coups led to the proclamation of a republic in March 1924, followed by more military dictatorships.

A measure of stability was attained with Venizelos' return to power in 1928. He pursued a policy of economic and educational reforms, but progress was inhibited by the international Great Depression. By the early 1930s, power struggles between Venizelos, who now led the antiroyalist Liberal Party, and Panayiotis Tsaldaris, who led the monarchist Popular Party, had reached a height. In March 1933 Venizelos lost the general elections to the Popular Party, and the new government began to make preparations for the restoration of the monarchy.

In March 1935 Venizelos and his supporters staged an unsuccessful coup, resulting in

his exile to Paris where he died a year later. In November 1935 King George II was restored to the throne by a rigged plebiscite, and he made the right-wing general Ioannis Metaxas prime minister. Nine months later, Metaxas assumed dictatorial powers with the king's consent under the pretext of preventing a communist-inspired republican coup.

WW II

Metaxas' grandiose vision was to create a Third Greek Civilisation based on its glorious Ancient and Byzantine past, but what he actually created was more a Greek version of the Third Reich. He exiled or imprisoned opponents, banned trade unions and the KKE (Kommunistiko Komma Ellados, the Greek Communist Party), imposed press censorship, and created a secret police force and a fascist-style youth movement. But Metaxas is remembered chiefly for his reply of *ochi* (no) to Mussolini's request to allow Italians to traverse Greece at the beginning of WW II, thus maintaining Greece's policy of strict neutrality. The Italians invaded Greece but were driven back into Albania.

A prerequisite of Hitler's plan to invade the Soviet Union was a secure southern flank in the Balkans. The British, realising this, asked Metaxas if they could land troops in Greece. He gave the same reply as he had given the Italians, but died suddenly in January 1941. The king replaced him with the timorous Alexander Koryzis, who agreed to British forces landing in Greece and committed suicide when the Germans invaded.

German troops marched through Yugoslavia and invaded Greece on 6 April 1941. Despite ferocious fighting by Greek, British, Australian and New Zealand troops, the whole country was under Nazi occupation within a month. King George II and his government went into exile in Egypt. Throughout the occupation the civilian population suffered appallingly, many dying of starvation. The Nazis rounded up over half the Jewish population of Greece and transported them to death camps.

Numerous resistance movements sprang up. The three dominant ones were ELAS

(Ellinikos Laikos Apeleftherotikos Stratos), EAM (Ethnikon Apeleftherotikon Metopon) and EDES (Ethnikos Dimokratikos Ellinikos Syndesmos). Although ELAS was founded by communists, not all of its members were left-wing, whereas EAM consisted of Stalinist KKE members who had lived in Moscow in the 1930s and harboured ambitions of establishing a postwar communist Greece. EDES (Ethnikos Dimokratikos Ellinikos Syndesmos) consisted of right-wing and monarchist resistance fighters. Often these groups fought one another with as much venom as they fought the Germans.

By 1943 Britain had begun speculating on the political complexion of postwar Greece. Winston Churchill wanted the king back and was afraid there would be a communist takeover, especially after ELAS and EAM formed a coalition and declared a provisional government in the summer of 1944. The Germans were pushed out of Greece in October 1944, but the communist and monarchist resistance groups continued fighting one another.

Civil War
On 3 December 1944, the police fired on a communist demonstration in Syntagma Square. The ensuing six weeks of fighting between the left and the right were known as the Dekembriana (December) Days, the first round of the civil war, and only the intervention of British troops prevented an ELAS-EAM victory. An election held in March 1946 and boycotted by the communists was won by the royalists, and a rigged plebiscite put George II back on the throne.

In October the left-wing Democratic Army (DA) was formed, which resumed the fight against the monarchy and its British supporters, marking the beginning of the second round of the civil war. The DA recruited thousands of members, and using guerrilla tactics occupied land along the Albanian and Yugoslav borders under the leadership of Markos Vafiades.

By 1947 the USA had replaced Britain as Greece's 'minder' and, inspired by the Truman Doctrine which aimed to contain the spread of Soviet influence, gave large sums of money to the anti-communist coalition government. The government made communism illegal and implemented the Certificate of Political Reliability (proof that the carrier was not left-wing), which remained valid until 1962 and without which Greeks couldn't vote and found it almost impossible to get work. The extremely bitter civil war dragged on until October 1949, when Yugoslavia fell out with the Soviet Union and cut off the DA supply lines. Vafiades was assassinated by a group of his Stalinist underlings and the DA capitulated.

More Greeks had been killed in the civil war than had been killed in WW II; thousands were homeless, many had been taken prisoner or exiled, and the DA had taken some 30,000 Greek children from northern Greece to Eastern-bloc countries, ostensibly for protection. The country was in an almighty mess politically and economically.

Reconstruction & the Cyprus Issue
General elections were held in 1950. The system of proportional representation resulted in a series of unworkable coalitions, and the electoral system was changed to majority voting in 1952 – which excluded the communists from future governments. The next election was a victory for the newly formed right-wing Greek Rally (Ellinikos Synagermos) party led by General Papagos, who had been a field marshal during the civil war. General Papagos remained in power until his death in 1955, when he was replaced by Constantine Karamanlis, the minister of public works.

Greece joined NATO in 1951, and in 1953 the USA was granted the right to operate sovereign bases in Greece. Intent on maintaining a right-wing government in Greece, the USA gave generous aid and even more generous military support. Living standards of Greeks improved during the 1950s, although it remained a poor country. The new tourist industry also began bringing in revenue.

Cyprus occupied centre stage in Greece's

foreign affairs, and has remained there to this day. Since the 1930s, Greek Cypriots (four-fifths of the population) had demanded enosis, while Turkey maintained its claim to the island ever since the British occupied it in 1914 (it became a British crown colony in 1925). After a new outbreak of communal violence between Greek and Turkish Cypriots in 1954, Britain stated its intention to make Cyprus an independent state.

The right-wing Greek EOKA (National Organisation of Cypriot Freedom Fighters) began guerrilla activities against the British administration. In 1959, however, Greece and Turkey accepted independence, and in August 1960 Cyprus became a republic with Archbishop Makarios as president and Turkish Fasal Kükük as vice president. This didn't really solve the issue, as the EOKA continued its activities while Turkish Cypriots clamoured for partition of the island, and the prospect of civil war in Cyprus remained real.

Back in Greece, George Papandreou, a former Venizelos supporter, founded the broadly based EK (Centre Union) in 1958, but an election in 1961 returned the ERE (National Radical Union), Karamanlis' new name for Papagos' Greek Rally party, to power for the third time in succession. Papandreou accused the ERE of ballot-rigging – probably true, but the culprits were almost certainly right-wing, military-backed groups (rather than Karamanlis) who feared communist infiltration if the EK came to power. Political turmoil followed, culminating in the murder, in May 1963, of Grigorios Lambrakis, the deputy of the communist EDA (Union of the Democratic Left). All this proved too much for Karamanlis, who resigned in protest at the king's visit to Britain while Cyprus remained an issue and left the country.

Despite the ERE's sometimes desperate measures to stay in power, an election in February 1964 was won by the EK. Papandreou wasted no time in implementing a series of radical changes. He freed political prisoners and allowed exiles to come back to Greece, reduced income tax and the defence budget, and increased spending on social services and education. Papandreou's victory coincided with King Constantine II's accession to the Greek throne, and with a renewed outbreak of violence in Cyprus which erupted into a full-scale civil war before the UN intervened and installed a peace-keeping force.

The Colonels' Coup

The right in Greece was rattled by Papandreou's tolerance of the left, fearing that this would increase the EDA's influence. The climate was one of mutual suspicion between the left and the right, each claiming that the other was conspiring a takeover. Finally, Papandreou decided the armed forces needed a thorough overhaul, which seemed fair enough, as army officers were more often than not the perpetrators of conspiracies. King Constantine refused to cooperate with this, and Papandreou resigned. Two years of ineffectual interim governments followed before a new election was scheduled for May 1967.

The election was never to be. A group of army colonels led by George Papadopoulos and Stylianos Patakos staged a coup d'état on 21 April 1967. In December King Constantine tried an unsuccessful counter-coup after which he fled the country. A military junta was established with Papadopoulos as prime minister.

The colonels imposed martial law, abolished all political parties, banned trade unions, imposed censorship, and imprisoned, tortured and exiled thousands of Greeks who opposed them. Suspicions that the coup had been aided by the CIA remain conjecture, but criticism of the coup, and the ensuing regime, was certainly not forthcoming from either the CIA or the US government. In June 1972 Papadopoulos declared Greece a republic (confirmed by rigged referendum in July) and appointed himself president.

In November 1973 students began a sit-in at Athens' Polytechnic college in protest against the junta. On the night of 16 November tanks stormed the building, injuring many and killing at least 20. On 25 November Papadopoulos was deposed by the thuggish Brigadier Ioannidis, head of the military security police.

In an effort to engender public support, Ioannidis mounted a coup in Cyprus in July 1974. The plan was to assassinate President Archbishop Makarios and unite Cyprus with Greece, but Makarios got wind of the plan and escaped. The junta installed Nikos Sampson, a former EOKA leader, as president, and Turkey reacted by invading the island.

The junta, realising they'd made the ultimate blunder by putting Greece's claim to Cyprus in jeopardy, removed Sampson and threw in the towel. However, the Turks continued to advance until they occupied the northern third of the island, forcing almost 200,000 Greek Cypriots to flee their homes for the safety of southern Cyprus.

After the Colonels

The army now called Karamanlis from Paris to clear up the mess in Greece. An election was arranged for November 1974 (won handsomely by Karamanlis' New Democracy party), the ban on communist parties was lifted, Andreas Papandreou (son of George) formed PASOK (the Panhellenic Socialist Union), and a plebiscite voted 69% against restoration of the monarchy.

(Ex-King Constantine, who now lives in London, didn't revisit Greece until the summer of 1993. The New Democracy government sent missile boats and a transport plane to follow his yacht. Nonetheless the ex-king said he and his family enjoyed the holiday, and he had no wish to overthrow the Greek constitution.)

Karamanlis' New Democracy (ND) party won the elections again in 1977, but his personal popularity began to decline. One of his biggest achievements before accepting the largely ceremonial post of president was to engineer Greece's entry into the European Community (EC), which involved jumping the queue ahead of other countries who had been waiting patiently to be accepted. On 1 January 1981 Greece became the 10th member of the EC.

The Socialist 1980s

In October 1981 Andreas Papandreou's PASOK party won the election with 48% of the votes, giving Greece its first socialist government. PASOK promised removal of US air bases and withdrawal from NATO.

Seven years into government, these promises remained unfulfilled (although US military presence was reduced), unemployment was high and reforms in education and welfare had been limited. Women's issues had fared better, though: the dowry system was abolished, abortion legalised, and civil marriage and divorce were implemented. The crunch came in 1988 when Papandreou's love affair with air hostess Dimitra Liani (whom he subsequently married) hit the headlines, and PASOK became embroiled in a financial scandal involving the Bank of Crete.

In July 1989 an unlikely coalition of conservatives and communists took over to implement a *katharsis* (campaign of purification) to investigate the scandal. In September it ruled that Papandreou and four former ministers be tried for embezzlement, telephone tapping and illegal grain sales. The trial of Papandreou came to an end in January 1992 with his acquittal on all accounts.

Into the 1990s

Elections in 1990 brought the ND back in power with a majority of only two seats, and with Constantine Mitsotakis as prime minister. Intent on redressing the country's economic problems of high inflation and high government spending, the government imposed austerity measures which included a wage freeze for civil servants and steep increases in public-utility costs and basic services. It also implemented a privatisation programme aimed at 780 state-controlled enterprises; OTE (the telecommunications company), electricity and Olympic Airways were first on the list. The government also cracked down on tax evasion, which is still so rife it's described as the nation's favourite pastime.

The austerity measures sparked off a

series of strikes in the public sector in mid-1990 and again in 1991 and 1992. The government's problems were compounded by an influx of Albanian refugees (see the People section later in this chapter), and the dispute over the name Macedonia for the southern republic of former Yugoslavia (see the Macedonia section in the Northern Greece chapter).

By late 1992 corruption allegations were being made against the government and it was claimed that Cretan-born Mitsotakis had a large, secret collection of Minoan art; in mid-1993 there were allegations of government telephone tapping. Former Mitsotakis supporters began to cut their losses: in June 1993 Antonis Samaras, the ND's former foreign minister, founded the Political Spring party and called upon ND members to join him. So many of them did that the ND lost its parliamentary majority and hence its capacity to govern.

An early election was called for October, in which Andreas Papandreou's PASOK party won 47% of the vote against 39% for ND and 5% for Political Spring. Because of the majority voting system, this translated into a handsome majority for PASOK in parliament. The victory was no surprise but the margin was, and showed the deep level of dissatisfaction with the government's austerity measures. The people chose to ignore

74-year-old Papandreou's heart condition and generally poor health, and the scandals that had plagued the closing stages of his government in the late 1980s.

On assuming office, Papandreou appointed his wife as chief of staff, his son George as deputy foreign minister, his wife's cousin as deputy minister of culture, and his personal physician as minister of health. He announced the renationalisation of public transport and an end to the privatisation of telecommunications, which made it seem unlikely he would be able to meet the EC's directives to cut the huge public debt.

MYTHOLOGY

Mythology was an integral part of the lives of all ancient peoples. The myths of Ancient Greece are the most familiar to us, for they are deeply entrenched in the consciousness of Western civilisation.

The myths were accounts of the lives of the deities whom the Greeks worshipped. The Greeks had many deities, including 12 principal ones, who lived on Mt Olympus. The myths are all things to all people – a rollicking good yarn, expressions of deep psychological insights, words of spine-tingling poetic beauty and food for the imagination. They serve a timeless universal need, and have inspired great literature, art and music, providing archetypes through

Demeter

Poseidon

Ares

Hestia

which we can learn much about the deeper motives of human behaviour.

No-one has the definitive answer as to why or how the myths came into being, but many are allegorical accounts of historical facts.

The Olympian family were a disparate lot despite being related. The next time you have a bowl of corn flakes give thanks to **Demeter** the goddess of vegetation. The English word 'cereal' for products of corn or edible grain derives from the goddess' Roman name, Ceres. In Greek the word for such products is *demetriaka*. Demeter was worshipped as the goddess of earth and fertility.

Poseidon, god of the sea and earthquakes, was most at home in the depths of the Aegean where he lived in a sumptuous golden palace. When he became angry (which was often) he would use his trident to create massive waves and floods. Ever intent upon expanding his domain, he challenged Dionysos for Naxos, Hera for Argos and Athena for Athens.

Ares, god of war, was a nasty piece of work – fiery tempered, bloodthirsty, brutal and violent. In contrast **Hestia**, the goddess of the hearth, symbol of security, happiness and hospitality, was as pure as driven snow. She spurned disputes and wars and swore to be a virgin forever.

Hera was not a principal deity; her job was a subservient one – she was Zeus' cupbearer.

Athena, the powerful goddess of wisdom and patron of Athens, is said to have been born (complete with helmet, armour and spear) from Zeus' head, with Hephaestus acting as midwife. Unlike Ares, she derived no pleasure from fighting, but preferred settling disputes peacefully using her wisdom; however, if need be she went valiantly into battle.

Hephaestus was worshipped for his matchless skills as a craftsman. When Zeus decided to punish men he asked Hephaestus to make a woman. So Hephaestus made Pandora from clay and water, and, as everyone knows, she had a box, from which sprang all the evils afflicting humankind.

Apart from one misdemeanour, Hephaestus' character seems to have been exemplary. During the Trojan War Athena asked the god to make her a new suit of armour. Poseidon, on hearing this, teased Hephaestus by saying that when Athena came to his forge she would expect him to make mad passionate love to her. As Athena wrested herself from the eager Hephaestus, he ejaculated against her thigh. She removed his seed with wool and threw it away, and Gaea, who happened to pass by, was inadvertently fertilised. When Gaea's unwanted offspring was born, Athena brought him up, and he eventually became King Erichthonius of Athens.

Hera

Athena

Hephaestus

Apollo

The 12 Principal Deities

Name	*Qualities*	*Attributes*
Zeus	supreme deity	thunderbolt
Hera	marriage, childbirth	cuckoo, peacock
Demeter	fertility	sheaf of wheat
Poseidon	sea, earthquakes	trident
Ares	war	armour
Hestia	domesticity	hearth
Athena	wisdom	owl
Hephaestus	fire, industry	hammer, anvil
Apollo	music, poetry	bow, lyre
Artemis	hunting, chastity	she-bear, stag
Hermes	commerce	winged sandals
Aphrodite	love, beauty	dove

Olympian Creation Myth

According to mythology the world was a great shapeless mass called Chaos. From Chaos came forth Gaea, the Mother Earth. She bore a son Uranus, the Firmament, and their subsequent union produced three 100-handed giants and three one-eyed Cyclopes. Gaea dearly loved her hideous offspring, but not so Uranus, who hurled them into Tartarus (the underworld).

The couple then produced the seven Titans, but Gaea still grieved for her other children. She asked the Titans to take vengeance upon their father, and free the 100-handed giants and Cyclopes. The Titans did as they were requested, castrating the hapless Uranus, but Kronos (the head Titan), after setting eyes on Gaea's hideous offspring, hurled them back into Tartarus, whereupon Gaea foretold that he (Kronos) would be usurped by one of his own offspring.

Kronos married his sister Rhea, but wary of his mother's warning, he swallowed every child Rhea bore him. When Rhea bore her sixth child, Zeus, she smuggled him to Crete, and gave Kronos a stone in place of the child, which he duly swallowed. Rhea hid the baby Zeus in the Dikteon cave in the care of three nymphs.

On reaching manhood, Zeus, determined to avenge his swallowed siblings, became Kronos' cupbearer and filled his cup with poison. Kronos drank from the cup, then disgorged first the stone and then his children Hestia, Demeter, Hera, Poseidon and Hades, all of whom were none the worse for their ordeal. Zeus, aided by his regurgitated brothers and sisters, deposed Kronos, and went to war against the Titans who wouldn't acknowledge him as chief god. Gaea, who still hadn't forgotten her imprisoned, beloved offspring, told Zeus he would only be victorious with the help of the Cyclopes and the 100-handed giants, so he released them from Tartarus.

The Cyclopes gave Zeus a thunderbolt, and the three 100-handed giants threw rocks at the Titans, who eventually retreated. Zeus banished Kronos, as well as all of the Titans except Atlas (Kronos' deputy), to a far-off land. Atlas was ordered to hold up the sky.

Mt Olympus became home sweet home for Zeus and his unruly and incestuous family. Zeus, taking a fancy to Hera, turned himself into a dishevelled cuckoo whom the unsuspecting Hera held to her bosom, whereupon Zeus violated her, and Hera reluctantly agreed to marry him. Their honeymoon on Samos lasted 300 years – could this explain Zeus' future infidelities? They had three children Ares, Hephaestus and Hebe. ■

Apollo, god of the sun, and **Artemis**, goddess of the moon, were the twins of Leto and Zeus. Many qualities were attributed to Apollo, for the Ancient Greeks believed that the sun not only gave physical light, but that its light was symbolic of mental illumination. Apollo was also worshipped as the god of music and song, which the ancients believed were only heard where there was light and security. Artemis was worshipped as the goddess of childbirth and protector of children; yet, paradoxically, she asked Zeus if he would grant her eternal virginity. She was also the protector of suckling animals, but loved to hunt stags!

Hermes was born of Maia, daughter of Atlas and one of Zeus' paramours. He had an upwardly mobile career. His first job was as protector of the animal kingdom. As the chief source of wealth was cattle, he therefore became the god of wealth. However, as civilisation advanced, trade replaced cattle as the main source of wealth, so Hermes became god of trade. However, a prerequisite for good trade was good commerce, so he became the god of commerce. To progress in commerce a merchant needed to be shrewd, so this attribute was assigned to Hermes. Later it was realised that to excel in commerce one needed to use the art of persuasion, so Hermes was promoted to god of oratory.

Last but not least of the 12 principal deities was the beautiful **Aphrodite**, goddess of love, who rose naked out of the sea. Her *tour de force* was her magic girdle which made everyone fall in love with its wearer. The girdle meant she was constantly pursued by both gods and goddesses – the gods because they wanted to make love to her, the goddesses because they wanted to borrow the girdle. Zeus became so fed up with her promiscuity that he married her off to Hephaestus, the ugliest of the gods.

Hades never made it to Mt Olympus, but his job was nevertheless an important one. Hades' dominion was the vast and mysterious underworld (Tartarus). He was the benevolent god who gave fertility to vegetation and who yielded precious stones and metals. But he was also the feared guardian of a dark realm, from which no-one, having once journeyed, ever returned.

A number of the countless lesser gods were powerful but never made it to Zeus' inner circle. Pan, the son of Hermes, was born with horns, beard, tail and goat legs. His ugliness so amused the other gods that eventually he escaped to Arcadia where he danced, played his shepherd's pipe and watched over the pastures, shepherds and herds. Dionysos, son of Hera and Zeus, was even more hideous at birth – horned and crowned with serpents. His parents boiled

Artemis

Hermes

Aphrodite

him in a cauldron, but he was rescued by Rhea, and banished to Mt Nysa in Libya where he invented wine. He eventually returned to Greece where he organised drunken revelries and married Ariadne, daughter of King Minos.

In addition to the gods the Ancient Greeks revered many beings who had probably once been mortal, such as King Minos, Theseus and Erichthonius. Intermediaries between gods and humans, such as the satyrs, also appear in the myths. The satyrs lived in woods and had goat horns and tails; they worshipped the god Dionysos, so, appropriately, they spent much of their time drinking and dancing. Nymphs lived in secluded valleys and grottoes and occupied themselves with spinning, weaving, bathing, singing and dancing – Pan found them irresistible. The Muses, of which there were nine, were nymphs of the mountain springs; they were believed to inspire poets, artists and musicians.

Finally, mention should be made of the three crones Tisiphone, Aledo and Megara – sometimes called the Furies – whose job it was to deal with grievances from mortals, and punish wrongdoers. They had dogs' heads, snakes' hair, bloodshot eyes, coal black bodies and bats' wings and carried brass-studded scourges. It was considered unlucky to call them by name – they had to be called the Eumenides – the kindly ones!

GEOGRAPHY

Greece, at the southern extremity of the Balkan peninsula, is the only member of the EC without a land frontier with another member. To the north, Greece has land borders with Albania, Macedonia and Bulgaria, and to the east with Turkey.

Greece consists of a peninsula and about 1400 islands, of which 169 are inhabited. The land mass is 131,900 sq km and Greek territorial waters occupy 400,000 sq km. The islands are divided into six groups: the Cyclades, the Dodecanese, the islands of the North-Eastern Aegean, the Sporades and the Saronic Gulf islands. The two largest islands, Crete and Evia, do not belong to any group. In Greece, no area is much more than 100 km from the sea. The much indented coastline has a total length of 15,020 km.

Roughly four-fifths of Greece is mountainous, with most of the land over 1500 metres above sea level. The Pindos range, which is an offshoot of the Dinaric Alps, runs north to south through the peninsula, and is known as the backbone of Greece. The mountains of the Peloponnese and Crete are part of the same formation. The marked variety of the terrain above water continues

Pan (right)   Dionysos   The Procession of Dionysos and Ariadne

underwater along the sea bed, which millions of years ago formed a projection of the land. The highest mountain is Mt Olympus (2917 metres). Greece does not have many rivers, and none which are navigable. The largest ones are utilised for hydro-electricity and irrigation. The five principal rivers are the Pinios, Akheloos, Aliakmoni, Aoos and Arakhthos, all of which have their source in the Pindos range in Epiros. The long plains of the river valleys, and those between the mountains and the coast, are the only low-lands. The mountainous terrain, dry climate and poor quality soil restricts agriculture to less than a quarter of the land. Greece is, however, rich in minerals, with reserves of oil, manganese, bauxite and lignite.

A recent report by the Greek Ministry of Agriculture stated that due to denudation of the forests, 85 cubic metres of soil was washed away from hill slopes per annum. Epiros and Macedonia, in Northern Greece, still have extensive forests; the denudation and the ensuing soil erosion occurs from Thessaly southwards. This is partly because the flora here is inclined to be of highly inflammable pinewoods and resinous evergreen shrubs.

Ancient Greece had extensive forests, but since time immemorial grazing by goats has been a cause of forest depletion. Also, up until this century, there was widespread felling of trees for boat building. But the denudation worsened as forests were cut down for building and industrial purposes, and until recently, for fire wood. The main cause in recent years has been forest fires – both the work of arsonists and those which have been accidentally lit; latest statistics show that 25,000 hectares is burned every year. The Ministry of Agriculture has embarked on a reafforestation programme, citing Israel, where barren wasteland has been transformed into orchards and woodland, as an example of what can be achieved.

CLIMATE

The climatic figures in the table below are for Athens, but Greece has regional variations in climate (see the climate charts on the following page). Southern Greece may be up to 4°C warmer than the north.

FLORA & FAUNA

Greece is endowed with a variety of flora unrivalled in Europe. Wild flowers in Greece are spectacular. There are over 6000 species, including 100 varieties of orchids, and some species which are unique. One factor which encourages the profusion of wild flowers in Greece is the limited use of chemical fertiliser – up to three times less than most other European countries.

The region with the most wild flowers is the arid and mountainous Mani area in the Peloponnese. During spring in this region, the valleys are carpeted with wild flowers which seem to sprout even from the rocks. This profusion is due to the area's aridity, which means very little land is cultivated, so the landscape is left in a wild state for nature

	Jan	Feb	Mar	Apr	May	Jun
Daylight hours/day	10	11	13	14	15	16
Average temperature	8	9	10	15	20	25
Rainfall mm/month	54	46	32	21	19	12
Sunshine hours/day	5	5	7	9	11	15
	Jul	Aug	Sep	Oct	Nov	Dec
Daylight hours/day	15	13	12	11	10	10
Average temperature	28	28	23	18	14	10
Rainfall mm/month	4	8	16	44	63	72
Sunshine hours/day	12	11	9	6	5	4

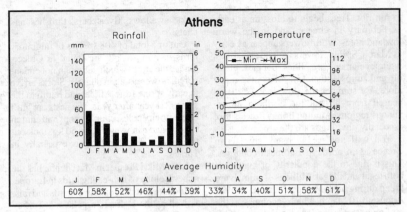

Athens

Rainfall

Temperature

Average Humidity

J	F	M	A	M	J	J	A	S	O	N	D
60%	58%	52%	46%	44%	39%	33%	34%	40%	51%	58%	61%

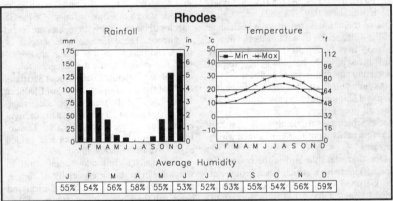

Rhodes

Rainfall

Temperature

Average Humidity

J	F	M	A	M	J	J	A	S	O	N	D
55%	54%	56%	58%	55%	53%	52%	53%	55%	54%	56%	59%

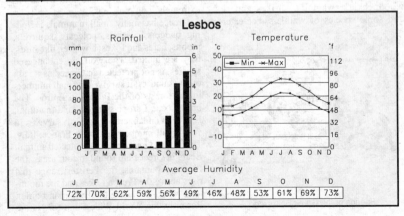

Lesbos

Rainfall

Temperature

Average Humidity

J	F	M	A	M	J	J	A	S	O	N	D
72%	70%	62%	59%	56%	49%	46%	48%	53%	61%	69%	73%

to run riot. Trees begin to blossom as early as February in Greece, and in the warm lowland areas, wild flowers appear as early as March. Spring flowers include anemones, white cyclamens, iris, lilies, poppies, gladioli and tulips – there are of course many more. By summer the flowers have disappeared from all but the northern mountainous regions. Autumn brings flowers too; especially ubiquitous are the crocuses.

You will not see as many animals in Greece as in northern European countries. This is due to the popularity of hunting – both legal and illegal. Millions of animals are killed during the long 'open' season, from 20 August to 10 March, which encompasses the bird migratory period. At the Hellenic Wildlife Hospital (☎ 0297-22 882), on Aegina, 80% of the animals treated have been shot. Of the 400 species of wild birds in Greece, only 35 may be legally hunted, but many birds brought to the hospital belong to protected and sometimes rare species.

As far as birds are concerned, Greece has the usual ubiquitous little brown jobs that are seen all over Europe. But it also has some species which are sufficiently distinctive and therefore easily identifiable, and some which are rare.

One unmistakable bird is the hoopoe (a type of kingfisher), which has a prominent black-tipped crest and black and white striped wings. Greece has most species of woodpeckers, wagtails, shrikes and tits and some species of warblers, bee-eaters, larks, swallows, flycatchers, thrushes and chats.

Out of a total of 408 species of migratory birds in Europe, 240 are found in Greece. One is the stork, which, although not endangered, is decreasing in number. Storks arrive in early spring from Africa, and return to the same nest year after year. The nests are built on electricity poles, chimney tops and church towers, and can weigh up to 50 kg; look out for them in northern Greece, especially in Thrace.

Lake Mikri Prespa, in Macedonia, has the richest colony of fish-eating birds in Europe, including egrets, herons cormorants and ibis, as well as the Dalmation pelican – Turkey and Greece are now the only countries in Europe where this bird is found. Of the 38 species of birds of prey, 36 species are found in Greece. These include nine species of hawk and falcon, most of which are migratory. Amongst these are the Peregrine falcon and the rare Eleonora falcon. About 350 pairs (60% of the world's population) of Eleonora falcons nest on the remote Sporades island of Piperi. The last 15 surviving pairs of royal eagles nest at the Evros delta in Thrace. Egyptian and Griffon vultures and golden eagles live in the mountainous regions.

Two easily identifiable wading birds to watch for in wetlands, especially in Thrace, are the avocet, which has a long upcurved beak, and the black-winged stilt, which has extremely long pink legs.

Greece has many small mammals including badgers, weasels, polecats, squirrels, rabbits, hares and foxes; however, like birds, they are hunted. The wolf, an endangered species, is not protected in Greece as it is in other countries; it survives in small numbers in the forests of the Pindos in Epiros. The brown bear, Europe's largest land mammal, is also an endangered species. It survives in very small numbers in Spain, France, Italy, Turkey and Greece and is a protected animal. Bears in Greece are found in four areas: the Pindos mountains, the Peristeri range that rises above the Prespa Lakes and the mountains which lie along the Bulgarian border. Recently, the World Wide Fund for Nature

1988: Σώστε την ελληνική ΑΡΚΟΥΔΑ....

οι φίλοι της ελληνικής ΑΡΚΟΥΔΑΣ

Friends of the Greek Bears logo

(WWF) ran a project in the Pindos range to research ways to guarantee the bears' survival in Greece.

One disgraceful practice which still occasionally occurs in Greece (but not to the extent that it does in Turkey) is the capturing of bear cubs to be trained as dancing bears. The mother bear is killed and her cub is trained to dance. The bear is often kept chained up in poor conditions with a ring through its nose and upper lip. Two organisations, the UK-based Libearté and the Greek Arcturos are working with local authorities to stamp out this illegal practice.

One of the pleasures of island hopping in Greece is watching the dolphins as they follow the boats. Although there are many dolphins in the Aegean, the striped dolphins have recently been victims of *murbilivirus* – a sickness which affects the immune system. Research into the virus is being carried out in the Netherlands.

Europe's rarest mammal, the monk seal, was once very common in the Mediterranean, but it's now on the brink of extinction in Europe – it survives in slightly larger numbers in the Hawaiian islands. There are only about 350 left in Europe, all of which live in Greece: about 30 in the Ionian Sea and the rest in the Aegean. Until recently the seals were killed by fisherman because they damaged fishing nets. The monk seal requires a gently sloping sandy beach on which to give birth; unfortunately tourists

Loggerhead turtle digging her nest

'require' these beaches for sunbathing, so fewer and fewer are available for the seals. The Hellenic Society for the Study & Protection of the Monk Seal (☎ 01-364 4164), Solomnou 35, Athens 10682, has a seal rescue centre on Alonissos, and the WWF funds seal-watch projects on Kefallonia, Ithaki and Lefkada.

The waters around Zakynthos and Kefallonia are home to the last large sea turtle colony in Europe, that of the loggerhead turtle. Each female turtle comes onto land to lay her eggs, which she buries in the sand. After hatching, the baby turtles have to make their way to the sea, but only three or four make the distance, faced not only with natural hazards, but cars, discos and beach parties. For details on how you can avoid contributing to the loggerhead's demise, see the Ionian Islands chapter. Other reptiles you will come across in Greece are frogs, lizards and tortoises. For information on snakes in Greece see the Health section in the Facts for the Visitor chapter.

Greece's national parks are the Vikos-Aoos Park in Epiros, the Olympus National Park on the borders of Thessaly and Macedonia, the Parnassos and Iti National Parks in Central Greece and the Parnitha National Park in Attica. All of these have refuges and some have marked hiking trails. Greece also has a National Marine Park off the coast of Alonissos in the Sporades.

Save Our Seals logo

Greece is – belatedly – becoming environmentally conscious, although, regrettably, it is often a case of closing the gate after the horse has bolted. The various societies for animal protection in Greece are listed in the *Athenian* magazine.

GOVERNMENT

Since 1975, democratic Greece has been a parliamentary republic with a president as head of state. The president and parliament, which has 300 deputies, have joint legislative power. The government is made up of a cabinet comprising a prime minister and 22 ministers.

Greece is divided into regions and island groups. The regions of the mainland are the Peloponnese, Central Greece (officially called Sterea Ellada), Epiros, Thessaly, Macedonia and Thrace. The island groups are the Cyclades, Dodecanese, North-Eastern Aegean, Sporades and Saronic Gulf, all in the Aegean Sea, and the Ionian, which is in the Ionian Sea. The large islands of Evia and Crete do not belong to any group. For administrative purposes these regions and groups are divided into prefectures (*nomos* in Greek).

ECONOMY

Traditionally, Greece is an agricultural country, but the importance of agriculture to the economy has declined rapidly since WW II. Some 43% of the workforce are now employed in services (contributing 55% of GDP), 29% in agriculture (contributing 16%), and 28% in industry (contributing 29%). Tourism is by far the biggest industry; shipping comes next. The eight million tourists who visit Greece each year contribute about about US$2.5 billion to the economy.

The previous government's austerity measures went down like a lead balloon with the Greek people, leading to a huge election victory for Andreas Papandreou's opposition PASOK party in the October 1993 general elections. But this hasn't solved the problem that austerity measures are still needed if Greece is to comply with EC economic directives, which are a condition for achieving integration with the more affluent community members. The measures are also likely to push up unemployment, which is officially running at 8% but is unofficially estimated to be several per cent higher. Greece has the second-lowest income per capita of all the EC countries after Portugal.

Inflation and the state budget deficit have become a bigger problem than ever as the unification of Europe draws near. Inflation is running at more than three times the EC average, and the budget deficit, which is threatening to get out of control at 14.5% of GDP, stands in stark contrast to the 5% demanded by the EC.

POPULATION

The population of Greece is about 10 million; about 88% live on the mainland. The population of the city of Athens is 885,800 but the population of greater Athens, which encompasses almost the whole Attic basin, is over three million. The other large cities and their populations are Thessaloniki (406,500), Piraeus (196,400), Patras (142,200) and Iraklion (102,400).

PEOPLE

It is doubtful that any Greek alive today is directly descended to an Ancient Greek. Contemporary Greeks are a mixture of all of the invaders who have occupied the country since ancient times. Today, there are a number of distinct ethnic minorities living in the country.

Roman Catholics, who originate from the Genoese and Franks, live mostly in the Cyclades, especially on the island of Syros, where they make up 40% of the population. The Franks dominated the island from 1207 AD to Ottoman times.

About 300,000 Muslims live in western Thrace; they are ethnic Turks who were exempt from the population exchange of 1923. There are also small numbers of Turks on Kos and Rhodes which, along with the rest of the Dodecanese, did not become part of Greece until 1947.

There are small Jewish communities in several large towns. In Ioannina, Larissa, Halkidi and Rhodes they date back to the

Roman era, and in Thessaloniki, Kavala and Didimotikho, from the 15th-century exiles from Spain and Portugal. In 1429, 20,000 exiled Jews arrived in Thessaloniki and by the 16th century they constituted the major part of the population. In 1941 the Germans entered Thessaloniki and rounded up 46,000 Jews who were taken by cattle car to Auschwitz, most never to return. These Jews consisted of more than half the entire Jewish population of Greece and 90% of Thessaloniki's Jews. The small number of Jews in Athens are mostly German Jews who came over with King Otho in the 1830s. Today there are only about 5000 Jews living in Greece.

Very small numbers of Vlach and Sarakatsani shepherds live a semi-nomadic existence in Epiros. They take their flocks to the high ground in summer and return to the valleys in winter. The Vlachs originate from the country which is now Romania; the origins of the Sarakatsani are uncertain.

You will come across Gypsies everywhere in Greece, but especially in Macedonia, Thessaly and Thrace. There are large communities of Gypsies in the Thracian towns of Alexandroupolis and Didimotikho.

The shedding of years of hardline Stalinism and isolation in Albania have left that country in turmoil and the people in a state of abject poverty. Consequently, thousands of Albanians have been illegally crossing the poorly guarded border post into Greece. Police deported 90,000 in 1991, but many returned. In early 1993, police estimated there were about 130,000 illegal Albanians in Greece, but other sources put the number as high as 600,000. The Greek government claims that the Albanian authorities are encouraging this exodus, and the government in Tirana accuses Greece of violating human rights in its treatment of the refugees.

EDUCATION

State education for Greek children begins at the age of seven, but most Greeks, if they can afford to, send their children to a private kindergarten at the age of five. Primary school classes are larger than those in most European countries -- usually 30 to 35 children. Primary school hours are short (8 am to 1 pm), but children get a lot of homework.

At 11 years of age children enter the *gymnasio*, and at 15 they may leave school, or enter the *lykeio*, from where they take university entrance examinations. Although there is a high percentage of literacy, many parents and pupils are dissatisfied with the education system, especially beyond primary level. The private sector therefore flourishes, and even relatively poor parents struggle to send their children to one of the country's 5000 *frontistiria* (intensive coaching colleges for the teaching of English). Parents deem this necessary, as secondary school children receive only two hours a week tuition in English in the state schools. Parents complain that the education system is grossly underfunded, and resembles that of Third World countries. The main complaint is lack of modern teaching aids in both gymnasia and lykeio.

Grievances reached a height in 1991, when lykeio students staged a series of sit-ins in schools throughout the country, and organised protest marches. In 1992, gymnasia pupils followed suit, and the government responded by making proposals which called for stricter discipline and a more demanding curriculum. More sit-ins followed, and in the end the government changed its plans and is currently reassessing the situation.

Boy reciting Homer from a scroll held by his teacher

ARTS

The origins of many of the arts in modern Europe can be traced back to Ancient Greece.

Art & Architecture

The marble figurines of the Cycladic Age were regarded as crude and primitive in the 19th century, but in the early 20th century these elegant simple forms became sources of inspiration for Brancusi, Epstein, Modigliani and Picasso. The largest collection of these figurines is housed in the Cycladic & Ancient Greek Art Museum in Athens (see the Athens chapter for details about this museum).

The magnificent vibrant frescoes with which the Minoans decorated their palaces reveal a highly developed sense of colour and design. The best examples of these are the Akrotiri collection in the National Archaeological Museum in Athens. Columns have always been a feature of European architecture, and although the Ancient Egyptians used columns before the Greeks, it is Greek columns which have most influenced European architects. During Archaic and Classical times the columns of Greek temples developed into Doric, Ionic and Corinthian orders. Doric columns, which first appeared in the 7th century, did not have a base, and their capitals consisted of a circular support, beneath a square slab. Ionic columns, which first appeared in the 6th century, had ornate bases and voluted capitals. Corinthian columns, which first appeared in the 5th century, were fluted, with quite elaborate capitals which resembled leaves.

During the Archaic period the monumental sculptures of standing male *kouros* and female *kore* evolved. They were characterised by stiff formal poses, and countenances with enigmatic smiles. Although still highly idealised, figures in the 5th century were depicted in more naturalistic poses. The marble, gold and ivory (chryselephantine) statues developed at this time. The most famous of these was *Pallas Athena*, which took pride of place in the Parthenon. By the 4th century both the poses and countenances of sculpted figures had become highly expressive.

In Byzantine times, art was restricted to

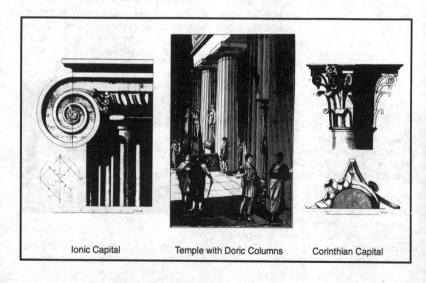

Ionic Capital   Temple with Doric Columns   Corinthian Capital

the painting of icons, mosaics and fresco painting, all of which were adornments in churches. Fresco painting superseded mosaics in the 13th century when Byzantium was in decline and mosaics became too costly. All Greek Orthodox churches are festooned with icons, which are small paintings of holy figures and saints; in Greek the word icon means image. The painting of an icon is considered a sacred task, and is revered not for its artistic merit, but for the sacredness of the subject and of the person who painted it. Even so, one of the most highly regarded painters of the Middle Ages, Domenikos Theotokopoulos (El Greco), reaped his inspiration from icon paintings.

As with art, religion was also the focus of architecture during Byzantine times. The basic structure of a Greek Orthodox church is a circular dome upon a square. By the 11th century, churches had come to be regarded as symbols of the Heavenly Order, so were embellished with images of Christ as Panocrator on the dome, the loftiest part of the church, with the apostles encircling its base.

After Independence, King Otho embarked upon a rebuilding programme in which neoclassical architecture was prevalent. These beautiful buildings with pastel hued façades, wrought-iron balconies and porches of Ionic columns were being replaced with characterless concrete blocks during the 1960s. However, in recent years, strict building laws have been imposed, and many of the surviving neoclassical buildings have been restored, and new ones in neoclassical style have been erected.

After Independence the development of the visual arts fell into three distinct categories:

Kouros

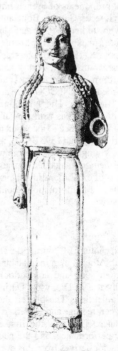

Kore

icon painting, folk or naive painting and mainstream European. Icon painting continues in a timeless tradition. The most renowned naive painter is Theophilos (1873-1934), who was born on Lesbos, but lived most of his life in Volos and Athens. The best examples of his work can be seen at the Theophilos Museum in Ano Volos.

Nikos Hadzikyriakos-Ghikas (born 1906) is the most highly acclaimed of contemporary Greek artists. He studied at the Sorbonne and has exhibited in London, Paris, New York, Athens, Berlin, Milan and elsewhere, and has works in the Tate Gallery, Musée d'Art Moderne, and the Metropolitan Museum. Ghikas' paintings are a highly personal and lyrical style of cubism. Other major 20th-century Greek painters are Spiros Papaloukas (1892-1957) and Constantinos Maleas (1879-1928), who were the foremost proponents of French Impressionism in Greece; George Bouzianis (1885-1959), who studied in Paris and Munich and was an expressionist painter; Nikos Engonopoulos (1910-86), who was Greece's pre-eminent surrealist; and Yiannis Speropoulos (born 1912), an abstract painter who was awarded the UNESCO prize at the 1960 Venice Biennale. The National Picture Gallery in Athens has works by all of these artists. One of Greece's first women painters was Maria Dessyla (1893-1987), and many emerging young Greek artists are women.

The *Athenian* magazine carries listings and revues of exhibitions in Athens, and is a good source of information about up and coming artists.

Drama

In the 6th century BC, during the Dionysion festival in Athens, men in goatskins used to take part in song and competitions at the ancient theatre of Dionysos. During one of these competitions Thespis left the ensemble, took centre stage and embarked on a solo performance. This was the first ever true dramatic performance, and the name Thespian for actor derives from this event.

Aeschylus (525-456 BC) is the so-called 'father of tragedy'; his best known work is *Oresteia* trilogy. Sophocles (496-406 BC) is regarded as the greatest tragedian. He is thought to have written over 100 plays, of which only seven major works survive. These include *Ajax*, *Antigone*, *Electra*, *Trachiniae* and his most famous play, *Oedipus Rex*. His plays dealt mainly with tales from mythology, and consisted of complex plots, and highly contrasting characters. Sophocles won first prize 18 times at the Dionysion festival, beating Aeschylus in 468 BC, whereupon Aeschylus went off to Sicily in a huff.

Euripides (485-406 BC), another famous tragedian, was more popular with the people than either Aeschylus or Sophocles, as his plots were considered more exciting. He wrote 80 plays of which 19 are extant (although one, *Rhesus*, is disputed). His most famous works are *Medea*, *Andromache*, *Orestias* and *Bacchae*. Euripides won the Dionysion festival competition five times. Aristophanes (427-387 BC) in contrast wrote comedies – often ribald – which dealt with topical issues. His play *The Wasp* ridicules Athenians who went to law over trivialities; *The Birds* pokes fun at Athenian gullibility towards charlatans; and *Plutus* deals with the unfair distribution of wealth. You can see plays by the Ancient Greek playwrights at the Athens and Epidaurus festivals (see the Athens and Peloponnese chapters for details), and at various other festivals around the country.

Film

Greeks of today are avid cinema goers, although most of the films shown are North American or British. The Greek film industry is in the doldrums. This is largely due to inadequate government funding, which is compounded by the type of films the Greeks produce. Greek films have a reputation for being slow moving, with complex themes involving symbolism and ambiguities. Although they are well made and the cinematography is often outstanding, they are too avant-garde to have mass appeal.

Greece's most acclaimed film director is

Theodore Angelopoulos, whose films include *The Beekeeper*, *Alexander the Great*, *Travelling Players*, *Landscapes in the Mist* and *The Hesitant Step of the Stork*. All have received awards at both national and international festivals.

Literature

The first, and greatest, Ancient Greek writer was Homer, author of the *Iliad* and *Odyssey*. Nothing is known of Homer's life or where or when he lived, or whether, as it is alleged, he was blind. The historian Herodotus placed the date of Homer as the 9th century BC, and no scholar since has proved or disproved this.

Herodotus was the author of the first historical work about Western civilisation. However, because of his highly subjective account of the Persian Wars he is regarded as the 'father of lies' as well as the 'father of history'. The historian Thucydides was more objective in his approach, but took a high moral stance. He wrote an account of the Peloponnesian Wars, and also the famous *Melian Dialogue*, which chronicles the talks between the Athenians and Melians prior to the Athenian siege of Melos. Pindar (518-

The Legacy of the Ancient Greek Philosophers

Western civilisation is indebted to the Ancient Greek philosophers – it is from the thoughts and deliberations of philosophers such as Socrates, Plato and Aristotle that our intellectual and philosophical heritage is derived. In an endeavour to arrive at some form of a universal or absolute knowledge, Plato recorded dialogues on perception and knowledge allegedly spoken by his master, Socrates. Our knowledge of Socrates is limited to the writings of his contemporaries, in particular, Plato – Socrates himself recorded nothing in writing, confining his teachings to conversations, or discourses.

Philosophical enquiry in Greece, and particularly Athens, was concerned with the pursuit of reason and truth, or an enquiry into the nature of existence. It was an attempt to find rational answers for phenomena which had previously been explained by a recourse to myths.

Athens in the 5th century BC was experiencing something of an intellectual revolution. A consequence of the formation of the city-states was that citizens were actively encouraged to engage in intellectual enquiry and to consider and debate the political, cultural and moral affairs which affected the whole community. This intellectual milieu gave rise to the Sophists. The Sophists were itinerant teachers of oratory who were concerned with *ideas*. They promoted lively debates, using their finely honed skills in the art of oratory to consider the concerns of the day – the nature of right and wrong, the value (or otherwise) of democracy and similar philosophical pursuits. Their craftily constructed arguments and clever dialogue frequently confounded their listeners: the Sophists had the capacity to render what would normally be considered sound, unsound, and vice versa, causing some disquiet amongst the populace.

Into this intellectual ferment arrived Socrates. Socrates employed his phenomenal intellect and wisdom to counter the arguments of the Sophists. His form of dialogue has become known as the dialectic. This entailed playing something of a devil's advocate. The hapless opponent who took on Socrates' genius and wit would find to their delight the great philosopher conceding to their arguments – only to discover that, as Socrates broke their argument down into smaller segments, the path of their enquiry would lead, almost inevitably, to an absurdity.

Socrates was primarily concerned with a quest for absolute truth, as opposed to the relativism of the Sophists, who argued that circumstances determined the nature of right and wrong. Socrates alleged that we do not perceive with our sense organs, but through them. Our sense organs are simply the instruments of our perception. There must, therefore, Socrates concluded, be some other faculty of which we are possessed which enables us to assess sense data. This, Socrates concluded, was the mind, or soul.

Socrates was extremely unpopular with some of his contemporaries, who charged him with corrupting the youth of Athens and ridiculing the structures and premises on which society was based. He was brought to trial in 399 BC, convicted, and forced to drink hemlock, his death a consequence of his conviction that only by a search for absolute truth can we attain virtue. ■

438 BC) is regarded as the pre-eminent lyric poet of Ancient Greece. He was commissioned to recite his odes at the Olympic Games. The greatest writers of love poetry were Sappho and Alcaeus, both of whom lived on Lesbos in the 5th century. Sappho's poetic descriptions of her affections for other women gave rise to the term lesbianism.

In Byzantine times, poetry, like all of the arts, was of a religious nature. During Ottoman rule poetry was inextricably linked with folk songs, which were not written down, but endured through an oral tradition. Many of these songs were composed by the klephts, and told of the harshness of life in the mountains, and of their uprisings against the Turks.

Dionysios Solomos (1798-1857) and Andreas Kalvos (1796-1869), who were both born on Zakynthos, are regarded as the first modern Greek poets. Solomos' work was heavily nationalistic and his *Hymn to Freedom* became the Greek national anthem. At this time there were heated debates amongst writers, politicians and educators about whether the official language should be demotiki or katharevousa. Demotic was the spoken language of the people and katharevousa was an artificial language loosely based on Ancient Greek. Almost all writers favoured demotic, and from the time of Solomos, most wrote only in that language. The highly acclaimed poet Constantine Cavafy (1863-1933) was less concerned with nationalism, being a resident of Alexandria, in Egypt; he wrote many love poems.

The most renowned 20th-century Greek poets are George Seferis (1900-71), who won the Nobel prize in 1963, and Odysseus Elytis (born 1911), who won the same prize in 1979. Seferis drew his inspiration from the Greek myths, whereas Elytis' work is surreal. Angelos Sikelianos (1884-1951) was another poet who drew inspiration from Ancient Greece, particularly Delphi, where he lived. His poetry is highly evocative, and includes incantatory verses, emulating the Delphic oracle. Yiannis Ritsos is another highly acclaimed Greek poet; his work draws on many aspects of Greece – the landscape, mythology and social issues. The most celebrated 20th-century Greek novelist is Nikos Kazantzakis. See the Books & Maps section in the Facts for the Visitor chapter for a commentary on his works.

Music & Dance

The folk dances which you will see performed in Greece today, derive from the ritualistic dances which were performed in Ancient Greek temples. One of these dances, the *syrtos*, is depicted on Ancient Greek vases, and there are references to dances in Homer's works. Many Greek folk dances, including the syrtos, are based on a circle formation, which derives from ancient times, when dancers formed a circle in order to seal themselves off from evil influences.

Each region of Greece has its own dances, but one dance you'll see performed everywhere is the *kalamatiano* which originated in Kalamata in the Peloponnese. Chances are you won't be in Greece long before you are asked to join in the kalamatiano – it's the

Greek dancers

dance where dancers stand in a row with their hands on one anothers' shoulders.

Singing, and the playing of musical instruments, like dance, have been an integral part of life in Greece since ancient times. Cycladic figurines holding musical instruments resembling harps and flutes date back to 2000 BC. Musical instruments of Ancient Greece included the lyre, lute, *piktis* (pipes), *kroupeza* (a percussion instrument), *kithara* (a stringed instrument), *aulos* (a wind instrument), *barbitos* (similar to a violincello) and the *magadio* (similar to a harp).

If Ancient Greeks did not have a musical instrument to accompany their songs they imitated the sound of one. It is believed that unaccompanied Byzantine choral singing derived from this custom.

The *bouzouki*, which you will hear everywhere in Greece, is a mandolin-like instrument similar to the Turkish *saz* and *baglama*. It is one of the main instruments of *rembetika* music – the Greek equivalent to the American Blues. The name rembetika may come from the Turkish word *rembet* which means outlaw. Opinions differ as to the origins of rembetika, but it is probably a hybrid of several different types of music. One source was the music which emerged in the 1870s in the 'low life' cafés called *tekédes* (hashish dens), of urban areas, and especially ports. Another source was the Arabo-Persian music played in sophisticated Middle Eastern music cafés *(café amán)* in the 19th century. Rembetika was popularised in Greece by the refugees from Asia Minor.

The songs which emerged from the tekédes had themes concerning hashish, prison life, gambling, knife fights etc, whereas café amán music had themes of erotic love. These all came together in the music of the refugees, from which a subculture of rebels, called *manges*, emerged. The *manges* wore showy clothes even though they lived in extreme poverty. They worked long hours in menial jobs, and spent their eve-

nings in the tekédes, smoking hashish and singing and dancing. Although hashish was illegal, the law was rarely enforced until Metaxas did his 'clean up' job in 1936. It was in a teké in Piraeus that Markos Vamvakaris, now acknowledged as the greatest *rembetis*, was discovered by a recording company in the 1930s.

Metaxas' censorship meant that themes of hashish, prison, gambling and the like disappeared from recordings of rembetika in the late 1930s, but continued clandestinely in some tekédes. This polarised the music, and the recorded stuff, stripped of its 'meaty' themes and language, became insipid and bourgeois; it even adopted another name – *laiko tragoudi* – to disassociate it from the illegal stuff. WW II brought a halt to recording, but a number of composers appeared at this time, probably inspired by hardship. Amongst them were Apostolos Kaldaras, Yiannis Papaioanou, Yiorgos Mitsakis and Manolis Hiotis, and one of the greatest women rembetika singers, Sotiria Bellou.

During the 1950s and 1960s rembetika became increasingly popular, but less and less authentic; it had become glitzy and commercialised. But Mikis Theodorakis and Manos Hadzidakis, two outstanding composers of Greek popular music (including rembetika), appeared at this time. The best of Theodorakis' work is the music which he set to the poetry of Seferis, Elytis and Ritsos.

During the junta years, many rembetika clubs were closed down, but in the 1980s there was a revived interest in genuine rembetika – particularly amongst students and intellectuals – and a number of clubs have opened in Athens. These clubs play host to many rembetika greats, such as Sotiria Bellou, as well as newcomers to the scene.

Since Independence Greece has followed mainstream developments in classical music. Performances by both national and international musicians may be heard at the Athens Concert Hall.

CULTURE
Traditional Lifestyle
Greece is steeped in traditional customs. Name days (celebrated rather than birthdays), weddings and funerals all have great significance. On someone's name day an open house policy is adopted and refreshments are served to wellwishers who stop by to give gifts. Weddings are highly festive occasions, with dancing, feasting and drinking sometimes continuing for days.

Greeks tend to be more superstitious than other Europeans. Tuesday is considered an unlucky day because on that day the Byzantine Empire fell to the Ottoman Turks. Many Greeks will not sign an important transaction, get married or begin a trip on that day. Greeks also believe in the 'evil eye', a superstition prevalent in many Middle Eastern countries. If someone is the victim of the evil eye, then bad luck will befall them. The bad luck is the result of someone's jealousy, therefore one should avoid being too complementary about things of beauty, especially new born babies. To ward off the 'evil eye', Greeks often wear a piece of blue glass, resembling an eye, on a chain around their necks.

Avoiding Offence
The Greeks' reputation for hospitality is not a myth. Greece is probably the only country in Europe where you may be invited into a stranger's home for coffee, a meal or even to spend the night. This can often lead to a feeling of uneasiness in the recipient if the host is poor, but to offer money is considered offensive. The most acceptable way of saying thank you is through a gift, perhaps to a child in the family. A similar situation arises if you go out for a meal with Greeks; the bill is not shared as in northern European countries, but paid by the host.

When drinking wine it is the custom to only half fill the glass. It is bad manners to empty the glass, so it must be constantly replenished. When visiting someone you will be offered coffee and it is bad manners to refuse. You will also be given a glass of water and perhaps a small serve of preserves. It is the custom to drink the water, then eat the preserves and then drink the coffee.

Personal questions are not considered rude in Greece, and if you react as if they are you will be the one causing offence. You will be inundated with queries about your age, salary, marital status etc – expect commiserations if you are over 25 and not married!

If you go into a *kafeneion*, *taverna*, shop or similar it is the custom to greet the waiters or assistant with *ka-li-ME-ra* (good day) or *ka-li-sp-ER-a* (good evening) – likewise if you meet someone in the street.

You may have come to Greece for sun, sand and sea, but if you want to bare all, other than on a designated nude beach, remember that Greece is a traditional country, so take care not to offend the locals.

Sport
Greek men are football and basketball mad, both as spectators and participants. If you happen to be eating in a taverna on a night when a 'big' match is being televised, expect indifferent service.

RELIGION
About 97% of Greeks belong to the Greek Orthodox Church. The rest of the population is split between Roman Catholic, Jewish and Muslim. Philipi, in Macedonia, is reputedly the first place in Europe where St Paul preached the gospel. This was in 49 AD, and during the next five years he preached in Athens, Thessaloniki and Corinth.

The Greek Orthodox Church, which is closely related to the Russian Orthodox Church and together with it forms the third-largest branch of Christianity (Orthodox means 'right belief'), was founded in the 4th century by Constantine the Great, who in 313 AD was converted to Christianity by a vision of the Cross. Until that time Christianity had not been tolerated by the Romans.

By the 8th century, there were a number of differences of opinion between the Pope in Rome and the Patriarch of Constantinople, as well as increasing rivalry between the two. One dispute was over the wording of the Creed. The original Creed stated that the

Holy Spirit proceeds 'from the Father' which the Orthodox Church adhered to, whereas Rome added 'and the Son'. Another bone of contention concerned the celibacy of the clergy. Rome decreed priests had to be celibate; in the Orthodox Church, a priest could marry before he became ordained. There were also differences in fasting: in the Orthodox Church, not only was meat forbidden during Lent, but wine and oil were also.

By the 11th century these differences had become irreconcilable, and in 1054 the Pope and the Patriarch excommunicated one another. Ever since, the two have gone their separate ways as the (Greek/Russian) Orthodox Church and the Roman Catholic Church.

During Ottoman times membership of the Orthodox Church was one of the most important criteria in defining a Greek, regardless of where he or she lived. Also, the church was the principal upholder of Greek culture and traditions.

Religion is still integral to life in Greece, and the Greek year is centred around the festivals of the church calendar. Most Greeks, when they have a problem, will go into a church and light a candle to the saint they feel is most likely to help them. On the islands you will see hundreds of tiny churches dotted around the countryside. Most have been built by individual families in the name of their selected patron saint, as thanksgiving for God's protection.

If you wish to look around a church you must observe a strict code of dress. Women must wear skirts that reach below the knees, men must wear long trousers and arms must be covered. Regrettably many churches are kept locked nowadays, but it's usually easy enough to locate caretakers, who will be happy to open them up for you.

LANGUAGE

The Greek language is probably the oldest European language, with an oral tradition of 4000 years, and a written tradition of approximately 3000 years. Its evolution over the four millennia was characterised by its strength during the golden age of Athens and the Democracy (mid-5th century BC); its use as a lingua franca throughout the Middle Eastern world, spread by Alexander the Great and his successors as far as India during the Hellenistic period (330 BC to 100 AD); its adaptation as the language of the new religion, Christianity; its use as the official language of the Eastern Roman Empire; and its eventual proclamation as the language of the Byzantine Empire (380-1453).

Greek maintained its status and prestige during the rise of the European Renaissance and was employed as the linguistic perspective for all contemporary sciences and terminologies during the period of Enlightenment. Today, Greek constitutes a large part of the vocabulary of any Indo-European language, and much of the lexicon of any scientific repertoire.

The modern Greek language is a southern Greek dialect which is now used by most Greek speakers both in Greece and abroad. It is the result of an intralinguistic influence and synthesis of the ancient vocabulary combined with lexemes from Greek regional dialects – namely Cretan, Cypriot and Macedonian.

Greek is spoken throughout Greece by a population of around 10 million, and by some five million Greeks who live abroad.

Stress

All Greek words of two or more syllables have an acute accent which indicates where the stress falls. For instance, άγαλμα is pronounced A-ghal-ma, statue, and αγάπη is pronounced a-GHA-pi, love.

Greetings & Civilities

Hello.
   ya-su   Γειά σου.
Goodbye.
   an-di-o   Αντίο.
Good morning.
   kali-me-ra   Καλημέρα.
Good afternoon.
   he-rete   Χαίρετε.
Good evening/
   night.
   kali-spe-ra/   Καλησπέρα/
   kali-ni-hta   καληνύχτα.

Greek Alphabet & Pronunciation

Greek	Pronunciation Guide		Example		
A α	a	as the 'a' in 'father'	αγάπη	aghapi	love
B β	v	as in 'vine'	βήμα	vima	step
Γ γ	gh	like a rough 'g'	γάτα	ghata	cat
	y	as in 'yes'	για	ya	for
Δ δ	TH	as in 'there'	δέμα	THema	parcel
E ε	e	as in 'egg'	ένας	enas	one (m)
Z ζ	z	as in 'zoo'	ζώο	zoo	animal
H η	i	as in 'feet'	ήταν	itan	was
Θ θ	th	as in 'throw'	θέμα	thema	theme
I ι	i	as in 'feet'	ίδιος	idjos	same
K κ	k	as in 'kite'	καλά	kala	well
Λ λ	l	as in 'leg'	λάθος	lathos	mistake
M μ	m	as in 'man'	μαμά	mama	mother
N ν	n	as in 'net'	νερό	nero	water
Ξ ξ	x	as in 'ox'	ξύδι	ksithi	vinegar
O o	o	as in 'hot'	όλα	ola	all
Π π	p	as in 'pup'	πάω	pao	I go
P ρ	r	as in 'road'	ρέμα	rema	stream
		a slightly trilled 'r'	ρόδα	roda	tyre
Σ σ, ς	s	as in 'sand'	σημάδι	simadi	mark
T τ	t	as in 'tap'	τόπι	topi	ball
Υ υ	i	as in 'feet'	ύστερα	istera	after
Φ φ	f	as in 'find'	φύλλο	filo	leaf
X χ	h	like the 'ch' in the Scottish loch, or like a rough 'h'	χάνω	hano	I lose
			χέρι	heri	hand
Ψ ψ	ps	as in 'lapse'	ψωμί	psomi	bread
Ω ω	o	as in 'hot'	ωρα	ora	time

Please.
sas paraka-lo Σας παρακαλώ.

Thank you.
sas efhari-sto Σας ευχαριστώ.

Many thanks.
sas efhari-sto po-li Σας ευχαριστώ πολύ.

That's fine. You're welcome.
i-ne en-da-ksi Είναι εντάξει.
paraka-lo Παρακαλώ.

Yes.
ne Ναι.

No.
o-hi Οχι.

Excuse me.
si-gno-mi Συγγνώμη.

Sorry. (excuse me, forgive me)
si-gno-mi Συγγνώμη.

How are you?
pos i-ste? Πώς είστε;

Well, thanks.
ka-la efhari-sto Καλά ευχαριστώ.

Essentials

I (don't) understand.
(THen) katala-ve-no (Δεν) καταλαβαίνω.

I don't speak...
THen mi-la-o... Δεν μιλάω...

Combinations of Letters

The combinations of letters shown here are pronounced as follows:

Greek	Pronunciation Guide		Example		
ει	i	as in 'feet'	είδα	iTHa	I saw
οι	i	as in 'feet'	οικόπεδο	ikopeTHo	land
αι	e	as in 'bet'	αίμα	ema	blood
ου	u	as in 'mood'	που	pu	where
μπ	b	as in 'beer'	μπάλα	bala	ball
	mb	as in 'amber'	κάμπος	kambos	forest
ντ	d	as in 'dot'	ντουλάπα	dulapa	wardrobe
	nd	as in 'bend'	πέντε	pende	five
γκ	g	as in 'God'	γκάζι	gazi	gas
γγ	ng	as in 'angle'	αγγελία	angelia	classified
γξ	ks	as in 'minks'	σφιγξ	sfinks	sphynx
τζ	dz	as in 'hands'	τζάκι	dzaki	fireplace

The pairs of vowels shown above are pronounced separately if the first has an acute accent, or the second a dieresis,

γαϊδουράκι	gaiduraki	little donkey
Κάιρο	kairo	Cairo

Some Greek consonant sounds have no English equivalent. The υ of the groups αυ, ευ and ηυ is generally pronounced 'v'.

The Greek question mark is represented with the English equivalent of a semicolon ';'.

Do you speak English?			Australia		
mi-la-te angli-ka?	Μιλάτε Αγγλικά;		*afstra-li-a*	Αυστραλία	
Does anyone speak English?			England		
mi-la-i ka-nis angli-ka?	Μιλάει κανείς Αγγλικά;		*a-ngli-a*	Αγγλία	
			New Zealand		
Where are the toilets?			*ne-a zilan-THi-a*	Νέα Ζηλανδία	
			the USA		
pu i-ne i tua-le-tes?	Πού είναι οι τουαλέτες;		*ino-me-nes poli-tee-es*	Ηνωμένες Πολιτεύεσ	
Where are you from?			How old are you?		
			po-so hro-non i-se?	Πόσων χρονών είσαι;	
apo pu i-ste?	Από πού είστε;		I am...years old.		
I am from...			*i-me...hro-non*	Είμαι...χρονών.	
i-me a-po...	Είμαι από...				

Small Talk

What is your name?
pos sas le-ne?   Πώς σας λένε;
My name is...
me le-ne...   Με λένε...
Are you married?
i-ste pandre-me-nos? (m)   Είστε παντρεμένος;
i-ste pandre-me-ni? (f)   Είστε παντρεμένη;
Just a minute.
mia sti-ghmi   Μια στιγμή.

Emergency

Help!
vo-i-thia!   Βοήθεια!
Go away!
fi-ghe!   Φύγε!
Call a doctor!
fo-na-kste e-na ya-tro!   Φωνάξτε ένα γιατρό!
Call the police!
tilefo-ni-ste stin astino-mi-a!   Τηλεφωνήστε στην αστυνομία!
Where is the police station?
pu i-ne o astinomi-kos stath-mos?   Που είναι ο αστυνομικός σταθμός;

Passport Details

name
o-noma   όνομα
address
THi-e-fthinsi   διεύθυνση
date of birth
imeromi-ni-a yje-ni-seos   ημερομηνία γεννήσεως
place of birth
to-pos ye-ni-seos   τόπος γεννήσεως
age
ili-ki-a   ηλικία
sex
fi-lon   φύλο
nationality
ethni-ko-tita   εθνικότητα
passport
THiava-ti-rio   διαβατήριο
visa
a-THia i-so-THu   άδεια εισόδου

Getting Around

I want to go to...
the-lo na pa-o sto/sti...   Θέλω να πάω στο/στη...
I would like to book a seat to...
tha i-thela na kli-so the-si ya to...   Θα ήθελα να κλείσω θέση για το...

What time does the...leave/arrive?
ti o-ra e-rhete/apoho-ri to...?   Τι ώρα έρχεται/αποχωρεί το...;
the (air)plane
aero-pla-no   αεροπλάνο
the boat
pli-o   πλοίο
the bus (city)
leofo-ri-o ya tin bo-li   λεωφορείο (για την πόλη)
the bus (intercity)
leofo-ri-o ya ta pro-a-stia   λεωφορείο (για τα προάστια)
the train
tre-no   τραίνο
the tram
tram   τραμ

How long does the trip take?
po-so THia-rki i THia Thro-mi?   Πόσο διαρκεί η διαδρομή;
Passengers must...
i taksi-THio-tes pre-pi...   Οι ταξιδιώτες πρέπει...
change trains
na-la-ksun tre-na   ν'αλλάξουν τραίνα
change platforms
na-la-ksun pla-tfo-rmes   ν'αλλάξουν πλατφόρμες
The train is delayed/cancelled.
to tre-no kathi-ste-rise/aki-ro-thike   Το τραίνο καθυστέρησε/ακυρώθηκε.

I would like...
tha i-thela...   Θα ήθελα...

a one-way ticket
  isi-ti-rio ho-ris   εισιτήριο χωρίς
  epistro-fi   επιστροφή
a return ticket
  isi-ti-rio met   εισιτήριο μετ'
  epistro-fis   επιστροφής
two tickets
  THi-o isi-ti-ria   δύο εισιτήρια
a student's fare
  mathiti-ko isi-ti-rio   μαθητικό
     εισιτήριο
1st class
  pro-ti the-si   πρώτη θέση
2nd class
  THef-teri the-si   δεύτερη θέση

Where can I hire a
  bicycle?
  pu bo-ro na ni-kia-   Πού μπορώ να
  so e-na po-THi-   νοικιάσω ένα
  lato/afto-ki-nito?   ποδήλατο/αυτοκίνη
     το;

How much is it...?
  po-so ko-sti-zi...?   Πόσο κοστίζει...;
daily/weekly
  ime-ri-sia/   ημερήσια/
  evTHoma-   εβδομαδιαία
  THi-e-a

Directions

Where is...?
  pu i-ne to/o/i...?   Πού είναι
     το/ο/η...;

How do I get to...?
  pos bo-ro na   Πώς μπορώ να
  pa-o sto/sti...?   πάω στο/στη...;
Is it far from/near
  here?
  i-ne makri-a/   Είναι
  ko-nda   μακριά/κοντά
  ap e-THo?   απ'εδώ;
Can you show me
  (on the map)?
  bo-ri-te na mu   Μπορείτε να μου
  THi-ksete   δείξετε
  sto ha-rti?   στο χάρτη;

Go straight ahead.
  pi-ghe-nete ef-thi-a   Πηγαίνετε ευθεία.

Turn left...
  stri-pste ariste-ra...   Στρίψτε
     αριστερά...
Turn right...
  stri-pste THe-ksia...   Στρίψτε δεξιά...
at the next corner
  stin e-po-meni   στην επόμενη
  gho-ni-a   γωνία
at the traffic lights
  sta fo-ta tis tro-   στα φώτα της
  he-as   τροχαίας

behind
  pi-so   πίσω
in front of
  mpro-sta a-po   μπροστά από
far
  makri-a   μακριά
near
  ko-nda   κοντά
opposite
  a-pe-nandi   απέναντι

Around Town

I'm looking for...
  psa-hno...   Ψάχνω για...
a bank
  mia tra-peza   μια τράπεζα
the city centre
  to ke-ndro tis po-lis   το κέντρο της
     πόλης
the...embassy
  tin...pre-svi-a   την...πρεσβεία
the market
  tin agho-ra   την αγορά
the museum
  to mu-si-o   το μουσείο
the police
  tin astino-mi-a   την αστυνομία
the post office
  to tahiTHro-mi-o   το ταχυδρομείο
a public toilet
  THimo-ti-kes tua-   δημοτικές
  le-tes   τουαλέτες
the telephone centre
  to tilefoni-ko ke-   το τηλεφωνικό
  ntro   κέντρο

I want to exchange
some money/
travellers'
cheques.

the-lo si-na-laghma/
the-lo na eksaryi-ro-so ori-sme-nes aksiTHjoti-kies
epita-ghies
Θέλω
συνάλλαγμα/Θέλω
να εξαργυρώσω
ορισμένες
ταξιδιωτικές
επιταγές.

I want to phone...
the-lo na tilefo-ni-so...
Θέλω να
τηλεφωνήσω...

What time does it
open/close?
ti o-ra a-ni-yi/
kli-ni?
Τι ώρα
ανοίγει/κλείνει;

beach
para-li-a
παραλία

castle
ka-stro
κάστρο

cathedral
katheTHri-kos na-os
καθεδρικός ναός

church
ekli-si-a
εκκλησία

market
agho-ra
αγορά

monument
mni-mi-o
μνημείο

mosque
dza-mi
τζαμί

old city
pa-lia po-li
παλιά πόλη

ruins
e-ri-pia
ερείπια

stadium
sta-THio
στάδιο

statues
a-gha-lmata
αγάλματα

Accommodation

I am looking for...
psa-hno ya to/ti...
Ψάχνω για το/τη...

Where is a...hotel?
pu i-ne e-na...
ksenoTHo-hi-o?
Πού είναι
ένα...ξενοδοχείο;

cheap
fti-no
φτηνό

good
ka-lo
καλό

nearby
kondi-no
κοντινό

clean
katha-ro
καθαρό

What is the address?
pia i-ne i THi-ef-thinsi?
Ποια είναι η
διεύθυνση;

I would like...
tha-ithela...
Θά ήθελα...

a single room
e-na THo-ma-tio ya e-na a-tomo
ένα δωμάτιο για
ένα άτομο

a double room
e-na THo-ma-tio ya THio a-toma
ένα δωμάτιο για
δύο άτομα

a room with a bath-
room
e-na THo-ma-tio me ba-nio
ένα δωμάτιο με
μπάνιο

a bed
e-na kre-va-ti
ένα κρεβάτι

I'm going to stay
for...
tha ka-thi-so ya...
Θα καθίσω για...

one day
mi-a me-ra
μία μέρα

two days
THi-o me-res
δύο μέρες

How much is it per
night/per person?
po-so ko-sti-zi ya ka-the vra-THi/ya ka-the a-tomo?
Πόσο κοστίζει
για κάθε βραδυά
κάθε άτομο;

Does it include
breakfast?
simberila-mva-ni kie proi-no?
Συμπεριλαμβάνει
και πρωϊνό;

Can I see it?
bo-ro na to THo?
Μπορώ να το δω;

I don't like this
room.
THen ma-re-si a-fto to THo-ma-tio
Δεν μ'αρέσει
αυτό το δωμάτιο.

Are there any
cheaper rooms?
  i-pa-rhun fti-no-tera Υπάρχουν
  THo-ma-tia? φτηνότερα
δωμάτια;
Where is the bath-
room?
  pu i-ne to ba-nio? Πού είναι το
μπάνιο;
It's expensive.
  i-ne po-li akri-vo Είναι πολύ
ακριβό.
I am/We are
leaving now.
  fe-vgho/fe-vghume Φεύγω/Φεύγουμε
  to-ra τώρα.
clean
  katha-ro καθαρό
dirty
  vro-mika(o) βρώμικα(ο)
electricity
  ilektri-smos ηλεκτρισμός
excluded
  ekse-ri-te εξαιρείται
fan
  anemis-ti-ras ανεμιστήρας
included
  simberila-mva-nete συμπεριλαμ–
βάνεται
key
  kli-THi κλειδί
pillow
  maksi-la-ri μαξιλάρι
sheet
  se-ndo-nia σεντόνια
shower
  dus ντους

Food
breakfast
  pro-ghevma πρόγευμα
lunch
  ghe-vma γεύμα
dinner
  THi-pno δείπνο
I would like the set
lunch, please.
  tha i-thela to ki-rio Θα ήθελα το
  ge-vma sas κύριο γεύμα, σας
  paraka-lo παρακαλώ.

I am a vegetarian.
  i-me horto-fa-ghos Είμαι χορτοφάγος.
I don't eat meat.
  THen tro-gho kre- Δεν τρώω κρέας.
  as
beer
  bi-ra μπύρα
Greek coffee
  elini-kos ka-fes ελληνικός καφές
mineral water
  metali-ko ne-ro μεταλικό νερό
tea
  tsa-i τσάι
wine
  kra-si κρασί

Shopping
How much is it?
  po-so kosti-zi? Πόσο κοστίζει;
  po-so ka-ni? Πόσο κάνει;
(informal)
I would like to
buy...
  the-lo nayo-ra-so... Θέλω
ν'αγοράσω...
I'm just looking.
  a-plos ki-ta-o απλώς κοιτάω.
Do you accept
credit cards?
  THe-heste pistoti- Δέχεστε
  kjes ka-rtes? πιστωτικές
κάρτες;
Could you lower
the price?
  bo-ri-te na mu ka- Μπορείτε να μου
  nete fti-no-teri κάνετε φτηνότερη
  ti-mi? τιμή;
clothing
  ruhi-smos ρουχισμός
small
  mi-kro μικρό
big
  me-gha-lo μεγάλο
more
  peri-so-tero περισσότερο
less
  li-gho-tero λιγότερο

Health

I'm...
i-me...	Είμαι...

diabetic
THiaviti-kos (m)	διαβητικός
THiaviti-kja (f)	διαβητικιά

epileptic
epile-pti-kos (m)	επιληπτικός
epile-pti-kja (f)	επιληπτικιά

asthmatic
asthmati-kos (m)	ασθματικός
asthmati-kja (f)	ασθματικιά

I'm allergic to...
i-me aleryji-kos (m) sta...	Είμαι αλλεργικός στα...
i-me aleryji-kja (f) sta...	Είμαι αλλεργικιά στα...

antibiotics
andivioti-ka	αντιβιωτικά

penicillin
peniki-li-ni	πενικιλλίνη

diarrhoea
THi-a-ria	διάρροια

Time & Dates

What time is it?
ti o-ra i-ne?	Τι ώρα είναι;

It is...am/pm.
i-ne...i o-ra pro mesi-mvri-as (a.m.)/ me-ta mesi-mvri-a(n)(p.m.)	Είναι...η ώρα, προ μεσημβρίας (π.μ.)/μετά μεσημβρία(ν) (μ.μ.).

in the morning
to pro-i	το πρωί

in the afternoon
to a-po-yevma	το απόγευμα

in the evening
to vra-THi	το βράδυ

Monday
THe-fte-ra	Δευτέρα

Tuesday
tri-ti	Τρίτη

Wednesday
te-ta-rti	Τετάρτη

Thursday
pe-mpti	Πέμπτη

Friday
paraske-vi	Παρασκευή

Saturday
sa-va-to	Σάββατο

Sunday
ki-ria-ki	Κυριακή

January
ianu-a-rios	Ιανουάριος

February
fevru-a-rios	Φεβρουάριος

March
ma-rtios	Μάρτιος

April
a-pri-lios	Απρίλιος

May
ma-ios	Μάιος

June
i-u-nios	Ιούνιος

July
i-u-lios	Ιούλιος

August
a-vghustos	Αύγουστος

September
se-pte-mvrios	Σεπτέμβριος

October
o-kto-vrios	Οκτώβριος

November
no-e-mvrios	Νοέμβριος

December
THe-kie-mvrios	Δεκέμβριος

today
si-mera	σήμερα

tonight
a-po-pse	απόψε

now
to-ra	τώρα

yesterday
hthes	χθες

tomorrow
a-vrio	αύριο

Numbers & Amounts

0
mi-THen	μηδέν

1
e-na	ένα

2			30	
THi-o	δύο		*tri-a-nda*	τριάντα
3			40	
tri-a	τρία		*sa-ra-nda*	σαράντα
4			50	
te-sera	τέσσερα		*pe-ni-nda*	πενήντα
5			60	
pe-nde	πέντε		*e-ksi-nda*	εξήντα
6			70	
e-ksi	έξη		*evTHo-mi-nda*	εβδομήντα
7			80	
e-pta	επτά		*o-ghTHo-nda*	ογδόντα
8			90	
o-hto	οχτώ		*ene-ni-nda*	ενενήντα
9			100	
e-ne-a	εννέα		*eka-to*	εκατό
10			1000	
THe-ka	δέκα		*hi-lia*	χίλια
20			one million	
i-kosi	είκοσι		*e-na ekato-mi-rio*	ένα εκατομμύριο

Facts for the Visitor

VISAS & EMBASSIES

Nationals of the USA, Canada, Australia, New Zealand and EC countries are allowed to stay in Greece for up to three months without a visa.

Greek Embassies

Following is a selection of Greek diplomatic missions abroad:

Albania
Rruga Frederik Shiroka, Tirana (☎ 342 90)

Australia
9 Turrana St, Yarralumla, Canberra ACT 2600 (☎ 062-73 3158/3011)

Bulgaria
Klement Gottwald 68, Sofia (☎ 02-44 37 70)

Canada
76-80 Maclaren St, Ottawa, Ontario K2P OK6 (☎ 613-238 6271)

Cyprus
Byron Boulevard 8-10, Nicosia (☎ 02-44 1880)

Denmark
Borgergade 16, 1300 Copenhagen (☎ 01-11 4533)

Egypt
18 Aisha el Taymouria, Garden City, Cairo (☎ 02-355 1074)

France
17, rue Auguste Vacquerie, 75116 Paris (☎ 01-47.23.72.28)

Germany
Koblenzer Str 103, 5300 Bonn 2 (☎ 228-83010)

Ireland
1 Upper Pembroke St, Dublin 2 (☎ 01-767 254)

Italy
Via S Mercadante 36, Rome 00198 (☎ 06-854 9630)

Japan
16-30 Nishi Azabu 3-chome Minato-ku, Tokyo 106 (☎ 03-403 0871/2)

New Zealand
235-237 Willis St, 8th Floor, Wellington (☎ 04-84 7556)

Netherlands
Koninginnegracht 37, The Hague (☎ 070-363 87 00)

South Africa
995 Pretorius St, Pretoria 0083 (☎ 012-437 352)

Spain
Avenida Doctor Arce 24, Madrid 28002 (☎ 01-564 4653)

Sweden
Riddargatan 60, 11457 Stockholm (☎ 08-663 7577)

Switzerland
Jungfraustrasse 3, 3005 Bern (☎ 31-44 1637)

Turkey
Ziya-ul-Rahman Sokak 9-11, Gazi Osman Pasa, Ankara (☎ 04-136 8860)

UK
1A Holland Park, London W11 3TP (☎ 071-727 8040)

USA
2221 Massachusetts Ave NW, Washington DC 20008 (☎ 202-667 3169)

Visa Extensions

If you wish to stay in Greece for longer than three months apply at a consulate abroad or at least 20 days in advance to the Aliens Bureau (☎ 01-770 5711), Leoforos Alexandras 173, Athens. Take your passport and four passport photographs along. You may be asked for proof that you can support yourself financially, so keep all your bank exchange slips (or the equivalent from a post office). These slips are not always automatically given – you may have to ask for them. The Aliens Bureau is open from 8 am to 1 pm on weekdays. Elsewhere in Greece apply to the local police authority. You will be given a permit which will authorise you to stay in the country for a period of up to six months. Many travellers overcome this red tape by briefly visiting Turkey and then re-entering Greece.

Turkish-Occupied North Cyprus

Greece will refuse entry to people whose passport indicates that they have visited Turkish-occupied North Cyprus since November 1983. This can be overcome if, upon entering North Cyprus, you ask the immigration officials to stamp a piece of paper (loose-leaf visa) rather than your passport. If you enter North Cyprus from the Greek Republic of Cyprus (only possible for a day visit) an exit stamp is not put into your passport.

Foreign Embassies in Greece

All foreign embassies in Greece are in Athens. There are consulates of various countries in Thessaloniki, Patras, Corfu, Rhodes and Iraklion. See the relevant chapters for details. Foreign embassies in Athens (telephone code 01) include:

Albania
    Karachristou 1, Athens 11521 (☎ 723 4412)
Australia
    Dimitrou Soutsou 37, Athens 11521 (☎ 644 7303)
Bulgaria
    Strattigou Kallari 33A, Psychikon, Athens 15452 (☎ 647 8105)
Canada
    Genadiou 4, Athens 11521 (☎ 723 9511)
Cyprus
    Herodotou 16, Athens 10675 (☎ 723 7883)
Egypt
    Leoforos Vasilissis Sofias 3, Athens 10671 (☎ 361 8612)
France
    Leoforos Vasilissis Sofias 7, Athens 10671 (☎ 361 1663)
Germany
    Leoforos Vasilissis Sofias 10, Athens 15124 (☎ 369 4111)
Ireland
    Leoforos Vasileos Konstantinou 7, Athens 10674 (☎ 723 2771)
Israel
    Marathonodromou 1, Psychikon, Athens 15452 (☎ 671 9530)
Italy
    Sekeri 12, Athens 10674 (☎ 361 1722)
Japan
    Leoforos Messogion 2, Athens 11527 (☎ 775 8101)
Netherlands
    Vasileos Konstantinou 5-7, Athens 10674 (☎ 723 9701)
New Zealand
    Semitelou 9, Athens 11521 (☎ 777 0686)
South Africa
    Kifissias 124, Athens 11510 (☎ 692 2125)
Turkey
    Vasilissis Georgiou B 8, Athens 10674 (☎ 724 5915)
UK
    Ploutarhou 1, Athens 10675 (☎ 723 6211)
USA
    Leoforos Vasilissis Sofias 91, Athens 11521 (☎ 721 2951)

DOCUMENTS

To enter Greece you need a valid passport or, for EC nationals, travel documents (identity cards). It is necessary to produce your passport when you register in a hotel or pension in Greece. You will find that many accommodation proprietors will want to keep your passport during your stay. This is not a compulsory requirement; they only need it long enough to take down the details.

If you want to rent a car or motorbike you will need an International Driving Permit or, if you are from an EC country, an EC driving licence. An International Driving Permit can be obtained before you leave home or from the ELPA (Greek Automobile Touring Club) on production of a national driving licence, passport and photograph. See the Useful Organisations section later in this chapter for contact details.

CUSTOMS

There are no longer duty-free restrictions within the EC. This does not mean, however, that customs checks have been dispensed with; random searches are still made for drugs.

Arrival

Upon entering the country from outside the EC, customs inspection is usually cursory for foreign tourists. There may be spot-checks, but you probably won't even have to open your bags. A verbal declaration is usually all that is required. At the time of writing, however, the EC governments were considering changes to the following duty-free allowances, so check with the Greek National Tourist Office (GNTO) or Greek Embassy before you arrive in Greece.

You may bring into Greece duty free 200 cigarettes or 50 cigars; one litre of spirits or two litres of wine; 50 grams of perfume; 250 ml of eau de cologne; one camera (still or video) and film; a pair of binoculars; a portable musical instrument; a portable radio or tape recorder; a typewriter; sports equipment and dogs and cats (with a veterinary certificate).

Importation of works of art and antiquities

is free, but they must be declared on entry, so that they can be re-exported. Import regulations for medicines are strict; if you are taking medication, make sure you get a statement from your doctor before you leave home. It is illegal, for instance, to take codeine into Greece without an accompanying doctor's certificate.

An unlimited amount of foreign currency and travellers' cheques may be brought into Greece. However, if you intend to leave the country with foreign banknotes in excess of US$1000, you must declare the sum upon entry. You may import 100,000 dr and export up to 20,000 dr.

Restrictions apply to the importation of windsurfers into Greece. See the Activities section later in this chapter for more details.

Vehicles

Cars can be brought into Greece for four months without a carnet; only a Green Card (international third party insurance) is required. When you enter Greece, your vehicle will be registered in your passport, in order to prevent you leaving the country without it.

Departure

The chances are no checks will be made on your baggage and no questions asked when you leave Greece. But it is strictly forbidden to export antiquities (anything over 100 years old) without an export permit. This crime is second only to drug smuggling in the penalties imposed. It is an offence to remove even the smallest article from an archaeological site, and if an antiquity is found in a traveller's luggage the article will be confiscated and prosecution may follow.

The place to apply for an export permit is Antique Dealers & Private Collections Section, The Archaeological Service, Polignotou 13, Athens.

MONEY

Banks will exchange all major currencies, in either cash, travellers' cheques or Eurocheques. To get Eurocheques you need a European bank account and usually have to

wait at least two weeks to receive the cheques. The best known travellers' cheques in Greece are Thomas Cook and American Express. A passport is required to change travellers' cheques, but not cash.

Commission charged on the exchange of banknotes and travellers' cheques varies not only from bank to bank but from branch to branch. It's less for cash than for travellers' cheques. The lowest charges levied are 200 dr for cash (banknotes only; no coins) with a value of up to 20,000 dr, and 400 dr for cash with a value above 20,000 dr.

For travellers' cheques the commission levied is 350 dr up to 20,000 dr, 450 dr for amounts between 20,000 and 30,000 dr, and a flat rate of 1.5% is levied on amounts over 30,000 dr. No commission is charged on Eurocheques.

All post offices have exchange facilities for banknotes, travellers' cheques and Eurocheques, and charge less commission than banks. It is usually quicker to change money at a post office than in a bank. Many travel agencies and hotels will also change money, travellers' cheques and Eurocheques at bank rates, but their commission charges are higher.

All major credit cards and Eurocheques are acceptable, but only in the larger, more expensive establishments. Some C class hotels accept credit cards, but D and E class hotels rarely do. Restaurants which accept credit cards tend to be the more expensive or tourist-orientated ones. Visa, Access (MasterCard) and Eurocard are the most widely accepted credit cards.

You can get a cash advance on a Visa card at the Commercial Bank of Greece and on Access (MasterCard) at the National Bank of Greece. Some branches of these banks – and others – have automatic teller machines which operate 24 hours a day.

There are restrictions on the amount of drachmas you may bring in or take out of Greece. See under Customs earlier in this chapter for details.

International Transfers

If you run out of money or need more for

whatever reason, you can instruct your bank back home to send you a draft. Specify the city and the bank as well as the branch that you want the money sent to. Also, a transfer to a tiny bank on a remote island is obviously going to be more difficult than to the head office in Athens. If you have the choice, select a large bank and ask for the international division.

Money sent by telegraphic transfer (which usually involves costs of US$20 or more, but ask) should reach you within a week; by mail, allow at least two weeks. When it arrives, it will most likely be converted into drachmas – you can take it as it is or buy travellers' cheques. US citizens can also use Western Union, which has offices in Athens, Piraeus and Thessaloniki.

Currency

The unit of currency is the drachma. Coins come in denominations of one, two, five, 10, 20, 50 and 100 dr. Bank notes come in 50, 100, 500, 1000 and 5000 dr. Sometimes 5000 dr notes are difficult to change in remote areas.

Exchange Rates

A$1	=	140.5 dr
C$1	=	161.1 dr
DM1	=	116.2 dr
NZ$1	=	94.5 dr
US$1	=	188.3 dr
UK£1	=	320.6 dr
Y100	=	180 dr

Costs

Greece is no longer dirt cheap. A rock-bottom daily budget would be 3000 to 4000 dr, and would mean hitching, staying in youth hostels or camping, and only occasionally eating in restaurants and taking a ferry. Renting decent rooms, eating at restaurants and taking buses and ferries regularly would cost about 7000 to 8000 dr a day. Prices vary quite a lot between islands: Mykonos and Hydra are the most expensive; the cheapest tend to be the less well-known ones.

Almost all museums and ancient sites will grant a 50% reduction with an International Student Identification Card (ISIC). Otherwise visits to sites and museums quickly cut into your budget. Apart from a few exceptions where entry is free, most small museums charge 400 dr, and major sites and museums cost between 1000 and 1500 dr. Most museums and ancient sites are free on Sunday and public holidays.

Tipping

In restaurants the service charge is included in the bill but it is the custom to leave a small amount. The practice is often just to round off the bill. Likewise for taxis – a small amount is appreciated.

Bargaining

Bargaining is not done to the extent that it is further east, and prices are fixed in large shops, but it is worth trying in souvenir shops, and is expected at outdoor markets. You can certainly try bargaining for hotel rooms and domatia during the off season.

WHEN TO GO

Greece has quite marked climatic variations. Northern Macedonia and northern Epiros have a climate similar to the Balkans, with freezing winters and very hot, humid summers.

The Attica peninsula, the Cyclades, Dodecanese, Crete and the central and eastern Peloponnese have a more typically Mediterranean climate with hot dry summers and milder winters. Snow is very rare in the Cyclades (in 1992 it snowed on Paros for the first time in 15 years), but the high mountains of the Peloponnese and Crete are covered in snow during the winter, and it does occasionally snow in Athens.

In July and August (the high season) the mercury can soar to 40°C in the shade just about anywhere in the country; the beaches are crowded, the ancient sites are swarming with tour groups and in many places accommodation is booked solid. The *meltemi* wind – a mixed blessing – also occurs daily during these months, and intermittently during September. It is a northerly wind that sweeps the east coast of mainland Greece (including Athens) and the Aegean islands, especially the Cyclades. The wind is caused by air pressure differences between North Africa and the Balkans. It certainly reduces humidity, but plays havoc with ferry schedules and sends everything flying – from beach umbrellas to washing hanging out to dry.

The western Peloponnese, western Sterea Ellada, south-western Epiros and the Ionian islands escape the meltemi and has less severe winters than northern Greece, but has the highest rainfall. The North-Eastern Aegean islands, Halkidiki and the Pelion peninsula fall somewhere between the Balkan-type climate of northern Greece and the Mediterranean climates. Crete stays warm the longest – you can swim off its south coast from mid-April to November.

December and January can be very cold everywhere, and February is often rainy. But, before deciding against a winter holiday in Greece, it is worth considering its skiing possibilities (see the Activities section later in this chapter for details). There are also occasional winter days with clear blue skies and sunshine when it is perfect for exploring ancient sites, which you may be lucky enough to have to yourself. November and March are changeable, with sunny days interrupted by windy or showery weather.

You have probably deduced from all this that the best months for visiting Greece are April to mid-June, and September and October. With the exception of Crete, the sea in April is perhaps a little too cold for most people, but it is still warm enough for swimming in October. Beaches and ancient sites are not so crowded; it's easier to find accommodation and you'll pay less for it.

WHAT TO BRING

Bring camera film, suntan oil and moisterising and cleansing creams, as they are expensive in Greece, as well as paperbacks if you read a lot (see the Books & Maps section later in this chapter).

Sturdy shoes are essential for clambering around ancient sites and wandering around historic towns and villages, which tend to have lots of steps and cobbled streets. Footwear with ankle support is preferable for trekking, although many visitors get by with trainers.

A day pack is useful to take belongings to the beach, and for sightseeing or trekking. A compass is useful and sometimes essential if you are going to trek in remote areas, as is a whistle, which you can use should you become lost or disorientated. A torch (flashlight) is not only needed for exploring caves, but comes in useful during occasional power

---

Student Cards

An ISIC (International Student Identity Card) is a plastic ID-style card with your photograph. These cards are widely available from budget travel agencies (take along proof that you are a student). In Athens you can get one from the International Student & Youth Travel Service (ISYTS; (☎ 01-323 3767), 2nd floor, Nikis 11.

Some travel agencies in Greece offer discounts on organised tours to students. However, there are no student discounts for travel within Greece, but Olympic Airways gives a 25% discount on domestic flights which are part of an international flight. Turkish Airlines (THY) gives 55% student discounts on its international flights. There are flights from Athens to Istanbul and Izmir. Most shipping lines to Cyprus, Israel and Egypt from Piraeus give a 20% student discount and a few of the lines from Greek to Italian ports do so. If you are under 26 years but not a student, the FIYTO (Federation of International Youth Travel Organisation) card gives similar discounts. Many budget travel agencies issue FIYTO cards including the International Student & Youth Travel Service, Nikis 11, Athens (☎ 01-323 3767); London Explorers Club, 33 Princes Square, Bayswater, London W2 (☎ 071-792 3770) and SRS Studenten Reisse Service, Marienstrasse 23, Berlin. ■

cuts. If you like to fill a washbasin or bathtub (a rarity in Greece), bring a universal plug as Greek bathrooms rarely have plugs. Otherwise an empty film container can double up as a plug.

If you visit in July and August it's prudent to pack a foam bedroll and lightweight sleeping bag: many camp sites have covered areas for tourists without tents to sleep under. Clothes pegs and a washing line are often, but not always, available in budget accommodation, so bring them along just in case. Whether or not you are going to self-cater, a plastic food container, plate, cup, cutlery, bottle opener, water container and an all-purpose knife are useful, not only for picnics, but for food you take with you on long boat trips. In summer a sun hat and sunglasses are essential (see the Health section later in this chapter).

You will only need light clothing – preferably cotton – during the summer months. But if you are going to climb Mt Olympus (or any other high mountain) you will need a sweater and waterproof jacket, even in July and August. During spring and autumn you will need a light sweater or jacket for evenings. In winter you will need a heavy jacket or coat, warm sweaters, winter shoes or boots, and an umbrella.

TOURIST OFFICES

If you would like tourist information about Greece, contact the the Greek National Tourist Organisation. It is known by the initials GNTO abroad and EOT (Ellinikos Organismos Tourismou) in Greece.

Local Tourist Offices

The address of the head office of the EOT is Amerikis 2, Athens 10564 (☎ 1-322 3111). There are about 25 EOT offices throughout Greece. Most EOT staff speak English, but they vary in their enthusiasm and helpfulness. All of the offices have maps, glossy brochures and information on transport and accommodation. In addition to EOT offices, there are also municipal tourist offices which serve the same function.

Tourist Police

In 1991 the tourist police, which had ceased operating in 1984, were resurrected. The tourist police work in cooperation with the regular Greek police and EOT. At each tourist police office there is at least one member of staff who speaks English. Hotels, restaurants, travel agencies, tourist shops, tourist guides, waiters, taxi drivers and tourist bus drivers all come under the jurisdiction of the tourist police. If you think that you have been ripped off by a member of staff of any of these businesses report it to the tourist police and they will investigate. If you need to report a theft, loss of passport etc, then go to the tourist police first, and they will act as interpreters between you and the regular police.

The tourist police not only help in times of trouble, they also fulfil the same functions as the EOT and municipal tourist offices, dispensing maps and brochures, and giving information on transport. They are particularly helpful in finding accommodation for tourists. At present their uniform is the same as the regular police – navy with a flat hat – but soon they may be given a different uniform.

Foreign Representatives

Tourist offices abroad include:

Australia
    51 Pitt St, Sydney NSW 2000 (☎ 02-241 1663)
Bulgaria
    Greek Press & Information Office, Klement Gottwald 68, Sofia (☎ 02-441 340)

Greek National Tourist Organisation logo

Canada
    1233 Rue de la Montagne, Suite 101, Montreal,
    Quebec H3G 1Z2 (☎ 541-871 1535)
Italy
    Via L Bissolati 78-80, Rome 00187
    (☎ 06-474 4249)
Netherlands
    Leidsestraat 13, Amsterdam NS 1017
    (☎ 020-254 212)
Turkey
    Olympic Airways, Cumhuriyet Caddessi 171A,
    Istanbul (☎ 212-132 9426)
UK
    4 Conduit St, London W1R ODJ
    (☎ 071-73 45997)
USA
    Olympic Tower, 645 5th Ave, New York, NY
    100022 (☎ 212-421 5777)

USEFUL ORGANISATIONS

Most of the organisations of interest to travellers have their headquarters in Athens. Some of these follow.

Accommodation

The Greek Youth Hostel Association (☎ 01-323 4107) is affiliated with the International Youth Hostel Federation (IYHF). The address is 7th floor, Dragatsaniou 4, Athens. You may buy an IYHF card here, although at most Greek youth hostels you can stay without a card.

Student Travellers

Apart from selling tickets for air, sea and road travel, the Information Centre, International Student & Youth Travel Service (☎ 01-323 3767), 2nd floor, Nikis 11, Athens, also issues student cards, if you have documents proving you are a student.

Mountaineering Clubs

Ellinikos Orivatikos Syndesmos (EOS – Greek Alpine Club; ☎ 01-321 2429/2355) is the largest and oldest Greek mountaineering and trekking organisation. Its headquarters are at Plateia Kapnikareas 2, Athens. The headquarters of the Hellenic Federation of Mountaineering Clubs (☎ 01-323 4555; fax 01-323 7666) are at Karageorgi Servias 7, Athens 10563. Both of these organisations are underfunded and staffed by volunteers,

but if you call or visit between 7 and 9 pm on a weekday evening, there should be someone there.

Automobile Associations

ELPA (☎ 01-779 1615) is the Greek automobile club; its headquarters are on the ground floor of Athens Tower, Messogion 2-4, Athens 11527. The ELPA offers reciprocal services to members of national automobile associations on production of a valid membership card. If your vehicle breaks down, dial 104.

Gay & Lesbian Travellers

Greece is a popular destination for gay travellers. The address of the Greek Gay Liberation Organisation is PO Box 2777, Athens GR 10022. The Athens gay switchboard number is ☎ 01-324 9660. The *Spartacus International Gay Guide*, published by Bruno Gmünder (Berlin), is a good international directory of gay entertainment venues in Europe.

For lesbians, the comprehensive international guide *Women Going Places* (Women Going Places Productions, 1992) is recommended.

Disabled Travellers

If mobility is a problem and you wish to visit Greece, the hard fact is that most hotels, museums and ancient sites in Greece are not wheelchair accessible. This is partly due to the uneven terrain of much of the country, which, with its abundance of stones, rocks and marble, presents a challenge even for able-bodied people.

If you are determined, then take heart in the knowledge that disabled people do come to Greece for holidays. But the trip needs careful planning, so get as much information as you can before you go. The British-based Royal Association for Disability and Rehabilitation (RADAR) publishes a useful guide called *Holidays & Travel Abroad: A Guide for Disabled People*, which gives a good overview of facilities available to disabled travellers in Europe. Contact RADAR (☎ 071-637 5400) at 25 Mortimer St, London W1N 8AB.

Lavinia Tours (☎ 031-23 2828; fax 031 21 9714), Egnatias 101 (PO Box 11106), Thessaloniki 54110, specialises in arranging travel for disabled travellers. The managing director, Eugenia Stravropoulou, has travelled widely both in Greece and abroad in her wheelchair.

BUSINESS HOURS

Banks are open Monday to Thursday from 8 am to 2 pm, and Friday from 8 am to 1 pm. Some banks in large towns and cities open from 3.30 to 6.30 pm in the afternoon and on Saturday mornings.

Official opening times for post offices are Monday to Friday from 7.30 am to 7.30 pm, but there are many variations on this. Main city post offices stay open until 8.30 pm and also open from 9 am to 3 pm on Saturday and 9.30 am to 1 pm on Sunday. Certain sections within the post office, such as fax facilities and parcel collection, often close at 2.30 pm, and some regional post offices close as early as 2 pm.

OTE offices (for long-distance and overseas telephone calls) are usually open from 7 am to 11 pm, seven days a week, but in some large cities they are open 24 hours and some regional offices are only open from 7.30 am to 3 pm on weekdays.

Shops open from 8 am to 1.30 pm and 5.30 to 8.30 pm on Tuesday, Thursday and Friday,

and from 8 am to 2.30 pm on Monday, Wednesday and Saturday, but these times are not always strictly adhered to; in tourist resorts and busy ports, many shops open seven days a week. *Periptera* (street kiosks) are open from early morning until late at night. Opening times of museums and archaeological sites vary, but most are closed on Monday.

PUBLIC HOLIDAYS

All banks and shops and most museums and ancient sites close during public holidays. National public holidays in Greece are:

1 January – New Year's Day
6 January – Epiphany
First Sunday in Lent
25 March – Greek Independence Day
Good Friday
Easter Sunday
1 May – Spring Festival
15 August – Feast of the Assumption
28 October – Ochi Day
25 December – Christmas Day
26 December – St Stephen's Day

FESTIVALS & CULTURAL EVENTS

The Greek year is a succession of numerous festivals and events, some of which are religious, some cultural, others an excuse for a good knees up, and some a combination of all three. The following is by no means an exhaustive list, but it covers the most important events, both national and regional. If you're in the right place at the right time, you'll certainly be invited to join in the revelry.

January

Feast of Agios Vasilios (Feast of St Basil) The year kicks off with this festival on 1 January. A church ceremony is followed by the exchanging of gifts, singing, dancing and feasting; the New Year pie (*vasilopitta*) is sliced and the person who gets the slice containing a coin will supposedly have a lucky year.

Epiphany Epiphany (the Blessing of the Waters), on 6 January, commemorates Christ's baptism by St John and is celebrated throughout Greece with religious ceremonies, when waters (seas, lakes and rivers) are blessed and crosses immersed in them. The largest ceremony takes place at Piraeus.

Gynaecocracy On 8 January this custom takes place in villages in the prefectures of Rodopi, Kilkis and Seres in northern Greece. On this day the sexes reverse roles: the women spend the day in kafeneia and other social centres where men congregate, and the men stay at home to do housework.

February-March

Carnival The Greek carnival season takes place during the three weeks before the beginning of Lent (the 6½ week period before Easter which is traditionally a period of fasting). The carnivals are ostensibly Christian pre-Lenten celebrations, but many derive from pagan festivals. There are many regional variations, but fancy dress, feasting, traditional dancing and general merrymaking prevail. Patras' carnival is the largest and most exuberant, with elaborately decorated chariots parading through the streets.

The most bizarre carnival takes place on the island of Skyros where the men transform themselves into grotesque 'half-man, half-beast' creatures by donning goat-skin masks and hairy jackets. Other carnivals worth catching are those at Naoussa in Macedonia, Athens Veria, Zakynthos and Kefallonia.

Shrove Monday (Clean Monday) On the Monday before Ash Wednesday (the first day of Lent), people take to the hills throughout Greece to have picnics and fly kites.

March

Independence Day The anniversary of the hoisting of the Greek flag by Bishop Germanos at Moni Agia Lavra is celebrated on 25 March with parades and dancing. Germanos' act of revolt marked the onset of the War of Independence. Independence Day coincides with the *Feast of the Annunciation*, so is also a religious festival.

March-April

Easter In the Greek Orthodox religion, Easter is the most significant festival, and emphasis is placed on the Resurrection rather than on the Crucifixion, so it is a joyous occasion. The festival commences on Good Friday with the procession of a shrouded bier (Christ's funeral bier) through the town or village. On Saturday evening the 'Christos anesti' (Christ is risen) mass takes place. At midnight, packed churches are plunged into darkness to symbolise Christ's passing through the underworld.

The ceremony of the lighting of candles which follows is the most significant moment in the Orthodox year, for it symbolises the Resurrection. Its poignancy and beauty are spellbinding. If you are in Greece at Easter you should endeavour to attend this ceremony, which ends with the setting off of fireworks and candle-lit processions through the streets.

The Lenten fast ends on Easter Sunday with the cracking of red-dyed Easter eggs and an outdoor feast of roast lamb followed by Greek dancing. The day's greeting is '*Christos anesti*' (Christ is risen), to which the reply is '*Alithos anesti*' (Truly He is risen).

On both Palm Sunday (the Sunday before Easter) and Easter Sunday, St Spiridon (the mummified patron saint of Corfu) is taken out for an airing and joyously paraded through the town. He is paraded again in Corfu town on 11 August.

Feast of Agios Georgios (Feast of St George) The feast day of St George, Greece's patron saint, and patron saint of shepherds, takes place on 23 April

or the Tuesday following Easter (whichever comes first). It is celebrated at several places but with particular exuberance in Arahova, near Delphi.

May

May Day On the first day of May there is a mass exodus from towns to the country. During picnics, wild flowers are gathered and made into wreaths to decorate houses.

Anastenaria On 21 May this fire-walking ritual takes place in Langadas near Thessaloniki. Barefooted villagers clutching icons dance on burning charcoal without sustaining injury. See the Northern Greece chapter for more details about this ritual.

June

Navy Week This naval festival is celebrated in mid-June in fishing villages and ports throughout the country. Volos and Hydra have unique adaptations of these celebrations: in Volos there is a re-enactment of the departure of the *Argo*, for legend has it that Iolkos (from where Jason and the Argonauts set off in quest of the Golden Fleece) was near the city of Volos. Hydra commemorates Admiral Andreas Miaoulis, who was born on the island and was a hero of the War of Independence. There is a re-enactment of one of his naval victories, accompanied by feasting and fireworks.

Feast of St John the Baptist This feast day on 24 June is widely celebrated. Wreaths made on May Day are kept until this day, when they are burned on bonfires.

July

Feast of Agia Marina (Feast of St Marina) This feast day is celebrated on 17 July in many parts of Greece, and is a particularly important event on the Dodecanese island of Kassos.

Feast of Profitis Ilias (Feast of the Prophet Elijah) This feast day on 20 July is celebrated at the hilltop churches and monasteries dedicated to the prophet, especially in the Cyclades.

August

Assumption Greeks celebrate this day with family reunions, so on the few days prior to 15 August it seems that the whole population is on the move; try to avoid travelling at this time. In particular avoid the island of Tinos at this time. Due to its miracle-working icon of Panagia Evangelistria, it becomes a place of pilgrimage for thousands, who come to be blessed, healed or baptised, or just for the excitement of being there. Many are unable to find hotels and sleep out on the streets.

September

Genesis tis Panagias (the Virgin's Birthday) On 8 September this day is celebrated throughout Greece with religious services and feasting.

Exaltation of the Cross This is celebrated on 14 September throughout Greece with processions and hymns.

October

Feast of Agios Demetrios This feast day is celebrated in Thessaloniki on 26 October with wine drinking and revelry.

Ochi (No) Day Metaxas' refusal to allow Mussolini's troops to traverse Greece in WW II is commemorated on 28 October. It is celebrated with remembrance services, military parades, folk dancing and feasting throughout the country.

December

Christmas Day Although not as important as Easter, Christmas is still celebrated with religious services and feasting. Nowadays much 'Western' influence is apparent, with Christmas trees, decorations and presents.

Summer Festivals & Cultural Performances

In Summer cultural festivals take place throughout Greece. The most important ones are the Athens Festival (June to September) with drama and music performances in the Theatre of Herodes Atticus, and the Epidaurus Festival (July to September) with drama performances in the ancient theatre at Epidaurus. Others cultural festivals include the Philipi & Thassos Festival (July and August); the Renaissance Festival in Rethymnon (July and August); the Dodoni Festival in Epiros (August); the Olympus Festival at Katerini and Litohora, in August; the Hippocratia Festival on Kos (August); and the Patras Arts Festival (August and September).

Summer is also the time for drunken revelries at wine festivals where, for a nominal admission charge, you can drink as much as you like. The biggest one is at Dafni, near Athens; others are held at Rethymnon and Alexandroupolis.

During September and October Thessaloniki hosts a string of festivals and events, including the International Trade Fair and the Feast of Agios Demetrios (details on the latter in the list above).

Sound & Light performances begin in April in Athens and Rhodes city, and end in October. In Corfu town the performances begin in May and end in September.

Greek folk dances are performed in

Athens and Corfu town from mid-May to September and Rhodes from May to October.

POST & TELECOMMUNICATIONS

Post offices *(tachidromio)* have yellow signs outside so are easy to spot – post boxes are also yellow. Greek post is generally reliable, but if you are sending something important, it is advisable to send it registered post.

Postal Rates

The postal rate for postcards and airmail letters to destinations within the EC is 90 dr for up to 20 grams and 140 dr for up to 50 grams. Elsewhere the rate is 120 dr up to 20 grams and 170 dr up to 150 grams. Post within Europe takes five to eight days and to the USA, Australia and New Zealand, nine to 11 days. Periptera (kiosks) also sell stamps, with a 10% surcharge.

Sending Mail

Do not wrap a parcel until it has been inspected at a post office. In Athens take your parcel to the Parcel Post Office (☎ 01-322 8940), Stadiou 4, and elsewhere to the parcel counter of a regular post office.

Receiving Mail

Mail can be sent poste restante (general delivery) to any main post office. The service is free of charge, but you are required to show your passport. Ask your friends and relatives

to write your family name in capital letters and underline it, and to mark the envelope 'poste restante'. It is a good idea to ask the post office clerk to check under your first name as well, if expected letters cannot be located. After one month, uncollected mail is returned to the sender. If you are about to leave a town and expected mail hasn't arrived, ask at the post office to have it forwarded to your next destination, c/o poste restante. See the Post & Telecommunications section in the Athens chapter for addresses of post offices which hold poste restante mail.

Parcels are not delivered in Greece; they must be collected from the parcel counter at a post office and in Athens from the Parcel Post Office.

Telephone

The Greek telephone service is maintained by the public corporation known as Organismos Telepikoinoniou Ellados, which is always referred to by the acronym OTE (pronounced O-tay). Telephone booths with a blue strip on top are for local calls and those with an orange strip are for long-distance calls. A local call costs 10 dr; the booths with blue strips only take 10 dr coins and do not give change; the ones with orange strips take 10, 20 and 50 dr coins. There are no telephone cards in Greece. The telephones in these booths are often out of order, but there are several other (preferable) options for making calls. Most hotel foyers have red payphones from which local calls can be made – they take 10 dr coins.

Direct-dial international and long-distance calls are easiest made from OTE offices; these can be found in every town. They contain cubicles equipped with meters; a counter clerk tells you which cubicle to use, and payment is made after completion of the call. Villages and remote islands without OTE offices almost always have at least one metered phone for long-distance and international calls – usually in a shop, kafeneion or taverna.

Another option is to use a periptero telephone. Almost every periptero has a telephone; these are usually metered (ask for 'me me-tri-TI'), and can be used for local, long-distance and direct-dial international calls. There is a small surcharge, but it is considerably less than that charged by hotels.

An advantage of periptero telephones over booths is that you do not need coins – you make the call first and then pay the periptero owner after completion. Hotel telephone surcharges are quite high. Rates for one unit are 13.5 dr in deluxe hotels, 12.5 dr in A class hotels, 11.5 dr in B class hotels, 10.5 dr in C class hotels and 10 dr in D and E class establishments.

Reverse charge (collect) calls can be made from an OTE office. The time you have to wait can vary considerably, from a few minutes to two hours. If you are using a private phone to make a reverse-charge call, dial the operator (domestic ☎ 132; international ☎ 161).

To call overseas, dial 00 which is the Greek overseas access code, followed by the country code for the country you are calling, then the local area code (dropping the leading zero if there is one) and then the number. Some country codes are:

Australia	– 61
France	– 33
Italy	– 39
Japan	– 81
Netherlands	– 31
New Zealand	– 64
Turkey	– 90
UK	– 44
USA & Canada	– 1

Fax, Telex & Telegraph
Telegrams can be sent from any OTE office; larger offices have telex facilities. Main city post offices have fax machines, but sending a fax is expensive.

TIME
Greece is two hours ahead of GMT/UTC and three hours ahead on daylight saving time, which begins at 12.01 am on the last Sunday in March, when clocks are put forward one hour. Clocks are put back an hour at 12.01 am on the last Sunday in September.

So, when it is noon in Greece it is also noon in Istanbul, 10 am in London, 11 am in Rome, 2 am in San Francisco, 5 am in New York and Toronto, 8 am in Sydney and 10 pm in Auckland.

ELECTRICITY
Electricity is 220 V, AC 50 Hz, and plugs are the standard continental type with two round pins. All hotel rooms and domatia have power points and most camping grounds have an electric supply.

LAUNDRY
Large towns and some islands have laundrettes, which charge about 1000 dr a load whether you do it yourself or have it service-washed. Hotel and room owners will usually provide you with a wash tub if requested.

WEIGHTS & MEASURES
Greece uses the metric system. Liquids – especially barrel wine – are often sold by weight rather than volume; 959 grams of wine, for example, is equivalent to 1000 ml.

Remember that, like other Continental Europeans, Greeks indicate decimals with commas and thousands with points.

BOOKS & MAPS
People & Society
Of the numerous festivals held in Greece one of the most bizarre and overtly pagan is the carnival held on the island of Skyros. The definitive book on the subject is *The Goat Dancers of Skyros* by Joy Coulentianou.

The Cyclades, or Life Amongst the Insular Greeks by James Theodore Bent (first published 1885; hardback) has stood the test of time and is still the greatest English-language book about the Greek islands. It relates the experiences of the author and his wife during a year of travelling around the Cyclades in the late 19th century. Sadly, the book is out of print. (The Hellenic Book Service may have a second-hand copy; see the Bookshops section later in this chapter.)

Time, Religion & Social Experience in Rural Greece by Laurie Kain Hart (paperback) is a fascinating account of village traditions which are still alive and well, beneath the tourist veneer. *Portrait of a Greek Mountain Village*, by Juliet du Boulay, is in similar vein, based on the author's personal experience of living in an isolated village.

A Traveller's Journey is Done (paperback) and *An Affair of the Heart* (paperback), by Dilys Powell, wife of archaeologist Humfry Payne, are very readable, affectionate insights into village life in the Peloponnese during the 1920s and 1930s when Payne was excavating there.

Road to Rembetica: Music of a Greek Subculture – Songs of Love, Sorrow and Hashish by Gail Holst is an exploration of the intriguing subculture which emerged from the poverty and suffering of the refugees from Asia Minor.

The Colossus of Maroussi by Henry Miller (paperback) is now regarded as a classic. With senses heightened, Miller relates his travels in Greece at the outbreak of WW II with feverish enthusiasm. Another book which will whet your appetite if you are contemplating a holiday in Greece is *Hellas: A Portrait of Greece* by Nicholas Gage (paperback).

Vanishing Greece by Clay Perry with an introduction by Patrick Leigh Fermor (hardback) is a large and expensive book of magnificent photographs of the landscapes and people of rural Greece. But the message of the book is a sad one: that the rural culture of Greece, little changed since Homer's time, is fast vanishing.

History & Mythology

A Traveller's History of Greece by Timothy Boatswain & Colin Nicholson (paperback) is probably the best choice for the layperson who wants a good general reference to the historical background of Greece. It gives clear and comprehensive coverage from Neolithic times to the present day. *Modern Greece: A Short History* by C M Woodhouse (paperback) is in a similar vein, although it has a right-wing bent; Woodhouse makes no attempt to hide his glee at the fall of PASOK in 1990. The book covers the period from Constantine the Great to 1990.

Mythology is an intrinsic part of life in Ancient Greece, and some knowledge of it will enhance your visit to the country. One of the best publications on the subject is *The Greek Myths* by Robert Graves (paperback, two volumes) which retells and interprets the adventures of the principal gods and heroes worshipped by the Ancient Greeks. The two volumes of Homer's *Odyssey* and *Iliad* translated by E V Rien (paperbacks) are possibly the best translations of these epics – Homer's account of the Trojan War and Odysseus' (Ulysses') subsequent adventures. *Ovid's Metamorphoses* translated by A D Melville (paperback) is a beautiful poetic interpretation of the Greek myths. Ovid (Publius Ovidius Naso) was a Roman who lived in the 1st century BC.

Women in Athenian Law and Life by Roger Just (hardback) is the first in-depth study of the role of women in Ancient Greece.

The Argonautica Expedition by Theodor Troev (paperback) encompasses Greek mythology, archaeology, travel and adventure. It relates the voyage undertaken by the author and his crew in the 1980s following in the footsteps of Jason and the Argonauts. The aim of the expedition was to investigate the possibility that maritime and cultural links had existed between what is now the Bulgarian coast and other points in the ancient world.

Mary Renault's novels provide an excellent feel for Ancient Greece. *The King Must Die* and *The Bull from the Sea* (both paperback) are vivid tales of Minoan times. *Mistras and Byzantine Style and Civilisation* by Sir Steven Runciman (paperback) and *Fourteen Byzantine Rulers* by Michael Psellus (paperback) are both good introductions to the Byzantine Age – a period of the country's history which is often overlooked by visitors to Greece.

Farewell Anatolia and *The Dead are*

Waiting by Dido Soteriou (paperbacks) are two powerful novels focusing on the population exchange of 1923. Soteriou was born in Asia Minor in 1909 and was herself a refugee.

The Villa Ariadne by Dilys Powell is centred around the dwelling of the title, which was built by Sir Arthur Evans and still stands near Knossos. Many people who were prominent in the shaping of modern Crete were either residents or guests at this house at one time or another, so the book is a very readable account of recent Cretan history. Crete played a pivotal role during WW II and many books have been written about this period of the island's history. *The Cretan Runner* by Georgios Psychoundaki (translated by Patrick Leigh Fermor; paperback) is a graphic account of this traumatic time – the author was active in the island's resistance movement.

In a similar vein *The Jaguar* by Alexander Kotzias (paperback) is a moving story about the leftist resistance to the Nazi occupation of Greece. Although a novel, it is packed with historical facts. *Greek Women in Resistance* by Eleni Fountouri (paperback) is a compilation of journals, poems and personal accounts of women in the resistance movement from the 1940s to 50s. The book also contains poignant photographs and drawings.

Eleni by Nicholas Gage (paperback) is an account by the author of his family's struggle to survive the horrors of the civil war, and his mother's death at the hands of the Communists. It was made into a film in 1985.

The third volume of Olivia Manning's Balkan trilogy *Friends & Heroes* (paperback) has Greece as a setting. It is based on the author's own experiences as the wife of a British Council lecturer, and is a riveting account of the chaos and confusion among the émigré community fleeing the Nazi invasion of Europe. *The Flight of Ikaros* (paperback) by Kevin Andrews is another classic. The author relates his travels in Greece during the 1940s civil war. *Greece in the Dark* by the same author is a perceptive account of his life in Greece during the junta years.

Poetry

Sappho: A new translation by Mary Bernard is the best translation of this great ancient poet's works.

Collected Poems by George Seferis (paperback), *Selected Poems by Odysseus Elytis* (paperback) and *Collected Poems by Constantine Cavafy* are all excellent translations of Greece's three greatest modern poets.

Novels

The most well known and widely read Greek author is the Cretan writer, Nikos Kazantzakis, whose novels are full of drama and larger-than-life characters. His most famous works are *The Last Temptation*, *Zorba the Greek*, *Christ Recrucified* and *Freedom or Death*, all of which are available in paperback. The first two have been made into films.

The Mermaid Madonna and *The School-mistress with the Golden Eyes* are two passionate novels by the writer Myrivilis Stratis. Their settings are two villages on the island of Lesbos, the writer's birthplace. *When the Tree Sings* by Stratis Haviaras (paperback) is a beautifully lyrical and impressionistic novel inspired by the author's experiences as a young boy in Greece during the traumatic years of the 1940s.

If you want to experience the ambience of Greece before you leave home, the Australian author Beverley Farmer has two collections of short stories, *Home Time* and *Milk* (McPhee Gribble/Penguin), many of which are set in Greece. A common theme in her work is the experience of foreigners who endeavour to make their home in Greece. The stories are beautifully written and make compelling reading.

Travel Books

During the 19th century many books about Greece were written by philhellenes who went to the country to help in the struggle for self determination. *Travels in Northern Greece* by William Leake is an account of Greece in the last years of Ottoman rule. Leake was the British consul in Ioannina during Ali Pasha's rule. The English painter and writer Edward Lear of *The Owl and the Pussy Cat* fame spent some time in Greece in the mid-19th century and wrote *Journeys of a Landscape Painter*.

Lawrence Durrell is the best known of the 20th-century philhellenes – he spent an idyllic childhood on Corfu. His evocative books *Prospero's Cell* (paperback) and *Reflections on a Marine Venus* (paperback) are about Corfu and Rhodes respectively. His coffee-table book *The Greek Islands* (hard and paperback) is one of the most popular books of its kind. Even if you disagree with Durrell's opinions and attitudes about the islands, you will probably concede that the photographs are superb. *My Family and Other Animals* by Gerald Durrell (paperback) is an hilarious account of the Durrell family's chaotic and wonderful life on Corfu – Gerald and Lawrence were brothers.

Patrick Leigh Fermor is another ardent philhellene, who now lives in Kardamili in the Peloponnese. His highly acclaimed book *The Mani* (paperback) is an account of his adventures in the Mani peninsula during the 1950s, when many traditional customs were still in evidence. By the same author, *Roumeli* (paperback) relates travels in northern Greece. *Deep into Mani* by Peter Greenhalgh & Edward Eliopoulis (paperback) is a journey through the same area some 25 years after Fermor's book about the Mani was written. If you are going to explore the Mani, this book (as well as those by Fermor) will greatly aid your appreciation of the region, which is one of the most strikingly beautiful and captivating in Greece.

Travels in the Morea by Nikos Kazantzakis (paperback) is a highly readable account of the great writer's travels through the Peloponnese in the 1930s.

Under Mount Ida: A Journey into Crete by Oliver Burch is a compelling portrayal of this diverse and beautiful island – full of insights into the landscape, history and people.

If you are planning a trip to Mt Athos (the Holy Mountain), and wish to get the most out of the experience, some preliminary reading is essential. The most informative and interesting accounts are *The Station* by Robert Byron (paperback) and *Athos: the Holy Mountain* by Sidney Loch (paperback).

Travel Guides

The world's first travel writer was the Ancient Greek traveller, Pausanias, who, in the 2nd century BC, wrote *The Guide to Greece*. Umpteen editions later it is now available in English in paperback.

For archaeological buffs the *Blue Guides* (paperbacks) are hard to beat. They go into tremendous detail about all the major sites, and many of the lesser known ones. They have separate guides for Greece and Crete. In contrast *Ebdon's Odyssey* (paperback) by John Ebdon is a highly entertaining and irreverent account of travels in Greece.

Lonely Planet's *Trekking in Greece* by Marc S Dubin is an in-depth guide to Greece's mountain paths, complemented with excellent maps.

Insight Guides' *Greece* contains Insight's usual beautiful and evocative photographs and intelligent commentaries on Greek culture, although it's a little short on practical

travel information – a great souvenir which will help you to invoke those holiday memories when you return home.

If you are going to live for any length of time in Athens then you will find *Athens: A Survival Handbook* by Stephanie Ginger & Christopher Klint (paperback) useful. It was published in 1985 so is now a bit out of date, but much of the information is still relevant.

Other guides aimed at independent travellers are Rough Guide's *Greece* and the Let's Go guide to *Greece & Turkey*.

Finally if you are an inveterate island hopper, the *Thomas Cook Guide to Greek Island Hopping* gives comprehensive listings of ferry times throughout Greece.

Botanical Field Guides

The Flowers of Greece & the Aegean by William Taylor & Anthony Huxley is the most comprehensive field guide to Greece. The Greek writer, naturalist and mountaineer George Sfikas has written many books on wildlife in Greece, some of which have been translated into English. Amongst them are *Wildflowers of Greece*, *Trees & Shrubs of Greece*, *Medicinal Plants of Greece* and *Wildflowers of Mt Olympos*. All are available in paperback.

Bookshops

The bookshops in Greece with the most comprehensive selections of foreign-language books (including English) are in Athens and Thessaloniki (see these sections). All the other major towns and tourist resorts have bookshops which sell some foreign-language books. Imported books are expensive, but the Greek publishers Evstathiadhis publish low-priced English translations of books by Greek authors in paperback, and books about Greece by foreign authors.

Abroad, the best bookshop for new and second-hand books about Greece, written in both English and Greek, is the Hellenic Book Service, 91 Fortress Rd, Kentish Town, London NW5 1AG (☎ 071-267 9499). It stocks almost all of the books recommended here, and will take mail or telephone orders.

Maps

Unless you are going to trek or drive, the maps given out by the EOT will probably suffice, although they are not 100% accurate. On islands where there is no EOT there are usually tourist maps for sale for around 300 dr, but again, these are not 100% accurate.

If you are going to trek, then the best available topographical survey maps of Greece are the *Karta Nomos* (1:200,000), published by the Ethniki Statistiki Ipiresia (National Statistical Office). There are 52 sheets; each covers a single administrative area. Relief is shown by colour tints with contours at 200-metre intervals. All names are given in Greek script only. The maps may be bought at the Athens Statistical Service Office, Likourgou 14, 3rd floor, near Omonia (show your passport). The maps cost UK£9.95 a sheet at Stanfords in London (see page 78). Lonely Planet's *Trekking in Greece* has over 40 contoured sketch maps which should suffice for most of the standard treks.

Under present Greek government regulations, larger scale topographic surveys published by the military authorities are not available to the general public. All is not lost however, as a series of walking maps (1:50,000) based on the military topographical maps are published in the bimonthly EOS magazine *Korfes*. Copies of these maps may be purchased in Greece at the EOS office (☎ 01-246 1528), Plateia Agiou Vlassiou 16, Aharnes (a suburb of Athens).

Areas covered to date are the most popular trekking and climbing areas in Greece. The latest ones have names in both Greek and Latin script; the earlier editions have names in Greek only. These maps cost UK£2.50 a sheet at Stanfords.

The best motoring map of the Greek mainland is the Bartholomew/RV Euromap (1:800,000), and for the islands and the Peloponnese, the 15 Freytag & Berndt maps. These maps cost UK£4.95 and UK£5.50 respectively at Stanfords.

Whichever maps you wish to purchase you will have less hassle if you do so before arriving in Greece. Every map of Greece available to the general public is stocked by Stanfords, 12-14 Long Acre, London WC2E 9LP (☎ 071-836 1321; telex 21667; fax 071-836 0189). Stanfords accepts telephone orders with payment by Access (MasterCard) or Visa.

MEDIA
Newspapers & Magazines
Greeks are great newspaper readers. There are 15 daily newspapers, of which the most widely read are *Ta Nea*, *Kathimerini*, and *Eleftheros Typos*.

English-language newspapers are the daily *Athens News* (120 dr) which carries world news and Greek news, and the *Weekly Greek News* (200 dr), which carries predominantly Greek news. English-language magazines are *Greece's Weekly* (300 dr) which is heavy on economic and political issues and the monthly *Athenian* (475 dr), a high-quality magazine with articles on politics, the arts, travel, theatre, cinema, and gallery and museum listings. The centrefold is the *Athenian Organiser* – a comprehensive list of useful telephone numbers, such as museums, galleries, libraries, cultural organisations, etc. The last few pages of *Greece's Weekly* magazine is a listings section (called the 'Polyguide', which is similar to the *Athenian Organiser*.

These publications are widely available in Athens and some of the major resorts, as is almost every British newspaper (the day after publication). The *Herald Tribune*, the

European and many international magazines including *Time*, *Newsweek* and the *Economist* are also available.

Radio & TV
Greece has two state-owned radio channels, ET ONE and ET TWO. On ET ONE there are three different programmes. The first two programmes are devoted to popular music and news, and the third programme has mostly classical music. ET TWO broadcasts mostly popular music. News in English can be heard on the First Radio Programme (412 kHz) at approximately 7.30 am on weekdays and 7.15 am on weekends. There are news bulletins daily in English at about 2.25 pm on ERT 2 the precise time of the English-language news bulletins depends on the duration of the Greek bulletins which precede them. Local radio stations – both legal and illegal – are increasing at such an alarming rate that the mountains around Athens have been compared to pin cushions, they have so many radio masts sticking out of them. The best frequencies to pick up the BBC World Service in Athens are:

GMT	
3 am to 7.30 am	9.41 MHz (31-metre band)
	6.05 MHz (49-metre band)
	15.07 MHz (19-metre band)
7.30 am to 6 pm	15.07 MHz (19-metre band)
6.30 pm to 11.15 pm	9.41 MHz (31-metre band)
	6.05 MHz (49-metre band)

As far as Greek TV is concerned, quantity rather than quality is the operative word. There are six TV channels: ET1, ET2, ET3, ANTENNI, MEGA and New channel. ANTENNI broadcasts CBS news at 6.30 am on weekdays and 7 am on weekends. All channels show many English and US serials and films with Greek subtitles.

FILM & PHOTOGRAPHY
Major brands of film are widely available, although expensive. A 36-exposure film costs around 1500 dr, and an additional 2500 dr to develop. Because of the brilliant sunlight in summer, it's a good idea to use a polarising lens filter.

Never photograph a military installation or anything else that has a sign forbidding photographs. Greeks usually love having their photos taken but, of course, it's polite to ask first.

HEALTH

There is at least one doctor on every island in Greece and larger islands have hospitals. Pharmacies in Greece are able to dispense medicines which in most European countries are only available on prescription, so for minor ailments you could first consult a pharmacist. Citizens of EC countries are covered for free treatment in public hospitals within Greece on presentation of an E111 form. Enquire at your national health service or travel agent in advance. Emergency treatment is free to all nationalities in public hospitals. In an emergency, dial 166.

All this sounds fine, but although medical training is of a high standard in Greece, the health service is underfunded and one of the worst in Europe. Hospitals are overcrowded, hygiene is not always what it should be and relations are expected to bring in food for the patient – which could be problematic for a tourist. Conditions and treatment are better in private hospitals, but they're expensive. All this means that a good medical insurance policy is essential.

Predeparture Preparations

Health Insurance A travel insurance policy to cover theft, loss, medical problems and personal liability is a must. There is a wide variety of policies and your travel agent will have recommendations. The international student travel policies handled by STA or other student travel organisations are usually good value. Some policies offer lower and higher medical expense options. Check the small print:

Some policies specifically exclude 'dangerous activities' which can include scuba diving, motorcycling, mountaineering, and even trekking. If such activities are on your agenda then you don't want that sort of policy.

You may prefer a policy that pays doctors or hospitals direct rather than you having to pay on the spot

and claim later. Make sure you keep all documentation. Some policies ask you to call back (reverse charges) to a centre in your home country, where an immediate assessment of your problem is made.

Check if the policy covers ambulances or helicopter rescue, and an emergency flight home. If you have to stretch out, you will need two seats and somebody has to pay for them!

Medical Kit A small, straightforward medical kit is a wise thing to carry. A possible kit includes:

• A mild analgesic, such as Panadol – for pain or fever
• Antihistamine – useful as a decongestant for colds, allergies, to ease the itch from insect bites or stings or to prevent motion sickness
• Kaolin preparation or similar – for possible stomach upsets
• Antiseptic, Mercurochrome and antibiotic powder or similar 'dry' spray – for cuts and grazes
• Calamine lotion – to ease irritation from bites or stings
• Bandages and Band-aids – for minor injuries
• Scissors, tweezers and a thermometer (note that mercury thermometers are prohibited by airlines)
• Insect repellent, sunscreen, suntan lotion

Warning Codeine, which is commonly found in headache preparations, is banned in Greece; check labels carefully, or risk prosecution. Due to the strict regulations applying to the importation of medicines into Greece, obtain a certificate from your doctor which outlines any medication you may have to carry into the country with you.

Health Preparations If you wear glasses or contact lenses, take a spare pair and your prescription in case of loss. Whilst poets since time immemorial have waxed lyrical about the dazzling light of Greece, on a more practical level, too much sunlight, whether it's direct or reflected (glare), can damage your eyes. It is very important to wear good sunglasses. Make sure they're treated to absorb ultraviolet radiation – if not, they'll do more harm than good as they'll dilate your pupils and make it easier for ultraviolet light to damage the retina.

If you require a particular medication, take an adequate supply, as it may not always be available in remote areas. The same applies to oral contraceptives. Take prescriptions with the generic rather than the brand name, which may not be available locally, as it will be easier to obtain replacements.

A medical emergency pendant containing relevant health history details is worth having if your medical condition is not easily recognisable (heart trouble, diabetes, asthma, allergic reactions to antibiotics etc).

Immunisations These are only an entry requirement for Greece if you're coming from an infected area – yellow fever and cholera are the most likely requirements.

Basic Rules

Food & Water Tap water is safe to drink in Greece, but if you prefer mineral water, it is widely available. You might experience mild intestinal problems if you're not used to copious amounts of olive oil; however, you'll get used to it and current research says it's good for you.

If you don't vary your diet, are travelling hard and fast and missing meals, or simply lose your appetite, you can soon start to lose weight and place your health at risk. Fruit and vegetables are good sources of vitamins and Greece produces a greater variety of these than almost any other European country. Both are reasonably cheap – most varieties cost less than 300 dr a kg.

Medical Problems & Treatment

By far the biggest health risk in Greece comes from the intensity of the sun; take care against sunburn, heat exhaustion and dehydration. Use a sunscreen and take extra care to cover areas that don't normally see sun, eg your feet. It is a good idea to use zinc cream or some other barrier cream for your nose and lips. Calamine lotion is good for mild sunburn. Greeks claim that yoghurt applied to sunburn is soothing.

Heat Exhaustion Dehydration or salt deficiency can cause heat exhaustion. Take time to acclimatise to high temperatures and make sure you drink enough – don't rely on feeling thirsty to indicate when you should drink.

Very dark yellow urine or not needing to urinate is a danger sign. If you go for a walk in Greece wear a sun hat and be sure to take sufficient water with you. Salt deficiency is characterised by fatigue, lethargy, headaches, giddiness and muscle cramps, and in this case salt tablets may help.

Heatstroke This serious, and sometimes fatal, condition can occur if the body's heat-regulating mechanism breaks down and the body temperature rises to dangerous levels. Long continuous periods of exposure to high temperatures can leave you vulnerable to heatstroke. You should avoid excessive alcohol or strenuous activity when you first arrive in a hot climate.

The symptoms of heatstroke are feeling unwell, not sweating very much or at all and high body temperature (39°C to 40°C). When sweating has ceased, the skin becomes flushed and red. Severe throbbing headaches and lack of coordination will also occur, and the sufferer may become confused or aggressive. Eventually the victim will become delirious or convulse. Hospitalisation is essential, but meanwhile get patients out of the sun, remove their clothing, cover them with a wet sheet or towel and fan them continually.

Hypothermia Although everyone associates Greece with heat and sunshine, even in summer, the high mountainous regions can be cool. There is snow on the mountains from November to April. On the highest mountains in the north, snow patches can still be seen in June. Keeping warm whilst trekking in these regions in spring and autumn can be as much of a problem as keeping cool in the lower regions in summer. Too much cold is as dangerous as too much heat, particularly if it leads to hypothermia. Cold combined with wind and moisture (ie soaking rain) is particularly risky. If you are trekking at high altitudes or in a cool, wet environment, be prepared.

Hypothermia occurs when the body loses heat faster than it can produce it and the core temperature of the body falls. It is surprisingly easy to progress from very cold to dangerously cold through a combination of wind, wet clothing, fatigue and hunger, even if the air temperature is above freezing. It is best to dress in layers – silk, wool and some of the new artificial fibres are all good insulating materials. A hat is important, as most heat is lost through the head. A strong, waterproof outer layer is essential, as keeping dry is vital. Carry basic supplies, including food that contains simple sugars to generate heat quickly, and lots of fluid to drink.

Symptoms of hypothermia are exhaustion, numb skin (particularly toes and fingers), shivering, slurred speech, irrational or violent behaviour, lethargy, stumbling, dizzy spells, muscle cramps and violent bursts of energy. Irrationality may take the form of sufferers claiming that they are warm and trying to take off their clothes.

To treat hypothermia, first get the patient out of the wind and rain, remove their clothing if it's wet and replace it with dry, warm clothing. Give them hot nonalcoholic liquids and some high-kilojoule, easily digestible food. This should be enough for the early stages of hypothermia, but if it has gone further it may be necessary to place victims in a warm sleeping bag and get in with them. Do not rub patients, place them near a fire or remove their wet clothes in the wind. If possible, place a sufferer in a warm, but not hot, bath.

Motion Sickness Sea sickness can be a problem in Greece, as the Aegean is unpredictable and can get very rough when the meltemi wind is up. For all types of motion sickness, eating lightly before and during a trip will reduce your chances of being inflicted. Fresh air helps, so you'll fare better on the deck of a ferry rather than inside. Also, try to find a place that minimises disturbance – near the wing on an aircraft, close to midship on boats, near the centre on buses. Looking at a steady reference point like the horizon can help, whereas reading or cigarette smoke don't. Commercial antimotion-sickness preparations, which can cause drowsiness, have to be taken before the trip commences; when you're feeling sick it's too late. Ginger is a natural preventative and is available in capsule form.

Diarrhoea A change of water, food or climate can all cause the runs, but diarrhoea caused by contaminated food or water is more serious. Despite all your precautions, you may still have a bout of mild travellers' diarrhoea. A few rushed toilet trips with no other symptoms is not indicative of a serious problem.

Moderate diarrhoea, involving half a dozen movements a day, is more of a nuisance. Dehydration is the main danger with diarrhoea, particularly for children, so fluid replenishment is the number one treatment. Weak black tea with little sugar, soda water, or soft drinks allowed to go flat and diluted 50% with water are all good.

Sexually Transmitted Diseases (STDs) Sexual contact with an infected partner spreads diseases. Although abstinence is the only 100% preventative, using condoms is also effective. Gonorrhoea and syphilis are the most common of these diseases: in men, sores, blisters or rashes around the genitals, discharges or pain when urinating are common symptoms. Symptoms may be less marked or not observed at all in women. Syphilis symptoms eventually disappear completely but the disease continues and can cause severe problems in later years. Antibiotics are used to treat gonorrhoea and syphilis. There are numerous other STDs, for most of which effective treatment is available. There is no cure for herpes or for HIV/AIDS. Always practising safe sex using condoms is the most effective preventative; it is impossible to detect the HIV-positive status of an otherwise healthy looking person without a blood test. Condoms (in Greek *kapotes* – ka-PO-tes) are widely available in Greece. They are sold in pharmacies and periptera.

HIV/AIDS can be contracted through infected blood transfusions. It can also be spread by dirty needles, so vaccinations, acupuncture, tattooing and ear and nose piercing can be as dangerous as intravenous drug use if the equipment is not clean.

There are no STD clinics in Greece, but the Andreas Syngrou Hospital (☎ 01-723 9611), Dragoumi 5, Athens (behind the Hilton Hotel), specialises in the treatment of STDs. Treatment is free, but telephone to find out when the out-patient clinic is open. Elsewhere go to the local hospital.

Mosquitoes These can be a nuisance in Greece, but most people get used to mosquito bites after a few days as their bodies adjust and the itching and swelling become less severe. Avoid bites by covering bare skin and using an insect repellent.

Insect repellents and green coils are widely available. Some, but by no means all, places to stay have insect screens on windows. One of the most effective deterrents is a small two-pronged electronic device on which a thin tablet is placed. Some hotels supply these, or they can be purchased in shops.

Ticks If you plan to spend most of your time on beaches or in bars, ticks will probably not be a problem. However, if you will be walking or trekking, you may well pass through a tick-infested area. Examine yourself and your clothes, and remove ticks with alcohol, vaseline or oil. Salt or a lighted cigarette end will also persuade them to let go. Don't pull them off, as the bite could become infected.

Scabies & Lice In some budget-end accommodation places, where laundering of linen may be less than scrupulous, you may be at risk of a scabies or lice infestation. Remedies with various degrees of effectiveness are available over the counter in Greece. All bedding and clothing must be washed in very hot water.

Bee & Wasp Stings Although there are a lot of bees and wasps in some areas of Greece, their stings are usually painful rather than dangerous. Calamine lotion will give relief or ice packs will reduce the pain or swelling.

Jelly Fish & Sea Urchins Watch out for sea urchins around rocky beaches; if you get some of their needles embedded in your skin, olive oil will help to loosen them. If they are not removed they will fester. Be wary also of jellyfish, particularly during the months of September and October. Although they are not lethal in Greece, their stings can be painful. Suggested cures for jellyfish stings are ammonia, papain meat tenderiser, urine or vinegar.

Snakes Greece's only poisonous snake is the adder, but it is so rare that you hardly ever hear of anyone being bitten. Snakes like to sunbathe on dry stone walls, so take care if you need to climb over one of these.

In the unlikely event of snakebite, keep the victim calm and still, wrap the bitten limb tightly, as you would for a sprained ankle, and then attach a splint to immobilise it. Then seek medical help. Tourniquets and sucking out the poison are now comprehensively discredited.

Sheepdogs These dogs are trained to guard penned sheep from bears, wolves and thieves. They are often underfed and sometimes ill-treated by their owners. They are almost always all bark and no bite, but if you are going to trek into remote areas, you should consider having rabies injections. You are most likely to encounter these dogs in the mountainous regions of Epiros and Crete.

Wandering through a flock of sheep over which one of these dogs is vigilantly (and possibly discreetly) watching is simply asking for trouble.

Women's Health
Gynaecological Problems Poor diet, lowered resistance through the use of antibiotics for stomach upsets, and even contraceptive pills can lead to vaginal infections when travelling in hot climates. Maintaining good personal hygiene, and wearing skirts or loose-fitting trousers and cotton underwear will help prevent infections.

Yeast infections (thrush), characterised by

a rash, itch and discharge, can be treated with vinegar, yoghurt, or even a lemon-juice douche. Nystatin suppositories are the usual medical prescription. Trichomonas is a more serious infection; symptoms are a discharge and a burning sensation when urinating. If a vinegar-water douche is not effective, medical attention should be sought. Flagyl is the prescribed drug. In both cases, male sexual partners must also be treated.

Some women experience irregular periods when travelling because of the upset in routine. Don't forget to take time zones into account if you're on the pill. If you run into intestinal problems, the pill may not be absorbed. Ask your physician about these matters before you go.

WOMEN TRAVELLERS

Many women travel alone in Greece and, as the crime rate is low, they are often safer than they would be in most European countries. This does not mean that you should be lulled into complacency; bag snatching and rapes do occur, but with no more frequency than in most other countries.

The biggest nuisance to foreign women travelling alone are the guys the Greeks have nicknamed *kamaki*. The word means 'fishing trident' and refers to the kamaki's favourite pastime, which is 'fishing' for foreign women, in order to have a sexual encounter, which they can boast to their friends about.

They will approach and say something like 'Where do you come from?' or 'Do you like Greece?'. A woman looking at a map gives them a good reason to approach and offer help. Ignoring them at this stage does not always work because kamaki enjoy a challenge. They'll follow you for a while, but give up eventually. Unfortunately, in your efforts to shake them off, you've probably walked in the opposite direction to the way you wanted to go, and are hopelessly lost, so out will come the map again...

Dressing conservatively helps to a certain extent to keep kamaki at bay, as does looking as if you know where you are going, even if you haven't got a clue. However, these men

are very much in the minority, and are a hassle rather than a threat. The majority of Greek men treat foreign women with respect, and are genuinely helpful.

DANGERS & ANNOYANCES
Theft

Crime – especially theft – is low in Greece, but unfortunately it is on the increase. The worst area is Omonia in Athens – keep track of your valuables here and at the flea market which gets very crowded. The vast majority of thefts from tourists are still committed by other tourists, and not by Greeks. Bearing this in mind, the biggest danger of theft is probably in dormitory rooms in hostels and on camp sites. So make sure you do not leave valuables unattended in such places. If you are staying in a hotel room, and the windows and door do not lock securely, ask for your valuables to be locked in the hotel safe – hotel proprietors are happy to do this.

Bar Scams

A warning needs to be given to solo male travellers about an unpleasant practice which is currently largely confined to Athens, although there have been one or two occurrences in other cities. The practice follows this pattern: a male traveller enters a bar and buys a drink; the owner then offers him another drink. Women appear, more drinks are provided and the visitor relaxes as he realises that the women are not prostitutes, just friendly Greeks. The crunch comes at the end of the evening when the traveller is presented with an exorbitant bill – a despicable way of inveigling money out of solo male travellers. One Englishman I met was £90 poorer at the end of one such evening.

Drugs

Greek drug laws are the strictest in Europe. Greek courts make no distinction between possession and pushing. The minimum sentence for even a small quantity of dope is seven years.

Lightning

Recent fatalities have highlighted the

When in Crete....
Behaviour that might be perfectly appropriate at a Mardi Gras celebration in Brazil or a nightclub in Soho will probably not be appreciated in a small Greek village. This was recently highlighted in an incident on the island of Crete when an English woman was arrested and detained for three nights for 'immoral dancing' in a local bar. An increase in the number of tourists arrested in Greece in recent years would suggest that many travellers are ignoring the first precept of travel – the visitor is a privileged guest, and the customs and mores of the host country should be observed and respected. Perhaps the recent trend towards 24-hour bars and concomitant increased retsina consumption may be partly responsible for the increase in 'inappropriate' behaviour. Whatever, before you decide to practise the lambada on the table top at that groovy little local taverna – remember – relatives at home might be jealous of those postcards of azure seas and long sandy beaches, but they will certainly prefer these to requests for bail! ∎

---

dangers of trekking in exposed areas during electrical thunderstorms. If you are caught in a thunderstorm, seek shelter, preferably in a low-lying area.

WORK
Unemployment in Greece is high so the chances of a foreigner finding lucrative employment are slim. If you wish to take up permanent employment in Greece then the most widely available option is teaching English. A TEFL (Teaching English as a Foreign Language) certificate or a university degree is an advantage but not essential. In the UK, look through the *Times Educational Supplement* or Tuesday's edition of the *Guardian* newspaper – in other countries, contact the Greek embassy. EC nationals don't need a work permit; however, if they intend to stay longer than three months, they will require a residence permit. Nationals of other countries do require a work permit.

Another possibility is finding a job teaching English once you are in Greece. You will see *frontistiria* (language schools) everywhere. Strictly speaking, you need a licence to teach in these schools, but many will employ teachers without one. The best time to look around for such a job is late summer.

If you are an EC national, an employment agency worth contacting is Working Holidays, Pioneer Tours (☎ 01-322 4321), Nikis 11, Athens. Penny Economou, the manager, is friendly and helpful and speaks excellent English. This agency offers hotel, bar, and au pair work, fruit picking etc. EC nationals can

also make use of the OAED (Organismos Apascholiseos Ergatikou Dynamikou), the Greek National Employment Service, in their search for a job. The OAED has offices throughout Greece.

Another alternative is to look through the classifieds of the English-language newspapers, or put an advertisement in yourself. The notice board at Compendium bookshop (see Bookshops under Athens) often advertises jobs. The other option is to look for non-taxable casual work – ask around restaurants and bars in tourist areas. In autumn and winter many foreigners are employed in harvesting and agricultural work. From November to February, there is work picking oranges in the Peloponnese, especially around the towns of Argos and Nafplion. Crete has the longest season, and the greatest number of crops, so work is available here from November to May. Try the Archanes region in late summer for work during the grape harvest. Youth hostels are good places to make enquiries about casual work.

ACTIVITIES
Windsurfing
Windsurfing is the most popular water sport in Greece. Chrissi Akti on Paros, and Vassiliki on Lefkada vie for the best windsurfing beaches. According to an Australian magazine, Vassiliki is one of the best places in the world to learn the sport, but you'll see sailboards for hire on almost every beach, except the least developed ones. Hire charges are around 1500 dr an hour. If you are a novice,

most places which rent equipment also give instruction.

Windsurfers may only be brought into Greece if a Greek national residing in Greece guarantees that it will be taken out again. To find out the procedure for arranging this, contact the Hellenic Windsurfing Association, Filellinon 7, Athens (☎ 323 0330).

Water Skiing

Water skiing is also popular. Islands with water-ski centres are Chios, Corfu, Crete, Kythera, Lesbos, Poros, Skiathos and Rhodes.

Snorkelling & Diving

Snorkelling is enjoyable just about anywhere off the coast off Greece. Especially good places are Monastiri on Paros, Velanio on Skopelos, Paleokastritsa on Corfu, Telendos Island (near Kalimnos) and anywhere off the coast of Kastellorizo.

Diving is a another matter. Any kind of underwater activity using breathing apparatus is strictly forbidden, other than under the supervision of a diving school. This is to protect the many antiquities in the depths of the Aegean. There are diving schools on the islands of Rhodes, Evia, Corfu and Mykonos, and Halkidiki and Glyfada (near Athens) on the mainland. If you wish to dive at Glyfada contact the Aegean Dive Shop (☎ 01-894 5409; fax 01-898 1120), Pandora 31, Glyfada.

Trekking

The topography of Greece is over 50% mountainous. It could be a trekkers' paradise, but there is one drawback. Like all organisations in Greece the EOS (Ellinikos Orivatikos Syndesmos), the Greek Alpine Association, is grossly underfunded. Most EOS staff are volunteers who have full-time day jobs. Consequently, many of the paths in Greece are overgrown and inadequately marked. Don't be put off by this, however, as the most popular routes are well walked and maintained. For trekking in more remote places, see Lonely Planet's *Trekking in Greece*.

On small islands it's fun to discover pathways for yourself. You are unlikely to get into danger as settlements or roads are never far away. You will encounter a variety of paths: *kalderimi* are cobbled or flagstone paths which date back to Byzantine times, and linked settlements. Sadly, many have been bulldozed to make way for roads. Donkey/mule paths are identifiable by droppings and brown dust on the paths. They are used by farmers, are easy to walk along, and usually lead to a settlement, field or farm. Goat tracks are also identified by droppings; these paths are useful, as goats follow contours and zigzag up slopes – they never charge straight uphill. They can be very narrow and tricky to negotiate, but widen as they approach 'home' – a compound or enclosure.

Skiing

Greece is one of the cheapest places in Europe to participate in this sport; it has around 20 resorts. There are no foreign package holidays to these resorts; they are used mainly by Greeks. Most have all the basic facilities and are a pleasant alternative to the glitzy resorts of Western Europe. The

season depends on snow conditions but is approximately from January to the end of April. Pick up a copy of *GREECE Mountain Refuges & Ski Centres* from an EOT office. Information may also be obtained from the Hellenic Skiing Federation (☎ 01- 524 0057; fax 01-524 8821), PO Box 8037, Omonia, Athens 10010.

Courses

The YWCA (XEN in Greek; (☎ 01-362 6971), Amerikis 11, Athens, has courses in painting, photography, cookery, jewellery-making and Greek dancing for men and women. The Athens Centre (☎ 01-701 2268), Arhimidous 49, the Hellenic American Union (☎ 01-362 9886) and the YWCA all run Greek language courses. The Athens Centre uses the most up-to-date teaching methods and its courses include attending cultural events, excursions to ancient sites, museums, cinemas and theatres. The cost for the 60-hour course, which may be spread over one to three months, is 50,000 dr. For other courses, information may be obtained from EOT offices and Greek embassies.

HIGHLIGHTS
Ancient Sites

Greece has more ancient sites than any other country in Europe. Don't miss the well-known ones such as the Acropolis, Delphi, Epidaurus, Olympia, Mycenae and Delos, but also seek out some of the lesser known ones, where you will encounter only a handful of other visitors. These include the Sanctuary of the Great Gods on Samothrace, Ancient Dion near Mt Olympus, Dodoni near Ioannina and Lato near Agios Nikolaos on Crete.

Historic Towns

Two of Greece's most spectacular medieval cities are the deserted Byzantine city of Mystra and the still-inhabited Byzantine city of Monemvassia. Both cities are in the Peloponnese.

The old town of Rhodes is the finest surviving example of a fortified medieval town. The Kastro quarter of Naxos town, on Naxos, where archways span the narrow stepped alleyways of whitewashed Venetian houses, is tranquil and beautiful. The Chora of Folegandros is one of the prettiest of the archetypal Cycladic towns; it has dazzling white cubic architecture and narrow winding streets. The 13th-century village of Pyrgi, on Chios, is visually the most unusual village in Greece – the exterior walls of the houses are decorated with striking black-and-white geometrical patterns. Mesta, also on Chios, is an evocative fortified medieval village. The old quarter of the Thracian town of Xanthi has the best preserved houses from the Turkish era.

Museums

First on everyone's list should be the National Archaeological Museum in Athens. Amongst its vast collection are the celebrated finds which Heinrich Schliemann unearthed at Mycenae, and the Minoan frescoes from Akrotiri, on the island of Thira. The Archaeological Museum in Thessaloniki houses exquisite treasures from the graves of the Macedonian royal family. The Archaeological Museum in Iraklion houses finds from the Neolithic to the Roman periods, but its star attraction is the Minoan collection.

Less well known, but nevertheless outstanding museums are Nafplion's Popular Art Museum, the Folklore Museum in Thessaloniki and the Cycladic Art Museum in Athens.

Hotels

You should stay in at least one traditional settlement. The most atmospheric ones are in the Mani. The Captain's House in Emboreiòs, Halki, in the Dodecanese group, is an outstanding place to stay: a turn-of-the-century ex-admiral's house with antique furniture, a tranquil garden and charming owners. Another lovely place is the Pension Ulla in Skopelos town, which has oak-beamed ceilings and brass bedsteads. One of the most charming places to stay on the Cyclades is the Petra Holiday Villas on Ios. The huge rooms are in traditional Cycladic style with stone floors, dazzling white walls, tasteful wall-hangings and ornaments.

Restaurants

The Petakos Taverna in Gythio, in the Peloponnese, resembles a labourer's café, but the food is delectable, and prices are low. All of the restaurants described in this guide which are in Patitiri, Alonissos, in the Sporades group, serve excellent fish dishes. If you are in Thessaloniki and want a splurge or two (or three!) go to Ouzeri Aristotelou, Ta Nisia Taverna or Saul Modiano Restaurant. In Ermoupolis, on Syros, climb the steps to the Folia Taverna. It's worth the effort to eat at one of the best restaurants in the Cyclades; prices are very reasonable.

Two restaurants worth seeking out in Iraklion, on Crete, are Ippocampos Ouzeri, which has delicious reasonably priced *mezedes* (hors d'ouevres; singular *meze*), and the up-market Giovanni Taverna, where you can enjoy delectable well-prepared food in elegant surroundings.

Beaches

Out of high season, especially if you have your own transport, Sithonia, the middle prong of the Halkidiki peninsula, is worth exploring for long stetches of fine sandy beaches. In the Peloponnese, the western coast of the Messini peninsula, from Kyparissia to Methoni, is studded with sandy beaches. Zaga Beach, at Koroni, on the eastern side of the same peninsula, is one of the most gorgeous – and longest – beaches in Greece.

The islands of Paros, Naxos, Ios and Mykonos have the best beaches in the Cyclades. Unfortunately a lot of people know this, so finding a secluded spot requires legwork. The coasts of Thassos and Lemnos, both in the North-Eastern Aegean group, boast many sandy beaches. Other exceptional beaches are those on the small island of Elafonissi; Porto Katsiki and Vassiliki on Lefkada, in the Ionian group; Psili Ammos on Patmos, Armenistis on Ikaria and Eristos on Tilos, in the Dodecanese group; and Pahia Ammos on Samothrace and Skala Eressos on Lesbos, in the North-Eastern Aegean group.

ACCOMMODATION

There is a range of accommodation in Greece to suit every taste and pocket. All places to stay are subject to strict price controls set by the tourist police. By law, a notice must be displayed in every room, which states the category of the room and the price for each season. The price includes 4.5% community tax and 8% VAT.

Accommodation owners may add a 10% surcharge for a stay of less than three nights, but this is not mandatory. A mandatory charge of 20% is levied if an extra bed is put into a room. During July and August, accommodation owners will charge the maximum price, but in spring and autumn, prices will drop by up to 20%, and perhaps even more in winter. These are the times to bring your bargaining skills into action.

Rip-offs rarely occur, but if you suspect you have been exploited by an accommodation owner, report it to either the tourist police or regular police and they will act swiftly. I only needed to resort to this action once, and I was quickly reunited with my drachma.

Camping

There are around 320 camp sites in Greece. They are operated by the EOT and various private enterprises. Most operate from April to October, but a few are open year round. The EOT publishes an annual booklet listing all of the country's camp sites and their facilities. The sites are classed A, B or C according to the facilities offered, and prices vary accordingly. The price ranges per night are adults: 620 to 850 dr; children up to 12 years: 380 to 570 dr; there is no charge for children under four years. Cars are 160 to 200 dr; small tents are 600 to 720 dr and large tents are 950 to 1280 dr. Between May and mid-September it is warm enough to sleep outside, but you will need a lightweight sleeping bag, as temperatures drop considerably overnight. Also, it is wise to have a foam pad to lie on and a waterproof cover for your sleeping bag.

Camping other than at an official site is illegal, but the rule is not always strictly enforced. If you do decide to take a chance on this, be absolutely sure you are not camping on private land, and clear up all rubbish when you leave. If you are told to move by the police, do so without protest, as the law is occasionally enforced in this matter. A couple of years ago a UK tourist was arrested for vagrancy whilst camping on a beach on Crete. Freelance camping is more likely to be tolerated on islands which don't have camp sites. A wise thing to do before freelance camping anywhere in Greece is to ask around. Other campers and even locals can advise on what the situation is.

Hostels

There are YWCA hostels (women only) in Athens and Thessaloniki. There are currently 17 IYHF (International Youth hostel Federation) hostels in Greece. They are mostly very casual places and IYHF cards are rarely asked for. Most have a curfew, usually sometime between 10 pm and midnight. Greece also has some unofficial youth hostels, which are run on similar lines to the IYHFs. Both official and unofficial hostels charge between 800 and 1200 dr per night for a dormitory bed.

In Athens there are a number of student hostels. These vary considerably in their standards of cleanliness. Some are well-run, friendly places, whilst others are veritable fleapits. They offer a variety of low-priced accommodation, ranging from singles to dormitory beds. Almost all of them have a bar serving reasonably priced drinks and snacks.

Mountain Refuges

There are 55 mountain refuges in Greece, on the mainland, Crete and Evia. They are operated by the EOS or the SEO. The EOT publication *GREECE Mountain Refuges & Ski Centres* has details about each refuge. Prices range from 1000 to 1500 dr per person, depending on the facilities – some are very basic.

Domatia

Domatia originally consisted of a makeshift bed put up in a rural family's home so they could play host to travellers in summer to supplement their meagre income.

Nowadays, many domatia are purpose-built appendages to the family house. Domatia are the first accommodation choice of most budget travellers, but over the last few years they have gone up-market and some of the new ones have fully equipped kitchen areas. On the whole, standards of cleanliness are high in domatia. The décor runs the gamut from cool grey marble floors, coordinated pine-wood furniture, pretty lace curtains and tasteful pictures on the walls, to ones so full of kitch, you are almost afraid to move in case you break an ornament.

Domatia are classified A, B and C. The price range is 1860 to 3500 dr for a single, 2390 to 5100 dr for a double, 3460 to 6050 dr for a triple, depending on the class and whether bathrooms are shared or private. In some domatia, you may be charged between 300 and 400 dr for hot water. Domatia are found throughout the mainland and on almost every island which has a permanent population; an exception is large cities on the mainland. Most domatia operate between the months of April and October, but a few stay open year round.

From June to September domatia owners are out in force, touting for customers. They meet buses and boats, shouting 'room, room'. Nowadays they quite often have photographs of the accommodation on offer. On islands which become inundated with tourists during the summer months, it is folly not to take up an offer. Be wary of domatia owners who 'bend the truth' regarding the location of their accommodation. This trick is particularly prevalent on the islands of Mykonos and Thira, where owners may tell you the accommodation is in the centre of town, and then drive you to somewhere out in the sticks. If you are at all dubious, insist they show you on a map the exact location of their place.

In spring and autumn you are less likely to be met by a domatia owner, in which case you can ask the tourist police, or the staff at a tourist office, to find you a room. Alternatively, simply walk around the streets looking for domatia signs, which are usually prominently displayed in Greek, English and German. On very remote islands the best source of information for domatia is usually a kafeneion or *pantopoleion*, an all-purpose shop found in remote areas.

Hotels

Hotels in Greece are divided into five categories: deluxe, A, B, C, D and E. Hotels are categorised according to the size of the room, whether or not they have a bar, and the ratio of bathrooms to beds, rather than standards of cleanliness, comfort of the beds and friendliness of staff – all elements which may be of greater relevance to guests. As one would expect, deluxe, A and B class hotels have many amenities, private bathrooms and constant hot water. C class hotels have a snack bar, rooms have private bathrooms, but hot water may only be available at certain times of the day. D class hotels may or may not have snack bars, most rooms will share bathrooms, but there may be some with private bathrooms, and they may have solar-heated water, which means hot water is not guaranteed. E classes do not have a snack bar, bathrooms are shared and you may have to pay extra (300 or 400 dr) for hot water, or there may be none at all.

In some deluxe, A and B class hotels breakfast is included during the high season, and in a few, half-board is obligatory. With the exception of deluxe class, prices are controlled by the tourist police. Rates in D and E class hotels are comparable with domatia. In a C class hotel, expect to pay between 5000 and 8000 dr for a single in high season, 7000 to 10,000 dr for a double and 8000 to 12,000 dr for a triple; In a B class expect to pay 6000 to 10,000 dr; 8000 to 12,000 dr; and 10,000 to 15,000 dr. In an A class hotel, expect to pay 10,000 to 15,000 dr; 14,000 to 18,000 dr; and 17,000 to 22,000 dr. In deluxe class hotels, the sky's the limit!

Pensions

Pensions in Greece are indistinguishable from hotels. They are classed A, B or C. An A class pension is equivalent in amenities and price to a B class hotel, a B class pension is equivalent to a C class hotel and a C class pension is equivalent to a D or E class hotel.

Traditional Settlements

Traditional settlements are old buildings of architectural merit, which have been renovated and converted into tourist accommodation. These are terrific places to stay, as, although they have all the modern amenities, they remain architecturally unchanged and are traditionally furnished. But they are expensive – most are equivalent in price to an A or B class hotel. The EOT publishes a leaflet with details of these places and you may reserve a room through them. There are traditional settlements on the islands of Thira, Psara and Chios, the Mani and Pelion peninsulas, and Monemvassia.

Apartments

Self-contained family apartments are available in some hotels and domatia. There are also a number of purpose-built apartments, particularly on the islands, which are available for either long or short-term rental. Prices vary considerably according to the amenities offered. In Athens look in the *Weekly Greek News* classifieds where apartments to let are advertised by individuals and estate agents. Also look at the notice board at Compendium Bookshop (see the Bookshops section in the Athens chapter). In other large towns and cities the tourist police should be able to help. In rural areas and islands, ask in a kafeneion or pantopoleion.

FOOD

Even the most dedicated Grecophile could not pretend that Greek food is one of the world's great cuisines, although it is not as consistently awful as a lot of visitors would have you believe. There are restaurants in

Greece which serve delectable food which does compare favourably with the world's great cuisines, but they are thin on the ground. The old joke about the Greek woman who on summer days used to shout to her husband 'come and eat your lunch before it gets hot' is based on truth, for food is invariably served lukewarm. Greeks simply prefer it this way, but if you cannot get used to it, then eat grilled food which is cooked fresh to order, and therefore served hot. On the plus side, ingredients are usually fresh, and produced locally, and frozen food is still a rarity.

When you eat out in Greece, many elements come into play to enhance the evening. Fast food has infiltrated Greece but it remains an anomaly in a country where food is ordered in a leisurely manner, and there are rests between dishes. As the evening progresses the music (often live) gets louder and the conversation more animated, often continuing until early morning.

Everyone in Greece eats out regularly, whatever their social or economic status. One gets the impression that despite a flagging economy, enjoying life is still of paramount importance in Greece. A large proportion of the enjoyment comes from eating, drinking and being with friends. The conviviality engendered is unique, and tourists are invariably invited to join in the fun. Add to this, the surroundings, which in summer means being outdoors, perhaps under a vine arbour, on a terrace overlooking the sea and a star-spangled sky. Even if the food and wine on such an evening compare unfavourably with those of other countries, in such a rarefied atmosphere, they taste wonderful. Many a visitor to Greece has proved this, by bringing home a bottle of retsina, only to discover that out of its indigenous environment, it does indeed taste ghastly!

Incidentally, one integral part of eating out in Greece disappeared overnight on 5 May 1992. In the midst of overwhelming domestic and international crises, the Greek government made the momentous decision to ban plastic tablecloths in all eating estab-

lishments. The reason given was to improve the quality of tourist services. But plastic tablecloths had been as enduring a part of eating out in Greece as lukewarm food and retsina.

By law every eating establishment must display a written menu including prices. Wherever you eat in Greece, bread will automatically be put on your table. The price of this bread is usually between 50 and 150 dr depending on the category of the restaurant. Greek bread is excellent – crusty with a soft centre.

The taverna is only one of Greece's many eating places, although there tends to be overlap between the different types of establishments. Some don't seem to be able to decide exactly what they are, and have signs outside proclaiming simultaneously to be a taverna, restaurant and *psistaria* (char-grill restaurant).

Tavernas

The taverna is usually a traditional place with a rough and ready ambience (before the ban, they used plastic tablecloths). In most tavernas a menu will be displayed in the window or on the door, but it is unlikely that tables will have individual menus. You will be invited into the kitchen to peer into the pots and point to what you want. This is not merely a privilege for tourists, Greeks also do it: they know the difference between a *gemista* and a *giouvetsi* and a *stifado* and a *salingaria*, but they want to see a tavernas's version of these dishes. Tavernas usually only open in the evening around 8 pm and often stay open till the early hours. Some tavernas are closed on Sunday.

Restaurants

A restaurant (*estiatorion*) is more sophisticated than a taverna, with white damask tablecloths, smart waiters and printed menus at each table – often with a translation in English. They serve 'ready food' which is usually displayed in containers on a counter. A restaurant may also have a charcoal grill. Some restaurants open in the morning to serve breakfast, and remain open all day, whilst others open for lunch (between 1 and 3 pm) and again in the evening for dinner (between 8 pm and 1 am); some close on Sunday. Restaurants which specialise in spit roast and charcoal grilled food – usually lamb, pork or chicken – are called psistaria.

Ouzeria
An *ouzeri* serves ouzo. In the more traditional establishments, this will be served with a small plate of titbits – perhaps a few olives, a slice of feta and a gherkin. But ouzeria are becoming trendy and sometimes have menus offering a large choice of mezedes and main courses.

Snack Bars
Snack bars are good places for a cheap quick bite. They usually sell *giros* (grilled meat in pitta bread), souvlaki, cheese, spinach and custard pies and *tost* which is toast served with a variety of fillings.

Galaktopoleia
A *galaktopoleion* (milk shop; plural galaktopoleia) sells dairy produce including milk, butter, yoghurt, rice pudding, cornflour pudding, custard, eggs, honey and bread. It may also sell home-made ice cream in a variety of flavours – look for the sign *pagoto politiko* displayed outside. Most have a sit-down area and serve coffee and tea. They are excellent and cheap places for breakfast. They usually open very early in the morning and close in the early evening.

Zaharoplasteia
A *zaharoplasteion* (patisserie; plural zaharoplasteia) sells cakes (both traditional and Western-type cream cakes), chocolates, biscuits, sweets, coffee, soft drinks and, possibly, alcoholic drinks. Sometimes it has chairs and tables, sometimes it's a takeaway.

Kafeneia
A *kafeneion* (plural kafeneia) is often regarded by foreigners as the last bastion of male chauvinism in Europe. It is characterised by bare light bulbs, nicotine-coated walls, smoke-laden air, rickety wooden tables and raffia chairs, and is frequented by middle-aged and elderly Greek men in cloth caps, who occupy themselves either fiddling with worry beads, playing cards or backgammon, or having heated political discussions. Traditionally women never entered a kafeneion, but in the large cities, this situation is gradually changing.

In rural areas it's a different matter: women are rarely seen inside a kafeneion. Whether a women traveller goes into a kafeneion or not is very much a matter of personal choice. Whenever I have done so I have been treated courteously. If you feel inhibited about entering one, there is usually outside seating, where you will feel less intrusive. Kafeneia originally only served Greek coffee, but nowadays most also serve soft drinks, Nescafé, beer and ouzo. Prices are low – around 70 dr for Greek coffee and 150 dr for Nescafé. Most are open all day every day, but some close during siesta time (roughly from 3 to 5 pm).

Other Places to Eat
Infiltrations from other countries include *pizzeria*, *creperies* and *gelateria*. The latter sells Italian-style ice cream in a variety of flavours.

Meals
Breakfast Most Greeks will make do with a Greek coffee and perhaps a cake or pastry for breakfast. If you want something more substantial, restaurants and milk shops serve a variety of breakfasts. These include bread with butter, jam or honey, eggs, or the budget travellers' favourite, yoghurt *(yiaourti)* with honey. In tourist ghettos you will see 'English Breakfast' on menus.

Lunch The midday meal is eaten late – between 1 and 3 pm. It can be either a light snack or a complete meal. The main meal can be taken at either lunch or dinner time. As Greeks enjoy eating, they often have two large meals a day.

Dinner The evening meal is eaten late – usually from 9 pm onwards. A full dinner in

Greece begins with mezedes, followed by a main course which may consist of ready food or grilled meat or fish. Only very posh restaurants or ones pandering to the tourist trade have Western-style desserts on the menu. Greeks tend to eat cakes separately in a galaktopoleion rather than as part of their lunch or dinner.

Greek Specialities

Mezedes In a simple taverna there will often be only three or four *mezedes* on offer: perhaps *taramosalata* (pâté made from smoked fish roe), *tzatziki* (yoghurt dip with cucumber and garlic), *elies* (olives) and *feta* (white goat cheese). In an ouzeri or restaurant there is usually a wider range.

Cold varieties may include *oktapodi* (octopus), *garides* (shrimps), *kalamaria* (squid), *dolmades* (stuffed vine leaves), *melitzanosalata* (aubergine (eggplant) dip) and *mavromatika* (black-eye beans). Hot mezedes may include *keftedes* (meatballs), *fasolia* (broad white beans), *loukanika* (small sausages), *tiropitta* (small cream-cheese pie), *spanakopitta* (small spinach pie), *bourekaki* (small meat pie), *kolokythakia* (deep-fried courgette), *melitzana* (deep-fried aubergine) and *saganaki* (fried cheese). It is quite acceptable to make a full meal of these instead of having a main course. Three or four plates of mezedes are equivalent in price and quantity to one main course.

Main Courses The most common main courses are moussaka (layers of eggplant, minced meat and potatoes topped with cheese sauce and baked), *pastitsio* (macaroni with minced meat and béchamel, baked), dolmades (cabbage or vine leaves stuffed with mincemeat or rice and served in an egg or lemon sauce) and gemista (either tomatoes or green peppers (capsicums) stuffed with minced meat or rice). Other main courses include *giouvetsi* (lamb or veal with pasta), *stifado* (meat stewed with onions), *souzoukaki* (meatballs in tomato sauce) and *salingaria* (snails in oil with herbs). The ubiquitous Greek or village salad *horiatiki*

salata is always eaten as a side dish by Greeks, but many budget-conscious tourists choose it as a main dish. It consists of peppers, onions, olives, tomatoes and feta cheese.

Fish is usually sold by weight in restaurants, and is not as cheap or as widely available as it used to be. The Mediterranean has been overfished – sometimes legally, to satisfy a growing demand from restauranteurs in large cities, and sometimes illegally by dynamiting. One fish however which has remained reasonably priced and widely available is kalamaria (squid) which is deep fried in batter, and at 600 to 800 dr for a generous plate full, is a tasty and nourishing choice for the budget traveller. Other reasonably priced fish (less than 1000 dr a portion) are *marides* (whitebait) and *gopes* which are similar to sardines. Slightly more expensive are oktapodi (octopus), *bakaliaros* (cod), *ksifias* (swordfish) and *glossa* (sole). A little further up the price scale are *barbounia* (red mullet), *lithrinia* (bass) and at the top is *astakos* (lobster) at around 6000 dr a kg.

Fish is usually grilled or fried, but more imaginative fish dishes include *gouvetsi* (shrimp casserole) and mussel or octopus *saganaki* (fish in tomato and cheese sauce) and *psarosoupa* (fish soup). As Greece does not have many rivers and lakes, freshwater fish are not widely available, although reasonably priced *pestrofa* (trout) is available in Epiros, from Lake Pamvotis in Ioannina, the Aoos River in Zagoria, and also from the Prespa Lakes in Macedonia.

Desserts & Cakes Greek cakes and puddings include *baklava* (layers of filo pastry filled with honey and nuts), *loukoumades* (fritters with honey or syrup), *kataifi* (chopped nuts inside shredded wheat soaked in honey), *rizogalo* (rice pudding), *loukoumi* (Turkish delight), *halva* (sesame seed paste) and *pagoto* (ice cream). Tavernas and restaurants usually only have a few of these on the menu. The best places to go for these delights are galaktopoleia or zaharoplasteia.

Snacks Favourite Greek snacks include

pretzel rings sold by street vendors, small souvlakia sticks, giros (sliced grilled meat in pitta bread, with tomato, onion and dressing), *souvlaki pitta* (pitta bread rolled around grilled meat), tost (toasted sandwiches), tiropitta (small cream-cheese pie), *bougatsa* (custard filled pastry), spanakopitta (spinach pie) and *sanduits* (sandwiches). Nuts are also widely available. Street vendors sell a wide variety of nuts for 200 to 300 dr a bag – pistachio nuts are particularly good.

Vegetarian Food

There is only a handful of vegetarian restaurants in Greece. If you merely want to minimise your consumption of meat, you will have no problem, as many Greek dishes consist of beans and vegetables in which meat is used as a mere flavouring. Otherwise, fried vegetables are safe bets, as olive oil is always used for frying – never lard. Greek salads are cheap, tasty, substantial and nourishing. Other options for vegetarians are yoghurt, rice pudding, cheese pies, spinach pies and nuts.

Fruit

Greece has many varieties of fruit. Particularly good are *sika* (figs), *rodakina* (peaches), *stafilia* (grapes), *karpouzi* (watermelon), and *kerasia* (cherries). Tavernas and restaurants sometimes have fruit on the menu for dessert. If you are on a tight budget, then the fruit of the wild-growing, prickly pear tree is very good. But be careful when peeling it, as the needles in the fruit's skin can very easily become embedded in your skin. Fig trees also grow wild.

DRINKS
Nonalcoholic Drinks

Coffee & Tea Greek coffee is the national drink. The beverage is a legacy of the Ottoman rule and, until the Turkish invasion of Cyprus in 1974, it was called Turkish coffee in Greece. It is served with the grounds, without milk in a small cup. Connoisseurs claim there are at least 30 variations of Greek coffee, but most people get by with knowledge of only three. These are *glyko* (sweet), *metrio* (medium) and *sketo* (no sugar).

The next most popular coffee is instant, called Nescafé (which it usually is). Ask for Nescafé *meh ghala* (pronounced me GA-la) if you want it with milk. In summer Greeks drink Nescafé chilled, with or without milk and sugar – this version is called *frappé*. In summer if you want hot Nescafé, specify this, otherwise you will automatically be served *frappé*.

Espresso and filter coffee are served only in trendy coffee shops. Cappuccino is more often seen on menus, but tends to be the Viennese rather than the Italian version. Or at least, the Greek version of a Viennese cappuccino, which is a disgusting concoction of black instant coffee with synthetic cream floating on top, which you'll pay through the nose for – at least 350 dr. If you want an Italian cappuccino, make sure that is what the café serves before you make your order.

If you order tea it will in all probability be made with a tea bag.

Soft Drinks Coca-Cola, Pepsi, Seven-Up, Sprite and Fanta are available everywhere in both cans and bottles. Fresh fruit juices – especially orange – are also available.

Water Tap water is safe to drink in Greece, but if you prefer it, bottled spring water is widely available in 750 ml (75 dr) and 1.5 litre (150 dr) bottles. Bottled sparkling mineral water is rarely seen.

Alcohol

Greeks rarely get drunk. The most plausible explanation for this is that they never drink without eating. Another explanation is that they eat food which has been cooked in olive oil and this inhibits alcohol absorption.

Beer The only widely available beers are Amstel and Henninger. Both are available in bottles and cans. Bottles are cheaper than cans; Amstel is cheaper than Henninger. Imported lagers, stouts and beers are available in tourist areas – usually in music bars and discos. Ones that you might spot are Newcastle Brown, Carlsberg, Castlemaine XXXX and Guinness.

Wine According to mythology the Greeks invented wine. And certainly, throughout the ancient world, Greece was renowned for its good wine. After your first glass of retsina you may well ask what went wrong. Well, a lot of water – or wine – has gone under the bridge since the days when the ancients held drunken revelries in honour of Dionysos, god of wine.

The quality of wine began to deteriorate during the Byzantine period, and went from bad to worse. But the combination of foreign tourists visiting Greece, and the urban Greeks' desire to become more 'Western-ised' led to a demand for higher quality wines. In 1969 legislation was passed on wines, and since then things have improved significantly. Large private wineries led the way by introducing new technology, and now cooperative wineries and small individual growers are following suit.

Popular and reasonably priced Greek labels include Rotonda, Kambas, Boutari (its best is Naoussa), Calliga and Lac des Roches. Slightly more expensive, but of good quality, are the Achaia-Clauss wines from the Peloponnese. The best, and most expensive wines, are those produced by the Porto Carras estate in Halkidiki. Good wines are produced on Rhodes and Crete; other island wines worth sampling are those from Samos (immortalised by Lord Byron), Thira, Kefallonia and Paros. *Aspro* is white, *mavro* is red and *kokkinelli* is rosé.

Most Greeks will tell you that you can't beat retsina. This wine is so called because the barrels in which it ferments are lined with pine resin. Originally, this was done to preserve the wine and to mask its poor flavour. Nowadays, the custom continues, because Greeks have become accustomed to it that way.

The flavour of retsina has been likened to many unpalatable substances, the most common being turpentine. But there are a number of reasons why it is advantageous to

acquire a taste for this wine: it is cheap – around 250 dr a half litre; it rarely causes a hangover; and it neutralises the effects of excessive olive-oil consumption. These days retsina is available in bottles, but the best (and the worst) still comes from the barrel. Many traditional tavernas serve retsina from the barrel; look for the barrels lining the walls and ask for *heema*, which means loose.

If you would like to participate in a modern-day Dionysian drunken revelry, then several wine festivals take place in Greece during the summer. The biggest is held at Dafni, near Athens, from mid-June to mid-September. For a nominal admission fee you can drink an unlimited amount of wine.

Strong Liquor Imported spirits and liqueurs are widely available – at a price. If you are budgeting, then stick with national drinks. Aniseed flavoured Ouzo, which is distilled from grape stems, is the most popular aperitif in Greece. It is similar to the Middle Eastern *arrack*, Turkish *raki* and French Pernod. It is clear and colourless, but turns white when water is added. The Cretan equivalent is called *raki*.

Greek brandies are categorised by stars. Five and seven stars are good quality and eminently acceptable. The most reputable brands are Metaxa, Votrys and Otys.

Self-Catering

Eating out in Greece is often as much an entertainment as a gastronomic experience, so to self-cater is to sacrifice a lot. All towns and villages of any size have well-stocked supermarkets, fruit and vegetable stalls, bakeries, and a weekly *laiki agora* (popular market – a market for the people rather than a wholesale market). Many towns also have huge indoor food markets which have fruit and vegetable stalls, butcher, dairy and delicatessen shops, all under one roof.

Only in very remote villages and remote islands is food availability limited. In such places, there may only be one all-purpose shop – a *pantopoleion*. This shop will stock only a limited amount of meat, vegetables, fruit and bread, but it will always have tinned foods, so you won't go hungry.

ENTERTAINMENT

Large cities have cinemas (outdoor in summer), theatres, classical concerts, rock gigs, discos and jazz clubs. Discos also abound in tourist ghettos. In cinemas films are shown in the original language (usually English) with Greek subtitles.

Folk Dancing

The pre-eminent folk dancers in Greece are the ones who perform at the Dora Stratou Theatre on Filopappos Hill in Athens; performances take place nightly in summer. Another highly commendable place is the Old City Theatre, Rhodes City, where the Nelly Dimoglou Dance Company performs during the summer. Folk dancing is an integral part of all festival celebrations and there is often impromptu folk dancing in tavernas.

Arts Festivals

Arts festivals are held around the country during the summer. The most important is the Athens Festival, where plays, operas, ballet and classical music concerts are staged at the Theatre of Herodes Atticus. This festival is held in conjunction with the Epidaurus Festival, where Ancient Greek dramas are performed at the theatre at Epidaurus. Other cities which host cultural festivals include Ioannina, Patras and Thessaloniki.

Spectator Sports

Soccer (football) is the most popular sport in Greece. The season lasts from September to the middle of May and matches are played on Wednesday and Sunday, and are often televised. Entry to a match costs around 1200 dr. Fixtures and results are given in the *Weekly Greek News*.

THINGS TO BUY

Greece produces a vast array of handicrafts. A good place to see what is available is the Centre of Hellenic Tradition, Pandrossou, Plaka (see the Athens chapter).

Antiques

It is illegal to buy, sell, possess or export any antiquity in Greece (see Customs). However, there are antiques and 'antiques'; a lot of items only a century or two old are regarded as junk, rather than part of the national heritage. These items include handmade furniture and odds and ends from rural areas in Greece, ecclesiastical ornaments from churches and items brought back from far-flung lands, many by admirals. Good hunting grounds for this 'junk' are Monastiraki and the flea market in Athens; the Piraeus Sunday morning market (see Piraeus section) and the *paliatzoures* (junk) shop in Gythio (see the Gythio section in the Peloponnese chapter).

Rugs

Flokati are thick woollen rugs, unique to Greece. The best quality rugs last a lifetime and are still hand woven. When finished they are placed in water for at least three days; this softens the wool. They may then be dyed, or left in their natural colour.

Arahova are brightly coloured and patterned wool rugs, named after the town in Sterea Ellada from where they originated. They make attractive wall-hangings or bedspreads. Many villages in Crete, notably Kritsa, produce and sell brightly coloured woven rugs.

Ceramics

You will see ceramic objects of every shape and size – functional and ornamental – for sale throughout Greece. The best places for high quality handmade ceramics are Athens, Rhodes and the island of Skyros.

If you have taken a fancy to an ancient vase in a museum collection, there are artists in Greece who produce hand-painted replicas of museum items (see the Agios Nikolaos section in the Crete chapter).

Leather Work

You will see leather goods for sale throughout Greece; most are made from leather imported from Spain. The best place for buying leather goods is Hania, on Crete.

However, bear in mind that the goods are not as high quality or as good value as those available in Turkey.

Jewellery

You could join the wealthy North Americans who spill off the cruise ships onto Mykonos to indulge themselves in the high-class gold jewellery shops there. But although gold is good value in Greece, and designs are of a high quality, it is still beyond the capacity of most tourists' pockets. If you prefer some-thing more reasonably priced, go for filigree silver jewellery. Ioannina is the filigree jewellery centre of Greece, but you will see it for sale in shops throughout the country.

Bags

Tagari bags are woven wool bags – often brightly coloured – which hang from the shoulder by a rope. If you think they are a bit passé (a relic from the hippy era), minus the rope they make attractive cushion covers.

Getting There & Away

You can get to Greece by air, rail, road and sea. Whichever way you're travelling, make sure you take out travel insurance. This not only covers you for medical expenses and luggage theft or loss, but also for cancellations or delays in your travel arrangements, under certain circumstances (you might fall seriously ill two days before departure, for example). Cover depends on your insurance and type of ticket, so ask both your insurer and your ticket-issuing agency to explain where you stand. Ticket loss is also (usually) covered by travel insurance. Make sure you have a separate record of all your ticket details – or better still, a photocopy. Buy travel insurance as early as possible. If you buy it the week before you fly, you may find, for example, that you're not covered for delays to your flight caused by strikes or industrial action.

Paying for your ticket with a credit card often provides limited travel insurance, and you may be able to reclaim the payment if the operator doesn't deliver. In the UK, for instance, credit-card providers are required by law to reimburse consumers if a company goes into liquidation and the amount in contention is more than UK£100. Ask your credit-card company what it's prepared to cover.

AIR

In Greece, air travel is experiencing something of an upheaval. The flag carrier, Olympic Airways, is Greece's only airline. It was originally owned by Aristotle Onassis, but in 1975 it was taken over by the state, and since then has been debt ridden. The government now wants to privatise it but alleges that the airline has two or three times more staff than it needs, so these must be got rid of first. Realising it cannot just give staff the boot without social repercussions, the government has decided to put an end to the Olympic Airways monopoly.

New airline companies are being formed

thick and fast and Olympic Airways is happily passing on to them efficient, well-trained staff. These new airlines will initially operate only air taxi and freight services, but no doubt some will eventually compete with Olympic Airways, and operate scheduled international and domestic passenger flights.

Meanwhile, another change came about in 1992 which in the immediate future is going to have a much greater impact upon flights into Greece, and its tourist industry as a whole. On 1 November 1992 work started on the construction of Greece's new Spata international airport in Attica, 24 km from Athens.

The government racked its brains to find a way to help meet the construction costs of this new airport, and came up with the brilliant idea of introducing an airport tax of 2500 dr. This tax came into effect in November 1992 and applies to all international incoming and outgoing flights, and almost all domestic flights. This means that if you fly to and from Greece you will pay 5000 dr, which will be added to the price of your ticket when you purchase it. European tour companies are up in arms about this, as are all the people involved in the tourist industry in Greece. But it is the Greek people who will be most affected, because the geography of the country means they depend heavily on domestic flights to move quickly from one part of the country to another.

Greece has 16 international airports. Athens, Thessaloniki, Iraklion (Crete), Rhodes and Corfu take scheduled flights, although the majority, of course, are into and out of Athens. If you are flying to Greece on a scheduled flight from outside Europe, you will be limited to Athens.

Within Europe, there are a limited number of flights to all of the other airports with Olympic Airways and/or the flag carrier of the particular country the flight is from. There are flights to Thessaloniki from Budapest, Frankfurt, Cyprus, London, Munich,

Air Travel Glossary

Apex Apex, or 'advance purchase excursion' is a discounted ticket which must be paid for in advance. There are penalties if you wish to change it.

Baggage Allowance This will be written on your ticket: usually one 20 kg item to go in the hold, plus one item of hand luggage.

Bucket Shop An unbonded travel agency specialising in discounted airline tickets.

Bumped Just because you have a confirmed seat doesn't mean you're going to get on the plane – see Overbooking.

Cancellation Penalties If you have to cancel or change an Apex ticket there are often heavy penalties involved; insurance can sometimes be taken out against these penalties. Some airlines impose penalties on regular tickets as well, particularly against 'no show' passengers. See the Getting Around chapter for details of cancellation penalties levied on domestic Olympic Airways flights.

Check In Airlines ask you to check in a certain time ahead of the flight departure (usually 1½ hours on international flights). If you fail to check in on time and the flight is overbooked the airline can cancel your booking and give your seat to somebody else.

Lost Tickets If you lose your airline ticket an airline will usually treat it like a travellers' cheque and, after enquiries, issue you with another one. Legally, however, an airline is entitled to treat it like cash and if you lose it then it's gone forever. Take good care of your tickets.

No Shows No shows are passengers who fail to show up for their flight, sometimes due to unexpected delays or disasters, sometimes due to simply forgetting, sometimes because they made more than one booking and didn't bother to cancel the one they didn't want. Full fare passengers who fail to turn up are sometimes entitled to travel on a later flight. The rest of us are penalised (see Cancellation Penalties).

Overbooking Airlines hate to fly empty seats and since every flight has some passengers who

Paris, Sofia, Stuttgart and Vienna; to Iraklion from Frankfurt and Cyprus; to Rhodes from Cyprus; and from Rome to Corfu.

Greece's other international airports are at Mykonos, Thira (Santorini), Hania (Crete), Kos, Karpathos, Samos, Skiathos, Khristoupolis (for Kavala), Preveza (for Lefkada), Kefallonia and Zakynthos. These airports are used exclusively for charter flights which are mostly from the UK, Germany and the Scandinavian countries. Charter flights also fly to all of Greece's other international airports. Athens is one of the major centres in Europe for budget airfares.

In Greece, as with everywhere else, remember always to reconfirm your onward or return bookings by the specified time – usually 72 hours before departure on international flights. If you don't, there's a real risk that you'll turn up at the airport only to find that you've missed your flight because it was rescheduled, or that you've been reclassified as a 'no show', which can mean the airline has cancelled your booking and given the seat to someone else. Lonely Planet has received several letters from people who've found themselves in this embarrassing and inconvenient predicament, so be warned.

Buying a Plane Ticket

If you are flying to Greece from outside Europe, the plane ticket will probably be the most expensive item in your budget, and buying it can be an intimidating business. There is likely to be a multitude of airlines and travel agents hoping to separate you from your money, and it's always worth putting aside some time to research the current state of the market. Start early: some of the cheapest tickets have to be bought months in advance, and some popular flights sell out early.

Discounted tickets are available in two distinct categories: official and unofficial. Official ones are advance-purchase tickets, budget fares, Apex, Super-Apex or whatever other name the airlines care to tack on them in order to put, as it is so succinctly

fail to show up (see No Shows) airlines often book more passengers than they have seats. Usually the excess passengers balance those who fail to show up but occasionally somebody gets bumped. If this happens guess who it is most likely to be? The passengers who check in late.

Reconfirmation At least 72 hours prior to departure time of an onward or return flight you must contact the airline and 'reconfirm' that you intend to be on the flight. If you don't do this the airline can delete your name from the passenger list and you could lose your seat. You don't have to reconfirm the first flight on your itinerary or if your stopover is less than 72 hours. It doesn't hurt to reconfirm more than once.

Restrictions Discounted tickets often have various restrictions on them – advance purchase is the most usual one (see Apex). Others are restrictions on the minimum and maximum period you must be away, such as a minimum of 14 days or a maximum of one year. See Cancellation Penalties.

Tickets Out An entry requirement for many countries is that you have an onward or return ticket, in other words, a ticket out of the country. If you're not sure what you intend to do next, the easiest solution is to buy the cheapest onward ticket to a neighbouring country or a ticket from a reliable airline which can later be refunded if you do not use it.

Transferred Tickets Airline tickets cannot be transferred from one person to another. Travellers sometimes try to sell the return half of their ticket, but officials can ask you to prove that you are the person named on the ticket. This is unlikely to happen on domestic flights, but on an international flight tickets may be compared with passports.

Travel Periods Some officially discounted fares, Apex fares in particular, vary with the time of year. There is often a low (off-peak) season and a high (peak) season. Sometimes there's an intermediate or shoulder season as well. At peak times, when everyone wants to fly, not only will the officially discounted fares be higher but so will unofficially discounted fares or there may simply be no discounted tickets available. Usually the fare depends on your outward flight – if you depart in the high season and return in the low season, you pay the high-season fare. ■

expressed, 'bums on seats'. These can be purchased either from travel agents or direct from the airline. These tickets often have restrictions on them – advance purchase is the most usual one. Others are restrictions on the minimum and maximum period you must be away, such as a minimum of 14 days and a maximum of one year.

Unofficial tickets are simply discounted tickets that the airlines release through selected travel agents. Don't go looking for discounted tickets straight from the airlines: they are only available through travel agents. Airlines can, however, supply information on routes and timetables, and their low-season, student and senior citizens' fares can be very competitive.

Return tickets usually work out cheaper than two one-way tickets – often much cheaper: in some cases, a well-planned return ticket can be *cheaper* than a one-way ticket.

Round-the-World (RTW) tickets have become very popular in recent years. The airline RTW tickets are often real bargains, and can work out to be no more expensive or even cheaper than an ordinary return ticket. Prices start at about UK£850, A$1800 or US$1300 depending on the season. The official airline RTW tickets are usually put together by a combination of two airlines, and permit you to travel anywhere you want on their route systems so long as you don't backtrack. Other restrictions are that you (usually) must book the first sector in advance and cancellation penalties then apply. There may be restrictions on how many stops you are permitted, and usually the tickets are valid for 90 days up to a year from the date of the first outbound flight. An alternative type of RTW ticket is one put together by a travel agent using a combination of discounted tickets.

Generally you can find discounted tickets at prices as low as or even lower than Apex or budget tickets. Phone around the travel agents for bargains. Find out the fare, the route, the duration of the journey, the stopovers allowed, and any restrictions on the ticket.

Charter Flights

Charter-flight tickets are usually the cheapest of all – and the most restrictive. These tickets are for seats left vacant on airlines which have been block booked by package-tour companies. However, certain conditions apply on charter flights to Greece: they must be accompanied by accommodation vouchers, which are issued routinely by travel agents but are not meant to be used. These are issued merely as a way of getting around the Greek laws regarding charter flights: even if the hotel on the voucher exists, it is doubtful whether these vouchers would be accepted. The law came into existence during the 1980s because so many impoverished scruffs from Western Europe were coming to Greece on cheap charter flights, and sleeping rough on beaches and in parks.

With a charter ticket you can visit Turkey and re-enter Greece, but you *cannot* use the return flight. Several countries (Greece included) which benefit greatly from charter-flight traffic have enacted this regulation which prohibits charter passengers from leaving the charter-destination country for the duration of their stay. Thus, if you fly to Athens on a charter flight and then legally enter Turkey (ie have your passport stamped), the officials at the airport in Athens will not allow you to board your return charter flight. You will have to pay for another whole ticket to get home. (If you just take a day excursion into Turkey, and the Turkish immigration officials do not stamp your passport, you will have no problem boarding your return charter flight.) The regulation is enforced so that the charter-destination country reaps all the benefits of the low charter fare and the tourist dollars which they anticipate will be spent in the country. This regulation does not apply to regular or excursion-fare flights.

Charter-flight tickets are only valid for up to four weeks, and usually have a minimum-stay requirement of at least three days. If you want to stay longer than four weeks, half a return charter flight ticket can be more economical than a one-way scheduled flight ticket, so it may be worthwhile forfeiting the return portion of the ticket.

Check the travel sections of major newspapers or the ads in popular travellers' magazines for charter-flight deals. More information on charter flights is given later in this chapter under specific point of origin headings.

Courier Flights

Another option (sometimes even cheaper than a charter flight) is a courier flight. This deal entails accompanying freight or a parcel which will be collected at the destination. You might also be able to fly one-way. The drawbacks are that your time away may be limited to one or two weeks, your luggage is usually restricted to hand luggage (the parcel or freight you carry comes out of your luggage allowance), and you may have to be a resident of the country which operates the courier service and apply for an interview before they'll take you on (dress conservatively if you do have to attend an interview).

Travel Agents

You may discover when you start ringing around that those impossibly cheap flights, charter or otherwise, are 'fully booked', but the agency just happens to know of another one that 'costs a bit more'. Or the flight is on an airline notorious for its poor safety standards and leaves you in the world's least favourite airport in mid-journey for 14 hours (where you're confined to the transit lounge because you do not have a visa). Or the agents may claim to have the last two seats available for Greece for the whole of July, which they will hold for a maximum of two hours. Don't panic – keep ringing around.

If you are flying to Greece from the USA, South-East Asia or the UK, you will probably find that the cheapest flights are being advertised by obscure agencies whose names haven't yet reached the telephone directory – the proverbial bucket shops. Many such firms are honest and solvent, but there are a few rogues who will take your money and disappear, only to reopen elsewhere a month or two later under a new name. If you feel suspicious about a firm, don't give them all the money at once – leave a deposit of 20% or so and pay the balance when you get the ticket. If they insist on cash in advance, go somewhere else or be prepared to take a big risk. Once you have booked the flight with the agency, ring the airline to check that you have a confirmed booking on the flight.

You may decide to pay more than the rock-bottom fare by opting for the safety of a better known travel agent. Firms such as STA, which has offices worldwide, Council Travel in the USA or Travel CUTS in Canada offer good prices to Europe (including Greece), and are unlikely to disappear overnight, leaving you clutching a receipt for a nonexistent ticket.

Use the fares quoted in this book as a guide only. They are approximate and based on the rates advertised by travel agents at the time of going to press, and are likely to have changed by the time you read this.

Travellers with Special Needs

If you've broken a leg, you're a vegetarian or require a special diet, are travelling in a wheelchair, taking a baby, terrified of flying, or whatever, let the airline staff know as soon as possible so that they can make the necessary arrangements. Remind them when you reconfirm your booking (at least 72 hours before departure) and again when you check in at the airport. It may also be worth ringing around the airlines before you make your booking to find out how they can handle your particular needs.

Children aged under two travel for 10% of the standard fare (or free, on some airlines) as long as they don't occupy a seat. They don't get a baggage allowance, either. 'Skycots' should be provided by the airline if requested in advance; these will take a child weighing up to about 10 kg. Children aged between two and 12 years can usually occupy a seat for half to two-thirds of the full fare, and do get a baggage allowance. Push chairs can often be taken as hand luggage.

To/From the UK

British Airways, Britannia Airways, Olym-pic Airways, Dan Air and Kenya Airways have direct flights from London to Athens; there are at least 30 flights a week. The first four airlines are relatively expensive, with fares costing around UK£330 one-way and Apex returns between UK£279 and UK£544, depending on the season and how long you wish to be away. The Kenya Airways flight is a leg of the London/Nairobi flight, and is more reasonably priced, at UK£240. In addition to the direct flights, there are heaps of connecting flights. The cheapest is probably Czechoslovak Airlines (CSA). On this flight there is a four-hour stopover in Prague, which is arguably Europe's most beautiful city, so not a bad place to be stuck in – if you have a Czech visa (or are a resident of a country which doesn't require one) you can hop on an airport bus and have a quick stroll around. On- the-spot visas are not issued.

Olympic Airways has three direct flights from London to Thessaloniki (UK£227/242 to UK£502 one-way/return). Most scheduled flights from London leave from Heathrow airport, but a few leave from Gatwick.

London is Europe's major centre for discounted fares. The following are the addresses of some of the most reputable agencies selling discount tickets.

Campus Travel
  52 Grosvenor Gardens, SW1 (☎ 071-730 3402); tube: Victoria
STA
  74 Old Brompton Rd, SW7 (☎ 071-937 9921); tube: South Kensington
Trailfinders
  194 Kensington High St, W8 (☎ 071-937 5400); tube: High St Kensington

Prices quoted by these agencies for flights to Athens at the time of writing were: Trailfinders (UK£95/179 one-way/return); STA (UK£80/140); Campus Travel (UK£75/139). These were discounted scheduled flights, not charters.

Two London-based courier flight companies are Polo Express (☎ 081-759 5383) and Courier Travel Service (☎ 071-351 0300).

At the time of writing Polo Express' flights to Athens cost UK£99 return with the choice of being away one or two weeks. The Polo Express personal baggage allowance is a generous 23 kg.

The listings magazines *Time Out* and *City Limits*, the Sunday papers, the *Evening Standard* and *Exchange & Mart* carry ads for cheap fares. Also look through the Yellow Pages for travel agency ads and look out for the free magazines and newspapers widely available in London, especially *TNT*, *Southern Cross* and *Trailfinder* – you can pick them up outside the main train and tube stations. Some travel agents specialise in flights for students aged under 30 and travellers aged under 26 (you need an ISIC card or an official youth card). But whatever your age you should be able to find something to suit your pocket. You can also telephone the Air Travel Advisory Bureau (☎ 071-636 5000) for information about current charter-flight bargains.

Most British travel agents are registered with ABTA (Association of British Travel Agents). If you have paid for your flight to an ABTA-registered agent who then goes out of business, ABTA will guarantee a refund or an alternative. If an agency is registered with ABTA, its advertisement usually says so.

In areas of London with large numbers of ethnic Greeks, there are travel agencies which specialise in package holidays and charter flights to Greece. Their prices may well be as competitive as those offered by the more centrally located agencies, and their service is often more courteous. Worth trying are:

Anemone
    109 Myddleton Rd, N22 (☎ 081-889 9207)
Blue Island Holidays
    Green Lanes, Winchmore Hill, N21
    (☎ 081-360 3400)
Byzantium Travel
    196 Seven Sisters Rd, N4 (☎ 071-281 0091)
Dayrise Holidays Ltd
    69 Chalk Farm Rd, NW1 (☎ 071-485 6444)
Hermes Travel
    8 Wordsworth Parade, Green Lanes, N8
    (☎ 081-881 0268)

Typical charter fares to Athens from London are UK£70/100 one-way/return in the low season and UK£90/120 in the high season. Many budget travel agencies offer flights to the islands as well as to Athens. Examples of shoulder-season (spring and autumn) return charter fares to the islands are Corfu (£125), Crete (£139), Kos (£149) and Rhodes (£139).

Charter flights to Greece also fly from Birmingham, Luton, Manchester and Newcastle. Look in the Yellow Pages and local press for ads.

In Athens, budget fares to London are around 40,000/67,000 dr one-way/return.

To/From Europe

Athens is linked to every major city in Europe by either Olympic Airways or the flag carriers of each country.

Though London is the discount capital of Europe, Amsterdam, Frankfurt, Berlin and Paris are also major centres for cheap airfares.

To/From the Netherlands
In Amsterdam try:

Budget Air
    Rokin 34 (☎ 627 12 51)
ILC Reizen
    NZ Voorburgwal 256 (☎ 020-620 51 21)
Malibu Travel
    Damrak 30 (☎ 623 68 14)
NBBS
    Rokin 38 (☎ 624 09 89) or Leidsestraat 53
    (☎ 638 17 36)

To/From Germany
For cheap air tickets in Frankfurt, try SRID Reisen (☎ 069-43 01 91), Berger Strasse 118. In Berlin, Alternativ Tours (☎ 8 81 20 89), Wilmersdorfer Strasse 94 (U-Bahn: Adenauerplatz), specialises in discounted fares to just about anywhere in the world. SRS Studenten Reise Service, at Marienstrasse 23 (U-Bahn and S-Bahn: Friedrichstrasse), offers flights at discounted student (aged 34 or less) or youth (aged 25 or less) fares. Travel agents offering unpublished cheap flights advertise in *Zitty*, Berlin's fortnightly entertainment magazine.

To/From France In Paris, one-way discount charter flights to Athens cost around 700FF. You can contact SOS Charters (☎ 1-49.59.09.09) for more information, or go to one of the many travel agencies, which include:

Council Travel
    31, rue St Augustine (☎ 42.66.20.87)
Selectour Voyages
    29, rue de la Huchette (☎ 43.34.55.30)
Voyages et Découvertes
    21, rue Cambon (☎ 1-42.61.00.01)

Athens to Europe Typical budget fares to various European cities from Athens are:

Destination	One-Way/Return
Amsterdam	45,000/73,000 dr
Copenhagen	48,000/75,000 dr
Frankfurt	44,000/67,000 dr
Geneva	40,000/62,000 dr
Hamburg	48,000/78,000 dr
Madrid	49,000/78,000 dr
Milan	40,000/67,000 dr
Munich	39,000/64,000 dr
Paris	49,000/75,000 dr
Zurich	39,000/62,000 dr

To/From Turkey

Olympic Airways, Turkish Airlines and Gulf Air share the Istanbul/Athens route, with at least one flight a day. The Gulf Air flight is a leg of the Bahrain/Athens service. Fares are US$222 one-way (55% student discounts available); return tickets are from US$236 to US$314, depending on the season.

Turkish Airways flies once a week from Izmir to Athens. The fare is US$201 one-way (55% student discount) and US$213 to US$284 return. There are no direct flights from Ankara to Athens; all flights go via Istanbul.

To/From Cyprus

Olympic Airways and Cyprus Airways share the Cyprus/Greece routes. From Larnaca there are daily flights to Athens (CY£154/163 one-way/return); five a week to Thessaloniki (CY£168/207); three a week to Iraklion (CY£123/131); and in summer, four

a week to Rhodes (CY£116/123). All of these flights have a 55% student discount.

From Paphos, Cyprus Airways flies to Athens once a week in winter, and twice a week in summer (CY£154/163).

To/From Albania

From Tirana, Olympic Airways flies three times a week to Athens (US$156/229 one-way/return); once a week to Ioannina (US$123/164); and once a week to Thessaloniki (US$123/164).

To/From the USA

The North Atlantic is the world's busiest long-haul air corridor, and the flight options to Europe – including Greece – are bewildering. These include advance purchase, budget fares, Apex, Super-Apex and charter. New York has the most direct scheduled flights to Athens. They are: Trans World Airlines (TWA) (11 flights a week), Olympic Airways (daily flights) and Delta Airlines (four flights a week). The fare on Olympic Airways is US$1040 one-way; Apex return fares range from US$935 to US$1291, depending upon the season, and how long you want to be away.

Direct scheduled flights to Athens from other east-coast cities include those from:

Boston
    four flights a week (one Olympic Airways and three TWA, prices similar to New York)
Chicago
    two flights a week (Olympic Airways, US$1635 one-way)
St Loius
    three flights a week (TWA, US$1645 one-way)
Washington
    three flights a week (Delta Airlines, US$1109 one-way)

On the west coast, the only direct connection with Athens is the heavily booked United Airlines daily flight from Los Angeles for US$2077 one-way. For Apex return fares, contact the relevant airlines.

There are connecting flights to Athens from many other US cities. On these flights you change planes at New York's John F

Kennedy airport. In addition, most of the European national airlines fly from New York (and some from other cities) to their home countries, and then on to Athens. These connections usually mean a stopover of three or four hours.

For flight bargains scan the *New York Times*, *LA Times*, *Chicago Tribune* and *San Francisco Chronicle Examiner*. All of these produce weekly travel sections in which you'll find any number of travel agents' ads. Council Travel and STA have offices in major cities nationwide. Access International in New York offers discounts to Europe from over 50 cities in the USA.

One-way fares can work out very cheap on a stand-by basis. Airhitch (☎ 212-864 2000) specialises in this sort of thing, and can get you to Europe one-way for US$160 (from the east coast); US$269 (from the west coast); and US$229 (from elsewhere in the USA).

On a courier flight, a New York-Europe return will cost about US$250/500 or less (about US$100 more from the west coast) in the low/high season. For more information about courier flights from the USA contact Council Travel in New York (☎ 212-661 1450) or Los Angeles (☎ 310-208 3551), and Discount Travel International in New York (☎ 212-362 3636) and San Francisco (☎ 415-292 7801). Call two or three months in advance, at the beginning of the calendar month.

If courier flights to Athens are not available, take a flight to London from where there are many cheap flights to Greece. The *Travel Unlimited* newsletter, PO Box 1058, Allston, MA 02134, publishes details of the cheapest airfares and courier possibilities for destinations all over the world from the USA and other countries, including the UK. It's a treasure-trove of information. A single monthly issue costs US$5, and a year's subscription costs US$25 (US$35 outside the USA).

From Athens to the USA From Athens, bargain flights to the USA are widely advertised. Fares quoted in mid-1992 by budget travel agencies were:

Destination	One-Way/Return
Atlanta	86,000/136,000 dr
Chicago	76,000/113,000 dr
Los Angeles	95,000/149,000 dr
New York	69,000/103,000 dr

Travel agents in Athens who sell low-priced flights to the USA include Consolas Travel (☎ 01-325 4932), Eolou 100, and Periscope (☎ 01-322 1515/4874), Filellinon 22. Consolas Travel also have offices in Iraklion (☎ 081-288 847) and Thessaloniki (☎ 031-238 910).

To/From Canada

From Canada there are two Olympic Airways flights a week from Montreal (C$1768/1813 to C$2207 one-way/return); Toronto (C$1079/1591 to C$1976); and Winnipeg (C$1301/1460 to C$2207). There are no direct flights from Vancouver, but there is a large number of connecting flights via Toronto, Amsterdam, Frankfurt and London on Canadian Airlines, KLM, Lufthansa and British Airways. The stopovers are between 1¼ (Lufthansa) and four hours. Fares are C$1501/1548 to C$2428.

In addition, some European national airlines fly from Montreal to their home countries, and then on to Athens. Two which are worth investigating, because they are likely to be cheaper than the others, are the Czechoslovak Airline (CSA) flight from Montreal to Athens, and the Lot-Polish Airlines flights from both Toronto and Winnipeg to Athens.

Budget flights are also available from Canada. Travel CUTS has offices in all major cities including: Toronto (☎ 416-979 2406); Vancouver (☎ 604-681 9136); and Edmonton (☎ 403-488 8487). Scan the budget travel agents' ads in the *Toronto Globe & Mail*, the *Toronto Star* and the *Vancouver Province*.

For courier flights originating in Canada, contact FB On Board Courier Services

☎ 514-633 0740 in Toronto or Montreal, or ☎ 604-338 1366 in Vancouver.

At the time of writing, budget travel agencies in Athens were advertising flights to Toronto for 69,000/102,000 dr one-way/return and to Montreal for 82,000/ 98,000 dr.

To/From Australia

There are two identically priced Olympic Airways flights a week from Sydney and Melbourne to Athens. The one-way excursion fare is A$1559 in the high season and return fares range from A$2099 in the low season, to A$2499 in the shoulder season and A$2599 in the high season. Because so many ethnic Greeks live in Australia, Olympic Airways sometimes has some special offers. Phone numbers of Olympic Airways offices in Australia are: Adelaide (☎ 08-212 7794); Melbourne (☎ 03-602 5400/5699/5798); and Sydney (☎ 02-251 1047).

Several airlines have connecting flights from Sydney to Athens. With the stopover cities and stopover times in brackets they are: Thai Airways (Bangkok, 3½ hours – transfer to Olympic Airways); Gulf Air (Bahrain, one hour); Singapore Airlines (Singapore, two hours); and Qantas Airways (Bangkok 3½ hours – transfer to Olympic Airways).

STA and Flight Centres International are Australia's major dealers in cheap fares. Check the travel agents' ads in the Yellow Pages and ring around.

The Saturday travel sections of the *Sydney Morning Herald* and Melbourne's *Age* newspaper have many ads offering cheap fares to Europe (including Greece), but don't be surprised if they happen to be 'sold out' when you contact the agents: they're usually low-season fares on obscure airlines with conditions attached. It also pays to check special deals in the ethnic Greek press, such as *Greek Cosmos*, *Neos Pirsos* and *Neos Kosmos* in Melbourne, and the *Greek Herald* and *Kosmos* is Sydney.

From Athens to Australia At the time of writing, flights to Sydney were being advertised for 140,000/269,000 dr one-way/return by the budget travel agencies in Athens.

To/From New Zealand

There are no direct flights from New Zealand to Athens, though there are connecting flights via Sydney, Melbourne, Bangkok and Singapore on Olympic Airways, United Airlines, Qantas Airways, Thai Airways and Singapore Airlines.

To/From Asia

To/From Hong Kong There are no direct flights from Hong Kong to Athens but there are a large number of connecting flights via Bangkok, Singapore, Bahrain and Bombay on Thai Airways, Singapore Airlines, Gulf Air, Bangladesh Biman Airlines, Cathay Pacific and British Airways. On some of these you change to an Olympic Airways flight to Athens. The fare is HK$9140/ 15,150 one-way/return. Hong Kong is the discount plane ticket capital of Asia, and its bucket shops are as unreliable as those of other cities. Ask the advice of other travellers before buying a ticket.

To/From Thailand From Bangkok, Olympic Airways flies four times a week to Athens, and Thai Airways twice a week. In addition there are around 15 connecting flights a week via Singapore, Dhaka, Karachi, Cairo, Bahrain and Copenhagen on Singapore Airlines, Biman Airlines, Pakistan Airlines, Egypt Air, Gulf Air and Scandinavian Airlines. Most have five or six-hour stopovers, but the Biman Airlines stopover in Dhaka is under two hours. The direct flights cost 27,335/31,590B one-way/return, but check out the prices of the Asian airlines, which are bound to be cheaper.

To/From India From Bombay, Biman Airlines has two direct flights a week to Athens; the one-way fare is Rs 15,642. There are five connecting flights via Bahrain, Addis Ababa, Karachi and Frankfurt on Gulf Air, Ethiopian Airlines and Delta Airlines. Gulf Air has the shortest stopover time.

There are no direct flights from Delhi to Athens, although there are seven connecting flights a week via Bombay, Karachi, Bahrain and Frankfurt on Air India, Pakistan Airlines,

Gulf Air and Delta Airlines. The Apex fare is the same as the Bombay-Athens flight, but you may have more chance of finding a cheaper discounted flight in Delhi. Try Delhi Student Travel Services in the Imperial Hotel, Janpath.

LAND
To/From Turkey
Bus Daily buses travel between Istanbul and Athens (23 hours) via Alexandroupolis (7½ hours) and Thessaloniki (14½ hours). In Istanbul the buses leave from the Anadolu Terminali (Anatolia Terminal) at the Topkapı *otogar* (bus station). Travelling from Greece the one-way fare is 10,000 dr from Athens, 6000 dr from Thessaloniki and 4000 dr from Alexandroupolis. Students are granted a 15% reduction and children aged under 12 years, a 50% reduction. See the Getting There & Away sections for each city for information on where to buy tickets. (See the Alexandroupolis Getting There and Away section for alternative ways of getting to Turkey by public transport.)

British passport holders need a visa to visit Turkey. This cannot be obtained in advance, but is payable on arrival. The cost is UK£5. Most other citizens of Western countries, including Australia, Canada, New Zealand and the USA, don't require a visa, nor do visitors from Japan.

If your passport is due to expire within three months you may not be admitted into Turkey.

Train There are daily trains between Athens (11,600 dr) and Istanbul, via Thessaloniki (9000 dr), Alexandroupolis (5000 dr) and many more places en route. This service is incredibly slow and the train gets uncomfortably crowded. There are often delays at the border and the journey can take up to 35 hours. You'd be well advised to take a bus. Inter-Rail passes are valid in Turkey but Eurail passes are not.

Car & Motorbike Greece has two border crossings with Turkey. One is at Kipi, 43 km north-east of Alexandroupolis. The other one is at Kastanies, 139 km north-east of Alexandroupolis. If your goal is Istanbul, then Kipi is the shortest route. But if you continue north to Kastanies, you will have the opportunity of seeing the fascinating towns of Soufli and Didimotikho, in Greece, and Edirne (ancient Adrianople) in Turkey.

Hitching If you want to hitchhike to Turkey, try to get a lift from Alexandroupolis right through to Turkey as you cannot hitchhike across the border.

To/From Bulgaria
Bus There is a twice-weekly bus between Athens and Sofia (15 hours; 5500 dr) via Thessaloniki (7½ hours; 2200 dr). Student and child discounts are available.

Train There is a daily train between Sofia and Athens (18 hours; 12,600 dr) via Thessaloniki (nine hours; 10,000 dr).

Car & Motorbike The Bulgarian crossing is at Promahona, 145 km north-east of Thessaloniki and 50 km from Seres.

Hitching If you want to hitchhike to Bulgaria try getting a lift from Thessaloniki or Seres straight through to Sofia, as lifts beyond Seres are difficult to come by.

To/From Albania
Bus The best connection to Albania is through Ioannina. Catch an early morning bus from Ioannina to the Albanian border at Kakavia. You must arrive at the border before noon to connect with the regular Albanian bus on to Tirana. Otherwise it should be possible to get a taxi to Gjirokastra (in Albania) or Saranda. In the other direction, the bus to Kakavia leaves Tirana at 3.30 am. Buy tickets from a kiosk behind the Palace of Culture (north side). At the time of writing there were plans to start a bus connection between Korça (Koritsa in Greek) and Thessaloniki, via Florina.

Car & Motorbike Greece has two borders

with Albania. The main one is 60 km north-west of Ioannina. Take the main Ioannina-Konitsa road and at the junction at Kalpaki turn left. This road leads to the border town of Kakavia. The other border crossing is nine km west of Kotas – a village on the Florina-Kastoria road. This road leads to the border town of Korça. Check with the tourist police in Greece whether it is possible to enter Albania in a private vehicle.

To/From the Former Yugoslav Republic of Macedonia

Train Coming from the Former Yugoslav Republic of Macedonia you can take a local train from Skopje to Gevgelija, the Greek border station (206 km, four daily, 2½ hours) and look for a Thessaloniki train from there. Alternatively, there's a daily afternoon train at around 3.30 pm between Bitola and the Greek border (Kremenica). There you change to a connecting Greek train which carries you slowly into Florina, Greece. The ticket office at the Bitola train station will only sell you a ticket as far as the border (US$1). Putnik or Feroturist can sell you a through ticket to Florina for about US$5 or you can buy the onward ticket directly from the Greek conductor at the border itself (about US$2). By the time you get to Florina, all the banks will be closed (there's a one-hour time difference), so plan ahead and bring some drachma from Western Europe.

Car & Motorbike There are two border crossings with the Former Yugoslav Republic of Macedonia. One is at Evzoni, 68 km north of Thessaloniki. This is the main highway to Skopje which continues to Belgrade, capital of former Yugoslavia, and now in war-torn Serbia. The other border is at Niki, 16 km north of Florina. This road leads to Bitola, and continues to Ohrid, the tourist mecca of former Yugoslavia.

To/From Europe

If you are travelling overland by bus, train or car from Western Europe to Greece, it will be necessary to cross various borders, so remember to check whether you require visas for those countries before leaving home. For instance, Australians will need a visa to travel through France.

Bus Eurolines, a division of National Express (the largest UK bus line), has an enormous network of European destinations. Their headquarters is in the UK (☎ 071-730 0202), at 52 Grosvenor Gardens, Victoria, London SW1.

Eurolines' agents in European cities which have services to Athens (via Thessaloniki) include:

Deutsche Touring, Am Römerhof 17, 6000 Frankfurt
   90 (☎ 069-7 90 30)
Deutsche Touring, Arnulfstrasse 3, Munich
   (☎ 089-59 18 24)
Eurolines/Budgetbus , Rokin 10, Amsterdam
   (☎ 020-627 51 51)
Eurolines , 55 rue St Jacques, 75005 Paris
   (☎ 1-43.54.11.99)
Lazzi Express, Via Tagliamento 27, Rome
   (☎ 06-841 74 58)

Some of the routes to Greece (including the UK service) go through Croatia and Bosnia-Hercegovina, in what was Yugoslavia. Check on the current situation if you want to travel on one of these routes. From the UK the journey takes around 56 hours and costs UK£121/206. In addition to the year-round ex-Yugoslav route, there is a summer-only service to Greece from the UK via France and Italy, with a ferry crossing from Ancona to Patras. The cost is the same as the other service and includes the ferry ticket. Other prices to Greece include Paris-Athens (800FF) and Rome-Athens (L120,000).

Destinations and prices of one-way tickets from Athens include: London 36,500 dr; Amsterdam 36,300 dr; Munich 26,300 dr; and Frankfurt 29,000 dr. For Eurolines' agents in Greece see the Getting There & Away sections for Athens and Thessaloniki.

Train Unless you have a Eurail pass or an Inter-Rail pass or are under 26 years old and eligible for a reduced-price fare, travelling to

Greece by train is expensive: around UK£350 return from the UK.

Eurail passes can only be bought by residents of non-European countries and are supposed to be purchased before arriving in Europe. However, they can be purchased in Europe so long as your passport proves that you've been there for less than six months, but the outlets where you can do this are limited. French National Railways (☎ 071-493 9731), 179 Picadilly, London, is one such outlet. Check the *Eurail Traveller's Guide* which comes with the pass for other outlets. If you've lived in Europe for more than six months, you are eligible for an Inter-Rail pass, which is a better buy.

Eurail passes are valid for unlimited travel on national railways and some private lines in Austria, Belgium, Denmark, Finland, France (and Monaco), Germany, Greece, Hungary, Italy, Luxembourg, the Netherlands, Norway, Portugal, Ireland, Spain, Sweden and Switzerland (which includes Liechtenstein). Great Britain is not covered. Eurail is also valid on some European ferry routes, including those between Italy and Greece.

Eurail passes offer reasonable value to people aged under 26. A Youthpass is valid for 2nd-class travel for one month (US$470 or UK£294) or two months (US$640 or UK£384). The Youth Flexipass, also for 2nd class, is valid for 15 days in a two-month period (US$420 or UK£254).

The corresponding passes for those aged over 26 are available in 1st class only. The Flexipass (five versions) costs from US$280 (UK£168) for five days in a 15-day period up to US$610 (UK£366) for 14 days within a one-month period. The standard Eurail pass (also five versions) costs from US$430 (UK£270) for 15 days unlimited travel, up to US$1150 (UK£726) for three months. Two or more people travelling together (minimum three people between 1 April and 30 September) can get good discounts on a Saverpass, which works like the standard Eurail pass.

If you lose your Eurail pass before you get to Europe, you cannot claim a refund. If your pass is lost or stolen once you are in Europe, you may apply for a duplicate, but only if the original pass was already validated and you can prove it by showing a validation slip. A police report is also necessary and a US$25 re-issuance fee applies. The catch with losing a Flexipass is that they assume you've been travelling every day since the validation (even if you haven't), so if your number of flexible days is equal to or exceeded by the number of days since the pass was validated, you won't be able to claim anything at all. There is at least one Eurail Aid Office (where duplicates are issued) in each country participating in the scheme; addresses are listed in the *Eurail Traveller's Guide*.

Inter-Rail passes are available to residents of European countries. The normal Inter-Rail card is limited to travellers under 26 years of age and costs UK£180 for one month. Terms and conditions vary slightly from country to country. In all cases, however, there is only a discount of around 50% in the country in which the Inter-Rail pass was purchased.

Cards are valid for 2nd-class rail travel in all countries covered by Eurail, plus Bulgaria, the Czech and Slovak republics, Morocco, Poland, Romania, Turkey and former Yugoslavia.

There is also an Inter-Rail card for people aged 26 or over, imaginatively called the Inter-Rail 26+. This is nowhere near as good a deal. Not only are costs higher (UK£180 for 15 days or UK£260 for one month), but the card is also more restricted: it is not valid in Britain or Spain and it gives discounts on fewer ferry routes. The Inter-Rail card for under 26 year olds is valid in France, Italy, Portugal and Spain, but the Inter-Rail 26+ is not.

European rail passes are only worth buying if you plan to do a reasonable amount of travelling within a short space of time: Eurail itself reckons that its passes only start saving money after 2400 km of travel within a two-week period – a distance just short of that from London to Athens. Certainly think twice about buying one if most of your travelling is going to be confined to Greece, because the rail network is limited and slow. (See the train section in the Getting Around chapter.)

When weighing up the options, you should consider the cost of other cheap ticket deals. Travellers aged under 26 years can pick up BIJ (Billet International de Jeunnese) tickets which cut fares by up to 50%. Various agents issue BIJ tickets in Europe, including Eurotrain (☎ 071-730 3402), 52 Grosvenor Gardens, London SW1. In Athens, BIJ tickets are issued by Voyages Wasteels Hellas (☎ 01-324 0622/2038/3039), Xenofontos 14 (near Plateia Syntagmatos Syntagma Square).

Cheap deals aside, rail services from Western Europe to Greece have been severely disrupted by events in former Yugoslavia. The direct route to most Western European cities was via Belgrade, but this service was suspended at the time of writing, so check the current situation. The most straightforward alternative route is to take a train to Italy and then a ferry to Greece. Trains run from major destinations throughout Europe directly to major Italian cities. Trains also link up with ferries from Brindisi (Italy) to Greece.

Due to the increased number of passengers, the trains through Italy have been more heavily booked and crowded than ever – so plan well ahead. A more complicated and longer route is to get a train to Budapest, then another one to Bucharest, from where there are trains to Thessaloniki and Athens, via Sofia, thus doing a big loop around the trouble spots.

Car & Motorbike Once again the troubles in former Yugoslavia have put paid to the most direct route for motorists driving from Western Europe to Greece. The route coming from the UK was Ostend, Brussels, Salzberg and then down the Yugoslav highway through Zagreb, Belgrade and Skopje and crossing the border to Evzoni. An alternative route was to take the longer scenic road down the coast via Split and Dubrovnik. The inland route added up to 3150 km and 50 hours non-stop driving.

The alternative is to drive to an Italian port and get a ferry to Greece. Coming from the UK this means driving through France where petrol and road tolls are exorbitant. In Italy, petrol prices have been deregulated, so are not as expensive as they used to be, but you must pay tolls on the autostrade.

SEA
To/From Turkey

There are five regular ferry services between Turkey's Aegean coast and the Greek islands. Although the boats get crowded during summer, they are still a more pleasant way of getting from one country to the other than the train or bus. Prices, however, are subject to frequent increases. Travellers have recently reported that the port departure tax for Turkey has been increased to a hefty 10,000 dr.

Tickets for all ferries to Turkey must be bought a day in advance. You will almost certainly be asked to turn in your passport the night before the trip. The next day, before you board the boat, you'll get it back. (See the relevant sections under individual island entries for more information about the following trips.)

Rhodes to Marmaris Small car ferries run between Rhodes and Marmaris daily except Sunday (usually late afternoon) from April to October and less frequently in the winter. In the high season tickets cost 6000/10,800 dr one-way/return. Recent reports from travellers suggest that prices have been increased to 14,600 dr.

Chios to Çesme Boats run daily (except Monday) between Chios and Çesme from mid-July to mid-September. In spring and autumn there are boats thrice weekly on Tuesday, Thursday and Sunday. In winter there is one boat a week, on Thursday, if the weather allows and if there are sufficient passengers to make the trip worthwhile. Tickets cost 7000/9500 dr one-way/return, including the port tax.

Kos to Bodrum Several boats daily ply

between Kos and Bodrum. At the time of writing the cost quoted by the travel agencies in Kos was 5000/10,000 dr which included the port tax. The Turkish boat owners tend to ask for more.

Lesbos to Ayvalik From late May to September there are daily boats between Lesbos and Ayvalik. In spring, autumn and winter, boats operate about once or twice a week, weather permitting. Tickets cost 6000/8000 dr one-way/return.

Samos to Kuşadası In summer there are daily boats to Kuşadası (for Ephesus) from Samos town and three a week from Pythagorion on Samos' south coast. There is no scheduled service in winter, but this may change. Tickets cost 5000/9000 dr one-way/return. This price includes the 1250 dr Turkish port tax.

To/From Italy
Events in former Yugoslavia mean that ferries to Greece from Italy are more popular than ever, so the earlier you make a reservation the better.

For more information about the following services, see the Patras, Igoumenitsa, Corfu and Kefallonia sections. In the UK, reservations can be made on almost all of these ferries at Viamare Travel Ltd (☎ 071-431 4560; fax 071-431 5456), Graphic House, 2 Sumatra Rd, London NW6 IPU.

Brindisi to Corfu, Igoumenitsa, Patras & Kefallonia The major companies operating ferries from Brindisi are: Adriatica (☎ 52 38 25), Viale Regina Margherita 13 (open from 9 am to 1 pm, 4 to 7 pm), and on the 1st floor of the *stazione marittima*, where you must go to check in; Hellenic Mediterranean Lines (☎ 52 85 31), Corso Garibaldi 8; Fragline (☎ 2 95 61), Corso Garibaldi 88; and Marlines (☎ 2 78 84), c/o Il Globo, Corso Garibaldi 97.

Adriatica and Hellenic operate the most expensive services, but they're also the most reliable. They are the only lines which officially accept Eurail passes, which means you pay only L25,000. If you want to use your Eurail pass, it is important to reserve some weeks in advance, particularly in summer. Even with a booking in summer, you must still go to the Adriatic or Hellenic embarkation office in the stazione marittima to have your ticket checked.

There are numerous other lines, but as the companies change hands and names, it is best to arrive in Brindisi and shop around if you are looking for a cheaper fare.

Discounts are available for travellers under 26 years of age and some companies offer discounts to Inter-Rail card holders. Note that fares increase by 50% in July and August. Ferry services are also increased during this period. Average high-season prices in deck class at the time of writing were: Adriatica and Hellenic to Corfu/Igoumenitsa: L105,000; Marlines for the same destination: L85,000 and to Patras: L90,000 (this company offers a 10% discount to students); and Fragline to Corfu/Igoumenitsa: L60,000, and Patras: L105,000. In cooler weather deck class can be unpleasant.

Tickets for airline-type seats cost around L10,000 more than deck-class tickets. The cheapest cabin accommodation costs around L30,000 more than deck class in low season and L45,000 more in high season.

Fares for cars are L90,000 in the high season.

At the time of writing a catamaran service commenced operation between Brindisi and Igoumenitsa via Corfu. The plans are that it will operate daily from mid-July to early September and less frequently in the low season. The one-way fare is 10,000 dr in low season and 14,500 dr in high season. Children aged under two years travel free and those between two and 12 pay half price. Return tickets attract a 15% reduction on outgoing and return travel.

Ancona to Patras In Ancona, all ferry operators have booths at the stazione marittima, off Piazza Candy. Here you can pick up timetables and price lists and make bookings. Most lines offer a 10% discount on return fares. Prices listed are for one-way deck class in the high season.

Minoan Lines (☎ 5 67 89) operates ferries to Igoumenitsa, Corfu, Kefallonia and Patras for L96,000. Karageorgis Lines (☎ 20 10 80) has ferries to Patras for L96,000. Marlines (☎ 5 00 62) goes to Igoumenitsa and Patras (L82,000).

Otranto to Corfu Ferries leave Otranto for Corfu and Igoumenitsa. For information and reservations, go to the stazione marittima at the port.

To/From Cyprus, Israel & Egypt
For information about agents for the following services in Greece, see the Piraeus, Iraklion and Rhodes sections.

Limassol to Rhodes, Crete & Piraeus In summer, at least three boats a week travel between Piraeus and Limassol in Cyprus. The boat operated by Arkadia Lines sails once a week via Rhodes, and the ones operated by Stability Lines sail twice a week via Rhodes; one of these is also via Iraklion (Crete). From Limassol, deck class to Piraeus costs CY£60 and takes 28 hours. The prices are the same for Iraklion and Rhodes.

In Limassol, the agent for Arkadia Lines is Salamis Tours (☎ 05-155 555), 247 28 October Ave; and the agent for Stability Lines is Vergina Lines (☎ 05-143 978), 3B Olymbion St, Honey Court 7.

Haifa to Limassol, Rhodes, Crete & Piraeus Both the Stability Lines and the Arkadia Lines boats from Piraeus to Limassol continue to Haifa (11 hours from Limassol), and then retrace their routes. Stability Lines' agent in Haifa is J Capsi Ltd (☎ 04-67 4444), Haatzmauth Rd, PO Box 27. Arkadia Lines' is Mano Seaways Ltd (☎ 04-53 1631), 39/41 Hameginim Ave.

Egypt to Haifa, Limassol, Rhodes & Piraeus The Stability Lines' boat which

goes via Rhodes (but not Crete) continues from Haifa to Port Said in Egypt (15 hours from Limassol).

To/From Albania
In 1993 a weekly small boat was operating between Corfu and Albania (Saranda). If this is still the case it should be widely advertised by travel agents; otherwise enquire at the EOT.

To/From Croatia
Jadrolinija lines used to operate a weekly car ferry service, from mid-June to mid-September, from Patras to Venice via Igoumenitsa, Corfu, Dubrovnik, Korcula, Starigrad, Hvar, Split, Zadar, Rab and Rijeka. This service was suspended in 1991 because of the war in Croatia, and in late 1993 it had not resumed. Any EOT or GNTO should be able to tell you if this is still the case.

TOURS
If a sun, sand and sea package holiday doesn't appeal to you, but you would like to holiday with a group, there are several companies which organise special interest holidays. UK-based companies which organise trekking holidays in Greece for less than UK£600 (including the airfare) are: Exodus Expeditions (☎ 081-675 5550); Ramblers Holidays (☎ 0707-33 1133); and Sherpa Expeditions (☎ 081-577 7187). Exodus Expeditions agents worldwide include: Australia (☎ 02-956 7766); New Zealand (☎ 09-524 5118); and Canada (☎ 416-979 2406).

The UK-based Explore Worldwide (☎ 0252-31 9448) organises reasonably priced small group holidays which include visits to many of the country's ancient sites.

Two UK companies which organise up-market holidays in Greece are Peregrine Holidays Ltd (☎ 0865-51 1642), who specialise in birdwatching and wild-flower holidays costing between UK£850 and UK£1130, and Wine Dark Sea (☎ 0764-70107) who specialise in cultural holidays in

Crete which cost between UK£760 and UK£1445.

If you wouldn't mind a sun, sand and sea holiday, but don't like crowded tacky resorts, UK companies specialising in package holidays to unspoilt areas of Greece include: Timsway (☎ 0293-55 4441); Laskarina (☎ 062-982 4881); Greek Islands Sailing Club (☎ 0932-22 0416); Simply Ionian (☎ 081-995 1121) and Simply Crete (☎ 081-994 4462).

For information on sailing and trekking holidays in Greece, see the relevant sections in the Getting Around chapter.

See the Skyros and Folegandros sections for specialist holidays on those islands.

LEAVING GREECE

Departure Taxes

The departure tax for air travellers is 2500 dr. However, this amount is included in the initial cost of your ticket, and is therefore not payable at the airport on departure (unless, of course, you buy your ticket at the airport). See the Air section at the beginning of this chapter for more information concerning airport taxes.

Port taxes vary from 1500 to 3000 dr depending on which port you leave from, although Lonely Planet has received unsubstantiated reports from travellers that the Turkey port tax is now 10,000 dr.

Getting Around

AIR

Greece has an extensive domestic air network – far larger than most countries of its size. Olympic Airways operates large aircraft between many major towns on the mainland and the large islands. Its affiliate, Olympic Aviation, operates 18, 30 and 50-seater aircraft between Athens and some of the smaller islands, as well as inter-island flights.

In the past, flights to popular islands have been heavily booked during July and August, making early bookings essential, but the new 2500 dr airport tax may have an effect on this. (See the Air section in the Getting There & Away chapter for more information about this tax.) Excluding the tax, airfares work out approximately 2½ times the cost of bus and ferry travel. Tickets may be bought at any Olympic Airlines office and many travel agencies. The head office of Olympic Airways in Athens (☎ 01-966 6666) is at Leoforos Syngrou 96. Olympic Airways accepts the following credit cards: American Express, Visa, MasterCard, Diners Club and Eurocard.

Domestic Olympic Airways tickets are non-transferable. If a passenger cancels a reservation between 24 and eight hours prior to departure, a cancellation charge of 30% of the fare is imposed. If the cancellation occurs within eight hours of departure or the passenger does not show up for the flight, the cancellation charge is 50% of the fare. Different conditions may apply for special fares – check this where you purchase your ticket. Travel insurance will generally cover you if you have to cancel due to ill health or an emergency; check your policy.

On all Olympic Airways flights the free baggage allowance is 15 kg. When the domestic flight is part of an international journey, the passenger is entitled to the international free baggage allowance on the domestic sector. When the tickets for domestic travel are sold and issued outside Greece, the free baggage allowance is 20 kg.

A 25% student discount is only available on domestic Olympic Airways flights if the flight is part of an international journey. Smoking is prohibited on all Olympic Airways domestic flights.

Mainland Flights

There are nine airports on the mainland (including Athens). All domestic flights on the mainland serve Athens, except for the Thessaloniki-Ioannina service (five per week, 50 minutes, 7400 dr). See the table in

---

Mainland Intercity Flights
One-way fares (excluding airport taxes), frequency and duration of flights from Athens are:

City	Flights/Week	Duration	Fare
Alexandroupolis	10	55 mins	13,700 dr
Ioannina	12	75 mins	11,600 dr
Kalamata	9	50 mins	8000 dr
Kastoria	4	80 mins	11,900 dr
Khristoupolis	7	60 mins	13,600 dr
Kozani	5	80 mins	10,600 dr
Preveza	5	80 mins	9600 dr
Thessaloniki	37	50 mins	13,700 dr

this section for details of flights to mainland cities from Athens.

Mainland to Island Flights

Flights operate from Athens to 21 islands, and from Thessaloniki to Hania and Iraklion on Crete, Lemnos and Mytilini (Lesbos) in the North-Eastern Aegean group, and Rhodes, in the Dodecanese group. See the table below for details.

Inter-Island Flights

There are year-round inter-island flights between Rhodes and Iraklion, Karpathos, Kassos, Kastellorizo and Kos; between Karpathos and Kassos; between Lemnos and Mytilini; between Sitia (Crete) and Karpathos; and between Zakynthos and Kefallonia. All other inter-island flights operate only during the summer months. Some of the short inter-island flights are

---

Flights from Athens & Thessaloniki to the Greek Islands

One-way fares (excluding airport taxes), frequency and duration of flights from **Athens** are:

Island	Flights/Week	Duration	Fares
Chios	30	40 mins	9200 dr
Corfu	21	50 mins	15,900 dr
Crete (Hania)	25	45 mins	12,100 dr
Crete (Iraklion)	46	45 mins	14,400 dr
Crete (Sitia)	2	85 mins	16,900 dr
Karpathos	3	50 mins	19,200 dr
Kefallonia	7	60 mins	11,600 dr
Kos	14	50 mins	13,700 dr
Kythera	7	50 mins	8500 dr
Lemnos	23	60 mins	9900 dr
Leros	7	55 mins	15,100 dr
Lesbos (Mytilini)	24	45 mins	11,600 dr
Milos	12	45 mins	7800 dr
Mykonos	42	45 mins	9900 dr
Naxos	25	50 mins	11,600 dr
Paros	40	45 mins	10,300 dr
Rhodes	35	55 mins	17,800 dr
Samos	28	60 mins	11,300 dr
Skiathos	42	50 mins	9500 dr
Skyros	4	50 mins	11,000 dr
Syros	14	35 mins	9700 dr
Thira (Santorini)	39	55 mins	12,300 dr
Zakynthos	14	60 mins	11,300 dr

This information is for flights between 14 June and 26 September. Outside these months, the numbers of flights to the islands drops considerably. This is especially so for Mykonos, Paros, Skiathos and Thira.

One-way fares (excluding airport taxes), frequency and duration of flights from **Thessaloniki** are:

Island	Flights/Week	Duration	Fares
Chios	2	50 mins	18,000 dr
Crete (Hania)	1	75 mins	21,800 dr
Crete (Iraklion)	2	75 mins	21,800 dr
Lemnos	7	70 mins	10,200 dr
Lesbos (Mytilini)	7	85 mins	16,000 dr
Rhodes	2	80 mins	23,500 dr

exempt from the airport tax. The one-way fares, frequencies and duration of flights can be found in the table below.

BUS

All long-distance buses on both the mainland and the islands are operated by KTEL (Koinon Tameion Eispraxeion Leoforeion), a collective of private bus companies. Drivers take great pride in their buses, staking out a little territory where they sit, and adorning it with icons, pin-ups, psychedelic love hearts and plastic mobiles.

The bus network is comprehensive and major routes have frequent services. With the exception of towns in Thrace, which are reached by buses from Thessaloniki, all of the large towns on the mainland, including those in the Peloponnese, are served by frequent buses from Athens. The islands of Corfu, Kefallonia and Zakynthos can also be reached directly from Athens by bus, and the fare includes the price of the ferry ticket.

Villages in remote areas are often served by only one or two buses a day. These operate for the benefit of school children and people going into the nearest town to shop, rather than for tourists. These buses leave the villages very early in the morning and return early in the afternoon. On islands where the capital is inland rather than a port, buses always meet the boats. Some of the very remote islands have not yet acquired a bus, but most have some sort of motorised transport even if it is only a bone-shaking three-wheel truck.

In large and medium-size towns there is usually a central covered bus station with seating, waiting rooms, toilets, a shop selling snacks and drinks, and a snack bar selling pies, cakes and coffee. In some larger towns and cities, there may be more than one bus station, each serving different destinations. In small towns and villages the 'bus station' may be no more than a bus stop outside a kafeneion or taverna which doubles up as a booking office: here a timetable will be displayed and tickets will be sold. In very remote areas the timetable may only be in Greek, but in most booking offices timetables are in both Greek and Roman script. The timetables give both the departure and return times – useful if you are making a day trip. The times will be given using the 24-hour clock system.

When you buy a ticket you will be allotted a seat, and the seat number will be noted on the ticket. The seat number is indicated on the back of each seat of the bus, not on the back of the seat in front; this causes confusion amongst Greeks and tourists alike. You may board a bus without a ticket, as it is possible to purchase a ticket on board on a popular route, but during high season, this may mean you have to stand. Keep your ticket for the duration of the journey as it will be checked several times en route.

Turn up in good time to buy your ticket –

Inter-Island Flights			
Island	*Flights/Week*	*Duration*	*Fares*
Iraklion-Mykonos	3	70 mins	12,400 dr
Iraklion-Rhodes	5	40 mins	13,200 dr
Iraklion-Thira (Santorini)	3	40 mins	8200dr
Karpathos-Kassos	4	15 mins	2400 dr
Karpathos-Rhodes	14	40 mins	8200 dr
Karpathos-Sitia	1	35 mins	8200 dr
Kefallonia-Zakynthos	1	30 mins	3,300 dr
Kastellorizo-Rhodes	4	45 mins	7,900 dr
Kos-Rhodes	3	30 mins	7500 dr
Lemnos-Mykonos (Mytilini)	3	50 mins	8,500 dr
Mykonos-Rhodes	3	70 mins	12,500 dr
Rhodes-Thira (Santorini)	4	60 mins	12,300 dr

at least 20 minutes before departure to make sure you get a seat. Buses often leave a few minutes before their scheduled time of departure – another reason to give yourself plenty of time. Don't board the bus until you have told the driver your destination and have ensured that your luggage has been placed into the appropriate hold, otherwise there is just a slight chance it may go into the wrong hold and end up in the wrong town, or be left behind.

The buses are comfortable and, although not all are air-conditioned, they all have either curtains or blinds which you can pull down for shade from the sun. Buses do not have toilets on board and neither are refreshments available, so make sure you take sufficient water with you. On long journeys, buses stop about every three hours for toilet needs, snacks or meals. Smoking is prohibited on all buses in Greece. Only the chain-smoking drivers dare to ignore the no-smoking signs.

Fares are reasonably priced, with a journey costing approximately 1100 dr per 100 km. Some examples of fares are Athens-Thessaloniki, 7½ hours, 5500 dr; Athens-Patras, three hours, 2400 dr; and Athens-Volos, 5¼ hours, 3500 dr.

TRAIN

Greece's rail system is under the auspices of the state-owned Hellenic Railways Organisation, OSE (Organismos Siderodromon Ellados). Greece did not get a railway system until 1881, making it the last country in Europe to do so. The service is restricted and slow, and is confined to the mainland (including the Peloponnese), but is cheaper than the bus service. The standard-gauge north-bound line runs up eastern Greece via Larissa to Thessaloniki. Just north of Athens, a branch runs to Halkida on Evia. At Thessaloniki there is a branch west to Florina and Skopje (in the Former Yugoslav Republic of Macedonia) and on to Munich. Two branches run north from Thessaloniki: one to Idomeni and Belgrade (in former Yugoslavia), where the line splits; the other to Pro-

mahonas and Sofia (Bulgaria) and on to Moscow.

The rambling eastern branch runs through Thrace to Alexandroupolis, north along the Turkish border to Kastanies, then into Turkey and on to Istanbul. At Larissa there is a branch line to Volos and from Volos a branch line to Kalambaka via Trikala.

A narrow-gauge railway runs west from Athens to the Peloponnese. At Corinth the line splits. One line continues west to Patras, with a branch line from Diakofto to Kalavryta (a spectacular trip not to be missed), then south to Pyrgos and Kalamata, with branch lines to Killini (for boats to Zakynthos and Kefallonia, in the Ionian group), and Olympia. The other line from Corinth runs south to Argos then west to Tripolis. An express train runs from Athens to Thessaloniki, but even this takes 6½ hours. There are two classes: 1st and 2nd. Some examples of costs are: Athens-Thessaloniki, eight hours, 3960/2640 dr (1st/2nd class); Athens-Patras, five hours, 1750/1150 dr; and Athens-Volos, five hours, 3000/2000 dr.

In summer, make reservations at least three days in advance, otherwise you will end up standing for part, if not the whole, of the journey. There is nothing attached to seats to indicate that they are reserved. This sometimes causes hassles – you may find your reserved seat already occupied, or if you haven't made a seat reservation, you may be booted out of a seat just as you've settled down.

A few large towns have OSE booking offices in the centre of town; otherwise purchase your ticket at a train station. There is a 20% reduction on return tickets. A reduction of 30% is granted to groups of no less than 10 people. Eurail and Inter-Rail cards are valid in Greece, but because the network is so limited, it's hardly worth purchasing one of these if you are only going to use it in Greece. If you already have one of these rail passes, you must still make a reservation. You cannot simply board the train without prebooking.

Tourist cards are available in Greece to individual passengers, families and groups of up to five people. They are valid for 10, 20 or 30 days and entitle the holder to make an unlimited number of journeys on all the rail routes. The prices of the cards depend on the number of passengers and the duration of validity – enquire at an EOT, OSE booking office or train station. Senior cards are available to passengers over 60 years of age on presentation of their IDs or passports. They cost 12,000 dr for 1st-class travel and 8000 dr for 2nd class, and are valid for one year from the date of issue. These cards entitle passengers to a 50% reduction on train travel plus five free journeys per year. Free journeys may not be taken 10 days before or after Christmas or Easter, or between 1 July and 30 September.

TAXI

Taxis are widely available in Greece except on very small or remote islands. They are reasonably priced by European standards, especially for three or four people sharing costs. The starting rate is 200 dr and then 94 dr per km outside a built-up area. Additional costs (on top of the per km rate) are 200 dr from an airport, 100 dr from a train or bus station and 40 dr for each piece of luggage. Intercity taxis do not have meters so you should always settle on a price before you get in. Almost all taxi drivers in Greece speak English, many having lived in Australia or America.

CAR & MOTORBIKE

If your first introduction to Greece is Athens, the chances are you will soon be cursing cars like you've never done before. Despite the fact that Greeks have the second-lowest standard of living of all EC countries, there are more cars per head of population in Athens than any other Mediterranean city – one vehicle to 3.1 residents.

Ironically, measures to cut down on pollution from cars have increased the number of vehicles on the roads. A rule imposed in 1980 which specified that cars with odd and even number plates could only be used on alternating days, was intended to reduce the number of cars used in Athens. However, it resulted in many families purchasing a second car (with the requisite odd or even number plate). At the beginning of 1993 all cars in use in central Athens had to have catalytic converters. This was promoted by a 1991 regulation reducing import taxes on cars with catalytic converters, if a vehicle at least 15 years old was scrapped. Many low-income families then became car owners for the first time by buying an old banger and trading it in for a new 'clean car'.

The problem of too many cars in Athens is compounded by the lack of a proper metro system (other than the Piraeus-Kifissia line), which in most cities of comparable size transports the bulk of commuters. In addition to this, the general standard of driving is atrocious: speed limits, traffic signals, no-parking signs and pedestrians are largely ignored.

The terrible driving evident in Athens is mirrored throughout the country – statistics show Greece has the highest car accident fatality rate in Europe. Seven people are killed every day, and on weekends the number rises to 30. The greatest cause of accidents is speeding in the wrong lane. Motorbike riders are just as reckless as car drivers and make a lot more noise – this is equated with masculinity, so it has become standard procedure to remove silencers.

In an effort to bring some order to this chaos, new, much stricter, traffic laws came into operation in 1992 (see the following section).

Having your own wheels enables you to explore off the beaten track, but bear in mind that roads in very remote areas are often dirt or poorly maintained asphalt – main roads are OK. Obtain a good road map before you set off.

There are six stretches of highway in Greece where tolls are levied. They are: Athens-Corinth, Corinth-Patras, Athens-Lamia, Lamia-Larissa, Larissa-Thessaloniki and Thessaloniki-Evzoni. Tolls are either 400 or 500 dr for a car and just under half these amounts for a motorbike.

If you are going to take a car on an island-hopping trip, enquire as to the state of the roads at your prospective destination – cars are useless on some of the smaller islands which have next to no roads. Almost all islands are served by car ferries, but these are expensive. Some examples of rates are: Piraeus to Hania (Crete): 9200 to 12,030 dr (inclusive of taxes) depending on the size of the vehicle; Rhodes: 11,130 to 14,610 dr; and Lesbos: 10,360 to 13,560 dr. Ferry charges for motorbikes also depend on size; a large bike will cost about the same as a 3rd-class passenger ticket.

Petrol prices in Greece increased three times whilst this book was being researched. At the time of writing they were Super: 200 dr a litre; regular and unleaded: 190 dr; and diesel: 120 dr. Unleaded petrol is widely available.

See the Documents section in the Facts for the Visitor chapter for information regarding licence requirements for EC nationals and travellers from other countries.

Road Rules

It is hoped that the new traffic laws will engender greater respect for road rules. In Greece, as throughout Continental Europe, you drive on the right and overtake on the left. Outside built-up areas, traffic on a main road has priority at intersections. In towns, vehicles coming from the right have priority. Seat belts must be worn in front seats, and in back seats if the car is fitted with them. Children under 12 years are not allowed in the front seat. It is compulsory to carry a first-aid kit, fire extinguisher and a warning triangle, and it is forbidden to carry cans of petrol. Helmets are compulsory for motorcyclists if the motorbike is 50 cc or more.

Outside residential areas the speed limit is 120 km/h on highways, 90 km/h on other roads and 50 km/h in built-up areas. The speed limit for motorbikes up to 100 cc is 70 km/h and for larger motorbikes, 90 km/h.

Drivers exceeding the speed limit by 20% are liable for a fine of 10,000 dr; by 40% incurs a 30,000 dr fine. Other offences and fines include:

- driving on the wrong side of the road – 20,000 dr
- going through a red light – 50,000 dr
- violating priority at crossroads – 20,000 dr
- overcrowding a vehicle – 10,000 dr
- use of undipped headlights in towns – 10,000 dr
- illegal reversing – 5000 dr

Drink driving laws are strict – a blood alcohol content of 0.05% is liable to incur a penalty, and over 0.08% is a criminal offence.

The police are empowered to fine traffic offenders, but payment cannot be made on the spot. The police officer who imposes the fine will tell the offender where to pay.

If you are involved in an accident and no-one is hurt, the police will not be required to write a report, but it is advisable to go to a nearby police station and explain what happened. A police report may be required for insurance-claim purposes. If an accident involves injury, a driver who does not stop and does not inform the police may face a prison sentence.

See the Useful Organisations & Publications section in the Facts for the Visitor chapter for information about the Greek Automobile Club (ELPA).

Rental

Car If the deadly driving has not put you off getting behind a wheel in Greece, then perhaps the price of hiring a car will. Rental cars are widely available, but are more expensive than most other European countries. Most of the big, multinational car-hire companies are represented in Athens and large towns, on large islands and at international airports. The smaller islands often have only one car-hire outlet which may be a multinational or Greek company.

Prebooked and prepaid rates are always cheaper, and there are fly/drive combinations and other programmes that are worth looking into. Transhire (☎ 071-978 1922), Unit 16, 88 Clapham Park Rd, London SW4 7BX, is a reasonably priced London-based company with whom you can arrange car hire in Greece. At the time of writing, its rates for July, August and September were: Suzuki

Alto and Fiat Panda – UK£90/169 three days/one week; Ford Fiesta and Fiat Uno – UK£99/169; Ford Escort (4 door) – UK£111/ 210; and Suzuki Jeep 4WD – UK£165/320. The prices include unlimited mileage, third-party insurance, Collision Damage Waiver (CDW) and local taxes.

If you decide to hire a car while you are in Greece, check if the quoted price includes unlimited mileage (it often doesn't). CDW will not be included in the quoted price and costs between 1700 and 2600 dr extra a day, depending on the type of car. Without CDW you will be responsible for the first 1,000,000 to 4,000,000 dr (depending on the type of car) worth of damage if the accident was not your fault, and the full amount if it was. The rates quoted will also be exclusive of 18% VAT (on the Dodecanese islands the VAT is 13%). If you are going to take the car into another country or onto a ferry you will require advance written authorisation from the hire company. Unless you pay with a credit card, most hire companies will require a minimum deposit of 20,000 dr per day.

In Greece, local companies are of course cheaper than the multinational ones, but you must be careful about the condition of the vehicle. At the time of writing, prices (exclusive of CDW and VAT) charged by the multinational companies were around 28,000 to 53,000 dr (depending on the type of car) per day in the low season and 34,000 to 66,000 dr in the high season. Local companies charge around 22,000 to 35,000 dr in the low season and 27,000 to 44,000 dr in the high season. See the Getting Around sections for cities and islands for details of places to rent cars.

The minimum driving age in Greece is 18 years, but most car-hire firms have a minimum age of 23 years, although a few will rent to 21 year olds.

Motorbike Mopeds and motorcycles are available for hire on every island except the smallest and most remote ones, and to a lesser extent on the mainland. Vespa scooters used to be widely available but these are now being replaced by Japanese models; most of the larger motorbikes available are also now Japanese. In many cases maintenance has been minimal so, before you hire a machine, check it thoroughly – especially the brakes: you'll need them!

Greece is not the best place to initiate yourself into motorcycling. Apart from the reckless drivers with whom you will be sharing the road, the roads are hilly and badly maintained in remote areas. Every year many tourists have motorcycle accidents in Greece. Take care!

Rates are around 3000 dr per day for a moped or 50 cc motorbike to 5000 dr per day for a 250 cc motorbike. Out of season these prices drop considerably, so use your bargaining skills. By October it is sometimes possible to hire a moped for as little as 1200 to 1500 dr per day. Most motorcycle hirers include third party insurance in the price, but it is wise to check this. This insurance will not include medical expenses; see the warning following.

Warning If you are planning to hire a motorcycle or moped, check that your travel insurance covers you for injury resulting from a motorbike accident. Many insurance companies don't offer this cover. Check the fine print!

Purchases

Greece has no car industry and imported cars are heavily taxed. Several firms in Athens are authorised to buy and sell tax-free cars in transit. One is Auto Imports, Liossion 220. Other possibilities are Transco (☎ 01-959 4827), Syngrou 336, and Kyriakos (☎ 01-922 2746), Syngrou 144. You will pay at least 400,000 dr for a decent secondhand small car.

BICYCLE

Greeks have not caught on to cycling, which isn't surprising considering the hilly terrain. Tourists are beginning to cycle in Greece, but if you decide to do so you'll need strong leg muscles. You can hire bicycles in a few places, but they are not as widely available as cars and motorbikes. Prices range from

Cycling in the Lap of the Gods

Intrepid cyclist Paul Hellander battled snow, high winds and curious canines on his recent cycling trip from Ioannina, in northern Greece, to Patras, in the north-west corner of the Peloponnese:

Greece is not the kind of place with which one would normally associate enjoyable cycling in Europe. It has high mountains, it can be very hot in summer and it has drivers whose road sense can leave much to be desired. Nonetheless, I am pleased to say that cycling is alive and well in Greece – though not necessarily by the Greeks themselves.

Greeks who ride bikes belong to one of two categories: elderly gentlemen who trundle around the provincial towns on antiquated, but adequate relics of a bygone age or youngsters whose only means of transportation, or recreation, is on two wheels. The bicycle-commuter or recreational off-roader seem to be unknown entities in Greece.

First a word about transporting a bike overseas. I took the mountain bike with me to Amsterdam with a view to doing some cycling in Europe. The bike was carefully packed in a large packing carton, marked 'Fragile, Bike' and so on. On arrival, I discovered that the rear wheel had been damaged in transit, making my first day's ride into Amsterdam central bumpy to say the least. Conversely on the return leg from Athens to Adelaide (Australia), I simply handed the bike as it was (with the handlebars turned sideways and pedals removed) and it received only one or two minor scratches. Bubble wrap around the frame would have prevented this.

Ioannina was a good place from where to set out: it is quite high up in the mountains and to get to the sea there is only one direction – down! Apart from a short climb out of the basin in which Ioannina lies, it is a long, fast downhill run to the plains, following the valley through which the wild Louros River flows. The road is smooth and there is relatively little traffic. Though not designated as a cycle track, there is a wide band at the side of the road on which cyclists can comfortably ride. This accompanied me for 90% of the way. At an average speed of 23 kp/h, I soon reached the orange groves in the prefecture of Arta and my meeting with the Ambracian Gulf followed a welcome lunch at the little village of Menidi: 97 km in 4¾ hours!

A short 27-km run after an extended lunch brought me to my first night's stop at Amfilochia in the bottom corner of the Ambracian Gulf.

The following morning started with a long climb out of Amfilochia as I skirted Mt Thyamon and Lake Ambracia in the direction of the impressive River Acheloos dam project. There were no serious hills and the traffic was light, but I had several encounters with dogs which obviously were not used to the sight of a multicoloured cyclist entering their territory. There were no other cyclists on the road, though the owner of a roadside stall informed me that he regularly saw columns of Italian, Swedish and German cyclists travelling this way during the summer months.

I passed Agrinio and entered the climb up to the Kleisoura Gap – the only way through to the marshy coastal plain leading to the small town of Messolongi where Lord Byron died of pneumonia in 1824 after bravely defending the struggles of the Greek patriots in the War of Independence against the Turks.

On the slow climb out of Messolongi and on to what I knew would be the difficult part, I got a hint of what was brewing on the Gulf of Corinth over the other side of the mountains. Strong headwinds whirling like dervishes through the gaps in the mountains found their mark: a struggling and tiring cyclist looking forward to completing the last 37 km of the day and the softness of a welcoming bed.

Have you ever tried cycling down a steep hill and the headwind just won't let you? Not only that, there is a 200-metre drop down to the sea on your right, down which the vicious winds threaten at any moment to deposit you unceremoniously! This was how I ended my journey, very late and almost in darkness.

Paul Hellander – Australia

800 to 3000 dr per day, depending on the type and age of the bike. Bicycles are carried free on most ferries.

HITCHING

Success at hitching a lift varies a lot depending on which part of the country you are in. It is difficult to get a lift just outside the large cities, particularly Athens, but in remote areas and islands with poor public transport it is relatively easy. On country roads it is not unknown for someone to stop and ask if you want a lift without you even having to stick out a thumb. In remote areas you can't afford to be fussy about the mode of transport, as it may be a tractor or a spluttering three-wheel truck.

As far as women hitching alone are concerned, Greece is probably safer than most countries for them to do so, but the element of risk still exists. This risk is less on the islands (especially small sparsely inhabited ones) than it is on the mainland. Ideally it would be better to hitch with a companion, preferably a male one. Many travellers enjoy the freedom of hitchhiking, despite the potential risks involved. The information provided here does not constitute an unconditional recommendation by Lonely Planet.

WALKING

Unless you have come to Greece just to lie on a beach, the chances are you will do quite a bit of walking. Because of the hilly terrain many villages and towns, including Athens, are at least in part pedestrianised with hilly, narrow, cobbled and stepped streets. You will also do a lot of walking if you visit archaeological sites and ruined fortresses. See the What to Bring, Health and Trekking sections in the Facts for the Visitor chapter.

BOAT
Ferry

For most people, travelling in Greece is synonymous with island hopping, which means making use of the extensive ferry network. Approximately 15 ferry-boat companies operate in Greece, but apart from 1st class,

prices are fixed by the government so you will pay the same for a ticket regardless of who owns the boat. Ferries do, however, vary in comfort, size, facilities offered and how long it takes them to get to a particular island.

The hub of the Greek ferry network is Piraeus, the port of Athens. Ferries leave here for the Cyclades, Dodecanese, the North-Eastern Aegean and Argo-Saronic islands and Crete. Athens' second port is Rafina, 70 km away from the city and connected by an hourly bus service.

Ferries leave Rafina for several of the Cyclades and North-Eastern Aegean islands, as well as Kos and Rhodes in the Dodecanese, all of which can also be reached from Piraeus. The only island in the groups mentioned so far which cannot be reached from Piraeus is the Cycladic island of Kea, which can only be reached from Lavrion, a port in Attica; it's easily reached by bus from Athens.

Ferries for the Ionian islands leave from the Peloponnese ports of Patras (for Kefallonia, Ithaki, Paxoi and Corfu) and Killini (for Kefallonia and Zakynthos); from Astakos (for Ithaki and Kefallonia) and Mytikas (for Lefkada and Meganisi), both in Sterea Ellada; and from Igoumenitsa in Epiros (for Corfu).

Ferries for the Sporades islands leave from Volos, Thessaloniki, Agios Konstantinos and Kymi on Evia. The latter two ports are easily reached by frequent bus from Athens. In addition, some of the North-Eastern Aegean islands have connections with Thessaloniki, as well as Piraeus. The odd ones out are Thassos which is reached from Kavala, and Samothrace which is reached from Alexandroupolis year round, and also has a high-season connection with Kavala. For more details on ferry services, see the table in this section, as well as the relevant port and island sections throughout the book.

Ferry timetables change from year to year and season to season, and ferries are subject to delays and cancellations at short notice due to inclement weather, strikes or boats conking out. No timetable is infallible, although the one given out by the EOT in

Major Ferry Routes from Mainland Greece Ports

This table shows the high-season deck-class prices at the time of writing. It should be considered a guide only: fares can change at short notice and sailing times can also vary, according to how many islands are visited en route and prevailing weather conditions. For more up-to-date information, contact the EOT or local port police.

Cyclades

	Piraeus	Rafina
Andros	–	3 hours
	–	(1516 dr)
Tinos	5½ hours	–
	(2700 dr)	
Mykonos	6½ hours	6 hours
	(2600 dr)	(2451 dr)
Syros	4½ hours	4½-6 hours
	(2400 dr)	(2100 dr)
Naxos	6 hours	–
	(2500 dr)	
Paros	5 hours	–
	(2225 dr)	
Ios	8-10 hours	–
	(3100 dr)	
Folegandros	10-12 hours	–
	(3100 dr)	
Thira (Santorini)	12 hours	–
	(3100 dr)	
Serifos	4½ hours	–
	(2500 dr)	
Sifnos	5½ hours	–
	(2400 dr)	

Crete

	Piraeus
Iraklion	12 hours
	(3850 dr)
Sitia	14 hours
	(4800 dr)
Hania	12 hours
	(3756 dr)

Dodecanese

	Piraeus
Rhodes	12-18 hours
	(4400 dr)
Astypalea	16 hours
	(2800 dr)

North-Eastern Aegean

	Piraeus
Samos	12½ hours
	(3610 dr)
Chios	10 hours
	(3142 dr)
Lesbos	15 hours
	(3700 dr)

Ionian

	Igoumenitsa	Patras	Killini
Corfu	1½ hours	10 hours	–
	(620 dr)	(3500 dr)	
Kefallonia	–	4 hours	–
		(1500 dr)	
Ithaki	–	6 hours	–
		(2050 dr)	
Zakynthos	–	–	1½ hours
			(780 dr)

Sporades

	Volos	Agios Konstantinos
Skiathos	3 hours	3½ hours
	(1800 dr)	(2243 dr)
Skopelos Town	4½ hours	5½ hours
	(2200 dr)	(2617 dr)
Alonissos	5 hours	6 hours
	(2400 dr)	(2886 dr)
Skyros	4¼ hours	–
	(7588 dr)	

Saronic Gulf

	Piraeus
Aegina	1½ hours
	(715 dr)
Poros	3½ hours
	(1200 dr)
Hydra	4½ hours
	(1500 dr)
Spetses	5½ hours
	(1750 dr)

Evia	Glyfa	Arkitsa	Oropou	Agia Marina	Rafina
Agiokambos	30 minutes (250 dr)	–	–	–	–
Loutra Edipsou	–	one hour (500 dr)	–	–	–
Eretria	–	–	30 minutes (200 dr)	–	–
Nea Styra	–	–	–	40 minutes (413 dr)	–
Marmari	–	–	–	–	1½ hrs (707 dr)
Karystos	–	–	–	–	2½ hrs

Athens is updated monthly, and is as accurate as far as is humanly possible. The guys to go to for the most comprehensive ferry information are the local port police (*limenarheio*), whose offices are always on or near the quayside. They have up-to-the-minute information on all the vessels which are due to sail into the port under their jurisdiction.

If you are going to do a lot of island hopping and you enjoy poring over timetables, you may decide it is worth buying the *Greek Travel Pages*. This is a weighty tome which is published monthly, primarily for the tourist industry, but it may be bought from Eleftheroudakis bookshop, Nikis 4, Athens, for 2000 dr. If you don't want to spend this much money, most hotels and travel agencies are willing to let you look through their copies. In addition to ferry timetables, the publication has timetables for trains and aeroplanes as well as pages and pages of useless information which you can tear out to lighten the load.

Throughout the year there is at least one ferry a day from a mainland port to the largest and most popular islands in each group, and during the high season (from June to mid-September) there are considerably more. Ferries sailing from one island group to another are not so frequent, and if you want to do this you'll need to plan carefully, otherwise you may end up having to backtrack to Piraeus to catch a ferry from there.

The large ferries usually have three or four classes: 1st class has air-conditioned cabins and a posh lounge and restaurant; 2nd class has smaller cabins and sometimes a lounge; tourist class gives you a berth in a communal area and 3rd (deck) class gives you access to a room with 'airline' seats, a snack bar-cum-lounge and, of course, the deck, and usually a self-service restaurant.

At a few remote islands, the arrival of a ferry boat is a once or twice-weekly occurrence which provides a lifeline to the sparse population. Witnessing the arrival of a ferry at such an island is an interesting spectacle, as it is one of the most exciting events of the week. It seems as if the whole population – including at least one tail-wagging dog – turns out to meet the ferry. Arriving and departing relations are warmly embraced, sacks of vegetables and crates of drinks are unloaded quickly and haphazardly, and high-tech and industrial appliances are carried off with the utmost care. All this takes place amidst frantic arm waving and much shouting and general pandemonium, in a frantic effort to ensure that the ferry arrives on time at the next island – which invariably it does not. It is well to remember on such occasions that chaos is a Greek word and the Greeks invented drama. Eventually, the task completed, the ferry departs and the island slips back into its customary tranquillity. ■

Greece – Major Ferry Routes

A 1st-class ticket can cost as much as flying and varies from one vessel to another: tourist class costs about 25% more than 3rd class and 2nd class just under double. Children under four travel free, between four and 10 pay half fare and over 10 pay full fare. Unless you state otherwise, when purchasing a ticket, you will automatically be given deck class. As deck class is what most tourists opt for, it is those prices which will be quoted in this book. All tickets are subject to an embarkation tax of 140 dr, 250 dr for NAT (the seaman's union) and 8% VAT.

Given that ferries are prone to delays and cancellations, do not purchase a ticket until it has been confirmed that the ferry is leaving, as getting a refund usually proves to be either impossible or a lot of hassle. If you need to reserve car space, however, it would pay to purchase your ticket prior to the day of departure.

Also bear in mind that travelling time can vary considerably from one ferry to another, depending on how many islands are called at on the way to your destination. For example, the Piraeus-Rhodes trip can take between 12 and 18 hours depending on the ferry. Before buying your ticket, check how many stops the boat is going to make, and its estimated arrival time.

Agencies selling tickets line the waterfronts of most ports, but rarely is there one which sells tickets for every boat, and often an agency is reluctant to give you information about a boat they do not sell a ticket for. This means you have to check the timetables displayed outside each agency to find out which ferry is next due to depart – or ask the port police. In high season, a number of boats may be due at a port at around the same time, so it is not beyond the realms of possibility that you might get on the wrong boat. The crucial thing to look out for is the name of the boat; this will be printed on your ticket, and in large lettering on the side of the vessel (in English).

If for some reason you haven't purchased a ticket from an agency, makeshift ticket tables are put up beside a ferry about an hour before departure. Tickets can also be purchased on board the ship, after it has sailed. If you are waiting at the quayside for a delayed ferry, unless you have it on good authority when it is due to arrive, don't lose patience and wander off. Ferry boats, once they have finally docked, can demonstrate amazing alacrity – blink and you may miss the boat.

Once on board the fun really begins – in high season, chaos reigns. No matter how many passengers are already on the ferry, more will be crammed on. Children get separated from parents, bewildered black-shrouded grannies are steered through the crowd by teenage grandchildren, people almost get knocked over by backpackers, dogs get excited and bark and everyone rushes to procure a seat. As well as birds in cages and cats in baskets there is almost always at least one truck of livestock on board – usually sheep, goats or cattle – who will vociferously make their presence known. I once travelled on a ferry which had a deck full of donkeys, and another time I shared my passage with a truck full of lions which were part of a travelling circus.

Greeks travelling third class usually make a beeline for the lounge/snack bar, whereas tourists often make for the deck where they can sunbathe. In high season you need strong nerves and lungs to withstand the lounge/snack bar which usually has at least two TVs turned on full blast, each tuned into a different channel, and suffering from interference which causes a loud crackling sound. At least two people will have radios turned on at full volume, and everyone will be engaged in loud conversation. Smoke-laden air adds the final touch to this delightful ambience. Unlike on other public transport in Greece, smoking is not prohibited on ferries.

On overnight trips, backpackers usually sleep on deck in their sleeping bags – you can also roll out your bag between the 'airline' seats. If you don't have a sleeping bag, claim an 'airline' seat as soon as you board. Leave your luggage on it – as long as you don't leave any valuables in it, it will be safe, and no-one will move it. The noise on board usually dies down around midnight so you should be able to snatch a few hours' sleep. Outside the peak season, ferries can be very quiet and subdued places; sometimes it may seem as if you are the only passenger on board.

The food sold in the snack bars ranges from mediocre to inedible, and the choice is limited to packets of biscuits, sandwiches, very greasy pizzas and cheese pies. Most large ferries also have a self-service restaurant where the food is OK, although more expensive than what you would normally pay, with main courses around 900 to 1200 dr. If you are budgeting, have special dietary requirements, or are at all fussy about what you eat, then take some food along with you.

Inter-Island Boat

In addition to the large ferries which ply between the large mainland ports and island groups, there are smaller boats which link two, three or four islands in a group, and occasionally, an island in one group with an island in another. These boats always used to be caïques – sturdy old fishing boats – but gradually these are being replaced by new purpose-built boats, which are usually called express or excursion boats. Tickets tend to cost more than those for the large ferries, but the boats are jolly useful if you're island hopping.

Taxi Boat

Taxi boats are small boats which transport people to beaches around an island which are inaccessible or difficult to get to by land. Most islands have at least one of these boats; some owners charge a set price for each person, others charge a flat rate for the boat, and this cost is divided by the number of passengers. Either way, prices are usually quite reasonable.

Hydrofoil

Hydrofoils are an alternative to ferries for reaching some of the islands. They take half the time and cost twice the price, and do not take cars or motorbikes. Some routes operate only during high season, and according to demand, and all are prone to cancellations due to inclement weather. One well-established service is between Piraeus and the Saronic Gulf islands. Some hydrofoils continue from the Saronic Gulf islands to Porto Heli, Tolo and Nafplion in the Peloponnese and some to Leonidio, Kyparissia, Monemvassia, Neapoli (all in the Peloponnese) and then on to the island of Kythera.

Another well-established service (summer only) is between Thessaloniki and the Sporades; some call in at Moudania on the Halkidiki peninsula. From Moudania there are hydrofoils to Alonissos which continue on to either Volos or Agios Konstantinos. In addition the Sporades are also served by hydrofoils from Volos and Agios Konstantinos.

The Dodecanese has a well-established service between Rhodes and Kos and a high-season service between Rhodes, Leros and Samos. Occasionally in high season hydrofoils link Rhodes with Halki, Tilos, Nisyros, Karpathos and Kastellorizo, but these routes are very much at the whim of the hydrofoil operators and are not scheduled services. A very irregular high-season service runs between Rafina and the Cyclades islands of Andros, Tinos, Mykonos and Naxos, but it is so prone to cancellations due to bad sea conditions that it may be discontinued. Some examples of hydrofoil prices are: Agios Konstantinos to Skopelos (5324 dr) and Alonissos (5577 dr); from Piraeus to Hydra (2700 dr) and Spetses (3000 dr). Tickets cannot be bought on board hydrofoils – buy them in advance from an agent.

Catamaran

Catamarans are the new guys on the inter-island travel scene. In 1991 C/M *Catamaran I* began operating from Flisvos (a port eight km east of Piraeus) to the Cyclades islands of Syros, Tinos, Mykonos, Paros and Naxos then on to either Ios and Thira or Amorgos and the Minor islands (Donoussa, Koufonisi, Iraklia and Shinoussa) or Sikinos, Folegandros and Ios. This comfortable air-conditioned craft costs around twice as much as the ferries.

Yacht

Despite the disparaging remarks about 'yachties' amongst tourists, yachting is *the* way to see the Greek islands. Nothing beats it for the peace and serenity of sailing the open sea, and the freedom of being able to visit remote and uninhabited islands.

The free EOT booklet *Sailing the Greek Seas*, although long overdue for an update, contains lots of information about weather conditions, weather bulletins, entry and exit regulations, exit and entry ports and guide-books for yachters. You can pick up the booklet at any GNTO office either abroad or in Greece.

If you are not rich enough to buy a yacht there are several other options open to you. You can hire a bare boat (a yacht without a crew) if two crew members have a sailing certificate. Prices start at around US$70 per day per person. Otherwise you can charter a boat with a skipper for around US$120 per day per person (meals included). Yacht charter companies operating in and around Athens and Piraeus include:

Aegean Sailing
    Makariou 2, Alimos, Attica (☎ 01-982 0670)

Aegean Yachts
    Poseidonos 10, Glyfada, Attica (☎ 01-893 2001)
Alfa Levante Yachts
    Vasilissis Sofias 12, Athens (☎ 01-721 9360)
Archipelagos Clippers
    Amalias 26, Athens (☎ 01-324 2132/3/4)
Basil Conyoyannis
    Zea Marina 5A, Piraeus (☎ 01-451 2010/8820)
Bibi's Yacht Cruises
    Vasileos Pavlou 91, Piraeus (☎ 01-413 0654)
Captain Kondos Cruises
    Ipitou 21, Athens (☎ 01-322 0400)
Destinations
    Amalias 26, Athens (☎ 01-324 2132/3/4)
Fine Yachting Travel
    Koundouriotou 145, Piraeus (☎ 01-412 0414)
Ghiolman Yachts
    Filellinon 7, Athens (☎ 01-323 3696)
G M Yachting
    Makariou 2, Alimos, Attica (☎ 01-981 5619)
Hellenic Island Holidays
    Apollonos 12, Athens (☎ 01-983 6465)
Seahorse
    Alkyonidon 83, Voula, Attica
    (☎ 01-895 2212/6220)
Seaways Sailing
    Irakeos 23, Glyfada, Attica (☎ 01-963 3356)

There are many more yacht charter companies in Greece; the EOT can give you some addresses. Also check out the Dodecanese chapter in this book.

A number of UK-based holiday companies offer holidays sailing around the Greek islands. You can book holidays with them either exclusive or inclusive of the airfare to Greece. Some of these include:

Frances McCulloch
    60 Fordwych Rd, London NW2 3TH
    (☎ 081-452 7509)
Greek Islands Sailing Club
    66 High St, Walton-on-Thames, Surrey KT12
    1BU (☎ 0932-220416)
Tenrag Yacht Charters
    Bramling House, Bramling, Canterbury, Kent
    CT3 1NB (☎ 0227-721874)
World Expeditions
    8 College Rise, Maidenhead, Berkshire SL6 6BP
    (☎ 0628-74174)

LOCAL TRANSPORT
To/From the Airport
In recent years Olympic Airways has been cutting down on buses to domestic airports. Where this service still exists, buses leave the Olympic Airways office approximately 70 minutes before departure. These days, especially on the smaller islands, often the only way to reach the airport is by taxi. This means that in at least one case (Karpathos to Kassos) you will fork out more for the taxi than the flight. Passengers are required to arrive at an airport one hour before departure of a domestic flight.

Transport to and from each international airport in Greece is covered within the Getting Around section of the relevant city.

Bus
Most Greek towns are small enough to get around on foot. The only ones where you may need to take a local bus are Athens, Piraeus and Thessaloniki. The procedure for buying tickets for local buses is covered in the Getting Around section for each city.

Underground (Subway)
Athens is the only city in Greece with an underground – and a very limited one at that. Athens' meagre one-line electric train runs from Piraeus (the port of Athens) to Kifissia, a northern suburb, with 21 stations in between. It hardly warrants being called an underground system although the section in the city centre is subterranean. In mid-1992 work started on a long-awaited proper underground for the city, and it has been estimated it will take six years to complete. Athens' town planners have stated its construction will create traffic havoc in the city – so what's new?

Taxi
For a long time Athens' taxi drivers had a bad reputation amongst tourists. Criticisms of them included gross ignorance of their city, refusing to take customers, rudeness and overcharging. In mid-1992 much tougher penalties came into existence for cab drivers who commit serious breaches of the law. Penalties include suspension of the cab driver's licence for one month, and removal of number plates for up to three days for minor offences. For serious offences, penal-

ties increase to six months' suspension and two months' plate removal.

Since the decree some tourists have noticed a marked improvement in the behaviour of taxi drivers in Athens and rip-offs are less frequent, although are not unheard of. See the Dangers & Annoyances section in the Athens chapter. If you have a complaint about a taxi driver, take the cab number and report your complaint to the tourist police. Taxi drivers in other towns in Greece are, on the whole, friendly, helpful and honest.

Taxis in towns and cities have meters. The starting rate for taxis in built up areas is 200 dr, then 48 dr per km between 5 am and midnight, and 94 dr between midnight and 5 am. Additional charges are 200 dr from an airport, 100 dr from a train or bus station and 40 dr for each piece of luggage.

TOURS

As befits a country whose major industry is tourism, Greece has countless tour companies intent upon parting tourists from their drachmas. It is always cheaper to see things independently; tours are only worth considering if your time is very limited. The most well-established tour companies are CHAT, GO Tours and Key Tours, all based in Athens. They each organise almost identical tours which include: Delphi (two days, 19,000 dr); ancient Corinth, Mycenae, and Epidaurus (two days, 20,000 dr); Delphi and Meteora (three days, 50,000 dr); and ancient Corinth, Mycenae, Epidaurus, ancient Olympia and Delphi (four days, 68,000 dr). For the addresses of these companies and details of some of their other tours, see the Athens chapter.

Organised Treks

Trekking Hellas, Filellinon 7, Athens 10557 (☎ 01-323 4548; fax 325 1474; London agent – Zoe Holidays, 34 Thornhill Rd, Surbiton KT6 7TL (☎ 081-390 7623) is a well-established company which specialises in small group treks on the Greek mainland. They will also organise 'tailor-made' treks on either the mainland or islands for groups of four or more people. Some examples of their treks are: Mt Helmos (four days, 40,000 dr); Ziria mountain range (three days, 18,000 dr); and Mt Taygetus (three days, 48,000 dr; seven days, 64,000 dr).

Other tours are recommended throughout the book.

Top: View from the Acropolis, Athens (JB)
Left: The Erechtheion, Athens (JB)
Right: The Parthenon, Acropolis, Athens (BD)

Top: The Theatre of Herodes, Acropolis, Athens (DH)
Left: The Parthenon, Athens (VB)
Right: Entrance to the Acropolis, Athens (RH)

Athens Αθήνα

The perpetual 'high' which the novelist Henry Miller experienced during his travels in Greece did not flag when he came to the capital. In the *Colossus of Maroussi* Miller waxed lyrical about the extraordinary quality of the city's light and rhythm.

Few visitors today, however, share his bubbling enthusiasm. Most, after the obligatory visit to the Acropolis and the National Archaeological Museum, beat a hasty retreat. For, although its glorious past and its influence on Western civilisation have imbued the city of Athens with emotional evocations commensurate with those of Rome and Jerusalem, it is a city which few fall in love with. These reactions are understandable, for, on entering Athens, you are confronted with its least appealing attributes of concrete urban sprawl, industrialisation and pollution.

To appreciate Athens, explore it with an adventurous, inquisitive spirit; don't dwell on its shortcomings, and, most importantly, be aware of the city's traumatic history – take a little time to reflect upon its long and troubled life. Unlike most historic capital cities, Athens does not have a history of continuous expansion; it is one characterised by glory, followed by decline and near annihilation, and then resurgence in the 19th century, when it became the capital of independent Greece.

The historical event which, more than any other, was responsible for the Athens of today took place in 1923 when the population almost doubled overnight with the arrival of refugees from Turkey. This sudden influx necessitated the hasty erection of concrete apartment blocks.

The expansion of Athens in all directions began at this time, and was perpetuated during the 1950s and 1960s when the country began the transition from an agricultural to an industrial nation. Young people began to flock to the city from the islands and rural areas, and this movement of the population has continued ever since. Now, the city's suburbs are clambering up the surrounding mountains.

Yet Athens has many redeeming qualities. The city is bounded on three sides by Mts Parnitha (1413 metres), Pendeli (1109 metres) and Hymettos (1026 metres). The last of these was once famed for its violet sunsets, which now, more often than not, are obliterated by the city's appalling pollution. At least one of these mountains can be glimpsed from almost every street in the city. Within the city there are no less than eight hills, of which the most prominent are Lykavitos (277 metres) and the Acropolis (156 metres).

If you wander off the main thoroughfares onto side streets, sooner or later you will encounter steps giving access to one of these eight hills. These steps are not only pleasant escape routes from the traffic-congested streets, but also serve as accesses to stunning panoramas. Athens improves considerably when viewed from a height enhanced by a backdrop of the glistening water of the Saronic Gulf – its boundary on the fourth side.

Travelling east, Athens is the last European city in the Mediterranean. King Otho and the middle class which evolved after Independence might have been intent upon

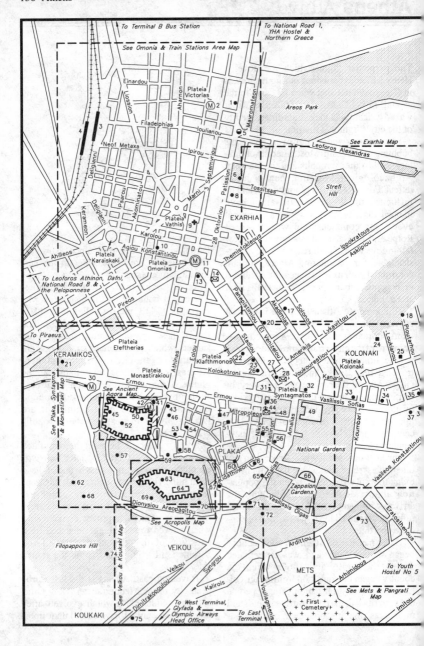

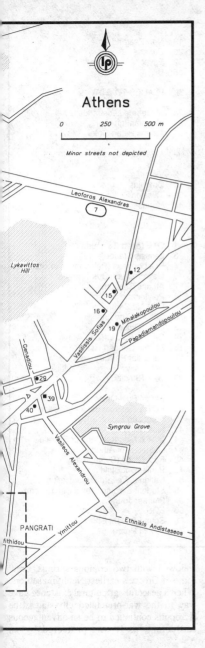

Athens

0   250   500 m

Minor streets not depicted

Leoforos Alexandras

7

Lykavittos
Hill

12

15

16

19 Mihalakopoulou

Vasilissis Sofias

Papadiamandopoulou

Genadiou

29

39

40

Vasileos Alexandrou

Syngrou Grove

PANGRATI

Ymittou

Ethnikis Andistaseos

fithidou

making Athens European in every sense of the word, but influences of Asia Minor are still immediately palpable. There are raucous street vendors on every square, and bustling, colourful, outdoor markets reminiscent of Turkish bazaars are ubiquitous.

There are many other reminders of the proximity of the Orient. Dwellings have balconies cascading with geraniums, jasmine or hibiscus and most of the city's streets and squares are fringed by orange trees. Courtyards and little gardens shaded by vines and palm trees and the few remaining 19th-century, red-tiled Turkish houses also lend a touch of exotica. Some of the older parts of the city have a ramshackle Third-World feel about them. Yet, in contrast, there are salubrious areas with elegant neoclassical mansions, which more prosperous northern European capitals would be hard pushed to match. Also, with their treasures and gloomy interiors, the numerous little Byzantine churches provide a visual respite from the concrete that often surrounds them.

The city of Athens stimulates not only with its visual images. The evocative perfumes of incense drifting from churches and flower-strewn balconies, the mouth-watering aromas from meat roasting over glowing charcoal, the distinctive strains of Greek music with its roots in the music of Asia Minor and the Middle East, all have their impact on the senses.

Another endearing aspect of the city is the congeniality of Athenians in contrast to the anonymity you can experience in many Western capitals. Within a week of staying in Athens the chances are you'll be passing the time of day, or stopping for a chat with some of its inhabitants.

Perhaps most significant of all is that, wherever you are in the centre of the city, the Acropolis, with its transcendent and compelling aura, is omnipresent. This serves as a constant reminder that, whatever pitfalls, trials and tribulations have befallen the city, its status as the birthplace of Western civilisation is indubitable.

MUSEUMS

6   National Archaeological &
     Numismatic Museums
17   Theatre Museum
22   City of Athens Museum
26   National Historical Museum
33   Benaki Museum
34   Goulandris Museum of Cycladic &
     Ancient Greek Art
37   Byzantine Museum
38   War Museum
40   National Art Gallery
     (Ethnike Pinakotheke)
43   Museum of Traditional Greek
     Ceramics
58   Museum of the University
59   Paul & Alexandra Kanellopoulos
     Museum
60   Centre of Folk Arts & Traditions
61   Greek Folk Art Museum
65   Jewish Museum

ANCIENT SITES

21   Keramikos
45   Temple of Hephaestus
46   Library of Hadrian
50   Stoa of Attalos
52   Ancient Agora
53   Roman Agora
54   Tower of the Winds
57   Areopagus Hill
62   Hill of the Pnyx
63   Acropolis
64   Parthenon
66   Zappeion
67   Monument of Lysikrates
69   Theatre of Herodes Atticus
70   Ancient Theatre of Dionysos
71   Arch of Hadrian
72   Temple of Olympian Zeus
73   Roman Stadium
74   Monument of Filopappos

EMBASSIES

12   Australia
15   USA

19   New Zealand
29   Canada
32   Egypt
35   UK

■   PLACES TO STAY

24   St George Lycabettus Hotel
25   Athenian Inn
39   Athens Hilton Hotel

Ⓜ   METRO

2   Victorias
11   Omonias
30   Thission
42   Monastirakiou

OTHER

1   OTE (open 24 hours)
3   Larissis Station
4   Peloponnese (Peloponissou) Station
5   Mavromateon Bus Terminal
7   Athens Stadium
8   Polytechneion
9   First Aid Centre
10   National Theatre
13   OTE (Omonia)
14   Central Post Office
16   Athens Concert Hall
18   Funicular Railway
20   University
23   OTE (Stadiou)
27   Box Office
28   Parcel Post Office
31   EOT & National Bank of Greece
36   American Express
41   Flea Market
44   EOT & General Bank of Greece
47   Cathedral of Athens
48   Post Office (Syntagma)
49   Parliament Building
51   National Welfare Organisation
55   Student & Youth Travel Service and
     Pioneer Tours
56   EOS
68   Sound & Light Show
75   Tourist Police

HISTORY
Early History

The early history of Athens is inextricably interwoven with mythology, making it impossible to disentangle fact from fiction. What is known is that the Acropolis, endowed with two copious springs, drew some of Greece's earliest Neolithic settlers. When a peaceful agricultural existence gave way to the war-orientated city-states, the Acropolis continued to be an advantageous settlement, as it was protected by an

Athena & the Olive Tree

According to mythology, Kekrops, a Phoenician, came to Attica where he founded a city on a huge rock near the sea. The gods of Olympus proclaimed that the city should be named after the deity who could produce the most valuable legacy for mortals. Athena and Poseidon contended. Athena produced an olive tree, symbol of peace and prosperity. Poseidon struck a rock with his trident and a horse sprang forth, which symbolised all the qualities of strength and fortitude for which he was renowned. Athena was the victor, for the gods proclaimed that her gift would better serve the citizens of Athens than the arts of war personified by Poseidon's gift.

The olive tree came to be held in such high esteem that, in the 6th century BC, the archon of Athens, Solon, passed a law that anyone found cutting one down would be executed. To this day, olive groves, more than any other vegetation, epitomise the Greek landscape, and the protein-rich olive is a staple of the Greek diet. ■

amphitheatre of mountains, and its summit was an excellent vantage point from which to spot potential invaders.

By 1400 BC, Athens had become a powerful Mycenaean city and, unlike the cities of Mycenae, Pylos and Tiryns, it survived the Dorian invasion of Greece in 1200 BC. But it couldn't escape the dark age that enveloped the rest of Greece, and very little is known of this period.

After its emergence from the dark age in the 8th century BC, a period of peace followed, both for Athens and the surrounding united towns. During this time the city became the artistic centre of Greece, excelling particularly in ceramics. The geometric designs of the dark-age vases evolved into a narrative style, depicting scenes from everyday Athenian life and from mythology. This pottery subsequently became known as the Protoattic style.

By the 6th century BC, Athens was ruled by aristocrats, generals and the *archon* (chief magistrate). Position in the hierarchy depended on wealth, which was gained either from commerce or agriculture. Labourers and peasants had no say in the functioning of the city. In 594 BC the reform-oriented Solon became the archon.

Solon is perhaps best known today for his maxim of 'nothing in excess'. He implemented many reforms which were beneficial to the poor, and so is regarded as the harbinger of Athenian democracy. His most significant reforms were the annulment of all debts and the implementation of trial

by jury. However, despite Solon's reforms, conflict between the wealthy aristocracy and the lower classes continued, leading to the benevolent tyrant Peisistratos seizing power in 560 BC.

Peisistratos built up a formidable navy, much to the consternation of the other city-states. But Peisistratos' initiatives went further than military supremacy. He inaugurated the Festival of the Great Dionysia, which was the precursor of Attic drama. He also constructed many splendid sacred and secular buildings

Peisistratos was succeeded by his son Hippias, who was much more of a tyrant in the modern sense of the word. Athens only managed to overthrow this oppressor in 510 BC, by swallowing its pride and accepting the help of King Kleomeus of Sparta. Although Sparta's role was that of arch rival to Athens, the latter often found it necessary to call upon Sparta for help.

Athens' Golden Age

After Athens was successful in subduing once and for all the powerful Persian Empire in the battles of Salamis and Plataea (again, with the help of Sparta) its power knew no bounds.

In 477 BC Athens established a confederacy on the sacred island of Delos and insisted on a tribute from many islands to fund their protection against the Persians. This sounds suspiciously like a protection racket, for in reality, Persia by that time was not much of a threat anyway. The demand was an example of Athens' determination to dominate at all costs. In 461 BC this treasury was moved to Athens and it was largely with this money that Pericles, who ruled from 461 to 429 BC, transformed the city, and the Classical Age reached its pinnacle in what has become known as Athens' golden age.

Most of the monuments you see on the Acropolis today date from Pericles' time. The principal architects of this building programme were Iotinus, Kallikrates and Mnesicles. Drama, music and literature also reached unprecedented heights in the tragedies of Aeschylus, Sophocles and Euripides. The sculptors Pheidias and Myron and the historians Herodotus, Thucydides and Xenophon, who laid the foundations for all future historians, were also active at this time.

Rivalry with Sparta
Sparta didn't take a back seat and allow Athens to revel in its glory, however. It continued to ruffle and chide. The increasing jockeying for power between the two led to the Peloponnesian Wars (from 431 to 404 BC). These protracted wars, which were nominally won by Sparta, left the city-states depleted and Athens was never to return to its former glory. Art and literature had declined irretrievably, yet the 4th century BC produced three of the West's greatest orators and philosophers in Socrates, Plato and Aristotle. The degeneracy into which Athens had fallen was perhaps best epitomised in the ignominious death sentence passed on Socrates for the 'crime' of defending free speech.

Athens' days of glory were now numbered. In 338 BC, along with the other city-states of Greece, it was conquered by Philip II of Macedon. After Philip's assassination, his son Alexander the Great, being a cultured young man, favoured Athens over other city-states, upon which he imposed rigid rule. However, after his untimely death, Athens passed in quick succession through the hands of several of his generals.

The Romans
After the Romans conquered Greece, Athens continued to be a major seat of learning, and many wealthy young Romans attended Athens' schools. At this time anybody who was anybody in Rome spoke Greek. The Roman emperors, particularly Hadrian, graced Athens with many grand buildings.

After the subdivision of the Roman Empire into east and west, Athens remained an important cultural and intellectual centre, but after the Emperor Justinian closed its schools of philosophy in 529 AD, the city declined into nothing more than an insignificant outpost of the Byzantine Empire.

Between 1200 and 1450, Athens was invaded by Franks, Catalans, Florentines and Venetians – all opportunists preoccupied only with grabbing for themselves principalities from the Byzantine Empire.

Ottoman Rule & Independence
In 1456, Athens was captured by the Turks, and nearly 400 years of Ottoman rule followed, during which time the city became a mere garrison town. The Acropolis became the home of the Turkish governor, the Parthenon a mosque and the Erechtheion a harem.

In the early stages of the War of Independence (1821-27), fierce fighting broke out in the streets of Athens, with the city changing hands several times between Turks and Greek liberators. In 1833 a Bavarian garrison took over and remained until 1835. In 1834 Athens had superseded Nafplion as the capital of independent Greece and King Otho set about transforming the sparsely populated, war-scarred town into something worthy of a capital. Bavarian architects created a city of imposing neoclassical buildings, tree-lined boulevards, flower gardens and squares. Many of these buildings have sadly been demolished, but you can see the best surviving examples on Vasilissis Sofias.

The 20th Century
Athens grew steadily throughout the latter half of the 19th and early 20th centuries, and, indeed, enjoyed a brief heyday as the 'Paris of the eastern Mediterranean'. But this prestigious role came to an abrupt end in 1923 with the Treaty of Lausanne. This treaty

resulted in nearly a million refugees from Turkey descending on Athens – an event which marked the beginning of its much-maligned concrete sprawl.

Athens, along with the rest of Greece, suffered appallingly during the German occupation of WW II. During this time more Athenians were killed by starvation than by the enemy. This suffering was perpetuated in the civil war.

During the 1950s the city experienced another population explosion, when, with the help of US aid, a radical industrial pro-gramme was embarked upon. Many people migrated from the islands and mainland vil-lages to Athens.

The colonels' junta, with characteristic insensitivity, tore down many of the crum-bling old Turkish houses of Plaka and the imposing neoclassical buildings of King Otho's time. In recent years, however, as successive governments have become more conservation-conscious, remaining old buildings of architectural merit are being restored. The sleazy bars, night clubs and strip joints of Plaka have been closed down and many of its streets have become pedes-trian ways.

ORIENTATION
If you pick up a free map from the EOT, and don't wander off into outlying suburbs, you shouldn't spend too much time being lost in Athens. From almost everywhere in the city its two most prominent landmarks – the Acropolis and Lykavitos Hill – can be seen, and these help immensely in orientation. Greeks are friendly and helpful, and almost anyone you ask will be able to direct you to Syntagma (say SYN-tag-ma).

Central Athens
Central Athens is roughly diamond shaped, with Plateia Omonias at the northern tip, Plaka at the southern, Plateia Syntagmatos at the eastern and Plateia Monastirakiou at the west.

Plateia Syntagmatos (Syntagma Square)
Πλατεία Σύνταγμα   This square is the city centre. If you take the bus from the airport and wish to stay in Plaka (the area with the highest concentration of hotels), alight here. Syntagma is a very pleasant introduction to the city, despite the manic speed at which the traffic zooms around it necessitating great care when crossing the road. It is a large, paved square, planted with orange, oleander and cypress trees. It is flanked by luxury hotels, banks, airline offices and expensive coffee shops and is dominated by the old royal palace, which since 1935 has been the seat of the Greek parliament.

Plaka   Πλάκα
This district to the south-west of Syntagma is easily reached by walking along Mitropoleos and turning left on either Nikis or Voulis. Plaka is the old Turkish quarter of Athens and virtually all that existed of the city when Athens was declared the capital of independent Greece. Its narrow labyrinthine streets nestle into the north-eastern slope of the Acropolis, and most of the city's ancient sites are contained within, or a short distance from, it. Although touristy in the extreme, Plaka retains much of its picturesque charm.

Plateia Omonias (Omonia Square)
Πλατεία Ομονίας   This, Athens' other main square, is one km north-west of Syntagma. If you come from Piraeus on the metro you may wish to alight here, and if so your first impression of the city will not be a very favourable one. But take heart, Athens doesn't come any worse than Omonia, and most of the city is considerably more appeal-ing. Where Syntagma is peopled with well-heeled businessmen and trendy young people, with a brisk purposefulness to their step, Omonia is seedy (see Dangers & Annoyances later). Omonia is the most daunting place in which to arrive in Athens. Fortunately, all the streets radiating from it are signposted in English as well as Greek in the metro shopping area, where you will emerge when you get off the train. Within this shopping area, there are public toilets, a bank, OTE and a post office.

Central Athens' two main streets, Stadiou

and Panepistimiou (which is also called El Venizelou) run between Syntagma and Omonia; both have restaurants, shops and cinemas. Athens University is halfway along Panepistimiou on the eastern side (*panepistimiou* means 'university').

Plateia Monastirakiou (Monastiraki Square) Πλατεία Μοναστηρακίου This square can be reached within 10 minutes from Syntagma, either by walking along Ermou or Mitropoleos. These two are the main streets of the commercial quarter. Ermou is lined with fashion and textile shops and Mitropoleos is the best place in Athens to buy carpets and flokati rugs. Halfway along Mitropoleos is a large square, which is dominated by the city's cathedral. Plateia Monastirakiou is where you will find the famous Flea Market; it is also the metro stop for Plaka.

Athinas and Eolou are the main streets leading from Monastiraki to Omonia. About three-quarters of the way up Athinas is the huge indoor meat market and adjoining fish market; opposite is the outdoor fruit-and-vegetable market. Stores along the streets bordering the markets sell cheeses, nuts, herbs, honey, dried fruits and cold meats. On Eolou most stores sell cut-price clothing and street vendors offer items such as sheets, towels, tablecloths and underwear.

Beyond the Centre

Around Syntagma Venturing now beyond the diamond, on the eastern side of Syntagma, are the National Gardens – a park of subtropical trees and ornamental ponds. Adjoining its southern side are the more formally laid-out Zappeion Gardens. South of here are the Arch of Hadrian and the Temple of Zeus. You will see these vast monumental structures on your right, if you enter the city on either the bus from Piraeus or the airport bus. Running south from here is Vouliagmenis, which leads to the East airport terminal. Skirting the western side of the National and Zappeion gardens is Leoforos Amalias, which, south of Hadrian's

Arch, becomes Leoforos Syngrou and leads to the West terminal.

Running eastwards from Syntagma, and skirting the northern end of the National Gardens, is Vasilissis Sofias – named after the consort of King George I. This is one of Athens' most imposing streets and was built by the Bavarian architects brought in by King Otho. A number of its neoclassical buildings are now embassies. Several of the city's most important museums are also along here. To the north of Vasilissis Sofias, flanking Lykavitos Hill, is the opulent residential district of Kolonaki. Here are high-rent apartment blocks, private art galleries, expensive coffee shops and restaurants and ultra-trendy boutiques. Kolonaki has long been the favoured address of Athenian socialites. More recently it has become a popular area with gays, who frequent its sophisticated bars.

Around Plaka South of the Acropolis is Filopappos Hill, and flanking it are the pleasant residential districts of Veikou and Koukaki. To the east, on the other side of Leoforos Syngrou, is the district of Mets, which still has some delightful old Turkish houses. North-east of Mets is Pangrati. Both are pleasing, residential neighbourhoods, but unfortunately are almost bereft of hotels.

North of Omonia Venturing north from Omonia the seediness gradually recedes and, beyond Plateia Vathis (Vathi Square), gives way to a respectable, if somewhat characterless neighbourhood. Athens' two train stations are at the western extremity of this area, on Deligianni. The National Archaeological Museum is in the eastern extremity, on 28 Oktovriou-Patission, which is a continuation of Eolou. The area's main square is Plateia Victorias. The district has a number of student hostels, which are a cross between youth hostels and budget hotels.

Just south of the National Archaeological Museum is the Athens Polytechneion. This establishment has university status, with faculties for fine arts and engineering subjects, whereas most students at Athens University read law or medicine. The Polytechneion has a tradition for being the spawning ground for radical thinking and alternative cultures. This was epitomised in the student sit-in of 1973 in opposition to the junta.

Squashed between the Polytechneion and Strefi Hill is the area of Exarhia, where many students live. In the last decade police have cleaned the place up, and it is now tame in comparison with what it used to be like. Nevertheless, it still has a lively atmosphere with graffiti-daubed walls and lots of bohemian-looking professors and rebellious-looking students milling around. Not surprisingly, it has the city's highest concentration of music clubs and fast-food joints.

North-west of Omonia is Plateia Vathis. Running north from here is Liossion, and up at No 260 is one of the city's two intercity bus stations (Terminal B). The other one (Kifissiou) is even further out, to the north-west of the city.

West of Plateia Monastirakiou Beyond Plateia Monastirakiou, Ermou becomes tattier. This is Athens at its most clapped out, with a ramshackle Third-World feel. There are lots of second-hand shops with a bizarre array of bric-a-brac overflowing onto the pavements.

INFORMATION
Tourist Offices
EOT's head office (☎ 322 3111) is at Amerikis 2, but this office does not normally deal with enquiries from the general public. The National Bank of Greece, Karageorgi Servias 2, Syntagma, has an EOT information desk (☎ 322 2545) which opens Monday to Friday from 8 am to 2 pm and from 3.30 to 8 pm, and Saturday from 9 am to 2 pm. The Hellenic Chamber of Hotels (☎ 323 7193), which gives out a list of Athens' hotels, also has a desk in this bank, open Monday to Friday from 8.30 am to 2 pm.

The General Bank of Greece, Ermou 1, Syntagma, also has an EOT information desk (☎ 325 2667/8), which opens Monday to Friday from 8 am to 8 pm and Saturday from 8 am to 2 pm. Suburban and intercity bus

timetables, ferry timetables, maps and copies of *This Week in Athens* can be obtained at both EOT desks. The EOT office (☎ 969 9590) at the East terminal is open Monday to Friday from 9 am to 7 pm and Saturday from 10 am to 5 pm.

Tourist Police
The head office (☎ 902 5992) of the tourist police is at Dimitrakopoulou 77, Veikou. It is open 24 hours a day, but it's quite a trek from the city centre – take trolley bus No 1, 5 or 9 from Syntagma. The tourist police also have a 24-hour information service (☎ 171). You can call them for general tourist information or in an emergency – someone who speaks English is always available.

Money
The National Bank of Greece, Karageorgi Servias 2, Syntagma, is open Monday to Thursday from 8 am to 2 pm and from 3.30 to 6 pm, Friday from 8 am to 1.30 pm and from 3 to 6.30 pm, Saturday from 9 am to 3 pm and Sunday from 9 am to 1 pm.

American Express (☎ 324 4975/6/7/8/9), Ermou 2, Syntagma, is open Monday to Friday from 8.30 am to 5.30 pm, and Saturday from 8.30 am to 1.30 pm. It has a free poste-restante service for both card and noncard holders. At the airport the East terminal exchange bureau is open 24 hours a day.

Post & Telecommunications
Athens' Central Post Office (☎ 321 6023) is at Eolou 100, Omonia, just east of Plateia Omonias (postcode 10200). Poste restante may be sent here, or to the other large post office on Syntagma Square (on the corner of Mitropoleos; postcode 10300). Both are open Monday to Friday from 7.30 am to 8 pm, Saturday from 7.30 am to 2 pm and Sunday from 9 am to 1.30 pm. There is also a post office in the underground station under Plateia Omonias which will hold poste restante mail. Opening hours are the same as the Central Post Office, but this office is not open on Sundays.

Parcels for abroad that weigh over one kg must be taken to the Parcel Post Office

(☎ 322 8940), Stadiou 4. To find it, walk through the arcade on the east side of Stadiou, and turn right. Parcels should not be wrapped until after inspection.

The OTE office, at 28 Oktovriou-Patission 85, is open 24 hours a day. There are also offices at Stadiou 15 and on the southeast corner of Omonia; both of these offices are open from 7 am to 11.30 pm daily. There is also an office at Athinas 50 which is open Monday to Friday from 7 am to 10 pm. Some useful telephone numbers include:

General telephone information   (☎ 134)
Numbers in Athens & Attica   (☎ 131)
Numbers elsewhere in Greece   (☎ 132)
International telephone information   (☎ 161 or 162)
International telegrams   (☎ 165)
Domestic operator   (☎ 151 or 152)
Domestic telegrams   (☎ 155)
Wake-up service (☎ 182)

Foreign Embassies
See the Facts for the Visitor chapter for a list of foreign embassies in Athens.

Cultural Centres
Following is a list of international cultural centres in Athens:

British Council
    Plateia Kolonakiou 17 (☎ 363 3215)
French Institute of Athens
    Sina 31 (☎ 361 5575)
Goethe Institute
    Omirou 14-16 (☎ 360 8111)
Hellenic American Union
    Massalias 22 (☎ 362 9886)
Norwegian Institute
    Erechtheiou 30 (☎ 923 1351)
Spanish Cultural Institute
    Skoufa 31 (☎ 360 3568)

From time to time all of these cultural centres give concerts, film shows and exhibitions. All major events are listed in the various English-language publications.

Travel Agencies
Most budget travel agencies are on Filellinon, Nikis and Voulis. The international Student & Youth Travel Service (SYTS) (☎ 323 3767), Nikis 11 (2nd floor), is the city's official student and youth travel service specialising in tickets for domestic and international air, sea and land travel. It also issues ISICs (student cards) and has information on cheap accommodation. Pioneer Tours (☎ 322 4321), also at Nikis 11, sells discounted air tickets, international bus tickets and has luggage storage for 200 dr a day. Magic Bus (☎ 323 7471), Filellinon 20, no longer operates its own buses to Europe but is an agent for Eurolines, and also sells discount air tickets (see also the Getting There & Away chapter).

Laundry
There's a self-service laundrette at Angelou Geronta 10 in Plaka, another one at Psaron 9 near Plateia Karaiskaki and another south of here at Kolokinthous 41 on the corner of Leonidou.

Bookshops
English-language paperbacks, travel guides, feminist books, maps etc are available at Pantelides Books (☎ 362 3673), Amerikis 11; Eleftheroudakis (☎ 322 9388), Nikis 4; and Compendium (☎ 322 1248), Nikis 28. Compendium stocks some Lonely Planet guides and has a second-hand book section and a predominantly English-language notice board with information about jobs, accommodation and courses in Athens.

French, German, English, Italian and Spanish books are available at Kauffmann (☎ 322 2160), Stadiou 28, and The Booknest (☎ 323 1703), Panepistimiou 25-29.

One of the best places to purchase international newspapers and magazines, as well as English-language Greek publications, is the periptero outside McDonald's, on Syntagma Square.

Emergency
For the fire brigade ring ☎ 199. For emergency medical treatment ring the tourist police (☎ 171) and they will tell you the location of the nearest hospital. Hospitals give free emergency treatment to tourists. For hospitals with out-patient departments

on duty call ☎ 106; for the telephone number of an on-call doctor ring ☎ 105 (from 2 pm to 7 am); for a pharmacy open 24 hours call ☎ 107; and for first-aid advice phone ☎ 166. US citizens can ring ☎ 721 2951 for emergency medical aid.

Dangers & Annoyances

Pickpockets Plateia Omonias' loiterers may cause you to clutch at your possessions, despite reminding yourself of Greece's low crime rate. Sadly, it is prudent to do this, for recently Omonia has gained a reputation for pickpockets, although as yet nothing like the scale of equivalent areas in most other European cities.

Slippery Surfaces Many of Athens' pavements and other surfaces underfoot are made of marble and become incredibly slippery when it is wet, so if you are caught in the rain, be very careful how you tread.

Hotel Touts It is the normal procedure for owners of student hostels in Athens to employ touts to meet tourists who have arrived by train. All of the hostels recommended in the Places to Stay section in this chapter do so, and it often saves a lot of hassle to take up an offer. However, before doing so ask to see the hostel leaflet. This will have a picture of the hostel, information about the facilities offered and (very importantly) a map showing its location. Be very suspicious of a tout who cannot show you a leaflet. Always agree upon a price in writing before taking up an offer.

Taxi Drivers Despite the new tougher penalties for offences (see Local Transport in the Getting Around chapter) the reformed behaviour of Athens' taxi drivers may have been short-lived. A traveller has reported that a taxi driver tried to charge him 6000 dr for a ride between the East and West airport terminals – a price which was shown on the meter. If you take a taxi in Athens agree on the price before you get in. If the driver still attempts to rip you off, ask to see the official tariff list (which every driver must keep in the cab) and point out the error. If there is still a dispute over the fare, take the driver's number and report the infringement to the tourist police.

WALKING TOUR

Despite gross commercialism, Plaka holds a compelling fascination and is still the most picturesque part of the city. The labyrinthine streets have no particular pattern, but follow the undulating terrain, making getting lost inevitable.

This walk is along some of Plaka's main thoroughfares, passing some of the well-known sites. Without detours it will take about 45 minutes.

Pollution

The infamous *nefos* (cloud) is the ominous grey mass that can often be seen hovering over Athens. It obliterates the wondrous violet sunsets that Athenians were once so proud of, and is having a dire effect upon the population. A World Health Organisation report stated that in 1984-85 Athens had smog levels seven times above the acceptable limit – in Europe only Tirana, the capital of Albania, has higher smog levels. The pollution is caused by motor vehicles, industries (mostly oil refineries and steel chemical works) and lack of green areas.

In the heatwave which hit Athens in the summer of 1987 the deaths of 2000 elderly Athenians were directly linked to pollution.

The Greek government has set up 10 stations around Athens to monitor air pollution and has implemented other measures in an effort to reduce the pollution levels.

All this has probably left you wondering whether to steer clear of the city altogether, or to pack a gas mask, but all in all it is probably worth enduring the pollution for as long as it takes to see the legacies of the birthplace of Western civilisation. ■

The walk begins at the former royal palace, now the **Parliament Building**, which flanks the eastern side of Syntagma. The palace was designed by the Bavarian architect F von Gartner and was built in 1836-42.

The building remained the royal palace until 1935, when it became the seat of the Greek parliament, and the royal family moved to a new palace on the corner of Vasileos Konstantinou and Herod Atticus. Since the abolition of the monarchy in 1974 this building has been the presidential palace.

The word *syntagma* means 'constitution' in Greek, and the square's name dates from 1843 when Athenians staged a protest here, calling for a constitution and refusing to move until one was granted by King Otho from the balcony of the royal palace. This protest seems to have set a precedent, for the square has been a favourite location for many protests and rallies since. In 1944 the first round of the civil war began here. Known as *Dekembriana* ('December days'), it was followed by a month of fierce fighting between the communist resistance and the British forces. In 1954 the first demonstration demanding the union (*enosis*) of Cyprus with Greece took place here. At general elections political parties hold their campaign meetings on the square and traditionally protest marches end up here.

The parliament building is guarded by the much photographed *evzones* (Greek for 'guards'). Their somewhat incongruous uniform of short kilts and pom-pom shoes is the butt of much surreptitious mickey-taking by sightseers. Their uniform is based on the attire worn by the *klephts*, the mountain brigands who fought so ferociously in the War of Independence. Every Sunday at 10.45 am the evzones perform a full changing-of-the guard ceremony.

Standing with your back to the parliament building you will see ahead of you, to the right, the **Hotel Grande Bretagne**. This, the most luxurious and grandest of Athens' hotels, was built in 1862 as a 60-room mansion for accommodating visiting dignitaries. In 1872 it was converted into a hotel and became the place where the crowned heads of Europe and eminent politicians stayed. The Nazis made it their headquarters during WW II. On Christmas Eve 1944, Winston Churchill was staying there, having been summoned over to help resolve the Dekembriana fighting, when a bomb was discovered in the hotel sewer during a routine inspection.

To begin the walk, cross over Leoforos Amalias and take the main pathway across the middle of the square. At the other side you will see the post office ahead of you to your left. Make for it by crossing the road at the zebra crossing ahead of you. At the post office turn right onto Mitropoleos, and take the first turn left onto Nikis. Continue along here to the crossroads with Kidathineon, a pedestrian walkway and one of Plaka's main thoroughfares.

Turn right and a little way along you will come to the **Church of Metamorphosis** on Plateia Satiros; opposite is the **Museum of Greek Folk Art**. Continue along here, and after Plateia Plakas, the square with the

---

Odoriferous Origins

When the capital was moved from Nafplion to Athens, so the story goes, Otho, who was not yet king, set about finding a suitable location for a home. The decision was a difficult one, compounded by the number of malarial swamps in Athens at that time. The first choice was the Acropolis, the idea being to use the front of the Parthenon as the entrance and blow up the rest and build the palace in its place. Fortunately, Otho's father, King Ludwig I of Bavaria, quashed that idea. Eventually hunks of meat were placed around the area which had been designated as central Athens. The palace was erected on the site where the meat with the least amount of mosquito larvae was found. ■

outdoor tavernas, take the first turn left onto Adrianou, another of Plaka's main thoroughfares. At the top turn right, and this will bring you to the square with the **Choregic Monument of Lysikrates**. (The word 'choregic' comes from *choregos*, which was a wealthy citizen who financed choral and dramatic performances.) This intact circular monument was built in 334 BC to commemorate a contest win in a choral festival. An inscription on the architrave states:

Lysikrates of Kykyna, son of Lysitheides, was Choregos; the tribe of Akamantis won the victory with a chorus of boys; Theon played the flute; Lysiades of Athens trained the chorus; Evainetos was archon.

The reliefs on the monument depict the battle between Dionysos and the Tyrrhenian pirates, whom the god had transformed into dolphins. It is the earliest known monument where Corinthian capitals were used externally. It stands in a cordoned-off archaeological site which is part of the **Street of Tripods**. It was here that winners of ancient dramatic and choral contests dedicated their tripod trophies to Dionysos. In the 19th century the monument was incorporated into the library of a French Capuchin convent, in which Byron stayed in 1810-11 and wrote *Childe Harold*. The convent was destroyed by fire in 1890. Recent excavations around the monument have revealed the foundations of other choregic monuments.

Facing the monument, turn left and then right onto Epimenidou. Ascend the steps, and at the top turn right onto Thrasilou, which skirts the Acropolis. Where the road forks, veer left and this path takes you into the area called Anafiotika, the highest part of Plaka. Here the little white cubic houses resemble those of the Cyclades; olive-oil cans brimming with flowers bedeck the walls of their tiny gardens. The houses were built by the people from the tiny island of Anafi, who were used as cheap labour in the building of Athens after Independence.

Continue to the end of the winding path, descend the steps to the right and follow the curving pathway which emerges onto

Choregic Monument of Lysikrates

Pratiniou. Turn left and soon you will see ahead of you a yellow-ochre building with brown shutters. This is the old university at Tholou 5, which was built by the Venetians. The Turks used it as public offices and it was Athens University from 1837 to 1841. Recently restored, it is now the **Museum of the University**, and includes some wonderful, old anatomical drawings, gruesome-looking surgical instruments etc. It is open Monday to Friday from 9 am to 1 pm. Admission is free.

Go to the end of Tholou and turn left onto Panos. At the top of the steps on the left is a restored 19th-century mansion which is now the **Paul & Alexandra Kanellopoulos Museum**. Retracing your steps, go down Panos to the ruins of the **Roman Agora**, then turn left onto Polygnotou and walk to the crossroads. Opposite, Polygnotou continues to the **Ancient Agora**. At the crossroads, turn right and then left onto Poikilis, then immediately right onto Areos. On the right are the remains of the **Library of Hadrian** and next to it the **Museum of Traditional Greek Ceramics**, which is open Tuesday to Sunday from 10 am to 2 pm. Admission is 200 dr. The museum is housed in the **Mosque of Tzistarakis** which was built in 1759. After Independence it lost its minaret and was used as a prison; it has been a museum since 1958. Calligraphic inscriptions may be seen above the doorway.

Ahead is **Plateia Monastirakiou**, which is named after the little church which stands there. To the left is the metro station and the **Flea Market**. Plateia Monastirakiou is Athens at its noisiest, most colourful and chaotic, teeming with street vendors selling nuts, coconut sticks and fruit – a good place to pick up a snack, if you are feeling peckish.

Turn right just beyond the mosque, onto Pandrossou. This street is a relic of the Turkish bazaar which once occupied the area; today it is full of souvenir shops, selling everything from cheap kitsch to high-class jewellery and clothes. The street is named after King Kekrop's daughter, Pandrosos, who was the first priestess of Athens. At No 89 is Stavros Melissinos, the 'poet sandal-maker' of Athens who names the Beatles, Rudolph Nureyev and Jackie Onassis amongst his customers and is in every guidebook on Greece from Tokyo to Toronto. Fame and fortune have not gone to his head, however – he still makes the best value sandals in Athens, costing between 1500 and 3000 dr per pair.

Pandrossou leads to **Plateia Mitropoleos** and the **Cathedral of Athens**. The cathedral has little architectural merit, which isn't surprising, considering that it was constructed from the masonry of over 50 razed churches and from the designs of several architects. Next to it stands the much smaller, and far more appealing, old cathedral of **Agios Eleftherios**. Turn left after the cathedral, and then right onto Mitropoleos and walk along here back to Syntagma.

THE ACROPOLIS

Athens exists because of the Acropolis, and the Acropolis is the most important ancient monument in the Western world. For these reasons alone it is rightly on the top of most people's 'sightseeing in Athens' lists. But unless you visit out of season you will have to contend with many other sightseers, many of whom will be in groups led by raucous guides. If you visit early in the day you will escape them to some extent. Be sure to wear comfortable shoes as the Acropolis' terrain consists of uneven, very slippery marble.

There is only one entrance to the Acropolis, but there are several approaches to this entrance. Either walk or take bus No 230 along Dionysiou Areopagitou to just beyond the Theatre of Herodes Atticus, where a path right leads to the entrance. Otherwise, take the path that is a continuation of Dioskouron, in the north-west corner of Plaka.

The Acropolis, crowned by the Parthenon, stands sentinel over Athens, visible from almost everywhere within the city. Its monuments of Pentelic marble gleam white in the midday sun and gradually take on a honey hue as the sun sinks. At night they are floodlit and seem to hover above the city. No matter how harassed you may become in Athens, a sudden unexpected glimpse of this magnificent sight cannot fail to uplift.

But, inspiring as these monuments are, they are faded remnants of Pericles' city, and it takes a great leap of the imagination to begin to comprehend the splendour of his creations. Using the mass of wealth he had accumulated from the tributes paid by subject states, Pericles spared no expense – only the best in materials, architects, sculptors and artists was good enough for a city dedicated to the cult of Athena, tutelary goddess of Athens. The city was a showcase of colossal buildings, lavishly coloured and gilded, and of gargantuan statues, some of bronze, others of marble plated with gold and encrusted with precious stones.

The Acropolis archaeological site (☎ 323 6665) is open Monday to Friday from 8 am to 5 pm; Saturday, Sunday and holidays from 8.30 am to 3 pm. The **Acropolis Museum** is

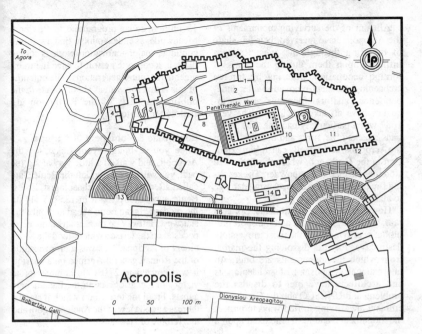

Acropolis

1	Erechtheion	9	Site of the Altar of Rome & Augustus
2	Porch of the Caryatids	10	Parthenon
3	Monument of Agrippa	11	Museum
4	Beulé Gate	12	Wall of Kimon
5	Propylaia	13	Theatre of Herodes Atticus
6	Site of the Athena Promachos	14	Site of Asklepion
7	Temple of Athena Nike	15	Ancient Theatre of Dionysos
8	Entrance Court	16	Site of Stoa of Eumenes

open Tuesday to Friday from 8 am to 5 pm, Saturday, Sunday and holidays from 8.30 am to 3 pm and Monday from 11 am to 5 pm. The combined admission fee is 1500 dr (free on Sunday and public holidays).

History

The Acropolis was continuously inhabited from Neolithic times. The cult of Athena began during the Mycenaean Age; the first temples were built on the Acropolis (which means 'high city') at this time. All of the buildings of the Acropolis were reduced to ashes by the Persians on the eve of the Battle of Salamis (480 BC).

People lived on the Acropolis up to the late 6th century BC, but in 510 BC the Delphic oracle declared that it should be the province of the gods. When Pericles set about his ambitious rebuilding programme, he transformed the Acropolis into a city of temples which has come to be regarded as the zenith of Classical Greece, and the golden age of Athens.

All four of the surviving monuments of the Acropolis have received their fair share of battering through the ages. Ravages inflicted upon them during the years of foreign occupation, pilfering by foreign archaeologists, inept renovation after Independence, visitors' footsteps and earthquakes have all taken their toll. The year 1687 was a particularly bad one. The Venetians attacked the Turks and opened fire on the Acropolis, accidentally causing an explosion in the Parthenon, where the Turks had stored an arsenal of gunpowder. The resulting fire blazed for two days, causing damage to all of the buildings.

However, the most recent menace of acid rain, caused by industrial and transport pollution, is proving to be the most irreversibly destructive, for it is dissolving the marble from which the monuments are built. An international symposium of archaeologists and architects have met to discuss the problem, and UNESCO and the Greek government are striving to find ways to protect the monuments, and have embarked upon a

15 million dollar programme to this end. Meanwhile, as endeavours to find a solution continue, major renovation work is taking place in a concerted effort to save the monuments for future generations. The outcome of this is that some areas are off limits to the public and parts of the Parthenon are enclosed in scaffolding.

Beulé Gate & Monument of Agrippa

Once you've bought your ticket for the Acropolis and walked a little way along the path, you will see on your left the Beulé Gate called after the French archaeologist, Ernest Beulé, who uncovered it in 1852. Walk up the modern zigzag ramp ahead and onto the stairway. Halfway up there is an eight-metre pedestal on the left, on which stood the Monument of Agrippa. This was a bronze statue of the Roman general Agrippa on a chariot; it was erected in 27 BC to commemorate victory in a chariot race in the Panathenaic games. From the terrace on which it stands, there is a good view of the Ancient Agora and the Temple of Hephaestus.

The Acropolis in Classical times

Propylaia

The Propylaia was the towering entrance to the Acropolis in ancient times. Built by Mnesikles in 437-432 BC its architectural brilliance ranks with that of the Parthenon. It consists of a central hall, with two wings on either side. Each section had a gate, and these five gates were in ancient times the only entrances to the 'upper city'. The middle gate (the largest) opened onto the Panathenaic Way. The western portico of the Propylaia must indeed have been imposing, consisting of six double columns, Doric on the outside and Ionic on the inside – the fourth column along has been restored. The ceiling of the central hall was painted with gold stars on a dark blue background. The north wing was a picture gallery (pinakotheke) and the south wing was the antechamber to the Temple of Athena Nike.

The Propylaia is aligned with the Parthenon, and it is the earliest example of a building designed in relationship to another. It remained intact until the 13th century and then various occupiers added appendages to it. In the 17th century it was struck by lightning and gunpowder stored by the Turks exploded, causing considerable damage. Heinrich Schliemann paid for the removal of one of its appendages – a Frankish tower – in the 19th century. Reconstruction took place between 1909 and 1917 and there was further restoration after WW II. Once you're through the Propylaia, there is a stunning view of the Parthenon ahead.

The Panathenaic Way was the route taken by the Panathenaic Procession, which was the climax of the Panathenaia, the festival held to venerate the goddess Athena. The origins of the Panathenaia are uncertain. According to some accounts it was initiated by Erichthonius, according to others, by Theseus. There were two festivals: the Lesser Panathenaic Festival took place annually, and the Great Panathenaic Festival was held every fourth anniversary of the goddess' birth.

The Great Panathenaic Festival began with dancing, followed by athletic, dramatic and musical contests. The Panathenaic Procession, which took place on the final day of the festival, began at the Keramikos and ended at the Erechtheion. Men carrying animals sacrificed to Athena headed the procession, followed by maidens carrying rhytons (horn-shaped drinking vessels). Behind them were musicians playing a fanfare for the girls of noble birth who followed, proudly holding aloft the sacred peplos (a glorious saffron shawl which had been painstakingly woven by maidens). Taking up the rear were old men bearing olive branches. The grand finale of the procession was the placing of the peplos on the statue of Athena Polias in the Erechtheion.

Temple of Athena Nike

Turning right on leaving the Propylaia, you will be able to view the exquisitely proportioned little Temple of Athena Nike (to which visitors have no access), which stands on a platform perched atop the steep south-west edge of the Acropolis overlooking the Saronic Gulf. It is of Pentelic marble and was built by Kallikrates in 427-424 BC. The building is almost square, with four graceful Ionic columns at either end. Its frieze, of which only fragments remain, consisted of scenes from mythology on the east and south sides, and scenes from the Battle of Plataea (479 BC), and Athenians fighting Boeotians and Persians on the other sides. Parts of the

---

A Tragic Homecoming
According to legend the Temple of Athena Nike is built on the spot where Aegeus awaited the return of his son Theseus from his expedition to slay the minotaur. Theseus had told Aegeus if he succeeded in his mission he would return in a boat with a white sail. But he forgot, and Aegeus, seeing a black sail, assumed his son had been killed and threw himself into the sea. ∎

Athena

frieze are in the Acropolis Museum. The platform was surrounded by a marble parapet of relief sculptures; some of these are also in the museum, including the beautiful one of Nike fastening her sandal.

The temple housed a statue of the goddess Athena; in her right hand was a pomegranate (symbol of fertility) and in her left a helmet (symbol of war). The temple was entirely dismantled by the Turks in 1686 so that a large gun could stand on the platform. It was carefully reconstructed between 1836 and 1842, but was taken to pieces again in 1936 because the platform was crumbling. The platform was reinforced and the temple rebuilt.

Statue of Athena Promachos

In ancient times only the pediment of the Parthenon was visible from in front of the Propylaia; the rest was obscured by numerous statues and two sacred buildings.

Continuing ahead along the Panathenaic Way you will see, to your left, a line of foundations of pedestals of statues which once lined the path. One of them, about 15 metres beyond the Propylaia, is the foundation of the gigantic statue of Athena Promachos (*promachos* means 'champion'). The nine-metre-high statue was the work of Pheidias, and symbolised Athenian invincibility against the Persians. The helmeted goddess was holding a shield in her left hand and a spear in her right. It was said that on a clear day the spear tip and helmet crest, gleaming in the sun, could be seen by sailors in the Cape of Sounion. The statue was carted off to Constantinople in 426 AD by the Emperor Theodosius. By 1204 it had lost its spear, so the hand appeared to be gesturing. This led the inhabitants to believe that the statue had beckoned the crusaders to the city, so they smashed it to pieces.

Parthenon

You have now reached the Parthenon, the monument which more than any other epitomises the glory of Ancient Greece. The name Parthenon means 'virgin's apartment'. It is the largest Doric temple ever completed in Greece, and the only one to be built completely, apart from its wooden roof, of Pentelic marble (marble from the Pentelikon mountain, near Athens). It is built on the highest part of the Acropolis, halfway between the eastern and western boundaries.

The Parthenon had a dual purpose – to house the great statue of Athena which had been commissioned by Pericles, and to be treasury for the tribute money which had been moved from Delos. It was built on the site of at least four earlier temples, dedicated to the worship of Athena. It was designed by Iktinos and Kallikrates, under the surveillance of Pheidias, to be the pre-eminent monument of Pericles' Acropolis. Building began in 447 BC and was completed in time for the Great Panathenaic Festival of 438 BC.

The temple consisted of eight fluted Doric columns at either end and 17 at each side. To achieve perfect form, its lines were ingeniously curved to counteract inharmonious optical illusions. Thus the foundations are slightly concave and the columns slightly convex, to make both look straight. Supervised by Pheidias, the sculptors Agorakritos

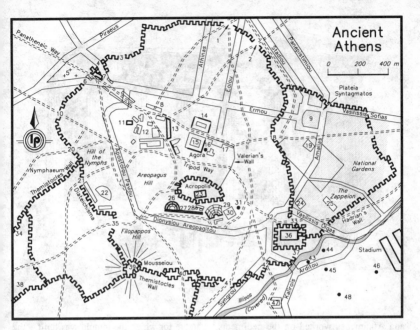

Ancient Athens

1	Acharnian Gate
2	North East Gate
3	Eriai Gate
4	Dipylon Gate
5	Keramikos
6	Sacred Gate
7	Pompeion
8	Stoa Poikile
9	Garden of Theophrastos
10	Peiraic Gate
11	Temple of Hephaestus
12	Metroon
13	Stoa of Attalos
14	Library of Hadrian
15	Roman Agora
16	Tower of the Winds
17	Pantheon
18	Diochares Gate
19	Lyceum
20	Demian Gate
21	Melitides Gate
22	Hill of the Pnyx
23	Parthenon
24	Gymnasium
25	Baths
26	Theatre of Herodes Atticus
27	Stoa of Eumenes
28	Asklepion
29	Theatre of Dionysos
30	Odeon of Pericles
31	Monument of Lysikrates
32	Arch of Hadrian
33	Hippades Gate
34	North Long Wall to Piraeus
35	Dipylon above Gate
36	Temple of Olympian Zeus
37	Diomeian Gate
38	South Long Wall
39	Monument of Filopappos
40	South Gate
41	Halade Gate
42	Itonian Gate
43	Kallirhoë Fountain
44	Agrai Metroon
45	Artemis Agrotera
46	Ardettos Hill
47	Hadrian's Gymnasium
48	Poseidon Helikonios

The Parthenon

and Alkamenes worked on the pediments, frieze and the metopes. All of the sculptures they created were brightly coloured and gilded. They consisted of 92 sculptured metopes, 44 statues and a frieze which went all the way round.

The metopes on the eastern side depicted Athenians fighting giants (the *gigantions*), and on the western side Theseus leading the Athenians into battle against the Amazons. Those on the southern side represented the contest of the Lapiths and Centaurs at the marriage feast of Pierithoos. The Ionic frieze measuring 159.5 metres ran all around the Parthenon. Much of it was damaged by an explosion in 1687, but the greatest existing part (just over 75 metres) consists of the much publicised Elgin Marbles, now in the British Museum.

The ceiling of the Parthenon, like that of the Propylaia, was painted blue and gilded with stars. At the eastern end was the *cella* (inner room of a temple), the holy of holies, into which only a few privileged initiates could enter. Here stood the chryselephantine statue for which the temple was built – the Athena Parthenos (*parthenos* means 'virgin') which was considered one of the wonders of the ancient world. The statue was designed by Pheidias and completed in 432 BC. It was of gold plate over an inner wooden frame, and stood, with its pedestal, almost 12 metres high. The face, hands and feet were made of ivory, and the pupils of the eyes were jewels. The goddess was clad in a long dress of gold on the breast of which was the head of Medusa carved in ivory. In her right hand she held a carved Victory (statuette of Nike – the Goddess of Victory) and in her left a spear; at the base of the spear was a serpent. On her head was a helmet on top of which was a sphinx with griffins in relief at either side. In 426 BC the statue was taken to Constantinople and disappeared. There is a Roman copy (the Athena Varvakeion) in the National Archaeological Museum.

Erechtheion

Although the Parthenon was the most impressive monument of the Acropolis, its function was more that of a showpiece and a treasury than a sanctuary for worship. The Erechtheion was far more an expression of the spirituality of the ancients. It was also far more bound up with the mythological origins of the city, and housed the cults of Athena, Poseidon and Erichthonius.

Following the Panathenaic Way around the northern portico of the Parthenon, you will see the Erechtheion to your left. It is immediately recognisable by its much-photographed **Caryatids**, the six larger-than-life maidens who take the place of columns to support its southern portico. They are so called because the models for them were women from Karyai in Laconia.

The Erechtheion was begun in 421 BC after the outbreak of the Peloponnesian Wars, but the work was halted by Pericles' unexpected death from the plague, and it was not completed until 395 BC. It is named after Erichthonius, the mythical king of Athens, who the ancients believed was buried beneath where the temple stands (to find out about Erichthonius' unconventional conception, see the Mythology section in the Facts about the Country chapter). The temple also stands on the spot where, according to mythology, Athena and Poseidon contested for possession of ancient Athens.

The Erechtheion is architecturally the most unusual monument of the Acropolis. Whereas the Parthenon is considered the supreme example of Doric architecture, the Erechtheion is considered the supreme example of Ionic. It was ingeniously built on several levels, to counteract the unevenness of the ground beneath. It consists of three basic parts, all of different dimensions. They are the main temple, the northern porch and the southern porch.

The main temple is of the Ionic order and is divided into two cellas: one is dedicated to Athena, the other to Poseidon; thus the temple represents a reconciliation of the two deities after their contest. In Athena's cella was the statue of Athena Polias holding a shield on which was a gorgon's head. It was this statue on which the sacred peplos was placed at the culmination of the Panathenaic

The Caryatids

Festival. The statue was illuminated by a golden lantern placed at its feet. The lantern had an asbestos wick which only required oil once every 12 months.

The northern porch consists of six graceful Ionic columns; on the floor are fissures supposedly cleft by Poseidon's trident. This porch leads into the **Temenos of Pandrossos**, where, according to mythology, the sacred olive brought forth by Athena grew. To the south of here was the **Kekropion** – King Kekrop's burial place.

The southern porch is that of the Caryatids, which prop up a heavy roof of Pentelic marble. The ones you see are plaster casts – the originals (except for one removed by Lord Elgin) are in the site's museum.

Acropolis Museum

This museum is to the south-east of the Parthenon. It houses a collection of sculptures and reliefs from the site. Ones to look out for in particular are the original Caryatids; the relief of Athena Nike fastening her sandal; and the pieces of the Parthenon frieze which Lord Elgin left behind.

Noteworthy sculptures include the one of a bull being devoured by a lioness, and of a man carrying a calf on his shoulders. Also not to be missed are the large collection of 6th-century BC kore (statues of maidens), which were dedicated to Athena. Each kore holds an offering to the goddess. One can see in these statues a development from the very stiff formal early ones, through to the grace and naturalism of the later ones. The development is evidenced in the increasing realism of their smiles, the flow of their drapery and their poses. Note their intricate headdresses, which are especially fascinating.

SOUTH SLOPE OF THE ACROPOLIS

The entrance to the south slope of the Acropolis is on Dionysiou Areopagitou. The site (☎ 323 6665) is open Tuesday to Friday from 8 am to 5 pm; Saturday, Sunday and holidays from 8.30 am to 3 pm and Monday from 11 am to 5 pm. Admission is 400 dr.

Ancient Theatre of Dionysos

The Ancient Theatre of Dionysos is built on the southern slope of the Acropolis. A theatre was first built on this site sometime during the 6th century BC, after the tyrant Peisistratos had introduced the Festival of the Great Dionysia to Athens. These festivals took place in March or April and consisted of contests where men clad in goatskins sang and performed dances. Everyone attended,

Dionysos

and the watching of performances was punctuated by feasting, revelry and generally letting rip.

By the 5th century BC, the festival consisted of performances of dramas by Aeschylus, Sophocles and Euripides, with some light relief provided by the bawdy comedies of Aristophanes. Only men performed, so they also took the female roles. Performances often started at dawn and ended at sunset, and could include as many as three tragedies and two comedies. Audiences were often paid by politicians to attend – if only present-day governments were as generous to the arts! If an audience didn't like a performance, they often pelted the actors with cheese and rotten fruit.

The theatre was originally made of wood, but between 342 BC and 326 BC, it was reconstructed in stone and marble by Lycurgus. The auditorium had a seating capacity of 17,000 consisting of 64 tiers of seats, of which around 20 survive. Apart from the front row, the seats were built of Piraeus limestone and were occupied by ordinary citizens, although women were confined to the last few rows. The seating was cleverly designed so everyone had a good view without being restricted by the person in front. The front row consisted of 67 thrones built of Pentelic marble; these were reserved for festival officiators and important priests. The most impressive one, which was in the middle, was reserved for the Priest of Dionysos, who sat shaded from the sun under a canopy. You will spot this seat easily as the lion-claw feet at either side are remarkably well preserved.

In Roman times, as well as for performances of plays, the theatre was also used for state events and ceremonies. These included the crowning of distinguished citizens, military displays and, on a less elevated level, cockfights.

The reliefs – mostly of headless figures – at the rear of the stage, depict the exploits of Dionysos, and date from the 2nd century BC. The westernmost one shows Dionysos seated on a throne in the theatre – some columns of the Parthenon can just be made out in the background. The two hefty, hunched up guys who have managed to keep their heads, are *selini*. Selini were worshippers of the mythical Selinos, the debauched father of the satyrs, whose chief attribute seems to have been an outsize phallus, and whose pastime was charging up mountains in lecherous pursuit of nymphs. In between harassing nymphs he was Dionysos' mentor.

Asklepion & Stoa of Eumenes

Directly above the Theatre of Dionysos, wooden steps lead up to a pathway. If you turn left at the top of the steps you will come to the Asklepion, which was built around a sacred spring. The worship of Asklepios, the god of healing, began in Epidaurus and was introduced into Athens in 429 BC. During this time a plague was sweeping the city – the same plague that carried off Pericles. Patients performed a ritual, believed to invoke the god and so effect a cure.

Beneath the Asklepion is a long colonnade, which is the Stoa of Eumenes. It was built by Eumenes II, King of Pergamon (197-159 BC), as a shelter and promenade for the audience of the theatre.

Theatre of Herodes Atticus

The path continues in a westerly direction from the Asklepion to the Theatre of Herodes Atticus built in 161 AD. Herodes Atticus was a wealthy Roman who built the theatre in memory of his wife Regilla. It was excavated in 1857-58 and completely restored in 1950-61. Performances of drama, music and dance are performed here during the Athens Festival. The theatre is only open to the public during performances.

Panagia Chrysospiliotissa

If you retrace your steps back to the Theatre of Dionysos, you will see an indistinct rock-strewn path leading to a grotto in the cliff face. In 320 BC Thrasyllos made this grotto into a temple dedicated to Dionysos. Today it is the tiny Panagia Chrysospiliotissa (Chapel of our Lady of the Cavern). It is a poignant little place with old pictures and icons on the walls. Above the chapel are two Ionic columns which are the remains of Thrasyllos' temple.

ANCIENT AGORA

From the 6th century BC the Agora was the hub of the city. It was devastated by the Persian attack of 480 BC, but a new agora was built in its place almost immediately after the Athenians returned to their city. By Pericles' time it was flourishing and continued to do so until 267 AD, when it was raided by a Germanic people from Scandinavia known as Herulians. By the 19th century an attractive Turkish quarter was standing on the site; this was demolished by archaeologists after Independence. If they'd had their way the archaeologists would have also knocked down the whole of Plaka, which was also Turkish.

The Agora is a large site bounded by Areopagus Hill in the south, the Athens-Piraeus metro line to the north, Plaka to the east and Leoforos Apostolou Pavlou to the west. The area has been excavated to Classical, and in parts, to prehistoric levels.

In Classical times the Agora was the meeting place of the city and all roads led there. One can imagine a lively crowded place resounding with the voices of traders, administrators, business people and philosophers – Socrates spent much time here expounding his philosophy. In 49 AD St Paul disputed daily in the Agora, intent upon winning converts to Christianity. It was also the centre of social life, for Athenian men that is – women at this time were largely confined to household duties. The only women who had a life outside the home were priestesses.

Nowadays, the Agora looks like a huge bombsite, and to visualise how it must have been in Classical times requires an even greater feat of imagination than that needed when visiting the Acropolis. Exceptions to the ruined look of the place are the Temple of Hephaestus, the Stoa of Attalos and the Church of the Holy Apostles.

There are several entrances to the site. The most convenient is the southern entrance at the western end of Polygnotou (see the

1 Stoa Poikile	10 Stoa of Attalos
2 Stoa of Basileios	11 Stoa of the Giants
3 Entrance	12 New Bouleuterion
4 Mosaic showing reconstruction of	13 Metroon
Agora	14 Odeon of Agrippa
5 Altar of the Twelve Gods	15 Tholos
6 Stoa of Zeus Eleutherios	16 Middle Stoa
7 Temple of Hephaestus	17 Sewer
8 Temple of Apollo	18 Church of the Holy Apostles
9 Temple of Ares	

Walking Tour section earlier). The site (☎ 321 0185) is open Tuesday to Sunday from 8.30 am to 3 pm and admission is 800 dr.

Stoa of Attalos

If you want to make any sense of the site the museum here, which borders the eastern end of the Agora, is a good place to begin your visit.

The original stoa was built by King Attalos II of Pergamum (159-138 BC). It was two storeys high and had two aisles. It housed expensive shops and was a popular stamping ground for wealthy Athenians. People also gathered here to watch the Panathenaic Procession which crossed diagonally in front of the stoa. It was authentically reconstructed in 1953-56 by the American School of Archaeology. The only deviation was that the original façade was painted red and blue and the reconstructed one has been left in natural Pentelic marble. The stoa has a series of 45 columns which are Doric on the ground floor and Ionic on the upper gallery.

The stoa is now a museum and on the ground floor are exhibits of vases and sculptures from the site including interesting everyday objects such as a child's potty (chamber pot), a toy animal on wheels, household grills and ovens. On the upper floor is a model of the Agora.

On a more mundane level there are toilets and a drinking fountain at the northern end of the stoa.

Temple of Hephaestus

This temple at the western edge of the Agora was surrounded by foundries and metalwork shops, as Hephaestus was the god of metalworkers. It was one of the first buildings of Pericles' rebuilding programme and is the best preserved Doric temple in Greece. It was built in 449 BC by Iktinos, who was also one of the architects of the Parthenon. It has 34 columns; the frieze on the eastern front depicts nine of the Twelve Labours of Herakles. In 1300 AD it was converted into the **Church of Agios Georgios**. The last service held here was on 13 December 1834, in honour of King Otho's arrival in Athens.

Unlike the Parthenon, the monument does not evoke a sense of wonder, but is nevertheless a pleasant place to wander around as herbal scents permeate the air. In Roman times a garden surrounded the temple and this has been reproduced as nearly as possible to its appearance in antiquity.

To the north-east of the Temple of Hephaestus are the foundations of the **Stoa of Zeus Eleutherios**; it was here that Socrates expounded his philosophy. Further north are the foundations of the **Stoa of Basileios** and the **Stoa Poikile** (Painted Stoa). These two are presently inaccessible to the public. The Stoa Poikile was so called because of its murals, which were painted by Polygnotes, Mikon and Panainos and depicted mythological and historical battles. At the end of the 4th century BC, Zeno taught his phlegmatic philosophy here, and his dis-

Hephaestus

ciples became known as Stoics, thus giving us the word 'stoic'. To the south-east of the Temple of Hephaestus was the **New Bouleuterion**, or council house, where the Senate (originally created by Solon) met. To the south of here was the circular **Tholos** where the heads of government met.

Church of the Holy Apostles

This charming little church, which stands near the southern entrance, was built in the early 11th century to commemorate St Paul's teaching in the Agora. In 1954-57 it was stripped of its 19th-century additions and restored to its original form. It contains some fine Byzantine frescoes.

THE KERAMIKOS

The Keramikos was the city's cemetery from the 12th century BC to Roman times. It was discovered in 1861 during the construction of Odos Pireos. Despite its seedy location, on Odos Ermou, beyond Monastiraki, it is one of the most verdant and tranquil of Athens' ancient sites and a habitat for tortoises and frogs. The latter may be seen in the damp areas flanking the brook Eridanos which flows through the site.

The entrance to the site (☎ 346 3552) is at Ermou 148. It is open Tuesday to Friday from 8 am to 5 pm; Saturday, Sunday and holidays from 8.30 am to 3 pm; and Monday from 11 am to 5 pm. The combined admission is 400 dr.

Sacred & Dipylon Gates

Once you have entered the site you will see the museum to the left and ahead of you half to the right, a knoll, which you should make for first because on top is a plan of the site. From here a path leads off to the right to the remains of the city wall, which was built by Themistokles in 479 BC, and rebuilt by Konon in 394 BC. To the right (east) the foundations of two gates can be seen.

The first, the Sacred Gate, spanned the Sacred Way and was the one by which pilgrims from Eleusus entered the city during the annual Eleusian Procession. The Dipylon Gate, to the east of the Sacred Gate, was the city's main entranceway and was where the Panathenaic Procession began. It was also the stamping ground of the city's prostitutes who gathered there to offer their services to jaded travellers.

From a platform outside the Dipylon Gate, Pericles gave his famous speech extolling the virtues of Athens and honouring those who died in the first year of the Peloponnesian Wars. The speech stirred many more to go to battle – and so to their deaths.

Between the Sacred and the Dipylon gates are the foundations of the **Pompeion**. This building was used as a dressing room for the participants of the Panathenaic Procession, and also served as a storehouse for the chariots and equipment used in the procession.

Street of Tombs

Retracing your steps, the Street of Tombs leads off the Sacred Way. This avenue was reserved for the tombs of Athens' most prominent citizens. The surviving stele are now in the National Archaeological Museum, and what you see are replicas. They consist of an astonishing array of funerary monuments, and their bas-reliefs warrant more than a cursory examination.

Ordinary citizens were buried in the areas bordering the Street of Tombs. One very well-preserved stele shows a little girl with her pet dog. You will find it by going up the stone steps at the northern side of the Street of Tombs. On the lateral way which runs from the south-east corner of the street of tombs, is the site's largest stele depicting two sisters, Demetria and Pamphile. Pamphile is seated beside Demetria who is standing.

Oberlaender Museum

The site's Oberlaender Museum is named after its benefactor Gustav Oberlaender who was a German-American stocking manufacturer. It contains stele and sculpture from the site, an impressive collection of vases and terracotta figurines.

ROMAN ATHENS
Tower of the Winds & Roman Agora

These are next to one another to the east of the Ancient Agora and north of the Acropolis.

The well-preserved Tower of the Winds was built in the 1st century BC by a Syrian astronomer named Andronikos. The octagonal monument of Pentelic marble is an ingenious construction which functioned as a sundial, weather vane, water clock and compass. Each side represents one of the points of the compass, and has a relief of a figure floating through the air, which depicts the wind associated with that particular point. Beneath each of the reliefs are the faint markings of sundials. The weather vane, which disappeared long ago, was a bronze triton (a spiral shell) which revolved on top of the tower. The Turks, not ones to let a good building go to waste, turned the tower into a hostelry for a band of Whirling Dervishes.

The entrance to the Roman Agora is through the well-preserved **Gate of Athena Archegetis** which is flanked by four Doric columns. It was erected sometime in the 1st century AD, financed by Julius Caesar.

The rest of the Roman Agora appears to the layperson as little more than a heap of rubble. To the right of the entrance are the foundations of a 1st-century public latrine. In the south-east area are the foundations of a propylion and a row of shops.

The site (☎ 321 0185) is open Tuesday to Sunday from 8.30 am to 3 pm. Admission is 400 dr.

Roman Stadium

The last Athenian monument with Roman connections is the Roman Stadium, which lies in a fold between two pine-covered hills between the neighbourhoods of Mets and Pangrati. The stadium was originally built in the 4th century BC as a venue for the Panathenaic athletic contests. By Roman times its function had been debased to the extent that, at the Emperor Hadrian's inauguration, 1000 animals were baited there. Shortly after this horrific event the seats had been rebuilt in Pentelic marble by Herodes Atticus. After hundreds of years of disuse the stadium was completely restored in 1895 by a wealthy Greek benefactor – Georgios Averoff. The following year the first Olympic Games of modern times were held here. It is a faithful replica of the Roman Stadium, comprising seats of Pentelic marble for 70,000 spectators, a running track and a central area for gymnastic contests – the stadium is in daily use.

City of Hadrian

The Roman emperor Hadrian had a great affection for Athens. Although, like all Roman emperors, he did his fair share of spiriting the city's movable Classical artwork to Rome, he also embellished the city with many monuments influenced by Classical architecture. However, grandiose as these monuments are, they lack the refinement and artistic genius of the Classical monuments. Yet they are an integral part of the city, and are so colossal that you cannot fail to notice them.

The site (☎ 922 6330) is open Tuesday to Sunday from 8.30 am to 3 pm. Admission is 200 dr.

Library of Hadrian

This library is to the north of the Roman Agora. The building, which was of vast dimensions, was erected in the 2nd century AD and included a cloistered courtyard bordered by 100 columns. As well as books the building had music and lecture rooms and a theatre. The library is at present inaccessible to visitors.

Arch of Hadrian

This lofty monument of Pentelic marble – now blackened by the effluent of exhausts – stands where traffic-clogged Vasilissis Olgas and Amalias meet. It was erected by Hadrian in 132 AD, to mark the boundary between the ancient city and Roman city. On the north-west frieze is the inscription, 'This is Athens, the Ancient city of Theseus'; on the south-east frieze is inscribed, 'This is the city of Hadrian, and not of Theseus'.

Temple of Olympian Zeus

This is the largest temple in Greece and took over 700 years to build. It was begun in the 6th century BC by Peisistratos, to keep the people occupied, so they wouldn't have the time or energy to plot against him, but it was abandoned through lack of funds.

Various other leaders had stabs at completing the temple, but gave up; it was left to Hadrian to complete the work in 131 AD. It consisted of 104 Corinthian columns with diameters of 1.7 metres and 17 metres high, of which 15 remain standing – the fallen column was blown down in a gale in 1852. Hadrian put a colossal statue of Zeus in the cella and in typical immodest fashion one of himself, of equal dimensions, next to it – both went missing long ago. Although darkened by pollution, and lacking the beauty of the Classical monuments, the temple is impressive because of the sheer size of the columns.

BYZANTINE ATHENS
Churches

Byzantium has only a meagre representation

in Athens, as, by the time of the split in the Roman Empire, it was a provincial town which had been overtaken by Thessaloniki. However Athens does have a few Byzantine churches worth looking at. The **Church of Agios Eleftherias** on Plateia Mitropoleos is considered the most beautiful of the city's churches. It is Athens' old cathedral and is now overshadowed by the much larger new cathedral. It is partly built of Pentelic marble and decorated with an external frieze of bas-reliefs of symbolic beasts.

The **Church of Kapnikarea** is another small church of the 11th century; it stands halfway down Ermou. The dome is supported by four large Roman columns. The **Church of Aghioi Theodoroi** is another 11th-century church of note; it stands just off Plateia Klafthmonos which is about halfway up Stadiou. It has a tiled dome and the walls are decorated with a terracotta frieze of animals and plants. Other churches worth peering into are the **Church of the Holy Apostles** (see Ancient Agora earlier) and the **Church of Agios Dimitrios** (see West of the Acropolis later on page 163).

MUSEUMS
National Archaeological Museum

This museum (☎ 821 7717/24), which was opened in 1874, is supreme amongst the city's museums. Despite all the pilfering by foreign archaeologists in the 19th century, it still manages to have the world's finest collection of Greek antiquities. It is so crammed with treasures that to do the place justice you need to visit several times. The following is intended as only a brief description of the general layout of the museum, focusing on some of the most important, spectacular, intriguing or quirky exhibits. At the time of writing a number of the rooms were closed. Several guidebooks to the museum are on sale in the foyer.

The museum is at 28 Oktovriou-Patission 44 and is open Tuesday to Friday from 8 am to 5 pm; Saturday, Sunday and holidays from 8.30 am to 3 pm and on Monday from 11 am to 5 pm. Admission is 1500 dr (free on Sunday and public holidays). To reach the museum take trolley bus No 2, 4, 5, 11 or 12 from Syntagma.

Hall of Mycenaean Antiquities The museum's *tour de force* is the Hall of Mycenaean Antiquities where gold gleams at you from everywhere. The chief exhibits are from the six shaft graves of Grave Circle A at Mycenae. Shaft graves were rectangular pits about six metres deep. The pit bottom was covered with pebbles, and stone walls measuring about 1½ metres high were built around the sides. After the body and treasures were placed in the pit, it was covered with tree trunks which rested upon the top of the stone wall. The pit was then filled with soil. Graves one to five were excavated by Heinrich Schliemann in 1874-76 and the sixth by Stamatakis in 1886-1902. Just beyond case 25 are four grave stele, two on each side. On the back of the one nearest case 25 are two pictures of Grave Circle A; one shows a reconstruction of the site. The five cases beyond the stele – numbers three, four, 23, 24 and 27 contain the most valuable finds from these shaft graves. Most famous of all is the golden **Mask of Agamemnon** in case three; it has subsequently been proven to be the death mask of a king who died three centuries before Agamemnon.

In the centre of the hall, cases 28 and 29 contain objects from the third grave, including gold sheets which covered the bodies of two royal babies. On the left, cases five and six contain finds from Grave Circle B (from 1650 to 1550 BC) which was outside the citadel at Mycenae. In case five is an unusual rock-crystal vase in the shape of a duck: its head and neck are gracefully turned back to form a handle. On the right, against the blue partition, is the head of a woman, possibly a sphinx or goddess, carved in limestone with brightly painted lips, eyes and fringe. It is a rare example of a Mycenaean sculpture in the round and dates from the 13th century BC. On the other side of the partition are fragments of frescoes from the palace at Mycenae; they reveal a strong Minoan influence.

Case 30, also in the centre, contains mis-

National Archaeological Museum

cellaneous finds from Mycenae, including a delightful little ivory carving of two voluptuous-looking women and a child; they may be Demeter, Persephone and Iacchus. On the right, just beyond here, is the famous **Warrior Vase** which, along with the Mask of Agamemnon, Schliemann rated as one of his greatest finds. It depicts men leaving for war and a woman waving them goodbye.

The rest of the hall is devoted to other Mycenaean sites. On the left, case nine contains tablets with inscriptions in Cretan Linear B script. In case 15, on the right, are objects from Tiryns, including the famous **Tiryns Treasure** believed to have been taken by a looter who robbed rich tombs: it is thought he must have forgotten where he buried the treasure. Back in the centre, case 32 contains the famous gold cups from the tholos tomb at Vaphio which depict the taming of wild bulls. These magnificent cups are regarded as amongst the finest examples of Mycenaean art.

Toward room 21, at the far end of the hall, is an explanation in English on the right-hand wall of the three different types of Mycenaean graves: shaft graves, chamber tombs and tholos tombs. The latter are the most elaborate and impressive, and the entrance to one of them, the **Treasury of Atreus**, has been reconstructed around the doorway at this end of the hall. To the right, are some slabs which decorated the façade of this treasury.

Cycladic Collection Room six, to the right of the Hall of Mycenaean Antiquities, is devoted to Cycladic art. At the western end is the largest Cycladic figurine yet found; it is almost life-size, and was found on the island of Amorgos. On the top wall are fragments of frescoes, including one of a delicately painted seascape with flying fish. On the right side are cases of pottery painted with lovely free-flowing designs depicting flowers, fish and birds.

Cases 56, 57 and 58 contain attractive clay 'frying pans' from early Cycladic cemeteries on Syros. They are black with inlaid intricate spiral, circle, triangle and star patterns in white. If you're wondering why on earth these people took frying pans to the grave with them, they are so called merely because of their shape. Their function remains obscure – on the wall, in English, are several possible explanations for their use.

Neolithic Collection In room five, to the left of the Hall of Mycenaean Antiquities, are Neolithic finds, mainly from Thessaly, and also a case containing pottery, figurines and jewellery from Troy. These finds were presented to the museum by Sophie Schliemann, wife of Heinrich. Particularly beautiful is the necklace of delicate gold beads.

Archaic Sculpture Rooms seven to 14, entered from the left side of the vestibule, contain Archaic sculpture. The main feature of room seven is the huge sepulchral amphora (a jar with two handles and a narrow neck) dating from 760 BC and found in the Keramikos. It is considered *the* masterpiece of the geometric style of pottery.

The chief exhibit in room eight is the huge Kouros of Sounion (600 BC). This was a

votive offering (offering to the gods) found in the Temple of Poseidon at Sounion. On the right, as you enter room nine, is the torso of a kore with elaborately folded drapery. Opposite is the Nike of Delos (550 BC), which unlike the stiff formalised poses of earlier kore looks as if it's dancing a jig, despite being minus hands and feet. To the left, at the end of the room, is one of the most beautiful of the museum's kore. It is a graceful tomb statue of a young girl called Phrasikleia (540 BC). Traces of colour can still be seen on its surface; don't fail to notice the elegant sandals.

Room 10 contains gravestones from the 6th century and two well-preserved sphinxes, one from Piraeus (540 BC) and the other from Sparta (570 BC). In Room 11 is the torso of another colossal kouros (540 BC) found at Megara, Attica. Also in this room are some grave stele, including a particularly well-preserved one of the warrior Aristion which has some traces of remaining colour.

Room 13 is dominated by the sepulchral kouros, named Kroisos. To the left of this sculpture is the base of a kouros found in the Keramikos; it has reliefs on three sides. One side shows four clothed youths mischievously provoking a fight between a cat and dog; another side shows nude youths wrestling; and the third side shows youths playing a ball game. Behind the screen is another base: on one of its sides are nude youths playing a game which looks similar to hockey; the other two sides depict chariot scenes.

Room 14 is given over to provincial stele monuments. The gravestone by Alxenor is one of the finest in the room and bears an endearing, if egocentric, inscription by the artist: 'Alxenor the Naxian made me. Admire me'.

Classical Sculpture In room 15, the bronze statue of **Poseidon of Artemision** (450 BC) is one of the masterpieces of the museum. Poised to hurl his trident (now missing), more than any other statue of Poseidon, it epitomises the god's strength and unlimited power. The statue was hauled from the sea off Cape Artemision in 1928.

Just within the door of this room is the beautiful and well-preserved Relief from Eleusis (440 BC). It depicts Demeter, accompanied by her daughter Persephone, giving Triptolemos an ear of wheat to sprout.

Room 16 contains Classical grave monuments, most of which were found in Attica. Room 17 contains classical votive sculpture.

Room 17 gives access to rooms 19 and 20, which contain more examples of votive sculpture. Room 20 consists mostly of Roman copies of Classical Greek statues. At the far end is the statue of Varvakeion Athena, which was made in about 200 BC. It is the most famous copy – much reduced in size – of the statue of Athena Parthenos by Pheidias. Room 18 contains late 5th and early 4th-century sepulchral monuments.

Late Classical & Hellenistic Sculpture In room 21, the central hall, your eye will be drawn to another outstanding piece – the 2nd-century bronze statue of the Horse & Jockey of Artemision, which was found with the statue of Poseidon. It is a remarkably animated piece of sculpture; especially impressive is the jockey's anxious expression.

At the time of writing room 22 was undergoing reorganisation. In rooms 23 and 24 there are more grave stele. Those in room 24

show a development from low to high relief; some even feature three-dimensional figures. In the centre of this room is an unusual grave monument (540 BC) consisting of a floral column supporting a cauldron decorated with griffins.

Room 25 is mostly devoted to charming diminutive reliefs of nymphs. They are not individually labelled but on the wall is an explanation, in English, of their function. On the left, just before room 26, is a highly unusual votive relief of a snake and a huge sandal on which is carved a worshipping figure. It dates from 360 BC and is believed to depict the 'Hero of the Slipper' who was worshipped near the Theatre of Dionysos. Rooms 26 and 27 contain more votive reliefs.

Room 28 contains the last funerary monuments of Attica. These were extremely realistic, particularly the Grave Monument of Aristonautes (330 BC), which was found in the Keramikos. Another remarkable monument in this room is the large sepulchral relief of a Black boy attempting to restrain a frisky horse. Found near Larissis Station in 1948, it dates from the second half of the 3rd century and is a powerful piece of unprecedented realism, especially apparent in the leg muscles of both the horse and boy and the magnificent drapery. In the centre of the room is the famous statue, Ephebos of Antikythera (340 BC); the amazingly realistic eyes have an hypnotic effect. Behind this

Demeter's Gift

In mythology, Demeter (the goddess of earth and fertility) received kindness from King Keleus of Eleusis, and help from her son Triptolemus, when she was looking for her daughter Persephone who had been abducted by Hades. As a reward she gave Triptolemus an ear of wheat, a plough and a winged chariot and told him to travel the world and teach humans about agriculture. This seems more like delegating work than reciprocating kindness and help, but such were the perverse and manipulating ways of the deities. ■

statue, to the right, is a head of a bronze statue probably of the Elean boxer Satyros. He certainly looks a nasty piece of work in contrast to the calm 'other world' expressions of the heads surrounding him.

Room 29 is dominated by the statue of Themis (the goddess of justice). Behind her is a head of Alexander the Great which has graffitied cheeks (these additions were added later). Next to him is a head of the orator Demosthenes who looks very perplexed. Also of note is the statue of the Gaul warrior whose animated aggressiveness is in marked contrast to the serene repose of Themis.

In room 30 there is light relief provided by the comic masks on the right, though some of their expressions are as menacing as they are funny. A little way down in the middle of the room is a delightful and sensitive statue of a naked boy with his hand on a goose – note his gentle smile and the apparent softness of his skin. Dominating the room is yet another statue of the sea god, this time Poseidon of Melos (140 BC), which was found on Milos in 1877. Behind this statue is the bronze head of a very melancholy looking guy; it was found on Delos. To the right is the amusing statue of Aphrodite, Pan & Eros. Pan is making amorous advances towards Aphrodite, who is about to clobber him with her sandal.

Room 34, is built to simulate an open-air sanctuary, displaying objects from the **Sanctuary of Aphrodite**, which was west of the monastery of Dafni and close to the Sacred Way. Room 36 houses the **Karapanos Collection**, which includes a chariot from the Roman period. Room 37 is the first of the bronze rooms to be opened. To the left a case shows casting techniques; another shows burial offerings. In the middle is a bronze statue of a youth (337 BC) which was found in the Bay of Marathon. At the time of writing the remaining rooms on the ground floor were closed for reorganisation.

Thira Exhibition If you're running out of time or energy, or both, you will find the Thira collection (which on no account should be missed) by walking straight ahead at the top of the stairs. In the first room is a display of pottery from Akrotiri on the island of Thira (Santorini). Beyond is the celebrated exhibition of the frescoes which were unearthed at Akrotiri by the Greek archaeologist, Spyridon Marinatos.

The frescoes are more varied and better preserved than the Minoan frescoes found on Crete. Extremely beautiful and harmonious in both colour and form, they give a comprehensive insight into the everyday life of the Minoans. They include two boxing youths, a youth holding two strings of fish, women performing religious rites, pastoral scenes of herdsmen, women carrying vases on their heads, as well as prancing antelopes and graceful lilies. The most unusual is the Ship Fresco which shows a flotilla of ships sailing from one coastal town to another. The frescoes will remain here until a suitable museum has been built on Thira.

Pottery Collection On leaving the Thira exhibition, turn left to reach the first of the pottery rooms, which house the world's most comprehensive collection of Ancient Greek pottery. The collection traces the development from the Bronze Age, through the Protogeometric and Geometric period, to the beginning of simple decorative motifs. In the 8th century BC human figures and flora and fauna were introduced into pottery for the first time. In the 7th century, myths were introduced and in the 6th century the famous Attic Black-Figured pottery was developed. By the middle of the 5th century Black-Figured pottery had been superseded by Red-Figured pottery, which reached its apex under Pericles. There are comprehensive explanations in English at the beginning of each room.

Numismatic Museum To reach the Numismatic Museum, turn left at the top of the stairs, and walk through room 56. This vast collection comprises 400,000 coins, from Ancient Greek, Hellenic, Roman and Byzantine times. Only a fraction are on display at any one time. Coins particularly to look out

Top: Gerolimena Bay, the Mani, Peloponnese (RH)
Left: The Corinth Canal, Peloponnese (BD)
Middle: The Pantanassa Convent, Mystra, Peloponnese (RH)
Right: The Church of St Spyridon, old Kardamyli, Messinia, Peloponnese (RH)
Bottom: The fortress, Methoni, Messinia, Peloponnese (RH)

Top: View of Kapsali from Chora's kastro, Kythera (RH)
Left: Taygetos Gorge near Kardamyli, Messinia, Peloponnese (RH)
Right: The main street, Monemvassia, Lakonia, Peloponnese (RH)

for are the **Owl Coins** of Classical Athens and the **Macedonian Coins**.

The Numismatic Museum is open Tuesday to Sunday from 8.30 am to 3 pm and entry is 400 dr.

Benaki Museum

This museum (☎ 361 1617) contains the sumptuous and eclectic collection of Antoine Benaki, who was the son of an Alexandrian cotton magnate named Emmanual Benaki. These exhibits were accumulated during Antoine's 35 years of avid collecting in Europe and Asia. In 1931 he turned the family house into a museum and presented it to the Greek nation.

The ground floor is devoted to ancient and medieval arts. It includes Bronze Age finds from Mycenae and Thessaly; two early works by El Greco; ecclesiastical furniture brought from Asia Minor by refugees; pottery, copper, silver and woodwork from Egypt, Asia Minor and Mesopotamia; and a reconstruction of a Muslim reception hall.

The 1st floor is devoted to the 17th to 19th centuries, and includes a reconstruction of a 17th-century room in a Rhodes mansion. Also on display are some Byron memorabilia, relics from the War of Independence, letters of Eleftherios Venizelos (who was a close friend of Emmannual Benaki) and the poet George Seferis, exquisite embroidery from the islands and Chinese ceramics. In the basement is a stunning collection of Greek regional costumes.

The museum has a pleasant rooftop café from where there are good views. It's on the corner of Vasilissis Sofias and Koumbari, and is open daily from 8.30 am to 3 pm. Admission is 200 dr.

Goulandris Museum of Cycladic & Ancient Greek Art

This museum (☎ 801 5870) was opened by Dolly Goulandris as a memorial to her husband. The building is modern and the finds are beautifully displayed, lit and labelled. Although the exhibits cover all periods from Cycladic to Roman times, the emphasis is on the Cycladic civilisation (from 3000 to 2000 BC). The 230 exhibits include the folded-arm, marble figurines, which are generic of that period, and inspired many 20th-century artists with their simplicity and purity of form.

The museum is the next one along from the Benaki Museum, at Neofytou Douka 4, just round the corner from Vasilissis Sofias. It is open Monday, Wednesday, Thursday and Friday from 10 am to 3.30 pm. Admission is 200 dr.

Byzantine Museum

The museum (☎ 721 1027) is housed in the Villa Ilissia, an attractive, mock-Florentine mansion erected around a peaceful courtyard reminiscent of a cloister. It was built in 1848 by the architect A Zachosfor Sophie de Marbois, duchesse de Plaisance (1785-1854). The daughter of a French diplomat, Sophie was an ardent philhellene. Bored with Parisian society of the 19th century, she left her statesman husband to live in Greece, where she befriended War of Independence leaders and brigands.

The museum contains a large collection of Christian art from the 4th to the 19th century. Unfortunately, the labelling is in Greek only, so if you want fully to understand what's what you'll have to buy one of the catalogues (from 600 to 800 dr). Otherwise, make for the right wing first, which contains icons and frescoes arranged in chronological order. This will help you to get the rest of the collection in perspective.

The exhibits begin with early Byzantine sculptures. By the 16th century the sculptures show a marked Italian influence. Room four is a reconstruction of an 11th-century Byzantine church, which is beautiful in its simplicity. In contrast, the reproduction of a post-Byzantine church, in room five, is elaborately decorated. The bishop's throne in this room was brought to Athens by refugees from Asia Minor. The 1st floor contains mostly icons and frescoes.

The museum is at Vasilissis Sofias 22 and is open Tuesday to Sunday from 8.30 am to 3 pm. Admission is 1000 dr.

Greek Folk Art Museum

This museum (☎ 322 9031) contributes greatly to the understanding of the life and culture of Greece in times gone by. It houses a superb collection of secular and religious folk art mainly from the 18th and 19th centuries. On the 1st floor is embroidery, pottery, weaving and puppets. On the 2nd floor is a reconstructed traditional village house with paintings by the primitive artist Theophilos of Lesbos. Greek traditional costumes are displayed on the 3rd and 4th floors. The museum is at Kidathineon 17, Plaka, and is open Tuesday to Sunday from 10 am to 2 pm. Admission is 200 dr.

National Art Gallery

The emphasis in this gallery (☎ 723 5938) is on Greek painting and sculpture from the 19th and 20th centuries AD, but there are also some 16th-century works and a few works by European masters, including paintings by Picasso, Marquet and Utrillo and Magritte's sculpture The Therapist.

Paintings by the primitive painter Theophilos are displayed on the mezzanine floor and 20th-century works are on the 1st floor. The 2nd floor has mostly 19th-century paintings, with one room of earlier works, which includes three El Greco paintings.

Greek sculpture of the 19th and 20th centuries is effectively displayed in the sculpture garden and sculpture hall which are reached from the lower floor. There are several works by Y Halepas (1851-1937) who was one of Greece's foremost sculptors.

The gallery is at Vasileos Konstantinou 50 (opposite the Hilton Hotel) and is open Tuesday to Saturday from 9 am to 3 pm and Sunday from 10 am to 2 pm. Admission is 150 dr.

War Museum

This museum (☎ 723 5263) is a relic of the colonels' junta. Even if you find war repugnant, you may, despite your better judgement, find this museum interesting. As Greece has been plagued by wars since time immemorial, a look around helps to get the country's history in perspective. All periods from the Mycenaean to the present day are covered, in models of battles, weapons, maps, armour, pictures etc.

Uniforms are displayed in the basement where there is also a café. In the grounds are a tank and seven military aircraft. The museum is at Vasilissis Sofias 24, just beyond the Byzantine Museum.

It is open Tuesday to Saturday from 9 am to 2 pm; 9.30 am to 2 pm on Sunday. Entry is free.

Centre of Folk Arts & Traditions

A small but well-displayed collection of costumes, embroideries, pottery, musical instruments etc can be seen in this museum (☎ 324 3987) at Angelika Hatzimichali 6, Plaka. Opening times are Tuesday and Thursday from 9 am to 9 pm and on Wednesday, Friday and Saturday from 9 am to 1 pm and 5 to 9 pm. Entry is free.

Paul & Alexandra Kanellopoulos Museum

This museum (☎ 324 3987) houses a small but fascinating collection of exhibits. It is a private collection owned by the Kanellopoulos family and housed in a renovated neoclassical mansion. The exhibits include pieces from Cycladic, Minoan and Classical times, Attic vases, Byzantine jewellery and embroideries, Persian jewellery from the 5th century BC, icons, coins etc. The museum is on the corner of Theorias and Panos, Plaka.

Opening times are Tuesday to Friday from 8.30 am to 3 pm. Admission is 400 dr.

National Historical Museum

This museum (☎ 323 7617) has exhibits from Byzantine and medieval times, royal portraits, photographs etc, but mostly memorabilia from the War of Independence, including Byron's helmet and sword. There is also a series of paintings by D Zographis depicting events leading up to the war. It is housed in the old parliament building at Plateia Kolokotroni, Stadiou. Theodoros Deligannis, who succeeded Trikoupis as prime minister of Greece, was assassinated on the steps of the building in 1905.

The museum is open Tuesday to Friday from 9 am to 1.30 pm and Saturday, Sunday and holidays from 9 am to 12.30 pm. Admission is 200 dr.

City of Athens Museum

This museum (☎ 324 6164) is housed in what was the original royal palace where King Otho and his consort Amalia lived for a few years during the 1830s. It retains some original furniture and costumes and personal objects which belonged to the royal couple. Also included in the collection are paintings, prints and models of Athens in the 19th century.

The museum is at Paparigopoulou 7 and is open on Monday, Wednesday Friday, Saturday and holidays from 9 am to 1.30 pm. Admission is 100 dr.

Jewish Museum

In this museum (☎ 323 1577) is an impressive collection of religious and folk art, and documents, of the Jewish community of Greece, which can be traced back to the 3rd century BC. It includes a reconstruction of a synagogue. The museum is housed on the 3rd floor of a 19th-century building at Amalias 36.

Opening times are Sunday to Friday from 9 am to 1 pm and entry is free.

Theatre Museum

Aspiring Thespians may be interested in visiting this museum (☎ 362 9430), which contains theatre memorabilia from the 19th and 20th centuries. Exhibits include photographs, costumes, props and reconstructions of dressing rooms of Greece's most celebrated 20th-century actors. The museum is at Akadimias 50. Opening times are Monday to Friday from 9 am to 3 pm and Sunday from 10 am to 1 pm. Admission is 150 dr.

HILLS OF ATHENS
Lykavitos Hill

The name means Hill of Wolves and derives from ancient times when the hill was in remote countryside and wolves menaced the flocks of sheep that grazed there. Today, it is

no longer remote or inhabited by wolves, but rises out of a sea of concrete to offer the finest views in Athens. From the summit there are panoramic views – depending on the mood of the nefos – of the city, the Attic basin, the surrounding mountains and the islands of Salamis and Aegina. From the top of Odos Loukianou a path leads to the summit. Alternatively, you can take the **funicular railway** from the top of Ploutarhou (175/275 dr, one-way/return).

There is a café halfway up the path and a restaurant (expensive) on the top. Also on the summit is the little **Chapel of Agios Giorgios**. The chapel is floodlit at night and from the streets below looks like a vision from a fairy tale. The **Lykavitos Open-Air Theatre**, to the north-east of the summit, is used mostly for performances of jazz and rock during the Athens Festival.

West of the Acropolis

To the west of the Acropolis are several hills. If you turn right when you leave the Acropolis you will come to **Areopagus Hill** (115 metres) reached by steps hewn into the rock. According to mythology, it was here that Ares was tried by the council of the gods for the murder of Halirrhothios, son of Poseidon.

The hill is also important historically, because the Council of the Areopagus, which was formed in the 7th century, used to assemble here to conduct murder trials. By the 4th century the Council of Areopagus also dealt with crimes of treason and corruption.

In 51 AD, St Paul delivered his famous 'Sermon to an Unknown God' from Areopagus Hill and gained his first Athenian convert, Dionysos, who became patron saint of the city. From the summit there are good views of the Ancient Agora. The hill is composed entirely of slippery rock so wear sensible shoes and tread carefully.

Filopappos Hill, which is also called the Hill of the Muses, can be reached from the Dionysos Taverna on Dionysiou Areopagitou. From here a series of paths leads up the tree-clad hill. On the top is the **Monument of Filopappos** built in 114-116 AD in honour of Julios Antiochus Filopappos, who was a prominent Roman consul and administrator. On a clear day the plain and mountains of Attica and the Saronic Gulf can be seen.

Continuing north-west along the main path you will reach the **Church of Agios Dimitrios**, which contains some fine frescoes. It was sensitively restored in 1951-57. Above here is the rocky **Hill of the Pnyx** (109 metres). This was the meeting place of the Democratic Assembly in the 5th century BC. Among the great orators who addressed assemblies here were Aristides, Demosthenes, Pericles and Themistokles.

To the north-west of the Hill of the Pnyx is the **Hill of the Nymphs** (104 metres) on which stands an observatory built in 1842. It is open to visitors on the last Friday of each month.

PARKS

Athens is sadly lacking in parks. Only three are large enough to be worthy of a mention and a visit.

National Gardens

These gardens are a delightful shady refuge from the blazing Athenian summer and are the favourite haunt of Athens' many stray cats. They were formerly the royal gardens and were designed by Queen Amalia as the palace gardens.

The garden contains subtropical trees, ornamental ponds with waterfowl, and a **Botanical Museum** (signposted) which houses interesting drawings, paintings and photographs. Entrances to the gardens are on Vasilissis Sofias and Leoforos Amalias.

Zappeion Gardens

These gardens are laid out in a network of wide walkways around the Zappeion Hall, which was built in the 1870s with money donated by the wealthy Greek-Romanian benefactor, Constantine Zappas. Until the 1970s the Zappeion Hall was used mainly as an exhibition hall. During Greece's presidency of the EC it was used for council of Europe meetings.

Areos Park

This pleasant park is north of the National Archaeological Museum on Leoforos Alexandras. It is a large, well laid-out park with wide, tree-lined avenues, one of which has a long line of statues of heroes of the War of Independence.

Athens' First Cemetery

Athens' First Cemetery (Proto Nekrotafeion Athinon) although not strictly a park nonetheless bears more than a passing resemblance to one. In the absence of an adequate number of real parks in Athens one should be grateful for any expanse of greenery. Athenian families, who come to attend the graves of departed loved ones, certainly seem to take this attitude, for they turn the duty into an outing by bringing along a picnic. It's a peaceful place to stroll around and the resting place of many famous Greeks and philhellenes.

To get there, walk south along Leoforos Syngrou passing the Temple of Zeus and turn left onto Athanassiou Diakou. At the busy intersection, cross the road and take Anapafseos which runs south. The cemetery gates are at the end of the road. You'll know when you are near because of all the stone masons, flower shops and shops choc-a-bloc with cemetery paraphernalia. This paraphernalia includes everything from life-size figures of Christ to miniature picture frames, for the Greeks put photographs of the deceased on the gravestones. All this, and the cemetery itself, are evidence that the Greeks throw themselves into the matter of death with the same enthusiasm with which they embrace life.

The cemetery is well kept and most of the tombstones and mausoleums are lavish in the extreme. Some are kitsch and sentimental, others are beautiful works of art, with pieces created by the foremost Greek sculptors of the 19th century. One example is the *Sleeping Maiden* by Y Halepas which is the tomb of a young girl – someone places a red rose in her hand every day.

Amongst the cemetery's famous residents' are the writers Rangavis (1810-92) and Soutsos (1800-68); the politician Chari-laos Trikoupis (1832-96); the archaeologists Heinrich Schliemann (1822-90) and Adolph Furtwängler (1853-1907); the benefactors Antoine Benake, Georgios Averoff and Theodore Singros; and heroes of the War of Independence, Sir Richard Church (1784-1873), Kolokotronis (1770-1843), Makrigannis and Andoutsos. Schliemann's mausoleum is decorated with scenes from the Trojan War. Located near the entrance is a memorial – poignant in its simplicity – to the 40,000 citizens who died of starvation during WW II.

ACTIVITIES
Skiing
The nearest ski resorts to Athens are on Mt Parnassos. One of the biggest is at Kalaria, where there are four pistes. The season lasts from mid-December to March or April depending on the weather. The ski department at Klaoudatos, the big department store on Athinas, organises excursions to the resort. The excursion buses leave for Parnassos from the stadium in Athens every morning at 5.40 am. If you wish to spend some time at the resort, Klaoudatos will also make a hotel reservation for you. Both ski hire and use of the chair lifts cost 2500 dr per day.

Tennis
There are several tennis clubs in Athens. The most central one is the Athens Tennis Club (☎ 923 2872), Vasilissis Olgas 2. This is a very exclusive club for members only, but if you're spending some time in Athens it may be worth making some enquiries. Other clubs are AOK Tennis Club, Kifissia (☎ 801 3100); and the Attica Tennis Club, Filothei (☎ 681 2557). In addition there are tennis courts at many of the EOT beaches on the Attica coast.

Golf
The nearest golf club to Athens is the Glyfada Golf Club (☎ 894 6820).

Other Sports Clubs
Addresses of other sports clubs include:

Gliding
   Gliding Club of Athens, Pafsaniou 8
   (☎ 723 5158)
Horse Riding
   Horse Riding Club of Athens, Gerakas
   (☎ 661 1088)
   Horse Riding Club of Greece, Paradissos
   (☎ 682 6128)
Jogging
   Hash House Harriers Jogging Club, Kifissia
   (☎ 808 0565)

Bird Watching
Keen bird watchers may like to contact the Hellenic Ornithological Society (☎ 361 1271), Benaki 53, Athens.

Language Courses
The following all have Greek-language courses: the Hellenic American Union (☎ 362 9886) Massalias 22; the YWCA (XEN) (☎ 362 4291) Amerikis 11; and the Athens Centre (☎ 701 2268) Arhimidous 49. The Athens Centre has the most up-to-date teaching methods and the course includes outings to theatres, cinemas, museums and ancient sites. Its 60-hour course costs 50,000 dr and may be taken over one or two months. Courses at the other two institutes are considerably cheaper – about half the price.

Organised Tours
The three established companies which run organised tours around Athens are CHAT (☎ 322 3137), Stadiou 4; GO Tours (☎ 322 5951/2/3/4/5), Voulis 31-33; and Key Tours (☎ 923 3166/3266), Kalirois 4. They all offer similar tours and prices. They include a half-day sightseeing tour of Athens (5000 dr), which does nothing more than point out all the major sights, and Athens by Night (5000 to 7000 dr).

The companies also have one-day tours to Cape Sounion (3700 dr); Delphi (9200 dr, 11,400 dr with lunch); ancient Corinth, Mycenae and Epidaurus (10,200 dr, or 12,400 dr with lunch); and Aegina, Poros and Hydra (9000 dr including lunch). These trips are only worth considering if your time is limited because it's much more fun and much cheaper to do them independently. Most hotels and travel agencies will take bookings for these tours, but check on how much commission they charge as it can be anything from 10 to 20%.

FESTIVALS
Athens Festival
The state-sponsored Athens Festival is the city's most important cultural event, running from mid-June to the end of September. It includes classical music concerts and dance performances by national and international orchestras and dance companies.

The main attraction is the performances of Ancient Greek dramas staged at the Theatre of Herodes Atticus. The plays are performed in modern Greek but somehow not understanding the language doesn't seem to matter. The atmosphere is charged, the setting is superlative, with the Acropolis, the Monument of Filopappos and the Temple of Olympian Zeus all floodlit. There are also performances at the Lykavitos Theatre, the open-air amphitheatre in Piraeus, and the Theatre of Epidaurus – special buses run here from Athens (see also the Nafplion and Epidaurus sections in the Peloponnese chapter).

Tickets sell out quickly, so try to buy yours as soon as possible. They can be bought at the Box Office (☎ 322 1459), Stadiou 4 (in the arcade). Opening times are Monday to Friday from 8.30 am to 1.30 pm and from 6 to 8.30 pm. Tickets may also be purchased on the day of the performance at the theatre box offices, but queues tend to be very long. There are student discounts for most performances on production of an ISIC.

Alternative Athens Festival
Over the last few years a privately sponsored alternative festival has run concurrently with the established festival. This festival features jazz and rock artists and Athens is becoming a respected international pop and jazz venue. Venues include the Lykavitos Theatre, the Panathinaikos Football Stadium on Leoforos Alexandras and the clubs listed under Live Music in the Entertainment section later in this chapter. Tickets for these performances can be purchased at the box offices of the respective venues and at major music shops. The EOT does not give out a schedule of the alternative festival, but events are listed in the English-language newspapers, as well as being widely advertised on posters.

PLACES TO STAY
Athens is a noisy city. Greeks are gregarious by nature and talk vociferously. Greek drivers are fond of their horns and although it is illegal to sound a car horn between 11 am and midnight, this law, like most driving laws, is often violated. Nightlife goes on till late. If you wander around the streets of Athens at any hour of the night, you will see people on the streets and cars on the roads. Greeks catch up on lost sleep during an afternoon siesta and you may be tempted to do the same. In the hotel recommendations, I have tried, as far as possible, to recommend hotels which are on side roads or pedestrian ways. Where I have recommended a hotel which is on a main thoroughfare, you can try asking for a room at the back. All of the prices quoted are for the high season. In the off season, you may be able to negotiate a discount.

The highest concentration of hotels is in and around Plaka. Most of the hotels in this area are within walking distance of Syntagma and Monastiraki, so are convenient if you're arriving by bus from the airport or by bus or metro from Piraeus. They are also convenient for most of the sights. This means that in July or August they fill up quickly, so it is wise to make a reservation in advance. Otherwise, once you arrive, start telephoning around to save yourself a long walk. Almost every periptero has a public telephone and you don't need to have the correct change to make a call.

The area around the train stations has many student hostels which are really budget hotels catering for backpackers. Generally speaking, these places are stopping-off points for travellers who arrive in Athens after a gruelling three or four-day train journey from northern Europe and want somewhere to crash and recuperate before making for the islands. So the owners lay on many amenities, creating within their hotels a microcosm of the city outside. All of the ones recommended have bars (serving breakfasts, snacks and cheapish drinks), TV, travel agencies, currency exchange and 24-hour hot showers. There's a great camaraderie among the backpackers staying in these places.

The area isn't interesting, but it's only a short trolley-bus ride from Syntagma and is within walking distance of Plateia Victorias metro station and the train stations.

There are many cheap hotels which are virtually bordellos in the streets close to Omonia. Although you wouldn't be in any danger staying in one of them, they are best avoided, unless you are prepared to be an involuntary eavesdropper into the seedier aspects of Athenian night life.

If you arrive in the city late and cannot find anywhere to stay, don't be tempted to sleep out as it is illegal and could be dangerous. You will be better off going to one of the many all-night cafés, some of which are recommended in Places to Eat later.

Camping

There are no camp sites in central Athens. *This Week in Athens* lists all 17 camp sites in Attica. The nearest one to the city centre is *Athens Camping* (☎ 581 4113/4 or 582 0353), Leoforos Athinon 198, seven km from the centre on the right side of the road. It has hot water, a minimarket and snack bar and is open year round. To reach the site take an Elefsina bus from Plateia Eleftherias. From Piraeus take bus No 802 or 845. By car follow the signposts for Dafni and the Peloponnese.

Two other camp sites near the city are *Acropolis Camping* (☎ 807 5253), 16 km north at the Athens-Lamia crossing, Nea Kifissia, and *Dionissiotis Camping* (☎ 807 1494), 18 km north on the national road, also at Nea Kifissia. Another camp site which is fairly close to Athens is the one at Dafni (see

the Dafni section later). There are also several camp sites on the Apollo coast (see the Coast Rd to Sounion and Cape Sounion sections later).

Places to Stay – bottom end
Plaka, Syntagma & Monastiraki The *YWCA* (XEN) for women only (☎ 362 4291), Amerikis 11, is a friendly, well-run place with singles/doubles for 3500/4000 dr with shared bathrooms, and triples for 1700 per person. There are laundry facilities and a snack bar.

Festos Hostel (☎ 323 2455), Filellinon 18, has clean, tidy rooms. The per-person costs are 1700 dr in doubles and 1550 dr in triples/quads; dorm beds are 1200 dr; all have shared bathrooms. The lively bar sells good-value breakfast, lunch and dinner with one vegetarian dish daily. Its travel agency sells ferry tickets to Italy and Crete and discounted air tickets. The English-speaking staff are friendly and helpful. Check out is 9 am and curfew is 2 am. Walking from Syntagma the hostel is on the right.

John's Place (☎ 322 9719), Patroou 5, has small, basic and reasonably clean singles/doubles/triples with shared bathrooms for 2500/4000/5000 dr. From Syntagma walk along Mitropoleos and Patroou is off to the left. *George's Guesthouse* (☎ 322 6474), Nikis 46, has dorm beds for 1700 dr and doubles/triples for 2700/3000 dr with shared bathrooms. Take the first turning left from Mitropoleos.

Kouros Hotel (☎ 322 7431), Kodrou 11, which is classed as a pension, is one of the cheapest hotels in the heart of Plaka. It's a beautiful 200-year-old house on a quiet street. Inside, the hotel is dingy but reasonably clean and has lots of character, with some lovely high moulded ceilings. Singles/doubles with shared bathrooms are 3500/4500 dr. Check out is 11 am. From Syntagma walk along Mitropoleos and turn left onto Voulis, which becomes Kodrou.

The E class *Hotel Solonion* (☎ 322 0008), Tsangari 11-13, is dilapidated, but clean and cheap. Rooms cost 3000/4000/5000 dr with

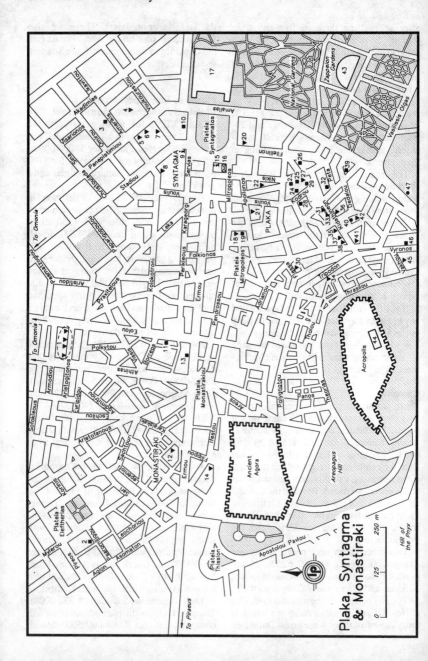

Plaka, Syntagma & Monastiraki

■   PLACES TO STAY

2	Hotel Capri
3	XEN
10	Hotel Grande Bretagne
11	Tempi Hotel
13	Hotel Hermion
19	John's Place
23	Hotel Myrto
24	Hotel Adonis
25	George's Guesthouse
26	Festos Hostel
28	Acropolis House Pension
29	Kouros Hotel
32	Phoebus Hotel
39	Hotel Solonion
46	Byron Hotel

▼   PLACES TO EAT

1	Meat Market Tavernas
4	Apotsos Ouzeri
5	Floca Coffee Shop
6	Zonar's Coffee Shop
7	Brazilian Coffee Shop
8	Far East Restaurant
12	O Marias Taverna
14	Ipiros Taverna
18	Peristeria Taverna
20	Syntrivani Restaurant
21	Milk Shop (Apollonos 11)
22	Milk Shop (Nikis 26)
27	Epic Restaurant
30	Eden Vegetarian Restaurant
31	The Cellar
33	Milk Shop (Kidathineon 10)
34	To Gerani Ouzeri
35	O Kostis Taverna
36	Michiko Japanese Restaurant
37	Milk Shop (Kidathineon 30)
38	To Kosmikon
41	Taverna Damigos
42	Tristato Cafe
45	Taverna Theofilos

OTHER

9	EOT, National Bank of Greece & Hellenic Chamber of Hotels
15	EOT & General Bank of Greece
16	Post Office
17	Parliament (Old Royal Palace)
40	Self-Service Laundrette
43	Zappeion
44	Parthenon
47	Arch of Hadrian

shared bathrooms. Walk west along Kidathineon and turn left at Asteriou, of which Tsangari is a continuation. *Byron Hotel* (☎ 323 0327/0325/3554), Vyronos 19, is a presentable, no-frills D class hotel, with rooms for 4500/6600/9900 dr with private bathrooms. Vyronos is a reasonably quiet street at the southern end of Plaka. To get there walk in a westerly direction along Kidathineon, continue along the first block of Thespidos, then turn left onto Sellev and continue straight ahead to Vyronos.

In the area of Monastiraki, the D class *Tempi Hotel* (☎ 321 3175), Eolou 29, is a cheery place with a friendly English-speaking owner. It has clean rooms and the ones at the front have balconies overlooking a little square with a church and a flower market. Rooms are 2500/4000/5000 dr with shared bathrooms. Check out is at 11 am and there is no curfew. This part of Eolou is pedestrianised. To reach the hotel, walk along Ermou from Syntagma and turn right onto Eolou.

If you continue along Ermou, you will come to the newly renovated *Hotel Hermion* (☎ 321 2753), Ermou 66c, where very pleasant singles/doubles with shared bathrooms are 3500/4500 dr. The *Hotel Capri* (☎ 325 2091/2085), Psaromiligou 6, Plateia Eleftherias, is further from Syntagma, in a grimy part of town, but it's still convenient for the sights. It has agreeable rooms with pale-blue walls, and a well-stocked bar with a dart board, table tennis and roof garden. Rooms are 3200/4800/5400 dr with private bathrooms. Coming from Piraeus on the metro get off at Thission Station, take Agion Asomaton and turn right onto Psaromiligou. From Syntagma walk along Ermou to Plateia Thission.

Veikou & Koukaki To reach these pleasant residential neighbourhoods either walk south from Dionysiou Areopagitou or take trolley bus No 1, 5 or 9 from the west side of Syntagma. *Marble House Pension* (☎ 923 4058 or 922 6461), Zini 35A, Koukaki, is one of Athens' nicest budget accommodations. Monica, the French manager, is

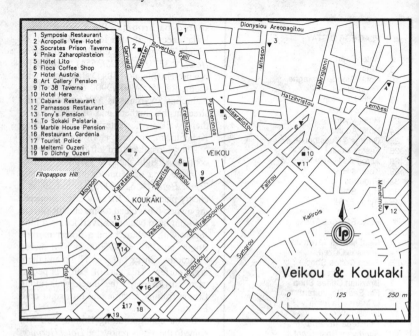

1 Symposia Restaurant
2 Acropolis View Hotel
3 Socrates Prison Taverna
4 Pnika Zaharoplasteion
5 Hotel Lito
6 Floca Coffee Shop
7 Hotel Austria
8 Art Gallery Pension
9 To 38 Taverna
10 Hotel Hera
11 Cabana Restaurant
12 Parnassos Restaurant
13 Tony's Pension
14 To Sokaki Psistaria
15 Marble House Pension
16 Restaurant Gardenia
17 Tourist Police
18 Meltemi Ouzeri
19 To Dichty Ouzeri

Veikou & Koukaki

friendly and helpful. Rates for the immaculate rooms are 4000/6100/7400 dr with private bathrooms and 3300/5600/6700 dr with shared bathrooms. The pension is on a quiet cul-de-sac off Zini. Get off the trolley bus at the Zini stop on Odos Veikou, or walk westwards along Odos Dimitrakopoulou and turn left onto Zini and the cul-de-sac is the first turning left.

Tony's Pension (☎ 923 6370/0561), Zaharitsa 26, Koukaki, is a clean, well-kept pension with a congenial atmosphere. Tony, the owner, speaks English and is helpful. The rooms are 5000/7000/8000 dr with private bathrooms. Beautifully furnished and well-equipped two-person studio apartments are also available for long or short-term rental. They cost from 6000 to 8000 dr in winter and 8000 to 12,000 dr in summer, depending on your length of stay. Zaharitsa is two blocks north-west of Dimitrakopoulou. If you take a trolley bus get off at the Drakou stop on Odos Veikou.

The *Art Gallery Pension* (☎ 923 8376/ 1933), Erechthiou 5, Veikou, is another very pleasant and clean place. The rates are 4000/5000/6000 dr with private bathrooms. To get to the pension walk west along Dionysiou Areopagitou, turn left onto Mitseon and right onto Hatzihristou and Erechthiou is the third turning left.

Hotel Lito (☎ 923 1768/0743), Misaraliotou 15, has a gloomy foyer and passageways, but the rooms are clean with adequate furniture and comfortable beds. Rates are the same as those at the Art Gallery Pension. To reach the hotel turn left onto Kariatidon from Dionysiou Areopagitou and the hotel is opposite the bottom of this road.

Mets & Pangrati *Joseph's House* (☎ 922 1160 or 923 1204), Markou Mousourou 13, is the only hotel in Mets and a long-time favourite with backpackers. It is housed in a dilapidated old building with lots of character. The room rates are 2500/5000 dr for

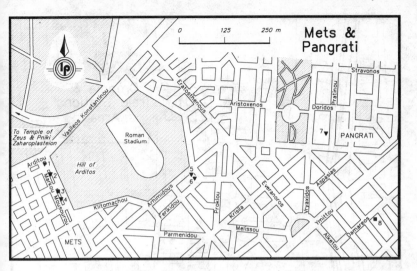

1	Stadio Music Bar		5	O Virinis Taverna
2	Manesis Taverna		6	O Megaritis Taverna
3	Joseph's House		7	Oikogeneiaki Taverna
4	Cafe Odeon		8	Youth Hostel No 5

doubles/triples with shared bathrooms. There's a kitchen with a refrigerator and cooker, washing and drying facilities, a small lending library and a friendly, pampered cat. To get here take trolley bus No 2, 4 or 11 from the west side of Syntagma, and get off at the stadium stop, or walk south along Amalias, turn left onto Olgas, then right onto Vasileos Konstantinou and almost immediately left onto Markou Mousourou.

Athens' *Youth Hostel No 5* (☎ 751 9530) Damareos 75, Pangrati, is an excellent unofficial hostel. Dorm beds are 1200 dr and double rooms are 1400 dr per person. Breakfast, which is 500 dr, includes a very tasty omelette. There is 24-hour hot water and the use of a washing machine for 500 dr. The hostel is locked at midnight, but if you want to stay out later you can ask for a key. Yiannas, the owner, keeps the place very clean, speaks six languages, is genial and helpful and if you need a job he may be able to offer you one.

The hostel is open year round and is heated in winter. Check out is 10 am and there is free luggage storage for guests. The hostel is 1½ km from Syntagma. To walk there go through the National Gardens, cross Vasileos Konstantinou, walk along Eratosthenous to Ymittou, cross over to Alketou, turn left onto Damareos and the hostel is along here on the right. Otherwise take trolley bus No 2 or 11 from Syntagma.

North of Omonia This section covers Exarhia, the areas around the train stations and Plateia Victorias.

Hostel Aphrodite (☎ 881 0589), Einardou 12, is one of Athens' best student hostels. It is very clean, with dazzling, white walls and

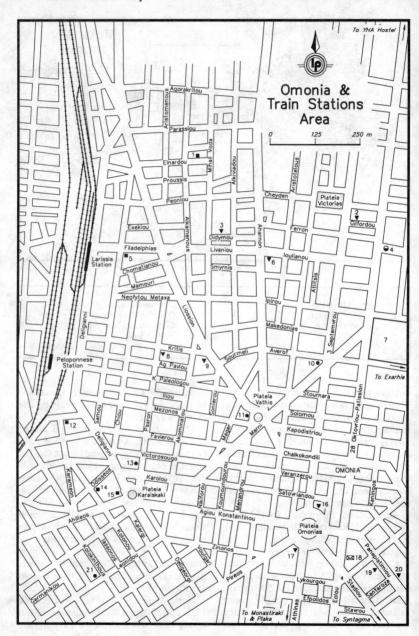

Omonia & Train Stations Area

To YHA Hostel

0   125   250 m

To Exarhia

To Monastiraki
& Plaka

To Syntagma

1	Hostel Aphrodite
2	Zorbas Hostel
3	Taverna I Kriti
4	Mavromateon Bus Terminal
5	Oscar Hotel
6	Dafni Taverna
7	National Archaeological Museum
8	Psistaria
9	O Vaggelis Taverna
10	Rodon Club
11	WC
12	Hotel Mystras
13	Laundrette
14	Rio Hotel
15	Crystal Hotel
16	Neon Cafe
17	Cafe Brettania
18	Central Post Office
19	Snack Bar (below Greek Ecology Party offices)
20	Ideal Restaurant
21	Laundrette

good-sized rooms, many with balconies. The hostel also has a sun terrace. For singles/doubles/triples with shared bathrooms it costs 2800/4000/4800 dr; or there are some slightly cheaper rooms with shared bathrooms. Dorm beds are 1000 dr.

The basement bar has Brazilian wall-hangings, a wide variety of reasonably priced drinks and a large choice of breakfasts, served between 5.30 and 11.30 am. Its travel agency sells a ticket giving unlimited travel between many Cycladic islands for 20 days, for less than a return ticket to one island. The English-speaking staff are helpful and knowledgeable about Athens. From the train stations cross over the road and take Filadelphias, turn left onto Alkamenous and right onto Einardou and the hostel is on the left. Take trolley bus No 2, 5, 9 or 12 to Plateia Victorias from Syntagma. From Piraeus you can catch the metro to Plateia Victorias.

Zorbas Hostel (☎ 823 2543), Gilfordou, is a lovely old house with cheery red-and-white rooms. Doubles/triples/quads with private bathrooms are 3600/5400/7200 dr. Dorm beds are 1500 dr. All rooms have private

showers. Continental breakfast is 500 dr and English breakfast is 750 dr. Gilfordou is a small street just east of Plateia Victorias.

The *Hotel Mystras* (☎ 522 7737/1807), Kerameon 26, has clean, nicely furnished rooms for 3200/4800/5400/7200 dr a single/double/triple/quad. From Larissis Station walk south to Kerameon and the hotel is on the left. Nearby, the *Hotel Rio* (☎ 522 7075), Odisseos 13, has decent singles/doubles/triples for 2500/3800/4800 dr with private bathrooms. Walk down Kerameon and turn left onto Odisseos and the hotel is on the right.

Museum Hotel (☎ 360 5611/2/3), Bouboulinas 16, is a long-established hotel behind the National Archaeological Museum. It's an agreeable place with unadorned, but pleasant rooms. The rates are 3900/5300/6360 dr with private bathrooms. From Syntagma take trolley bus No 2, 4, 5 or 11.

The *Hotel Exarchion* (☎ 360 3296/1256/8684), Plateia Exarheion, is in the hub of studentsville. It's a modern hotel and the light, airy rooms have large French windows which open onto balconies. The room rates are 4000/5300 dr for singles/doubles with private bathrooms. The square can be noisy during the night so try to get a room at the back. To get to the hotel from the National Archaeological Museum walk a little way south and turn left at Stournari, which leads to Plateia Exarheion.

The *Hotel Orian* (☎ 362 7362/7116/0191 or 360 5193), Emmanual Benaki 105, is at the base of Strefi Hill. It's a well-kept, clean hotel with bright airy, rooms and a roof terrace with plants and good views. The rooms cost 3200/4200 dr with shared bathrooms. Next door is the co-managed *Hotel Dryades* which has the same telephone numbers. It is also well kept and clean, with wood-panelled rooms costing 4200/6200 dr with private bathrooms. The friendly, courteous manager speaks English. To get to these hotels take bus No 230 from the west side of the National Gardens (south of Syntagma) or if you are feeling energetic, walk up Emmanual Benaki which runs east from

1	Kostoyiannis Taverna
2	Cafe
3	Museum Hotel
4	Hotel Dryades
5	Hotel Orian
6	Green Door Music Club
7	Ach Marie Club
8	AN Club
9	Cheap Café
10	Hotel Exarchion
11	Ouzeri I Gonia
12	Taverna Efimero
13	Ouzeri I Aegli
14	Neopolis Restaurant
15	Monasteri Restaurant
16	Dardovsovos Taverna
17	Taverna Ta Bakiria

Stadiou, just south of Omonia – but be warned it's a steep uphill trek.

Kypseli Athens' only *YHA Hostel* (☎ 822 5860) is at Kypselis 57. It's an OK hostel but quite a trek north from the centre, so telephone first to check if there's a bed. Dorm beds are 1200 dr. A IYHF membership card is required, but if you don't have one you can buy a day permit (500 dr) or join on the spot (2500 dr). The hostel does not have cooking facilities or a snack bar. There is a midnight curfew and the hostel is closed for cleaning between 10 am and 1.30 pm. It is open year round. Take trolley bus No 2, 4 or 9 from Syntagma to the Zakynthou stop.

Places to Stay – middle

Plaka The *Acropolis House Pension* (☎ 322 2344/6241), Kodrou 6-8, is a beautifully preserved, 19th-century mansion which retains many original features. The rooms are attractively furnished, spacious and centrally heated, and have air-con and 24-hour hot water. Singles/doubles/triples with private bathrooms are 5600/7600/9900 dr. Rooms with shared bathrooms are less attractive and cost 5400/7100/8800 dr. From Syntagma take the second turning left along Mitropoleos onto Voulis, and the hotel is on the right where Voulis becomes Kodrou. On the opposite side of Kodrou at No 3, the modern *Hotel Adonis* (☎ 324 9737/8) has comfortable rooms and a lovely roof garden, with splendid views. The rooms cost 6200/8000/10,300 dr with private bathrooms. The price includes breakfast.

The C class *Phoebus Hotel* (☎ 322 0142/3), Peta 12, has spacious immaculate rooms which are more reminiscent of an English country cottage than central Athens. The rates are 5800/7400/8800 dr with private bathrooms. Walk up Nikis, cross over Kidathineon, and you will see the hotel on the left.

The *Hotel Mytro* (☎ 322 7237 or 323 4560), Nikis 40, is another pleasant, mid-range option. Singles/doubles/triples/quads with private bathrooms are 6700/8300/10,300/12,200 dr. The owner speaks excellent English and is a tour guide, so is a mine of information on Athens. The hotel is on the right coming from Mitropoleos.

Veikou & Koukaki The *Acropolis View* (☎ 921 7303/4/5; fax 923 0705; telex 219 936), on the corner of Rovertou Galli and Webster 10, Veikou, has a beautiful location tucked into a quiet corner between Filopappos Hill and the Acropolis. The nicely furnished rooms have individually controlled air-con, balconies and telephones. The rates are 8200/10,900/13,000 dr with private bathrooms. A buffet breakfast is included in the price. There are stunning views from the roof terrace.

Just south of this hotel, the *Hotel Austria* (☎ 923 5151; fax 902 5800), Mouson 7, has comfortable rooms with balconies and telephones. The rates are 8700/10,900 dr for singles/doubles. There are free parking areas near these two hotels. To reach the hotels by public transport take bus No 230 from Syntagma, get off at the Theatre of Herodes Atticus, then cross over Dionysiou Areopagitou and walk south down Garivaldi.

At the other side of Veikou the C class *Hotel Hera* (☎ 923 6683/5618; telex 223 941), Falirou 9, is a modern hotel with a spacious lobby incorporating a coffee bar, TV lounge, breakfast room and French windows opening out onto a garden. There is also a roof garden with a snack bar. The tastefully furnished rooms have direct-dial telephones, a music system, air-con and central heating. During a very cold winter it was the warmest hotel I stayed at in Athens. The room rates are 8100/11,500/13,800 dr with private bathrooms. The hotel has a private indoor car park. Take trolley bus No 1, 5 or 9 and get off at the bottom of Makrygianni.

Around the Train Stations If you would like to stay near the train stations but want something more luxurious than a student hostel then the newly renovated *Crystal Hotel* (☎ 523 1083; telex 216 566 NIDO; fax 522 3755), Ahilleos 4, is a good-value, mid-range hotel. The comfortable, carpeted rooms have direct-dial telephone, radio, central heating and air-con. The rates, which include breakfast, are 7770/12,000/15,000 dr with private bathrooms. The hotel, which has a well-stocked bar, a TV corner and a restaurant which serves Greek and international dishes, is on Plateia Karaiskaki, which is west of Omonia and south of the train stations. Take trolley bus No 1 from the east side of Syntagma, or from outside the train stations.

The new *Oscar Hotel* (☎ 883 4215), on the corner of Samou and Filadelphias opposite Larissis Station, is a superior B class hotel which could easily pass for a deluxe one. The hotel has a bar, cafeteria, snack bar, restaurant, car park and rooftop garden with a small swimming pool. The rooms have air-con, telephones, stereo music and balconies; TV is available on request. The cost is 9300/13,400/16,600 dr (including breakfast); all rooms have private bathrooms and some have bathtubs.

Kolonaki This posh area predictably doesn't have any budget accommodation, or indeed, much accommodation at all. If you can afford it, it is a very agreeable place to stay, as it's away from the the hustle and bustle of the centre, and very near the many museums on Vasilissis Sofias.

The B class *Athenian Inn* (☎ 723 8097/ 9552/8756; telex 224 092 INN GR; fax 721 5614), Haritos 22, is a small but distinguished place, which was reputably a favourite of Lawrence Durrell. It's on a quiet street in the heart of Kolonaki, and has a cosy, friendly intimacy which is often lacking in hotels of this category. The rooms are unpretentious but comfortable with air-con and pretty pictures of island scenes on the walls. The cost, which includes breakfast, is 11,000/14,500/17,900 dr. Haritos is five blocks north of Vasilissis Sofias, and just north-east of Plateia Kolonakiou. You can take bus No 023 from opposite the Parliament Building on Vasilissis Sofias.

Places to Stay – top end

If you are wealthy then *the* place to stay in Athens is, and always has been, the deluxe *Hotel Grande Bretagne* (☎ 322 5312; telex 219 615; fax 322 8034), on Syntagma. It ranks amongst the most famous and grand hotels in the world and is the only Athens' hotel with a rich history (see the Walking Tour section earlier). It has undergone much expansion since it first became a hotel in 1872 and is constantly being renovated, but still has an old-world grandeur. The elegantly furnished rooms have air-con, minibar, satellite TV and video and there is 24-hour room service. The rates are 34,900/ 41,700 dr for singles/doubles. Children under 12 years of age sharing their parents' room may stay free of charge.

St George Lycabettus Hotel (☎ 729 0711; telex 214 253; fax 729 0439), Kleomenous 2, has a prime location at the foot of Lykavitos Hill. It's a deluxe hotel, but has only 150 rooms, so prides itself on being friendlier and having a personal touch. The rooms are spacious and light, with minibars, local and satellite TV and large windows and balconies.

Prices, which depend on the view from the window, start from 16,500/21,000/26,300 dr. The price includes a buffet breakfast.

Despite its small size it has all the facilities you would expect of a luxury hotel. The hotel is directly north of Plateia Kolonakiou, at the western end of Kleomenous and is on the No 023 bus route from Vasilissis Sofias.

The *Athens Hilton* (☎ 722 0201; telex 215 808; fax 721 3110) is just east of Kolonaki at Vasilissis Sofias 46, in the district of Ilissia. This vast concrete edifice, at the junction of Vasilissis Sofias and Vasileos Konstantinou, is not particularly appealing, but, once inside, nothing has been spared in expense and aesthetics. It has lashings of marble and bronze, public areas with enormous chandeliers and carpets which were especially designed by eminent Greek artists. The room rates are US$208/242 a single/double and suites cost from US$412. There is no charge for children, regardless of their age, sharing a room with their parents.

The deluxe *Athens Ledra Marriott* (☎ 934 7711; telex 223 465 MAR GR; fax 935 8603) is at Syngrou 115, in the district of Kallithea, south of Koukaki. It drips with opulence and gets top marks for its premier chandelier – the largest I've ever seen, but maybe I just haven't stayed in enough deluxe hotels. Each room has colour TV with in-house films, direct-dial telephone, individual thermostat-controlled air-con, 24-hour room service and soundproofing. The rates are US$260/280 a single/double for deluxe rooms and U$200/ 220 for standard rooms. There is a rooftop swimming pool, four bars, three restaurants – one, the Koria Kai serves Poly- nesian, Cantonese and Japanese food. The hotel is some way out of the centre at Syngrou 115 – 10 minutes' drive south of Syntagma.

The posh leafy suburb of Kifissia has a number of luxury hotels. The A class *Theoxenia Hotel* (☎ 801 2751/65) on the corner of Filadelfeos and Kolokotroni has a taverna, restaurant and a swimming pool. Singles/ doubles cost 10,000/13,800 dr.

The A class *Semiramis Hotel* (☎ 808 8101), Harilaou Trikoupi 48, has a restaurant, disco and swimming pool. Rates are 17,000/23,250 dr.

The A class *Grand Chalet* (☎ 808 4837/

8/9), Kokinara 38, is similarly endowed and has rates of 24,300/27,100 dr.

The deluxe *Pentelikon Hotel* (☎ 808 0311; fax 801 0314), Deligianni 66, is an exquisite place built in traditional style with a swimming pool and a lovely garden. All of the beautifully furnished rooms have minibars and satellite TVs. Rates are 42,000/48,100 dr for singles/doubles and suites are 115,000 dr; breakfast is a staggering 5100 dr.

PLACES TO EAT

Plaka is the area which springs most readily to mind when tourists contemplate eating out in Athens. Indeed, it does have good restaurants in all price ranges, which are patronised as much by locals as by tourists. But it also has some establishments which pander exclusively to the tourist trade. In these places the food tends to be bland and mediocre, the portions are skimpy and the prices high. You'll be serenaded by bouzouki players, whose rendering of rembetika songs is often an antiseptic watered-down travesty of the genuine thing, and their gratuity will come out of your bill. These places are pretty easy to spot, for, apart from the bouzouki players, they will have waiters at their entrances who try just that bit too hard to lure you into their establishments.

Nothing quite matches the picturesqueness of Plaka for outdoor eating in summer, but every neighbourhood of Athens has its good eating places. These are often small friendly unpretentious tavernas in obscure little streets, which have been in the same family for generations. Pangrati, Veikou, Koukaki, Exarhia and the area around the train stations are all promising neighbourhoods to explore and to find places, which, in the absence of other tourists, will make you feel that you've made a personal discovery.

Places to Eat – bottom end

Plaka, Syntagma & Monastiraki Plaka's restaurants range from very expensive to workers' cafés. Monastiraki is a good place for cheap giros; the last block of Mitropoleos

before Plateia Monastirakiou is lined with cafés selling this fare. Syntagma consists mostly of expensive patisseries.

Peristeria Taverna, Patroou 5, serves traditional Greek dishes. Chicken with potatoes, moussaka and meatballs are all 650 dr and draught retsina is 450 dr. Most evenings you will be serenaded by a singing guitarist, with the songs become increasingly maudlin as the evening progresses, but who cares after a few retsinas. In summer the tables spill out onto the car park opposite. To reach Patroou, walk along Mitropoleos from Syntagma and turn left onto Patroou.

Nearby, the old-fashioned milk shop, at Apollonos 11, is one of my favourite places in Athens for breakfast or a snack. Its homemade cheese-and-spinach pie is unbeatable in quality and costs 300 dr for a generous slice. Delicious gooey cakes, home-made rice pudding and yoghurt are similarly priced and excellent cappuccino is 200 dr. The shop is open from 6.30 am to 9 pm Monday to Saturday, and until 2 pm on Sunday. Apollonos is one block south of Mitropoleos.

Kidathineon has a large choice of eateries. Walking in a westerly direction from Nikis, just beyond the Greek Folk Art Museum, is the cellar restaurant at Kidathineon 21, Plaka. The restaurant is rough and ready and always packed. Tasty stewed meat-and-vegetable dishes are 700 dr and draught retsina is 250 dr. The restaurant is open in the evenings only, and is closed during June, July and August. A little further along, on the right, on the corner of Moni Asteriou, is another cellar restaurant (called *The Cellar*). Prices are similar to those at No 21. Nearby, the milk shop at No 10 is a good place for breakfast.

Of the tavernas on Plateia Plakas, *O Kostis*, Kidathineon 18, has the tastiest and most reasonably priced food. Stuffed tomatoes are 550 dr, moussaka is 750 dr and lamb with potatoes is 850 dr. *To Kosmikon*, on the corner of Kidathineon and Adrianou, is an unpretentious psistaria with delicious eggplant salad, taramosalata and tzatziki for 350 dr, chicken, pork and beef shish kebabs are 750 dr and a generous giros is 800 dr. Next door, at No 30, the milk shop is another good place for a low-priced breakfast.

Opposite, at No 41, the lively atmospheric *Taverna Damigos* claims to be the oldest taverna in Plaka. It was opened in 1865 by the Damigos family and framed family photographs bedeck the walls. Its speciality is bakaliarakia (950 dr) which is deep-fried cod served with skordalia (garlic sauce). The fish – salted cod, imported from Iceland – was once a luxury of the poor, but is now regarded as a tasty dish for everyone. The milk shop next door, at No 43, has delicious takeaway crepes: savoury ones cost from 350 to 500 dr and sweet ones are 230 to 350 dr.

To Gerani Ouzeri, Tripodon 14, is one of Plaka's most genuine eateries, with an oak-beamed ceiling, marble tables and wicker chairs. There is also a terrace. It specialises in mezedes which are brought to you on a tray for you take your pick: dolmades and kalamaria are both 500 dr, flaming sausages are 600 dr and draught red retsina is 400 dr. The ouzeri is open for lunch and dinner. To get there, walk along Thespidos, which is the westerly continuation of Kidathineon, and turn right onto Tripodon.

If you continue along Tripodon, and turn right at the crossroads, you will come to *Eden Vegetarian Restaurant*, Flessa 3, one of only two vegetarian restaurants in Athens (for details of the other see Omonia, Places to Eat – bottom end). Imaginative dishes are created with mushrooms, spinach, avocados and lots more. Soya chilli con carne is 800 dr, soya moussaka is 750 dr and spinach pie with feta cheese is 550 dr. The restaurant has a welcoming open fire in winter and a rooftop garden in summer. It is open from noon to midnight.

Syntrivani Restaurant, Filellinon 5, is a tranquil oasis, entered by a long passageway which takes you away from the busy street outside. In summer there is a delightful garden with a fountain *(syntrivani* means 'fountain'). The menu is extensive and prices are reasonable. Moussaka, meatballs and dolmades are all 800 dr. The restaurant is open from 11 am to 10 pm in winter and till midnight in summer.

Epic Restaurant, Nikis 46, is a pleasant, unassuming place which specialises in grilled meats and fish. Chicken is 600 dr, sardines are 500 dr, and lamb chops are 1000 dr. The little milk shop at Nikis 26 is another good breakfast place where you can get fried eggs for 120 dr, yoghurt for 140 dr, and Nescafé for 130 dr.

Ipiros Taverna, at Filippou 16 in the Flea Market, has cheap tasty food. The outdoor tables in summer are great for watching the market's hustle and bustle.

Another old Athens taverna with loads of atmosphere is the cavernous *Sigalas Taverna*, Plateia Monastirakiou 2. The taverna, established in 1879, has huge barrels of retsina lining its walls. Tzatziki, aubergine dip and taramosalata are all 270 dr, and moussaka and stuffed tomatoes are both 620 dr. The taverna is open from 6 am to 2 am every day. To get there walk west along Mitropoleos and turn right onto Plateia Monastirakiou and it's on the right – it's the building with the four old-fashioned, wrought-iron lamps outside.

Lastly in this area *O Marias Taverna*, Christokoridou 3, is rough and ready and in the most run-down part of town, but the food is good and cheap. Meatballs are 500 dr and chicken and chips are 550 dr. Walk west along Ermou from Monistaraki and turn right at the Pella Inn, then take the first left and you'll see the restaurant on the left.

Veikou & Koukaki These two areas have some lovely, authentic neighbourhood tavernas and restaurants. The milk shop at Veikou 77 has a good selection of cakes for between 200 and 300 dr.

One of the cheapest restaurants in the area is *Restaurant Gardenia*, Zini 31, Koukaki, on the corner of Dimitrakopoulou. Grilled sardines are 500 dr, chicken casserole is 650 dr and stifado is 700 dr. On the opposite side of the road *Melteni Ouzeri*, Zini 26, is a lovely place with white, stucco walls, marble-topped tables and blue-painted wooden chairs, all of which give the place a Cycladic-island feel. In summer, an outside eating area is shielded from the traffic by large pot plants. There is a choice of 40 delicious mezedes dishes and a mixed plate of five or six costs between 800 and 900 dr.

To 38 Taverna, Veikou 38, is another good-value establishment. When I went there I had the most expensive item on the menu, which was a very generous helping of crispy fried cod, which cost 800 dr. The restaurant is lively, rough and ready and very popular. There is no name on the door, and it's on the premises of a barber's shop; facing the barber's shop, it is the door to the left. It is open every evening from 8 pm, but closes from 1 June to 15 September.

Cabana Restaurant, Petmeza 5, is a reasonably priced restaurant and grill between Falirou and Syngrou. It has a good choice of vegetarian dishes. *To Sokaki Psistaria*, Argyriou 6, is one of the nicest psistaria in the area. Tzatziki, taramosalata and aubergine salad are all 300 dr, grilled chicken is 600 dr, other grilled meats are 900 dr, retsina is 250 dr and Amstel is 200 dr. Walking west along Veikou it's up an alleyway to the right.

There is no shortage of grocers and greengrocers in Veikou and Koukaki. There's a well-stocked delicatessen at Veikou 47 and a good bakery next door at No 45.

Mets & Pangrati One of my favourite places to go in Athens for coffee and cake is the *Pnika Zaharoplasteion*, Syngrou 1, just south of the Temple of Zeus. It is spotlessly clean and the fact that it is completely untouristy is reflected in the prices and unadorned interior. Just south of here on the other side of busy Vasileos Konstantinou *Parnassos Restaurant*, Menehmou 2, is a large, clean, honest-to-goodness Greek restaurant with no concessions to tourists; it's a popular lunch-time venue with mechanics from the nearby garages on Syngrou. Dishes are typical Greek fare (mostly casseroles) and a filling meal with beer or retsina will cost between 1200 and 1500 dr.

O Megaritis Taverna is a lovely, bright cheery taverna with a glowing old-fashioned stove in winter, and a roof garden in summer; it has been run by the Megaritis family for around 100 years. The food is superb; dolmades in a thick piquant lemon sauce, meatballs in tomato sauce and stifado are all 800 dr. Walk a little way along Arhimidous from Plateia Plastira, and turn left at O Virinis Taverna; O Megaritis Taverna is next door. *O Virinis Taverna* is also commendable and just slightly more expensive. You can take trolley bus No 2, 4 or 11 from the west side of Syntagma to Plateia Plastira.

On Markou Mousourou in Mets there is a butcher, a greengrocer and an excellent bakery at No 26 which sells very good spinach-and-cheese pies. There's a *laiki agora* (common market) on Arhimidous on a Friday.

Omonia Athens' second vegetarian restaurant, which is really more of a snack bar, is below the Greek Ecology Party offices at Panepistimiou 57. The food is delicious and amazingly good value. Large portions of wholemeal pizzas, cheese pies and spinach pies are 300 dr; main dishes, which are mostly vegetable stews served with brown rice, are 500 dr. It is hectic downstairs, but peaceful upstairs. At the back of the snack bar there is a well-stocked health-food shop.

The *Athens Meat Market*, on Aristogitonos, between Athinas and Eolou, must resemble a vegetarian's vision of hell, with carcasses of every animal fit for human consumption hanging from hooks. However, adventurous carnivores should try one of the tavernas here. Most are open 24 hours, except Sunday. They serve traditional meat dishes such as patsas (tripe soup), podarakia (pig-trotter soup) as well as more prosaic meat stews such as stifado and meatballs. The dishes cost between 500 and 1000 dr.

Café Brettania, Plateia Omonias, on the corner of Athinas, is one of the nicest things about Omonia: it's the perfect place for breakfast or a snack. The décor is pleasant, with marble tables and wrought-iron chairs, the food is great and the waiters are courteous. It has a large variety of beverages: cappuccino is 350 dr and soft drinks are 200 dr. The café is open 24 hours and free entertainment is provided by the clientele who get more and more weird as the night progresses.

On the other side of Omonia, the *Neon Café*, in a beautiful neoclassical building, used to be a rough-and-ready joint frequented by chain-smoking, card-playing old men. It has been completely refurbished and is now an up-market, self-service cafeteria with a pleasing décor of pastel walls, moulded ceilings, chequered floor and marble tables. It is probably the only eating place in Athens with a no-smoking area. The salad bar has a choice of 20 ingredients: a mixed salad plate is 610 dr. Pastas with a good choice of sauces are 880 dr and fish is 900 dr.

Exarhia In Exarhia the clientele in the tavernas are, not surprisingly, mostly students, with a smattering of professors and other academic and arty-looking people. Many of these tavernas are in spruced-up, neoclassical buildings. There is also a good number of trendy ouzeria in the area.

If you fancy a snack before visiting the National Archaeological Museum, the café at Bouboulinas 34 behind the museum has a mixed meze plate for two for 800 dr and toasted sandwiches with a large choice of fillings for between 200 and 300 dr. The café is closed on Sunday. There are lots of other cafés and fast-food places in Exarhia, where you can grab a giros or souvlaki. West of the square and still near the museum, the café at Soultani 13, on the corner of Solomou, has a 'greasy spoon' image, but serves tasty food. The café is open from noon to 11.30 pm and is closed on Sunday.

Exarhia also has a good choice of more up-market tavernas. *Dardovsovos Taverna*, Isavron 29B, is at the eastern extremity of Exarhia. The food here is some of the most scrumptious I've tasted in Athens. The taverna elevates even the humble fried potato to gastronomic heights, serving it thin, crisp and golden. The chicken casserole with mushrooms is highly commendable at 800 dr; retsina is 300 dr. The restaurant is open from 8.30 pm to 1 am (closed on Sunday). To get there, it's either a long trek up Harilaou Trikoupi from Akadimias and then turn right after No 110, or you can take

bus No 230 from Syntagma and get off at the Kaladroumou stop.

The crumbling plaster walls, marble-top tables, raffia chairs and polished-wood floorboards add up to a very attractive ambience at *Taverna Efimero*, Methonis 58. Mezedes range in price from 250 to 400 dr each. Main courses are also very good and range from 800 to 1000 dr.

Nearby the *Ouzeri I Aegli*, Methonis 43, has a cheery interior. There is a large choice of mezedes ranging in price from 400 to 600 dr; main courses are from 800 to 1000 dr. There is outdoor eating in a little garden in summer. *Ouzeri I Gonia*, Arahovis 59, on the corner of Emmanual Benaki, has pretty décor and a good range of tasty meze dishes priced between 350 and 750 dr; ouzo is 350 dr a bottle.

Taverna Ta Bakiria, Mavromihali 119, has a lovely traditional décor with brass and copper trays and ceramic dishes hanging on the walls. It has a good choice of grilled meats, and very tasty casseroles delicately flavoured with herbs and wine, ranging from 900 to 1100 dr. *Neopolis Restaurant*, Zoodochou Pigis 72, on the corner of Kalidromiou, is a large restaurant with a huge choice of typical Greek dishes. Lamb with potatoes is 800 dr and beef with aubergines is 900 dr.

For self-caterers there are lots of greengrocers, grocers and butchers on just about every street in Exarhia and the large supermarket at Harilaou Trikoupi 113 takes all major credit cards. There is a good bakery at Emmanual Benaki 64 and a laiki agora on Kalidromiou on Saturday.

Around the Train Stations Wherever you choose to eat in these areas you will find the lack of tourist hype refreshing; it's a million miles from the strategically placed menus and restaurant touts of Plaka.

Just north of Plateia Vathis *O Vaggelis Taverna*, Liossion 21 (the entrance is round the corner on Sahini), is an honest-to-goodness, unpretentious traditional taverna which serves tasty meat-and-vegetable stews at low prices and draught red retsina for 250 dr.

There is outdoor eating in a garden in summer.

Further north *Dafni Taverna*, Ioulianou 65, has a rustic ambience and an outdoor eating in a walled garden in summer.

Taverna I Kriti, Didymou 30 (off Alkiviadou), is a pleasant neighbourhood taverna patronised by locals of all ages; it's a good choice for a quiet, relaxed evening. Tzatziki, taramosalata and aubergine dip are all 350 dr, grilled meats are between 750 and 1000 dr. The psistaria, Psaron 48 (opposite the church on Plateia Pavlou), serves tasty, herb-flavoured beef souvlaki for 900 dr, roast chicken for 650 dr and draught retsina for 350 dr.

There is a large supermarket at Psaron 41 and loads of greengrocers, grocers, fish and butcher shops in the area. There is a laiki agora on Psaron on Wednesday, and another one on Alkamenous on Saturday.

Places to Eat – middle

Plaka, Syntagma & Monastiraki This area has some atmospheric teashops, coffee shops and patisseries which are not by any means cheap, but are nice places to go for a treat.

Tristato Café, in Plaka on the corner of Dedalou and Angelou Geronta, is a 1920s-style coffee shop which is very popular with young Athenians and has a good atmosphere. Filter coffee is 350 dr and cheesecake and chocolate cake are both 450 dr. *Floca*, on Panepistimiou (in the arcade) near Syntagma, is the most central of this chain of coffee-and-pastry shops. The first Floca opened in Athens in 1939, and there are now 14 of them in the city. Greek coffee is 350 dr, filter coffee is 485 dr, croissants 400 dr, baklava 450 dr and Western-style cakes between 500 and 600 dr. Nearby, the *Brazilian*, Voukourestiou (between Panepistimiou and Stadiou) is another popular and long-established coffee shop, with prices and fare similar to Floca. The same goes for *Zonar's* at Panepistimiou 9.

Taverna Theofilos, Vakhou 4, is another Plaka restaurant of long standing, having opened in the early 1940s. It's a cosy little place with walls like blackboards, which are completely covered with graffiti. A large, striped tom cat adds to the charm. Tzatziki and fava (chick-pea dip) are both delicious. A three-course meal will cost between 2000 to 2500 dr per person. To reach the taverna, from the Monument of Lysikrates take the first turning right off Vironos.

Apotsos Ouzeri, Panepistimiou 10 (in an arcade opposite Zonar's), is Athens' oldest ouzeri having opened in 1900. It is a popular lunch-time venue with journalists and politicians. It has a large choice of mezedes ranging in price from 400 to 1000 dr. The ouzeri is only open at lunch times: Monday to Friday from 11 am to 5 pm, Saturday from 11 am to 4 pm (it's closed Sunday).

Veikou If you are a Floca fan then there is a *Floca* coffee shop at Veikou 1. Just a short walk from Dionysiou Areopagitou *Socrates Prison*, Mitseon 20, is a delightful restaurant with an Art Nouveau interior and 19th-century Parisian posters on the walls; there is outdoor eating in a garden in summer. The restaurant is not named after the philosopher, but after the owner, whose name is also Socrates, and who reckons the restaurant is his prison. There is a choice of 14 meze dishes ranging in price from 200 to 550 dr. Main dishes range from 800 to 1300 dr. The restaurant is closed from 10 to 31 August.

To Dichty, near the corner of Veikou and Olympiou 2, is an up-market ouzeri with a nautical bent: fishing nets and lifebuoys hang on the walls. It has a large selection of wonderfully imaginative mezedes such as mussels with fried cheese (900 dr) and kalamaria in red wine (650 dr). To reach Olympiou walk south-west along Veikou and turn left.

Mets & Pangrati Over in Mets, *Manesis Taverna*, Markou Mousourou 3, is another very attractive taverna with an imaginative menu. Inside, the white stucco walls are graced with ceramic plates and large, heavily framed mirrors. There is eating in a garden in summer, which the Egyptian manager, Halim, tells me is the most beautiful garden in Athens, but as I have only eaten here in a snowy February, I can't vouch for this.

There are two fixed-price menus. Menu A costs 2200 dr and consists of a meze plate followed by a main dish then fresh fruit. Menu B costs 2000 dr and is a meze-only plate, followed by fruit for dessert. Red house wine is included in both menus. The taverna is on the left walking south along Markou Mousourou.

Café Odeon, Markou Mousourou 19, is the nearest I've found in Athens to a Parisian café, probably because Alegos the owner is married to a French woman. Cappuccino is 400 dr, espresso coffee is 280 dr, soft drinks are 250 dr, ouzo is 300 dr, Heineken 350 dr, spirits 750 dr and cocktails 1000 dr. You can enjoy your drink while listening to jazz tapes. The café is open from 10 am to 2 am everyday. Take trolley bus No 2, 4 or 11 from Syntagma and get off at the Stadium stop for Markou Mousourou.

Oikogeneiaki Taverna, Pratinou 5, Pangrati, has some unusual dishes which you will not find in the average taverna. They include snails stewed with onions and herbs and spicy sausages in a stew. A filling meal with beverage will cost between 2000 and 2500 dr. To reach the taverna take trolley bus No 2, 4 or 11 to Plateia Plastira, walk east along Elthidou and turn left onto Pratinou.

Exarhia *Kostoyiannis Taverna*, Zaimi 37, near the National Archaeological Museum, is a long-time favourite with well-heeled Athenians. It's a large restaurant with a tasteful décor. Prices range from 1100 to 1500 dr.

Places to Eat – top end

Following is a selection of Athens' top-end, blow-the-budget restaurants. The resort of Glyfada also has a range of top-end restaurants. See under the Coast Road to Sounion section later in this chapter.

Plaka & Syntagma Athens has a number of oriental restaurants, but there are two which are favourites with the city's expatriate Japanese.

One of these is *Michiko Japanese Restau-*

rant, Kidathineon 27, which is housed in Plaka's largest surviving mansion. It has a shady front garden featuring lanterns and an ornamental pool. Starters range from 600 to 1400 dr, sushi dishes are 3000 dr and bento dishes are 4000 dr. The other one is the *Far East Restaurant*, Stadiou 7, which has a spacious, elegant oriental interior and serves Korean, Japanese and Chinese cuisine. Appetisers include steamed meat dumpling (950 dr) and spring rolls (950 dr). Main courses include satay beef (2700 dr) and lemon duck (2650 dr). The restaurant has a large selection of imported and Greek non-resinated wines starting at 2600 dr.

Ideal Restaurant, Panepistimiou 46 (next to the Ideal Cinema), is a long-established favourite with Athenians and has been rebuilt after a devastating fire. The interior is Art Deco and the menu is a mixture of Greek, Turkish and European dishes. The average price for a full meal with beverage is 4000 dr.

The *GB Corner*, at the Hotel Grande Bretagne, serves international and Greek cuisine, including Hungarian goulash and Athenian tripe soup. A full meal will cost about 6000 dr.

Veikou South of the Acropolis *Symposia Restaurant* (☎ 922 3521), Erehthiou 46, in a restored 1920s house, is one of Athens' most elegant restaurants. There is a large selection of Greek wines. Only come here if you are rich or have something very special to celebrate – a full meal with beverage will set you back from 8000 to 9000 dr. It is recommended that you make a reservation.

Kifissia If you want to do serious damage to your credit cards you could head for the posh northern suburb of Kifissia where there are many up-market restaurants. As it's quite a trek out here telephone first to find out if a restaurant is open, and whether a reservation is required.

At all the ones listed here you'll pay between 4000 and 8000 dr for a full meal.

The *Blue Pine Restaurant* (☎ 807 7745), Tsaldari 37, has an interesting and varied menu including sweetbreads, eggplant dumplings and curries. The *Belle Helene* (☎ 806 7994), Poleologou 1, specialises in steak and fish dishes. The restaurant is in an attractive park.

Lotofagos (☎ 801 3201), Agios Lavras 4, has a buffet of international dishes. The restaurant is behind the underground station. *Moustakas* (☎ 801 4584), on the corner of Harilaou and Trikoupi, serves traditional Greek fare.

Ilissia & Kallithea The Athens Hilton, in the district of Ilissia, just east of Kolonaki, has several restaurants. Its *Ta Nissia Restaurant*, which specialises in mezedes and fish dishes, is very popular with well-heeled Athenians. Dinner here will cost around 6000 dr. You will pay a similar price at the *Kona Kia* at the Athens Ledra Marriott, in the district of Kallithea, south of Koukaki. This is a Polynesian restaurant complete with a waterfall.

ENTERTAINMENT
Cinema

Athenians are avid cinema-goers and it's not such a bad idea for travellers to attend cinemas either, as they are cheaper here than in northern European capitals and just as comfortable. Most cinemas show British and US recent releases in their original language. The two areas with the highest concentration of cinemas are the main streets running between Syntagma and Omonia and the Patission and Plateia Amerikis area.

The major cinemas in central Athens are the *Apollon* (☎ 323 6811), Stadiou 19; *Astor* (☎ 323 1297), Stadiou 28; *Ally* (☎ 363 2789), Akadimias 64; *Ideal* (☎ 362 6720), Panepistimiou 46; *Asty* (☎ 322 1925), Koria 4; and *Titania* (☎ 361 1147), on the corner of Panepistimiou and Themistokleous. The Asty shows mostly avant-garde films; the Titania shows second-run films from 10 am to 10 pm. The others show mostly first-run films (usually British or US, with Greek subtitles). Shows start at approximately 7, 9 and 11 pm.

Outside the central area the *Ilion* (☎ 881 0602), on the corner of Troias 34 and 28 Oktovriou-Patission, shows foreign-language (ie not English or Greek) films which are often cult or avant-garde. The *Greek Cinema Club* (☎ 361 2046), Kanaris 1, Kolonaki, regularly shows avant-garde films, both Greek and international. The Ideal Cinema, which is the most luxurious cinema, with the best sound system, often has an after-midnight show on Saturday. All the major cinemas have listings in the *Athens News* and *Weekly Greek News*. Admission costs are between 600 and 800 dr.

Most of the indoor cinemas close from the end of May to mid-September. In summer they are replaced with outdoor cinemas which tend to change location every year. New films are not shown in these cinemas, so you can see old favourites again. Going to the outdoor cinema tends to be a social occasion more than anything, so there's a lot of audience noise. There are two showings per evening: the early show starts around dusk and the late show about 11 pm.

Theatre

Athens has a dynamic theatre scene, but naturally most performances are in Greek. If you are a theatre buff you may enjoy a performance of an old favourite, provided you know the play well enough. *The Week in Athens* has a cursory listing, but the listings in the *Athenian* are more comprehensive. They both state when a performance is in English – which happens occasionally.

Greek Folk Dancing

In summer, performances of Greek folk dances are given by the Dora Stratou Dance Company at their own theatre (☎ 921 4659) on Filopappos Hill. The company was formed many years ago and has gained an international reputation for authenticity and professionalism. Performances are held nightly at 10.15 pm from May to October. Tickets may be bought at the door and cost 1500 dr. The theatre is signposted from the western end of Dionysiou Areopagitou.

Concerts & Contemporary Dance

There are frequent classical-music concerts, by both international and Greek performers, at the *Athens Concert Hall* (☎ 722 1164), Vasilissis Sofias (next to the US Embassy). Occasional dance performances and jazz concerts are also given here. Classical-music concerts are performed at the *Pallas Theatre* (☎ 322 4434), Voukourestiou 1, and operas are performed at the *National Opera* (Ethniki Lyriki Skene) (☎ 361 2461), Akadimias 59. Dance performances are also given at the *Athens College Theatre* (☎ 647 4676), Stefanou Delta, Psyhiko.

If anything big is happening, posters will be displayed, and tickets will be for sale at the box office at Stadiou 4. The English-language newspapers and the *Athenian* publish listings.

Sound & Light Show

Athens' endeavour at this spectacle is not one of the world's best, but it is an enduring and integral part of the Athens tourist scene, so if you don't want to miss it, here is the information. Performances in English, French and German take place every evening from the beginning of April until the end of October on the Hill of the Pnyx (☎ 322 1459). During the performance lights are played onto the monuments of the Acropolis to an accompanying historical narration, music and sound effects. The lights are the most exciting part of the performance. Check at the EOT for times of the English-language performances. Tickets cost 1000 dr. You can either walk along Dionysiou Areopagitou or take bus No 230.

Music Bars

Although most of the following recommendations are too small to warrant being called discos, most have a dance floor of sorts. One of the most central is *Oggies Bar*, Filellinon 17, where there is an English DJ who plays Western pop. There is no cover charge and beer is 500 dr, spirits 800 dr and cocktails 1100 dr. Close by and similarly priced is *Disco Absolute* at Filellinon 23. Further south, *Steven's Pub*, Dionysiou Areopagitou

3 on the corner of Tziteon, is a good place to meet other travellers. Draught beer is 400 dr a pint and cocktails are 800 dr. Western pop music is played and there's a small dance floor.

Over in Mets, *Stadio*, on the corner of Markou Mousourou and Ardittou, is a favoured venue of Athenian sophisticates. There's an outside roof terrace in summer with good views of the Acropolis. There's no cover charge but drinks are expensive. In Kolonaki *The Cave*, Haritos 6, looks like a real cave with a few strategically placed helmets for added authenticity. Music is techno and jazz only. Cocktails are 800 dr and beer is 500 dr.

The highest concentration of music bars is in Exarhia. The *Green Door Music Club*, Kalidromiou 52, is one of the most popular with Athens' students. There's no name on the door but it is next to the periptero on the left, as you walk south along Kalidromiou. There are several other music bars on Kalidromiou, between Zosimadou and Zoodochou Pigis; just walk along flapping your ears and enter whichever one takes your fancy.

If you want to hear some good music without having your eardrums perforated and have a conversation at the same time, then try the *Passenger Club*, 1st Floor, Mavromihali 168. The music is mellow (mostly jazz and R&B), with no hard rock or heavy metal. Cocktails are 1000 to 1200 dr, spirits and beer 700 dr. The nearby *Enalax Club*, Mavromihali 139, is another friendly place. It plays a wide variety of music including jazz, rembetika and Greek folk music. Cocktails are 750 dr. The club is closed during June, July and August.

Gay Bars

A popular bar with gays (male) is *Alexander Club*, Anagnostopoulou 44, Kolonaki. It's a relaxed, friendly place and is open every night from 9 pm to 2 am throughout the year. Another popular gay bar is *Granazi Bar*, Lembesi 20, which is south of Hadrian's Arch and east of Syngrou.

Discos

Discos proper are mostly out towards the airport and function only in summer. One exception is *Disco Easy Way*, Imitou 219, where you can hear loud Western rock music. If you're over 25 you may feel geriatric here. Cocktails and spirits are 1000 dr and soft drinks are 500 dr. There is no cover charge. The disco is closed from May to September. To get there, walk south along Markou Mousourou, turn left onto Imitou and it's a little way along on the right, or you can take trolley bus No 4. Two of the most popular and enduring of the discos near the airport (East terminal) are *Aerodhromio* which has an open-air dance floor and is opposite the international airport and *Akrotiri* on Odos Kosmasi also near the airport. At these places you can expect to pay at least 3000 dr for admission which includes the first drink.

Live Music

The best place to hear international bands is the *Rodon Club* (☎ 524 7427), Marni 24. Good places to hear live rock music by Greek bands are the *Ach Maria Club* (☎ 363 9217), Solomou 20 and the *AN Club*, Solomou 13-15, in Exarhia. If anything exciting is going on at any of these places you'll see posters all over Exarhia. Big concerts are listed in the *Weekly Greek News*.

Rembetika Clubs

Athens has a good number of rembetika clubs, but most close down from May to September. Performances in these clubs start at around 11.30 pm; most do not have a cover charge but drinks are expensive – often as much as 3000 dr. Clubs open up and close down with great rapidity – telephone to check if a club is still open. The biggest concentration of clubs is in and around Exarhia.

Taxima (☎ 363 9919), Isavron 29, is a well-established, friendly club in a traditionally furnished neoclassical house. Past performers include Vassilis Yianissis (violin) Dimitris Anagnostopoulos (bouzouki), Areti Bellou (guitar) and Babis Goles (vocal). The club is closed on Sunday. *Rembetiki Istoria*

(☎ 642 4937), Ippokratous 181, is also popular and plays host to some top musicians. The club is closed on Monday.

Frangosyriani (☎ 360 0693), Arahovis 57, has the reputation of being one of the most authentic clubs. Nikos Argyropoulos & Company is the group which performs most often here. It is closed on Thursday. *Kavouras* (☎ 361 0202), Themistokleous 64, is another club in a neoclassical house. It is closed on Sunday. *Minore* (☎ 823 8630), Notara 34, is popular with young people and there's lots of dancing. It closes on Monday.

A more central club is the newly opened *Rembetiki Stoa Athanaton* (☎ 321 4362), Sofokleous 19, in the central meat market. Unusually for a rembetika club, it is open afternoons from 3 to 6 pm and reopens at midnight until 6 am. Hondronakos and Koulis Skarpelis perform here. It is closed on Sunday.

Spectator Sports

Football Of the 18 teams in the Greek First Division Football League, six are in Athens. They are Aek, Apollon, Ethnikos, Olympiakos, Panathinaikos and Panionios. Aeks play at the Nea Philadelphia Stadium; Apollon at Rizoupolis; Athinikos at Vasileos Georgiou 39, Piraeus; Panionios at Nea Smyrni; and Panathinaikos at the Athens Stadium, Leoforos Alexandras 160, just north of Lykavitos Hill. Olympiakos plays at the Karaiskaki Stadium in Piraeus. Matches are played on Wednesday and Sunday and are often televised. Entry to a match costs an average of 1200 dr. The football season lasts from September to the middle of May. Fixtures and results are given in the *Weekly Greek News*.

Horse Racing Horse racing takes place at the Faliro Race Course on Syngrou. Ring ☎ 941 7761 to find out when meetings take place.

THINGS TO BUY
Flea Market

This market is the first place which springs to most people's minds when they think of buying things in Athens. The Flea Market is a commercial area which stretches both east and west of Plateia Monastirakiou and consists of shops selling goods running the whole gamut from high quality to trash. However, when most people speak of the Athens Flea Market, they are referring to the outdoor flea market which takes place on a Sunday morning. This market spills over into Plateia Monastirakiou and all the way down Ermou to the entrance to the Keramikos.

A visit to Athens isn't complete without a visit to this market. It's good fun, so long as you don't mind being jostled by crowds, hooted at by cars and motorbikes, having your aesthetic sensitivities assaulted and not finding the bargain of the week. All manner of things are on sale – new, second-hand, third-hand and fourth-hand. There's everything from clocks to condoms, binoculars to bouzoukis, tyres to telephones, giant evil eyes to jelly babies and wigs to welding kits. Wandering around the market you'll soon realise that Greece is top of the league of European countries when it comes to mass-produced kitsch. If you're looking for a plastic jewellery box with a psychedelic picture of the Virgin Mary on the lid, which plays 'Never on a Sunday' when you open it, you might just be in luck at the Flea Market.

Flokati Rugs

Most of Athens' flokati-rug shops are on or around Mitropoleos. Karamichos Mazarakis Flokati, Voulis 31-33, has the largest selection. Before you commit yourself look at the back of the rug, as the best ones are evenly tufted rather than in clumps.

Traditional Handicrafts

The Centre of Hellenic Tradition, Pandrossou 36, Plaka, has a display of traditional and modern handicrafts from each region of Greece. Most of the items are not for sale, but if you have a look around you will get an idea of what is available. Amidst all the treasures is a charming café serving drinks and snacks.

The National Welfare Organisation, Ipatias 6, Plaka, was formed to develop and preserve rural Greek handicrafts. On sale are rugs, pottery, copper, woodwork and embroidery. The prices are high but the goods are of the best quality.

Leather Sandals

Good-quality leather sandals may be bought from Stavros Melissinos, Pandrossou 89 (see the Walking Tour section earlier).

Wall-Hangings

Moda (next to the Monument of Lysikrates), on Odos Sellev, Plaka, is a workshop specialising in beautiful, hand-woven wall-hangings; many depict island scenes. Prices start at 5500 dr.

GETTING THERE & AWAY
Air

Located nine km south-east of the city, Athens' airport, Ellinikon, has two terminals with separate entrances 1½ km apart: the West terminal for all Olympic Airways flights and the East terminal for all other flights. For Olympic Airways flight information ring ☎ 936 3363 and for all other airlines ring ☎ 969 9466/7. There is luggage storage (open 24 hours; 200 dr per piece) at the East terminal, 100 metres to the right of the exit. For information about domestic flights from Athens see the Getting Around chapter. The head office of Olympic Airways (☎ 966 6666) is at Leoforos Syngrou 96. The most central Olympic Airways branch office (domestic: ☎ 929 2235; international: ☎ 929 2555) is at Othonos 6.

Athens is one of Europe's major centres for buying discounted air tickets. There are dozens of travel agents on Filellinon, Nikis and Voulis which sell low-priced air tickets to Europe and the USA. For some recommendations see the Travel Agencies section under Information at the beginning of this chapter. Athens' airline offices include:

Air Canada (☎ 322 3206)
Air France (☎ 323 8507)
Alitalia (☎ 322 9414)
Biman-Airlines (☎ 324 1116)
British Airways (☎ 325 0601)

Cyprus Airways (☎ 324 6965)
Czechoslovak Airlines (☎ 323 0174)
Delta Airlines (☎ 323 5242)
Gulf Air (☎ 322 6684)
Kenya Airways (☎ 323 7000)
KLM (☎ 322 2208)
LOT-Polish Airways (☎ 322 1121)
Qantas Airways (☎ 360 9411)
South African Airways (☎ 321 6411)
Thai Airways (☎ 324 3241)
Turkish Airlines (☎ 322 1035)
TWA (☎ 322 6451)

Bus

The EOT gives out an intercity bus schedule.
Athens has two main intercity bus stations.
Terminal B is at Liossion 260. To get there
take bus No 024 from the entrance to the
National Gardens on Amalias. Buses run
every 15 minutes from 5 am to midnight. The
table below shows the destination, journey
time, fare and frequency of buses which
leave from this terminal:

Agios Konstantinos – 2½ hours, 2000 dr, hourly
    buses
Delphi – three hours, 1950 dr, five buses daily
Edipsos – 3½ hours, 1800 dr, three buses daily
Halkida – 1½ hours, 900 dr, half hourly buses
Karpenissi – six hours, 3200 dr, two buses daily
Kymi – 3½ hours, 1950 dr, six buses daily
Trikala – 5½ hours, 3600 dr, seven buses daily
Volos – 5¼ hours, 3500 dr, nine buses daily

Terminal A is at Kifissou 100. To get there
take bus No 051 from the corner of Zinonos
and Menandrou, near Omonia. The table following shows the destination, journey time,
fare and frequency of the buses which leave
from this terminal:

Astakos – five hours, 3400 dr, two buses daily
Corfu – 11 hours, 6050 dr (including boat ticket),
    three buses daily
Corinth – 1½ hours, 1000 dr, hourly buses
Epidaurus – 2½ hours, 1650 dr, two buses daily
Gythio – 5½ hours, 3000 dr, four buses daily
Igoumenitsa – 8½ hours, 5450 dr, three buses daily
Ioannina – 7½ hours, 4850 dr, 10 buses daily
Kalamata – 4½ hours, 2850 dr, 10 buses daily
Kefallonia – eight hours, 4721 dr, five buses daily
Lefkada – 5½ hours, 4100 dr, four buses daily
Loutraki – 1½ hours, 1000 dr, eight buses daily
Monemvassia – seven hours, 3700 dr, one bus daily
    (9.30 am)

Nafplion (via Mycenae) – 2½ hours, Mycenae 1400
    dr, Nafplion 1700 dr, hourly buses
Patras – three hours, 2400 dr, hourly buses
Pyrgos (for Olympia) – five hours, 3500 dr, 10 buses
    daily
Sparta – 4½ hours, 2500 dr, seven buses daily
Thessaloniki – 7½ hours, 5500 dr, nine buses daily
Zakynthos – seven hours, 3920 dr (including boat
    ticket), three buses daily

Buses for most destinations in Attica leave
from the Mavromateon terminal at the junction of Alexandras and 28 Oktovriou-
Patission, 250 metres north of the National
Archaeological Museum.

Train

Trains for northern Greece and Europe leave
from Larissis Station, Odos Deligianni. Destinations, journey times, fares and frequency
are:

Alexandroupolis – 14 hours, 4800 dr (2nd class), 7200
    dr (1st class), two trains daily
Larissa – five hours, 1880 dr (2nd class), 2820 dr (1st
    class), 12 trains daily
Paleofarsala – 5½ hours, 1500 dr (2nd class), 2250 dr
    (1st class), nine trains daily
Platy – seven hours, 2400 dr (2nd class), 3600 dr (1st
    class), eight trains daily
Thessaloniki – eight hours, 2640 dr (2nd class), 3986
    dr (1st class), seven trains daily

In addition there are three express trains
daily to Thessaloniki. The journey takes six
hours and tickets cost 4230 dr (2nd class),
6340 dr (1st class).

Trains for the Peloponnese leave from
Peloponnese (Peloponissou) Station, Pelop-
onnissou 3. Destinations, journey times,
fares and frequency are:

Corinth – two hours, 600 dr (2nd class), 850 dr (1st
    class), 12 daily
Kalamata – seven hours, 2200 dr (2nd class), 3300 dr
    (1st class), five daily
Kyparissia – 8½ hours, 1950 dr (2nd class), 2930 dr
    (1st class), nine daily
Patras – five hours, 1150 dr (2nd class), 1750 dr (1st
    class), seven trains daily

The two stations are very close to one

another. To reach them take trolley bus No 1 from Syntagma. The stop is the same for both stations, but to get to Peloponnese Station cross over the metal bridge at the southern end of the Larissis Station.

There is baggage storage at Larissis Station: opening times are 6.30 am to 9.30 pm and the cost is 200 dr per piece. Information may be obtained, and advance bookings made at the following EOS offices: Filellinon 17 (☎ 323 6747); Sina 6 (☎ 363 4402); and Karolou 1 (☎ 524 0647).

Car & Motorbike

If you want to travel north from Athens get to National Rd 1 which begins north of Nea Kifissia. To get there from central Athens take Vasilissis Sofias from Syntagma. To get to the Peloponnese take National Rd 8, which begins beyond Dafni. To get there take Agiou Konstantinou from Omonia.

Most car-rental firms are on Syngrou. Just Rent a Car (☎ 923 9104), Syngrou 43, is one of the most reliable Greek companies. Other outlets include:

Avis
    Amalias 48 (☎ 322 4951)
Budget
    Syngrou 8 (☎ 921 4771)
Eurodollar Rent A Car
    Syngrou 299 (☎ 922 9672)
Hertz
    Vouliagmenis 567A (☎ 994 2854)

Campervan hire outlets are Camper Caravans (☎ 323 0552), Nikis 4 and I Galatoulas Co (☎ 581 2103), Athinon 330. Motorbikes may be rented from Rent a Moto (☎ 342 3918), Plateia Thission.

Hitching

Athens is the most difficult place in Greece to hitchhike from. Your best bet is to ask the truck drivers at the Piraeus cargo wharves. Otherwise, for the Peloponnese, take a bus from Plateia Eleftherias to Dafni, where National Rd 8 begins. For northern Greece take the metro to Kifissia, then a bus to Nea Kifissia and walk to National Rd 1.

GETTING AROUND
To/From the Airport

Blue-and-yellow, double-decker express buses A and B run between the city and the East and West terminals (the destination is written on the front of the bus). The main bus stops in Athens are at Amalias, opposite the National Gardens, just south of Syntagma and on the west side of Stadiou, just south of Omonia. In high season if there's sufficient demand the buses continue to Plateia Vathis and Plateia Karaiskaki. Before Syntagma, the buses stop at Stiles (south of the Temple of Olympian Zeus) which is useful if you intend to stay in Veikou or Mets. From 6 am to midnight the buses run every 20 minutes and the fare is 160 dr; from midnight to 6 am there is one bus an hour and the fare is 200 dr. Always purchase tickets from the booths adjacent to the stops prior to your journey. During rush hour the journey can take up to an hour. At other times, it should take about 30 minutes.

Passengers for the West terminal also have the option of the following Olympic Airways buses, which leave from the Olympic Airways terminal at Syngrou 96 (every 30 minutes, 6.30 am to 8.20 pm, 160 dr): bus No 133 from Othonos on Syntagma (every 15 minutes, 5.40 am to midnight, 75 dr); bus No 122 from Vasilissis Olgas in front of the Zappeion Gardens (every 15 minutes, 5.30 am to 11.30 pm, 75 dr).

A taxi to or from either airport terminal to central Athens costs around 1500 dr.

Buses & Trolley Buses

Many of Athens' ancient sites are close to one another in, or around, Plaka and many of the museums are on Vasilissis Sofias near Syntagma. So if you are in Athens to see the sites the chances are you will only need to use public transport occasionally.

Blue-and-white buses serve Athens and the suburbs. They are frequent till midnight and run hourly on many routes throughout the night. Green bus No 040 goes from Syntagma to Piraeus every 20 minutes during the day and hourly during the night. Trolley buses serve the city, and have comfortable upholstered seats (the buses have uncomfortable wooden seats).

There is a flat fare of 75 dr throughout the city on both buses and trolley buses. Tickets must be purchased before you board, either at a transport kiosk or periptero. Most, but not all periptera sell tickets. The same tickets can be used on either buses or trolley buses. Tickets may be bought in blocks of 10, but there is no discount for bulk buying. Once you enter a bus or trolley bus you must validate the ticket by putting it into a machine; the penalty for failing to do so is 1500 dr. Travel cards are available which are valid from the first day of each month to the last, and cost 2500 dr.

Metro

Athens' metro is simple to understand and you cannot get lost as there is only one line, which is divided into three sections: Piraeus to Omonia, Omonia to Perissos and Perissos to Kifissia. The stations are: Piraeus, Faliro, Moschato, Kalithea, Petralona, Thission, Monastiraki, Omonia, Plateia Victorias, Attiki, Agios Nikolaos, Kato Patissia, Perissos, Pefkakia, Nea Ionia, Iraklion, Irini, Maroussi and Kifissia. The price of a ticket for travel within one or two sections is 75 dr and for three sections 100 dr. There are ticket machines and ticket booths at all stations. The machines for validating tickets are at the platform entrances. As with bus tickets the penalty for travelling without having a validated ticket is 1500 dr. The trains run every five minutes between 5 am and midnight.

A new metro system is currently under construction.

Taxis

Athens' taxis are yellow. If you see an Athenian standing on the edge of the pavement tearing their hair out, waving an arm, bellowing and looking as if they are having a nervous breakdown, the chances are they will be trying to get a taxi at rush hour. Despite the large number of taxis you will see careering around the streets of Athens at rush hour, it is incredibly difficult to get one.

To hail a taxi, stand on a pavement and bellow your destination at every one which passes. If a taxi is going your way the driver will stop (or may stop) even if there are already passengers inside. This does not mean the fare will be shared: each person will be charged the fare shown on the meter. If you get in one which does not have other passengers, make sure the meter is switched on. Don't set off before agreeing on a price; you shouldn't have to pay more than 600 dr for anywhere within the city, but remember prices double between midnight and 5 am. It sometimes helps if you can point out your destination on a map – many Athens' taxi drivers are extremely ignorant of their city.

If it is absolutely imperative that you get somewhere on time (eg to the airports), and you want to go by taxi it is advisable to book a radio taxi – you will be charged 300 dr extra but it's worth it. The radio taxis operating out of central Athens are:

Enossi (☎ 644 3345)
Ermis (☎ 411 5200)
Erta (☎ 346 7137)
Ikaros (☎ 513 2316)
Kosmos (☎ 493 3811)
Omonia (☎ 502 0145)
Proodos (☎ 643 3400)
Sata (☎ 862 5407)

For more information about Athens' taxi drivers, including their legendary reputation and how they are (hopefully) mending their ways, see the Taxi section in the Getting Around chapter.

Car

Driving in Athens is hair-raising, so if you're behind a wheel, keep your wits about you and keep calm. Parts of Eolou and Plaka are pedestrian ways and most streets in the centre operate a one-way system. Fortunately, all escape routes are very clearly sign-posted.

Greeks have a cavalier attitude towards driving laws, but contrary to what you will see, parking *is* illegal alongside kerbs marked with yellow lines, where street signs prohibit parking and on pavements and pedestrian malls. Athens has numerous small car parks, but these are not sufficient for the large number of cars used in the city. A large multistorey car park is presently under construction in Odos Amerikis. The 'odd-even' registration plate restriction operating in central Athens (see the Car & Motorbike section in the Getting Around chapter) does not apply to foreigners until the 41st day of driving in the city.

For details of car and motorcycle rental agencies in Athens, see the previous Getting There & Away section.

Cycling in Athens

I was determined to cycle through the centre of a city that from appearances point of view is decidedly non-cyclist-friendly. No cycle tracks exist, to my knowledge, and only a few hardy souls and foreign cyclists would dare to enter the maelstrom of traffic that surges through the streets of Athens 24 hours a day. I couldn't have been more surprised. Cycling around Plateia Omonias (Omonia Square), up Stadiou and into Plateia Syntagmatos (Syntagma Square) presented no more problems than riding through King William St in my home city of Adelaide, Australia, on my way home from work after 5 pm. Yes, you have to be alert and cycle confidently with the flow; you must indicate your intentions clearly and not hesitate; you need to use common sense and cycle with care, but it was rewarding to be able to 'do' Athens and then to visit the old streets of Plaka using a mode of transport that is eminently suited to this form of tourism. Parked up on the Acropolis, perched on my bike and enjoying the view (no smog that day) gave me a sense of achievement.

Cycling in central Athens, though not for the nervous amongst us, is quite definitely a goer.

Paul Hellander – Australia

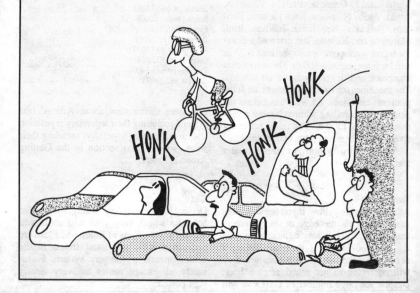

Bicycle

The sports department of Klaoudatos, the large department store on Athinas, near Omonia, hires out high-quality mountain bikes for 3000 dr per day.

Around Athens

PIRAEUS Πειραιάς

Piraeus (in Greek Pi-re-AS) is the port of Athens, the main port of Greece and one of the major ports of the Mediterranean. It's the hub of the Aegean ferry network, the centre for Greece's maritime export-import and transit trade and the base for its large merchant navy. Nowadays, Athens has expanded sufficiently to meld imperceptibly into Piraeus, the road linking the two passing through a grey, urban sprawl of factories, warehouses and concrete apartment blocks. Piraeus is as bustling and traffic-congested as Athens, without any of the latter's redeeming qualities. It's not a place in which many visitors want to linger; most come merely to catch a ferry.

History

The history of Athens and Piraeus has always been inextricably linked. Piraeus has been the port of Athens since Classical times, when Themistokles transferred his Athenian fleet of ships from the exposed port of Phaleron (modern Faliro) to the security of Piraeus. After his victory over the Persians, at the battle of Salamis in 480 BC, Themistokles fortified Piraeus' three natural harbours. In 445 BC Pericles extended these fortifying walls to Athens and Phaleron. The Long Walls, as they were known, were destroyed by the Spartans in the Peloponnesian Wars, but rebuilt in 394 BC.

Piraeus was a flourishing commercial centre during the Classical Age, but by Roman times it had been overtaken by Rhodes, Delos and Alexandria. During medieval and Turkish times it diminished to a tiny fishing village, and by the time of Independence it was home to less than 20 people. Its resurgence began in 1834 when Athens became the capital of independent Greece. By the early 20th century it had superseded the island of Syros as Greece's principal port. In 1923 its population was swollen by 100,000 refugees from Turkey. The Piraeus which evolved from this influx and was vividly portrayed in the film *Never on a Sunday* had a seedy, romantic appeal, with its bordellos and hashish dens exuding rembetika music.

These places have long since gone and beyond its façade of smart, new shipping offices and banks, Piraeus is now just plain seedy.

Orientation

Piraeus is 10 km south-west of central Athens. It has three harbours. The largest is the Great Harbour (Megas Limin), from where all the ferries leave. The Zea Marina (Limin Zeas) is where yachts owned by millionaires berth and the departure point for hydrofoils (excluding those to Aegina). North-east of here is the picturesque Mikrolimano whose name means small harbour; it is brimming with private yachts.

Whatever your mode of transport, the chances are that when you arrive in Piraeus it will be at the northern end of the Great Harbour. This harbour is skirted by Akti Kondili on its northern side, Akti Kalimassioti at the northern end of its eastern side, Akti Poseidonos a bit further south and Akti Miaouli still further south. Between the latter two is the main square of Plateia Karaiskaki, which abuts onto Akti Tzelepi. Another large square, Plateia Themistokleous, is at the northern end of Akti Miaouli.

Ferries for Crete leave from both the far western end of Akti Kondili and the middle of Akti Miaouli; for the Eastern Cyclades they leave from Akti Kondili and the southern end of Akti Poseidonos; for the Central and Western Cyclades, from the eastern end of Akti Kondili, Akti Poseidonnos and Akti Tzelepi; for the Saronic Gulf islands, from

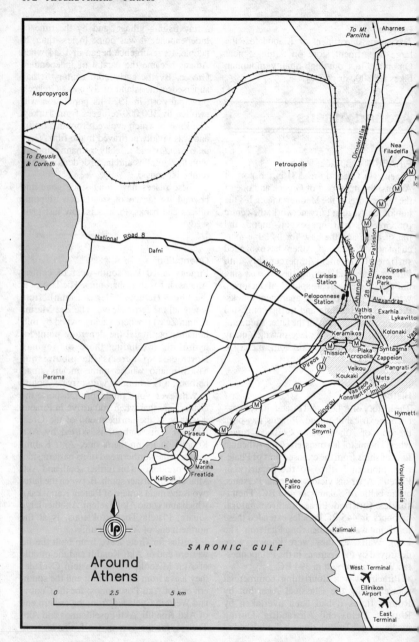

Around
Athens

just south of Plateia Karaiskaki; and for the Dodecanese, from the middle of Akti Miaouli. International ferries leave from the southern end of Akti Miaouli.

Confused? It gets worse, because ferries do not always leave from the quay allotted to them. When you buy your ticket ask the agent where the ferry will be leaving from and leave yourself plenty of time to locate it, ideally one hour. If you are running short of time most ferries have a temporary ticket table set up alongside the point at which they are moored. All ferries display a clock face showing their departure time, and have their ports of call written in English above their bows.

The metro station is at the top end of Akti Poseidonos, but the entrance is round the corner on Alipedou. The train station for the Peloponnese is one block up from the metro. The train station for northern Greece is at the opposite side of the harbour. To reach there turn left at the top of Akti Kalimassioti onto Akti Kondili and left again at the end of here.

Both the bus station and the bus stop for the airport buses are on Plateia Karaiskaki, but the bus stop for bus No 040 to Athens is on Vasileos Konstantinou. To reach there walk up Vasileos Georgiou Androutsou to Plateia Korai and turn right onto Vasileos Konstantinou, which in time-honoured Greek fashion has two names; its other name is Iroon Politechniou.

It's a 20-minute walk from the northern end of the Great Harbour to Zea Marina. To reach it walk south along Akti Miaouli and turn left onto either Skouze, Filellinon or Trikoupi.

Information

Piraeus' EOT (☎ 413 5716) is very inconveniently situated at Zea Marina. Why it should be here and not at the Great Harbour defies imagination. Do millionaire yacht owners really require the services of the EOT more than poverty-stricken backpackers? Its opening times are Monday to Friday from 7.30 am to 2 pm. The telephone number of Piraeus' port police is ☎ 417 2657.

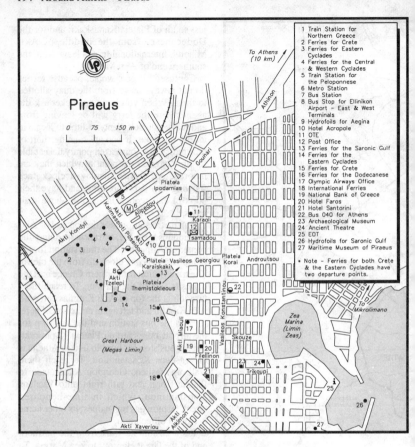

Piraeus

0   75   150 m

To Athens
(10 km)

Athinon

Gounari

Akti Kondyli

Akti Karaiskaki Poseidonos

Karaoli

Tsamadou

Plateia
Ipodamias

(M)

Alipedou

Plateia Vasileos Georgiou
Karaiskaki

Plateia
Korai

Androutsou

Akti
Tzelepi

Plateia
Themistokleous

Akti Miaouli

Vasileos Konstantinou

Skouze

Zea
Marina
(Limin
Zeas)

To
Mikrolimano

Great Harbour
(Megas Limin)

Filellinon

Trikoupi

Akti
Alkimon

Akti Xaveriou

1 Train Station for
   Northern Greece
2 Ferries for Crete
3 Ferries for Eastern
   Cyclades
4 Ferries for the Central
   & Western Cyclades
5 Train Station for
   the Peloponnese
6 Metro Station
7 Bus Station
8 Bus Stop for Ellinikon
   Airport – East & West
   Terminals
9 Hydrofoils for Aegina
10 Hotel Acropole
11 OTE
12 Post Office
13 Ferries for the Saronic Gulf
14 Ferries for the
   Eastern Cyclades
15 Ferries for Crete
16 Ferries for the Dodecanese
17 Olympic Airways Office
18 International Ferries
19 National Bank of Greece
20 Hotel Faros
21 Hotel Santorini
22 Bus 040 for Athens
23 Archaeological Museum
24 Ancient Theatre
25 EOT
26 Hydrofoils for Saronic Gulf
27 Maritime Museum of Piraeus

• Note – Ferries for both Crete
  & the Eastern Cyclades have
  two departure points.

Money The National Bank of Greece is at the southern end of Akti Miaouli, but there's a plethora of more conveniently situated banks on the waterfront further north. They're mostly big and flashy – you can't miss them.

Post & Telecommunications The main post office is on the corner of Tsamadou and Filonos, just north of Plateia Themistokleous. It's open Monday to Friday from 7.30 am to 8 pm. The OTE is just north of here at Karaoli 19 and is open 24 hours a day. The postcode for Piraeus is 18501 and the telephone code is 01.

Archaeological Museum

If you have time to spare in Piraeus then you shouldn't miss this museum. It's well laid out and contains some important and interesting finds from Classical to Roman times. These include some very fine tomb reliefs dating from the 4th to 2nd century BC. The star piece of the museum is, however, the magnificent statue of Apollo, the *Piraeus Kouros*. It is the oldest larger than life size hollow bronze statue yet found. It dates from around 520 BC and was discovered, buried in rubble, in 1959. The museum (☎ 452 1698) is at Trikoupi 31 and is open Tuesday to

Sunday from 8.30 to 3 pm. Admission costs 400 dr.

Maritime Museum of Piraeus

This is another interesting museum. The collection spans the history of the Greek navy from ancient times to the present day, with drawings and plans of battles, models of ships and battle scenes and uniforms and war memorabilia. There is a display of naval weapons in the grounds of the museum. The museum (☎ 451 6822) is on Akti Themistokleous at Zea Marina. To reach it, continue along Trikoupi from the Archaeological Museum and turn right. Opening times are Tuesday to Saturday from 8.30 am to 1 pm. Admission is 100 dr.

Places to Stay – bottom end

There's no reason why anyone should stay in Piraeus when Athens is so close. If you do get stuck don't attempt to sleep out, for Piraeus is the most dangerous place in Greece to do so.

Many of the budget hotels are geared more towards accommodating sailors than tourists, but the D class *Hotel Acropole* (☎ 417 3313/7587), Gounari 7, is one of the few which caters for backpackers. The tidy but plain rooms are 3500/5500/6500 dr a single/double/triple with shared bathrooms. Gounari is the main thoroughfare running inland from Plateia Karaiskaki. The hotel is just a little way up on the left, and is very convenient for all the transport options.

Another reasonable budget place is the D class *Hotel Faros* (☎ 452 6317/8), Notara 141, where singles/doubles are 3000/4400 dr with private bathrooms. Notara is parallel with Akti Miaouli two blocks inland. Nearby, the *Hotel Santorini* (☎ 452 2147), Trikoupi 6, has decent rooms for 4000/5700/6840 dr with private bathrooms.

Places to Stay – middle

The B class *Castella Hotel* (☎ 411 4735/6/7), Vasilissis Pavlou 75, has air-con rooms, a bar, restaurant and a roof garden with a view of Mikrolimano. Singles/doubles are 9100/13,850 dr. Vasilissis Pavlou is the stretch of waterfront beyond Mikrolimano.

Places to Stay – top end

Most of Piraeus' best hotels are on the waterfront near Mikrolimano. The B class *Hotel Cavo D'Oro* (☎ 412 2210), Vasilissis Pavlou 19, has air-con rooms, a restaurant and disco. Rates are 10,000/14,000 dr for singles/doubles.

Piraeus' most expensive hotel is the plush B class *Hotel Mistral*, Vasilissis Pavlou 105. Rates are 12,900/16,900 dr for singles/doubles.

Places to Eat

If all you want is a quick bite before catching a ferry, then there are several reasonably priced places on Akti Poseidonos and along Gounari. On the other hand, if you fancy a splurge before commencing your island hopping, or as a grand finale to your holiday, there are a number of good, but expensive, restaurants around Zea Marina and Mikrolimano. One highly commendable restaurant is the elegant *Deligiannis*, Akti Koundouriotou 1, where a three-course meal will cost around 3000 dr but is well worth it. Akti Koundouriotou is the waterfront between the two harbours.

Entertainment

The Piraeus open-air marble amphitheatre features drama and dance performances as part of the Athens Festival (see Festivals in the Athens section earlier). The theatre is on the Hill of Kastela behind the Mikrolimano.

Anifori (☎ 411 5819), Vasileos Georgiou Androutsou 47, is a lively rembetika club. Performances begin at 10.30 pm (it's closed on Sunday).

Things to Buy

Piraeus Flea Market Many locals will tell you that this market is infinitely better than its famous counterpart in Athens. As well as stalls selling junk, there are small shops selling high-quality jewellery, ceramics and antiques. The market is held on Sunday mornings on Alipedou and Skilitsi, near

Plateia Ipodamias. To reach it, from the metro-station entrance turn left and walk up Alipedou.

Getting There & Away

Air For information about domestic flights see the Getting Around chapter and for information about the airport see the Athens Getting There & Away section. The Olympic Airways office (☎ 452 0968 or 929 2797/8) is at Akti Miaouli 27.

Bus There are no intercity buses to or from Piraeus – you must go to one of the intercity bus stations in Athens. See Getting There & Away in the Athens section earlier.

Train Trains to the Peloponnese and northern Greece leave from each of Piraeus' train stations respectively. To locate the stations see Orientation earlier.

Ferry (Domestic) The following islands and island groups are linked to Piraeus by ferries: Crete, the Cyclades (except Kea), the Dodecanese (Kastellorizo, Agathonisi, Lipsi, Nisyros and Tilos cannot be reached directly – ferries change in Rhodes), the Saronic Gulf and the North-Eastern Aegean (except Thassos and Samothrace; for Psara and Inousses ferries change on Chios). The EOT in Athens gives out a ferry schedule which is updated weekly.

The following information applies only to the high season (from June to mid-September). There are daily ferries to the Cycladic islands of Kythnos, Serifos, Sifnos, Milos, Kimolos, Syros, Mykonos, Paros, Naxos, Ios and Tinos; two or three ferries a week to Iraklia, Shinoussa, Koufonisi, Donoussa, Amorgos, Folegandros, Sikinos, and Anafi; and one ferry a week to Andros (see also the Rafina and Lavrion sections later in this chapter). In the shoulder season (April, May and October) ferry schedules are reduced to some extent and in winter they are reduced considerably.

Rhodes, Kos, Kalymnos, Leros and Patmos in the Dodecanese have daily ferries from Piraeus; Astypalea, Karpathos, and Kassos have two or three a week. The North-Eastern Aegean Islands with daily ferries from Piraeus are Chios, Lesbos, Ikaria and Samos. Lemnos has two or three connections a week. There are year-round daily ferries to all of the Saronic Gulf islands. There are daily ferries to Crete (Iraklion) year round and in the high season daily ferries to Hania, four or five a week to Rethymnon and two or three a week to Kastelli (via Monemvassia, Neapoli, Gythio, Kythera and Antikythera).

If you want to take a car on board a ferry then it is advisable to buy a ticket in advance from an agent in Athens. Otherwise, wait until you get to Piraeus; agents selling ferry tickets are thick on the ground around Plateia Karaiskaki.

See the Boat section in the Getting Around chapter and the Getting To/From sections of each island for more information.

Ferry (International) In summer there are at least three ferries a week from Piraeus to Haifa in Israel (via Crete, Rhodes and Limassol in Cyprus). One of the boats is operated by Arkadia Lines, and the others by Stability Lines. One of Stability Lines' boats continues to Port Said in Egypt. The fares from the various ports in Greece are usually the same, despite the fact that Rhodes is considerably nearer to the ferries' destinations than Piraeus. Both lines offer 20% student (up to 28 years), youth (up to 25 years) and return-ticket discounts. One-way, deck-class prices from Greece to Limassol are 15,500/13,000 dr in the high/low season, to Port Said 20,000 dr and to Haifa 25,000 dr. Port taxes are US$17.

The boats begin operating in early April and stop at the end of October. The high season is from the beginning of June until mid-September. Buy tickets for Limassol and Haifa from Arkadia Lines (☎ 324 8158/8168/8178), Amalias 34, Athens, or from Stability Lines (☎ 413 2392/2395 or 451 0500), Sachtouri 11, Piraeus. Buy tickets for Port Said at the latter. Tickets may also be bought in the UK at Viamare Travel (☎ 081-452 8231), 33 Mapesbury Rd,

London NW2 4HT. For more information see the Ferry section in the Getting There & Away chapter.

Hydrofoil There are year-round, daily hydrofoils from the Zea Marina to the Saronic Gulf islands of Aegina, Hydra, Poros and Spetses. Some of these also call at Ermione, Porto Heli, Leonidio, Tolo, Nafplion, Monemvassia and Neapolis in the Peloponnese and the island of Kythera. In addition, at least hourly hydrofoils leave from Akti Tzelepi to Aegina. Buy tickets at the kiosks adjacent to the departure points. For more information see the hydrofoil section in the Getting Around chapter and the Getting To/From sections of the individual islands.

Catamaran The C/M *Catamaran* operates between the port of Flisvos, eight km east of Piraeus, and the major Cycladic islands. See individual island entries in the Cyclades chapter for details.

Getting Around

To/From the Airport Express buses run between Akti Tzelepi and both Athens' airport terminals every 20 minutes from 6 am to midnight (160 dr) and every 90 minutes from midnight to 6 am (200 dr). A taxi costs about 1500 dr.

Bus Bus No 040 (a green one) goes from Vasileos Konstantinou to Syntagma every 20 minutes during the day and hourly during the night. This bus can take up to 45 minutes to get from Athens to Piraeus; the metro is quicker.

Metro See the Athens Getting Around section for information about the Athens-Piraeus metro.

DAFNI Δαφνή
Dafni Monastery

This monastery, 10 km north-west of Athens, along the busy and industrialised road to Corinth, is Attica's most important Byzantine monument. It is built on the route of the Sacred Way and on the site of an ancient Sanctuary to Apollo. Its name derives from the daphne laurels which were sacred to Apollo.

The monastery's 11th-century church contains some of Greece's finest mosaics, regarded as some of the most outstanding in Greece. They were executed at a time when the artistic and intellectual achievements of Byzantium had reached unprecedented heights. Paradoxically, the empire was at its least secure and about to be bombarded from the east by the Seljuk (pre-Ottoman) Turks (a great dynasty which preceded the Ottoman Empire) and from the west by the Normans. However, it was neither of these groups of invaders who destroyed the monastery, but, typically, the crusaders who sacked it in 1205. It was rebuilt and occupied by monks until the time of the War of Independence, after which it was used as army barracks and a lunatic asylum. Much restoration has taken place since.

The mosaics on the church walls depict saints and monks, the ones on the dome depict apostles, prophets and guardian archangels. Exquisite though these mosaics are, they fade into insignificance once the visitor has gazed upon the Christos Pantocrator (Christ in Majesty) which occupies the centre of the dome. This masterpiece of Byzantine art will overwhelm even a confirmed atheist, so remarkable is the fierce and resolute expression of Christ. The monastery is open daily from 8.30 am to 3 pm, and entry is 500 dr.

Wine Festival

If the penetrating glare of the Pantocrator has not hypnotised you into unrelenting piety and abstention, then you can leave this cloistered world behind and amble along to Dafni's annual wine festival, which is held in the grounds adjacent to the monastery. This, Greece's wildest drinking binge where you can consume as much as you like, is held between August and mid-September. So long as your priority is quantity rather than quality when it comes to wine drinking, you'll have the time of your life. Eat before

The Abduction of Persephone

According to mythology Hades fell in love with Persephone, daughter of Demeter, the goddess of wheat and fertility. Zeus was reluctant to give his consent to a marriage, as he knew it would upset Demeter who doted upon her daughter. So Hades abducted Persephone and imprisoned her in his underworld (the world of the dead). Distraught Demeter searched everywhere for her daughter, but to no avail, so in revenge she cursed the soil so that it became infertile.

In her search for Persephone she came in disguise to Eleusis and was treated kindly by King

Keleus. His son, Triptolemos, recognised her and told her that his brothers, Eumolpus and Eubuleus, had seen Hades carrying her daughter into the underworld. Demeter implored the gods to return Persephone to her. This they promised to do, providing the girl had not eaten anything while in the underworld, for, once having partaken of the food of the dead, no-one can return to the world of the living.

But Persephone had eaten a piece of pomegranate which Hades had given her as a token of his love. Zeus, however, managed a compromise whereby Persephone could spend nine months of the year with her mother on earth, and the other three months with Hades in the underworld. Demeter lifted her curse, apart from the three-month period when Persephone had to return to the underworld. During this time the earth's soil became infertile again. In thanks to King Keleus and Triptolemus, Demeter gave permission for her principal temple in Greece to be built at Eleusis. ■

you go to the festival as you have to pay for the food and it's not very good. The festival grounds are open daily from 7.45 pm to 12.30 am. Entry is 300 dr.

Places to Stay

Near the monastery is *Dafni Camping* (☎ 581 1563) which charges 800 dr per person and 500 dr per tent.

Getting There & Away

From Plateia Eleftherias in Athens, buses leave every 20 minutes en route to Elefsina. The 25-minute journey costs 75 dr.

ELEUSIS Ελευσίνα

The ruins of ancient Eleusis (also called Elefsina) are 12 km further along the road south from Dafni and on the same bus route.

The ancient city of Eleusis was built around the **Sanctuary of Demeter**. The site dates back to Mycenaean times when the cult of Demeter began.

The myth of Persephone and Demeter is both an allegory of the death of vegetation in winter and its rebirth in spring, and of human

immortality, for Persephone's return to earth shows that death (entry into the underworld) is not annihilation. This is of course an oversimplification of the myth, which, like all myths, is complex, obscure and contradictory. Sometimes mother and daughter were depicted as two separate entities, sometimes Persephone became identical with Demeter. Whatever, Demeter (and/or her daughter Persephone), personification of life, death and rebirth, and thus the cycle of the seasons, was worshipped at Eleusis. The myth is a universal and timeless one, mirrored in the Egyptian myth of Isis and Osiris and in the Christian resurrection.

The cult of Demeter at Eleusis became one of the most important cults in Ancient Greece. By Classical times it was celebrated in a huge annual festival, when thousands of pilgrims came to be initiated into the Eleusian mysteries. In procession, they walked from the Acropolis to Eleusis along the Sacred Way, which was lined with statues and votive monuments. Initiates were sworn to secrecy on punishment of death, and, not one, during the 1400 years that the sanctuary functioned, disclosed its secrets. The sanctuary was closed by the Roman emperor Theodosius in the 4th century AD.

After Delphi, the sanctuary was the most important in Ancient Greece, but today, although it is of immense archaeological significance, it is uninspiring. This inability to invoke any feelings of wonder and awe within the layperson is largely due to its grubby industrial surroundings. A visit to the site's **museum** first, will help you to make some sense of the ruins. Both the site and museum are open Tuesday to Sunday from 8.30 am to 3 pm. Admission is 400 dr. Get a bus either from Plateia Eleftherias or from the stop at Dafni.

MONI KAISSARIANIS
Μονή Καισσαριανής

This 11th-century monastery, five km east of Athens and at a height of 341 metres, is idyllically set amid pines, plane and cypress trees on the slopes of Mt Hymettos. The air is permeated with the aroma of herbs which grow on the mountain. Bees have fed on these herbs since ancient times and the honey once made by the monks was famous.

The source of the river Ilissos is on a hill above the monastery. Its waters were once believed to cure infertility and were sacred to Aphrodite; a temple dedicated to her stood nearby. The spring feeds a fountain on the eastern wall of the monastery, where the water gushes from a marble ram's head (this is a copy; the 6th-century original is in the National Archaeological Museum).

Surrounding the courtyard of the monastery are a mill, bakery, bathhouse and refectory. The church is dedicated to the Presentation of the Virgin and is built to the Greek-cross plan. Four columns taken from a Roman temple support its dome. The 17th-century frescoes in the narthex are the work of Ioannis Ipatos. Those in the rest of the church date from the 16th century, and were painted by a monk from Mt Athos.

To appreciate the tranquillity of the monastery, try to visit on a weekday, for at weekends it swarms with picnicking Athenians. The grounds are open until sunset

and the monastery buildings are open Tuesday to Sunday from 8.30 am to 3 pm; admission is 500 dr. To get to the monastery take bus No 224 from Plateia Kaningos (at the north end of Akadimias) to the terminus. From here it's about a 30-minute walk to the monastery.

Attica Αττική

Attica, a *nomos* of Sterea Ellada, contains more than just the capital and its port of Piraeus. There are several places of interest, most of which can be reached by orange buses from the Mavromateon bus terminal.

COAST ROAD TO CAPE SOUNION

This road skirts Attica's Apollo coast. It's a beautiful coastline of splendid beaches and stunning sea vistas which has been spoilt by overdevelopment. Many of the beaches are either EOT pay beaches or belong to hotels. The beaches are resplendent with boats and water-sports equipment for hire, tennis and volley-ball courts and children's playgrounds.

The first resort you'll encounter travelling south is **Glyfada**, Attica's largest resort, which becomes overrun with package tourists in summer, who are joined by half the population of Athens at weekends. In addition, Glyfada has a permanent population of wealthy expatriates. Loads of bars and discos and noisy air traffic complete the picture – you'd be better off staying on the bus.

If you should find yourself here, Glyfada has some good up-market restaurants. *Moskva* (☎ 894 2524), Vyzaniou 1 (Glyfada's central square), is a posh Russian restaurant with an extensive menu. A three-course dinner will cost around 6000 dr. The similarly priced *Psaropoulos* (☎ 894 5677), Kalamon 2 (at the Glyfada Marina), is a popular seafood restaurant of long standing.

Voula Camping (☎ 01-895 2712) is an EOT site just south of Glyfada.

The next resort south, **Vouliagmeni,** is

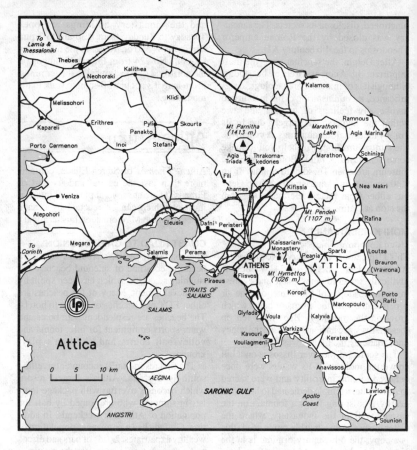

more up-market with a yacht marina, water-ski school and an EOT beach. *Hellenic Camping Varkiza Beach* (☎ 01-897 3613/4/5) is just north-east of Vouliagmeni at Varkiza. There are other resorts on the way to Cape Sounion, all of which have lots of weekend villas owned by well-to-do Athenians. However, between the resorts it's still possible to find almost deserted stretches of beach. Cape Sounion, 70 km from Athens, is at the south-eastern tip of Attica.

Getting There & Away

If your destination is Sounion then take one of the *paraliako* (coastal) buses which leave hourly on the half-hour (two hours, 800 dr) from the Mavromateon bus terminal in Athens. The buses also stop on Filellinon, on the corner of Xenofondos, 10 minutes later, but by this time they're usually very crowded.

There are additional buses from outside the Zappeion Gardens which go to Glyfada and Vouliagmeni.

INLAND ROAD TO CAPE SOUNION

The inland road to Cape Sounion passes through the Mesogeia (which means 'middle land') region, renowned for its red soil which yields fine olives and vines. **Peania**, a village 18 km east of Athens in the eastern foothills of Mt Hymettos, was the birth place of the orator Demosthenes (384-322 BC). Little remains of the ancient town and visitors come today not for ruins but to look around the **Vorres Museum** (☎ 01-664 2520/4771), which houses folklore items, prints and pictures, and an impressive collection of contemporary Greek paintings. Some pieces of modern sculpture stand in the courtyard.

Plateia Vasileos Konstantinou is Peania's main square. To reach the museum from here walk down Demosthenous (which has the ND (New Democracy) building on the corner and the post office next to it). At the bottom turn right onto Dimihounta, walk to the top and turn left onto Diadohou Konstantinou and a little way along you will see a sign pointing straight ahead to the museum. The museum is only open on Saturday and Sunday from 10 am to 2 pm. Admission is 100 dr. As it's a bit of a trek out here, telephone first to check that it is open.

The **Koutouki Cave** (☎ 01-664 2108), 510 metres above sea level on the eastern slopes of Mt Hymettos and four km west of Peania, is the most accessible of the caves in Attica. It was discovered in 1926 and has an impressive array of stalactites and stalagmites which are very effectively lit. The cave is signposted from Peania. It is open daily from 10 am to 5.30 pm. Admission is 350 dr. Again, telephone first to check that the cave is open.

Koropi, seven km south of Peania, is the largest of the villages of Mesogeia and is a lively market town, noted for its retsina. Its **Church of the Transfiguration**, on the road to Markopoulo, is one of the oldest churches in Attica and contains the remains of 10th-century frescoes. The road continues to **Markopoulo**, an unremarkable town except for its bakers and churches. It is said the best bread in Attica is baked here, and several of its small churches contain attractive 17th-century frescoes. The road south continues to Lavrion and Sounion.

Getting There & Away
Take one of the inland *mesogiaki* buses bound for Sounion from the Mavromateon terminal in Athens. They leave hourly on the hour and take 2¼ hours to get to Sounion.

CAPE SOUNION Ακρί Σούνιο
Temple of Poseidon
The Ancient Greeks chose their temple sites carefully, with prime considerations being the site's natural beauty and appropriateness to the god to whom the temple was dedicated. Nowhere is this more evident than at Cape Sounion, where the Temple of Poseidon stands on a craggy spur that plunges 65 metres into the sea. The temple was built in 444 BC at the same time as the Parthenon. It is constructed of local marble from Agrilesa and its slender columns – of which 16 remain – are Doric. It is thought that the temple was built by the architect of the Temple of Hephaestus in Athens' ancient Agora.

The temple appears gleaming white when viewed from the sea and is discernible from a long distance. It gave great comfort to sailors in ancient times: they knew that once they'd spotted it, they were nearly home. The view from the temple over the sea is equally impressive, for on a clear day Kea, Kythnos and Serifos can be seen to the south and Aegina and the east coast of the Peloponnese to the west. The site also contains scanty remains of a propylaia, a fortified tower and, to the north-east, a 6th-century temple to Athena.

If you wish to indulge the sentiments of Byron's lines from *Don Juan*:

> Place me on Sunium's marbled steep,
> Where nothing save the waves and I,
> May hear our mutual murmurs sweep...

You'll have to visit early in the morning before the tourist buses arrive. Byron was so taken by Sounion that he carved his name on one of the columns, and many others followed suit. The site is open Monday to Saturday from 9 am to sunset and on Sunday from 10 am to sunset. Admission is 600 dr.

Places to Stay & Eat There are two camp sites at Cape Sounion. They are *Camping Vakchos* (☎ 0292-39 571/262) and *Sounio Camping* (☎ 0292-39 358). Both are on the road to Lavrion.

The café at the site is expensive and although there are several tavernas on Sounion Beach, none are very cheap so you may like to bring along a picnic.

Getting There & Away
Bus You can take either the inland or coastal bus to Cape Sounion. See the Coast Rd to Sounion and the Inland Rd to Sounion sections for information.

LAVRION Λαύριο
Lavrion is an unattractive industrial town on the east coast of Attica, 10 km north of Sounion. It is only worth a mention because it is the departure point for ferries to the island of Kea. The town has definitely seen better days. In ancient times its silver mines, worked by slaves, were so productive that they helped finance Pericles' building programme. The island of Makronisos opposite the port was used as a place of exile during the civil war. With time to spare you could visit the **Mineralogical Museum** (☎ 0292-26 270), Plateia Iroon Politechniou. It's open Wednesday, Saturday and Sunday from 10 am to noon. Admission is 50 dr.

Getting There & Away
Bus Take one of the hourly buses from the Mavromateon terminal in Athens (1½ hours, 650 dr).

Ferry In the high season there are ferries to Kea every morning and evening from Monday to Friday. On Saturday and Sunday there are six a day. For exact times call the port police (☎ 0292-25 249). Tickets cost 950 dr. Three ferries a week continue to Kythnos (1645 dr).

RAFINA Ραφήνα
Rafina, on Attica's east coast, is Athens' main fishing port and second port for passenger ferries. It's much smaller than Piraeus,

has considerably less ferry traffic and so is far less confusing and crowded. Fares are 20% cheaper, but as the bus fare from Athens to Rafina is 300 dr you won't end up saving very much. If you prefer buses to boats, then sailing from Rafina cuts down on the time you spend on the ferry.

The port police (☎ 22 888) are in a kiosk near the quay. Agencies selling tickets are along the ramp leading to Plateia Plastira. Rafina's telephone code is 0294 and the post code is 19009.

There are frequent bus connections with Athens so there is no need to spend the night here. However, should you wish to do so, *Cococamp* (☎ 22 794) is a camp site on the beach two km north of the port. The D class *Hotel Corali* (☎ 22 477), on the central square of Plateia Plastira, is a good value budget hotel with singles/doubles/triples for 3000/5000/7000 dr. Walk up the ramp from the quayside to reach the square. Another D class hotel, *Hotel Akti* (☎ 24 776), Vithinias 14, is similarly priced. To reach this hotel turn left at the top of the ramp.

Getting There & Away
Bus There are buses every three-quarters of an hour from the Mavromateon terminal in Athens (one hour, 300 dr).

Ferry There are two or three ferries a day to Karystos (two hours, 1320 dr) and Marmari (1½ hours, 750 dr) in Evia, Andros (two hours, 1500 dr), Tinos (four hours, 2064 dr) and Mykonos (five hours, 2450 dr); one a day to Paros (five hours, 2200 dr) and Naxos (six hours, 2250 dr); three a week to Syros (3½ hours, 2060 dr) and two a week to Agios Efstratios (13 hours, 2500 dr), Lemnos (14 hours, 3500 dr) and Kavala (19 hours, 5000 dr) and one a week to Kos (13 hours, 3700 dr) and Rhodes (15 hours, 4300 dr).

MARATHON REGION
Marathon Μαραθώνας
The unremarkable little town of Marathon sprawls in the Marathon plain 42 km northeast of Athens. Its eminence stems from the Battle of Marathon (490 BC) when 9000

Greeks and 1000 Plataeans managed to defeat around 25,000 Persians, thanks to the ingenious tactics of Miltiades. He altered the conventional formation of the phalanx (lines of soldiers in battle) so there were fewer soldiers in the centre, but more in the wings. This lulled the Persians into thinking that the Greeks were going to be a pushover. They easily broke through the soldiers in the centre, but were defeated by the large number of unforeseen soldiers in the wings. At the end of the battle 6000 Persians lay dead and only 192 Greeks. The story goes that after the battle a runner was sent to Athens to announce the victory and after shouting *Enikesame!* ('We won!') he col-lapsed in a heap and never revived – the origins of today's Olympic marathon foot race.

The Battle of Marathon quashed the Persians' plans to conquer Athens and then make inroads into Europe. Although the Persians were to attack again (for the final time) 10 years later, the Battle of Marathon was regarded as a decisive one because it proved that the Persians were not invincible.

Marathon Tomb

This burial mound stands just 350 metres from the Athens-Marathon road, four km before the town of Marathon. In Ancient Greece, victims of battles were returned to their families for private burial, but as a sign of honour the 192 men who were killed at Marathon were cremated and buried in this collective tomb. The mound is 10 metres high and 180 metres in circumference. The tomb site is signposted from the main road and is open Tuesday to Sunday from 8.30 am to 3 pm. The **Marathon Museum**, nearer to the town, has the same hours and admission is 400 dr.

Lake Marathon

This is an enormous lake eight km to the west of Marathon town. Part of it has been made into a dam of Pentelic marble which was completed in 1926. It collects the water from the numerous streams which flow down Mt Parnitha and until 1956 was the sole supplier of water to Athens. It's an awesome sight and is thought to be the only dam in the world with marble walls.

Ramnous Ραμνούς

The ruins of the ancient port of Ramnous are 15 km north-east of Marathon town. It's an evocative, overgrown and secluded little site, standing on a plateau overlooking the sea. Among the ruins are the remains of a Doric **Temple of Nemesis** (435 BC), which once contained a huge statue of the goddess. Nemesis was the goddess of retribution and mother of Helen of Troy. I wonder what retribution she meted out to her wayward daughter for her capers with Paris. There are also ruins of a smaller 6th-century temple dedicated to Themis, goddess of justice. The site is open Tuesday to Sunday from 8.30 am to 3 pm and admission is free.

Schinias Σχινιάς

Schinias, south-east of Marathon, is a good, albeit popular beach; it's long and sandy and fringed by pine trees. If you come here on a weekday you'll find it a lot less crowded than at weekends. The camp site, *Camping Marathon* (☎ 0294-55 587), is on the way to the beach.

Getting There & Away

There are hourly buses from the Mavro-mateon terminal to Marathon (one hour, 480 dr). The tomb, the museum and Schinias Beach are within short walking distances of bus stops (tell the driver where you want to get out). There are no buses to Lake Marathon or Ramnous; you really need your own transport.

BRAURON Βραύρωνα

In Brauron (in modern Greek Vravrona, pro-nounced Vra-vr-ON-a) is the **Sanctuary of Artemis**. Brauron is on the east coast of Attica, just outside the modern village of Vravrona, 40 km from Athens and eight km from the Mesogian town of Markopoulo. According to mythology, Brauron was one of the League of Twelve Cities of King Kekrops, founder of Athens. Remains from

The Wrath of Artemis

Artemis has several aspects. She was the goddess of childbirth and protector of animals – especially she-bears and stags, but is also known as the virgin goddess of the moon and the hunt. When King Agamemnon sacrificed a stag before his expedition to Troy Artemis became so enraged that she punished him by preventing the expedition from leaving until he sacrificed his daughter Iphigenia to her. In the nick of time, the goddess took pity on the girl, rescued her and fled with her to Tauris, where Iphigenia became a priestess in a sanctuary to the goddess.

Meanwhile, Iphigenia's brother, Orestes, had murdered his mother Klytaemnestra and was being pursued by the Furies. On the advice of an oracle he was told that he could make amends for his crime by introducing the cult of Artemis to the Greeks. This he was to do by bringing an image of the goddess to the country. So he set off for the Sanctuary of Artemis at Tauris and was reunited with his sister. Together they stole an image of Artemis and thus introduced the worship of the goddess to Greece. ■

as early as 1700 BC have been discovered on the site. It first became a sanctuary to Artemis during the time of the tyrant Peisistratos, who made the worship of Artemis the official religion of Athens.

The sanctuary was built at Brauron. Euripides' Iphigenia plays and Goethe's play *Iphigenie auf Tauris* are based on this myth.

The cult centred around a festival held every four years, when prepubescent girls performed a ritual dance, dressed as bears. At the site are the ruins of the dormitories where the girls stayed, the Temple of Artemis, a stone bridge and the shrine of Iphigenia. The site's **museum** (☎ 0294-71 020) houses interesting finds from the sanctuary and the surrounding area. Both site and museum are open Tuesday to Sunday from 8.30 am to 3 pm. Admission is 400 dr. The hours and days may be reduced in the winter, so during this time enquire at the EOT in Athens or call the museum.

Getting There & Away

The site is a hassle to get to as there are no direct buses from Athens. Take either the 6 am Sounion bus (via Markopoulo) or the 1.30 pm Lavrion bus from the Mavromateon terminal to Markopoulo (six km south-west of Brauron). From here you can either change to a local bus headed for Vravrona (6.45 am and 2 pm, 150 dr), or walk to the site. Bear in mind that if you get the later bus you won't have long at the site. An alternative is to get a bus from outside the Thission metro station to the village of Loutsa, five km north of Vravrona, and then walk from there.

Peloponnese Πελοπόννησος

The Peloponnese (Pe-lo-PO-nis-os in Greek) is the southernmost section of the Balkan peninsula. Since the late 19th century, due to the construction of the Corinth Canal, it has for all intents and purposes been severed from the mainland – the only link is via the narrow Isthmus of Corinth. The region is divided into seven prefectures: Corinthia, Argolis, Achaia, Elia, Arcadia, Messinia and Lakonia.

The Peloponnese is a region of outstanding natural beauty, with lofty mountains valleys of orange groves and cypress trees, and a disproportionate number of the mainland's best beaches. The diversity of the landscape is mirrored in the legacies left behind by the many civilisations which took root in the region: Ancient Greek sites, crumbling Byzantine cities and Frankish and Venetian fortresses are found in profusion. The area of the Mani, a peninsula in the south of the Peloponnese, has an additional attraction: the remnants of fortified tower houses built as refuges from clan wars from the 17th century onwards.

The Ionian island of Kythera is also covered in this chapter because it is most easily reached from the Peloponnese.

History & Mythology

The name Peloponnisos derives from the mythological hero, Pelops, and the word for island, *nisos*, so literally translated it means Island of Pelops. The region's medieval name was the Morea (*mouria* is Greek for mulberry tree), possibly because of its similarity in shape to a mulberry leaf, or because mulberry trees grow so well in the area.

The deities may have resided on Mt Olympus, but they made frequent jaunts into the Peloponnese, so it is a region rich in myths and Pelops features in many of these.

Since ancient times the Peloponnese has taken a major role in Greek history. When the Minoan civilisation declined after the 15th century BC, the focus of power in the ancient Aegean world moved from Crete to the hill fortress palaces of Mycenae and Tiryns in the Peloponnese. As elsewhere in Greece, the Dorian invasion resulted in a dark age for the region. When it emerged from this dark age in the 7th century BC, Sparta, Athens' arch rival, had superseded Mycenae as the most powerful city in the Peloponnese. The period of peace and prosperity under Roman rule (146 BC to around 250 AD) was shattered by a series of invasions by Goths, Avars and Slavs.

The Byzantines were slow to make inroads into the Peloponnese, and were not firmly established until the 9th century. In 1204, after the fall of Constantinople to the crusaders, the crusader chiefs William de Champlitte and Geoffrey de Villehardouin came to the region and divided it into 12 fiefs which they parcelled out to various barons of France, Flanders and Burgundy. These fiefs were overseen by de Villehardouin, self-appointed Prince of Morea (as the region was by then called).

The Byzantines gradually won back the Morea, and from there even retrieved Constantinople in 1261. Although the Byzantine Empire as a whole was now in terminal decline, a glorious renaissance took place in the Morea, centred on Mystra, which Byzantine Emperor Michael VIII Palaeologus made the region's seat of government.

Peloponnese

0   15   30 km

The Morea fell to the Turks in 1460 and hundreds of years of power struggles between the Turks and Venetians followed. The Venetians had long coveted the Morea and had succeeded in establishing trading ports at Methoni, Pylos, Koroni and Monemvassia.

The War of Independence began in the Peloponnese – Bishop Germanos of Patras raised the flag of revolt near Kalavryta on 25 March 1821. But the Egyptian army under the leadership of Ibrahim Pasha brutally restored Turkish rule in 1825.

In 1827 the Triple Alliance of Great Britain, France and Russia (moved by Greek suffering and the activities of the philhellenes – Byron's death in 1824 was particularly influential) came to the rescue of the Greeks by fighting the Egyptian-Turkish fleet at point-blank range in the decisive Battle of Navarino, ending Turkish domination of the area.

The Peloponnese became part of the independent state of Greece, and Nafplion in Argolis became the first national capital. However, after the assassination in 1831 of Kapodistrias, Greece's first president, on the steps of the town's Church of St Spyridon,

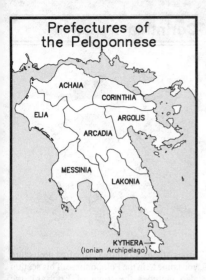

Prefectures of the Peloponnese

ACHAIA

CORINTHIA

ELIA

ARGOLIS

ARCADIA

MESSINIA

LAKONIA

KYTHERA
(Ionian Archipelago)

the new king Otho moved the capital to Athens.

In WW II, Kalavryta, in Achaia, suffered an abhorrent atrocity when all its male inhabitants were killed by the Germans.

The civil war (1944-49) caused widespread destruction and in the 1950s many inhabitants of the villages migrated to Athens, Australia and the USA. More recently, the towns of Corinth and Kalamata have suffered devastating earthquakes. Both are still in the throes of recovery.

Getting There & Away

Air The domestic airport at Kalamata in Messinia is the only airport in the Peloponnese.

Bus From Athens there are buses to most towns in the Peloponnese. For details see

Pelops

Pelops was the son of the conniving Tantalos, who invited the gods to a feast and served up the flesh of his son to test their power of all-knowing. Of course, the omniscient gods knew what he had done and refrained from eating the flesh. However, Demeter, who was in a tizz over the abduction of her daughter, Persephone, by Hades, accidentally ate a piece of Pelops' shoulder. Fortunately, the gods reassembled Pelops, and fashioned another shoulder of ivory. Tantalos was suspended from a fruit tree overhanging a lake, and was thus punished with eternal tantalising thirst.

Pelops took a fancy to the beautiful Hippodameia, daughter of Oinomaos, King of Elia. Oinomaos, who was a champion chariot racer, was told by an oracle that his future son-in-law would bring about his death. Oinomaos announced that he would give his daughter in marriage to any suitor who defeated him in a chariot race, but that he would kill those who failed – a fate which befell many suitors. Pelops took up the challenge and bribed the king's charioteer, Myrtilos, to take a spoke out of a wheel of the king's chariot. The chariot crashed during the race and Oinomaos was killed, so Pelops married Hippodameia and became King of Elia; the couple had two children, Atreus and Thyestes. Atreus became king of Mycenae and was the father of that kingdom's greatest king, Agamemnon. Pelops' devious action is blamed for the curse on the Royal House of Atreus which ultimately brought about its downfall. ■

Ancient coin depicting chariot race

Getting There & Away in the Athens chapter. There are also buses from Ioannina in northern Greece and the Ionian island of Lefkada (both via the Rio-Andirio ferry) to Patras. If you don't have your own transport, travelling by bus is a pleasant means of exploring the Peloponnese. There are adequate services to all but the most remote areas.

Train The rail network in the Peloponnese is narrow-gauge. There are two main lines: Athens-Corinth-Diakofto-Patras-Pyrgos-Kyparissia-Kalamata; and Athens-Corinth-Mycenae-Argos-Tripolis-Kalamata. In addition there are four branch lines: Diakofto-Kalavryta (rack and pinion); Pyrgos-Olympia; Pyrgos-Katakolo; and Kavassila-Killini.

Car & Motorbike If you are travelling from Athens to the Peloponnese with your own transport, you have the choice of the New National Road (a toll highway) or the slower Old National Road which hugs the coast and has fine views of the Saronic Gulf. Coming from north-west Greece, you can enter the Peloponnese via the Rio-Andirio ferry.

Ferry Patras is one of Greece's major ports with ferries to Corfu (Greece) and Brindisi, Bari and Ancona (Italy). Killini, south-west of Patras, has ferry connections with Kefallonia and Zakynthos. Ferries for Crete (Kastelli) and Piraeus leave from Monemvassia and Gythio, stopping at Kythera and Antikythera.

Hydrofoil In July and August, hydrofoils plying between Piraeus and the Saronic Gulf islands call at some ports on the east coast of the Peloponnese, including Porto Heli, Tolo, Nafplion, Monemvassia and Neapoli. See the Getting Around chapter for details.

Corinthia Κορινθία

From Athens, Corinthia is the first prefecture you come to in the Peloponnese. This section also includes the town of Loutraki, the village and ancient site of Perachora, and Lake Vouliagmeni, for although they are north of the Corinth Canal, they belong to the prefecture of Corinth.

CORINTH Κόρινθος
Modern Corinth (in Greek CO-rin-thos, population 22,700), the capital of Corinthia, is just six km west of the Corinth Canal. The town moved here after the former site was destroyed by an earthquake in 1858. The new town was in turn wrecked by an equally violent earthquake in 1928 and damaged by yet another one in 1981.

The modern town is unprepossessing, with rubble and dust from road construction and unattractive sturdy concrete buildings, constructed to withstand future earthquakes. It only warrants an overnight stay because of its proximity to ancient Corinth. Old Corinth lingers on as a mere village near the ancient site.

Orientation & Information
It is not difficult to find your way around Corinth. The post office is at Adimantou 33 and the OTE is on the corner of Kolokotroni and Adimantou. Corinth's telephone code is

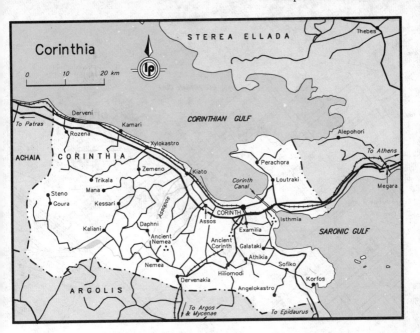

Corinthia

0   10   20 km

STEREA ELLADA
Thebes
CORINTHIAN GULF
To Patras
Derveni
Kamari
Rozena
Xylokastro
Alepohori
ACHAIA CORINTHIA
Zemeno
Kiato
Perachora
To Athens
Trikala
Mana
Corinth
Canal
Loutraki
Steno
Kessari
Megara
Goura
CORINTH
Kaliani
Daphni
Assos
Examilia
Isthmia
SARONIC GULF
Ancient
Nemea
Ancient
Corinth
Galataki
Athikia
Sofiko
Nemea
Hiliomodi
Korfos
Dervenakia
Angelokastro
ARGOLIS
To Argos
& Mycenae
To Epidaurus
Steno

0741 and the postcode is 20100. The National Bank of Greece is at Ethnikis Antistaseos 7.

There is no EOT in Corinth. The tourist police (☎ 23 282), Ermou 51, are open daily from 8 am to 2 pm and 5 to 8 pm. The regular police (☎ 22 143) are in the same building.

Places to Stay – bottom end

Corinth Beach Campground (☎ 27 967/8) is about three km west of the town centre. Any buses going to ancient Corinth will drop you off at the camp site. The *Blue Dolphin Campground* (☎ 25 766/7) is three km from ancient Corinth on the beach. To reach this site take the bus to Lecheon from the bus stop on Koliatsou, just off Ethnikis Antistaseos.

The *Belle-Vue Hotel* (☎ 22 088), Damaskinou 41, has clean and tidy single/double/triple rooms for 2500/3000/4500 dr with shared bathrooms. The C class *Hotel Corinthos* (☎ 26 701/2/3 or 23 693), Damaskinou 26, has pleasant single/double rooms for 5400/6500 dr with private bathrooms and balconies. There are a good number of other hotels on the same street.

Places to Stay – middle

The C class *Hotel Konstantatos* (☎ 22 120 or 25 311), on Damaskinou, has elegant furnishings, though you may find the stuffed fox in the middle of the lounge a bit disconcerting. Room rates are 7000/8500 to 10,000 dr with private bathrooms.

Places to Eat

Restaurant To 24 Hours on Agiou Nikolaou (near the train station) serves wonderful food. This place never closes.

The lively *Taverna O Thodorakis* on the waterfront has fried sardines and fried kalamaria for 700 dr and Greek salad for 500 dr. The taverna is open every evening. *Taverna O Anaxagoras*, Agiou Nikolaou 31, at the opposite end of the waterfront, specialises in mezedes, ranging from 300 to

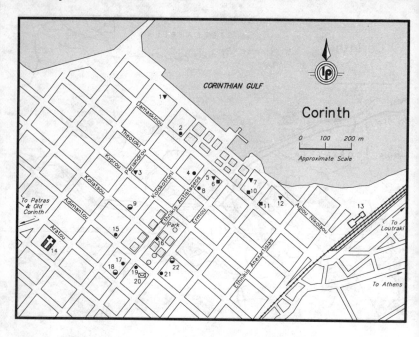

Corinth

CORINTHIAN GULF

0   100   200 m

Approximate Scale

To Patras & Old Corinth

To Loutraki

To Athens

■ PLACES TO STAY

6   Belle-Vue Hotel
10 Hotel Corinthos
11 Hotel Konstantatos

▼ PLACES TO EAT

1   Taverna O Anaxagoras
3   Food Market
5   Kanata Restaurant
7   Taverna O Thodorakis
12 Restaurant To 24 Hours

OTHER

2   Cinema
4   Town Hall
8   National Bank of Greece
9   Bus Stop for Lecheon
    (for Blue Dolphin Campground)
13 Train Station
14 Agios Pavlos Church
15 OTE
16 Taxi Rank
17 Gregorios Lagos
18 Bus Station for Nafplion, Sparta,
    Kalamata, Tripolis etc.
19 Rent a Car
20 Post Office
21 Tourist Police
22 Bus Station for Ancient Corinth,
    Loutraki, Athens etc.

400 dr. The taverna is open for lunch and dinner. The *Kanata Restaurant*, Damaskinou 41, is open all day. There's a 15% discount for guests at the Belle-Vue Hotel. Corinth's food market is on the corner of Kyprou and Periandrou.

Getting There & Away

Bus Corinth has two intercity bus terminals. One is on the corner of Aratou and Ethnikis Antistaseos. Buses leave here every hour for Nafplion (1¼ hours, 720 dr) via Mycenae (45 minutes, 440 dr) and Argos (one hour, 600 dr). There are nine buses to Tripolis (1½ hours, 1000 dr); eight buses a day to Sparta (three hours, 1550 dr); and seven to Kalamata (four hours, 2650 dr).

Corinth's other bus terminal is on the corner of Ermou and Koliatsou. From here there are half-hourly buses to Athens (1½ hours, 1000 dr) and Loutraki (20 minutes, 170 dr), hourly buses to ancient Corinth (20 minutes, 140 dr), and seven buses a day to Nemea (one hour, 500 dr).

Train There are 11 trains a day to Athens (two hours, 550 dr). On the line which skirts the north and west coasts, there are seven trains a day to Patras (3½ hours, 750 dr); five to Pyrgos (5½ hours, 1310 dr); and four to Kyparissia (6½ hours) and Kalamata (7½ hours, 1650 dr). On the inland line, there are three trains a day to Argos (one hour, 390 dr) Tripolis (2½ hours, 690 dr) and Kalamata (5½ hours, 1650 dr).

Car There are two car-rental outlets, Rent a Car (☎ 25 573), Adimantou 39, or Gregorios Lagos (☎ 22 617), Ethnikis Antistaseos 42.

ANCIENT CORINTH & ACROCORINTH

The sprawling ruins of ancient Corinth are seven km south-west of modern Corinth. Towering 575 metres above them is the massive fortified bulk of Acrocorinth.

Allow a whole day to see both ancient Corinth and Acrocorinth. Most people come on a day trip from modern Corinth but there are tavernas and a few domatia in the village near the ancient site – look for the signs. There is also a restaurant at Acrocorinth.

The site (☎ 0741-31 207) is open daily from 8 am to 6 pm. The on-site museum is open the same times from Tuesday to Sunday and from 11 am to 6 pm on Monday. Admission to the site (including the museum) is 1000 dr.

History

During the 6th century BC, Corinth was one of Ancient Greece's wealthiest cities, with a population of 750,000. It owed its wealth to a unique and strategic position on the Isthmus of Corinth, which meant it was able to build twin ports, one on the Aegean Sea (Kenchreai) and one on the Ionian Sea (Lecheon). From these ports it traded throughout the entire Mediterranean. It survived the Peloponnesian Wars, flourished under Macedonian rule, but was sacked by the Roman consul Mummius in 146 BC for revolting against Roman rule. In 44 BC Julius Caesar began rebuilding the city and once again it became a prosperous port.

During Roman times when Corinthians weren't clinching business deals, they were paying homage to the Aphrodite in a temple dedicated to her (which meant they were having a rollicking time with the temple's sacred prostitutes, both male and female). St Paul, perturbed by the Corinthians' wicked ways, spent 18 fruitless months preaching here.

Sisyphus' Eternal Penance

If you make the trek up to Acrocorinth from ancient Corinth, spare a thought for Sisyphus. According to mythology, Sisyphus, king of Corinth, witnessed Zeus' abduction of Aegina, and reported this to her father, the river god Asophus. As an eternal penance, Sisyphus was condemned by Zeus to push a rock to the top of Acrocorinth for his indiscretion, whereupon it would instantly roll down and have to be pushed up again. ■

Ancient Corinth
Exploring the Site Earthquakes and sackings by a stream of invaders have left little standing in ancient Corinth, and what's left is mostly from the Roman era. An exception is the 5th-century BC Doric **Temple of Apollo**, the most prominent ruin on the site. To the south of this temple is a huge **agora**, or forum, bounded at its southern side by the foundations of a **stoa**, built to accommodate the bigwigs who were summoned here in 337 BC by Philip II, to sign oaths of allegiance to Macedon. In the middle of the central row of shops is the **bema**, a marble podium, from which Roman officials addressed the people.

At the eastern end of the forum are the remains of the **Julian Basilica**. To the left (north) is the **Lower Peirene Fountain** – the Upper Peirene fountain is on Acrocorinth. According to mythology, Peirene wept so much when her son Kenchrias was killed by Artemis that the gods, rather than let all the ensuing water go to waste, turned her into a fountain. In reality, it's a natural spring which has been utilised since ancient times and still supplies old Corinth with water. The water tanks are concealed within a fountain house with a six-arched façade; through the arches you will see the remains of frescoes on the walls. To the west of the fountain, steps lead to the **Lecheon Road**, which was the main thoroughfare to the port of Lecheon. On the right (east) side of the road is the **Peribolos of Apollo**, a courtyard flanked by Ionic columns, some of which have been restored. Near by is a **public latrine**, of which some seats remain.

The site's **museum** houses statues, mosaics, figurines, reliefs and friezes.

Acrocorinth Ακροκόρινθος
Earthquakes and invasions compelled the people of ancient Corinth to retreat to Acrocorinth, a sheer bulk of limestone which was one of the finest natural fortifications in Greece. The original fortress was built in ancient times and was coveted and strengthened by streams of invaders. The ruins are a medley of imposing Roman, Byzantine, Frankish, Venetian and Turkish ramparts, harbouring remains of Byzantine chapels, Turkish houses and mosques. It's a wonderfully atmospheric and fascinating place to explore.

On the higher of Acrocorinth's two summits is the **Temple of Aphrodite**, where the sacred courtesans who so raised the ire of St Paul catered to the desires of the insatiable Corinthians. Little remains of the temple, but the views are tremendous.

The site is open Tuesday to Sunday from 8.30 am to 6 pm. Admission is 400 dr.

Getting There & Away
Buses to ancient Corinth leave Corinth on the hour every hour; they return on the half hour. There are no direct buses to Acrocorinth. If you have your own car you can drive up, otherwise it's a strenuous 1½-hour walk, which you should try to do in the early morning before it gets too hot. Taxis charge 1000 dr one way from ancient Corinth to Acrocorinth.

CORINTH CANAL
The idea of a canal cutting through the Isthmus of Corinth and thus joining the Ionian to the Aegean Sea was first proposed by the tyrant Periander, founder of ancient Corinth. The enormity of the task defeated him, so instead he built a paved slipway across which sailors dragged small ships on rollers, a method which was used until the 13th century.

In the intervening years, many leaders, including Alexander the Great and Caligula, toyed with the canal idea, but Nero was the one who actually began digging. In AD 67 in true megalomaniacal fashion, using a golden pick-axe, he struck the first blow himself, then left it up to 6000 Jewish prisoners to do the hard work. However, the project was soon halted by invasions of Gauls. Finally, in the 19th century (1883-93), a French engineering company dug the canal.

The Corinth Canal cuts through solid rock, is over six km long and 23 metres wide, and the vertical sides rise 90 metres above the water. The canal did much to elevate

Piraeus to the status of a major Mediterranean port. It's an impressive sight, particularly when a ship is going through.

Getting There & Away

You can reach the canal by taking a Loutraki bus from modern Corinth to the canal bridge. Any buses or trains between Corinth and Athens will of course also pass over the canal.

ISTHMIA Ισθμια

At the south-western end of the canal is the site of ancient Isthmia. There is little of interest here for the novice, but archaeological buffs will marvel at the remains of the **Sanctuary of Poseidon** as well as those of a defensive wall and **Roman theatre**. As with Nemea, Delphi and Olympia, ancient Isthmia was renowned as one of the sites of the Panhellenic Games, and the excellent **museum** at the site (open daily except Tuesday) contains various ancient athletic exhibits.

The modern village of Isthmia lies a short distance to the east of the ancient site.

LOUTRAKI Λουτράκι

Loutraki (population 6823) lounges between a pebble beach and the tall cliffs of the Gerania mountains, just six km north of the Corinth Canal. It was once a traditional spa town patronised by elderly and frail Greeks, and is still a major producer of bottled mineral water. However, the town was devastated by the 1981 earthquake, and subsequent reconstruction has resulted in its reincarnation as a tacky resort with modern characterless hotels. Loutraki hardly warrants an overnight stay, but you may like to stop off here, en route from Corinth to Perachora, to taste the celebrated water which gushes from a fountain on the main street.

Getting There & Away

There are half-hourly buses from Corinth to Loutraki (20 minutes, 170 dr) and from Athens there are eight buses a day (1½ hours, 1000 dr). From Loutraki there are buses every hour to Perachora (20 minutes, 140 dr).

PERACHORA Περαχώρα

The village of Perachora (population 1425), 13 km north of Loutraki, stands on a plateau a little way inland from the sea. The road continues west to **Lake Vouliagmeni**, a lagoon linked to the sea by a narrow channel. There are several inexpensive fish tavernas on its shore.

Beyond the lake are the ruins of **ancient Perachora** which were excavated by Humfry Payne from 1930 to 1933. Payne was accompanied by his wife, Dilys Powell, who gives an interesting account of her stay in the area in her book *An Affair of the Heart*. At the site are the ruins of an agora, a stoa, and an 8th-century temple in a **Sanctuary to Hera**. A visit to the site is, however, more worthwhile for the views of the surrounding mountains.

Getting There & Away

From Loutraki there are hourly buses to Perachora (20 minutes, 140 dr) and in July and August one bus a day at 10 am (returning at 1 pm) to Vouliagmeni (500 dr return).

NEMEA Νεμέα

Ancient Nemea lies four km north-east of the modern village of the same name. According to mythology, Herakles carried out the first of his Twelve Labours here – the slaying of the lion which had been sent by Hera to destroy Nemea. The lion became the constellation Leo; each of the Twelve Labours is correlated to a sign of the zodiac.

Like Olympia, Nemea was not a city but a sanctuary, and venue for the biennial Nemean games, held in honour of Zeus. These games were one of the Great Panhellenic festivals. Only three columns of the 4th-century BC Doric **Temple of Zeus** remain; other remains include a bathhouse and hostelry. The site's **museum** is excellent and includes models of the site and explanations in English.

At the **stadium**, which is 500 metres back along the road, you can see the athletes' starting line and distance markers. The site and museum (☎ 0746-22 739) are open Tuesday to Sunday from 8.30 am to 3 pm. Admission to both is 500 dr.

Getting There & Away
There are seven buses a day to the village of Nemea from Corinth (one hour, 500 dr); ask the driver to let you off at the site, which is four km before the village.

Argolis Αργολίδα

Argolis is the easternmost of the prefectures of the Peloponnese. This region, which has some very significant archaeological sites, is comprised primarily of a peninsula which effectively divides the Saronic Gulf from the Argolic Gulf.

Within its borders are Mycenae, Tiryns, Argos and Epidaurus.

MYCENAE Μυκήνες
The modern village of Mycenae (in Greek Mi-KI-nes) has little to recommend it other than its proximity to the ancient site, two km to the north. The village is geared towards the hordes of day-tripping tourists who stop en route to ancient Mycenae, but does offer a few accommodation options if you wish to stay overnight. It's a small village consisting of a single street. There's no bank, but there's a post office at the ancient site where you can

exchange currency. Mycenae's telephone code is 0751 and the postcode is 21200.

Places to Stay – bottom end
There are two camp sites at Mycenae. *Camping Mycenae* (☎ 66 247) is near the bus stop in Mycenae village and *Camping Atreus* (☎ 66 221) is near the Corinth-Argos road.

Mycenae's *YHA Hostel* (☎ 66 285) is above the Restaurant Iphigenia on the main road. Beds are 800 dr per person and an IYHF card is required. It's a small hostel so ring first to check it's not full. The charming C class *Belle Helene Hotel* (☎ 66 255) has comfortable singles/doubles for 3000/5700 dr. The renowned amateur archaeologist Heinrich Schliemann (see under Ancient Mycenae) stayed here while excavating at the site, and other famous guests have included Claude Debussy and Virginia Woolf. The bus stop is outside the hotel.

Further up the hill, the *Hotel Klitemnistra* (☎ 66 451) has double/triple rooms for 4000/5000 dr.

Places to Stay – top end
A more expensive option is the B class *La Petit Planete* (☎ 66 240 or 27 729), on Leoforos Tsounta. Rates are 7000/9000 dr for singles/doubles. The hotel has a restaurant and bar.

Places to Eat
The restaurants cater for the day-trippers, and are nothing special. The *Restaurant Iphigenia* and the *Restaurant Menelaos* seem the best of the bunch.

Getting There & Away
Bus Mycenae is served by buses from Nafplion (three per day, one hour, 350 dr) and Argos (six per day, 30 minutes, 250 dr). Most of the buses stop at both the village and the ancient site. Otherwise you can get one of the hourly Corinth-Argos buses which will drop you off on the main road from where you can walk to the site.

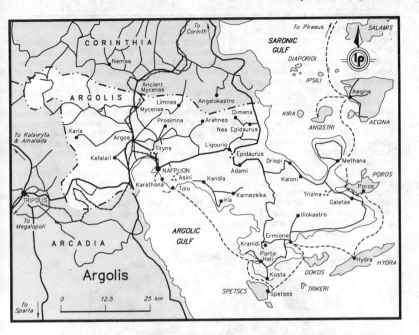

Argolis

Train The Mycenae train station is at Fichtio, two km from the village. It is on the Corinth-Kalamata line.

ANCIENT MYCENAE

In the barren foothills of Mt Agios Ilias (750 metres) and Mt Zara (600 metres) stand the sombre and mighty ruins of ancient Mycenae, vestiges of a kingdom which for 400 years (1600-1200 BC) was the most powerful in Greece, holding sway over the Argolid (the modern-day prefecture of Argolis) and influencing the other Mycenaean kingdoms.

The site (☎ 0751-66 585) is open Monday to Friday from 8 am to 5 pm and Saturday and Sunday from 8.30 am to 3 pm. Admission to the citadel and the Treasury of Atreus is 1000 dr.

History & Mythology

To everyone, Mycenae is synonymous with Homer and Schliemann. In the 7th century BC, Homer told in his epic poems, the *Iliad* and the *Odyssey*, of 'well-built Mycenae, rich in gold', poems which until the 19th century were regarded as nothing more than gripping and beautiful legends. Then in the 1870s the amateur archaeologist Heinrich Schliemann (1822-90), despite derision from professional archaeologists, struck gold, first at Troy, and then at Mycenae.

In Mycenae, myth and history are inextricably linked. According to Homer's epics and Aeschylus's *Oresteia*, Mycenae was founded by Perseus, the son of Danae and Zeus. Perseus' greatest heroic deed was the killing of the hideous snake-haired Medusa, whose looks petrified in both senses of the word. The dynasty of Perseus was eventually overthrown by Pelops, a son of Tantalus. The Mycenaean Royal House of Atreus was probably descended from Pelops, although myth and history are so intertwined, and the genealogical line so complex, no-one knows

The Life of Heinrich Schliemann

Heinrich Schliemann is often dismissed as too eccentric and monomaniacal to be taken seriously in the dry, academic world of archaeology – someone who was driven more by impulse than carefully correlated facts. Despite his gross inaccuracies in dating his finds, Schliemann must be acknowledged as the archaeologist who proved that the kingdom of Mycenae had existed and was not merely a product of Homer's imagination.

The life of Heinrich Schliemann was as dramatic, fantastic and eventful as any of Homer's tales. He was born in the Baltic German state of Mecklenburg in 1822. His father was a feckless womaniser and drunkard whose long-suffering wife died when Schliemann was only nine years old. Forced to leave school at 14, Schliemann got a job stacking crates in a local grocery store. Five years later he'd had enough, and set off to seek his fortune. He walked to Hamburg and got a job as a ship's boy on a vessel bound for Venezuela. The ship was wrecked off the Dutch Frisian island of Texel; against all odds Schliemann survived and wandered into Amsterdam half-naked, half-dead and destitute.

With a thirst for both knowledge and money, he worked for various trading companies in Holland and studied obsessively in his spare time. One of his passions was languages; modern European languages he learnt in six weeks, but Ancient Greek took him a while longer. By the age of 24 he was working for an international Dutch trading company, and in 1846 he was appointed their representative in St Petersburg. Already fluent in English, Portuguese, French, Dutch, Spanish and Italian, he was now able to add Russian to his repertoire.

The alleged death mask of Agamemnon

for certain. Whatever, the House of Atreus, through means fair and foul (but mostly foul), was by the time of Agamemnon the most powerful of the Achaeans (Homer's name for the Greeks). Despite this, it even-

tually came to a sticky end, thus fulfilling the curse which had been put on it due to Pelops' misdeeds.

To find out about this downfall we must turn to Homer, of whom little is known other

Over the next 20 years Schliemann made a considerable amount of money in various business enterprises. One particularly lucrative one was as a private banker in California during the gold rush. By the time he was 40, he had so much money in the bank he decided it was time to indulge a fantasy which had obsessed him for many years. Since his time in Amsterdam, he had steeped himself in Greek mythology and was convinced that Homer's epics were, albeit loosely, based on fact. In 1868 he decided to prove this, but wanted a sympathetic partner to help him. He wrote to a friend, a bishop in Athens, asking him to find him a suitable wife. The bishop came up with a number of likely candidates, including 17-year-old Sophia Engastromenos (later the family name was changed to Kastomenos). When they met, Schliemann asked her a number of questions. The two crucial ones were: Could she recite some of Homer by heart? And would she like to travel? The highly intelligent Sophia passed the test, they were married and she was whisked off to Hissartik (ancient Ilios, alias Troy) in Asia Minor to assist Schliemann in his excavations. In his overenthusiasm Schliemann dug too deep and uncovered treasures which belonged to a pre-Homeric period, not that of King Priam as he believed. The same happened in Mycenae, where he excavated next. The gold mask which he unearthed and excitedly proclaimed as the death mask of Agamemnon actually belonged to a king who lived three centuries earlier.

His marriage to Sophia was a happy one; she accompanied him in all his expeditions, ever-supportive, hard-working and enthusiastic. Marriage did not, however, diminish Schliemann's eccentricities and obsessions – the Schliemanns' house, on Odos El Venizelou in Athens (built by the esteemed German architect, Ernst Ziller) was named Iliou Melathron (Palace of Troy) and their son and daughter were called Agamemnon and Andromache.

Appropriately, his mausoleum in Athens' First Cemetery, designed by Ziller, is adorned with scenes from the Trojan War.

One of the biggest archaeological mysteries of postwar years has been the whereabouts of Priam's Treasure – Schliemann's name for the treasures he uncovered at Troy has stuck even though they belong to a much earlier king. Schliemann donated the gold to Berlin, where it went on display in the Ethnological Museum. In 1945 when the Red Army occupied Berlin the collection disappeared. Some people believed the gold had been melted down, others that it had been sold on the black market by Soviet soldiers. Another rumour was that it was stored in a vault at the Pushkin Museum in Moscow, although Russia repeatedly denied this. Then in August 1993 Russian Culture Minister Yevgeni Siderov stated that he had seen and touched the treasures which had indeed been hidden in Russia on orders from the Kremlin at the end of WW II.

Talks are presently taking place between Bonn and Moscow over the many artworks which disappeared during WW II, and Schliemann's gold will be amongst those discussed. Presently the Russians, Germans, Turks and Greeks are all laying claims to Priam's Treasure. ∎

Heinrich Schliemann

than he lived sometime around 800 BC and was a bard who told tales of events which had happened hundreds of years earlier. These tales were passed down to him by word of mouth from other bards, all of whom would have altered and added to the tales. So Homer's tales cannot be taken as accurate accounts of historical events, but rather as myths, which nonetheless give us an inkling of what life was like in those far-off times.

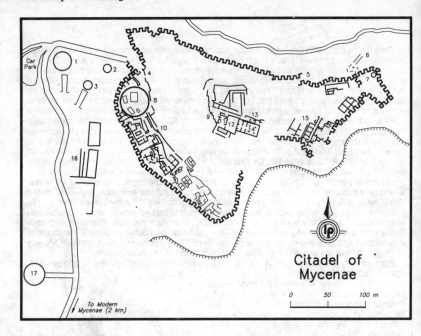

Citadel of Mycenae

0   50   100 m

To Modern Mycenae (2 km)

1	Grave Circle B	10	Houses
2	Tomb of Klytaemnestra	11	Throne Room
3	Tomb of Aegisthus	12	Great Court
4	Lion Gate	13	Agamemnon's Death Chamber
5	Postern Gate	14	Megaron
6	Drain	15	Artisans' Quarters
7	Cistern	16	Merchants' Houses
8	Grave Circle A	17	Treasury of Atreus
9	Agamemnon's Palace		

The historical facts are that Mycenae was first settled by Neolithic people in the 6th millennium BC. Sometime between 2100-1900 BC, during the old Bronze Age, Greece was invaded by people of Indo-European stock who had crossed Anatolia via Troy to Greece. This new wave of invaders brought an advanced culture to the then primitive Mycenae and other mainland settlements. This new civilisation is now referred to as the Mycenaean, named after Mycenae, its most powerful kingdom. The other kingdoms included Pylos, Tiryns, Corinth and Argos in the Peloponnese; evidence of Mycenaean civilisation has also been found at Thebes and Athens.

The city of Mycenae consisted of a fortified citadel and surrounding settlement. Due to the sheer size of the walls of the citadel (13 metres high and seven metres thick), the Ancient Greeks believed that they must have been lifted by a Cyclops, one of the giants described by Homer in the *Odyssey*.

Archaeological evidence indicates that

The Trojan War & the Fall of the House of Atreus

In his epic poems, the *Iliad* and the *Odyssey*, Homer related the events of a crucial period in Mycenaean history – the Trojan War and its aftermath. Homer called Troy Ilium (hence the epic's title *Iliad*). The 10-year war took place around 1250 BC between the Achaeans and the Trojans, during the reign of Mycenae's King Agamemnon and Troy's King Priam.

Agamemnon's brother, Menelaus, King of Sparta, had suffered great humiliation when his beautiful wife Helen wasabducted by Paris, the son of King Priam of Troy. Menelaus sought the advice of Nestor, King of Pylos, the oldest and wisest of the Mycenaean kings, who told him that nothing less than a combined force of all the armies of Greece would be sufficient to get Helen back. So, accompanied by Agamemnon, Menelaus visited all the princes and heroes in the land to ask for their assistance. Amongst them were Odysseus, King of Ithaca (Ithaki), Patroclus, Achilles and Nestor. Agamemnon, as the most powerful and richest king in Greece, headed the Greek expedition to Troy. Fighting on the Trojan side were Paris, his brother Hector and Priam. The war dragged on for 10 years, during which time Hector killed Patroclus, Achilles killed Hector and Paris killed Achilles, and still there was no end in sight. Odysseus then came up with the idea of the wooden horse filled with soldiers. That's the way Homer reported it.

While all this was going on in Troy, back in Mycenae, Agamemnon's wife, Klytaemnestra, had taken a lover, Aegisthus. On his return to Mycenae, Agamemnon was greeted lovingly by his wife (despite his being accompanied by his Trojan concubine, Cassandra). However, later while he was taking a bath, Klytaemnestra, assisted by her lover, stabbed him to death. Orestes, her son, then avenged the murder of his father by murdering her, and so the Mycenaen Royal House of Atreus came to its dramatic end. ■

Trojan Horse

---

around 1200 BC the palaces of the Mycenaean kingdoms were destroyed. A long held theory was that the destruction was the work of Dorian invaders. Later evidence shows that the decline of the Mycenaean civilisation was symptomatic of a general turmoil which was taking place at that time around the Mediterranean. The great Hittite Empire in Anatolia, which had reached its height between 1450-1200 BC, was now in decline, as was the Egyptian civilisation. The Mycenaeans, Hittites and Egyptians had all prospered through trade with one another, but by the end of the 1200s this trading had ceased. Many of the great palaces of the Mycenaean kingdoms were destroyed 150 years before the Dorians came to Greece. But whether the destruction was the work of outsiders, or was due to internal division

between the various Mycenaean kingdoms, remains unresolved.

Exploring the Site

The **Citadel of Mycenae** is entered through the **Lion Gate**, so called because above the lintel is a relief of two lionesses supporting a pillar. This motif is believed to have been the insignia of the Royal House of Atreus.

Once inside the citadel you will find **Grave Circle A** on the right. This was the royal cemetery and contained six grave shafts. Five were excavated by Schliemann in 1874-76 and the magnificent gold treasures he uncovered are now in the National Archaeological Museum in Athens. In the last grave shaft Schliemann found a well-preserved gold mask with some flesh still clinging to it. In a state of fervour he sent a telegram to the Greek king stating 'I have gazed upon the face of Agamemnon'. The mask turned out to be that of an unknown king who had died some 300 years before Agamemnon.

To the south of Grave Circle A are the remains of a group of houses. In one of these was found the famous **Warrior Vase** which Schliemann regarded as one of his greatest finds.

The main path leads up to Agamemnon's palace, centred around the **Great Court**. The rooms to the north were the private royal apartments. One of these rooms is believed to be the chamber in which Agamemnon was murdered. Access to the **throne room**, west of the Great Court, would originally have been facilitated by a large staircase. On the south-east side of the palace is the **megaron** (reception hall).

On the northern boundary of the citadel is the **Postern Gate** through which, it is said, Orestes escaped after murdering his mother. In the far north-eastern corner of the citadel is the **secret cistern** which can be explored with the aid of a torch – but take care, the steps are slippery.

Until the late 15th century BC, the Mycenaeans put their royal dead into shaft graves. They then devised a new kind of entombment – the tholos tomb, which was shaped like a beehive. The approach road to Mycenae passes to the right of the best preserved of these, the **Treasury of Atreus** or tomb of Agamemnon. A 40-metre-long passage leads to this immense beehive-shaped chamber. The stone blocks from which it was built reduce in size as the structure tapers to its central point.

Further along the road on the right is **Grave Circle B**, and nearby are the tholos tombs of Aegisthus and Klytaemnestra.

Getting There & Away

Buses depart several times daily for both ancient and modern Mycenae from Nafplion and Argos. See the Getting There & Away section under (modern) Mycenae for details.

ARGOS Αργος

Argos (AR-ghos, population 20,000) is the oldest continuously inhabited town in Greece, but vestiges of its past glory lie mostly beneath the prosaic modern town. The ruins which have been excavated are perhaps only of interest to aficionados. Nevertheless, Argos is a convenient base from which to explore the sites of Argolis, and has a refreshing lack of tourist hype. It is also a major transport hub for buses. Incidentally, Argos is a good place to find a job picking oranges.

Orientation & Information

Argos' showpiece and focal point is the magnificent central square, Plateia Agiou Petrou with seats, fancy Art Nouveau lights, citrus and palm trees and the impressive Agios Petros church. However, beyond here, Argos deteriorates into an unremarkable workaday town.

The central square is 500 metres from the train station. To get to the square, walk straight up Filellinon to a five-road intersection. Continue straight ahead up Makariou to a junction with a large church on the left. Continue along the same road, which veers slightly to the right, to a fork in the road (the OTE is in the middle of this folk). Take the left fork, which is Vasileos Georgiou, and you will come to Plateia Agiou Petrou.

There are two bus stations in Argos. The Athens bus station is near the central square. With your back to the ticket office turn right and take the second right onto Vasilissas Olgas (passing the Archaeological Museum on your right) which leads to Plateia Petrou. The Arcadia-Lakonia bus station is at Pheothonos 24. To reach here from the Athens bus station, turn left from the ticket office, take the first right and then the first left and it's along this road on the right.

The post office is at Danaou 16. This street runs off the central square, by the Hotel Telessila. The OTE office is at Nikitara 8, just off the east side of the central square.

Argos' postcode is 21200 and the telephone code is 0751. The National Bank of Greece is a little way along Nikitara from the

· central square. Argos' hospital (☎ 27 831) is on Odos Corinth, which runs off the north side of the central square. There is no EOT or tourist police in Argos. To contact the regular police, call ☎ 27 222.

Archaeological Museum

Even if you're just passing through Argos try to visit the Archaeological Museum on Vasilissas Olgas. The contents include some outstanding Roman mosaics and sculptures, Neolithic, Mycenaean and geometric pottery and bronze objects from Mycenaean tombs. The museum (☎ 28 819) is open Tuesday to Sunday from 8.30 am to 3 pm. Admission is 400 dr.

Roman Ruins

Argos' Roman ruins are on both sides of Odos Tripolis, which is the main Argos-Tripolis road. From the central square walk along Danaou and turn right onto Theatron to reach this road. On the west side is an enormous **theatre** which could seat up to 20,000 people (even more than the famous theatre at Epidaurus). It dates from Classical times but was greatly altered by the Romans. Nearby are remains of a 1st-century AD **odeion** (indoor theatre), and **Roman baths**. The site is open every day from 8.30 am to 3 pm. Admission is free.

A footpath leads, in 45 minutes of hard slog, from the theatre up to the **Fortress of Larissa**, a conglomeration of Byzantine, Frankish, Venetian and Turkish architecture, standing on the foundations of the city's principal ancient citadel.

The **Sanctuary of Apollo & Athena** and the nearby remains of a **Mycenaean necropolis**, where some chamber tombs and shaft graves have been excavated, lie to the north of the Roman ruins. The hill to the north-east of these ruins is the site of a small, ancient citadel and an early Bronze Age settlement. It is now crowned by the chapel of Agios Elias. To reach these ruins from the Roman ruins, walk north along Odos Tripolis and turn left at the intersection with Tsokri. From the central square, walk up Vasileos Konstantinou, which becomes Tsokri.

Places to Stay

The cheapest hotel in Argos is the D class *Hotel Theoxenia* (☎ 27 370), Tsokri 31, where airy and clean single/double/triple rooms are 2500/3950/5470 dr with shared bathrooms. From the central square walk up Vasileos Konstantinou, which becomes Tsokri. Another pleasant budget hotel is the E class *Hotel Apollon* (☎ 27 908 or 28 021), Papaflessa 11 (Papaflessa is just north of Nikitara, near the central square. The rates here are 3500/6000/8000 dr for rooms with private bathrooms; singles/doubles with shared bathrooms are 3000/5000 dr.

The C class *Hotel Telessila* (☎ 28 351), on the central square, has singles/doubles for 3500/5000 dr with private bathrooms and 2500/4000 dr with shared bathrooms. Just north-east of the central square the D class *Hotel Palladion* (☎ 27 346, 28 235 or 22 968), Vasilissis Sophias, has agreeable single/double rooms for 4000/6000 dr with private bathrooms. The C class *Hotel Mycenae* (☎ 28 569/332), on the central square, has large and comfortable rooms for 6400/9500/11,400 dr.

Places to Eat

The *Restaurant Aigli*, on the central square near the Hotel Mycenae, serves well-prepared food in pleasant surroundings. The nameless zaharoplasteion (patisserie), on the corner of Vasilissas Olgas near the Athens bus station, has a large choice of reasonably priced cakes. Argos' food market is on Vasileos Konstantinou.

Getting There & Away

Bus From Argos' Athens bus station there are half-hourly buses to Nafplion (30 minutes, 250 dr); hourly buses to Athens (2½ hours, 1550 dr); six buses a day to Mycenae (25 minutes, 250 dr); and two buses a day to Nemea (one hour, 400 dr).

From the Arcadia-Lakonia bus station there are nine buses a day to to Tripolis (1¼ hours, 800 dr); eight to Sparta (2½ hours, 1250 dr); three to Leonidio (three hours, 950 dr); and one a day at 10 am to Andritsena (3½ hours, 1700 dr).

Train There are four trains to Athens (three hours, 900 dr) via Mycenae (10 minutes, 100 dr), Nemea (45 minutes, 200 dr) and Corinth (one hour, 400 dr). There are three trains a day to Kalamata (3½ hours, 1000 dr) via Tripolis (one hour, 550 dr).

NAFPLION Ναύπλιο

Nafplion (NAF-pli-o, population 9000), 12 km south-east of Argos on the Argolic Gulf, is capital of the prefecture and has been a major port since the Bronze Age. So strategic was its position that it had three fortresses: the massive principal fortress of Palamidi, the smaller Its Kale ('Inner Castle' in Turkish) and the diminutive Bourtzi on an islet north of the old town.

Nafplion is one of Greece's most alluring cities. In the old town, narrow streets of elegant Venetian houses and gracious neoclassical mansions are watched over by the towering Palamidi Fortress.

Dispossessed of its eminence as capital of Greece after Kapodistrias' assassination by the Maniot chieftains, Constantine and George Mavromichaelis, Nafplion settled back a more comfortable role as a peaceful seaside resort. With good bus connections, the city makes a pleasant base from which to explore Argolis' many ancient sites.

Like Argos, Nafplion is a good place to find casual work, picking either oranges or apricots.

Orientation

The old town occupies a narrow promontory with the Its Kale fortress on the southern side, and the promenades of Bouboulinas and Akti Miaouli on the north side. The principal streets of the old town are Amalias, Vasileos Konstantinou, Staikopoulou and Kapodistriou. The old town's central square is Plateia Syntagmatos (Syntagma Square), which is at the western end of Vasileos Konstantinou. The bus station is on Syngrou, the street which separates the old town from

the new. The main street of the new town is 25 Martiou, which is an easterly continuation of Staikopoulou.

Information

Nafplion's post office is on Syngrou, and the OTE is on the northern side 25 Martiou. Nafplion's postcode is 21100 and the telephone code is 0752. The National Bank of Greece is on Plateia Syntagmatos. The Municipal Tourist Office (☎ 24 444) is in the town hall, just south of the western end of Bouboulinas. The amiable and helpful tourist police (☎ 28 131) are at the southern end of Syngrou – follow the road as it curves right.

Palamidi Fortress

This vast citadel stands atop a 215-metre-high rock. Within the outer walls are three separate Venetian fortresses, which were built between 1711 and 1714, but were seized by the Turks only a year after completion. Above each of the gates of the citadel is the Venetian emblem of the Lion of St Mark. During the War of Independence, the Greeks, under the leadership of the venerable klepht chief, Theodore Kolokotronis, besieged the citadel for 15 months, before the Turks surrendered. In the new town, just north of the OTE, stands a splendid equestrian statue of Kolokotronis, who was known as the Grand Old Man of the Morea.

The fortress affords terrific views, but access is by seemingly endless steps (around 1000), beginning just south-east of the bus station – climb early in the day and take some water with you. Alternatively, there is a three-km road to the fortress; a taxi costs 500 dr one way. The fortress (☎ 28 036) is open Monday to Friday from 8 am to 5 pm, and Saturday and Sunday from 8 am to 3 pm. Admission is 400 dr.

Museums

Nafplion's **Popular Art Museum** (☎ 28 379) won the European Museum of the Year award in 1981 for its superlative displays of traditional textile-producing techniques (with in-depth explanations in English) and

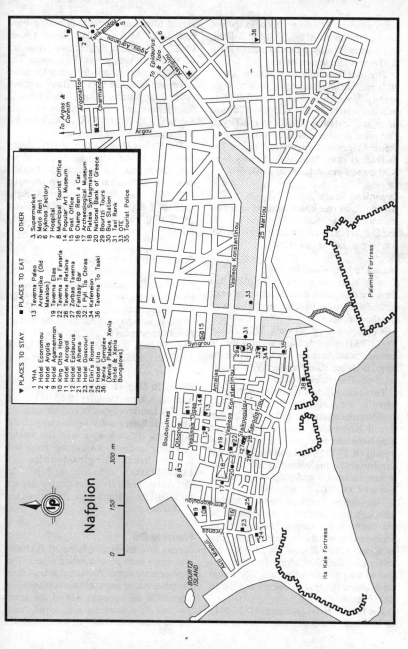

Nafplion

0   150   300 m

BOURTZI ISLAND

Palamidi Fortress

Its Kale Fortress

To Argos & Corinth

To Epidaurus & Tolo

PLACES TO STAY
1 YHA
2 Hotel Economou
4 Hotel Argolis
9 Hotel Agamemnon
10 King Otto Hotel
11 Hotel Acropol
12 Hotel Epidaurus
21 Hotel Athena
23 Hotel Dioscouri
24 Elini's Rooms
36 Xenia Complex
   (Xenia Palace, Xenia
   Hotel & Xenia
   Bungalows)

PLACES TO EAT
13 Taverna Paleo
   Archantiko (Old
   Mansion)
19 Taverna Elias
22 Taverna Ta Fanaria
26 Taverna Retsina
27 Zorbas Taverna
28 Fantasy Bar
32 I Pyli Tis Chiras
34 Kafeneion
36 Taverna To Tsaki

OTHER
3 Supermarket
5 Moto Rent
7 Kyknos Factory
8 Municipal Tourist Office
14 Popular Art Museum
15 Post Office
16 Champ Rent a Car
17 Archaeological Museum
18 Plateia Syntagmatos
20 National Bank of Greece
29 Bourtzi Tours
30 Bus Station
31 Taxi Rank
33 OTE
35 Tourist Police

folk costumes. The museum is in the old town on the corner of Ipsilandi and Sofroni, and is open Tuesday to Sunday from 9 am to 2.30 pm. Admission is 400 dr.

The **Archaeological Museum** (☎ 27 502) on Plateia Syntagmatos is in an 18th-century Venetian building. The collection includes pottery from Neolithic to Classical times and finds from Mycenae and Tiryns. The prize piece is a virtually intact suit of bronze Mycenaean armour from Tiryns. The museum is open Tuesday to Sunday from 8.30 am to 3 pm. Admission is 400 dr.

Organised Tours
Bourtzi Tours (see Entertainment) organises tours to Mystra (7500 dr); Mycenae, Corinth and Delphi (12,000 dr); Kalavryta (8000 dr); and Hydra and Spetses (4200 dr).

Places to Stay – bottom end
There are no camp sites in Nafplion, but there are many sites at the beach resorts east of Nafplion (see Beaches in the Around Nafplion section).

Nafplion's very pleasant *YHA Hostel* (☎ 27 754) is in the new town some 20 minutes' walk from the bus station (see the map). Beds are 800 dr and an IYHF card is required. The curfew is 11 pm.

The D class *Hotel Economou* (☎ 23 954), opposite the youth hostel, has agreeable double/triple rooms for 4000/4500 dr with shared bathrooms; doubles with private bathrooms are 5000 dr. Nearby the *Hotel Argolis* (☎ 27 721), on Leoforos Argou, has comfortable single/double rooms with private bathrooms and plant-strewn balconies for 4000/5500 dr.

The highest concentration of domatia (although there aren't that many) are in the old town on the narrow streets between Staikopoulou and the Its Kale fortress. One of these, *Elini's Rooms* (☎ 27 036), has lovely pine-furnished rooms for 5000 dr a double with private bathrooms. The rooms are between the Hotel Dioscuri and the Its Kale fortress.

The D class *Hotel Epidaurus* (☎ 27 541), on Ipsilandi, has doubles for 5000 dr with shared bathrooms or 6300 dr with private bathrooms. At the C class *Hotel Athena* (☎ 27 695), Plateia Syntagmatos, rates are 4000/5600 dr with private bathrooms. The rooms are pokey so only try here if the other places are full. The C class *Hotel Acropol* (☎ 17 796), Vasilissis Olgas 9, has friendly management and clean single/double/triple rooms for 4000/5800/7000 dr with private bathrooms, including breakfast.

The D class *Hotel Lito* (☎ 28 093) Zygomata 28, at the southern (top) end of Farmakopoulou, has comfortable singles/doubles with shared bathrooms for 4700/5600 dr and doubles with private bathrooms for 8000 dr. The *King Otto Hotel* (☎ 27 585), Farmakopoulou 3, is similarly priced.

Places to Stay – middle
The C class *Hotel Dioscouri* (☎ 28 550), on the corner of Zygomata 6 and Vyronos, has immaculate rooms for 6700/8900/10,000 dr, including breakfast. Even greater luxury awaits those who can afford it at the B class *Hotel Agamemnon* (☎ 28 021/2; fax 28 022), Akti Miaouli 3. Rates are 9820/15,580/20,670 dr for half board, which is mandatory.

Places to Stay – top end
Nafplion's *Xenia Complex* (☎ 28 991/2; fax 28 987) has three types of accommodation. The *Xenia Palace* is deluxe class with all the trimmings commensurate with this rating, including a disco, swimming pool and private beach. Singles/doubles are 13,500/17,000 dr and suites are 31,400 dr. The A class *Xenia Hotel* has singles/doubles for 9500/11,900 dr and *Xenia Bungalows* are 17,000 dr.

Places to Eat
Zorbas Taverna, Staikopoulou 30, is one of Nafplion's most popular eating places. The appropriately named *Fantasy Bar* next door has great snacks and cocktails at reasonable prices. On the opposite side of the street *Taverna Ta Fanaria* is also good, with similar prices to Zorbas. Just south of here is

the *Taverna Retsina*, on Kapodistriou, which is also a popular place.

Taverna Ellas, on the corner of Plateia Syntagmatos and Vasileos Konstantinou, is a good place for people-watching as you tuck into hearty Greek staples such as meatballs, chicken in tomato sauce and moussaka. *Taverna Palaeo Archantiko* (Old Mansion), on the corner of Ipsilandi and Sofroni, is full of character and serves tasty dishes such as squid, stuffed tomatoes and swordfish.

The nameless kafeneion at Syngrou 14 is a good place for breakfast, with yoghurt and honey, fresh crusty bread and Nescafé for 400 dr. Nearby, *I Pyli Tis Chiras* is a cheap, rough and ready taverna. For a change try the traditional *Taverna To Tsaki* (The Fire Place) on 25 Martiou in the new town. An excellent meal here of Greek salad, souvlaki, chips and retsina will set you back about 1700 dr.

Entertainment

From mid-June to the end of August, Ancient Greek dramas are performed at the Theatre of Epidaurus (30 km from Nafplion) in conjunction with the Athens Festival. Tickets may be bought in Nafplion at Bourtzi Tours (☎ 22 691 or 25 010), Syngrou 4. Sale of tickets begins 10 days before each performance. For more information see the Epidaurus section. On the evenings of performances, Bourtzi Tours runs buses to Epidaurus from Nafplion, as does the KTEL bus syndicate. There's competition between the two, so check which is cheaper.

There are two discos in Nafplion: *Disco Idol* is on the corner of Syngrou and Flessa and *Disco Memory* is next door. There are several music bars on Bouboulinas.

Getting There & Away

Bus From Nafplion there are hourly buses to Athens (2½ hours, 1700 dr); half-hourly buses to Argos (30 minutes, 220 dr); hourly buses to Tolo (30 minutes, 220 dr); four a day to Porto Heli (two hours, 1000 dr); and three a day to Mycenae (one hour, 380 dr), Epidaurus (40 minutes, 380 dr) and Galatas (for Poros; two hours, 1050 dr).

Car & Motorbike Cars can be hired from Champ Rent a Car (☎ 24 930), on Staikopoulou, west of Plateia Syntagmatos. A reliable motorbike-hire outlet is Moto Rent (☎ 27 183 or 25 642), Tsilikanidou 3, in the new town.

Hydrofoil During July and August, every day except Sunday, hydrofoils depart from Nafplion for Zea Marina (Piraeus; four hours, 4980 dr) via Tolo (20 minutes, 760 dr), Porto Heli (50 minutes, 2050 dr), Spetses (one hour, 2060 dr), Ermione (1½ hours, 2130 dr), Hydra (two hours, 2390 dr), Poros (2½ hours, 2990 dr), Methana (three hours, 3480 dr) and Aegina (three hours, 3580 dr). Tickets can be bought at Bourtzi Tours.

AROUND NAFPLION
Beaches

The nearest sandy beach to Nafplion is **Karathona Beach**, at the far side of the Palamidi Fortress. There is no access from the fortress. To get to this beach, you can either walk (one hour) or take a bus out of town on 25 Martiou, which doubles back to the coast.

Further around the coast there's a line of beaches beginning with **Asini**, nine km from Nafplion, followed by **Tolo**, **Drepano**, **Plaka**, **Kadia** and **Iria**. Tolo, 11 km from Nafplion, is the most developed, with watersports equipment for hire.

Places to Stay Most of the hotels along this stretch of coast are block-booked by package holiday companies, but there's a plethora of prominently signposted camp sites.

Near Asini Beach there's *Kastraki Camping* (☎ 59 386/7); at Tolo there's *Lido I* (☎ 59 489), *Lido II* (☎ 59 396), *Sunset Camping* (☎ 59 566), *Stars* (☎ 59 226), *Tolo Plaz* (☎ 59 133) and *Xeni* (☎ 59 338); at Plaka there's *Plaka Beach* (☎ 92 294/395), *Argolis Beach* (☎ 92 228) and *Triton* (☎ 92 128). The telephone code for all of these camp sites is 0752.

At Iria Beach, 27 km from Nafplion, there is *Iria Beach Camping* (☎ 0753-91 253) and *Poseidon* (☎ 0753-91 341).

Ancient Asini Ασίνη

The ruins of ancient Asini, on a rocky headland just one km inland from Asini Beach, offer a diversion from sunbathing and swimming. There are remains of an acropolis, Mycenaean tombs, Roman baths and Venetian fortifications.

Tiryns Τίρυνθα

The ruins of Homer's 'wall-girt Tiryns' are four km north-west of Nafplion. The walls of Tiryns are the apogee of Mycenaean architectural achievement (or paranoia), being even more substantial than those at Mycenae. In parts they are 20 metres thick, and the largest stones are estimated to weigh 14,000 kg. Within the walls are secret stairways, vaulted galleries and hidden storage chambers. Frescoes from the palace are now in the National Archaeological Museum in Athens. Tiryns' setting is less awe-inspiring and atmospheric than Mycenae's, but on the plus side it's far less visited. The site (☎ 0752-27 502) is open Monday to Friday from 8 am to 7 pm, and Saturday and Sunday from 8.30 am to 3 pm. Admission is 500 dr. The ruins stand to the right of the Nafplion-Argos road.

Reconstruction of Tiryns

Asklepios with Hygeia

Getting There & Away

There are hourly buses from Nafplion to Tolo (30 minutes, 220 dr) via Asini.

Any Nafplion-Argos bus will drop you outside the ancient site of Tiryns.

EPIDAURUS Επίδαυρος

Epidaurus (Ep-EE-dav-ros), 30 km east of Nafplion, is one of the most renowned of Greece's ancient sites. Epidaurus was a sanctuary of Asklepios, the god of medicine. The difference in the aura here, compared with that of the war-orientated Mycenaean cities, is immediately tangible. Henry Miller wrote in *The Colossus of Maroussi* that Mycenae 'folds in on itself', but Epidaurus is 'open, exposed...devoted to the spirit'. Certainly Epidaurus seems to emanate joy, optimism and celebration.

History & Mythology

Legend has it that Asklepios was the son of Apollo and Koronis. Whilst giving birth to Asklepios, Koronis was struck by a thunder bolt and killed. Apollo took his son to Mt Pelion where the physician Chiron instructed the boy in the healing arts.

Apollo was worshipped at Epidaurus in Mycenaean and Archaic times, but by the 4th century BC, he had been superseded by his son, and Epidaurus became acknowledged as the birthplace of Asklepios. Although there were sanctuaries to Asklepios throughout Greece, the two most important ones were at Epidaurus and on the island of Kos. The fame of the sanctuary spread far and wide, and in 293 BC, when a plague was raging in Rome, Livy and Ovid came to Epidaurus to ask for medicinal aid.

The treatments provided at the sanctuary involved diet instruction, herbal medicines, and occasionally even surgery, with a bit of magic thrown in for good measure.

Asklepios' attributes are a serpent and staff. The serpent, by renewing its skin, symbolises rejuvenation, and the staff symbolises Asklepios walking all over the land rendering aid. It is believed that licks from snakes were one of the curative practices at the sanctuary.

The sanctuary also served as a place of entertainment. Every four years the Festival of Asklepieia took place at Epidaurus, when dramas were staged and athletic competitions held.

Theatre

These days it is the 3rd-century theatre, not the sanctuary, that is the crowd-puller at Epidaurus. It is one of the best preserved of Classical Greek buildings, and is renowned for its amazing acoustics. The theatre is built of limestone and will seat up to 14,000 people. Its entrance is flanked by restored Corinthian pilasters.

The Festival of Epidaurus takes place here each year in July and August. See the Entertainment section for details.

Museum

The museum is between the sanctuary and the theatre. It houses statues, stone inscriptions recording miraculous cures, surgical instruments, votive offerings and plans and partial reconstructions of the sanctuary's once elaborate tholos. After the theatre, the tholos is considered to have been the site's most impressive building and fragments of beautiful, intricately carved reliefs from its ceiling are also on display.

Sanctuary

The vast ruins of the sanctuary are likely to be less crowded than the theatre. In the south, is the huge **Katagogeion**, which was a hostelry for pilgrims and patients to the sanctuary. West of here is the large **banqueting hall**, in which the Romans built an **odeion**. It was in this building that the Festival of Asklepieia took place. Opposite here is the **stadium**, venue for the festival's athletic competitions.

To the north are the foundations of the **Temple of Asklepios** and next to it the **abaton**. As with present-day alternative medicine the therapies practised here seemed to have depended on the influence of the mind upon the body. It is believed that patients were given a pep talk by a priest on the powers of Asklepios, and then put to sleep in the abaton to dream of a visitation by the god. The dream would hold the key to the healing process.

To the east is the **Sanctuary of Egyptian Gods**, which is an indication that the cult of Asklepios was an adaptation of the cult of Imhotep – Imhotep was worshipped in Egypt for his healing powers. To the west of the Temple of Asklepios are the remains of the **tholos**, built in 360-320 BC. The function of the tholos is unknown.

One gets a strong impression walking around the sanctuary that its lovely setting in the green foothills of Mt Arahneo, its air redolent with the fragrance of herbs and pine trees, would in itself have had a beneficial effect upon the ailing. Considering the state of Greece's current health system, perhaps they ought to resurrect this centre.

Places to Stay

Although most visitors come to Epidaurus on a day trip, there are a small number of accommodation options if you want to stay overnight. The B class *Xenia Hotel* (☎ 0753-22 003/4/5) at the site charges 7000/10,000 dr for singles/doubles. At the village of Ligourio, four km north of Epidaurus on the main road to Nafplion, there are a couple of cheaper options; the *Hotel Koronis* (☎ 0753-22 267) and the *Hotel Asklepios* (☎ 0753-22

251) are both on the Nafplion-Epidaurus road and charge similar rates of around 2500/4000 dr for single/double rooms.

Places to Eat
In Ligourio the *Restaurant Oasis* on the main road serves reasonably priced Greek staples.

Entertainment
From 26 July to 30 August each year, during the Festival of Epidaurus, ancient dramas are performed at the Epidaurus theatre. Performances start at 9 pm and tickets may be bought at Epidaurus (☎ 0753-22 006) on Thursday, Friday and Saturday from 9.30 am to 1 pm and 6 to 9 pm; the Athens Festival box office (see Entertainment in the Athens chapter); or Bourtzi Tours, Nafplion (see the Nafplion section in this chapter). Tickets cost 1200/1500/2000/2500 dr depending on the seat. Students pay 600 dr.

Getting There & Away
There are three buses a day from Nafplion to Epidaurus (40 minutes, 380 dr) via Ligourio (350 dr).

Achaia Αχαία

The prefecture of Achaia lies between Argolis and Elia; its capital is Patras. Achaia owes its name to the Achaeans, the Indo-European branch of migrants who settled in mainland Greece and brought forth the Mycenaean civilisation. The coast of Achaia consists of a string of resorts which are more popular with Greeks than with tourists. Inland are the high peaks of Mt Panahaiko, Mt Erimanthos and Mt Helmos.

It takes about two hours to drive from Corinth to Patras along the New National Highway. The Old National Road which skirts the coast is longer but affords the best views. Whichever road you choose, you should stop off at the pleasant village of Diakofto, and ride the fantastic Diakofto-Zahlorou-Kalavryta rack and pinion railway. Overnight stops at Zahlorou and Kalavryta are also highly recommended.

DIAKOFTO Διακοφτό
Diakofto (Dee-a-kof-TO), 80 km from Corinth and 55 km from Patras, is a delightful and serene village, tucked between steep mountains and the sea, amid lemon and olive groves.

Orientation & Information
Diakofto's layout is easy to figure out. The train station is in the middle of the village; to reach the waterfront cross over the railway track, and walk down the road straight ahead. If you turn right here you will come to pebbly Egali Beach after one km.

To reach the central square, walk along the road opposite the station and veer right. Turn right here to reach the post office which is on the left. The National Bank of Greece is a little further along on the right and the OTE is 300 metres beyond here, on the left. Diakofto's postcode is 25100 and the telephone code is 0691. There is no EOT or tourist police in Diakofto.

Diakofto-Kalavryta Railway
This rack and pinion railway roller coasts its way through the chasmic Vouraikos Gorge, rising 700 metres in 22½ km. It was built by an Italian company between 1885 and 1895, and is a remarkable engineering accomplishment. The original steam engines were replaced in the early 1960s by diesel cars, but the old steam engines can still be seen outside the Diakofto and Kalavryta stations.

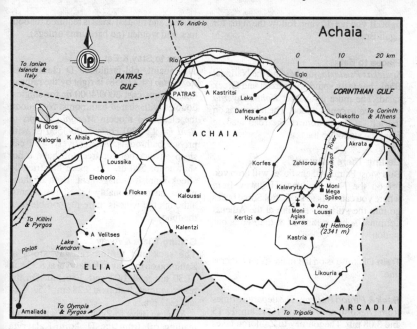

The line crosses narrow bridges and goes through tunnels and along precariously overhanging ledges. Below, the Vouraikos river tumbles over massive boulders. The journey from Diakofto to Kalavryta, stopping en route at Zahlorou, takes about 1½ hours. See under Diakofto's Getting There & Away section for departure times.

It's possible to walk through the gorge along the track. Ensure that you don't arrive at a tunnel at the same time as the train, however! There are a few flat grassy areas along the route which are ideal for camping. If you are camping and you eat at the Romantza Restaurant in Zahlorou you can use the shower there. Water should be carried, although of course water and meals are available at Zahlorou, the halfway point.

Places to Stay

Diakofto's D class *Hotel Lemonies* (☎ 2850 or 3950) has agreeable single/double rooms for 3000/4000 dr with private bathrooms.

The hotel is on the right halfway down the road to the sea. *Hotel Helos* (☎ 41 236), also D class, on the central square, is similarly priced.

Diakofto's nicest accommodation is the lovely C class *Chris Paul Hotel* (☎ 41 715/855; fax 804 5669), which is managed by a friendly Greek-Australian couple. The air-con single/double/triple rooms cost 5420/9378/11,866 dr including breakfast. The hotel is near the train station and is well signposted.

The *Pension Galini* (☎ 41 829 or 42 872/053), near Egali Beach, consists of 23 well-equipped apartments in extensive grounds, with flowerbeds, lemon groves and a sports field. The prices are 6000/9000 dr for two/three people, and 11,000 dr for four or five people. To reach the apartments from the train station cross the track and turn immediately right (at the periptero). After one km, turn left at the signpost for Egali Beach and the pension is signposted to the right. If you are driving, follow the signs for Egali Beach.

Places to Eat

Soulekas Psistaria, just beyond the National Bank, has tasty souvlaki, tzatziki and Greek salad. The more up-market *Kohili Taverna* serves well-prepared food. The taverna is on the left, at the bottom of the road leading from the station to the sea.

Getting There & Away

Bus Most Patras-Athens buses will drop you off on the New National Highway from where you can walk to Diakofto. Some buses go into the village – enquire at the Athens' Terminal A bus station or at the Patras bus station.

Train Diakofto is on the main Athens-Patras line.

Rack & Pinion Railway The departure times from Diakofto are 7.45 and 10.42 am; 12.15 and 3.08 pm. The journey to Zahlorou takes 50 minutes and costs 210 dr. To Kalavryta from Diakofto, it takes about 1½ hours and costs 350 dr.

ZAHLOROU Ζαχλωρού

The picturesque and unspoilt settlement of Zahlorou, the halfway stop on the Diakofto to Kalavryta line, straddles both sides of the river and railway line.

Moni Mega Spileo Μονή Μέγα Σπήλαιο
A steep three-km path (signposted) leads from Zahlorou to the Moni Mega Spileo (Monastery of the Great Cavern). The original monastery was destroyed in 1934 when gunpowder stored during the War of Independence exploded. The new monastery houses illuminated gospels, relics, silver crosses, jewellery and the miraculous icon of the Virgin Mary, which, like numerous icons in Greece, is said to have been painted by St Luke. It was supposedly discovered in the nearby cavern by St Theodore and St Simeon in 362 AD. A monk will show visitors

around, and modest dress is required for both men and women (no bare arms or legs).

Places to Stay & Eat

The quaint, old-fashioned D class *Hotel Romantzo* (☎ 22 758) is right by the railway line. Rooms cost 3000/4000 dr for singles/ doubles with shared bathrooms. Next door, the clean and modern *Messinia Rooms to Rent* (☎ 22 789) costs 2500/3500 dr with private bathrooms. Alternatively, you can sleep on the roof for free and have a hot shower for 500 dr. This place has friendly Greek-Finnish management. Both of these places have reasonably priced restaurants, although the wine is more memorable than the food.

Getting There & Away

The rack and pinion railway stops at Zahlorou on the way to Kalavryta at 8.33 and 11.30 am; and 1.03 and 3.56 pm. On the return journey, it stops at 9.28 am; 1.57, 4.48 and 5.47 pm.

You can drive to Zahlorou on a dirt road, leading off from the Diakofto-Kalavryta road.

KALAVRYTA Καλάβρυτα

Kalavryta (Ka-LA-vri-ta, population 1800, elevation 756 metres) is a cool mountain resort, with copious springs and shady plane trees. Two relatively recent historical events have assured the town a special place in the hearts of all Greeks. The revolt against the Turks began when, on 25 March 1821, Bishop Germanos of Patras raised the banner of revolt at the monastery of Agias Lavras, six km from Kalavryta. And on 13 December 1943, in one of the most abhorrent atrocities of WW II, the Nazis set fire to the town and massacred all its male inhabitants over 15 years old in a reprisal against resistance activity. The total number killed was 1436. The hands of the cathedral clock stand eternally at 2.34, the time the massacre began.

Orientation & Information

Opposite the train station a large mural reads 'Kalavryta, founder member of the Union of

Martyred Towns, appeals to all the world to fight for world peace'. To the right of the mural is Odos Syngrou, which after one block becomes Odos 25 Martiou; to the left is Odos Konstantinou. The central square, Plateia Eleftherias, is between these two streets, two blocks up from the train station. The bus station is on the left side of Kallimani. From the train station walk up Syngrou and turn right at Hotel Maria onto Kallimani. The post office is on the main square and the OTE is on Konstantinou. Kalavryta's postcode is 25001 and the telephone code is 0692. The National Bank of Greece is on 25 Martiou, just before the central square. There is no EOT or tourist police in Kalavryta

Martyrs' Monument

This huge cross on a hill of pine and cypress trees above the town is an imposing and poignant shrine to those who were massacred. Follow the signpost from the station, which will take you to Odos 13 Dekemvriou. Just beyond the cemetery, on the left, a paved path and steps lead up to the shrine.

Places to Stay

There is no camp site in the area, but freelance camping may be tolerated.

The cheapest hotel in Kalavryta is the D class *Hotel Paradissos* (☎ 22 303), on Kallimani, where tidy singles are 2000 dr with shared bathrooms; attractive doubles/triples with private bathrooms are 5000/6000 dr. The *Hotel Maria* (☎ 22 296), Syngrou 2, has comfortable singles/doubles for 4000/5000 dr with private bathrooms; the price includes breakfast.

The B class *Hotel Filoxenia* (☎ 22 493/422), on Kallimani, is a lovely place with wood panelling and traditional brass light fittings. Rates are 5485/7968 dr with private bathrooms. Walk one block up Syngrou from the train station and you'll come to Hotel Maria on the right. To reach the other two hotels turn right at Hotel Maria onto Kallimani.

The B class *Hotel Kalavrita* (☎ 22 712/845) is another attractive hotel with stucco

walls and embroidered wall-hangings. Single/double/triple/quad rooms here are 6000/9000/13,500/18,000 dr with private bathrooms. The hotel is behind the train station.

Places to Eat

The *Taverna O Elotos*, on 25 Martiou opposite the church, is large, bright and cheerful. Main meals range between 800 and 1000 dr.

The cosy little *Bytina Taverna*, opposite the bus station, has hearty meals at a similar price. The taverna has a quaint décor of brass bells and caged birds and an owner with a clock fetish; there are no less than eight on the wall. I ate there on the night daylight saving began, and each clock was carefully taken down and lovingly washed and polished, before having its pointers changed – the clocks got far more attention than the customers.

There are grocers, butchers and greengrocers on 25 Martiou. On Saturday there is a laiki agora (market) just down from the ski centre.

Getting There & Away

Bus There are five buses a day to Patras (1000 dr) and two buses a day to Athens, leaving at 9 am and 4.45 pm.

Train The narrow-gauge train to Diakofto (via Zahlorou) leaves at 9.06 am; 1.35, 4.26 and 5.25 pm.

Taxi Kalavryta's taxi rank (☎ 22 127) is on the central square.

AROUND KALAVRYTA
Moni Agias Lavras

The original 10th-century monastery was burnt by the Nazis. The new monastery has a small museum where the banner standard is displayed along with other monastic memorabilia. There is no bus to the monastery so you must either walk the six km from Kalavryta or take a taxi.

Limni Kastrion Cave

This cave, 16½ km south of Kalavryta near

the village of Kastria, is two km long and has 13 subterranean lakes linked by waterfalls and a profusion of stalactites hanging high above. The cave is usually open daily from 9.30 am to 4.30 pm, although it is advisable to telephone first (☎ 0692-31 262) to check. At the time of writing, there was one bus a day to Kastria – check the schedule at the bus station. A taxi to the cave from Kalavryta will cost about 4000 dr return.

Ski Centre

The ski centre (elevation 1650-2100 metres), with nine pistes and one chair lift, is 14 km east of Kalavryta on Mt Helmos. It has a cafeteria and first-aid centre but no overnight accommodation. The ski centre has an office in Kalavryta (☎ 22 661; fax 22 415), on 25 Martiou. Opening times are Monday to Friday from 7 am to 3 pm. Several outlets on Odos Konstantinou rent skis for approximately 2000 dr per day. There is no bus to the centre from Kalavryta; a taxi will cost around 2000 dr.

Mt Helmos Refuge

The EOS-owned *B Leondopoulos Mountain Refuge* is situated at 2100 metres on Mt Helmos. A marked footpath leads to the refuge from the ski centre (one hour), another leads from the village of Ano Loussi (1½ hours), on the way to Kastria. If you would like to stay in the refuge, or would like more information on walks or climbs on Mt Helmos, talk to EOS representative Charilaos Ermeidis (☎ 22 346 or 23 043) in the Zaharoplasteion Ermeidis, on 25 Martiou, Kalavryta.

Mavroneri Waterfall

This waterfall, which plungers into a ravine on the northern side of Mt Helmos, is one of a number of places in Greece which is claimed to be the source of the River Styx, across which the dead must journey before they can enter Hades, the world of the dead.

It is possible to trek to the waterfall from the EOS refuge of B Leondopoulos on Mt Helmos (two hours) or from the village of Peristera (five hours). Peristera is one of a cluster of remote mountain villages lying west of a road which runs south from Akrata, about 10 km east of Diakofto.

With your own transport you may like to explore this remote region (buses are very infrequent).

For more information about trekking to the waterfall, contact the Egio branch of the EOS (☎ 0691-25 285), on the corner of Satiriou Pontou and Aratou, Egio. Egio is on the coast, 13 km west of Diakofto.

PATRAS Πάτρα

Patras (in Greek PA-tra, population 142,200), Greece's third-largest city and principal port for boats to Italy and the Ionian islands, sees many tourists in transit, but less who stay. This impulse to beat a hasty retreat is understandable, for the city lacks any immediate appeal.

Patras was destroyed by the Turks during the War of Independence, and under Kapodistrias, was rebuilt on a grid plan, with ornate neoclassical buildings, wide arcaded streets and large squares. However, 150 years on, this once grand city is now in need of a major facelift – everything looks dusty, crumbling and neglected.

Orientation

Patras' grid system facilitates orientation. The waterfront is Iroon Politechniou at the north-eastern end, Othonos Amalias in the middle and Akti Dimeon further west. Customs is at the eastern end of the waterfront, and the main bus station and the train station are on Othonos Amalias. Most of the agencies selling ferry tickets are on Iroon Politechniou and Othonos Amalias. The main thoroughfares of Agiou Dionysiou, Riga Fereou, Mezonos, Korinthou and Odos Kanakari run parallel to the waterfront. The main square is Plateia Trion Symahon, opposite the train station.

Information

Tourist Offices The EOT (☎ 42 3866, 42 0303/4/5 or 42 9046) is just outside customs. The helpful English-speaking staff give out a free map and have information on bus, train and boat schedules. It is open every day from 7 am to 9.30 pm. The tourist police (☎ 22 0902/3) on Patreos are extremely helpful and courteous. They give out the same information as the EOT and are open 24 hours a day.

Money The National Bank of Greece is on Plateia Trion Symahon. In summer the opening times are Monday to Thursday from 8 am to 2 pm and 6 to 8.30 pm; Friday from 8 am to 1.30 pm and 6 to 8.30 pm; and Saturday and Sunday from 11 am to 1 pm and 6 to 8.30 pm. In winter it is closed on weekends. American Express is represented by Albatros Travel (☎ 22 0993/4609), Othonos Amalias 48.

Post & Telecommunications The main post office is on the corner of Zaimi and Mezonos. It is open Monday to Friday from 7.30 am to 8 pm; Saturday from 7.30 am to 2 pm; and Sunday from 9 am to 1.30 pm. There is a mobile post office outside customs which is open Monday to Saturday from 8 am to 8 pm and Sunday from 9 am to 6 pm. Patras' postcode is 26001.

The main OTE office is on the corner of Dimitriou Gounari and Odos Kanakari, in the western part of the city. It is open 24 hours a day. There is also an OTE at customs which is open every day from 7.30 am to 6.30 pm and 7.30 to 10.30 pm. Patras' telephone code is 061.

Foreign Consulates Foreign consulates in Patras include:

Germany
    Mezonos 98 (☎ 22 1943)
UK
    Votsi 2 (☎ 27 6403)

Bookshop The Press Agency Book Store (☎ 27 7396), Agiou Nikolaou 32, sells English-language books, newspapers and magazines.

Laundry The self-service Plintirios Laundrette is on Trion Navarhon 74, in the west part of the city. It's open Monday to Friday from

9 am to 9 pm; Saturday from 9 am to 1 pm (closed Sunday). In August it's open from 8 am to 3 pm and 5 to 9 pm.

Emergency There is a First Aid Centre (☎ 27 7386) on the corner of Karolou and Agiou Dionysiou.

Kastro
Like many Greek cities, Patras improves the higher up you get. If you clamber up the steps at the end of Agiou Nikolaou, you will reach the kastro (fortified hill). The area huddled around the fortress is quite picturesque in contrast to the area nearer the port, and there are great views over to the Ionian islands of Zakynthos and Kefallonia.

Archaeological Museum
This small museum (☎ 27 5070) is well laid out with labelling in English. The collection includes finds from Mycenaean, Hellenic and Roman times such as grave objects, sculpture, figurines, a mosaic and a lovely disc of blue glass in an ivory frame which was found in a Roman house in Patras. The museum is at Mezonos 42. Opening times are Tuesday to Sunday from 8.30 am to 3 pm. Admission is 400 dr.

Achaia Clauss Winery
This winery, in a lovely hillside setting nine km south-east of Patras, produces some of Greece's finest wines. It was founded in 1854 by the Bavarian Gustav Clauss, who made a dark red wine, Mavrodaphne (Black Daphne), named after the object of his unrequited love; you will be given a sample on arrival. There are free tours of the winery between 7.30 am and 1 pm and 4 to 7 pm (10 am to 4.30 pm in the off season). Take bus No 7 from the corner of Kolokotroni and Odos Kanakari.

Places to Stay – bottom end
Kavouri Camping (☎ 42 8066/2145), two km east of customs, is the closest camp site to Patras. Take bus No 1 from Agios

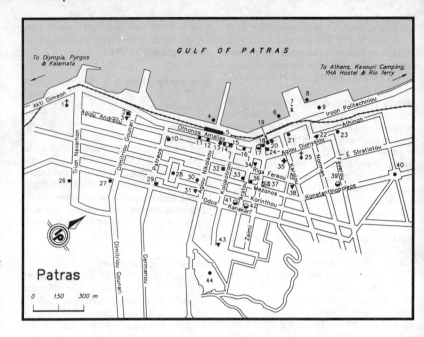

Dionysios church. Further along the road near the Rio ferry, which is nine km northeast of Patras, are *Rio Camping* (☎ 99 1585/1450/3388) and *Rio Mare* (☎ 99 2263). For these sites take bus No 6 from Odos Kanakari.

Patras' pleasant *YHA Hostel* (☎ 42 7278), Iroon Politechniou 68, is in a 19th-century mansion, 1½ km east of the customs building. Beds in dormitories are 1100 dr and roof space is 800 dr. Breakfast is 300 dr. There is no curfew and an IYHF card is not required. To reach the hostel walk in an easterly direction along Iroon Politechniou.

The *Pension Nicos* (☎ 27 6183), on the corner of Patreos 3 and Agiou Andreou 121 (a westerly continuation of Agiou Dionysiou), is the best of the budget hotels and the only one which caters to the needs of backpackers – others double up as bordellos. It's a delightfully ramshackle place with cheery rooms and a friendly owner. Singles/doubles are 1800/3000 dr, triples/quads are 3200/

4500 dr with shared bathrooms, and doubles/triples are 4000/4500 dr with private bathrooms.

Other respectable options are the C class *Hotel Acropole* (☎ 22 4213/4235), Othonos Amalias 39, with rooms for 3500/5500 dr and *Hotel Marie* (☎ 33 1302/1324), on Dimitriou Gounari, where rates are 4100/5500 dr.

Places to Stay – middle

The B class *Hotel Rania* (☎ 22 0114/0537/0435), Riga Fereou 53, has immaculate rooms for 7000/11,286 dr. The *Hotel Adonis* (☎ 22 4213/4235; fax 22 6971), Zaimi 9, opposite the bus station, has plush, tastefully furnished single/double/ triple aircon rooms for 7700/9800/12,300 dr, including breakfast.

Places to Stay – top end

Patras' best hotels are outside the town on the

■ PLACES TO STAY

2	Hotel Marie
10	Pension Nicos
15	Hotel Acropole
24	Hotel Adonis
32	Hotel Rania

▼ PLACES TO EAT

3	Thalassia Restaurant
31	Nicolaros Taverna
34	Osteria Taverna
38	Harlofix Costos Restaurant
43	Maria Vegetarian Restaurant

OTHER

1	Agios Andreas Church
4	Boats to Ionian Islands
5	Train Station
6 & 8	Boats to Italy
7	GNTO
9	Customs
12	Albatros Travel (Agent for American Express)
13	Plateia Trion Symahon

14	National Bank of Greece
17	Main Bus Station
25	Agios Dionysios Church
26	Plintirios Laundrette
27	OTE
28	Plateia Vasileos Georgiou
29	Tourist Police
30	Press Agency Book Store
33	Plateia Olgas
35	First Aid Centre
36	Archaeological Museum
37	Post Office
39	Bus Station for Lefkada & Messolongi
40	Plateia Agias Sofias
41 & 42	Bus Stops for Nos 6, 7 & 8 Buses
44	Kastro

FERRY LINE CENTRAL OFFICES

11	Marlines
16	Karageorgis
18	Ionic
19	Strintzis & European Lines
20	Fragline
21	Adriatica
22	Minoan
23	Hellenic Mediterranean

coast. The B class *Achaia Beach* (☎ 99 1801) is on the coast at Paralia Proastiou, three km south-west of Patras. It has a bar, restaurant, swimming pool and nightclub. Singles/doubles are 10,000/11,500 dr.

The B class *To Tzaki Hotel* (☎ 42 8303/25/47/69; fax 42 6750) on the same stretch of coast has a bar, restaurant and TV lounge. Doubles are 13,300 and suites are 22,500 dr.

The most luxurious hotel in the vicinity is the A class *Porto Rio* (☎ 99 2102) at Rio, nine km north-east of Patras. The hotel has two restaurants, a nightclub, two swimming pools, tennis courts and a health studio. Singles/doubles are 11,500/14,700 dr and suites are 24,500 dr.

Places to Eat

You can eat well in Patras so long as you avoid the overpriced tourist traps along the waterfront. *Nikolaros Taverna*, Agiou Nikolaou 50, and *Harlofix Costos Restau-*rant, Riga Fereou 3, both serve good value, traditional food. The *Maria Vegetarian Restaurant* (☎ 62 2108), Kolokotroni 79, is excellent. Nut roast with yoghurt topping is 550 dr, spaghetti with mushrooms and cream is 730 dr and large salad is 600 dr. The restaurant is in a neoclassical mansion at the top of Kolokotroni. As it's such a long trek up here, telephone to make sure it's open.

The green-shuttered *Osteria Taverna*, Aratou 5, has traditional décor and serves delicious food. Main courses are around 900 dr. The *Thalassia Restaurant*, Agiou Andreou 128, specialises in seafood and is one of those rare Greek restaurants which shines like a beacon in the midst of all the places dishing up moussaka and souvlaki. The highly recommended mixed seafood platter, costing 1500 dr, consists of king prawns, mussels, kalamaria and whitebait. Other dishes include shrimp saganaki (1100 dr), king prawns (1700 dr) and seafood spaghetti (1800 dr).

Entertainment

The **Patras Carnival** in January and February is Greece's most riotous celebration. High spirits and euphoria envelop the city, as elaborately decorated floats and people in fancy dress parade through the streets. The **Patras Arts Festival**, held in the summer, features events staged at the Roman odeion, at the kastro. The EOT and tourist police will be able to give you information.

Getting There & Away

Bus From the main bus station on Othonos Amalias there are at least hourly buses to Athens (three hours, 2400 dr); 10 a day to Pyrgos (two hours, 1200 dr); four a day to both Ioannina (four hours, 2800 dr) and Kalavryta (1000 dr); three a day to both Thessaloniki (9½ hours, 5500 dr) and Delphi (1350 dr); two a day to both Kalamata (four hours, 2700 dr) and Tripolis (four hours, 2050 dr); and one a day to Killini (summer only, 1½ hours, 950 dr) Four buses a day to the Ionian island of Lefkada (2150 dr) leave from a small bus station at the corner of Faverou and Konstantinopoleos.

Take bus No 6 from Odos Kanakari for the Rio-Andirio ferry (30 minutes, 50 dr).

Train There are seven trains a day to Athens (five hours, 1300 dr) via Diakofto (one hour, 280 dr) and Corinth (2½ hours, 750 dr); seven a day to Pyrgos (two hours, 630 dr); and four trains a day to Kalamata (six hours, 1200 dr).

Ferry (Domestic) From Patras there are daily ferries to the Ionian islands of Kefallonia (four hours, 1500 dr), Ithaki (six hours, 2050 dr) and Corfu (10 hours, 3500 dr – see also under International Ferries). The telephone number of Patras' port police is ☎ 34 1002.

Rio-Andirio Ferry This ferry plies between Rio, nine km north-east of Patras, and Andirio, every 15 minutes between 7 am and 11 pm (15 minutes, 76 dr; car 600 dr).

Ferry (International) In summer there is at least one boat a day from Patras to the Italian ports of Brindisi (19 hours), Bari (17½ hours) and Ancona (33 hours) via Igoumenitsa and Corfu. It is possible to stop over in Corfu free of charge, so long as you specify you wish to do so when you buy your ticket. A few of the boats go nonstop to Brindisi and Ancona. There is one boat a week to Ortona.

At the time of writing the cost of low/high season one-way deck-class tickets on all lines to Brindisi was 9800/15,800 dr. On most lines to Brindisi, Inter-Rail pass holders travel free but must pay 1500 dr port tax. The cost to Ancona was 9800/12,800 dr, with the exception of Marlines (9300/12,100 dr), and to Bari 7000/9000 dr. On all lines, bicycles travel free. The periods designated as high and low season vary between companies, but is always sometime between mid-June and mid-September.

In high season one boat a week goes from Patras to Limassol in Cyprus (42 hours, 17,500 dr) via Crete (Iraklion) and Rhodes. Boats to Italy leave from two points on the waterfront. See the Patras map.

The addresses and routes of the central offices or representatives of the ferry lines operating out of Patras are:

Adriatica
  Othonos Amalias 8 (☎ 42 1995): Brindisi via Igoumenitsa and Corfu
Fragline
  Othonos Amalias 5 (☎ 27 7676): Brindisi via Igoumenitsa and Corfu
Hellenic Mediterranean
  On the corner of Sarantoporou & Athinon (☎ 42 9520): Brindisi via Kefallonia and Ortona via Igoumenitsa and Corfu
Ionic
  Othonos Amalias 25 (☎ 22 6053): Ancona via Igoumenitsa and Corfu
Karageorgis
  Othonos Amalias 32 (☎ 27 4554): Ancona nonstop
Marlines
  Othonos Amalias 56 (☎ 22 6666): Ancona via Igoumenitsa and Corfu, and Limassol via Crete and Rhodes
Minoan
  On the corner of Norman 1 & Athinon (☎ 42 1500): Ancona via Igoumenitsa and Corfu

Strintzis & European Lines
  Othonos Amalias 14 (☎ 27 7783): Ancona and
  Bari via Igoumenitsa and Corfu

Getting Around
Bus Local bus Nos 6, 7 and 8 leave from bus
stops on either side of Aratou (see map).

Car Car-hire outlets include: Ansa (☎ 27
7329), Votsi 2; Europcar (☎ 62 1360), Agiou
Andreou 6; Eurodollar (☎ 22 4609),
Othonos Amalias 48; and Hertz (☎ 22 0990),
Karolou 2.

Elia   Ηλεία

Elia, in the western Peloponnese, is one of
its most fertile prefectures, watered by the
river Alfios, the 'Sacred Alph' in Samuel
Taylor Coleridge's *Kubla Khan*. Its valleys
are speckled with vine, orange and olive
groves, clusters of cherry and walnut trees,
and fields of corn, wheat and vegetables. The
prime tourist attraction is the site of ancient
Olympia.

PYRGOS Πύργος
The capital of the prefecture is Pyrgos (population 22,000), 98 km south-west of Patras,
and 24 km from Olympia. It's an unattractive
agricultural town with nothing of interest to
the visitor, but unfortunately it can't be
avoided as it's the connecting point for buses
and trains to Olympia. The bus and train
stations are about 100 metres apart. The bus
station is on Manolopoulou and the train
station is just a short walk away. If you get
stuck in Pyrgos overnight, try the C class
Hotel Olympos (☎ 0621-23 650/1/2), on the
corner of Vasileos Pavlou and Karkavitsa, or
the C class *Hotel Pantheon* (☎ 0621-97 468),
Themistokleous 7. Both are near the train
station and charge around 7000 dr a double.

Getting There & Away
Bus From the bus station there are 16 buses
to Olympia on weekdays, between 5.15 am
and 9 pm; 14 on a Saturday, between 5.15 am
and 7.30 pm; and nine on a Sunday, also
between 5.15 am and 7.30 pm (30 minutes,
260 dr). There are 10 buses a day to both
Athens (five hours, 3500 dr) and Patras (two
hours, 1200 dr); seven a day to Lehena (one
hour, 350 dr); four a day to Kyparissia (one
hour, 750 dr); three a day to Killini at 6 and
10.30 am and 2.35 pm (50 minutes, 700 dr);
three a day to Tripolis (four hours, 1800 dr),
Kalamata (two hours, 1400 dr), and
Andritsena (1½ hours, 750 dr).

Train Seven trains a day chug to Patras (two
hours, 630 dr); six a day to both Athens
(seven hours, 1650 dr) and Kyparissia (1¼
hours, 300 dr); five to Olympia (36 minutes,
200 dr); and four to Kalamata (3¼ hours,
650 dr).

OLYMPIA Ολύμπια
The site of ancient Olympia lies just half a
km east of the modern village of Olympia (in
Greek O-lim-BEE-a). Modern Olympia
panders unashamedly to the tourist trade: its
main street is lined with souvenir and coffee
shops, and restaurants. But despite this overt
commercialism, it's a relaxing and pleasant
place stay. This is largely due to its alluring
setting in a hollow dotted with stately
cypress trees and meadows of long grass and
flowers, encircled by the soft green foothills
of Mt Kronion. Nikos Kazantzakis wrote that
there was 'no landscape which so per-
severingly invites peace and reconciliation'.

The ancient site is of course the major

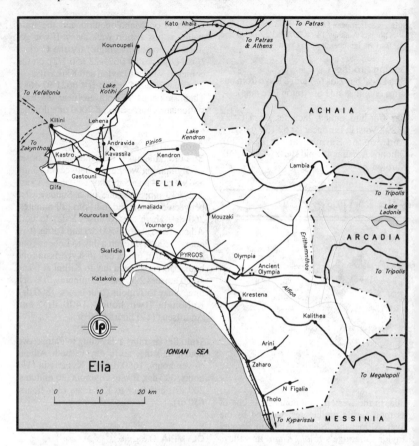

Elia

attraction here, but you may also like to visit the **Historical Museum of the Olympic Games**, which has a collection of commemorative stamps and literature covering the games. The museum is at the western end of the village, two blocks south of Praxitelous Kondili. It is open Tuesday to Sunday from 8.30 am to 3 pm. Admission is 400 dr.

Orientation

The modern village lies along the main Pyrgos-Tripolis road, which is called Praxitelous Kondili. In the centre of town, Odos Douma, which branches off Praxite-lous Kondili, leads to the train station. The bus stops for Pyrgos and Tripolis are opposite one another, on Praxitelous Kondilia, a little east of the turn-off for the train station.

Information

Olympia's outstanding Municipal Tourist Office (☎ 23 100/125) is on Praxitelous Kondili, by the bus stops. The staff give out a good map of the village, have comprehensive information on bus, train and ferry schedules (from Killini and Patras) and exchange currency. It is open daily from 8.30 am to 10 pm in July and August and until

8.15 pm in winter. There are no tourist police; the regular police (☎ 22 100) are behind the tourist office.

To reach the post office walk along Praxitelous Kondili towards ancient Olympia from the bus stops and take the first turn right. The OTE is on Praxitelous Kondili, just a little beyond the turn-off for the post office. Olympia's postcode is 27065 and the telephone code is 0624. The National Bank of Greece is on the corner of Praxitelous Kondili and Stefanopoulou. The hospital (☎ 22 222) is signposted from the church at the western end of the village.

Places to Stay – bottom end

The nearest camp site to Olympia is *Camping Diana* (☎ 22 314/425), 250 metres from the centre of the village. It is a superior site with a pool and costs 800 dr per person and 500 dr for a small tent. There is a 10% reduction for students. A sign by the National Bank of Greece points the way to the site. Other sites near Olympia are *Camping Olympia* (☎ 22 745), one km along the road to Pyrgos and *Camping Alphios* (☎ 22 950), one km from Praxitelous Kondili, signposted from the Pyrgos side of the village.

Olympia's *YHA Hostel* (☎ 22 580), Praxitelous Kondili 18, has dorm beds for 800 dr; hot showers are 150 dr. There is no curfew and an IYHF card is not required. The hostel is open from March to November.

There are a good number of domatia in Olympia. The *Pension Achilleys* (☎ 22 562), Stefanopoulou 4, has clean and cosy single/double/triple rooms for 2000/3500/4000 dr with shared bathrooms. Walking towards Pyrgos, turn left at the National Bank of Greece and the pension is on the right. A little further up this street you will come to the plant-festooned *Pension Poseidon* (☎ 22 567), Stefanopoulou 9, where very agreeable single/double rooms are 3000/4500 dr with shared bathrooms.

The D class *Hotel Hermes* (☎ 22 577) has pleasant rooms for 3000/4000/5500 dr with private bathrooms. Coming from Pyrgos the hotel is on the right 500 metres before the village. A little nearer to the village, just

before the church, is the C class *Hotel Oinomaos* (☎ 22 056), which is an incredible bargain with light, spacious and attractively furnished rooms for 3000/3500/4700 dr with private bathrooms. The hotel is open all year, but in summer caters for package-tour groups.

Places to Stay – middle

The luxurious A class *Hotel Andonios* (☎ 22 348/9) has a commanding position above the southern side of the village, offering all-embracing views from its balconies. Rates are 9000/16,000 dr for singles/doubles; all rooms have private bathrooms, air-con, TV and radio. To reach the hotel take the road by the side of the church at the Pyrgos end of the village.

Places to Stay – top end

The A class *Hotel Amalia* (☎ 22 190/1) on the Pyrgos-Olympia road has a restaurant, swimming pool and roof garden. Singles/doubles are 13,200/17,900 dr.

Another A class is the *Best Western Hotel Europa International* (☎ 22 650/700/306; fax 23 166), which is very close to the ancient site. This opulent place has a bar, restaurant, swimming pool tennis court and horse riding. Singles/doubles are 13,600/18,900 dr.

Places to Eat

Restaurants in Olympia cater predominantly to bus tour groups so don't expect too much. One that has managed to retain a traditional taverna ambience is *Taverna O Barba Fotis*, 500 metres back along the road to Pyrgos, next to the Hotel Hermes. The *Pension Poesidon*, on Stefanopoulou, has a summer-only outdoor taverna serving grilled foods. *Taverna Praxitelous*, next door to the police station, is a favourite with locals.

For self-caterers there are several supermarkets along Praxitelous Kondili and a good baker and greengrocers on Spilopoulou, near the church.

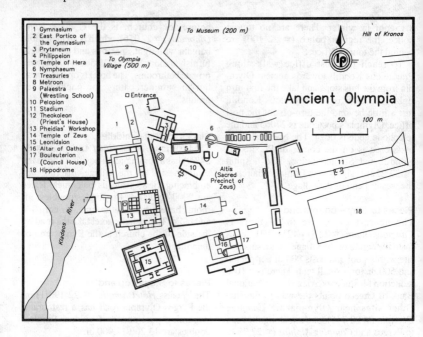

1 Gymnasium
2 East Portico of the Gymnasium
3 Prytaneion
4 Philippeion
5 Temple of Hera
6 Nymphaeum
7 Treasuries
8 Metroon
9 Palaestra (Wrestling School)
10 Pelopion
11 Stadium
12 Theokoleon (Priest's House)
13 Pheidias' Workshop
14 Temple of Zeus
15 Leonidaion
16 Altar of Oaths
17 Bouleuterion (Council House)
18 Hippodrome

To Museum (200 m)

Hill of Kronos

To Olympia Village (500 m)

□ Entrance

Ancient Olympia

0   50   100 m

Altis (Sacred Precinct of Zeus)

Kladeos River

Getting There & Away

Bus On weekdays there are 15 buses to Pyrgos between 6.30 am and 8.15 pm; on Saturday there are 12 and on Sunday nine (30 minutes, 260 dr). There are three buses a day to Tripolis (four hours, 1500 dr).

Train There are five trains a day to Pyrgos (36 minutes, 200 dr).

ANCIENT OLYMPIA

Ancient Olympia was a complex of temples, priests' dwellings and public buildings and the venue of the Olympic Games, which took place every four years. During these games the city-states were bound by *ekeheiria* (a sacred truce) to stop beating the hell out of one another, and compete in races and sports. City-states which contravened this truce, which lasted for three months, were heavily fined.

The site is open Monday to Friday from 8 am to 7 pm and Saturday and Sunday from 8.30 am to 3 pm. Admission is 1000 dr (free on Sunday and public holdiays).

History & Mythology

The origins of Olympia date back to Mycenaean times. The Great Goddess, identified with Rea, was worshipped here in the 1st millennium BC. By the Classical era, Rea had been superseded by her son Zeus. A small regional festival, which probably included athletic events, was introduced here sometime in the 11th century BC. However, the first official quadrennial Olympic Games were held in 776 BC and by 676 BC they were open to all male Greeks, reaching their height of prestige in 576 BC. The games were held in honour of Zeus, who was popularly acclaimed as their founder. They took place at the time of the first full moon in August.

The athletic festival lasted five days and included wrestling, chariot and horse racing, the pentathlon (consisting of wrestling, discus and javelin throwing, long jump and running) and the pancratium (a vicious form of fisticuffs). The winners were presented with prizes of olive wreaths.

Originally only Greek-born males were allowed to participate, but later Romans were permitted. Slaves and women were not allowed to enter the sanctuary as either participants or spectators, and any women who were discovered trying to sneak in were thrown from a nearby rock.

The event served purposes besides athletic competition. Writers, poets and historians were given the opportunity to read their works to a large audience, and citizens of the various city-states were able to meet one another. Traders clinched business deals and city-state leaders were brought together in an atmosphere of festivity, conducive to resolving their differences through discussions, rather than battles.

The games continued during the first years of Roman rule, although by this time their importance had declined, and thanks to Nero, were less edifying. In 67 AD, Nero entered the chariot race with 10 horses, ordering that the other competitors could have no more than four. Despite this advantage he toppled to the ground and abandoned the race, but in a politic move by the judges was still declared the winner.

The games were held for the last time in 394 AD after which they were banned by Emperor Theodosius I, as part of a purge of pagan festivals. In 426 AD Theodosius II decreed that the temples of Olympia be destroyed.

The modern Olympic Games were instituted in 1896 and, other than during WW I and WW II, have been held every four years in different cities around the world. The Olympic flame is lit at the ancient site, and carried by runners to the city where the games are held.

Exploring the Site

Ancient Olympia is well signposted from the modern village. The entrance to the site is just beyond the bridge over the Kladeos river (a tributary of the Alfios). Thanks to The-

Discus thrower

odosius II and various earthquakes, very little remains of the magnificent buildings of ancient Olympia, and a visit is worthwhile more for the idyllic setting than for the ruins.

On entering the site the first ruin encountered is that of the **gymnasium**, which dates from the 2nd century BC. Just south of here is the partly restored **palaestra**, or wrestling school, where the contestants practised and were trained. The next building was the **theokoleon** (the priests' house), behind which was the workshop where Pheidias sculptured the gargantuan chryselephantine **Statue of Zeus**, one of the Seven Wonders of the Ancient World. The workshop was identified by archaeologists due to the discovery of tools and moulds. Beyond the theokoleon is the **leonidaion**, an elaborate structure which accommodated dignitaries.

The **altis**, or **Sacred Precinct of Zeus**, lies to the left of the path. Its most important building was the immense 5th-century Doric **Temple of Zeus** in which stood Pheidias' statue. The 12-metre-high statue was removed to Constantinople by Theodosius II, where it was destroyed in a fire in 475 BC.

The temple consisted of 13 lateral columns and six at either end, none of which are standing.

The **stadium** lies to the east of the altis and is entered through an archway. Little survives of the 200-metre track, although the start and finish lines and the judges' seats remain. The stadium could seat at least 30,000 spectators; slaves and women spectators had to be content with watching from the Hill of Kronos. South of the stadium was the **hippodrome**, where the chariot contests took place.

To the north of the Temple of Zeus was the **pelopion**. This was a little wooded hillock which contained an altar to Pelops. It was surrounded by a wall and the remains of its Doric portico can still be seen. Many artefacts which are now on display in the museum were found buried in the hillock.

North of here is the 6th-century Doric **Temple of Hera**, which is the site's most intact structure. Hera was worshipped along with Rea until the two were superseded by Zeus.

To the east of this temple is the **nymphaeum**. This monument was erected by the wealthy Roman banker Herodes Atticus in 156-160 AD. Typical of buildings financed by Roman benefactors it was a grandiose construction consisting of a semicircular building with Doric columns, flanked at each side by a circular temple. The building contained statues of Herodes Atticus and his family. Despite its elaborate appearance the Nymphaeum had a practical purpose: it was a fountain house which supplied Olympia with fresh spring water.

From the Nymphaeum a row of 12 **treasuries** stretched to the stadium. These had the appearance of miniature temples and each one was erected by a city-state for use as a storehouse. These buildings marked the northern boundaries of the Altis; the remains are reached by ascending a flight of stone steps.

At the bottom of these steps are the scant remains of the 5th-century BC **metroon**, a temple dedicated to Rea, the mother of the gods. Apparently the ancients worshipped Rea in this temple with orgies.

To the west of the Temple of Hera are the foundations of the **philippeion**. This was a circular construction with Ionic columns built by Philip of Macedon to commemorate the Battle of Khaironeia (338 BC), where he defeated a combined army of Athenians and Thebans. The building contained statues of Philip and his family.

North of the Philippeion was the **prytaneum**, which was the magistrate's residence. Here the winning athletes were entertained and feasted.

To the south of the Temple of Zeus is the **bouleuterion**, or council house, where competitors swore at the **Altar of Oaths** to obey the rules decreed by the Olympic Senate.

Reconstruction of Olympia

Museum

The museum is 200 metres north of the site, on the opposite side of the road. The star piece is the 4th-century Parian marble statue of **Hermes of Praxiteles**, a masterpiece of Classical sculpture, from the Temple of Hera. Hermes was given the task of taking the infant Dionysos to Mt Nysa, and the statue portrays the god in repose.

Other important exhibits are a sculptured **Head of Hera** and the pediments and metopes from the Temple of Zeus. The eastern pediment depicts the chariot race between Pelops and Oinomaos, the western pediment shows the fight between the Centaurs and Lapiths and the metopes depict the Twelve Labours of Herakles.

The museum is open Tuesday to Friday from 8 am to 5 pm, Saturday and Sunday from 8.30 am to 3 pm and Monday from 11 am to 5 pm. Admission is 1000 dr.

KILLINI Κυλλήνη

The shabby little port of Killini (Ki-LEE-ni), 78 km south-west of Patras, is the jumping-off point for ferries to Kefallonia and Zakynthos. If you get stuck in Killini, the tourist/port police (☎ 0623-92 211) at the quay will point you in the direction of the available accommodation.

Getting There & Away

Bus & Train One bus a day leaves Patras for Killini and there are at least three buses a day from Pyrgos (50 minutes, 700 dr). There are supposedly seven trains a day on the Kavassila-Killini branch line (35 minutes), but this line is subject to even more delays and cancellations than is the norm in Greece. An alternative is to get a bus from Patras to Lehena (on the main Patras-Pyrgos road) and take a local bus to Killini (11.20 am and 2.45 pm, 20 minutes, 70 dr). A taxi from Lehena to Killini costs around 1500 dr.

Boat Depending on the season there are between three and seven boats a day to Zakynthos (1½ hours, 780 dr) and two boats every day to Poros on Kefallonia (1½ hours, 925 dr).

Arcadia Αρκαδία

Peaceful, pastoral and picturesque Arcadia is the central prefecture of the Peloponnese. Its name evokes images of grassy meadows, forested mountains, gurgling streams and shady grottoes. It was a favourite haunt of Pan, who played his pipes, watched over herds and frolicked with nymphs in this sunny and bucolic idyll.

Almost enclosed within high mountains, Arcadia was in ancient times cut off from the ubiquitous battles and intrigues which plagued the rest of Greece, enabling its people to live in tranquillity. Unlike its neighbours, it has no renowned ancient or Byzantine site (though it has several little known ones), so remains a backwater of crumbling medieval villages, remote monasteries and Frankish castles, visited only by determined tourists.

TRIPOLIS Τρίπολη

Tripolis (pronounced TRI-po-lee, population 21,337) is the capital, and only town of any size in the prefecture. With a dearth of attractions it's not a place to linger, but it's a major transport hub for the Peloponnese so you may have to pass through. Tripolis has a tragic recent history: in 1821 it was taken by Kolokotronis and its 10,000 Turkish inhabitants massacred. Three years later the town was recaptured by the Turks, who burnt it to the ground before withdrawing in 1928.

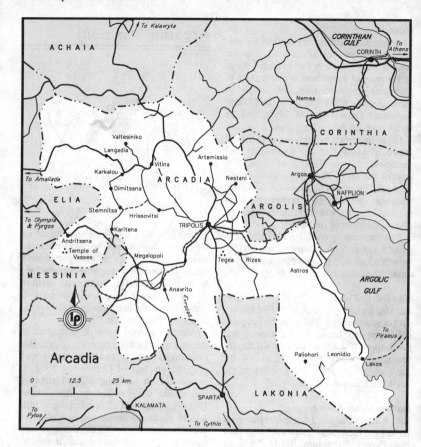

Arcadia

0   12.5   25 km

Orientation & Information

The town's central square is Plateia Kolokotroni. To get here from the train station, walk straight ahead along Lagopati and turn left onto Venizelou. The Arcadias bus station is on Plateia Kolokotroni; from here buses leave for Athens, Pyrgos and various Arcadian villages. Buses for Kalamata, Pylos and Sparta leave from the Messinia & Lakonia bus terminal on Plateia Agiou Vasiliou, one of Tripolis' other large squares. Odos Vasileos Georgiou, running west from Plateia Kolokotroni, leads to Plateia Agiou Vasiliou

The post office and OTE are just off Plateia Agiou Vasiliou. Tripolis' postcode is 22100 and the telephone code is 071. The National Bank of Greece is on Plateia Agiou Vasiliou.

There is a Municipal Tourist Office (☎ 23 9392) in the town hall on Ethnikis Antistaseos, which runs off Plateia Agiou Vasiliou. There is no tourist police; the regular police (☎ 22 2411) are on Ethnikis Antistaseos.

Places to Stay

If you get stuck in Tripolis overnight, the

cheapest hotel is the E class *Hotel Ikinouria* (☎ 22 2463), on Ligouriou, where singles/doubles are 2000/4000 dr. Ligouriou is the road to Sparta, which runs off Plateia Kolokotroni; the hotel is on the left. The C class *Galaxy Hotel* (☎ 22 5195/6/7), on Plateia Agiou Vasiliou, has pleasant singles/doubles for 5000/6700 dr. The B class *Hotel Arcadia* (☎ 22 5551/2/3), on Plateia Kolokotroni, has single/double rooms for 5800/10,000 dr.

Places to Eat

A plethora of cafés and restaurants on and around Plateia Kolokotroni and Plateia Agiou Vasiliou will stave off hunger if you hang around in Tripolis long enough to need a meal.

Getting There & Away

Bus From the Arcadias bus station there are 13 buses a day to Athens (three hours, 1900 dr); eight to Megalopoli (40 minutes, 420 dr); three to both Pyrgos (three hours, 1800 dr) and Argos (1¼ hours, 900 dr); and two to both Dimitsana (1½ hours, 850 dr) and Andritsena (one hour, 900 dr). There is one bus a day from Monday to Friday to/from Stemnitsa, leaving Tripolis at 1.30 pm. For Karitena take the Andritsena bus.

From the Messinia & Lakonia bus terminal there are nine buses a day to Sparta (1½ hours, 700 dr); six to Kalamata (two hours, 1050 dr); and two to Pylos (three hours, 1650 dr).

Frequent local buses (blue) leave from Plateia Kolokotroni for Tegea.

Train Tripolis is on the main Athens-Kalamata line, with four trains a day to Athens (4½ hours, 1650 dr) via Argos (1½ hours, 340 dr) and Corinth (2½ hours, 600 dr). All but one of these trains stop at all of the intermediate stations (see the Getting Around section at the beginning of this chapter). There are three trains a day to Kalamata (three hours, 600 dr).

AROUND TRIPOLIS
Ancient Tegea

Ancient Tegea (Τεγέα), eight km south of Tripolis, was the most important city in Arcadia in Classical and Roman times. It was constantly bickering with its arch rival Mantinea, and fought a long war with Sparta, to which it finally capitulated and was allied to in the Peloponnesian Wars. Tegea was laid waste in the 5th century AD, but rebuilt by the Byzantines, who called it Nikli. The ruins of the city lie scattered around the modern village of Tegea (also called Alea).

The bus from Tripolis stops outside Tragea's **museum**, which houses thrones, statues and reliefs from the site, including fragments of the pediment from the 4th-century Doric **Temple of Athena Alea**. The temple's pediment was regarded as one of the greatest artworks of its time. The museum is open Tuesday to Sunday from 8.30 am to 3 pm. Admission is 300 dr.

MEGALOPOLI Μεγαλούπολη

Despite its grandiose name, Megalopoli (Me-gha-LO-po-lee), which means Great City, is a drab town, suffering from a bad dose of pollution from its large hydroelectric plant. It's another Peloponnese town to get out of quickly, and is only worth a mention because it's an important junction, sitting astride the Pyrgos-Tripolis and Kalamata-Tripolis road, with bus connections to a number of destinations in the Peloponnese.

Getting There & Away

There are eight buses a day to Athens (4½ hours, 2400 dr) via Tripolis (30 minutes 420 dr) and Kalamata (one hour, 650 dr) and two to Andritsena (1¼ hours, 420 dr).

CENTRAL ARCADIA

Between Tripolis and Andritsena is a tangle of medieval villages, precipitous ravines and narrow winding roads, woven into valleys of dense vegetation, beneath the peaks of the Menalon mountains. This is the heart of Arcadia, an area which has some of the most breathtaking scenery in the Peloponnese. Driving or trekking, the possibilities for discovering remote settlements and idyllic camping and picnic spots are endless, but even using local buses, three of the area's most beautiful villages are within reach. These are Karitena, Stemnitsa and Dimitsana, all on the 37-km stretch of road which joins the southern Pyrgos-Tripolis road via Megalopoli and Andritsena with the northern one via Olympia.

There's no organised camping in the area, but unofficial camping is OK; just bear in mind the region is high above sea level and nights are chilly, even in summer.

Karitena Καρίταινα

Just three km north of, and high above, the Megalopoli-Andritsena road is the gorgeous medieval village of Karitena (Kar-IT-ena, population 320), aptly called the 'Toledo of Greece'. A path and steps leads from the central square to the village's 13th-century **Frankish castle** atop a massive rock.

Karitena's 13th-century church of **Agios Nikolaos** has well-preserved frescoes. The church is locked, but if you ask around, someone will direct you to the caretaker. From the church a path leads down to the Frankish bridge which spans the river Lousios (a tributary of the Alfios) – the bridge features on 5000 dr notes. Karitena has one hotel, the D class *Hotel Karitena* (☎ 0791-31 203), where singles/doubles are 2000/3700 dr.

North of Karitena the road runs to the east of the Lousios Gorge. After 10 km, just south of the small village of Elliniko, a dirt track to the left leads in 1½ hours of walking to the site of **ancient Gortys**, on the west side of the gorge, and reached by a bridge. Gortys was an important city from the 4th century BC. Most of the ruins date from Hellenistic times, but to the north of these ruins are the remains of a sanctuary to Asklepios.

Getting There & Away Most of the buses from Megalopoli, Pyrgos and Tripolis to Andritsena do the three-km detour to Karitena, but a few will drop you off on the main road from where it's an arduous uphill walk to the village. Get up-to-date information on where the buses will stop from the respective bus stations.

Stemnitsa Στεμνίτσα

Stemnitsa (Stem-NIT-sa, altitude 1000 metres), 15 km north of Karitena, is another lovely village of stone houses and Byzantine churches. Just north of the village a path to the left leads in just over an hour to **Moni Agiou Ioanni tou Prodromou**. A monk will show visitors the chapel's splendid 14th and 15th-century frescoes. From here paths lead to the deserted monasteries of **Palaeo** and **Nea Philosophou** and also south along the riverbank to the site of ancient Gortys – the monks at Prodromou will point the paths out to you.

Stemnitsa has one hotel, the very pleasant C class *Hotel Triokolonion* (☎ 0795-81 297), with singles/doubles for 3600/7000 dr with private bathrooms.

Getting There & Away From Monday to Friday a bus leaves Tripolis for Stemnitsa (via Hrissovitsi) at 1.30 pm.

Dimitsana Διμιτσάνα

Built amphitheatrically on two hills at the beginning of the Lousios Gorge, Dimitsana (Dim-it-SAN-a, population 600), 11 km north of Stemnitsa, is yet another delightful medieval village. Despite its remoteness and small size, Dimitsana played a significant role in the country's struggle for self-determination. Its Greek school, founded in 1764, was one of the spawning grounds for the ideas which led to the uprisings against the Turks. Its students included Bishop Germanos of Patras, and the Patriarch Gregory V who was hanged by the Turks in retaliation for the Greeks' massacre of the Turks in Tripolitsa (Tripolis). The village also had a number of gunpowder factories and a branch of the Philiki Etairia (the 'friendly society' which was founded in Odessa in Russia in 1814), where Greeks met in secret to discuss the revolution.

From those heady days prior to Independence, Dimitsana has become a sleepy Arcadian village where the most exciting event of the day is the arrival of the bus from Tripolis. Two points of interest for tourists, apart from the beauty of the village and its surroundings, are the **Folk Museum** and **library**, on Odos Nikolaou Makri (open daily from 8 am to 2 pm; free admission) and the **Moni Aimialon**, three km south on the road to Stemnitsa (open daily from 9 am to 2 pm).

Dimitsana has one hotel, the C class *Hotel Dimitsana* (☎ 0795-31 518), where singles/doubles are 3500/4800 dr with private bathrooms. The hotel is just south of the village, on the main road coming from Stemnitsa.

Getting There & Away There are two buses a day from Tripolis to Dimitsana at 1.45 and 6 pm (1½ hours, 800 dr).

ANDRITSENA & THE TEMPLE OF VASSES

Andritsena (Ανδρίτσαινα) (And-RIT-sena, population 900), 81 km west of Tripolis and 65 km south-east of Pyrgos, is a charming village perched 765 metres up a mountainside. Crumbling stone houses with rickety wooden balconies flank its narrow cobbled streets, and a stream gushes through its central square, where old men sit outside the Apollon Kafeneion, shaded by an enormous plane tree.

The post office, OTE and bank are all near the central square. Andritsina's postcode is 27061 and the telephone code is 0626. The village's only concession to tourism is its small **Folk Museum**, which is open every day from 11 am to 1 pm and 5 to 6 pm. Admission is free. Most people come to Andritsena in order to visit the Temple of Vasses, 14 km away.

Temple of Vasses

The Temple of Vasses, 14 km south of Andritsena, stands on a hill (1200 metres) overlooked by Mt Paliavlakitsa. The road from Andritsena climbs steadily along a mountain ridge, through increasingly dramatic scenery, to the most isolated temple in Greece.

The well-preserved temple was built in 420 BC by the people of nearby Figalia, who dedicated it to Apollo Epicurus (The Helper) for delivering them from pestilence. Designed by Iktinos, the architect of the Parthenon, it combines Doric and Ionic columns and a single Corinthian column – the earliest example of this order.

At the time of writing the temple was enclosed in an immense marquee while restoration work was being carried out. Whether or not this is still the case, a visit to the site is worthwhile for the breathtaking setting. The site is not enclosed and admission is free.

There are no buses to Vasses – you must take a taxi from Andritsena which will cost around 2500 dr. It's usually possible to find people in the central square to share with.

From Vasses a dirt road continues for 11 km to the village of **Perivolia**, from where a track leads in two km to the little village of **Ano Figalia**, which is built on the site of ancient Figalia.

Places to Stay

Andritsena has two hotels. The D class *Hotel Pan* (☎ 22 213) has comfortable doubles for 3200/4000 dr. The hotel is on the road coming from Pyrgos. At the opposite side of the village, the B class *Theoxenia Hotel* (☎ 22 219/235/270) charges 6800/10,300 dr for singles/doubles, including breakfast.

Places to Eat

Most of Andritsena's eateries are on the central square. Meals are also served at the *Theoxenia Hotel*.

Getting There & Away

There are two buses a day to Andritsena from Megalopoli (1¼ hours, 650 dr), Pyrgos (1½ hours, 750 dr) and Tripolis (two hours, 950 dr); and one bus a day from Argos (3½ hours, 1700 dr).

Messinia   Μεσσηνία

The prefecture of Messinia has the loveliest beaches in the Peloponnese. Between the long swathes of golden sand fringing its coast, and the mountainous backdrop of the Taygetos range, lie fertile plains of citrus and olive groves, fig trees and vines, and even, in places, banana trees. Numerous fortresses, the legacies of successive invaders, dot the countryside.

KALAMATA   Καλαμάτα

Kalamata (Ka-la-MA-ta, population 30,000) is the capital of Messinia and the second largest city in the Peloponnese. 'Calamitous Kalamata' aptly sums up this hapless city: the old town was almost totally destroyed by the Turks during the War of Independence and rebuilt unimaginatively by French engineers in the 1830s, and on 14 September 1986, Kalamata was devastated by a severe earthquake which registered up to 6.2 on the Richter scale. Twenty people lost their lives, hundreds were injured and over 10,000 homes were destroyed. The destruction is still very much in evidence, in the rubble and dust, derelict buildings, concrete skeletons of new buildings and construction work.

The most pleasant parts of Kalamata are the stone, pebble and shingle beach, and the kastro and the old houses around its base. To reach the latter, walk up Ipapandi from Plateia 25 Martiou. Kalamata's Archaeological Museum and Folk Museum were both severely damaged in the earthquake and remain closed.

Orientation

The old town around the kastro is picturesque and the waterfront of Odos Navarinou which extends eastwards from the town is lively, but the interminably long (actually three km), wide dusty streets between are hellish. The main streets linking the old town with the waterfront are Faron and Aristomenous. On Aristomenous are the two large squares of Plateia Georgiou and Plateia Konstantiadokou.

The train station is at the end of Sideromikou Stathmou. The bus station is inconveniently located at the north-western edge of town. To get to the local bus terminal from here walk south along Artemidos and cross the third bridge over the river. Continue straight ahead to Plateia 25 Martiou where you can get a No 1 bus to the waterfront.

Information

Kalamata's Municipal Tourist Office (☎ 21 959) is on Odos Makedonias (the road signposted to Athens). The tourist police (☎ 23 187), Aristomenous 46, are open daily from 8 am to 2 pm. The regular police are in the same building.

To reach the post office at Iatropoulou 4, take Sideromikou Stathmou which branches off Plateia Georgiou, turn right onto Iatropolou and the post office is on the left. It's open Monday to Friday from 7.30 am to 2 pm. The OTE is on the western side of Aristomenous, just north of Plateia Georgiou. It's open 24 hours. Kalamata's postcode is 24100 and the telephone code is 0721.

There are several banks on Aristomenous including the National Bank of Greece opposite the OTE; there is another branch on the waterfront on the corner of Ariti and Navarinou. Euphoria, Faron 210, sells English-language newspapers and books.

Kastro

Looming over the town is the 13th-century kastro, which remarkably survived the

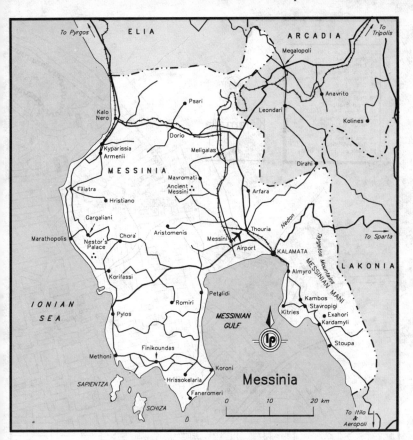

Messinia

ravages of the 1986 earthquake. Excellent views are afforded from the battlements. The kastro is the site of an annual summer **festival**, which includes cultural events such as contemporary musical performances and plays.

Places to Stay – bottom end
Despite the daunting picture I've painted you might decide to use Kalamata as a base for exploring Messini. Kalamata has a string of camp sites along its waterfront, all reached by taking the No 1 bus. They are *Camping Patista* (☎ 29 525); *Elite Camping* (☎ 27

368); *Camping Fare* (☎ 29 520); and *Maria's Sea & Sun Camping* (☎ 41 314). The last of these is in a lovely setting shaded by tamarisk trees and edging onto the beach, four km east along Navarinou. The site has a minimarket, bar and restaurant and charges 700 dr per person and 500 dr per tent; hot showers are 50 dr. The site also has some bungalows which sleep two people and cost 4000 dr.

Near the train station, the D class *Hotel George* (☎ 27 225), on the corner of Dagre and Frantzi 5, has tidy single/double rooms for 2500/3500 dr. Near the waterfront, the D

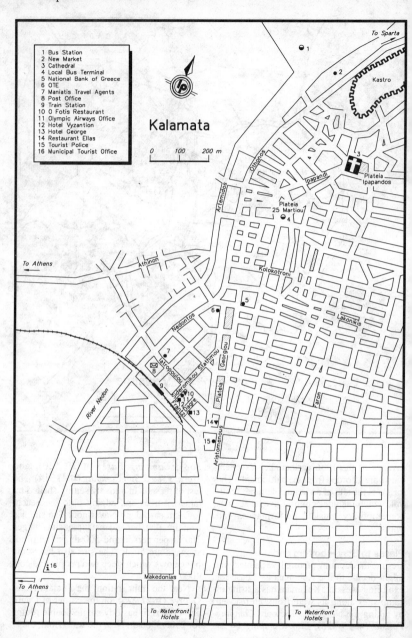

1 Bus Station
2 New Market
3 Cathedral
4 Local Bus Terminal
5 National Bank of Greece
6 OTE
7 Maniatis Travel Agents
8 Post Office
9 Train Station
10 O Fotis Restaurant
11 Olympic Airways Office
12 Hotel Vyzantion
13 Hotel George
14 Restaurant Ellas
15 Tourist Police
16 Municipal Tourist Office

Kalamata

0   100   200 m

To Sparta

Kastro

Plateia
Ipapandos

Othonos

Ipapandi

Artemidos

Plateia
25 Martiou

To Athens

Athinon

Kolokotroni

Nedontos

Lakonikis

Iatropoulou

Sidiromikou Stathmou

Georgiou

Plateia

Faron

Plateia Dagre

Aristomenous

River Nedon

To Athens

Makedonias

To Waterfront
Hotels

To Waterfront
Hotels

class *Hotel Nevada* (☎ 82 429), Santa Rosa 9, has clean singles/doubles/triples for 2600/4000/5000 dr with shared bathrooms. On the opposite side of the road the D class *Hotel Avra* (☎ 82 759), Santa Rosa 10, has comfortable rooms for 3000/4000/5000 dr with shared bathrooms. To reach these hotels walk up Faron from the waterfront and take the first left onto Santa Rosa.

The cheapest of the waterfront hotels is the D class *Hotel Plaza* (☎ 82 590), Navarinou 117, where spotless attractively furnished, balconied rooms have rates of 4000/6500/7500 dr.

Places to Stay – middle

The C class *Hotel Vyzantion* (☎ 86 824/5 or 83 251), Sideromikou Stathmou 13, has a cool interior of traditional furniture and heavy brocade drapes. The prices are 6400/7800/9000 dr for rooms with private bathrooms; the price includes breakfast.

On the waterfront the palatial C class *Haikos Hotel* (☎ 88 902/924/946/968; fax 23 800), Navarinou 115, has carpeted and attractively furnished rooms for 7000/8000/8500 dr. Further along the waterfront the C class *Hotel Floisbos* (☎ 82 177/282), Navarinou 135, has agreeable rooms for 7500/9500/11,500 dr.

The B class *Filoxenia Hotel* (☎ 23 166/7/8) overlooks the beach at the eastern end of Navarinou. It has a restaurant, bar, swimming pool and disco. Rates are 8500/ 11,700 dr for singles/doubles and suites are 23,250 dr.

Places to Stay – top end

The A class *Hotel Elite Village* (☎ 25 015, 22 434 or 85 303; fax 84 369), Navarinou 2, is Kalamata's best hotel with restaurants, bars, a swimming pool and disco. Single/double rooms are 15,300/19,200 dr and suites are 37,000 dr.

Places to Eat

There are numerous eating places in Kalamata but many of these are fast-food joints. If you prefer a more traditional ambience try *O Fotis Restaurant* on Sideromikou Stathmou, near the train station.

The *Restaurant Ellas*, Aristomenous 28, is a wonderful cavernous place which is definitely pre-earthquake. Main meals are under 800 dr. If you want to concoct a meal yourself, Kalamata's large new food market is across the bridge from the bus station. Kalamata is noted for its olives, olive oil and figs.

Getting There & Away

Air From Kalamata's airport (☎ 69 442) there are daily flights in summer to Athens (8000 dr). In winter these drop to two a week on Saturday and Sunday. The Olympic Airways office (☎ 22 376/724) is at Sideromikou Stathmou 17.

Bus From Kalamata's bus station there are nine buses a day to Koroni (1½ hours, 520 dr) and Pylos (1½ hours, 620 dr). There are also nine buses a day to Athens (4½ hours, 2850 dr) via Megalopoli (650 dr), Tripolis (950 dr), Argos (1600 dr) and Corinth (2650 dr). There are five buses a day to Methoni (1½ hours, 750 dr); three of these continue to Finikoundas (two hours, 850dr); four to Itilo (two hours, 850 dr); two to Patras (four hours, 2700 dr) via Pyrgos (two hours, 1700 dr), and Sparta (2½ hours, 750 dr) via Artimisia (320 dr), and Mavromati (1½ hours, 330 dr).

Train Kalamata is the end of the line for both branches of the Peloponnese railway. On one branch there are four trains a day to Athens (seven hours, 2200 dr) via Tripolis (2½ hours, 650 dr), Argos (four hours, 940 dr) and Corinth (5¼ hours, 1250 dr). On the other branch there are also four trains a day to Athens (11 hours, 2200 dr), via Kyparissia (two hours, 450 dr), Pyrgos (3¼ hours, 650 dr) and Patras (5½ hours, 110 dr).

Getting Around

To/From the Airport Kalamata's airport is 10½ km west of the city. There is no airport shuttle bus and a taxi will cost approximately 1000 dr.

Bus The No 1 is Kalamata's only local bus. It does a valiant job plying frequently between Plateia 25 Martiou and the Hotel Filoxenia, at the eastern end of the waterfront, making its way south along Aristomenous and Faron. There is a flat fare of 110 dr.

Car & Motorbike Cars can be rented from Maniatis Travel Agents (☎ 25 300 or 27 694), Iatropoulou 1 (opposite the post office). The staff at Kalamata's ELPA office (☎ 82 166), Faron 155, are very helpful. Motorbikes can be hired from Bastakos Motorbikes (☎ 26 638), Faron 190.

LANGADA PASS

The 63-km road from Kalamata to Sparta is one of the most scenically spectacular roads in Greece. The road twists and turns as it cuts through the Taygetos mountains, by way of the Langada Pass. The highest point of the pass is 1524 metres, after which it begins descending through the **Langada Gorge** to the village of Trypi. To the north of this gorge is the spot where the ancient Spartans used to throw babies who were surplus to requirement – that is, too weak or deformed to become good soldiers. It is possible to travel by bus along this route, but you'll have to change buses in Artemisia.

There are two hotels in Trypi; both are D class. The *Keadas Hotel* (☎ 0731-98 222) has singles/doubles for 4400/5800 dr. The *Hotel Trypi* (☎ 0731-25 387) is similarly priced.

PYLOS Πύλος

Pylos (PI-los, population 2500), on the coast 51 km south-west of Kalamata, sits at the southern end of an immense bay. It was in this bay on 20 October 1827 that the British, French and Russian fleets, under the command of Admiral Codrington, fired at point-blank range on Ibrahim Pasha's Turkish and Egyptian fleet, sinking 53 ships and killing 6000 men, with negligible losses on the Allies' side.

This was the Battle of Navarino, the decisive battle in the War of Independence, and one which was not meant to have been a battle at all. The presence of the Allied fleet was intended merely to coax Ibrahim Pasha and his fleet into leaving, but things got out of hand; George IV on hearing the news described it as a 'deplorable misunderstanding'.

Pylos (formerly Navarino) also has another claim to fame due to its close proximity to the archaeological site of Nestor's Palace.

History aside, Pylos, with its huge natural harbour almost enclosed by the Sfakteria islet, a delightful tree-shaded central square, two castles and surrounding pine-covered hills, is one of the most picturesque towns in the Peloponnese.

Orientation & Information

The bus station is on the central square, Plateia Trion Navarchon, which is at the bottom of the road coming from Kalamata, and just back from the waterfront. The post office is on Odos Nileos; with your back to the bus station, turn left to reach it. Take the first left beyond the post office to reach the OTE. Pylos' postcode is 24001 and the telephone code is 0723. The National Bank of Greece is on the central square. There is no EOT or tourist police in Pylos. The regular police (☎ 22 316) are between the square and the waterfront.

Castles

Pylos has two castles, one at each side of the bay. **Palaeokastro** is six km north of Pylos at the other side of the bay, but it's in such a state of ruin that it's hardly worth the effort to get there. In contrast, **Neo Kastro** is right in town and is in good nick, having been used as a prison until this century. Within its walls are a citadel, a mosque converted into a church and a courtyard surrounded by dungeons. Soon a marine archaeological museum will open at the castle, to house finds from the wrecks of the Turkish and Egyptian ships – the underwater exploration of the bay is being funded by UNESCO. The castle is open daily from 8 am to 3 pm and admission is free. To reach the castle entrance, walk up the road from the central square signposted to Methoni, and you will come to a sign pointing right.

Organised Tours

Sapienza Travel (☎ 23 207), on the waterfront next to the Miramare Hotel, organises tours of the Bay of Navarino and the island of Sfakteria for 3000 dr. On the trip around the island, stops are made at memorials to admirals of the Allied ships. Stops are also made in the bay to look down at the wrecks of the sunken Turkish ships, discernible in the clear waters. It's worth checking the cafés around the waterfront to see if any boat owners are offering cheaper tours.

Places to Stay – bottom end

The nearest camp site to Pylos is *Navarino Beach Camping* (☎ 22 761), six km north of Pylos on Gialova Beach. Take a Kyparissia bus from Pylos.

There are a few domatia on the approach road to Pylos from Kalamata – look for the signs. The cheapest hotel is the pleasant D class *Hotel Navarino* (☎ 22 564). Rates are 3000/4000 dr for singles/doubles with shared bathrooms. From the bus station, walk to the waterfront, turn left and the hotel is on the left.

The C class *Hotel Galaxy* (☎ 22 780), on Plateia Trion Navarchon, has reasonable rooms for 5000/7000/8400 dr. The C class *Arvaniti Hotel* (☎ 23 050/341), on Nileos beyond the post office, is a better choice with spacious rooms for 5500/7000/8400 dr.

Places to Stay – middle

The nicest hotel in this price range is the C class *Hotel Karalis Beach* (☎ 23 021/022), with tasteful, traditional furniture and lots of marble and plants. The room rates are 6000/12,000/13,500 dr. The hotel is below the castle, almost overhanging a rocky beach; turn left from the central square onto the waterfront and continue for 200 metres. The C class *Karali Hotel* (☎ 23 021/2), Kalamatas 26, is a another luxurious place with rooms for 8000/10,000/12,000 dr. The

hotel is on the Kalamata-Pylos road, on the left approaching Pylos.

Places to Eat

The *Ta Adelfia*, below the Navarino Hotel, is a popular place with outdoor eating overlooking the bay. The restaurant is open for lunch and dinner.

The *O Grigaris Restaurant* serves tasty low-priced dishes in a garden. From the bus station turn right and follow the square around towards the waterfront, turn right at the Santa Rosa Café on the central square, follow the road around and you'll come to the restaurant.

After your meal order a coffee and cake and watch the world go by at *Krinos Zaharoplasteion* on the central square. There are supermarkets, fruit and vegetable stalls, a baker (at No 38) and psistaria on lively Odos Ipiskoupou. To get there, turn right at the bus station and ascend the wide steps straight ahead.

Getting There & Away

There are nine buses a day to Kalamata (1½ hours, 600 dr); six to Kyparissia (two hours, 750 dr), via Nestor's Palace (30 minutes, 200 dr) and Chora (35 minutes, 220 dr); five to Methoni (15 minutes, 140 dr); four to Finikoundas (45 minutes, 300 dr); and two to Athens (seven hours, 3500 dr).

Getting Around

Motorbike Sapienza Travel (☎ 23 207), on the waterfront next to the Miramare Hotel, rents mopeds and 50 cc motorbikes.

AROUND PYLOS
Nestor's Palace

This is supposedly Homer's 'sandy Pylos' where Telemachos (with Athena disguised as Mentor) was warmly welcomed when he came to enquire of the wise old King Nestor if he knew the whereabouts of his long lost father, Odysseus, King of Ithaca.

The palace, originally a two-storey building, is the best preserved of all the My-cenaean palaces. Its walls stand a metre high, giving the visitor a good idea of the layout of a Mycenaean palace complex. The main palace, in the middle, was a vast building of many rooms. The largest was the **Throne Room**, from where the king dealt with all state business. In the centre of the room was a large circular hearth surrounded by four ornate columns which supported a 1st-floor balcony. Some of the fine frescoes which were discovered in the room are now in the museum in the nearby village of Chora (see the following section). Rooms surrounding the throne room include the sentry box, pantry, waiting room, a vestibule and, most fascinating of all, a bathroom with a terracotta tub still in place.

The most important find at the site were around 1200 **Linear B script tablets**, which were the first found on the mainland. Some of them are in the museum at Chora.

The site was excavated later than the other Mycenaean sites, between 1952 and 1965. An excellent guidebook by Carl Blegen, who led the excavations, is on sale at the site for 500 dr.

Nestor's Palace is 17 km north of modern Pylos. It is open Monday to Saturday from 8.30 am to 3 pm and Sunday from 9.30 am to 2.30 pm. Admission is 400 dr.

Chora Χώρα
Chora's excellent little **Archaeological Museum**, three km north-east of Nestor's Palace, includes finds from the site and other Mycenaean artefacts from Messinia. The most notable pieces are the frescoes from the throne room at Nestor's Palace. The museum is open Monday, Wednesday and Saturday from 8.45 am to 3 pm and Sunday from 9.30 am to 2.30 pm. Admission is 400 dr.

Getting There & Away
The Kyparissia bus from Pylos stops at Nestor's Palace and Chora.

METHONI Μεθώνη
Methoni (Meth-ON-ee, population 1300), 12 km south of Pylos, was one of the seven cities offered to Achilles by Agamemnon, and Homer described it as 'rich in vines'. These days it's a pretty seaside town, with a

crowded sandy beach, and a magnificent 13th-century fortress. This vast fortification, uncharacteristically, does not perch on a hill, but is on a promontory, surrounded on three sides by the sea, and separated from the mainland by a moat. The medieval port town of Methoni which stood within its walls was the Venetian's first and longest held occupancy in the Peloponnese, and a stopover point for pilgrims en route to the Holy Land. In medieval times, the twin fortresses of Methoni and Koroni were known as 'the Eyes of the Serene Republic'.

Orientation & Information
Methoni consists of two main streets. Arriving by bus from Pylos, facing straight ahead you will see a fork in the road. The left fork leads to the beach, and the right fork is Methoni's shopping street. The post office and OTE are next door to one another on the left side of the beach road. The National Bank of Greece is on the right side of the shopping street.

There is no EOT or tourist police in Methoni. The regular police (☎ 22 316) are on a side street off the beach road; look for the sign before the post office and OTE.

Fortress
This splendid fortress, a supreme example of military architecture, is vast, wild and romantic and you'll need at least half a day to explore it thoroughly. Within the walls are a Turkish bath, a cathedral, houses, a cistern, parapets and underground passages – see how many Lion of St Mark insignias you can spot. A short causeway leads from the fortress to the diminutive octagonal Turkish castle standing on an adjacent islet – bring a torch to explore the interior. The site is open Monday to Saturday from 8 am to 7 pm and on Sunday from 8 am to 6 pm. Admission is free. Facing the sea at the beginning of the beach, turn right to reach the castle entrance.

Places to Stay – bottom end
Camping Methoni (☎ 31 228) is a reasonable site 600 metres beyond the Methoni Beach Hotel, which is at the beginning of the beach.

Hotel Dionysos (☎ 31 317) is an elegant E class establishment. Rates are 2600/3600 dr for singles/doubles with shared bathrooms. Taking the right fork from the bus stop, the hotel is on the left. The rooms of *Tsonis Dimitrios* (☎ 31 640/588), next door above Cafeteria George, are spotless and well furnished. Double/triple rates are 5800/6800 dr, with use of a communal kitchen. Family apartments are also available. There are many other domatia signs on this road and on the beach road.

Places to Stay – middle

The *Albatros Hotel* (☎ 31 160/170) is a very up-market D class place. The tastefully furnished rooms have a refrigerator, fan and balcony with a sun canopy. Rates are 6200/7560/9000 dr with private bathrooms. The hotel is next to the post office.

The C class *Hotel Castello* (☎ 31 300/280) is a new hotel with beautifully furnished and balconied rooms with views of the castle, and a garden ablaze with roses and dahlias. Doubles are 7500 dr and family apartments are 11,000 dr. Walk down the beach road and look for the hotel sign pointing left.

If you walk a little way along the beach you will come to the new C class *Hotel Giota* (☎ 31 191/290), with light, modern rooms costing 6000/8000/9600 dr.

The B class *Methoni Beach Hotel* (☎ 31 455/415), at the beginning of the beach, was a once-luxurious hotel which has retained its dignity, but is now a bit the worse for wear. Singles/doubles are 8000/9600 dr .

Methoni's best hotel is the B class *Hotel Amalia* (☎ 31 129/193/195/233), standing in splendid isolation on a hill, with wonderful views of Methoni and the fortress. The hotel has lots of cool marble; rooms are luxuriously furnished and each one has a balcony and a flower-bedecked terrace. Rates are 8000/11,600/13,300 dr with breakfast. The hotel is 250 metres up a dirt road (drivable) from the beach. The road begins just beyond the camp site.

Places to Eat

The *Restaurant Oinouses*, on the beach 100 metres beyond the Hotel Giota, serves tasty reasonably priced food.

The *Louise* is an excellent restaurant on the shopping street. Locals I spoke to recommended *Klimateria Restaurant*, opposite the Castello Hotel, but when I visited Methoni it was temporally closed.

Getting There & Away

A bus timetable is pinned on the door of the newsagent just down from the bus stop. There are seven buses to Pylos (15 minutes, 140 dr) and four to Finikoundas (30 minutes, 200 dr). There are no direct buses to Koroni – change buses in Finikoundas.

FINIKOUNDAS Φοινικούντας

Finikoundas, midway between Methoni and Koroni, is a fishing village rapidly developing into a holiday resort with a reputation for good windsurfing. Currently it is patronised more by backpackers than package tourists. With no archaeological sites or cultural diversions, the beach is it in Finikoundas. From the bus stop walk straight ahead to reach the waterfront.

Places to Stay

Camping Ammos (☎ 0723-71 262), two km west of Finikoundas, is a pleasant camp site with water sports. There are a number of domatia in the village and two appealing mid-range hotels. *Hotel Finikoundas* (☎ 71 308), by the bus stop, has single/double/triple rooms for 6000/8000/9000 dr. Turning left at the waterfront you will come to the *Hotel Porto* (☎ 71 457), which has the same rates.

Getting There & Away

There are three buses a day to Kalamata via Methoni and Pylos and two a day to Koroni at 6 am and 4.30 pm. If the lousy bus service tempts you into taking a taxi, charges are 1500 dr to Methoni and 2000 dr to Koroni.

KORONI Κορώνη

Koroni (Ko-RO-nee, population 1380), the

second 'Eye of the Serene Republic', is 35 km south-east of Methoni and 43 km south-west of Kalamata. It's a delightful medieval town, built on a promontory, with pastel-coloured tiled Venetian houses clambering uphill to its castle. The castle, most of which is taken up by the **Timiou Prodromou Convent**, is tame compared with Methoni's, but is a tranquil place to stroll around, with pleasing views of the Messinian Gulf and the Taygetos mountains. Koroni's main attraction is its superlative **Zaga Beach**, a long sweep of golden sand.

Orientation & Information
Facing the church, from the bus station turn left for Koroni's main street; you will pass the post office on the way. The OTE is on the left side of the main street coming from the bus terminal. Koroni's postcode is 24004 and the telephone code is 0725. To get to Zaga Beach, ascend the steps to the right of the church opposite the bus stop, turn left onto Odos Maisonos, and look for the beach sign pointing left; the entrance to the castle is on the way to the beach. To reach the harbour turn right from the bus station, take the first right and then turn right again at the waterfront.

Koroni does not have an EOT or tourist police.

Places to Stay
Camping Koroni (☎ 22 119) is a super site with a restaurant, bar, minimarket, swimming pool, kitchen and wash room. Rates are 800 dr per person and 650 dr per tent. Coming from Kalamata the site is on the left side of the road – buses stop out the front.

The E class *Hotel Diana* (☎ 22 134/313) has clean single/double/triple rooms for 2000/4000/5500 dr with shared bathrooms. From the bus station turn right, take the first right and the hotel is on the left. The D class *Flisvos Hotel* (☎ 22 238), overlooking the harbour, has comfortable doubles for 4000 dr with private bathrooms.

The *Koroni Pension* (☎ 22 385/448) is above the Symposium Restaurant. Both are owned by the amiable George, a Greek-American who is extremely helpful to tourists. The spacious and clean rooms are 2500/4000 dr with private bathrooms and use of a communal kitchen. The pension is on the right side of the main street.

At the beginning of Zaga Beach, *Andreas Koutsoukos* (☎ 22 262) rents luxurious rooms above his taverna. Double/triple/quad rates are 6000/7000/8000 dr. The rooms have air-con, music channels, telephone, refrigerator, hot plates, an electric mosquito device and a private bathroom.

Places to Eat
One of Koroni's nicest restaurants is *Symposium*, on the main street, owned by the aforementioned George. Moussaka and meatballs are 700 dr and a seafood combination plate (whitebait, kalamaria and prawns) is 950 dr. George makes at least five vegetarian dishes every day.

Getting There & Away
There are nine buses a day to Kalamata (1½ hours, 520 dr) and two buses a day to Finikoundas.

MESSINIAN MANI
Messinian Mani, or outer Mani, is the area of the prefecture bordered by the Taygetos mountains and the west coast of the Mani peninsula, Kalamata, at the head of the peninsula, and Itilo, about halfway down its west coast. The indented coast is speckled with superb beaches. As you travel south from Kalamata, the towers, a unique feature of the Mani, begin to appear, a foretaste of what awaits on the peninsula of Lakonian or inner Mani. The scenery is a stunning blend of sea and mountains; especially noteworthy are the vistas between Almyro and Kambos and the descent from the village of Stavropigi to Kardamyli. There are many camp sites along this stretch of coast, unlike the inner Mani, which has none.

Kardamyli Καρδαμύλη
Kardamyli (Kar-da-MEE-lee, population 300) was another of the seven cities offered to Achilles by Agamemnon. It's a lovely

Top: View from Ancient Delphi, Sterea Elláda (GA)
Left: Ancient Delphi, Sterea Elláda (GA)
Right: Timber-framed house in the old quarter of Varousi, Trikala, Thessaly (RH)

Top: On the way to Meteora, Thessaly (RH)
Left: Man and donkey, Meteora, Thessaly (RH)
Right: Agios Stefanos (St Stephen Convent), Meteora, Thessaly (RH)

place with an atmospheric and derelict old quarter, and a picturesque new village where the buildings have remained faithful to traditional styles.

Orientation & Information Kardamyli sits astride the main Kalamata-Areopoli road. The central square, Plateia 22 Martiou 1821, is at the northern end of the main thoroughfare. The bus stops are opposite one another in the centre of the village. The post office is a little beyond the bus stops, on the left, walking south towards Stoupa. To get to Kardamyli's pebble-and-stone beach walk back along the road towards Kalamata and look for the sign pointing left, beyond the bridge. To get to Old or 'Upper' Kardamyli turn right just before the bridge.

There is no OTE, but Morgan Holidays (☎ 73 220/520; fax 73 190), 150 metres south of the bus stop, on the left, has a metered telephone. Kardamyli's postcode is 24022 and the telephone code is 0721. There is no EOT or tourist police, but the staff at Morgan Holidays are helpful.

Taygetos Gorge Ξαράδρα Ταύγετου
The bridge at the beginning of the village, coming from Kalamata, crosses the mouth of the Taygetos Gorge. You can trek up the gorge for 2½ hours to reach the deserted Monastery of the Saviour. Alternatively you can trek down the gorge in four to five hours. To do this take the 6.15 am bus from Kardamyli to the mountain village of Exahori. Opposite the bus stop a path leads to the vicinity of a village called Kolibetseika, from where a path leads down into the gorge. These two treks are strenuous – strong footwear is essential, and you should take plenty of water. Morgan Holidays hope to organise treks into this scenically spectacular gorge in the near future.

Places to Stay You will see a number of domatia signs along the main road. *Olivia Koumounakou* (☎ 73 326/623) rents immaculate doubles for 5000 dr with private bathrooms. Opposite are the equally agreeable rooms of *Statis Bravacos* (same telephone number as Olivia's rooms), where double/triple rooms cost 6000/7500 dr. To get to these rooms, walking towards Stoupa, turn right opposite the post office, and look for two white houses.

Continuing to the end of this road, a right turn will bring you to a charming stone building which is *Lela's Taverna & Rooms* (☎ 73 541). A little name-dropping won't go amiss here, for Lela is the former housekeeper of author Patrick Leigh Fermor. The tasteful and modern single/double/triple/quad rooms cost 4500/6000/7000/8000 dr with private bathrooms. Incidentally, Mr Fermor still lives in Kardamyli.

Back on the main road, *Villa Vlachos* (☎ 73 220/520; fax 73 190), above Morgan Holidays, has attractive rooms with polished wood floors and ceilings. Double/triple rates are 5900/6500 dr with private bathrooms; two-bedroom apartments are 8000 dr.

At the Kalamata end of town, the rooms of *Stavros & Katina Papadea* (☎ 73 445) are large and beautifully furnished with double/triple rates of 5700/6000 dr. Walk along the main road towards Kalamata and turn left at the sign for Kardamyli Beach. The rooms are a distinctive red brick building on the right. Back on the main road, continuing towards Kalamata, you will come to *Castle Pension* (☎ 73 226/396) on the right. The pension is a beautiful stone building with black wrought-iron balconies. The gorgeous double/triple/quad rooms are 6700/7800/9160 dr with private bathrooms.

Places to Eat *Lela's Taverna*, below her rooms of the same name, gets glowing reports from both locals and tourists. Tables and chairs are laid out on a terrace with great sea views. The *Gelateria*, opposite the central square, has delicious ice cream for 130 dr a scoop, yoghurt with fruit and honey for 350 dr and filter coffee for 150 dr.

Getting There & Away Kardamyli is on the main Kalamata-Itilo bus route.

Getting Around Morgan Holidays has car, motorbike and mountain-bike hire.

Stoupa Στούπα

Stoupa, 10 km south of Kardamyli, is undergoing a metamorphosis from fishing village to holiday resort for discriminating package tourists intent on seeking out the 'unspoilt Greece'. For the moment it's still worth a visit, and although it's not as picturesque as Kardamyli, it does have two superlative beaches, separated by a headland. Like Kardamyli, Stoupa also has literary connections. Nikos Kazantzakis lived here for a time and based the protagonist of his novel *Zorba the Greek* on a man who worked as a supervisor at a coal mine in Pastrova, near Stoupa.

Orientation & Information Stoupa is one km west of the main Kalamata-Areopoli road. From the bus turnaround point, with your back to the mountains, walk straight ahead to reach the sea. To the right is the larger of Stoupa's two beaches – a glorious crescent of golden sand. The road which skirts this beach continues over the headland to the other beach.

Stoupa's development as a resort has been so rapid that its amenities have yet to catch up. As yet it has no bank, post office or OTE. Until this is rectified, Katerina's Supermarket, to the left of the main beach, has currency exchange and an OTE telephone. Stoupa's postcode is 54054 and the telephone code is 0721. Stoupa has no EOT or tourist police.

Places to Stay Avoid Stoupa in July and August when accommodation is monopolised by package-tour operators. *Camping Kala Goria* (☎ 54 319), above the small beach, is a well-kept site with a children's playground, minimarket and a bar. Rates are 600 dr per person and 400 dr per tent.

Panorea Rooms (☎ 54 323/386), on the road between the two beaches, are basic but clean, and cost only 2500 dr a double with

shared bathroom and kitchen. If there are two or more of you, seek out Thanasis, who you will find in a small office (more a hole in the wall, no telephone) at the beginning of the large beach. The wacky Thanasis is the champion of independent and out-of-season travellers, renting a variety of houses in Stoupa; none are purpose-built and he doesn't let to tour groups. The houses are available year round for short and long-term rental and cost 5000/6700 dr for two/three people and 10,000/11,000 dr for four/six people.

Petros Nikolareas Furnished Apartments (☎ 54 063) are pleasant, comfortable and good value. Double/triple apartments are 5000/8500 dr. Facing the sea from the bus stop, take the road which forks left, and you will come to the rooms on the right. *Maistreli Apartments* (☎ 54 595) are spacious, clean and attractive. Rates are 8000 dr for two/three people and 13,500 dr for five/six people. From the bus stop walk straight ahead towards the sea and the apartments are on the left.

The C class *Stoupa Hotel* (☎ 54 308/485) has agreeable double/triple rooms for 6000/7200 dr. The hotel is on the right side of the approach road to Stoupa.

Places to Eat The *Ippokampos Taverna* has superlative chicken roll stuffed with herbs for 850 dr, small/large mezedes for 650/1400 dr and stuffed tomatoes, moussaka or pastitsio for 650 dr. The taverna is on the road leading from the bus stop to the sea.

Akrogiali Taverna, at the beginning of the large beach, also serves good, reasonably priced food.

Getting There & Away Stoupa is on the main Kalamata-Itilo bus route. Some buses will drop you off at the bus turnaround in the village; others will drop you on the main road from where it's a 1½ km walk to the beaches.

Lakonia   Λακωνία

Lakonia is the south-east prefecture of the Peloponnese; Sparta is its capital. Despite playing a prominent role in ancient history, Lakonia has few remains from this time. King Menelaus (husband of Helen, of Troy fame) was, if we are to believe Homer, a powerful Mycenaean king, yet Lakonia, unlike the other centres of the Mycenaean civilisation, has yielded no ruins of a palace kingdom. After the decline of the Mycenaean civilisation, the Dorians invaded from the north, ushering in a dark age and driving out the descendants of the Mycenaeans. It was from the Dorians that the mighty Spartans of the Classical Age were descended. Ancient Sparta has been found, but it is the most uninspiring ruin in the whole of Greece.

However, what Lakonia lacks in ancient ruins, it makes up for in medieval and later ones: in the glorious Byzantine churches and monasteries of Mystra, the evocative medieval town of Monemvassia and the bizarre tower settlements of inner Mani. All of these are enhanced by a superb landscape of the towering Taygetos peaks and the vast fertile Lakonian plain, where roads are fringed with orange, mulberry and cypress trees.

LAKONIAN MANI

Although the region loosely referred to as the Mani begins south of Kalamata in Messinia, the Lakonian Mani, which begins at the village of Itilo, is most indicative of the region. This separation between [ ] Mani (also known as the outer [ ] Lakonian Mani (also known as in.... had many implications when Greece was occupied by foreign powers. Such was the formidable reputation of the inhabitants of the inner Mani, that foreign occupiers, thought they were best left alone.

Grey rock, mottled with defiant clumps of green scrub and the occasional stunted olive or cypress tree characterise the bleak mountains of inner Mani. The lower slopes are terraced, for wherever possible this unyielding soil has been cultivated. A curious anomaly is the profusion of wild flowers which mantles the valleys in spring, exhibiting nature's resilience and defiance by seeming to sprout forth even from the rocks. The indented coast has sheer cliffs plunging into the sea, and rocky outcrops sheltering pebbled beaches. This wild and barren landscape is broken only by the settlements of austere and imposing stone towers, mostly abandoned, but still standing sentinel over the region.

History

The people of the Mani regard themselves as direct descendants of the Spartans. After the decline of Sparta, citizens who were loyal to the principles of Lycurgus, founder of Sparta's constitution, chose to withdraw to the mountains rather than serve under foreign masters. Later, refugees from the occupying powers joined these people, who became known as Maniots, from the Greek word *mani* (mania). The Maniots claim they are the only Greeks not to have succumbed to foreign invasions. This may be somewhat exaggerated, but the Maniots have always enjoyed a certain amount of autonomy and a distinctive way of life.

Until Independence, the Maniots lived in clans led by chieftains. Fertile land was so scarce that it was fiercely fought over by the growing number of Maniots; blood feuds were a way of life, and families constructed towers to use as hideouts.

The Turks failed to subdue the Maniots, who eagerly participated in the War of Inde-

Lakonia

0   10   20 km

pendence. However, after 1834 they were reluctant to give up their own independence and become part of the new kingdom.

To this day the Maniots are regarded by other Greeks as fiercely independent, royalist and right wing. In fact, the word 'laconic' originates from this formidable region of the Peloponnese. But don't be deterred from visiting the region by descriptions of the Maniots as hostile, wild and hard people. Contact with the outside world and lack of feuding have had a mellowing effect, and these days the Maniots are as friendly and hospitable as Greeks elsewhere.

Information

The telephone code for the Lakonian Mani (including Areopoli) is 0733.

Itilo & Neo Itilo

Itilo (Οίτυλο) (IT-ee-lo), 29 km south of Stoupa, was the medieval capital of the Mani, but was superseded by Areopoli, 11 km to the south, in the last century. Coming from Messinian to Lakonian Mani, Itilo is where you will change buses.

The village is now a crumbling and tranquil backwater, severed in two by a ravine which was traditionally regarded as the border between outer and inner Mani. Standing above the ravine is the massive 17th-century **Castle of Kelefa** from which the Turks attempted to constrain the Maniots. It's worth a scramble around; you can't miss it – it's on a hill above the road leading down to Neo Itilo. Nearby, the **Monastery of Dekoulou** has colourful frescoes in its church. Neo Itilo, four km down the road, is a quiet secluded bay with superb views and a pebble beach.

Places to Stay Unofficial camping may be permitted on the north side of Neo Itilo Bay.

The *Adonos Pension* (☎ 59 237) is Itilo's only place to stay. Reasonable rooms are 3000/4000 dr with shared bathrooms, and very basic rooms are 2000/3000 dr. Coming from Kalamata the rooms are on the left as you approach Itilo. If you ask, the bus driver will drop you outside; otherwise it's a tiring uphill trek.

Neo Itilo has two places to stay. The *Galarie Pension* (☎ 59 390), on the left coming from Itilo, has double/triple rooms with large balconies and beautiful furniture for 7000/8000 dr with private bathrooms. Further along the same road the plush and outrageously expensive C class *Hotel Itilo* (☎ 51 300) has rates of 11,000/17,000 dr for singles/doubles. These prices are for halfboard, which is obligatory. Excluding the last two weeks of July and all of August there is a 35% discount for stays of one week or more.

Places to Eat Itilo's only eating place is the *Garden Taverna* on the central square by the bus stop. My meal here of souvlaki, Greek salad and retsina came to 1300 dr.

Getting There & Away There are three buses a day to Areopoli and three a day to Kalamata. The Itilo-Areopoli bus stops at Neo Itilo.

Limeni Λιμένι
The road continues to the little fishing village of Limeni (Li-ME-nee), where the *Limeni Rooms & Restaurant* (☎ 51 458) has

comfortable doubles for 5000 dr and the restaurant is reasonably priced. The next restaurant (nameless but under a bamboo shade) is more expensive but serves excellent fish dishes. The road continues for another three km to Areopoli.

Areopoli Αρεόπολη
Areopoli (Ar-e-O-po-lee, population 900), capital of the Mani, is aptly named after Ares, the god of war. Dominating the central square is a statue of Petrobey Mavromichaelis who proclaimed the Maniot insurrection against the Turks. Constantine and George Mavromichaelis, who assassinated Kapodistrias, Greece's first president, belonged to the same family. The town retains many other reminders of its rumbustious past.

In the narrow, cobbled streets of the old town, grim tower houses stand proud and vigilant. Stroll around here during siesta time when the heat and the silence make it especially evocative.

Also take a look at the unusual reliefs above the doors of the **Church of Taxiarchai**, on Kapetan Matapan, which depict feuding archangels and signs of the zodiac.

Orientation & Information The bus stop is in front of the Nicolas Corner Taverna on Plateia Athanaton, the town's central square. The post office and OTE are on the corner of the central square and Kapetan Matapan, the main thoroughfare through the old town. Areopoli's postcode is 23062 and the telephone code is 0733. To reach the National Bank of Greece walk along Kapetan Matapan and turn right at the first church onto Odos P Mauromichali; the bank is a little way along here on the left. It is open only on Tuesday and Thursday, from 9 am to noon.

Areopoli does not have an EOT or tourist police.

Places to Stay – bottom end The cheapest rooms are those of *Perros Bathrellos* (☎ 51 205), 70 metres along Kapetan Matapan, on the left, above a nameless taverna – look for the domatia sign. The basic but clean single/double/triple rooms cost 2000/3000/4000 dr with shared bathrooms.

If you continue along Kapetan Matapan to the Church of Taxiarchai, you will see a sign pointing left to *Tsimova Rooms* (☎ 51 301). These cosy rooms, bedecked with knick-knacks, family photos and icons, are in a 300-year-old renovated tower, owned by George Versakos. The prices are 4000/5000/8000/10,000 dr for singles/ doubles /triples/quads with private bathrooms; plainer single/double rooms across the road go for 2000/3000 dr. George will proudly show you his mini-museum of daggers, pistols, a stele and ancient coins. His friendly daughter Popi speaks good English.

In the new town the *Hotel Mani* (☎ 51 269) has comfortable single/double/triple rooms for 4650/6200/8000 dr with private bathrooms. The hotel is 40 metres beyond the National Bank.

Places to Stay – middle At the end of Kapetan Matapan a sign points right to the *Kapetanakas Tower* (☎ 51 233), which is an EOT traditional settlement. It is austere and authentic, emanating the spirit of the traditional Mani. Rates are 7278/9122 dr for doubles/triples with shared bathrooms and 10,200/12,644 dr with private bathrooms.

At the Church of Taxiarchai a sign points right to the *Londas Pension* (☎ 51 360), another 300-year-old tower. The rooms have white-washed stone walls, wood-beamed ceilings, marble floors and plant-strewn terraces. Doubles/triples are 11,000/16,000 dr, including breakfast.

Places to Eat The *Nicolas Corner Taverna*, on the central square, serves tasty Greek staples. The taverna is open all day. The nameless taverna below the rooms of Perros Bathrellos, on Kapetan Matapan (see Places to Stay), is also commendable. The *Europa Psistaria* on the central square serves succulent grilled food. There is a supermarket at the beginning of Kapetan Matapan.

Getting There & Away The bus office (☎ 51 229) is inside the Nikolas Corner Taverna. There are four buses to Gythio (30 minutes, 320 dr); three to Itilo (20 minutes, 150 dr) via Limeni; two buses to Gerolimenas (30 minutes, 300 dr) via Pyrgos Dirou; two buses to the Dirou Caves (15 minutes, 140 dr); one to Lagia (40 minutes, 460 dr) via Kotronas; and three a week on a Monday, Wednesday and Friday to Vathia (350 dr, 40 minutes).

Dirou Caves Σπήλαιο Διρού
These extraordinary caves can be reached by taking a turn-off four km from the village of Pyrgos Dirou, eight km south of Areopoli.

The caves were inhabited by Neolithic people, but abandoned after an earthquake. They were rediscovered in 1900 and systematic exploration was undertaken by the speleologists Ioannis and Anna Petrochilos in 1949. Experts believe the caves may extend as far north as Sparta.

Tourists glide along the subterranean river of the caves in small duralinox boats. The half-hour trip is an awe-inspiring journey through narrow tunnels and immense caverns. The myriad clusters of stalactites and stalagmites have fittingly poetic names such as the Palm Forest, Crystal Lilly and the Three Wise Men. The last part of the trip is on foot.

The caves are open every day from 8 am to 6 pm from June to September and every-day from 8 am to 3 pm from October to May. Admission is 1500 dr. There are long queues in summer so arrive early; if you arrive after 4 pm you may not get in. For information telephone ☎ 52 222/3.

Places to Stay Many people visit the caves on a day trip from Areopoli or Gythio, but there is accommodation closer to the caves, at Pyrgos Dirou and on the road leading down to the caves. Possibly the cheapest are those at *Kambinara Domatia & Restaurant* (☎ 52 256), where tidy singles/doubles/triples are 2000/3000/5000 dr with shared bathrooms. They are two km from the cave on the right coming from Pyrgos Dirou. The nearest hotel to the cave is the D class *To*

Panorama (☎ 52 280), one km from the caves on the right. Comfortable doubles with private bathrooms are 5000 dr.

Places to Eat The restaurant at *Kambinara Domatia & Restaurant* (see Places to Stay) excels in grilled food. There is a reasonably priced restaurant at the cave.

Pyrgos Dirou to Gerolimenas

Journeying south down Mani's west coast from Pyrgos Dirou (Πύργος Διρού) to Gerolimenas, one enters a striking landscape of stark barren mountains, broken only by deserted settlements of mighty towers. From one of these, Stavri, reached by turning right from the main road, you can trek in 40 to 50 minutes over rough terrain to the **Castle of Maina**, on the Tigani promontory. This Frankish castle was built by William II de Villehardouin in 1248. Back on the main road, Kita, with a plethora of towers, is worth a stroll around. Although the 17 km between Pyrgos Dirou and Gerolimenas there is only one place to stay: the *Tsitsiris Castle Guest House* (☎ 56 297) at Stavri – a traditional settlement in a restored tower house. Rooms have air-con, music channels and telephones. Double/triple/quad rates are 7280/9230/10,600 dr. The guesthouse has a restaurant and bar and is well signposted from the main road.

Gerolimenas Γερολιμένας

Gerolimenas (Ye-ro-li-ME-nas) is a tranquil fishing village built around a sheltered bay, on the south-western tip of the peninsula. There's something irresistible about this place – perhaps the omnipresent gentle rhythmic sound of the waves lapping the pebble shore. The village has a post office with currency exchange (open Monday to Friday from 8 am to 2 pm), but no bank or OTE.

Walk to Ano & Kato Boutari From the village walk back along the road towards Pyrgos Dirou. About 100 metres beyond the Hotel Agrogiali a road off to the right with the street sign Mantoivaloi leads in two km

to the almost deserted village of Ano (Upper) Boutari. The **Church of Agios Stratigos** here has a well-preserved cycle of frescoes mostly dating from the 12th century. A little further on at the village of Kato (Lower) Boutari, the **Anemodoura Tower**, built around 1600, is thought to be one of the earliest Maniot towers.

Places to Stay The E class *Hotel Akrotenaritis* (☎ 54 205) has singles/doubles/triples for 1500/2500/3500 dr with shared bathrooms. The hotel is at the bus stop. The D class *Hotel Akrogiali* (☎ 54 204), overlooking the beach, charges 3000/4800/5800 dr for rooms with private bathrooms, and 19,000 dr for modern two-room apartments.

Places to Eat Both hotels have similarly priced restaurants. There is a well-stocked supermarket on the road behind the Hotel Akrogiali.

Gerolimenas to Porto Kagio

South of Gerolimenas the road continues for four km to the small village of Alika, where it divides. One road leads east to Lagia and the other south to Vathia and Porto Kagio. The southern road follows the coast, passing some pebbly beaches, and then climbs steeply inland to Vathia (VA-thee-a), the most dramatic and awesome of all the traditional Mani villages, comprising a cluster of closely packed tower houses perched on a lofty rock.

Beyond Vathia the road continues to climb, offering intoxicating views. At 12 km from Alika the road descends to the indented coastline with rocky outcrops sheltering yet more pebble beaches. A turn-off right leads to two sandy beaches at Marmari, on the west coast. The road continues to the fishing hamlet of Porto Kagio (Πόρτο Κάγιο) on the shore of an almost circular bay.

Places to Stay At Vathia another wonderful traditional settlement awaits those who can afford it. *Vathia Towers* (☎ (54 229) is an austere and dramatic place to stay. Single/double/triple/quad rooms are 7780/10,212/12,666/13,878 dr. It is the only place to stay in Vathia, and is open all year.

Porto Lagio has one place to stay: the new *Akroteri Domatia* (no telephone), overlooking the beach. The rooms are immaculate with marble floors, tasteful furniture, private bathrooms and balconies. The cost is 7000 to 10,000 dr a double depending on size, position etc. The village has three tavernas all specialising in fish dishes.

Lagia to Kotronas

Approached from Alika, Lagia (Λάγια), at 400 metres above sea level, is a formidable-looking place. It was once the chief town of south-east Mani, but now the village is permeated with a strange aura of insularity and brooding, as if the ghosts of the Mani of old still linger in its deserted towers.

From Lagia the road winds down, with spectacular views of the little fishing harbour of **Agios Kyprianos** – just a short diversion from the main road. The next village along is **Kokala**, a busy and friendly little place with two pebble beaches. The bus stop is in front of Synantisi Taverna.

After Kokala the road climbs once more, and in four km there are more beaches at the sprawling village of **Nyfi**. A turn-off to the right leads to the sheltered beach of **Alipa**. Continuing north, a turn-off on the main road, just beyond Flomochori, descends in three km to **Kotronas**, the last village on the east coast of the peninsula.

Places to Stay There is no accommodation in Lagia but there are three possibilities in Kokala. *Marathos Domatia*, above the taverna, on the beach nearest to Lagia, has doubles for 3000 dr with shared bathrooms and 4000 dr with private bathrooms. Further along the road *Pension Kokala* (☎ 58 307) has comfortable double/triple rooms for 3500/4300 dr.

On a hill overlooking the sea are the superlative *Papa's Rooms* (☎ 58 290) called after their owner, the jovial Papa Georgiou, who is the local priest. The double/triple/quad rooms are a hefty 8000/10,000/12,000 dr, but Papa is not averse to a little bargaining. To reach the rooms go up the dirt track (drivable) opposite Synantisi Taverna in the centre of the village by the bus stop.

At Nyfi, the *Pension Nifi* (☎ 58 242) has pleasant doubles with shared bathrooms for 3500 dr. The pension doesn't have a sign but it's a distinctive cream and brown building, above a taverna on the right, at the beginning of the village.

Places to Eat In Kokala, the *Marathos Taverna* on the beach, below the rooms of the same name, has good reasonably priced food. Further along the road, *Restaurant Monaxia*, signposted on the right, is Kokala's best restaurant.

Kotronas Κοτρώνας

Around Kotronas (KO-tro-nas) the barrenness of the Mani gradually gives way to relative lushness, with olive groves and cypress trees. Kotronas is a lively little place which positively bustles after Mani's half-deserted tower villages. Its main thoroughfare leads straight to the waterfront where the bus does a turn around. To the left is a bay with a small sandy beach.

The post office is on the right side of the main thoroughfare as you go towards the sea. The islet off the coast can be reached by a causeway. Walk inland along the main thoroughfare and turn left at the fork. Take the first left, and walk across the wasteground to a narrow road which soon degenerates into a path which leads to the causeway. On the island there are ruins surrounding a well-kept little church.

Places to Stay The *Adelfia Pansion* (☎ 53 209) is the unmissable pink, yellow, blue and red building on the right of the main road as you go towards the sea. Rates for the cheery single/double/triple rooms are 2000/3000/3500 dr with shared bathrooms. Above a taverna overlooking the beach the *Kotroni Domatia* (☎ 53 269/246) has doubles with shared bathrooms for 3100 dr.

Kotronas' other place to stay is the palatial

and well-equipped *Kotronas Bay Bungalows* (☎ 53 400). Each bungalow accommodates up to four people and costs 15,000 dr. To reach the bungalows turn left at the waterfront and follow the road which skirts the bay.

Places to Eat The *Kotroni Taverna*, below the rooms of the same name, has tasty reasonably priced grilled food. The *Kotronas Bay Bungalows* plans to open a restaurant. There are two minimarkets and a baker on the main street.

SPARTA Σπάρτη

If the city of the Lacedaemonians were destroyed, and only its temples and the foundations of its buildings left, remote posterity would greatly doubt whether their power were ever equal to their renown

Thucydides

Sparta (in Greek SPAR-ti, population 12,000) is the capital of Lakonia. Ancient Sparta produced no great artists, writers, historians, philosophers or monuments of beauty, but is renowned for the privations its citizens were compelled to endure. It is from Sparta that our word 'spartan' is derived. These days most people come to Sparta to visit Mystra, only six km away.

Orientation

You won't get lost in Sparta, for the modern city, constructed in 1834, is laid out on a grid system, with two main thoroughfares. Paleologou runs north to south through the town, and Lykourgou runs east to west. These two streets intersect in the middle of town. The central square, Plateia Kentriki, is one block west of the intersection. The bus station is on Vrasidou. To get to the central square from

A Spartan Existence

Lycurgus, traditionally considered the founder of ancient Sparta's constitution, military institutions and education system, described the Spartans as 'free and independent', their laws commanding them to 'conquer or to die'.

The bellicose Spartans sacrificed all the finer things in life for military expertise. At birth male children were examined by the city council. Those deemed too weak to become good soldiers were left to die of exposure on a hillside. The others remained in the care of their mothers until the age of seven when they were taken away to undergo tough military training. As well as the beatings inflicted on them as part of an endurance test, boys had to wrestle one another and participate in athletic competitions and rigorous physical exercises. They wore only a thin garment and went barefoot, even in winter, and were given insufficient food in order to encourage them to steal, as a test of survival. If they were discovered, they were punished not for the crime but for being caught.

At the age of 20 they became soldiers and remained so until they were 60. They were allowed to marry at 30 but had to continue living in the army barracks. Married couples could only meet occasionally for the purpose of procreation.

Although girls remained with their mothers, they were also subjected to tough physical training so that they would give birth to healthy sons. ■

Statue of barefooted Spartan warrior

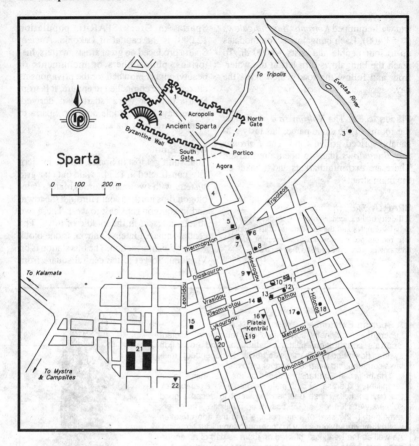

Sparta

To Tripolis

Evrotas River

Acropolis

Ancient Sparta

North Gate

Byzantine Wall

South Gate

Portico

Agora

0   100   200 m

To Kalamata

Thermopylon

Dioskouron

Vrasidou

Kleomvrotou

Lykourgou

Leonidou

Paleologou

Tripoleos

Dafnou

Hilonos

Menelaou

Plateia Kentriki

Othonos Amalias

To Mystra & Campsites

here turn left onto Paleologou and right onto Lykourgou.

Information

The post office is at Kleomvrotou 12, one block north of the intersection. The OTE is between Lykourgou and Kleomvrotou, one block east of Paleologou. Sparta's postcode is 23100 and the telephone code is 0731. Sparta's excellent EOT (☎ 24 852) is in the town hall on the main square. The tourist police (☎ 26 229) are at Hilonos 8, one block east of the museum.

The National Bank of Greece is on the right side of Paleologou (when you face north).

Exploring the Site

To witness the accuracy of Thucydides' prophecy, have a wander around ancient Sparta's meagre ruins. Walk north along Paleologou and at the top you will meet with a large statue of a belligerent looking King Leonidas, standing in front of a football stadium. To the left of the stadium a path leads to the southern gate of the **acropolis**. Pathways lead from here to the forlorn ruins standing amid olive groves. A path left leads

■ PLACES TO STAY

5 Hotel Cecil
13 Hotel Maniatis
14 Laconia Hotel
15 Cyprus Hotel

▼ PLACES TO EAT

6 Psistaria
9 Diethnes Restaurant
16 Averof Restaurant
22 Dionysos Taverna

OTHER

1 Church (Ancient Sparta)
2 Theatre (Ancient Sparta)
3 Sanctuary of Artemis Orthia
4 Football Stadium
7 John Coumantaros Art Gallery
8 National Bank of Greece
10 Bus Station
11 Post Office
12 OTE
17 Archaeological Museum
18 Tourist Police
19 EOT
20 Bus Stop for Mystra
21 Cathedral

to the 2nd or 3rd-century BC **theatre**, the site's most discernible ruin. Along the road to Tripolis a path leads to the **Sanctuary of Artemis Orthia**. Like most of the deities in Greek mythology, the goddess Artemis had many aspects, one of which was Artemis Orthia. In earliest times this aspect of the goddess was honoured through human sacrifice. The Spartans supplanted this activity for the only slightly less gruesome one of flogging young boys in honour of the goddess.

Museum & Gallery

Sparta's **Archaeological Museum**, just east of Paleologou, includes votive sickles which Spartan boys dedicated to Artemis Orthia, heads and torsos of various deities, a statue of Leonidas and stele and masks. The museum is open Tuesday to Saturday from

8.30 am to 3 pm and Sunday from 9.30 am to 2.30 pm. Admission is 1000 dr.

The **John Coumantaros Art Gallery**, Paleologou 123, has an impressive permanent collection of 19th and 20th-century French and Dutch paintings and also holds exhibitions of works by contemporary Greek painters. It's open Tuesday to Saturday from 9 am to 3 pm and Sunday from 10 am to 2 pm. Admission is free.

Places to Stay

Camping Mystra (☎ 22 724) and *Camping Castleview* (☎ 93 384) are both on the Sparta-Mystra road. Both have good facilities and charge similar rates.

The E class *Cyprus Hotel* (☎ 26 590), Leonidou 66 (on the corner of Lykourgou), is ramshackle but clean, with a helpful, English-speaking owner. There are comfortable common areas for meeting and chatting to other travellers. The rates are 3000/4000/5400 dr for singles/doubles/triples with shared bathrooms. The D class *Hotel Cecil* (☎ 24 980), Paleologou 125, has cosy rooms for the same price.

The more luxurious C class *Laconia Hotel* (☎ 28 951), Paleologou 61, has singles/doubles for 4000/7000 dr. The palatial C class *Hotel Maniatis* (☎ 22 665 or 29 991; fax 29 994), Paleologou 72, has immaculate rooms with air-con, automatic telephone and music programme. Rates are 5700/7200/8500 dr.

Places to Eat

The psistaria at Paleologou 124 sells low-priced grilled meat; pork is 600 dr. The *Averof Restaurant*, on the corner of Paleologou and Lykourgou, has tasty Greek staples – moussaka, pastitsio and meatballs are all 700 dr. The *Diethnes Restaurant*, Paleologou 105, is a long-established place with chicken and potatoes for 700 dr and moussaka for 750 dr.

For an unspartan splurge make for *Dionysos Taverna*, Menelaou 79, two blocks south-west of the main square. Pork or chicken in red wine is 1200 dr and oven-baked veal with feta is 1400 dr. In summer, you can eat in an attractive garden. There are many supermarkets on Paleologou.

Getting There & Away

From Sparta's bus station on Vrasidou there are nine buses a day to Athens (five hours, 2500 dr) via Argos (2½ hours, 1250 dr) and Corinth (four hours, 1550 dr); five a day to Gythio (one hour, 570 dr); four a day to Neapoli (four hours, 1300 dr) and Tripolis (1¼ hours, 680 dr); two a day to Kalamata (2½ hours, 750 dr); and one a day to Gerolimenas (three hours, 1100 dr).

Frequent buses for Mystra (30 minutes, 200 dr) leave from a bus stop just round the corner from Lykourgou, on Agissilaou. You can also take this bus for the camp sites. The EOT gives out a schedule, and the main bus station has the times written on their board.

MYSTRA Μυστράς

The captivating ruins of the once splendid town of Mystra (Mis-TRAS), crowned by an impregnable fortress, spill down from a spur of Mt Taygetos.

History

The fortress of Mystra was built by Guillaume de Villehardouin in 1249. When the Byzantines won back the Morea from the Franks, Emperor Michael VIII Palaeologus made Mystra its capital and seat of government. It soon became populated by people from the surrounding plains seeking refuge from invading Slavs. From this time, until the last despot, Demetrios, surrendered it to the Turks in 1460, a despot of Morea (usually a son or brother of the ruling Byzantine emperor) lived and reigned at Mystra.

During the rule of the despots, whilst the empire plummeted into decline elsewhere, Mystra experienced a renaissance. A school of humanistic philosophy was founded by Gemistos Plethon (1355-1452), whose enlightened ideas attracted intellectuals from all corners of Byzantium. After Mystra was ceded to the Turks, Plethon's pupils moved to Rome and Florence, where they made a significant contribution to the Italian Renaissance. Art and architecture also flourished, evidenced in the splendid buildings and vibrant frescoes of Mystra.

Mystra declined under Turkish rule. It was captured by the Venetians in 1687 and it thrived once again with a flourishing silk industry and a population of 40,000. It was recaptured by the Turks in 1715, and from then on it was downhill all the way. It was burned by the Russians in 1770, the Albanians in 1780 and Ibrahim Pasha in 1825. Not surprisingly, at the time of Independence it was in a very sorry state, virtually abandoned and in ruins. Since the 1950s much restoration work has taken place.

Exploring the Site

You will need a whole day to do Mystra justice: wear sensible shoes, bring plenty of water and begin at the upper entrance to the site, rather than the lower, so that you will be walking down, rather than uphill. The site is divided into three sections: the **Kastro** (the fortress on the summit), the **Upper Town** (hora), and the **Lower Town** (kato hora).

Upper Town From opposite the upper-entrance ticket office a path (signposted kastro) leads up to the fortress, which was built by the Franks and extended by the Turks. The path going down from the ticket office leads to **Agia Sofia**, which served as the palace church; some of its frescoes survive. Descending the steps from here a T-junction is reached, and a left turn leads to the **Nafplion Gate**, which was the main entrance to the town. Near the gate is the huge **Palace of the Despots**, a complex of several buildings, constructed at different times. The vaulted audience room, the largest of its buildings, was added in the 14th century. Its façade was painted, and its window frames were highly ornate, but hundreds of years of neglect have robbed it of its former grandeur. It is presently being restored.

From the palace a winding, cobbled path

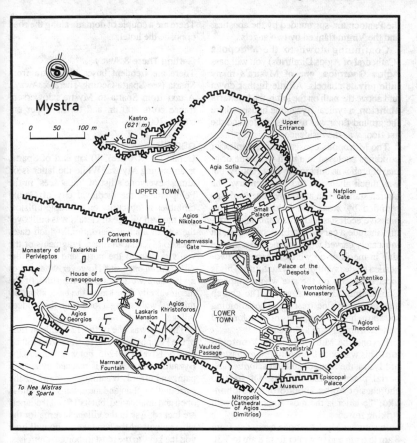

Mystra

Kastro
(621 m)

0   50   100 m

Upper
Entrance

Agia Sofia

UPPER TOWN

Nafplion
Gate

Agios
Nikolaos

Small
Palace

Convent
of Pantanassa

Monemvassia
Gate

Monastery of
Perivleptos

Taxiarkhai

House of
Frangopoulos

Palace of the
Despots

Aphentiko

Vrontokhion
Monastery

Agios
Georgios

Laskaris
Mansion

Agios
Khristoforos

LOWER
TOWN

Agios
Theodoroi

Vaulted
Passage

Evangelistria

Marmara
Fountain

To Nea Mistras
& Sparta

Episcopal
Palace

Museum

Mitropolis
(Cathedral
of Agios
Dimitrios)

leads down to the **Monemvassia Gate**, which was the entrance to the lower town.

Lower Town Once through the Monemvassia gate, turn right to reach the well-preserved 14th-century **Convent of Pantanassa**; the nuns who live here are the only inhabitants of Mystra. The building has beautiful stone-carved ornamentation on its façade and the capitals of its columns. It's an elaborate perfectly proportioned building, which is never overstated. Its exquisite, richly coloured 15th-century frescoes are amongst the finest examples of late-Byzan-

tine art. From the columned terrace on the northern façade there is a wonderful view of the pancake-flat and densely cultivated plain of Lakonia.

The path continues down to the **Monastery of Perivleptos**, which is built into a rock. Its 14th-century frescoes are equal to those of Pantanassa, and have been preserved virtually intact. Each of the scenes in the frescoes is an entity in itself – enclosed in a simple symmetrical shape. The overall effect is of numerous icons, placed next to one another, relating a visual narrative. The church has a very high dome. In the centre is the Pantocrator, surrounded by the apostles, and the Virgin flanked by two angels.

Continuing down to the **Mitropolis** (Cathedral of Agios Dimitrios) you will pass **Agios Georgios**, one of Mystra's many little private chapels. A little further down and above the path on the left is the **Laskaris Mansion**, a typical Byzantine house, where the ground floor was used as stables and the 1st floor was the residence.

The Mitropolis consists of a complex of buildings enclosed in a high wall. The original church was built in the 13th century, but was much altered in the 15th century. The church stands in an attractive courtyard surrounded by stoas and balconies. Its impressive ecclesiastical ornaments and furniture include a carved marble iconostasis, an intricately carved wood throne and a marble slab in the floor on which is carved a two-headed eagle (symbol of Byzantium). This is located exactly on the site where Emperor Constantine XI was crowned. The church also has some fine frescoes. The adjoining **museum** houses fragments of sculpture and pottery from Mystra's churches.

Beyond the Mitropolis is the **Vrontokhion**. This was once the wealthiest monastery of Mystra, the focus of cultural activities and burial place of the despots. Of its two churches of **Agios Theodoroi** and **Aphentiko**, the latter is the most impressive, with striking frescoes.

In summer Mystra is open every day from 8 am to 6 pm and in winter from 8 am to 3.30 pm. Admission is 1000 dr; students from EC countries are admitted free on production of an ISYC card. Outside the lower entrance to Mystra there is a *kantina* (mobile café), which sells snacks and delicious fresh orange juice for 250 dr.

Places to Stay

Most people visit Mystra on a day trip from Sparta, but there is limited accommodation in the village of **Nea Mystra**, near the site. The B class *Hotel Byzantion* (☎ 0731-93 309), near the central square, has singles/doubles/triples for 5000/7000/8000 dr.

There are a couple of domatia along the road opposite the hotel.

Getting There & Away

There are frequent buses to Mystra from Sparta (see Sparta Getting There & Away). A taxi from Sparta to Mystra's lower entrance costs 800 dr, and to the upper entrance, 1000 dr.

GERAKI Γεράκι

Geraki (Ye-RA-kee), 40 km east of Sparta, is an unsung Mystra. While the latter is on almost everyone's list of 'must sees' in the Peloponnese, the medieval city of Geraki crumbles in obscurity on a remote hillside. The modern village of Geraki was built over the site of ancient Geronthrai, which dates back to Mycenaean times. Fragments of the walls remain to the north and east of the village in an open site. However, what makes a visit here worthwhile are the ruins of the medieval city four km to the east, about 50 minutes' walk along a road from the modern village.

The city was one of the 12 Frankish fiefs of the Peloponnese. The fortress was built by Jean de Nivelet in 1245, but was ceded to the Byzantines in 1262. It is reached by a steep path, and affords breathtaking views of the surrounding plain and mountains. The site is open and unattended, but its 15 small chapels are locked. Ask in the village taverna for the whereabouts of the caretaker, who will give you the keys to the most important churches. There is no accommodation in Geraki, but it's easy enough to visit on a day trip from Sparta.

Getting There & Away

If you are driving, the road to Geraki is signposted to the right a little way out of Sparta along the Tripolis road. There are several buses a day from Sparta to the modern village (45 minutes, 400 dr).

GYTHIO Γύθειο

Once the port of ancient Sparta, Gythio (YI-thee-o, population 4054) is an attractive fishing town with a bustling waterfront of

19th-century pastel-coloured buildings, behind which crumbling old Turkish houses clamber up a steep wooded hill.

Orientation & Information

The bus station is at the northern end of the town. To reach the waterfront of Akti Vasileos Pavlou walk straight ahead with the park on your left. The town's central square, Plateia Mavromichali, is halfway along the waterfront. The quay is opposite this square. Beyond this square, the waterfront road veers left and then right. A little way along this stretch, a causeway leads to Marathonisi islet.

The post office is on Odos Ermou. From the bus station office turn right (walking away from the park) then veer right onto Herakles. Walk past the OTE office on the corner of Herakles and Kapsali and take the second turn left onto Ermou. The post office is on the right. Gythio's postcode is 23200 and the telephone code is 0733.

To reach the National Bank of Greece, turn left from the bus station. There is a health clinic (☎ 22 001/2/3) on the waterfront between Plateia Mavromichali and the causeway.

There is no EOT or tourist police in Gythio. The regular police (☎ 22 100) are on the waterfront between the bus station and Plateia Mavromichali.

Things to See

According to mythology, the tranquil pine-shaded **Marathonisi islet** is ancient Kranae where Paris (prince of Troy) and Helen (wife of Menelaus) consummated that affair which caused a bit of a ruckus back in Mycenaean times. The islet's 18th-century tower once belonged to the wild Mavromichaelis family, Maniot rebels who played a part in the assassination of Kapodistrias, Greece's first president, in Nafplion. The tower now houses a tame **museum**. The islet is a perfect spot for a picnic. Gythio has an **ancient theatre**, but don't expect another Epidaurus. This one is minuscule, but it is well preserved. To reach it follow directions for the post office, continue along Ermou and turn right onto Archaiou Theatrou. Walk to the end of here and turn left and the theatre is on the right next to an army camp.

Places to Stay – bottom end

There are four camp sites near Gythio, all on the coast, on the road to Areopoli. They are *Meltemi* (☎ 22 833 or 23 260), *Gythion Beach* (☎ 23 441), *Mani Beach* (☎ 23 450/1) and Kronos (☎ 24 124). The 'camping' bus stops at all of these sites except Kronos, which is three km from the nearest bus stop.

Amongst the cheapest of Gythio's numerous domatia are the rooms of *Tassos & Georgia Kalathis* (☎ 22 504), whose quaint, ramshackle house has clean doubles/triples/quads for 2000/3000/4000 dr. Turn right at Plateia Mavromichali onto Tzannibi Gregoraki and look for the signs.

Koutsouris Rooms to Rent (☎ 22 321) are lovely, cosy rooms with small kitchens and private bathrooms. Singles/doubles/triples are 2000/3000/4000 dr. Guests have the use of a delightful garden with citrus trees and five tortoises. Walk up Tzannibi Gregoraki, turn right at the church with the clock tower and the rooms are on the left.

The *Bougainvillaea Rooms* (no telephone), Herakles 22 (next to the OTE and buried beneath bougainvillea), is an outstanding domatia. The owner, Greek-Canadian Kim Brummel, has a variety of double rooms ranging from 2000 to 4000 dr. All are spotless with nice homely touches.

Gythio's cheapest hotel is the dilapidated but clean *Hotel Aktaion* (☎ 22 294), where rooms are 3500/4500/5500 dr with shared bathrooms. The foyer is chock-a-block with the kindly but eccentric owner's unusual paintings. The hotel is the first along the waterfront, coming from the bus station.

Further along the waterfront, between Plateia Mavromichali and the causeway, the *Saga Pension* (☎ 23 220) has immaculate, rooms for 4000/5000/6000 dr with private bathrooms. The pension has a car park.

Places to Stay – middle

The B class *Cavo Grosso Bungalows* (☎ 22

774/897 or 23 488/823) are near Mavro-
vouni Beach, two km south of Gythio. The
two-room bungalows have bathrooms,
lounge and kitchen facilities and there is a
restaurant, café and TV lounge. The cost is
12,800 dr.

Places to Eat
Most of the waterfront tavernas are tourist
traps. One local told me he wouldn't eat in
any of them if he was paid to. The workers'
café-like *Petakos Taverna* is Gythio's best
taverna. The woman who does the cooking
here should be famous for her wonderful,
delicately herb-flavoured dishes. Blackeye
bean and spinach stew is 500 dr, chicken with
potatoes and cannelloni are both 550 dr, arti-
choke stew is 650 dr and excellent draught
wine is 250 dr. The restaurant is open for
lunch and dinner. To reach it, walk north
along the waterfront, on the road signposted
to Skala, and the restaurant is in the town's
stadium on the right.

The *To Taka Café* is even more rough and
ready; it's a butchers shop by day and in the
evenings serves superb charcoal grilled
souvlaki for 120 dr and chicken for 1400 dr
a kg. Turn right onto Ermou from Herakles
and the café is on the left.

The *Om Café* is owned by a French couple
with a flair for creating unusual dishes –
tomato stuffed with tuna, egg and parsley is
650 dr, salad Nicoise is 800 dr, and grapefruit
stuffed with prawns and crab is 1300 dr – it's
OK to just pop in for a drink. The café is a
laid-back place where unobtrusive jazz, Brazilian folk and classical music is played –
sometimes live. The café is on the right side
of Tzannibi Gregoraki, coming from Plateia
Mavromichali.

There's a good supermarket between the
bus station and the OTE and a laiki agora on
Ermou on Tuesday and Friday mornings.

Things to Buy
While you are in Gythio take a look in the
fascinating antique-cum-junk shop near the
police station. It sells traditional farming
tools, household appliances, small items of
furniture (some of hand-carved wood),
church ornaments, pottery, old stamps and
coins.

Getting There & Away
Bus There are six buses a day to Areopoli
(30 minutes, 330 dr); five to Athens (5½
hours, 2750 dr) via Sparta (one hour, 570 dr);
four to the camp sites along the Areopoli
road; four to Kalamata, two via Sparta and
two via Itilo; three to the Dirou Caves (one
hour, 400 dr); two to Gerolimenas (two
hours, 750 dr); and one to Monemvassia (two
hours, 1625 dr).

Ferry The F/B *Ionion* is the only large ferry
which calls at Gythio. In theory it is meant
to arrive at 11 pm on Monday and Thursday
and go to Kapsali on Kythera (three hours,
740 dr); Antikythera (1862 dr); and Kastelli
on Crete (seven hours, 2400 dr). In reality it
is usually 3 or 4 am when it arrives in Gythio.
Fortunately the café on the quay stays open
until the ferry arrives.

On its return the ferry calls at Gythio on
Tuesday and Friday at 3.45 pm, from where
it goes to Agia Pelagia on Kythera; Neapoli
(four hours, 1384 dr); Monemvassia (five
hours, 1853 dr); and Piraeus (13 hours, 3485
dr). For tickets and information go to the
helpful Rozakis Travel Agency (☎ 22
229/207), on the waterfront just before
Plateia Mavromichali. The port police (☎ 22
262) are on the waterfront just before the
causeway.

Getting Around
Car & Motorbike There are no car-hire
outlets in Gythio. Motorbikes can be rented
from Super Cycle Moto (☎ 24 407/001), a
little way up Tzannibi Gregoraki from
Plateia Mavromichali.

GEFYRA & MONEMVASSIA
Monemvassia (Mon-em-vas-EE-a)
(Μονεμβασσία), 99 km from Sparta, is a
massive rock which rises dramatically out of
the sea, off Lakonia's east coast. It is reached
by a causeway from the mainland village
of Gefyra (Γέφυρα) (also called Nea
Monemvassia). In summer, Gefyra and

Monemvassia brim over with tourists, but the extraordinary impact of one's first encounter with the medieval town of Monemvassia, and the delights of exploring it, override the effects of tourism. The poet Yiannis Ritsos, who was born and lived for many years in Monemvassia, wrote of it, 'This scenery is as harsh as silence'.

From Gefyra, Monemvassia looks nothing more than a huge rock rising out of the sea, with a fortress on top, and a few scattered buildings at sea level. But cross the causeway and walk along the curving road by the sea for 20 minutes and you will come to a narrow tunnel in a massive fortifying wall. The tunnel is L-shaped so you cannot see to the other side. After you enter, you will emerge into the magical town of Monemvassia, totally concealed until that moment.

Unlike Mystra, Monemvassia's houses are inhabited, albeit, mostly by weekenders from Athens.

History

The island, appropriately called the Gibraltar of Greece, was part of the mainland, until separated by a devastating earthquake in 375 AD. Its name means 'single entry' (*moni* – single, *emvasia* – entry), as there is only one entry to the medieval town. During the 6th century, barbarian incursions forced the inhabitants of the surrounding area to retreat to the natural fortress of the huge rock. By the 13th century, it had become the principal commercial centre of Byzantine Morea, complementary to Mystra, the spiritual centre. It was famous throughout Europe for its highly praised Malvasia (also called Malmsey) wine.

Later came a succession of invasions from Franks, Venetians and Turks. During the War of Independence it was the scene of an abhorrent massacre of its Turkish inhabitants, upon their surrender, following a three-month siege by the Greek army.

Orientation & Information

All practicalities can be dealt with in Gefyra. The main street is 23 Iouliou which skirts the coast and leads to the causeway. The bus station is on 23 Iouliou, just a short walk from the causeway. The post office is on the left side of Odos Spartis; walking away from the causeway it's on the left; the National Bank of Greece is next door. The OTE is at the top of 28 Oktovriou, which is a turn-off right from 23 Iouliou. Monemvassia's postcode is 23070 and the telephone code is 0732.

There is no EOT or tourist police in Monemvassia or Gefyra. However, Greek Australian Peter Derzolis, the manager of Malvasia Travel Agency (☎ 61 752/432/445), just up from the bus station, is extremely helpful and sells ferry and air tickets, has currency exchange and rents cars and motorbikes.

Medieval Town

The narrow, cobbled main street is lined with souvenir shops and tavernas, flanked by winding stairways which weave between a complex network of stone houses with walled gardens and courtyards. The main street leads to the central square and the **Cathedral of Christ in Chains**, dating from the 13th century. Opposite is the **Church of Agios Pavlos**, built in 956 AD and now a small **museum**. Just above it is the **Church of Mirtidiotissa**, virtually in ruins, but still with a small altar and a defiantly flickering candle. Overlooking the sea is the recently restored, whitewashed 16th-century **Panagia Chrysaphitissa**.

The **fortress** (signposted) and upper town are reached by ascending steps off to the left, shortly after entering the old town. The upper town is now a vast and fascinating jumbled ruin, except for the **Church of Agia Sophia**, which perches on the edge of a sheer cliff.

Places to Stay – bottom end

Camping Paradise (☎ 61 680) is a very pleasant, well-shaded site, next to a beach with a minimarket, bar and disco. It is 3½ km south of Gefyra.

In Gefyra there are numerous domatia – look for the signs on the approach road from Molai and also on 28 Oktovriou beyond the bus station.

Gefyra's cheapest hotel is the newly renovated E class *Hotel Akrogia* (☎ 61 360), next to the National Bank of Greece. Single/double rooms cost 2600/3900 dr with private bathrooms. The D class *Hotel Aktaion* (☎ 61 234), by the causeway, is also pleasant with rooms for 2900/4000/5000 dr with private bathrooms.

The C class *Hotel Minoa* (☎ 61 224/398/209), also by the causeway, has dazzling white walls, lots of cool grey marble and spacious nicely furnished rooms. Rates are 5400/7400/9500/11,680 dr for singles/doubles/triples/quads.

Places to Stay – middle

Villas Trougakos (☎ 61 177), signposted from the Molai-Gefyra road, is a complex of modern, tastefully furnished apartments. The prices are 11,500 dr for two or three people and 15,000 dr for four people.

There are no budget places to stay in Monemvassia. All of the highly desirable places are expensive, impeccably restored traditional settlements. They include *Malvasia Guest Houses* (☎ 61 113/435/323), with singles/doubles/triples/quads for 6000/8400/13,350/17,800 dr (including breakfast) and *Byzantino* (☎ 61 254/351/562; fax 61 331), with doubles/triples/quads for 12,500/14,000/16,000 dr. If you would like to rent a room in a private house you can make a reservation through Malvasia Travel Agency, but expect to pay around 8000 dr a double. Staying in Monemvassia is a memorable experience, for the allure of the town increases at night under the stars.

Places to Eat

Gefyra In Gefyra, *Taverna Nikolas*, just up from Malvasia Travel Agency, serves tasty, reasonably priced dishes. *T' Agnantio Taverna*, 100 metres further along the road, is highly recommended.

Monemvassia In Monemvassia, *To Kanoni*, on the right of the main street, has an imaginative and extensive menu. Starters include mushrooms with cream, and cheese and ham crepes; main dishes include

tagliatelli with spinach, mixed fish dish (for four people) and mixed grill (for two people). Deserts include yoghurt with honey, and plums stuffed with walnuts. There is also a wide range of unresinated Greek wines ranging from 700 to 2500 dr.

Getting There & Away

Bus None of the bus services to/from Gefyra are direct; all involve a change of bus in the small town of Molai. However, it is possible to purchase a ticket right through to your final destination. There are three buses a day to Athens (seven hours, 3250 dr) via Sparta (2½ hours, 1150 dr) and Tripolis (3½ hours, 1550 dr); and one bus a day (summer only) to Gythio (1½ hours, 850 dr).

Ferry The F/B *Ionion*, the unpunctual old tub which also serves Gythio, is the only ferry which calls in at Monemvassia. See the Gythio Getting There and Away section, and subtract five hours from the sailing time to Piraeus, and add five hours for the sailing times to Crete, to estimate the sailing times from Monemvassia. Buy tickets from Malvasia Travel Agency.

Hydrofoil In summer there are five flying dolphins a week to Kythera (one hour, 3200 dr) and Leonidio (one hour, 3000 dr) and three a week to Piraeus (four hours, 6050 dr) via Gerakas, Kyparissi, Spetses, and Hydra.

Getting Around

Car & Motorbike These can be rented from Malvasia Travel Agency (see under Orientation & Information). The medieval town of Monemvassia is inaccessible to cars and motorbikes, but there is a parking area outside the entrance to the town.

NEAPOLI Νεάπολη

Neapoli (Neh-A-po-lee) is the southernmost port of the Peloponnese on the tip of the easternmost peninsula. It's an undistinguished place and only worth a mention because it's the major jumping-off point for the island of Kythera, and frequent caïques make the crossing to the small island of

Elafonissi, which lies west of Neapoli and north of Kythera. If you get stuck in Neapoli overnight it shouldn't be too difficult to find a room at a hotel or domatia.

Getting There & Away
Bus There are four buses a day to Neapoli from Sparta (four hours, 1400 dr).

Ferry The F/B *Martha* leaves Neapoli every day at 9 am for Agia Pelagia on Kythera, with additional sailings at 4.30 pm on Monday, Wednesday and Friday, and 3.30 pm on Sunday. The F/B *Ionion* includes Neapoli on its meander down the Peloponnese coast en route to Crete. It sails to Kastelli on Crete via Agia Pelagia (Kythera), Gythio and Kapsali (Kythera) at 6.30 pm on Monday and 4.50 on Thursday. The Thursday sailing calls at Antikythera. On Tuesday at 12.30 pm the same ferry sails to Agia Pelagia (Kythera), Monemvassia, Gerakas, Kyparissi and Piraeus and on Saturday it sails to Monemvassia and Piraeus at 8 pm. Bear in mind that the F/B *Ionion* is subject to delays (see Gythio Getting There & Away).

Hydrofoil In summer there are hydrofoils every day except Monday at 7.15 am to Piraeus via Spetses, Hydra and Poros.

ELAFONISSI Ελαφονήσι
Elafonissi sees few foreign tourists, but is popular with Greeks who pop over from the mainland for fish lunches in summer, particularly on Sunday. The island's main attraction, apart from the fish blowouts, is its superb beaches, which the Greeks liken to the those of the South Seas – and they're not exaggerating.

Elafonissi's telephone code is 0732.

The island has no hotels but there are a couple of pensions, the *Elafonisos* (☎ 49 268) and *Liaros* (☎ 49 271/2), and a few domatia. There is no official camp site, but you may find it possible to camp unofficially.

Getting There & Away
Caïque In summer, caïques ply between Elafonissi and Neapoli several times a day.

Kythera Κύθηρα

The island of Kythera (KI-thi-ra, population 4000), south-west of Neapoli, is approximately 30 km long and 18 km wide. This somewhat anomalous island is geographically an extension of the Peloponnese, historically part of the Ionian archipelago and administered from Piraeus. It survives economically on remittances from the many islanders who have emigrated to 'Big Kythera', as these expats call Australia.

According to mythology, the island was the birthplace of Aphrodite, who rose fully grown out of the sea foam where Zeus had thrown Cronus' sex organ after castrating him. The goddess then re-emerged in Cyprus, so both islands claim to be her birthplace.

Birth of Aphrodite

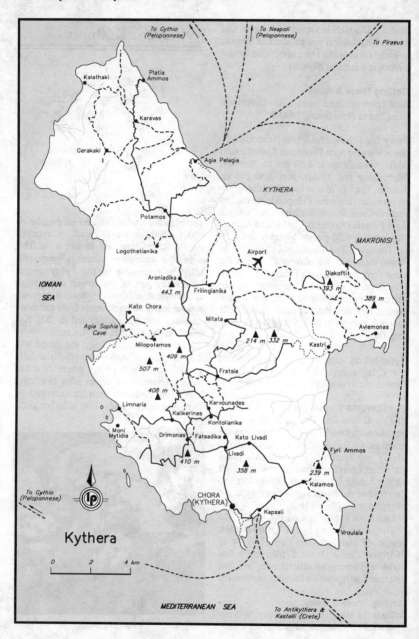

To Gythio
(Peloponnese)

To Neapoli
(Peloponnese)

To Piraeus

Kalathaki

Platia
Ammos

Karavas

Gerakaki

Agia Pelagia

KYTHERA

Potamos

MAKRONISI

Logothetianika

Airport

Diakofti
393 m

389 m

IONIAN
SEA

Aroniadika
443 m

Frilingianika

Kato Chora

Mitata

Avlemonas

Agia Sophia
Cave

214 m 332 m

Kastri

Milopotamos
409 m

507 m

Fratsia

408 m

Karvounades

Limnaria

Kalikerines

Kontolianika

Moni
Mytidia

Drimonas Fatsadika

Kato Livadi

Fyri Ammos

410 m

Livadi

239 m

358 m

Kalamos

To Gythio
(Peloponnese)

lp

CHORA
(KYTHERA)

Kapsali

Vroulaia

Kythera

0   2   4 km

MEDITERRANEAN SEA

To Antikythera &
Kastelli (Crete)

Until recently Kythera was little visited by foreign tourists, partly through inaccessibility, but also through the islanders' indifference to the tourist industry. However, in recent years the EOT has begun making efforts to attract tourists to Kythera, but it's still an island for those who want to get away from it all. Don't turn up in Kythera in July or August without a hotel reservation, as the island does not have an abundance of accommodation, particularly at the budget end of the market. Domatia owners don't tend to meet the boats as they do on most islands.

Kythera consists of a plateau of rolling hills giving way to high cliffs. There are two ports, Agia Pelagia on the north-east coast, and Kapsali in the south. The capital of the island is Chora (also called Kythera). The island's main road cuts through the centre, joining the two ports and several settlements between.

Getting To/From Kythera

Air In summer there are daily flights to Athens (50 minutes, 8500 dr) at 10.20 am and 4.30 pm, except Monday when there is one flight at 12.50 pm. The Olympic Airways office (☎ 33 362) is on the central square in the town of Potamos, 22 km north of Chora. Reservations may also be made at Conomos Travel (☎ 33 490/321), opposite the quay at Agia Pelagia, Kythera Travel in Chora and Rama Travel (☎ 31 561) on the waterfront in Kapsali. The airport is out in the sticks in the east part of the island.

Ferry The F/B *Martha* sails at least once a day from Agia Pelagia to Neapoli. The F/B *Ionion* leaves Agia Pelagia at 8 pm on Monday for Gythio, Kapsali (Kythera) and Kastelli (Crete) and at 6.30 pm on Friday. The Friday sailing also calls at Antikythera. At 2 pm on Tuesday it leaves Agia Pelagia for Monemvassia, Gerakas, Kyparissi and Piraeus, and on Saturday it leaves at 6.45 pm for Neapoli, Monemvassia and Piraeus. It leaves Kapsali at 2.20 am on Tuesday and Saturday for Kastelli on Crete; Saturday's sailing includes Antikythera. On Saturday at noon, it leaves Kapsali for Gythio, Agia

Pelagia (Kythera), Neapoli, Monemvassia and Piraeus. Note that the F/B *Ionion* is often subject to delays.

In summer there are often small boats from Agia Pelagia to Elafonissi. Enquire at the port police about these.

Hydrofoil In summer, there are hydrofoils from Agia Pelagia on a Monday, Tuesday, Wednesday, Thursday and Saturday to Piraeus (five hours, 6000 dr) via Monemvassia, Gerakas, Kyparissi, Spetses and Hydra.

Getting Around Kythera

Bus Kythera's bus service is deplorable – the worst for an island of its size. In summer a bus leaves Agia Pelagia at 8 am, stopping at all the villages on the main road, and arriving at Kapsali at 9.30 am. At 11.30 am it leaves Kapsali and does the same journey in reverse. During the school term, buses are more frequent, but are naturally monopolised by school children. There is no airport bus, but it's usually easy to find someone to share a taxi with. Not surprisingly there are many taxis on the island and hitching is fairly easy.

Car & Motorbike Cars can be hired from Tserigo Rent Car (☎ 31 363/030/836), on the main street in Chora. Panayiotos, at Moto Rent (☎ 31 600) on Kapsali's waterfront, rents well-maintained mopeds for 1300 to 1700 dr and motorbikes for 3500 to 4000 dr.

CHORA (KYTHERA)

Chora (Χώρα), the capital of Kythera, and also known by the same name as the island, perches on a long slender ridge, two km uphill from Kapsali. It's an attractive settlement, with white, blue-shuttered houses and a central square planted with hibiscus, bougainvillea and palm trees.

Orientation & Information

Most practicalities can be dealt with in Chora. The central square is Plateia Dimitriou Stati and the main street runs south from here. The post office is on the left, at the southern end of this street. To reach the

OTE climb up the steps by the side of Kythera Travel on the central square, and follow the signs. Kythera's postcode is 80200 and its telephone code is 0735. The National Bank of Greece is on the central square. The police station (☎ 31 206) is signposted from the southern end of the main street.

Kythera does not have a tourist office or tourist police but the helpful, amiable and English-speaking Panayiotos unofficially offers information to tourists. Panayiotos is based at his Moto Rent office (☎ 31 600) on the waterfront in Kapsali, but also has branch offices in Chora (☎ 31 004) and Agia Pelagia (no telephone). The staff at Kythera Travel (☎ 31 390/490) on Chora's central square are also helpful.

Kastro

Chora's Venetian kastro is at the southern end of town, beyond the police station. It's not especially impressive, but if you walk to its southern extremity, passing the white-washed Church of Panagia, you will come to the edge of a sheer cliff, from where there is a stunning bird's-eye view of Kapsali and the hills and coast beyond.

Museum

The town's interesting little museum is just north of the central square. In one room there are some gravestones of British soldiers and their infant children who died on the island in the 19th century (Kythera was part of Britain's Ionian Protectorate from 1815-64). Dominating the other room is a large stone lion and in a cabinet to the right, a charming terracotta figurine of a woman and child. The museum is open Tuesday to Saturday from 8.45 am to 3 pm and Sunday from 8.30 am to 2.30 pm. Admission is free.

Places to Stay – bottom end

Chora's cheapest accommodation is *Georgiou Pissi Pension* (☎ 31 070/210), where singles/doubles are 2000/3000 dr with shared bathrooms. Walk south along the main street and look for the blue and white sign on the left. Attractive rooms at *Pension*

Ketty (☎ 31 318/232) go for 5000 dr a double with private bathrooms. Walk south along the main street, take the first left after the arch and turn left at the top of the steps. The new *Castelli Rooms* (☎ 31 069) are spacious, and immaculate, with kitchen areas, private bathrooms and shared terraces with breathtaking views. Rates are 6000 dr a double. You will see a sign at the southern end of the main street, just before the road forks.

Places to Stay – middle

The opulent B class *Hotel Margarita* (☎ 31 694/5) is an authentically renovated 19th-century mansion. Rates are 9200/14,000 dr for singles/doubles. The rooms are traditionally furnished and have air-con, TV, telephone and private bathrooms. The hotel is down the steps opposite Zorba's Psistaria on the main street.

Places to Eat

On the main street, *Zorba's Psistaria* serves tasty grilled food. *Restaurant Mirtoon* is probably Kythera's best restaurant. It is on the main Kapsali-Chora road, but can also be reached through the web of Chora's narrow streets – locals should be able to direct you.

To Apaggio Snack Bar with tables on the central square has rice pudding, toasted sandwiches, home-made cakes, cheese pies and mezedes (evenings only). It also has that rarity in Greece – filter coffee (250 dr). If you order this the waiter may pull a face, but if you insist will reluctantly make it.

KAPSALI Καψάλι

Kapsali, Kythera's southern port, is an appealing, bustling little place with two beaches separated by a headland. Facing inland from the ferry quay, the larger beach stretches to the left, skirted by the road which leads to Chora. There is a third beach which is small and secluded. To reach this, on the road to Chora take the first left along a dirt track, from where steps lead down to the beach. Another road inland and parallel to the waterfront road is also signposted Chora. The two roads merge just outside Kapsali. Canoes (300 dr per hour), pedal boats and surf boards (both 800 dr per hour) and water-skis (3000 dr per hour) can be hired from Panayiotis at Moto Rent, on the waterfront.

Kapsali's port police (☎ 31 222) are next to Moto Rent.

Places to Stay – bottom end

Kythera's one camp site, *Camping Kapsali* (☎ 31 580), is a pleasant site shaded by pine trees. The rates are 540 dr per person and tent. The site is 300 metres from Kapsali's quay and is signposted from the inland road which leads to Chora.

There are not many places to stay in Kapsali. Try *Irene Megapoudi Rooms* (☎ 31 340), which are large and clean with private bathrooms and cost 5780/6700 dr for doubles/triples. The rooms are at the far end of the road skirting the large beach – look for a bamboo-shaded terrace with cacti plants.

Places to Stay – top end

For a touch of luxury try the B class *Raikos Hotel* (☎ 31 629), a complex of striking white buildings on a hill between Kapsali and Chora. The rooms are dazzling white with vibrant flower arrangements; the effect is one of understated elegance. The air-con rooms have radio, telephone, minibar, kitchen area and balconies and cost 22,000/31,000 dr for doubles/triples including breakfast. The hotel has a pool.

Places to Eat

Kapsali isn't exactly overflowing with culinary delights. The most popular restaurant with locals is *Restaurant Zerbas* at the quay.

Getting There & Around

See the relevant sections at the beginning of the Kythera section.

AGIA PELAGIA Αγία Πελαγία

Kythera's northern port of Agia Pelagia has more places to stay than Kapsali, but is not so attractive. With your back to the quay, the rather tatty waterfront is to the right. At the beginning of the quay there is a room-finding office (no telephone), which only operates in

July and August. Agia Pelagia's port police (☎ 33 280) are next to O Vatis Taverna.

Places to Stay – bottom end

Agia Pelagia's cheapest rooms are *Alexandra Megalopoulou's Rooms* (☎ 33 282). The clean, simply furnished rooms are 3600 dr a double with shared bathrooms. They are opposite the quay above the Faros Taverna. *Pari Gerakiti's Rooms* (☎ 33 462) are clean and pleasant with double/triple rates of 6000/6500 dr with private bathrooms. Turn left from the quay and walk along the road which skirts the sea and look for a white building with green shutters. The very pleasant D class *Hotel Kythera* (☎ 33 321), owned by Mike and Freda from Australia, has very comfortable, spotless singles/doubles for 4500/6500 dr with private bathrooms. The hotel is opposite the quay next to the Faros Taverna.

Places to Stay – middle

The beautiful *Filoxenia Apartments* (☎ 33 610/100) each have a bedroom, lounge and kitchen. Rates for doubles/triples/quads are 12,000/14,500/15,000 dr. Turn left from the quay and look for a white building with blue shutters, on the right.

Places to Eat

O Vatis Taverna serves tasty low-priced Greek staples. The taverna is on the waterfront just to the right of the quay. *Faros Taverna*, opposite the quay, is also recommended.

Getting There & Around

See the Getting To/From Kythera and Getting Around Kythera entries at the beginning of the Kythera section for details on local transport and ferry departures from Agia Pelagia.

MILOPOTAMOS Μυλοπόταμος

Milopotamos is one of the island's most alluring villages, with several places of interest nearby; unfortunately it doesn't have any accommodation. The village's central square is flanked by a church and kafeneion. After a leisurely coffee here, you can stroll down to the **Neraida** (water nymph) waterfall. From the square, continue along the road and take the right fork, and in just under 100 metres a path on the right leads down to the waterfall. It's a magical spot, with luxuriant greenery, shady plane, maple and poplar trees and a wooden picnic bench.

To reach the abandoned **kastro** of Milopotamos, take the left fork after the church, and follow the sign for Kato Chora (lower village). The road leads to the centre of Kato Chora, from where a portal with the insignia of St Mark leads into the atmospheric and slightly spooky kastro, with derelict houses and well-preserved little churches (locked of course). Like the kastro in Chora this one also ends abruptly at a precipice.

The **Cave of Agia Sophia** was first explored by Ioannis and Anna Patrochilos of Dirou Cave fame. Sometime in the 12th century, the cave was converted into a chapel and dedicated to Agia Sophia, who, according to legend, visited the cave with her daughters Pistis, Elpis and Agape (Faith, Hope and Charity). At the entrance are some well-preserved frescoes. The cave is reached by a two-km road and a steep path from Milopotamas. The very irregular opening times are pinned on a signpost to the cave,

just beyond Milopotamos' central square. Admission is 500 dr and includes a guided tour.

ANTIKYTHERA Αντικύθηρα

The tiny island of Antikythera (population 115), 38 km south-east of Kythera, is the most remote island in the Aegean and definitely one for the reclusive. It has one settlement (Potamos), one doctor, one police officer, one teacher (with five pupils), one metered telephone and one monastery, but there is no post office or bank. Antikythera's telephone code is 0735.

Places to Stay & Eat

Currently the only accommodation for tourists is 10 basic rooms in two purpose-built blocks, which only operate in the summer. There is a kafeneion in Potamos and there are plans to open a restaurant.

Getting There & Away

The F/B *Ionion* calls twice a week: at 4 am on a Sunday when it's bound for Kastelli on Crete and at 10.15 pm the same day on its way to Piraeus via Kythera, Gythio, Neapoli and Monemvassia. If the sea is choppy the ferry does not stop at Antikythera, so this is not an island for tourists on a tight schedule.

Central Greece

Central Greece, comprising Sterea Ellada and Thessaly, has three principal attractions: the ancient site of Delphi, the amazing rock 'forest' and monasteries of Meteora and the verdant Pelion peninsula.

Sterea Ellada
Στερεά Ελλάδα

Sterea Ellada is bordered by Thessaly and Epiros to the north and the narrow Corinth and Patras gulfs in the south. The region acquired the name Sterea Ellada (Greek Continent) in 1827, because it was the only continental portion of the newly formed Greek state – the Peloponnese was classed as an island.

The island of Evia, separated from the mainland by a narrow gulf, and a jumping-off point for the Sporades islands, is covered in the Sporades chapter.

ATHENS TO THEBES

If you have your own transport and intend travelling from Athens to Delphi you have a choice of two routes: the main highway or the old mountain road to Thebes; the latter is a turn inland just west of Eleusis. Along the way you can take a turn-off left to the 4th-century BC **Fortress of Aigosthena**, and have a swim at nearby **Porto Germenon**, on the north coast of the Gulf of Corinth. The fortress is well preserved, with its towers still standing. Within the walls are two Byzantine churches.

Porto Germenon is a pleasant low-key resort with a pebble beach, inexpensive fish tavernas and one hotel, the C class *Hotel Egosthenion* (☎ 0263-41 226).

Back on the Thebes road, two km beyond the turn-off for the Fortress of Aigosthena and Porto Germenon, you will see the **Fortress of Eleutherai** on a hill to the right. This fortress also dates from the 4th century BC, but is less impressive than Aigosthena. The fortress stands at the entrance to the pass over Mt Kythairon. According to mythology, the baby Oedipus was left to perish on this mountain.

If you are a battle buff you may like to make the five-km detour to the remains of **Plataea**, which overlooked the plain where the famous Battle of Plataea (479 BC) took place. The remains are reached by turning left at **Erithres**.

THEBES Θήβα

Thebes (THEE-va, population 18,712), 87 km north-west of Athens, figured prominently in history and mythology, and the two are inextricably linked. The tragic fate of its royal dynasty, centred around the myth of Oedipus, rivalled that of Mycenae.

Thebes' telephone code is 0262.

History

After the Trojan War, Thebes became the dominant city of the district of Boeotia. In 371 BC the city was victorious in a battle against Sparta, which had hitherto been invincible. In 336 BC Thebes was sacked by Alexander the Great for rebelling against Macedonian control; 6000 Thebans were killed and 30,000 taken prisoner.

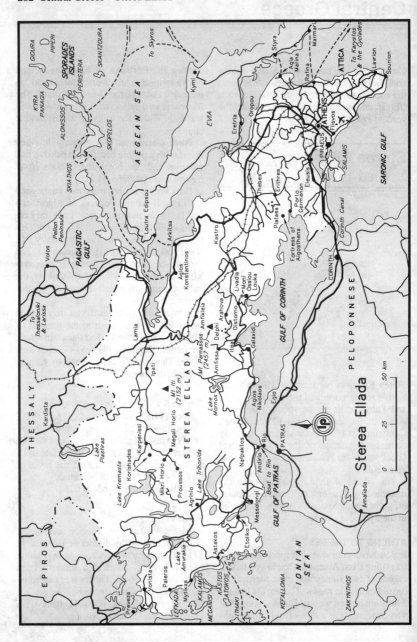

Oedipus Rex

Whilst wandering the countryside, Oedipus, who had been adopted at birth, unwittingly murdered his real father, the king of Thebes, thus widowing his natural mother, the Queen Jokasta. He then gained access to Thebes by answering a riddle posed by the Sphinx who resided at the entrance to the city – the Sphinx ate anybody who couldn't come up with the answer. On being outwitted by Oedipus, the Sphinx killed herself.

As a reward for getting rid of this vexatious creature, the Thebans gave Oedipus the hand in marriage of his newly widowed mother, Queen Jokasta. As mother and son had lived apart since Oedipus' birth, neither knew the identity of the other. When an oracle enlightened them, the queen took her own life, and Oedipus, in an act of self-mortification, gouged out his eyes and wandered the country as a blind beggar.

The riddle, in case you're wondering, was 'What creature has four legs in the morning, two at midday, and three in the evening, and is at its weakest when it has the most?' The answer is man – man crawls on all fours as a baby, walks upright when mature and uses a cane in old age! ■

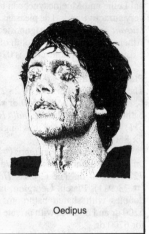

Oedipus

Archaeological Museum

Present-day Thebes is a drab provincial town with few vestiges of its past glory, but it does have an impressive Archaeological Museum. The collection includes pottery from prehistoric and Mycenaean times, Linear B tablets found in the Mycenaean palaces and some Mycenaean clay coffins, which are unique to mainland Greece. The museum is open Tuesday to Sunday from 8.30 am to 3 pm. Admission is 400 dr. It's at the northern end of Odos Pindarou, which runs parallel to Epaminondou, where the bus station is located.

Places to Stay – bottom end

If you get stuck in Thebes there are three hotels to choose from. The D class *Dionyssion Melathron* (☎ 27 855), on the corner of I Metaxa and Kadmou, has singles/doubles with shared bathrooms for 4000/5000 dr and 5000/6000 dr with private bathrooms. Kadmou is parallel to Epaminondou, one block to the west.

The C class *Neobe Hotel* (☎ 27 949), Epaminondou 63, has singles/doubles with shared bathrooms for 3500/5500 dr and doubles with private bathrooms for 6500 dr.

Places to Stay – middle

The C class *Meletiou Hotel* (☎ 27 333), at 56-58 Epaminondou, has singles/doubles for 7500/10,000 dr.

Getting There & Away

There are hourly buses from both Athens (1½ hours, 900 dr) and Livadia (45 minutes, 550 dr).

LIVADIA Λειβάδεια

Livadia (population 17,500) is on the Athens-Delphi road, 45 km north-west of Thebes. The town flanks both sides of a gorge through which the River Erkinas flows. A 14th-century Frankish castle overlooks Livadia from Profitis Elias hill.

The town's main claim to fame is as the site of the oracle of Trophonios. According to legend, the ordeal one had to go through in order to consult this oracle resulted in a permanent look of fright. First, the pilgrim drank from the fountain of Lethe (Waters of Forgetfulness) and then of the Mnemosyne (Waters of Remembrance). They were then lowered into a hole in a cave and left there for days on end to commune with the oracle.

Springs, which are supposedly the original Lethe and Mnemosyne, can be seen in a very attractive park. The pleasant *Xenia Restaurant* in the park is signposted from the Athens-Delphi road, just south of the town.

Livadia's telephone code is 0261.

Places to Stay

The D class *Hotel Erkyna* (☎ 28 227), Lappa 6, has rooms for 2500/3500 dr with shared bathrooms. The B class *Levadia Hotel* (☎ 23 611), Plateia L Katsoni, has singles/doubles for 8500/12,220 dr.

The C class *Hotel Philippos* (☎ 24 931/2), on Odos Athinon, has singles/doubles for 7220/10,150 dr. The C class *Hotel Elikon* (☎ 23 911), Plateia Georgiou, has singles/doubles with shared bathrooms for 5200/6200 dr and doubles with private bathrooms for 6700 dr.

Getting There & Away

There are frequent buses from Livadia to Athens, Thebes, Delphi and Distomo (for Moni Ossiou Louka).

PATRAS TO DELPHI

The 153-km route from Patras to Delphi is via the Rio-Andirio ferry. From Andirio, where there is an imposing fortress, the road skirts the north shore of the Gulf of Corinth, passing a number of seaside towns and villages before turning inland at Itea. The coast is more popular as a holiday destination with Greeks than with foreign tourists.

Nafpaktos, nine km east of Andirio, is a little resort with an attractive harbour, a good beach and a well-preserved Venetian castle. It sits in a lush region with a backdrop of pine-covered mountains. Nafpaktos was known as Lepanto in medieval times and it was here that the famous naval battle of Lepanto took place, in 1571.

Nafpaktos has several hotels and there are two camp sites between it and Andirio, *Platanitis Beach* (☎ 0634-31 555) and *Dounis Beach* (☎ 0634-31 565). There is another camp site, *Doric Camping* (☎ 0266-31 722), further east along the coast at **Agios Nikolaos**.

Galaxidi, further along the road, is perhaps the prettiest town along this coast. It was a prosperous caïque-building centre in the 19th century, and some fine stone mansions survive from this time.

Its Naval Museum houses models of ships, marine paintings and paraphernalia from the War of Independence.

Galaxidi has a number of hotels and *Galaxidi Camping* (☎ 0265-41 530) is just west of town.

Itea, 17 km further along the road, is a less attractive, commercial and market town. The main road turns inland here for Delphi and Amfissia and a minor road continues for two km to **Kira**. This was ancient Kirrha, the port of Delphi, which was destroyed by the Amphyctionic Council in the First Sacred War (595-586 BC). Kira has a good beach and two camp sites, *Kaparelis Camping* (☎ 0265-32 330) and *Ayannis Camping* (☎ 0265-32 555).

Getting There & Away

The Patras-Delphi bus goes along this stretch of coast. There are six buses a day from Delphi to Itea and five a day from Itea to Nafpaktos, stopping at the coastal towns along the way.

DELPHI Δελφοί

Modern Delphi (Del-FEE, population 250) is 178 km north-west of Athens. It has nothing especially to recommend it other than as a handy jumping-off point for the ancient site. Odos Vasileos Pavlou & Frederikis, its main thoroughfare, is lined with hotels, souvenir shops and restaurants.

Orientation & Information

Almost everything you'll need in Delphi is on Vasileos Pavlou & Frederikis. The bus stop is here next to the Taverna Kastri. The post office, OTE and the National Bank of Greece are also on this street. The ancient site is 1½ km back along the main road to Arahova.

Delphi's Municipal Tourist Office (☎ 82 900) is at Vasileos & Pavlou Frederikis 44. Opening times are Monday to Saturday from

8 am to 3 pm, with additional opening hours of 6 to 8 pm during July and August.

In summer the bank opens from 6 to 7.30 pm in addition to normal hours. Delphi's postcode is 33054; the telephone code is 0265.

Places to Stay – bottom end

Delphi's nearest camp site is *Apolon Camping* (☎ 82 750/762), 1½ km west of modern Delphi. *Delphi Camping* (☎ 28 944/363) is four km down the Delphi-Itea road.

Finding a room in Delphi does not present any problems, as hotels are plentiful.

The *YHA Hostel* (☎ 82 268), Apollonos 29, is one of Greece's best. It is run by a helpful and courteous woman from New Zealand, and has double rooms for 3500 dr and dorm beds for 1000 dr. The hostel is open from March to November. Apollonos runs north of Vasileos Pavlou & Frederikis.

Places to Stay – middle

Most of Delphi's hotels are on Vasileos Pavlou & Frederikis. The D class *Hotel Athina* (☎ 33 054), Vasileos Pavlou & Frederikis 51, has nicely furnished single/double rooms for 3300/4500 dr with shared bathrooms and 5500 dr for doubles with private bathrooms.

The C class *Hotel Pan* (☎ 82 294), at No 53, has pleasant rooms for 3700/6000 dr with private bathrooms. The opulent C class *Hotel Hermes* (☎ 82 318/163/641), Vasileos Pavlou & Frederikis 29, has spacious, tastefully furnished singles/doubles/triples for 5600/7200/8500 dr with private bathrooms. This hotel has spectacular views down to the Gulf of Corinth. The pleasant C class *Hotel Parnassos* (☎ 82 321) at No 30 is similarly priced and also has good views.

Places to Stay – top end

Delphi's most luxurious hotel is the A class *Hotel Amalias* (☎ 82 101/2/3/4/5; fax 82 033), on Apollonos. The hotel has a bar, café, restaurant and a swimming pool. Rates are 13,200/17,900 dr for singles/doubles.

Another plush place is the A class *Hotel Vouzas* (☎ 82 232/4), Vasileos Pavlou &

Frederikis 1. Singles/doubles here are 13,200/16,800 dr. The hotel has a bar, restaurant and roof garden.

Places to Eat

The *Taverna Vakhos*, Apollonos 31, next door to the youth hostel, serves tasty Greek staples. Main meals cost around 850 dr. The *Taverna Kastri*, which doubles up as the bus station office, is also commendable, and is similarly priced to the Vakhos.

Getting There & Away

Bus There are seven buses a day from Delphi to Amfissa (30 minutes, 260 dr); six to Itea (30 minutes, 260 dr) and Arahova (20 minutes, 150 dr); five to Athens (three hours, 1950 dr); one direct bus to Patras (1350 dr) and two via Itea. For Thebes, take a bus to Livadia from where there are frequent buses. The bus to/from Athens gets very crowded in the summer, so turn up early to buy a ticket.

Train The nearest train station to Delphi is at Livadia, on the Athens-Thessaloniki line. This is only worth considering if you have a rail pass.

ANCIENT DELPHI

Of all the ancient sites in Greece, to most people, Delphi is the one with the most potent 'spirit of place'. Built on the slopes of Mt Parnassos, overlooking the Gulf of Corinth and extending into a valley of cypress and olive trees, Delphi's setting is stunning, but even so, its allure lies more in the awe it invokes than in its landscape. The ancients regarded Delphi as the centre, or navel, of the world, for according to .nythology Zeus released two eagles at opposite ends of the world and they met here.

The site is open Monday to Friday from 8 am to 6 pm and Saturday and Sunday from 8.30 am to 3 pm. Admission is 1000 dr (free on Sunday and public holidays).

History

Delphi reached its height as a sanctuary dedicated to Apollo, when multitudes of pilgrims

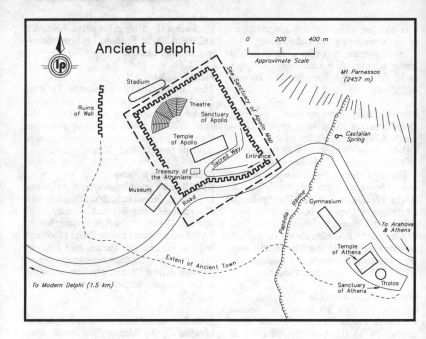

bearing expensive votive gifts came to ask advice of its oracle. The Delphic oracle was believed to be Apollo's mouthpiece, and was the most powerful in Greece. Battles were fought, marriages took place, journeys were embarked upon and business deals clinched on the strength of its utterances.

During early Mycenaean times, the earth goddess Gaea was worshipped at Delphi, and it is believed the oracle originated at that time. Later Delphi became a sanctuary to Themis, then Demeter and later Poseidon, but by the end of the Mycenaean period, Apollo had replaced the other deities. The oracle was a priestess over 50 years of age, who sat on a tripod at the entrance to a chasm from which emitted vaporous fumes. The priestess inhaled these fumes which induced a frenzy. Her seemingly unintelligible utterances in answer to a pilgrim's question were translated into verse by a priest.

In summer Apollo was worshipped at Delphi, but in winter, he and the oracle took a rest and Dionysos stepped into his place. As everywhere, the god of wine was honoured with merrymaking and feasting, which must have come as a welcome relief from the serious business of trying to comprehend the oracle's cryptic and grave messages.

Following battles between the city-states, the oracle was showered with treasures from the victors and accused of partiality from the defeated. Not surprisingly, the sanctuary became a hotbed of chicanery, coveted for its priceless treasures. It was eventually the cause of Greece's demise at the hands of the Macedonians.

Delphi was protected by a federation of Greek states called the Amphyctionic Council. However, the surrounding territory belonged to the city of Krisa, who took advantage of this by charging visitors an exorbitant fee for the privilege of disembarking at its port of Kirrha. This angered the city-states, especially Athens, who called upon the Amphyctionic Council to do something about it. The result was the First Sacred War (595-586 BC) which resulted in the council destroying Krisa and its port.

The council now took control of the sanctuary, and Delphi became an autonomous state. The sanctuary enjoyed great prosperity, receiving tributes from numerous benefactors, including the kings of Lydia and Egypt. Struggles for its control ensued, and Delphi passed from one city-state to another, resulting in further sacred wars.

The Third Sacred War was precipitated by a dispute between Thebes and Phocis, in 356 BC, over control of the sanctuary. Philip II, the king of Macedon, seized the opportunity to exert power over the city-states by acting as arbitrator in this war. He brought an end to the conflict and, in 346 BC, the sanctuary again came under the protection of the Amphyctionic Council. Philip now took Phocis' place in the council, which had probably been his intention all along.

The Fourth Sacred War broke out in 339 BC when the Amphyctionic Council declared war on Amfissa because it had staked a claim to the sanctuary. The council appealed to Philip for help. Philip saw this as an opportunity to bring his formidable army into Greece, and, in so doing, not only destroyed Amfissa, but fought, and defeated, a combined army of Athenians, Thebans and their allies in the Battle of Khaironeia, in Boeotia. Philip had now achieved his ambition – control of Greece.

In 191 BC Delphi was taken by the Romans and the oracle's power dwindled. It was consulted on personal, rather than political issues. Along with the country's other pagan sanctuaries, it was abrogated by Theodosius in the late 4th century AD.

Exploring the Site

The **Sanctuary of Apollo** is on the left of the main road as you walk towards Athens. From the entrance, at the site of the old **Roman agora**, steps lead to the **Sacred Way**, which winds up to the foundations of the Doric **Temple of Apollo**.

Once you have entered the site, you will

The Delphi Oracle

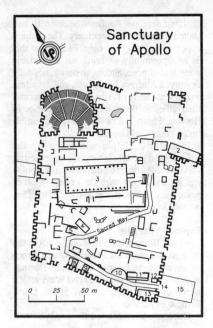

Sanctuary of Apollo

1   Theatre
2   Stoa of Attalos
3   Temple of Apollo
4   Bouleuterion (Council House)
5   Athenian Treasury
6   Knidos Treasury
7   Thebes Treasury
8   Siphnos Treasury
9   Sicyon Treasury
10 King of Argos Monument
11 Votive offering of Lacedemonians
12 Site of Bull of Corcyra
13 Votive offering of Athens
14 Main Entrance
15 Roman Agora (Market Place)

pass on your right the pedestal which held the statue of a bull dedicated by the city of Corcyra (Corfu). Further along are the remains of monuments erected by the Athenians and Lacedemonians. The semicircular structures on either side of the Sacred Way were erected by the Argives (people of Argos). The one to the right was the **King of Argos Monument**, which was built in the 4th century BC.

In ancient times the Sacred Way was lined with treasuries and statues given by grateful city-states, including Thebes, Siphnos, Sicyon, Athens and Knidos, in thanks to Apollo for helping them win battles. The **Athenian treasury** has been reconstructed. To the north of this treasury are the foundations of the **bouleuterion** (council house).

The 4th-century Temple of Apollo dominated the entire sanctuary. Inside the cella was a gold statue of Apollo and a hearth where an eternal flame burned. On the temple architrave were inscriptions of the wise utterings of Greek philosophers, such as 'Know Thyself' and 'Nothing in Excess'. The chasm from which the priestess inhaled vapours has not been found; all that is known is that it was somewhere within the temple.

Above the temple is the well-preserved 4th-century **theatre**, which was restored by the Romans. From the top row of seats there are magnificent views. Plays were performed here during the Pythian Festival, which, like the Olympic Games, was held every four years. From the theatre another path leads up to the **stadium**, the best preserved in all of Greece.

From the Sanctuary of Apollo, walk towards Arahova and you will come to the **Castalian spring** on the left, where pilgrims had to cleanse themselves before consulting the oracle. Opposite is the **Sanctuary of Athena** (free admission), where Athena Pronaia was worshipped. This is the site of the 4th-century **tholos**, the most striking of Delphi's monuments. It was a graceful circular structure of 20 columns on a three-stepped podium – three of its columns have been re-erected. The purpose of the Tholos is unknown.

Museum
Ancient Delphi amassed a considerable treasure-trove, and this is reflected in its magnificent museum collection. On the landing is the **omphalos**, a sculpted cone

Top: The mosaic courtyard at the ancient site of Pella, Macedonia (RH)
Left: Monastery of Dionysiou, Mt Athos Peninsula, Macedonia (DH)
Right: View of Kavala and the aqueduct, Macedonia (RH)

Top: Onion domes of the Russian monastery St Pandeleimon, Athos, Macedonia (DH)
Bottom: View of Mt Athos, Macedonia (DH)

which once stood at what was considered the navel of the world – the spot where the eagles released by Zeus met. In the second room along from here are two 6th-century **kouroi**. To the right of this room is displayed parts of the frieze from the **Siphnian treasury**, which depicts the battle between the gods and the giants, and the gods watching the fight over the corpse of Patroclus during the Trojan War.

In the rooms to the left are fragments of metopes from the **Athenian treasury** depicting the Labours of Herakles, the Exploits of Theseus and the Battle of the Amazons. Further on you can't miss the large **Acanthus Column**, with three women dancing around it. In the end room is the celebrated life-size **Bronze Charioteer**, which commemorates a victory in the Pythian Games of 478 or 474 BC.

The museum (☎ 0265-82 313) is open Tuesday to Friday from 8 am to 6 pm; Saturday and Sunday from 8.30 am to 3 pm and Monday from 11 am to 6 pm. Admission is 1000 dr.

Getting There & Away

Buses between Arahova and modern Delphi will drop you at the site. See Getting There & Away under modern Delphi for details.

AROUND DELPHI
Mt Parnassos Ορος Παρνασσός
There are two ski centres on Mt Parnassos, both with overnight accommodation. The largest is the EOT centre at Fterolakkas (1750 metres), which also has facilities higher up at Kelaria (1950 metres). For more information contact the EOT in Delphi or Athens or the ski centre (☎ 22 689/694/695). The centre is 24 km from Arahova and 17 km from Amfikleia. The Athens department store, Klaoudatos, organises trips to this ski centre. For more information, see Skiing in the Activities section of the Athens chapter.

The second centre is at Gerondovrahos. For more information contact Athens Ski-Lovers Club (☎ 01-643 3368), Sarantapichou 51, Athens, or Nikos Georgakos

(☎ 0267-31 391) in Arahova. The centre is 25 km from Arahova and 34 km from Delphi.

Getting There & Away There is no public transport to either centre – you'll need to take a taxi or hitch from Delphi or Arahova.

Arahova Αράχωβα
Arahova (Ar-A-ho-va, population 2700, altitude 960 metres) is built on a rocky spur of Mt Parnassos, 10 km from Delphi on the main Athens-Delphi road. The main street is flanked by shops selling embroideries, handwoven goods, flokati rugs and other souvenirs. The town is also noted for its cheese, honey and a pleasantly tasting unresinated red wine.

Despite this overt flaunting of its assets to the passing tourists, Arahova is a charming town and an alternative base to modern Delphi from which to visit the ancient site. In the little alleys bordering the main street, stone houses cling to the steep hillside. The **Festival of Agios Georgios** is held in the town on St George's day (23 April). However, if this date falls during Lent, the festival is postponed until Easter Tuesday. It's a joyous occasion with feasting and folk dancing.

Orientation & Information The main thoroughfare is Odos Delphion which is flanked by three squares. The bus station is at the Celena Café opposite the central square. The post office, OTE and EOT (☎ 31 630/692) are all on Plateia Xenias, one block west of the central square. Arahova's postcode is 32004 and the telephone code is 0267.

Places to Stay & Eat The D class *Hotel Apollon* (☎ 31 427), Delphion 20, has pleasant, spotless single/double rooms for 3000/5300 dr, with shared bathrooms. The lovely centrally located C class *Arahova Inn* (☎ 31 353/134/497; fax 31 134) is one of the town's newest hotels. Rooms cost 7000/11,000 dr. The hotel also has a bar, restaurant and central heating.

The older B class *Hotel Xenia* (☎ 31 230/1/2), Plateia Xenia, also has a bar, restaurant and central heating. The rates are 8000/11,000 dr for singles/doubles.

The town also has some rooms to rent in private houses where you'll pay around 5000 dr a double. For information about these enquire at the Celena Café.

O Karmalis Taverna, Delphion 51, serves tasty low-priced Greek staples.

Getting There & Away The five buses a day which run between Athens and Delphi stop at Arahova. In addition there are eight local buses to Delphi (20 minutes, 150 dr).

MONI OSSIOU LOUKA
Μονή Οσσίου Λουκά

The Moni Ossiou Louka (Monastery of St Luke Stiris) is eight km east of the village of Distomo, which lies just south of the Athens-Delphi road. Its principal church contains some of Greece's finest Byzantine frescoes.

The monastery is dedicated to a local hermit who was canonised for his healing and prophetic powers. The monastic complex includes two churches. The interior of the principal one of **Agios Loukas** is a glorious symphony of marble and mosaics. There are also icons by Mikhail Damaskinos, the 16th-century Cretan icon painter.

In the main body of the church the light is partially blocked by the ornate marble window decorations. This creates striking contrasts of light and shade which greatly enhance the atmosphere. The crypt where St Luke is buried also contains fine frescoes. The other church, **Theotolos** (Church of St Mary), built in the 10th century, has a less impressive interior.

The monastery is in an idyllic setting, with breathtaking vistas from its leafy terrace. There is a taverna in the monastery grounds. Opening times are 8 am to 2 pm daily and also from 4 to 6 pm from May to September. Admission is 600 dr, and modest dress is required (no shorts).

Places to Stay
Ossiou Louka is a hassle to get to by public transport, so if you get stuck, there are a couple of budget hotels in Distomo, includ-ing the D class *Hotel America* (☎ 0267-22 079), J Kastriti 1, where singles/doubles are 3000/4000 dr with shared bathrooms. Nearby, the D class *Hotel Koutriaris* (☎ 0267-22 268), on the central square of Plateia Ethnikis Antistassis, has singles/doubles for 3100/4200 dr with shared bathrooms.

Getting There & Away
There is one direct bus a day from Athens which leaves Bus Terminal B at 10.30 am (3½ hours, 1300 dr). Otherwise you can take the Delphi bus from Athens and get off at the turn-off for Distomo, from where you can take a taxi nine km to the monastery. From Livadia there are 11 buses a day to Distomo (45 minutes, 400 dr) and one to the monastery at 1.30 pm (one hour, 550 dr). There are hourly buses to Athens from Livadia (two hours, 1100 dr).

AGIOS KONSTANTINOS
Αγιος Κωνσταντίνος

Agios Konstantinos, on the main Athens-Thessaloniki route, is one of the three mainland ports which serve the Sporades islands (the other two are Thessaloniki, in the prefecture of Macedonia, and Volos, in Thessaly; see the next section).

There are a number of hotels in the town, but, with judicious use of buses from Athens to the port, you will probably not need to stay overnight before catching a Sporades-bound ferry or hydrofoil. If you get stuck, try the *Hotel Poulia* (☎ 0235-31 663).

Getting There & Away
Bus Buses depart hourly for Agios Konstantinos from Athens Terminal B bus station (2½ hours, 2000 dr).

Ferry There are daily ferries from Agios Konstantinos to Skiathos (3½ hours, 2243 dr); Skopelos town (5 ½ hours, 2617 dr); and Alonissos (six hours, 2886 dr).

Hydrofoil Hydrofoils depart daily for Skiathos (1½ hours, 3469 dr); Skopelos town

(5324 dr); and for Alonissos (three hours, 5577 dr).

LAMIA TO KARPENISSI

If you have the time an exploration of the mountainous region west of the city of Lamia is worthwhile. The attractive village of **Ipati**, 25 km from Lamia and eight km south of the Lamia-Karpenissi road, has the remains of a fortress and is the starting point for treks on Mt Iti (2152 metres).

This mountain is the focus of the Iti National Park, established in 1966. It's a verdant region with forests of fir and black pine. In mythology, Mt Iti was where the dying Herakles built his own pyre and was burned to death. Whilst the mortal elements in Herakles perished, the immortal Herakles joined his divine peers on Mt Olympus.

From Ipati it's a four-hour walk along a marked path to the mountain's *Trapeza Refuge* (1850 metres). For information about this refuge contact the Lamia EOS (☎ 0231-26 786), Ipsilandou 20, Lamia.

Ipati has two hotels. The D class *Hotel Panhellinion* (☎ 0231-59 640) has singles/doubles with shared bathrooms for 1600/3600 dr. The C class *Hotel Panorama* (☎ 0231-59 222) has rooms with shared bathrooms for 2700/3300 dr and doubles with private bathrooms for 3800 dr.

Ipati is served by frequent buses from Lamia.

KARPENISSI Καρπενήσι

Karpenissi (population 5000, altitude 960 metres) is in the foothills of Mt Timfristos (2315 metres), 82 km west of Lamia. The town is not especially attractive, but is situated in a beautiful well-wooded region which the EOT brochures tout as the 'Switzerland of Greece'. There are many opportunities for trekking, and, if you have your own transport, exploration of some delightful mountain villages.

Karpenissi's telephone code is 0237.

Places to Stay

Karpenissi has one D class hotel, the *Hotel Panhellinion* (☎ 22 330), Sp Tsitsara 9,

where singles/doubles are 2500/3500 dr with shared bathrooms. The C class *Hotel Galini* (☎ 22 914), R Fereou 3, has rooms with private bathrooms for 3000/6200 dr. In the same class, the *Hotel Helvetia* (☎ 22 465), Zinopolou 33, has rooms with shared bathrooms for 4000/4600 dr and with private bathrooms for 5800/6400 dr and the *Anessis Hotel* (☎ 22 840), Zinopoulou 44, has rooms for 5800/6400 dr with private bathrooms.

The B class *Mont Blanc* (☎ 22 322), Vasileos Pavlou & Frederikis, has singles/doubles with shared bathrooms for 3000/5000 dr and with private bathrooms for 5500/8000 dr.

The Mt Timfristos Refuge of *Takis Flengas* (☎ 0237-22 002), at 1840 metres, can be reached along a 12-km road from Karpenissi, or is a 2½-hour walk along a path. If you wish to stay at the refuge, contact the Karpenissi EOS (☎ 0237-23 051), Georgiou Tsitsara 2, Karpenissi.

Getting There & Away

There are two buses a day from Athens to Karpenissi (six hours, 3200 dr).

AROUND KARPENISSI

From Karpenissi a scenic mountain road leads south for 37 km to the village of **Proussos**. Along the way there are several delightful villages. The charming village of **Korishades** has well-preserved mansions and is five km south-west of Karpenissi, reached by a turn-off right along the Proussos road. **Mikri Horio** and **Megali Horio** are 12 km further along the road.

The **Monastery of the Virgin of Proussiotissa**, just before the village of Proussos, has a miracle-working icon. There are more icons, wood carvings and ecclesiastical ornaments in the monastery's 18th-century church. A small number of monks live at the monastery and pilgrims flock there in August for the Feast of the Assumption.

Places to Stay

The D class *Hotel Antigone* (☎ 0237-41 221) at Megali Horio has singles/doubles with private bathrooms for 3900/7300 dr. The

Agathidis Pension (☎ 0237-91 248) at Proussos has rooms with private bathrooms for 4000/6500 dr.

Thessaly   Θεσσαλία

Thessaly is the proud possessor of two of Greece's most extraordinary natural phenomena: the giant rock pinnacles of Meteora and the riotously fertile Pelion peninsula. On a more modest scale it also has the beautiful Vale of Tembi. Travelling north from Thessaly to Macedonia, whether by road or train, you will pass through this 12-km-long vale, which is a narrow passageway between Mts Olympus and Ossa. The road and railway line share the vale with a river, whose richly verdant banks contrast dramatically with the sheer cliffs at either side. If you have your own transport there are viewpoints at the most scenic spots.

The vale has also been a favoured place for invaders of Greece. The Persian King Xerxes gained access to central Greece via Tembi in 480 BC, as did the Germans in 1941.

VOLOS Βόλος

Industrial Volos (VO-los, population 71,400) is Thessaly's main port. Destroyed by an earthquake in 1955, and rebuilt with sturdy quake-proof structures, it has little to recommend it, other than serving as a good base from which to explore the enchanting Pelion peninsula, or to catch a ferry or hydrofoil to the Sporades islands and Evia. In mythology, Volos was ancient Iolkos from where Jason and the Argonauts set sail on their quest for the Golden Fleece.

Orientation

The waterfront is Argonafton; running parallel to it are the city's main thoroughfares of Iasonos, Dimitriados and Ermou. The central square of Plateia Riga Fereou is just west of these streets. To the west of here is the train station; the bus station is south-west of that.

Information

The EOT (☎ 24 915, 23 500 or 37 417) is on the southern side of Plateia Riga Fereou. The exceedingly helpful staff give out town maps, information on bus, ferry and hydrofoil schedules, and have a list of hotels in all categories in the whole of Thessaly. Opening times are Monday to Friday from 7 am to 2.30 pm and 6 to 8.30 pm; Saturday, Sunday and holidays from 5.30 to 8.30 pm. In the off season (September to May) opening hours are 7 am to 2 pm, Monday to Friday. The tourist police (☎ 27 094) are in the same building as the regular police at 28 Oktovriou 179.

The post office is at Pavlou Mela 45. Opening times are Monday to Friday from 8.30 am to 3 pm. The OTE is at Eleftheriou Venizelou 22 and is open from 6 am to midnight every day. Volos' postcodes are 38321, 38333 or 38334). The telephone code is 0421. Volos' General Hospital (☎ 24 531/2/3/4) is in the eastern part of town near the Archaeological Museum.

Archaeological Museum

This excellent museum, in the south-east of town (see map), has a comprehensive collection of finds from the area. Especially impressive is the large collection of painted grave stele from the nearby Hellenistic site of Dimitrias. The museum is open Tuesday to Sunday from 8.30 am to 3 pm. Admission is 400 dr.

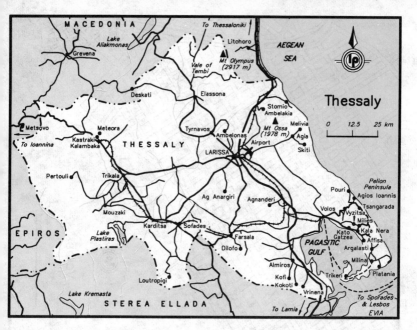

Thessaly

Places to Stay – bottom end

The nearest camp sites to Volos are at Kato Gatzea, 18 km away, on the west coast of the Pelion peninsula. They are *Camping Marina* (☎ 22 277), *Camping Hellas* (☎ 22 267) and *Sikia Fig Tree Camping* (☎ 22 279). The buses to Milies and Platania pass all three.

There is no shortage of hotels in Volos and finding a room is fairly easy. The D class *Hotel Xeni* (☎ 37 814 or 34 729), Iasonos 93, has well-kept single/double/triple rooms for 2630/3600/4800 dr with shared bathrooms and 2880/4900/5900 dr with private bathrooms. Also agreeable is the D class *Hotel Agra* (☎ 25 370 or 28 980), Solonos 5, on the corner of Iasonos. Rates are 2500/3500/4500 dr with shared bathrooms, and 3500/4500/5500 dr with private bathrooms.

Two very similar C classes with comfortable but unadorned rooms are the *Hotel Santi* (☎ 33 341/2/3), Topali 13, on the corner of Iasonos, where rates are 4500/6770/8120 dr and *Admitos Hotel* (☎ 21 117/8/9), Athan-

assiou Diakou 3, where rooms go for 4500/5600/6700 dr.

Places to Stay – middle

The B class *Hotel Electra* (☎ 33 671/2/3), Topali 22, has immaculate rooms overlooking a quiet pedestrian street. Rates are 6430/9480/11,370 dr. Volos' poshest hotel is the B class *Park Hotel* (☎ 36 6511/2/3/4/5), Deligiorgi 2. The stylish rooms have air-con, direct-dial telephone, radio and balcony. Rates are 7080/10,360/12,730 dr.

Places to Eat

The *Charama Restaurant*, Dimitriados 49, serves very tasty dishes. The cavernous old *Athinaik Taverna*, Eleftheriou Venizelou 1A, has low-priced food.

Argonafton, on the waterfront, is lined with tavernas and ouzeria which specialise in fish dishes. Locals give top marks to *Ouzeri Nautilia*, Argonafton 1, at a busy traffic intersection. If you eat here be sure to

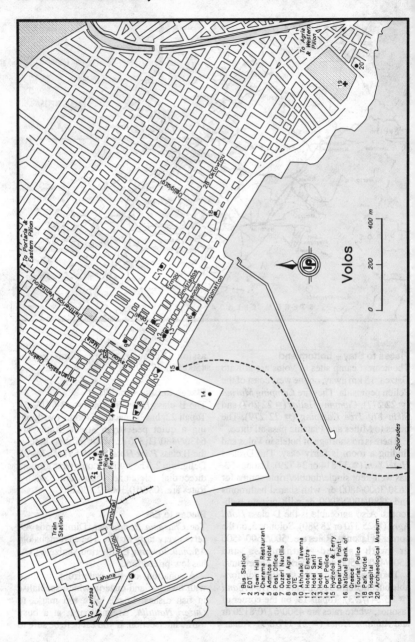

Volos

To Agria
& Western
Pilion

To Portaria &
Eastern Pilion

Train Station

To Larissa

To Sporades

Plateia
Riga
Fereou

0   200   400 m

1 Bus Station
2 EOT
3 Charama Restaurant
4 Admitos Hotel
5 Town Hall
6 Post Office
7 Ouzeri Naultia
8 Hotel Agra
9 OTE
10 Athinaiki Taverna
11 Hotel Electra
12 Hotel Santi
13 Hotel Xeni
14 Port Police
15 Hydrofoil & Ferry
   Departure Point
16 National Bank of
   Greece
17 Tourist Police
18 Park Hotel
19 Hospital
20 Archaeological Museum

sample the local firewater, *tsipouro*, which is similar to ouzo, but more potent. It costs 300 dr for a small bottle, plus titbits – just mind the traffic when you get up to leave.

Getting There & Away

Bus From the bus station there are 10 buses a day to Athens (five hours, 3500 dr); nine a day to Larissa (one hour, 700 dr); and four a day to both Thessaloniki (4 hours, 2350 dr); and Trikala (3½ hours, 1500 dr).

Buses to the major villages of the Pelion peninsula are as follows: 11 a day to Kala Nera, of which seven continue on to Affisa; 10 a day to Makrinitsa (via Portaria); seven to Vyzitsa (via Milies); six to Milina (via Argalasti and Horto), three of which continue to Platania; three a day to both Zagora (via Hania) and Agios Ioannis (via Tsangarada). Buses also run to many of the smaller villages, but often only two or three times a day. Check the board at the bus station.

Train There are 13 trains a day to Larissa for connections to Athens and Thessaloniki. There is one direct train a day to Athens and three to Thessaloniki. Seven trains a day go to Kalambaka via Trikala.

Ferry There are daily ferries from Volos to Trikeri (Pelion; 1½ hours, 900 dr); Skiathos (three hours, 1800 dr); Glossa (Skopelos; 3½ hours, 2200 dr); Skopelos town (4½ hours, 2200 dr); Alonissos (five hours, 2400 dr); and twice weekly to Kymi (Evia; eight hours, 5300 dr). At the time of writing there was a ferry to Lesbos (10 hours, 3753 dr) on a Sunday; check with the EOT to see if this is still sailing.

Hydrofoil There are daily hydrofoils to Skiathos (one hour, 3469 dr); Glossa (Skopelos) (1½ hours, 3978 dr); Skopelos town (two hours, 4231 dr); and Alonissos (three hours, 4743 dr).

Getting Around

Car Cars can be rented from Europcar (☎ 36

238), Iasonos 79, and Theofanidis Hellas (☎ 32 360), Iasonos 137.

PELION PENINSULA Πήλιο Ορος

The well-watered Pelion peninsula lies to the east and south of Volos. It consists of a mountain range, of which the highest peak is Mt Pliassidi (1651 metres). The inaccessible eastern flank consists of high cliffs which plunge dramatically into the sea. The gentler western flank coils around the calm sea of the Pagasitic Gulf, and is fringed by sand and pebble beaches.

The interior is a green wonderland where trees hanging heavy with fruit vie with wild olive groves, forests of horse chestnut, oak, walnut, eucalyptus and beech trees to reach the light of day. Ivy, convolvulus and other trailing plants drape around tree trunks and create tangles of thick undergrowth in an orgy of fertility, more reminiscent of a tropical jungle than a European landscape.

In ancient times the mountains of the Pelion were known as the 'healing mountains' because on their slopes grew (and still grow) medicinal plants such as henbane, nightshade, bittersweet, hemlock and meadow saffron. The enchanting landscape is enhanced by a backdrop of sparkling sea which is almost always in sight.

The villages tucked away in this profuse foliage are characterised by whitewashed, half-timbered houses with overhanging balconies and grey slate roofs, and cobbled mule paths winding around their vibrant gardens. Flagstone squares harbouring little Byzantine churches and sculpted fountains shaded by enormous gnarled plane trees are another feature of these settlements.

With your own transport you can see a great deal of the peninsula in one day. If you're using buses, two or three days should be allowed: no single bus route goes around the whole peninsula, so it is impossible to tour the coast and inland villages in one day.

Many of the places to stay in the Pelion are traditional mansions which have been tastefully converted into pensions. They are wonderful places to spend a night or two, but they don't come cheap.

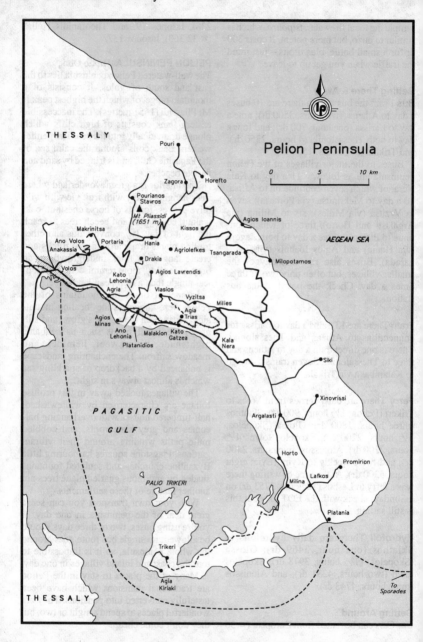

Pelion Peninsula

0   5   10 km

THESSALY

Pouri

Zagora   Horefto

Pourianos
Stavros
▲ Mt Pliassidi
(1651 m)

Makrinitsa   Kissos   Agios Ioannis

Ano Volos   Portaria   Hania   AEGEAN SEA
Anakassia
                    Agriolefkes   Tsangarada
Volos   Drakia
          Kato   Agios Lavrendis   Milopotamos
          Lehonia
Agria   Vlasios
                    Vyzitsa   Milies
Agios   Agia
Minas   Trias
Ano   Kato
Lehonia   Gatzea   Kala
Platanidios   Nera
Malakion

PAGASITIC   Siki

GULF   Xinovrissi

                    Argalasti

                    Horto
                              Promirion
PALIO TRIKERI   Milina   Lafkos

                    Platania

Trikeri

Agia
Kiriaki

THESSALY   To
          Sporades

The Pelion has an enduring tradition of regional cooking. Be sure to try some of the local specialities, such as *fasolada* (bean soup), *kouneli stifado* (rabbit stew), *spetsofai* (a spicy stew of sausages and peppers), and *tyropsomo* (cheese bread).

History & Mythology
In mythology the Pelion was inhabited by centaurs – reprobate creatures who took delight in deflowering virgins.

The Turkish occupation did not extend into the inaccessible central and eastern parts of the Pelion, and as a result the western coastal towns were abandoned in favour of mountain villages. In these remote settlements, culture and the economy flourished; silk and wool were exported to many places in Europe. Like other remote areas in Greece it became a spawning ground for ideas which culminated in the War of Independence.

Getting There & Away
Buses to the villages of the Pelion leave from the Volos bus station (see Volos' Getting There & Away section).

Volos to Makrinitsa
Taking the north-eastern route from Volos, the road climbs to the villages of **Anakassia** and **Ano Volos**. The former is four km north-east of Volos. In its central square is the **Theophilos Museum**, housed in an 18th-century mansion. The museum features the works of the primitive painter Theophilos (1873- 1934) who lived for many years in Volos. It's open Monday to Friday from 8 am to 2 pm. Admission is free.

Portaria, the next village, is 13 km from Volos. True to form, its plateia has a splendid old plane tree, and the little 13th-century church of **Panagia of Portaria** has fine frescoes. A fork to the left in the village leads to Makrinitsa, 17 km from Volos.

Makrinitsa Μακρινίτσα
Makrinitsa (Mak-rin-IT-sa), clinging to a mountainside at an elevation of 750 metres, is aptly called the Balcony of Pelion. The traditional houses were built with three storeys at the front and only one at the back, giving the impression they are stacked on top of one another. It is one of the loveliest of the Pelion villages, but is also the most touristy. However, as it is closed to traffic, it remains tranquil. There's a car park at the entrance to the village and if you've come by bus this is where you will alight. To get to the central square walk straight ahead along the cobbled main street. The square has an old hollow plane tree, a sculpted marble fountain and the little church of **Agios Ioannis**.

Places to Stay The *Domatia Makropoulou* (☎ 99 016/073) is one of the cheapest places to stay in Makrinitsa. The simply furnished, spotless double/triple rooms are 5800/6900 dr. Walk up the path by the side of Restaurant Gallini, on the central square, continue along the path and you will come to the domatia on the right. On the way you will pass the *Archontiko Diomidis Pension* (☎ 99 430/090), a traditional mansion with lots of wall-hangings, brass and ceramic ornaments and carved wood furniture. Rates are 7500 dr a double.

The *Pension Xiradaki* (☎ 99 250) is a beautiful old stone mansion, with minimal but tasteful traditional décor. Single/double/triple/quad rates are 5900/10,200/12,600/13,700 dr, with breakfast. Look for the pension sign pointing left on the main street.

Places to Eat Try the reasonably priced *Restaurant Gallini* on the central square for excellent spetsofai, fasolada and kouneli stifado. A main course should cost around 900 dr.

Makrinitsa to Tsangarada
Back on the main Volos-Zagora route the road continues to the modern village of **Hania**, where there's a *YHA Hostel* (☎ 0421-24 290) which only opens in July and August. Just two km from here is the ski resort of **Agriolefkes**, where there is a Ski Centre (☎ 39 136) which has three downhill runs and one cross-country run. Information can be obtained either from the EOT in Volos

or the Volos EOS (Greek Alpine Club) at Dimitriados 92 (☎ 25 696).

From Hania the road zigzags down through chestnut trees to a road junction. The left turn leads to **Zagora**, the largest of the Pelion villages and a major fruit-growing centre.

Horefto, eight km downhill from Zagora, is a popular resort with a long sandy beach. North of Zagora, **Pouri**, another charming village, spills down a steep mountainside.

Back at the road junction, the right turn leads through a series of villages to Tsangarada. The route is one of the most scenically spectacular in the Pelion. The most delightful of the villages is **Kissos**, which is built on steep terraces. Its 18th-century Church of Agia Marina has fine frescoes. From Kissos, a six-km road leads down to the coastal resort of **Agios Ioannis**.

Tsangarada Τσαγκαράδα
Tsangarada (Ts-an-ga-RA-da), nestling in oak and plane forests, is an extremely spread-out village comprising the four separate communities of Taxiartis, Paraskevi, Agios Stefanos and Agkiziaki. The largest is Paraskevi, which is just north of the main Volos-Milies-Tsangarada road. The bus stops near the central square of Plateia Paraskevis. The plane tree on this square is reputedly the largest and oldest in Greece – locals claim it is 1500 years old. No doubt this is an exaggeration, but whatever its age it's a magnificent specimen with a girth of 14 metres.

The small seaside resort of **Milopotamos**, with a sheltered beach, is eight km down the road from Tsangarada.

Places to Stay There are several domatia on the main road near Plateia Paraskevis. The *Konaki Pension* (☎ 49 481), further along the road on the right (beyond the turn-off for Milopotamos), is a traditional mansion with double/triple rates of 6700/8000 dr. Further along on the opposite side of the road the *Paradissos Pension* (☎ 49 551/209) is a lovely place run by two friendly and enthusiastic brothers. The immaculate, cosy

single/double/triple rooms are 7000/9600/ 11,000 dr. If you'd rather be on the coast, then Milopotamos has a few domatia.

Places to Eat The *Paradissos Restaurant* (at the pension of the same name) is excellent. Their home-made apple and cherry preserve (sold in 500-gram jars) is ambrosia to anyone with a sweet tooth.

Volos to Milies & Vyzitsa
After leaving Volos the west-coast road passes through the touristy villages of **Agria**, **Kato Lehonia** and **Ano Lehonia**. Several roads off to the left lead to one of the most beautiful areas of Pelion; the road from Ano Lehonia to **Vlasios** is particularly lovely. Right turns lead to the seaside resorts of **Platanidios**, **Malakion** and **Kato Gatzea**. Further along the coast road at **Kala Nera**, 19 km from Volos, there is a turn-off left for Tsangarada. A little way along here, a turn-off left leads through apple orchards to the spread-out village of Milies (*milies* is Greek for apple trees).

Milies Μηλιές
Built in the late 16th century, Milies (Mi-li-ES) was a rich agricultural centre, prospering on olive oil, fruit and silk production. Like most of the Pelion it enjoyed semi-autonomy and, largely due to its excellent school, it played a major role in the intellectual and cultural awakening that led to independence.

Milies was the birthplace of Anthinos Gazi (1761-1828) who raised the Thessalian revolt in 1821. Shortly after independence a railway line was built between Volos and Milies and it became a prosperous centre of commerce. *Little Smokey*, the steam train which used to chug along this route, was retired long ago, but there is talk of reintroducing a train as a tourist attraction. Meanwhile, the train station and line are still there, and the latter is delightful to walk along. To reach the station from Milies' central square, facing towards Vyzitsa (the next village along), turn left at the clock tower, walk across the car park and take the cobbled path by the side of Aigli Taverna.

The station is worth a look whether or not you are going to walk along the track.

The **Milies Folk Museum**, which houses a display of local crafts, is on the right beyond the central square.

Places to Stay The *Old Station Guest House* (☎ 86 425), by the station in Milies, is an old stone house with traditional furnishings. Doubles go for 7800 dr.

Places to Eat The setting of the *Old Station Guest House Restaurant* is idyllic and the food is tasty and reasonably priced. The gastronomic highlight of Milies is the scrumptious tyropsomo (cheese bread). You can buy it at the bakery on the main Volos-Tsangarada road, just before the Milies turn-off.

Vyzitsa Βυζίτσα

Just two km beyond Milies is the peaceful little village of Vyzitsa (altitude 550 metres). Cobbled pathways wind between its traditional slate-roof houses. To reach Vyzitsa's shady central square follow the signs to the Kontos Mansion.

Places to Stay Vyzitsa has several domatia where doubles average 6000 dr – look for the signs. The *Karagiannopoulos Mansion* (☎ 86 373) is a beautiful place; the lounge has a carved-wood ceiling and stained-glass windows. Rates are 5950/10,210/12,600/13,700 dr with breakfast. The mansion is on the road coming from Milies.

The *Kontos Mansion* (☎ 86 793) is equally appealing, and is the village's largest. Rates are 6400/10,300/13,300/15,300 dr. The pension is signposted to the right from the bus terminal.

Places to Eat The *Thetis Kafeteria*, just beyond the bus terminal, is a serene place, with tables and chairs on a patio shaded by walnut trees. Tasty desserts start at around 300 dr and cocktails are 800 to 1000 dr. The best of the tavernas on the central square is *The Cave of the Centaur*, where delicious main courses start at less than 900 dr. The

name is in Greek – look for the taverna furthest away from the path.

South to Platania

Continuing south from Kala Nera the bus goes as far as Platania. Although not as fertile as the northern part of the peninsula, the southern part of the Pelion is still attractive, with pine-forested hills and olive groves. The road passes inland through the large unexceptional inland village of **Argalasti**, and then forks – the left fork continues inland, the right goes to the coastal resorts of **Horto** and **Milina**. The road heads inland from Milina and then south to Platania.

Platania Πλατανιά

Platania (Plat-ani-A) is a popular resort with a good sand and pebble beach. It's a fun place to spend a day or two, although it's quite developed. Les Hirondelles Travel Agency (☎ 71 231) rents a variety of water-sports equipment. Rates are 500 dr an hour for canoes and 600 dr for pedalos; water-skis are 8000 dr and scooters are 2500 dr for 30 minutes. Daily motor-boat hire costs between 8560 and 47,200 dr depending on size and horsepower. Turn left at the sea to reach the agency.

Places to Stay *Kastri Beach Camping* (☎ 54 248) is at Kastri Beach, five km east of Platania. Look for the sign pointing left on the approach road to Platania.

Louisa Camping (☎ 65 660) is just 500 metres before Platania.

The cheapest hotel in Platania is the D class *Hotel Platania* (☎ 71 250/266) where pleasant single/double/triple rooms are 3000/5700/6900 dr with private bathrooms and 4000/4800 dr for doubles/triples with shared bathrooms. Turn left at the sea to reach the hotel. Another agreeable option is the D class *Hotel des Roses* (☎ 71 230/268), by the bus terminal. Rates are 4500/5400 dr with shared bathrooms; doubles with private bathrooms are 6000 dr.

The C class *Hotel Drossero Akrogiali* (☎ 71 210/211) has doubles/triples for

5700/6800 dr with private bathrooms. Turn right at the sea to reach this hotel.

Places to Eat *To Steki Restaurant* has a large choice of well-prepared dishes. A Greek salad will cost about 500 dr and main courses are less than 800 dr. Turn left at the sea to reach this place.

Getting There & Away See the Getting There & Away section under Volos for bus services to Platania.

Hydrofoil Hydrofoils sail daily in summer from Platania to Skiathos (1975 dr), Glossa (Skopelos; 1975 dr), Skopelos town (2914 dr), and Alonissos (2914 dr). Tickets can be purchased from Les Hirondelles Travel Agency (☎ 71 231).

Getting Around Les Hirondelles Travel Agency rents 50 cc motorbikes for 3500 dr, 70 cc for 4130 dr, 100 cc for 4720 dr and 125 cc for 5900 dr (excluding insurance).

TRIKALA Τρίκαλα

Trikala (TRI-ka-la, population 45,000) is ancient Trikki, reputed birthplace of Asklepios, god of healing. It's a bustling agricultural town, through which flows the river Lethaios, and is a major hub for buses. Whilst Trikala's attractions hardly warrant a special trip, the chances are if you're exploring central Greece you'll eventually pass through here en route to somewhere.

Orientation & Information

Trikala's main thoroughfare is Asklepion. Facing the river, turn left from the bus station to reach Plateia Riga Ferou at the northern end of Asklepion. The train station is at the opposite end of Asklepion, 600 metres from Plateia Riga Ferou.

To reach the central square of Plateia Iroon Politechniou turn right at Plateia Riga Ferou and cross the bridge over the river. The post office is at Saraphi 13; turn left at the central square and it's a little way along on the left. To reach the OTE walk along the left side of the central square and turn left onto 25

Martiou. The OTE is a little way along here on the right at the far side of a small square.

Trikala's postcode is 42100 and the telephone code is 0432. The National Bank of Greece is on the central square. Trikala does not have an EOT or tourist police; the regular police (☎ 32 777) are on the corner of Kapodistiou and Asklepion.

Things to See

At the time of writing the **Fortress of Trikala** was closed for restoration. In any case it's worth a wander up to the gardens which surround it for the views – and there's a pleasant café. Walk 400 metres up Saraphi from the central square and look for the sign pointing right. To get to Trikala's old Turkish quarter of Varousi, turn sharp right at the sign for the fortress. It's a fascinating area of peaceful narrow streets and fine old houses with overhanging balconies. At the other side of town the Turkish mosque languishes in a state of extreme dilapidation – its roof has sprouted trees! From the bus station, turn right and you'll reach the mosque in 250 metres.

Places to Stay – bottom end

Trikala isn't a tourist centre so finding accommodation is easy. The cheapest place is the gloomy E class *Hotel Panellinio* (☎ 27 644) on Plateia Riga Ferou. Rates are 3500/4500 dr for doubles/triples with shared bathrooms The *Hotel Palladion* (☎ 28 091) (classed as a pension), Vyronos 4, is a more agreeable cheapie, with clean single/double/ triple rooms for 3500/5500/ 6500 dr with shared bathrooms. The hotel is behind Plateia Riga Ferou's Hotel Achillion.

The C class *Hotel Dina* (☎ 27 267/145/6), on the corner of Asklepion and Karanasiou 38, has immaculate rooms with air-con, telephone and balconies for 5500/7000/8395 dr. The hotel is 60 metres down from Plateia Riga Ferou, on the right.

Places to Stay – middle

The palatial B class *Hotel Achillion* (☎ 28 192), on Plateia Riga Ferou, has singles/ doubles/triples for 7400/8800/10,600 dr.

Places to Stay – top end

The B class *Hotel Divani* (☎ 27 286), on Plateia Kitrilaki, overlooking the river, is Trikala's best hotel. Singles/doubles are 12,000/15,000 dr and suites are 24,000 dr.

Places to Eat

There are several cheap eating places around the bus station and characterless fast-food joints and cafés line Asklepion. An exception is the traditional *Kalkantera Zaharaplasteion*, Asklepion 51, where home-made cakes and Nescafé are both 150 dr. The shop is on the left, walking from Plateia Riga Ferou.

The outdoor café at the fortress is very pleasant, with an ornamental pond where extremely vigorous fountains play – watch how you go, or you'll get a soaking. Soft drinks are 200 dr and Nescafé is 300 dr.

Getting There & Away

Bus From Trikala's bus station there are 20 buses a day to Kalambaka (30 minutes, 350 dr); seven to Athens (5½ hours, 3600 dr); six to Thessaloniki (5½ hours, 2400 dr); four to Volos (3½ hours, 1500 dr); and two to Ioannina (3½ hours, 1800 dr).

Train Trikala is on the Volos-Kalambaka line. There are seven trains a day in each direction.

KALAMBAKA Καλαμπάκα

Kalambaka (Ka-lam-BA-ka, population 5700) is almost entirely modern, having been devastated by the Nazis in WW II. Its chief claim to fame is its proximity to Meteora. It takes a whole day to see all of the monasteries of Meteora, so you'll need to spend the night in either Kalambaka or the village of Kastraki, which is closer to the rocks.

Orientation & Information

The central square is the hub of the town and the main thoroughfares of Rodou, Trikalon, Ioanninon, Kastraki and Vlachava radiate from it. Kalambaka's other large square is Plateia Riga Ferou – Odos Trikalon connects the two. The post office and OTE are both on Ioanninon. Kalambaka's postcode is 42200 and the telephone code is 0432. The National Bank of Greece is on Plateia Riga Ferou.

The bus station is on the right side of Rodou walking from the central square. Arriving, most buses stop on the central square to let passengers alight. To get to the train station from the central square walk along Trikalon, take the right fork after Plateia Riga Ferou, turn right at Kondili and the station is opposite the end of this road.

There is no EOT in Kalambaka. The tourist police (☎ 22 109/813) are at Hagipetrou 10, near the bus station.

Places to Stay – bottom end

There are several camp sites in the area. *Theopetra Camping* (☎ 81 405/6) and *Camping Philoxina* (☎ 24 446) are on the Trikala-Kalambaka road. *Meteora Garden* (☎ 22 727) is three km from Kalambaka on the Kalambaka-Ioaninna road.

Possibly the cheapest rooms in Kalambaka are those of *Mrs Argyroula Karakanta* (☎ 22 136), Epirou 47. The basic, but OK single/double/triple rooms are 2000/2500/3000 dr with shared bathrooms. Next door, *Eleni Karogorou Rooms* (☎ 22 162), Epirou 45, are immaculate and cost 3000/4500 dr with private bathrooms. Walk along Ioanninon from the central square, and Epirou is a turn-off to the right; the rooms are on the left.

Koka Roka Rooms (☎ 24 554), at the beginning of the path to Agia Triada Monastery, are clean and nicely furnished and cost 3500 dr for doubles with shared bathrooms and 4200 dr with private bathrooms. The owner is a friendly Greek-Australian. From the central square, walk 500 metres to the top of Vlachava, and you'll come to the rooms on the left.

Kalambaka's cheapest hotel is the E class *Hotel Astoria* (☎ 22 213 or 23 557), Kondili 93. The clean pine-furnished double/triple rooms cost 4000/5000 dr with shared bathrooms and 5000 dr for doubles with private bathrooms. The hotel is on the road opposite the train station. The D class *Hotel Meteora*

(☎ 22 367), Ploutarhou 14, is a charming and cosy place, with rooms for 4000/6500 dr with private bathrooms. The price includes breakfast. From the central square, walk along Kastraki, and Ploutarhou is the second turn right.

The C class *Hotel Odission* (☎ 22 320), on Kastraki, has light spacious rooms; rates are 5400/7200/9300 dr including breakfast. The *Hotel Helvetia* (☎ 23 041/800), Kastraki 45, has very pleasant single/double/triple rooms for 5500/6600/7920 dr.

Places to Stay – middle
The B class *Famissa Hotel* (☎ 24 117 or 22 163; fax 24 615), Trikalou 103, has rates of 9000/13,000 dr for singles/doubles. All the rooms have balconies, radio and direct-dial telephone. The hotel has a restaurant and bar.

Places to Stay – top end
Trikala's most luxurious hotel is the A class *Hotel Amalia* (☎ 81 216/7; fax 81 457), three km from the town on the main Trikala-Kalambaka road. Singles/doubles are 13,200/17,900 dr and suites are 35,800 dr. The hotel has a bar, restaurant and swimming pool.

Places to Eat
Koka Roka Taverna, below Koka Roka Rooms (see Places to Stay), serves tasty low-priced food. *Taverna Stathmos*, Kondili 56, is also good value. *Taverna Opuros* excels in charcoal grilled dishes; their generous mixed grill is 950 dr. The taverna is on the right side of Trikalon, near the central square.

Getting There & Away
Bus From Kalambaka there are very frequent buses to Trikala, four to Volos and three to Ioannina. There are five buses a day to Metamorphosis (via Kastraki); they leave from Kalambaka's central square.

Train There are seven trains a day to/from Volos via Trikala, Karditsa and Farsala.

Getting Around
Motorbike Motorbikes can be hired from *Moto Service* (☎ 23 526), on Odos Meteoron. From the central square, walk along Ioanninon, turn right at the post office and the outlet is on the right. The cost is 3500 dr for 50 cc motorbikes.

METEORA Μετέωρα
Meteora (Me-TE-ora) is an extraordinary place. The massive pinnacles of smooth rocks with holes in them like Emmenthal cheese are ancient and yet, paradoxically, could be a setting for a science fiction story. The monasteries are the icing on the cake in this already strange and beautiful landscape.

Each monastery is built around a central courtyard surrounded by monks' cells, chapels and refectory. In the centre of each courtyard stands the *katholikon* (main church).

History
The name Meteora derives from the verb *meteorizo*, which means to suspend in the air. Many theories have been put forward as to the origins of this 'rock forest', but it remains a geological enigma.

From the 11th century, solitary hermit monks lived in the caverns of Meteora. By the 14th century, Byzantine power was on the wane and incursions into Greece were on the increase, so monks began to seek peaceful havens away from the bloodshed. The inaccessibility of the rocks of Meteora made them an ideal retreat, and the less safe the monks became, the higher they climbed, until eventually they were living on top of the rocks.

The earliest monasteries were reached by climbing articulated removable ladders. Later, windlasses were used so monks could be hauled up in nets, and this method was used until the 1920s. A story goes that when apprehensive visitors enquired how frequently the ropes were replaced, the monks' stock reply was 'When the Lord lets them break!' These days access to the monasteries is by steps hewn into the rocks. Some

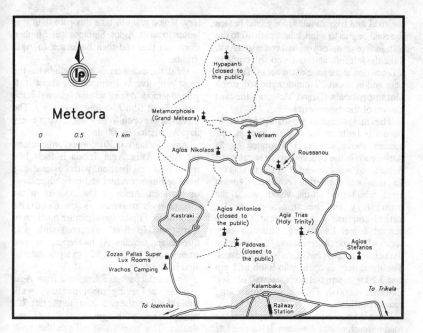

Meteora

0   0.5   1 km

Hypapanti
(closed to
the public)

Metamorphosis
(Grand Meteora)

Varlaam

Agios Nikolaos

Roussanou

Kastraki

Agios Antonios
(closed to
the public)

Agia Trias
(Holy Trinity)

Agios
Stefanos

Padovas
(closed to
the public)

Zozas Pallas Super
Lux Rooms

Vrachos Camping

Kalambaka

To Trikala

To Ioannina

Railway
Station

windlasses can still be seen (you can have a good look at one at Agia Triada), but they are now used for hauling up provisions.

Activities

Meteora Adventures operates a rock-climbing school for beginners, and rock-climbing packages in the Meteora region for both beginner and advanced climbers. The school is located at the entrance of Vrachos Camping in Kastraki. For further information contact Meteora Adventures, Attention Jane Balistreri & Michael Klein, Kastraki PO Box 4, 42200 Kalambaka. The fax No is 432-23 134.

Monasteries

The monasteries are linked by asphalt roads, but the area is best explored on foot on the old paths, where they still exist. There will be precious moments between the roaring tour buses when you'll hear only bees humming, birds singing and the jingling of

goat bells; all immensely evocative in this awe-inspiring landscape. Strict dress codes are enforced. Women must wear skirts below their knees, men must wear long trousers and arms must be covered.

A dirt track leads in 15 minutes from Kastraki to the **Monastery of Agios Nikolaos**. To reach it walk to the end of the main road in Kastraki which peters out to a dirt track. After about 10 minutes the path crosses a stream bed and then a fork branches left. Take this steep path, which veers left at the top to bring you to the road below Agios Nikolaos.

The Monastery of Agios Nikolaos was built in the 15th century. The superlative frescoes in its katholikon were painted by the monk Theophanes Strelizas from Crete. Especially beautiful is the one of Adam naming the animals. The monastery is open every day from 9 am to 6 pm. Admission is 300 dr.

On leaving Agios Nikolaos turn left onto

the road and five minutes along, just before the road begins to wind, take a path off to the left. In five minutes you will come to a fork. Take the left fork and soon you will come to a T-junction at the base of the rocks. Turn left here and in about 20 minutes you will reach **Metamorphosis** (Grand Meteora), the best known of the monasteries.

The majestic and imposing Metamorphosis is built on the highest rock at 613 metres above sea level. Founded by St Athanasios in the 14th century, it became the richest and most powerful of the monasteries, thanks to the Serbian emperor, Symeon Uros, who turned all his wealth over to the monastery and became a monk. Its katholikon has a magnificent 12-sided central dome. Its striking, although gory, series of frescoes *Martyrdom of Saints* depict the persecution of Christians by the Romans. The monastery is open from 9 am to 1 pm and 3.20 to 6 pm, but is closed on Tuesday. Entrance is 600 dr. There is a kantina selling snacks outside.

From Metamorphosis turn right on the road to reach nearby **Varlaam**. It has fine late Byzantine frescoes by Frangos Kastellanos. Varlaam is open from 9 am to 1 pm and 3.30 to 6 pm (closed on Friday). Admission is 300 dr.

On leaving Varlaam walk back to the main road and veer right. In about 15 minutes you will come to a fork: right is signposted to Roussanou and left to Agios Stefanos. Take the left fork and in about 10 minutes you will come to a signpost pointing right to Roussanou. A 10-minute walk along this path will lead to the **Convent of Roussanou**; access is across a vertiginous bridge. The katholikon features more gory frescoes. Roussanou is open from 9 am to 6 pm every day. Admission is 300 dr.

After Roussanou you have the choice of either a short walk to the Agios Nikolaos-Metamorphosis road or going back along the path and continuing along the road to Agia Triada. If you decide to do this you will reach Agia Triada in about 45 minutes (you may be able to hitch a lift on this stretch). A path leads down to Kalambaka from this monastery. If you want to take this path then it is better to visit Agios Stefanos (St Stephen Convent) first and then backtrack to Agia Triada.

Of all the monasteries **Agia Triada** has the most primitive and remote feel about it. It gained temporal fame when it featured in the James Bond film *For Your Eyes Only*. The monastery is open from 9 am to 6 pm every day. Admission is 300 dr.

Agios Stefanos is 30 minutes further along the road. After Agia Triada it feels like returning to civilisation, with business-like nuns selling souvenirs and even videotapes of Meteora. Amongst the exhibits in the monastery's **museum** is an exquisite embroidered Epitaphios (picture on cloth of Christ on His Bier), executed with gold threads and sequins. Agios Stefanos is open from 9 am to 1 pm and 3.20 to 6 pm. Admission is 300 dr.

To find the path to Kalambaka from Agia Triada, on leaving the monastery walk straight ahead; the path is off to the left. It's well marked with red arrows, dots and slashes. The monks will tell you this walk takes 10 minutes, but unless you're James Bond or have the agility of a mountain goat, it'll take you around 30 minutes. On the walk there are tremendous views of the rocks at close quarters, where you see not only their dramatic contours but the details of their strata. The path ends near the Koka Roka Taverna in Kalambaka.

KASTRAKI Καστράκι

The small village of Kastraki (Kas-TRA-ki) nestles at the foot of the rocks, two km from Kalambaka. If you decide to stay here *Vrachos Camping* (☎ 22 293), next door to Zozas Pallas Super Lux Rooms, has excellent facilities and a swimming pool.

Zozas Pallas Super Lux Rooms really are luxurious. Singles/doubles are 3000/4000 dr with private bathrooms. The rooms are on the left (west side) of the Kalambaka-Kastraki road. There are more domatia in the centre of the village. Kastraki is on the Kalambaka-Metamorphosis bus route.

Northern Greece Βόρεια Ελλάδα

Northern Greece comprises the regions of Macedonia, Thrace and Epiros. With thickly forested mountains and tumbling rivers they resemble the Balkans more than they do other parts of Greece. Northern Greece offers great opportunities for trekking, but it is an area where you don't have to go into the wilds to get off well-worn tourist tracks, for its towns are little visited by foreign holiday makers. Unlike the unglamorous and noisy towns of the Peloponnese and central Greece, many of which serve as transport hubs to get out of quickly, most towns in northern Greece have considerable appeal, with atmospheric old quarters of narrow streets and wood-framed houses.

Macedonia Μακεδονία

Macedonia is the largest prefecture in Greece, and its capital, Thessaloniki, is Greece's second city.

With abundant and varied attractions it's surprising that more travellers don't find their way to here. Tucked up in the right-hand corner are the beautiful Prespa Lakes, one of Europe's most important bird sanctuaries. To the south, Mt Olympus, Greece's highest peak, at 2917 metres, rises from a plain just six km from the sea. The unsung towns of Edessa, Veria and Florina unfold their charms to only the occasional visitor. For archaeological buffs there is Alexander the Great's birthplace of Pella; the sanctuary of Dion, where Alexander made sacrifices to the gods; Vergina, where the Macedonian kings (apart from Alexander) were buried; and Philipi, where the battle which set the seal on the future of the Western world was fought. Macedonia is also the site of the Monastic Republic of Athos.

History

Since 1991, the history of Macedonia has become inextricably linked with events in former Yugoslavia.

What's in a name? An awful lot if you are Greek and the name is Macedonia. In January 1992, the Yugoslav Republic of Macedonia declared its full independence. Ever since this pronouncement the Greek government has protested vociferously, insisting that the new country change its name before the European Community (EC) grants recognition. In May 1992, Greece stated it would recognise the republic's independence and cooperate with it to ensure stability in the region, so long as its name did not include the word Macedonia. In response, the EC recognised Macedonia in June 1992, provided that it adopt another name. Amongst the Greek people, the issue has resulted in a surge of unprecedented nationalism with slogans throughout the country declaring 'Macedonia is Greek, always was, is, and always will be'.

The Greeks' objections to the name Macedonia are twofold. They believe that it is an infringement of their cultural heritage, and they read into it undercurrents of territorial claims. They say Macedonia is, and always has been, a Greek name. The 'Greekness' of Alexander the Great, the greatest of Macedonian kings, is indisputable. After all, it was he who spread Greek

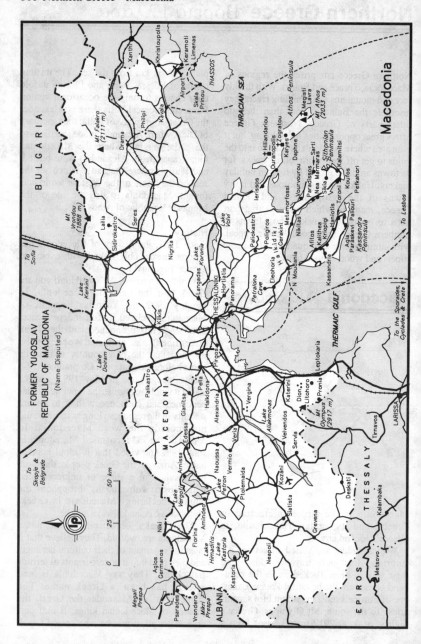

culture to India and the Middle East, and in so doing established Greek as the international language of the ancient world.

Whether Alexander the Great's ancestors were Greek is a different matter. The ethnic origins of the ancient Macedonians has, since the beginning of recorded history, been a conundrum, for it seems that Macedonia has always been a mélange of languages and nationalities.

However, the definition of what constitutes a Greek lies more in a unifying culture and language than in ethnography. In 337 BC, Philip II bound all Greeks together when he invited them to sign a treaty at the Isthmus of Corinth, uniting them against the enemy, Persia. Greeks regard this occasion as the birth of Hellenism, which against all odds has survived to this day.

After Alexander's death, Macedonia continued to be part of Greece, until, with the rest of the country, it came under Roman domination. When the Roman Empire split in the 4th century AD, Macedonia, traversed by the Via Egnatias (the long straight road which linked Rome to Byzantium), became a powerful region with a relatively stable population. This stability came to an end in the 7th century AD when it was invaded by Serbs, who were followed by Bulgars and Muslims. During Byzantine times, Samuel, a Slav Macedonian king, fought against the Byzantines, and his army made inroads into Macedonia. In the 14th century the Serb Stefan Dusan (ruled 1331-55) occupied all of Macedonia, except Thessaloniki. This occupation was short-lived as it was quickly superseded by the Ottoman conquest.

All this coming and going inevitably added to the ethnic mix which already existed. However, throughout Ottoman rule in Macedonia, as in the rest of Greece, a strong Greek identity remained intact, nurtured through religion and culture.

The Greeks' concern about claims on the territory of Macedonia stem from the late 19th century, when the Ottoman Empire was on the point of collapse. At this time, countries welling over with nationalistic fervour were poised to pick up the spoils. The Serbs

made no secret of the fact that they coveted Macedonia, but a much greater threat came from King Ferdinand of Bulgaria.

This volatile situation culminated in the two Balkan Wars (1912-13). In the first Balkan War, the Serbs, Bulgarians and Greeks fought the Turks, and in the second round the Serbs and Greeks fought the Bulgarians. The second Balkan War was ended by the Treaty of Bucharest which ceded 52% of Macedonia to Greece, 38% to Serbia and 18% to Bulgaria. In both world wars Bulgaria fought against Greece and in WW II parts of Macedonia were occupied by Bulgaria who implemented a policy of enforced 'Bulgarianisation'. After the victory of the Allies in WW II, the threat from Bulgaria was replaced by one from Yugoslavia.

In April 1945, Tito proclaimed the Socialist Republic of Macedonia. Greece is convinced that Tito did this to strengthen his southern flank and that his ultimate ambition was to create an independent Macedonian state which would include the Greek province of Macedonia, and the Bulgarian region of Macedonia known as Pirin. Greece says it was too busy fighting the civil war to protest at the time, a situation that Tito was only too aware of. Incidentally, during the civil war the Greek communists forcibly evacuated many children from Macedonia to Eastern-bloc countries, ostensibly for protection, but undoubtedly also for indoctrination.

In 1952 a Macedonian grammar was published in Tito's republic and in 1968 the republic acquired the autocephalous Macedonian church. To Greece, these factors added credence to its suspicions.

Greece continued to protest against the name Macedonia throughout 1992 and into 1993. Then in April 1993, Macedonia was admitted to the UN under the temporary name of the Former Yugoslav Republic of Macedonia, which doesn't exactly trip off the tongue. Greece has given its approval of this name.

To this day there are people in Greek villages on the borders of Bulgaria and the new republic who speak Macedonian. This is one of the south Slavonic group of languages, which is a dialect of Bulgarian, with some Turkish, Greek, Albanian and Vlach words. An offshoot of the present nationalistic fervour is that a minority of these people are coming out and saying 'I am Macedonian' and demanding greater autonomy for Macedonian-speaking Greeks within Greece. The country is not without other ethnic minorities. Could it be that Greece, in its much ado about Macedonia, has inadvertently opened a Pandora's box?

THESSALONIKI Θεσσαλονίκη

Thessaloniki (Thess-alo-NI-ki, population 406,500) was the second city of Byzantium and is the second city of modern Greece. However, being second does not mean that Thessaloniki lies in the shadow of, or tries to emulate, the capital. It is a sophisticated city with a distinct character of its own, which is very different from Athens. It has a lively nightlife, good restaurants and, although it doesn't have the impressive ancient monuments of the capital, it has several good museums, a scattering of Roman ruins and superlative Byzantine churches.

Thessaloniki sits at the top of the wide Thermaic Gulf. The oldest part of the city is the Kastra, the old Turkish quarter, whose narrow streets huddle around a Byzantine fortress on the slopes of Mt Hortiatis.

Thessaloniki is best avoided during festival time (September and October), as accommodation is almost impossible to find, and prices are increased by at least 20%. At other times finding a room should not present any problems.

History

Like almost everywhere in Greece, Thessaloniki has had not only its triumphs but more than its fair share of disasters; as with Athens, an awareness of these helps greatly in one's appraisal of the city.

The city was named Thessaloniki in 316 BC by the Macedonian general, Kassandros, after his wife, daughter of Philip II and half-sister of Alexander the Great. While Philip was successfully expanding his territory in

Thessaly, his wife gave birth to their daughter. When he arrived home Philip announced that the child would be called Thessaloniki, which means 'Victory in Thessaly'.

After the Roman conquest in 168 BC Thessaloniki became the capital of the province of Macedonia. Thessaloniki's geographical location on the Thermaic Gulf and its position on the Via Egnatias promoted its development. It was also an important staging post on the trade route to the Balkans.

The Roman emperor Galerius made it the imperial capital of the eastern half of the Roman Empire, and after the empire split it became the second city of Byzantium, and flourished as both a spiritual and economic centre. Inevitably, its strategic position brought attacks and plunderings by Goths, Slavs, Muslims, Franks and Epirots. In 1185 it was sacked by the Normans, and in 1204 made a feudal kingdom under Marquis Boniface of Montferrat. In 1246 it was reunited to the Byzantine Empire. After several sieges it finally capitulated to Ottoman rule when Murad II staged a successful invasion in 1430.

In 1492, 20,000 Jewish exiles from Spain and Portugal settled in Thessaloniki. These immigrants boosted the city's trade, and brought about many improvements and, by the 16th century, Jews constituted the major part of the population. However, there are now very few Jews living in the city for in WW II, 46,000 of Thessaloniki's Jews were deported to death camps in Auschwitz.

Along with the rest of Macedonia, Thessaloniki became part of Greece in 1913. In August 1917 a fire broke out in the city and, as there was no fire brigade, the flames spread quickly, destroying 9500 houses and rendering 70,000 inhabitants homeless. The problem of homelessness was exacerbated by the influx of refugees from Asia Minor after the 1923 population exchange. During the late 1920s the city was carefully replanned and built on a grid system with wide streets and large squares.

In 1978 Thessaloniki experienced a severe earthquake. Most of the modern buildings were not seriously damaged, but the Byzantine churches suffered greatly and most are still in the process of being restored.

Orientation

Thessaloniki's waterfront of Leoforos Nikis stretches from the port in the west, to the White Tower in the east. North of the White Tower are the exhibition grounds where Thessaloniki's annual International Trade Fair is held; the university campus is north of here. The city's other principal streets of Mitropoleos, Tsimiski and Ermou run parallel to Nikis. Egnatias, the next street up, is the city's main thoroughfare and most of Thessaloniki's Roman remains are between here and Odos Agiou Dimitriou. The city's two main squares are Plateia Eleftherias, and Plateia Aristotelous, both of which abut the waterfront. The central food market is between Egnatias, Irakliou, Aristotelous and Dragoumi. Plateia Eleftherias is one of the city's local bus terminals, although the main terminal is at Plateia Dikastirion. The train station is on Monastiriou, a westerly continuation of Egnatias. The city does not have one general intercity bus station; there are several terminals for different destinations. The airport is 16 km south-east of the city.

Kastra, the old Turkish quarter, is north of Odos Athinas and just within the ramparts.

Information

Tourist Office The EOT (☎ 27 1888), Plateia Aristotelous 8, is open Monday to Friday from 8 am to 8 pm and Saturday from 8 am to 2 pm.

Tourist Police The Tourist Police (☎ 54 8907) are at Egnatias 10, but the entrance to the building is around the corner on the left side of Tandalidou. The office is open from 7.30 am to 11 pm from October to March and 24 hours from April to September.

Money The National Bank of Greece, Tsimiski 11, is open Monday to Friday from 8 am to 2 pm and 6 to 8 pm, on Saturday from 8 am to 1.30 pm and on Sunday from 9.30 am to 12.30 pm.

American Express (☎ 26 9984) is repre-

sented by Doucas Tours, Plateia Eleftherias. Services are for card holders only. Opening hours are Monday to Friday from 8.30 am to 2 pm and 5.30 to 8.30 pm, and Saturday from 8.30 am to 1.30 pm.

Post & Telecommunications The main post office is at Tsimiski 45. It's open Monday to Friday from 7.30 am to 8 pm, Saturday from 7.30 am to 2.15 pm and Sunday from 9 am to 1.30 pm. Thessaloniki's postcode is 54101.

The OTE is at Karolou Dil 27 and is open 24 hours. Thessaloniki's telephone code is 031.

Foreign Consulates Foreign consulates in Thessaloniki include:

Germany
    Karolou Dil 4a (☎ 23 6315)
Netherlands
    Komninon 26 (☎ 22 7477)
UK
    El Venizelou 8 (☎ 27 8006, 26 9984)
USA
    Nikis 59 (☎ 26 6121)

Australia, New Zealand and Canada are represented by the UK Consulate.

Mt Athos Permits After obtaining a letter of recommendation from your consulate, permits to the monastic region of Mt Athens can be obtained from the Ministry of Macedonia & Thrace (☎ 27 0092), on Plateia Diikitiriou. For further information about applying for permission to visit this area, see the section on Mt Athos later in the chapter.

Bookshops Molho, Tsimiski 10, has a comprehensive stock of English-language books, magazines and newspapers. Malliaris Kaisia, Aristotelous 9, also has many English-language publications.

Laundries Wash & Go, just north of Agiou Dimitriou, is a trendy place with magazines and a soft-drink machine. Walk up Tritis Septemvriou, turn left onto Agiou Dimitriou and look for the sign pointing right. It's open

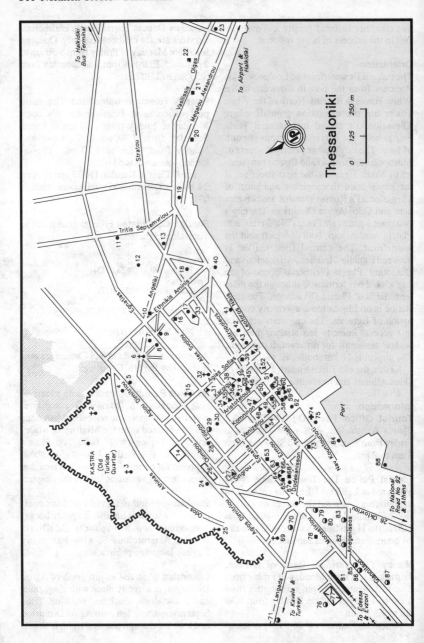

Thessaloniki

0   125   250 m

■ PLACES TO STAY

10	ABC Hotel
16	YHA Hostel
20	Macedonia Palace Hotel
21	Hotel Queen Olga
22	Hotel Metropolitan
39	YWCA
53	Hotel Atlas
55	Tourist Hotel
56	Electra Palace Hotel
57	Continental Hotel
63	Hotel Averof
65	Hotel Atlantis
68	Hotel Acropol
73	Astor Hotel
78	Capsis Hotel

▼ PLACES TO EAT

27	Life Restaurant
31	Patsas Ilias
33	Brothers' Taverna
34	Ta Spata Psistaria
35	Alexis the Greek
44	Ta Nisia Taverna
46	Ouzeri Aristotelous
47	Babel Snack Bar
48	O Loutros Fish Taverna
54	Saul Modiano
61	Olymbos Naoussa Restaurant
64	Nameless Snack Bar
66	Ta Nea Ilisia

◖ BUS STATIONS

29	Local Bus Station
70	Langadas Bus Station
71	Kavala Bus Station
76	Alexandroupolis Bus Station
79	Veria Bus Station
80	Katerini Bus Station
82	Florina Bus Station
83	Pella, Kastoria, Volos & Edessa Bus Station
85 & 86	Athens & Trikala Bus Station
87	Ioannina Bus Station

OTHER

1	Monastery of Vlatadon

2	Church of Nikolaos Orfanos
3	Church of Ossios David
4	Atatürk's House
5	Show Avantaz
6	Church of Agios Georgios
7	Bianca Laundrette
8	Arch of Galerius
9	Egnatia Tours
11	Traffic Disco
12	International Trade Fairground
13	Archaeological Museum
14	Church of Agios Dimitrios
15	Church of the Panagia Akheiropoietos
17	Plateia Navarinou
18	Society for Macedonian Studies Art Gallery
19	Natali Cinema
23	Folklife & Ethnographical Museum of Macedonia
24	Ministry of Macedonia & Thrace
25	Church of Agia Ekaterini
26	Plateia Diikitiriou
28	Roman Agora
30	Plateia Dikastirion
32	Church of Agia Sofia
36	OTE
37	OSE
38	EOS
40	White Tower
41	USA Consulate
42	Entasis Music Bar
43	Museum of the Macedonian Struggle
45	Post Office
49	National Bank of Greece
50	Magic Bus
51	Plateia Aristotelous
52	EOT
58	Doucas Tours
59	UK Consulate
60	Olympic Airways Office
62	Plateia Eleftherias
67	Tourist Police
69	Church of the Dodeka Apostoloi
72	Plateia Demokratias (also called Plateia Vardari)
74	First Aid Centre
75	Nomikos Lines
77	Plateia Galopourou
81	Train Station
84	Ferry Departure Point
88	Hydrofoil Departure Point

Monday to Saturday from 9 am to 2.30 pm and 4.30 to 8.30 pm; Sunday from 9 am to 4.30 pm.

Bianca Laundrette, on Antoniadou, has a more utilitarian ambience. Walk up D Gournari from the Arch of Galerius and Antoniadou is a turn-off to the right. It's open Monday to Friday from 8 am to 2 pm. Both laundrettes charge 1000 dr a load for wash and dry.

Emergency There is a first-aid centre (☎ 53 0530) at Nav Kountourioti 6, near the port. The largest public hospital is Ippokration (☎ 83 0024), Konstantinoupoleos 49.

Archaeological Museum

In 1977 one of Greece's most eminent archaeologists, Professor Andronikos, was excavating at Vergina near Thessaloniki when he found an unlooted tomb which turned out to be that of King Philip II of Macedon. The spectacular contents of this tomb, now on display in this museum, are comparable to the grave treasures of Mycenae. Among the exhibits are exquisite gold jewellery, bronze and terracotta vases, tiny ivory reliefs of intricate detail, and a solid gold casket with lion's feet, embossed with the symbol of the royal house of Macedonia, which contained the bones of Philip II. The most mind-boggling exhibit is the bones themselves, which are carefully laid out to reconstruct an almost complete skeleton. There is something very uncanny about looking at someone who until that moment was just a name in a history book.

The opening hours of the museum (☎ 83 0538) are Tuesday to Friday from 8 am to 5 pm, Saturday, Sunday and holidays from 8.30 am to 3 pm and Monday from 11 am to 5 pm. Admission costs 1000 dr. The museum is opposite the entrance to the exhibition grounds. To get there either walk east along Tsimiski or take bus No 3.

Folklife & Ethnological Museum of Macedonia

This museum (☎ 83 0591), housed in a beautiful 19th-century mansion, is one of the best of its kind in Greece. As well as elaborate costumes and intricate embroideries the collection also includes traditional agricultural and craft tools.

The upstairs exhibition is titled 'Thessaloniki 1913 to 1919'. Life in the city at that time is presented through blown-up photographs taken by Fred Boissonas, a pioneer photographer and philhellene. The exhibition also includes eye-witness accounts (translated into English) of the fire of 1917.

The museum is at Vasilissis Olgas 68, and is open on Monday and Wednesday from 9.30 am to 5.30 pm and Tuesday, Friday, Saturday and Sunday from 9.30 am to 2 pm; it's closed on Thursday. Admission is 150 dr. It is 15 minutes' walk from the Archaeological Museum, or you can take eastbound bus No 5, 7 or 33 and get off at the Fleming stop.

White Tower

This 15th-century tower is both the city's symbol and most prominent landmark. During the 18th century it was used as a prison for insubordinate janissaries, the elite troops of forcibly converted Christian boys, who became servants of the sultan. In 1826, at the order of Mahmud II, many of the janissaries were massacred in this tower and thereafter it became known as the bloody tower. After independence it was whitewashed as a symbolic gesture to expunge its function during Turkish rule. The whitewash has now been removed and it has been turned into a very fine **Byzantine Museum** (☎ 26 7832) , with splendid frescoes and icons.

In the pleasant museum café a 30-minute audiovisual show is shown every hour between 10 am and 4 pm (except at 2 pm).

The museum is open on Monday from 11 am to 5 pm, Tuesday to Friday from 8 am to 5 pm and Saturday, Sunday and holidays from 8.30 am to 3 pm; admission is 500 dr.

Other Museums

The **Museum of the Macedonian Struggle** (☎ 22 9778) charts through models, pictures and diagrams the story of the liberation of Macedonia from the Ottomans and the threat of Bulgarian nationalism. The museum is at

Proxenou Koromila 23, in what was the Greek Consular building when Macedonia was still part of the Ottoman Empire. Proxenou Koromila runs parallel to, and between, Mitropoleos and Nikis. Opening times are Monday to Friday and Sunday from 9 am to 2 pm and in addition on Monday and Wednesday from 5 to 7 pm. It is closed on Saturday. Admission is free.

The **Society for Macedonian Studies Art Gallery** has a permanent collection consisting of some 200 paintings, drawings and engravings by eminent 20th-century Greek artists. The gallery is on the 6th floor of the same building as the State Theatre of Northern Greece and the Aristoteleion cinema. It is open Sunday to Friday from 9 am to 2 pm. Admission is free.

Kemal Atatürk, the founder of the Republic of Turkey, was born in Thessaloniki in 1881. The Turkish timber-framed house where he was born and spent his childhood has been faithfully restored and is now a museum called **Atatürk's House**.

A visit is a bit of a cloak and dagger affair, but is worth the effort. You must ring the bell of the Turkish Consulate building (around the corner on Agiou Dimitriou); you will be asked to show your passport, and then someone will show you around. The museum is open every day from 2 to 6 pm. Admission is free.

Roman & Byzantine Thessaloniki

Thessaloniki has few remaining Roman ruins, but its churches span every period of Byzantine art and architecture, and were once the city's foremost glory. Not withstanding the extensive damage they have received due to fire and earthquakes, and their conversion to mosques, a visit to the most renowned ones is still worthwhile. You can see the Roman remains and the major churches in a circular walk.

The **Roman agora**, in the upper part of Plateia Dikastirion, is reached by crossing Egnatias from Aristotelous. Excavations began in the 1970s and are still in progress, so the site is cordoned off from the public;

so far the odeion and two stoas have come to light.

From the north-east corner of this site, walk up Agnotou Stratiottou, cross over Olimbou, walk straight ahead, and you will see the 5th-century **Church of Agios Dimitrios** on the opposite side of the road.

Dimitrios was born in the city in the 3rd century and became an eminent scholar, and an early convert to Christianity. He was martyred on the orders of Galerius, who was not a Christian and ruthless in his persecution of those who were. Several claims of appearances of Dimitrios' ghost in warrior-like guise at apposite moments during sieges caused the enemy to flee in terror. This, coupled with claims of miraculous cures at the site of his martyrdom, gained him a sainthood. The church, Greece's largest, was built on the site where he was martyred.

The church was converted into a mosque by the Turks who plastered over the interior walls. When it was restored to the Christians again, it was discovered to have the finest mosaics of all the city's churches.

The frescoes and the building received extensive damage in the fire of 1917. However, five 8th-century mosaics have survived and can be seen on either side of the altar. The church is open to the public Sunday to Friday from 9.30 am to 2.30 pm and 5.30 to 9.30 pm, and from 9.30 am to 3 pm on Saturday.

On leaving the church turn left and walk along Agiou Dimitriou till you come to Odos Dragoumi, which leads off to the right. Walk down here until you reach Filipou, and you will see ahead the 3rd-century **Church of Agios Georgios**, the oldest of Thessaloniki's churches. It is a Roman brickwork rotunda, which was originally intended as a mausoleum for Galerius, but never fulfilled this function. Constantine the Great transformed it into a church. The minaret from its days as a mosque remains. At the time of writing the church was still closed while restoration work was taking place.

Walk a little way around the church and turn right onto D Gounari, and you will see ahead the imposing **Arch of Galerius**, which was erected in 303 AD to celebrate the emperor's victories over the Persians in 297 AD. Its eroded bas-reliefs depict battle scenes with the Persians. Turn right onto Egnatias, and then left to reach the 8th-century **Church of Agia Sofia**, on Agias Sofias, which emulates its renowned namesake in Istanbul. The dome has a striking mosaic of the Ascension.

On leaving the Church of Agia Sofia, retrace your steps back to Egnatias, cross the road, and continue a little way up Agias Sofias to the **Church of the Panagia Akheiropoietos**, on the right. This church, built in the 5th century, is an early example of basilican form; some mosaics and frescoes remain. The name means 'made without hands' and derives from the 12th century, when an icon supposedly miraculously appeared in the church. So many icons in Greece have appeared miraculously, one wonders if perhaps God is a frustrated artist.

Several of the smaller churches are also worth a look at. They include the 13th-century **Church of Agia Ekaterini**, the **Church of the Dodeka Apostoloi** (Church of the Twelve Apostles) and the 4th-century **Church of Nikolaos Orfanos**, which has exquisite frescoes. The little 5th-century **Church of Ossios David**, in Kastra, was allegedly built to commemorate Galerius' daughter, Theodora, whose clandestine baptism took place while her father was on one of his campaigns.

Kastra & the Ramparts

The Turkish quarter of Kastra is all that is left of 19th-century Thessaloniki. The original ramparts of Kastra were built by Theodosius (379-475 AD), but were rebuilt in the 14th century.

Kastra's streets are narrow and steep, with lots of cobbles and steps, flanked by timber-framed houses, with overhanging upper storeys and tiny whitewashed dwellings with shutters. From Kastra there are stunning views of modern Thessaloniki and the Thermaic Gulf. To reach here, either take bus No 22 or 23 from Plateia Eleftherias, or walk north along Agia Sophias, which becomes

Dimadou Vlatadou after Athinas. At the top of here turn right onto Odos Eptapirgiou.

Organised Tours

Doucas Tours (☎ 26 9984/5/6/7), El Venizelou 8, has a half-day tour of Thessaloniki for 3500 dr. Their full-day 'Alexander the Great Tour' visits Pella, Vergina, Veria and Edessa. Other tours include Meteora, Kavala and Philipi and a cruise around the Athos peninsula. All of these tours cost between 6000 and 7000 dr.

Festivals

Thessaloniki hosts a string of festivals in September and October, which are held in the exhibition grounds. First is the International Trade Fair, which is followed by a cultural festival which includes film shows, Greek song performances and culminates in the celebration of St Dimitrios Day on 26 October, followed by military parades on Ochi Day on 28 October.

Places to Stay – bottom end

There are no camp sites close to Thessaloniki; the nearest ones are on the crowded beaches at Perea and Agia Triada, 20 and 22 km away respectively. Take bus Nos 67, 69 or 72 from Plateia Dikastirion.

Thessaloniki's *YHA Hostel* (☎ 22 5946), Alex Svolou 44, has dorm beds for 1200 dr. The doors are locked between 11 am and 6 pm, and there is an 11 pm curfew. An IYHF card is required.

The *YWCA* (XEN in Greek) (☎ 27 6144), Agias Sofias 11, is clean and well run: dorm beds are 1500 to 2000 dr, double rooms are 3000 dr. Only women can stay here.

The *Hotel Atlantis* (☎ 54 0131), Egnatias 14, has pokey, but clean double/triple rooms for 2500/3500 dr with shared bathrooms. The D class *Hotel Acropol* (☎ 53 6170), Tandalidou 4, is Thessaloniki's best budget hotel. It's clean, quiet and owned by a friendly English-speaking family. The single/double/triple rooms cost 3300/4500/

6000 dr with shared bathrooms. The hotel is just beyond the tourist police entrance.

Another quiet option is the D class *Hotel Averof* (☎ 53 8498), Leontos Sofou 24, around the corner from Egnatias. The attractive pine-furnished rooms cost 3300/5500/6500 dr with shared bathrooms. The D class *Hotel Atlas* (☎ 53 7046), 40 Egnatias, has clean, carpeted singles/doubles for 3000/4000 dr with shared bathrooms (shower 400 dr); doubles with private bathrooms are 6000 dr. This is a nice hotel, but the rooms at the front get a lot of traffic noise.

The D class *Tourist Hotel* (☎ 27 6335/0501 or 28 4768), Mitropoleos 21, has pleasant rooms and a spacious lounge with comfortable armchairs and a TV. The cost is 3400/5200 dr for singles/doubles with shared bathrooms and 6900/8100 dr for doubles/triples with private bathrooms. Walk east along Egnatias, turn right onto El Venizelou, walk to Plateia Eleftherias, turn left onto Mitropoleos and the hotel is at the end of the block on the left, at the corner of Komninon. The C class *Continental Hotel* (☎ 27 7553), Komninon 5, charges 3500/5500/6500 dr for singles/doubles/ triples with shared bathrooms, and 5500/8000/9000 dr with private bathrooms. All of the rooms have a refrigerator and the ones with private bathrooms have colour TV and air-con. The hotel has an idiosyncratic lift which should be donated to an industrial archaeological museum. To reach this hotel, turn right at the Tourist Hotel.

Places to Stay – middle

The C class *ABC Hotel* (☎ 26 5421), Angeliki 41, has 102 rooms all with private bathrooms, telephone and a balcony. Singles/doubles are 8000/12,500 dr including breakfast. The hotel is at the eastern end of Egnatias. Further east the modern B class *Hotel Queen Olga* (☎ 82 4621; fax 83 0550), Vasilissis Olgas 44, has cosy rooms with a warm mellow décor and private bathrooms, radio, colour TV, minibar and air-con; the rates are 10,150/12,400 dr. This hotel has a car park. Travelling east, the hotel is on the right. A little further along, on the opposite side of the road, the B class *Hotel Metropolitan* (☎ 82 4221), Vasilissis Olgas 65, has attractively furnished rooms with private bathrooms, telephone and radio. The price for singles/doubles/triples is 11,250/15,800/19,500 dr including breakfast. All of the middle-range hotels recommended so far have bars and restaurants.

The B class *Capsis Hotel* (☎ 52 1321/421; fax 51 0555), Monastiriou 18, 200 metres east of the train station, is the city's largest hotel with 428 rooms. It has two standards of rooms: business-class single/double rooms with colour TV, radio, telephone and air-con cost 15,600/20,000 dr; standard rooms are plainer but have everything except the telephone and cost 10,400/15,200 dr. The hotel has a roof garden, pool, health studio, sauna, hairdressers, boutiques, bars and restaurants.

The *Astor Hotel* (☎ 52 7121; telex 41 2655 ASTO GR), on the corner of Tsimiski and Salamos, is modern and bright with lots of brass and cream marble. Room rates are 14,000/19,000/23,000 dr which includes breakfast.

Places to Stay – top end

Thessaloniki's A class *Electra Palace Hotel* (☎ 23 2221; fax 23 5947), Plateia Aristotelous 9, has an impressive façade in the style of a Byzantine palace. The interior is a tasteful combination of Byzantine and modern décor. All rooms have a telephone, air-con, minibar, colour TV, three-channel music radio and a hair dryer. The cost for singles/doubles is 17,900/22,500 dr including breakfast. The hotel has two restaurants and a bar.

Thessaloniki's only deluxe-class hotel is the *Macedonia Palace Hotel* (☎ 83 7520/620/720; telex 41 2162 MP GR), Megalou Alexandrou. The hotel lacks the grandeur of some of Athens' luxury hotels and from the outside it could be mistaken for a large apartment block, but inside it has lots of black and grey marble, giving it a touch of cool tranquil elegance. Singles/doubles are 20,000/25,000 dr and suites are 50,000 dr. The hotel overlooks the sea just beyond the White Tower.

Places to Eat – bottom end

There are lots of fast-food places and snack bars in Thessaloniki where you can get a giros, pizza or cheese pie for around 300 dr. *Babel Snack Bar*, Komninon 18, is a good place for a snack or breakfast with reasonably priced crepes, pies, toasted sandwiches and filter coffee. The nameless snack bar at Egnatias 24 has delicious chocolate pie for 300 dr.

The bright and busy *Life Restaurant*, Filipou 1, on the corner of Syngrou and Filipou, offers a rarity in Greece – instant service. The menu is large and the food well prepared: moussaka, pastitsio and spaghetti are all 650 dr. The restaurant is open every day for lunch and dinner. Another popular place with similarly priced Greek staples is *Ta Nea Ilisia* on Leontis Sofou, opposite the Hotel Averof.

For a lively evening try the long-established *O Loutros Fish Taverna*, in an old Turkish *hammam* (bathhouse) on Komninon, near the flower market. Don't be misled by the rough and ready ambience – this taverna has a cult following. If you go there you could be rubbing shoulders with politicians, professors and actors. Excellent fish dishes cost around 600 to 800 dr. The taverna is always crowded and there are often spontaneous renderings of rembetika music, usually on Tuesday and Thursday evenings.

For an ethnic experience go to the *Patsas Ilias* tripe shop at Egnatias 102, where you can have a bowl of hearty tripe soup for 500 dr; other reasonably priced Greek staples are also available.

Alexis the Greek, Aristotelous 26, is an unpretentious little ouzeri which serves excellent fish dishes: mussel saganaki, mussel soup and kalamaria are all 800 dr. Next door at the popular *Ta Spata Psistaria*, Aristotelous 28, a tasty meal of giros, chips, aubergine salad, fried courgettes and retsina will cost about 1700 dr.

The *Olymbos Naoussa Restaurant*, Leoforos Nikis 5, is a time-honoured restaurant whose dilapidated grandeur is offset by sparkling white damask tableclothes and napkins. It was once the city's premier restaurant and still has a loyal following amongst the older generation. It's a little pricier than the restaurants so far recommended but still manages to squeeze in to the bottom end of the market. Egg and lemon soup is 660 dr, delicately herb-flavoured rice with mussels is 820 dr and chicken casserole is 850 dr. It is only open for lunch and is closed at weekends.

The *Brothers' Taverna* (name in Greek), Plateia Navarinou 9, is another place which is always packed. It has a pleasing ambience, with enlarged pictures of old Thessaloniki on the walls; their very tasty kebabs cost around 1000 dr.

Places to Eat – middle & top end

The *Ouzeri Aristotelous* has first-rate mezedes, which include cuttlefish stuffed with cheese for 1200 dr, fried eggplant with garlic for 360 dr and whitebait in sauce for 750 dr. The food here is rich and filling, so three mezedes per person is sufficient, and you should try to balance the oily dishes with the more bland ones. The restaurant, which has a Parisian ambience with marble-top tables, is in an arcade off the left side of Odos Aristotelous as you walk towards the waterfront – look for the wrought-iron gate at the entrance to the arcade. It's open from 12.30 to 4.30 pm and from 8.30 pm to 3 am, and is closed on Sunday.

Ta Nisia Taverna, Koromila 13, is another wonderful place. It has white stucco walls, a wood-beamed ceiling, lots of plants, and pretty plates on the walls. The unusual and imaginative mezedes include cuttlefish with spinach in wine for 1200 dr and little triangles of pastry filled with eggplant for 200 dr each. The restaurant is open for lunch and dinner, but is closed on Sunday.

The *Saul Modiano* is one of Thessaloniki's most elegant restaurants, with purple velvet upholstered chairs. Imaginative dishes start at 1200 dr. Unlike most Greek restaurants, the elegance doesn't end when you enter the loo – the women's toilet provides cotton-wool buds, make-up remover pads, perfume, and hand and body lotion. The restaurant is in an arcade off the northern side of Irakliou, between I Dragoumi and El Venizelou; the arcade is next to Stoa Fast Food Café.

Entertainment

Discos & Music Bars *Milos* (☎ 52 5968), Andreou Georgiou 56, is a huge old mill which has been converted into an entertainment complex with an art gallery, restaurant, a bar and a live music club (classical and rock). Andreou Georgiou is off the map in a grim part of town. Either take a westbound bus No 31, or walk down 26 Oktovriou from Plateia Vardari to Andreou Georgiou, which is off to the right next to the petrol station at 26 Oktovriou 36. Milos is a spruce cream and terracotta building, 250 metres along on the right.

Live bouzouki and Greek folk are played at *Show Avantaz*, Agiou Dimitriou 156 (opposite the Turkish Consulate). There is no cover charge and cocktails and spirits cost 1200 dr. The club is open from 11 pm to 4 am nightly, but closes from June to September.

One of Thessaloniki's biggest winter discos is *Traffic* on Tritis Septemvriou, two blocks down from Egnatias on the right. *L'apogée* at Ethnikis Anithstasis 16 and *Troll*, almost next door, are lively winter discos in the eastern part of town (off the map) – any taxi driver will be able to take you there.

Thessaloniki's summer discos are out towards the airport – the hippest are *Swing* and *Amnesia*. Back in the centre *Loft*, Pavlou Mela 40, is a popular music bar with an arty décor. *Entasis*, Koromila 29, is a male and female gay bar.

Cinema Thessaloniki's cinemas showing first-run English-language films include the *Olympian* on Plateia Aristotelous, *Aristoteleion*, opposite the White Tower, and *Cinema Pallas*, at Nikis 69. *Natali* is an open-air summer cinema on Megalou Alexandrou.

Things to Buy

Thessaloniki's women have a reputation for being the most chic in Greece, so, to supply a demand, Thessaloniki has many clothes and shoe shops selling ultra-fashionable gear. Bargains can be found along Egnatias and the shops around the indoor food market, and you can pick up high-quality stuff on Tsimiski. Also look out for vendors on Tsimiski, some of whom sell trendy handmade jewellery at reasonable prices.

Getting There & Away

Air The Olympic Airways office (☎ 23 0240) is at Nav Koundouriti 3. The airport phone number is ☎ 42 5011.

Domestic There are at least seven flights a day to Athens (13,700 dr), six a week to Lemnos (9900 dr), four a week to Ioannina (7400 dr) and two a week to both Iraklion (21,800 dr) and Rhodes (23,500 dr).

International International flights to/from Thessaloniki include:

Budapest – two a week
Cyprus – three a week
Frankfurt – two a day
London – three a week
Munich – one a day
Paris – four a week
Sofia – two a week
Vienna – one a day

Bus Most of Thessaloniki's bus terminals are near the train station. Frequent buses for Athens and Trikala leave from Monastiriou 65 and 67, opposite the train station. Buses for Alexandroupolis leave from Koloniari 17, Plateia Galopourou, behind the train station. Buses for Pella, Edessa, Volos and Kastoria leave from Anageniseos 22 and for Florina from Anageniseos 42. Ioannina buses leave from Christoupipsou 19 (off Giannitson). Buses for Veria leave from 26 Oktovriou 10. The Katerini bus station is a turn-off right (heading west) just beyond the

Veria station. Kavala buses leave from Langada 69.

All buses for the Halkidiki peninsula leave from Karakassi 68 which is in the eastern part of the city and off this book's map but on the EOT map. To reach the Halkidiki terminal take bus No 10 to the Botsari stop (near Odos Markou Botsari).

To Europe & Turkey Buses also leave for many cities in Europe, as well as for Istanbul. Tickets may be bought from Magic Bus (☎ 26 3566), Tsimiski 32, who are an agent for Eurolines.

Train All trains leave from the station on Monastiriou (☎ 51 7000). There are nine trains a day to Athens (7½ hours, 3960/2640 dr 1st/2nd class), eight to Edessa (two hours, 640 dr), four of which continue to Florina (four hours, 1100 dr). There are five trains a day to Alexandroupolis (2100/4000 1st/2nd class) and three trains to Volos (4½ hours, 1300 dr). Only Athens has an express service, which takes six hours and costs 6000 dr. Tickets may be bought at the train station or the OSE office (☎ 27 6382), Aristotelous 18. The station has a National Bank of Greece, a post office, an OTE, and a restaurant which is open 24 hours. Luggage storage is 200 dr per piece, per day.

To Europe & Turkey Trains leave Thessaloniki for many destinations in Europe, though the present situation in former Yugoslavia is disrupting many schedules, as trains bound for central and Western Europe have to pass through Serbia and Croatia. There is one train a day to Istanbul which takes at least 18 hours (9000 dr).

Car The ELPA (Greek Automobile Club; ☎ 42 6319) is at Vasilissis Olgas 228. Cars may be hired from Budget Rent a Car (☎ 27 4272), Angelaki 15, and InterRent-Europcar (☎ 82 6333), G Papandreou 5, among others.

Ferry A ferry sails on Saturday throughout the year to Lesbos (15 hours, 5000 dr), Lemnos (eight hours, 3000 dr) and Chios (18 hours, 5000 dr). In summer there are boats on Monday and Friday to Iraklion, on Crete (6300 dr). Both go via Paros and Thira; the one on Friday also stops at Tinos and Mykonos.

Thessaloniki's port authority police telephone number is ☎ 53 1504. Ferry tickets may be purchased from Nomikos Lines (☎ 52 4544/522/736), Koundourioti 8.

Hydrofoil In summer there are four hydrofoils a week to the Sporades islands of Skiathos (3½ hours, 5599 dr), Skopelos (4½ hours, 6450 dr) and Alonissos (five hours, 6449 dr). Tickets can be purchased from Egnatias Tours (☎ 22 3811), Kambouniou 9.

Getting Around
To/From the Airport Thessaloniki's airport is 16 km south-east of town. There is no Olympic Airways transfer service. Public bus No 78 plies to and from the airport; it leaves from in front of the train station and costs 115 dr. A taxi to or from the airport costs 1100 dr.

Bus Orange articulated buses operate within the city and blue buses and orange single buses operate both within the city and out to the suburbs. There is a flat fare of 75 dr within the city.

On the articulated orange buses you buy a ticket from the conductor sitting next to the door. On the single buses you buy the ticket from a machine on the bus, which is not very user friendly. It will take five, 10, 20 and 50 drachma coins, but does not give change. There are three different tickets for the three zones: 75 dr within the city, 100 dr for the suburbs and 115 dr for outlying villages. Books of 12 tickets are available and monthly travel cards cost 2800 dr.

Taxi Thessaloniki's taxis are blue and white and the procedure for hailing one is the same as in Athens – stand on the edge of the pavement, and bellow your destination at every one which passes. For a radio taxi telephone ☎ 21 7218.

AROUND THESSALONIKI
Panorama & Hortiatis

Panorama (Πανόραμα) is a village nine km east of Thessaloniki on the slopes of Mt Hortiatis, overlooking the gulf. It's a pleasant enough place, but don't expect an unspoilt mountain village as it's full of smart villas owned by wealthy city dwellers, plus a large modern shopping mall, and lots of trendy coffee shops.

Hortiatis (Χορτιάτης), six km further on, has more of a mountain village feel about it. You may even spot some genuine village phenomena like a donkey, an old red-roof dwelling, or a herd of goats between the villas. Just beyond the village square there are several tavernas which sell good souvlaki.

If you continue along the winding main road for another 2½ km you will come to a large kafeneion on the right. Opposite here (signposted) is a marked path which leads in 1½ hours to a mountain refuge 1000 metres up Mt Hortiatis. From the refuge there are paths to remote mountain villages. If you would like to stay at the refuge contact the Thessaloniki SEO (Association of Greek Climbers; ☎ 22 4710), Plateia Aristotelous 5, Thessaloniki.

Getting There & Away To get to Panorama take bus No 57, 58 or 61 from Plateia Dikastirion; the No 61 continues on to Hortiatis.

Langadas Λαγκαδάς

The village of Langadas, 12 km north-east of Thessaloniki, is famous for the fire-walking ritual *anastenaria* which takes place on 21 May, the feast day of St Constantine and his mother, St Helena. The fire walkers, or *anastenarides* (groaners) believe the ritual originated in the village of Costi (an abbreviation of Constantinos) in eastern Thrace. The story is that in 1250 AD the Church of St Constantine caught fire and the villagers, hearing groans from the icons, entered the church, retrieved them, and escaped unscathed. The icons were kept by the families concerned, and descendants and devotees honoured the saint each year by performing the ritual. In 1913 when the village was occupied by Bulgarians the families fled to the villages of Serres, Drama and Langadas, taking the icons with them.

The anastenarides step barefoot onto burning charcoal. Holding the icons and waving coloured handkerchiefs, they dance whilst emitting strange cries, accompanied by drums and lyres. They believe they will not be burned, because God's spirit enters into them. Each year new fire walkers are initiated.

The church condemns the ritual as pagan, and indeed the celebration seems to have in it elements of the pre-Christian worship of Dionysos. If you would like to see this overtly commercial but intriguing spectacle, it begins at 7 pm – turn up early to get a ringside seat. Frequent buses leave for Langadas from the terminal at Irinis 17, near Odos Langada in Thessaloniki.

PELLA Πέλλα

Pella (PE-la), most famous as the birthplace of Alexander the Great, lies in the plain of Macedonia astride the Thessaloniki-Edessa road. Its star attraction is its marvellous mosaics. King Archelaos (ruled 413-399 BC) moved the Macedonian capital from Aigai to Pella, although Aigai remained the royal cemetery.

The mosaics, most of which depict mythological scenes, are made from natural coloured stones and the effect is one of subtle and harmonious blends and contrasts. They were discovered in the remains of houses and public buildings, on the north (right, coming from Thessaloniki) side of the road. Some are *in situ* and others are housed in the museum. Also on the north side of the road is a courtyard laid out with a black and white geometric mosaic, and six re-erected columns.

The **museum**, which is at the southern side of the site, is one of Greece's best on-site museums. In Room 1, there's a reconstruction of a wall from a house at Pella, and a splendid circular table inlaid with intricate floral and abstract designs, which it is thought belonged to Philip II. In Room 2 are the mosaics which have been lifted from the site.

The site and museum (☎ 0382-31 160/278) are open Tuesday to Saturday from 8.30 am to 3 pm. Admission to the site (including museum entry) is 400 dr. There is a drinking fountain outside the museum, and a kafeneion next to the north side of the site.

Getting There & Away

There are frequent buses to Pella from Thessaloniki (40 minutes, 420 dr). If you use the bus and wish to visit Pella and Vergina in one day, after visiting Pella, take a Thessaloniki bus back along the main road, and get off at Halkidona, from where you can pick up a bus to Vergina.

MT OLYMPUS Ορος Ολυμπος

Mt Olympus, chosen by the ancients as the abode of their gods, is Greece's highest and most awe-inspiring mountain. It has around 1700 plant species, some of which are rare and endemic. The lower slopes are covered with forests of holm oak, arbutus, cedar and conifers, the higher ones with oak, beech, black and Balkan pine. The mountain also maintains a varied bird life. In 1937 it became Greece's first national park.

In August 1913, Christos Kakalos, a native of Litohoro, and the Swiss climbers, Frederic Boissonas and Daniel Bood-Bovy, were the first mortals to reach the summit of Mytikas (2917 metres), Olympus' highest peak.

Litohoro Λιτόχωρο

The village of Litohoro (Lee-TO-ho-ro, altitude 305 metres) is the place to make for if you wish to climb Olympus. The village developed in the 1920s as a health resort for the tubercular; later it settled comfortably into its role as 'base camp' for climbing Olympus. However, in recent years it has once again begun to promote its health resort image. This has resulted in difficulties in finding a hotel room in July and August, particularly at weekends, as they are occupied by the frail, the unfit and the chain smokers, who couldn't climb the Acropolis, let alone the mighty mount.

Orientation Litohoro's main road is Agiou Nikolaou, which, if you are coming from Thessaloniki or Katerini, is the road by which you will enter the village; it leads up to the central square of Plateia Kentriki. On the right side of this road is a large army camp. The road to Pronia, where the main trail up Olympus begins, is a turn-off to the right, just before the central square.

The bus terminal is just south of Plateia Kentriki on Agiou Nikolaou.

Information The post office is on Plateia Kentriki. The OTE is on Agiou Nikolaou, almost opposite the turn-off for Pronia. Litohoro's postcode is 60200 and the telephone code is 0352. The National Bank of Greece is on Plateia Kentriki. The police station (☎ 81 100/1) is on the corner of the road to Pronia. There is a health centre (☎ 22 222) five km away, at the turn-off for the village from the main coastal highway.

Due to a lack of government funding Litohoro's EOT office was not open at the time this book was researched, so a friendly helpful person was replaced by an unfriendly, unhelpful computer in the office window. The computer waxed lyrical about the beauties of Olympus, but didn't tell you how the hell to get up there. The office is a wooden building on Agiou Nikolaou, just before the turn-off for Pronia.

The EOS (Hellenic Alpine Club; ☎ 81 944) in Litohoro has helpful English-speaking staff who give information about Olympus and a free pamphlet giving details of some of the treks. To get to this office, when you are facing inland on Agiou Nikolaou, turn left opposite the Myrto Hotel and follow the signs. The office is open Monday to Friday from 9 am to 1 pm and 6 to 8.30 pm, and on Saturday from 9 am to 1 pm. It's closed on Sunday. The EOS has three refuges on Olympus.

The SEO (Association of Greek Climbers; ☎ 82 300) also gives information, but you are more likely to find someone who speaks

English at the EOS. To get to the SEO, walk along the road to Pronia and take the first turn left and first left again. The SEO office is open from 6 to 10 pm every day, and has one refuge on Olympus.

Places to Stay There's a plethora of camp sites along the coast around the turn-off for Litohoro. They include *Olympios Zeus* (☎ 22 115/6/7), *Olympos Beach* (☎ 22 112 or 81 437) and *Minerva* (☎ 22 177/8). All of these sites have good facilities and a taverna, snack bar and minimarket. All these sites have the same telephone area code as Litohoro: 0352.

Litohoro's clean, well-run *YHA Hostel* (☎ 81 311 or 82 176) charges 900 dr for a bed and 400 dr for linen. Single/double rooms are 1800/3000 dr. Motorbike rental is 2400 dr, bicycle rental is 720 dr, mountain-clothing hire is 550 dr, mountain-boot hire 500 dr and left-luggage storage is 300 dr. Maps and books on Olympus are on sale at the hostel. The warden, Kostas Irandos, is an experienced mountaineer. He doesn't suffer fools, but if you are a serious trekker, and genuinely interested in Olympus he is an invaluable source of information. You will find the hostel by following the signs from Plateia Kentriki.

Litohoro's cheapest hotel is the clean, well-kept D class *Hotel Markesia* (☎ 21 831/2), which costs 3750/4500/5400 dr for singles/doubles/triples with private bathrooms. From Plateia Kentriki, facing inland, turn left onto 28 Oktovriou and the hotel is along here on the left. The pleasant C class *Hotel Aphrodite* (☎ 81 415), on Plateia Kentriki, has rooms for 4000/5200/6500 dr with private bathrooms. The D class *Park Hotel* (☎ 81 252), next to the army camp and on the right side of Agiou Nikolaou as you face inland, has single/double rates of 4000/4500 dr.

Litohoro's poshest hotel is the C class *Mytro Hotel* (☎ 81 398/498), where all the rooms have a telephone, private bathrooms and balconies and cost 4500/5500/6700 dr. The hotel, which is on Agiou Nikolaou, near the central square, has a lovely wood-panelled Tyrol-style TV lounge-cum-bar.

Places to Eat *Olympos Taverna*, on Agiou Nikolaou opposite the Park Hotel, is good value with meals for 650 dr. *Deas Psistaria*, next to the OTE, has generous portions of charcoal grill chicken for 750 dr. *To Pazari*, just down from the Hotel Markesia on 28 Oktovriou, specialises in fish dishes; fried sardines are 650 dr and fried kalamaria is 750 dr.

Getting There & Away There are many buses from the intercity bus station in Katerini to Litohoro (200 dr) and nine a day between Thessaloniki and Litohoro. Athens-Thessaloniki and Volos-Thessaloniki buses will drop you off on the main highway, from where you can catch the Katerini-Litohoro bus.

Litohoro train station is on the Athens-Volos-Thessaloniki line (nine trains a day) but the station is close to the coast nine km from Litohoro, so you must walk from the station to the main road (150 metres) to pick up the Katerini-Litohoro bus.

Getting Around Motorbikes and bicycles can be hired at the Litohoro YHA. See under Places to Stay for details.

Mt Olympus Trails

The following trails by no means exhaust the possibilities on Olympus, but they are the ones which between the months of June and September can be tackled by anyone who is fit – no mountaineering experience or special equipment is required. It takes two days to climb Olympus, spending one night at a refuge. However, if you are a keen trekker you'll want to spend longer exploring the mountain – it really deserves more than a couple of days.

You will need to take warm clothing as it can become very cold and wet, even in August. Sunblock cream is also essential as much of the climbing is above the tree line. Climbing boots are the most suitable footwear, but sturdy shoes or trainers will suffice. A good topographical map of the region is essential. The relevant Korfes map of the Olympus region is probably the best available. Maps can be obtained from the youth hostel in Litohoro.

Do your homework before you begin the trek by talking with someone at the EOS or SEO (see Information in the previous section on Litohoro). Let them know how long you plan to trek and when you will return. Bear in mind that Olympus is a high and challenging mountain – it has claimed its share of lives.

For more comprehensive trekking information on Mt Olympus, including detailed trail descriptions, see Lonely Planet's *Trekking in Greece*.

Litohoro to Pronia The most popular trail up Olympus begins at Pronia (Πρόνοια), a tiny hamlet 18 km from Litohoro. It has a car park, basic taverna and a source of water, but no telephone and there is no bus service. The EOS-owned Dimitris Boundolas Refuge (Refuge D) is halfway along the Litohoro-Pronia road at Stavros (930 metres). It is open from April to November. If you plan to do the six-hour trek from Diastavrosi to the SEO refuge you may wish to stay here.

Most people either opt to drive, hitch or take a taxi (4500 dr) to Pronia, but if you have sufficient stamina, you can trek there along an 18-km marked trail, which follows the course of the Ennipeas River. The strenuous four-hour trek is over sharply undulating terrain but offers glorious views. It begins beyond the cemetery in Litohoro and ends just before the taverna at Pronia. Just one km before Pronia you can can look at the ruined **Monastery of Agiou Dionisos** which was built at the beginning of the 16th century and blown up by the Turks in 1828. It was rebuilt only to be blown up again by the Nazis in 1943 who believed resistance fighters were using it as a hide out.

Pronia to Spilios Agapitos (Refuge A) The trail begins just beyond the taverna in Pronia; you must fill up with water here as it is the last source before Spilios Agapitos (Σπήλαιο Αγαπητός). The trail is well maintained and well used – there is no chance of getting lost and you will meet other trekkers along the way. It is possible to go up on a mule (5000 dr) – contact the EOS for details. The trail is a steep path which passes first through thick forests of deciduous trees and then through conifers. It takes around 2½ hours to reach the refuge.

Refuge A (☎ 0352-81 800) can accommodate up to 90 people. It has cold showers and serves very good meals from 6 am to 9 pm, both to guests and to those people just popping in. The warden, Kostas Zolotas, speaks fluent English, is an experienced mountaineer and will be able to answer any questions you may have. The cost of staying at the refuge, which is open from May to October, is 1200 dr a night (900 dr for Alpine Club members). If you wish to stay during July and August it is advisable to make a reservation either through the EOS in Litohoro or Thessaloniki, or by telephoning the refuge.

Refuge A to Mytikas (Via Kaki Skala) The path to Mytikas (Μύτικας) begins just behind Refuge A. Fill up with water because there is no source beyond here. The last of the trees thin out rapidly; the path is still marked by red slashes and once again it is easy to follow. After one to 1½ hours you will come to a sign pointing right to the SEO refuge. To reach Mytikas continue straight ahead. The path now zigzags over the scree for another hour before reaching the summit ridge. From the ridge there is a 500 metre drop into the chasm of **Kasania** (the Cauldron).

Just before the drop, in an opening to the right, is the beginning of **Kaki Skala** (Rotten Stairway), which leads in 40 minutes of rock scrambling to the summit of Mytikas; the route is marked by red slashes on the rocks. The route keeps just below the drop into Kasania, although at a couple of places you can look down into the cauldron – a dramatic sight. If you have never done rock scrambling before take a look at Kaki Skala and decide then and there if you want to tackle it. Many turn back at this stage, but just as many novices tackle Kaki Skala. If you decide against it, all is not lost, for if you turn left at the summit ridge, an easy path leads in 15 to 20 minutes to Skolio peak (2911 metres), Olympus' second highest peak.

Mytikas to SEO Refuge (Giossos Apostolides) After you've admired the breathtaking views from Mytikas, signed the summit book and said a prayer of thanks to the gods for helping you up, and another, asking them to help you down, you are faced with the choice of returning to Refuge A via Kaki Skala or going on to the *SEO Refuge* of Giossos Apostolides. At 2720 metres this is the highest refuge in the whole of the Balkans with a stunning panorama of the major peaks of Olympus. The refuge has beds for 90 people and meals are served. It has no showers or natural drinking water, but bottled water is sold; it is much less visited than Refuge A. The EOS *Refuge C*, called Christos Kakkalos, is nearby, and has beds for 18 people; it is only open during July and August.

Neither of these refuges has a telephone. To get to them you can return via Kaki Skala to the path signposted to the SEO Refuge; this path is called Zonaria and leads to the refuge in one hour. Alternatively, you can descend Mytikas via **Louki Couloir**, which begins just north of the summit and is another 45-minute rock scramble. A few experienced climbers claim Louki Couloir is easier than Kaki Skala, but the general consensus is that it is more difficult – it is certainly more sheer and prone to rock falls. At the bottom of Louki Couloir you meet up with the Zonaria path. Turn left onto the path and you will reach the SEO lodge in 20 minutes.

SEO Refuge to Diastavrosi The refuge is on the edge of the Plateau of the Muses and from here a well-maintained path leads in 4½ hours to Diastavrosi (Διασταύρωση), on the Pronio-Litohoro road. From the plateau the path goes along a ridge called Lemon (Neck) with the Enipeau ravine on the right and the Papa Rema ravine on the left. After one hour you arrive at Skoula summit (2485 metres) and from here it is 1½ hours to

Petrostrounga (the stony sheepfold). The next stretch of path leads through woodland to a small meadow known as **Barba** and from here it is 40 minutes to Diastavrosi, which is 14 km from Litohoro.

Ancient Dion Δίον

Recently discovered ancient Dion is an extensive, well-watered site at the foot of Mt Olympus, just north of Litohoro and 16 km south of Katerini. It was the sacred city of the Macedons, who gathered here to worship the Olympian gods. Alexander the Great made sacrifices to the Olympic gods here, before setting off to conquer the world.

Dion's origins are unknown but there is evidence that an earth goddess of fertility was first worshipped here. Later, other gods were worshipped, including Asklepios, the god of medicine. The most interesting discovery so far is the evocative **Sanctuary to Isis**, the Egyptian goddess, in a lush low-lying part of the site. Its votive statues were found virtually intact with traces of colour remaining. Copies of these statues have been placed in the positions of the originals, which are now in the site's museum. Also worth seeking out is the magnificent well-preserved mosaic floor, dating from 200 AD, which depicts the **Dionysos Triumphal Epiphany**. During the Olympos Festival which takes place during August plays are performed at the reconstructed theatre at the site.

The site's **museum** (☎ 0351-53 206) is well laid out with a large collection of statues and votive offerings from ancient Dion; labelling is in English and Greek. On sale at both the site and the museum is a pamphlet in English about Dion. It costs 300 dr and without this the site will have little meaning, for as yet labelling and signposts are nonexistent.

The site is open Monday to Friday from 8 am to 6 pm and Saturday, Sunday and holidays from 8.30 am to 3 pm. Admission is 500 dr. The museum's opening times are Tuesday to Sunday from 8 am to 5 pm and Monday from 12.30 to 5 pm. Admission is 400 dr.

Places to Stay As it is a bit of a hassle to get to Dion, you may wish to stay overnight in the modern village. The pleasant C class *Dion Hotel* (☎ 53 336) is on the main road in (modern) Dion, near the bus stop. Singles/doubles with private bathrooms are 3550/5500 dr.

Getting There & Away There are no buses from Litohoro to Dion; you must first go to Katerini from where there are 12 buses a day (150 dr). The Dion bus terminal is 400 metres from Katerini's intercity bus station. To reach it, walk out of the intercity bus station, cross the road, and walk along Odos Karaiskaki, which is signposted to the centre. Continue along here for 150 metres and you will come to a crossroad; turn left onto Odos Pangari Tsaldari.

Walk a little way along here to a T-junction and turn right – the road is still called Tsaldari. Walk 100 metres along here and you will come to a five-road intersection. Cross over the road to Restaurant Olympos, make a right turn and take the second turn left onto Kosma Ioannou. Continue up here for 40 metres and you will come to the Dion bus station on the left, opposite the Orfeas cinema.

Once in the village of modern Dion, both the site and museum are clearly signposted.

VERIA Βέροια

Most people merely pass through Veria (VER-ia, population 37,000), 75 km west of Thessaloniki, en route to the ancient site of Vergina. But Veria, capital of the nome of Imathia, is a fascinating town, with some curious little churches and many houses from the Turkish era.

Orientation & Information

The town's two main squares, Plateia Antoniou and Plateia Orologiou, are one km apart. Connecting them are the town's two main thoroughfares: the modern Odos Venizelou which halfway along becomes Odos Mitropoleos, and the traditional Vasileos Konstantinou (also called Odos Kentriki). To reach Plateia Antonios from the

intercity bus station, walk out of the station onto Odos Iras, turn right and immediately left onto Malakous, and the square is a little way along here with Venizelou and Vasileos Konstantinou both running off to the left. The train station is quite a way from the town centre on the road to Thessaloniki.

The post office is at Mitropoleos 33 and the OTE at No 45. Veria's postcode is 59100 and the telephone code is 0331. The National Bank of Greece is on the corner of Mitropoleos and Ippokratous. There is no tourist office or tourist police; the regular police (☎ 22 391/233) are next door to the post office on Mitropoleos.

Things to See

The most interesting part of Veria is the old Turkish quarter. For a short walk around this area, begin by walking down Vasileos Konstantinou from Plateia Antoniou. The narrow and winding Vasileos Konstantinou is the commercial street of old Veria, flanked by old-fashioned tailor shops, bookbinders, kafeneia and antique shops. Halfway along on the right is a huge ancient-looking plane tree and opposite is the dilapidated **Old Metropoleos Cathedral**. To reach the residential part of the old Turkish quarter, turn right at the plane tree onto Odos Goudi.

Many of the old houses here are built of wattle and daub with overhanging first floors. Where the road forks, turn left onto Odos Panagiou Dexia. Along here on the right is the **Church of Panagiou Dexia**. This is one of the town's many churches built in the 17th and 18th centuries when Turkish law forbade Christian worship, so the churches were camouflaged as houses.

At the bottom of Panagios Dexias, turn left onto Dimosthenous and take the right fork to reach the footbridge over the river. From here there are pretty views of the river which flows through a verdant gorge. Retrace your steps to Dimosthenous and take the first turn right onto Southou, which leads back to Vasileos Konstantinou. Turn right and you will come to the crumbling old **Mosque of Orta Tzami** on the left, set back from the road.

Continue a little further along to reach Plateia Orologiou.

On the other side of town on Odos Kontogiorgaki, between the Macedonia Hotel and Odos Paster, there are more Turkish houses and the **Church of Agios Stefanos**, which was also camouflaged as a house.

The **Archaeological Museum** is in this part of town on Leoforos Anixou. It contains some finds from the tombs of Vergina and Levkadia. The museum is open from 8.30 am to 3 pm from Tuesday to Sunday. Admission is 400 dr. To reach it, take any of the roads running east from Venizelou, which will bring you to Leoforos Anixos.

Places to Stay – bottom end

The best value of Veria's five hotels is *Hotel Veroi* (☎ 22 866 or 23 566) on Plateia Orologiou. The hotel is very clean with large comfortably furnished single/double rooms with balconies, costing 3500/5500 dr with private bathrooms. The nearest hotel to the bus station is *Hotel Vasilissa Vergina* (☎ 22 301 or 24 886), which has singles/doubles for 4600/7000 dr with private bathrooms. The hotel is on the corner of Plateia Antoniou and Venizelou.

The C class *Hotel Politimi* (☎ 64 902/946/924), Megalou Alexandrou 35, has rooms for 5200/6500 dr with private bathrooms. At the *Hotel Villa Elia* (☎ 26 800/1/2), Elias 16, room rates are 5800/7100 dr with private bathrooms. Both Elias and Megalou Alexandrou are left turns off Venizelou, coming from Plateia Antonios.

Places to Stay – middle

The best of Veria's hotels is the B class *Hotel Macedonia* (☎ 66 902/946/924/968; fax 66 902), Kontogiorgaki 50. The spacious, tastefully furnished rooms are 7900/9900 dr with private bathrooms. To reach it walk along Venizelou, turn left onto Elias and right at the Top Café, onto Paster; the hotel is at the end of here on the right.

Places to Eat

Giros, souvlaki and pizza establishments are ubiquitous, but finding other food is more difficult. *Thalassina Taverna*, Odos Tsoupeli, has a good choice of fish dishes. A generous full meal will cost about 1700 dr. The taverna is on a quiet side street with out-door eating under a grape arbour. Coming from Plateia Antonios, Tsoupeli is the third turn right along Venizelou. The *Café Kostas*, close to the Hotel Veroi, on Plateia Orologiou, has good cheese and spinach pie for 200 dr.

Getting There & Away

Bus Frequent buses leave from Veria's intercity bus station for Thessaloniki (920 dr), Edessa (600 dr) and the ancient site of Vergina (190 dr).

Train There are six trains a day in either direction on the Thessaloniki-Veria-Edessa-Florina line.

VERGINA Βεργίνα

The ancient site of Vergina (Ver-GEE-na), 11 km south-east of Veria, is ancient Aigai, the first capital of Macedon. The capital was later transferred to Pella, but Aigai continued to be the royal burial place. Philip II was assassinated here in 336 BC at the wedding reception of his daughter, Kleopatra.

To fully appreciate the significance of the discoveries, you need to visit Thessaloniki's Archaeological Museum, where the magnificent finds of Philip II's tomb are displayed, along with Philip II himself! Unfortunately, Philip's tomb is off limits to visitors as it is still being excavated.

The ruins of ancient Vergina are spread out, but well signposted from the modern village of the same name. The **Macedonian Tomb**, 500 metres uphill from the village, has a façade of four Ionic half columns. Inside is a marble throne. Continue 400 metres further up the road to reach the ruins of an extensive palatial complex, built as a summer residence for King Antigonos Gonatas (278-240 BC). The focal point of the site is a large Doric peristyle which was surrounded by pebble mosaic floors. One of the mosaics, with a beautiful floral design, is well preserved and *in situ*. A large oak tree on the highest point of the site affords some welcome shade.

Both this site (☎ 0331-92 337) and the Macedonian tomb are open Tuesday to Saturday from 8 am to 3 pm and Sunday from 8.30 am to 3 pm. Entrance to both is free. There is a café opposite the Macedonian tomb.

EDESSA Εδεσσα

Edessa (population 16,000) is the capital of the nome of Pella. Extolled by Greeks for its many waterfalls, it is little visited by foreign tourists. Until the discovery of the royal tombs at Vergina, Edessa was believed to be the site of the ancient Macedonian city of Aigai.

Orientation

Edessa's intercity bus station is on the corner of Filipou and Pavlou Mela. To reach the town centre cross over Filipou and walk straight ahead along Pavlou Mela to the T-junction, and turn right onto Egnatias. Almost immediately the road forks: the left fork continues as Egnatias; the right fork is Demokratias. These two streets, along with Filipou, are the town's main thoroughfares.

The train station is opposite the end of 18 Oktovriou. To reach the town centre from here walk straight ahead up 18 Oktovriou for 400 metres to a major road junction. From here the biggest waterfall (Katarrakton) is signposted sharp left; veer half right for Demokratias.

Information

There is no EOT or tourist police; the regular police are on Iroon Polytechniou, which runs between Filipou and Democrias, but the only police officer who speaks English is not very helpful.

The post office is at Democrias 26. The OTE is on Agiou Dimitrios. To reach it turn right from Pavlou Mela, by the Hotel Pella, and it's signposted off to the left. Edessa's postcode is 58200 and the telephone code is 0381. The National Bank of Greece is at Democrias 1.

Waterfalls

Edessa stands on an escarpment in the foothills of Mt Vermion. Its main attraction is the numerous streams and waterfalls which flow through the town. These culminate in the biggest waterfall, called **Katarrakton**, which plunges dramatically down a cliff to the agricultural plain below. The cliff is mantled with abundant vegetation and there are wonderful views of the vast plain which extends all the way to Thessaloniki. The numerous streams which flow under the town's little stone bridges are fringed by pedestrian ways and charming little parks with outdoor cafés.

Places to Stay – bottom end

Edessa's cheapest hotel is the D class *Hotel Olympion* (☎ 23 485), on Democrias. The tidy single/double rooms cost 2500/3500 dr with shared bathrooms. From the bus station, cross Filipou and walk up Pavlou Mela to the T-junction and you will see the hotel on the right. Diagonally opposite is the D class *Hotel Pella* (☎ 23 541), Egnatias 30, with rooms for 3000/4000 dr with private bathrooms.

The D class *Hotel Elena* (☎ 23 218/951), Plateia Timenidon, has light and airy rooms for 3300/6000 dr with private bathrooms. From the bus station turn right at Filipou, walk three blocks to the road junction with signposts to the waterfalls and Florina, turn right onto Arkranteleimonos and you will see the hotel a little way along here on the left.

Places to Stay – middle

Edessa's best hotel is the B class *Hotel Katarraktes* (☎ 22 300/1/2), where rates are 7000/9200 dr. The hotel has comfortable, traditionally furnished rooms with private bathrooms and balconies. Follow the signposts for the waterfall, and look for the hotel on the left, just before Katarrakton.

Places to Eat

A very good psistaria (the owners say it is the town's only psistaria, but this might be a bit of an exaggeration) is the *Tzingas Brothers Taverna/Psistaria*, 26 Filipou, opposite the bus station. Chicken is 450 dr, roast beef is

500 dr and giros is 700 dr. The town's most traditional taverna is *Taverna Rolio*, Agiou Dimitriou 5, near the OTE. Scrumptious fried courgettes and fried peppers are 200 dr, Greek salad is 500 dr, meatballs are 700 dr and souvlaki is 800 dr.

Getting There & Away

Bus From the main bus station there are many buses to Thessaloniki, six a day to Veria and three a day to Athens. Four buses a day go to Florina and Kastoria from a second bus station, marked by a bus sign at the corner of Egnatias and Pavlou Mela.

Train There are six trains a day both ways on the Thessaloniki-Florina line. The stretch between Edessa and Florina is particularly beautiful as it skirts the western shore of Lake Vergokitida. The journey is meant to take 1½ hours, but Greek trains being what they are, it can take twice as long.

FLORINA Φλώρινα

The mountain town of Florina (FLO-ri-na, population 12,500) is the capital of the nome of Florina. Tourists used to come to Florina only because it was the last town in Greece before the Yugoslav border, but it's a lively town, and a pleasant place for an overnight stopover if you are touring the area.

If you enjoy your stay in Florina you're in good company. Greece's most famous film director, Theodore Angelopoulos, loves Florina (although it is not his birthplace). Two of his films, *Alexander the Great* and *The Hesitant Step of the Stork* were made on location here.

Florina is the only place from which you can take a bus to the Prespa Lakes.

Orientation & Information

The main street is Pavlou Mela, which leads to the central square of Plateia Georgiou Modi. To reach here from the train station, walk straight ahead with the Archaeological Museum on your left. From Plateia Georgiou Modi, turn right onto Stefanou Dragmou to reach the intercity bus station which is 250 metres along on the left. If you turn left from

Plateia Georgiou Modi, onto 25 Martiou, you will reach the river. Odos Megalou Alexandrou is straight ahead from the square.

The post office is at Kalergi 22; walk along Stefanou Dragoumi towards the bus station and Kalergi is off to the left. The OTE is at Tyrnovou 5. Walking along Pavlou Mela from the train station, Tyrnovou is a turn-off to the left. Florina's postcode is 53100 and the telephone code is 0385.

There is no EOT or tourist police; the regular police telephone number is ☎ 22 100.

Archaeological Museum

The museum is in a modern building near the train station. It is well laid out, but labels are in Greek only. The curator will show you around but his English is limited. Downstairs there is pottery from the Neolithic, early Iron Age and Bronze Age and grave stele and statues from the Roman period. Upstairs there are some Byzantine reliefs and fragments of frescoes, and finds from an as yet unidentified town built by Philip II, discovered on the nearby hill of Agiou Karalambos. The museum is open Tuesday to Saturday from 8.30 am to 3 pm. Admission is 400 dr.

Riverside

Old Florina occupied both river banks and many Turkish houses and neoclassical mansions survive. The town has a thriving artistic community, and the Society for the Friends of Art of Florina has restored one of the neoclassical mansions on the river bank, which is now the **Museum of Modern Art**, Leoforos Eleftheriou 103. The museum houses a permanent collection of works by contemporary Greek artists and hosts frequent exhibitions.

It is open from 6.30 to 9.30 pm on Monday, Wednesday and Saturday, and 10 am to 1.30 pm on Sunday. Admission is free. To reach the museum walk down 25 Martiou, cross the bridge over the river and turn right. Even if you are not interested in art, this is a pleasant walk along the river bank.

Places to Stay – bottom end

Florina has only one D class hotel, the *Hotel Ellenis* (☎ 22 671/2), Pavlou Mela 39. It's clean enough if you can tolerate the bizarre décor of red-carpeted walls (yes, walls) and plastic 'wood' panelling. The single/double room rates are 4000/6000 dr with private bathrooms. Coming from the train station the hotel is on the left. Up a notch, the C class *Hotel Antigone* (☎ 23 180/490/1/2), Arianou 1, has slightly jaded but pleasant rooms for 4300/6500 dr. Turn right onto Stefanou Dragmou, from Plateia Georgiou Modi, and the hotel is 200 metres along on the left, close to the bus station.

Places to Stay – middle

The B class Hotel Lyngos (☎ 28 322/3), Tagmatarchou Naoum 1, just north of Plateia Georgiou Modi, has spacious and comfortable single/double rooms for 5000/8250 dr.

Places to Stay – top end

The B class *King Alexander* (☎ 23 501/2), in an elevated position above town on Leoforos Nikis, has luxurious singles/doubles for 7200/10,600 dr.

Places to Eat

The *Taverna Okostatis*, 25 Martiou 18, serves tasty grilled food which is reasonably priced, despite the taverna's elegant ambience. Aubergine salad is 200 dr, Greek salad is 450 dr, roast chicken is 550 dr and souvlaki is 650 dr. *Restaurant Olympos*, Megalou Alexandrou 22 (on the right as you walk from the square) has a large choice of well-prepared low-priced ready food. Bean and aubergine stews are 350 dr and stuffed peppers and stuffed tomatoes are 550 dr. There is outdoor eating in a pretty courtyard. Both of these restaurants are near Plateia Georgiou Modi and are open for lunch and dinner.

Getting There & Away

Bus From the main bus station there is one bus a day to Athens (leaving at 8.30 am), six buses a day to Thessaloniki, seven to Kozani, three to Kastoria (via Amindeo) and two a day to Agiou Germanos (for the Prespa Lakes) at 7.45 am and 2.30 pm.

Train (Domestic) Florina is at the end of the Thessaloniki-Veria-Edessa line. There are six trains a day in both directions. The approximate journey time from Thessaloniki is four hours, but it can take longer.

Train (International) See the Getting There & Away chapter for details on going to the Former Yugoslav Republic of Macedonia from Florina.

PRESPA LAKES

In the mountainous north-west corner of Greece, at an altitude of 850 metres, are the two lakes of Megali Prespa (Great Prespa) and Mikri Prespa (Little Prespa). The lakes are separated by a narrow strip of land. The area is one of outstanding natural beauty and is little visited by foreign tourists. The road from Florina passes through thick forests and lush meadows with grazing cattle; if you have your own transport there are lots of picnic tables.

Mikri Prespa has an area of 43 sq km and is almost entirely in Greece, except for the south-western tip which is in Albania. Megali Prespa is the largest lake in the Balkans; the biggest part is in former Yugoslavia (1000 sq km); 38 sq km is in Greece and a small part in the south-west is in Albania. Much of the shore of Megali Prespa is of precipitous rock, which rises dramatically from the chilly blue water. The Prespa area became a national park in 1977.

Mikri Prespa Μικρή Πρέσπα

This lake is a wildlife refuge of considerable interest to ornithologists. It is surrounded by thick reed beds where numerous species of birds, including cormorants, pelicans, egrets, herons and ibis, nest. The lake's islet of **Agiou Achilios** has ancient Byzantine remains; boat operators will take you across for a nominal fee.

Psarades Ψαράδες

The village of Psarades, on Megali Prespa,

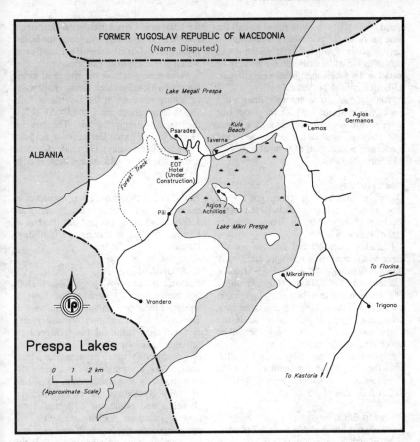

FORMER YUGOSLAV REPUBLIC OF MACEDONIA
(Name Disputed)

Lake Megali Prespa

Kula Beach

Psarades

Taverna

Agios Germanos

Lemos

ALBANIA

Forest Track

EOT Hotel (Under Construction)

Agios Achillios

Pili

Lake Mikri Prespa

To Florina

Mikrolimni

Vrondero

Trigono

Prespa Lakes

0   1   2 km

(Approximate Scale)

To Kastoria

70 km from Florina, is a picturesque village which still has a number of old wattle- and-daub houses. Before WW II Psarades was a thriving fishing village with a population of over 1000, but it's now home to little more than 100 people. Many of the remaining middle-aged men in the town were victims of the enforced evacuation of children during the civil war. Some spent as long as 10 years in Albania or Hungary.

Orientation & Information The village of Psarades has no bank or post office, but Philipos Papadopoulos, the owner of the grocery shop on the village square, will exchange cash. There is no OTE but a few of the tavernas have metered telephones. Germanos Papadopoulos, the owner of Taverna Paradosi, speaks excellent English having spent many years in Canada. He'll be happy to give information about the village.

Megali Prespa Μεγάλη Πρέσπα
Local fishermen will take you on a lake trip, where you'll get good views of Albania and former Yugoslavia, as well as seeing many birds. Pandelis Sialtsis (☎ 51 272) will take you on a 40-minute trip for 1500 dr. Modern

speed boats will whiz you round in half the time for twice the price, but it's much more fun to go in Pandelis' boat which looks almost as old as he does. He can usually be found at the lake shore; otherwise villagers will direct you to his home.

You can take a pleasant walk along a dirt track, which skirts the lake for about one hour, before going inland through a forest. The track begins at the unfinished (and apparently abandoned) EOT hotel across the lake from Psarades.

Places to Stay

There is no official camp site but you may be able to camp freelance at Kula Beach on the southern shore of Megali Prespa, five km east of Psarades.

Psarades' only official domatia are the clean and comfortable rooms of *Lazaros & Helen Christianopoulos* (☎ 0385-51 327), which cost 3600/4000 dr for singles/doubles. The rooms are above the family taverna, at the far end of the village. Several other families rent rooms unofficially, so if the Christianopoulos' rooms are full you will be directed to another place to stay.

If you don't mind being away from the lakes the village of Agios Germanos has one place to stay, the *Pension I Prespes* (☎ 0385-51 320). Doubles are 5200 dr.

Places to Eat

Five tavernas line the waterfront at Psarades. They all dish up excellent fresh fish, straight from the lake. Menus and prices seem to be identical; small fish are 570 dr and carp and trout are 850 dr.

Getting There & Away

Bus The only town with a direct bus link to the lakes is Florina. At the time of writing there was no bus to Psarades but check this with the bus station in Florina as the schedule might change. There are two buses on weekdays to Agiou Germanos village, 16 km east of Psarades. The buses leave Florina at 7.45 am and 2.30 pm. These buses stop at the road junction between the two lakes: left leads to Kula Beach and Psarades and right leads to

the villages of Lemos and Agiou Germanos. Another bus bound for Pili meets the buses. If you get this bus ask to be off at Kula Beach, which is five km from Psarades.

From here you have the choice of either hitching a lift to Psarades, a long uphill walk, or asking someone at the taverna at Kula Beach to telephone for a taxi (☎ 51 247) – they will willingly do this. The bus for Florina leaves Agiou Germanos at 6.15 am and 4 pm on weekdays. On a Saturday there is only one bus at 7.15 am and there is none on Sunday.

Taxi If you decide to use a taxi for part of or the whole journey, prices from Psarades are 1500 dr to Lemos (to pick up the bus to Florina), 6000 dr to Florina and 7000 dr to Kastoria.

KASTORIA Καστοριά

Kastoria (Kas-to-ri-A, population 17,000) lies between Mts Grammos and Vitsi in western Macedonia, 200 km north-west of Thessaloniki. It is regarded by many Greeks as their most beautiful town. Indeed its setting is exemplary, occupying the isthmus of a promontory which projects into a tree-fringed lake, surrounded by mountains. Its architecture is also outstanding, consisting of many Byzantine and post-Byzantine churches and numerous 17th and 18th-century mansions, called *arkhontika*, because they were the homes of the *arkhons* – the town's leading citizens. In Kastoria the arkhontika were the dwellings of rich fur merchants.

The town has a long tradition of fur production. Jewish furriers (refugees from Europe) came to Kastoria because of the large numbers of beaver living by the lake. They carried out their trade with such zeal that by the 19th century the beaver was extinct in the area. The furriers then began to import scraps of fur. There is still a fur industry here; you will see fur workshops, warehouses and shops all over town.

Orientation

Kastoria's intercity bus station is on 3

Septemvriou, one block inland from the lakeside. To reach the town centre from here, with your back to the station office turn left and walk to Plateia Davaki which is one of the city's main squares. Odos Mitropoleos, the town's main commercial thoroughfare, runs south-east from here to the other main square of Plateia Omonias (Omonia Square).

Information

Kastoria's EOT (☎ 24 484) is in the town hall on Odos Ioustinianou, which runs north-east from Plateia Davaki. The staff are helpful and give out lots of brochures, maps and information.

The post office is at the northern end of Leoforos Megalou Alexandrou, which skirts the lakeside. The OTE is on Agiou Athanasiou which runs off Plateia Davaki just north of Mitropoleos. Kastoria's postcode is 52100 and the telephone code is 0467.

The National Bank of Greece is on 11 Novembriou, just north of Plateia Davaki.

Byzantine Churches

Many of the numerous churches in Kastoria were originally private chapels attached to the arkhontika houses. Almost all of the churches are locked and gaining access to them is something of a Byzantine experience in itself. The key man (literally) for the ones around Plateia Omonias is Christos Philikas. If you can track him down he will be happy to open them up for you – ask around the kafeneia on the square. Another possibility is the Byzantine Museum's curator who may be able to contact someone who can show you some of the churches.

Even if you don't manage to get a look inside any churches, all is not lost, for some of them have external frescoes. One such church is the **Taxiarkhia of the Metropolis**, on Plateia Pavlou Mela, south of Plateia Omonias, which has a 13th-century fresco of the Madonna and Child above the entrance. Inside the church is the tomb of Pavlos Melas, a Macedonian hero who was killed by Bulgar terrorists during the struggles which culminated in the Balkan Wars. Melas' life is

documented in Thessaloniki's Museum of the Macedonian Struggle. Many streets in Macedonia are named Pavlou Mela in memory of this hero.

Museums

The new **Byzantine Museum** houses outstanding icons from many of the town's churches. It will help you to appreciate the churches if you visit this museum first. It is adjacent to the Xenia du Lac Hotel on Plateia Dexamenis. Opening times are 8 am to 2 pm Monday to Friday. Admission is 400 dr.

Most of the surviving arkhontika are in the southern part of the town in the area called Doltso. The most important ones are the Emmanouil, Basara, Natzi, Vergoula, Skoutari, Papia and Papaterpou mansions – named after the families who once lived in them.

One of the arkhontika has been converted into the **Kastorian Museum of Folklore**. The 530-year-old house belonged to the wealthy Neranzis Alvazis family. It is sumptuously furnished and has displays of ornaments, kitchen utensils and tools. The museum is open every day from 8.30 am to 6 pm. Admission is 200 dr. The guidebook at the museum is a bit steep at 1000 dr and probably unnecessry.

Lakeside Walk

A pretty tree-shaded nine-km road skirts the promontory. The lake is fringed by reeds which are the habitat of frogs and turtles and many species of birds. On the lake you will see many species of water fowl and great crested grebe.

Just under halfway is the **Monastery of Mavriotissa**. Father Gabriel, the resident monk, will give you a guided tour. Next to the monastery is the 11th-century **Church of St Mary** and the 16th-century **Church of St John the Theologian**. Both churches are liberally festooned with frescoes and icons, and are usually open. Beside the monastery there is a reasonably priced restaurant, which is the only source of refreshment on the walk. Begin the walk on the road to the hospital (see the map on page 332).

Kastoria

Places to Stay – bottom end

There is a free camp site in the grounds of the Mavriotissa Monastery (see Lakeside Walk).

Kastoria's cheapest hotel is the D class *Hotel Palladion* (☎ 22 493), Mitropoleos 40. The single/double rates are 1800/2700 dr with shared bathrooms. The C class *Hotel Acropolis* (☎ 22 537), Grammou 14, has tidy rooms for 2920/3550 dr with shared bathrooms and 3225/4220 dr with private bathrooms. The C class *Hotel Anesis* (☎ 29 410), Grammou 10, has clean and comfortable rooms for 3200/5000/6000 dr with

private bathrooms. To reach these two hotels from the bus station, facing the lake turn left, then take the first left onto Finikis Terias, then right at the T-junction and the hotels are on the left.

The C class *Hotel Kastoria* (☎ 29 453), Leoforos Nikis 122, has nicely furnished rooms with private bathrooms for 3500/6000 dr. It's in a prime location overlooking the lake at the north-eastern edge of town. The *Hotel Keletron* (☎ 22 676), 11 Novembriou 52 (an easterly continuation of Grammou), has comfortable rooms for 4000/5500 dr with private bathrooms.

The *Hotel Orestion* (☎ 22 257), Plateia Davaki 1, is a superior C class with very pleasant rooms for 5640/7330 dr with private bathrooms.

Places to Stay – middle

Kastoria's A class *Xenia Du Lac Hotel* (☎ 22 565), Plateia Dexamenis, is one of Greece's best Xenia's. It's in a quiet part of town and good value at 6772/10,380 dr with private bathrooms.

Places to Eat

One of the town's best restaurants is the bright and modern *Restaurant Omonoia* on Plateia Omonias, with meals under 650 dr. Nearby the *Mantziaris Restaurant*, Valala 8, is also good and cheap. *Restaurant Klimataria*, Orestion 6, is an old-fashioned, no-frills restaurant with a large choice of ready food. To reach the restaurant walk along 11 Novembriou towards the lake. In the same part of town, *Restaurant Orestion*, Ermou 37, is a nice, unpretentious little place which dishes up tasty low-priced ready food.

Getting There & Away

Air The airport is 10 km south of Kastoria. There are three flights a week from Kastoria to Athens (11,900 dr) on Monday, Wednesday and Friday. The Olympic Airways office (☎ 22 275 or 23 125) is at Leoforos Megalou Alexandrou 15.

Bus From Kastoria's intercity bus station there are six buses a day to Thessaloniki, five a day to Edessa and two to Athens.

HALKIDIKI Χαλκιδική

The Halkidiki peninsula is a large blob to the south-east of Thessaloniki, from which three long 'fingers' extend into the Aegean. The two large lakes of Koronia and Volvi separate the peninsula from the rest of Macedonia.

Halkidiki boasts 500 km of coastline, with superb sandy beaches, surrounded by calm, aquamarine sea. Unfortunately, these assets have been ruthlessly exploited and the two fingers of Kassandra and Sithonia consist of either luxurious holiday complexes for the rich and famous, or package tourist ghettos. The easternmost 'finger' of Halkidiki is the Monastic Republic of Mt Athos (Holy Mountain).

Halkidiki is not a place for budget or independent travellers as virtually all accommodation is booked solid throughout the summer. If you are camping then a visit is more practicable, as Halkidiki has many camp sites, which, even if they are bursting at the seams, are unlikely to turn you away. The free *Guide to Halkidiki* available at the Thessaloniki EOT lists most of these sites.

This guide aptly describes Halkidiki as one of 'the most dymanically (sic) developing areas of the country'.

Northern Halkidiki

The **Petralona Cave**, 56 km south-east of Thessaloniki in northern Halkidiki, has stalactites and stalagmites and is where the 700,000-year-old Neanderthal skull (evidence of one of Europe's earliest inhabitants) was found. The cave is open daily from 8.30 am to 4.30 pm. Admission is 550 dr. Doucas Tours (see Organised Tours in the Thessaloniki section) sometimes have tours to the caves.

The **Archaeological Museum** at Poligiros, capital of Halkidiki, houses finds from the peninsula's ancient sites including the Sanctuary of Zeus at Aphytis and the ancient city of Acanthos. The museum is open Tuesday to Sunday from 8.30 am to 3 pm. Admission is 400 dr.

Getting There & Away A bus goes to Petralona Cave at 1 pm every day, but does not return the same day. To get back to Thessaloniki you must walk or hitch to the village of Eleohoria, five km south, from where you can pick up a bus to Thessaloniki. All buses to the Sithonia 'finger' stop at Poligiros.

Kassandra Peninsula

The Kassandra (Κασσάνδρα) peninsula is less beautiful than the Sithonian peninsula. Its commercialism is horrendous and, even if you're not averse to package tourists, roaring motorbikes, fast-food joints and discos, you're unlikely to find accommodation. However, if you can't resist the lure and have a tent, there are lots of camp sites.

Getting There & Away There are 13 buses to Kalithea (1150 dr) on the east coast; 11 buses to Pefkahori (1500 dr), also on the east coast, via Kriopigi and Haniotis; seven buses to Paliouri (1650 dr) and three buses to Agia Paraskevi, both on the southern tip. All the buses leave from the bus terminal at Odos Karakassi 68 in Thessaloniki.

Sithonian Peninsula

Sithonia (Σιθωνία) is an improvement on Kassandra, even in the journey there. The landscape en route is quite spectacular with sweeping vistas of thickly forested hills.

An undulating road makes a loop around Sithonia, skirting wide bays, climbing into the pine-forested hills and dipping down to the resorts. Travelling down the west coast there are good stretches of sandy beach between **Nikitas** and **Paradissos**. Beyond here, **Nea Marmaras** is Sithonia's biggest resort, with a very crowded beach. The gigantic monstrosity of Porto Carras sits at one side of the bay. This is a luxury holiday complex for 3000 guests built by the wine-producing magnate John G Carras and modelled on Spanish Marbella – ugh.

Beyond Nea Marmaras the road climbs into the hills from where dirt roads lead down to several beaches and camp sites. **Toroni** and **Koufos** are small resorts at the south-west tip. The latter is a picturesque little place with a good beach. The southern tip of Sithonia is still relatively isolated and is scenically the most spectacular region of Halkidiki (excluding the Athos peninsula) – rocky, rugged and dramatic. As the road rounds the south-east tip, Mt Athos comes into view across the gulf, further adding to the spectacular vistas. In this region the resort of **Kalamitsi** has a gorgeous sandy beach.

Continuing up the east coast, the bus does a little two-km detour inland to the pleasant village of **Sikia**, which has less tourist hype than the coastal resorts. Back on the coast the resort of Sarti is next along the route.

Sarti Sarti has not succumbed entirely to the package-tourist industry and has a good laid-back atmosphere. From its beach there are splendid views of Mt Athos.

The town consists of two streets: one is the waterfront and the other is parallel and one block inland. The bus terminal is on the latter – a timetable is pinned to a nearby tree. There is no tourist office but the staff of Koutras Travel (☎ 0375-41 553), near the bus terminal, are helpful and speak English. The agency organises half-day mule treks in the mountains for 3500 dr, and Mt Athos cruises for 1700 dr.

Places to Stay If you decide to stay, *Sarti Beach Camping* (☎ 0375-41 450) is not only a camp site, but a holiday complex with a variety of accommodation. At their hotel, doubles with private bathrooms go for 6000 dr. Three and four-person bungalows are 10,000 and 12,000 dr respectively. Motorbikes can be rented at this camp site; 50cc cost 3000 dr. Travelling north it's on the right side of the main approach road – buses stop outside.

On the opposite side of the road *Motel, Hotel* or *Villa Phillis* (☎ 0375-41 360) – it's one place, it just can't decide what it is – has a friendly Greek-Australian owner and pleasant double/triple rooms for 6000/7000 dr. There are many domatia further north along this road.

Places to Eat The *Pergola Café Restaurant* in Sarti is a great place where you can have a drink, a snack or a full meal; it's open all day till late evening. Their pergola plate has a bit of everything – meatballs, kalamaria, souvlaki – and is excellent value at 1000 dr. From the bus stop turn left opposite Koutras Travel and you'll see the restaurant on the right – painted purple, grey and orange.

Getting There & Away Buses to Halkidiki leave from the bus terminal at Odos Karakassi 68 in Thessaloniki . There are six buses a day to Nea Marmaras (1650 dr); and five buses to Sarti (2300 dr). Most of the Sarti buses do a loop around the Sithonian peninsula enabling you to see the magnificent southern tip.

Secular Athos (Athos Peninsula)

Most of the easternmost of the three prongs of the Halkidiki peninsula is occupied by the Athonite monasteries. You will probably only want to pass through secular Athos to see the monasteries. The beaches are admittedly very fine in parts, but they have long been developed for the package-tour indus-

try. Soulless resorts based on large hotels with no interest in, or of interest to, independent travellers are dotted along the coast. **Ierissos** is one of the few real towns, notable mainly for being the terminus for the irregular boat serving the east-coast monasteries, but you can't enter Athos this way. The **canal** dug across the peninsula by the Persian King Xerxes in the 5th century BC for his invasion fleet is featured proudly on most maps, but it was filled in centuries ago and there's precious little for the untrained eye to see.

Ouranopolis Ουρανόπολη Ouranopolis is the village at the end of secular Athos. The most obvious feature of the village is the 14th-century **tower** built to guard what was then a dependency of Vatopediou monastery. A building in a side street, one block back from the waterfront, is, despite appearances, actually early 20th century. It once housed a monastic copper works (now a pharmacy). Most of the rest of the village was founded in 1922 by refugees from Asia Minor.

As well as the ferry for pilgrims to Athos, boats from here run tourist trips along the coast of Mt Athos for those unwilling or unable (by reason of gender – see following) to set foot there. Ouranopolis' postcode is 63075, and the telephone code is 0377.

Places to Stay & Eat There are domatia and a few hotels, including the D class *Hotel Galini* (☎ 71 217), one block back from the coast road. It has singles/doubles for 3500/4800 dr with shared facilities – you take breakfast in the family's dining room behind the small grocer's shop they run beneath the hotel rooms.

The D class *Hotel Akrogiali* (☎ 71 201), on the waterfront, has singles/doubles for 4000/6400 dr. The prominent B class *Xenia* (☎ 71 264/5) has more up-market singles/ doubles for 5000/10,000 dr. The hotel has a bar and restaurant.

There are a number of restaurants facing the sea on the beach; between these and the road, not far away from the tower, *O Kokkinos* is reasonably priced and has good fish dishes.

Research for the following section on Mt Athos was undertaken by David Hall.

Agio Oros (Holy Mountain) – Mt Athos
Αγιον Ορος

This semiautonomous monastic area occupies most of the Athos peninsula. To set foot here is to step back in time – literally by 13 days, because the Athonite community still uses the Julian calendar – and metaphorically by 500 years, as this is a remnant of the Byzantine Empire, which otherwise ended with the fall of Constantinople in 1453.

Setting foot here, however, is not straightforward; foreign men can stay in the monasteries for four nights (extendible up to six) after completing some formalities (see Obtaining a Permit later in this section). Visitors walk from monastery to monastery, enjoying the landscape (Athos is also called 'The garden of the Virgin Mary') on the way, experiencing a little of the ascetic life of the monks. Despite some of the rigours associated with a visit to the Holy Mountain, this unique experience can be a very enriching one.

Women cannot enter the area at all. The closest approach they can make to the monasteries is to view them from one of the round-trip cruises. Boats carrying women must keep at least 500 metres offshore.

History Hermits gravitated to Mt Athos from the very early years of the Byzantine Empire. The first monastery on Athos, Megisti Lavra, was founded in 961-963 AD by St Athanasius with support from the emperor, Nikephoros II Phokas; the next emperor, John Tsimiskes, granted Athos its first charter. The Athonite community flourished under the continuing support of the Byzantine emperors, who issued decrees reinforcing its status. The most notorious decree was that made under Constantine IX Monomachus barring access to women, beardless persons and female domestic animals. This is still in force, except that it is no longer a requirement to be bearded. Hens (for eggs) are tolerated; birds are apparently too lowly to be included in the ban.

Monasteries continued to be founded, particularly when Christians from outside the area came in during the first crusades. By 1400 there were said to be 40 monasteries, including foundations by Bulgarians, Russians and Serbian princes. The Athos community submitted to Turkish rule after the fall of Constantinople, but retained its semi-independent status. The last monastery to be founded was Stavronikita, in 1542. The community declined over the centuries to the present 20 ruling monasteries.

In the Greek War of Independence (1821-1829) many monasteries were plundered and entire libraries burned by Turkish troops. Fires have in any case been a common occurrence during the centuries, due to the candles and oil lamps used in the wooden buildings. The present constitution of Athos dates from 1924. It was guaranteed by the 1975 Greek constitution, and recognises Athos as a part of Greece (all the monks, regardless of their origin, must become Greek nationals), with the Iera Synaxis (Holy Council, composed of one representative from each of the 20 monasteries) responsible for all internal administration.

Obtaining a Permit Only 10 foreign adult males may enter per day, but unrestricted numbers of Greek men may enter. Start the procedure early, particularly for summer visits, when you may have to wait weeks for a place – make a reservation. Athos can get quite crowded at weekends.

You can start the process in Athens or Thessaloniki, but you are supposed to complete the paperwork in the city in which you started it. As you have to be in northern Greece anyway, it is simplest to start in Thessaloniki.

Ordained clergymen should have an introduction from their bishop, and need permission to visit Athos from the Ecumenical Patriarchate of Constantinople – apply via the Metropolis of Thessaloniki, Vogatsikou 5 (☎ 031-227 677).

Applying in Thessaloniki You need a letter of recommendation from your consulate. There are a number of foreign consulates listed under the Thessaloniki section. The UK Consulate also acts for Australians, Canadians and New Zealanders.

Some consular hours are: UK – Monday to Friday from 9 am to 2 pm; and USA – Tuesday and Thursday from 9 am to noon. Try telephoning the US Consulate (☎ 26 6121/0716) if you need your letter of recommendation urgently.

The British charge the highest consular fees in Greece for letters of recommendation – UK£15 payable in drachma. Pious but poor Canadians should therefore use their embassy in Athens (if this doesn't require a special journey). The US Consulate doesn't levy a charge.

Take your letter of recommendation to the Ministry of Macedonia & Thrace (opening hours 10 am to 2 pm, Monday to Friday) on Plateia Diikitiriou (follow El Venizelou up from the waterfront). In Room 222 (1st floor, east wing), Directorate of Political Affairs, the staff exchange your letter of recommendation for a permit to enter Athos on a particular date. This completes the paperwork, as it is no longer necessary to get a further note from the Aliens' Police.

In busy seasons, the ministry may give you a date for your visit several weeks or even months away. You can reserve a place from outside Greece either via your consulate or by contacting directly the Ministry of Macedonia & Thrace (☎ 031-27 0092), Directorate of Political Affairs, Room 222, Plateia Diikitiriou, Thessaloniki, 54123.

Applying in Athens First obtain your letter of recommendation from the consular section of your embassy. Consular fees for this (payable in drachma) are: British UK£15; US gratis; Canadian C$10; Australian A$25 (ask for a *note verbale*, which sounds like a contradiction in terms).

Take your letter of recommendation to the Ministry of Foreign Affairs, Zalakosta 2, to obtain a permit, or *diamonitirion*, to enter Athos on a specific date. No further paperwork is required.

It is also possible to make an advance reservation for a particular date via your embassy.

Orientation & Information There is no land access from secular Greece; all visitors enter the Athonite community by boat from Ouranopolis to Daphne, the small port of Athos. This has a port authority building, police and customs, post office, a couple of general stores selling food and religious artefacts made on Athos and a café. There is no OTE office, but one of the shops has a telephone with a meter. The only other town is Karyes, the administrative capital, which includes the headquarters building of the Holy Council, an inn, post office, OTE office, doctor and a couple of shops. There are no tourist police, but there is a regular police station in Karyes.

The remaining settlements are the 20 monasteries and dependent religious communities, which range from *skites* (SKI-tess), resembling villages, to the isolated dwellings of hermits – the total population of monks and resident laymen is about 1600. In addition to Karyes and Daphne, police are based at St Pandeleimon, Megisti Lavra, Agia Anna, Zografou and Hiliandariou.

The landscape is dominated in the south by the white peak of Mt Athos itself; the northerly part is densely wooded. Wildlife abounds; the small population of monks and absence of any industry (apart from some logging) have virtually turned the area into a reserve.

Leave video cameras behind – they're prohibited on Athos.

Exploring Athos Once you have obtained your diamonitirion (permit to stay in the monasteries), you are free to roam. There are few proper roads, and not many vehicles – you get around on foot, following the old paths, or by boat.

A caïque leaves Agia Anna every day at 9 am for Daphne, serving intermediate west-

Visitors & the Monastic Life

Don't imagine that all the monks are simple, otherworldly men. Although some of the hermits in the south of the peninsula are, to put it politely, weird, many of the monks in the monasteries are highly educated men very familiar with the outside world – you will come across monks who spend much of their life outside the monasteries, as university professors or missionary doctors.

The monks have not chosen their way of life primarily for the benefit of visitors. Your reception will vary from correct but distant to warm and hospitable, and this partly depends on you. Every aspect of your behaviour in a monastery will be under close scrutiny (even if you think everyone is ignoring you) and will be eagerly discussed by the monks (they are apparently great gossips).

Certain behaviour is expected of you. Wear long trousers, not shorts, everywhere on Athos. Inside the monasteries, do not wear a hat, do not smoke or behave arrogantly (for example by singing or whistling); it is polite to wear long-sleeved shirts. When you meet a monk along the way, greet him by saying '*evloite*' (ev-lo-YEE-teh, literally 'bless me'); the usual response is the blessing *o kyrios* ('the Lord'). Photography is often forbidden within monasteries, and never photograph a monk without his permission.

Remain dressed on the way to and from the washrooms, and even in them. Exposing skin is a big no-no, so attempt to wash with your shirt on, unless the guest quarters have enclosed showers to preserve modesty. Do not swim within sight of a monastery, however hot and sweaty you feel after walking; not only is this forbidden, but raw sewage is discharged into the apparently welcoming sea.

The monasteries have a common ground plan; from the outside, each resembles a fortified castle having one gateway for access. In the central courtyard is the katholikon (monastery church), frequently coloured blood-red, and behind this is the *trapeza* (refectory). Most monasteries now accommodate only a fraction of the monks they once did, and have abandoned, derelict sections; some of these are being renovated with the aid of EC funds for heritage protection.

The monastic day begins at sunset, which is midnight in the Byzantine time kept in the monasteries (distrust the clocks, which must be adjusted every day). This is when the outer gate is shut, and it is not reopened until daybreak. When you reach a monastery, head for the guest quarters, *arhontariki* (usually signposted), and find the guestmaster. The monks traditionally welcome visitors by offering them home-distilled *tsipouro* and *loukoumi*, or perhaps coffee. The guestmaster will show you to a two to 10-bedded guest room.

Visitors are not expected to participate completely in the monastic religious life (just as well, since the most important services take place during the night), and some monasteries do not permit the non-Orthodox within the church; you should, however, if permitted, attend the morning and evening services which usually precede the mealtimes (it's bad form to sneak straight into the refectory for the food).

Services are indicated by a monk walking round the monastery striking a *simandro*, a large wooden plank, with a mallet in a distinctive rhythm. Those unfamiliar with Orthodox rituals will find the services bewildering. Monks shuffle in and out apparently at random, some stand, some sit, for no apparent reason, icons are kissed, and they, and the worshippers, have censers of burning incense shaken at them. The only music permitted is that of the human voice (heavenly in some monasteries, diabolical in others), and the liturgical language used is an archaic form of Greek. The apparently endless repetition of some sections has a hypnotic effect.

Religious practice on Athos derives from the 14th-century Hesychast movement, according to which the divine light radiated at the Transfiguration can be perceived by certain practices of meditation and repetitive chanting.

---

coast monasteries or their arsenals (landing stages for monasteries not immediately by the sea), returning from Daphne every afternoon. A more irregular caïque serves points on the east coast (theoretically three times a week, weather permitting on this exposed coast) between Ierissos and Mandraki, the harbour for Megisti Lavra. Another service

around the south connects Mandraki and Agia Anna. The caïques are inexpensive; for example, at the time of writing the trip from Daphne to Dionysiou cost 200 dr.

Unless you travel exclusively by boat, you should be reasonably fit and prepared to walk for several hours a day in the heat. Carry water with you, and, as food often

If the non-Orthodox are permitted in the church, they will usually be confined to the exonarthex, the outer porch (the double narthex is a peculiarity of the Athos churches). When there is no service in progress some monasteries make a point of showing non-Orthodox visitors the church interior – most of them are stuffed with more relics and icons than you can shake a censer at.

The monks dine twice a day, or only once on the frequent fasting days. The simple vegetarian meals rely heavily on produce from the monastery gardens, occasionally supplemented by fish. Common accompaniments to the cooked vegetables include home-baked bread, olives, eggs and cheese (where did that come from?). Some monasteries serve very palatable wine with the meals, an uncharacteristic epicurean touch.

In some monasteries, non-Orthodox visitors eat separately from the monks, and at others they eat with them. The latter has the advantage that you see a little more of the life of the monastery, but the disadvantage that you must stop eating as soon as the monks rise and leave, no matter how much remains. The refectories are frequently decorated with frescoes, and during the meal, a monk rapidly reads out scriptures. On fasting days the monks normally provide some light refreshment for their guests; it may look meagre, but remember, the monks have nothing.

Older books classify the monasteries into coenobite or idiorhythmic type, depending on whether communal life is centrally or more loosely organised. This distinction is now obsolete: the last idiorhythmic monastery, Pandokratoros, became coenobite on 8 June 1992 (Byzantine calendar), among much feasting and celebration.

The lives of monks who live in skites, clusters of houses around a church, are not as strict as those of the monks who reside in the monasteries. Monks in the skites have more free time, and produce most of the Athos artefacts sold in Daphne and Karyes. One of the houses acts as the guest quarters, and visitors are received hospitably. Some *kelloi*, literally cells, but more like small farmhouses, and usually accommodating two to four monks, also receive guests. The hermits, of course, usually keep to themselves.

The accommodation offered by the monasteries can be spartan, the food frugal, and you won't meet any female form of life more highly evolved than a chicken, but you will have been in exalted company. The Byzantine emperor, John VI Cantacuzenus, on his enforced abdication in 1354, became a monk on Athos for the rest of his life. Rasputin, the Mad Monk (an unfair name, as technically speaking he wasn't a monk) walked here in 1891 from Siberia, a journey of 2000 miles.

David Hall

becomes an obsession among visitors, take extra supplies, such as biscuits and dried fruit (chocolate, the hiker's usual emergency supply of calories, is a dumb thing to carry in hot weather).

Other useful things to take include a torch (flashlight), compass, the best map of Athos you can find (a 1:50,000 map showing con-

tours is available through Stanfords of London; ☎ 071-836 1321), a whistle (in case you get lost), a small shaving mirror (not all monastic washrooms have mirrors) and mosquito coils.

You can only spend one night in each monastery. Some of the heavily visited ones near Karyes request that you telephone them

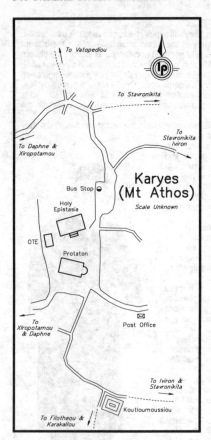

To Vatopediou

To Stavronikita

To Stavronikita
Iviron

To Daphne &
Xiropotamou

Karyes
(Mt Athos)

Bus Stop

Scale Unknown

Holy
Epistasia

OTE

Protaton

To
Xiropotamou
& Daphne

Post Office

To Iviron &
Stavronikita

Koutloumoussiou

To Filotheou &
Karakallou

in advance to be sure of a place (the numbers are displayed in the Holy Epistasia (Holy Council building) where you wait for the diamonitirion), but this can be a frustrating experience, as the telephone is not answered for many hours of the day during periods of rest and meditation. You must reach the monastery before sunset, as the gate is then shut, and not opened for anyone.

In **Karyes** you should see the 10th-century **Protaton**, the basilican church opposite the Holy Epistasia, which contains a number of treasures including paintings by Panselinos, the master of the Macedonian

School. Karyes itself is a strange place – like a ghost town, with many derelict buildings testifying to a former grander era. If you've had a long day, you may decide to stay at the monastery of **Koutloumoussiou** in Karyes. Otherwise, you should now decide on your itinerary.

A popular route is to head for one of the monasteries on the east coast, and then to continue to Megisti Lavra, returning to Daphne on the west coast. This can involve some lengthy walks unless you use the caïques, but these can be unreliable on the east coast.

From Karyes, you can walk to **Stavronikita** or **Iviron** on the coast, to continue by caïque, or coastal paths (easier to follow than the inland paths). Alternatively, from Karyes you can walk to **Filotheou** along a pleasant shady path (spring water available) in about 3½ hours. About 30 minutes further on is **Karakallou**. Beyond here the old Byzantine path has been converted into a road, and you face a 5½-hour walk along it (unless a monastic vehicle gives you a lift) to **Megisti Lavra**.

Not only is this the oldest monastery on Athos, it is the only one to remain undamaged by fire during its history. Its 10th-century structure therefore protects a number of treasures, including frescoes by Theophanes of Crete and the tomb of St Athanasius, the founder.

A caïque leaves Megisti Lavra at about 3 pm for the skiti Agia Anna. Alternatively, you can follow the path around the wilderness of the south end of the peninsula. You come to the skiti of **Kerasia**, and subsequently **Agia Anna**, either of which (although Agia Anna has a better reputation for hospitality) can be used as a base for climbing **Mt Athos** (2033 metres).

This climb should not be undertaken lightly, and it is wise not to attempt it alone. It also wouldn't hurt to inform someone of your plans before setting off. Remember that it will be cold at the top, and you will need to take food and water. Water is available from a well at the chapel of Panagia (Virgin Mary), a short distance below the summit.

You can return to Daphne by caïque from Agia Anna.

Another route is to head from Karyes to see the architecturally interesting monasteries on the west coast, including the spectacular Simonas Petras, clinging to a cliff like a Tibetan lamasery. From Karyes you climb over the central spine of the hills and head down again. You'll come first to **Xiropotamou**, which has newly renovated guest rooms (still lit by oil lamps) and serves good food and wine to guests separately from the monks. A path leads from here to Daphne; you can follow the coastal path from here or take the daily caïque leaving at 12.30 pm for Agia Anna calling at Simonas Petras, Grigoriou, Dionysiou and Pavlou. Alternatively, from Karyes you could head for Filotheou and then take a path to Simonas Petras from there.

Simonas Petras, sometimes called Simopetra, is an awesome sight from its sea-level arsenal. From here it's a stiff climb to the monastery. Its outside walls are surrounded by wooden balconies – you walk along these from the guest rooms to the washroom, seeing the sheer drop beneath your feet. Swallows nest in the eaves and delight in vertiginous swoops to the sea. You can't normally get outside the monasteries to experience Athos at night – standing on these balconies in the dark listening to the swallows and staring down at the light of a solitary fishing boat is a magical experience.

From Simonas Petras you can descend to a coastal path which branches off the path to the arsenal at a small shrine. The path brings you to **Grigoriou**, which has a very pleasant position by the sea, and a comfortable guesthouse by the harbour outside the main monastery building. This has electric light and the rare luxury of showers.

The coastal path from here onwards is quite strenuous, as it climbs and descends three times before coming to **Dionysiou**, another cliff-hanger of a monastery resembling Simonas Petras in some ways. One of the treasures of its katholikon (main church), in a separate chapel, is an age-blackened icon claimed as the oldest in Athos. It is said to

have been carried round the walls of Constantinople to inspire its successful defence against a combined siege by the Persians and Avars in 626. The coastal path from here continues to Pavlou and Agia Anna.

A road less travelled by takes in the monasteries north of Karyes. You can walk from Karyes to **Vatopediou**, on the coast – this picturesque monastery is an oddity in that it keeps to the European calendar. When Athos was at its height, Vatopediou had a celebrated school (now in ruins). A coastal path leads on to Esfigmenou, and further on, little visited because of its isolation, is **Hiliandariou**, a Serbian foundation still inhabited by Serbs and noted for its hospitality.

Halfway between the east and west coasts is the Bulgarian monastery, **Zografou**, (which means 'the Painter', named for a miraculous icon not painted by human hands). On the west coast, the most northerly monastery is **Dohiariou**, which is considered to have some of the best architecture on Athos.

Coming south on the coastal path you reach **Xenofondos** and then **St Pandeleimon**, the Russian monastery (which welcomes visitors with tea). This enormous building used to accommodate over 1000 monks, who came in swarms from Russia in the 19th century. Most of the distinctive Russian-style buildings date from that period – and many are now derelict. The monastery was once renowned for the quality of its singing; this has been through a low point in the recent past, but is happily picking up again. These west-coast monasteries or their arsenals are served by the Ouranopolis-Daphne ferry.

Many alternative routes are possible using the network of old Byzantine paths – most of these have been recently marked by the Thessaloniki Mountaineering Club, but unmarked logging tracks make it amazingly easy to get lost in the woods. Monks' paths which cross vehicle tracks and lead directly to (or away from) monasteries are marked at the roadside by small crosses.

Getting There & Away Entry is by boat from

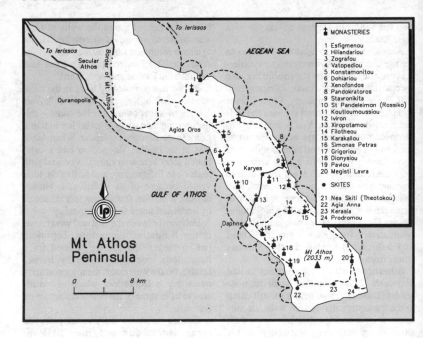

Ouranopolis, which is accessible by bus from Thessaloniki's Halkidiki terminal at Karakassi 68. There are seven buses a day (2½ hours, 1600 dr). The first bus (6 am) from Thessaloniki arrives in time for the boat; otherwise you need to stay overnight in Ouranopolis. This gives you a chance to buy easily carried food, and find somewhere to store unwanted gear (probably for a fee). Take only the bare minimum to Athos, as you'll have to lug it round all the time.

You may prefer to store unneeded baggage in Thessaloniki – when you return from Athos to Ouranopolis, the bus to Thessaloniki is waiting for the boat, and you may miss it while recovering luggage. Also, you might want to leave Athos via the west-coast boat to Ierissos – no big advantage if all your worldly goods are in Ouranopolis.

Entering Athos The boat, usually the small car ferry *Axion Esti*, leaves Ouranopolis at 9.45 am for Daphne (560 dr). You must surrender your Athos entry permit and passport on boarding. The journey takes about two hours; some intermediate stops are made for monks and other residents, but you can't get off before Daphne. Once there, an apparently clapped-out bus waits to take you to Karyes for 350 dr.

In the main square of Karyes, walk up the steps of the Holy Council building (flying the flag of the Byzantine Empire) and wait for the Byzantine bureaucracy to return your passport and issue your diamonitirion – this costs 5000 dr, but the monasteries do not expect any further donations for accommodating you for the next four nights. The diamonitirion can be extended (for a further two days) in Karyes at the end of the four days.

Leaving Athos The daily boat to Ouranopolis leaves Daphne at noon – there is a fairly rigorous customs check to ensure that you're not walking off with any antiquities (even visiting clerics have been known to snaffle valuable relics). The morning caïque from Agia Anna arrives in Daphne in ample time for the Ouranopolis boat. The irregular east-coast caïque is an alternative exit to Ierissos.

KAVALA Καβάλα

Kavala (Ka-VA-la, population 57,000), 163 km east of Thessaloniki, is one of the most attractive of Greece's large cities. It spills gently down the foothills of Mt Simbolon to a commodious harbour. The old quarter of Panagia nestles under a massive Byzantine fortress.

Modern Kavala is built over ancient Neopolis which was the port of Philipi. Mehmet Ali (1769-1849), who became Pasha of Egypt and founder of the last Egyptian royal dynasty, was born in Kavala. Like Athens and Thessaloniki, its population was almost doubled by the population exchange with Asia Minor.

Orientation

Kavala's focal point is its central square of Plateia Eleftherias. The town's two main thoroughfares, Eleftheriou Venizelou and Erythrou Stavrou run west from here parallel with the waterfront Ethnikis Andistassis. The old quarter of Panagia occupies a promontory to the south-east of Plateia Eleftherias. To get to this quarter, walk east along Eleftheriou Venizelou from Plateia Eleftherias, turn left at the T-junction and take the first right (signposted Panagia and the castle).

The intercity bus station is on the corner of Mitropoleos Kavalas and Filikis Eterias, near the Thassos ferry quay.

One of the town's most prominent landmarks is an imposing aqueduct which was built during the reign of Suleiman the Magnificent (1520-66).

Information

Tourist Office The EOT (☎ 22 2425/8762 or 23 1653) is on the west side of Plateia Eleftherias. The helpful staff give out a map of the town, have information on transport and have a list of the town's hotels with prices.

They also have information on the summer drama festivals at Philipi and Thassos.

Opening times of the office are Monday to Friday from 7 am to 2.30 pm and 5 to 8 pm; Saturday from 8 am to 1 pm; it's closed on Sunday.

Tourist Police The tourist police (☎ 22 2905) are in the same building as the regular police at Omonia 119.

Money The National Bank of Greece is on the corner of Omonia and Dragoumi. There are many other banks in this area, but none have extended opening hours.

Post & Telecommunications The main post office is at the corner of Mitropoleos Kavalas and Erythrou Stavrou and is open Monday to Friday from 7.30 am to 8 pm. Kavala's postcode is 65403. The OTE is at the corner of Andistassis and Averof. It is open from 6 am to midnight in summer and 6 am to 11 pm in winter. Kavala's telephone code is 051.

Bookshop The Papadogianis Bookshop at Omonia 46 on the corner of Aminta stocks international newspapers and magazines and a few English-language paperbacks – if you're a Barbara Cartland fan, you could be in luck.

Panagia Παναγία

The pastel-coloured houses in the narrow tangled streets of the Panagia quarter are less dilapidated than those of Thessaloniki's Kastra and the area is less commercialised than Plaka.

Its most conspicuous building is the **Imaret**, a huge structure with 18 domes, which overlooks the harbour from Odos Poulidou. In Turkish times the imaret was a hostel for theology students. It has recently been restored and is now a pleasant café (see Places to Eat). Within the café are some cabinets displaying memorabilia from

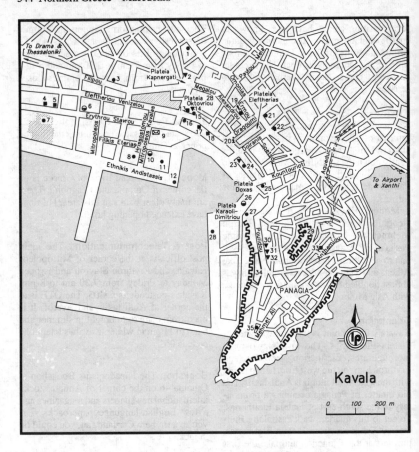

Kavala

0   100   200 m

Mehmet Ali's time. The carefully restored Turkish house where Mehmet Ali was born is now open to the public. If you ring the bell the caretaker will show you around; along with other rooms, you will see Ali's harem. The house is at the southern end of Poulidou. Nearby is an equestrian statue of Ali.

Museums
Kavala's **Archaeological Museum** houses well-displayed finds from ancient Amphipolis, between Thessaloniki and Kavala. Amphipolis was a colony of Athens, and a gold-rush town with mines on Mt Pangaeum.

The finds include sculpture, jewellery, grave stele, terracotta figurines and vases. The museum is at the western side of town on Erythrou Stavrou. Opening times are Tuesday to Sunday from 8.30 am to 3 pm. Admission is 400 dr.

The **Municipal Museum of Kavala** is also worth a visit. On the ground floor are pictures and sculptures by contemporary Greek artists including a large collection of works by Polygnotos Vagis (1894-1965), who was born in Potamia on Thassos, and emigrated to America where he gained an international reputation.

■ PLACES TO STAY

4	Hotel Nefeli
5	Hotel Esperia
13	Hotel Panorama
17	Hotel Acropolis
18	Hotel Galaxy
19	Hotel Attikon
33	Giorgos Alvanos Rooms

▼ PLACES TO EAT

2	Michalakis Taverna
14	Café Andreadi
23	Ta Plakakia Restaurant
30	Taverna Faros
31	Psaria Steki
32	Antonios Restaurant

OTHER

1	Tourist Police
3	Municipal Museum of Kavala
6	Bus Stop for Alexandroupolis
7	Archaeological Museum
8	Olympic Airways Office
9	Main Post Office
10	Bus Station
11	OTE
12	Ferry & Hydrofoil Departure Point for Thassos
15	Alkyn Travel Service
16	Budget Rent a Car
20	EOT
21	National Bank of Greece
22	Papadogianis Bookshop
24	Tzatzala Travel Agency
25	Nikos Miliades Shipping Agency
26	Local Bus Station
27	Zolotis Travel Agency
28	Ferry Departure Point for Aegean Islands (except Thassos)
29	Byzantine Fortress
34	Imaret
35	House of Mehmet Ali

On the upper floor is a superb folk-art collection with costumes, jewellery, handicrafts, household items and tools. At the time of writing the museum was at Filipou 4, but its collection has outgrown these premises, so it is due to move sometime in the near future. Enquire about the new premises at the EOT.

Places to Stay – bottom end

Ireni Camping (☎ 22 9776) is two km east of Kavala on the coast road, and *Alexandros Camping* (☎ 31 6347) is further along the road at Nea Kavala. At Keramoti there is *Keramoti Camping* (☎ 0591-5279). *Batis Kavala Camping* (☎ 22 7151) is three km west of Kavala at Batis Beach.

The best deal for budget travellers is the cosy rooms in the beautiful 300-year-old house rented by *Giorgos Alvanos* (☎ 22 8412/1781), Anthemiou 35, in Panagia. Single/double rates are 2200/3100 dr.

The *Hotel Attikon* (☎ 22 2257), Megalou Alexandrou 8, is pretty dire and is only included because there is a dearth of budget accommodation in Kavala. Rates are 2500/3500 dr with shared bathrooms. *Hotel Acropolis* (☎ 22 3543), Eleftheriou Venizelou 53, is marginally better and has singles with shared bathrooms for 3500 dr and doubles with private bathroom for 5500 dr.

The C class *Hotel Panorama* (☎ 22 4205), Eleftheriou Venizelou 26 C, has reasonable singles/doubles for 3500/5000 dr with shared bathrooms and 6000/7500 dr with private bathrooms. On the waterfront the *Hotel Nefeli* (☎ 22 7440/1/2/3/4), Leoforos Erythrou Stavrou 50, has pleasant single/double rooms for 5500/7000 dr with private bathrooms. The C class *Hotel Esperia* (☎ 22 9621/2/3/4/5), Erythrou Stavrou 42, is similarly priced.

Places to Stay – middle

The B class *Hotel Galaxy* (☎ 22 4812/4541/4605), Eleftheriou Venizelou 27, is Kavala's best hotel, with spacious, attractively furnished single/double rooms for 8500/11,800 dr. All rooms have air-con, refrigerator, telephone, radio and private bathrooms.

There are many mid-range hotels on the stretch of coast just south-west of Kavala. The B class *Blue Bay Hotels* (☎ 71 777/800/1/2) is on the beach at Nea Iraklitsa. It has a restaurant, bar, roof garden and swimming pool. Rates are 8000/10,000 dr for singles/doubles and 14,100 dr for bungalows. The B class *Egeon Strand Hotel* (☎ 71 897/8; fax

71 947), also on Nea Iraklitsa Beach, has singles/doubles for 8000/11,000 dr. It doesn't have a swimming pool but has a sauna, solarium, gymnasium and hydromassage.

Places to Stay – top end
The most luxurious hotel in the vicinity of Kavala is the A class *Tosca Beach Hotel* (☎ 22 4856/5053) which has doubles for 11,800 dr and suites for 21,800 dr. The hotel is five km south-west of Kavala at Myrmigia Beach.

Places to Eat
Kavala's restaurant scene is a vast improvement on its accommodation. There are three popular restaurants on Poulidou, opposite the imaret. The first is *Taverna Faros*; their fried mussels at 600 dr are delectable. Another one, *Psaria Steki*, has souvlaki for 600 dr and mussels in tomato sauce for 650 dr. *Antonios Restaurant*, next door, is also recommended by locals.

Ta Plakakia Restaurant, Doiranis 4, near Plateia Eleftherias, is a rough and ready place with a huge choice of low-priced dishes. The *Michalakis Taverna*, Kassandrou 3, on Plateia Kapnergati, is more up-market. Don't be put off by their tacky murals and folksy wall-hangings – the food is good.

The *Café Andreadi*, on a side street off Eleftheriou Venizelou, has good cheese pies and custard pies for 180 dr and filter coffee for 150 dr. The café in the Imaret is in a lovely serene setting around a courtyard of fruit trees. Espresso, cappuccino, fruit juice and beer are all 300 dr, ice cream is 500 dr and mixed mezedes is 1000 dr.

If you want to concoct a picnic there are fruit vendors everywhere and a food market between Spetsou and Omonia.

Getting There & Away
Air Kavala shares Khristoupolis Airport with Xanthi. There is one flight a day to Athens (13,600 dr) at 8.15 pm. The airport is 29 km south-east of Kavala.

Bus From the intercity bus station there are half-hourly buses to Xanthi (one hour, 700 dr); hourly buses to Keramoti (500 dr, one hour); and Thessaloniki (two hours, 750 dr). For Philipi take one of the frequent Drama buses and ask to be let off at the ancient site of Philipi (20 minutes, 220 dr).

Buses for Alexandroupolis (four hours, 1950 dr), which originate in Thessaloniki, do not leave from the intercity bus station, but from outside the Dore Café (☎ 22 7601), Erythrou Stavrou 34, from where you buy a ticket.

To/From Turkey There are two buses every day except Friday and Sunday from Kavala to Istanbul (5500/9300 dr one-way/return). They leave at 5.30 am and 6.30 pm. You can buy tickets from Alkyn Travel Service (☎ 83 6251 or 22 2533) on Eleftheriou Venizelou, next door to the Hotel Panorama.

Train The nearest train station to Kavala is at Drama, 30 km away. Drama is on the Thessaloniki-Alexandroupolis line and there are four trains a day in either direction. There is a frequent bus service between Kavala and Drama.

Car Budget Rent a Car (☎ 22 8785/4961) is on the 1st floor of Eleftheriou Venizelou 35, opposite the Hotel Panorama.

Ferry There are ferries every hour from Kavala to Skala Prinos (1½ hours, 400 dr) on Thassos. The 2 and 8.30 pm ferries continue to Limenas. Ferries go direct to Limenas every 45 minutes (480 dr, 45 minutes) from the small port of Keramoti, 46 km south-east of Kavala.

In summer there are ferries from Kavala to Samothrace (four hours, 2100 dr) on Monday at 10 am; Wednesday at 2 pm; Friday at 5 pm; and Saturday at 3 pm. Buy tickets from Zolotis Travel Agency (☎ 83 5671). There are ferries to Lemnos (five hours, 2300 dr) on Monday at 6 pm; Tuesday at 8 pm; Wednesday at 8 am; Friday at 10 pm and Saturday at 8.30 pm. The Friday ferry continues to Lesbos, Chios, Samos, Patmos,

Leros, Kalymnos, Kos and Rhodes. The Saturday boat continues to Lesbos, Chios and Rafina (in Attica). Buy tickets from Nikos Miliades Shipping Agency (☎ 22 6147/3421/0067), Karaoli-Dimitrou 36.

Hydrofoil There are six hydrofoils a day to Thassos (30 minutes, 1045 dr). Purchase tickets at the departure point at the port. There are hydrofoils to Lesbos on Tuesday, Thursday and Saturday (13,000 dr). Tickets can be bought from Tzatzala Travel Agency (☎ 22 3322/2005), Venizelou 9.

Getting Around

To/From the Airport There is no Olympic Airways bus to the airport. A public bus leaves from the intercity bus station at 6.20 pm every evening.

PHILIPI Φίλιπποι

The ancient site of Philipi (FEE-li-pee) lies 15 km inland from Kavala astride the Kavala-Drama road. The original city was called Krenides. Philip II seized it from the Thasians in 356 BC because it was in the foothills of Mt Pangaion, and there was 'gold in them thar' hills', which he needed to finance his battles to gain control of Greece.

During July and August a **Festival of Drama** is held at the site's theatre. Information about this can be obtained from the EOT in Kavala. The site (☎ 051-51 6470) and museum (☎ 051-51 6251) are both open Tuesday to Sunday from 8.30 am to 3 pm. Admission to each is 400 dr.

History

A visit to Philipi is worthwhile more for the significance of the events which happened there than for what can be seen, so some knowledge of its history is essential. Philipi is famous for two reasons: it was the scene of one of the most decisive battles in history, and it was the first European city to accept Christianity.

By the 1st century AD, Greece had become the battleground for factions of the Roman republic, and Philipi was coveted for its strategic position on the Via Egnatias.

Julius Caesar's death at the hands of the republicans Cassius and Brutus had created a power vacuum. Eager to fill this gap, the two most powerful armies of Rome (with 80,000 men per side) met in battle on the plain of Philipi. One side was led by the imperial Mark Antony (great nephew of Julius Caesar) and Octavian, and the other by Julius Caesar's assassins. Octavian was the victor, causing Cassius and Brutus to commit suicide. The battle set the seal on the future of a new Rome which was to be imperialist (and as things turned out, Christian as well).

Octavian, after this victory, waged another famous battle (the Battle of Actium) in 31 AD, where he fought his former ally Mark Antony and Antony's consort, Cleopatra. Again, Octavian was the victor (and again the defeated committed suicide) and so now in control, he established an autocracy, and became Augustus, first emperor of Rome.

Neopolis (present-day Kavala), the port of Philipi, was the landing stage in Europe for travellers from the Orient. And so it was here that St Paul came in 49 AD to embark upon his conversion of the pagan Europeans. His overzealous preaching landed him in prison; a misadventure which was going to be repeated many times in the future.

Exploring the Site

Despite being the first Christian city in Europe, the people of Philipi didn't have much luck in their church-building endeavours. The 5th-century **Basilica A** was the first church built in the city, but it was wrecked by an earthquake shortly after completion. The remains of this church can be seen on the north side of the site (left coming from Kavala), near the road and to the east of the theatre.

Their next attempt was the 6th-century **Basilica B**, on the southern side of the site, next to the large and conspicuous forum. This church was an ambitious attempt to build a church with a dome, but the structure was top heavy and collapsed before it was dedicated. In the 10th century its sole remaining part, the narthex, was made into a church – several of its Corinthian columns can be seen.

Philipi's best preserved building is the **Theatre**, which isn't Roman but was built by Philip II. Also in good nick are 50 marble latrines at the southern end of the forum. The site's **museum**, on the north side, houses both Roman and Christian finds from Philipi, and also Neolithic finds from the nearby site of Dikili Tach.

Getting There & Away
Buses between Kavala and Drama will let passengers off at the ancient site (20 minutes, 220 dr).

Epiros   Ηπειρος

Epiros occupies the north-west corner of the Greek mainland. To the north is Albania; to the west is the Ionian Sea and Corfu. Its port of Igoumenitsa is a jumping-off point for ferries to Corfu and Italy. The high Pindos mountains form the region's eastern boundary, separating it from Macedonia and Thessaly.

The road from Ioannina to Kalambaka cuts through the Pindos mountains and is one of the most scenically spectacular in Greece, particularly the section between Metsovo and Kalambaka, which is called the Katara pass. In northern Epiros the Vikos-Aoos National Park is a wilderness of lofty mountains, cascading waterfalls, precipitous gorges, fast-flowing rivers and dense forests harbouring villages of slatestone houses. These settlements are known as the Zagros villages.

History
In early times Epiros' remote mountainous terrain was divided into tribes who were unaffected by, and oblivious to, what was happening in the rest of the country. Eventually one tribe, the Molossi, became so powerful that it dominated the whole region, and its leader became king of Epiros. The most renowned of these was King Pyrrhus (319-272 BC), whose foolhardy fracas in Italy against the Romans gave rise to the phrase 'Pyrrhic victory' – a victory achieved at too great a cost.

King Pyrrhus came to an undignified end. After unsuccessful attempts to gain control of Macedonia and parts of Rome he decided to have a go at Argos. On entering the city an old woman threw a tile at him from her rooftop which hit him on the head and killed him.

Epiros fell to the Turks in 1431, although its isolation ensured it a great degree of autonomy. It became part of independent Greece in 1913 when the Greek army seized it from the Turks during the second Balkan War. During WW II many Greeks took to the mountains of Epiros in a strong resistance movement. When the resistance split into the factions which culminated in the civil war, Epiros was the scene of heavy fighting. During this time, as in Macedonia, many children from Epiros were forcibly evacuated to Eastern-bloc countries by the communists.

IOANNINA Ιωάννινα
Ioannina (YAH-nee-na, population 90,000) is the capital and largest town of Epiros, and the gateway to the Vikos-Aoos National Park. It stands on the western shore of Lake Pamvotis, which is the site of a tranquil island. During the Ottoman rule Ioannina became a major commercial and intellectual centre and one of the largest and most important towns in Greece. The city reached

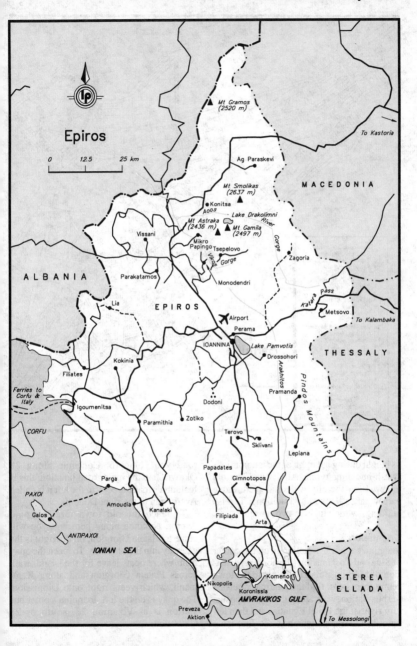

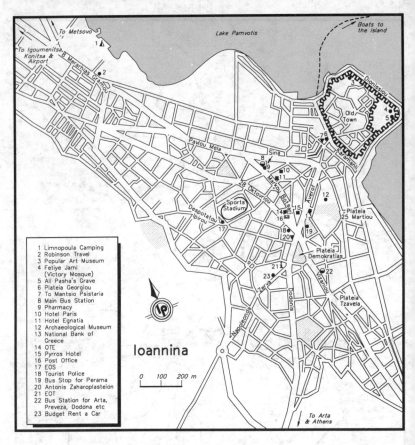

Ioannina

1	Limnopoula Camping
2	Robinson Travel
3	Popular Art Museum
4	Fetiye Jami (Victory Mosque)
5	Ali Pasha's Grave
6	Plateia Georgiou
7	To Mantsio Psistaria
8	Main Bus Station
9	Pharmacy
10	Hotel Paris
11	Hotel Egnatia
12	Archaeological Museum
13	National Bank of Greece
14	OTE
15	Pyrros Hotel
16	Post Office
17	EOS
18	Tourist Police
19	Bus Stop for Perama
20	Antonis Zaharoplasteion
21	EOT
22	Bus Station for Arta, Preveza, Dodona etc
23	Budget Rent a Car

its height during the reign of the ignominious swash-buckling tyrant Ali Pasha. The old town within the city walls has picturesque narrow lanes flanked by traditional Turkish buildings, which include two mosques.

Orientation

Ioannina's main bus station is on the corner of Sina and Zossimadon (the northern extension of Markou Botsari). To get to the town centre from here, find the pharmacy outside the bus station, walk along the road opposite, turn right at the Hotel Egnatias and then left onto 28 Oktovriou which is the first main road you come to. Continue along 28 Oktovriou to the major road junction; this is Ioannina's main street – to the left it is called Averof and to the right Dodonis.

To reach the old town turn left onto Averof, continue along here and you will come to Plateia Giorgiou; on the right is the gateway into the old town. To reach the quay from where boats leave for the island, walk across Plateia Giorgiou and along Karamanli, which veers right onto Dionissiou. The quay is on the left. Ioannina's other bus station is at Vizaniou 28, south of 28 Oktovriou.

Ali Pasha

Ali Pasha, one of the most flamboyant characters of recent Greek history, was born in 1741 in the village of Tepelini in Albania. In 1787 the Turks made him Pasha of Trikala and by 1788 he ruled Ioannina. His life was a catalogue of brigandage, murder, warfare and debauchery.

Tales abound about Ali. He supposedly had a harem of 400 women, but as if that were not enough he was also enamoured of Kyra Frosyni, his eldest son's mistress. When she rejected his amorous overtures, she and 15 other women were put into sacks and tipped into the lake.

Ali's sons seem to have taken after their father: one was a sex maniac who was in the habit of raping women; the other had the more innocuous hobby of collecting erotic literature.

Ali's lifelong ambition was to break away from the Ottoman Empire and create an independent state. In 1797 he collaborated with Napoleon, but in 1798 he wrested Preveza from the French. In 1817 he courted the British who rewarded him with Parga.

In 1822 Sultan Mahmud II decided he'd had enough of Ali's opportunistic and fickle alliances and sent his troops to execute him. The 82-year-old Ali took refuge on the 1st floor of the guesthouse of Agios Panteleimon monastery on the island, but was killed when the troops fired bullets at him through the ceiling from below. Ali was then beheaded, and his head paraded around Epiros before being buried in Constantinople (Istanbul) – the rest of his body was buried in Ioannina. ■

Information

The EOT is on Napoleonda Zerva 2. Turn right at the bottom of 28 Oktovriou onto Dodonis and you will come to it on the right set back on a square. Most people come to Epiros to trek in the mountains and Ioannina is a good place to get information or arrange an organised trek; the EOT has information on the Vikos Gorge trek. The office is open from 7.30 am to 2.30 pm and 5.30 to 8.30 pm Monday to Friday, and 9 am to 2 pm on a Saturday. The tourist police (☎ 25 673 or 26 226) are opposite the post office on 28 Oktovriou.

If you wish to trek in more remote areas than the Vikos Gorge then talk to someone at the EOS (☎ 22 138), Despotatou Ipirou 2. The office is open Monday to Friday in the evening from 7 to 9 pm.

The OTE and post office are on 28 Oktovriou. Ioannina's postcodes are 45221 and 45444. The telephone code is 0651.

Museums

Archaeological Museum This is an excellent museum which is spacious and well laid out. In the first room on the right there is a collection of Paleolithic tools, including a 200,000 BC hand axe from Kokkinopolis, near Preveza. Also in this room are finds from Dodoni including two charming bronze statuettes of children; one is throwing a ball and the other is holding a dove. Another delightful piece is a terracotta rattle in the shape of a tortoise.

The far room on the left houses a permanent exhibition of 19th and 20th-century paintings, sculpture and prints, including some mildly risqué nudes in amongst the stuffy portraits of local dignitaries. Don't miss the beautiful little terracotta sculpture entitled *Two Friends* by T Chrisochoidou. The museum (☎ 33 357) is in a small park set back from the east side of Averof. It is open Tuesday to Sunday from 8.30 am to 3 pm. Admission is 400 dr.

Popular Art Museum This museum (also called the Municipal Museum; ☎ 26 356) is housed in the Aslan Pasha mosque, in the old town. Its eclectic collection includes local costumes and photographs of old Ioannina. It's open Tuesday to Friday from 8.30 am to 3 pm. Admission is 400 dr.

To Nisi (The Island) Το Νησί

This traffic-free island is a serene place to wander around. It has four monasteries and a whitewashed village which was built in the 17th century by refugees from the Mani in the Peloponnese. It also has some domatia (see Places to Stay).

The **Panteleimon Monastery**, where Ali was killed, houses a small **museum**. It was temporally closed at the time of writing due to damage caused when a tree fell onto it during a storm. In July 1992 Greek culture minister Anna Psarouda-Benaki ordered the funding of 55 million drachmas for repairs to the museum. This caused an outcry amongst Greek feminists who stated it was inappropriate for a woman minister to support a museum which commemorates a man who put women into sacks and drowned them.

The monastery is signposted, as are all the other monasteries on the island.

Organised Treks
Robinson Travel (☎ 29 402; fax 0651 27071), 8 Merarhias Gramou 10, specialises in treks to remote areas of Epiros. The treks are of eight, 10, 12 and 15 days' duration and they cost approximately 10,000 dr per day inclusive.

Every Sunday between October and June the Ioannina EOS (see Information) organises a one-day trek in the Pindos mountains. Anyone is welcome and the cost is approximately 1500 dr per person.

Festival
During July and August a Festival of Ancient Drama takes place at the restored theatre at the nearby site of Dodoni. Information may be obtained from the EOT in Ioannina.

Places to Stay – bottom end
Limnopoula Camping (☎ 25 265) is on the edge of the lake, two km north-west of town. The cost is 500 dr per person and 380 dr per tent. The site has a restaurant and bar. To reach it either walk west along along Pavlou Mela onto Griva Mavogiani and continue along here onto Merarhias Gramou and look for the sign pointing right, or take a Perama-bound bus from Plateia Eleftherias.

The *Hotel Paris* (☎ 20 541), Tsirigoti, has clean single/double rooms for 3000/4500 dr with shared bathrooms. The hotel is near the main bus station.

On the island *Delas Sotinos* (☎ 73 494)

rents pleasant doubles for 4000 dr. From the quay walk straight ahead along Monachon Nektarou and the rooms are on the right. Another possibility are the rooms of *Varvara Vasilios* (☎ 24 396). Walk up Monachon Nektarou and take the first turn right onto Venizelou. Keep on this road to the end (where you will encounter a stone wall), turn right and at the junction turn left onto Melet Archiereos. The rooms are 40 metres along on the left. Single/double rates are 3000/4000 dr.

Back in Ioannina proper, the C class *Hotel Egnatias* (☎ 25 667), near the main bus station, has comfortable, but unadorned singles/doubles for 5000/7000 dr, with private bathrooms. The C class *Pyrros Hotel* (☎ 27 652), Gounari 3, has rates of 5000/6800 dr with private bathrooms; some rooms have TV. Gounari is opposite the clock tower on Averof.

Places to Stay – middle
Ioannina's most luxurious hotel is the B class *Xenia* (☎ 25 087/8), Dodonis 33. Singles/doubles are 9000/12,500 dr. The hotel has a bar and restaurant.

Places to Eat
There are several eating places on Plateia Giorgiou. The nicest is *To Mantsio Psistaria*, opposite the entrance to the old city. For a more memorable meal in a picturesque setting, head for the island, where there are several good tavernas specialising in fish dishes – you choose your meal live from tanks. As the island is small it's an easy matter to look at all of the tavernas before making your choice.

Apostolos & Telem Balaiadis Restaurant near the Panteleimon Monastery (Ali Pasha Museum) is a favourite with locals. Trout is 880 dr, frogs legs and crayfish are both 1400 dr a kg. While in Ioannina don't miss the local speciality, bougatsa (custard tart); *Antonis Zaharoplasteion*, at 28 Oktovriou 5, serves a particularly good one for 250 dr.

Things to Buy
Ioannina has for a long time been a centre for

Top: The statue of Cleopatra, Delos, Cyclades (DH)
Left: Whats on the menu? Naxos Town, Cyclades (DH)
Right: View of Thira (Santorini), Cyclades (VB)

Top: Paros, Cyclades (VB)
Middle: Fira, Thira (Santorini), Cyclades (DH)
Bottom: Mykonos Town, Mykonos, Cyclades (DH)

the manufacture of fine filigree silver. Shops selling this type of jewellery line Averof and Odos Karamanli. Prices start at around 3000 dr for rings and earrings.

Getting There & Away

Air There is at least one flight a day to Athens (11,600 dr) and flights to Thessaloniki (7400 dr) on Friday, Saturday, Sunday and Monday. The Olympic Airways office (☎ 26 218) is on the right side of Dodonis as you walk towards the EOT.

Bus From the main bus station there are 10 buses a day to Igoumenitsa (2½ hours, 1200 dr); eight to Athens (eight hours, 4850 dr) and Konitsa (two hours, 800 dr); five to Thessaloniki, (seven hours, 4000 dr); four to Metsovo (1½ hours, 700 dr); two to Trikala (3½ hours, 1700 dr) and one to Parga (three hours, 1500 dr). Buses to the Zagros villages also leave from this bus station. The schedule is as follows: Papingo villages (Monday, Wednesday and Friday at 5 am and 3 pm, Sunday 9.30 am); Tsepelovo (Monday to Friday at 6 am and 3 pm, with an additional bus in summer at 9 am on Monday, Wednesday and Friday); Monodendri (Monday to Friday at 5.30 am and 4 pm).

From Ioannina's other bus station, at Vizaniou 28, there are 10 buses a day to Arta (2½ hours, 1200 dr); and two buses a day to Patras (4½ hours, 2800 dr). Buses also leave here for Preveza, Parga and Dodoni (see the Dodoni Getting There & Away section for details on this bus).

To Albania See the Getting There & Away chapter for information on going to Albania from Ioannina.

Car Budget Rent a Car (☎ 25 102) is at Napoleonda Zerva 24.

Getting Around

To/From the Airport Ioannina's airport is five km north-west of town on the road to Perama. Take No 8 bus from the bus stop just south of Averof, near the clock tower.

Boats to the Island There are boats every half-hour to the island (10 minutes, 150 dr).

AROUND IOANNINA

Perama Cave Σπήλαιο Περάματος
This cave (☎ 0651-23 440 or 21 521), four km north of Ioannina, is one of the largest in Greece. It was discovered in 1940 by locals searching for a hiding place from the Nazis, and explored by the speleologists Ioannis and Anna Petrochilos, who also explored the Dirou Caves in the Peloponnese. The Perama Cave is second in Greece only to the Dirou Caves in its astonishing array of stalactites and stalagmites. It consists of many chambers and passageways and is 1100 metres long. It's open from 8 am to 5 pm. Admission is 400 dr.

Getting There & Away Take the No 8 bus from near the clock tower to the village of Perama, from where the cave is signposted. The buses run every 20 minutes.

DODONI Δωδώνη
Dodoni, 21 km south-west of Ioannina, is Epiros' most important ancient site. It lies in a fertile valley at the foot of Mt Tomaros and is one of Greece's most evocative ancient sites.

Site opening times change frequently, so enquire at the EOT in Ioannina. Admission is 400 dr.

The *Pension Andromachi* (☎ 0651-91 196) is in the village of Dodoni, near the site.

History

An earth goddess was worshipped here as long ago as 2000 BC. She spoke through an oracle which was reputedly the oldest in Greece. By the 13th century BC Zeus had taken over and it was believed he spoke through the rustling of leaves from a sacred oak tree. Around 500 BC a temple to Zeus was built, but only the foundations and a few columns of this and other smaller temples remain. The oracle was the most important in Greece until it was superseded by the Delphic oracle.

Exploring the Site

The site's colossal 3rd-century BC **theatre**, an ambitious project overseen by King Pyrrhus, has been restored, and is now the site of the Festival of Ancient Drama (see under Festivals in the Ioannina section for details). To the north of the theatre a gate leads to the **acropolis**; part of its once substantial walls are still standing. To the east of the theatre are the foundations of the **bouleuterion** (council house) and a small temple dedicated to Aphrodite. Close by are the scant remains of the **Sanctuary of Zeus**. This sacred precinct was the site of the oracle of Zeus and the sacred oak.

Christianity also left its mark on Dodoni, as evidenced by the remains of a 6th-century AD Byzantine basilica, which was built over the remains of a sanctuary dedicated to Herakles.

Getting There & Away

The bus service to Dodoni is pretty abysmal considering it's Epiros' major ancient site. There are buses from Ioannina on Monday, Tuesday, Wednesday, Friday and Saturday at 6.30 am and 4.30 pm. There are no buses on a Thursday and only one bus on a Sunday at 6 pm, which returns at 6.45 pm.

Buses leave from Ioannina's Vizaniou bus station for the village of Dodoni, and return at 7.30 am and 5.30 pm. An alternative is to get a Zotiko bus which stops 1½ km from the site. This bus leaves the Vizaniou bus station on Monday, Wednesday and Friday at 5.30 am and 2 pm and returns at 7.15 am and 4.30 pm. If your interest in archaeology is not so great as to get you out of bed at dawn, then a taxi will cost around 4500 dr return.

ZAGORIA & THE VIKOS GORGE

The 46 Zagros villages lie north of Ioannina in the region of Zagoria (Ζαγόρια). As with many inaccessible mountainous areas in Greece, the Zagros villages maintained a high degree of autonomy in Turkish times, so their economy and culture flourished.

An outstanding feature of the villages is their architecture. The houses are built entirely of slate from the surrounding mountains – a perfect blending of nature and architecture. With their winding cobbled and stepped streets the villages could have leapt straight out of a Grimm's fairy tale. Some of the villages are sadly depopulated, with only a few elderly inhabitants, whilst others, like Monodendri and Tsepelovo, are beginning to thrive on the new-found tourism in the area.

Good roads connect most of the villages and with a car you could see many of them in one day.

The Vikos-Aoos National Park encompasses much of the area. Within the park is the Tymfi Massif which is part of the north Pindos range and comprises Mts Astraka, Gamila and Tsouka Rossa, the Vikos Gorge and the Aoos River Gorge. It's an area of outstanding natural beauty and is becoming popular with trekkers. So far it is untouched by mass tourism, but several companies organise treks in the region, including the British-based Exodus Expeditions and Robinson Travel Agency in Ioannina.

The area is thickly forested; hornbeam, maple, willow and oak predominate, but there are also fir, pine and cedar trees. Bears, wolves, wild boar, wild cat, wild goat and the rare Rissos quadruped roam the mountains. Vlach and Sarakatsani shepherds still live a seminomadic existence taking their flocks up to high grazing ground in the summer and returning to the valleys in the autumn.

The telephone code (excluding Konitsa) for the Zagros villages is 0653. For information about buses to the Zagros villages, see Ioannina's Getting There & Away section.

Vikos Gorge Χαράδρα του Βίκου

The focal point of the region is the 10-km-long Vikos (VEE-kos) Gorge, which begins at the village of Monodendri (elevation 1090 metres), at the southern end of the gorge. Monodendri is 38 km north of Ioannina, and is reached by a turn-off right from the main Ioannina-Konitsa road.

The Vikos Gorge is the most trekked gorge in Greece, after the Samaria Gorge on Crete. It doesn't require any special expertise but it is a strenuous trek of around 7½ hours ending at the village of Mikri Papingo. Climbing boots are the best footwear, but trainers will suffice. Before you come to Monodendri visit the EOT or the EOS in Ioannina, either of whom will give you a map of the gorge, and answer any questions you may have.

At the far end of Monodendri there is a spectacular view down into the gorge from the 15th-century **Monastery of Agia Paraskevi**. The descent into the gorge is down a steep marked path between the village and the monastery. Once in the gorge, it's a four-hour trail to the end, from where a trail up to the right leads in 2½ hours to the settlement of **Mikri (Small) Papingo**. The larger settlement of **Megali (Large) Papingo** is two km west of here. Klima spring, about halfway along the gorge, is the only source of water, so take plenty along with you.

Places to Stay & Eat Monodendri's choicest accommodation is the lovely traditional *Monodendri Pension & Restaurant* (☎ 61 233), where doubles are 6500 dr. The restaurant serves reasonably priced, well-prepared food. The pension is in the middle of the village. Another pleasant place is the *Vikos Pension* (☎ 61 232), with doubles for 7000 dr. There are also rooms available in private houses – enquire at the restaurant.

The EOT have converted four 19th-century dwellings in the Papingo villages into traditional guesthouses (☎ 41 088/125). Doubles cost 12,000 dr. But if your drachmas don't stretch to this, there are domatia in Megali Papingo where singles/doubles cost around 3500/6000 dr, or the similarly priced *Agnandi's Rooms* (☎ 41 123) in Mikri Papingo. The villages have tavernas, and stores where you can stock up on provisions.

Mt Gamila Refuge
From Mikri Papingo there is a good marked path to the Gamila Refuge (1950 metres) (also called Rodovoli Refuge) which is owned by the EOS club in Megali Papingo

(☎ 41 138/230), from whom you must get the key. Water is available at the refuge and, if it is fully booked, you can camp on the front porch.

From this refuge there are marked trails to Drakolimni (Dragon) Lake (1½ hours) and to the village of Tsepelovo (four hours). For rock climbers there are over 20 routes up Mt Astraka. The EOS in Ioannina gives out a leaflet detailing these.

Tsepelovo Τσεπέλοβο
Tsepelovo is a delightful Zagros village, 51 km north of Ioannina. There are many opportunities for scenic day walks from the village.

Places to Stay The *Gouris Pension* (☎ 81 214/288) is an immaculate place where doubles cost 4000 dr. The enterprising owner, Alexis Gouris, also runs a grocery shop and restaurant in the village. He speaks excellent English and is very knowledgeable about treks in the area, and will happily pass on information to tourists. From the village bus stop, take the road leading uphill to the left from the square to reach Alexis' shop and rooms.

Alexis' new 55-bed B class hotel, complete with swimming pool, located just outside the village, should be open by the time you are reading this.

Konitsa Κόνιτσα
Konitsa (KO-neet-sa, population 2900), 64 km north of Ioannina, is the largest settlement in the area. It's a lively market town and a good base from which to explore northern Zagoria.

Orientation & Information The bus station is on the central square, where you will also find the post office and the National Bank of Greece. There is no EOT or tourist police. Konitsa's postcode is 44100 and the telephone code is 0655.

Walk to Stomiou Monastery Μονή Στομίου This scenic walk along the Aoos River Gorge takes about one hour. Cross the stone bridge at the beginning of the town (coming from Ioannina), turn left and follow the Aoos River to the waterfall. Cross the bridge and follow the path up to the monastery. Occasionally there is a lone monk in residence here who shows visitors around the monastery, but even if you find it locked, the walk is worth it for the tremendous views.

Places to Stay & Eat *To Dentro Restaurant & Rooms* (☎ 22 055 or 23 001), 500 metres before the town centre on the Ioannina road, is Konitsa's best deal. It has beautifully furnished, spotless doubles/triples for 4000/4500 dr with shared bath, and triples with private bathrooms for 6000 dr. Ioannis, the jovial owner, can advise on local walks. If you ask, the bus driver will drop you off at the rooms. To Dentro also has the best restaurant in town. Spaghetti bolognese is 800 dr, trout is 1000 dr and their speciality, grilled feta with chilli, is 400 dr.

If the To Dentro is full or doesn't suit, the *Hotel Egnatias* (☎ 22 083), next to the bus station, has drab singles/doubles for 3000/4500 dr.

Getting There & Away From Monday to Friday there are eight buses to Konitsa (two hours, 800 dr) from Ioannina, and on Saturday and Sunday, there are four buses.

METSOVO Μέτσοβο
The village of Metsovo (MET-sov-a, population 2800, elevation 1116 metres) sprawls down a mountainside just south of the Katara pass, at the junction of Epiros, Thessaly and Macedonia, 58 km from Ioannina and 90 km from Trikala. The inhabitants are descendants of Vlach shepherds, most of whom have hung up their crooks to make a living in the tourist trade.

Metsovo has many tourist trappings: locals dressed in traditional costumes, local handicrafts, a regional cuisine, stone-built mansions, invigorating air, a superb mountain setting and good conditions for skiing. Some visitors find the village twee and artificial, while others are enamoured of its undeniable and considerable charm.

History
Originally a small settlement of shepherds, the inhabitants of Metsovo were granted many privileges in Ottoman times, as reward for guarding the mountain pass upon which Metsovo stands. This pass was the only route across the Pindos range, and the Metsovite guards' vigilance facilitated the passage of Ottoman troops. The privileges led to Metsovo becoming an important centre of finance, commerce, handicraft production and sheep farming. A school was established in the town in 1659 at a time when Greek teaching schools were not allowed in other parts of the country.

Metsovo's privileges were abolished in 1795 by that spoilsport, Ali Pasha. In March of 1854 it suffered considerable destruction by Ottoman troops led by Abdi Pasha. But Metsovo was lucky in that it had many prosperous benefactors: locals who had gone on to achieve national and international recognition. The most famous of them were George Averoff (1815-99) and Michael Tositsa (1885-1950). Both bequeathed considerable amounts of money to Metsovo, which was used to restore the town to its former glory and finance several small industries.

Orientation & Information
Orientation in Metsovo is easy as there is only one main thoroughfare. Coming from Kalambaka the town is a turn-off to the left from the Katara pass. The main thoroughfare loops down to the central square, passing many restaurants, hotels and souvenir shops. A maze of stone pathways winds between the fine, traditionally built houses.

The bus stop is on the central square in front of Café Diethnes. The post office is on the right side of the main thoroughfare walking from the central square. To reach the OTE, walk along the road opposite the bus station, keep veering right and you will come to the OTE on the right. Metsovo's postcode is 44200 and the telephone code is 0656. The

National Bank of Greece is on the far side of the central square.

There is no EOT or tourist police; the regular police (☎ 41 233/222) are on the right, a little way along the road opposite the bus stop.

Things to See

The **Tositsa Mansion**, the restored mansion of the Tositsa family, has been turned into a Folk Museum, and is a faithful reconstruction of a wealthy 19th-century Metsovon household, with exquisitely handcrafted furniture, artefacts and utensils. The museum is about halfway up the main street. Opening times are Friday to Wednesday from 8.30 am to 1 pm and 4 to 6.30 pm. Wait at the door until the guide opens it and lets you in (every half-hour). Admission is 400 dr.

The 14th-century **Monastery of Agiou Nikolaos** stands in a gorge below Metsovo. Its chapel has post-Byzantine frescoes and a beautiful carved wood iconostasis. The monastery is a 30-minute walk from Metsovo and is signposted to the left, just beyond the Hotel Athinea.

The **Averoff Gallery** was financed by George Averoff's three children. It houses a permanent collection of 19th and 20th-century works by Greek painters and sculptors. To reach the gallery turn left at the far side of the central square and the gallery is on the right. It's open Tuesday to Sunday from 9 am to 1.30 pm and 5 to 7.30 pm. Admission is 200 dr.

Activities

Metsovo's ski centre (☎ 41 211) is on the right side of the main Kalambaka-Ioannina highway, just before the turn-off for the town. There is a taverna at the centre and an 82-seat ski lift, two downhill runs and a five-km cross-country run. Ski hire is available in Metsovo.

Places to Stay – bottom end

Metsovo's hotels, predictably, have a folksy ambience, right down to the town's one E class establishment. The E class *Hotel Athinea* (☎ 41 332), on the central square, is old but clean, and the woven rugs on the floors add a homely touch. Single/double/triple/quad rooms cost 3500/5500/7500/8500 dr with private bathrooms. The D class *Hotel Acropolis* (☎ 41 672) has traditional furniture, wooden floors and ceilings and colourful wallhangings. Rates are 5000/7500 dr for doubles/triples with private bathrooms. Look out for it on the right at the beginning of the road down to Metsovo.

Places to Stay – middle

The C class *Hotel Egnatias* (☎ 41 263/900; fax 41 485) has cosy rooms with fitted carpets, wood-panelled walls and balconies. Singles/doubles/triples are 6250/7500/9000 dr. The hotel is on the right side of the main road as you approach the central square.

On the opposite side, further up the hill, the C class *Hotel Bitouni* (☎ 41 217/545) has immaculate rooms and a charming lounge with a flagstone floor, brass plates, embroidered cushions and carved wood coffee tables. Rates are 6250/7500/9000/10,500 dr.

The C class *Hotel Apollon* (☎ 41 844/833; fax 42 110) is Metsovo's newest hotel. The gorgeous, carpeted rooms cost 6950/8800/10,950/15,200 dr. To reach the hotel, walk along the road opposite the bus station and look for the sign pointing right.

Places to Eat

The *Athenea Restaurant* (in the hotel of the same name; see Places to Stay) has tasty, reasonably priced food. The *Taverna To Spitiko*, on the left side of the main street coming from the central square, serves low-priced local dishes; a mixed cheese plate for two people is 1300 dr.

The 1st-floor *Taverna Metsovitiko Saloni* is an up-market establishment with a beautiful interior of traditional carved wood furniture and colourful wall-hangings. A full meal with wine will cost around 2000 dr. The restaurant is just up from the post office. The *Tsoulias Zaharoplasteion*, opposite the post office, serves cakes, rice pudding and corn-flour pudding; everything including Nescafé is 150 dr.

Things to Buy

Craftshops selling both high quality stuff and kitsch are ubiquitous in Metsovo. The old-fashioned food shop opposite the bus stop sells local cheeses, for which the town is famous.

Getting There & Away

From Metsovo there are six buses to Thessaloniki, four to Ioannina and four to Trikala (via Kalambaka).

IGOUMENITSA Ηγουμενίτσα

The west-coast port of Igoumenitsa (Ig-ou-men-IT-sa, population 6000), 100 km from Ioannina, is a purely functional place from which to get ferries to Corfu and Italy. Ferries used to also sail to Dubrovnik in former Yugoslavia, but this service had been suspended at the time of writing.

Orientation

The ferries for Italy and the domestic ferries for Corfu leave from two separate quays quite close to one another on the waterfront of Ethnikis Antistaseos. To get to the bus station turn left from both ferry quays, walk along Ethnikis Antistaseos, turn right onto 23 Fevrouariou and two blocks inland turn left onto Kyprou; the bus station is a little way along on the left.

From the waterfront turn right onto Evangelistrias (one block beyond 23 Fevrouariou) and the post office and OTE are next to one another on the right. Igoumenitsa's postcode is 46100 and the telephone code is 0665.

The Ionian Bank, on the corner of El Venizelou, is the most convenient bank. To reach it from the Corfu quay, turn left; from the Italian quay turn right.

Information

The EOT (☎ 22 227), on the waterfront beside the Italian quay, is open every day from 7 am to 2.30 pm. The tourist police office (☎ 22 222) is on the waterfront almost opposite the Corfu quay.

Places to Stay & Eat

Most ferries leave Igoumenitsa in the morning so you may have to stay overnight here on the evening before your departure. Walk two blocks up El Venizelou from the waterfront, turn right at Kyprou, cross over the road and you'll come to the D class *Hotel Lux* (☎ 22 223), with singles/doubles for 2500/3800 dr with shared bathrooms and 3700/4400 dr with private bathrooms. On the waterfront the *Hotel Acropol* (☎ 22 342) has OK rooms for 3000/4500 dr with shared bathrooms (hot shower 300 dr). The hotel is just beyond the turn-off for the bus station.

The D class *Egnatias* (☎ 23 648/455) has comfortable rooms for 4000/5000 dr with private bathrooms. Cross over Kyprou from El Venizelou and the hotel is on the right. A little way along the road to Parga (signposted from the waterfront) the C class *Hotel Epirus* (☎ 22 504 or 23 474) has very pleasant rooms for 6000/8800 dr with private bathrooms.

The *To Astron Restaurant*, El Venizelou 9, and the *Restaurant Nikolas*, on the corner of 23 Fevrouariou and Gregoris Lambraki, serve reasonably priced, tasty food.

Getting There & Away

Bus From Igoumenista's bus station there are nine buses to Ioannina (2½ hours, 1200 dr); five to Parga (one hour, 600 dr); three to Athens (eight hours, 5450 dr); two to Preveza (2½ hours, 1350 dr); and one to Thessaloniki (eight hours, 4500 dr).

Ferry & Catamaran There are ferries every hour to Corfu between 5 am and 10 pm (1½ hours, 620 dr). Agencies opposite the quay sell tickets. Most of the ferries to/from Italy also stop at Corfu.

To Italy There are around six ferries a day from Igoumenitsa to Brindisi (11 hours, 9800/15,800 dr low/high season). There is at least one ferry a day to Bari (13 hours, 6000/8000 dr low/high season) and Ancona (24 hours, 9800/12,800 dr low/high season); five ferries a week to Otranto (nine hours, 7000/9500 dr low/high season), and three a week to Ortona (24 hours, 13,500/16,500 dr low/high season). Some of the ferries to Ancona go direct, but all of the others go via Corfu (two hours) where some lines allow you to stop over free of charge. Most of the boats leave in the morning between 6 and 8 am and you must turn up at the port at least two hours before departure.

All of the central ticketing offices are on Ethnikis Antistaseos. Hellenic Mediterranean (for Ortona) are at No 32 (☎ 25 682 or 22 180; Adriatica (for Brindisi) are at No 58 a (☎ 22 952/679); Anek (for Ancona) are at No 34 (☎ 22 104/158); and Marlines (also for Ancona are at No 42 (☎ 23 301/911). For other lines, go to Chris Travel Agency at No 60 (☎ 25 351/2/3/4/5).

At the time of writing a daily catamaran service had commenced between Igoumenitsa and Brindisi via Corfu (3½ hours 10,000/14,500 dr low/high season; the price is the same if the ferry is boarded in Corfu). Check with the EOT if this service is still operating.

PARGA Πάργα

Parga (PAR-ga), 77 km north of Preveza and 48 km south of Igoumenitsa, spills down to a rocky bay, flanked by coves, and islets. Add to this a Venetian castle and the long pebble and sand Valtos Beach and you have somewhere truly alluring. So it will come as no surprise to be told that it's overrun with tourists, and that hotels, domatia and travel agents have swamped the once serene fishing village.

Orientation & Information

The bus station is at Odos Alexandrou Varga 18 and the post office is in the same building. Turn left at the bus station and walk straight ahead at the crossroads onto Odos Vasila and you will come to the National Bank of Greece and the OTE; continue along this street to reach the waterfront. Parga's postcode is 68200 and the telephone code is 0684. There is no EOT or tourist police; the regular police (☎ 31 222) are in the same building as the post office and the bus station.

Nekromanteion of Aphyra

Just about every travel agent in Parga advertises trips to Nekromanteion (Νεκρομαντείο) . The trip takes you up the Acheron River from where you continue on foot to the Nekromanteion. According to mythology this river was the River Styx across which the old boatman, Charon, rowed the dead. Until the departed had taken this journey they could not enter Hades (the world of the dead) and so were in a state of limbo.

The Nekromanteion was the ancients' venue for the equivalent of a modern-day seance. They believed the spot to be the Gate of Hades, and so it became an Oracle of the Dead and a Sanctuary to Hades and Persephone. Pilgrims came here with votive offerings in the hope that the souls of the departed would communicate with them through the oracle. The maze-like Nekromanteion is fascinating to explore. The trip costs around 1500 dr.

Places to Stay – bottom end

There are three camp sites on the coast just north of Parga, all signposted from the Parga-Igoumenitsa road. The first is *Parga Camping* (☎ 31 161), followed by *Elia Camping* (☎ 31 130) and lastly *Enjoy Camping* (☎ 31 171).

One of Parga's nicest hotels is the D class *Hotel Agiou Nektarios* (☎ 31 150) on the corner of the main Preveza-Igoumenitsa road and the turn-off to Parga. The cosy single/double rooms cost 4500/6500 dr with private bathrooms. To reach the hotel from the bus station turn left and left again at the crossroads and the hotel is on the right.

If you turn right at the crossroads you'll be on Odos Spiros Livada which is lined with hotels and domatia. The D *Hotel Paradisos* (☎ 31 229), on the left along here, has comfortable rooms for 5000/7500 dr.

Places to Stay – top end

The B class *Vlatos Beach Hotel* (☎ 31 610/005/065), on the beach at Vlatos, has singles/doubles for 9000/10,800 dr. The hotel has a café and restaurant. The B class

Parga Beach Hotel (☎ 31 410/293; fax 31 412), on Parga Beach, has rates of 7000/10,600 dr.

The *Lichnou Beach Hotel* (☎ 31 257/422/157) has rates of 9000/13,000 dr. The last two hotels mentioned both have a bar, restaurant and tennis court. Vlatos Beach is just north of Parga and Lichnou Beach is just south.

Places to Eat
The nameless psistaria at Alexandrou Varga 4 has generous portions of roast chicken for 650 dr and souvlaki for 800 dr. Turn left from the bus station, go straight ahead at the crossroads and it's on the left.

Getting There & Away
Bus From Parga's bus station there are five buses a day to both Igoumenitsa (one hour, 600 dr) and Preveza (two hours, 900 dr) and one to Ioannina (three hours, 1500 dr).

Excursion Boat The small Ionian island of Paxi lies just 20 km off the coast. In summer there are daily excursion boats to the island (1200 dr) from Parga. The excursions are widely advertised by Parga's travel agents.

PREVEZA Πρέβεζα
Preveza (PRE-ve-za), built on a peninsula between the Ionian Sea and the Gulf of Amvrakikos, is a purely functional place where ferries ply over a narrow strait to Aktion. To get to the bus station from the quay, walk inland along Odos Kon Kariotaki (opposite the ELPA mobile office) and you will come to the OTE on the right. Turn right here onto Leoforos Irinis and the intercity bus station is along here on the right. The EOT, post office and National Bank of Greece are in a row on the waterfront – turn right from the quay.

Preveza's telephone code is 0682 and the postcode is 48100.

Places to Stay
There is little to detain the visitor in Preveza, but should you get stuck, the nearest camp site is *Indian Village* (☎ 22 382). Turn left from the quay and it's 2½ km along the road.

The cheapest hotel is the pleasant D class *Hotel Urania* (☎ 27 123 or 24 304), Leoforos Irinas, where singles/doubles/triples are 4000/6500/7500 dr with private bathrooms. The hotel is on the right walking towards the bus station. The palatial C class *Hotel Dioni* (☎ 27 381/2/3), Plateia G Papageorgiou, has rooms for 6800/8800/10,600 dr with private bathrooms. Turn right from the quay, and the hotel is signposted to the left, just beyond the ELPA office. There are several eateries along the waterfront.

Getting There & Away
Air There are at least five flights a week (20 minutes, 9600 dr) from Preveza airport to Athens. The airport is sometimes called Lefkada or Aktion. The Olympic Airways office (☎ 28 674) is on the corner of Spiliadou and Balkou. The airport is seven km south of Preveza.

Bus From the intercity bus station there are nine buses a day to Ioannina (two hours, 1300 dr); five to Parga (two hours, 900 dr) and Arta (one hour, 600 dr); two to Igoumenitsa (2½ hours, 1350 dr); and three to Athens (six hours, 4100 dr).

Ferry The Preveza-Aktion ferry plies to and fro every half-hour (60 dr per person; 530 dr per car).

AROUND PREVEZA
Nikopolis Νικόπολη
In 31 BC, Octavian (later Emperor Augustus of Rome) defeated Mark Antony and Cleopatra in the famous Battle of Actium (present-day Aktion). To celebrate this victory, Octavian built Nikopolis, which means 'City of Victory' and populated it by forcible resettlement of people from surrounding towns and villages. It was plundered by Vandals and Goths in the 5th and 6th centuries, but rebuilt by Justinian. It was sacked again by the Bulgars in the 11th century, after which nobody bothered to rebuild it.

Little is left of the walls built by Augustus, but the Byzantine walls and a theatre survive, and there are remains of temples to Mars and Poseidon (an appropriate choice of gods for the warmongering Octavian), an aqueduct, Roman baths and a restored Roman odeion. The immense site sprawls over both sides of the Preveza-Arta road. It is open Tuesday to Sunday from 9 am to 3 pm. Admission is 400 dr. The Preveza-Arta buses stop at the site.

ARTA Αρτα

Arta (population 18,000), the second-largest town of Epiros, is 76 km south of Ioannina and 50 km north-east of Preveza. The town is built over the ancient city of Ambracia which King Pyrrhus of Epiros made his capital in the 4th century BC. In the 14th century AD the Frankish despot of Epiros made it his seat of government. Despite this distinguished past the town has no outstanding attractions and most people whiz through en route from Patras to Ioannina (via the Rio-Andirio ferry). However, if you do decide to stop off you'll find a pleasant town devoid of any tourist hype.

Arta's telephone code is 0646.

Things to See

The town's most distinguished feature is its fine 18th-century **stone-arched bridge**, which crosses the River Arahthos. The prominent 13th-century **fortress** in the north-east part of town has good views from its ramparts.

Arta also has several churches of note: the 13th-century **Church of Panagia Parigoritissa**, overlooking Plateia Skoufa, just south of the central square of Plateia Kilkis, is a well-preserved, striking building. The churches of **Agios Vasilios** and **Agia Theodora** have attractive ceramic decorations on their exterior walls. Both of these churches are just west of the main thoroughfare of Odos Pyrrhus, which runs south from the fortress to the central square.

Places to Stay & Eat

The town has two C class hotels: the *Hotel Cronos* (☎ 22 211), Plateia Kilkis, has singles/doubles for 5200/6800 dr with private bathrooms; the *Hotel Amvrakia* (☎ 28 311) has singles/doubles for 4000/5500 dr with private bathrooms. The Amvrakia is at Priovolou 13; this street is one block east of Pyrrhus. The more expensive B class *Xenia* (☎ 27 413) is in a superb setting inside the grounds of the fortress. Singles/doubles here with private bathrooms are 5500/7200 dr.

There are several restaurants on Plateia Kilkis.

Getting There & Away

Ioannina-Patras buses stop in Arta. There are five buses a day between Preveza and Arta (one hour; 600 dr).

Thrace Θράκη

Thrace is the north-eastern region of Greece and the backwater of the mainland. If you ask Greeks from elsewhere what it has to offer, chances are most will reply 'nothing', and some will add in words weighted with meaning 'and Turks live there'. The Turkish population of Thrace, along with the Greek population of Constantinople and the Turkish islands of Gokçeada and Bozcaada were exempt from the 1923 population exchange. This phenomenon alone sets the area apart from the rest of Greece. The landscape is dotted with the slender minarets of mosques, villages of red-roofed houses in

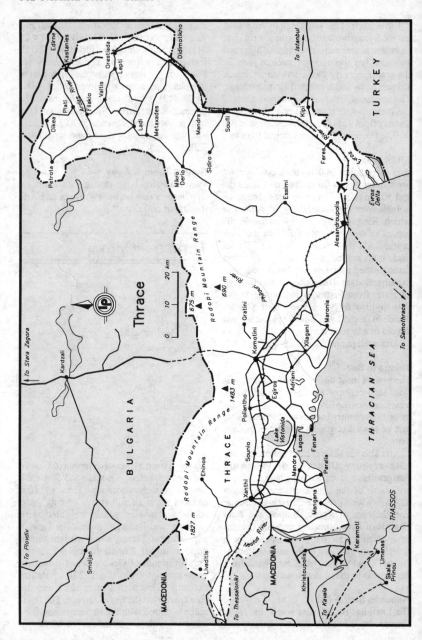

in Turkish-style, there is a more pronounced Turkish influence in the food, and a greater proliferation of Eastern-style bazaars and street vendors.

Besides being of ethnographical interest the region has some picturesque towns and a varied landscape. It has a long coastline interspersed with wetlands and a hinterland of mountains (the Rodopi range) covered in thick forest and undergrowth. The mountains are punctuated by valleys through which flow several rivers. The most important is the River Evros, which marks the boundary with Turkey. Between the coast and the mountains is a fertile plain where sunflowers, grown for their oil, create a pretty foreground to the mountainous backdrop. Tobacco is also grown, to supply a thriving industry – although the rest of Europe is giving up the noxious weed, amongst Greeks smoking is increasing at an alarming rate. Another feature of the area is its large number of storks. Look out for their huge untidy nests on high extremities of buildings.

History

The earliest Thracian tribes were of Indo-European extraction, and the ethnic and cultural origins of the region have more of an affinity with Bulgaria and Turkey than Greece. During the 7th century BC, the Thracian coast was conquered by the most powerful Greek city-states, but during the 6th and 5th centuries BC it was subjugated by the Persians.

After the Persian defeat at the Battle of Plataea, Thrace was governed by Athens. In 346 BC Philip II of Macedon gained control. During Roman times it was an insignificant backwater, but after the split of the empire, the region developed culturally and economically, because of its strategic position on the Via Egnatias. Later, its fate was similar to that of pretty much everywhere else in Greece, with invasions by Goths, Huns, Vandals and Bulgars and finally the Turks in 1361.

In 1920 the Treaty of Sèvres decreed that all of Thrace become part of the modern Greek state, but after the 1923 population exchange, Greece lost Eastern Thrace to Turkey.

XANTHI Ξάνθη

Travelling east from Thessaloniki or Kavala, Xanthi (HAN-thee, population 31,000) is the first town you will come to in Thrace. The old town of Xanthi has many beautiful well-maintained Turkish dwellings from the 19th century. Xanthi is a lively and flourishing town where Turks make up 10% of the population, and live amicably side by side with the Greeks. The town is the centre of Thrace's tobacco-growing industry.

Orientation & information

The main thoroughfare is 28 Oktovriou, which runs north to south through the town. Halfway along here is Plateia Eleftherias, and just west of here on Odos Iroon is a huge fascinating indoor food market. The main bus station is at the northern end of this food market and the bus station for Kavala is opposite the southern end on Odos Eklission. The train station is two km from town – just off the main Kavala-Xanthi road.

If you continue up 28 Oktovriou from Plateia Eleftherias, you will come to the central square of Plateia Kentriki, with a prominent clock tower on its western side. To reach the old town from here, continue north along Vasileos Konstantinou. The post office is at A Giorgiou 16, and the OTE is at Michael Vordou 2; both streets lead west from Plateia Kentriki. Xanthi's postcode is 67100 and the telephone code is 0541. Walk one block up Vasileos Konstantinou, turn right and you'll see the National Bank of Greece on the left. The Olympic Airways office (☎ 22 944) is at Michael Vordou 4, near the OTE.

There is no tourist office or tourist police in Xanthi, but the regular police (☎ 22 100), at 28 Oktovriou 223, will do what they can to help, dragging in an English speaker off the street if necessary.

Old Xanthi

Old Xanthi is built on a hillside overlooking the modern town. The narrow winding streets have some lovely neoclassical mansions which once belonged to wealthy tobacco merchants. The more modest dwellings also have considerable charm; most are pastel coloured, and have overhanging timber framed first floors.

Two of the old town's mansions which adjoin one another have been converted into the **Museum of Xanthi**. They were built for the Coumtzogli brothers, who were tobacco magnates. The museum is well laid out and exhibits include traditional agricultural and household implements, carpets, embroidery and jewellery. Whilst in the museum cast your eyes upwards to the ceilings, which are amazing. Some are of carved wood, others are painted with intricate designs. Also don't miss the antique toilet upstairs (no longer usable). The bowl is decorated both inside and out with elaborate floral designs.

Labelling of exhibits is in Greek, but the friendly curator, Deodoros Tserpistolis, will do his best to explain things, although his English is limited. The museum is at Antika 7 and is open every day from 10 am to 1 pm and 6 to 8 pm (in winter from 5 to 7 pm). Admission is 100 dr.

Places to Stay – bottom end

The D class *Lux Hotel* (☎ 22 341 or 23 004), Georgiou Stavriou 18, near Plateia Kentriki, has single/double rooms at 2500/3000 dr with shared bathrooms. Coming from Vasileos Konstantinou, turn right at the National Bank of Greece to reach the hotel.

The town's two clean and comfortable C class hotels are better options. The *Hotel Dimokritus* (☎ 25 111), 28 Oktovriou 41, near Plateia Kentriki, has rates of 4600/5700/6900 dr with private bathrooms. The *Hotel Xanthippion* (☎ 77 061/2/3/4/5), 28 Oktovriou 212, has single/double rates of 4600/5600 dr with private bathrooms. This hotel has a car park, and is at the southern end of town.

Places to Stay – middle

Xanthi's best hotel is the modern B class *Hotel Nestos* (☎ 27 531/2/3/4/5). The rooms go for 7500/9500 dr with private bathrooms.

The hotel is one km south of the town centre. Coming from Kavala by road, it's on the right as you enter the town. This hotel also has a car park.

Places to Eat

Locals rate the *Klimataria Restaurant* on Plateia Kentriki as the town's best eating place. It has a large selection of ready food: stuffed peppers, stuffed aubergines and chicken stew are all 650 dr.

Students hang out at *Taverna Xanthi* which has outdoor eating in a walled garden. A huge meal of souvlaki, chips, Greek salad and Amstel beer will cost about 1550 dr. Walk to the top of Vasileos Konstantinou and you will see a sign pointing left to the taverna.

On Vasileos Konstantinou there are many zaharoplasteia selling Turkish cakes and confectionery. One of the best is *Anestis*, at the northern end of the street on the right.

Getting There & Away

Air Xanthi shares Khristoupolis Airport with Kavala in Macedonia (see the Kavala section for flight details). The airport is 47 km away.

Bus From the main bus terminal there are eight buses to Komotini (45 minutes, 450 dr) and seven to Thessaloniki (four hours, 2500 dr). There are no direct buses to Alexandroupolis; you must change buses at Komotini. Seven buses go to Kavala (one hour, 600 dr).

Train There are five trains a day to both Alexandroupolis (610 dr) and Thessaloniki (1500 dr). The 7.20 pm eastbound train goes to Istanbul. Train tickets may be purchased either at the station, or from the OSE agent, Tarpidis Tours (☎ 22 277 or 27 840), Tsaldari 5, which is in the Agora Nousa (an indoor shopping precinct) just east of Plateia Kentriki. A taxi to the station costs 400 dr.

Getting Around

To/From the Airport There are no Olympic Airways buses to Khristoupolis. A taxi costs 5000 dr. Alternatively you can take a Kavala-bound bus to the town of Khristoupolis, and take a taxi to the airport which is 12 km away.

KOMOTINI

Komotini (population 35,000), 57 km east of Xanthi, is the capital of the prefecture of Rodopi. Its population is half Greek and half Turkish. It lacks the character of Xanthi and is unremarkable except for its outstanding **Archaeological Museum** (☎ 0531-22 411), Simeonidi 4, which houses well-displayed finds from little-known ancient sites in Thrace, most notably Abdera and Maronia.

The latter was Homer's Ismaros, where Odysseus obtained the wine which he used to intoxicate the Cyclops Polyphemus. Whilst in this drunken state, Polyphemus had a stake driven into his one remaining eye by villagers who sought revenge for his misdeeds. (The scant remains of the ancient site of Maronia are near the modern village of Maronia, 31 km south-east of Komotini.) The museum is well signposted and opening times are Tuesday to Sunday from 9 am to 3 pm. Admission is 400 dr.

Komotini's telephone code is 0531.

Places to Stay

The nearest camp site to Komotini is *Fanariou Komotinis Camping* (☎ 0535-31 217/270). The site is by the sea near the village of Fanari, about 26 km south-west of Komotini.

If you get stuck in Komotini, finding a place to stay shouldn't be a problem. Amongst the possibilities are the E class *Hotel Hellas* (☎ 22 055), Dimokritou 31, where singles/doubles with shared bathrooms are 2500/3400 dr. The *Pension Olympos* (☎ 37 690/1/2/3), Orfeus 35, has singles/doubles with shared bathrooms for 4400/6100 dr and with private bathrooms for 5500/8600 dr. The *Democritus Hotel* (22 579), Plateia Vizinou 8, has singles/doubles for 5500/7300 dr with private bathrooms.

Komotini's best hotel is the B class *Chris & Eve Mansion* (☎ 23 787, 28 946 or 29 777; fax 26 979). This is a posh place with posh amenities, including a swimming pool, sauna and gymnasium. Rates are 6800/9100

The blinding of the cyclops Polyphemus

dr for singles/doubles and suites are 13,500 dr. The hotel is three km from Kavala on the Komotini-Alexandroupolis road.

Getting There & Away

There are frequent buses from Komotini to Xanthi and Alexandroupolis. Eight buses a day travel between Kavala and Komotini (45 minutes, 450 dr).

ALEXANDROUPOLIS Αλεξανδρούπολη

Alexandroupolis (Alex-and-ROU-pol-is, population 34,000), the capital of the prefecture of Evros, is a modern, dusty and prosaic town with a heavy military presence, and there is no reason why anyone should wish to visit other than to transit east to Turkey, or to catch the ferry to Samothrace.

Alexandroupolis' hotels get surprisingly full, as for some unfathomable reason Greek holiday makers flock here in July and August, and their numbers are swelled by overlanders, who descend upon the town en route to Turkey. During these months try to continue your journey to Samothrace or Turkey; otherwise, make an accommodation reservation in advance.

Orientation

The town is laid out roughly on a grid system, with the main streets running east to west, parallel with the waterfront, where the lively evening *volta* (promenade) takes place. The waterfront is Karaoli Dimitriou at

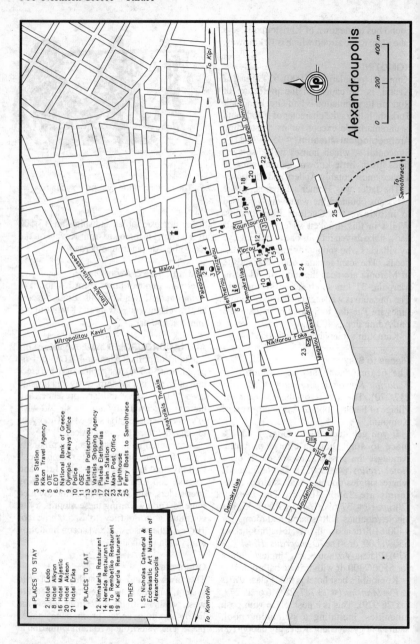

Alexandroupolis

PLACES TO STAY
2 Hotel Lido
8 Hotel Alkyon
16 Hotel Majestic
20 Hotel Akteon
21 Hotel Erika

▼ PLACES TO EAT
12 Klimataria Restaurant
14 Nereida Restaurant
18 To Rembetiko Restaurant
19 Kali Kardia Restaurant

OTHER
1 St Nicholas Cathedral &
  Ecclesiastic Art Museum of
  Alexandroupolis
3 Bus Station
4 Kikon Travel Agency
6 OTE
7 EOT
9 National Bank of Greece
10 Olympic Airways Office
11 OSE
13 Plateia Politechnou
15 Vatitsis Shipping Agency
17 Plateia Eleftherias
22 Train Station
23 Main Post Office
24 Lighthouse
25 Ferry Boats to Samothrace

the eastern end, and Megalou Alexandrou at the western. The town's most prominent landmark is the large 19th-century lighthouse on the middle of the waterfront. The two main squares are Plateia Eleftherias and Plateia Politechniou. Both are just one block north of Karaoli Dimitriou.

The railway station is on the waterfront just south of Plateia Eleftherias and east of the port from where boats leave for Samothrace. The intercity bus station is at Eleftheriou Venizelou 36, five blocks inland. The local bus terminal is on Plateia Eleftherias.

Information

The Municipal Tourist Office (☎ 24 998) is in the town hall on Demokratias. The helpful staff dispense maps and have information on accommodation and transport.

The main post office is on the waterfront on the corner of Nikiforou Foka and Megalou Alexandrou. The OTE is on the corner of Mitropolitou Kaviri and Eleftheriou Venizelou. Alexandroupolis' post- code is 68100 and the telephone code is 0551. The National Bank of Greece is at Demokratias 246. The police (☎ 26 418) are at Karaiskaki 6. The port police telephone number is ☎ 26 468.

Ecclesiastic Art Museum of Alexandroupolis

This outstanding museum is one of the best of its kind in the country. It contains a priceless collection of icons and ecclesiastical ornaments brought to Greek Thrace by refugees from Asia Minor. Unfortunately due to a cutback in government funding the museum is unable to keep regular opening hours, but if you ring the bell of the offices next door, someone will show you around. Entrance is free. The museum is in the grounds of the St Nicholas Cathedral.

Festival

Alexandroupolis has a wine festival during July and August. It takes place at Camping Alexandroupolis camp site, on the coast, three km west of town.

Places to Stay

Camping Alexandroupolis (☎ 28 735) is on the beach three km west of the town. It's a clean well-run site with good facilities. Take a local bus from Plateia Eleftherias to reach the site.

The *Hotel Ledo* (☎ 28 808), Paleologou 15, is an outstanding D class hotel with comfortable single/double/triple rooms for 1800/2500/3200 dr with shared bathrooms and 3400/3800 dr for doubles/triples with private bathrooms. The hotel is one block north of the bus station. Another low-priced hotel is the D class *Hotel Majestic* (☎ 26 444), Plateia Eleftherias 7, where rooms are 2250/3380/4500 dr with shared bathrooms. Even closer to the port is the E class *Hotel Akteon* (☎ 28 078). This ramshackle place has loads of character and is a long-time favourite with backpackers. The double/ triple/quad rooms are 4000/5000/6000 dr.

The C class *Hotel Alkyon* (☎ 27 465), Moudanion 1, has palatial rooms for 4800/6700/8140 dr with private bathrooms. To reach the hotel walk west along Megalou Alexandrou and turn right at Kritis. Another good choice in this price range is the *Hotel Erika* (☎ 31 691), which is a very superior D class where single/double room rates are 5000/7300 dr. All rooms have private bathrooms, telephone, TV and balconies. The hotel is on the corner of Karaoli Dimitriou and Kountourioti.

Places to Eat

One of the town's cheapest restaurants is *To Rembetika*, Plateia Eleftherias 8, where sardines and kalamaria are both 600 dr. The *Kali Kardia Restaurant*, Karaoli Dimitriou 100, is also commendable. A very tasty meal here will cost about 1600 dr.

Klimataria Restaurant, on Plateia Politechniou, has a large selection of ready food at low prices: moussaka is 660 dr, stuffed vegetables are 670 dr and lamb with vegetables is 750 dr. *Neraida Restaurant*, diagonally opposite the Klimataria, is also good, and similarly priced.

Getting There & Away

Air The Olympic Airlines office (☎ 26 361) is at Ellis 4. Alexandroupolis has a domestic airport, which is seven km east of town, near the village of Loutra. The airport serves Athens only, with a daily flight at 7.20 pm; the cost is 13,700 dr.

Bus From Alexandroupolis' bus station there are frequent buses to Soufli, Didimotikho, Orestiada and Komotini. There are five buses a day to Thessaloniki (six hours, 3200 dr) via Kavala. There are no direct buses to Xanthi; you must change buses in Komotini.

To Turkey There are daily OSE buses to Istanbul, leaving at 10 am. The journey takes six or seven hours and tickets cost 4000 dr. Buy them from the OSE office on Plateia Politechniou. In addition, two buses operated by a private bus company go to Istanbul on a Friday, leaving at 2.30 and 6 am. Tickets cost 5000 dr and may be bought at a number of travel agencies including Kikon Travel Agency (☎ 25 455), Eleftheriou Venizelou 68.

Otherwise you can take a bus from the intercity bus station to Kipi (three departures a day) the border town, which is 43 km from Alexandroupolis. You cannot walk across the border but it is easy enough to hitch across – you may be lucky and get a lift all the way to Istanbul. Otherwise take a bus from Ipsala (five km beyond the border) or from Keşan (30 km beyond the border).

Train There are two trains a day to/from Athens and intermediate stations (15 hours, 7200/4800 dr, 1st/2nd class). Five trains a day do the journey to/from Thessaloniki (seven hours, 4000/2100 dr, 1st/2nd class). There are also three trains a day to Kastanies via Didimotikho and Orestiada.

To Turkey There is one train a day to Istanbul, which leaves Alexandroupolis at 9 pm. Tickets cost 5000 dr and the journey can take 10 hours. The train is hot and crowded in summer; the bus is a marginally better choice.

Ferry In July and August the sailing times to Samothrace are 8 am and 3 pm on Monday; 8 pm and 5 pm on Wednesday; 9 am and 3 pm on Thursday; 8 and 10 am and 5 pm on Friday; 8 am and 3 pm on Saturday and 8.30 am, noon and 5 pm on Sunday. In spring and autumn there are two sailings a day and in winter, one. Tickets may be purchased from Vatitsis Shipping Agency (☎ 26 721, 23 512 or 22 215), Kyprou 5 (opposite the port). Tickets cost 1120 dr and the trip takes two hours.

Getting Around

To/From the Airport There is no airport shuttle bus. Take a Loutra-bound bus from Plateia Eleftherias.

EVROS DELTA Δέλτα Εβρου

The Evros Delta, 20 km south-east of Alexandroupolis, is ecologically one of Europe's most important wetlands; 300 species of birds have been recorded including the last 15 surviving pairs of royal eagles, and more than 200,000 migrating waterfowl spend part of their winter here. Unfortunately the wetlands are in a highly sensitive area due to their proximity to Turkey, and at the time of writing permission from the security police in Alexandroupolis was required in order to visit. Contact the regular police or the municipal tourist office for further information.

ALEXANDROUPOLIS TO DIDIMOTIKHO

North-east of Alexandroupolis the road, railway line and River Evros run close together, skirting the Turkish border. This is a highly sensitive area with many signs prohibiting photography. It's also a lush and attractive region with fields of wheat and sunflowers, and forests of pine trees.

Feres, 29 km north-east of Alexandroupolis, has an interesting 12th-century Byzantine church called **Panagia Kosmosoteira**; it is signposted from the main road.

Continuing north, the little town of **Soufli**, 67 km north-east of Alexandroupolis and 31 km south of Didimotikho, has lots of character, and has retained a number of its Turkish wattle-and-daub houses. It is renowned in Greece for its production of silk. This is because the mulberry tree, upon which the silkworms feed, used to thrive in the region. Unfortunately, most of the mulberry trees have been chopped down to make way for crops, but the town still has one silk-producing factory.

Soufli also has an interesting **Folk Museum** with a display of silk-producing equipment. The museum is signposted from the town's main through road, but opening times are subject to change.

If you decide to spend the night in Soufli the D class *Egnatia Hotel* (☎ 22 001), Vasileos Georgiou 225, has singles/doubles for 1900/2700 dr with shared bathrooms. The most up-market place to stay is the C class *Hotel Orpheus* (☎ 22 305), on the corner of Vasileos Georgiou and Tsimiski. Rates are 5900/7800 dr with private bathrooms.

Soufli is on the Alexandroupolis-Didimotikho bus and train routes.

DIDIMOTIKHO Διδυμότειχο

Didimotikho (Did-im-OT-iko, population 8500) is the most interesting of the towns north of Alexandroupolis, although few tourists venture here. The town's name derives from the double walls which once enclosed it (*didima* – 'twins', *tikhos* – 'walls'). In Byzantine times it was an important town. When it fell to the Turks in 1361, Murad I made it the capital. In 1365 he transferred the capital to Adrianople (present-day Edirne). The town's most prominent landmark is a large mosque, with a pyramidal shaped roof, on Plateia Kentriki. The town's population consists of 15% Turks and also a number of Gypsies.

Orientation & Information

Orientation is easy in this small town, as almost everything you need is on or near Plateia Kentriki, the central square, which you can't miss because of the mosque. The OTE and the National Bank of Greece are on Plateia Kentriki and the post office is just north of here; walk along Vasileos Alexandrou, and take the first left onto Kolokotroni, and it's on the right. Didimotikho's telephone code is 0553 and the postcode is 68300.

To get to Plateia Kentriki from the bus station, walk along the road straight ahead, and turn right onto Odos Venizelou, which is the town's main thoroughfare – the square is at the end of here. From the railway station turn left, and keep walking to 25 Maiou, and continue along here to Venizelou. There is no tourist office or tourist police.

Things to See

Didimotikho is yet another place to wander in. With the mosque on your left, walk straight ahead from Plateia Kentriki to the picturesque, tree-shaded Plateia Vatrahos (Frog Square in English), so named because of its frog-shaped fountain. Continue ahead up Odos Metaxa. In this area are many Turkish timber-framed houses. Continue uphill to the **Cathedral of Agiou Athanasios**. Next to the cathedral are some well-preserved sections of the town's Byzantine walls.

If you walk back down Metaxa, and turn left onto Odos Vatatzi, you will come to the **Folk Museum** on the right. This is an outstanding museum, with displays of Thracian costumes, 19th and early 20th-century agricultural equipment and household implements, and a reconstructed kitchen from a 1920s house. The museum is open Monday to Friday from 5 to 8 pm.

Building of the mosque on Plateia Kentriki was started by Murad I and finished by his son, Bayezid, in 1368. It is the oldest and largest mosque in Europe. Its minaret, which has two intricate ornate balconies, has lost its top, all the windows are smashed and the walls are crumbling, but it is still obvious that it must once have been a fine building.

Places to Stay

Didimotikho has two hotels. The D class *Hotel Anesis* (☎ 22 050) has tidy single/double rooms for 3700/4400 dr with private bathrooms. The owners aren't exactly a bundle of laughs, but maybe they're just not used to foreigners. The hotel is on the left side of Vasileos Alexandrou, coming from Plateia Kentriki. The other option is the posh B class *Hotel Plotini* (☎ 23 400/416 or 22 251/111), Agias Paraskevi 1, two km south of town on the road to Alexandroupolis – approaching the town it's on the left.

Places to Eat

Fast-food and cheap souvlaki places are on Venizelou. The two best tavernas are *Vangelis Taverna* on Odos Vasileos Georgiou, south of Venizelou, and *Taverna Kipsilaki* which is opposite the OTE. Both specialise in grills and have similar prices; chicken is 650 dr and souvlaki is 750 dr. Taverna Kipsilaki also has low-priced ready food at lunch times.

Didimotikho has some fine old kafeneia; the one at the top of Kolokotroni looks as if it's jumped straight out of the museum, which is opposite. The one on Plateia Vatrahos has tables and chairs set under shady plane trees.

Getting There & Away

There are many buses a day from Alexandroupolis to Didimotikho (two hours, 1050 dr). There are also at least three trains a day from Alexandroupolis (three hours, 700 dr).

NORTH OF DIDIMOTIKHO

From Didimotikho the road continues for another 20 km to **Orestiada** (population 13,000). This town was built in the 1920s to house refugees who came from Turkey during the population exchange. It's a modern town with little character. If you get stuck it has a couple of budget hotels. The cheapest one is the D class *Hotel Acropolis* (☎ 22 277), Vasileos Konstantinou 46, where singles/doubles are 3700/4500 dr with private bathrooms. The C class *Hotel Vienna* (☎ 22 578 or 29 190), Orestou 64, has rates of 4400/8000 dr with shared bathrooms and 7500/9900 dr with private bathrooms.

The best hotel is the *Hotel Electra* (☎ 23 540), A Pantazinou 50. The rooms here cost 7200/10,360 dr and suites are 17,000 dr.

It's another 19 km to **Kastanies**, Greece's northern road-border point into Turkey. Unless you're planning to continue to Turkey there's little point coming here.

If you cross the border into Turkey the first town you'll arrive at is the eastern Thracian town of **Edirne**, nine km from Kastanies. The town (formerly called Adrianople) is overlooked by most tourists and retains much of its traditional character, making it well worth a visit. If you want to cross the border here by bus the municipal tourist offices in Alexandroupolis will provide you with information.

Cyclades Κυκλάδες

The Cyclades personify all the elements which spring most readily to mind when reference is made to the Greek islands: dazzling white buildings offset by vividly coloured wooden balconies and brilliant blue church domes, bathed in refulgent light, fringed by golden beaches and residing in an aquamarine sea.

Goats, sheep and some cattle are raised on the mountainous and barren islands of the Cyclades. Naxos is the only one sufficiently fertile to produce a surplus of crops for export. Many islanders still fish for a living, but tourism is becoming the dominant source of income.

Some of the Cyclades, like Mykonos, Paros, Thira and Ios, have vigorously embraced the tourist industry, engulfing their coastlines in sun lounges, umbrellas and water-sports hire equipment. Others, such as Andros, Kea, Kythnos, Serifos and Sifnos, are not heavily visited by foreign tourists, but because of their proximity to the mainland are popular as weekend and summer holiday retreats for Athenians.

Tinos stands alone; it is not a holiday island, but the country's premier place of pilgrimage – a Greek Lourdes. Other islands like Anafi and the tiny islands which lie east of Naxos, are little more than clumps of rock, with tiny depopulated villages and few tourists.

The Cyclades lie close to one another and are quite small compared with islands in other groups, making them ideal for an island-hopping holiday. It is best to avoid the island group during July and August as accommodation is hard to come by at this time, so the chances are you'll have to spend some nights sleeping on a beach.

The Cyclades are more prone to the northwesterly *meltemi* wind than any other island group.

History

The Cyclades have been populated since at least 5000 BC. Around 3000 BC Phoenician colonists settled on the islands and their advanced culture heralded the Cycladic civilisation. During the Early Cycladic Age (3000-2000 BC) people began living in houses, built boats and began mining obsidian on the island of Milos, which was exported throughout the Mediterranean. It was also during this time that the famous Cycladic marble statues were sculpted.

During the Middle Cycladic Age (2000-1500 BC) the islands were occupied by the Minoans. Around the 15th century BC, at the beginning of the Late Cycladic Age (1500-1100 BC), the Cyclades passed to the Mycenaeans. The Dorians followed but by the 8th century BC, Archaic culture was burgeoning. After the Greek victory over Persia, the Cyclades became part of the Delian League and so were incorporated into the Athenian empire, thus suffering the onerous annual tax which was imposed by Athens.

In 190 BC the islands were conquered by the Romans and trade links were established with many parts of the Mediterranean, bringing prosperity.

In 1204, the Frankish vanquishers gave the Cyclades to Venice, who parcelled the islands out to opportunistic aristocrats. The most powerful of these was Marco Sanudo

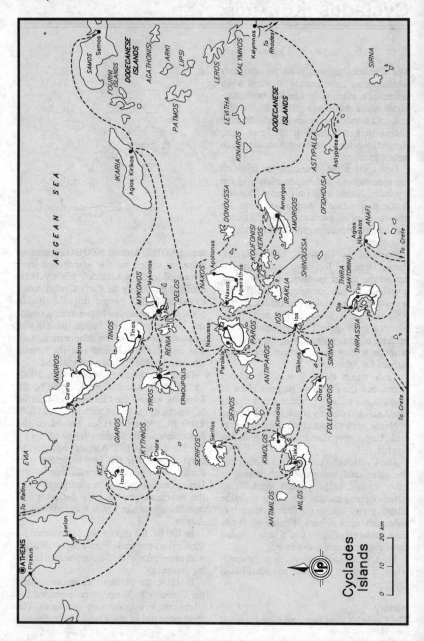

Cyclades Islands

0   10   20 km

(self-styled Duke of Naxos), who acquired Naxos, Paros, Amorgos and Folegandros.

The islands were brought under Turkish rule in 1453. Neglected by the Ottomans they became a backwater, prone to pirate raids – hence the labyrinthine character of their towns, which was meant to disorientate attackers. On some islands the population moved inland to escape the pirates, while on others, the inhabitants would brave it out on the coast. The Cyclades' participation in the War of Independence was minimal, but they became havens for people fleeing from islands where insurrections against the Turks had led to massacres.

Tourists started visiting the islands in great numbers in the 1970s. Before this influx, the Cyclades had suffered from depopulation and many islanders lived in abject poverty.

Getting To/From the Cyclades

For more detailed travel information than is outlined in the following brief section, see the relevant sections under individual island entries.

Air Milos, Mykonos, Naxos, Paros, Syros and Thira have daily connections with Athens. Mykonos and Thira have three flights a week to Iraklion and four to Rhodes.

Ferry The Cyclades are the closest major island group to Piraeus, and they are also clustered relatively close to one another. Ferry services to and from Piraeus and between subgroups of islands within the group are frequent. The most frequently visited of the group, Mykonos, Naxos, Paros, Ios and Thira, are in the centre of the archipelago, and all have daily connections with Piraeus and with one another. Mykonos also has daily connections with Rafina.

Thira has a daily connection with Crete (Iraklion) and a once-weekly connection with Sitia (Crete) via Agios Nikolaos. Ios and Naxos have twice-weekly links with Iraklion.

Paros, the ferry hub of the Aegean, has at least four ferries a day to Piraeus in summer and an almost daily connection with the

Cycladic marble figurine

North-East Aegean island of Samos, via Ikaria. Mykonos and Naxos have once-weekly connections with Samos. Andros, the most northerly island in the group, is served only from Rafina. Tinos, to the south-east of Andros, has good connections with both Piraeus and Rafina. Syros has at least two ferries a day to Piraeus.

Kea, Kythnos, Serifos, Sifnos and Milos are often referred to as the Western Cyclades. Kythnos, Serifos, Sifnos and Milos are served every day from Piraeus by the F/B *Sifnos* and F/B *Milos* and Kea is served by daily ferries from Lavrion. Getting from the Western Cyclades to the rest of the group is not so easy; the most frequent connection is on the small daily Paros-Sifnos ferry.

The less visited islands of Amorgos, Sikinos and Folegandros have four or five ferries a week to Piraeus, and the island of

Anafi has only two or three. Sikinos and Folegandros have a once-weekly connection with Sitia (Crete) via Agios Nikolaos.

Hydrofoil & Catamaran During July and August a hydrofoil connects Rafina with Andros, Tinos, Mykonos and Naxos. This craft is often cancelled because of rough seas. The C/M *Catamaran* connects Flisvos (a port eight km east of Piraeus) with Syros, Tinos, Mykonos, Paros and Naxos and continues to either Ios, Sikinos, Folegandros and Thira, or Amorgos, Koufonisi, Shinoussa and Iraklia. Hydrofoils and catamaran fares are about twice as much as ferry fares.

Getting Around the Cyclades

Air There are inter-island flights between Mykonos and Thira.

Bus The most frequently visited islands of the group have excellent bus services. The smaller and less visited ones have adequate services. The very smallest ones, Anafi, Donoussa, Koufonisi, Shinoussa and Iraklia, do not have public transport.

Car, Motorbike & Bicycle Car hire is available on Milos, Tinos, Mykonos, Naxos, Paros and Thira. Motorbike and moped hire is available on almost all of the islands, but bicycle hire is available on very few – see details under the entries for Naxos and Thira.

Ferry, Hydrofoil & Catamaran Island hopping within the Cyclades archipelago is fairly easy; for more information see the relevant sections under individual island entries.

Andros Ανδρος

Andros (AND-ros) is the most northerly of the Cyclades. It is also one of the most fertile, being second only to Naxos in both this respect and its size. Citrus and olive trees and vines sprout forth from its fecund soil. Andros is unusual in this archipelago in that it has retained its pine forests and mulberry woods. Other distinctive features of the island are its dovecotes (although Tinos has more) and dry stone walls, constructed in an ingenious and elaborate manner.

Getting To/From Andros (Island)

Ferry From Andros there are several ferries a day to Rafina (three hours, 1516 dr), Tinos and Mykonos, and four or five a week to Syros. Three times a week the F/B *Ionian Sun* goes from Andros to Kos and Rhodes, once via Nisyros and Tilos and once via Astypalea and Kalymnos. Andros' port police telephone number is ☎ 22 250.

Hydrofoil A hydrofoil links Andros with Rafina, Tinos, Mykonos and Naxos every day except Sunday.

Getting Around Andros (Island)

There are around six buses a day between Gavrio and Andros town, via Batsi.

GAVRIO Γαύριο

The port of Andros is Gavrio, on the west coast, and the capital is Andros town, on the east coast. Gavrio is a characterless place: neither a bustling workaday port or tourist resort. However, in high season, you may find accommodation more easily here than at the resort of Batsi or Andros town. The ferry quay is in the middle of the waterfront and the bus stop is right next to it. Turn right from the quay and walk along the waterfront to reach the OTE and turn left to reach the post office. Andros' telephone code is 0282 and the postcode is 84500. Andros doesn't have a tourist office or tourist police.

Places to Stay – bottom end

The island's only camp site, *Camping Andros* (☎ 71 444), is in Gavrio. It has a restaurant, minimarket, bar and swimming pool. The site is 300 metres from the waterfront up the Batsi road, but the site's van meets all ferries.

If you decide to stay look for domatia

Andros

0   3   6 km

signs along the waterfront, or try the *Aphrodite Hotel* (☎ 71 209/233) where attractive singles/doubles are 4500/6500 dr with private bathrooms. To reach the hotel (which is classed as a pension) turn right from the quay, walk along the waterfront and turn left onto the road signposted to Batsi. The hotel is just over 100 metres up on the left.

· Places to Stay – middle
The B class *Andros Holiday Hotel* (☎ 71 443/384), overlooking the beach, is considered by many to be Gavrio's best hotel. It has à restaurant, bar, tennis court, sauna, jacuzzi

and gymnasium. Rates are 9500/14,000 dr for singles/doubles.

Places to Eat
One of Gavrio's best restaurants is the reasonably priced *Restaurant O Valmas*. Turn right from the quay, and then left one block before the Batsi road.

BATSI Μπατσί
Batsi, on the west coast, eight km south of Gavrio, is Andros' major resort. The attractive little town encircles a bay with a fishing

harbour at one side and a good sandy beach at the other.

Places to Stay & Eat

Scan the waterfront for domatia signs. Alternatively, the *Skouna Hotel* (☎ 41 315/240), overlooking the beach, has very pleasant rooms for 4000/6000 dr with private bathrooms. *Karanassos Hotel* (☎ 41 480), also overlooking the beach, has singles/doubles for 4500/6500 dr with private bathrooms.

Taverna Tikalo, one block back from the harbour, serves reasonably priced tasty fish dishes.

ANDROS TOWN

Andros town is on the east coast, 35 km from Gavrio. It could not by any stretch of the imagination be described as a beautiful town, but its situation is striking, as it extends onto a long narrow headland.

Orientation & Information

The bus station is on Plateia Goulandri. To the left of here, as you face the sea, is the marble-surfaced main pedestrianised thoroughfare. Along here you will find the post office, OTE and National Bank of Greece. If you walk along the main thoroughfare towards the sea you will come to Plateia Kairi, the central square, beyond which is the headland. Steps lead down to beaches from both sides of the square. The street which traverses the promontory ends at Plateia Riva, where there is a bronze statue of an 'Unknown Sailor'. The ruins of a Venetian fortress stand at the tip of the headland.

Museums

Andros town has two outstanding museums, both endowed by Basil Goulandris, a wealthy ship owner and Andriot. The **Archaeological Museum** is just north of Plateia Kairi. The contents include the Parian marble 1st-century BC Hermes of Andros and finds from Andros' two ancient cities of Zagora and Paleopolis. The museum is open Tuesday to Sunday from 8.30 am to 3 pm. Admission is 400 dr.

The **Museum of Modern Art** has a collection of 20th-century Greek and European paintings. Opening times are Wednesday to Monday from 10 am to 2 pm and 6 to 9 pm.

Places to Stay & Eat

Best value of Andros town's hotels is the C class *Hotel Egli* (☎ 22 303), just off the right side of the main thoroughfare, between the two squares. Rates are 6500 dr a double with private bathrooms. *Restaurant Stathmos*, on Plateia Goulandri, has tasty low-priced fare.

AROUND THE ISLAND

The **Agios Petros Tower** is a huge, imposing circular watch tower, dating at least from Hellenistic times, but possibly earlier. It is a 30-minute walk to the tower from Camping Andros camp site – look for the signpost for Agios Petros, which is also the name of a village. Continuing along the coast road to Batsi, there is a turn-off left which leads in five km to the 12th-century **Moni Zoodohou Pigis**; a few nuns still live here. **Paleopolis**, on the coast road, nine km south of Batsi, is the site of ancient Andros, where the Hermes of Andros was found. The remains are scant, but the setting is lovely, and there is a beach. Beyond here the main road strikes inland for Andros town. From the village of Mesaria it's a strenuous two-hour walk to the 12th-century **Moni Panahrandou**, the island's most important and largest monastery.

Tinos Τήνος

Tinos (TEE-nos, population 9000) is a green and mountainous island, though less so in both respects than its close neighbour Andros. The celebrated Church of Panagia Evangelistria sets the tone of its capital, while more modest churches, unspoilt hill villages and ornate whitewashed dovecotes are the attractions of rural Tinos.

Not only is Tinos an important centre of Greek Orthodoxy, it also has a sizeable Roman Catholic population, the result of its long occupation by Venetians. The Turks only succeeded in wresting the island from

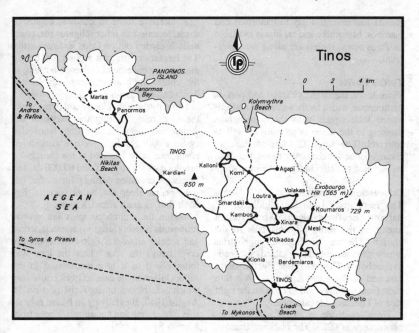

the Venetians in 1715, long after the rest of the country had surrendered to Ottoman suzerainty.

Getting To/From Tinos (Island)

Ferry There are several ferries a day from Tinos to Piraeus (5½ hours, 2700 dr) via Syros, and two to Rafina (five hours, 2220 dr) via Andros. Coming from Rafina, the ferry continues from Tinos to Mykonos. Tinos' port police (☎ 22 348) are on the waterfront near the quay.

Hydrofoil & Catamaran Every day except Sunday, during July and August, a hydrofoil connects Tinos with Mykonos and Naxos; and with Rafina via Andros. On the same days the C/M *Catamaran* connects Tinos with Piraeus (Flisvos) via Syros; and with Mykonos, Paros and Naxos. It continues to either Ios, Sikinos, Folegandros and Thira or Donoussa, Amorgos (both Katapola and Aegiali), Koufonisi, Shinoussa and Iraklia.

Getting Around Tinos (Island)

From Tinos town there are frequent buses to

The Miracle-Working Icon of Panagia Evangelistria
In 1822 the whereabouts of a miracle-working icon appeared in a dream to the nun, Pelagia, at the Convent of Kechrovouniou. Workers unearthed the icon, Panagia Evangelistria (Our Lady of the Assumption), and a church was built on the site where it was found. Tiniots began attributing miraculous cures to the icon and the church became an important place of pilgrimage. On the feasts of the Annunciation and Assumption (25 March and 15 August) pilgrims, amongst them the afflicted and dying, come in their thousands to revere the Panagia Evangelistria. ∎

Kionia and several a day to Panormos and Kambos. Motorbike and car hire is available in Tinos town; outlets are along the waterfront.

TINOS TOWN

Tinos town, the island's capital and port, is picturesque, with a lively waterfront and animated little streets with shops and stalls catering to the needs of pilgrims as well as tourists. The huge Church of Panagia Evangelistria watches over the action from its elevated position in the centre of town.

Orientation & Information

The ferry quay is in the middle of the harbour. Leoforos Megaloharis, straight ahead, is the route pilgrims take to the church. The narrow Odos Evangelistrias which is to the right (facing inland) also leads to the church. The post office is at the southeast end of the waterfront; to reach it turn right from the quay. The OTE is on the right side of Leoforos Megaloharis.

Tinos' postcode is 84200 and the telephone code is 0283. The National Bank of Greece is on the waterfront just beyond Evangelistrias. The bus station is just to the right of the quay. The town beach of Agios Fokas is a 20-minute walk south from the waterfront.

Tinos does not have a tourist office or tourist police. To reach the regular police (☎ 22 255) turn right from the ferry quay and left at the Hotel Possidonion and look for the sign.

Church of Panagia Evangelistria

Εκκλησία της Παναγίας Ευαγγελίστριας
This church is a glorious neoclassical confection of white and cream. The ornate façade has an upper and lower colonnade of graceful white columns. The final approach is up carpeted steps, which must be a relief to the pious souls who choose to crawl there. Step inside for an ecclesiastical extravaganza, including of course the miracle-working icon, dripping with gold, silver, jewels and pearls, and surrounded by votive gifts from grateful recipients of its powers.

A lucrative trade in candles, copies of icons, incense and other religious paraphernalia is carried out on Odos Evangelistrias. The largest candles cost around 500 dr and after a very ephemeral existence burning in the church they are gathered up, melted down and sold again.

Not only the frail, elderly and dying make the pilgrimage; during the feasts of the Annunciation and Assumption Tinos also swarms with children, for it is considered auspicious to be baptised at the church – a privilege which costs around 60,000 dr. The hotels are crammed during pilgrimages, but most people sleep out, either because they can't find, or can't afford, a room.

Within the church complex are several **museums** housing religious artefacts, icons, and secular artworks. Below the church, a crypt marks the spot where the icon was found. Next to it is a mausoleum to the sailors killed on the *Elle*, a Greek cruise ship which was blown up in Tinos port on 15 August 1940, allegedly by an Italian submarine. The church and museums are open from 8 am to 8 pm.

Archaeological Museum

The Archaeological Museum (☎ 22 670), just below the church on Leoforos Megaloharis, contains a mosaic, Roman sculptures, a 1st-century sundial designed by Andronikos of Kyrrhos and impressive clay pithoi. Opening times are Tuesday to Sunday from 8 am to 3 pm. Admission is 400 dr.

Places to Stay

Avoid Tinos at pilgrimage times, unless you want to join the huddled masses who sleep on every available horizontal space.

Camping Tinos (☎ 22 344 or 23 548) is a very pleasant site with good facilities just south of the town. Follow the signs from the waterfront.

Look for domatia signs along Evangelistrias and other streets leading inland from the waterfront. The best of the town's few D class establishments is the *Hotel Eleana* (☎ 22 561) which has well-kept doubles for 6500 dr with private bathrooms.

From the quay turn right and then left at the Hotel Possidonion and you'll come to the hotel, opposite the Church of Agios Ioanni. Another D class, the *Hotel Aigli* (☎ 22 240), opposite the quay, is similarly priced.

The C class *Hotel Meltemi* (☎ 22 881/2/3), on Megaloharis, has light, airy single/double rooms for 5000/6000 dr with private bathrooms. The C class *Hotel Delfinia* (☎ 22 289), on the waterfront, has pleasant singles/doubles for 5500/7500 dr with private bathrooms. The C class *Oasis Hotel* (☎ 23 055 or 22 455), on Evangelistrias, is similarly priced. The long-established B class *Hotel Tinion* (☎ 22 261) has spacious doubles for 8500 dr with bathrooms. The hotel is on the way to the camp site, which is signposted from the waterfront.

Places to Eat

Eating places are nothing special on Tinos. The best I found was *Kypos Taverna*; from the quay turn right, then left at the Hotel Possidonion and take the third turn left. A full meal with retsina will cost about 1600 dr.

AROUND THE ISLAND

At **Kionia**, four km north-west of Tinos town, there are several small beaches, the nearest one overlooked by the enormous Tinos Beach Hotel. The site of the **Sanctuary of Poseidon and Amphitrite**, just before the hotel, dates from the 4th century BC. The Tiniots worshipped Poseidon because they believed he banished the snakes which once inundated the island. The site is an open one.

At **Porto**, eight km east of Tinos town, there is a good sandy beach that doesn't get overcrowded. **Kolymvythra**, on the north coast, has two lovely sandy beaches. Further along the coast there is a small beach at **Panormos Bay** from where the distinctive green marble quarried in nearby **Marlas** and **Panormos** (also called Pyrgos) was once exported. Panormos is a picturesque village where sculptors still carve the marble. Figurines and other marble artefacts are on sale. You can take the bus to Panormos village,

from where it's a pleasant three-km walk to the bay.

The ruins of the **Venetian Fortress of Exobourgo**, on a 565-metre hill, stand sentinel over a cluster of unspoilt hill villages. The fortress, built on an ancient acropolis, was where the Venetians made their last stand against the Turks. The ascent can be made from several villages, but the shortest is from Xinara (take a Kambos bus). It's a steep climb but the views are tremendous.

Mykonos Μύκονος

Mykonos (MEE-kon-os, population 4500) is the most visited and most expensive of all Greek islands and the one with the most sophisticated nightlife. It is the undisputed gay capital of Greece. The days when Mykonos was the number-one rendezvous for the world's rich and famous may be over but I'd like to bet Mykonos still has more poseurs per square metre than any other Mediterranean holiday spot. Depending on your temperament you'll either be captivated or take one look and leave before your feet have had a chance to touch dry land. Barren, low-lying Mykonos would never be in the running in a Greek island beauty competition, but it does have superb beaches and is the most convenient jumping-off point for the sacred island of Delos.

Getting To/From Mykonos (Island)

Air Mykonos has at least eight flights a day to Athens (9900 dr), one to Thira (7700 dr) and three a week to Rhodes (12,500 dr) and Iraklion (12,400 dr). The Olympic Airways office (☎ 22 490/5) is on Plateia Agios Loukas.

Ferry Mykonos has daily connections with Rafina (six hours, 2451 dr) via Tinos and Andros; Piraeus (6½ hours, 2600 dr) via Tinos and Syros; and Naxos, Paros, Ios and Thira. Around four ferries a week operate between Mykonos and Amorgos. Three times a week the F/B *Ionian Sun* goes from

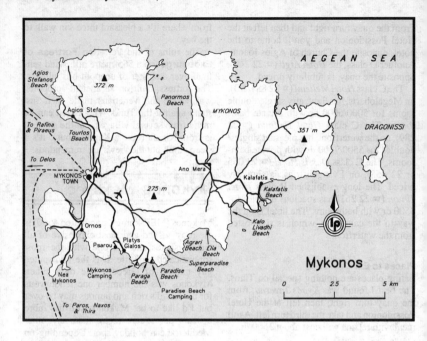

Mykonos to Kos and Rhodes, once via Nisyros and Tilos and once via Astypalea and Kalymnos. There is a once-weekly connection with Samos via Ikaria. The port police (☎ 22 218) are on the waterfront, above the National Bank of Greece.

Excursion Boat These boats leave for Delos (30 minutes, 1400 dr return) between 8 and 10 am and return between noon and 2 pm. Aris Giannakakis Tours (☎ 22 089 or 23 244/689) on the waterfront and Portes Travel, Panachrantou 12, (among others) have guided tours of Delos (4500 dr).

Hydrofoil & Catamaran Every day except Sunday a hydrofoil connects Mykonos with Naxos, and with Rafina via Andros and Tinos.

Also on these days the C/M *Catamaran* connects Mykonos with Piraeus (Flisvos) via Syros and Tinos, and with Naxos via Paros. Twice a week it connects Mykonos with Ios,

Sikinos, Folegandros, Thira, Donoussa, Amorgos, Koufonisi, Shinoussa and Iraklia.

Getting Around Mykonos (Island)
To/From the Airport Mykonos' airport is about 3 km south-east of the town centre. A shuttle bus operates between the airport and the town.

Bus Mykonos has an excellent bus service. Frequent buses leave the North Bus Station for Agios Stefanos (via Tourlos), Ano Mera Elia, Kalo Livadhi and Kalafatis, and from the South Bus Station for Agios Giannis, Psarou, Platys Gialos, Paradise Beach and the airport.

Car & Motorbike Most car and motorbike-rental firms are around the South Bus Station. The biggest is Pegasus Rent-a-Car (☎ 23 760). They have cars from 11,000 to 20,000 dr per day. They also rent motorbikes for 2500 to 5000 dr per day.

Caïque There are frequent caïques from Mykonos town to Superparadise, Agrari and Elia beaches and from Platys Gialos to Paradise, Superparadise, Agrari and Elia beaches.

MYKONOS TOWN

The warren-like arrangement of Cycladic villages reaches its apex in Mykonos town, the island's port and capital. Some visitors are enamoured with this, others find it claustrophobic and can't wait to get out – which is easier said than done. You'll have a fair old dance trying to get orientated. Just when you think you've succeeded, you will discover you are at the opposite end of the town to where you thought you were; the throngs of people you have to elbow your way around add to the frustration. However, even the most claustrophobic misanthrope surely couldn't deny that Mykonos town is beautiful. The town is an elaborate tableau of chic boutiques, chimerical houses with brightly painted wooden balconies, and geraniums, clematis and bougainvillea cascading down whiter than white walls – all just a little too perfect for some tastes.

Orientation

The waterfront is to the right of the ferry quay (facing inland) beyond the scrappy town beach. The central square of Plateia Manto Mavrogenous (usually called Taxi Square) is a little further south along the waterfront.

Mykonos town has two bus stations: the North Bus Station is behind the OTE office (see Information) and the South Bus Station is at the beginning of the road to Ornos. The quay for boats to Delos is at the western end of the waterfront. South of here is Mykonos' famous row of windmills (now defunct) and the Little Venice quarter where balconies hang over the sea.

Information

Mykonos has no tourist office. When you disembark from the ferry you will see ahead a long low building which contains four numbered offices. No 1 is the Hotel Reservation Department (no telephone) which is open from 8 am to midnight; No 2 is the Association of Rooms & Apartments (☎ 24 860), which is open from 10 am to 6 pm; No 3 is Camping Information; and No 4 is the Tourist Police (☎ 22 482), which has variable opening times. The first two will help you find accommodation.

The post office is between the town beach and the central square. The OTE is just north of the town beach. Mykonos' postcode is 84600 and the telephone code is 0289. The National Bank of Greece is further around the waterfront.

Museums

Mykonos town has three museums. The **Archaeological Museum**, near the quay, houses pottery from Delos and some grave stele and jewellery from the island of Renia (the necropolis of Delos). The chief exhibits are a pithos featuring a Trojan War scene in relief, and a statue of Herakles. Opening times are Tuesday to Saturday from 9 am to 3 pm and Sunday and holidays from 9.30 am to 2.30 pm. Admission is 400 dr.

The **Marine Museum** houses interesting and well-displayed nautical paraphernalia. Opening times are 10.30 am to 1 pm and 6.30 to 9 pm daily. Admission is 200 dr.

The excellent **Folklore Museum**, housed in an 18th-century sea captain's mansion, features a large collection of memorabilia, a reconstructed 19th-century kitchen and a bedroom with a four-poster bed.

There's also a somewhat macabre stuffed pelican, the erstwhile Petros, who was run over by a car in 1985. He was hastily supplanted by Petros II, who you will no doubt meet during your wanders around town. Petros I nose dived onto Mykonos during a storm in the mid-1950s and the islanders regarded him as a lucky mascot, which indeed he was, as he heralded Mykonos' status as the premier Cycladic resort. The museum, which is near the Delos quay, is open Monday to Saturday from 5.30 to 8.30 pm. Entrance is free.

Panagia Paraportiani

Of Mykonos' many churches, the Panagia Paraportiani is the most famous. It is actually four little churches amalgamated into one: a sparkling white, lumpy asymmetrical building which seems to have been cobbled together without rhyme or reason, and yet the result is one of great beauty. The interplay of light and shade on the multifaceted structure creates subtle nuances of white. It's a photographers' delight.

Organised Tours

Excursion boats operators run day trips to the sacred island of Delos. See the entry under Getting To/From Mykonos (Island) for details.

Places to Stay – bottom end

Mykonos has two camp sites: *Paradise Beach Camping* (☎ 22 582; fax 24 350) on Paradise Beach and *Mykonos Camping* (☎ 24 578) on Paraga Beach (10 minutes' walk from Platys Gialos Beach). Both sites have good facilities and minibuses which meet the boats.

The prices of Mykonos' hotels will leave you gob smacked – they're around double most other places in Greece. In addition to this, some have management which will overwhelm you with their indifference. If you are brave enough to set foot on the island without a reservation between June and September, and are offered suitably priced accommodation when you arrive, take it. Otherwise seek the assistance of the organisations referred to in the information section.

Angela's Rooms (☎ 22 967), on Plateia Mavrogenous, is one of the cheapest places in town; rates are 5800/8000 dr for doubles/triples with private bathrooms. The delightfully old-world D class *Hotel Apollon* (☎ 22 223), on the waterfront, is run by two genteel (but business-like), elderly ladies. Rates are 5000/7000/8000 dr for singles/ doubles/triples with private bathrooms.

The E class *Hotel Olympia* (☎ 22 964), just up from the South Bus Station, is good value with rates of 6000/7000 dr for doubles/

triples with private bathrooms. The D class *Hotel Carboni* (☎ 22 217), on Andronikou Matogianni, has attractive pine-furnished single/double rooms for 6000/7000 dr with private bathrooms. The D class *Hotel Phillipi* (☎ 22 294), Kalogera 32, has immaculate rooms for 5500/10,500/13,000 dr with private bathrooms. The hotel has a delightful garden. Nearby, *Rooms Chez Maria* (☎ 22 480) has traditional touches like old family pictures and fancy lightshades. Doubles/ triples are 6000/8000 dr.

Places to Stay – middle

The C class *Hotel Delos* (☎ 22 312/517), next to the post office, has a bright and cheerful décor. Rates are 11,200/14,100 dr for doubles/triples with private bathrooms. The *Hotel Delphines* (☎ 22 317), on Mavroganni, is another attractively furnished place. Rates are 10,800/13,500/16,200 dr.

Places to Stay – top end

If you want to indulge in a little Mykonite luxury, the A class *Hotel Lito* (☎ 22 207/918) is where the celebs used to stay in the island's heyday. Rates are 15,000/18,000/22,500 dr. For more top-end hotel listings, see under Beaches later in this section.

Places to Eat

The high prices charged in most of Mykonos' eating establishments are not always indicative of quality or quantity. *Jackpots*, near the Delos quay, is one of the cheapest eateries, with prices starting at 600 to 700 dr. *Nico's Taverna*, nearby, is popular, although service can be brusque when it's busy and by the time you've been presented with your bill you may have forgotten what you've eaten. Prices are comparable with Jackpots. *Ta Kiouria Restaurant* is also good value, with a full meal including retsina costing around 1700 dr. *Taverna Antonini*, Plateia Manto Mavrogenous, is also not beyond the budget traveller's pocket, with well-prepared Greek staples costing from 700 to 1000 dr.

The *Sesame Kitchen*, next to the Marine Museum, serves mostly vegetarian dishes at reasonable prices.

Entertainment

Chances are that, unless you've come to Mykonos only to visit Delos, you'll want to sample some of the nightlife which leaves all other Greek islands in the shade. New places come and go but the following are perennials. The *Windmill Disco* and *Scandinavian Bar*, near the Panagia Paraportiani, vie for selling the cheapest drinks. Both are rowdy and get packed. The *City Disco*, nearby, is considered the wildest of them all, with a nightly drag show. The *Rainbow Disco*, on Mitropoleos, is another loud and crowded place with a very young clientele. *Pierro's Bar*, near Matogianni, used to be exclusively gay but now gets a mixed crowd. *Remezzo*, near the Archaeological Museum, is a more sophisticated disco with an older clientele.

The atmospheric waterfront *Thalami Bar* features exclusively Greek music. For a classy, sedate ambience try *Montparnasse Bar* or *Kastro Bar*, both in Little Venice. They play classical music at sunset. The *Gallery Bar* is also an agreeable, civilised place. If you're roomless or an insomniac, head for the *Yacht Club* which is open 24 hours.

AROUND THE ISLAND
Beaches

The nearest beach to Mykonos town is the postage-stamp sized, crowded **Tourlos**, two km to the north. **Agios Stefanos**, two km beyond here, is larger but just as crowded. Unless you're pushed for time, jump on a bus to **Platys Gialos**, on the south-west peninsula. The beach is long and sandy but inevitably crowded because of its proximity to town. From here caïques ply back and forth to the island's best beaches further around the south coast. They are **Paradise**, **Superparadise**, **Agrari** and **Elia** – nudism is accepted on all of them. Superparadise is where you'll find the hunks without trunks – it's the nudist gay beach. Elia is the last caïque stop, so is the least crowded. The next beach along, **Kalo Livadhi**, is also relatively uncrowded.

Beaches on the north coast are prone to the meltemi. The best one is **Panormos Beach**, reached along a road or a path just before Ano Mera.

Places to Stay – top end There are many splurge hotels around Mykonos' coast. The A class *Petinos Beach* (☎ 24 310/1; fax 23 680), on the beach at Platys Gialos, has a swimming pool, a bar and a wide variety of water sports. Doubles are 26,500 dr. The A class *Princess of Mykonos* (☎ 23 031/806 or 24 713/735; fax 23 031), at Agios Steganos, is touted as Jane Fonda's favourite Mykonos hangout. The building is in traditional Cycladic style with loads of amenities. Single/double rates are 24,000/27,900 dr.

Ano Mera Ανω Μέρα

The pleasant, unhyped village of Ano Mera, seven km east of Mykonos town, is the only inland settlement on the island. Its 6th-century **Moni Panagia Tourliani** has a very fine stone carved bell tower, an ornate wood iconostasis carved in Florence in 1775 and some fine 16th-century icons of the Cretan School; there is a small **museum**.

Surprisingly this inland village has one of the island's best hotels, the A class *Ano Mera Hotel* (☎ 22 404; fax 24 814). The hotel has a swimming pool, restaurant and disco. Singles/doubles are 18,500/21,000 dr.

Delos Δήλος

Despite its diminutive size, Delos is one of the most important archaeological sites in Greece, and certainly the most important in the Cyclades archipelago – in fact, the Cyclades are so named because they form a circle (*kuklos*) around Delos. Lying just a few km off the west coast of Mykonos, the sacred island of Delos is the mythical birthplace of Apollo and Artemis.

Apollo

History
Delos was first inhabited in the 3rd millennium BC. In the 8th century BC, the annual Delia festival was established on the island to celebrate the birth of Apollo. For a long time the Athenians coveted Delos, seeing its strategic position as one from where they could control the Aegean, and by the 5th century BC it had come under their jurisdiction.

After Athens defeated the Persians it established the Delian League in 477 BC, and its treasury was kept on the island. It carried out a number of purifications, decreeing that no one could be born or could die on Delos, thus strengthening its control over the island.

Delos reached its height in Hellenistic times, becoming one of the three most important religious centres in Greece and a flourishing centre of commerce. It traded throughout the Mediterranean and was populated with wealthy merchants, mariners and bankers from as far away as Egypt and Syria. These inhabitants built temples to the various gods worshipped in their countries of origin, although Apollo remained the principal deity worshipped on the island.

The Romans made Delos a free port in 167 BC which brought even greater prosperity, but by then it had become debased and was the most lucrative slave market in the Mediterranean. In 88 BC it was sacked by Mithridates and 10,000 inhabitants were massacred. From then on Delos was prey to pirates, and later, also to looters of antiquities.

Getting To/From Delos
See Excursion Boat under Mykonos for schedules and prices.

THE SITE
Orientation & Information
Landing is at a small modern quay, just south of the **Sacred Harbour**.

Many of the most significant finds from Delos are in the National Archaeological Museum in Athens, but the on-site **museum** has a modest collection.

It is not possible to stay overnight on Delos, and the boat schedule allows you only three hours there. Bring plenty of water and, if you want, some food, because the island's cafeteria is poor value. Wear a hat and sensible shoes.

Entrance to the site costs 1000 dr (including entrance to the museum).

Exploring the Site
Following is an outline of some of the significant archaeological remains on Delos. For further information, obtain one of the several guides to the site which are on sale at the ticket office.

If you have the energy it's a good idea to begin your visit by climbing Mt Kythnos (113 metres), to the south-east of the harbour. This will give you a vantage point from where you can observe Delos' layout. On

   Top: Dolphin frieze, Knossos, Crete (DH)
Middle: Knossos, Crete (VB)
Bottom: Knossos, Crete (VB)

   Top: The small village of Loutro, Crete (VB)
Bottom: General store, Sitia, Crete (DH)

clear days there are terrific vistas of the surrounding islands.

You reach the path by walking through the **theatre quarter**. Delos' wealthiest inhabitants built their houses here in the precincts of the **Theatre of Delos**. The houses were built around peristyled courtyards. Mosaics, apparently a status symbol, were the most striking feature of each house and it is from these that their present names have been derived. These colourful mosaics are exquisite works of art, mostly representational and offset by intricate geometric borders. The most lavish of the dwellings were the **House of Dionysos**, named after its mosaic depicting the wine god riding a panther, and the **House of Cleopatra**, where headless statues of the two owners were found and are now in the museum. The **House of the Trident** was one of the grandest of the houses; the **House of the Masks**, which was probably a hostelry for actors, has another mosaic of Dionysos resplendent astride a panther. The **House of the Dolphins** has another exceptional mosaic.

The theatre dates from 300 BC and had a large cistern, the remains of which can be seen; it which supplied much of the town with water. The houses of the wealthy had their own cisterns – essential appendages as Delos was almost as parched and barren then as it is today.

On the descent from Mt Kythnos you can explore the **Sanctuaries of the Foreign Gods**. Here, at the **Shrine to the Samothracian Great Gods**, the Kabeiroi (the twins Dardanos and Aeton) were worshipped. At the **Sanctuary of the Syrian Gods** there are remains of a theatre from where an audience watched orgies held in honour of the Syrian deities. There is also an area where Egyptian deities, including Serapis and Isis, were worshipped.

The **Sanctuary of Apollo**, to the north of the harbour, contains temples dedicated to him. It is also the site of the much photographed **Terrace of the Lions**. These proud beasts carved from marble were votive offerings from the people of Naxos, presented to Delos in the 7th century BC. Their function was to guard the sacred area. To the east of them is the **Sacred Lake** (dry since 1925) where, according to legend, Leto gave birth to Apollo.

The Birth of Apollo & Artemis

The twins Apollo and Artemis were the children of Leto and Zeus. Leto was one of Zeus' countless mistresses and, like all the others, she was relentlessly pursued by the jealous Hera. Eventually Leto arrived on Delos which at that time was a piece of loose rock knocked here and there by the vagaries of the Aegean Sea. However, when Leto arrived Poseidon anchored the island to the bottom of the sea.

This must have been a great relief to Leto, as she was about to give birth. Artemis was born first and apparently made amazingly rapid progress, for she assisted at the birth of her brother Apollo the following day. His progress seems to have surpassed even that of his sister, for within a few hours of his birth he had grown into a handsome youth.

It was just as well that the twins thrived, for after their births Leto set off again, with Hera in hot pursuit. ■

Leto with the twins Apollo and Artemis

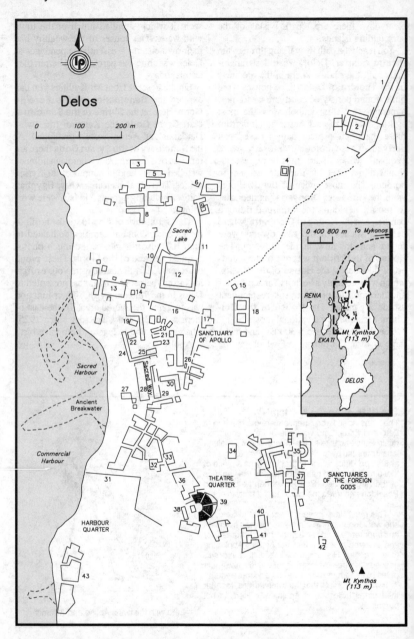

Delos

0   100   200 m

Sacred
Lake

Sacred
Harbour

Ancient
Breakwater

Commercial
Harbour

SANCTUARY
OF APOLLO

Sacred Way

HARBOUR
QUARTER

THEATRE
QUARTER

SANCTUARIES
OF THE FOREIGN
GODS

Mt Kynthos
(113 m)

0   400   800 m   To Mykonos

RENIA

EKATI

Mt Kynthos
(113 m)

DELOS

1	Stadium
2	Gymnasium
3	House of Comedians
4	Sanctuary of Archegetes
5	House of Diadumenos
6	Lake House
7	Hill House
8	Institution of the Poseidoniasts
9	Palaestra
10	Terrace of the Lions
11	Roman Wall
12	Agora of the Italians
13	Stoa of Poseidon
14	Dodekatheon
15	Tourist Pavillion
16	Stoa of Antigonas
17	Sanctuary of Dionysos
18	Museum
19	Temple of Artemis
20	Poros Temple
21	Temple of the Athenians
22	Keraton
23	Temple of Apollo
24	Stoa of the Naxiots
25	House of the Naxiots
26	Monument of the Bulls
27	Agora of the Competialists
28	Stoa of Philip V
29	South Stoa
30	Agora of the Delians
31	Wall of the Triarus
32	House of Cleopatra
33	House of Dionysos
34	House of Hermes
35	Sanctuary of the Syrian Gods
36	House of the Trident
37	Shrine of the Egyptian Gods
38	Cistern
39	Theatre of Delos
40	House of the Dolphins
41	House of the Masks
42	Sacred Cave
43	Warehouses

Syros Σύρος

Many tourists come to Syros (SEE-ros, population 19,000) merely to change ferries, which is a pity because its capital, Ermoupolis, is a beautiful city.

During the 19th century a combination of fortuitous circumstances resulted in Ermoupolis becoming the major port of Greece. It was long ago superseded by Piraeus, but is still the Cyclades' largest city and its capital, with a population of 14,000.

Syros' economy does not depend on tourism. It has a ship-building industry and repair yard, four textile factories, dairy farms, and a horticultural industry which supplies the rest of the Cyclades with plants and flowers.

History

During the Middle Ages Syros was the only Greek island with an entirely Roman Catholic population, the result of conversions by the Franks who took over the island in 1207. This gave it the support and protection of the West (particularly the French) during Ottoman times.

Syros remained neutral during the War of Independence and thousands of refugees from islands ravaged by the Turks fled here. These people brought their Orthodox religion with them and built a new settlement on a hill (now called Vrodado) and the port town of Ermoupolis. After Independence Ermoupolis became the commercial, naval and cultural centre of Greece. Today Syros' Catholic population is 40% and the Orthodox, 60%. The city's grand churches and neoclassical mansions are testimonies to its former grandeur.

Getting To/From Syros

Air Syros has at least two flights a day to Athens (9700 dr). The Olympic Airways office (☎ 26 244/309) is on Akti Papagou.

Ferry Syros has at least two ferries a day to Piraeus (4½ hours, 2400 dr), Tinos and Mykonos; four to Rafina (4½ to six hours depending on the route, 2100 dr); at least one to Paros and Naxos; and at least four a week to Amorgos. Syros' port police (☎ 22 690 or 28 888) are at the eastern side of the waterfront.

Catamaran Every day except Sunday the C/M *Catamaran* connects Syros with Piraeus (Flisvos) and with Tinos, Mykonos,

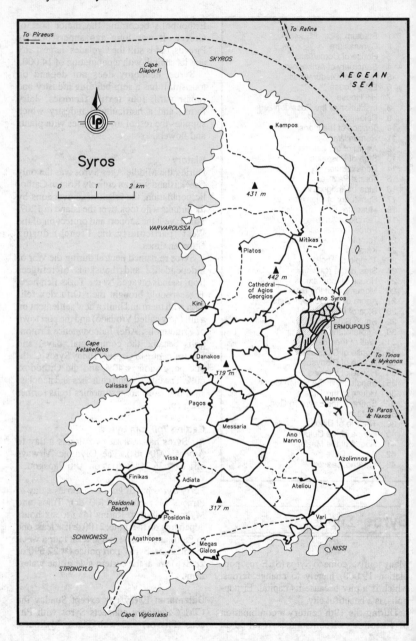

Syros

0   1   2 km

Paros and Naxos, continuing to either Ios, Sikinos, Folegandros and Thira, or Donoussa, Amorgos, Koufonisi, Shinoussa and Iraklia.

Getting Around Syros

Frequent buses do a southern loop around the island from Ermoupolis, calling at all the beaches mentioned in the text. Cars can be hired from Eurocar (☎ 25 968), Plateia Kanari. The Team Work Agency (see Organised Tours under Ermoupolis) organises many tours around the island.

ERMOUPOLIS Ερμούπολη

As the boat sails into Syros' port of Ermoupolis you will see the Catholic settlement of Ano Syros to the left, and the Orthodox settlement of Vrodado to the right. Spilling down from them both and skirting the harbour is Ermoupolis; all in all it's an impressive sight.

Orientation

All boats dock at the west side of the bay. To reach the central square of Plateia Miaouli, turn right and then left onto El Venizelou. The post office and OTE are both on this square.

Information

At the time of writing Syros' EOT (☎ 26 725) was temporarily housed in the town hall on Plateia Miaouli. The tourist police (☎ 22 610) are in a side street between Kalomnopoulou and Vokotopoulou. Team Work Agency (see Organised Tours) is an efficient, helpful travel agency.

Syros' postcode is 84100 and the telephone code is 0281. The National Bank of Greece is on Kalomnopoulou, east of Plateia Miaouli. The bus station is by the quay, on the west side of the harbour.

Ano Syros Ανω Σύρος

Vrodado and Ermoupolis merge into one another, but Ano Syros is quite different – a typical Cycladic settlement of narrow alleyways and whitewashed houses. It's fascinating to wander around and has splendid

views over to neighbouring islands. On the way up take a look at the **Orthodox Cemetery of Agios Georgios**, which has ostentatious mausoleums reminiscent of Athens' First Cemetery. The finest of Ano Syros' Catholic churches is the Baroque **Cathedral of St George**. Close by is the **Capuchin Monastery of St Jean**, founded in 1535 to minister to the poor. Ano Syros was the birthplace of Markos Vamvakaris, the celebrated rembetika singer. To reach Ano Syros walk up Odos Omirou.

Other Sights

Plateia Miaouli is bustling Ermoupolis' hub of activity. It's flanked by palm trees and cafés and overlooked by the town hall, a magnificent neoclassical building designed by the German architect Ernst Ziller. The small **Archaeological Museum** is in the town hall. It houses a mediocre collection of vases, grave stele, heads and torsos – hardly worthy of the capital of the Cyclades. Opening times are Tuesday to Sunday from 8.30 am to 3 pm. Admission is free.

The **Apollon Theatre** (closed for restoration at the time of writing), on Plateia Vardaki, was designed by the French architect Chabeau and is a replica of La Scala in Milan. In Syros' heyday it hosted an Italian opera season. From the **Church of Anastasis**, on top of Vrodado hill, there are terrific views. To reach here walk up Louka Ralli.

Organised Tours

For tours to areas of interest on Syros, contact Team Work Agency (☎ 23 400 or 22 866), on the eastern waterfront at Plateia Kanari.

Places to Stay

Syros is not as popular as most of the Cycladic islands, so finding accommodation is usually not too much of a hassle. The aforementioned Team Work Agency has a room-finding service.

The convivial *Tony's Rooms to Let* (no telephone), Vokotopoulou 3, is a favourite with backpackers. The large, clean single/double/triple rooms have rates of 2300/3200/

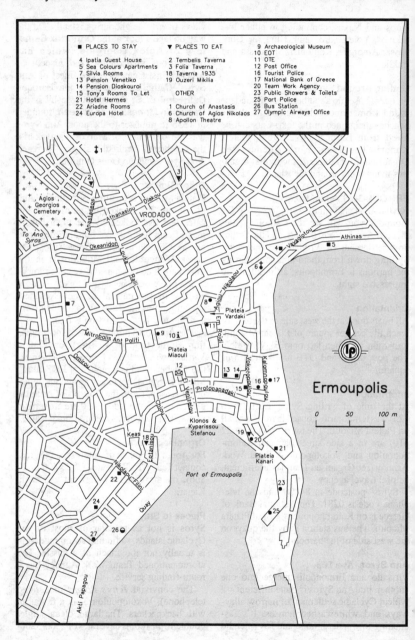

■ PLACES TO STAY

4 Ipatia Guest House
5 Sea Colours Apartments
7 Silvia Rooms
13 Pension Venetiko
14 Pension Dioskouroi
15 Tony's Rooms To Let
21 Hotel Hermes
22 Ariadne Rooms
24 Europa Hotel

▼ PLACES TO EAT

2 Tembelis Taverna
3 Folia Taverna
18 Taverna 1935
19 Ouzeri Mikilia

OTHER

1 Church of Anastasis
6 Church of Agios Nikolaos
8 Apollon Theatre

9 Archaeological Museum
10 EOT
11 OTE
12 Post Office
16 Tourist Police
17 National Bank of Greece
20 Team Work Agency
23 Public Showers & Toilets
25 Port Police
26 Bus Station
27 Olympic Airways Office

Ermoupolis

0   50   100 m

Port of Ermoupolis

4400 dr with shared bathrooms and a communal kitchen. From Eleftheriou Venizelou turn right onto Protopapadaki, and then left onto Vokotopoulou, and the rooms are on the left.

Close by, *Pension Diaskouroi* (☎ 22 530), on Klonos & Kyparissou Stefanou, is a lovely old building with a colonnaded terrace. The comfortable rooms are 2500/ 3500 dr for singles/doubles with shared bathrooms and 4500/6000 dr for doubles/triples with private bathrooms. Just beyond here, *Pension Venetiko* (☎ 28 596), Em Roidi 2, has attractive, simply furnished rooms costing 3500 dr for doubles with shared bathrooms.

Silvia Rooms (☎ 81 080), Omirou 38, is a 19th-century mansion with spotless, elegantly furnished rooms. Rates are 3000/ 4200/5500 dr with shared bathrooms.

Ipatia Guest House (☎ 23 575), Vavagiotou 3, is a wonderful 1870s neoclassical mansion. The rooms have brass bedsteads, stone floors and wood-panelled ceilings – ask if you can take a peek at the magnificent painted ceiling in the family quarters. Rates are 4000/6888 dr for singles/doubles with shared bathrooms and 4800/8000 dr with private bathrooms. From Plateia Vadaki continue to the Church of Agios Nikolaos and the guest house is a little further along, on the left. *Ariadne Rooms* (☎ 81 307), Nikolaou Filini 9, is an up-market domatia comprising stylish apartments with modern décor, kitchens and private bathrooms. Rates are 5800/ 6800/8500 dr.

The C class *Europa Hotel* (☎ 28 771) is housed in the island's former municipal hospital. It is built around a central courtyard, which has a beautiful pebble mosaic. The immaculate rooms have rates of 6000/8500/ 10,200 dr with private bathrooms. The hotel is signposted from the quay. The B class *Hotel Hermes* (☎ 23 011/012), Plateia Kanari, has comfortable rooms for 5700/ 9150 dr and deluxe rooms with TV and air-con for 7200/9500/11,400 dr.

The luxurious *Sea Colours Apartments* (☎ 25 961 or 23 400; fax 23 508) has two-person studios for 9500 dr and four-person apartments for 12,000 dr. Follow directions

for Ipatia Guest House, go down the steps opposite, and Sea Colours is a little way along on the right.

Places to Eat

Ermoupolis has some excellent restaurants. The *Folia Taverna*, Athanasiou Diakou 2, is one of the best eating places in the Cyclades, serving delectable, imaginatively prepared dishes at reasonable prices. A full meal with retsina will cost about 1400 dr. To reach the taverna walk up Omirou and turn right onto Okaenidon. Walk to the end of here, turn left and then right onto Athanasiou Diakou, and the restaurant is along here on the left where the road curves.

Another first-rate place is *Taverna 1935*, on Eptanisou. Its cavernous interior has a wood-beamed ceiling and huge wine barrels lining the wall. Prices are similar to the Folia. From the waterfront walk one block up Keas, turn left and the restaurant is on the right.

Tembelis Taverna, Anastaseos 17, below the Church of Anastasis, is also good value. Another commendable place is *Ouzeri Mikilia*, on the waterfront.

If you have a sweet tooth be sure to try some loukoumia (Turkish delight) while on Syros; it's supposed to be the best in Greece. There is a food market on Odos Chiou.

Entertainment

Lili's Taverna (off the map), in Ano Syros, features live rembetika music at weekends. It's a famous place, so anyone in Ano Syros will be able to direct you. Plateia Miaouli has loads of cafés and bars. Most popular is the *Piano Bar*, where cocktails and spirits cost around 900 dr.

GALISSAS Γαλησσάς

The west-coast resort of Galissas has the island's best beach – a 900-metre crescent of sand, shaded by tamarisk trees. Armeos, a short walk away, is an official nudist beach. Despite the fact that hotels and domatia are mushrooming at alarming rates here, Galissas still has a good laid-back feel.

Places to Stay – bottom end

Syros' two camp sites are both at Galissas. *Camping for Two* (☎ 42 052/321) has the most facilities – everything from motorbike rental to minigolf, and barbecues to bungalows. Its minibus meets the ferries. The other site is *Yianna Camping* (☎ 42 941/418).

Karmelina Rooms (☎ 42 320) are clean and tidy and cost 3365 dr a double with shared bathrooms and communal kitchen. The same family own sparkling new apartments which cost 6000/8200 dr for doubles/triples. The domatia are on the right of the main road coming from Ermoupolis (beyond the branch road to the beach). Opposite are the pleasant *Despina Studios* (☎ 42 333), with private bathrooms and a communal kitchen. Rates are 5500 dr a double. Almost next door are the more luxurious *Corali Rooms* (☎ 42 926 or 85 536), with rates of 7500 dr for two-person apartments with private bathrooms.

Dendrinos Rooms (☎ 42 469) are tastefully bedecked with batik wall hangings, Cycladic figurines and stone reliefs. Rates are 5800/7800 dr for doubles/triples with private bathrooms. The rooms are on the left of the road to the Camping for Two camp site (signposted).

Places to Stay – middle

Hotel Benois (☎ 42 833/944/333), at the entrance to the beach, is an attractive C class hotel. Rates are 6000/8500/10,200 dr for singles/doubles/triples with private bathrooms.

The A class *Dolphin Bay Hotel* (☎ 42 924; fax 42 843) is a large unmissable cluster of buildings to the left of the beach as you face the sea. The rooms have satellite TV, music, private safe and other amenities. Singles/doubles are 8600/14,200 dr.

Places to Eat

Stelios Restaurant, overlooking the beach, serves tasty reasonably priced food for less than 1000 dr.

OTHER BEACHES

South of Galissas there are more beaches. All have domatia and some have hotels. The first one is **Finikas**, with a small beach shaded by trees. The next one, **Posidonia**, is more appealing, with a sand and pebble beach shaded by tamarisk trees. A little further south, **Agathopes** has a low-key sandy beach. On the south coast, **Megas Gialos** is a tranquil place with two sand beaches. **Vari**, the next bay along, has a sand beach but is more developed.

Naxos   Νάξος

Give me again your empty boon,
Sweet Sleep – the gentle dream
How Theseus 'neath the fickle moon
Upon the Ocean stream
Took me and led me by the hand
To be his Queen in Athens land.

He slew the half-bull Minotaur
In labyrinthine ways.
But, threadless, had he come no more
From out my father's maze:
Yet I who taught his hands this guile
Am left forlorn on Naxos Isle.

**Dionysiaca XLVII by Nonnos
(translated by Roger Lancelyn Green)**

Naxos (NA-xos, population 20,000) is where Theseus disloyally dumped Ariadne after she helped him in his efforts to slay the Minotaur (half-bull, half-man) on Crete. However, she didn't pine for long as she was

Ariadne

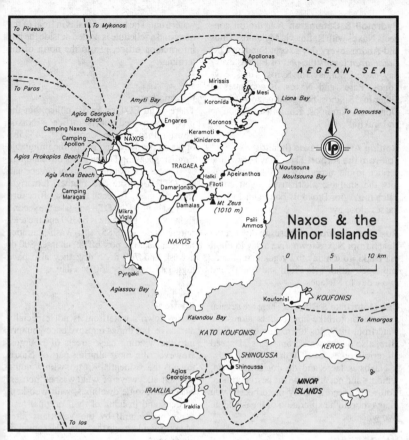

Naxos & the Minor Islands

0   5   10 km

soon ensconced in the arms of Dionysos. The island is the Cyclades' biggest and most fertile, producing olives, citrus fruits, corn and potatoes. Its Mt Zeus (1010 metres) is the archipelago's highest peak. Rugged mountains and green valleys add up to one of the most scenic islands of the group. Naxos is popular, although not as heavily visited as Mykonos, Thira and Paros.

Getting To/From Naxos (Island)

Air Naxos' airport only began operating in 1992. There are daily flights to Athens (11,600 dr). There is as yet no Olympic Airways office; the airline is represented by Orbit Travel Services (☎ 22 454) on the waterfront in Naxos town.

Ferry Naxos has daily ferries to Piraeus (six hours, 2500 dr), Mykonos, Paros, Ios and Thira; almost daily connections with Iraklia, Shinoussa, Koufonisi and Amorgos; twice weekly with Folegandros, Sikinos, Donoussa and Iraklion (Crete); and a once-weekly connection with Samos. Naxos' port police (☎ 22 340) are on the waterfront just south of the quay.

Hydrofoil & Catamaran A hydrofoil connects Naxos with Rafina via Mykonos, Tinos and Andros every day except Sunday. C/M *Catamaran* leaves the port of Flisvos every day except Sunday for Syros, Tinos, Mykonos, Paros and Naxos. It continues to either Ios, Sikinos, Folegandros and Thira or Donoussa, Amorgos, Koufonisi, Shinoussa and Iraklia.

Getting Around Naxos (Island)

To/From the Airport There may be a shuttle service to the airport by the time this book hits the shelves; alternatively, you could catch the Agios Prokopis-bound bus, which passes close by.

Bus There are frequent buses to Agia Anna Beach from Naxos town, five a day to Filoti via Halki, four a day to Pyrgaki, Apollonos and Apeiranthos (via Filoti and Halki), and two a day to Melanes.

Car, Motorbike & Bicycle There are several car and motorbike-hire outlets along the waterfront in Naxos town. Sun Cycle Bike Hire, also on the waterfront, rents 21-speed all-terrain bikes for 1800 dr.

Naxos is large and the roads are steep, winding and not always in the best condition. You really need a sturdy motorbike if you plan a thorough exploration of the island on two wheels.

NAXOS TOWN

Naxos town, on the west coast, is the port and island capital. It's a large town divided into two neighbourhoods, Bourgos, where the Greeks lived and Kastro, on the hill above, where the Venetian Catholics lived. A causeway to the north of the port leads to the islet of Palatia and the unfinished Temple of Apollo, Naxos' most famous landmark. The unappealing northern shore of Naxos town is called Grotta – nicknamed Grotty by some tourists. Just south-west of the town is the glorious sandy beach of Agios Georgios.

Orientation

The ferry quay is at the northern end of the

waterfront. The bus terminal is in front of the quay and a schedule is posted outside the bus information office, just to the north of the terminal.

Information

There is no EOT or tourist police, but the privately owned tourist office – Naxos Tourist Information Centre (☎ 24 358), opposite the quay, and run by the inimitable English-speaking Despina – is outstanding.

To reach the National Bank of Greece and the OTE (opposite one another) turn right from the quay. To reach the post office turn left just beyond the OTE and take the second right. Naxos' postcode is 84300 and the telephone code is 0285. Pro-Wash Laundry Service, near the post office, charges 800 dr a wash and 700 dr to dry; they also have luggage storage for 150 dr a day.

Kastro

Naxos town's waterfront is not especially attractive, but things improve once you turn into the winding back streets of Bourgos. However, the most alluring part of Naxos town is the residential Kastro, with winding stepped alleyways of whitewashed houses. These handsome dwellings, with well-kept gardens and insignia of their original residents, were built by the Venetians after Marco Sanudo made the island the capital of his duchy.

Stroll in Kastro during siesta time to capture fully its hushed, medieval atmosphere. The well-stocked **Archaeological Museum** (signposted) is here, housed in a former school where Nikos Kazantzakis was briefly a pupil. The contents include the usual collection of torsos and funerary stele, vases, vases and more vases, as well as Hellenistic and Roman terracotta figurines and, more interestingly, some early Cycladic figurines. The museum is open Tuesday to Sunday from 8.30 am to 3 pm. Admission is 400 dr. Close by, the **Sanoudos Palace** and the **Roman Catholic cathedral** are worth taking a look at.

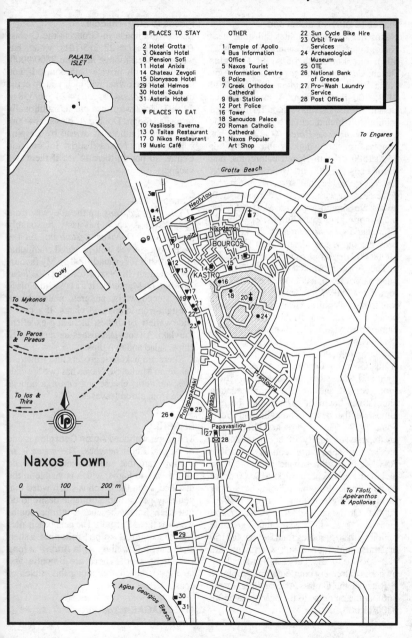

PLACES TO STAY
2 Hotel Grotta
3 Okeanis Hotel
8 Pension Sofi
11 Hotel Anixis
14 Chateau Zevgoli
15 Dionyssos Hotel
29 Hotel Helmos
30 Hotel Soula
31 Asteria Hotel

▼ PLACES TO EAT
10 Vasilissis Taverna
13 O Tsitas Restaurant
17 O Nikos Restaurant
19 Music Café

OTHER
1 Temple of Apollo
4 Bus Information
  Office
5 Naxos Tourist
  Information Centre
6 Police
7 Greek Orthodox
  Cathedral
9 Bus Station
12 Port Police
16 Tower
18 Sanoudos Palace
20 Roman Catholic
  Cathedral
21 Naxos Popular
  Art Shop

22 Sun Cycle Bike Hire
23 Orbit Travel
  Services
24 Archaeological
  Museum
25 OTE
26 National Bank
  of Greece
27 Pro-Wash Laundry
  Service
28 Post Office

PALATIA
ISLET

To Engares

Grotta Beach

Neofytou

Agiou Nikodemou

BOURGOS

Quay

To Mykonos

KASTRO

To Paros
& Piraeus

To Ios &
Thira

Pentouria

Protopapadaki

Dionyssou

Papavasiliou

Naxos Town

0   100   200 m

To Filoti,
Apeiranthos
& Apollonas

Agios Georgios Beach

Places to Stay – bottom end

Naxos has three camp sites, all quite near Naxos town. They are *Camping Naxos* (☎ 23 501), one km south of Agios Georgios Beach; *Camping Maragas* (☎ 24 552), Agia Anna Beach; and *Camping Apollon* (☎ 24 117), 700 metres from Agios Prokopios Beach. All the sites have good facilities and minibuses which meet the boats.

The *Dionyssos Hotel* (☎ 22 331) has simply furnished single/double rooms for 1500/2500 dr with shared bathrooms, and dorm beds for 900 dr. Nearby, the *Hotel Anixis* (☎ 22 112) has attractive rooms for 3800/5350 dr with private bathrooms. Both hotels are signposted from Market St, the main thoroughfare of Bourgos. The slightly dilapidated *Okeanis Hotel* (☎ 22 436/826), near the quay, has clean rooms for 3000/5000/6000 dr with private bathrooms.

The *Pension Sofi* (☎ 23 957/077), in a quiet part of town, has spotless double/triple rooms for 5800/7000 dr with private bathrooms and balconies. The owner meets most boats – his red van displays the pension's name. Otherwise, it's a 350-metre walk from the quay.

There are many domatia and hotels near Agios Georgios Beach. From the port turn right and walk along the waterfront. At the fork, veer left, and soon the accommodation alternatives begin in earnest. On the left, almost at the beach, you will find *Hotel Soula* (☎ 23 637). The owner, Nikos Polykretis, has a variety of accommodation: nicely furnished hotel rooms are 5500/7000/9000 dr with private bath, breakfast included; apartments are 7000/10,000 dr for doubles/triples. Another building has simply furnished single/double rooms for 3000/5000 dr. On the same street, the C class *Hotel Helmos* (☎ 22 455) is another agreeable option with cosy rooms for 4500/6500/8150 dr; three and four-person apartments are 12,500/14,000 dr. The English-speaking owner is extremely courteous and helpful.

Rates at the C class *Asteria Hotel* (☎ 23 866), at the entrance to the beach, are 5500/8300/11,000 dr.

Places to Stay – middle

Best of the hotels in Grotta is the C class *Hotel Grotta* (☎ 22 215/101), which has well-furnished rooms; rates are 7800/9000/10,500 dr with private bathrooms. If you telephone, the owner will pick you up at the quay. The *Chateau Zevgoli* (☎ 24 525/358 or 22 993), in Kastro, has plush, traditionally furnished rooms. Doubles/triples are 14,000/15,000 dr. The hotel is owned by Despina who runs the Naxos Tourist Information Centre, so pop in there to see if there is a vacancy.

Places to Eat

O Tsistas Restaurant, up the alleyway from Zas Travel Agency, has tasty reasonably priced food. *O Nikos Restaurant*, on the waterfront, serves well-prepared traditional Greek dishes for around 1000 dr. My favourite restaurant in Naxos town is *Vasilissis Taverna*, on Market St. It's a cosy little place with stucco walls, pictures, plates, black wrought-iron lamps and plants. It serves a wide variety of dishes, including excellent souvlaki. All souvlaki dishes are served with chips, salad and two dips.

There are bakeries, grocers and fruiterers galore on Market St. Naxos has two specialities: *kefalotiri* cheese and *citron*, a liqueur made from citron leaves.

BEACHES

The aforementioned **Agios Georgios** is one of Naxos' finest beaches. The water is so shallow here that you feel you could wade all the way to Paros, which is visible in the distance – and the beach is so crowded that you may get an uncontrollable desire to do just that. Sandy beaches continue southwards as far as **Pyrgaki**. The next beach after Agios Georgios is **Agios Prokopios**, a sheltered bay, followed by **Agia Anna** – a long stretch of sand. There are domatia and tavernas strung out all along this stretch of coast.

THE TRAGAEA Τραγαία

The lovely Tragaea region is a vast plain of

olive groves and unspoilt hamlets harbouring numerous little churches. **Filoti**, on the slopes of Mt Zeus, is the region's largest village. From the beginning of the village (coming from Naxos town), a dirt road leads off right into the heart of the Tragaea. Following this road, you will come to the isolated hamlets of **Damarionas** and **Damalas**.

From Damalas it's a short walk back to the main road and the picturesque village of **Halki**, which has several towerhouses. These were built by aristocratic families as refuges and lookout posts in times of pirate raids and internecine feuds. The best preserved is the **Grazia Pirgos**; to reach it turn right at the **Church of Panagia Protothronis** (with fine frescoes), which is on the main road near the bus stop.

APEIRANTHOS Απείρανθος

Apeiranthos is a handsome, austere village of stone houses and steep winding streets paved with marble. Its inhabitants are descended from refugees who fled Crete to escape Turkish repression. On the right of the village's main thoroughfare (coming from the Naxos town-Apollonas road) is an **Archaeological Museum** with a small collection of local finds. The museum is open Tuesday to Sunday from 8.30 am to 2 pm. Admission is free. On the left there is a basic taverna with glorious views from its outside terrace. Apeiranthos does not have any accommodation.

APOLLONAS Απόλλωνας

Apollonas, on the north coast, was once a tranquil fishing village but is now a fully fledged resort. It has a small sand and a larger pebble beach. Hordes of day- trippers pour in to see the gargantuan 7th-century **kouros**, which lies in an ancient quarry a short walk from the village. It is signposted to the left as you approach Apollonas on the main inland road from Naxos town. This remarkable 10½-metre-long statue is unfinished, apparently abandoned because it had cracked.

If you wish to stay, Apollonas is amply provided with tavernas and domatia.

The inland route from Naxos town to Apollonas winds through breathtaking mountainscapes – a highly commendable trip. If you have your own transport you can return to Naxos town via the west-coast road. This passes through a wild and sparsely populated part of the island with awe-inspiring sea vistas; several tracks along the way lead down to secluded beaches.

Minor Islands

Between Naxos and Amorgos there is a chain of small islands variously called the 'Minor Islands', 'Back Islands' and 'Lesser Islands'. Only four of the islands have a permanent population: **Donoussa** (Δονούσα), **Koufonisi** (Κουφονήσι), **Iraklia** (Ηράκλεια) and **Shinoussa** (Σχοινούσσα).

The islands were densely populated in antiquity, as evidenced by the large number of graves which have been found. In the Middle Ages they were uninhabited except for corsairs and goats, and after Independence a few intrepid souls from Naxos and Amorgos reinhabited them. These days each has a tiny population. Up until a few years ago their only visitors were Greeks returning to their roots, but they now see a small number of independent tourists, mostly backpackers. The joys of visits to these islands lie in their splendid beaches, slow pace of life, and opportunities for walks along donkey paths.

Donoussa is the most northerly of the group, and the furthest away from Naxos. The others are clustered together, a short distance from the south-east coast of Naxos. Each has an OTE, telephone and post office, but the latter establishments should not be depended on for currency exchange; it's wise to take drachma with you.

The islands have domatia and tavernas at their ports, but don't expect anything fancy. In addition, accommodation is available at

Shinoussa's inland capital (which is also called Shinoussa).

Getting To/From the Minor Islands

There are two ferries a week from Piraeus to each of the islands: one via Syros, Paros and Naxos and the other via Syros, Tinos and Mykonos. In summer, a local ferry links the islands about four times a week with Amorgos and Naxos.

During July and August C/M *Catamaran* connects Piraeus (Flisvos) to Donoussa, Amorgos, Koufonisi, Shinoussa and Iraklia.

Amorgos Αμοργός

Elongated Amorgos (Am-or-GOS, population 1800) is the most easterly of the Cyclades. It's too far off the beaten track for package-tour operators but gets overrun with latter-day hippie types who stay throughout the summer. However, like Ios to the west, it's working hard to clean up its image, having recently sprouted a posh B class hotel at Aegiali. With rugged mountainscapes and an extraordinary cliff-hanging monastery,

Amorgos is still an enticing and worthwhile island for those wishing to venture off the well-worn Mykonos-Paros-Thira route. Amorgos has two ports, Katapola and Aegiali; the capital, Amorgos town, is northeast of Katapola.

Getting To/From Amorgos (Island)

Most ferries stop at both Katapola and Aegiali, but check if this is the case with your ferry. In summer there are daily ferry links with Naxos, Koufonisi, Shinoussa, and Iraklia. There are five ferries a week to Piraeus (10 hours, 2700 dr); three a week to Paros, Syros, Mykonos, Tinos and Donoussa; and two to Astypalea, in the Dodecanese. The C/M *Catamaran* links Amorgos with Piraeus (Flisvos) via Koufonisi, Shinoussa, Iraklia, Naxos, Paros, Mykonos, Tinos and Syros twice a week.

Getting Around Amorgos (Island)

There are frequent buses from Katapola to Amorgos town, Moni Hozoviotissas and Agia Anna Beach, and one or two a day to Aegiali and Paradisi beaches. Check the schedules of these last two, because roads on

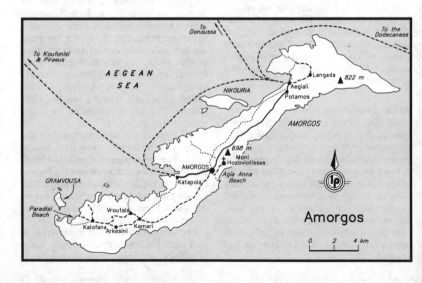

Amorgos are being improved, and this will no doubt have an advantageous effect upon the bus service. From Aegiali there are frequent buses to Langada.

KATAPOLA Κατάπολα

Katapola, the principal port, occupies a large bay in the most verdant part of the island. A smattering of remains from the ancient city of Minoa (a Cretan settlement) lie above the port. Amorgos has also yielded many finds from the Cycladic civilisation: the largest Cycladic figurine in the National Archaeological Museum in Athens was found in the vicinity of Katapola. The quay leads straight onto the central square and the waterfront is to the left of here. Katapola does not have a tourist office or tourist police; the regular police (☎ 71 210) are on the central square.

Places to Stay & Eat

Camping Amorgos (☎ 71 257) is just back from the northern end of the waterfront. Turn left from the quay (facing inland).

Domatia owners meet the ferries. *Pension Amorgos* (☎ 71 214) has spotless doubles with shared bathrooms for 4500 dr and with private bathrooms for 6000 dr. From the quay walk past the central square and you'll see it on the right. The C class *Hotel Minoa* (☎ 71 480/481) has comfortable doubles with private bathrooms for 7000 dr. The hotel is signposted from the waterfront.

There's a cluster of tavernas around the quay serving typical Greek fare. Try *Restaurant Minos* for a reasonably priced meal. Facing inland turn right from the quay to reach the taverna.

AMORGOS TOWN

Amorgos town, 400 metres above sea level and six km inland from Katapola, is a typical Cycladic village. The bus stop is on a square at the beginning of the village. The OTE is just beyond here on the main thoroughfare and the post office is further up the same road. Amorgos' telephone code is 0285 and its postcode is 84008. There are no hotels or pensions in Amorgos town but there are domatia – look for the signs along the main thoroughfare.

AEGIALI Αιγιάλη

Aegiali is Amorgos' other port. It's got more of a laid-back feel to it than Katapola and a far superior beach which stretches to the left of the quay as you face inland.

Places to Stay & Eat

As in Katapola, domatia owners meet the ferries. The C class *Hotel Mike* (☎ 71 252), opposite the quay, was Aegiali's first hotel and is now a bit dilapidated. Doubles with private bathrooms are 7000 dr. Just back from the beach *Lakki Pension* (☎ 73 244; fax 73 393) has immaculate doubles with private bathrooms for 7500 dr. The pension has a delightful garden, and a taverna and bar.

The posh B class *Egialis Hotel* (☎ 73 244/393; fax 73 244) is in an elevated position above Aegaili Beach. All rooms have a telephone, radio and balcony with great views. The cost is 9100/11,250 dr for singles/doubles.

AROUND THE ISLAND

A visit to the 11th-century **Moni Hozoviotissas** is the principal sightseeing excursion on Amorgos and is unreservedly worthwhile, as much for the spectacular scenery, as for the monastery itself. The dazzling white monastery clings precariously to a cliff face above the east coast. A handful of monks still live there and one will show you around. The contents include a regulatory miracle working-icon, which was found in the sea below the monastery – having arrived there, unaided, from either Asia Minor, Cyprus or Jerusalem, depending on which legend you hear. It's a splendid walk to the monastery from Amorgos town, or you can take a bus.

Pebbled **Agia Anna Beach**, on the east coast, just south of Moni Hozoviotissas, is the nearest decent beach to both Katapola and Amorgos town. **Paradisi**, on the west coast, is a delightful unspoilt beach. **Langada** is the most picturesque of the villages which lie inland from Aegiali – well worth a morning's respite from the beach to explore.

Paros Πάρος

Paros (PA-ros, population 9000) is an attractive island, with its softly contoured terraced hills of vineyards, fruit trees and olive groves, culminating in Mt Profitis Ilias (770 metres). It is popular with both backpackers and tourists (package and otherwise) who crave style and can't afford Mykonos.

Paros is famous for its pure white marble – no less than the Venus de Milo herself was created from it. Parian marble ensured that Paros prospered from the early Cycladic Age onwards. Trading in marble continued to flourish during the Hellenic and Roman periods and it was occasionally used later – Napoleon's tomb is a Parian marble creation.

The island of Antiparos ('before' Paros) lies one km south-west of Paros.

Getting To/From Paros

Air There are at least five flights a day to Athens (10,300 dr). The Olympic Airways office (☎ 21 900) in Paroikia is on the right side of Propona as you come from the waterfront.

Ferry Paros is the ferry hub of the Cyclades with daily connections to Piraeus (five hours, 2225 dr), Naxos, Ios, Thira, Mykonos and Sifnos; almost daily with Syros, Amorgos, Ikaria, Samos and Iraklion (Crete); and at least two a week with Sikinos and Folegandros. The port police (☎ 21 240) are just back from the northern waterfront, near the post office.

Catamaran Every day except Sunday C/M *Catamaran* links Paros with Piraeus (Flisvos) via Mykonos, Tinos and Syros; and

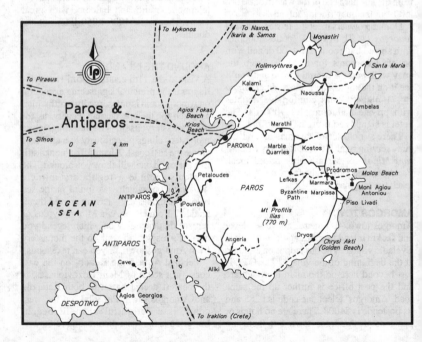

Architectural Animosity

Legend has it that St Helen, mother of Constantine the Great, had a vision of the True Cross whilst praying in a small church where the Ekatontapyliani now stands. She promised to build a magnificent church on the site, but died before fulfilling this promise.

Emperor Justinian authorised the construction of the church in the 6th century, commissioning Ignatius, an apprentice of Isidore of Miletus (architect of the Hagia Sophia in Constantinople), to design and build the church with Isidore acting as supervisor. The end product turned out to be so magnificent that Isidore was overcome with jealousy and pushed Ignatius off the roof; the tenacious Ignatius hung on to him, however, and the two fell to their deaths. A frieze depicting this sorry tale can be seen in the church's courtyard. ■

Naxos from where it continues to either Ios and Thira or Donoussa, Amorgos, Koufonisi, Shinoussa and Iraklia.

Getting Around Paros

Bus From the bus station in Paroikia there are frequent buses to Dryos (for Chrysi Akti) via Lefkas and Marpissa; Naoussa; Pounda (for Antiparos); and Aliki (for Petaloudes and the airport).

Car & Motorbike You can hire cars from Budget Rent-a-Car (☎ 22 302), on the northern waterfront in Paroikia. There are many motorbike-hire firms in Paroikia.

PAROIKIA Παροικία

The island's capital and port is Paroikia. The rather drab and messy waterfront conceals an attractive and typically Cycladic dazzling white old quarter.

Orientation & Information

As you disembark from the ferry, the white windmill in front of you is the Municipal Tourist Office (☎ 22 079). The staff have boat and bus schedules, maps and currency exchange. The central square is straight ahead past the windmill. The road on the extreme left leads to the northern waterfront, which has modern characterless hotels. The bus station is 50 metres along here from the quay; the post office is a little further along on the right. Paros' postcode is 84400.

Also on the left, but going inland, is the wide Odos Propona, which leads to the famous Church of Ekatontapyliani. The road on the right leads to the south-west water-

front, which is lined with cafés. The OTE is a little way along here on the left. Paros' telephone code is 0284.

The National Bank of Greece is on the central square. Opposite this bank is the Commercial Bank of Greece. The street between these two banks is the main thoroughfare of the old town. Both the north and south-west waterfronts skirt mediocre beaches.

Church of Ekatontapyliani (Our Lady of the Hundred Gates)

This church is the most splendid in the Cyclades. The building is actually three distinct churches: Agios Nikolaos, the largest, is in the east of the compound, and its columns of Parian marble and carved iconostasis are especially lovely; the other two churches are the Church of Our Lady, and the Baptistery. Only 99 doors have been counted and it is said that when the 100th is accounted for, Constantinople will return to Greece. Opening times are from 6 am to noon and 5 to 9 pm.

Archaeological Museum

This museum is behind the Church of the Ekatontapyliani. It has some interesting reliefs and statues, but the most important exhibit is a fragment of the 3rd-century Parian Chronicle, which lists the most outstanding artistic achievements of Ancient Greece. It was discovered in the 17th century by the Duke of Arundel's cleric, and most of it found its way to the Ashmolean Museum, Oxford. The museum is open Tuesday to

Saturday from 8.30 am to 3 pm. Admission is 400 dr.

Organised Tours

Tour agencies operate excursion boats from Paroikia to the island of Antiparos. See Getting To/From & Around Antiparos for details.

Places to Stay

The nearest camp site to Paroikia is *Camping Koula* (☎ 22 082), 500 metres along the northern waterfront. *Parasporos Camping* (☎ 21 944) is two km south of Paroikia – its minibus meets the boats. *Krios Camping* (☎ 21 705) is on Kryos Beach opposite the port – take a taxi boat from Paroikia.

The D class *Hotel Kypreou* (☎ 21 383), on the right side of Odos Propona, has comfortable single/double/triple rooms for 2500/3550/4000 dr with private bathrooms. The family also owns the sparkling new *Nikos Kypreos Apartments* nearby, where rates are 8000/10,000/12,000 dr for doubles/triples/quads.

Mimikos Rooms (☎ 21 437) have been a haven for backpackers for almost 20 years. The rooms are nicely furnished and very clean; rates are 5000/7000 dr for doubles/triples. Walk into the old town and follow the signs to To Tamariska Garden Restaurant, which is adjacent to the rooms.

The D class *Hotel Kontes* (☎ 21 096), behind the tourist office, has nice rooms with marble floors. Singles/doubles/triples are 4000/6000/7000 dr with private bathrooms. *Villa Aphrodite* (☎ 22 911) has a magnificent garden and immaculate doubles/triples with private bathrooms for 5600/6700 dr. Walk along the northern waterfront, turn right at the fenced off archaeological site, left at the Lido Hotel and the villa is on the right.

Icarus Rooms (☎ 21 695) has spotless, cosy doubles/triples for 7000/8000 dr. Walk along the northern waterfront and turn right at the Asterias Hotel. The co-managed *Hotel Stella* and *Hotel Fransiskes* have very agreeable single/double rooms for 4000/6000 dr with private bathrooms. Both hotels are 130 metres beyond the aforementioned fenced-off archaeological site.

The C class *Hotel Argonauta* (☎ 21 240), above the Commercial Bank of Greece, has lovely double/triple rooms for 11,000/14,200 dr, with private bath, telephone and balcony.

Places to Eat

Aligaraia Restaurant, on Plateia Fragkikou Itsantani, serves excellent traditional Greek fare with main courses for around 800 dr. From Hotel Kontes veer right and you will see the restaurant straight ahead. The laid-back *Stafedo Café* serves mostly vegetarian dishes. Prices start at 700 dr. Soothing classical music is played here in the morning – great if you're hung over. To reach the café walk along the south-west waterfront and turn left at the Salon Dior.

Continuing along the waterfront you will come to a small square on the left, with the excellent *Corfo Leon Restaurant*. A full meal including a beverage will cost about 1400 dr.

The long-established *May Tey Oriental Restaurant* serves imaginatively prepared food (no MSG is used). Starters include spring rolls at 450 dr. A vegetarian or chicken curry will cost from 900 to 1000 dr. The décor is authentic even down to the Siamese cat who stretches out on the sofa. Walk between the two banks into the old town, and continue straight ahead onto Odos Lochagou Kartianou; after the archway turn right, and the May Tey is on the left.

Entertainment

Most of Paroikia's bars are along the south-west waterfront. Further south, just before the road curves, there's a cluster of rowdy discos, including such home-away-from-home delights as the *Dubliner*, the *Down Under* and the *Londoner*. The *Pirate Bar*, on the old town's main drag, plays jazz tapes. Paroikia's outdoor cinema, *Cine Paros*, is just back from the northern waterfront.

NAOUSSA Νάουσα

Naoussa, on the north coast, has metamorphosed from a pristine fishing village to a multifaceted town that can't decide what it wants to be. Down at the harbour it's still a working village, with piles of yellow fishing nets, brightly coloured caïques, and little ouzeria with rickety tables and raffia chairs. Behind the central square (where the bus terminates) it is an exceptionally picturesque white village, with the surface of its narrow alleyways whitewashed with fish and flower motifs. To the left of the harbour, however, domatia and posh apartment blocks have mushroomed. Despite its identity crisis, Naoussa remains a relaxed place and its huge serrated bay has good beaches, served by taxi boats (350 dr). The best of these are **Kolimvythres**, which has strange rocks and **Monastiri**, which is nudist. **Santa Maria**, on the other side of the eastern headland, is good for windsurfing.

Places to Stay & Eat

Naoussa Camping (☎ 51 595) is at Kolimvythrès and *Surfing Beach* (☎ 51 013/181) is at Santa Maria. Both have good facilities and Surfing Beach has a surfing and water-ski school. Minibuses from both sites meet the ferries.

If you walk from the bus station towards the waterfront and turn left, you'll find *Pension Galini* (☎ 51 210) on the left. This charming little place has doubles with private bathrooms for 5980 dr. The owner also owns the attractive *Spiros Apartments* at Kolimvythres Beach, which cost 7500 dr a double.

The E class *Hotel Madaky* (☎ 51 475), on the central square, has pleasant double/triple rooms for 4600/6700 dr with shared bathrooms and 5000/5700 dr for singles/doubles with private bathrooms. In the heart of Naoussa town the *Pension Stella* (☎ 51 317) has rooms for 4400/8400 dr with private bathrooms. To reach it, walk inland from the central square, turn left at the post office and right at the pharmacy. *Limanaki Taverna*, at the harbour, serves tasty fish dishes. A full meal with retsina will cost about 1500 dr.

AROUND THE ISLAND
Lefkas to Marpissa & Moni Agiou Antoniou

Lefkas (Λευκάδα), 12 km south-east of Paroikia, is the island's highest and loveliest village. During the Middle Ages it was the island's capital. From its central square a signpost points to a well-preserved Byzantine paved path which leads in one hour of easy walking amidst delightful verdant countryside to the village of **Prodromos**, from where it is a short walk to either **Marmara** or **Marpissa** (Μάρπησσα). From Marmara it's a short walk to the pleasant sandy beach at **Molos**, where you can take a dip.

Alternatively, you can go to Marpissa, and puff and blow your way up a steep central path to the 16th-century **Moni Agiou Antoniou** (Μονή Αγίου Αντωνίου), atop a 200-metre-high hill. It was on this fortified summit that Paros' Venetian rulers were defeated by the Turks in 1537. The monastery and its grounds are locked, but there are breathtaking views over to Naxos, and Paros' east-coast villages. You'll definitely be in need of a dip after this exertion, and the crowded east-coast resort of **Piso Livadi** is just a short walk away.

Marathi Μαράθι

In ancient times Parian marble was considered the finest in the world, as its translucence extended to a depth of 3.5 mm compared to a mere 1.5 mm for Pentelic marble. The **marble quarries** at Marathi are now abandoned, but it's exciting, with the aid of a torch, to explore the three shafts. Take the Lefkas bus and get off at Marathi village, from where the quarries are signposted.

Petaloudes (Valley of the Butterflies)

In summer butterflies almost enshroud the copious foliage at Petaloudes (Πεταλούδες), eight km south of Paroikia. The 'butterflies' are actually tiger moths, but don't be put off by this – it's a very pretty sight. Many travel agents organise tours there from Paroikia, including excursions on donkeys (1200 dr).

Otherwise, you can take the Aliki bus and ask to be let off at the turn-off for Petaloudes.

Petaloudes is open during July and August from Monday to Saturday (9 am to 8 pm) and Sunday (9 am to 1 pm and 4 to 8 pm). Admission is 200 dr.

Beaches

Besides the beaches already mentioned, there is a decent beach at **Kryos**, accessible by frequent taxi boat (500 dr) from the capital. Paros' best beach is **Chrysi Akti** (Golden Beach), on the south-east coast – it's reputedly brilliant for windsurfing. There are lots of domatia and hotels.

Antiparos Αντίπαρος

Antiparos has long been regarded as a quiet alternative to Paros. However, development is happening at such a pace here that when you arrive you may well ask yourself not where are the domatia and hotels, but where are the dwellings of the inhabitants? Antiparos does have a permanent population of 650 who live in a very attractive village (also called Antiparos), but it's hidden in the middle of all the tourist accommodation.

Getting To/From & Around Antiparos

In summer there are frequent excursion boats from Paroikia on Paros to Antiparos. The trip takes 45 minutes and costs 680 dr. There is an hourly caïque service from Pounda on the west coast of Paros to Antiparos (15 minutes, 115 dr). The only bus service on the island is to the cave, in the centre of the island.

Orientation & Information

To reach the village centre, turn right from the quay, walk along the waterfront, and turn left at the yellow ochre periptero, onto the main street. The post office is on the left. Antiparos' postcode is 84007. At the top of the main street, turn left to reach the central square. The versatile little OTE, with currency exchange and ferry information (as well as telephones!), is just beyond here. Antiparos' telephone code is 0284.

To reach the atmospheric **Kastro**, another Marco Sanudo creation, turn right at the central square and go under the stone arch. Beach bums will direct you to the island's decent beaches. Nudism is only permitted on the camp-site beach.

Cave of Antiparos

Despite zealous looting of stalactites and stalagmites in years gone by, Antiparos' cave is still awe inspiring. A strange spectacle took place here in 1673 when the French ambassador, Marquis de Nointel, held Christmas Mass in the cave. He cajoled 500 Parians into attending, and commissioned a large orchestra to perform.

The cave is open every day from 10 am to 4 pm. Admission is 400 dr. Frequent buses from the village of Antiparos go to the cave or you can take one of the excursion boats which in summer leave from Antiparos village, Paroikia and Pounda. From the boat landing stage it's a steep 30-minute walk to the cave, or you can go up on a donkey.

Places to Stay

The island's well-equipped camp site, *Camping Antiparos* (☎ 61 221), is on a beach 800 metres north of the boat quay. Signs point the way.

Domatia are very much in evidence on Antiparos and there are also three hotels. Turn right from the port, and you'll see the D class *Hotel Anarghyros* (☎ 61 204) on the left. Rates are 3500/5500 dr for singles/doubles with private bathrooms. The D class *Hotel Mantalena* (☎ 61 220) is a little further along. Doubles with private bathrooms are 6500 dr. Just around the corner to the left is the C class *Hotel Chrissi Akti* (☎ 61 206), with similar prices.

Places to Eat

Taverna Gorgis, on the right of the main street, serves tasty Greek staples. Turn left at the top of the main road and you'll see *Marios Taverna* on the right, where you can order fresh, crispy kalamaria for around 700 dr.

Ios   Ιος

Ios (Eeos, population 1400) is the *enfant terrible* of the Greek islands; the apogee of sun, sand, sea and sex. Unless you're a raver you should avoid the 'Village' (Ios town), at least, between June and September.

On a more positive note Ios has superb beaches, an extremely pretty capital (the infamous Village), and cheap accommodation. It is also working hard to clean up its image. The travel agents at the port have free luggage storage, so backpacks do not litter the place, and free safe boxes to cut down on thefts.

Not only young hedonists holiday on Ios, but the young and 'old' (probably anyone over 25) are for the most part polarised. The young stay in the Village and the others at Gialos.

Ios has a very tenuous claim to being the burial place of Homer – his supposed grave is in the north of the island.

Getting To/From Ios (Island)

There is no commerical airport on Ios. Ios has daily ferry connections with Piraeus (eight to 10 hours, 3100 dr), Paros, Naxos, Mykonos and Thira; almost daily connections with Iraklion (Crete); and at least four a week with Sikinos and Folegandros. The C/M *Catamaran* sails twice a week from Ios to Thira; and to Piraeus via Mykonos, Syros and Tinos. To reach Ios' port police (☎ 91 264) turn right at Plateia Emirou, walk along the waterfront and you'll come to it on the right, just before the camp site.

Getting Around Ios (Island)

In summer packed buses trundle along the Gialos-Ios town-Milopotas Beach route every 15 minutes or so.

GIALOS, IOS TOWN & MILOPOTAS BEACH

Ios is nicely compact. The capital, Ios town (alias the Village) is one km inland from the port of Gialos (Γυαλός), and Milopotas

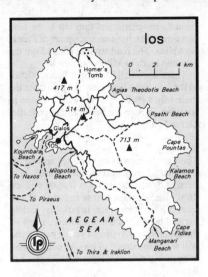

Beach (Μυλοπόταμος) is one km east of here. These are the island's only settlements. Gialos Beach, at the port, isn't at all bad – turn left at the quay to reach it. Koumbara Beach, a 20-minute walk west of Gialos, is less crowded and mainly nudist. Milopotas is a superb long curving sand beach, unrivalled, even in the beach-laden Cyclades.

Orientation & Information

From the ferry quay at Gialos walk straight ahead to reach the bus terminal on Plateia Emirou. From this square turn left, then immediately right and in just under 100 metres you'll come to steps on the right. These lead in 20 minutes to Ios town – or you can take the bus.

Once in Ios town, from the bus stop walk to the large church up to the left, and the National Bank of Greece is behind here. From the church, turn right onto one of the town's main thoroughfares, pass the Ios bakery, take the second turn left and you will see a sign pointing to the post office.

The OTE was due to move at the time of writing; its new location should be well signposted. Ios' postcode is 84001 and the telephone code is 0286. Continue along the main thoroughfare and turn left at the road junction to reach the central square of Plateia Sp Valeta. The road straight ahead from the bus stop leads to Milopotas Beach.

There is a small Municipal Tourist Office to the left of the boat quay in Gialos, but the main office (☎ 91 028) is by the bus stop in Ios town. Pick up the free information leaflet *Out of Time*.

Warning

There are numerous signs posted around the town warning against alcohol abuse – take heed of these warnings. On Ios you will see drinks for sale cheaper than anywhere else in Greece, but these are invariably locally brewed hooch. As a consequence, many of the apparently intoxicated young people you will see on the streets of Ios may not be drunk as such, but poisoned from drinking this bad liquor.

Places to Stay – bottom end

Ios Camping (☎ 91 329) is at Gialos. Turn right at Plateia Emirou, walk along the waterfront and you'll come to it on the right. There are three camp sites on Milopotas Beach. The first is *Stars* (☎ 91 302), the second *Milopotas* (☎ 91 554) and the third the spiffy *Far Out Camping* (☎ 91 468), with a restaurant, volley ball, basket ball, and tennis courts, wind-surf and water-ski hire and a minibus service to Ios town and Gialos.

In Gialos you will find domatia signs at the beginning of the road to Ios town, on the steps leading up to the town, and also along the waterfront. The C class *Hotel Poseidon* (☎ 91 091) has immaculate double/triple rooms for 6000/7200 dr. Walk along the waterfront and turn left at the Enigma Bar and the hotel is up the steps on the left.

If you walk towards Milopotas Beach from Ios town bus stop, you will see countless domatia signs. The *Hermes Rooms* (☎ 91 471) on the right, halfway between the village and the beach, are spotless. Room rates are 7000/8000 dr for doubles/triples with private bathrooms. The next place to stay along the road is the equally commendable *Petradi Rooms* (☎ 91 510). The rooms

have balconies and private bathrooms and cost 6000/7500/8500 dr for doubles/triples/quads. The establishment has a bar/restaurant and a terrace with wonderful views of Milopotas Beach and Thira.

Places to Stay – middle

If you want one splurge in the Cyclades you couldn't do better than *Petra Holiday Villas* (☎ 91 409). The luxurious open-plan apartments have tasteful furniture and ornaments, and well-equipped kitchens. Rates are 12,000 dr a double. The villas are on a hill above the far end of Gialos Beach.

The lovely C class *Far Out Hotel* (☎ 91 446/468; fax 91 088), on the left, between the village and Milopotas Beach, is a cluster of traditional-style white buildings. Rates are 7000/9000/12,000 dr for singles/doubles/triples.

Places to Stay – top end

Ios' most luxurious hotel is the B class *Ios Palace* (☎ 91 269/224), at·the end of Milopotas Beach closest to the Village. Rates are 12,100/15,800 dr for singles/doubles.

Places to Eat

At Gialos, *Restaurant Psarades* has excellent fish dishes at reasonable prices. The *Restaurant Polydoros*, on Koumbara Beach, is very popular. Moussaka, pastitsio and meatballs are 750 dr.

In Ios town, *Pithari Taverna*, beside the large church, serves low-priced traditional Greek fare. The *Captain's Table*, opposite the Dubliner Disco, satisfies the needs of gastronomically unadventurous Brits with tasty fish & chips for 900 dr. Close by, the *Red Lion Bar* (see Entertainment) has filled jacket potatoes for 400 to 700 dr, shepherds pie for 750 dr and chicken curry for 800 dr. When Italians come to Ios they won't eat anywhere except *Pinocchios*. Pizzas are 1500 to 2000 dr. Look for the signs pointing the way, and Pinocchio standing outside.

Entertainment

Ravers say the port is dull and older people say the Village is crazy, so take your pick. At the port, two bars which cater for a mixed age group are the *Frog Club*, near Plateia Emirou, and the *Enigma Cocktail Bar*, further around the waterfront. The *Marina Bar*, overlooking Gialos Beach, is one of the few places which plays Greek music.

In the village there's loads of choice. The *Kahlua Bar*, just beyond the central square, is a cosy friendly place. The *69 Disco*, nearby, is wild. The *Dubliner Disco*, just up from the bus stop, is a huge place reminiscent of an English (or Irish) pub. It has stone floors, wood-beamed ceilings, outdoor terraces and a small disco area; reasonably priced imported drinks are on sale. Opposite, at the *Red Lion Bar*, an English-language video plays every afternoon. At the *Ios Club* you can listen to classical music while watching the sunset. Turn left at Ios town bus stop (facing the church) and left again at the Sweet Irish Dream bar to get there. The club is something of a chameleon – after the sun's done its bit, it turns into a disco.

AROUND THE ISLAND

The beaches, along with the nightlife, are the lure of Ios. Vying with **Milopotas** for best beach is **Manganari Beach**, on the south coast, reached by excursion boats from Gialos. **Agias Theodotis Beach**, on the north-east coast, is more remote. Neither buses or boats go here, so it's either a three-hour trek across the island, or a bumpy motorbike ride.

Folegandros
Φολέγανδρος

Folegandros (Fo-LE-gan-dros, population 650) is one of the most alluring Greek islands (how could it be anything else, with such a wonderful name?). It's an island which bridges the gap between those which have lost their innocence to discos, bars, and every other tourist trap, and the small depopulated islands, which are on the brink of total abandonment. Since the early 1980s tourists have

been coming in increasing numbers to Folegandros. Despite this, as many of the inhabitants earn a living from fishing and agriculture as they do from tourism.

Folegandros' tourists tend to be those who want a taste of genuine island life rather than a nonstop party, and the locals, having seen what's happened to neighbouring Ios, are determined to keep it this way. Admittedly, Folegandros gets crowded during July and August, but come any other time and it's a blissful place. The island has several good beaches, and a striking landscape of cultivated terraces giving way to precipitous cliffs.

Cycladic School
The Cycladic School (founded on Folegandros in 1984) has courses in drawing, painting, Greek cookery, folk dancing and Hatha yoga. For information write to Anne & Fotis Papadopoulos (no telephone), Folegandros 84011, Cyclades, Greece.

Getting To/From Folegandros
Ferry From Folegandros five ferries a week go to Piraeus (10-12 hours, 3100 dr), Ios, Thira and Sikinos; around three a week go to Paros, Milos, Sifnos and Serifos; two a week leave for Naxos; and there is one a week to Sitia (Crete) via Agios Nikolaos.

Catamaran Once a week the CM *Catamaran* connects Folegandros to Piraeus (Flisvos) via Ios, Naxos, Paros, Mykonos, Tinos and Syros.

Getting Around Folegandros

The island bus meets all boats and makes frequent trips between Chora and Ano Meria, stopping at the road which leads down to Angali Beach. There are no taxis. In summer there are daily excursion boats from Karavostassi to Angali, Agios Nikolaos and Livadaki beaches.

KARAVOSTASSI Καραβοστάσι

All boats dock at the unremarkable harbour of Karavostassi, on the east coast. The capital is the concealed cliff-top Chora, four km inland. The island's only other settlement is Ano Meria, four km north-west of Chora.

Places to Stay

Camping Livadi (☎ 42 203) is on Livadi Beach, one km from Karavostassi. To reach the site turn left onto the cement road which skirts Karavostassi Beach.

There are several domatia in Karavostassi; if you are not offered a room when you get off the boat look for the signs. The C class *Aeolos Beach Hotel* (☎ 41 205), overlooking the beach, has immaculate doubles with private bathrooms for 7000 dr and suites for 10,000 dr.

CHORA Χώρα

Folegandros' captivating Chora is perhaps the most beautiful island capital in the Cyclades (apologies to Mykonos fans).

Orientation & Information

From the bus turnaround, facing away from the port, turn left and follow the curving road. An archway on the right leads into the Kastro; a left turn will bring you to three shady squares in a row. The third square is the central square; from here, take the second turn right, after Restaurant Platinis, to reach the combined post office and OTE, on Plateia Ant I Patsa. Folegandros' postcode is 84011; the telephone code is 0286. There is no bank.

Folegandros does not have a tourist office or tourist police. To reach the regular police (☎ 41 249), face the post office, turn left and then right and they're along here on the right.

The island's one travel agency is adjacent to the Kastro entrance. It sells ferry tickets and has currency exchange.

Things to See

Chora is an archetypal Cycladic village of dazzling white churches and sugar-cube houses. The medieval **Kastro**, a tangle of narrow streets, spanned by archways, dates from when Marco Sanudo ruled the island in the 13th century. The wooden balconies of its houses are ablaze with bougainvillea, azaleas and hibiscus and their external staircases are bedecked with potted geraniums and dozing cats. The newer village, outside Kastro, is just as pretty. On its first square are water troughs where donkeys come to drink. On the next square, the white circle painted on the ground is an old threshing floor. From the square where the bus does its turn around, a path leads up to the **Church of the Panagia**, from where there are splendid views.

Places to Stay

The owner of the nameless cafeteria (☎ 41 265), adjacent to the post office, rents doubles for 3600 dr. There are several more reasonably priced domatia near the police station. The cheapest hotel is the E class *Hotel Danassis* (☎ 41 230), an atmospheric place with stone floors and wood-beamed ceilings. Rates are 5600 dr a double with shared bathrooms. Enter the Kastro, walk straight ahead, and the hotel is on the left.

Nikos Rooms (no telephone) are lovely well-equipped apartments. Rates are 7500 dr a double. Turn right at Taverna Platinis on the central square, and the rooms are on the right. The comfortable C class *Hotel Odysseus* (☎ 41 239) has doubles for 6500 dr. Turn left after the police station and the hotel is on the left. The B class *Hotel Fani-Vevie* (☎ 41 237) has rates of 7000 dr a double. The hotel is at the beginning of the road to Ano Meria.

The C class *Folegandros*, on the square in Chora where the bus terminates, has large well-equipped apartments for 24,000 dr.

Places to Eat

Taverna Platinis, on the central square, is a lively place which serves good food. Main meals start at 700 to 800 dr. Prices are similar at *Taverna Nikos*, adjacent to the post office. The nameless cafeteria (see Places to Stay), opposite, is reasonably priced. A breakfast here of bacon and eggs and Nescafé will cost about 650 dr. Just beyond the entrance to Kastro there is a cheap souvlaki joint.

Entertainment

Delightfully traditional Chora might be, but the Folegandriots are not killjoys – the town does have one disco – a sign in town points the way.

AROUND THE ISLAND

Ano Meria Ανω Μεριά

The settlement of Ano Meria stretches for several km along either side of the road. There are reasons for this scattered layout. Northern Folegandros is more fertile than the south, but the landscape is also more open and visible from the sea, and hence too vulnerable to pirate raids. When pirates were no longer a threat, people moved to the north where the land was more favourable for cultivation. Each dwelling is in fact a farm surrounded by its terraced fields and grazing land. If you walk from Chora to Ano Meria you'll be rewarded with stunning sea and cliff vistas.

Places to Stay Ano Meria has tavernas but no official accommodation; however, rooms may be available in family houses – ask at a kafeneion.

Beaches

There is a pebble beach at Karavostassi, and also at Livadi Beach, the next bay around (follow the signs for Livadi Camping). The island's finest beach is sandy **Angali**, where there are several domatia and tavernas. Other good beaches are **Agios Nikolaos** and **Livadaki**, both north-west of Angali, and **Agios Georgios**, which is north-west of Ano Meria. A path from Ano Meria's Church

of Agios Andreas leads to Agios Georgios Beach. The walk takes about an hour.

Sikinos Σίκινος

For many years the neighbouring islands of Sikinos (SIK-in-os, population 300) and Folegandros were spoken of in the same breath as remote unspoilt islands. However, whereas Folegandros has 'taken off' (in the nicest possible way) and is now on the tourist map, Sikinos remains a backwater. Perhaps Folegandros does, only just, have the edge over Sikinos, with a more dramatic landscape, better beaches and a prettier capital. However, if your desire for a quiet unspoilt island takes precedence over all else, then Sikinos is a better choice.

There are two settlements, the port of Alopronia, and the capital, Sikinos town, which consists of the contiguous villages of Chora and Kastro. The fortified **Moni Zoodohou Pigis** stands on a hill above the town.

There is a combined post office and OTE in Sikinos town. Sikinos' postcode is 84010 and the telephone code is 0286. Both Alopronia and Sikinos town have a few domatia, and tavernas selling basic low-priced fare. Alopronia also has the new, very posh B class *Porto Sikinos* (☎ 51 220; fax 51 220), on the beach. Rates for doubles with private bathrooms are 10,000 dr. This establishment is built in traditional Cycladic style and has a bar and restaurant. Perhaps it is a sign that Sikinos has 'taken off'.

The principal excursion on Sikinos is the one-hour scenic trek south-west from Sikinos town to Episkopi. When the building at Episkopi was investigated by 19th-century archaeologists, the Doric columns and inscriptions led them to believe it had originally been a shrine to Apollo. However, it is now believed to be the remains of a 3rd-century AD mausoleum. In the 7th century, the ruins were transformed into a church. In the 17th century, the church was greatly extended to become Moni Episkopi. The church and monastery are no longer in use.

Getting To/From & Around Sikinos

The island bus meets all ferries and does several trips a day between Alopronia and Sikinos town. Sikinos has the same ferry schedule as Folegandros.

Thira (Santorini)
Θήρα (Σαντορίνη)

Thira (THEE-ra, population 7500), also known as Santorini, is regarded by many as the most spectacular of all Greek islands. Thousands of tourists come every year to gape at the caldera, vestige of what was probably the world's biggest volcanic eruption. Thira is unique, and should not be missed, but it gets very crowded, and is overly commercial in a tackier way than Mykonos. It is a strange island – a place where beaches are black, and rocks float and crumble at a touch. It is an island on which to sightsee, wonder, question and speculate, rather than experience traditional Greek island life, or relax on secluded beaches.

The main port of Thira is Athinios. This is a purely functional place, not a settlement. Buses meet all ferries and whisk passengers to Fira, the capital, which teeters on the lip of the caldera, high above the sea.

History

Dorians, Byzantines and Turks inhabited Thira, as they did all the other Cycladic islands, but it is the island's first inhabitants, the Minoans, and its geological peculiarities, that make Thira unique. In Greece you may well feel the earth move, for it is a country vulnerable to eruptions and earthquakes – mostly minor, barely detectable tremors. However, on Thira, the earth's movements have been so violent that they have caused the island to change shape drastically several times.

In 3000 BC, Minoans came to the island from Crete, and their settlement at Akrotiri dates from the height of their great civilisation. The island at that time was circular and called Stronghyle (the Round One). Sometime around 1450 BC a colossal volcanic eruption caused the middle of Stronghyle to sink, leaving a caldera of high cliffs – one of the world's most dramatic geological spectacles. The theory that this catastrophe destroyed not only Akrotiri but the whole Minoan civilisation has yet to be substantiated. Another theory, and one which has fired the imagination of writers, artists and mystics since ancient times, postulates that the island was part of the lost continent of Atlantis.

Major eruptions and earthquakes occurred in 236 BC, 197 BC (causing Palia Kameni island to appear), 1707 (causing Nea Kameni to appear), 1711, 1866, 1870 and 1925. The last serious earthquake occurred on Thira as recently as 1956, devastating the towns of Fira and Oia.

Getting To/From Thira

Air There are daily flights to Athens (12,300 dr) and Mykonos (7700 dr), three flights a week to Iraklion (8200 dr) and four flights a week to Rhodes (12,300). The Olympic Airways office (☎ 22 493) is in Fira, on the road to Kamari, one block east of 25 Martiou.

Ferry Thira has daily connections with Piraeus (12 hours, 3100 dr), Mykonos, Naxos, Paros, Ios and Crete (Iraklion); around five a week with Sikinos and Folegandros; around three a week with Milos, Serifos and Sifnos; twice a week with Thessaloniki; and once a week with Sitia (Crete) via Agios Nikolaos. There are daily boats from the town of Oia to Thira's satellite island of Thirassia. The port police (☎ 22 239) are on the west side of 25 Martiou, just north of Plateia Theotokopoulou.

Catamaran The C/M *Catamaran* sails to Thira once a week from Piraeus (Flisvos) via Tinos, Syros, Mykonos, Paros and Naxos.

Getting Around Thira

Bus Thira has a good bus service, but the vehicles do get packed. Buses leave Fira's bus station every hour for Akrotiri, Oia and Monolithos; every half hour for Kamari and every 20 minutes for Perissa. Buses leave Fira, Kamari and Perissa for the port of Athinios 1½ hours before most ferry departures.

Car, Motorbike & Bicycle Cars can be hired from Budget Rent-a-Car (☎ 22 990), in Fira, next to the Olympic Airways office. Fira has

many motorbike-rental firms. Bicycles can be hired from Kostos for 1000 dr per day. Turn right at the Commercial Bank and the office is on the right.

FIRA Φήρα

The commercialism of Fira has not diminished its all-pervasive dramatic aura. Walk to the edge of the caldera for spectacular views of the cliffs with their multicoloured strata of lava and pumice.

Orientation

Fira's central square is Plateia Theotokopoulou. The main thoroughfare of Odos 25 Martiou runs north to south through the town, intersecting this square. Neither street nor square is a pretty sight, as they consist almost entirely of travel agencies promulgating their offerings in garish advertisements.

Facing north on Plateia Theotokopoulou, turn left opposite the Commercial Bank of

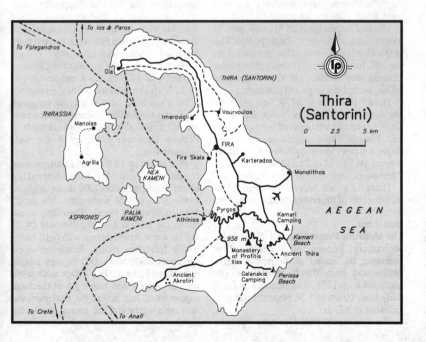

Greece, and at Hotel Tataki turn right onto Odos Erithrou Stavrou. This is the main commercial thoroughfare, lined with souvenir shops, bars and restaurants. Any turn left along here will bring you to the edge of the caldera. One turn left leads to the cable-car station (signposted) for Skala Fira (the port of Fira used by cruise ships and some excursion boats). Donkeys will also take you down, or you can walk down the 600 steps.

Information

Fira's long-awaited and promised EOT and tourist police had not materialised at the time of writing. Thira's police station (☎ 22 239) is north of the central square, on the right. Dozens of travel agencies ostensibly offer tourist information, but in reality most only want to part you from your money for the numerous excursions on offer. One of the most helpful agencies is Dakoutros Travel (☎ 22 958 or 23 246). It gives a 20% student discount on all excursions. To reach it, face north on Plateia Theotokopoulou, and turn right at the Commercial Bank of Greece.

The bus station is on 25 Martiou, just 50 metres south of Plateia Theotokopoulou. The post office is just north of the bus station on the left. To reach the OTE walk through the covered way at the right side of the post office, ascend the steps and turn right.

Thira's postcode is 84700 and the telephone code is 0286. The National Bank of Greece is on the left between the bus station and Plateia Theotokopoulou. American Express is represented by X-Ray Kilo Travel Agency (☎ 22 624 or 23 243/401) on Plateia Theotokopoulou.

There is a self-service laundrette 100 metres north of the central square on the left.

Museums

The **Museum Megara**, behind the Catholic Monastery, houses local memorabilia, including fascinating photographs of Fira before and immediately after the major earthquake of 1956. The museum is open daily from 10 am to 1.30 pm and 5 to 8 pm. Entrance is 300 dr.

The **Archaeological Museum**, opposite the cable-car station, houses finds from Akrotiri and ancient Thira, some Cycladic figurines and Hellenistic and Roman sculpture. Opening times are Tuesday to Sunday from 8.30 am to 3 pm. Admission is 400 dr.

Organised Tours

Tour agencies operate trips to Thirassia and the other islands around Thira. Check out the best deals with Fira's travel agents.

Places to Stay – bottom end

Fira's *Camping Santorini* (☎ 22 944) is a superb site with many facilities, including a restaurant and swimming pool. The cost is 800 dr per person and 200 dr per tent. It's 400 metres east of Plateia Theotokopoulou – look for the sign pointing the way.

Accommodation owners who meet the boats at the port of Athinios are more aggressive and persistent than they are on any other Greek island. Perhaps living on the edge of a tectonic plate has had an adverse effect upon them. Be wary of proprietors with accommodation in Karterados (a village three km south-east of Fira), who insist their accommodation is in Fira when you tell them that this is where you want to stay.

Fira has two youth hostels: the *Camares Hostel* (☎ 23 142) and the *Kontonari Hostel* (☎ 22 722). The latter has the best reputation. It has a snack bar, and an English-language video is shown every evening. Dorm beds are 900 dr at both hostels. Both are north of Plateia Theotokopoulou and are well signposted.

Villa Mari ι (☎ 22 092) has clean, pleasant rooms and a friendly English-speaking owner. Rates are 5000/7000 dr for doubles/triples with private bathrooms. It's on 25 Martiou, north of Plateia Theotokopoulou, above the laundrette. *Villa Haroula* (☎ 23 469) is a new establishment with light, beautifully furnished rooms. Singles/doubles/triples are 3000/5000/7000 dr with private bathrooms. From the bus station walk south for 100 metres, and turn right at the large supermarket. Just before the road narrows, turn right again and the rooms are on the right.

Pension Rousa (☎ 23 220), opposite the bus station, has agreeable rooms for 4000/5000/6000 dr with private bathrooms. Behind here, the D class *Hotel Santorini* (☎ 22 593/054) has simple but clean rooms for 5600/9600/11,500 dr with private bathrooms. The D class *Hotel Tataki* (☎ 22 389) has clean pleasant rooms and a tranquil flower-adorned courtyard. Room rates are 5600/9100 dr for singles/doubles with private bathrooms. Facing north on Plateia Theotokopoulou, turn left opposite the Commercial Bank and the hotel is on the left.

Places to Stay – middle & top end

The C class *Hotel Asimina* (☎ 22 034/989/035) has cosy, prettily furnished rooms for 8500/13,000/15,250 dr with private bathrooms. It's on Erithrou Stavrou, just beyond the Archaeological Museum.

The D class *Locos Hotel* (☎ 22 480), because of the views it commands, charges mid-range rates despite its low grade. The attractive double rooms are 10,500 dr with private bathrooms. Facing north on Plateia Theotokopoulou, turn left after the Commercial Bank, walk past the Hotel Tataki and turn left to reach this hotel.

The C class *Kallisti Thira Hotel* (☎ 22 317) has pleasant singles/doubles for 12,000/17,500 dr. The hotel is on the east side of 25 Martiou, south of Plateia Theotokopoulou. The *Pelican Hotel* (☎ 23 113/4; fax 23 514) has comfortable rooms. The focal point of the lounge is a tank full of very strange-looking fish. Room rates are 13,000/15,600 dr. To reach the hotel, facing north, turn right at the Commercial Bank on Plateia Theotokopoulou and the hotel is on the left.

Thira's largest and most luxurious hotel is the conspicuous A class *Santorini Palace* (☎ 22 771/781 or 22 868; fax 23 705), in Fira. The hotel has a restaurant, bar and swimming pool. The rates are 20,100/25,100 dr for singles/doubles.

Places to Eat

Fira is not blessed with good eating establishments. One of the the best of the bunch is *Nikolas Taverna*, on Erithrou Stavrou, which has delicious seafood dishes for 800 dr. The *Delphi Garden* is another of Fira's better eating places. Turn right at the Commercial Bank and it's on the right. *Koutouki Restaurant* specialises in grilled food. A full meal including Amstel will cost about 1700 dr. The restaurant is set back from the road, on the left of 25 Martiou, north of Plateia Theotokopoulou.

Entertainment

There's something to suit all tastes in Fira. The *Two Brothers Bar* is a favourite with backpackers. Facing north, turn left opposite the Commercial Bank, take the first left and it's on the right. One of Fira's best discos is the *Tithora Club* (on the steps down to Skala Fira), with a cave interior resplendent with a fountain. At sunset you can sip (pricey) cocktails to classical music at the *Kastro Bar*, opposite the Archaeological Museum. If you continue beyond here, and veer right, you will come to the *Eternity Bar*, where jazz music is played. You can hear Greek music at the lively *Apocalypse Club*; look for the signs on the left side of 25 Martiou, north of Plateia Theotokopoulou.

AROUND THE ISLAND

Karterados Καρτεράδος

Having probably put you off Karterados (see Fira Places to Stay), I have to admit it's a pleasant village with cheaper accommodation than Fira, so it's not a bad choice, as long as you don't mind the 20-minute walk into town.

Places to Stay On the main approach road from Fira, you will see a row of tavernas on the left. *Stavros Filitsis* (☎ 23 538), the proprietor of the last one (Taverna Neriada), owns 40 rooms in the village. Rates are 1500/3000/4500 dr with shared bathrooms and 2000/4000/6000 dr with private bathrooms; two-person apartments on a nearby beach are 8000 dr.

The *Hotel Karterados* (☎ 22 489) has pleasant rooms and a large terrace ablaze with bougainvillea. Singles/doubles with private bathrooms go for 6000/8000 dr. To get there, walk past the row of tavernas mentioned above to a stone windmill and take the small road straight ahead (the main road veers left). Take the first turn right, ascend the steps, take the first left, pass Hotel Ginoan, then veer right.

Ancient Akrotiri Παλαιό Ακρωτήρι

Ancient Akrotiri was a Minoan outpost. Excavations were begun in 1967 by the late Professor Spyridon Marinatos, who was tragically killed at the site in 1974. His excavations uncovered an ancient city which had been buried beneath volcanic ash – the best preserved prehistoric settlement in the Aegean. The buildings date to the late 16th century BC and some ruins are two and three storeys high. No skeletons or treasures have been found here, which indicates that the inhabitants were forewarned of the eruption and were able to escape.

A visit to Akrotiri is one of the highlights of Thira, but even so, the most outstanding finds from the site are the stunning frescoes which are at present on display in the National Archaeological Museum in Athens. Site opening times are Tuesday to Sunday from 8.30 am to 3 pm; admission is 1000 dr.

Ancient Thira Παλαιά Θήρα

Ancient Thira was first settled by the Dorians in the 9th century BC, but most of the ruins date from Hellenistic, Roman and Byzantine times. They include temples, houses with mosaics, the Agora, a theatre and a gymnasium. From the site there are splendid views. Opening times are Tuesday to Sunday from 9 am to 3 pm. Admission is free. From Perissa a path leads in 30 minutes to the site. If you're driving, there's a road from Kamari.

Monastery of Profitis Ilias

Μονή Προφήτη Ηλία

This monastery crowns Thira's highest peak, Mt Profitis Ilias (956 metres). Despite sharing the peak with the temporal appendages of radio and TV pilons and a radar station, it's worth the trek up here for the stupendous views. The monastery has an interesting **Folk Museum**. It can be reached on foot along paths from either the village of Pyrgos (1½ hours) or from ancient Thira (one hour).

Oia Οία

The fishing port of Oia was devastated by the earthquake of 1956 and has never fully recovered. Nevertheless, it's a dramatic and striking town and much quieter than Fira. Built on a steep slope of the caldera, many of its dwellings nestle in the niches hewn in the volcanic rock. From the bus turnaround turn left (following signs for the youth hostel), turn immediately right, take the first left, ascend the steps and walk across the central square to Odos Nikolaou Nomikou, which skirts the caldera and is the main thoroughfare.

Places to Stay & Eat Oia's exceptionally clean and comfortable *Youth Hostel* (☎ 71 290/1/2) has dorm beds for 1700 dr. The hostel is signposted from the bus stop. If you turn left onto Nikolaou Nomikou you will come to *Jack's Rooms & Apartments* (☎ 71 439/338), where doubles with private bathrooms cost 4000 dr, and luxurious troglodytic apartments are 15,000/22,000 dr for doubles/triples or quads. Just before these rooms, *Lauda Traditional Hostel* (☎ 71 204/157) has simple but tastefully furnished troglodytic single/double rooms for 6200/8500 dr with shared bathrooms, and apartments for 13,900 dr. Further along, the *Hotel Fregata* (☎ 71 221/276/105) and *Hotel Anemones* (☎ 71 220) both charge 7000 dr a double.

Restaurant Neptune, on Nikolaou Nomikou, serves tasty Greek staples. Stuffed aubergines are 800 dr and veal in tomato sauce is 950 dr.

Beaches

Thira's black sand beaches become unbearably hot, making a beach mat essential. **Kamari** and **Perissa**, on the east coast, are the best beaches, but they get crowded. Both have domatia, hotels and camp sites. *Kamari Camping* (☎ 31 453) is one km up the main road from Kamari Beach and *Galanakis Camping* (☎ 81 343) is on the beach at Perissa. *Monolithos*, further up the coast, is slightly less crowded, but you'd do better to walk north from here, where deserted stretches of beach can be found.

Thirassia & Surrounding Islands

Unspoilt Thirassia (Θηρασσιά) was separated from Thira by an eruption in 236 BC; its largest village, Manolas, has tavernas and domatia. The uninhabited islands of **Palia Kameni** and **Nea Kameni** are still volcanically active. There are daily boats from Oia to Thirassia. Palia and Nea Kameni can only be visited on excursions from Thira. A full day's excursion is 4000 dr and a half-day is 2000 dr. Shop around the numerous travel agents in Fira for the best deal.

Anafi Ανάφη

Diminutive and unpretentious Anafi (An-AF-ee, population 250) lies 30 km east of its spectacular and showy neighbour, Thira. It's an island which until recently was unknown or ignored by tourists. However, among the rapidly diminishing number of pristine Greek islands, Anafi is beginning to make its mark, and gets a trickle of visitors. It's an unassuming island with nothing to amaze except a slow-paced traditional way of life, and lack of any tourist hype – the ideal place to unwind. According to mythology, Anafi popped up from the sea at Apollo's command when Jason and the Argonauts were in dire need of dry land during a storm.

Anafi's little port is **Agios Nikolaos**. **Chora**, the capital, is a 20-minute walk from the port up a steep road. Chora has a post office. There are several pleasant beaches near Agios Nikolaos. There are no hotels on Anafi but the port and Chora have a few domatia and tavernas. Freelance camping may be tolerated. Anafi's 'sight' is **Moni Kalamiotissas**, in the extreme east of the island, near some scant remains of a sanctuary to Apollo. It's a three-hour walk from Chora to the monastery.

Getting To/From Anafi

At the time of writing, ferry service to Anafi was poor, with only two ferries a week from Piraeus (3600 dr). The F/B *Olympia Express* sailed to Anafi from Piraeus via Paros, Naxos, Ios and Thira and the F/B *Apollon Express* sailed via Syros, Paros, Naxos, Ios and Thira. There are also occasional excursions to Anafi from Thira.

Milos Μήλος

The volcanic island of Milos (MEE-los, population 5000), the most westerly island of the Cyclades, is overlooked by most foreign tourists. This is a pity because although it's not as extraordinary, visually, as the volcanic islands of Thira or Nisyros, Milos has some weird rock formations, hot springs, pleasant beaches and superb vistas. However, its most celebrated asset, the beautiful Venus de Milo (a 4th-century statue of Aphrodite) is far away in the Louvre (having lost its arms on the way there).

Since ancient times the island has been quarried for minerals, resulting in huge gaps and fissures in the landscape. From earliest times obsidian (a hard black volcanic glass, used for manufacturing sharp blades) was mined on the island, and exported throughout the Mediterranean. Nowadays, 35% of the population is employed in the mining industry.

Philokope, the ancient city of Milos, was one of the oldest settlements in the Cyclades. During the Peloponnesian Wars, Milos was the only Cycladic island to take Sparta's side. It paid dearly for this when the avenging Athenians massacred all adult male Melians (inhabitants of Milos), and enslaved the women and children.

Getting To/From Milos

Air There is at least one flight a day to Athens (7800 dr) from Milos. The Olympic Airways

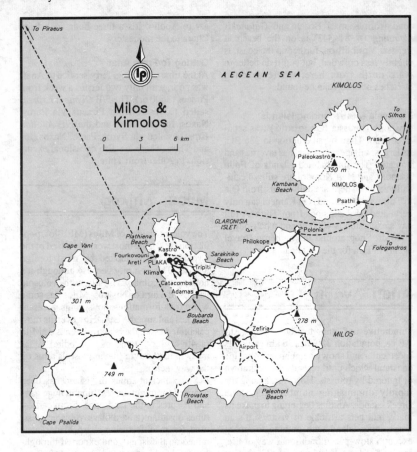

office (☎ 22 380) is at 11 Odos 25 Martiou, in Adamas.

Ferry There are daily ferries from Milos to Piraeus (seven hours, 2600 dr), almost daily to Sifnos, Serifos and Kythnos, and two to Folegandros, Thira and Sitia (Crete) via Agios Nikolaos. A small boat goes four times a day to the neighbouring island of Kimolos from Polonia, on Milos' east coast. Milos' port police (☎ 22 100) are on the waterfront near the OTE.

Getting Around Milos

There are frequent buses from Adamas to Plaka (via Tripiti), six a day to Polonia, four a day to Paleohori and three to Provatas.

Motorbikes and mopeds can be hired from Hotel Semiramis (see Adamis' Places to Stay). There are other outlets, as well as car-hire outlets, along the waterfront.

ADAMAS Αδάμαντας
Although Plaka is Milos' capital, the port of Adamas has most of the island's accommodation. Other than this Adamas has little to

offer, but the more alluring Plaka is just a short bus ride away.

Orientation & Information

From Adamas' quay, turn right onto the waterfront. The OTE, post office and National Bank of Greece are all along here on the left. Adamas' postcode is 84801 (the rest of Milos is 84800). The telephone code is 0287. The central square, with the bus stop and taxi rank, are at the end of this stretch of waterfront. Just beyond the square there is a major crossroad; the road to the right skirts the town beach and Odos 25 Martiou; straight ahead is the town's main thoroughfare, and the road to Plaka.

Milos' Municipal Tourist Office (☎ 22 445) is opposite the quay; pick up their useful booklet *Welcome to Milos Island*, which has a list of places to stay.

Organised Tours

Chronis Tours, at the Chronis Hotel (see Adamis Places to Stay), organises a tour of the island for 3200 dr.

Places to Stay – bottom end

The best of Adamas' three D class hotels is the *Hotel Semiramis* (☎ 22 117/8), with a delightful garden and comfortable doubles/triples for 7000/9500 dr with private bathrooms. Petros and Nikos, the friendly English-speaking owners, are a mine of information. Walk along 25 Martiou, take the road which branches left, and the hotel is on the left. The *Hotel Georgantas* (☎ 21 955), at the beginning of 25 Martiou, has doubles for 7500 dr. The *Hotel Delfini* (☎ 22 001) has pleasant single/double rooms for 5000/7500 dr with private bathrooms. Turn left from the quay to reach this hotel. Adamas also has many domatia, but no camp site, and freelance camping is not tolerated.

Places to Stay – middle

The best of Adamas' C class hotels is the *Chronis Hotel* (☎ 22 226), on the right side of 25 Martiou. It comprises stone-built bungalows in a lovely garden. The spacious rooms all have TV, refrigerator and tele-

phone. Rates are 7000/9000/12,000 dr for singles/doubles/triples.

Places to Eat

There is not an abundance of outstanding eating places in Adamas. On the waterfront, *O Floisvos* is recommended, with some meals for less than 750 dr. *Trapetselis Restaurant*, which overlooks the town beach, serves commendable, reasonably priced fish dishes.

PLAKA & TRIPITI

Plaka (Πλάκα), the capital, and the lower settlement of Tripiti (Τρυπητή), are contiguous. Plaka, which is four km uphill from Adamas, is a typical Cycladic town: labyrinthine, dazzling white and picturesque.

Milos Folklore Museum

This is an outstanding museum housed in a 19th-century mansion. The salon has pictures, a couple of gramophones, and a heating stove. The bedroom is chock-a-block with fascinating items: there are lacy bloomers hanging on the wall, a child's commode, and night attire laid out on a beautiful four-poster bed. Because of fear of pirate raids bedrooms were always at the rear of houses, and the inhabitants slept with guns under their pillows – what a life! The storeroom has tools for producing wine, and agricultural and fishing implements. Another room displays embroidery, applique work, crochet and weavings.

A sign from the bus turnaround in Plaka points to the museum. Opening times are 10 am to 1 pm daily, with additional opening hours of 6 to 8 pm from Tuesday to Saturday.

When you leave the Folklore Museum turn left to reach the **Church of Panagia I Kortiatissa**. From its terrace there are breathtaking views of Milos' north coast and Antimilos islet, uninhabited except for a rare breed of goat.

Kastro

At the bus turnaround, facing the direction from which you've come, turn right, and you will reach a path which leads up to the Frankish Kastro, built on the ancient acropolis. Inside the walls is the 13th-century **Church of Thalassitras**. It was on this hill that the final battle between the ancient Melians and Athenians took place. From its commanding position there are panoramas of almost the entire island.

Archaeological Museum

This museum is in Tripiti, on the right side of the road leading from Plaka to the much signposted catacombs. Don't miss the lovely, perfectly preserved terracotta figurine of Athena (which is not labelled) in the middle room. In the room to the left are some charming figurines from Philokope. The museum is open Tuesday to Sunday from 8.30 am to 3 pm. Admission is 400 dr.

AROUND PLAKA & TRIPITI
Roman Ruins

Plaka is built over the site of ancient Milos, which the Athenians destroyed. It was rebuilt by the Romans and there are some Roman ruins nearby, including the famous catacombs. On the road leading to the catacombs you will see a sign pointing right to the well-preserved **ancient theatre**. On the track leading to the theatre a rusting sign (in Greek) points left to where a farmer stumbled upon the Venus de Milo, in 1820. Opposite the sign there are remains of massive Doric walls. Back on the cement road, 50 metres further along, you will come to the sign for the 1st-century **catacombs**, one of Greece's earliest extant Christian monuments. A passage leads into a large chamber flanked by tunnels which contained the tombs. Opening times are 8.30 am to 3 pm, but they are closed on Wednesday and Sunday. Admission is 400 dr.

Klima Κλίμα

From the catacombs, the hamlet of Klima is a short walk away. With your back to the catacomb ticket kiosk, turn left and then right onto a path. In 100 metres you will come to steps which lead down to the hamlet. On the way down you will pass a chapel hewn into the rocks. Klima was the port of ancient Milos, but nowadays it's a charming unspoilt fishing hamlet, skirting a narrow seaweed beach. The whitewashed buildings, with brilliant blue, green and red doors and balconies, have boat houses on the ground floor and living quarters on the first floor. Klima has one hotel (with a restaurant), the D class *Hotel Panorama* (☎ 21 623 or 22 112), where doubles cost 6000 dr.

Plathiena Beach

Plathiena is a lovely sandy beach below Plaka. A walk from Plaka to Plathiena can take in detours to the tiny fishing hamlets of Areti and Fourkovouni. At Plaka walk towards the Kastro path and look for a well-maintained kalderimi to the left. After five minutes the path forks; take the left fork for Areti or the right fork for Plathiena. If you take the Areti path, in 15 minutes you will reach a track from where you can clamber down to to **Areti**. Turn right on the track and in a few minutes you will see **Fourkovouni**, to the left, which again, you can clamber down to.

Continuing along the track the landscape becomes surreal, with intense red and orange, and dazzling white volcanic rock – startling against a deep blue summer sky. Soon you will come to a crossroad; from here, the left turn leads to Plathiena and the right turn leads to the other branch of the kalderimi from Plaka.

AROUND THE ISLAND

The beaches of **Provatas** and **Paleohori**, on the south coast, are long and sandy. There are hot springs at Paleohori. **Polonia**, on the north coast, is a fishing village with a small beach, and domatia. It's also the jumping-off point for the island of **Kimolos**. This island lies off Milos' north-east coast, and is little visited by tourists. It has domatia and tavernas, as well as fine beaches.

The ancient site of **Philokope** is just three km inland from Polonia. Three successive levels of cities have been uncovered here – Early, Middle and Late Cycladic. The islet of **Glaronisia**, off the north coast, is a rare geological phenomenon composed entirely of hexagonic volcanic stone bars.

Kea Κέα

Kea (KEE-a, population 1600) is the nearest of the Cyclades to the mainland. In summer it's heavily visited by Athenians who come for both weekends and longer holidays. It's a green island with a profusion of almond and oak trees and fruit orchards. The port is Korissia, and the capital is Ioulis, which spills down a hill, five km inland.

Getting To/From & Around Kea
Kea can be reached from the mainland port of Lavrion, in Attica. There are at least two ferries every day and more at weekends. There is a once-weekly ferry between Kea and Kythnos.

There are around five buses a day from Korissia to Ioulis and Otzias (via Vourkari) and a much less frequent service to Pisses.

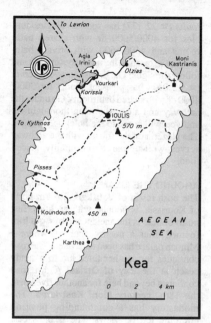

KORISSIA Κορησσία
Korissia is not especially attractive, but makes a satisfactory base. From the ferry quay, turn left and walk along the waterfront. Where the main road curves, another road leads straight ahead to skirt the town beach. If you continue a little beyond here you'll come to the nicer Gialiskari Beach.

Places to Stay
The large C class *Hotel Karthea* (☎ 31 222), just before the beach, has comfortable doubles for 6000 dr with private bathrooms. Most of the accommodation in Korissia is beyond here on the road which runs parallel to the beach. Here you will find the B class *Hotel Tzia Mas* (☎ 21 303/223) with singles/doubles for 7000 dr with private bathrooms. Nearby, *Pension Korissia* (☎ 21 484/355) has attractive doubles with private bathrooms for 6000 dr.

IOULIS Ιούλης
Ioulis is a delightful town of higgledy-piggledy alleyways and steps, and sweeping vistas. The bus turnaround is on a square from where an archway leads to Ioulis proper. The post office is on this square. Go through the archway to reach the main thoroughfare which is uphill to the right. The OTE is along here on the right. Ioulis' postcode is 84002 and the telephone code is 0288.

Things to See
The **Archaeological Museum**, on the main thoroughfare, houses local finds, mostly from Agia Irini. Opening times are Tuesday to Sunday from 8.30 am to 3 pm. If you continue walking beyond the museum you will come to a path which leads to the celebrated 6th-century granite-carved **Kea Lion**, a huge beast with a benevolent expression – a gentle giant.

Places to Stay & Eat
There are two hotels in Ioulis. The *Hotel*

Ioulis (☎ 22 177) has spotless singles/doubles for 4000/5000 dr with shared bathrooms and 4500/5500 with private bathrooms. Go through the archway, turn left and follow the signs. The E class *Hotel Filoxenia* (☎ 22 057) has pleasant rooms for 3000/4000 dr with shared bathrooms. Go under the archway and along the main thoroughfare, and you will come to the hotel on the right. The pizzeria on the square with the archway serves well-prepared reasonably priced food.

AROUND THE ISLAND

The posh resort of **Vourkari**, 2½ km north of Kourissia, is popular with yachties. Just north of here is the ancient site of **Agia Irini** (named after a nearby church), where a Minoan palace has been excavated. The road continues for another three km to a sandy beach at the **Bay of Otzias**. A dirt road continues beyond here for another five km to the 18th- century **Moni Kastrianis**. The monastery has a commanding position affording terrific views. The island's best beach, eight km south west of Ioulis, has the unfortunate name of **Pisses**. It is long and sandy and backed by a verdant valley of orchards and olive groves.

Places to Stay

The island's camp site, *Kea Camping* (☎ 22 132), is at Pisses Beach. There are also domatia and tavernas here.

The *Kea Beach Hotel & Bungalows* (☎ 22 144; fax 31 234) is on Koundouros Beach, two km south of Pisses Beach. The hotel complex has a bar, restaurant, disco and swimming pool. Rates are 8250/10,350 dr for sinlges/doubles and 19,000 dr for bungalows.

Kythnos Κύθνος

In contrast to Kea, Kythnos (KI-thnos), the next island south, is barren. Like Kea it attracts Athenian holiday-makers, although why is a bit of a mystery, because there's really little to enthuse about, unless you're desperate for a cure for rheumatism – Kythnos has the Cyclades' most potent **Thermal Baths**. The port of **Merihas** is an uninspiring place and the capital, **Chora**, 10 km inland, lacks the picturesque beauty of other Cycladic capitals. **Loutra**, four km from Chora, is where the baths are; it also has a sand and pebble beach. From Merihas it's four km to **Driopis**, which was the capital in the Middle Ages. It's a more attractive place than Chora, with red-tiled dwellings and winding streets. There are hotels and do-

matia in Merihas and Loutra. There are daily ferries from Kythnos to Piraeus (three hours, 1800 dr), Serifos, Sifnos and Milos and three a week to Lavrion (four hours, 1600 dr).

Serifos Σέριφος

First impressions of Serifos (SE-rif-os, population 1100) are of a barren, rocky island. However, on closer inspection there are pockets of greenery, where tomatoes and vines are cultivated. Serifos' port is Livadi, on the south-east coast. The island's white capital (also called Serifos) cascades down the hillside, appearing to cling on so as not to tumble into the sea.

Getting To/From & Around Serifos (Island)

Serifos has daily ferries to Piraeus (4½ hours, 2500 dr) via Kythnos; and to Milos via Sifnos. Around three ferries a week sail to Folegandros, Sikinos, Ios and Thira. There are frequent buses between Livadi and Serifos town.

LIVADI Λιβάδι

Attractive Livadi is built at the top end of a huge elongated bay. From the ferry, walk to the end of the quay and turn right to reach the waterfront and central square. Continue around the bay to reach the pleasant and shaded sandy beach. Karavi Beach, a 30-minute walk south, is more secluded and is the island's unofficial nudist beach. On the way you'll pass the crowded Livadakia Beach.

Places to Stay

Serifos' camp site is the well-maintained *Korali Camping* (☎ 51 500/073), at Livadakia Beach.

Captain George Rooms (☎ 51 274) is one of the best value domatia; doubles with private bathrooms are 6000 dr. The rooms are just beyond the central square on the left. The C class *Areti Hotel* (☎ 51 479/107; fax

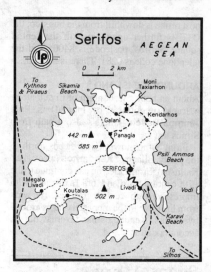

51 298) has pleasant rooms and management; doubles cost 7500 dr. Walk to the end of the quay and turn left up the steps to reach the hotel. The C class *Serifos Beach Hotel* (☎ 51 209/468) is a large pleasant place with similar rates. It's just back from the waterfront, beyond the central square. At the beach, the *Perseas Pension* (☎ 51 273) has doubles with private bathrooms for 7000 dr. A bit further along, the C class *Maistrali Hotel* (☎ 51 381/298) has lovely light and airy balconied rooms. Doubles are 12,000 dr.

Places to Eat

Benny's Restaurant, near the quay, is Livadi's 'in' eating place. A good filling meal will cost about 1700 dr. The *Cavo D'oro Restaurant*, near the Serifos Beach Hotel, and *Taverna O Stamatis*, at the beach, serve reasonably priced, well-prepared Greek fare.

SERIFOS TOWN

Dazzling white Serifos town is a delectable place, one of the most striking of the Cyclades' capitals. You can either take the bus or walk up steps from Livadi. The village is crowned by a ruined 15th-century Venetian fortress (reached by more steps). The post office is downhill from the bus stop; the OTE is further uphill, just off the central square. Serifos' postcode is 84005 and the telephone code is 0281. There is no bank.

AROUND THE ISLAND

About an hour's walk north of Livadi along a track (negotiable by moped) is **Psili Ammos Beach** – there's also a path from Sifnos town.

From Sifnos town a path heads north to the pretty village of **Kendarhos** (also called Kallitsos). From here you can continue to the 17th-century fortified **Moni Taxiarhon**, with impressive 18th- century frescoes. The walk from the town to the monastery takes around two hours. Kendarhos has tavernas but no accommodation.

Sifnos Σίφνος

Sifnos (SEEF-nos, population 2000) coyly hides its most alluring assets from those who pass by on a ferry. Take a glimpse, and you will assume it's as barren as Serifos, for the port resides in the most arid part of the island. Explore, and you'll find an attractive landscape of terraced olive groves, almond trees and oleander bushes, speckled with numerous dovecotes, whitewashed smallholdings and chapels.

Sifniot olive oil is highly prized throughout Greece. Perhaps this has something to do with the island's reputation for producing the country's best chefs. Local specialities include *revithia* (baked chickpeas) and *xynomitsithra* (a sheep's milk cheese). The island also produces superior pottery – something to do with the quality of its clay. You'll come across many shops selling locally produced ceramics.

Getting To/From & Around Sifnos

Sifnos has daily ferries to Milos, and Piraeus (5½ hours, 2400 dr) via Serifos and Kythnos; around three a week to Folegandros, Sikinos, Ios and Thira; and one a week to Crete (Agios Nikolaos and Sitia).

There are frequent buses between Apollonia and Kamares, Kastro and Platys Gialos. There are daily taxi boats from Kamares to Vathi.

KAMARES Καμάρες

Don't judge Sifnos by the port of Kamares, which is a singularly unprepossessing place, despite having a good sandy beach. There is a Municipal Tourist Office (☎ 31 804) opposite the quay. The staff are extremely helpful and will find accommodation for you.

Places to Stay & Eat

The C class *Stavros Hotel* (☎ 31 641), in the middle of the waterfront, has clean simply furnished doubles for 5000 dr with shared bath, and 6000 dr with private bathrooms. The co-owned *Kamari Pension* (☎ 31 710/641/382; fax 31 709) has attractive singles/doubles for 5000/7000 dr with private bathrooms.

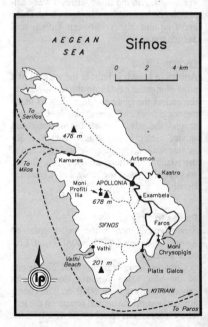

Restaurant O Boulis, on the waterfront near the church, serves well-prepared traditional Greek fare. A full meal with retsina should cost around 1700 dr.

APOLLONIA Απολλόνια

Apollonia, the modern capital of Sifnos, sprawls on a plateau five km uphill from the port. The bus stop is on the animated central square where you'll also find the post office, OTE and the National Bank of Greece. The **Museum of Popular Art** is also here. Opening times are 6 to 10 pm daily. Admission is 100 dr.

Places to Stay & Eat

The C class *Hotel Sophia* (☎ 31 238), just north of the central square, has light airy single/double rooms for 3500/5500 dr with private bathrooms. Another choice place to stay is the C class *Hotel Sifnos* (☎ 31 624), with immaculate single/double rooms for 6000/7500 dr with private bathrooms. From the central square (facing away from Kamares) turn right beyond the museum, and right again, and the hotel is on the right. The *Restaurant Sophia*, below the hotel of the same name, serves well-prepared food. Expect to pay about 1500 dr for a full meal and a beverage.

AROUND THE ISLAND

The pretty village of **Artemon** is just north of Apollonia. Not to be missed is the walled, cliff-top village of **Kastro**, three km from Apollonia; it's a magical place of buttressed alleys and whitewashed houses. The serene village of **Exambela**, just south of Apollonia, is said to be the birthplace of most of Sifnos' famed chefs.

The resort of **Platys Gialos**, 10 km south of Apollonia, has a long sandy beach, some hotels and domatia, and the island's only camp site, *Camping Platys Gialos* (☎ 31 786), in an olive grove behind the beach. The spectacularly situated **Moni Chrysopigis**, near Platys Gialos, was built to house a miraculous icon of the Virgin, spotted glowing in the sea by two fishermen. A path leads from the monastery to a beach with a taverna. **Vathi**, on the west coast, is a gorgeous unspoilt sandy bay with a few domatia and tavernas. There is no road access, but in summer there are daily taxi boats from Kamares.

Places to Stay

One of Sifnos' best hotels is the B class *Platys Gialos Hotel* (☎ 31 224/324; fax 31 325), at Platys Gialos. All rooms have air-con and rates are 15,000/18,000 dr for sinlges/doubles.

Crete Κρήτη

Crete is Greece's largest and most southerly island. It is divided into four prefectures, each with an administrative capital. From east to west the prefectures are: Lassithi (capital: Agios Nikolaos), Iraklion, Rethymnon and Hania; the capitals of these last three have the same names as the prefectures to which they belong. These capitals (which are the island's largest towns) are all on the north coast. Most of the south coast is too precipitous to support large settlements.

The scenery of Crete is tremendously varied. A mountain chain runs east to west across the island, consisting of three mighty ranges: the Mt Dikti range in the east, the Mt Ida (also called Mt Psiloritis) range in the middle and the Lefki Ori (White Mountains) in the west. These lofty mountains, which support an alpine flora, are dotted with agricultural plains and plateaus, and sliced by numerous dramatic gorges. Long sandy beaches speckle the coastline, and the east coast boasts Europe's only palm-tree forest.

Blessed with an auspicious climate and fertile soil, Crete is Greece's cornucopia, producing a wider variety of crops than anywhere else in the country. In the high Lassithi plateau, pears, apples, almonds, cereals, cabbages, onions, beans and potatoes are grown. In the east, near Ierapetra, thousands of greenhouses nurture cucumbers, tomatoes, aubergines and courgettes; while the coast west of Ierapetra is fringed by banana plantations and melon groves. On the southern Messara Plain there are fields of wheat and groves of lemon and orange trees. Grapes are grown all over the island, but the finest are produced in the Arhanes region, south of Iraklion.

The fertility and warm climate also produces an enormous variety of flora. *Wild Flowers of Crete* by George Sfikas is an excellent field guide.

Crete is visited not only for its scenery and beaches. The island was also the birthplace of Europe's first advanced civilisation, the

Minoan. If you intend to visit Crete's Minoan sites, a book on the subject will help immensely in your understanding of this great civilisation. One of the best is *Palaces of Minoan Crete* (paperback) by Gerald Cadogan.

Due to its size and distance from the rest of Greece, a folk culture evolved on Crete independent of the mainland. Vibrant Cretan weavings can be found for sale in many of the island's towns and villages. The traditional Cretan songs you will hear differ from those heard elsewhere in Greece. Called *mantinades*, these songs are highly emotive, expressing the age-old concerns of love, death and the yearning for freedom. Many of the older men on Crete dress traditionally in breeches tucked into knee-high leather boots, and black-fringed kerchiefs tied tightly around their heads.

The attractions of Crete have not gone unnoticed by tour operators, so the island has the dubious reputation of playing host to 24% of Greece's tourists. Package tourists tend to stay on the north coast between Hania and Agios Nikolaos, with the highest concentration east of Iraklion. However, the tour operators are now beginning to make inroads into the south-coast resorts, although as yet these are still visited predominantly by independent travellers, particularly backpackers.

The wild and rugged west coast of Crete was, until recently, little visited, but travel agents now organise day trips to this area.

To avoid the crowds it is best to visit in the low season. The climate on the south coast is so mild that swimming is possible from April to November.

History

Crete has been inhabited since Neolithic times (7000 to 3000 BC). However, to most people the history of Crete is synonymous with the Minoan civilisation. (The term 'Minoan', derived from the name of the legendary King Minos of Crete, was coined by the archaeologist, Sir Arthur Evans.)

The vestiges which have come down to us from the Minoans captivate not only the experts, but also those normally indifferent to ancient history and archaeology. It is the frescoes of the Minoans, more than any other of their legacies, which enamour the non-specialist. The message they communicate is of a society which was powerful, wealthy, joyful and optimistic.

Artistically the frescoes are superlative; the figures that grace them have a naturalism which is lacking in the contemporaneous Cycladic figurines, Ancient Egyptian artwork (which in certain respects they resemble), and the Archaic sculpture which came later. Compared with candle-smoke-blackened Byzantine frescoes, the Minoan frescoes, with their fresh, bright colours, look as if they were painted yesterday.

The frescoes depict a society in which all physical phenomena were unblemished. Gracing them are white-skinned women with elaborately coiffured glossy black locks. Proud, graceful and uninhibited, these women had hourglass figures and dressed in stylish gowns that revealed perfectly shaped breasts. The bronze-skinned men were tall, with tiny waists, narrow hips, broad shoulders and muscular thighs and biceps, and the children were slim and lissom. The Minoans also seemed to know how to enjoy themselves. They played board games, boxed and wrestled, played leap-frog over bulls and

over one another, and performed astonishing acrobatic feats.

The land the Minoans inhabited was one of abundance. Rivers brimmed with fish and waterfowl, fields were full of ripe wheat and vibrant flowers, graceful deer raced through forests and dolphins frolicked in the sea.

The Minoans were religious, as frescoes and models of people partaking in rituals testify. However, the Minoans' beliefs, like many other aspects of their society, remain an enigma. There is sufficient evidence to confirm that they worshipped bulls, but how and why is shrouded in mystery. There is also tentative evidence that all was not as it appears to be in those far-off times. There are hints of human sacrifice, and of a Draconian society which other races lived in fear of.

So what is fact and what is speculation? What is known is that early in the 3rd millennium BC, an advanced people migrated to Crete and brought with them the art of metallurgy. Many aspects of Neolithic culture lived on in the Early Minoan period (3000-2100 BC), but during the Middle Minoan period (2100-1500 BC), a society evolved which was unprecedented in its artistic, engineering and cultural achievements. It was during this time that sophisticated palatial complexes were built at Knossos, Phaestos, Malia and Zakros.

Also during this period the Minoans began producing their exquisite Kamares Ware pottery (see the Archaeological Museum entry under Iraklion) and intricate silverware, and established trade links with Egypt and Asia Minor, thus becoming a great maritime power.

Around 1700 BC, all four palace complexes were destroyed by an earthquake. However, undeterred, the Minoans built bigger and better palaces on the sites of the original ones, as well as settlements in other parts of the island.

Sometime around 1500 BC, when the civilisation was at its peak, the palaces were destroyed again, signalling the start of the Late Minoan period (1500-1100 BC). This destruction was probably caused by Mycenaean invasions, although the volcanic

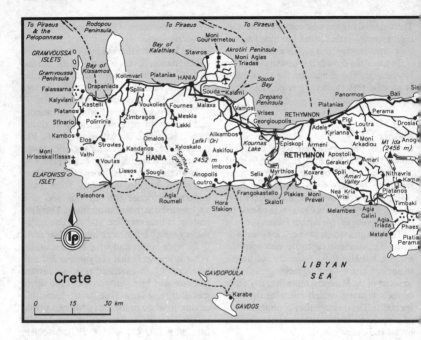

Crete

0   15   30 km

To Piraeus & the Peloponnese · *Rodopou Peninsula* · *To Piraeus* · *To Piraeus* · GRAMVOUSSA ISLETS · *Gramvoussa Peninsula* · *Bay of Kissamos* · *Bay of Kalathias* · *Moni Gourvernetou* · Stavros · *Akrotiri Peninsula* · *Moni Agias Triadas* · Falassarna · Kolimvari · Platanias · HANIA · *Souda Bay* · Panormos · Bali · Sis · Kalyviani · Drapaniada · Spilia · Souda – Kalami · *Drepano Peninsula* · Platanias · Perama · Platanos · Kastelli · Voukolies · Fournes · Malaxa · Vamos · Vrises · RETHYMNON · Sfinario · Polirrinia · Zimbragos · Meskla · Lakki · Georgioupolis · Adele · Pigi · Loutra · Drosia · Kambos · Elos · Strovles · Omalos · Alikambos · *Lefki Ori* · *Kournas Lake* · Episkopi · Armeni · Kyrianna · *Moni Arkadiou* · *Mt Ida (2456 m)* · Anogie · Moni Hrisoskalitissas · Vathi · Kandanos · Xyloskalo · Askifou · RETHYMNON · Apostoli · Gerakari · Amari · Voutas · *HANIA* · *2452 m* · Imbros · Selia · Myrthios · Koxare · Spili · *Amari Valley* · Nithavris · Kama · ELAFONISSI ISLET · Lissos · Sougia · *Samaria Gorge* · Anopolis · Loutro · Frangokastello · Plakias · *Moni Preveli* · *Nea Kria Vrisi* · Platanos · Paleohora · *Agia Roumeli* · *Hora Sfakion* · Skaloti · Melambes · *Agia Galini* · Timbaki · *Agia Triada* · Phaes · Matala · *Platia Perama*

GAVDOPOULA · *LIBYAN SEA* · Karabe · *GAVDOS*

---

eruption which took place on the island of Thira may also have had something to do with it. The Knossos palace was the only one to be salvaged. It was finally destroyed by fire around 1400 BC.

The Minoan civilisation was a hard act to follow. The war-orientated Dorians, who arrived in 1100 BC, were a pedestrian lot in comparison with the Minoans. The 5th century BC found Crete, like the rest of Greece, divided into city-states. The glorious Classical Age of mainland Greece made little impact on Crete. Neither did the island participate in the Persian Wars which plagued the mainland. The island was even passed unnoticed by Alexander the Great, so was never part of the Macedonian Empire.

By 67 BC Crete was subjugated to the Romans who, from their capital at Gortyn, ruled over their province of Cyrenaica, which encompassed not only Crete but large chunks of North Africa. Crete, along with the rest of Greece, became part of the Byzantine Empire in 395 AD. In 1210 it was occupied by the Venetians, who left legacies of mighty fortresses, ornate public buildings and monuments, and handsome nobles' and merchants' dwellings.

Many of the artists, writers and philosophers who fled Constantinople after it was conquered by the Turks in 1453 settled on Crete, and soon the Cretan School of Icon Painters was established. The painters of this school had a formative influence upon the young Cretan painter, Domenico Theotocopoulos, who moved to Italy where he became known as El Greco, one of the geniuses of the Renaissance.

Despite the massive Venetian fortifications which sprang up all over the island, by 1669 the whole of Crete was under Turkish rule. The first uprising against the Turks was led by Ioannis Daskalogiannis in 1770. This set the precedent for many more insurrections, and in 1898 the Great Powers intervened and made the island a British

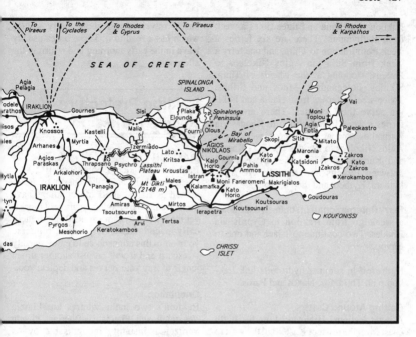

protectorate. It was not until 1913 with the signing of the Treaty of Bucharest that Crete was officially united with Greece, although the island's parliament had declared the de facto union in 1905.

On 20 May 1941 German parachutists landed on Crete. For the next 10 days the Allied forces of Britain, Australia, New Zealand and Greece fought ferociously, but hopelessly, in what became known as the Battle of Crete. There were heavy losses on both sides, but it was a nominal victory for the Germans. The Allied troops were evacuated by sea from Crete's south coast. The German occupation of Crete lasted until the end of WW II. As elsewhere in Greece resistance groups sprang up in the mountains. Amongst the bravest members of the Cretan resistance were the 'runners' who relayed messages on foot over the mountains. One of these runners, George Psychoundakis, wrote a book based on his experiences titled *The Cretan Runner*.

Getting To/From Crete

The following section provides a brief overview of air and boat options to/from Crete. For more comprehensive information, see the relevant sections at the end of entries to specific towns.

Air Crete has two international airports. The principal one is at Iraklion and there is a smaller one at Hania. In addition there is a domestic airport at Sitia. All three airports have flights to Athens, and Iraklion and Hania have flights to Thessaloniki. Iraklion also has flights to Rhodes, Mykonos and Thira, and Sitia has flights to Karpathos and Kassos.

Ferry (Domestic) Crete has ports at Iraklion, Hania, Agios Nikolaos, Sitia, Kastelli and Rethymnon. Following are high-season schedules; services are reduced by about half in the low season.

Direct daily ferries travel to Piraeus from

Iraklion and Hania and three times a week from Rethymnon. There are six ferries a week from Iraklion to Thira, and one ferry a week from Sitia via Agios Nikolaos to Piraeus, stopping at the islands of Thira, Sikinos, Folegandros, Milos and Sifnos. Twice-weekly ferries from Hania and Iraklion serve the Cyclades. There are three ferries a week from Iraklion to Rhodes via Karpathos, and at least two a week from Agios Nikolaos to Rhodes via Sitia, Kassos and Karpathos. Two ferries a week sail between Piraeus and Kastelli via Antikythera, Kythera and the Peloponnese.

Ferry (International) In summer, three boats a week go from Iraklion to Cyprus via Rhodes. Two continue to Israel and one to Egypt.

Hydrofoil In summer hydrofoils link Iraklion with Thira, Ios, Naxos and Paros.

Getting Around Crete
A good National Highway skirts the north coast from the town of Kastelli in the west to Sitia in the east. Frequent buses run along this road, linking all of the north-coast towns. Less frequent buses operate between the north-coast towns and resorts and places of interest on the south coast, via the mountain villages of the interior. These routes are Hania to Paleohora, Omalos (for the Samaria Gorge) and Hora Sfakion; Rethymnon to Plakias, Agia Galini, Phaestos and Matala; Iraklion to Agia Galini, Phaestos, Matala and the Lassithi plateau; Agios Nikolaos to Ierapetra; and Sitia to Ierapetra, Vai, Kato Zakros and Paleokastro.

There is nothing comparable to the National Highway on the south coast and parts of it are without any road at all, but where there are roads there are bus services. There is no road between Paleohora and Hora Sfakion, the most precipitous part of the south coast; a boat (daily in summer) connects the two resorts via Sougia and Agia Roumeli.

As well as the bus schedules given in each section in this chapter, clapped out 'village

buses' travel to just about every village which has a road to it. These buses usually leave in the early morning and return in the afternoon.

Iraklion Prefecture
Νομός Ηρακλείου

IRAKLION
Iraklion (I-RA-klee-o, population 102,000), Crete's capital, lacks the charm of Rethymnon or Hania, as its old buildings have been swamped by modern apartment blocks, yet it exudes a dynamism due to its frenetically paced, neon-lit streets. Immerse yourself in this atmosphere to enjoy the city – resist it and it will be just another urban jungle to fray your nerves and deplete you.

Orientation
Iraklion's two main squares are Plateia Venizelou and Plateia Eleftherias. Plateia Venizelou, instantly recognisable by its famous Morosini Fountain (better known as the Lion Fountain), is the heart of Iraklion and the best place from which to familiarise yourself with the layout of the city. A few steps south of the square there is an intersection of five important thoroughfares. They are: 25 Avgoustou which runs north to the Old Harbour (also called the Venetian Harbour); Dikeosinis which runs east to Plateia Eleftherias; Kalokerinou which runs west to Porta Hania (Hania Gate); 1866 (the market street) which runs south; and 1821, which runs to the south-west. Incidentally, the pedestrianised shopping street of Daidalou, one block north of Dikeosinis, is reputably the best place on Crete for busking. To reach Plateia Venizelou from the port, turn right, walk along the waterfront and turn left onto 25 Avgoustou.

Iraklion has three intercity bus stations. Station A, on the waterfront between the port and 25 Avgoustou, serves eastern Crete. The bus station for Hania and Rethymnon is opposite Station A. Station B, 50 metres beyond Hania Gate, serves Phaestos, Agia Galini, Matala and Fodele. To reach the city centre from Station B walk through the Hania Gate and along Kalokerinou. For details on bus schedules, see the Iraklion Getting There & Away section.

Information

Tourist Offices The EOT (☎ 22 8225/6081/8203; fax 22 6020) is at Xanthoudidou 1, just north of Plateia Eleftherias. Opening times are Monday to Friday from 8 am to 3 pm. The very helpful tourist police (☎ 28 3190) are at Dikeosinis 10. They are open from 7 am to 11 pm.

Money Most of the city's banks are on 25 Avgoustou, including the National Bank of Greece which is at No 35. The Credit Bank at No 94 has an automatic teller machine for Visa and American Express card holders. None of the banks open on afternoons or at weekends. American Express (☎ 22 2303 or 24 6202; fax 22 4717) is represented in by Adamas Travel Bureau, 25 Avgoustou 23. Opening hours are Monday to Saturday from 8 am to 5 pm.

Post & Telecommunications The central post office is on Plateia Daskalogiani. Turn onto Dikeosinis from Plateia Eleftherias, take the first turn left, and you will see the post office in front of you. Opening hours are 7.30 am to 8 pm Monday to Friday, 7.30 am to 2 pm on Saturday and 9 am to 1.30 pm on Sunday. There is a mobile post office at El Greco Park, just north of Plateia Venizelou, which is open from 8 am to 6 pm Monday to Friday and 8 am to 1.30 pm on Saturday. Iraklion's postcode is 71001.

The OTE is opposite the western side of El Greco Park, and is open from 6 am to midnight every day. Iraklion's telephone code is 081.

Foreign Consulates Foreign consulates in Iraklion include:

Germany
   Zagrafou 7 (☎ 22 6288)

Netherlands
   25 Avgoustou 23 (☎ 24 6202)
UK
   Papalexandrou 16 (☎ 22 4012)

Bookshop IEL (International Educational Library) Bookshop (☎ 28 9605), Handakos 71, has a good selection of English-language books.

Laundry There is a self-service laundrette at Merabelou 25. From Plateia Eleftherias walk along Xanthoudidou, take the second turn right after the Archaeological Museum and the laundrette is on the left. A wash and dry costs 1500 dr.

Emergency The Venizelion General Hospital (☎ 23 7502/7580) is on Leoforos Knossos, four km from the town centre, and one km before the ancient site of Knossos. To reach it take a Knossos-bound bus.

Luggage Storage There is a reliable luggage-storage facility (☎ 28 1750) in the basement of 25 Avgoustou 48. The cost is 300 dr per day. There are also luggage storage facilities at Bus Station A (200 dr) and the YHA hostel at Vironos 5 (guests 100 dr; non-guests 150 dr).

Archaeological Museum

This superlative museum (☎ 22 6092) is second in size and importance only to the National Archaeological Museum in Athens. If you are seriously interested in the Minoan civilisation, you will want to visit the museum more than once, but even a fairly superficial perusal of the contents requires a morning or an afternoon. Attention here is drawn only to a tiny fraction of the finds in the museum. The exhibits, arranged in chronological order, include pottery, jewellery, figurines, and sarcophagi, as well as the famous frescoes, mostly from Knossos and Agia Triada. All testify to the remarkable imagination and advanced skills of the Minoans.

Room 1 is devoted to the Neolithic and Early Minoan periods. Room 2 has a

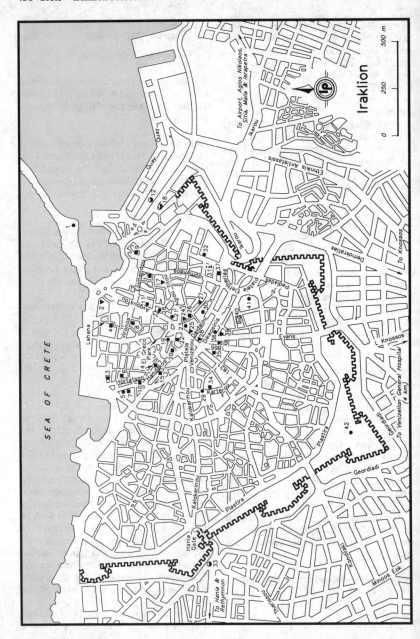

Iraklion

SEA OF CRETE

collection from the Middle Minoan period. Amongst the most fascinating exhibits are the tiny coloured glazed reliefs of Minoan houses from Knossos.

Room 3 contains the famous **Phaestos Disc**. The symbols inscribed on this 16-cm diameter disc have not been deciphered. The symbols, which look similar to Egyptian hieroglyphs, are separated into groups; it is possible that each group denotes a word or sentence. Also in this room are the famous **Kamares Ware Vases**, named after the sacred cave of Kamares where the ware was first discovered. Included amongst this collection are many examples of the lovely 'eggshell ware' (so called because of its fragility). One of the finest examples of Kamares Ware in this room is the libation vessel decorated with dolphins and shells.

Exhibits in Room 4 are from the Middle Minoan period. Most striking is the 20-cm black stone **Bull's Head**, which was a libation vessel. The bull has a fine head of curls, from which sprout horns of gold. The eyes of painted crystal are extremely lifelike. Another fascinating exhibit in this room is the elaborate **gaming board**, on which perhaps a Minoan version of draughts was played. Also in this room are relics from a shrine at the palace in Knossos, including two figurines of **Snake Goddesses**; one of the figurines is holding snakes, and another has them coiled around her. Snakes symbolised immortality for the Minoans.

Pottery, bronze figurines and seals are some of the exhibits displayed in Room 5. These include vases imported from Egypt and some Linear A and B tablets. The Mycenaean Linear B script has been deciphered, and the inscriptions on the tablets displayed here have been translated as household or business accounts from the palace at Knossos.

Room 6 is devoted to finds from Minoan cemeteries. Especially intriguing are two small clay models of groups of figures which were found in a tholos tomb. One depicts four male dancers in a circle, their arms around each other's shoulders. The dancers may have been participating in a funeral

■ PLACES TO STAY

4 Lena Hotel
6 Vergina Rooms
7 Rooms Mary
8 YHA Hostel
9 Lato Hotel
10 Hotel Rea
13 Hotel Irini
14 YHA Hostel
15 Christakos Rent Rooms
20 Pension Atlas
22 Hotel Hellas
26 Hotel Selena
30 Hotel Daedalos
34 Hotel Metropol
35 Cretan Sun Hotel
37 Astoria Hotel

▼ PLACES TO EAT

2 Ippocampos Ouzeri
17 La Parisienne Restaurant
24 Café Louzogoo
25 Restaurant Knossos
27 Giovanni Taverna
28 Loukoumades Café
38 Odos Theodasaki Tavernas
39 Restaurant Ionia

OTHER

1 Venetian Fortress (Rossa al Mare)
3 Historical Museum of Crete
5 IEL Bookshop
11 Adamis Travel Bureau
12 Bus Station for Hania & Rethymnon
16 National Bank of Greece
18 Bus Station A (for Eastern Crete)
19 OTE
21 Venetian Loggia (City Hall)
23 San Marco Basilica
29 Agias Ekaterini Museum
31 EOT
32 Archaeological Museum
33 Bus Station B (for Phaestos, Agia Galini, Matala & Fodele)
36 Tourist Police
40 Post Office
41 Olympic Airways Office
42 Nikos Kazantzakis' Grave

ritual. The other model depicts two groups of three figures in a room flanked by two columns. In each group two large figures are sitting, and another smaller figure is offering them libations. It is not known whether the large figures represent gods or departed mortals. On a more grisly level, there is a display of the bones of a horse. Horses, bulls and rams were sacrificed as part of Minoan worship, and this had been this particular horse's fate.

The finds in Room 7 include vases and lamps from villas excavated at Sklavocambos, Vathypetro and Tilisos. Also in this room are the three celebrated vases from Agia Triada. The **Harvester Vase**, of which only a fragment remains, depicts a light-hearted scene of young farm workers returning from olive picking. The **Boxer Vase** depicts Minoans indulging in two of their favourite pastimes – boxing and wrestling. The **Chieftain Cup** depicts a more cryptic scene: a chief holding a staff and three men carrying animal skins.

Room 8 has yet another eye-catching libation vessel. This one has a beautiful elongated shape and is decorated with shells and other marine life. In case 138, in Room 10, there are some delightful terracotta figurines. In case 143 there is a collection of idols including a child (headless) on a swing. Swinging was another pastime the Minoans seem to have greatly enjoyed; it may also have had some sort of religious significance.

Room 13 is devoted to Minoan sarcophagi. However, the most famous and spectacular of these, the **Sarcophagus from Agia Triada**, is upstairs in Room 14 (The Hall of Frescoes). This stone coffin, painted with floral and abstract designs, and ritual scenes, is regarded as one of the supreme examples of Minoan art.

The most famous of the Minoan frescoes are also displayed in Room 14. Frescoes from Knossos include the **Procession Fresco**, the **Griffin Fresco** (from the Throne Room), the **Dolphin Fresco** (from the Queen's Room) and the amazing **Bull-leaping Fresco**, with a seemingly double-jointed acrobat somersaulting on the back of a charging bull. Other frescoes here include the two lovely **Frescoes of the Lilies** from Amnisos, and fragments of frescoes from Agia Triada. Also in this room is a model of the Palace of Knossos. There are more frescoes in Rooms 15 and 16 including the famous **La Parisienne**, from Knossos. It is so named because the young woman portrayed has an upturned nose, pretty hairstyle and elegant attire.

The museum is on Xanthoudidou, just north of Plateia Eleftherias. Opening times are Monday to Friday from 8 am to 7 pm and Saturday, Sunday and holidays from 8.30 am to 3 pm. Admission is 1000 dr.

Historical Museum of Crete

The eclectic finds of this museum (☎ 28 3219) are housed in a 19th-century mansion. Downstairs is the large **Byzantine Collection** which includes vestments, ecclesiastical ornaments, icons, coins, jewellery and a reconstruction of a chapel.

On the 1st floor, one room is devoted to the author **Nikos Kazantzakis**, with displays of letters, manuscripts and books, and a reconstruction of his library. Another room relates the events of the **Battle of Crete** through photographs and other sources. A third room is devoted to **Emmanual Tsouderos**, who was born in Rethymnon and was prime minister in 1941.

On the 2nd floor there is an outstanding **Folklore Collection**. It includes embroidery, weavings, crochet, tapestry, jewellery and costumes. In the far room is an impressive wedding loaf: a huge oval with an intricate relief pattern of flowers.

The basement focuses on the construction and ornamentation of important secular and religious buildings from the Venetian and Turkish eras. The exhibits include tiles from a mosque, and a Turkish fountain from Hania, which the custodian will obligingly turn on for you.

The museum, which is just back from the western waterfront, is open Monday to Friday from 9 am to 3 pm and on Saturday from 9 am to 2 pm. It is closed on Sunday. Admission is 600 dr.

Other Sites

Iraklion burst out of its city walls long ago but these massive fortifications with seven bastions and four gates are still very conspicuous, dwarfing the concrete structures of the 20th century. The fortress was built by the Venetians between 1462 and 1562 and was so sturdy it withstood Turkish bombardments for 20 years. The 16th-century **Rocca al Mare**, another Venetian fortress, stands at the end of the Old Harbour's jetty. This fortress (☎ 24 6211) is open Tuesday to Sunday from 8.30 am to 3 pm. Admission is 400 dr.

Several other notable vestiges from Venetian times survive in the city. Most famous is the **Morosini Fountain** on Plateia Venizelou, which spurts water from four lions into eight ornate U-shaped marble troughs. The fountain, built in 1628, was commissioned by Francesco Morosini who was then Governor of Crete. Opposite is the three-aisled 13th-century **Basilica of San Marco**. It has been reconstructed many times and is now an exhibition gallery. A little north of here is the attractive reconstructed 17th-century **Venetian Loggia**. It was a Venetian version of a gentleman's club; a place where the male aristocracy went to drink and gossip.

The delightful **Bembo Fountain**, at the southern end of 1866, is shown on local maps as the Turkish Fountain, but it was actually built by the Venetians in the 16th century. It was constructed from a hotchpotch of building materials including an ancient statue. The ornate edifice adjoining the fountain was added by the Turks, and now functions as a snack bar.

The former Church of Agias Ekaterini is now a **Museum** (☎ 24 2111) housing an impressive collection of icons. Most notable are the six icons painted by Mikhail Damaskinos, the mentor of Domenico Theotocopoulos (El Greco). The museum is open Monday to Saturday from 10.30 am to 1 pm. In addition it opens on Tuesday, Thursday and Friday afternoons from 4.30 to 6.30 pm. Admission is 400 dr.

You can pay homage to Crete's most acclaimed contemporary writer, Nikos Kazantzakis (1883-1957), by visiting his tomb at the Martinengo Bastion (the fortress' best preserved bastion) in the southern part of town. The epitaph on his grave, 'I hope for nothing, I fear nothing, I am free', is taken from one of his own works.

Trekking

The Iraklion branch of the EOS (☎ 22 7609) is at Dikeosinis 53. It owns the Prinos Refuge on Mt Ida, which is reached by walking for 1½ hours along a footpath from the village of Melisses, 25 km from Iraklion.

Organised Tours

The Iraklion branch of Creta Travel (☎ 22 3749), Epimendou 20-22, has tours to Knossos and Iraklion's Archaeological Museum (3200 dr); Vathypetro Villa, the Arhanes villages, the Nikos Kazantzakis Museum and Thrapsano (4200 dr); Phaestos, Gortyn and Agia Triada (4400 dr); Gournia, Kritsa, Agios Nikolaos and Ierapetra (4600 dr); Lassithi plateau (4400 dr); Hania, Rethymnon and Arkadi Monastery (5700 dr); Zakros, Sitia and Vai (6400 dr); Samaria Gorge (6000 dr); and Spinalonga island and Agios Nikolaos (5600 dr).

Places to Stay – bottom end

There are two YHA hostels in Iraklion. The one which has been established the longest has new premises at Vironos 5 (☎ 28 6281). This clean, well-run hostel charges 900 dr for dorm beds and 2500 dr for double rooms. The hostel has a snack bar where breakfast and snacks are served. The second hostel (☎ 28 0858), at Handakos 24, has the same prices and also has a snack bar.

Two of Iraklion's cheapest budget hotels are close to El Greco Park. The *Hotel Hellas* (☎ 22 5121), Kantanoleon 11, has tidy single/double/triple rooms for 3000/3500/4500 dr with shared bathrooms. The *Pension Atlas* (☎ 28 8989), Kantanoleon 6, has clean, cheery rooms for 2500/3000/4000 dr with private bathrooms. Walk up 25 Avgoustou from the waterfront to the end of the Venetian Loggia, turn right and veer left, and you will come to the Hotel Hellas on the left. Follow the road as it veers left and you will come to the Pension Atlas on the right.

The area west of here, near the Historical Museum, has several budget places to stay. *Vergina Rooms* (☎ 24 2739), Hortatson 32, is a turn-of-the-century house with a small courtyard. The spacious rooms cost 2000/3500/5000 dr with shared bathrooms. Nearby, *Rooms Mary* (☎ 28 1135), Hortatson 67, has pleasant doubles for 3800 dr with shared bathrooms and 4500 dr with private bathrooms. On a side street just south of here, the *Hotel Rea* (☎ 22 3638), Kalimeraki 4, has clean, pleasant single/double rooms for 3500/4000 dr with shared bathrooms.

Further south and nearer Plateia Venizelou, *Christakos Rent Rooms* (☎ 28 4126), Eugenikou 12, has well-kept double/triple rooms for 4000/5000 dr with shared bathrooms. Eugenikou is a turn-off left along Handakos, as you come from 25 Avgoustou.

One of Iraklion's nicest and quietest budget hotels is the *Lena Hotel* (☎ 22 3280 or 24 826), Lahana 10, where spotless and comfortable single/double/triple rooms cost 2550/3700/5000 dr with shared bathrooms; doubles with private bathrooms are 5500 dr. Walk up 25 Avgoustou from the waterfront, take the second turn right onto Vironos and Lahana is the third turn right.

The *Cretan Sun Hotel* (☎ 24 3794), No 10 Odos 1866, has a shabby exterior, but the rooms are large and clean. Single/double rates are 3500/4500 dr with shared bathrooms. One drawback to this hotel is its noisy location overlooking the street market.

The C class *Hotel Daedalos* (☎ 22 4391/2/3/4/5), Daidalou 15, is reasonably priced for a mid-range hotel but at the time of writing it looked a bit shabby; the owner told me it was going to be completely redecorated in the near future. Singles/doubles/ triples are 5400/7400/9100 dr, breakfast included. Close by, the C class *Hotel Selena* (☎ 22 6377/8), Androgeo 7, has pleasant singles/doubles for 4500/7000 dr with private bathrooms. Androgeo is just north of Daidalou.

Places to Stay – middle

The C class *Lato Hotel* (☎ 22 8103/5001; fax 24 0350), Epimendou 15, has cosy, wood-panelled rooms. Rates are 8000/10,000/12,000 dr for singles/doubles/triples, including breakfast. The hotel has a car park. Epimendou is a turn-off left, a little way up 25 Avgoustou from the waterfront. The *Hotel Irini* (☎ 22 6407/9703/6561), Idomeneos 4, is a very superior C class with spacious rooms. Rates are 6900/10,200/11,900 dr, including breakfast. Walk along Epimendou from 25 Avgoustou, take the fourth turn right onto Idomeneos, and the hotel is on the right.

The C class *Hotel Metropol* (☎ 24 2330/4280), on Odos Karterou, has immaculate, attractively furnished rooms for 8313/10,418/12,524 dr. Walk up 1821 from Plateia Venizelou, take the second turn right onto Karterou, and the hotel is on the right.

Places to Stay – top end

The A class *Astoria Hotel* (☎ 22 9002), Plateia Eleftherias 11, has a restaurant, disco, swimming pool and roof garden. Singles/doubles are 12,900/13,800 dr.

The A class *Apollonia Beach Hotel* (☎ 82 1602) has a beach bar, restaurant, pool and a disco. Rates are 13,700/23,100 dr. The A class *Akti Zeus Hotel* (☎ 82 1503; fax 82 1252) is a huge place with just about every amenity imaginable. Rates are 14,250/18,900 dr. The last two hotels are on Linoperamata Beach, eight km west of Iraklion.

Places to Eat – bottom end

Iraklion has some excellent restaurants to suit all tastes and pockets. The highest concentration of tavernas is on Odos Theodasaki, a little street between 1866 and Odos Evans. They're all good so just take a look and see which one takes your fancy. Close by, the *Restaurant Ionia*, on the corner of Evans and Giannari, serves up delectable Greek staples. A main meal will cost less than 900 dr.

The *Ippocampos Ouzeri*, on the waterfront just west of 25 Avgoustou, is always busy. The large range of mezedes on offer are delicious and reasonably priced, starting at 300 dr.

The long-established *Restaurant Knossos*, Plateia Venizelou, is one of those traditional Greek establishments frequented by business people and academics. It's a sedate place with courteous, smartly dressed waiters and crisp white tablecloths. A large choice of well-prepared traditional Greek dishes is on offer. A meal with wine will cost around 2000 dr.

If during your travels in Greece you haven't yet tried loukoumades (fritters with syrup), then the unpretentious *Loukoumades Café* on Dikeosinis is a good place to sample this gooey confection. The *Café Louzogoo*, on Androgeo, is a stylish place with an Art Deco interior. It's a lot more tranquil than the crowded cafés around Plateia Venizelou. Nescafé and filter coffee are 350 dr, cappuccino is 450 dr, spirits are 800 dr and cakes are between 500 and 1000 dr.

Whether or not you're self catering, you'll enjoy a stroll up Odos 1866 (the market street). This narrow street is always packed, and stalls spill over with food of every description, including ornate Cretan wedding loaves. These loaves (smaller versions of the one on display at the Historical Museum of Crete) are not meant to be eaten, but rather, make an attractive decoration in a kitchen. Given an occasional spray with insecticide they will last for ages.

Places to Eat – middle

The *Giovanni Taverna* is a splendid place with elegant antique furniture and subdued lighting; in summer there is outdoor eating on a quiet pedestrian street. The food is traditional Greek, but carefully prepared with discriminating use of herbs and spices. From Plateia Venizelou walk one block up Daidalou, turn left onto Perdikari, take the first right onto Korai, and you will come to the taverna on the right. A delicious meal here, including half a carafe of red house wine, will cost about 2800 dr, and is worth every drachma.

La Parisienne Restaurant, Agiou Titou 7, is an up-market restaurant with a traditional Flemish décor. The menu includes boeuf au Beaujolais, coq au vin and Chateaubriand steak. Main courses range in price from 2200 to 5000 dr, and desserts from 800 to 1500 dr. Coming from the waterfront, turn sharp left immediately after the Loggia onto Agiou Titou. The restaurant is 100 metres along here on the left.

Getting There & Away

Air From Iraklion's airport there are at least five flights a day to Athens (14,400 dr); five flights a week to Rhodes (13,200 dr); and three flights a week to Mykonos (12,400 dr) and Thira (8200 dr). The Olympic Airways office (☎ 22 9191) is on Plateia Eleftherias.

Bus There are half-hourly buses to Rethymnon (1½ hours, 1000 dr) from the Rethymnon/Hania bus station opposite Bus Station A.

Destinations of buses which leave from Bus Station A are:

Agia Pelagia – 30 minutes, 400 dr, four buses daily
Agios Nikolaos – 1½ hours, 900 dr, almost half-hourly buses
Arhanes – 30 minutes, 220 dr, 12 buses daily
Ierapetra – 2½ hours, 1400 dr, eight buses daily
Lassithi plateau – two hours, 950 dr, two buses daily
Malia – one hour, 460 dr, half-hourly buses
Milatos – 1½ hours, 700 dr, two buses daily
Sitia – 3½ hours, 1900 dr, six buses daily

Destinations of buses which leave from Bus Station B are:

Agia Galini – 2½ hours, 1000 dr, eight buses daily
Anogia – one hour, 480 dr, six buses daily
Fodele – one hour, 460 dr, two buses daily
Lendas – three hours, 1050 dr, two buses daily
Matala – two hours, 1000 dr, seven buses daily
Phaestos – two hours, 850 dr, eight buses daily

Ferry (Domestic) There are two direct ferries a day between Piraeus and Iraklion (12 hours, 3850 dr). They depart from both Piraeus and Iraklion between 6.30 and 7.30 pm. There are six ferries a week to Thira (five hours, 3000 dr), four of which continue to Paros (3200 dr) and one to Naxos (3200 dr). There are three ferries a week to Rhodes (11 hours, 2500 dr) via Pigadia Karpathos.

Almost all of the travel agencies who sell ferry tickets are on 25 Avgoustou. Iraklion's port police telephone No is ☎ 24 4912.

Ferry (International) In summer, three boats a week go from Iraklion to Limassol on Cyprus (18,200 dr), via Rhodes. At the time of writing boats left on Monday at 9 am, Tuesday at 8 am and Friday at 10.30 am. The Tuesday boat continued on to Israel (25,000 dr) and Egypt (25,000 dr) and the Friday boat to Israel. These prices include port taxes of 3000 dr. Tickets may be bought from Ara Batzoglou Travel Bureau (☎ 22 6697/8), 25 Avgoustou 54, amongst others. As always the schedule changes from year to year so check with the EOT.

Hydrofoil In summer hydrofoils link Iraklion with Thira (2½ hours, 4000 dr), Ios (3½ hours, 5600 dr), Naxos (4½ hours, 6500 dr) and Paros (five hours, 6500 dr).

Getting Around
To/From the Airport Bus No 1 goes to/from the airport every 15 minutes between 6 am and 1 am. It leaves the city from outside the Astoria Hotel on Plateia Eleftherias.

Bus Local bus No 2 goes to Knossos every 15 minutes from Bus Station A. It also stops on 25 Avgoustou and 1821. The journey takes 20 minutes and costs 150 dr.

Car & Motorbike Most of Iraklion's car and motorbike-hire outlets are on 25 Avgoustou. Car-hire outlets include Autorent (☎ 28 4438/9497) at No 38; Avis (☎ 22 5421/9402) at No 58; Budget (☎ 22 1315 or 24 3918) at No 34; and Hertz (☎ 22 9702/9802) at No 44. Budget, Eurocar, Eurodollar, Hertz, Holiday Autos and InterRent all have offices at Iraklion airport.

The reliable motorbike outlet, Touring, has offices throughout Crete. The head office (☎ 28 0711/3211) is at 25 Avgoustou 18.

KNOSSOS Κνωσσός
Knossos (Knos-OS), five km from Iraklion,

was the capital of Minoan Crete. Nowadays it's the island's major tourist attraction.

In 1900 the ruins of Knossos were uncovered by the British archaeologist, Sir Arthur Evans. Schliemann had had his eye on the spot (a low flat-topped mound), believing an ancient city was buried there, but had been unable to strike a deal with the local landowner.

Evans was so enthralled by what he discovered, that he spent 35 years and £250,000 of his own money excavating and reconstructing sections of the palace. Some archaeologists have disparaged Evans' reconstruction, believing he sacrificed accuracy to his overvivid imagination. However, most non-specialists agree Sir Arthur did a good job and that Knossos is a knockout. Without these reconstructions it would be impossible to visualise what a Minoan palace looked like.

You will need to spend around four hours at Knossos to explore it thoroughly. The café at the site is rather expensive – you'd do better to bring a picnic along. The site (☎ 23 1940) is open Monday to Friday from 8 am to 7 pm and Saturday, Sunday and holidays from 8.30 am to 3 pm. Admission is 1000 dr.

History
The first palace at Knossos was built around 1900 BC. In 1700 BC it was destroyed by an earthquake and rebuilt to a grander and more sophisticated design. It is this palace which Evans reconstructed. It was partially destroyed again sometime between 1500 and 1450 BC. It continued to be inhabited for another 50 years before it was devastated once and for all by a fire.

The city of Knossos consisted of an immense palace, residences of officials and priests, the homes of ordinary people, and burial grounds. The palace, which covered an area of 22,000 sq metres, consisted of royal domestic quarters, public reception rooms, shrines, workshops, treasuries and storerooms built around a central court. Like all Minoan palaces, it also doubled up as a city hall; all the bureaucracy necessary for the smooth running of a complex society was carried out within its walls.

Exploring the Site

Numerous rooms, corridors, dogleg passages, nooks and crannies, and staircases prohibit a detailed described walk around the palace. However, Knossos is not a site where you'll be perplexed by heaps of rubble, trying to fathom whether you're looking at the throne room or a workshop. Thanks to Evans' reconstruction, the most significant parts of the complex are instantly recognisable (if not instantly found). On your wanders you will come across a good number of Evans' reconstructed columns; most are painted deep brown-red with gold-trimmed black capitals. These, like all Minoan columns, taper at the bottom.

It is not only the vibrant frescoes and mighty columns which impress at Knossos; keep your eyes open for the little details which are also evidence of a highly sophisticated society. These may well lead you to ask what humanity has been playing around at for the last 3000 years. Things to look out

The Myth of the Minotaur

The myth inspired by the labyrinth at Knossos indulges in even more perversion and horror than the average Greek myth. King Minos invoked the wrath of Poseidon when he failed to sacrifice a white bull to him. Poseidon's divine retribution caused Pasiphae, King Minos' wife, to fall in love with the animal.

In order to attract the bull, Pasiphae asked Daedalus, chief architect at Knossos and all-round handyman, to make her a hollow wooden cow structure. Concealed in this disguise the bull found her irresistible, and the outcome of their bizarre association was the Minotaur: a hideous monster who was half-man and half-bull.

King Minos asked Daedalus to build a labyrinth in which to confine the Minotaur and demanded that Athens pay an annual tribute of seven youths and seven maidens to satisfy the monster's huge appetite.

Theseus killing the Minotaur

Minos discovered that Daedalus had been instrumental in bringing about the union between his wife and the bull; eventually he locked up the architect and his son Icarus in the labyrinth. Daedalus made wings from feathers stuck together with wax and, wearing these, father and son made their getaway. As everyone knows, Icarus flew too close to the sun, the wax on his wings melted, and he plummeted into the sea off the island of Ikaria.

Meanwhile, the Athenians were enraged by the tribute demanded by Minos, so Theseus, prince of Athens, posed as a youth and schemed to kill the monster. He fell in love with Ariadne, the daughter of King Minos, and she gave him a ball of thread to unwind, to facilitate his exit from the labyrinth. Theseus succeeded in his mission and fled Crete with Ariadne, only to dump her on Naxos island on his way back to Athens. ■

Knossos Palace Ruins

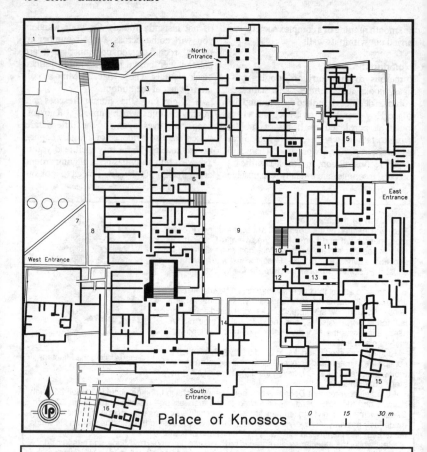

Palace of Knossos

1	Royal Road	9	Central Court
2	Theatral Area	10	Grand Staircase
3	Lustral Basin	11	Hall of the Double Axes
4	Bull Fresco	12	Water Chamber
5	Giant Pithoi	13	Queen's Megaron
6	Throne Room	14	Priest King Fresco
7	Western Court	15	South-East House
8	Corridor of the Procession Fresco	16	South House

for are the drainage system built with pipes angled in such a way as to prevent flooding; the placement of light wells to ensure the maximum amount of light possible entered where it was needed most; and the relationship of rooms to passages, porches, light wells and verandahs, to ensure rooms were kept cool in summer and warm in winter.

The usual entrance to the palace complex is across the Western Court and along the **Corridor of the Procession Fresco**. One wall of this corridor was painted with the

Procession Fresco which depicted a long line of people carrying gifts to present to the king; only fragments remain. A copy of one of these fragments, called the **Priest King Fresco**, can be seen to the south of the Central Court.

An alternative is to have a look at the Corridor of the Procession Fresco, but then leave it and walk straight ahead to enter the site from the northern end. If you do this you will come to the **theatral area**, a series of steps whose function remains unknown. It could have been a theatre from where spectators watched acrobatic and dance performances. Alternatively, the population could have gathered there to welcome important visitors arriving at Knossos via the Royal Road.

From the the theatral area the **Royal Road** leads off to the west. The road, Europe's first (Knossos has lots of firsts), was flanked by workshops and dwellings of ordinary people. The **lustral basin** is also in this area. Evans speculated that this was a basin where the Minoans performed a ritual purging by water, before participating in religious ceremonies. There are more of these basins at Knossos and they have also been found at the other palace complexes.

Entering the **Central Court** from the north, you will pass the relief **Bull Fresco** which depicts a charging bull. Relief frescoes were made by moulding wet plaster, and then painting it while still wet.

Also worth seeking out in the northern section of the palace is the **giant pithoi**. *Pithoi* were jars used for storing olive oil, wine and grain. Evans found over 100 of these huge jars at Knossos (some were two metres high). The raised patterns decorating the jars were inspired by the ropes which were bound around them so that they could be moved.

Once you have reached the Central Court, which in Minoan times was surrounded by the high walls of the palace, you can begin exploring the most important rooms of the complex.

From the northern end of the west side of the palace, steps lead down to the **throne room**. This room is fenced off but you can still get a good view of it. The centrepiece, the simple, beautifully proportioned throne, is flanked by the **Griffin Fresco**. Griffins were mythical beasts regarded as sacred by the Minoans. The floor of the room is paved, and there are stone benches around the wall. No rooms like this have been found in any of Crete's other palace complexes. Evans surmised that this was because it was built after the catastrophe which took place between 1500 and 1450 BC, when Knossos was the only palace to remain occupied.

The room is thought to have been a shrine, and the throne the seat of a High Priestess, rather than a king. Certainly, the room seems to emanate an aura of mysticism and reverence rather than pomp and ceremony. The Minoans did not worship their deities in great temples but in small shrines, and each palace had several of these.

On the 1st floor of this side of the palace is the section Evans called the **Piano Nobile**, for he believed the reception and state rooms were here. A room at the northern end of this floor displays copies of some of the frescoes found at Knossos.

Returning to the Central Court, from the middle of the eastern side of the palace the impressive **grand staircase** leads to the royal apartments which Evans called the Domestic Quarter. At the bottom of this staircase a right turn leads eventually to the **Hall of the Double Axes**. This was the king's megaron, a spacious double room in which the ruler both slept and carried out certain court duties. The room had a light well at one end and a balcony at the other to ensure air circulation. The room is so called because of double axe marks on its light well. These marks appear in many places at Knossos. The double axe was a sacred symbol to the Minoans. *Labrys* was Minoan for 'double axe' and our word labyrinth derives from this ancient word.

From the Hall of the Double Axes a passage leads to the **Queen's megaron**. The decoration of this room is delightful. Above the door is a copy of the **Dolphin Fresco**, one of the most exquisite Minoan artworks, and a blue floral design decorates the portal. Next to this room is the queen's bathroom complete with terracotta bathtub. For most people the *pièce de résistance* of the queen's suite of rooms is the **water chamber**, touted as the first ever to work on the flush principle. Don't look for the chain – water had to be poured down by hand. This marvel of Minoan plumbing is reached by a short passage from the Queen's megaron.

Getting There & Away

Regular buses operate from Iraklion. See Iraklion's Getting Around section for details.

MYRTIA Μυρτιά

The village of Myrtia (also called Varvari), 22 km south of Iraklion, was the birthplace of Nikos Kazantzakis' father, and the writer himself lived there for a time. The **Nikos Kazantzakis Museum** is on the central square of the village. The collection of the writer's personal mementoes is well displayed. A video show compiled from film clippings of the author's life is shown in Greek, German, French and English.

The museum is open Monday, Wednesday, Saturday and Sunday from 9 am to 1 pm and 4 to 8 pm, and on Tuesday and Friday from 9 am to 1 pm only. The admission is 400 dr.

The journey to the village passes through lovely vineyard country. The museum is signposted from the main road. Creta Travel (see Organised Tours under Iraklion) organises a tour which includes this museum and the villages of Arhanes and Thrapsano (4200 dr, excluding museum fee).

TILISOS Τύλισος

At the village of Tilisos (TIL-is-os), 13 km from Iraklion, there is a minor Minoan site where three villas dating from different periods have been excavated. The site is open Tuesday to Sunday from 8.30 am to 3 pm. Admission is 400 dr.

Continuing along the same road for another eight km you will come to the remains of another Minoan house, on the left. Called **Sklavocambos**, this house dates

from 1500 BC and is of simple construction; it was probably the villa of a local district governor

ARHANES Αρχάνες

The attractive village of Arhanes (Ar-HAN-es), strictly speaking the contiguous villages of Kato and Epano Arhanes, 16 km from Iraklion, lies in the heart of Crete's principal grape and wine-producing region. Recent excavations have revealed several Minoan remains in the vineyards surrounding the village. The most noteworthy is the elaborate **Vathypetro Villa**, in which a prosperous Minoan noble resided.

The many roomed villa included store-rooms, where wine and oil presses, a weaving loom and a kiln were discovered. The villa is five km from Arhanes, on the road going south – look for a signpost to the right. The site is not enclosed and there is no entrance fee.

Getting There & Away

There are 12 buses a day from Iraklion's Bus Station A to Arhanes (half an hour, 220 dr). There are no buses to Vathypetro; if you don't fancy the walk, then Creta Travel in Iraklion have a tour which includes a visit to the villa.

GORTYN Γόρτυνα

The archaeological site of Gortyn (also called Gortina and Gortys) lies 46 km south-west of Iraklion, and 15 km from Phaestos, in the plain of Mesara. It's a vast and wonderfully intriguing site with bits and pieces from various ages strewn all over the place. The site was a settlement from Minoan to Christian times. In Roman times Gortyn was the capital of the province of Cyrenaica.

The most significant find at the site was the massive stone tablets inscribed with the **Laws of Gortyn**, which date from the 5th century BC. The laws deal with just about every offence it is possible to imagine a human being committing. The tablets are on display at the site.

An important ruin at the site is the 6th-century **Basilica**, dedicated to Agios Titos, who was a protégé of St Paul and first bishop of Crete.

Other ruins at Gortyn include the 2nd-century AD **Praetorin** which was the residence of the governor of the province, a **Nymphaeum** and the **Temple of Pythian Apollo**. The site (☎ 081-22 6092) is open every day from 8.30 am to 3 pm. Admission is 400 dr. The ruins are on both sides of the main Iraklion-Phaestos road.

PHAESTOS Φαιστός

The Minoan site of Phaestos (Fes-TOS), 63 km from Iraklion, was the second most important palace city of Minoan Crete. Of all the Minoan sites it has the most awe-inspiring location, with all-embracing views of the Mesara plain and Mt Ida. The layout of the palace is identical to Knossos, with rooms arranged around a central court.

In contrast to Knossos, Phaestos has yielded very few frescoes; it seems the palace walls were mostly covered with a layer of white gypsum. Perhaps with such inspiring vistas from the windows the inhabitants didn't feel any need to have the beauties of nature reproduced inside. Evans didn't get his hands on the ruins of Phaestos, so although excavations have taken place here, there has been no reconstruction. Like the other palatial complexes there was an old palace here which was destroyed at the end of the Middle Minoan period. Unlike the other sites parts of this old palace have been excavated, and its ruins are partially superimposed upon the new palace.

Exploring the Site

The entrance to the new palace is by a magnificent, perfectly proportioned, 15-metre-wide **Grand Staircase**. The stairs lead to the west side of the **Central Court**. The best preserved parts of the palace complex are the reception rooms and private apartments which are to the north of the Central Court; excavations continue here. This section was entered by an imposing portal with half columns at either side, the lower parts of which are still *in situ*. Unlike the Minoan freestanding columns, these do not taper at

the base. The celebrated Phaestos disc was found in a building to the north of the palace. The disc is in Iraklion's Archaeological Museum.

Getting There & Away

There are eight buses a day from Iraklion's Bus Station B to Phaestos (two hours, 850 dr); and six from Matala (30 minutes, 150 dr) and Agia Galini (40 minutes, 250 dr).

AGIA TRIADA Αγία Τριάδα

Agia Triada (Ag-I-a Tri-A-da) is a small Minoan site, just three km west of Phaestos. Its principal building was smaller than the other royal palaces but built to a similar design. This, and the opulence of the objects found at the site, indicate that it was a royal residence, possibly a summer palace of the Phaestos rulers. To the north of the palace is a small town where remains of a stoa have been unearthed.

Finds from the palace now in Iraklion's Archaeological Museum include a sarcophagus, two superlative frescoes and three vases: the Harvester Vase, Boxer Vase and Chieftain Cup.

The site is open Tuesday to Sunday from 8.30 am to 3 pm. Admission is 400 dr. You can walk to Agia Triada in 30 minutes from Phaestos along a path through an orchard. The path heads west (towards the sea) along the base of the north side of the ridge which runs between the two sites.

MATALA Μάταλα

Matala (MA-ta-la), on the coast 11 km southwest of Phaestos, was one of Crete's hippie hangouts, but it now attracts a more varied bunch of tourists. However, you may still see the odd hippie casting a nostalgic eye up at the caves which made Matala famous. These versatile caves, hewn from the sandstone rock, have had a disparate collection of occupants (dead and alive) during their long history. The Romans used them as tombs, in the Middle Ages they were used as refuges from pirates, and during the 1960s hippies regarded them as desirable residences.

Matala is a decidedly tacky tourist resort,

but the sandy beach below the caves is one of Crete's best. The resort is a convenient base from which to visit Phaestos and Agia Triada.

Orientation & Information

Matala's layout is easy to fathom. The bus stop is on the central square, one block back from the waterfront. To reach the beach just walk a little way back the way the bus came and you'll see it to the left. There is a mobile post office near the beach, on the right of the main road as you come into Matala. The OTE is beyond here in the beach car park.

Places to Stay

Matala Community Camping is a reasonable site just back from the beach.

If you don't mind being away from where it's all happening, there are several pleasant accommodation options along the approach road to Matala; after seeing where it's all happening you may well decide you made the right decision to stay away. The bus stops outside the Hotel Europa, 600 metres before the centre of Matala. The *Pension Romantika* (☎ 42 357), opposite this hotel, has attractive rooms with fancy glass lights and marble floors. Single/double/triple rates are 3000/4000/4500 dr with private bathrooms.

If you get off the bus at Hotel Europa and walk back a little way to where the road forks right, you will see *Pension Pinelopi* (☎ 42 315), on the right. The rooms here are modern and spotless. Rates are 4000/5500 dr for doubles/triples with private bathrooms.

If you take the fork to the right, 40 metres along you will come to a dirt road leading off right. This leads to the *Pension Galini* (☎ 42 131) which is well away from the main road and very quiet. The comfortable double/triple rooms cost 3800/4000 dr with private bathrooms.

If you walk towards Matala from Hotel Europa (in the direction the bus is going) in 150 metres you will come to *Rent Rooms Koudouris* (☎ 42 731), on the left, with a colourful well-tended garden. The single/double/triple rooms are tastefully furnished

with rates of 3000/4000/4500 dr with private bathrooms.

If you decide to brave Matala proper, walk back along the main road from the bus station and turn right at the Zafiria Hotel. This street is lined with budget accommodation. One of the cheapest places is *Fantastic Rooms to Rent* (☎ 42 369), on the right. The comfortable double/triple rooms cost 3000/4500 dr with private bathrooms. The C class *Ava Marina Hotel* (☎ 42 125), also along here, is an immaculate place with singles/doubles for 4400/5500 dr with private bathrooms.

Back on the main road, walk a little way towards Phaestos and you will come to the C class *Hotel Fragiskos* (☎ 42 135/380), on the left. The very attractive single/double/triple rooms cost 4000/7500/9500 dr with private bathrooms. The hotel has a swimming pool. If you continue along the road you will come to *Tsiterakis Rooms* (☎ 42 784), also on the left – look for a one-storey cream building. The basic, clean double/triple rooms cost 3000/3600 dr·with shared bathrooms.

If you don't like the sound of Matala, then **Pitsidia Village**, 4½ km inland and seven km from Phaestos, is a quieter alternative for a base. There are no hotels but a good number of rooms. *Acropol Rent Rooms* (☎ 42 179) and *Pension Aretousa*, opposite, have agreeable doubles for 4000 dr with shared bathrooms. Both of these places are near the bus stop.

Places to Eat

The restaurants in Matala are poor value for money. *Restaurant Neosicos* is probably the best. A meal of kalamaria, chips, Greek salad and Amstel will set you back about 1500 dr. From the central square face towards the sea and turn left. Follow the road as it skirts the bay and you'll come to the taverna. If you don't mind a walk, *Restaurant Mystical View* has views which live up to its name and serves good food to boot. Walk two km back along the road to Phaestos, and you'll see the restaurant sign pointing left. The restaurant teeters high above Komos Beach.

Getting There & Away
There are seven buses a day between Iraklion and Matala (two hours, 1000 dr) and six a day between Matala and Phaestos (30 minutes, 150 dr).

MALIA Μάλια
The Minoan site of Malia (MAL-ee-a) is the only cultural diversion on the stretch of coast east of Iraklion, which otherwise has surrendered lock, stock and barrel to the package-tourist industry. Malia is smaller than Knossos and Phaestos, but like them consisted of a palace complex and a town. Unlike Knossos and Phaestos the palace was built on a flat fertile plain, not on a hill.

The site (☎ 22 462), which is three km east of the resort of Malia, is open Tuesday to Sunday from 8.30 am to 3 pm. Admission is 400 dr.

Exploring the Site
Entrance to the ruins is from the **West Court**. At the extreme southern end of this court there are eight circular pits which archaeologists think may have been used for storing grain. To the east of the pits is the main entrance to the palace which leads to the southern end of the **Central Court**. At the south-west corner of this court you will find the **Kernos Stone**, a disc with 34 holes around its edge. Archaeologists have so far been unable to ascertain its function. Possible explanations are that it was a libation table or a game.

The **central staircase** is at the north end of the west side of the palace. The **loggia**, just north of the staircase, is where religious ceremonies took place. Bang in the middle of the central court is a rectangular hole on which an altar stood. Most of the eastern side of the palace consisted of storerooms. The row of column bases at the northern end of the central court are the remains of a portico. Beyond them are two rows of three pillars which are believed to have supported a first-floor banqueting hall, beneath which was a kitchen.

Getting There & Away
Any bus going to/from Iraklion along the north coast will drop you off here.

Lassithi Prefecture
Νομός Λασσιθίου

AGIOS NIKOLAOS Αγιος Νικόλαος
The manifestations of package tourism gather momentum as they advance eastwards from Iraklion, reaching their zenith in Agios Nikolaos (A-yios Nik-O-la-os). In July and August the town's permanent population of 9000 is joined by 11,000 tourists. Most of these are sun-starved Brits; the lure of the *Lotus Eaters* and *Who Pays the Ferryman* (TV series which were filmed nearby) first dragged them in over a decade ago, and they've been arriving in ever-increasing numbers since.

However, Agios Nikolaos is more than just a collection of pleasure palaces to satisfy the ephemeral whims of the not-too-discriminating tourist. Before the advent of package holidays, Agios Nikolaos was a very attractive town in its own right. Its setting, built around the Bay of Mirabello, is exemplary. The lake in the centre of the town, surrounded by tavernas and cafés, adds the finishing touch to Agios Nikolaos' picturesque appeal.

To appreciate the town, visit in the low season, as during July and August places to stay are almost impossible to find and negotiating the streets is like being in a rugby scrum.

Orientation
To reach the central square and the lake, with your back to the bus station office turn right and take the first right onto Odos Sofias Venizelou. This street leads up to the central square of Plateia Venizelou. Continue straight ahead from this square onto Odos Koundourou. Turn left at the bottom of Koundourou and you will come to a bridge

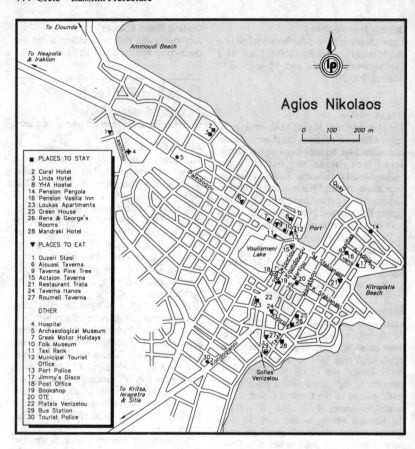

Agios Nikolaos

PLACES TO STAY
2 Coral Hotel
3 Linda Hotel
8 YHA Hostel
14 Pension Pergola
16 Pension Vasilia Inn
23 Loukas Apartments
25 Green House
26 Rena & George's Rooms
28 Mandraki Hotel

PLACES TO EAT
1 Ouzeri Stasi
6 Alouasi Taverna
9 Taverna Pine Tree
15 Actaion Taverna
21 Restaurant Trata
24 Taverna Itanos
27 Roumeli Taverna

OTHER
4 Hospital
5 Archaeological Museum
7 Greek Motor Holidays
10 Folk Museum
11 Taxi Rank
12 Municipal Tourist Office
13 Port Police
17 Jimmy's Disco
18 Post Office
19 Bookshop
20 OTE
22 Plateia Venizelou
29 Bus Station
30 Tourist Police

which separates the lake from the harbour. The tourist office is at the far side of the bridge.

Once over the bridge, if you turn right and follow the road as it veers left, you will come to the northern stretch of waterfront which is the road to Elounda. Most of Agios Nikolaos' largest and most expensive hotels are along this stretch of waterfront. If you turn right at the bottom of Odos Koundourou you will come to a stretch of waterfront with steps leading up to the right. These lead to streets which have the highest concentration of small hotels and pensions.

Information
The Municipal Tourist Office (☎ 22 357; fax 26 398) is open daily from 8.30 am to 9.30 pm from 1 April to 15 November. The efficient staff give out a good map and have currency exchange facilities. If you are brave enough to turn up in Agios Nikolaos in the high season, the staff will do a laudable job in endeavouring to find accommodation for you. The tourist police (☎ 26 900 or 22 321), Kondogianni 34, are also very helpful and are open 24 hours.

Money The Macedonia & Thrace Bank,

Plateia Venizelou 13, is open Monday to Thursday from 8 am to 2 pm and 6 to 8 pm; Friday from 8 am to 1.30 pm; and Saturday from 10 am to 2 pm. There are many other banks which are open normal hours.

Post & Telecommunications The post office, 28 Oktovriou 9, is open Monday to Saturday from 7.30 am to 2 pm. The OTE is at the corner of 25 Martiou and K Sfakianaki. It is open daily from 7 am to midnight. Agios Nikolaos' postcode is 72100 and the telephone code is 0841.

Bookshop There is a well-stocked English-language bookshop at Koundourou 5.

Emergency Agios Nikolaos' General Hospital (☎ 25 221) is between Lasithiou and Paleologou.

Museums

The **Folk Museum**, next door to the tourist office, has a well-displayed collection of traditional handicrafts, costumes and photographs. It is open Sunday to Friday from 10 am to 1.30 pm and 6 to 9.30 pm. Admission is 100 dr.

The **Archaeological Museum** (☎ 24 943), on Paleologou, is a modern building housing a large well-displayed collection from eastern Crete. It's open Tuesday to Sunday from 8.30 am to 3 pm. Admission is 400 dr.

Beaches

Agios Nikolaos' popularity is certainly not due to its beaches. The narrow strip of town beach, at the south-east end of M Sfakianaki, has more people than pebbles. Ammoudi Beach, on the road to Elounda, is best described as a nasty little beach. In the other direction there is a mediocre municipal beach along the western waterfront. Almyros, a pebble beach two km beyond here on the road to Sitia, is the best of the bunch in the immediate vicinity of the town. The sandy beach at the resort of Istron, 11 km further east, is the best of the lot along this stretch of coast. There are 14 buses a day to Istron from Agios Nikolaos.

Voulismeni Lake Λιμνη Βουλισμένη
This lake has inspired many legends and suppositions regarding its depth and origins. The locals have given it various names, including Xepatomeni (bottomless), Voulismeni (sunken) and Vromolimni (dirty). The lake isn't bottomless – it has a depth of 64 metres; the 'dirty' name came about because the lake used to be stagnant and so gave off quite a pong in hot weather. This was rectified in 1867 when a canal was dug linking it to the sea. Early this century the lake changed colour one day and gave off sulphurous vapours which asphyxiated the fish. This bizarre occurrence led to the belief that the lake was connected to the volcano on Thira. According to mythology Athena and Artemis enjoyed taking a dip in its waters.

Organised Tours

Many travel agencies in Agios Nikolaos organise tours to sites and nearby villages. One reliable agency of long standing is Agios Travel (☎ 26 149), Sofias Venizelou 19, just around the corner from the bus station. Its excursions include Spinalonga (1800 dr); Samaria Gorge (5000 dr); and Lassithi plateau and the Dikteon Cave (2700 dr). They also have one-hour (3000 dr) and two-hour (5000 dr) horse-riding excursions.

Places to Stay – bottom end

The nearest camp site to Agios Nikolaos is *Gournia Moon Camping* (☎ 0842-93 243). The site has a restaurant, snack bar and minimarket. It is almost opposite the Minoan site of Gournia (see the Around Agios Nikolaos section).

The Agios Nikolaos *YHA Hostel* (☎ 22 823), at Stratigou Koraka 3, was closed at the time of writing for a badly needed refurbishment. The *Green House* (☎ 22 025), Modatsou 15, is a favourite with backpackers. It is ramshackle, but clean, with a lush garden, four friendly cats and helpful English-speaking owners. Singles/doubles/triples are 1500/2000/2500 dr with shared bathrooms.

Walk up Tavla (a continuation of Modatsou) from the bus station, and you'll find it on the right. Just down from here are *Rena & George's Rooms* (☎ 28 059), Kyprou 15, on the corner of Tavla. The pleasant, clean single/double rooms here cost 2800/3500 dr with private bathrooms.

Pension Vasilia Inn (☎ 23 572/613), Ariadnis 6, has cosy, attractively furnished rooms. Rates are 3000/4000/5000 dr for singles/doubles/triples with private bathrooms. Follow directions for the Green House, turn right at Odos Evans, then first left onto Pasifias and first right onto Ariadnis and you will see the pension on the right. The *Pension Pergola* (☎ 22 452 or 28 152) has comfortable singles/doubles with private bathrooms for 4500/5500 dr. The pension overlooks the sea, two blocks beyond Ariadnis.

Loukas Apartments (☎ 23 169), Plateia Venizelou 13 (above the Macedonia & Thrace Bank), are light, airy and spacious and cost 5500/6600/8000 dr for doubles/triples/quads. The C class *Mandraki Hotel* (☎ 28 880), on Tavla, very near the bus station, has immaculate apartments. Rates are 5000/6000 dr for doubles/triples.

Over at the other side of town, on the northern waterfront, the C class *Linda Hotel* (☎ 22 130/4) has attractive singles/doubles for 4200/5700 dr with private bathrooms.

Places to Stay – middle

The large and opulent B class *Coral Hotel* (☎ 28 363/7), on the northern waterfront, has singles/doubles for 8300/13,600 dr. The hotel has a swimming pool, snack bar and restaurant.

Places to Stay – top end

North of Agios Nikolaos, on the road to Elounda, there are a number of luxury hotels. The deluxe *Minos Palace Hotel* (☎ 23 801; 23 816) is on a headland, just over two km from the town. It has extensive grounds with a swimming pool, sun terraces, gardens, beach bar and taverna. Rates are 20,000/25,100 dr for singles/doubles. The deluxe *St Nicolas Bay Hotel* (☎ 25 041/2/3; fax 24 556), nearby, has a private beach, two swimming pools, tennis courts and restaurants. Rates are 21,500/48,500 dr for singles/doubles and bungalows are 62,000 dr.

Places to Eat

Agios Nikolaos' waterfront tavernas are mostly expensive; head inland for better value eateries. *Ouzeri Stasi*, Lasithiou 23, has delicious mezedes. Meals are less than 1000 dr. It is just beyond the hospital and opens only in the evenings. *Roumeli Taverna*, on the corner of Metamorfoseos and Sofias Venizelou, is open all day. Prices are similar to the Ouzeri Stasi.

Taverna Itanos, Kyprou 1, is a lively and traditional taverna, with chicken for 550 dr, lamb for 730 dr and stifado for 900 dr. *Restaurant Trata*, on the corner of Sfakianaki and Tselepi, is a bright and cheerful restaurant with a roof garden. Prices are comparable with the Itanos.

The *Actaion Restaurant*, by the bridge, has the lowest prices of the waterfront establishments and also serves some of the best food. *Taverna Pine Tree*, Paleologou 18, specialises in charcoal grill food. Giant prawns are 1500 dr. *Alouasi Taverna*, at Paleologou 40, has traditional décor and a lovely garden. A large plate of delicious mezedes (enough for four people) is 1700 dr.

Things to Buy

Nic Gabriel makes handmade copies of ceramic objects from all the museums in Greece. He has a large selection in his workshop and can make items to order. His workshop is at Paleologou 28 (☎ 24 075).

Entertainment

Naturally, discos and bars abound in Agios Nikolaos. *Lipstick Disco*, overlooking the harbour, is one of the wildest. *Jimmy's Disco*, on the corner of Evans and Tselepi, is reputed to have the cheapest drinks.

Getting There & Away

Bus Destinations of buses from Agios Nikolaos' bus station are:

Elounda – 20 minutes, 150 dr, 19 buses daily
Kritsa – 15 minutes, 150 dr, 12 buses daily
Ierapetra – one hour, 480 dr, nine buses daily
Iraklion – 1½ hours, 900 dr, almost half-hourly buses
Istron – 30 minutes, 190 dr, 14 buses daily
Kroustas – 20 minutes, 220 dr, four buses daily
Lassithi plateau – three hours, 1250 dr, two buses daily
Plaka – 40 minutes, 240 dr, seven buses daily
Sitia – 1½ hours, 1000 dr, six buses daily

Ferry Agios Nikolaos has the same ferry schedule as Sitia. Ferry tickets can be bought from Agios Travel (see under Organised Tours), amongst others. The port police (☎ 22 312) are in the same building as the tourist office.

Getting Around
Car, Motorbike & Bicycle There are many car and motorbike-hire outlets on the northern waterfront. There is only one bicycle-hire outlet: Greek Motor Holidays (☎ 24 411), Paleologou 24. The cost is 1000 dr a day and 5000 dr a week.

GOURNIA Γουρνιά
The important Minoan site of Gournia (Gor-NYA) lies just off the coast road, 19 km south-east of Agios Nikolaos. The ruins, which date from 1550-1450 BC, consist of a town overlooked by a small palace. Gournia's palace was far less ostentatious than the ones at Knossos and Phaestos, and was the residence of an overlord rather than a king. The town is a network of streets and stairways flanked by houses whose walls stand up to two metres in height. Trade, domestic and agricultural implements found on the site indicate that Gournia was a thriving and busy little community.

The site (☎ 0841-22 462) is open Tuesday to Sunday from 8.30 am to 3 pm. Admission is free. Gournia is on the Sitia and Ierapetra bus routes from Agios Nikolaos. The bus stops right outside the site.

MONI FANEROMENI Μονή Φανερωμένης
Just two km before Gournia, on the Agios Nikolaos-Sitia road, a five-km gravel road leads off right to the late Byzantine Moni Faneromeni. This was one of the monasteries which played a leading role in the Cretan uprisings; a small number of monks still live here. A visit to the monastery is worthwhile for the stunning vistas down to the coast. If you wish to walk here ask to be let off the Agios Nikolaos-Sitia bus at Gournia Moon Camping.

KRITSA Κριτσά
Kritsa (Krit-SA) village perches 600 metres up a mountainside, 11 km from Agios Nikolaos. Hordes of tourists are bussed into the village every day in summer. The villagers exploit these invasions to the full, and craft shops of every description line the main streets.

However, beyond these shops where tourists rarely venture, Kritsa has remained authentic, with crooked streets of white-washed houses inhabited by friendly people. It deserves an overnight stay, as once the tour coaches have departed it is a tranquil place with superb views down to the Bay of Mirabello.

The village of **Kroustas**, five km south of Kritsa, is also charming and far less frequently visited by tourists. Kroustas has a taverna but no accommodation.

Church of Panagia Kera
This tiny triple-aisled 14th-century church is on the right one km before Kritsa on the Agios Nikolaos road. Its interior walls are almost entirely covered with detailed frescoes depicting scenes from the gospels. These frescoes are considered the most outstanding examples of Byzantine art on Crete. Unfortunately the church is on the package-tourist circuit so is usually packed. There's a reasonably priced snack bar next door. It's a good idea to sit here and wait for the opportunity to enter the church between visits by tour groups. The church is open Monday to Saturday from 9 am to 3 pm and Sunday from 9 am to 2 pm. Admission is 400 dr.

Places to Stay
Kritsa doesn't have any hotels, but there are several domatia. Coming from Agios

Nikolaos, 250 metres beyond the village sign you will see on the right the sign for *Rooms to Rent Argyro* (☎ 0841-51 613/174). Rates are 2000/3500/5500 dr for singles/doubles/triples with shared bathrooms. Further into the village, just beyond the bus station by a little white church on the left, you will see a 'Rooms to Rent' sign. These are the pleasant and clean rooms of the *Oikonomaki family* (☎ 51 291). Rates are 2000/2300 dr for singles/doubles. Almost opposite are *Kera Rooms* (☎ 51 045), owned by Maria Kokkini. These are modern, light and airy, and cost 2000/2500 dr with shared bathrooms.

Places to Eat

Unfortunately the good value prevailing in accommodation is not reflected in Kritsa's eating establishments. The most promising-looking place, *Taverna Ellena*, was closed for renovation at the time of writing. Keep going along the main road, and beyond the two signposts to Plateau Katharon, you'll come to Odos Kritsotopoulas; along here you'll find a sign pointing left to the taverna. Even if the food turns out to be unremarkable, the view from the taverna's outside terrace is stupendous.

The *Taverna Castello*, next to the post office, serves well-prepared food but it's not particularly cheap, with moussaka at 850 dr and a mixed grill at 1000 dr. The *Oasis Restaurant*, opposite the bus station, is slightly more expensive. The cafeteria behind the bus station which looks as if it might be cheaper isn't. The patisserie opposite Taverna Castello is a good place for people-watching; cakes are 300 dr and sandwiches are 700 dr.

Things to Buy

The myriad goods on sale in Kritsa runs the whole gamut from massproduced trash to exquisite handmade products, so careful scrutiny is in order before you part with your drachmas. Goods include leather sandals, hand-woven woollen bags, wall-hangings and rugs; crocheted, embroidered and appliqued tablecloths, ceramics and hand-painted copies of icons.

Getting There & Away

There are 12 buses daily from Agios Nikolaos to Kritsa (15 minutes, 150 dr) and four to Kroustas (20 minutes, 220 dr).

ANCIENT LATO

The ancient city of Lato (Λατώ, La-TO), four km north of Kritsa, is one of Crete's few non-Minoan ancient sites. Lato was founded in the 7th century BC by the Dorians and at its height was one of the most powerful cities on Crete. It sprawls over the slopes of two acropolises in a lonely mountain setting, commanding stunning views down to the Gulf of Mirabello.

The city's name derived from the goddess Leto whose union with Zeus produced Artemis and Apollo, both of whom were worshipped here.

Lato is far less visited than Crete's Minoan sites. It is open Tuesday to Sunday from 8.30 am to 3 pm. At the time of writing, entrance was free, but the keeper told me a charge may soon be made.

Exploring the Site

In the centre of the site is a deep well which is cordoned off. Facing the Bay of Mirabello, you will see to the left of the well some steps; these are the remains of a **theatre**.

Above the theatre was the **prytaneion**, where the city's governing assembly met. The circle of stones behind the well was a threshing floor. The columns next to it are the remains of a stoa which stood in the agora; in this area there are remains of a pebble mosaic. To the right a path leads up to the **Temple of Apollo**. A statue of the god once stood on the pediment in the temple.

Getting There & Away

Coming from Agios Nikolaos, you will find the beginning of the three-km dirt road to Lato signposted to the right, 200 metres after the sign for Kritsa. No buses go to Lato but the road is passable by car or motorbike. Alternatively, it is a delightful walk passing olive groves, and small holdings with chickens, sheep and goats.

Top: Gialos, Symi, Dodecanese (RH)
Left: View of the Acropolis and sea at Lindos, Rhodes, Dodecanese (DH)
Right: Bouka harbour, Kassos, Dodecanese (RH)

Top: Kastellorizo harbour, Kastellorizo, Dodecanese (RH)
Left: Autumn crocuses, Knights' Castle, Tilos, Dodecanese (RH)
Right: Moni Agiou Penteleimona, Tilos, Dodecanese (RH)

SPINALONGA PENINSULA

Χερσόνησος Σπιναλόγκας

Just before Elounda (coming from Agios Nikolaos), a sign points right to **ancient Olous** which was the port of Lato. The city stood on, and around, the narrow isthmus (now a causeway) which joined the southern end of the Spinalonga (Spin-a-LONG-a) peninsula to the mainland. Most of the ruins now lie beneath the water, and if you go snorkelling near the causeway you will see outlines of buildings, tops of columns etc. However, be warned, the water hereabouts seems to be a sea-urchins paradise. The peninsula is a pleasant place to stroll and near the causeway there is an early Christian mosaic.

SPINALONGA ISLAND

Νήσος Σπιναλόγκα

Spinalonga island lies just north of the Spinalonga peninsula. The island's fortress was built by the Venetians in 1579 to protect Elounda and Mirabello bays. It withstood Turkish sieges for longer than any other Cretan stronghold, finally surrendering in 1715, some 30 years after the rest of Crete. The Turks used the island as a base for smuggling. Following the reunion of Crete with Greece, Spinalonga became a leper colony. The last leper died there in 1953 and since then the island has been uninhabited. Among locals Spinalonga is still known as 'the island of the living dead'. It is rumoured that when catches were low fishermen in Elounda and Plaka would dock at Spinalonga and buy fish from the lepers at reduced prices. It seems the locals would rather have died of starvation than eat lepers' fish, but mixed with the main catch they were never to know.

The buildings flanking the cobbled streets within the massive stone walls are now in ruins. The island is fascinating to explore; it emanates an aura which is both macabre and poignant. The **cemetery**, with its open graves, is an especially strange place. Dead lepers came in three classes: those who saved up money from their government pension for a place in a concrete box; those whose

funeral was paid for by relations and who therefore got a proper grave; and the destitute, whose remains were thrown into a charnel house.

Getting There & Away

You can visit the island by excursion boats from Agios Nikolaos, or fishermen in Elounda and Plaka (a fishing village five km further north) do trips for 1000 dr per person. If you take the boat from Agios Nikolaos you will pass Bird island and Kri-Kri island, one of the last habitats of the kri-kri, Crete's wild goat. Both of these islands are uninhabited and designated wildlife sanctuaries.

ELOUNDA Ελούντα

There are magnificent mountain and sea vistas along the 11-km road from Agios Nikolaos to Elounda. The resort of Elounda (El-OON-da), which is considerably quieter than Agios Nikolaos, has an attractive harbour and a sheltered lagoon-like stretch of water formed by the Spinalonga peninsula.

Orientation & Information

Elounda's post office is opposite the bus stop. From the bus stop walk straight ahead to the clock tower and church which are on the central square. There is a small OTE office next to the church. Elounda's postcode is 72053 and the telephone code is 0841. The town doesn't have a tourist office or tourist police.

Places to Stay

Zaharenia Rooms (no telephone) has large, unadorned double/triple rooms for 2900/3500 dr with private bathrooms. The rooms are opposite the Church of Constantinos above Zoe designer T-shirt shop. *Elpis Rooms* (☎ 41 384), on the opposite side of the road, are more luxurious. Rates are 4000/4800 dr for doubles/triples with private bathrooms. The C class *Hotel Calypso* (☎ 41 316/967), overlooking the harbour near the central square, has comfortable doubles for 8000 dr.

Just south of Elounda, on the road to Agios Nikolaos, there are several deluxe hotels.

One of them is the *Astir Palace* (☎ 41 584/1/ 2/3/4; fax 41 783). Rates are 21,000/ 27,000 dr for singles/doubles and 31,100 dr for bungalows. The more expensive deluxe *Elounda Beach* (☎ 41 412/3; fax 41 373) is regarded by some as Crete's best hotel. It has a delightful garden, swimming pool, disco, cinema, jacuzzi and sporting amenities, including deep-sea diving. Singles/doubles are 28,000/ 35,000 and bungalows are 58,600 dr.

Places to Eat

The *Marilena Restaurant* on the central square and the Hotel Calypso's restaurant are both popular and good value.

Getting There & Away

There are 19 buses a day from Agios Nikolaos to Elounda (20 minutes, 150 dr).

LASSITHI PLATEAU Οροπέδιο Λασιθίου

The first view of the mountain-fringed Lassithi (La-SITH-ee) plateau, laid out like an immense patchwork quilt, is breathtaking. The plateau, 900 metres above sea level, is a vast expanse of pear and apple orchards, almond trees and fields of crops, dotted by some 7000 windmills. These are not conventional stone windmills, but slender metal constructions with white canvas sails, which, when they are unfurled, make the vistas even more magnificent. There are 20 villages dotted around the periphery of the plateau; the largest is **Tzermiado,** which has 1300 inhabitants.

The plateau, with its mineral rich soil, has been cultivated since Minoan times. The inaccessibility of the region made it a hotbed of insurrection during Venetian and Turkish rule. Following an uprising in the 13th century, the ruling Venetians drove out the inhabitants of Lassithi and destroyed their orchards. The plateau lay abandoned for 200 years.

Most people come to Lassithi on coach trips, but it deserves an overnight stay, for when the package tourists have departed clutching their plastic windmill souvenirs, the villages return to pastoral serenity. The telephone code for Lassithi is 0844.

Dikteon Cave Δικταίον Αντρον

Apart from the sheer pleasure of walking in and around the plateau, the principal sight of Lassithi is the Dikteon Cave, just outside the village of **Psychro** (Psi-HRO). Here, according to mythology, Rhea hid the newborn Zeus from Kronos, his offspring-gobbling father. The cave, which has both stalactites and stalagmites, was excavated in 1900 by the British archaeologist David Hogarth. Inside he found numerous votive offerings indicating that the cave was a place of cult worship. These finds are housed in the Archaeological Museum in Iraklion. Bring a torch along to explore the cave, and wear sensible shoes as the entrance is slippery. The path to the cave (signposted) is a turn-off to the left just beyond Psychro. Opening times are 8 am to 6 pm. Admission is 400 dr.

Places to Stay & Eat

Psychro is the best place to stay; it's near the cave and has the best views of the plateau. There are some clean, basic rooms signposted from the central square. The village's only hotel is the D class *Zeus Hotel* (☎ 31 284), where doubles are 4000 dr. The hotel is on the left side of the main road, going towards the cave from the central square.

There are three budget hotels, and domatia in Tzermiado. There are also domatia at the village of **Agios Georgios**, between Tzermiado and Psychro.

The *Zeus Hotel* in Psychro and the *Hotel Kourites* in Tzermiado have reasonably priced restaurants. The rough and ready taverna on the right side of Psychro's central square (as you face towards the cave) serves tasty low-priced food.

Getting There & Away

There are two buses a day from Iraklion (two hours, 950 dr) and Agios Nikolaos (three hours, 1250 dr) to the Lassithi plateau. Both buses go through Tzermiado, Agios Georgios, and Psychro and terminate at the Dikteon Cave.

SITIA Σητεία

Back on the north-coast road, Sitia (Si-TEE-a,

population 8000) is an attractive town which is a good deal quieter than Agios Nikolaos. A sandy beach skirts a wide bay at the eastern end of town. The main part of the town is terraced up a hillside; the buildings are a pleasing mixture of new and fading Venetian architecture.

Orientation & Information

The bus station is on the eastern waterfront. To reach the centre of town from here, facing the sea turn left onto Karamanli and walk along the waterfront to the central square of Plateia Agonostou, recognisable by its palm trees and statue of a dying soldier. Proceeding along the waterfront you will come to a small quay used by fishing boats; the large quay from where the ferries leave is 300 metres beyond here. If you arrive in Sitia by ferry turn left from the quay to reach the centre of town.

The post office is on Odos Therissou. From the central square (facing inland) turn left onto El Venizelou, and Therissou is a turn-off to the right. The OTE is on Odos Kapetan Sifis, which runs inland from the central square. Sitia's postcode is 72300 and the telephone code is 0843. The National Bank of Greece is on the central square.

There is a mobile Municipal Tourist Office on the central square which operates from May to October.

Archaeological Museum

Sitia's Archaeological Museum is a modern building which houses a well-displayed collection of local finds spanning all the ages from Neolithic to Roman, with emphasis on the Minoan. The museum (☎ 23 917) is on the left side of the road to Ierapetra. It is open Tuesday to Sunday from 8.30 am to 3 pm. Admission is 400 dr.

Festival

Sitia produces superior sultanas and a **Sultana Festival** is held in the town in the last week of August, during which wine flows freely and there are performances of Cretan dances.

Places to Stay

Sitia's *YHA Hostel* (☎ 22 693) is at Therissou 4, on the road to Iraklion. Beds cost 700 dr. Walking from the waterfront it's on the left.

Rooms to Rent (☎ 28 628), owned by Emmanual Leventeris, is a small holding with chickens, rabbits and a vegetable garden. The clean, simply furnished singles/doubles/triples cost 2000/2500/3000 dr with shared bathrooms. From the bus station, walk inland along the dirt road to your left and you'll see the rooms on the left – look for a single-storey white building with a blue sign. Mr Leventeris often meets the buses.

The D class *Hotel Arhontiko* (☎ 28 172 or 22 993), Kondilaki 16, is voted by many to be Crete's best budget hotel. It has beautiful, spotlessly clean rooms and a charming owner. Rates are 2500/3000/4000 dr with shared bathrooms. To reach this hotel walk inland along the street opposite the small fishing quay and you'll see a sign pointing to the hotel. Sitia doesn't have a camp site but it's sometimes possible to camp in the grounds of the youth hostel.

Places to Eat

Meraklis Taverna, almost opposite the post office, on Therassou, is lively, authentic, popular with locals and serves wonderful food. It's open all day and sometimes features live bouzouki music in the evenings. *To Kyma Café*, Venizelou 189, near the small quay, is another authentic eatery. It specialises in mezedes, which range in price from 350 to 650 dr.

Getting There & Away

Air From Sitia's tiny airport there is one flight a week to Athens (16,900 dr), Karpathos (8200 dr) and Kassos (6300 dr). All the flights leave on a Tuesday. The Olympic Airways office (☎ 22 270/596) is at Eleftheriou Venizelou 56.

Bus From Sitia there are six buses to Ierapetra (1½ hours, 700 dr); five buses to Iraklion (3½ hours, 1650 dr) via Agios Nikolaos (1½ hours, 850 dr); four to Vai (one hour, 340 dr); and two to Kato Zakros (one hour, 650 dr).

Ferry The F/B *Kimolos* leaves Sitia at 1 am on Wednesday for Kassos, Pigadia and Diafenes on Karpathos, Halki, Symi and Rhodes (11 hours, 2200 dr). At 3 pm on Thursday it leaves for Piraeus (14 hours, 4800 dr) via Agios Nikolaos, Thira, Sikinos, Folegandros, Milos and Sifnos.

Buy ferry tickets at Tzortzakis Travel Agency (☎ 25 080/090), Eleftheriou Venizelou 183. Walking from the central square the office is on the left just before the small quay.

Getting Around

To/From the Airport The airport (signposted) is just one km from the town. There is no airport bus and a taxi costs 400 dr.

Car & Motorbike Car and motorbike-hire outlets are mostly on the eastern waterfront near the bus station.

AROUND SITIA

Moni Toplou Μονή Τοπλού
The imposing Moni Toplou, 18 km from Sitia, looks more like a fortress than a monastery. It was often treated as such, being ravaged by both the Knights of St John and the Turks. Its star piece is an 18th-century icon by Ioannis Kornaros, one of Crete's most celebrated icon painters. The monastery is a three-km walk along a road, which branches off the Sitia-Vai road. The Sitia-Vai bus will drop you off at the beginning of the road.

Vai Βάι
The allure of sandy Vai (Vie) Beach, on Crete's east coast, 24 km from Sitia, is its celebrated palm-tree forest, which has around 5000 palm trees. It is wise to arrive here early to appreciate its undeniable beauty, because as the day gets underway the beach gets crowded. Most visitors who stake a territory on the main beach consist of families with buckets and spades, sunbeds, grannies and trannies – the works. To escape this ballyhoo you can clamber up and over a

rocky outcrop (to the left facing the sea) to a small secluded beach. Alternatively, you can go in the other direction where there is a path over a hill to a quiet beach frequented by nudists.

There are two tavernas at Vai but no accommodation. For more secluded beaches head north for another three km to the ancient site of **Itanos**. Below the site are several coves which are fine spots for swimming. There are four buses a day to Vai from Sitia (one hour, 340 dr).

ZAKROS & KATO ZAKROS

The village of Zakros (Ζάκρος, ZAK-ros), 45 km south-east of Sitia, is the nearest permanent settlement to the east-coast Minoan site of Zakros, which is five km away. It has domatia and one hotel, the C class Hotel Zakros (☎ 0843-28 479), where doubles with private bathrooms are 4500 dr. Kato Zakros, next to the site, is a gorgeous little seaside settlement with a pebble beach, domatia and tavernas; it is only inhabited in summer. In summer you can trek through a beautiful gorge from the village of Zakros to Kato Zakros.

Getting There & Away

There are two buses a day to Kato Zakros (via Paleokastro and Zakros) from Sitia (one hour, 650 dr). They leave Sitia at 11 am and 2.30 pm and return at 12.30 and 4 pm.

ANCIENT ZAKROS

Ancient Zakros, the smallest of Crete's four palatial complexes, was a major port in Minoan times, with trade links with Egypt, Syria, Anatolia and Cyprus. The palace dominated the town and, although considerably smaller than those at Knossos, Phaestos and Malia, like them, it consisted of royal apartments, storerooms and workshops flanking a central courtyard.

The town occupied a low plain, originally by a stream, the level of which has risen over the years so that some parts of the palace are submerged. The ruins are not well preserved, but a visit to the site is worthwhile for its wonderfully wild and remote setting. Zakros is on a much more human scale than the other palatial complexes, and one can imagine a peaceful seaside existence, a bit cut off from court life at Knossos. The site is open Tuesday to Sunday from 8.30 am to 3 pm. Admission is 400 dr.

IERAPETRA Ιεράπετρα

Ierapetra (Ye-RA-pet-ra, population 11,000), on the south coast, is Crete's most southerly major town. It was a major port of call for the Romans in their conquest of Egypt. After the tourist hype of Agios Nikolaos, the unpretentiousness of Ierapetra is refreshing. Ierapetra is a town whose business is agriculture not tourism.

Orientation

The bus station is on Lasthenous. With your back to the ticket office, turn right and continue walking along Lasthenous. About 50 metres along you'll come to a roundabout. A turn left here leads to the beach (signposted). Take the fourth road round (going anticlockwise) to reach the centre of town; this road is still Lasthenous. About 200 metres along you'll come to the central square of Plateia Eleftherias. On the right of the square is the National Bank of Greece.

If you turn right opposite the bank you will come to the OTE just one block away. Continuing straight ahead from this square you will come to Plateia Emmanual Kothri. Cross diagonally right here to come to the post office at Stylianou Chouta 3.

Information

The Municipal Tourist Office (☎ 28 658) is next door to the Archaeological Museum on Odos Adrianou Kostoula. To reach it turn right from Plateia Emmanual Kothri.

Ierapetra's postcode is 72200 and the telephone code is 0842.

Things to See

Ierapetra's one-room **Archaeological Museum** is for those with a short concentration span. Pride of place is given to an exquisite well-preserved statue of Demeter. However, unless you are an archaeological buff the otherwise meagre collection hardly justifies the 400 dr entrance fee. Opening times are Tuesday to Sunday from 8.45 am to 3 pm. The museum is next door to the tourist office on Adrianou Kostoula.

If you walk south along the waterfront from the central square you will come to the **Fortress**, which was built in the early years of Venetian rule and strengthened by Francesco Morosini in 1626. It is in such a fragile state that it's presently closed to the public. Just beyond the fortress is the pleasant little harbour with fishing boats. Striking inland from here you will come to the attractive old quarter which is a delightful place for a stroll. On your wanders around this quarter you'll come across a mosque and a Turkish fountain.

Beaches

Ierapetra has two beaches. The main town beach is near the harbour and the other beach stretches east from the bottom of Patriarchou Metaxaki. Both beaches have coarse grey sand.

Places to Stay – bottom end & middle

The nearest camp sites to Ierapetra are two sites adjacent to one another on the beach at the coastal resort of Koutsounari, seven km east of Ierapetra. They are *Ierapetra Camping* (☎ 0842-61 351) and *Koutsounari Camping* (☎ 0842-61 213). Both sites have a restaurant, snack bar and minimarket and charge identical prices. The Ierapetra-Sitia buses pass the sites.

The very pleasant *Katerina Hotel* (☎ 28 345) has a modern exterior which is deceptive as the interior has stucco walls and mock-traditional furniture. Doubles with private bathrooms are 5000 dr. To reach the hotel from the bus station, walk to the roundabout and turn left onto Odos Patriarchou Metaxaki (signposted to the beach). At the waterfront turn right and you'll see the hotel on the right.

Pension Lilian (☎ 24 442), Georgiou Giannakou 40, is a beautiful place with cosy rooms. Rates are 5800/6800 dr for doubles/triples with private bathrooms. From the bus station, walk along Lasthenous towards the town centre and you will come to the Hotel Creta; turn right here onto Georgiou Giannakou. The pension is along here on the right.

The C class *Ersi Hotel* (☎ 23 208), Plateia Eleftherias, has very comfortable rooms. Rates are 3500/6000/7000 dr for singles/doubles/triples. The hotel is on the right coming from the bus station. If you continue along Lasthenous and cross over Plateia Emmanual Kothri onto Kyrvra, and take the first turn right you will come to *Hotel Ligia* (☎ 28 881). This friendly family-run hotel is nicely furnished and all the rooms have a telephone and balcony. Rates are 3800/5500/6600 dr with private bathrooms.

Places to Stay – top end
The A class *Lyktos Beach Hotel* (☎ 61 280; fax 61 318), on the beach seven km east of Ierapetra, has many amenities including a gymnasium and swimming pool. Rates are 15,600/26,600 dr for singles/doubles.

Places to Eat
One of the cheapest restaurants in Ierapetra is the *Korali*, on the left side of Patriarchou Metaxaki as you walk towards the sea. A full meal with beverage will cost around 1300 dr. Another good value eatery is *Taverna Klemeraria*, Adrianou Kostoula 63. Adrianou Kostoula runs inland from Plateia Emmanual Kothri. The tree-shaded outdoor area of the kafeneion next to the post office on Plateia Emmanual Kothri is a pleasant place to sit and watch the world go by, whilst sipping a Nescafé or soft drink.

Getting There & Away
From Ierapetra's bus station there are nine buses a day to Agios Nikolaos (one hour, 480 dr) via Gournia and Istron; eight to Makri Gialos (30 minutes, 360 dr); and six to Sitia (1½ hours, 800 dr) via Koutsounari (for camp sites) and Mirtos (30 minutes, 200 dr).

AROUND IERAPETRA
The beaches to the east of Ierapetra tend to get crowded. For greater tranquillity, head for **Chrissi islet**, where there are good uncrowded sandy beaches. In summer an excursion boat (1500 dr) leaves for the islet every morning and returns in the afternoon.

Mirtos, on the coast 17 km west of Ierapetra, is a pleasant low-key resort with a decent dark sand beach. There are domatia and tavernas, and one hotel, the D class *Hotel Mirtos* (☎ 0842-51 225), where doubles are 4000 dr with private bathrooms. There are six buses a day from Ierapetra to Mirtos (30 minutes, 200 dr).

Rethymnon Prefecture
Νομός Ρεθύμνου

RETHYMNON Ρέθυμνο
Rethymnon (RETH-im-no, population 20,000) is Crete's third-largest town. A massive *fortezza* (fortress) looks down over an atmospheric old Venetian-Ottoman quarter which is a maze of narrow streets, graceful wood-balconied houses and ornate Venetian monuments; several minarets add a touch of the Orient. Despite architectural similarities to Hania, Rethymnon has a distinct character of its own. An added attraction is a long sandy beach right in town.

The site on which the town stands has been continuously inhabited since Neolithic times, but little remains of Rethymnon's ancient past. During Venetian times Rethymnon prospered, and was an artistic and intellectual centre, after a large number of refugees from Constantinople chose to settle there. In recent years many of Rethymnon's Venetian and Turkish buildings have been restored.

Orientation
Although Rethymnon is smaller than Hania, to the north-west, it is a town in which it is considerably more difficult to get your bearings. There are two bus stations, opposite one another on the corners of Moatsou and Demokratias. From the bus stations (with the Olympic Hotel on your left) walk straight ahead along Demokratias, cross over

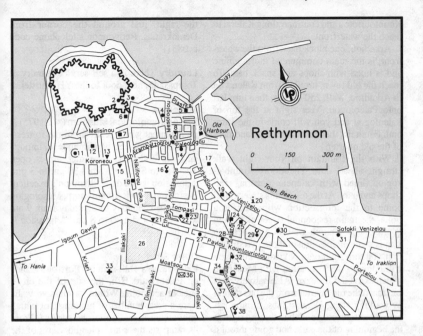

Rethymnon

0   150   300 m

■ PLACES TO STAY

4   Pension Anna
6   Eliza Rooms
7   Hotel Fortezza
12 Rent Rooms Ergina
17 Café Bar 67 Rooms
18 Rent Rooms Garden
19 Achillion Hotel
23 YHA Hostel
24 Pension Vrisinas
25 Hotel Minoa
34 Olympic Hotel

▼ PLACES TO EAT

8   Taverna Kyria Maria
13 Angela Ouzeri
15 Gounakis Restaurant & Bar
21 Taverna Ta Balkania
28 Ouzeri To Luhnari

OTHER

1   Fortress
2   Entrance to Fortress
3   Archaeological Museum
5   Historical & Folk Art Museum
9   Port Police
10 Rimondi Fountain
11 Plateia Iroon Politechniou
14 Motorbike Rental Firms
16 Nerandjes Mosque
20 Municipal Tourist Office
22 Minaret
26 Municipal Park
27 OTE
29 Kara Pasha Mosque
30 Car Hire Rental Firms
31 Happy Walker Travel Agency
32 National Bank of Greece
33 Hospital
35 Bus Station for Iraklion & Hania
36 Post Office
37 Bus Station for Agia Galini, Moni
    Arkadiou & Plakias
38 Veli Pasha Mosque

Kountouriotou and continue along Kalergi to reach the waterfront.

Arkadiou, one block back from the waterfront, is the main commercial thoroughfare and is lined with shops and snack bars. To reach the old town, turn left from Kalergi on to Arkadiou, walk 250 metres, then turn left onto Paleologou. Veer right at the top of Paleologou and you will come to the Rimondi Fountain, the most distinctive landmark of the old quarter.

With the fountain on your right walk straight ahead onto Theodoras Arambatzoglou, lined with kafeneia, ouzeria, craft shops and bars. At the top of this street you'll come to the intersection with Nikiforou Foka, the main residential street of the old quarter. The Church of the Annunciation stands at the intersection of these two streets.

If you turn right onto Nikiforou Foka you will come to the T-junction with Melisinou which skirts the fortezza. Alternatively, you can reach the old quarter from the bus station by walking along Demokratias, turning left onto Kountouriotou and then turning right at the beginning of the park, and going through a Venetian city gate onto Antistaseos.

To reach the small, almost circular Old Harbour (also called the Venetian Harbour), continue along Kalergi to the waterfront and turn left. Rethymnon's town beach stretches eastwards from the Old Harbour.

Information

Tourist Office To reach Rethymnon's Municipal Tourist Office (☎ 29 148 or 24 143) from the bus stations, walk along Kalergi to the waterfront, turn right and you'll come to it on the left.

Money The National Bank of Greece is on the corner of Demokratias and Kountouriotou. The Credit Bank, Pavlou Kountouriotou 29, has an automatic teller machine for Visa and American Express card holders.

Post & Telecommunications The post office is at Moatsou 21, to the west of the bus stations. Rethymnon's postcode is 74100. The OTE is at Pavlou Kountouriotou 28, on

the right, just around the corner from Demokratias. Rethymnon's telephone code is 0831.

Laundry There is a self-service laundry at Tompasi 45, next door to the YHA hostel.

Museums

The **Archaeological Museum** (☎ 29 975) is on the street which leads up to the fortress. The finds displayed here include an important coin collection. The museum is open Tuesday to Sunday from 8.30 am to 3 pm. Admission is 400 dr. Rethymnon's excellent **Historical & Folk Art Museum**, Mesologiou 28, is open Monday to Saturday from 9 am to 1.30 pm and 5.30 to 8 pm. Admission is 200 dr.

Other Sites

Rethymnon's 16th-century **Fortress** stands on Paleokastro Hill, the site of the city's ancient acropolis. Within its massive walls were a great number of buildings, of which only a church and a mosque survive. From its ramparts there are splendid views of the city and the coast.

The fortress is open every day from 9 am to 4.30 pm. Admission is 300 dr.

The old quarter is a wonderful place to stroll around. Amongst vestiges of Rethymnon's Venetian period are the **Rimondi Fountain** and just east of it is the 16th-century **Loggia**. At the southern end of Antistaseos is the well-preserved **Great Gate**, a remnant of the walls the Venetians built around the city to deter pirates. Turkish legacies in the old quarter include the mosque near the Great Gate and further along Antistaseos, the **Neradjes Mosque**, which was converted from a Franciscan Church. The **Mosque of Veli Pasha** is just south of the two bus stations, in the new town.

Trekking

The Happy Walker (☎ 22 446), Anca Travel, Sofokli Venizelou 21, has a programme of daily walks along remote mountain paths in the region. The walks are in small groups and cost between 4000 and 5000 dr per person.

Trekking Plan (☎ 20 123), Portaliou 81, organises treks in the Lefki Ori (for details see Hania's Organised Tours section). Rethymnon's chapter of the EOS (☎ 22 710/229) is above the post office on Moatsou.

Festivals
During July, Rethymnon hosts a **Wine Festival** in the municipal park. Admission is 400 dr. In the last few years a **Renaissance Festival** has taken place in Rethymnon during July and August. This festival features drama, dance, films and art exhibitions.

Places to Stay – bottom end
The nearest camp site is *Elizabeth Camping* (☎ 28 694), near Myssiria Beach, three km east of Rethymnon. The site has a taverna, snack bar and minimarket. To reach it take an Iraklion bus and ask to be let off at the site.

The *YHA Hostel* (☎ 22 848), Tompasi 41, is a friendly well-run place with a bar; beds are 700 to 800 dr. There is no curfew and an IYHF card is not required.

Café Bar 67 (☎ 51 283), Venizelou 67, has clean simply furnished singles/doubles for 2000/3000 dr. An outstanding domatia is *Rent Rooms Garden* (☎ 26 274) at Nikiforou Foka 82 in the heart of the old town. It is an impeccably maintained 600-year-old Venetian house with many original features and a gorgeous grape-arboured garden; doubles/triples are both 4500 dr with private bathrooms. Further west in the old town, *Rent Rooms Ergina* (☎ 29 474), Smirnis 4, has immaculate single/double/triple rooms for 4500/5800/7000 dr with private bathrooms. Walking north along Nikiforou Foka turn left onto Koroneou, and Smirnis is the fifth turn-off to the right, just before Plateia Iroon Politechniou. North of Nikiforou Foka, *Pension Anna* (☎ 25 586), Katehaki 5, on the left side of the road leading up to the fortress, has two-person studios for 5500 dr.

The E class *Achillion Hotel* (☎ 22 581), Arkadiou 151, has huge, nicely furnished rooms. Doubles/triples/quads are 5000/6000/7000 dr with shared bathrooms. The co-owned *Eliza Rooms*, Plastira 12, are modern, attractive rooms in a newly renovated

house. Doubles/triples are 6000/8000 dr with private bathrooms. *Pension Vrisinas* (☎ 26 092), Hereti 10, has pleasant double/triple rooms for 3600/5000 dr with shared bathrooms. Hereti is a little street off to the left from Arkadiou as you come from Kalergi. If everywhere else is full you may have luck at the *Hotel Minoa* (☎ 22 508), Arkadiou 62, where clean but characterless rooms cost 3600/4000/5500 dr with private bathrooms.

Places to Stay – middle
The B class *Hotel Fortezza* (☎ 21 551/2 or 23 828; fax 20 073), Melissinou 16, is a striking crenellated building with strawberry pink exterior walls. It has a snack bar, restaurant and swimming pool. Rates are 9600/13,100 dr for singles/doubles. The B class *Olympic Hotel* (☎ 24 761/2/3/4), on the corner of Moatsou and Demokratias, has comfortable rooms, a bar and a roof garden. Rates are 8000/11,500 dr.

Places to Stay – top end
The A class *Grecotel El Greco* (☎ 71 102/124; fax 71 215) is a huge place on the beach, eight km east of Rethymnon. It has lots of amenities including a restaurant, swimming pool, a water-sports centre and tennis courts. Rates are 11,500/21,700 dr.

Places to Eat
As usual there are many tourist-oriented restaurants on the waterfront. Around the Old Harbour the waiters block your way in their desperate efforts to cajole you into eating at their establishments. To find cheaper food and a more authentic atmosphere, wander down the little side streets back from the water.

One of Rethymnon's cheapest eating places is the untouristy *Taverna Ta Balkania*, at Igoum Gavriil 7. Main meals start at 550 dr. It's open 24 hours and is popular with local workers.

Taverna Kyria Maria, Diog Mesologiou 20, tucked behind the Rimondi Fountain, is a cosy, traditional taverna, serving tasty food. *Ouzeri To Luhnari*, Gerakari 41, is a pleasant place with reasonable prices. Well-prepared imaginative meze dishes range from 250 to 500 dr. Live Greek music is sometimes featured in the evenings.

Gounakis Restaurant & Bar, Koroneou 6, has superlative live Cretan music every evening, and often impromptu dancing. It also serves good traditional food. *Angela Ouzeri*, further along Koroneou, is a rough and ready place serving tasty, low-priced fish dishes and mezedes.

Entertainment

Rethymnon has many discos. *Disco Delfini*, opposite Walking Tours, is one of the most well established. *Caneli Club*, on Arkadiou, near the Old Harbour, reputedly has the cheapest drinks. The *Black Cat Bar*, below the fortress wall, is also reasonably priced. The *Fortezza Disco*, at the Old Harbour, is frequented by a hip young crowd. The *Gounakis Restaurant & Bar*, Koroneou 6, is the best place in Rethymnon to hear live Cretan music (see Places to Eat).

Getting There & Away

Bus From the Plakias bus station there are eight buses to Plakias (one hour, 610 dr); six buses to Agia Galini (1½ hours, 800 dr); four to Moni Arkadiou (30 minutes, 300 dr); and two a day to Preveli (610 dr). From the second bus station there are buses every half hour to Hania (one hour, 950 dr) and Iraklion (1½ hours, 1000 dr).

Ferry The F/B *Arkadi* leaves Piraeus on Monday, Wednesday and Friday at 7.30 pm and sails direct to Rethymnon (3400 dr). It leaves Rethymnon for Piraeus at 7.30 pm on Tuesday, Thursday, Saturday and Sunday. The telephone number of Rethymnon's port police is ☎ 29 950 or 24 823.

Getting Around

Car & Motorbike Car-hire firms are mostly around the eastern end of Arkadiou and the eastern waterfront. An exception is Budget (☎ 25 060; telex 29 1184), which is at Pavlou Kountouriotou 93. Most motorbike-rental firms are on Paleologou.

AROUND RETHYMNON

Moni Arkadiou Μονή Αρκαδίου

This 16th-century monastery stands in attractive hill country 23 km south-east of Rethymnon. The most impressive building of the complex is the Venetian Baroque church. Its striking façade has eight slender Corinthian columns and is topped by an ornate triple-belled tower. This façade features on the 100 dr note.

In November 1866 the Turks sent massive forces to quell insurrections which were gathering momentum throughout the island. Hundreds of men, women and children who had fled their villages used the monastery as a safe haven. When 2000 Turkish soldiers staged an attack on the building, rather than surrender, the Cretans set light to a store of gun powder. The explosion killed everyone, Turks included, except one small girl. This sole survivor lived to a ripe old age in a village nearby. A bust of this woman, and the abbot who lit the gun powder, stand outside the monastery.

The monastery is open every day and entry is free. The small **Museum** has an admission charge of 300 dr.

Getting There & Away At the time of writing buses from Rethymnon to the monastery (30 minutes, 300 dr) left at 6 and 10 am, noon and 2.30 pm. The return times were 7 and 11.15 am; and 1.15 and 4 pm.

Amari Valley Κοιλάδα Αμαρίου

If you have your own transport you may like to explore the enchanting Amari valley, which lies south-east of Rethymnon, between Mt Ida and Mt Kedros. This region harbours around 40 well-watered unspoilt villages set amid olive groves and almond and cherry trees.

The valley begins at the picturesque village of **Apostoli**, 25 km south-east of Rethymnon. The turn-off for Apostoli is on the coast three km east of Rethymnon. At Apostoli, the road forks, and then joins up again 38 km to the south, making it possible to do a circular drive around the valley; alternatively you can continue south to Agia

Galini. There is an EOS refuge on Mt Ida, a 10-km walk from the small village of **Kouroutes**, five km south of Fourfouras. For information contact the Rethymnon EOS (see Rethymnon section).

RETHYMNON TO PLAKIAS & AGIA GALINI

Heading south from Rethymnon, at eight km there is a turn-off right for the late Minoan cemetery of **Armeni**, two km before the modern village of Armeni. The main road passes through woodland, which gradually gives way to a bare and dramatic landscape. At 18 km there is turn-off right for **Selia**, **Rodakino** and **Frangokastello**, all in Hania prefecture, and a little beyond, another turn-off right for Plakias (this turn-off is referred to as the Koxare junction).

The main road continues through the mountain town of **Spili** (see Around Plakias), to **Agia Galini**. Taking the Plakias road, shortly after the village of **Koxare**, the road enters the dramatic two-km-long **Kourtaliotis Gorge**, with high cliffs of bare rock at either side. After Astomatis village there is a turn-off for Moni Preveli. The road continues through the village of **Lefkogia**, which has domatia and tavernas, then passes the turn-off right for Myrthios (two km) and enters Plakias.

PLAKIAS Πλακιάς

Plakias, with a mountain backdrop and a fine beach, was once a tranquil retreat for adventurous backpackers. Nowadays it's yet another resort which has been discovered by the package-tour operators. However, if you visit out of high season you can still experience its undeniable charm.

Orientation & Information

Orientation is easy in this little seaside town. One street skirts the beach and another runs parallel, one block back. The bus stop is in the middle of the waterfront. Plakias doesn't have a bank. In summer there is a mobile post office on the waterfront. Candia Tours Travel Agency, near the bus stop, has currency exchange. Plakias' postcode is 73001 and the telephone code is 0832.

Between Plakias and Preveli Beach there are several secluded coves popular with freelance campers and nudists. These coves are within walking distance of Plakias and Lefkogia (see Around Plakias).

Places to Stay

The new *Camping Apollonia*, on the right of the main approach road to Plakias, is a superb site with a restaurant, minimarket, bar and swimming pool. Rates are 650 dr per person and 400 dr per tent.

There is a *YHA Hostel* (☎ 31 202) in Myrthios, the pleasant hilltop village three km above Plakias. There are also domatia in this village.

One of the cheapest places to stay in Plakias is the rooms of *Antonis Stefanakis* (no telephone). Singles/doubles/triples are 1500/3300/4000 dr with shared bathrooms and a communal kitchen. To reach the rooms walk 200 metres straight ahead from the bus stop and they're on the right. *Morpheas Rent Rooms* (☎ 31 420), next to the bus stop, are light, airy and attractively furnished. Prices are 3000/5700/7000 dr with private bathrooms. The *Hotel Livicon* (☎ 31 216), next door, has tidy doubles/triples for 5500/6500 dr with private bathrooms.

Pension Afrodite (☎ 31 266) is one of Plakias' nicest places to stay. Spotless doubles/triples are 6000/7200 dr with private bathrooms. From the bus stop walk back a few steps and take the first left. At the T-junction turn left and then take the first right and you will come to the pension on the left.

Secret Nest Rooms (☎ 31 235), above the taverna of the same name, are cosy well-kept rooms with rates of 5700/6000 dr for doubles/triples with private bathrooms; double/triple apartments are 6000/7000 dr. To reach the rooms walk west along the waterfront from the bus station, veer right at the bakery, continue straight ahead and they are on the left.

Places to Eat

The *Secret Nest Taverna* (see Places to Stay)

is a traditional restaurant set away from the razzmatazz of the waterfront. *Taverna Corali*, on the waterfront, west of the bus station, serves tasty food, with main meals for around 600 dr. *Taverna Mitos*, opposite Camping Apollonia, is also commendable and similarly priced.

Getting There & Away

There are eight buses a day from Rethymnon to Plakias (one hour, 610 dr). From Plakias there are two buses to Agia Galini (1½ hours, 700 dr) and one to Hora Sfakion. The Agia Galini buses leave at 11 am and 6.30 pm. If these times are not convenient then you can take a bus from Plakias to the Koxare junction (referred to as Bale on bus timetables) and from there take a bus to Agia Galini. There are seven buses from Plakias to the Koxare junction and five buses from the junction to Agia Galini.

At the time of writing the 2.15 pm bus from Rethymnon went to Plakias first and then backtracked to Myrthios; other buses went only to Plakias. Check the current schedule at the bus station in Rethymnon. Alternatively, you can take a Plakias bus and ask to be let off at the turn-off to Myrthios, from where it's a two-km walk to the village.

AROUND PLAKIAS
Moni Preveli & Preveli Beach

The well-maintained Moni Preveli (Μονή Πρέβελη), 14 km east of Plakias, stands in splendid isolation high above the Libyan Sea. Like most of Crete's monasteries, it played a significant role in the islanders' rebellion against Turkish rule. It became a centre of resistance during 1866, causing the Turks to set fire to it and destroy its crops. After the Battle of Crete, many British, Australian and New Zealand soldiers were secretly sheltered here by Abbot Agathangelos, before their evacuation to Egypt. In retaliation the Germans plundered the monastery. In the monastery's small **museum** there's a candelabra presented by grateful British soldiers after the war.

The River Megalopotamos flows through the Kourtaliotis Gorge and enters the Libyan

Sea at Preveli Beach (Παραλία Πρέβελης), below the monastery. If you walk back along the road from the monastery, you will see a path off to the right which leads to the beach. The beach is fringed by vibrant oleander bushes and palm trees and is popular with freelance campers.

Places to Stay & Eat The nearby village of Lefkogia has several domatia and tavernas, and is a pleasant, relatively unspoilt base from which to explore the area.

Getting There & Away At the time of writing there were two buses a day between Moni Preveli and Rethymnon via Plakias. Check with the bus station in Rethymnon to see if this bus is still running. Otherwise take a Rethymnon-Plakias bus and ask to be let off at the road leading to Preveli (signposted), between the villages of Assomates and Lefkogia. From here it is a six-km walk to the monastery.

Spili Σπήλι

Spili (SPEE-lee), nine km west of the Koxare junction on the main Rethymnon-Agia Galini road, is a gorgeous mountain town with cobbled streets, rustic houses and plane trees. If you are tempted to stay the night there is one very pleasant hotel: the C class *Green Hotel* (☎ 0832-22 225/056), where singles/doubles are 3500/4500 dr with private bathrooms. The hotel is signposted from the bus stop. There are also several domatia in the town.

AGIA GALINI Αγία Γαλήνη

Agia Galini (A-ya Ga-LEE-nee) is another picturesque little town which has gone down the tubes due to an overdose of tourism. Still, it does boast 340 days of sunshine a year, and some places to stay remain open year round. It's a convenient base from which to visit Phaestos and Agia Triada, and although the town beach is mediocre, there are boats to more alluring beaches.

Orientation & Information

The bus station is at the top of Eleftheriou

Venizelou. To reach the central square, which overlooks the harbour, walk downhill along this street. The post office is on Eleftheriou Venizelou, 30 metres downhill from the bus station, on the left. The OTE is on the central square. Agia Galini's postcode is 74056 and the telephone code is 0832. Take the second turn left after the post office and you will find the agent for the National Bank of Greece. Opening times are 9 am to 1 pm and 5 to 9 pm.

Places to Stay

Agias Galini Camping (☎ 91 386/239) is next to the beach, 2½ km east of the town; it is signposted from the Iraklion-Agia Galini road. The site is well shaded and has a restaurant, snack bar and minimarket.

Rent Rooms Pella (☎ 91 213/143) has spacious and clean rooms. Rates are 5500/6000 dr for doubles/triples with private bathrooms. The rooms are co-owned with the Restaurant Megalonissos which is at the bus stop – the rooms are close by.

The D class *Hotel Selina* (☎ 91 273) has clean, cosy rooms. Singles/doubles/triples are 2800/4600/5500 dr with private bathrooms including breakfast. The Selina stays open year round. Opposite is the *Hotel Ariston* (☎ 91 285), where tidy rooms cost 3500/4000/4500 dr with private bathrooms. The hotel has a communal balcony, fragrant with jasmine.

To reach these hotels walk downhill from the bus station, turn left after the post office, take the second turn right onto Vasileos Ioannis and the hotels are at the bottom of here, just before the steps which lead down to the harbour. *Hotel Korali* (☎ 91 458) has pleasant rooms which cost 4000/5000 dr for doubles/triples with private bathrooms. Turn left after the post office and you'll come to the hotel on the left.

Places to Eat

The *Restaurant Megalonissis*, next to the bus stop, is one of Agia Galini's cheapest restaurants. English breakfast is 500 dr, and main meals start at 550 dr. The *Acropol Taverna*, at the top of Vasileos Ioannis, is reasonably

priced, with main meals for less than 1000 dr. Opposite, the *Greenwich Village Restaurant* is another popular place with similar prices.

Getting There & Away

Bus From Iraklion there are eight buses a day to Agia Galini (2½ hours, 900 dr). Six buses a day leave Agia Galini for Rethymnon (800 dr) and Phaestos (40 minutes, 200 dr); and two a day depart for Plakias (850 dr). You can also get to Plakias by taking a Rethymnon-bound bus and changing at Koxare. To get to Matala take an Iraklion-bound bus and change at the town of Mires.

Taxi Boat In summer there are daily taxi boats from the harbour to the beaches of Agios Giorgios and Agios Pavlos. These beaches, which are west of Agia Galini, are difficult to get to by land. Both are less crowded and far superior to the Agia Galini Beach.

Hania Prefecture
Νομός Χανιών

RETHYMNON TO HANIA

Leaving Rethymnon prefecture, the National Highway runs close to the sea. The road crosses the Petras river and then skirts a long stretch of sandy beach where there is a scattering of tavernas and domatia. The hotel development intensifies as it enters the pleasant resort of **Georgioupolis**, where the Almyros river (whose source is Kournas Lake) flows into the sea.

From Georgioupolis, a road (signposted Kournas) leads south in six km to the mountain-fringed **Kournas Lake**, a habitat to a large number of birds. The English painter and writer of limericks, Edward Lear, likened it to the English Lake District, commenting that it was 'Very fine and Cumberlandish'. There are several tavernas on its shore, and pathways for strolls.

There is no bus to Kournas Lake but you can take a Rethymnon-Hania bus and get off

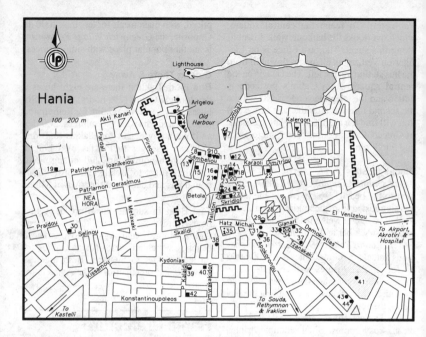

Hania

at Georgioupolis, from where some people hitch to the lake.

The National Highway continues to the alluring village of **Vrises** (VRIS-ess). The village is the junction for the road south to Hora Sfakion. There is one budget hotel and several domatia and tavernas. Vrises allegedly produces the best yoghurt in Crete. The road continues, bypassing the Drepano peninsula and, after passing the turn-off for the Souda ferry, enters Hania.

HANIA Χανιά

Hania (Han-YA, population 50,000), Crete's second city and former capital, has an Old Harbour with crumbling softly hued Venetian buildings which have an abundance of character and charm. Unfortunately this area also has an abundance of tourists.

Hania was first inhabited in Minoan times when it was called Kydonia; excavations of this ancient city began in 1960. It was a flourishing city-state during Hellenistic times and continued to prosper under the Romans. The city became Venetian at the beginning of the 13th century. The Venetians, who called the city La Canea, built a fortress to keep out marauding pirates and invading Turks. However, it did not prove very effective against the latter who took Hania in 1645 after a siege lasting only two months.

The Great Powers made Hania the island capital in 1898 and it remained so until 1971, when Iraklion became the capital.

Hania suffered severe bombardment during WW II. Notwithstanding, enough of the old town survived for Hania to be regarded by many as Crete's most beautiful city.

Orientation

Hania's bus station is on Kydonias, two blocks south-west of Plateia 1866, one of the city's principal squares. Halidon runs from Plateia 1866 to the Old Harbour. The fortress

PLACES TO STAY

4	Eugenia Rooms
8	George's Pension
9	Piraeus Hotel
15	Pension Amarylis
19	Pension Ideon
20	Pension Kydonia
22	Rooms to Rent Navarino
25	Rooms for Rent Petraki
26	Xenia Rooms & To Diporto Kafe Ouzeri
30	Villa Katerina
40	Hotel Samaria
42	Diana Rooms

PLACES TO EAT

5	Café Crete
6	Amfora Restaurant
10	Café-Eaterie Ekstra
13	Taverna Tamam
18	Kafe Ouzeri Rembetiko
23	Lukulos Restaurant

OTHER

1	Nautical Museum
2	Fagotto Jazz Bar
3	Carmela's Ceramic Shop
7	Mosque of the Janissaries
11	George Chaicalis Book Shop
12	Trekking Plan
14	Laundrette
16	Ideon Adron
17	UniKreta Travel Agency
21	Archaeological Museum
24	Orthodox Cathedral
27	Shoemakers
28	Food Market
29	Bus Stop for Souda
31	Plateia Venizelou
32	ANEK Office
33	National Bank of Greece
34	Post Office
35	EOT
36	Bus Stop for YHA Hostel
37	OTE
38	Plateia 1866
39	Bus Station
41	Public Garden
43	Olympic Airways Office
44	EOS

separates the Old Harbour (also called the Outer Harbour) from the crowded town beach in the quarter called Nea Hora. The Old Harbour waterfront is very lively in the evenings. Zambeliou, one block inland from here, is the old town's main thoroughfare. It's a narrow, winding street, lined with craft shops, budget hotels and tavernas. Hania's port of Souda is tucked into the base of the eastern side of the Akrotiri peninsula, six km south-east of the town.

If the town beach at Nea Hora is too crowded for your liking, there are better and marginally less crowded beaches just a few km west of Hania. You can reach these on foot or by local bus from Plateia 1866.

Information
Tourist Office For years Hania's EOT was in the Mosque of the Janissaries, at the Old Harbour. However, at the time of writing, the building was closed for renovation and the EOT (☎ 26 426) was dispensing information

from a 4th-floor office above the Agricultural Bank on Plateia 1866. The entrance to this building is around the corner from Plateia 1866 at Odos Kriari 40. Office opening times are Monday to Friday from 8 am to 3 pm.

Money The National Bank of Greece is on the corner of Tzanakaki and Gianari, opposite the food market. The Credit Bank, Halidon 106, has an automatic teller machine for Visa and American Express card holders.

Post & Telecommunications The central post office is at Tzanakaki 3, just up from the National Bank of Greece. It is open Monday to Friday from 8 am to 8 pm. Hania's postcode is 73100. The OTE is next door to the post office at Tzanakaki 5. Opening times are 6 am to 11 pm every day. Hania's telephone code is 0821.

Bookshop The George Chaicalis Book

Shop (☎ 26 408), at the bottom of Halidon, sells English-language newspapers, books and maps.

Laundry There is a self-service laundry at Ag Deka 18. A wash and dry costs 1000 dr.

Luggage Storage There is a luggage-storage facility at the bus station which charges 200 dr per piece.

Museums

Hania's **Archaeological Museum** (☎ 24 418), Halidon 21, is in the former Venetian Church of San Francisco, dating from the 16th century. The Turkish fountain in the grounds is a relic from the building's days as a mosque.

The museum houses a well-displayed collection of finds from western Crete dating from the Neolithic to the Roman era. Exhibits include statues, pottery, coins, jewellery and some impressive painted sarcophagi from the late-Minoan cemetery of Armeni (see the Rethymnon to Plakias & Agia Galini section). The museum is open Tuesday to Friday from 8.30 am to 3 pm. Admission is 400 dr.

The **Naval Museum** has an interesting collection of model ships, naval instruments and paintings and photographs. Opening times are Tuesday to Sunday from 10 am to 2 pm. Admission is 300 dr. The museum is at the Old Harbour.

Other Sites

The area to the east of the Old Harbour, just south of Tombazi, is the site of **Ancient Kydonia**; excavations are currently taking place here. The best preserved parts of the Venetian fortress' walls skirt the section of waterfront to the west of Tombazi. The **Lighthouse** which stands at the entrance to the harbour was built by the Venetians.

Whether or not you are self catering you should at least feast your eyes on Hania's turn-of-the-century covered **food market**; it makes all other food markets look like stalls at a church bazaar. It's a magnificent 19th-century cruciform building, selling meat,

fish, fresh and dried fruits, vegetables, cheeses, honey, olive oil, herbs and nuts.

Trekking

Trekking Plan (☎ 44 946 or 53 983), Karaoli Dimitriou 15, organises treks in the Lefki Ori. Prices for one-day treks start from 6000 dr (all inclusive) and five-day treks cost 65,000 dr (which includes meals, accommodation, transport and guide). The treks are in small groups and are led by experienced mountaineers.

Mountain Climbing

Hania's chapter of the EOS (☎ 24 647), Tzanakaki 90, is the place to go for information about serious climbing in the Lefki Ori and to make a reservation to stay at the mountain refuge at Kallergi, near the Samaria Gorge. The office is open Monday to Friday between 7 and 9 pm.

Sailing

Yachts (both bare boat and skippered) can be chartered from Cretan Sailing (☎ 40 863 or 28 117), Halidon 3.

Places to Stay – bottom end

The nearest camp site to Hania is *Hania Camping* (☎ 51 090), three km west of town on the beach. The cost is 600 dr for an adult and 430 dr for a tent. The site is pleasant and shaded and has a restaurant, bar and minimarket. Take a Kalamaki Beach bus (every 15 minutes) from the south-east corner of Plateia 1866 and ask to be let off at the camp site.

The *YHA Hostel* (☎ 53 565), Drakonianou 33, is a pleasant hostel charging 850 dr for a dorm bed. An IYHF card is not requested and there is no curfew. Reasonably priced breakfast and dinner is available. The hostel is some distance from the town centre; take the Agios Ionnis bus from the food market.

There are many pensions and domatia in and around Zambeliou. *Piraeus Hotel* (☎ 54 154), Zambeliou 14, has single/double/triple rooms for 2700/4200/6000 dr with shared bathrooms. If it's character you're after, you can't do better than *George's Pension* (☎ 43

542), Zambeliou 30, in a 600-year-old house with antique furniture; singles/doubles are 2000/3000 dr.

If you turn right near the bottom of Halidon onto Karaoli Dimitriou (the eastern extension of Zambeliou) and take the first right you will come to *Pension Kydonia* (☎ 57 179), Isodion 10. Rates are 2000/3000/4500 dr with shared bathrooms. If you continue along Karaoli Dimitriou you will come to the sign for *Rooms to Rent Navarino* (☎ 56 598), Sarpaki 67. The spotless rooms here cost 2300/3200 dr with shared bathrooms.

Back on Zambeliou, if you take the first turn left after George's Pension you will come to *Pension Amarylis* (☎ 56 797), Skufou 6. Doubles/triples are 5000/6000 dr with private bathrooms, and 4000/5000 dr with shared bathrooms.

There's a bevy of domatia on Betola. Rates at *Rooms for Rent Petraki* (☎ 43 562), at No 18, are 3500/5600 dr for singles/doubles with private bathrooms. On the other side of the road *Xenia Rooms* (☎ 53 430), at Betola 41, are tidy rooms costing 3000 dr a double with private bathrooms. The friendly, helpful owner has two more domatia on the same street, so he should be able to fix you up with something.

If you want to hop straight out of bed and onto an early morning bus bound for the Samaria Gorge, stay at the plant-festooned *Diana Rooms* (☎ 27 874), P Kalaidi 33, the nicest accommodation near the bus station. The rooms are light, airy and very clean. Singles/doubles/triples are 2000/3700/4500 dr with private bathrooms.

Eugenia Rooms (☎ 54 357 or 22 721) is a charming place tucked away in a little side street near the Naval Museum. Rates are 4000/5800/6800 dr with private bathrooms. Walk along the waterfront and turn left onto Angelou. Turn left opposite Fagotto Jazz Bar, and you'll see a sign to the rooms.

The Nea Hora area is easier for parking and has many accommodation bargains. The well-kept *Pension Ideon* (☎ 53 214), on Patriarchou Ioanikeiou, has rates of 2500/4000/5000 dr. *Villa Katerina* (☎ 25 183 or 58 940), Selinou 78, has brand-new, attractively furnished three and four-person apartments for 5000 dr, and doubles for 3000 dr. Coming from the town centre take the sixth turn right along Selinou to reach the villa.

Places to Stay – middle
The A class *Amfora Hotel* (☎ 42 998 or 43 132), in the same building as the restaurant of the same name, has lots of character. Singles/doubles are 8000/11,100 dr.

Places to Stay – top end
The B class *Hotel Samaria* (☎ 51 551/2/3/4/5; fax 51 525), on Kydonias near Plateia 1866, has a bar, café and roof garden. Rates are 11,300/16,100 dr.

Places to Eat
Taverna Tamam, Zambeliou 51, is excellent value. *Café-Eaterie Ekstra*, Zambeliou 8, serves carefully prepared Greek and international dishes for less than 1000 dr. The café is open all day. *To Diporto Kafe Ouzeri*, Skridlof 40, is one of the cheapest eating places in Hania, with main meals for around 700 dr. Despite its greasy-spoon ambience the food is good.

The *Amfora Restaurant*, near the Naval Museum, is one of the most reasonably priced of the waterfront restaurants. It serves mouth-watering meat and fish dishes; a full meal with wine will cost around 2000 dr. Mezedes are good value at *Kafe Ouzeri Rembetiko*, Agion Deka 5. Prices range from 700 dr for a small one to 1300 dr for a large one. If you fancy a change from Greek food *Lukulos Restaurant*, opposite the Archaeological Museum, is a popular Italian restaurant. Pizzas cost from 1000 to 1300 dr and spaghetti dishes are 650 to 800 dr. The authentic *Café Crete*, Kalergon 22, has live Cretan music and dancing every evening, and serves low-priced mezedes. For information about Hania's food market see the Things to See section.

Entertainment
The *Café Crete* (see Places to Eat) is the best place in Hania to hear live Cretan Music.

Ideon Adron, Halidon 26, is a music bar in a delightful garden. Hania's hippest disco, *Ariadne*, has a cool, sophisticated white-marble décor. Beer costs 900 dr and spirits and cocktails are 1500 dr. The disco is behind the Mosque of the Janissaries.

Fagotto Jazz Bar, on Angelou, is an atmospheric place with black and white photographs of jazz greats. Classical and jazz tapes are played, and sometimes there's live jazz in summer. Beer is 500 dr, spirits are 800 dr and cocktails are 900 dr.

In summer, performances of Cretan dances are held in Hania's fortress. They take place on a Thursday and begin at 9 pm.

Things to Buy

Good quality handmade leather goods are available from shoemakers on Skridlof, where shoes cost from 6000 dr. The old part of Hania has many craft shops. *Bizzarro*, at Zambeliou 19, sells exquisite handmade dolls in traditional Cretan dress. The prices start at 6500 dr. *Carmela's Ceramic Shop*, on Angelou, sells beautiful handcrafted jewellery and ceramics by young Cretan artists, who have revived ancient techniques and designs from both Greece and around the world.

Getting There & Away

Air From Hania's airport there are at least three flights a day to Athens (12,100 dr) and one flight a week (Tuesday) to Thessaloniki (19,500 dr). The Olympic Airways office (☎ 27 701/778) is at Tzanakaki 88. The airport is on the Akrotiri peninsula, 14 km from Hania.

Bus Buses depart from Hania's bus station for the following destinations:

Hora Sfakion – two hours, 1000 dr, four a day
Kastelli – one hour, 600 dr, 15 a day
Lakki – one hour, 330 dr, two a day
Moni Agias Triadas – 30 minutes, 300 dr, two a day
Omalos (for the Samaria Gorge) – one hour, 650 dr, four a day
Paleohora – two hours, 1000 dr, six a day
Rethymnon – one hour, 950 dr, every half hour
Skatoli – 2½ hours, 1200 dr, one a day

Sougia – two hours, 1000 dr, two a day (8.30 am and 1.30 pm)
Stavros – 30 minutes, 300 dr, four a day

Ferry A ferry leaves Hania's port of Souda at 7 pm every evening for Piraeus (12 hours, 3756 dr). Tickets can be bought at the ANEK office (☎ 23 636), opposite the food market. Another ferry leaves for Piraeus at 6.30 pm on Tuesday and Thursday. Minoan Lines (☎ 23 636), Halidon 8, sells tickets for this ferry. Souda's port police telephone no is ☎ 89 240.

Getting Around

To/From the Airport Olympic Airways buses leave from outside the Olympic Airways office 1½ hours before each flight.

Bus Local buses (blue) for the port of Souda and the YHA hostel leave from the food market; the ones for the beaches leave from Plateia 1866.

Car, Motorbike & Bicycle Hania's car-hire outlets include Avis (☎ 50 510), Tzanakaki 58; Budget (☎ 52 788), Kariaskaki 39; Eurocar (☎ 56 830 or 43 002), Tzanakaki 62B; and Maan (☎ 54 454 or 56 230), Arhontaki 10. Motorbike-hire outlets are mostly on Halidon. Mountain bicycles can be rented from Trekking Plan (☎ 44 946), Karaoli Dimitriou 15, for 1500 dr a day.

AKROTIRI PENINSULA

Χερσόνησος Ακρωτήρι

The Akrotiri (Ak-ro-TEE-re) peninsula, to the east of Hania, has several places of interest, as well as being the site of Hania's airport, port and a military base. At Souda, there is an immaculate **military cemetery**, where around 1500 British, Australian and New Zealand soldiers who lost their lives in the Battle of Crete are buried. To reach the cemetery take a Souda Port bus from outside the Hania food market.

If you haven't yet had your fill of Cretan monasteries there are three on the Akrotiri peninsula. The impressive 17th-century **Moni Agias Triadas** was founded by the

Venetian monks Jeremiah and Laurentio Giancarolo. The two were brothers, and converts to the Orthodox faith. The 16th-century **Moni Gourvernetou** (Our Lady of the Angels) is four km north of Moni Agias Triadas. This monastery has an ornate sculptured Venetian façade. Both of these monasteries are still inhabited by monks.

From Moni Gourvernetou a footpath leads in 30 minutes to the derelict **Moni Katholiko**, dedicated to St John the Hermit who lived in a cave nearby. The monastery is in the ravine of a dried-up riverbed. It is a short walk along the ravine to the sea.

There are two buses a day to Moni Agias Triadas from Hania bus station.

HANIA TO AGIA ROUMELI VIA THE SAMARIA GORGE

The road from Hania to the beginning of the Samaria (Sa-ma-RIA) Gorge is one of the most spectacular routes on the whole of Crete. It heads through orange groves to the village of **Fournes** where a left fork leads to **Meskla**. The main road continues to the village of **Lakki** (LA-kee), 24 km from Hania. This unspoilt village in the Lefki Ori mountains affords stunning views wherever you look. The village was a centre of resistance during the uprising against the Turks, and in WW II.

From Lakki a path leads down to the village of Meskla, which you will see nestling in the valley below. If you are based in Lakki and take this path, it is a five-km walk back to Fournes, from where you can catch a bus back to Lakki. The *Kri-Kri Restaurant & Rooms* (☎ 67 316), in Lakki, has comfortable singles/doubles for 2000/3000 dr with shared bathrooms. The restaurant serves good value meals. There are also domatia and tavernas in Meskla.

From Lakki the road continues to the Omalos plateau and Xyloskalo, where the Samaria Gorge begins. From Xyloskalo a five-km dirt track leads off to the left to the *Kallergi Refuge* (☎ 0821-54 560), from where several peaks of the Lefki Ori range can be climbed. To make reservations and for more information about the climbs, contact the EOS (☎ 24 647) in Hania.

Samaria Gorge Φαράγγι Σαμαριάς

It's a wonder the stones and rocks underfoot haven't worn away completely, given the number of people who trample through the Samaria Gorge. An early start helps to a certain extent to avoid the crowds, but during July and August even the early bus from Hania to the top of the gorge can be packed. However, despite the crowds a trek through this stupendous gorge is still indubitably worthwhile. The gorge is open between May and October; it is dangerous to enter outside these months as it is prone to flash floods.

At 18 km, the Samaria Gorge is the longest in Europe. It begins below the Omalos plateau and was formed by a river which flows between the Lefki Ori and Mt Volikas. Its width varies from 150 metres to three metres and its vertical walls reach 500 metres at their highest points. The gorge is the habitat of an inordinate number of wild flowers which are at their best in April (when the gorge isn't open) and May. Along with the islet of Kri-Kri, off the coast of Agios Nikolaos, the gorge is the last habitat of Crete's wild goat, the kri-kri – you're unlikely to spot one of these as they keep well away from trekkers. The gorge was made a national park in 1962 to save the kri-kri from extinction. Spending the night in the gorge is prohibited.

The trek from Xyloskalo to Agia Roumeli takes around six hours. Early on in the season it's sometimes necessary to wade through the stream which flows through the gorge, resulting in wet feet. Later, when the stream is sparse, it's possible to use rocks as stepping stones.

The gorge is reached by descending the steep Xyloskalo (wooden staircase). You can enter between 6 am and 3 pm; there is an admission charge of 1000 dr. The first section of the gorge is wide and rather like walking through a valley. At about six km you reach the abandoned village of Samaria where there are picnic tables. The inhabitants of this village were relocated when the gorge became a national park. After the village, the gorge narrows and becomes more dramatic. At 12 km the rock cliffs at either side are only three metres apart; this is the so-called **Iron Gates**, the narrowest part of the gorge.

The gorge ends just north of the almost-abandoned village of Old Agia Roumeli. From here the path continues to the small, messy and crowded resort of Agia Roumeli, with a much-appreciated pebble beach and sparkling sea.

What to Bring The bed of the gorge is stony so sensible footwear is essential (trainers are fine). The going is downhill all the way, but even so the trek is strenuous because of the distance covered and the strain of walking on stones and rocks. Wear a hat because part of the gorge is exposed.

There's no need to take water, for while it's risky to drink water from the stream which runs through the gorge, there are plenty of springs along the way which spurt delicious cool water straight from the rock. There is nowhere to purchase food in the gorge, so take some along.

Getting There & Away There are excursions to the Samaria Gorge from every sizeable town and resort on Crete. Most travel agents have two excursions: 'Samaria Gorge Long Way' and 'Samaria Gorge Easy Way'. The first comprises the regular trek from the Omalos plateau to Agia Roumeli. On the second one you are transported to Agia Roumeli, from where you walk as far as the Iron Gates. Some intrepid trekkers do the gorge in reverse, starting at Agia Roumeli, and ending at the Omalos plateau.

Obviously it's cheaper to trek the Samaria Gorge under your own steam. Hania is set the most convenient town from which to set off. Buses leave Hania's bus station for Xyloskalo at 6.15, 7.30 and 8.30 am and 1.30 pm; the journey takes one hour. If you intend to stay on the south coast ask for a one-way ticket (650 dr), otherwise you'll automatically be sold a return. Buses also travel from Rethymnon to Xyloskalo, leaving at 6.15 and 7 am (1600 dr); from Kastelli, leaving at

5, 6 and 7 am (1300 dr); and from Georgi-oupolis, leaving at 6.30 and 7.20 am and 3.30 pm (1000 dr).

AGIA ROUMELI   Αγία Ρούμελη
Agia Roumeli (A-ya Roo-MEL-ee) has little going for it, but if you have just trekked through the Samaria Gorge and are too exhausted to face a journey, there is one hotel, the posh B class *Hotel Agia Roumeli* (☎ 91 293), where singles/doubles are 5000/7000 dr with private bathrooms. There are also a number of domatia where you'll pay around 3500 dr for a double.

Getting There & Away
Five boats a day leave Agia Roumeli for Hora Sfakion (one hour, 800 dr) via Loutro. Sometimes the last boat does not call at Loutro, so check this, if this is where you wish to go. The arrival of the boat at Hora Sfakion is synchronised with the bus service to Hania. There are also daily boats from Agia Roumeli to Paleohora (two hours, 1200 dr) via Sougia (one hour, 690 dr).

LOUTRO   Λουτρό
The small but rapidly expanding fishing village of Loutro (Loo-TRO) lies between Agia Roumeli and Hora Sfakion. Loutro doesn't have a beach but there are rocks from where you can swim. There is one pension, the very comfortable *Porto Loutro* (☎ 0825-91 227), where doubles with private bathrooms are 6500 dr; there are plenty of domatia and tavernas.

From Loutro an extremely steep path leads up to the village of **Anopolis**, where there are also domatia. Alternatively, you can save yourself the walk by taking the Hania-Skatoli bus which calls in at Anopolis en route. The bus leaves Hania at 2 pm and returns the following morning, calling in at Anopolis at 7.30 am.

From Loutro it's a moderate 2½-hour walk along a coastal path to Hora Sfakion. On the way you will pass the celebrated **Sweet Water Beach**, named after fresh-water springs which seep from the rocks. Freelance campers spend months at a time here; even if you don't feel inclined to join them you won't be able to resist a swim in the translucent sea. Loutro is on the Hora Sfakion-Paleohora boat route.

HORA SFAKION Χώρα Σφακίων

Hora Sfakion (Sfa-KI-on) is the small coastal port where the hordes of walkers from the Samaria Gorge spill off the boat and onto the bus. As such, in high season it can seem like Picadilly Circus at rush hour. Hora Sfakion played a prominent role during WW II, as most of the Allied troops were evacuated by sea from the town after the Battle of Crete.

Orientation & Information

The ferry quay is at the west side of the harbour. From here walk to the waterfront, turn right and then left at the end to reach the square where the buses turn around. The post office is at the western end of the narrow street which runs parallel to the waterfront, one block inland.

Hora Sfakion's postcode is 73001. The OTE is opposite the post office; its telephone code is 0825. There is no EOT or tourist police; the regular police are on the square where the buses turn around.

There is a small pebble beach at the eastern end of the waterfront.

Places to Stay & Eat

The nicest accommodation in Hora Sfakion is the D Class *Hotel Stavros* (☎ 91 220), opposite the western end of the inland street. The rooms are spotless and the English-speaking owners are friendly and helpful. The single/double rooms are priced at 3500/4500 dr with private bathrooms. There are domatia and more hotels on the waterfront and inland street.

Most of the hotels have restaurants, but they tend to be overpriced; check the prices before ordering. The café belonging to the Hotel Stavros is a pleasant place for a drink or snack. For a tasty meal try the restaurant at the Hotel Samaria, on the waterfront. A full meal with Amstel will set you back about 1500 dr.

Getting There & Away

Bus There are five buses a day from Hora Sfakion to Hania (two hours 1000 dr); two to Plakias (three hours, 650 dr) via Frangokastello, which leave at 11.30 am and 5.30 pm; one to Rethymnon (four hours, 1000 dr) which leaves at 7.30 pm; and one to Kastelli (1300 dr) which leaves at 5 pm.

Boat In summer there are daily boats from Hora Sfakion to Paleohora (three hours, 1800 dr) via Loutro, Agia Roumeli and Sougia. On Monday, Wednesday, Thursday, Saturday and Sunday the boat leaves at 4.30 pm and on Tuesday and Friday it leaves at 7 pm. On Tuesday and Friday there is a boat to Gavdos island. Check this schedule with the EOT, Hania port police or Interkreta Travel Agency (☎ 41 393/050) in Paleohora, as it's liable to change from year to year. In addition there are four boats a day to Agia Roumeli (one hour, 800 dr) via Loutro.

AROUND HORA SFAKION

The road from Vrises to Hora Sfakion cuts through the heart of the Sfakia region, in the eastern Lefki Ori. The inhabitants of this region have long had a reputation for fearlessness and independence, characteristics they retain to this day. One of Crete's most celebrated heroes, Ioannis Daskalogiannis, was a Sfakiot. In 1770 Daskalogiannis lead the first Cretan insurrection against Ottoman rule. When help promised by Russia failed to materialise, he gave himself up to the Turks to save his followers. As punishment the Turks skinned him alive in Iraklion. Eye witnesses related that Daskalogiannis suffered this excruciating torture in dignified silence.

The Turks never succeeded in controlling the Sfakiots, and some of the fiercest fighting between Turks and mountain rebels took place in this rugged mountainous region. Cretans are regarded by other Greeks as being immensely proud and this characteristic reaches its apogee in the Sfakiot. Many folk tales and *rizitika* (local folk songs) were written by the Sfakiots, expressing their resistance to the Turks and struggle for self determination. These songs are still sung in the region today; one of the most popular is the *Song of Daskalogiannis*.

The village of **Imbros**, 23 km from Vrises, is at the head of the 10-km-long Imbros Gorge. This gorge is shorter than the Samaria Gorge but equal in beauty, and far less visited. If you would like to walk through it take any bus bound for Hora Sfakion from the north coast and get off at Imbros. Walk out of the village towards Hora Sfakion and a path to the left leads down to the gorge. The gorge path ends at the village of **Komitades**, from where it is an easy walk by road to Hora Sfakion. You can of course do the trek in reverse, beginning at Komitades. The Happy Walker does an organised trek through this gorge (see Rethymnon Organised Tours).

Frangokastello Φραγγοκάστελλο

Frangokastello (Frang-o-KAS-tel-o) is a magnificent fortress, 15 km east of Hora Sfakion. It was built by the Venetians in 1371 as a defence against pirates and rebel Sfakiots who seem to have resented the Venetian occupation as much as they did the Turkish. It was here in 1770 that Ioannis Daskalogiannis surrendered to the Turks. In 1828 many Cretan rebels, led by Hadzi Michali Daliani, were killed here by the Turks. Legend has it that at dawn on 17 May (the date of the massacre) the ghosts of Hadzi Michali Daliani and his followers can be seen riding along the beach. The castle overlooks a gently shelving sandy beach. Domatia and tavernas are springing up rapidly here, but it's still a relatively unspoilt little spot.

Getting There & Away There is one bus a day to Skatoli from Hania (2½ hours, 1200 dr), via Anopolis and Frangokastello. It leaves Hania at 2 pm and Skaloti at 7 am. There are two buses a day to Plakias from Hora Sfakion (650 dr) via Frangokastello; they leave at 11.30 am and 5.30 pm.

PALEOHORA Παλαιοχώρα

Paleohora (Pa-lee-o-HO-ra) was discovered by hippies back in the 1960s and from that day on its days as a tranquil fishing village were numbered. However, it remains a relaxing resort, favoured not only by backpackers, but families also, many with young children.

The little town lies on a peninsula, with a sandy beach exposed to the wind on one side and a sheltered rocky beach on the other. In the evenings the main street is closed to traffic and the tavernas move into the road, which becomes a playground for hordes of multinational children. The most picturesque part of Paleohora is the narrow streets huddled around the castle.

The ruins of the 13th-century Venetian castle are worth clambering up to for the splendid sea and mountain views. From Paleohora, a six-hour walk along a highly scenic coastal path leads to the small resort of **Sougia**, passing the ancient site of **Lissos** (five hours from Paleohora), which was a sanctuary to Asklepios.

Orientation

Paleohora's main street, El Venizelou, runs north to south. The bus stop is opposite the Lissos Hotel. Walking south along El Venizelou from the bus stop, several streets lead off left to the pebble beach. Boats leave from the old harbour at the northern end of this beach. At the southern end of El Venezelou, Odos Kontekaki, a turn-off right, leads to the gorgeous sandy beach, which is shaded by pine trees.

Information

The Municipal Tourist Office is in the town hall on El Venizelou. Opening times are 9 am to 2 pm and 5 to 9 pm daily.

The post office is on the road which skirts the sandy beach. The OTE is on the west side of El Venizelou, just north of Kontekaki. Paleohora's postcode is 73001 and the telephone code is 0823. The National Bank of Greece is on El Venizelou, north of the OTE.

Places to Stay – bottom end

Camping Paleohora (☎ 41 130/120) is 1½ km north-east of the town, near the pebble beach. The camp site has a taverna but no minimarket.

Rooms to Rent Anonymous, set in a dishevelled but charming garden and owned by the amiable English-speaking Manolis, is a terrific place for backpackers. The clean, simply furnished single/double/triple rooms cost 1500/2500/3200 dr with shared bathrooms. When you arrive, Anonymous, a large brown dog, will probably come to greet you. Walk up El Venizelou from the bus stop, turn right at the town hall, follow the road as it veers right, and the rooms are on the left.

The D class *Lissos Hotel* (☎ 41 266/122), El Venizelou 12, opposite the bus stop, also has a friendly English-speaking owner called Manolis. The hotel's ageing, but spotless doubles/triples are 3400/4800 dr with shared bathrooms, and 3700/4800 dr with private bathrooms; well-equipped studios are 5500/7500 dr. The hotel has a tranquil garden.

Marina Devoga Rooms (☎ 41 564), on Kontekaki, is another bargain. Rates are 3000/5000 dr for doubles/triples with shared bathrooms. *Pension Spamandos* (☎ 41 197), just south of the old harbour, has attractive rooms with rates of 3000/4000 dr for singles/doubles with shared bathrooms; doubles with private bathrooms are 5500 dr.

Oriental Bay Rooms (☎ 41 076), at the northern end of the pebble beach (on the way to the camp site), has immaculate singles/doubles for 3000/4000 dr with private bathrooms. The *Poseidon Pension* (☎ 41 374/115), next to the post office, has cosy rooms for 4000/4500 dr with private bathrooms. The co-owned *Poseidon Apartments* cost 5000/6500 dr for doubles/triples.

The *Hotel Aghas* (☎ 41 525/155), behind the outdoor cinema, has spacious, attractive double/triple rooms for 6500/7500 dr with private bathrooms. The C class *Polydoros Hotel* (☎ 41 068), on Kontekaki, has pleasant, but rather small single/double rooms for 5600/7900 dr with private bathrooms.

Places to Stay – middle

Paleohora's newest and poshest hotel is the C class *Pal Beach Hotel* (☎ 41 512/556), overlooking the sandy beach. The modern single/double rooms cost 7000/11,000 dr.

Places to Eat

The very popular *Dionysos Taverna*, on El Venizelou, serves superb low-priced food. The *Galaxy Restaurant*, next to the post office, is also good value, with main meals from 700 to 1000 dr. *Restaurant Small Garden*, behind the OTE, is a nice unpretentious little place with similar prices to the Galaxy. The *Pelican Taverna* has a prime position overlooking the old harbour. Their moussaka, at 600 dr, is commendable. *To Kati Allo*, on El Venizelou, is one of Paleohora's best psistarias. Pork souvlaki is 800 dr and lamb chops are 850 dr. *Pizzeria Niki*, on Kontekaki, serves very tasty, reasonably priced pizzas, and pasta dishes.

Entertainment

Most visitors to Paleohora spend at least one evening at the well-signposted outdoor cinema. Another option for a night out is the *Paleohora Disco*, next to the camp site.

Getting There & Away

Bus There are six buses a day to Hania from Paleohora (two hours, 1000 dr). At the time of writing buses left Paleohora at 7.30 am, noon, 1.30, 3.30, 5 and 7.30 pm.

Boat In summer there are daily boats from Paleohora to Hora Sfakion (three hours, 1800 dr) via Sougia (one hour, 690 dr), Agia Roumeli (two hours, 1200 dr) and Loutro (2½ hours). The boat leaves Paleohora at 8.30 am on Monday, Wednesday, Thursday, Saturday and Sunday and leaves Hora Sfakion for Paleohora at 4.30 pm. On Tuesday and Friday it leaves Paleohora at 8 am and returns from Hora Sfakion at 7 pm. On these days the boat also goes to the island of Gavdos (1900 dr). Boats leave every day at 10 am for Elafonissi (680 dr) and return at 4 pm. Tickets for all of these boats can be bought at Interkreta Travel Agency (☎ 41 393/050), Kontekaki 4.

Getting Around

Car & Motorbike Cars and Motorbikes can be rented from an outlet next door to Interkreta Travel.

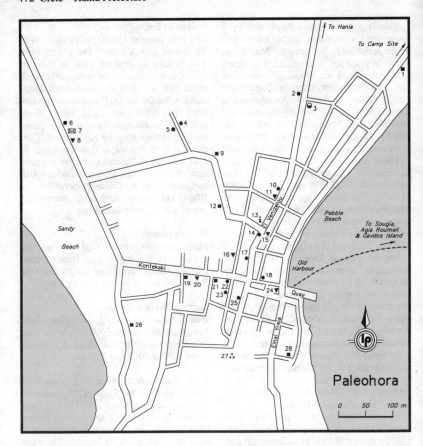

Paleohora

To Hania

To Camp Site

Pebble Beach

To Sougia,
Agia Roumeli
& Gavdos Island

Old Harbour

Quay

Sandy Beach

Kontekaki

El Venizelou

Einai Yreia

0   50   100 m

AROUND PALEOHORA

Sougia Σούγια

If Paleohora is too busy for you, you may prefer quieter Sougia, the next resort east along the coast. Sougia has a long pebble beach, domatia and tavernas. There is a coastal path to Paleohora (see the Paleohora section). There are two buses a day from Hania to Sougia (2½ hours, 1000 dr) at 8.30 am and 1.30 pm. Buses from Sougia to Hania leave at 7 am and 3.30 pm. Sougia is on the Paleohora-Hora Sfakion boat route.

Gavdos Island Νήσος Γαύδος

Gavdos island (GAV-dos, population 50), in the Libyan Sea, 65 km from Paleohora, is the most southerly place in Europe. The island has three small villages and pleasant beaches. There is a post office, OTE, one police officer and one doctor. Gavdos is an excellent choice for those yearning isolation and peace. The best source of information about the island is Interkreta Travel in Paleohora.

There are no hotels but several of the locals let rooms, and there are tavernas. There is no official camp site but camping freelance may be tolerated. Fishermen from

■ PLACES TO STAY

1   Oriental Bay Rooms
2   Lissos Hotel
5   Hotel Aghas
6   Poseidon Pension
9   Poseidon Apartments
12 Rooms to Rent Anonymous
19 Marina Devoga Rooms
21 Polydoros Hotel
26 Pal Beach Hotel
28 Pension Spamandos

▼ PLACES TO EAT

8   Galaxy Restaurant
11 Dionysos Taverna
15 To Kati Allo Psistaria
16 Restaurant Small Garden
20 Pizzeria Niki
24 Pelican Taverna

OTHER

3   Bus Stop
4   Outdoor Cinema
7   Post Office
10 National Bank of Greece
13 Town Hall & Municipal Tourist Office
14 Periptera (for foreign newspapers)
17 OTE
18 Police Station
22 Interkreta Travel Agency
23 Car & Motorcycle Rental
25 Port Police
27 Castle Ruins

Gavdos take tourists to the remote, uninhabited island of Gavdopoula.

Getting There & Away There are boats twice a week from Paleohora, Sougia and Hora Sfakion to Gavdos.

Elafonissi Ελαφονήσι
Elafonissi, at the southern extremity of Crete's west coast, is a seemingly endless beach of fine sand overlooked by Elafonissi islet, where there are more beaches. The water is so shallow you can wade out to the islet. Many freelance campers come to these beaches and there are also excursions from Hania. There is no accommodation or tavernas, but there are three cantinas in summer. The closest domatia are near Moni Hrisoskalitissas.

Moni Hrisoskalitissas
Μονή Χρυσοσκαλίτισσας
Moni Hrisoskalitissas (Mo-NEE Hris-o-ka-LEE-tiss-as), five km north of Elafonissi, is inhabited by two nuns. It's a very beautiful monastery perched on a rock, with splendid views of the coast. Hrisoskalitissas means 'Golden Staircase' and the name derives from a legend which claims that one of the 90 steps leading up to the monastery is made of gold. There are tavernas and domatia in the vicinity.

Getting There & Away In summer there is one bus a day from Kastelli to Elafonissi (800 dr) via Hrisoskalitissas. It leaves Kastelli at 8.30 am and returns at 4 pm. In summer there are boats every day from Paleohora (650 dr) to Elafonissi. They leave Paleohora at 10 am and return at 4 pm.

KASTELLI Καστέλλι
If you find yourself in the north-coast town of Kastelli (Kas-TEL-ee, population 3000), you've probably arrived by ferry from the Peloponnese or Kythera. While there is nothing remarkable about Kastelli, it's a pleasant and relaxed seaside town in which to while away a few days. The town also serves as a good base from which to explore Crete's west coast. Kastelli's beach hardly sparks off a string of superlatives, but it's adequate enough to rest up on if you've stumbled into town after a long ferry journey.

Orientation & Information
The port is three km west of town. In summer a bus meets the boat, otherwise a taxi costs 700 dr. The bus station in Kastelli is to the left of the main through road as you come from the port. To reach the town centre, with your back to the bus station office, turn left

and then first left onto Odos Amerikas. Take the second right onto Odos Skalidi to reach the central square.

The post office is on the north side of the main through road, beyond the bus station. The OTE is further along this road on the right. Kastelli's postcode is 73400 and the telephone code is 0822. The National Bank of Greece is at the far end of Skalidi, on the left walking from the central square. Kastelli has no EOT or tourist police. To reach the waterfront, walk north from the central square.

Places to Stay

Kastelli's *Camping Kissamos* (☎ 23 444/322) is a super site with a taverna, bar and pool. It also has reasonably priced domatia and apartments. The site is 150 metres west of the central square and well signposted.

One of the best deals in Kastelli is *Koutsounakis Rooms* (☎ 23 416), on the central square. The spotless, comfortable singles/doubles are 3000/4200 dr with private bathrooms. Opposite, the C class *Hotel Casteli* (☎ 22 140) has tidy rooms for 3000/5000 dr. *Argo Rooms for Rent* (☎ 23 563/322), Plateia Telonio, are spacious, tastefully furnished rooms for 4000/6000 dr with private bathrooms. From the central square, walk down to the seafront, turn left, and you will come to the rooms on the left. The C class *Hotel Kissamos* (☎ 22 086), on the north side of the main through road (west of the bus station) has nicely furnished, light and airy rooms for 4000/5000 dr with private bathrooms.

Places to Eat

The *Angelica Restaurant* is one of Kastelli's best restaurants. Vegetarian moussaka is 600 dr and lamb is 750 dr. Walk towards the sea from the central square and turn left one block before the waterfront; walk to the end of this road and you will see the restaurant ahead of you. The restaurant adjoining the *Hotel Castelli* serves reasonably priced Greek staples.

Getting There & Away

Bus From Kastelli there are 17 buses a day to Hania (600 dr). Buses leave for Omalos (for the Samaria Gorge, 650 dr) at 5, 6 and 7 am; for Elafonissi (800 dr) via Moni Hrisoskalitissas at 8.30 am; and for Falassarna (350 dr) at 9.30 and 10 am, and 4.30 pm.

Ferry The F/B *Ionian* is the only ferry which calls at Kastelli. In summer at the time of writing the ferry left Kastelli at 8 am on Tuesday and Friday bound for Piraeus via the islands of Antikythera and Kythera, and Gythio, Neapoli and Monemvassia in the Peloponnese. The ferry is subject to delays and the schedule changes from year to year so check with the EOT in Hania or at E Xirouchakis Travel Agency (☎ 22 655) on the central square in Kastelli, from where you can buy a ticket.

Getting Around

Car & Motorbike Motorbikes can be hired from *Rent From Antony* (☎ 22 909). Walk eastwards along the main through road, take the second turn left after the post office and the outlet is on the right. There are several car-hire outlets along Skalidi.

AROUND KASTELLI

Falassarna Φαλασάρνα

Falassarna (Fal-AR-sar-na), 16 km west of Kastelli, was a Cretan city-state in the 4th century BC. There are scant remains, and most people head to Falassarna for its superb beach, which is long and sandy and interspersed with boulders. There are several domatia at the beach. In summer there are three buses a day from Kastelli to Falassarna (350 dr).

Gramvoussa Peninsula

Χερσόνησος Γραμβουσών

North of Falassarna is the wild and remote Gramvoussa (Gram-VOO-sa) peninsula. There is a wide track, which eventually degenerates into a path, along its eastern side to the sandy beach of **Tigani**, on the west side of the peninsula's narrow tip. The beach is overlooked by the two islets of Agria (Wild) and Imeri (Tame) Gramvoussa. There is a ruined castle on Agria Gramvoussa. To reach the track take a west-bound bus from Kastelli and ask to be let off at the turn- off to the right for the village of Kalyviani (five km from Kastelli). Kalyviani is a two-km walk from the main road. Once at the village walk to the far end of the main street from where the path begins. The shadeless walk takes around three hours – wear a hat and take plenty of water.

Ennia Horia (Nine Villages) Εννιά Χωριά Ennia Horia is the name given to the mountainous region south of Kastelli, which is renowned for its chestnut trees. If you have your own transport you can drive through the region en route to Moni Hrisoskalitissas and Elafonissi, or with a little back tracking to Paleohora. Alternatively, you can take a circular route returning via the coast road. Whichever route you choose, you'll be rewarded with stunning vistas. In the beautiful village of **Elos**, a **Chestnut Festival** takes place on the third Sunday of October, when sweets made from chestnuts are eaten. The road to the region heads inland five km east of Kastelli.

Ancient Polirrinia

The ruins of the ancient city of Polirrinia (Πολυρρήνια, Po-lee-ren-EE-a) lie seven km inland from Kastelli, on a hill above the village of Polirrinia. The city was founded by the Dorians and was continuously inhabited until Venetian times. There are remains of city walls, and an aqueduct built by Hadrian. It's a scenic walk from Kastelli to Polirrinia, otherwise there is a very infrequent bus service – enquire about the current schedule at Kastelli's bus station. To reach the Polirrinia road, walk east along Kastelli's main through road, and look for the sign pointing right about 500 metres east of the bus station. The village of Polirrinia has a taverna but no accommodation.

Dodecanese Δωδεκάνησα

Strung along the coast of western Turkey, the Dodecanese (Do-de-KA-nis-a) archipelago is much closer to Asia Minor than to mainland Greece. Because of their strategic and vulnerable position these islands have been subjected to an even greater catalogue of invasions and occupations than the rest of Greece.

The name means 'Twelve Islands', but a glance at the map will show you that the group consists of quite a few more. The name originated in 1908 when 12 of the islands united against the newly formed Young Turk-led Ottoman Parliament which had taken away the liberties that the Dodecanese had been granted under the sultans. The 12 were: Rhodes, Kos, Kalymnos, Karpathos, Patmos, Tilos, Symi, Leros, Astypalea, Nisyros, Kassos and Halki.

The Dodecanese has had a more varied history than any other island group, but historic endowments are not the islands' only attractions. For those who like beaches and bars, there are the highly developed resorts of Rhodes and Kos. In contrast, the untouristy islands of Lipsi and Tilos have equally appealing beaches, without the crowds. For those who like to get off the beaten track and experience traditional island life, there are the far-flung islands of Agathonisi, Kassos and Kastellorizo. For those who like extraordinary landscapes, there is the volcanic island of Nisyros. Another attraction of the Dodecanese is its duty-free status, which means you can buy booze at a lower price than almost anywhere else in Europe.

History

The Dodecanese islands have been inhabited since pre-Minoan times; by the Archaic period Rhodes and Kos had emerged as the dominant islands of the group. Even when the islands were part of the Delian League, their distance from Athens gave them considerable autonomy and they were, for the most part, free to prosper unencumbered by

subjugation to imperial Athens. Following Alexander the Great's death, Ptolemy I of Egypt ruled the Dodecanese.

The Dodecanese islanders were the first Greeks to be converted to Christianity through the tireless efforts of St Paul, who made two journeys to the archipelago, and St John, who was banished to Patmos, where he received his revelation.

The early years of Byzantium were fortuitous for the islands, but by the 7th century AD they were subject to plundering by a string of invaders. By the early 14th century it was the turn of the crusaders – the Knights of St John of Jerusalem, or Knights Hospitallers. The Knights went on to become rulers of almost the whole of the Dodecanese, building mighty fortifications on every island, but not mighty enough to keep out the Turks in 1522.

The Turks were booted out by the Italians in 1912 during a tussle over possession of Libya. In contrast to the lax Turkish rule the Fascist Italian rulers were intent upon Italianising the islands. Inspired by Mussolini's grandiose vision of a vast Italian Mediterranean Empire, they made Italian the official language and prohibited the practice of Orthodoxy. True to the dictates of Fascism they constructed grandiose public buildings and monuments, in a style that was the

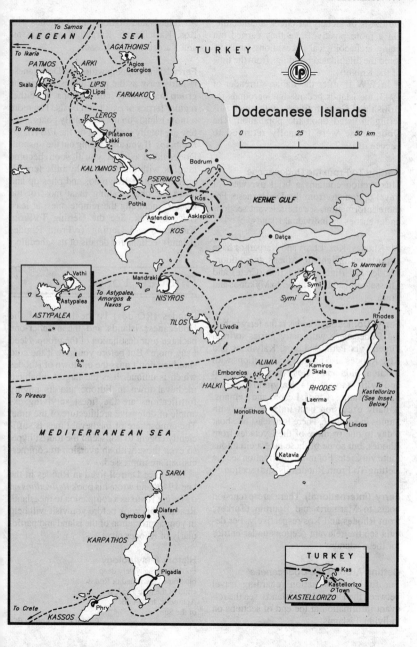

Dodecanese Islands

antithesis of archetypal Greek architecture. On a more positive note they carried out many archaeological excavations, and restored the dilapidated buildings from the time of the Knights.

In WW II, after the Italian surrender of 1943, the islands became battlegrounds for British and German forces, with much suffering inflicted upon the population. The Dodecanese were formally returned to Greece in 1947.

Getting To/From the Dodecanese

This section contains a brief overview of travel options to/from the Dodecanese. For more information, see the relevant sections under entries on individual islands.

Air Rhodes, Kos, Leros and Karpathos have airports with flights to Athens. In addition, Rhodes has flights to Iraklion (Crete) and Thessaloniki and in summer to Mykonos and Thira.

Ferry (Domestic) Rhodes is the ferry hub of the Dodecanese with daily ferries to/from Piraeus via Patmos, Leros, Kalymnos and Kos. Rhodes also has ferry connections with Iraklion, Sitia and Agios Nikolaos on Crete and with Kavala via Kalymnos, Leros, Patmos, Samos, Chios, Lesbos and Lemnos. A daily excursion boat links Patmos with Samos in summer. There is at least one boat a day to one or more of the Cyclades from Rhodes, but some of these take a circuitous route via Crete. For more information see the Getting To/From Rhodes (Island) section.

Ferry (International) There are excursion boats to Marmaris and Bodrum (Turkey) from Rhodes and Kos respectively. For details see the relevant sections under entries for these islands.

Getting Around the Dodecanese

For further information regarding travel between the Dodecanese islands, see the relevant information at the end of sections on individual islands.

Air Inter-island flights connect Rhodes with Kos, Kastellorizo, Karpathos and Kassos, and Karpathos with Kassos.

Ferry Island hopping within the Dodecanese is fairly easy as the principal islands in the group have daily connections by either regular ferries or excursion boats. The more remote islands do not have daily boats and a few are totally dependent on the F/B *Nissos Kalimnos*. If you are seeking out the unspoilt Dodecanese islands you'll soon become familiar with this trustworthy little ferry. It operates out of Kalymnos and plies up and down the chain calling in at most of the islands, including the remote ones, at least twice a week. See the Getting To/From Kalymnos and Getting To/From Rhodes (Island) sections for details of its schedule.

Rhodes Ρόδος

Rhodes (RO-dos) is the largest of the Dodecanese islands and the number-one package-tour destination of the group. Need I say more? But before you give it the cold shoulder, don't miss the old town of Rhodes which is unique. It is the largest inhabited medieval town in Europe and its mighty fortifications are the finest surviving example of defensive architecture of the time. The atmosphere of medieval times is sufficiently cogent to transcend the tourist hype, so even those with an aversion to commercialism are impressed.

Lawrence Durrell lived in Rhodes in the late 1940s and wrote his book *Reflections on a Marine Venus* as a companion to the island. Reading this book before you visit will help in your appreciation of the island and particularly of Rhodes city.

History & Mythology

Forth from the watery deep
blossomed the island of Rodos,
child of the love goddess
Aphrodite, to be bride
of the Sun.

Pindar (5th Century BC)

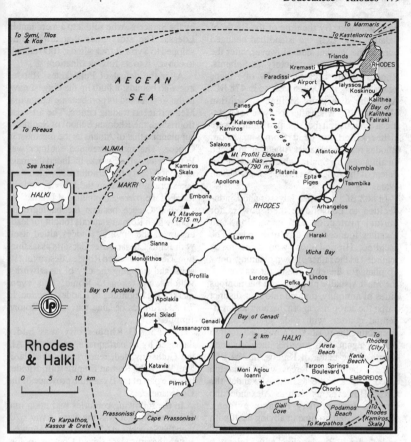

A few stone tools found in a cave in southern Rhodes are the only evidence that Rhodes was inhabited during Neolithic times. As elsewhere in Greece, the island's early history is interwoven with mythology. According to myth, the sun god Helios chose Rhodes as his bride and bestowed upon her light, warmth and vegetation. Their son, Kerkafos, had three sons, Kamiros, Ialyssos and Lindos, who divided the island into three parts and founded the cities that were named after them.

Although the Minoans and Mycenaeans had outposts on Rhodes, it was not until the arrival of the Dorians in 1100 BC that Rhodes began to exert its power and influence. The Dorians settled in the three cities of Kamiros, Ialyssos and Lindos and made each an autonomous state. They took advantage of trade routes to the East which had been established during Minoan and Mycenaean times, and soon the island was flourishing as an important centre of commerce in the Aegean. Largely through expediency and connivance, Rhodes continued to prosper until Roman times.

Rhodes was allied to Athens in the Battle of Marathon (490 BC), in which the Persians were defeated. By the time of the Battle of Salamis (480 BC), the island had changed over to the Persian side. However, after the unexpected Athenian victory at Salamis, Rhodes hastily became an ally of Athens again, joining the Delian League in 478 BC. After the disastrous Sicilian Expedition (416-412 BC), when after four years of fighting at Syracuse all the Athenian soldiers were either killed, or dead from starvation, Rhodes revolted against Athens and formed an alliance with Sparta, which it aided in the defeat of the Athenians in the Peloponnesian Wars.

In 408 BC, Kamiros, Ialyssos and Lindos decided to consolidate their powers for mutual protection and expansion, and together founded the city of Rhodes. The architect Hippodamos, who came to be regarded as the father of town planning, drew up plans for the city. The result was one of the most visually pleasing and harmonious cities of antiquity, divided into four distinct parts: the acropolis, agora, harbour and residential quarter, with wide straight streets connecting them. Rhodes now allied itself to Athens again, and together they defeated Sparta at the battle of Knidos, in 394 BC. Rhodes then joined forces with Persia and aided it in a battle against Alexander the Great. However, as soon as Alexander the Great's invincibility became evident, Rhodes wasted no time in allying itself with him. In the skirmishes following Alexander's death, Rhodes sided with Ptolemy I.

In 305 BC, Antigonus, one of Ptolemy's rivals, sent his son, the formidable Demetrius Poliorketes (the Besieger of Cities), to conquer the city. Rhodes had more than met its match, but it managed to repel Demetrius after a long siege. To celebrate this victory, the 32-metre-high bronze statue of Helios Apollo (Colossus of Rhodes), one of the Seven Wonders of the Ancient World, was built. The statue was traditionally thought to have straddled Mandraki Harbour but in recent years this has been disputed. Whatever, it only stood for 65 years before collapsing during an earthquake. It lay abandoned until 653 AD when it was chopped up by the Saracens, who sold it to a merchant in Edessa. The story goes that after being shipped to Syria, it took almost 1000 camels to convey it to its final destination.

After the defeat of Poliorketes, Rhodes knew no bounds: it built up the biggest navy in the Aegean and its port became a principal Mediterranean trading centre. The arts also flourished, the Rhodian School of Sculpture supplanting that of Athens as the foremost in Greece. The most esteemed sculptor was Pythocretes, whose works included the magnificent Victory of Samothrace, which now takes pride of place in the Louvre, and the relief of the *trireme* (warship) at Lindos.

When Greece became the battleground upon which Roman generals fought for leadership of the empire, Rhodes allied itself with Julius Caesar. After Caesar's assassination, Cassius besieged Rhodes, destroying its ships and stripping the city of its artworks, which were taken to Rome. This event marked the beginning of Rhodes' decline. In 70 AD Rhodes became part of the Roman Empire.

In 155 AD Rhodes city was badly damaged by an earthquake, and in 269 AD the Goths invaded, rendering further damage. When the Roman Empire split, Rhodes became part of the Byzantine province of the Dodecanese.

In the following centuries raid upon raid followed. First it was the Persians in 620, then the Saracens in 653; the Turks followed. When the crusaders seized Constantinople, Rhodes was given independence. Later the Genoese gained control. The Knights of St John of Jerusalem turned up in Rhodes in 1309 and ruled for just over 200 years until they were ousted by the Ottomans. Rhodes suffered several earthquakes during the 19th century, but greater damage was rendered in 1856 by a mighty explosion caused by gunpowder which had been stored and forgotten – almost 1000 people were killed and many buildings were wrecked. After 35 years of Italian occupation, along with the other Dodecanese, Rhodes became part of Greece in 1947.

Top: The Sanctuary of the Great Gods, Samothrace, North-Eastern Aegean Islands (DH)
Left: The 19th century church of the Taxiarchs, Mesta, Chios, North-Eastern
Aegean Islands (RH)
Right: Chora, Samothrace (RH)

Top: Village of Theologos, Thassos, North-Eastern Aegean Islands (RH)
Bottom: Ancient agora, Thassos, North-Eastern Aegean Islands (RH)

Getting To/From Rhodes (Island)

Air There are at least four flights a day to Athens (17,800 dr); at least two a day to Karpathos (8200 dr); five a week to Iraklion (13,200 dr); four a week to Thira (8200 dr); three a week to Kos (7500 dr), Kastellorizo (7900 dr) and Kassos (8200 dr); and two a week to Thessaloniki (23,500 dr). The Olympic Airways office (☎ 24 571/2/3/4/5) is at Ierou Lohou 9 in Rhodes city. The airport is 16 km south-west of the city.

Ferry (Domestic) Rhodes is the ferry hub of the Dodecanese. The following was the schedule at the time of writing, but it changes periodically so ask the EOT or tourist information office in Rhodes city for an up-to-date schedule.

Every day at noon the F/B *Ialyssos* or the F/B *Kamiros* leaves for Piraeus (18 hours, 4400 dr) via Kos (3½ hours, 2200 dr); Kalymnos (5½ hours, 2550 dr); Leros (7½ hours, 3100 dr); and Patmos (8½ hours, 3200 dr).

On Tuesday, Thursday and Saturday F/B *Rodos* goes direct to Piraeus (12 hours) at 6 pm. Tickets for the *Ialyssos*, *Kamiros* and *Rodos* can be purchased at the DANE Agency (☎ 30 930/942), Amerikis 95, in Rhodes city.

On Monday at noon the F/B *Agios Rafail* leaves for Kavala (8000 dr), on the mainland in the region of Macedonia, via Kos, Kalymnos, Leros, Patmos, Samos, Chios, Lesbos and Lemnos. Buy tickets at the Red Sea Agency (☎ 27 721 or 22 683) on Theodoraki (off Karpathou), in Rhodes city.

At 1 pm on Tuesday F/B *Ionian Sun* leaves for Rafina (17½ hours, 4400 dr) via Kos (3½ hours); Kalymnos (5½ hours); Astypalea (eight hours); Mykonos (13 hours); and Andros (16 hours). Buy tickets at Skevos Travel (☎ 22 461/354), Amerikis 111.

At 4 pm on Wednesday F/B *Kimolos* leaves for Piraeus via Halki (two hours, 1400 dr); Diafani and Pigadia (six hours, 2400 dr) on Karpathos; Kassos (7½ hours, 2500 dr); Sitia (11 hours, 2200 dr) and Agios Nikolaos (13 hours, 4100 dr) on Crete. From here the ferry continues to the Cycladic islands of Thira, Sikinos, Folegandros, Milos and Sifnos. See Agios Nikolaos' Ferry section for details. In the other direction (coming from Piraeus) the ferry calls at Symi, after Halki, and before Rhodes. Tickets can be bought from Kouros Travel (☎ 24 377), Karpathou 34.

The F/B *Milena* leaves at the same time for Piraeus via Pigadia (Karpathos), Iraklion (11 hours) and Thira (15 hours). Buy tickets from Kydon Agency (☎ 23 000 or 27 900), on Ethelondon Dodekanission (between Amerikis and Makariou).

On Thursday F/B *Ionian Sun* leaves at 1 pm for Tilos, Nisyros, Kos, Mykonos, Tinos, Andros and Rafina; buy tickets from the aforementioned Skevos Travel.

On Thursday at 3 pm and Friday at 10 pm the F/B *Milini* leaves for Piraeus via Iraklion, Thira and Paros; buy tickets from Kydon Agency.

On Monday and Friday at 3.30 pm the F/B *Nissos Kalimnos* leaves for Kastellorizo (six hours, 2100 dr). On Tuesday and Saturday at 10 am it leaves for Kalymnos (eight hours, 2600 dr) via Symi (two hours, 1000 dr), Tilos (3½ hours, 1700 dr), Nisyros (4½ hours, 1600 dr) and Kos (six hours, 2200 hours); buy tickets from Kydon Agency.

Ferry (International) Following are the schedules for international ferries from Rhodes.

To/From Cyprus & Israel In summer there are three ferries a week to Limassol (18 hours) and Haifa (30 hours). See Getting There & Away in the Piraeus section of the Athens chapter for more information. Buy tickets from Red Sea Agency (☎ 27 721 or 22 683), on Theodoraki, or Kouros Agency (☎ 24 377 or 22 400), Karpathou 34. The immigration and customs offices are on the quay.

To/From Turkey Small car ferries run between Rhodes and Marmaris daily (except Sunday) between April and October and less frequently in winter. At the time of writing passenger tickets cost 6000/10,800 dr one-way/return. Travellers have since reported that prices have increased to 14,600 dr. Buy tickets from Triton Holidays (☎ 30 657), Plastira 25 (between Mandraki and Makariou), to whom you must submit your passport on the day before your journey.

Excursion Boat There are excursion boats to Symi every day in summer (3000 dr return), leaving Mandraki at 9 am and returning at 6 pm.

Caïque For information about caïques to Halki from Rhodes, see the Getting To/From Halki section.

Hydrofoil If you believe the Dodecanese Hydrofoil Company brochure their hydrofoils link Rhodes to almost all of the Dodecanese, including Kastellorizo. The trouble with hydrofoils is that they sail (or don't sail) very much according to the vagaries of the weather. The only well-established service is to Kos (two hours, 4000 dr) which seems to operate throughout the season. In July and August there may also be hydrofoils to Leros (three hours), Patmos (3¼ hours), Symi (50 minutes) and Samos (3¾ hours). Enquire at Kouros Travel (☎ 24 377), Karpathou 34.

Getting Around Rhodes (Island)

To/From the Airport Thirteen buses a day travel between the airport (200 dr) and the West Side bus station. The first one leaves Rhodes at 6.50 am and the last one leaves at 9.30 pm. Coming from the airport the first one leaves at 7.15 am and the last one at 10.15 pm.

Bus Rhodes has a reasonable bus service. The EOT gives out a schedule. From the East Side bus station there are hourly buses to Faliraki (180 dr); nine a day to Lindos (650 dr); five a day to Kolymbia (300 dr); three a day to Psinthos (928 dr); and one a day to Genadi (750 dr).

From the West Side station there are half-hourly buses to Kalithea; 12 buses a day to Koskinou (170 dr); four to ancient Kamiros (600 dr); two a day to Petaloudes (500 dr); one a day to Monolithos (900 dr) via Kamiros Skala; and one a day to Embona (700 dr).

Car & Motorbike Car-hire outlets in Rhodes city include Alfa (☎ 20 253), 28 Oktovriou 5; Autorent (☎ 22 151), Ammochostou 10; Avis (☎ 24 990), Gallias 9; Hertz (☎ 92 902), Griva 16; InterRent (☎ 21 658), 28 Oktovriou 18; and Just Rent a Car (☎ 31 895), Orfanidi 45. Hertz, Avis, Inter Rent, Eurocar

and Budget have offices at the airport – compare prices as there is quite a lot of competition.

Motorbikes can be hired from Mike Moto (☎ 31 797), Plateia Evreon in the old town. There are also several outlets in the new town.

Bicycle The Bicycle Centre (☎ 28 315), Griva 39 (off the map), in the new town, is one of Greece's best bicycle-hire outlets. The daily rates are: three-speed bikes 800 dr; mountain bikes 1200 dr; tandems 1500 dr; and racing bikes 2000 dr. Baskets and baby seats are 100 dr. If you hire a bike for a week you get two days free. Griva is a left-hand branch off Alex Diakou, which is a westerly continuation of Papagou.

RHODES CITY

The heart of Rhodes city is the old town, enclosed within massive walls. The new town to the north is a monument to package tourism, with just about every hotel, restaurant and bar sporting stickers advertising holidays for the 18 to 30 year olds. You will have to venture into the new town to catch a bus or take a taxi and to deal with practicalities, but almost everything of interest lies within the walls of the old town.

Orientation

The old town is a confusing and fascinating mesh of Byzantine, Turkish and Latin architecture. Quiet, twisting alleyways are punctuated by large and lively squares. Odos Sokratous, which runs east to west, and its easterly continuation, Aristotelous, make up the old town's bustling main commercial thoroughfare. The old town's two main squares are also along here: Plateia Evreon, with a fountain decorated with bronze sea horses, at the eastern end of Aristotelous, and Plateia Hippocrates, with the distinctive Castellania fountain, at the eastern end of Sokratous. Acquainting yourself with Sokratous and these two squares will help to some extent with orientation, but you'll just have to accept that, as in many other places

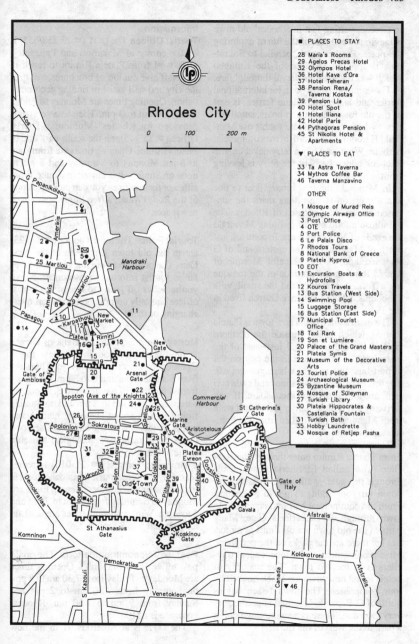

Rhodes City

0   100   200 m

■ PLACES TO STAY

28 Maria's Rooms
29 Agelos Precas Hotel
32 Olympos Hotel
36 Hotel Kava d'Ora
37 Hotel Teheran
38 Pension Rena/
   Taverna Kostas
39 Pension Lia
40 Hotel Spot
41 Hotel Iliana
42 Hotel Paris
44 Pythagoras Pension
45 St Nikolis Hotel &
   Apartments

▼ PLACES TO EAT

33 Ta Astra Taverna
34 Mythos Coffee Bar
46 Taverna Manzavino

OTHER

1 Mosque of Murad Reis
2 Olympic Airways Office
3 Post Office
4 OTE
5 Port Police
6 Le Palais Disco
7 Rhodos Tours
8 National Bank of Greece
9 Plateie Kyprou
10 EOT
11 Excursion Boats &
   Hydrofoils
12 Kouros Travels
13 Bus Station (West Side)
14 Swimming Pool
15 Luggage Storage
16 Bus Station (East Side)
17 Municipal Tourist
   Office
18 Taxi Rank
19 Son et Lumiere
20 Palace of the Grand Masters
21 Plateia Symis
22 Museum of the Decorative
   Arts
23 Tourist Police
24 Archaeological Museum
25 Byzantine Museum
26 Mosque of Süleyman
27 Turkish Library
30 Plateia Hippocrates &
   Castellania Fountain
31 Turkish Bath
35 Hobby Laundrette
43 Mosque of Retjep Pasha

in Greece, getting lost in Rhodes' old town is inevitable and part of the fun of exploring the place. Further north, parallel to Sokratous, is Ippoton (Avenue of the Knights) which was the main medieval thoroughfare.

The commercial harbour, for international ferries and large inter-island ferries, is east of the old town. Excursion boats, small ferries, hydrofoils and private yachts use Mandraki Harbour, to the north of the commercial harbour. When you buy a ferry ticket be sure to check which harbour the ferry is leaving from.

In Mandraki the two bronze deer (a doe and a stag) on stone pillars mark the supposed site of the Colossus of Rhodes. The grandiose public buildings lining Mandraki are a relic of Mussolini's era. In contrast, just north of Mandraki, at the eastern end of G Papanikolaou, is the graceful Mosque of Murad Reis. In the grounds of the mosque are a Turkish cemetery and the small Villa Cleobolus, where Lawrence Durrell lived in the 1940s.

The main square of the new town is Plateia Rimini, which is just outside the northern wall of the old town, and just west of the waterfront. If you arrive in the city on the airport bus, this is near where you get off. The tourist offices, bus stations and main taxi rank are all on or near this square. If you arrive by ferry, the square is just a short walk from Mandraki, but further from the commercial harbour.

There are eight gates into the old town. From Plateia Rimini enter through the New Gate (also called Eleftheria Gate). Once through the gate, walk south (passing Ippoton on your right) to get to Sokratous. From the commercial harbour, enter the old town through St Catherine's Gate. Many parts of the old town are off limits to motorists but there are car parks on the periphery. Most accommodation for independent travellers is in the old town. The majority of hotels in the new town are block booked by tour companies. The town beach begins north of G Papanikolaou and is predictably very crowded. There is a swimming pool in a park to the west of the EOT.

Information

Tourist Offices The EOT (☎ 23 255/655) is on the corner of Makariou and Papagou – walk west from Plateia Rimini to reach it. The staff give out lots of brochures, a map of the city and will assist in finding accommodation. Opening times are Monday to Friday from 7.30 am to 3 pm. The same service is provided by Rhodes' Municipal Tourist Office (☎ 35 945), on the south-east side of Plateia Rimini. Opening times are from 8 am to 8 pm Monday to Saturday and 8 am to noon on Sunday. It is closed in winter. From either of these offices you can pick up a copy of the *Rodos News*, a free English-language newspaper.

Tourist Police The tourist police (☎ 27 423) are in the old town just south of the New Gate. The police here are not very helpful as far as tourist information is concerned, so you're better off going to one of the tourist offices and only coming here to report overcharging or theft.

Money The main National Bank of Greece is on Plateia Kyprou in the new town. Opening times are Monday to Thursday from 8 am to 2 pm and 6 to 8 pm, on Friday from 8 am to 1.30 pm and 3 to 8.30 pm, on Saturday from 8 am to 2 pm and on Sunday from 9 am to noon. There are many more banks in the new town and there are two banks close to the Archaeological Museum in the old town.

American Express (☎ 21 010) is represented by Rhodos Tours, Ammochostou 18, in the new town. Summer opening times are Monday to Saturday from 9 am to 2 pm and 5 to 9 pm. Winter opening times are 8.30 am to 1 pm and 5 to 8 pm.

Post & Telecommunications The main post office is on Mandraki. Opening times are Monday to Friday from 7.30 am to 8 pm, on Saturday from 7.30 am to 2 pm and Sunday from 9 am to 1.30 pm. Rhodes' postcode is 85100.

The OTE is at Amerikis 91 in the new

town. It is open daily from 8 am to midnight. Rhodes' telephone code is 0241.

Foreign Consulates Foreign consulates in Rhodes include:

Germany
    Parodos Isiodou 12 (☎ 63 730)
Netherlands
    Alexandrou Diakou 27 (☎ 31 571)
Turkey
    Iroon Politechniou 12 (☎ 23 362)
UK
    25 Martiou 23 (☎ 24 963)

Laundries There are two self-service laundrettes in Rhodes: the Hobby Laundrette, at Platonos 31 in the old town and Lavomatique, at 28 Oktovriou 32 in the new town. This street is a westerly continuation of 25 Martiou. Both laundrettes charge around 1000 dr a load.

Emergency Rhodes' General Hospital (☎ 25 555 or 22 222) is at Erythrou Stavrou in the new town. Walk west along Eleftheriou Venizelou from the north-west corner of the old town and Erythrou Stavrou is a turn-off to the right.

Luggage Storage The New Market Pension on Plateia Rimini has luggage storage for 300 dr a day (12 hours). A luggage-storage facility is due to open next to Hobby Laundrette in the old town.

Old Town

The town is divided into two parts. In medieval times the Knights of St John lived in the Knights' Quarter and the other inhabitants lived in the Chora. The 12-metre-thick city walls are closed to the public, but you can take a guided walk along them, which starts at the courtyard of the Palace of the Grand Masters (800 dr). At the time of writing, the walks were on Tuesday and Sunday starting at 2.45 pm, but check the current schedule on display at the entrance to the palace.

Knights' Quarter The Knights of St John were a religious order of the church of Rome

founded in Amalfi in the 11th century. They went to Jerusalem initially to minister to the needs of the pilgrims who arrived there, and soon extended their duties to tending the poor and sick of the Holy Land. Over the years they became increasingly militant, joining forces with the Knights Templars and the Teutonic Knights of St Mary in battles against infidels.

The Knights of St John were expelled from the Holy Land with the fall of Jerusalem. They went first to Cyprus, and then to Rhodes, where they arrived in 1309. Through some medieval wheeler-dealing with the island's ruling Genoese admiral, Viguolo de Viguoli, they became the possessors of Rhodes.

The Knights stayed 213 years, during which time they transformed Rhodes into a mighty bulwark, standing at the easternmost point of the Christian West and safeguarding it from the Muslim infidels of the East. The Knights withstood two Muslim offensives in 1444 and 1480, but in 1522 Sultan Süleyman the Magnificent staged a massive attack with 200,000 troops. After a long siege the 600 Knights, plus 1000 mercenaries and 6000 Rhodians surrendered – hunger, disease and death having taken their toll.

The most appropriate place to begin your exploration of the old town is the imposing cobbled Avenue of the Knights. The street flanked by two archways consists of inns where the Knights lived. The Knights were divided into seven 'tongues' or languages, according to their place of origin: England, France, Germany, Italy, Aragon, Auvergne and Provence and each one was responsible for protecting a section of the bastion. The Grand Master, in overall charge, lived in the palace, and each tongue was under the auspices of a bailiff. The Knights were divided into soldiers, chaplains and ministers to the sick.

To this day the street exudes a noble and forbidding aura, despite the fact that modern offices now occupy most of the inns. Its lofty buildings stretch in a 600-metre-long unbroken wall of honey-coloured stone blocks, and its flat façade is punctuated by huge doorways and arched windows. The inns reflect the Gothic style of architecture of the Knights' countries of origin. They form a harmonious whole in their bastion-like structure, but on closer inspection each possesses graceful and individual embellishments, including coats of arms.

First on the right, at the eastern end of the Avenue of the Knights, is the **Inn of the Order of the Tongue of Italy** (1519); next to it is the **Palace of Villiers De L'isle Adam**. After Sultan Süleyman had taken the city, it was Villiers De L'isle who had the humiliating task of arranging the Knights' departure from the island. Next along is the **Inn of France** (1509), the most ornate and distinctive of all the inns. On the opposite side of the street is a wrought-iron gate behind which is a lush Turkish garden where a small fountain plays. Back on the right side is the **Chapelle Francaise** (Chapel of the Tongue of France), with a statue of the Virgin and Child in a recess. Next to it is the residence of the Chaplain of the Tongue of France. Across a narrow alleyway is the **Inn of Provence**, with four coats of arms forming the shape of a cross, and opposite is the **Inn of Spain**. These two are the last of the inns.

On the right is the most magnificent building of all, the 14th-century **Palace of the Grand Masters** (☎ 23 035). This is the most prominent building of the old town. It was destroyed in the gunpowder explosion of 1856 and the Italians rebuilt it in a grandiose manner, with a preposterously ostentatious interior, intending it as a holiday home for Mussolini. It is now a **museum**, containing sculpture, mosaics taken from Kos by the Italians, and sumptuous antique furniture. The palace is open Tuesday to Sunday from 8.30 am to 3 pm. Admission is 800 dr.

The **Archaeological Museum** (☎ 27 657), on the corner of Appellou and Ippoton, is housed in the 15th-century Knights' Hospital, a splendid structure built around a courtyard. In the time of the Knights, its infirmary had beds for 100 patients. The collection spans the period from Mycenaean times to the time of the Knights. Exhibits include a Head of Helios, vases and kouroi

from Kamiros, Mycenaean jewellery from Ialyssos, Knights' gravestones and two statues of Aphrodite. Lawrence Durrell was so enamoured of one of these statues that he named his *Reflections on a Marine Venus* after it. The museum is open Tuesday to Sunday from 8.30 am to 3 pm. Admission is 600 dr.

There are several smaller museums in this vicinity. The 11th-century Church of the Virgin of the Castle was enlarged by the Knights who made it into their cathedral. It is now the **Byzantine Museum**, and houses a collection of Christian artworks from early Byzantine times to the 18th century. It is open Tuesday to Sunday from 8.30 am to 3 pm. Admission is 400 dr.

Close by, the **Museum of the Decorative Arts** houses local pottery, furniture and costumes and a reconstruction of a room in a traditional Rhodian house. Opening times are Tuesday to Sunday from 8.30 am to 3 pm. Admission is 400 dr.

Chora This was where the ordinary folk lived during the time that the Knights ruled the roost. Until this century, Rhodes had a large Jewish population who lived in the south-east part of Chora. In 1943, after the Nazis had taken over from the Italians, almost all of these Jews were taken to Auschwitz, never to return. The synagogue on Dossiadou has a plaque on the wall commemorating the tragedy. The synagogue is still a place of worship for the small number of remaining Jews and is usually open in the morning. Close by, Plateia Evreon (full name Plateia Martiron Evreon, which means Square of the Jewish Martyrs) was named in memory of these Jews.

The Chora also has many Ottoman legacies. During Turkish times the churches in the old town were converted to mosques, and many more were built from scratch. You will come across these on your wanders, but most of them are in a state of dilapidation and are locked. The most important one is the pink-domed **Mosque of Süleyman**, with an elegant portal and a slender minaret. The mosque, at the western end of Sokratous, was built in 1522 in celebration of the Ottoman victory against the Knights. It was rebuilt in 1808. At the time of writing it was closed for restorations.

Opposite the mosque is the 18th-century **Turkish library** where many Islamic manuscripts are kept, including an illuminated Koran. It is sometimes open to the public – check the times on the notice outside.

The 18th-century **Turkish bath**, on Plateia Arionos, retains its original marble floors and basins. It offers a rare chance to have a Turkish bath in Greece – sexes are segregated. The baths are open Monday to Saturday from 5 am to 7 pm. Entrance is 500 dr on Monday, Tuesday, Thursday and Friday and only 150 dr on Wednesday and Saturday.

Places to Stay – bottom end

Rhodes' two camp sites are at Faliraki and Lardos (see the Beaches section).

The old town of Rhodes is well supplied with domatia and low-priced hotels so even in high season you should be able to find somewhere. The *Pythagoras Pension* (☎ 30 486), Pithagora 81, is a friendly laid-back place where you'll meet lots of backpackers. Beds in five-bed dorms cost 2000 dr. Walk south along Appellou from Sokratous, turn left at Platonos and right onto Pithagora and the pension is along here on the left.

Pension Rena (☎ 26 217), Pithagora 55, has tidy doubles for 4000 dr with shared bathrooms. Close by, along a little alleyway, *Pension Lia* (☎ 26 209), Pithagora 66c, has clean doubles/triples for 3500/4000 dr with shared bathrooms. The lovely honey-coloured marble floors make up for the ghastly floral wallpaper.

The E class *Hotel Spot* (☎ 34 737), Perikleous 21, has light airy rooms for 3000/4000 dr with private bathrooms. Perikleous runs south from Plateia Evreon. Close by, the *Pension Iliana* (☎ 30 251), Gavala 1, has clean, spacious singles/doubles/triples with private bathrooms for 3000/4000/5000 dr. The pension is an old house with character, which belonged to a Jewish family before

WW II. It has a small bar-cum-TV lounge, an outside terrace and a charming hotchpotch of bric-a-brac – look for the hotel signpost on Plateia Evreon.

The *Agelos Precas Pension* (☎ 27 846), Sokratous 41c, has pleasant doubles/triples for 3500/4000 dr with shared bathrooms and use of a kitchen. Beyond here, on the sixth turn-off to the left after the Castellania fountain, you will come to *Maria's Rooms* (☎ 22 169), at the western end of Menekleous. These immaculate, nicely furnished rooms, built around a quiet courtyard, cost 4000/5000 dr for doubles/triples with shared bathrooms and 5600/6700 dr with private bathrooms.

The *Hotel Tehran* (☎ 27 594), Sofokleous 41b, has comfortable rooms for 2000/4000/5000 dr with private bathrooms. The *Olympos Hotel* (☎ 28 279), Agion Fanourion 56, has agreeable doubles for 6000 dr with private bathrooms. Further south, the D class *Hotel Paris* (☎ 26 354 or 21 095), Agion Fanourion 88, has spacious rooms around a large tranquil courtyard, planted with orange and banana trees. Rates are 5000/8000/10,000 dr with private bathrooms.

The delightful D class *Hotel Kava d'Oro* (☎ 36 980), Kistiniou 15, in an 800-year-old house, is the closest hotel to the commercial harbour and one of the city's nicest budget places. It's spotlessly clean and has a friendly bar. Rates are 3000/4500/6000 dr with private bathrooms. In 1992 Michael Palin (of Monty Python fame) stayed here when he stopped off in Rhodes on his Pole to Pole journey for the BBC TV series. To reach the hotel from the commercial harbour, walk behind the row of shops opposite the harbour entrance, go through the narrow pedestrian gate, turn left, and the hotel is 50 metres along on the left. There is free parking nearby.

The D class *Hotel Anna Maria* (☎ 36 980 or 25 537), Papalouka 18, in the new town (off the map) has clean, pleasant rooms and charges 2000/3000/4500 dr with shared bathrooms. Reach it by walking west along Eleftheriou Venizelou from the north-west corner of the old town.

Places to Stay – middle

The *St Nikolis Hotel & Apartments* (☎ 34 561 or 36 238; fax 32 034) is the most luxurious accommodation in the old town. The rooms, with rough stucco walls and attractive furniture, cost 9000/14,000/17,000 dr, including breakfast; the well-equipped apartments sleep four people and cost 18,400 dr. The hotel is tucked away in the extreme south-west corner of the old town. It has a large garden and a roof terrace with terrific views of the old town.

Places to Stay – top end

Rhodes city's top-end hotels mostly skirt the beaches to the north and west of the old town. All of the hotels listed are off the map in this book. The A class *Avra Beach* (☎ 25 284/5) at Ixia has a restaurant, bar and swimming pool. Rates are 11,750/14,400 dr for singles/doubles. The deluxe *Grand Hotel Astir Palace* (☎ 26 284) is on Akti Miaouli which is the western waterfront of the city. The hotel has a bar, restaurant and swimming pools. Rates are 15,250/19,600 dr for singles/doubles, and 78,000 dr for suites.

The deluxe *Rodos Palace* (☎ 25 222 or 26 222; fax 25 350) is on the beach at Ixia, just south-west of Rhodes city. This vast place has loads of amenities. Rates are 15,500/21,500 dr for singles/doubles, 75,900 dr for bungalows and 112,000 dr for suites.

Places to Eat

Rhodes city doesn't overwhelm one with its culinary delights – its restaurants have gone the way of most in the tourist ghettos of Greece, serving bland food at inflated prices.

One of the city's most authentic and unpretentious places is south of the old town. Walk along Odos Canada and you will come to *Taverna Manzavino* which serves well-prepared, reasonably priced traditional Greek dishes. Their delicious beef stew in wine costs 950 dr.

In the old town *Ta Astra Taverna*, Appellou 41, is popular with locals and good value. Their 'Greek Plate' (a bit of everything) for 900 dr, will satisfy the hungriest traveller. To reach this place, take the second turn left along Sokratous, after passing the Castellania Fountain.

Taverna Kostas, Pithagora 62, is a little more expensive, but commendable. Kalamaria is 1000 dr, souvlaki and pork chops are 1200 dr and swordfish is 1400 dr.

The best (some say the only) cappuccino in Rhodes city can be had for 200 dr at the very pleasant and untouristy *Mythos Cafe Bar*, Evripidou 13-15, near the Castellania Fountain. The café also has a wide range of reasonably priced alcoholic beverages. Self caterers will find fruit and vegetable stalls, butchers and a fish market in the New Market on Plateia Rimini. *Paneri* (☎ 35 877), on Odos Fanouraki, in the new town, is an excellent health-food shop.

Entertainment

The Son et Lumière (☎ 21 922), in the grounds of the Palace of the Grand Masters, depicting the Turkish siege, is superior to most such efforts. The entrance is on Plateia Rimini and admission is 700 dr (students 350 dr, children 200 dr). There are performances in English every evening except Sunday. Check the times with the EOT.

The Nelly Dimoglou Dance Company gives performances of folk dances from all over Greece at the *Folk Dance Theatre* (☎ 20 157), on Adronikou, in the old town, just south of the Turkish bath. Performances are nightly except Saturday from May to October and begin at 9.20 pm. Admission is 1400 dr. The performances are highly professional, spirited and, along with the Dora Stratou Dance Company's in Athens, are the best in Greece. Greek dance lessons are also given here. Classical music recitals are given at the *National Theatre* (☎ 29 678) just north of Mandraki, near the eastern end of G Papanikolaou.

The city's cinemas include the *Rodon* behind the National Theatre, the *Dimotikou* on G Eustatheadi and the *Esperia* on 25 Martiou.

In the new town it seems that if a building is not a hotel or restaurant it's a disco or bar. You can dance under laser lights on a moving floor at *Le Palais Disco*, on 25 Martiou,

listen to live rock n' roll at the *Rock Box* at
Alex Diakou 65 and drink Castlemaine
XXXX beer at the *Down Under Bar* on
Orfanidou – all the staff here are Aussies.
The last two places are in the western part of
the new town.

Getting There & Around
See the Getting To/From and Getting Around
Rhodes (Island) entries at the beginning of
the Rhodes section.

ANCIENT CITIES
Lindos Λίνδος
The most famous of the ancient cities is
Lindos, but with 500,000 visitors a year it's
just a bit *too* famous.

The Acropolis of Lindos is built on a huge
rock 116 metres above sea level. Of the three
Doric settlements, Ialyssos, Kamiros and
Lindos, Lindos was the most important,
because of its excellent vantage point and
good natural harbour. It was first settled
around 2000 BC and is now a conglomeration of ancient, Byzantine, Frankish and
Turkish remains.

The most important ancient ruin is a 4th-
century BC **Temple to Athena**. The cult of
Athena was first established on Lindos as
early as the 10th century BC, so this temple

Athena

replaced earlier ones. After the founding of
the city of Rhodes, Lindos declined in commercial importance, but remained an
important place of worship. The ubiquitous
St Paul landed here en route to Rome. The
first fortress was built here in Byzantine
times and was strengthened by the Knights
and also used by the Turks.

It's a steep climb up the steps to the **acropolis** or you can ride up on a donkey (600 dr).
At the base of the final flight of steps look
out for the sculptor Pythocretes' relief of a
warship hewn out of the rock. A statue of
Poseidon originally stood on the deck of the
ship symbolising Lindos' naval superiority.
At the top of the steps you enter the acropolis
by a vaulted corridor. Once through here,
cross the 20-columned Doric stoa and ascend
the stairway to the remains of a 5th-century
BC propylaia, beyond which is the **Temple
to Athena**. Once at the top there are breathtaking views down to Lindos village. The
site is open Monday to Friday from 8.30 am
to 4.30 pm and Saturday and Sunday from
8.30 am to 2.30 pm. Admission is 1000 dr.

Lindos village, clustered below the
Acropolis, is an immaculate showpiece of
dazzling white 17th-century houses. Once
the dwellings of wealthy admirals, in recent
years many of the houses have been bought
and restored by foreign celebrities. The
village has been declared a National Historic
Monument, so new building is prohibited.

The conspicuous 15th-century Church of
Agia Panagia (St Mary) has fine 18th-
century frescoes. Lindos' sandy beach is
chock-a-block with bodies, beach umbrellas
and sunbeds. Forget about finding accommodation in Lindos, as almost all of it is
block-booked by package companies –
you're better off coming on a day trip from
Rhodes city.

Ialyssos Ιαλυσός
Like Lindos, Ialyssos, 10 km from Rhodes,
is a hotchpotch of Doric, Byzantine and
medieval remains. The Doric city of Ialyssos
was built on the flat-topped hill of Filerimos
(280 metres). A visit to the site is more
worthwhile for the views, than for the sparse

ruins. The hill was an excellent vantage point, so attracted successive invaders. All that remains from ancient times are the foundations of a 3rd-century BC **Temple of Athena Poliados & Zeus Poleas** and a 4th-century BC fountain, which was restored in 1926. A fortress was built in Byzantine times and later used by the Knights. Süleyman the Magnificent used it as his headquarters, during his siege of Rhodes city.

Also at the site are a restored monastery, the Church of our Lady of Filerimos and the subterranean Chapel of Agios Georgios. The Chapel is liberally embellished with frescoes.

The site is open Tuesday to Sunday from 8.30 am to 3 pm. Admission is 400 dr.

Getting There & Away No buses go to ancient Ialyssos. The airport bus, which leaves from Rhodes' West Side bus station, stops at Trianda, on the coast. Ialyssos is five km inland from here.

Kamiros Κάμειροσ

The extensive ruins of the ancient city of Kamiros stand on a hillside near the north-west coast, 34 km from Rhodes city. Unlike the other two ancient cities it has no Knight's castle. The groundplan of the city is clearly discernible. There is a partially reconstructed 3rd-century BC **Doric stoa** which bordered the agora, the foundations of a **Temple to Athena** and ruins of houses and wells. The site is open Tuesday to Sunday from 8.30 am to 3 pm. Admission is 400 dr. Buses travel from the West Side bus station in Rhodes city to Kamiros.

Don't confuse Kamiros with Kamiros Skala. The latter is the departure point for caïques to Halki, 15 km beyond the ancient site, and reached by the Monolithos bus.

PETALOUDES Πεταλούδες

This is another one of the 'must sees' on the package-tour itinerary. Numerous, silent and barely discernible 'butterflies' (actually *callimorpha quadripunctarea*) share this twee little gorge with an even greater number of noisy and conspicuous tourists. You wend your way through the narrow green gorge by crisscrossing wooden footbridges over a stream and pools. The butterflies are lured by the strong scent of styrax trees. Petaloudes is open daily from 9 am to 6 pm (from June to September). Admission is 200 dr. Buses to Petaloudes leave from the West Side bus station in Rhodes city.

BEACHES

Rhodes has some excellent beaches, many of which, although not all, get crowded. The best ones are on the east coast; the west coast is exposed and most of the beaches are pebble or stones. As far south as Lindos, hotels are mostly the domain of package tourists, so it's advisable to make visiting these beaches a day trip from Rhodes city. Frequent buses go down the coast as far as Lindos, but except for Faliraki, most of the beaches are a bit of a trek from the main road, where the bus stops are.

An atmosphere of decadence and grandeur linger on in the derelict Moorish-style buildings of the one time thermal spa at **Kalathea**, 10 km from Rhodes city. The spa was built by the Italians and occupies a pleasant shady park. Below are a number of coves which are good for snorkelling. **Faliraki Beach**, 15 km south of Rhodes city, is the island's premiere holiday resort. The main stretch of beach is crowded, but the bay at the extreme southern end is uncrowded and popular with nude bathers.

Diversions from the beach include the **Faliraki Snake House** (on the main road) with live reptiles and tropical fish (open 11 am to 11 pm; 350 dr), and the **Aqua Adventure** (Greece's longest waterslide), in the grounds of the huge Hotel Pegalos at the northern end of Faliraki.

Faliraki Camping (☎ 85 358) is a good site with a restaurant, bar, minimarket and swimming pool.

Just before Kolymbia, a right turn leads in five km of pine-fringed road to **Epta Piges** (Seven Springs), where there is a small and pretty artificial lake fed by the springs and flanked by profuse greenery. The lake can be reached either along a path or through a dark dank tunnel. Back on the coast, **Kolymbia** and **Tsambika** are fine beaches. Above Tsambika Beach, the hilltop Byzantine **Moni Tsambika** affords terrific views.

The fishing village of **Haraki**, 12 km south of Tsambika, has a gorgeous crescent-shaped pebble beach. Between here and Vlicha Bay there is a long stretch of beach with uncrowded spots. The celebrated **Lindos Beach** is the next along (see the Ancient Cities section). **Pefka**, just south of Lindos, has a good sandy beach. **Lardos** has Rhodes' second camp site, *St George Camping* (☎ 0244-44 203), with a bar, restaurant, disco and swimming pool.

From Lardos an almost uninterrupted beach of pebble, shingle and sand dunes extends down to **Plimiri**. Along this stretch, **Genadi** is the only resort of any size. South of here it's relatively easy to find deserted stretches of beach. Both Genadi and Plimiri have domatia.

In the extreme south, the remote **Prassonissi** (Green Island) is joined to Rhodes by a narrow sandy isthmus, with rough sea on one side and calm on the other. The isthmus is reached along an eight km dirt track from the inland village of Katavia.

Halki Χάλκη

Halki (HAL-kee, population 250) is a small island 16 km off the west coast of Rhodes. So far it has escaped the tourist development of its large neighbour. It's a barren and rocky island with no springs and only a few wells, so all the water has to be brought in by tanker from Rhodes. As with most of Greece's small islands the population has been greatly reduced by emigration. Many islanders moved to Tarpon Springs, Florida, where they established a sponge-fishing community. Along with regular fishing, sponge fishing had always been one of the islanders' main occupations.

Getting To/From Halki

Ferry At the time of writing, the F/B *Kimolos* left Halki for Symi and Rhodes on Wednesday mornings and left for Diafani and Pigadia on Karpathos and Kassos en route to Crete later the same day. There is no ticket office on Halki so buy your ticket on the ferry.

Caïque There are caïques from Kamiros Skala on Rhodes' west coast to and from Halki all year round. The boat leaves Kamiros Skala every day (except Sunday) at 2.30 pm. On Sunday it leaves at 9 am. The cost is 800 dr. To get to Kamiros Skala from Rhodes city take the 1.15 pm Monolithos bus from the West Side bus station. The caïque awaits the arrival of the bus before departing for Halki. Caïques from Halki to Kamiros Skala leave at 5.30 am to connect with the Rhodes city bus which arrives at Kamiros Skala at 7.30 am. There is no bus on Sunday; Sunday boats leave Halki at 4 pm.

Getting Around Halki

Halki has no cars, buses or taxis. The boat *Meltimi II* holds up to 12 people and may be hired for excursions to all of the island's beaches (10,000 dr) or to the nearby uninhabited islet of Alimia (15,000 dr), which has excellent beaches. Information about these excursions can be obtained at Costos Café on the waterfront.

EMBOREIOS Εμπορειός

Halki has only one settlement, the attractive little port town of Emboreios, built around a U-shaped bay, and consisting of imposing mansions, many now derelict. The town's most prominent building is Agios Nikolaos church, which has the tallest belfry in the Dodecanese, and an attractive black and white pebble mosaic courtyard.

Orientation

The ferry quay is in the middle of the harbour. There is one road out of Emboreios, beginning behind the post office. The road bypasses Podamos, which is the island's only sandy beach. You will see the beach from the road, and it is easily reached. This narrow cement road has the incongruous name of Tarpon Springs Boulevard (christened in gratitude to the ex-Halkiots in Florida, who financed its construction).

Information

There is a small tourist office (☎ 57 330) in a kiosk between the post office (opposite the quay) and the war memorial. The information available here is limited, but the staff will help you to find accommodation.

There is no OTE, but the minimarket behind the waterfront war memorial has a metered telephone. Halki's telephone code is 0241.

Places to Stay

The nicest place to stay on Halki is the *Captain's House* (☎ 57 201), a beautiful 19th-century mansion with period furniture and a tranquil tree-shaded garden. It is owned by a retired Greek sea captain and his British wife, Christine. Rates are 5000 dr a double with shared bathrooms. Reservations are essential in July and August, but you may be lucky and find space in the low season.

To reach the Captain's House, turn right at the quay and walk to the church. Climb the church steps, turn right at the top, and walk through the church grounds and out at the other side. Turn left and then immediately right to walk along a narrow alleyway. Take the left fork; you will pass on your left some white villas which belong to Laskarina Holidays. A little way along you will come to seven stone steps to the left. The Captain's House is at the top of these on the right.

Another lovely place is *Pension Cleanthi* (☎ 37 648 or 57 334), a 130-year-old yellow stone building, with light airy rooms. The rates are 5000 dr a double with private bathrooms; well-equipped studios are 5000 dr for two people and 10,000 dr for four people. The pension is on the road to Podamos Beach, just beyond the school.

Places to Eat

Several tavernas line the waterfront in Emboreios. *Omonoias Taverna*, to the right of

the port as you face inland, has succulent spit-roast lamb for 1100 dr. At the *Ioannis Taverna*, at the far left of the waterfront, a (large) meal of shrimps and rice, tzatziki and beer will set you back about 2200 dr.

The only taverna out of town is *Nick's Taverna* on Podamos Beach. The food is good here too, with main meals from 600 to 1100 dr.

AROUND THE ISLAND

Chorio Χωριό

Chorio is the inland town which was built to protect the islanders from pirate raids. At one time it was a thriving community of 3000 people, but it's now derelict and uninhabited. A narrow winding path leads from Chorio's churchyard to a Knights of St John castle. The chapel within the castle has late-Byzantine frescoes. Chorio is approximately a 30-minute walk along Tarpon Springs Boulevard from Emboreios.

At Chorio, if you take the left fork of Tarpon Spring Boulevard, and then take the first turn right onto a wide stony track, in about 30 minutes you will reach the secluded little cove of **Giali**, which has a stony, often wave-lashed beach.

Moni Agiou Ioanni Μονή Αγιου Ιωάννη

This monastery has an attractive courtyard, shaded by an enormous pine tree. There are no monks here now, but the shepherd-cum-caretaker, Dimitri, lives here with his family. Free beds are available for tourists, but you must take your own food and water. The monastery is a two-hour walk from Chorio. Take the right fork of Tarpon Spring Boulevard. Along the way there are views of many of the other Dodecanese islands and of Turkey.

Karpathos Κάρπαθος

The elongated island of Karpathos (KAR-pa-thos), midway between Crete and Rhodes, is traversed by a mountain range which runs north-south. For hundreds of

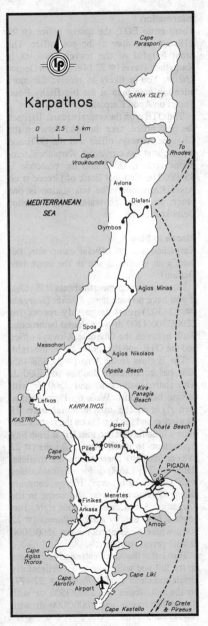

Karpathos

0   2.5   5 km

MEDITERRANEAN
SEA

years the north and south parts of the island were isolated from one another and so developed independently. It is even thought that the northerners and southerners have different ethnic origins. The northern village of Olymbos is of endless fascination to ethnologists for the age-old customs of its inhabitants. Despite having charter flights from northern Europe, Karpathos still has a long way to go before it becomes a tourist ghetto like Rhodes and Kos.

Despite its large size the island has a relatively uneventful history. Homer relates that the island (which he refers to as Krapathos) participated in the Troy campaign. Unlike almost every other Dodecanese island it was never under the auspices of the Knights of St John.

Karpathos is a wealthy island as it receives more money from emigrants living abroad (mostly in the USA) than any other Greek island. A devastating fire in 1983 destroyed much of the forest of northern Karpathos.

Getting To/From Karpathos

Air There are flights to Athens (19,000 dr) on Tuesday, Thursday and Saturday; to Kassos (2400 dr) on Wednesday, Friday and Sunday; and at least two every day to Rhodes (8200 dr). There is a flight on Tuesday to Sitia on Crete (8200 dr). The Olympic Airways office (☎ 22 150/057) is on the central square in Pigadia.

Ferry F/B *Kimolos* is the only inter-island ferry which calls at Diafani. Coming from Crete it arrives at Pigadia early on Wednesday morning and proceeds to Diafani, Halki (1426 dr), Symi (1991 dr) and Rhodes (2442 dr). It returns to Pigadia later the same day en route to Kassos, Crete (Sitia and Agios Nikolaos) Thira, Sikinos, Folegandros, Milos, Sifnos and Piraeus.

The F/B *Daliana* sails from Pigadia to Rhodes on Wednesday and Friday and to Crete (Iraklion), Thira and Piraeus on Wednesday and Sunday. The F/B *Lisithi* sails from Pigadia to Rhodes on Saturday and to Kassos, Crete (Sitia and Agios Nikolaos), Milos and Piraeus on Sunday.

Getting Around Karpathos

To/From the Airport There is no airport bus, and a taxi from Pigadia to the airport costs a hefty 2000 dr, which is a bit ironic when the airfare to Kassos is only 2400 dr. The taxi rank (☎ 22 705) is on Demokratias, just round the corner from Karpathou.

Bus Pigadia is the transport hub of the island, but the bus service is not brilliant. A schedule is pinned up at the bus station. There are three buses a day to Amopi (115 dr) and one bus to Finikes (400 dr) via Menetes and Arkasa. On Monday and Thursday there is a bus to Lefkos via Arkasa and Finikes. There is no bus between Pigadia and Olymbos.

Car & Motorbike By Circle (☎ 22 690/489), next door to the post office, is a reliable rental outlet. Prices for cars range from 7500 to 10,000 dr. Motorbikes range from 2000 dr for a 50 cc to 4500 dr for a 200 cc.

Excursion Boat In summer there are daily excursion boats from Pigadia to Diafani for 2500 dr return. There are also frequent boats to the beaches of Ahata, Kira Panagia and Apella for 1500 dr. Tickets can be bought from Karpathos Travel in Pigadia.

On a Sunday there is an excursion boat to the island of Kassos, for 3000 dr. Tickets can be bought at Olympos Travel (☎ 22 993) at the beginning of Apod Karpathou in Pigadia.

PIGADIA Πηγάδια

Pigadia (population 1300) is the island's capital and main port. The town is built on the edge of Vronti Bay, a four-km-long sandy beach. On the beach, surrounded by an enclosure, are the remains of an early Christian basilica. Pigadia is a lively place and, as it has excursion boats to many other places on the island, it serves as a good base.

Orientation

From the quay, turn right and take the left fork onto Apod Karpathou, Pigadia's main thoroughfare which leads to the central square.

Information

There is no EOT; the tourist police (☎ 22 218) are next door to the post office. The most helpful of the travel agencies is Karpathos Travel (☎ 22 148/754), on Demokratias. You're likely to receive far more attention here than at the big flashy Possi Travel on Apod Karpathou.

The OTE is on the central square. To reach the post office, take the road between the Olympic Airways office and the OTE and turn right at the crossroad. Karpathos' telephone code is 0245 and the postcode is 85700. The National Bank of Greece is on Apod Karpathou. The bus station is one block up from the waterfront, on Odos Demokratias.

Places to Stay

Karpathos has no official camp site, but there's an unofficial site in the north (see Diafani).

Domatia owners meet the boats at Pigadia. If you have no luck here, *Eftahia Georgiou* (☎ 22 302) rents large tidy rooms for 2200/3300/4200 dr with shared bathrooms. Walk between the Olympic Airways office and the OTE, and the rooms are on the right.

The E class *Hotel Avra* (☎ 22 388/485/528) has comfortable doubles for 3000 dr with shared bathrooms and 3500 dr with private bathrooms. Walk up Demokratias, turn right at the bus terminal onto 28 Oktovriou and the hotel is on the right. Continue a little further and turn left at Blue Sky Apartments to reach *Harry's Rooms* (☎ 22 188) on the left. These rooms are spotless. Rates are 2450/3600 dr for singles/doubles with shared bathrooms. If you continue along 28 Oktovriou you will come to the Karpathos Arts Centre on your right. Just beyond here are *To Kanaki Rooms* (☎ 22 908), where pleasant rooms are 3500/5000 dr with private bathrooms.

Turn left at the Arts Centre and 400 metres up the hill you will come to the delightfully kitsch and clean *Carlos' Rooms* (☎ 22 477) on the left. Rates are 2500/3500 dr with shared bathrooms and 3000/5000 dr with private bathrooms.

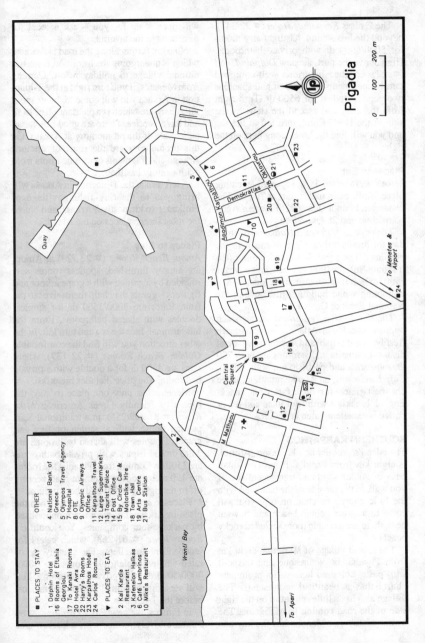

Pigadia

0   100   200 m

Quay

Vronti Bay

Central Square

M Mathéou

To Menetes &
Airport

To Aperi

PLACES TO STAY
1   Dolphin Hotel
16 Rooms of Ettahia
    Georgiou
17 Jo Kanaki Rooms
20 Hotel Avra
22 Harry's Rooms
23 Karpathos Hotel
24 Carlos' Rooms

PLACES TO EAT
2   Kali Kardia
    Restaurant
3   Cafeneion Halikas
6   Café Cambiros
10 Mike's Restaurant

OTHER
4   National Bank of
    Greece
5   Olympos Travel Agency
7   Hospital
8   OTE
9   Olympic Airways
    Office
11 Karpathos Travel
12 Large Supermarket
13 Tourist Police
14 Post Office
15 By Circle Car &
    Motorbike Hire
18 Town Hall
19 Arts Centre
21 Bus Station

The C class *Karpathos Hotel* (☎ 22 347), beyond the bus station, has light airy rooms for 5000/6000 dr with private bathrooms. High above the port, the new *Dolphin Hotel* (☎ 22 665) has luxurious well-equipped family apartments for 8000 dr and spacious two-person studios for 6500 dr. Turn right from the quay and ascend the steps by the side of the Hotel Coral, turn left at the top and you will find the hotel along here on the right.

Places to Eat

Mike's Restaurant is a superlative eating place. Tasty main meals start at 700 dr. The restaurant is on a side street between Apod Karpathou and 28 Oktovriou.

The popular *Kafeneion Halikas* is open all day for drinks but only serves meals in the evenings. The menu is limited; quite often it's only stifado (900 dr) and green beans (500 dr), but both are delicious. It's a crumbling white building, just beyond the National Bank of Greece.

The *Kali Kardia Restaurant*, on the beach opposite the Hotel Atlantic, serves superb freshly caught fish and inexpensive meat dishes; kalamaria and sardines are both 700 dr, moussaka and pastitsio are both 750 dr. *Café Lambrinos*, on Apod Karpathou, is the cheapest place for breakfast or a snack. English breakfast with fruit juice and tea or coffee is excellent value at 550 dr.

SOUTHERN KARPATHOS

The island's premier holiday resort, **Amopi**, is eight km from Pigadia. It has two small bays of golden sand and translucent sea. If you walk to the far side of the headland with the little church perched on top, you will come to a larger pebble beach and beyond here, there are a couple more secluded rocky beaches.

The inland village of **Menetes**, eight km from Pigadia, is picturesque and unspoilt with pastel-coloured houses. Its prominent church has a beautiful iconostasis. The village also has a little **museum** on the right side of the road coming from Pigadia. The owner of Taverna Manolis has the key and

will open it up for you – ask a local for directions to the taverna.

Nine km further along the road is **Arkasa**, which is undergoing the transition from traditional village to holiday resort. Coming from Menetes, if you turn right at the T-junction in Arkasa you will come to the unspoilt village square which is a pleasant place to sit and have a coffee. There are good beaches at either side of the promontory at Arkasa. On this promontory are the ruins of **ancient Arkasa** and fragments of mosaic floors from a 5th-century basilica.

A left turn at the T-junction in Arkasa will bring you to the tiny fishing village of **Finikes**, two km north of Arkasa, and one of the most serene places on the island.

Places to Stay

Amopi Beach Rooms (☎ 22 723) at Amopi are simply furnished, spotless rooms surrounded by a garden with a grape arbour and fig trees – guests may help themselves to the fruit. Rates are 3000/3500 dr for singles/ doubles with shared bathrooms. From the bus terminal, face the sea and turn left. In the other direction you will find the comfortable *Golden Beach Rooms* (☎ 22 137), where rates are 4500 dr for a double with a private bathroom. The price includes breakfast.

Menetes has only one place to stay, the rooms of friendly Greek-American *Mike Rigas* (☎ 81 269/255), in a traditional Karpathian house with a garden of figs and grapes. Doubles with shared bathrooms are 2400 dr and triples with private bathrooms are 3500 dr. Coming from Pigadia, the rooms are 150 metres down a cement road veering off to the right, just beyond the museum.

Places to stay are springing up all over the place in Arkasa, but most are monopolised by package-tour companies. You could try *Rooms Irene* (☎ 61 263), which caters for independent travellers. The prettily decorated single/double/triple rooms are 3000/ 4000/5000 dr with private bathrooms. You will see a sign pointing left to the rooms, just before the T-junction.

In Finikes, the new *Fay's Paradise* (☎ 61 308) are lovely rooms, with a kitchen area and private bathrooms. They cost 3000/4000/5000 dr. The rooms are on the left of the main road, beyond the little fishing harbour.

Places to Eat

In Amopi the *Golden Beach Restaurant* in front of the rooms of the same name serves tasty food. *Taverna Manolis* in Menetes serves reasonable food. A large giros with tomato and onion garnish is 700 dr. It's the village's only taverna – locals will direct you.

The *Restaurant Petaluda*, in Arkasa's central square, has kalamaria for 500 dr and swordfish for 800 dr.

Locals come from all over the island to eat at the excellent *Dimitrios Fisherman's Taverna* in Finikes. Red mullet and bass are 5000 dr a kg, lobster is 6400 dr; kalamaria is 400 dr a portion and swordfish is 800 dr. The taverna is opposite Paradise Rooms.

Other Beaches

The beautiful east-coast beaches of **Ahata**, **Kira Panagia** and **Apella** are most easily reached by excursion boat from Pigadia. **Lefkos**, on the west coast, is a tiny hamlet with three superb sandy beaches. Over the last few years it has become the 'in' place, not only with backpackers and nudists seeking out remote beaches, but also with small tour operators, so in July and August it gets crowded. However, at other times it's well worth a visit, and has plenty of reasonably priced domatia.

NORTHERN KARPATHOS

Diafani Διαφανέσ

Diafani is Karpathos' small northern port. There's no post office or bank but Nikos Travel Agency (☎ 51 410), on the waterfront, has currency exchange. There's no OTE, but there is a metered telephone in a café just back from the waterfront.

Olymbos Ολυμπος

Clinging to the ridge of barren Mt Profitis Ilias, four km above Diafani, is Olymbos (340 inhabitants), a living museum. Young women wear brightly coloured and embroidered skirts, waistcoats and headscarves and goatskin boots. The older women's apparel is more subdued but still distinctive. Interiors of houses are decorated with embroidered cloth and their façades with brightly painted ornate plaster reliefs. The inhabitants speak in a vernacular which contains some Doric words, and the houses have wooden locks of the kind described by Homer. Olymbos is a matrilineal society – a family's property passes down from the mother to the first-born daughter. The women still grind corn in windmills and bake bread in outdoor communal ovens.

Olymbos, alas, is no longer a pristine backwater with inhabitants living in a time warp, oblivious to the 20th century. Nowadays, hordes of tourists come to gape, and the inhabitants have naturally responded to this by opening souvenir shops. However, the traditional customs remain intact, and Olymbos is still a fascinating place to visit.

The bus turnaround is at the beginning of the village. Follow the road around to reach the main street which leads to the central square.

On the road between Olymbos and Diafani, a one-hour walk along a dirt road to the left will take you to the remote, barely inhabited village of **Avlona**. From here there is a path to **Vroukounda**, where there are the remains of a Doric settlement.

Festivals On 29 August a lively festival with feasting and dancing is held in Vroukounda's chapel of Agios Ioannis, which is in a cave.

Places to Stay

There's an unofficial camp site at Vananda Beach, 30 minutes' walk to the north of Diafani.

The *Golden Beach Hotel* (☎ 51 315), opposite the quay in Diafani, has tidy single/double/triple rooms for 1500/2500/3000 dr with shared bathrooms.

Pension Glaros (☎ 51 259/216) has clean nicely furnished rooms with wood-panelled ceilings. Rates are 2000/2500/3000 dr with shared bathrooms. From the quay you will spot the pension up to the left.

Just off the main street in Olymbos, the clean, simply furnished rooms at *Pension Olymbos* (☎ 51 252) cost 1300/2000/3000 dr with shared bathrooms. Just beyond the bus turna- around the simply and tastefully furnished *Mike's Rooms* (☎ 51 304) cost 3000 dr a double.

The new *Hotel Aphrodite* (☎ 51 307/454) has immaculate double/triple rooms for 4000/5000 dr with private bathrooms, including breakfast. To reach the hotel from the central square, walk down the steps opposite Taverna Parthenonas.

Places to Eat

In Diafani the *Golden Beach Taverna* below the hotel of the same name is good. Stuffed tomatoes, moussaka and kalamaria are all 700 dr and souvlaki is 1000 dr.

Olymbos has some culinary specialities. You may like to try *macarounis* which is handmade noodles mixed with grated cheese and onions, and fried. The *Olymbos Taverna* below the pension of the same name is excellent. Macarounis is 430 dr, green beans are 450 dr and moussaka and pastitsio are 680 dr. *Mike's Taverna* below his rooms has macarounis, moussaka and pastitsio for 400 dr. *Parthenonas Restaurant* on the central square has macarounis for 500 dr and stuffed vegetables for 750 dr. There is often live traditional Greek music here in the evening.

Getting Around

Bus A minibus meets the excursion boats from Pigadia at Diafani and transports people up to Olymbos for 400 dr. Otherwise you can make the strenuous 2½-hour uphill trek from Diafani through a ravine.

Excursion Boat In Diafani, Nikos Travel Agency takes tourists by small boat to nearby beaches for a nominal fee. Occasionally there are boat trips to the uninhabited islet of Saria where there are the remains of a Byzantine church.

Kassos Κάσσος

Kassos (KA-sos, population 1200), 11 km south of Karpathos, is a rocky little island of prickly pear trees, sparse olive and fig trees, dry stone walls, sheep and goats. It is one of the least visited islands of the Dodecanese and definitely one for the unspoilt-island aficionados amongst you.

If you tell Karparthians you're off to Kassos they'll tell you to take your knitting. But for travellers intent upon seeing something of traditional Greek life, and who enjoy walking, Kassos has a lot to offer. Remaining Kassiots realise that tourism is the only solution to address the problem of the island's rapidly falling population. However, they are fussy about what type of tourists they want, saying, 'We don't want long-haired youths or drunkards or drug takers'.

The recent commencement of a weekly excursion boat from Karpathos was met with some trepidation. Karpathos' tourism is pretty low key, compared with that of neighbouring Rhodes or Kos, but to Kassiots, Karpathos is Sodom and Gomorrah. 'Be careful who you send us' they warned. They relate with good humour that the first daytrippers to their island were a boat load of Jehovah's Witnesses.

History

Despite being diminutive and remote, Kassos has had as eventful and tragic a history as anywhere in Greece. During Turkish rule the island flourished. By 1820, it had a population of 11,000 and a large mercantile fleet. Mohammad Ali, Turkish Governor of Egypt, saw this fleet as a deterrent to his plan to establish a base on Crete from which to attack the Peloponnese and quell the uprising there. So on 7 June 1824, Ali's men landed on the island and killed an estimated 7000 inhabitants. This tragic event is commemorated each year on the day of the slaughter. Former Kassiots return from the USA and elsewhere to participate in the anniversary.

During the late 19th century many Kas-

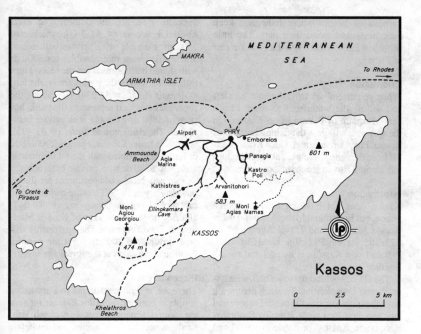

siots emigrated to Egypt. It is said that 5000 Kassiots helped build the Suez Canal. In this century many Kassiots have emigrated to the USA.

Getting To/From Kassos

Air In summer there are daily flights to Rhodes (8200 dr) and on Tuesday, Thursday and Saturday to Karpathos (2400 dr). The Olympic Airways office (☎ 41 444) is on Kritis. The tiny airport is 2½ km west of Phry.

Ferry F/B *Kimolos* calls in at Kassos twice a week, on its way to and from Rhodes. Its ports of call from Piraeus are Sifnos, Milos, Folegandros, Sikinos, Thira, Agios Nikolaos (Crete), Sitia (Crete), Kassos, Pigadia (Karpathos), Diafani (Karpathos) Halki, Symi, Rhodes and vice versa. At the time of writing, it left Piraeus at 8 am on Tuesday and left Rhodes at 4 pm on Wednesday. It leaves Kassos for Rhodes (2500 dr) at 4 am

on Wednesday and for Piraeus (4400 dr) at 11.30 pm on Wednesday. If the sea is rough (which it often is) the boat does not stop at Kassos.

Excursion Boat There are excursion boats from Karpathos to Kassos on Sunday in the summer. For details see the Getting To/From Karpathos section. In July and August there are daily excursion boats to Armathia islet (1500 dr return) from Phry.

Getting Around Kassos

To/From the Airport There is no airport bus; a taxi costs 400 dr.

Bus The island's one bus travels in a circuit to all of the villages from Phry. There is a flat fare of 150 dr.

PHRY Φρυ

Phry is the island's capital and port. The town's focal point is the picturesque old harbour of Bouka where fishermen keep their boats and mend their nets. The little suburb of Emboreios is less than one km east of Phry.

Orientation

When you disembark from the boat, turn left and follow the waterfront to reach Phry's central square of Plateia Iroon Kassou. On the way you will pass the fishing harbour of Bouka. Phry's main street, Odos Kritis, leads off from the central square. Take the first turn left along Kritis to reach the post office.

Information

Kassos does not have an EOT or tourist police, but Emmanual Manousos, who owns Kassos Maritime and Travel Agency (☎ 41 323/305; telex 292-506 K MEM GR), Plateia Iroon Kassou, is helpful and speaks English.

The OTE is behind the town hall, which is on Plateia Demokratias. To reach here, walk from the quay towards the central square and take the first turn right after To Panorama Restaurant. Kassos' postcode is 85800 and the telephone code is 0245.

The National Bank of Greece is represented by the supermarket at the beginning of Kritis. The bank will exchange travellers' cheques but does not give cash advances on credit cards. The port police (☎ 41 222) are on the left side of the road to Emboreios, and the police are a little further along on the right. The bus terminal is on Kritis, 50 metres from Plateia Iroon Kassou.

Phry has a little **museum**, facing the town hall; it's along the road to the left. I can't elucidate on its contents, because when I visited Kassos, the museum's caretaker was on holiday in Rhodes, and had taken the key with him.

Places to Stay

All of the island's accommodation is in Phry. *Ketty Markous Rooms* (☎ 41 613/498/216) are immaculate and cost 2700 dr a double with shared bathrooms and use of a kitchen. The rooms are beyond the police station on the way to Emboreios. Further along, on the opposite side, are the comfortable *Elias Koutlakis Rooms* (☎ 41 363), which cost 3500 dr a double with private bathrooms. *Maria Economou* rents doubles for 3000 dr with shared bathrooms. Take the second turn right on Kritis and the rooms are on the left.

Anessis Hotel (☎ 41 234/201), above the supermarket which represents the bank, has rates of 3800 dr a double with private bathrooms. The *Anagennisis Hotel* (☎ 41 495), on Plateia Iroon Kassou, charges 2900/3800 dr for singles/doubles with shared bathrooms, and 3930/5780 dr with private bathrooms.

Two new blocks of apartments are due to open in Phry in 1993. They are owned by the brothers *Georgiou Manousos* (☎ 41 047) and *Emmanual Manousos* of Kassos Maritime & Travel Agency. The apartments will cost around 10,000 dr for four people. Enquire about them at the travel agency.

Places to Eat

There are several restaurants in Phry and a couple in Emboreios. *Milos Restaurant* near the central square serves very fresh fish. Sardines are 3000 dr a kilo, red mullet is 4500 dr and lobster is 5000 dr. *Kassos Restaurant* on Plateia Demokratias is run by a co-operative of Kassiot women. A tasty meal here of chicken with potatoes, Greek salad and retsina will cost about 1500 dr.

AROUND THE ISLAND
Beaches

Kassos' best beach is the isolated and lovely pebbled cove of **Khelathros**, a 2½-hour walk south along a dirt road. Walking from Agia Marina to Arvanitohori, turn right on a dirt road to reach the beach. Where the dirt road forks, take the left downhill folk (the right fork leads to Agios Giorgios monastery). The beach has no facilities whatsoever. The less appealing beach of **Ammounda** is just beyond the airport. There are superb sandy beaches on the nearby uninhabited islet of **Armathia**.

Villages

You can walk from Phry to all of the island's other villages. **Agia Marina**, one km south-west of Phry, is a pretty village with a gleaming white and blue church. On 17 July, the **Festival of Agia Marina** is celebrated here. Many of the village's traditional houses have been restored by wealthy former Kassiots who spend the summer here. From Agia Marina the road continues to **Arvanitohori**, the island's most verdant village, with fig and pomegranate trees and gardens spilling over with frangipani and bougainvillea.

Poli, three km south-east of Phry, is the island's former capital, built on the ancient acropolis, of which there are scant remains. Melancholy **Panagia**, between Phry and Poli, has less than 50 inhabitants. Its once grand sea-captains' and ship-owners' mansions are now derelict.

Caves

Kassos has two caves. **Ellinokamara Cave** is enclosed by a Hellenic wall. To reach the cave walk along the road from Agia Marina to Arvanitohori. Just beyond the two disused windmills take a cement road which veers right and leads to the hamlet of Kathistres. Continue along the road and when it veers right, continue straight ahead on a stony path and take the steep dirt track veering off to the left. The cave is at the top on the right. The stalactite and stalagmite **Cave of Selai** is supposedly 1½ km beyond here, but I searched for it in vain. Mr Manousos told me there used to be a sign pointing to the cave, but the wind blew it down; he assured me a new sign would soon be erected.

Monasteries

The island has two monasteries. **Agias Mamas** (signposted), a four-km walk from the village of Poli, flourished until this century but is no longer inhabited. **Agiou Giorgiou** is a 2½-hour walk from Arvanitohori. Take the Khelathros Beach road and where the road forks, go right and up to reach the monastery. There are no monks, but there is a resident caretaker and 10 beds for visitors. Accommodation is free but as always it is courteous to leave a donation. On both of these walks you will be rewarded with fine panoramas of the island's stark and barren

mountainous landscape and the glistening sea. You will also pass numerous abandoned terraces, testimony to the days when Kassos was a thriving little island.

Kastellorizo
Καστελλόριζο

Tiny, rocky and barren Kastellorizo (Kas-tel-O-ri-zo), a mere speck on the map, is around 118 km east of Rhodes its nearest Greek neighbour and only 2½ km from the southern coast of Turkey.

Its official name is Megisti (The Biggest), for it is the largest of a group of 14 islets. The island draws more and more visitors each year as committed Grecophiles seek out unspoilt islands. In 1992 there was a proliferation of Italians as the island had been seductively portrayed in the Oscar-winning film *Mediterraneo*. The film featured a war-time love affair between an Italian naval commander and a Greek woman. The island's remoteness has so far ensured that its tourism is low key.

The island has no sandy beaches but there are rocky inlets from where you can swim in a crystal clear and calm sea – it's a great place for snorkelling.

History

The ghost town you see today is made all the more poignant by an awareness of the island's past greatness. Due to its strategic position, Dorians, Romans, pirates from Asia Minor and Africa, crusaders, Egyptians, Turks and Venetians have all landed on the shores of Kastellorizo. The 20th century has been no less traumatic with occupations by French, British and Italians.

In 1552 Kastellorizo surrendered peacefully to the Turks and so was granted special privileges, allowing it to preserve its language, religion and traditions. Its cargo fleet became the largest in the Dodecanese and the islanders achieved a high degree of culture and education.

Kastellorizo lost all strategic and economic importance after the 1923 population exchange. In 1928 it was ceded to the Italians who severely oppressed the islanders, and so the Kastellorizo diaspora began. Many islanders emigrated to Perth, Australia, where today some 10,000 people of Kastellorizo origin live.

Kastellorizo suffered severe bombardment during WW II, and English commanders ordered the few remaining inhabitants to abandon their island. They fled to Cyprus, Palestine and Egypt, but were not allowed to take any belongings with them. In October 1945, 300 islanders boarded the Australian ship *Empire Control* to return to Kastellorizo. Tragically, the ship burst into flames and 35 people lost their lives. Two months later the remaining refugees returned to their island to find that most of their houses had been destroyed by bombings and the remaining ones had been ransacked by the occupying troops. Not surprisingly more islanders emigrated.

Today Kastellorizo is home to just over 200 inhabitants. It is rumoured that if the population drops to less than 200 the island will become Turkish. Another rumour is that

the Greek government are toying with the idea of building a prison here to boost the population. Most of the houses which escaped the bombing in WW II stand empty. All this paints a very gloomy picture, but despite everything, Kastellorizo's waterfront is one of the liveliest in Greece, with impromptu singing and dancing taking place most evenings.

Getting To/From Kastellorizo (Island)

Air In summer there are daily flights to and from Rhodes (7900 dr), and in winter there are three a week; buy tickets from Dizi Tours.

Ferry The F/B *Nissos Kalimnos* is the only passenger boat that sails to Kastellorizo (six hours, 2100 dr). See the Getting To/From Rhodes (Island) section for its schedule.

Excursion Boat (From Turkey) In summer there are excursion boats from Kas, on the southern coast of Turkey, to Kastellorizo (Meis Adasi in Turkish). Making the trip the other way round is a different matter, because Kas is an official port of entry whereas Kastellorizo is not. However, unofficially, it is possible to go on a day excursion to Kas. Just keep your ears open and ask around.

Getting Around Kastellorizo (Island)

There is one bus on the island which is used solely to transport people to and from the airport (300 dr). The island has no taxis so make sure you don't miss the bus because it's a long uphill slog.

KASTELLORIZO TOWN

Kastellorizo town is the island's only settlement. The town is built around a U-shaped bay, its waterfront skirted with imposing, spruced-up three-storey mansions with wooden balconies. However, this alluring countenance eclipses back streets of abandoned and derelict houses overgrown with ivy, crumbling stairways and stony pathways winding between them.

Orientation & Information

The quay is at the eastern side of the bay. The central square of Plateia Ethelontou Kastellorizo abuts the waterfront, almost halfway round the bay. The post office and police station (☎ 29 068) are on the western side of the bay, just before the Hotel Megisti.

There is no OTE but Taverna Mavros, on Plateia Ethelontou Kastellorizo, has a metered telephone. Kastellorizo's postcode is 85111 and the telephone code is 0241. The National Bank of Greece is represented by Taverna International, on the waterfront beyond the central square. The port police are at the northern tip of the bay, beyond the ferry quay.

There is an EOT office on the eastern side of the waterfront but I have never found it open. Dizi Tours & Travel (☎ 49 239), three doors along from this office, is the island's only travel agency. Here you can buy Olympic Airways tickets, exchange travellers' cheques and get cash advances on American Express, Visa and MasterCard.

Things to See

The **Knights of St John Castle** stands on a hill to the east of the quay. A metal staircase leads to the top from where there are splendid views of the Turkish coast. The **museum** within the castle, houses a well-displayed eclectic collection, including folk costumes, frescoes, old pictures of Kastellorizo and a 19th-century sponge diver's suit. Opening times are Tuesday to Sunday from 8 am to 2.30 pm. Admission is free.

Just beyond the museum, steps down to the left lead to a pathway which skirts the coast. A little way along here you will come to some rough stone steps which clamber up the cliff face to a **Lycian tomb** with a well-preserved Doric façade. There are a number of these along the Turkish coast opposite, but this is the only one to have been found in Greece.

Excursions

Excursion boats operate trips to the **Islet of Ro**. See the feature in this section for more details.

The **Blue Cave**, on Kastellorizo's east coast, is spectacular. The name is derived from the blue appearance of the water in the cave, caused by refracted sunlight. Several boat owners run excursions here – look for the signs along the waterfront. The price is around 2000 dr per person.

Places to Stay

If you arrive by boat you will probably be offered a room when you disembark, otherwise the following budget options charge 4000 dr a double. *Rooms Kastraki* and *Pension Barbara* (☎ 29 295) are both along a narrow street (signposted Horafia and Mandraki), at the top of the eastern side of the harbour. Further around the bay, behind Plateia Australias, you will find *Rooms O Paradeisos* (☎ 29 074). The *Blue & White Pension* (no sign) is a popular place on the western side of the bay.

The *Pension Castelo* (no sign) is up a notch in comfort and price. Two-bedroomed family apartments are 10,000 dr and attractive, comfortable doubles are 6000 dr. Facing inland, walk across Plateia Ethel-

---

The Woman of Ro

The Islet of Ro, one of Kastellorizo's 13 satellites, has been immortalised along with its last inhabitant, Kyria Despina, alias the Woman of Ro, who died in 1982. Despina and her shepherd husband were the only inhabitants of Ro. When her husband died, Despina remained alone on the island, staunchly hoisting the Greek flag every morning, and lowering it in the evening, in full view of the Turkish coast. The Woman of Ro has become a symbol of the Greek spirit of indomitability in the face of adversity. There are excursion boats to the islet: look for signs along the waterfront at Kastellorizo town. There is a bust of Kyria Despina on Plateia Horafia. ■

ontou Kastellorizo and turn right at the palm tree. Walk across the wasteground and the pension is straight ahead. If you can't find the owner, Despina, try the Taverna Mavros where she works.

The island's only hotel, the B class *Hotel Megisti* (☎ 29 072) at the west side of the bay, is an opulent place with rates of 6000/10,000/12,000 dr.

Places to Eat

Restaurant Oraia Megisti, on Plateia Ethelontou Kastellorizo, serves excellent food. Main courses are around 1000 dr. *Restaurant Eftychia*, opposite, is also good with similar prices. Further along the waterfront *Taverna International* is also commendable. *Restaurant Platania* on Plateia Horafia (follow the signs for Horafia) is a nice unpretentious place. A full meal here will cost about 1500 dr.

Tilos Τήλος

Tilos (TEE-los, population 300) lies 65 km west of Rhodes city. It is less barren and rocky than Kassos, Halki or Kastellorizo, being blessed with springs and pockets of lush greenery, where almond, pomegranate, carob and walnut trees sprout forth. However, this agricultural potential is not utilised for, rather than work the land for a pittance, young Tiliots leave for the mainland or emigrate to Australia or the USA.

Tilos has superb beaches and many opportunities for walking, but is still unspoilt. Accommodation is good value and camping freelance is permitted on all of the island's beaches. The island has two settlements: the port of Livadia, and Megalo Chorio, eight km to the north. A third settlement, Mikro Chorio, was abandoned after WW II, and its derelict dwellings are intriguing to explore. It is reached by a turn-off left between Livadia and Megalo Chorio.

The 'mastadon' cave (see History) is north of here but is presently closed to the public. The staff at Tilos Travel Agency will tell you whether this is still the case.

History

You may be puzzled to see on sale here T-shirts declaring 'Tilos the Elephant Island'. They refer to the bones of mastadons which were found in a cave on the island. Mastadons were midget elephants which became extinct around 4600 BC.

Tilos is also known as the home of Irini, one of the greatest of ancient Greece's female poets, who lived here in the 4th century BC.

Elephants and poetry apart, Tilos' history followed the same catalogue of invasions and occupations as the rest of the archipelago. Locals insist that Tilos has a mass of subterranean treasures awaiting discovery. This was borne out by the discovery in late 1992 of tombs dating from 300 BC. The tombs are at Agios Antonios Beach – the owners of the Hotel Australia will direct you to them.

Getting To/From Tilos

The F/B *Ionian* and F/B *Nissos Kalimnos* are the only ferries with Tilos as a port of call. See the Getting To/From Rhodes (Island) section for details of their schedules. There may possibly be hydrofoils and excursion boats from Rhodes and Kos in high summer; enquire at travel agencies on these islands.

Getting Around Tilos

Tilos' only 'bus' is an orange 12-seater transit van, which does trips from Livadia's central square to Megalo Chorio and Eristos Beach (both 150 dr). Tilos Travel Agency rents 50 cc motorbikes for 2500 dr and four-seater motorboats for 5000 dr a day.

LIVADIA Λιβάδια

Livadia, with just 50 inhabitants, nestles at the edge of a large bay on the island's east coast. All the facilities tourists need are here, as well as most of the accommodation. A long pebble beach skirts the bay at the eastern end of the village. The pleasant Lethra Beach is about 30 minutes' walk in the other direction. Walking inland from the central square turn right at the 'Hotel Livadia' street. Continue along here and

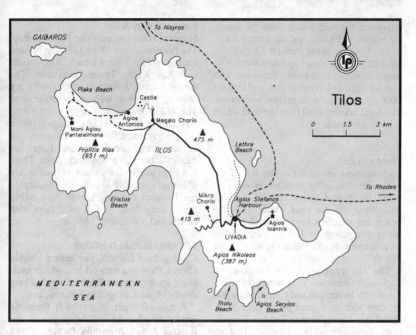

soon the road narrows to a dirt track. Beyond the last row of houses go through a wooden gate and continue along the pathway to reach Lethra Beach.

Orientation & Information
From the ferry quay turn left, and ascend the wide steps to the right; at the top walk straight ahead to reach Livadia's central square. The post office and OTE are in the same building on the central square. Tilos' postcode is 85002 and the telephone code is 0241. Both the port police (☎ 53 350) and the regular police (☎ 53 220) are in the large white building to the left of the quay. Tilos has no EOT but the English-speaking owner of Tilos Travel Agency (☎ 53 259) at the quay is helpful.

Places to Stay
Livadia is well provided with accommodation. The E class *Hotel Livadia* (☎ 53 266),

overlooking the central square, has tidy doubles for 2200 dr with shared bathrooms and 3000 dr with private bathrooms. At the western end of the beach you'll find *Rooms to Rent O Spiros* (☎ 53 339), where rates are 3400 dr a double with private bathrooms. Next door, *Paraskevi Rooms* (☎ 53 280) charges 2900 dr for doubles with shared bathrooms. The next one along, *Stamatos Rooms* (☎ 53 334), has doubles with shared bathrooms for 3100 dr. All of these places are clean and simply furnished. To reach the western end of the beach walk straight ahead across the central square from the quay and take the first turn left after Pension Perigali.

The *Pension Perigali* (☎ 53 398) has tastefully furnished single/double rooms for 2850/4800 dr with shared bathrooms. The *Casa Italiana Rooms* (☎ 53 253/259), opposite the quay, has immaculate double/triple rooms with private bathrooms and kitchen areas for 5000/6000 dr. *Yiannis Studios* (behind Yiannis Bar), at the other side of the village on the road which skirts the beach, are equally agreeable, and the same price.

The C Class *Hotel Irini* (☎ 53 293/359; fax 53 238) is the island's poshest hotel, with lovely stucco-walled rooms decorated with tasteful rugs and ceramic plates. Rates are 8000 dr a double with private bathrooms. The hotel is signposted from the road which follows the beach.

Places to Eat

The nameless restaurant to the left of the quay, at the base of the steps, serves well-prepared low-priced Greek staples. *Sophia's Restaurant*, on the road which skirts the beach, has excellent food. A Greek plate (a bit of everything) is 890 dr; other dishes include moussaka for 590 dr and souvlaki for 720 dr.

The cheapest place for breakfast is *Kafeneion Omonoias*, next to the post office. Toast with butter, jam and coffee is only 300 dr; they also have good pizzas for 650 dr. *Snack Bar Viyios*, next to Pension Perigali, is also good for breakfast or a snack. Try their speciality, french toast (250 dr), which comes dripping with syrup and sprinkled with cinnamon.

MEGALO CHORIO Μεγάλο Χωριό

Megalo Chorio, eight km north of Livadia, has a population of 150. It's a serene place of whitewashed houses crowned by the ruins of a **Knights' Castle**, from where there are stunning views of Plaka Bay, Gaidaros islet and Nisyros. The castle has an intact gateway, and a small chapel with some faded frescoes. In autumn, the site is strewn with purple crocuses which add vibrant splashes of colour to the grey stone. It's a steep 30-minute trek up to the castle; walk through the village, passing the grocery store on the left, and you will find the path on the left. Megalo Chorio's large **Church of Taxiarchis** has a black and white pebble mosaic courtyard and a highly ornate interior, including a beautiful gilded iconostasis. Someone in the town hall opposite will open up the church for you.

Places to Stay & Eat

Megalo Chorio has only two places to stay. The *Pension Sevasti* (☎ 53 237), just beyond the turn-off for Eristos Beach, is co-owned with Kali Kardia Taverna next door. The nicely furnished single/double rooms are only 2000/2830 dr with shared bathrooms. The *Milou Rooms and Apartments* (☎ 53 204/220), in the centre of the village opposite the grocery store, have kitchen areas and attractive traditional artefacts. Rates are 4200/5780 dr with private bathrooms. There is a large jungle-like garden with an aviary of budgerigars. *Kali Kardia Taverna*, next to the Pension Sevasti, serves reasonably priced tasty food. A full meal here with retsina will cost around 1400 dr.

AROUND MEGALO HORIO

Coming from Livadia, just before Megalo Chorio, there is a turn-off left, which leads in 2½ km to gorgeous **Eristos Beach**, a long swathe of sand, fringed by tamarisk trees.

A turn-off right (signposted) from the Eristos Beach road will bring you to the isolated **Agios Antonios Beach**. **Plaka Beach**, three km west of here, is a mixture of sand and pebbles, and is dotted with trees, making it an ideal camping spot. The 18th-century **Moni Agiou Penteleimona**, five km beyond Plaka Beach, is uninhabited but well maintained. It has fine 18th-century frescoes; one of them is quite surreal, depicting the monastery's founder, monk Laurentios, holding the monastery in his hands.

The monastery is kept locked but the island's minibus driver takes groups of visitors there on Sunday. The scenery on the way, and at the monastery itself, is spectacularly dramatic.

Places to Stay & Eat

Eristos Beach has three places to stay. The *Tropicana Taverna & Rooms* (☎ 53 242) has pleasant doubles/triples with shared bathrooms for 3000/3600 dr and the surrounding garden does indeed look tropical. Beyond here, a sign points left to *Nausika Taverna & Rooms*. The clean double/triple rooms are 3600/5000 dr with shared bathrooms.

The immaculate D class *Hotel Australia*, overlooks Agios Antonios Beach. Rates are 5000/5780/6780 dr for singles/doubles/triples with private bathrooms. The hotel is owned by four Greek-Australian brothers. Ferries are met by the hotel's red transit van. All of these places have restaurants serving well-prepared reasonably priced meals.

Nisyros Νίσυρος

The small island of Nisyros (NEE-see-ros, population 1000) lies between Tilos and Kos. The nucleus of the island is a dormant volcano, creating a curious anomaly whereby the island is waterless, yet fertile. The mineral-rich earth holds moisture and yields olives, vines, figs, citrus and almond trees – the Turkish name for the island was Intzirli Adasi (Fig Island). It is one of the strangest and most beautiful of all Greek islands, for its lush vegetation is combined with dramatic moonscapes.

The island has four settlements: Mandraki the capital, Pali, a fishing village, and the crater-top villages of Emboreios and Nikea. The island has not suffered such drastic population depletion as other small islands of the Dodecanese, because many of its men earn a living quarrying pumice.

Getting To/From Nisyros

Ferry Nisyros is one of F/B *Nissos Kalimnos*' ports of call. See the Ferry sections under Rhodes and Kalymnos for details of its schedule. Prices from Nisyros are: Kastellorizo 3680 dr, Rhodes 1550 dr, Kalymnos 890 dr, Tilos 720 dr and Kos 490 dr.

The F/B *Ionian Sun* also calls at Nisyros. See the Getting To/From Rhodes (Island) section for details of its schedule.

Excursion Boat In summer there is a daily

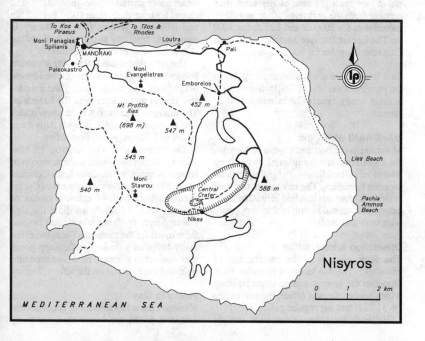

excursion boat from Kardamena on Kos to Nisyros and less frequently from Kos town.

Getting Around Nisyros

Bus As with most small islands the bus service is just adequate. There are at least two buses every day to the volcano (500 dr return), five buses to Pali and two buses on weekdays to Nikea and Emboreios, but none on weekends. A bus schedule is displayed outside Polyvotis Tours at the quay. Enetikis Travel (☎ 31 180; fax 31 168), on the right side of the main street, organises various bus excursions around the island.

Taxi There are two taxi companies: Bobby's Taxi (☎ 31 460) and Irene's Taxi (☎ 31 474). Prices of taxi journeys are as follows: Volcano (4000 dr), Emboreios (1500 dr), Nikea (2000 dr) and Pali (600 dr). An island tour is 6000 dr.

Motorbike & Bicycle Alpha Rent (no telephone) on the right side of the main road coming from the port rents 50 cc and 70 cc motorbikes for 2000 dr and 125 cc for 3000 dr. The Cactus Bar (see Mandraki Places to Eat) rents bicycles for 700 dr a day.

Taxi Boat There are taxi boats every day to the pumice-stone islet of Giali where there is a good sandy beach (20 minutes, 500 dr return).

MANDRAKI Μανδράκι

Mandraki is the port and capital of Nisyros. Its dwellings are traditional two-storey whitewashed buildings with brightly painted wooden balconies. The most attractive part is the web of streets huddled below the monastery. The central square is also very pretty with trees and cafés.

Orientation & Information

The ferry quay is at the eastern end of Mandraki. The bus terminal is at the quay. Opposite the quay is a large white building which houses the post office, the port police (☎ 31 222) and the regular police.

To reach the town centre walk straight ahead along the road which skirts the sea. Where the road forks, the right road leads to the sea-front square of Plateia Iroon and the main road continues straight ahead. The National Bank of Greece is represented by a store along here. The road continues to the small Plateia Aristotelous Fotiadou. Cross here and pass the town hall on the right. Nisyros does not have an OTE but one may be open soon. Meanwhile, Sakellazidis General Store, on a narrow street opposite the town hall, has a metered telephone. Nisyros' telephone code is 0242. Continue to the end of the main road and turn left to reach the central square of Plateia Elikomini. Nisyros has no EOT or tourist police.

Things to See

The 14th-century **Moni Panagias Spilianis** (Virgin of the Cave) is built on a cliff at the western end of town. Its star attraction is its chapel which is built into a cave in the cliff face and is crammed with the usual ecclesiastic paraphernalia. The monastery and chapel are open daily from 10.30 am to 3 pm and admission is free. The monastery is signposted from the street which skirts the cliff at the western end of the town.

The little **Historical & Popular Museum** houses an array of bric-a-brac (embroideries, old photographs, old books etc) and a reconstruction of an old kitchen in the basement. The museum is halfway up the steps which lead to the monastery. It is open daily from 10 am to 2.30 pm. Admission is free.

The **Paleokastro** (Old Kastro), 15 minutes' walk from Mandraki, is the acropolis of ancient Nisyros, which dates from Classical times. The impressive well-preserved Cyclopean walls are built of massive blocks of volcanic rock. To reach it follow the sign pointing right (walking inland) just beyond the turn-off for the museum. The route eventually becomes a donkey path. Keep going until you get to a cement road, and then turn right and the kastro is on the left.

Places to Stay

Mandraki has a fair amount of accommodation and prices are lower than on many islands. There are no camp sites on Nisyros. The cheapest accommodation is *Pension Drosia* (☎ 31 328/082), where clean rooms cost only 1500 dr a double with shared bathrooms and 2500 dr with private bathrooms. Walk along the main road and, where it forks, keep to the road which skirts the sea. Keep going and eventually you will come to the pension on the right.

The *Hotel Romantzo* (☎ 31 340) has comfortable single/double/triple rooms for 4000/4500/6500 dr with private bathrooms. Take the first turning left after leaving the quay and the hotel is a little way along on the right. Opposite here the pleasant *Three Brothers Hotel* (☎ 31 344) has doubles with private bathrooms for 4000 dr. If you continue along this road, you will come to the C class *Haritos Hotel* (☎ 31 322/122), where comfortable spacious rooms with direct-dial telephone and balconies cost 4500/6000/7500 dr with private bathrooms.

Nisyros' best hotel is the C class *Hotel Porfyris*, which has a swimming pool, bar and TV room. The rates are 5000/6500 dr for singles/doubles with private bathrooms, including breakfast. Walk along the main road into town and a sign on the left points to the hotel.

Places to Eat

Taverna Nissyros is a charming little place with reasonable prices. The restaurant is in a side street to the left of the main road as you come from the quay – look for the sign. *Restaurant Elikiomeni*, on the central square, is also commendable. A full meal here will come to about 1400 dr.

Karava Restaurant, next to Enetikos Travel on the main road, has an outdoor terrace overlooking the sea. Their tasty dishes include stuffed courgettes for 450 dr and rice and shrimps for 1200 dr. For breakfast, a snack or a drink, head for the trendy bamboo-roofed *Cactus Bar* where a variety of breakfasts cost from 600 to 800 dr. The bar is between Plateia Elikiomini and the Hotel Porfyris. While on Nisyros be sure to try the non-alcoholic local beverage called *soumada*, made from almond extract.

AROUND THE ISLAND
Volcano

Nisyros is on a volcanic line which passes through the islands of Aegina, Paros, Antiparos, Milos, Thira, Nisyros, Giali and Kos. The almost circular island originally culminated in a central mountain of some 1400 metres, but in a violent eruption in 1552 the centre collapsed, forming the fertile plain known as Lakki. Minor eruptions occurred in 1871, 1873, 1888 and 1933. The plain of Lakki is four km wide, and within it are five craters; the largest one is Stefanos, which is 25 metres high and 350 metres across.

A steep path descends into Stefanos where you can examine the multicoloured fumaroles at close quarters, listen to their hissing, and smell their sulphurous vapours. The steam which they emit has a temperature of 98°C and the surface of the crater is soft and hot, making sturdy footwear essential.

If you come to the crater by bus you'll be accompanied by hordes of day-trippers from Kos, who rather detract from the extraordinary sight. In any case the bus only allows you 35 minutes which is hardly long enough to wander around and savour a glass of soumada from the little café near Stefanos. It's a good idea to either walk to or from the crater. You can walk from either Nikea (see the Nikea section) or from Mandraki. From Mandraki follow directions for Paleokastro, but instead of turning right at the cement road, continue straight ahead onto a dirt track. The scenic walk takes about two hours.

Emboreios & Nikea

Emboreios (Εμπορειός) and Nikea (Νίκαια) are the two villages which perch on the rim of the volcano. From each, there are stunning views down into the caldera. Only 20 inhabitants linger on in Emboreios, and most of its old stone houses are derelict. It's a lonely and evocative place – exploring its narrow stepped streets you may come across one or two elderly women sitting on their doorsteps crocheting, and their husbands sitting outside the village's only kafeneion.

However, for the most part, the winding and stepped streets of Emboreios are empty, their silence disturbed only by the occasional braying of a donkey or the grunting of pigs. As you leave Emboreios on the asphalt road, a stepped kalderimi on the left leads in about one hour to Pali. At one point it intersects the asphalt road; turn left onto the road and you will come to the kalderimi again on the right.

In contrast to Emboreios, picturesque Nikea is well kept and buzzes with life – it does after all, have 60 inhabitants. It has dazzling white houses with vibrant gardens and a central square with a lovely pebble mosaic. From Nikea's other square of Plateia Nikolaou Chartofili, a steep path marked with red slashes leads in 30 minutes to the caldera. The village's main thoroughfare links the two squares. The bus terminal is on Plateia Nikolaou Chartofili.

Places to Stay & Eat Emboreios has no accommodation for tourists and no tavernas.

Nikea's only accommodation is a *Community Hostel* on Plateia Nikolaou Chartofili. Rates are 2000 dr a double with shared bathrooms. If you would like to stay here see Panayiotis Mastromikali (☎ 31 285), who is the owner of the only taverna in the village – it's on the right just up from Plateia Nikolaou Chartofili. The food is good at the taverna, and reasonably priced

Pali Πάλοι
The attraction of Nisyros does not lie in its beaches, but if you like to be near a beach, the fishing village of Pali, four km east of Mandraki, has the island's best. There is a stretch of pale sand before the village and a long stretch of dark volcanic sand beyond.

Places to Stay & Eat The C class *Hotel Hellenis* (☎ 31 453), just off the central square, has pleasant rooms for 4000 dr a double with private bathrooms. Paraskevi, the owner, serves up wonderful dishes in the restaurant adjoining the hotel. Paraskevi's shepherd husband, the charismatic Manolis, is an accomplished musician, and sometimes plays the lyre in the taverna.

Astypalea Αστυπάλαια

Astypalea (As-ti-PA-lee-a, population 1100) is the most westerly of the Dodecanese and its history, geographical position and architecture are more akin to the Cyclades than to the group it belongs to. It is 40 km from Kos, its nearest neighbour in the Dodecanese.

During the Middle Ages when the Knights of St John held sway over most of the Dodecanese, Astypalea was occupied by the Venetian Quirini family. In 1912 it was the first island in the archipelago to pass from the Turks to the Italians.

Astypalea is the only Greek island without snakes, so it will be popular with ophiophobes – St Patrick must have managed to get here (after ridding Ireland of snakes) before St Paul. The island consists of two land masses joined by a narrow seven-km-long isthmus.

Astypalea is still not visited by many foreign tourists, but has long been a popular holiday spot with city Greeks, many of whom have built summer villas here.

Getting To/From Astypalea (Island)
Ferry Lying betwixt the Cyclades and the Dodecanese, Astypalea misses out on the ferries that serve each group. The F/B *Nissos Kalimnos* visits once a week. At the time of writing, it left Kalymnos on Thursday at 9.45 am for Astypalea (two hours, 1500 dr) and returned to Kalymnos at 12.45 pm.

The F/B *Ionian Sun* arrives at Astypalea around midnight on Monday en route for Rhodes via Kalymnos and Kos, and returns at around 8 pm en route to Rafina via Mykonos, Tinos and Andros.

Ferries sail twice a week to/from Piraeus via the Cyclades islands (16 hours, 2800 dr): one via Syros, Paros, Naxos, Iraklia, Shinoussa, Koufonisi, Katapola (Amorgos), Aegiali (Amorgos) and Donoussa; and the other via Syros, Tinos, Mykonos, Donoussa, Katapola and Aegiali. At the time of writing the first ferry sailed at 1 pm on a Thursday and the second at 6.30 pm on a Sunday, but

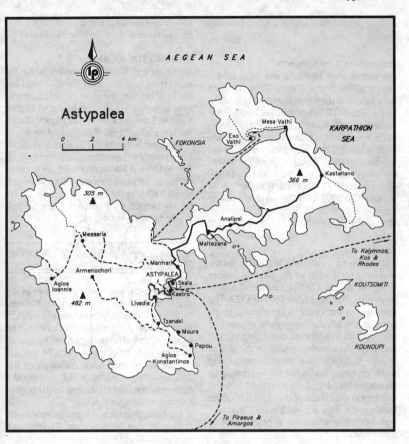

Astypalea

0   2   4 km

AEGEAN SEA

FOKONISIA

305 m ▲

Messaria

Armenochori

Agios
Ioannis

482 m ▲

Marmari

ASTYPALEA

Skala

Livadia   Kastro

Tzanaki

Moura

Papou

Agios
Konstantinos

Exo
Vathi   Mesa Vathi

KARPATHION
SEA

366 m ▲   Kastellano

Analipsi

Maltezana

To Kalymnos,
Kos &
Rhodes

KOUTSOMITI

KOUNOUPI

To Piraeus &
Amorgos

check the exact time of all ferries to/from Astypalea with the port police or a travel agent as they are likely to change from year to year.

Getting Around Astypalea (Island)

Bus There are four buses from Skala to Livadia (120 dr) and from Kastro and Skala to Maltezana (120 dr).

Excursion Boat There are excursion boats to many of the island's less accessible beaches and to nearby islets. Enquire about

these at Gournas Travel Agency on the waterfront in Astypalea town.

ASTYPALEA TOWN

The main settlement of the island is Astypalea town which is divided into two parts: the port of Skala (also called Pera Gialos) and uphill, the picturesque Kastro (also called Hora), topped by a fortress. Kastro consists of dazzling white cubic houses with wooden balconies that are far more reminiscent of the Cyclades than the Dodecanese. On the outskirts a line of derelict windmills adds to the charm. There is a small beach at Skala.

Orientation & Information

All ferries dock in Skala and from here a steep road leads up to Kastro. The post office is in Kastro at the top of the street leading to Skala. The OTE is beneath the Hotel Paradissos on the waterfront in Skala. Astypalea's postcode is 85900 and the telephone code is 0243. There is no bank on the island but the National Bank of Greece is represented by the store below the Aegean Hotel. There is no EOT or tourist police; the regular police (☎ 61 207) are in the same building as the port police (☎ 61 208), near the beginning of the road going up to Kastro.

Castle

The imposing castle which crowns Kastro was built on the site of the island's ancient acropolis by the Quirini family, who held sway over the island from 1207 to 1522. The entrance to the castle bears their coat-of-arms. In the Middle Ages the inhabitants of the island all lived within the castle walls but gradually the settlement outgrew them. The houses huddled close together within the walls are now in ruins but are fascinating to wander around and explore. Above the entrance is the church of the Our Lady of the Castle and within the walls is the Church of Agios Giorgios which has an ornate wooden iconostasis.

Places to Stay & Eat

Camping Astypalea (☎ 61 338) is three km east of Skala and is signposted from there.

Astypalea has four hotels; all are D class and they're all in Skala. The two nicest are the *Hotel Paradissos* (☎ 61 224) with singles/doubles for 3000/5000 dr and the D class *Hotel Vangelis* (☎ 61 281)with singles/doubles for 2500/4000 dr. Both hotels are on the waterfront. There are domatia in both Skala and Kastro; the owners meet the boats.

Astypalea's tavernas are much of a muchness. The nicest is *Taverna Akrogiali*, which has stuffed tomatoes and stuffed peppers for

550 dr and moussaka and pastitsio for 700 dr. The taverna is on the beach in Skala.

AROUND THE ISLAND

To the west of Skala, **Livadia** (Λιβάδια) is in the most verdant part of the island and has the best, but also the most crowded, beach. Less crowded beaches can be found further south at **Tzanaki**, **Moura** and **Papou**. Tzanaki is the island's unofficial nudist beach.

Marmari, north-east of Skala, has pleasant little bays for sunbathing and swimming. Beyond here at **Maltezana** there are remains of Roman baths with mosaics. **Exo Vathi** and **Mesa Vathi**, in the north of the island, are fishing hamlets with beaches. They are best reached by excursion boat.

Symi Σύμη

Symi (SEE-mi, population 2300) lies in the straits of Marmara, 24 km north of Rhodes, its nearest Greek neighbour and only 10 km from the Turkish peninsula of Dorakis. The island has an interior of jagged rocks, and an indented coast of precipitous cliffs, sheltering numerous small bays. Although on the decline, sponge fishing is still the island's main industry. Like Halki, Symi suffers from a severe water shortage.

Unspoilt, Symi is not. It gets an inordinate number of day-trippers from Rhodes, and several small tour companies monopolise most of the places to stay. It doesn't have a camp site, so is definitely not an island to turn up on in July and August without a reservation. Almost all of the inhabitants live in the capital, which is also called Symi. Apart from the beaches near Symi town, the other beaches dotted around the coast are only accessible by excursion boat. See under Excursion & Taxi Boats in the Getting Around Symi (Island) section.

History

Symi has a long tradition of both sponge diving and ship building. Homer records that Symi contributed three ships to the Trojan

AEGEAN SEA

To Tilos

To Rhodes

Cape Makria

CHONDROS

NIMOS ISLET

PLATI

Diapori Straits

OXIA

Kokkinochoma Bay

Cape Toli

Emboreios

Nos

Harani

Gialos

SYMI

Chorio

Agia Marina

249 m

Pedi Bay

Pedi

Agios Nikolaos

Agios Emilianos

Cape Kefalaki

Ladi Bay

Pidima

471 m

594 m

Georgiou Disalona Bay

SYMI

528 m

Nanou Bay

Kefalou Bay

Black Caves

Lopidia Bay

Marathounta Bay

Vathigialo Bay

Cape Merde

Panormitis

Moni Taxiarhis Mihail

Faneromenis Bay

Cape Parathiras

SESKIA ISLET

Symi

0   2   4 km

expedition – no mean feat considering that mighty Rhodes only managed to muster nine. During Ottoman times the island enjoyed virtual autonomy, and was granted the right to fish for sponges in Turkish waters. In return Symi supplied the sultan with first-class boat builders and top-quality sponges to keep himself and the ladies of his harem squeaky clean.

These factors, and a lucrative ship-building industry, brought prosperity to the island. Gracious mansions were built and culture and education flourished. By the turn of the century the population was 22,450 and the island was launching some 500 ships a year. The Italian occupation, the introduction of the steamship and Kalymnos' rise as the Aegean's principal sponge producer, put an end to Symi's prosperity.

On 8 May 1945 the treaty surrendering the Dodecanese islands to the Allies was signed on Symi.

Getting To/From Symi (Island)

Ferry Symi is a port of call for the F/B *Nissos Kalimnos*. Once a week (at the time of writing it was Tuesday) the F/B *Kimolos* leaves Piraeus for Rhodes via the Cyclades, Crete and Symi. See Rhodes' and Agios Nikolaos' (Crete) Ferry sections for schedule details.

Excursion Boat There are daily excursion boats to Symi from Rhodes' Mandraki Harbour (3000 dr return).

Getting Around Symi (Island)

Bus Symi's public transport consists of a couple of 12-seater vans. These run between Gialos and Pedi Beach (via Chorio) every half hour between 8 am and 6.30 pm and then once an hour till 11 pm. The bus stop in Gialos is about halfway along the left side of the harbour. There is a flat fare of 100 dr.

Motorbike Symi Natural Sponges Shop, on the right side of the harbour, doubles up as a motorbike-rental office with 50 cc mopeds for 3000 dr. Consider carefully before you hire, because the road network is limited –

you'd be wiser to keep your money or buy a sponge.

Excursion & Taxi Boat There are many excursions around the island. Symi Tours (see Information) organises truck (5000 dr) and boat trips (3000 dr) to the monastery. Their other trips include: round the island with beach barbecue (4000 dr) and Sesklia islet and barbecue (3000 dr). Taxi boats do trips to many of the island's beaches. Excursion and taxi boats leave from the top of the left side of the harbour.

SYMI TOWN

Symi town is one of the most beautiful places in the Dodecanese. The harbour is shaped like an elongated U with pastel-coloured neoclassical mansions heaped up the steep hills on either side. However, like Kastellorizo, behind the striking façade many of the buildings are derelict. The town is divided into two distinct parts: Gialos, the harbour, and Chorio, the original town which nestles around the kastro walls.

Symi town's beach is the crowded and pebbled Nos Beach. Turn left at the clock tower (facing the sea) and the beach is just beyond the boat-building yard. Emboreios Beach, a little beyond here, is preferable.

Orientation

Facing inland, the quayside skirts the right side of the harbour. Inter-island ferries dock at the tip of the quay, and excursion boats from Rhodes further in. Excursion boats to Symi's beaches leave from the top of the opposite side of the bay. The tree-shaded central square is at the top of the bay.

Information

Symi's Municipal Tourist Office is scheduled to open in the near future. There is no tourist police; the regular police are in the same building as the post office. Symi Tours (☎ 71 307) is a helpful travel agency. You'll find it at the top of the left side of the harbour, between the Ionian Bank and the National Bank of Greece.

Near the inter-island ferry quay you will

see a clock tower. Twenty metres to the left of this, steps lead up to the post office. To reach the OTE, facing inland, take the road by the left side of the central square and look for a sign pointing left. Symi's postcode is 85600 and the telephone code is 0241. The National Bank of Greece is at the top end of the left side of the harbour, squeezed between the Vigla Taverna and a souvenir shop. The **Symi Maritime Museum**, on the central square, should be open by the time this book hits the shelves.

Chorio

The Chorio, with its narrow, labyrinthine streets crossed by crumbling archways, is a fascinating place to explore. As you approach the area around the kastro, the once grand 19th-century neoclassical mansions give way to small, modest stone dwellings of the 18th century.

To reach Chorio take the stairway from Plateia Oekonomou, which is near the top of the left side of the waterfront; the steps are called Kali Strata (Good Stairs). At the top, cross over Odos Alithinis and continue straight ahead along Ioannidou. At the top of here turn right and follow the blue arrows to the **Museum of Symi**, which is a hotchpotch of archaeological and folklore finds.

The museum is open Tuesday to Sunday from 10 am to 2 pm. Admission is free.

If you turn right at the museum and then right again you will see the first of the blue arrows which point to the castle. Unfortunately these peter out before the castle is reached, but locals will direct you, if you ask for 'kastro'. The castle incorporates blocks from the ancient acropolis, which included a temple of Athena. From this vantage point there are splendid views down to the harbour.

Places to Stay – bottom end

One of the cheapest places to stay in Gialos is the ramshackle but clean *Hotel Glafkos* (☎ 71 358). Rates are 3000/4000 dr for doubles/triples with shared bathrooms. The hotel is on the street bordering the left side of the central square (facing inland). At the top of the left side of the harbour, *Rooms To Let Helena* (☎ 71 931/524/397) has nicely furnished doubles for 4500 dr with private bathrooms, and four-person apartments for 6500 dr. *Pension Les Katerinettes* is housed in a 19th-century building which was formerly the town hall where the treaty granting the Dodecanese to the Allies was signed. Some of the attractive rooms have magnificent painted wood ceilings. Doubles are 6000 dr. The pension is near the quay and is managed by Sunny Land Ltd Tourist & Travel Agency (☎ 71 320), a couple of doors away – contact them to make a reservation.

Places to Stay – middle

In Chorio, the B class *Hotel Village* (☎ 71 800; fax 71 802) has elegant carpeted and air-con rooms. Rates are 7500/8500 dr for doubles/triples including breakfast. The hotel is in the centre of Chorio at the bus stop.

The A class *Hotel Aliki* (☎ 71 665) is built in traditional style with attractively furnished rooms. Singles/doubles cost 8000/13,000 dr. Facing inland from the inter-island ferry quay, turn right, follow the waterfront and the hotel is on the left.

Places to Eat

Many of Gialos' restaurants cater for day-trippers and are mediocre. An exception is *Vassilis Restaurant* which serves carefully prepared dishes. Tasty main dishes cost between 650 and 1000 dr.

Restaurant Les Katerinettes, below the pension of the same name, has an international menu. Fried peppers and aubergines with feta are 650 dr, swordfish is 1300 dr and souvlaki is 1500 dr. They also have a large selection of desserts including apple tart at 490 dr.

In Chorio, *Dallaras Restaurant* serves generous portions of Greek staples at low prices. The restaurant is almost at the top of the steps from Gialos, on the left.

Things to Buy

Symi, along with Kalymnos, is one of the best places in Greece for buying sponges. It is also one of the best places for buying fresh herbs and spices. Shops selling these products line the quayside.

AROUND THE ISLAND
Beaches

Most of Symi's beaches are pebbled. Getting to many of them involves either a long walk on rough paths or taking an excursion boat. An exception is **Pedi Beach**, two km east of Chorio and easily reached by bus. It is in the most fertile part of the island with fruit trees growing in the valley behind the beach. It has some sandy stretches and is a burgeoning holiday resort, with hotels, domatia and tavernas.

Agios Nikolaos Beach, on the southern side of Pedi Bay, is less crowded and within walking distance of Pedi Beach. The small beach of **Agia Marina** is at the extreme north-eastern end of Pedi Bay. A path leads here from Chorio but excursion boats also make the trip. **Nanou Bay**, about halfway down the east coast, has a shingle beach. **Agios Emilianos** is a secluded beach on the west coast, also reached by excursion boat. **Marathounta Bay** is a stony beach within walking distance of Moni Taxiarhis Mihail (see the following section). Excursion boats ply between Gialos and the bay.

Moni Taxiarhis Mihail
Μονή Ταξιάρχηου Μιξαήλ

The large Moni Taxiarhis Mihail (Monastery of Michael of Panormitis) is in the striking, almost circular bay of Panormitis, where there is a small beach. The monastery is Symi's principal sight, so it's a stopping-off point for many of the day-trippers from Rhodes. A monastery was first built here in the 5th or 6th century, but the present building dates from the 18th century. It has a conspicuous and ornate bell tower and a pretty pebble mosaic courtyard, but the building is rather ostentatious looking and fails to evoke feelings of reverence It is dedicated to St Michael, the patron saint of Symi, who was adopted by Greek sailors to ensure a safe sea passage.

The monastery's church contains an intricately carved wooden iconostasis, frescoes, and an icon of St Michael which supposedly appeared miraculously at the site where the monastery now stands. The monastery complex contains a museum, restaurant and guest rooms. Beds cost 1500 dr; you cannot make a reservation and it tends to fill up with vacationing Greeks in July and August, but at other times you will have no difficulty getting a bed.

To reach Marathounta Bay from Moni Taxiarhis Mihail walk along the road which leads north to Chorio and a track leads off right to the bay.

Kos Κως

Kos (population 21,000) is the third-largest island of the Dodecanese. It lies 20 km north of Nisyros and only five km from the Turkish peninsula of Bodrum. Kos is one of the most well-watered and fertile islands of the Dodecanese.

The island rivals Rhodes in its tourist development and although its ruins are important and should not be missed, many of its beautiful beaches are now horrendous, with wall-to-wall sunbeds and beach umbrellas.

Pserimos is a small island between Kos and Kalymnos. It has a good sandy beach, but unfortunately becomes overrun with day-trippers from both of its larger neighbours.

History

Kos' fertile land attracted settlers from the earliest times. Many traces of Neolithic people have been found. So many people lived here by Mycenaean times that the island managed to muster up 30 ships for the Trojan War. In the 7th and 6th centuries BC Kos flourished as an ally of the powerful Rhodian cities of Ialyssos, Kamiros and Lindos. In 477 BC, Kos, after suffering in an earthquake and under subjugation to the Persians, joined the Delian League, and began to flourish once more. At this time Hippocrates (460-377 BC), the father of medicine, was born and lived on the island. After Hippocrates' death, a Sanctuary of Asklepios

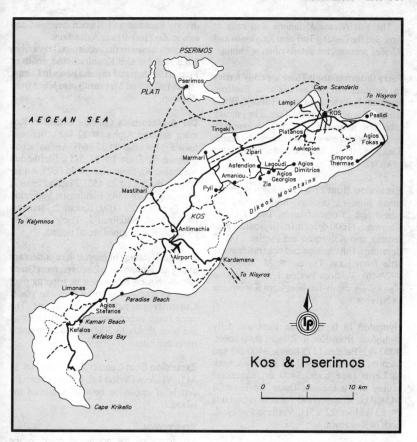

Kos & Pserimos

0   5   10 km

and a medical school were built, which perpetuated his teachings, and made Kos famous throughout the Greek world. During the time of Alexander the Great, and after his death, Kos continued to flourish.

Ptolemy II of Egypt was born on Kos and this secured the island the protection of Egypt, under which it became a prosperous trading centre. In 130 BC it came under Roman domination, and in the 1st century AD it was put under the administration of Rhodes, with whom from this time it shared the same vicissitudes, right up to the tourist deluge of the present day.

Getting To/From Kos (Island)

Air In summer there are daily flights to Athens (13,700 dr) and three flights a week to Rhodes (7500 dr). The Olympic Airways office (☎ 28 330/1/2 or 22 833) is at Vasileos Pavlou 22, Kos town.

Ferry (Domestic) Kos shares many ferry connections with Rhodes. The F/B *Ialyssos*, F/B *Kamiros*, F/B *Agios Rafail* and F/B *Ionian Sun* all have Kos and Rhodes amongst their ports of call. For details of their schedules see the Getting To/From Rhodes (Island) section.

The F/B *Nissos Kalimnos* also calls at Kos. See the Getting To/From Kalymnos and Rhodes sections for details of its schedule.

Ferry (International) There are daily ferries in summer from Kos town to Bodrum (ancient Halicarnassus) in Turkey. Boats leave at 8 am and return at 4 pm. The journey takes one hour and costs 5000 dr one-way and 10,000 dr return (these prices include the Turkish port tax). Many travel agents around town sell tickets.

Excursion Boat From Kos town there are many boat excursions, both around the island and to other islands. They include: Kalymnos (1600 dr return); Nisyros (2500 dr return); and Kalymnos and Pserimos (4000 dr return). Information and tickets are available from Exas Travel (☎ 28 545 or 23 992/646), Vasileos Pavlou 1 & 4. There is also a daily excursion boat from Kardamena to Nisyros.

Hydrofoil In high season there are daily hydrofoils from Kos to Rhodes (two hours, 4000 dr), Patmos (1½ hours, 3400 dr) and Samos (1¾ hours, 3500 dr) and five a week to Leros (one hour, 3400 dr). Agencies selling tickets include: Oscar Travel (☎ 28 543), Akti Kountourioti 1 and N Adroitakis (☎ 23 131 or 22 251), Vasileos Pavlou 2, both in Kos town.

Getting Around Kos (Island)

To/From the Airport At the time of writing there was an Olympic Airways bus from outside the Olympic Airways office to the airport which left two hours before the departures of Olympic Airways flights. Check if it's still operating. The airport is 26 km south-west of Kos town near the village of Antimachia.

Bus From the bus station at the corner of Pisandrou and Kleopatras there are five buses a day to Tingaki (120 dr); four to Pyli (150 dr); four to Kardamena (270 dr); three to Mastihari (250 dr); two to Kefalos (380 dr) via Paradise and Kamari beaches; and two to Zia (160 dr) via Asfendion.

Hourly buses to the Asklepion leave from a bus stop on Akti Kountouriotou, south of Plateia Eleftherias. Frequent buses to Lampi, Agios Fokas and Messaroto also leave from this stop.

Car & Motorbike Car-hire outlets in Kos town include: Alpha (☎ 22 488), Bouboulinas 23; National (☎ 22 864), Antinavarhou Ioannidi 3; Trust (☎ 23 315), Eleftheriou Venizelou 30; Sovereign (☎ 24 062), Amerikis 17; Budget (☎ 22 455), Plateia Plessa 2; Blue Sky (☎ 28 134), Eleftheriou Venizelou 49; Rena (☎ 28 009), Kanari 2; Stamatis (☎ 22 516), Nafclirou 1. There are many motorbike and moped rental outlets.

Bicycle Sightings of bicycle-hire outlets are as rare as sightings of cuckoos on most Greek islands, but on Kos you'll be tripping over bikes to rent – they're all over the place. Obviously you pay for what you get. The price range is between about 700 dr for an old bone shaker to 3000 dr for a top-notch mountain bike.

Excursion Boat Contact Exas Travel (☎ 28 545), Vasileos Pavlou 1 & 4, in Kos town for details of excursion boat trips around the island.

KOS TOWN

Kos town, on the north-east coast, is the capital of the island and the main port. The old town of Kos was destroyed by an earthquake in 1933, but the new town, although modern, is picturesque, with palms, pines, oleander and hibiscus sprouting everywhere. The castle of the Knights dominates the port, and ruins from Hellenistic and Roman times are strewn everywhere.

Orientation

The ferry quay is on the eastern side of the almost circular harbour. To get to the town centre walk to the waterfront keeping the castle to your left. Once at the waterfront of Akti Kountouriotou, turn right, and a little way along you will see a sign to the centre pointing left. Follow this to come to the central square of Plateia Eleftherias, flanked on its southern side by a large indoor fruit and vegetable market, on the northern side by the **Archaeological Museum**, and on the east side by the Defdar Mosque.

South of the castle, the waterfront is called Akti Miaouli. To reach here, walk along Finikon (also aptly called the Avenue of Palms) which is an easterly continuation of Akti Kountouriotou.

Information

Kos used to have an excellent Municipal Tourist Office on Akti Kountouriotou but this closed in 1992 due to lack of funds. Hopefully the office will open again because with around 100,000 tourists a year, if any island needs a tourist office it's Kos. The problem is compounded by the tourist police being fairly unhelpful when it comes to dispensing information to tourists. For what it's worth, they're in the large yellow government building with the clock tower, opposite the quay. The regular police (☎ 22 222) are in the same building. The port police (☎ 28 507) are on Akti Kountouriotou, south of Plateia Eleftherias.

The post office is on El Venizelou. To reach it walk up Vasileos Pavlou by the left side of the market and take the second left and it's two blocks along on the left. The OTE is at Vironos 6, just north of the post office. From Plateia Eleftherias walk one block up Vasileos Pavlou and turn left onto Xanthou. Kos' postcode is 85300 and the telephone code is 0242.

The National Bank of Greece is on the corner of Rigou Fereou and Antinavarhou Ioannidi, one block north of Plateia Eleftherias. The bus station is on the corner of Pisandrou and Kleopatras. Walk up Vasileos Pavlou from Plateia Eleftherias and turn right at the Olympic Airways office.

The Foreign Press Agency at Vasileos Pavlou 2 stocks a large selection of English-language newspapers and magazines. Kos' General Hospital (☎ 22 300) is at Hippocratous 32.

Archaeological Sites

Two factors contributed to Kos having such a wealth of archaeological sites. One was the earthquake of 1933 which brought to light the ruins and the other was the presence of the Italians who finished off what the earthquake had begun by carrying out excavation work and restoration – most of the ruins were, after all, Roman. Before you do anything, pay your respects to the **Hippocrates plane tree** beneath which the good people of Kos (and the EOT brochure) will tell you the great man taught. Plane trees don't usually live for more than 200 years – so much for the power of the Hippocratic oath – though in all fairness it is certainly one of Europe's oldest. The tree dominates the charming, cool Plateia Platanou where a fountain plays and there's the elegant **Mosque of Gazi Hassan Pasha** built in the 1780s. The square is at the extreme eastern end of Akti Kountouriotou.

From Plateia Platanou a bridge leads across Odos Finikon (Avenue of Palms) to the **Castle of the Knights**, another fine example of medieval military architecture. Along with Rhodes castle, and that of Bodrum, across the straits in Turkey, this impregnable fortress was the Knights' most stalwart defence against the encroaching Ottomans. The castle, which had massive outer walls and an inner keep, was built in the late 1300s. The keep was originally separated from the town by a moat, which is now the Avenue of Palms. The Knights used many blocks of stone and marble from ancient buildings, including the Askleplion, to build the castle. The castle is open Tuesday to Sunday from 8.30 am to 3 pm. Admission is 400 dr.

The **ancient agora**, to the south of Plateia Platanou, is, in typical Dodecanese fashion, a medley of ancient, Roman and Byzantine remains. On its western side was a massive 3rd-century BC stoa, of which some columns have been reconstructed. On the north side, near Plateia Platanou, are the ruins of a shrine of Aphrodite, temple of Hercules and a 5th-century Christian basilica. The site is not enclosed, and entry is free.

The other ruins lie mostly in the south part of the town. From Plateia Eleftherias, walk south to the end of Vasileos Pavlou, and you will arrive at the main thoroughfare of Grigoriou. Cross over here to the **casa Romana**, a lavish Roman villa which was restored by the Italians. One of the rooms has a lovely, delicately coloured fish mosaic. The villa is open Tuesday to Sunday from 8.30 am to 3 pm. Entrance is 400 dr. East of here is the **central thermea** (Roman baths). Further west along Grigoriou is the partially restored marble **odeion**, at the end of a road flanked by cypresses.

On the other side of Grigoriou is the site called the **Western Excavation**, fringed by the Dekumanus Maximus, an exposed section of paved Roman road. The large site has more paved Roman roads and remains of Greek and Roman houses and public buildings. They include the **nymphaeum** which consisted of once lavish public latrines, with a bathing pool in front of each one – was that not carrying personal hygiene a bit too far? Here also is the **xysto**, a large Hellenistic gymnasium, with some of its columns restored. Next to it is a Roman-era swimming pool. The site also has some very fine mosaics. Most notable are the *Judgement of Paris* and the *Abduction of Europa* (ie by Zeus).

The **Archaeological Museum** (☎ 28 326), Plateia Eleftherias, has many statues from Hellenistic and Roman times and a fine 2nd or 3rd-century AD mosaic in the vestibule. The museum is open Tuesday to Sunday from 8.30 am to 3 pm. Admission is 400 dr.

Places to Stay – bottom end

Kos' one camp site is *Kos Camping* (☎ 23 910/275). Along with the camp site on Patmos it's the nicest in the Dodecanese. It's run by the friendly English-speaking Gregoriadou family. It's a well-kept site in a shady olive grove, and has a taverna, snack bar, minimarket, kitchen, laundry, hot showers and bike and motorbike rental. Rates are 800 dr per person and 500 dr per tent. Their minibus meets almost all the ferries includ-

ing the 4 am one from Piraeus. The site is 2½ km along the eastern waterfront and is signposted from the port.

Try to avoid Kos in July and August when rooms are hard to come by. If you do visit in these months and you're offered a room at the port then take it and be grateful. If it doesn't suit, you can always hunt around the next day.

The cheapest hotel is the D class *Dodekanissos Hotel* (☎ 28 460 or 22 860), Ipsilandou 9. Unadorned clean and comfortable rooms are 2000/3000 dr for singles/doubles with shared bathrooms and 3000/5000 dr with private bathrooms. Follow directions for the National Bank of Greece, and the hotel is on the right, one block beyond here, on the corner of Ipsilandou and Riga Fereou. *Pension Alexis* (☎ 28 798), Irodotou 9, is also good value with clean singles/doubles for 3000/4500 dr with shared bathrooms. Walk along Akti Kountouriotou from the quay and turn left onto Megalou Alexandrou (signposted to the airport) and take the first right onto Irodotou.

Another bargain is the *Hotel Acropol* (☎ 22 244/448), Tsaladari 4, in an old house with a lush garden. Plain, but clean singles/doubles/triples are 3000/5000/6000 dr with shared bathrooms. Walking from the quay, Tsaladari is a turn-off to the left, one block before Megalou Alexandrou. The hotel is a little way up here on the right. The D class *Hotel Helena* (☎ 22 986), Megalou Alexandrou 5, has pleasant singles/doubles for 3500/6000 dr with private bathrooms.

Argyro Apartments, Odos Kleovoulou, are in a quiet residential part of town. The pleasant apartments with fully equipped kitchens and private bathrooms cost 4000/5000/6000 dr for singles/doubles/triples. Walk along Megalou Alexandrou to Theofrastou (with the Nefati snack bar on the corner) and turn right. Walk past the children's playground, turn right, cross the road and it's the second building on the right.

Places to Stay – middle

The B class *Theodorou Beach* (☎ 23 363/364), on G Papandreou, is a lovely hotel, with a cool spacious interior, and tastefully furnished rooms. Rates are 6500/8500/10,000 dr for singles/doubles/triples with private bathrooms. The hotel is just over one km along the eastern waterfront (on the way to Kos camping, which is signposted).

The A class *Ramira Beach* (☎ 28 489 or 22 891) is three km south-east of Kos town near Psalidi Beach. The hotel has a restaurant, swimming pool, tennis court and a shady garden. The attractively furnished singles/doubles are 8000/12,000 dr.

Places to Stay – top end

Most of Kos' top-end hotels are on the beaches to either side of Kos town, with a big concentration at Psalidi Beach, just southeast of town. The A class *Dimitra Beach Hotel* (☎ 28 581/2), at Psalidi, is a complex consisting of a hotel and attractive bungalows. The rates are 11,000/16,000 dr for singles/doubles and 21,800 dr for bungalows. The A class *Platanista Hotel* (23 749 or 25 452), also at Psalidi, is an architecturally interesting crenellated building. The well- furnished rooms cost 13,000/15,000 dr for singles/doubles.

Places to Eat

The *Mira Mare Restaurant*, Vasileos Geogiou 6a, is one of the few authentic restaurants left in Kos town. A mixed Greek plate for two is 4000 dr, a fish plate for two is 3500 dr, cod and chips are 700 dr and chicken and mushrooms are 750 dr. Vasileos Georgiou is an eastern continuation of Akti Miaouli on the eastern waterfront. The *Olympiada Restaurant*, behind the Olympic Airways office, is one of the best value restaurants in town, with good meals for under 900 dr. The *Anatolia Hammam Restaurant*, just north of Plateia Diagorais, is in a lovely setting on a natural rock terrace, overlooking the Western Excavation site. A large mixed grill is 1200 dr. All these restaurants are open for lunch and dinner.

The *Kathgorias Café Bar*, Vasileos Pavlou 7, is a traditional place with pancakes for 500 dr and yoghurt and honey for 350 dr. It's open from 8 am to 10 pm.

Entertainment

Discos are plentiful in Kos town. The greatest concentration are in the north part of town. Don't miss the nightly amazing laser light show at the *Playboy Disco* at Kanari 2. The disco has a 2001-type setting. Further north, *Heaven* and *Calua* are outdoor discos next to one another on Zouroudi; the latter has a swimming pool.

AROUND THE ISLAND

Asklepion Ασκληπιείον

The Asklepion (☎ 28 763), on a pine-covered hill four km south-west of Kos town, is the most important of Kos' ancient sites. The ruins occupy three different levels; from the top level there is a wonderful view of Kos town and Turkey. The Asklepion consisted of a religious sanctuary to Asklepios, the god of healing, a healing centre, and a school of medicine, where the training followed the teachings of Hippocrates.

Hippocrates was the first doctor to have a rational approach to diagnosing and treating illnesses. Before him, the treatment of the sick was bound up with jiggery pokery, and cures were left very much in the lap of the gods. Up until 554 AD people came from all over the Greek, and later the Roman world, to be treated here, as well as for medical training.

The propylaia, Roman-era public baths

Asklepios

and the remains of guest rooms are on the first level. A wide staircase leads to the next level in the middle of which is a 4th-century BC **Altar of Kyparissios Apollo**. West of this is the first **Temple of Asklepios**, which was built in the 4th century BC. To the east is the 1st-century BC **Temple to Apollo**; seven of its graceful columns have been re-erected. In the middle of the third level are the remains of the once magnificent 2nd-century BC **Temple of Asklepios**, the most important building of the Asklepion. The site is open from 8.30 am to 3 pm. Admission is 600 dr.

Getting There & Away Frequent buses go to the site, but it is very pleasant to cycle or walk here. Take Megalou Alexandrou out of Kos town. On the way to the site you will pass through the village of Platanos (also called Kermetes), where many of the inhabitants are of Turkish origin. The village has a mosque, and Turkish and Jewish cemeteries. Beyond the village, a lovely avenue of cypress trees leads to the Asklepion.

Beaches
Kos, like Rhodes, has good beaches, but most are crowded. There are mediocre beaches to both the north and south of the harbour in Kos town, but the nearest decent beach to the town is the crowded **Lampi Beach**, four km to the north-west. Further round the coast, **Tingaki**, 11 km from Kos town, has a good sandy beach. From here there are excursion boats to the small island of **Pserimos**, which also has decent beaches. **Marmari Beach**, four km west of Tingaki, is less crowded.

Mastihari, further south-west, retains considerable charm, despite rapid development over the last few years. It has a long sandy beach and secluded spots can be found amongst the sand dunes at its extreme western end. On the way to the dunes you will pass the foundations of an early Christian basilica. There are loads of domatia in Mastihari, as well as the D class *Hotel Fenareti* (☎ 51 396) and the *Pension Mastihari* (☎ 51 371), both with doubles for 5000

dr. There are excursion boats from Mastihari to Kalymnos.

Agios Fokas and **Empros Thermae**, south-east of Kos, are reasonable beaches; the latter has dark volcanic sand and hot mineral springs. **Kardamena**, on the south coast 27 km from Kos town, was once a lovely fishing and agricultural village, but it's degenerated into the island's premier resort and is best avoided. The island's best beaches are further down the coast, where the island narrows. Here is the long sandy **Paradise Beach**, and beyond it, **Kamari Beach** in Kefalos Bay. One side (the best one) of this bay is monopolised by Club Méditerranée. There are lots of domatia in the area.

Inland
Several attractive villages are scattered on the northern slopes of the Dikeos mountain range. At **Zipari**, 10 km from the capital, a road to the left (coming from Kos town) leads to **Asfendion**, from where most of these villages can be reached by car or on foot. The road straight ahead leads to the village of **Zia** which is quite touristy, but worth a visit because the surrounding countryside is lovely, and the village has a good taverna.

From Zia there is a path up to the highest peak of the Dikeos mountains (850 metres). The path is to the right of Zia's Kefalovrisi church, and the walk takes about one hour. From Asfendion, a turn-off left leads to the tiny and pristine villages of **Agios Georgios** and **Agios Dimitrios**; a right turn leads to **Lagoudi** village. From Lagoudi a dirt track leads to **Amaniou**, from where a road leads up to the ruins of the medieval village of old **Pyli**.

Kalymnos Κάλυμνος

Kalymnos (KA-lim-nos, population 14,500), only 2½ km south of Leros, is a mountainous, arid island, with the exception of the fertile valley of Vathi. Kalymnos is not

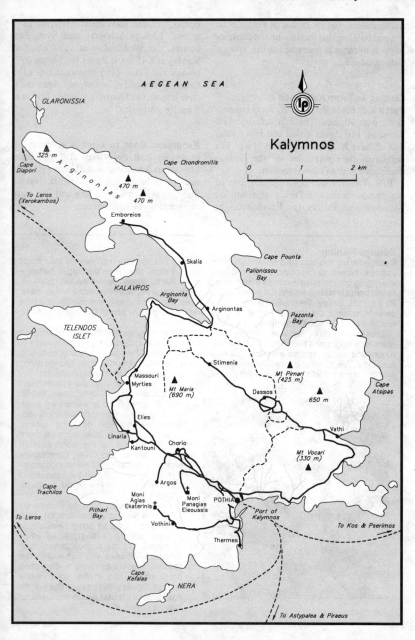

undiscovered, but its capital of Pothia is so big and bustling that tourists are not conspicuous. Kalymnos is renowned as the 'sponge fishing island'.

Getting To/From Kalymnos

Ferry Kalymnos shares many ferry connections with Rhodes. The F/B *Ialyssos*, F/B *Kamiros*, F/B *Agios Rafail* and F/B *Ionian Sun* all have Kalymnos as a port of call. For details of their schedules see the Getting To/From Rhodes (Island) section.

F/B *Nissos Kalimnos* operates out of Kalymnos. It leaves Pothia at 6 am on Monday and Friday for Rhodes (eight hours), via Kos (two hours); Nisyros (3½ hours); Tilos (4½ hours); and Symi (six hours). On Wednesday at 7.30 am and Sunday at 6.45 am it leaves for Samos (6½ hours) via Leros (1½ hours); Lipsi (2½ hours); Patmos (3½ hours); and Agathonisi (five hours). On Thursday it leaves Pothia at 6 am for Astypalea.

Excursion Boat In summer there is an excursion boat every day at 1 pm from Myrties to Xerokambos on Leros (1000 dr one-way); three a day from Pothia (two on Sunday) to Mastihari on Kos and one daily to Pserimos (1400 dr return).

Sponge Fishing

Sponge fishing has occupied Kalymniots since ancient times and was until recently their major industry. As well as the obvious one, sponges have had many other uses throughout history – everything from padding in armour to women's tampons. For hundreds of years the sponges were fished from the waters around Kalymnos, but as the industry grew, fishers ventured further away. By the 19th century divers sailed such great distances that they had to spend months at a time away from home, departing shortly after Easter and returning at the end of October. These two events were celebrated in religious and secular festivals.

Until the first diving suit was invented in the late 19th century, sponge divers were weighed down with stones and had to hold their breath under water. The early diving suits were made of rubber and canvas and were worn with a huge bronze helmet joined to an air pump by a long hose pipe. This contraption enabled divers to stay under the water for much longer. Sponge diving was perilous work and those who didn't die young invariably became paralysed or crippled.

For many years the fishing fleets dived for sponges off the Libyan coast, but Mr Gadaffi proved an unwelcoming host, exacting an exorbitant tax from the divers. Nowadays, the few remaining sponge fishers wear oxygen tanks and work much closer to home, in the north-eastern Aegean and around Crete. Contributory factors to the demise of the sponge industry has been overfishing in the Aegean and the availability of low-priced synthetic sponges.

Greeks are not ones to decline an excuse for feasting and celebration, even if the reasons for so doing have disappeared, so the festivals have been preserved. At the sponge factory near Plateia Eleftherias you can watch the process which transforms a disgusting black object into a nice pale yellow sponge. It goes without saying that Kalymnos is one of the best places in Greece for sponge buying. ■

Getting Around Kalymnos

Bus Pothia's bus schedule at the time of writing was as follows: to Massouri (150 dr) via Myrties, every two hours between 7 am and 9 pm; to Emboreios (300 dr) on a Monday, Wednesday and Friday at 8 am and 4 pm; to Vathi (200 dr) from Monday to Saturday at 6.30 am; 1.30 and 5 pm and on a Sunday at 7.30 am; 1.30 and 5 pm.

Taxi Shared taxis are an unusual feature of Kalymnos; they cost around twice as much as buses. A price list is displayed at the taxi rank on Plateia Kyprou. These taxis can also be flagged down en route.

Motorbike There are several motorbike-hire outlets along Pothia's waterfront. Thomas Souloumias' Rent a Motorbike (☎ 23 073), operating from the Kalymnos Tourist Shop on Plateia Dimarchou, has reasonable prices: 50 cc are 2000 dr and 80 and 90 cc are 2500 dr – bargain like mad out of season.

Excursion Boat There are daily excursion boats to Emboreios (1000 dr). Every Saturday an excursion boat from Myrties does a trip around the island and to the island of Pserimos (2000 dr).

POTHIA Πόθια

Pothia, the port and capital of Kalymnos, is where the majority of the inhabitants live. Although it's considerably bigger and noisier than most island capitals, Pothia is not without its charm, and makes a good base from which to explore the island.

Orientation

Pothia's waterfront is in the south-east part of town. The ferry quay extends from the southern side of the crescent shaped bay. To reach the centre of town walk to the end of the quay and turn right. Continue along the waterfront and you will come to the Cathedral of Agios Christos. Odos Venizelou, the main thoroughfare of Pothia's commercial area, stretches from here to Plateia Kyprou, the town's central square.

Information

The EOT (☎ 23 140) is in a building in the small park near the quay. The efficient English-speaking staff give out maps and have information on ferry and bus schedules.

The post office is on the northern continuation of Venizelou. The OTE is a few steps further up on the opposite side. Kalymnos' postcode is 85200 and the telephone code is 0243. The National Bank of Greece is in the middle of the waterfront.

The police (☎ 22 100) are north of Plateia Kyprou on the road parallel to Venizelou. The port police (☎ 29 304) are at the beginning of the quay, on the right as you face the sea. The bus station is just south of Agios Christos cathedral on the waterfront.

Archaeological Museum

This well-kept little museum (☎ 23 113) is housed in a neoclassical mansion which once belonged to a wealthy sponge merchant, Mr Vouvalis. In one room there are some Neolithic and Bronze Age finds. Other rooms are reconstructed as they were when the Vouvalis family lived there. In the study there are family portraits and in the lavish guest room are chandeliers, a beautiful gilded ceiling, richly upholstered furniture and a beautiful carpet. The museum is open Tuesday to Sunday from 10 am to 2 pm. Admission is free. It is near Plateia Kyprou and is well signposted.

Places to Stay

Two good choices for backpackers are the *Pension Greek House* (☎ 29 559 or 23 752), where cosy wood-panelled single/double/triple rooms are 2500/4000/5500 dr with private bathrooms and the pleasant *Katerina Rooms* (☎ 22 186), with rates of 2000/2500/3500 dr with shared bathrooms. These two places are quite close to one another in an area to the north-west of the quay.

The C class *Hotel Panorama* (☎ 23 138) has a lovely grey and white décor and pretty lace curtains. All of the rooms have balconies with fine views over the whole of Pothia. Prices are 3700/6000 dr for singles/doubles with private bathrooms. The hotel is just

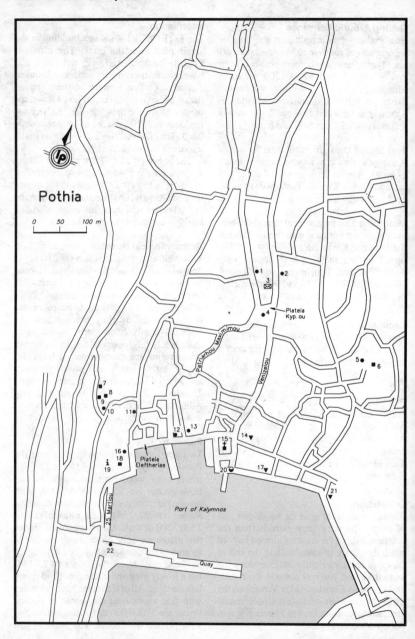

Pothia

0   50   100 m

1
2
3
4 • Plateia Kyp.ou
Patriarhou Maximimou
Venizelou
5 6
7
8
9
10
11
12
13
14
15
16
18
19 i Plateia Eleftherias
20
17
21
25 Martiou
Port of Kalymnos
22
Quay

beyond Katerina Rooms and is well sign-posted.

The *Hotel Themelina* (☎ 22 682), opposite the Archaeological Museum, is an outstanding place which inexplicably has a D rating. It's a well-preserved 19th-century mansion with a beautiful garden and a swimming pool. The spacious traditionally furnished rooms cost 3500/7000/9000 dr with private bathrooms. The C class *Olympic Hotel* (☎ 28 802/803), near the EOT, has comfortable but bland rooms for 6000/8500/10,200 dr, breakfast included.

Places to Eat

If you ask locals which is their favourite eating place, there's a good chance they will say the *Xefteries Taverna*. This unpretentious place hidden away in a back street behind the southern end of Venizelou has been in the same family for 85 years. The food is delicious and low priced. A meal of stifado, Greek salad and retsina will cost about 1500 dr. Of the fish tavernas on the western waterfront, *Uncle Petros' Taverna*, at the far end, is rated the most highly by locals. A full meal here including Amstel will cost about 1200 dr. Just east of the cathedral there is a large indoor food market selling fruit, vegetables and meat.

VATHI Βαθύς
Vathi, eight km north-east of Pothia, is one of the most beautiful and peaceful parts of the island. Vathi means 'deep' in Greek and refers to the slender fjord which cuts through high cliffs into a fertile valley. The region is divided into three small settlements: the one around the harbour is Rena, the middle one is Platanos and the third is Metorki. In the valley, narrow roads wind between citrus orchards.

There is no beach at Rena, but excursion boats take tourists to quiet little coves around the coast for 500 dr. In the cliff at the left side of the fjord there is a cave which you can swim to.

Places to Stay
Vathi has two places to stay, both at Rena. To the left as you face the sea is the C class *Hotel Galini* (☎ 31 241) where immaculate single/double/triple rooms are 2000/4000/4800 dr with private bathrooms and balconies. The owner is a friendly Greek-Australian.

The *Pension Manolis* (☎ 31 300 or 22 641), in an elevated position to the right of the harbour, has beautiful double rooms for 4500 dr with private bathrooms. There is a large communal kitchen and terraces surrounded by a lovely well-kept garden. The English-speaking Manolis is an official tour guide and very knowledgeable about walks in the area.

Places to Eat
The *Harbour Taverna* at Rena specialises in seafood. A meal of succulent giant prawns in garlic butter and wine, with chips will cost

about 1200 dr. The taverna is open for lunch and dinner.

POTHIA TO EMBOREIOS

The road from Pothia to the west coast passes the ruins of the **Castle of the Knights of St John**, on the left. The church within the castle has some faded frescoes. Chorio, the old capital of the island, is just beyond here, three km from Pothia. The **Pera Kastro** watches over Chorio; the 'pirate proof' village within its walls was inhabited until the 18th century, and a number of its little chapels are well preserved.

The road continues to the west coast and into package-tourist territory, particularly at **Myrties** and **Massouri**. Myrties is overlooked by the islet of **Telendos**, to which there are frequent boats. Myrties also has an excursion boat to Xerokambos on Leros (see the Getting To/From Kalymnos section).

Beyond Massouri the coast is less developed. The end of the road is **Emboreios** (Εμπορειός) which has a very pleasant pebble beach shaded by tamarisks, which only gets crowded in July and August. There are no hotels here, but several of the tavernas on and near the beach rent rooms for 4000 to 7000 dr a double.

TELENDOS ISLET Νήσος Τέλενδος

Tranquil and traffic-free Telendos (TEL-en-dos) islet, less than one km from the resort of Myrties, has a little hamlet at its quayside, Roman and early Christian ruins and a medieval fortress. Telendos' best beach is at the far side of the islet. To reach it, turn left from the quay, and follow the path over the ridge.

Places to Stay & Eat

Telendos has several domatia, all of which skirt the waterfront. Opposite the quay, *Pension & Restaurant Uncle George* (☎ 47 502 or 23 855) has light, airy single/double rooms for 2000/3000 dr with private bathrooms, including breakfast; four-person apartments are 5000 dr. Turn right at the quay and walk along the narrow cement road which skirts the waterfront. Soon this becomes a dirt track and 100 metres further

on you will come to *Galanommatis Fotini Rooms to Rent & Restaurant* (☎ 47 401), a distinctive green and white building. Rates here are 3000 dr a double with private bathrooms. Both of the restaurants serve well-prepared dishes. At each you'll pay around 1400 dr for a full meal with beer or wine.

Getting There & Away

Frequent caïques leave Myrties for Telendos (300 dr) between 7 am and 11 pm.

Leros Λέρος

Over the last few years the island of Leros (LE-ros) has received so much adverse publicity concerning its large psychiatric institution, that for me to go on about it would be to labour a point. Whether or not it is going to colour your impression of the island depends on your temperament; some tourists seem oblivious to it, whilst for others it negates anything positive that the island might otherwise have to offer.

Lakki is the main port of Leros, but smaller ferries and some excursion boats use Agia Marina port, and the excursion boat from Myrties on Kalymnos docks at Xerokambos. Platanos is the capital of Leros. Lakki is one of the best natural harbours in the Aegean and, during their occupation of the Dodecanese, the Italians chose it as their principal naval base in the eastern Mediterranean. Leros' deeply indented coast harbours numerous sheltered coves.

Getting To/From Leros

Air In summer there are daily flights to Athens (15,100 dr) and five a week in winter. The Olympic Airways office (☎ 22 844 or 24 144) is in Platanos, just before the turn-off for Panteli. The airport is in the north of the island near Partheni.

Ferry Leros shares many ferry connections with Rhodes. The F/B *Ialyssos*, F/B *Kamiros*, F/B *Agios Rafail* and F/B *Ionian Sun* all have Leros and Rhodes amongst their ports

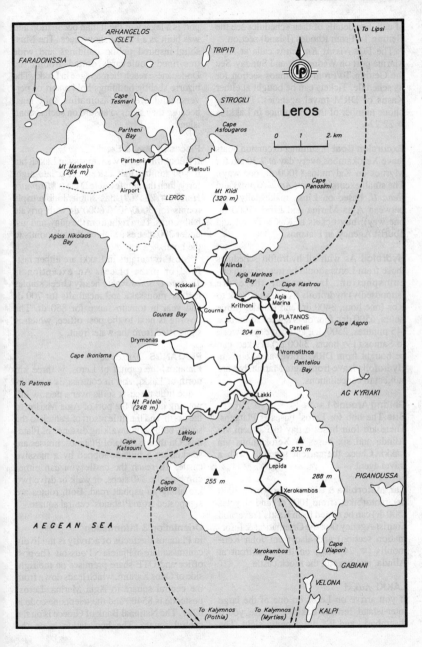

Leros

of call. For details of their schedules see the Getting To/From Rhodes (Island) section.

The F/B *Nissos Kalimnos* calls at Agia Marina port on Wednesday and Sunday. See the Getting To/From Kalymnos section for its schedule. Tickets can be bought at either Kastis or DRM travel agencies. The telephone number of the port police in Lakki is ☎ 22 224.

Excursion Boat In summer excursion boats leave Xerokambos every day at 7.30 am for Myrties on Kalymnos (1000 dr, one-way). The small excursion boats *Anna Express* and *Rena II*, based on Lipsi, make daily trips between Agia Marina and Lipsi (1000 dr, one-way); buy tickets at Kastis Travel and Tourist Agency, in Platanos.

Hydrofoil As with all hydrofoil schedules those from Leros should be treated with circumspection. In summer there are (supposedly) hydrofoils five days a week to Kos (one hour, 3400 dr) and Rhodes (three hours, 6500 dr); four days a week to Patmos (45 minutes, 2500 dr); and two days a week to Samos (1½ hours, 3400 dr). Tickets can be bought from DRM Travel and Tourism. Hydrofoils leave from Agia Marina, but are subject to cancellations.

Getting Around Leros

Bus The hub for Leros' buses is Platanos. There are four buses a day to Partheni via Alinda and six buses to Xerokambos via Lakki. Check the current schedule with a travel agent.

Car, Motorbike & Bicycle Cars (from 7000 dr), motorbikes (from 1000 dr) and bicycles (500 dr) can be rented from Kastis Travel and Tourist Agency (see the Orientation & Information section) and also from John Koumoulis (☎ 24 015), on the waterfront at Alinda, just beyond the mock castle.

LAKKI Λακκί
If you arrive on Leros on one of the large inter-island ferries, Lakki is where you'll disembark, and it's not a pretty sight. The

port is a legacy of the Italian occupation and was built as a Fascist show piece. The Mussolini-inspired public buildings and wide tree-lined boulevards dotted around the Dodecanese reach their apogee in Lakki. The bizarre shabby buildings hold a sort of perverse and creepy fascination, not least because they seem so absurd on such a small island.

Places to Stay & Eat
It's doubtful you'll want to stay in Lakki, but if you tumble half asleep off a late-night ferry, then the comfortable D class *Miramare Hotel* (☎ 224 69) has single/double/triple rooms for 3000/5000/6000 dr with private bathrooms. Turn right from the quay, and just under 300 metres a sign on the left points to the hotel.

Most restaurants in Lakki are either fastfood or pizza places. An exception is *Taverna O Sotos* where hearty Greek staples include moussaka and meatballs for 700 dr and veal in tomato sauce for 850 dr. The taverna is next to the post office, which is signposted from the waterfront.

PLATANOS Πλάτανος
Platanos, the capital of Leros, is three km north of Lakki, and in contrast, is a picturesque little place. It spills over a narrow hill pouring down to the port of Agia Marina to the north, and the little resort of Panteli to the south, both within walking distance of Platanos. On the east side of Platanos, houses are stacked up a hillside topped by a massive castle. To reach the castle you can either climb up the 370 steps, or walk or drive two km along an asphalt road. Both routes are signposted from Platanos' central square.

Orientation & Information
In Platanos the focus of activity is the lively central square of Plateia N Poussou. The post office and OTE share premises on the right side of Odos Xarami, which leads down from the central square to Agia Marina. Leros' postcode is 85400 and the telephone code is 0247. The National Bank of Greece is on the central square. The bus station is on the

Lakki-Platanos road, just before the central square. A laundrette, well signposted from the central square, charges 1000 dr for wash and dry.

Leros has no EOT or tourist police. The staff at Kastis Travel and Tourist Agency (☎ 22 500) on the waterfront at Agia Marina are helpful. Turn right at the bottom of Xarami and the agency is on the left. Another agency, DRM Travel and Tourism (☎ 23 502 or 24 303) has a room-finding service; turn left at the bottom of Xarami to reach this agency.

Places to Stay

The *Pension Platanos* (☎ 22 608), on the central square, has cheery pink-walled rooms with private bathrooms for 3000/3500/4000 dr. *Andreas Metias* (☎ 22 058 or 23 824) rents large immaculate, attractively furnished doubles for 3200 dr with shared bathrooms. Walk down Odos Xarami and look for the rooms to rent sign at the end of the high stone wall.

The C class *Elefteria Hotel* (☎ 23 550/145) has lovely rooms for 4200/5100/ 6500 dr with private bathrooms; studios are 5700 dr and family apartments are 7700 dr. It's on the left, coming from Lakki or Panteli, just before the bus station.

Places to Eat

Around Platanos' central square there are several places where you can get cheap giros or souvlaki. The *Garbo Restaurant* serves international cuisine and the friendly owners, Frank and Kath, are English. The food is well prepared and portions are large. English breakfast is 850 dr, vegetarian spaghetti bolognese is 650 dr, vegetable curry is 900 dr, fillet steak with butter and brandy sauce is 1500 dr and chocolate gateau with fresh cream is 350 dr. The restaurant is on the right side of Odos Xarami, coming from Platanos.

AROUND PLATANOS

The port of **Agia Marina** is bit run down, but a pleasant enough place, with a more genuine ambience than the resort of Alinda to the north. It's easy enough to walk from Agia Marina to Alinda, just three km north along the road. On this walk you will pass the little resort of **Krithoni**, and a cemetery where members of the British, Canadian and South African forces killed on the island in WW II are buried.

At **Alinda** there's a long crescent of sand and gravel beach. Continuing around the bay sheltered coves can be found. **Gourna**, on the west coast, has a sandy beach which slopes very gently into the sea. There's a small chapel here, built on an islet, and reached by a causeway. To reach Gourna Beach, take the Partheni road from Alinda, and there is a turn-off to the left.

Walking in the other direction from Platanos, you'll arrive at **Panteli**, a little fishing village-cum-holiday resort with a sand and shingle beach.

Places to Stay

The *Hotel Costantinos* (☎ 22 337/904), Krithoni, is a blue and white building above a supermarket, on the right, as you come from Agia Marina. The comfortable rooms are 5000 dr a double with private bathrooms. In Alinda the best deal for independent travellers is *Papafotis Pension* (☎ 22 247). The light and airy double/triple rooms cost 4000/4500 dr with private bathrooms. Coming from Krithoni, look for a cream and brown building, set back from the road, on the left.

In Panteli, *Pension Roza* (☎ 22 798) has pleasant double/triple rooms for 2700/4000 dr with shared bathrooms and 3500 dr for doubles with private bathrooms. The pension is on the left 100 metres along the waterfront. The *Pension Happiness* (☎ 23 498) has tasteful double/triple rooms with private bathrooms for 5000/6000 dr; it's on the left as you walk down the main road from Platanos. In Gourna there are several domatia and a seasonal taverna.

Places to Eat

Carnivores should make for *Chicken Lot* on the waterfront at Krithoni. Chicken is 650 dr and souvlaki and pork chops are 800 dr. On the waterfront in Alinda, *Finikas Taverna* has tasty Greek staples for less than 900 dr.

The *Restaurant Drossia*, below the Pension Roza in Penteli, is an unpretentious place serving good tasty food. Sardines are 600 dr, moussaka is 700 dr and Greek salad is 400 dr.

XEROKAMBOS Ξερόκαμπος

If you want to venture further afield than the beaches around Platanos, then Xerokambos Bay, in the south of the island, is a pleasant low-key resort with a beach that's a mixture of pebble, gravel and sand. Facing the water, if you walk to the left around the bay, there are some good spots for snorkelling.

Places to Stay

Leros' one camp site is Xerokambos' *Camping Leros* (☎ 23 372). It's a pleasant shady site, on the right, at the beginning of the village as you come from Lakki. The camp site has a diving club with equipment for hire, but you must show a certificate.

The pleasant *Maria Stamatia Rooms to Rent* (☎ 22 913) cost 2700 dr a double with shared bathroom and communal kitchen. They're on the left of the road coming from Lakki, just beyond the kafeneion/psistaria. Just 60 metres beyond here are *Michael Yanoukas Rooms* (☎ 23 148). The rooms are spacious and well kept, and cost 3000 dr a double, with shared bathroom.

Places to Eat

The nameless kafeneion/psistaria, on the left of the road as you come from Lakki, serves low-priced souvlaki. The *Tzilzifies Restaurant* on the beach serves reasonable food.

Patmos Πάτμος

Of all the smaller islands of the Dodecanese, Patmos (PAT-mos, population 1500) is the best known. The island is a place of pilgrimage for both Orthodox and Western Christians, for it was here where St John wrote his divinely inspired revelation (the Apocalypse). Once a favourite venue for the pious and hippies wishing to tune into its spiritual vibes, Patmos is now just as popular with sun and sea worshippers. The only remaining vestiges of the island's exclusiveness are the umpteen signs (often ignored) forbidding topless and nude bathing. If it's contemplation or tranquillity you're pining for, then stay on the ferry until it gets to Lipsi or Agathonisi.

History

In AD 95, St John the Divine was banished to Patmos from Ephesus by the pagan Roman emperor Dominian. Whilst residing in a cave on the island, St John wrote the *Book of Revelations*. In 1088 the Blessed Christodoulos, an abbot who came from Asia Minor to Patmos, obtained permission from the Byzantine emperor Alexis I Comnenus to build a monastery to commemorate St John. Pirate raids necessitated sturdy fortifications, and so the monastery looks like a mighty castle.

Under the duke of Naxos, Patmos became a semiautonomous monastic state, and achieved such wealth and influence that it was able to stand indomitable against Turkish oppression. In the early 18th century, a theology and philosophy school was founded by Makarios Kalogheras and flourished as a centre of excellence until the 19th century. Gradually the island's wealth polarised into secular and monastic entities; the secular wealth was acquired through ship building, an industry which diminished with the arrival of the steam ship.

Getting To/From Patmos

Ferry Patmos shares many ferry connections with Rhodes. The F/B *Ialyssos*, F/B *Kamiros*, F/B *Agios Rafail* and F/B *Ionian Sun* all have Patmos and Rhodes amongst their ports of call. For details of their schedules see the Getting To/From Rhodes Island section.

The F/B *Nissos Kalimnos* also calls in at Patmos on its way to Samos from Kalymnos. See the Getting To/From Kalymnos section for details of its schedule.

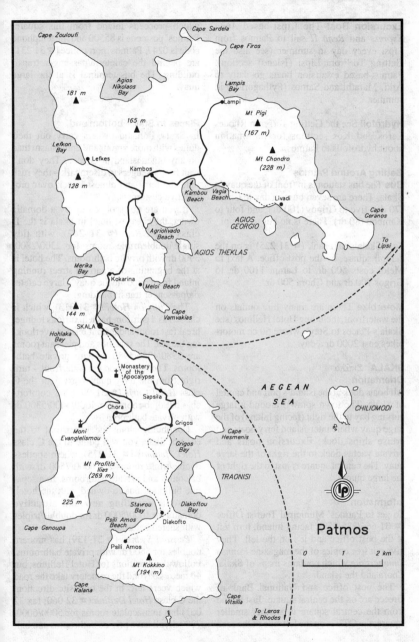

Cape Zouloufi
Cape Sardela
Cape Firos

Agios Nikolaos Bay

181 m

Lampis Bay
Lampi
Mt Pigi
(167 m)

165 m

Lefkon Bay
Lefkes
Kambos
Mt Chondro
(228 m)

128 m

Kambou Beach
Vagia Beach
Livadi

Cape Ceranos

AGIOS GEORGIO

Agriolivado Beach

AGIOS THEKLAS

To Lipsi

Merika Bay
Kokarina
Meloi Beach

144 m

Cape Vamvakias

SKALA

Hohlaka Bay

Monastery of the Apocalypse

Sapsila

Chora

Grigos

Moni Evanglelismou

Cape Hesmenis

Grigos Bay

AEGEAN SEA

CHILIOMODI

Mt Profitis Ilias
(269 m)

TRAONISI

225 m

Stavrou Bay

Psili Amos Beach

Diakoftou Bay

Cape Genoupa

Diakofto

Psili Amos

Mt Kokkino
(194 m)

Cape Kalana

Cape Vitsilia

To Leros & Rhodes

Patmos

0   1   2 km

Excursion Boat The Lipsi-based *Anna Express* and *Rena II* sail to Patmos from Lipsi every day in summer (see also the Getting To/From Lipsi (Island) section). Patmos-based excursion boats go daily to Arki, Marathi and Samos (Pythagorion) in summer.

Hydrofoil See the Getting To/From Rhodes Leros and Kos sections for information about hydrofoils to Patmos.

Getting Around Patmos
Bus The bus station is in front of the quay in Skala. There are seven buses a day to Chora (70 dr); five to Grigos (100 dr); and four to Kambou (80 dr). There is no bus to Lampi.

Taxi Skala's taxi rank (☎ 31 225) is on the central square, by the post office. A taxi to Meloi costs 500 dr, to Lampi 1100 dr, to Grigos 700 dr and Chora 500 dr.

Motorbike There are many hire outlets on the waterfront, including Hotel Hellinos (see Skala's Places to Stay), where 50 cc motorbikes cost 2000 dr a day.

SKALA Σκάλα
Orientation
All boats dock at the island's port and capital of Skala. The town sprawls around a large curving bay to the right (facing inland) of the large quay where inter-island ferry boats and cruise ships dock. Excursion boats and private yachts dock to the right of the large quay. The central square is just to the right of the large quay.

Information
To get to Patmos' Municipal Tourist Office (☎ 31 666/235/058), facing inland, turn left at the post office and it's on the left. They give out free copies of the magazine *Patmos Summertime* which contains maps of Skala, Chora and the island.

The post office and National Bank of Greece are on the central square. Just inland from the central square is another smaller square; the OTE is on the left side of the road which proceeds inland from this square. Patmos' postcode is 85500 and the telephone code is 0247. Patmos' port police (☎ 31 231) are behind the cafeteria/passenger transit building. The bus terminal is at the large quay.

Places to Stay – bottom end
In Skala, domatia owners carry out their duties with more vigour and enthusiasm than on any other island in Greece. They don't wait for passengers to disembark – they rush onto the ferry and almost knock over prospective customers.

If you are not scooped up by a domatia owner, the cheapest hotel in Skala is the D class *Hotel Rex* (☎ 31 242), with tidy single/double/triple rooms for 2300/2800/3900 dr with private bathrooms. The hotel is at the beginning of a narrow street running inland from opposite the quay's large cafeteria/passenger transit building.

The *Patmion Hotel* (☎ 31 313), which is classed as a pension, has a luxurious lounge, breakfast room and a front terrace overlooking the sea. The spacious and pleasant rooms are 3980/4980/5980 dr with private bathrooms. The hotel is on the waterfront – turn right from the ferry quay. Next door the C class *Hotel Chris* (☎ 31 001) has comfortable but drab rooms for 4000/4400/5300 dr with private bathrooms.

Continuing along the waterfront to the edge of Skala you will come to the C class *Hotel Hellinos* (☎ 31 275), where spotless double/triple rooms are 6000/7500 dr with balconies and private bathrooms. In a separate building, but co-owned with the hotel, are some sparkling new and attractive domatia for 4000/5000 dr for doubles/triples with shared bathroom.

Pension Sydney (☎ 31 139) has modern doubles for 5600 dr with private bathrooms. Follow the directions for Hotel Hellinos, but 40 metres beyond the cemetery take the road which veers left. In the opposite direction, the C class *Hotel Delfina* (☎ 32 060; fax 32 061) has immaculate rooms for 5000/6000/7200 dr; all have private bathrooms and balconies. Turn left from the quay and you will come to the hotel on the right.

Places to Stay – middle
The best hotel in Skala is the B class *Hotel Skala* (☎ 31 343/4), next to the Patmion Hotel. Rates for the very comfortable rooms are 7000/10,000/13,000 dr, including breakfast. The hotel has a lovely garden and a swimming pool.

Places to Eat
One of the nicest eating places in Skala is *Grigori's Taverna*, where tasty dishes are less than 1000 dr. The taverna is to the left of the quay as you face inland. *O Pantelis Taverna* has reasonably priced, tasty Greek staples. A meal of moussaka, cabbage salad, chips and Amstel should cost about 1200 dr. The taverna is one block back from the waterfront, behind the Café Bar Arion. *Polar Galateria*, just inland from the small square beyond the main square, has filter coffee for 250 dr, cappuccino for 280 dr, pies and pastries for 300 dr and ice cream (many flavours) for 130 dr. There are two excellent bakers on the small square; both sell cakes, cookies and pies, as well as bread. The fruit and vegetable market is nearby and well signposted.

MONASTERIES & CHORA
The immense Monastery of St John the Theologian, with its buttressed grey walls, crowns the island of Patmos. An asphalt road leads in four km from Skala to the monastery, but many people prefer to walk up the well-maintained cobbled path. The path passes the **Monastery of the Apocalypse**, built around the cave where St John received his divine revelation. Inside the cave you can see the rock which the saint used as a pillow, and the triple fissure in the roof, from which the voice of God issued, and which supposedly symbolises the Holy Trinity.

From the cave it's just another 15 minutes to the **Monastery of St John the Theologian**. The finest frescoes of the monastery are those in the outer narthex, which depict significant events in St John's life. The priceless contents in the monastery's **treasury** are second only to those in the monasteries of Mt Athos, and include icons, ecclesiastical ornaments, embroideries and pendants made of precious stones.

Monastery opening times change frequently, so it is best to check with the tourist office (see under Information), then visit as early as possible before the tour groups arrive. Admission is free.

Huddled around the base of the monastery are the immaculate whitewashed houses of **Chora**, many with handsome wooden doors. The houses are a legacy of the island's great wealth in the 18th and 19th centuries. Some of them have been bought and renovated by wealthy Greeks and foreigners. The village has a rather hushed atmosphere, and an air of exclusiveness.

NORTH OF SKALA
The pleasant tree-shaded **Meloi Beach** is just two km from Skala. It is reached by a turn-off from the main road going north.

Continuing two km north along the main road there's a turn-off right to the sandy and quiet **Agriolivado Beach**. The main road continues to the pleasant inland village of **Kambos** and then down to the shingle beach at **Kambou**, from where you can walk to the secluded **Vagia Beach**. The main road ends at **Lampi**, nine km from Skala, on the north coast. The beach here is composed of multi-coloured stones, but don't expect a psychedelic extravaganza (as I did when I read about this beach), because the stones are of very subtle hues. The beach is gorgeous, nonetheless, and vies with Psili Amos in the south of the island for best beach on Patmos.

Places to Stay
The *Patmos Flowers Camping* (☎ 31 821), at Meloi, is an outstanding site, with each pitch shaded by thick tall bamboo. The rates are 400 dr for an adult and 200 dr for a tent. The site has a minimarket, café bar and a communal kitchen with a refrigerator and sinks, but no cooker. The camp site is signposted from the quay in Skala. Buses

don't go to Meloi; a taxi from Skala will cost 500 dr.

Next to Taverna Meloi (which is well signposted) and very near the beach at Meloi, there are some basic but clean *Rooms* (☎ 32 382), owned by a smiling and gentle couple, who speak not a word of English. The rates are 2500 dr for a double with shared bathrooms. At Kambou the owners of George's Place Snack Bar (see Places to Eat) work as an unofficial room-letting agency, so if you pop in, they will put you in touch with a local domatia owner.

At Lampi, *Dolphin Rooms* (☎ 31 951) has doubles with private bathrooms for 5600 dr. The rooms are on the beach behind the To Delfini Restaurant.

Places to Eat
Taverna Meloi, on the beach at Meloi, is highly commendable. A full meal will cost about 1500 dr. The taverna is well signposted from the main road and is open for breakfast, lunch and dinner.

At Kambou, *George's Place Snack Bar*, at the far end of the beach, is owned by two friendly laid-back young men – one Greek, one English – and is almost a vegetarian snack bar, although it does have one or two token meat dishes. A variety of vegetable pies cost between 450 and 550 dr each, as do the salads. Their superb home-made apple pie is 450 dr, filter coffee is 250 dr and herb and fruit teas are 200 dr.

To Delfini Restaurant, on the beach at Lampi, specialises in fish dishes. A meal of whitebait, chips, Greek salad and Amstel should set you back about 1500 dr.

SOUTH OF SKALA
Grigos (Γρίγος), four km south-east of Skala, is a pleasant resort with a curving sandy beach, with canoe and windsurf rental. Sandy **Psili Amos Beach** to the south-west of Grigos is generally regarded as the island's best. No road leads here, and the easiest way to get to it is by excursion boat from Skala.

Places to Stay
The D class *Hotel Flisvos* (☎ 31 380), at Grigos, has simply furnished, clean doubles for 3500 dr with shared bathrooms and three-person apartments for 6700 dr. Facing the sea, the hotel is on the far right of the bay; you can reach it by walking along the beach. *Restaurant O Stamatis and Rooms* (☎ 31 302) has comfortable doubles with private bathrooms for 5600 dr, and large apartments for 10,000 dr. The rooms are on the beach at the end of the main road. Psili Amos has no accommodation.

Lipsi Λειψοί

Lipsi (Li-PSEE, population 650), 12 km east of Patmos, and 11 km north of Leros, is an idyllic little island where donkeys still outnumber cars and motorbikes, and there are as yet no discos or music bars. The cheery and friendly inhabitants busy themselves with fishing, agriculture, animal husbandry, and keeping happy the relatively small number of tourists who venture here.

The picturesque port town of Lipsi is the only settlement. Around the coast are excellent beaches. 'Taxis' (bone-shaking Nissan trucks) will transport you almost anywhere you want to go, but if you enjoy walking, the island is small enough to explore on foot in a few days.

Getting To/From Lipsi (Island)
Ferry The only inter-island ferry which calls at Lipsi is the F/B *Nissos Kalimnos*. See the Getting To/From Kalymnos section for details of its schedule.

Excursion Boat The *Rena II* and *Anna Express* do daily trips in the summer to Agia Marina on Leros and to Skala on Patmos. They leave sometime in the morning and return sometime in the afternoon – the time-table is displayed at the small quay. The one-way fare is 1000 dr. In addition, they both make early evening trips to Patmos and

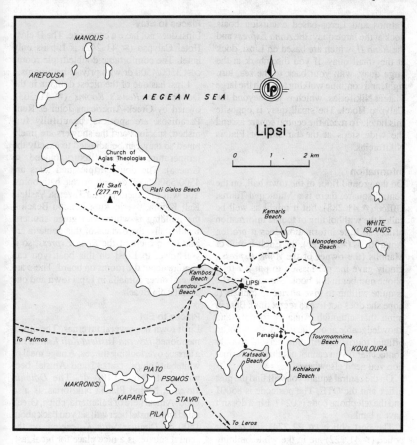

await the arrival of the large ferries from Rhodes and Piraeus, which usually arrive around 11 pm or midnight, then they return to Lipsi. The advantage of this is that you can get straight to Lipsi without having to spend the night on Patmos.

The *Anna Express* charges 2000 dr one-way for this trip and the *Rena II* charges 1500 dr. These two excursion boats, and others, also do trips to Arki and Marathi islands (2000 dr return) in the high season.

Getting Around Lipsi (Island)
Taxi The 'taxis' do (frequently bone-shak-

ing) trips to most of the island's beaches for around 500 dr per person.

Excursion Boat
Various excursion boats including the *Rena II* and *Anna Express* do trips to Lipsi's beaches, and to the uninhabited White Islands (1000 dr) which lie off the east coast. A return trip to these islands costs 1000 dr.

LIPSI TOWN
Orientation
All boats dock at Lipsi town, where there are two quays. The inter-island ferry boat and

Patmos and Leros-based excursion boats dock at the large quay; the *Anna Express* and the *Rena II*, which are based on Lipsi, dock at the small quay. If you disembark at the large quay, with your back to the sea, turn right, and continue walking to reach the large Plateia Nikiforias, which is just beyond the Calypso Hotel. The small quay is opposite this hotel. To reach the central square ascend the wide steps at the far side of Plateia Nikiforeias.

Information

On the ground floor of the town hall, on the central square, there is a Municipal Tourist Office (☎ 41 288), but it might as well be called the withholding of tourist information office, so little information does it proffer. Anna Rizos (☎ 41 225), the English wife of Manolis (the owner of the *Anna Express*), kindly gave me permission to put her telephone number in this book. She said that she is quite willing to give advice to tourists (I hope she does not live to regret this). Bear in mind that although Anna is friendly and knowledgeable about the island, she is not an official tourist information person, so only contact her if you cannot obtain the information you need elsewhere.

On the central square you will find the post office and the OTE. The postcode is 85001 and the telephone code is 0247. Lipsi doesn't have a bank.

The port police (☎ 22 224) and regular police (☎ 41 222) are in the white building at the base of the steps which lead up to the central square.

Museum

Lipsi's little museum shares a room with the tourist information office. Its underwhelming exhibits include a collection of pebbles from Belgium, Russia and Australia and plastic bottles filled with holy water from Mt Athos and the well of Samaria. Its labelling is exemplary – everything down to the tiniest pebble has been meticulously labelled in neat handwritten English. Entrance is free but its opening times, like that of the tourist office, are erratic.

Places to Stay

Lipsi does not have a camp site. The D class Hotel Calypso (☎ 41 242) is Lipsi's only hotel. The comfortable double/triple rooms cost 3500/4500 dr with private bathrooms.

Lipsi has one of the nicest domatia in the Dodecanese. *Rena's Rooms* (☎ 41 363), owned by Greek-Americans John & Rena Paradisos, are spotless, beautifully furnished, spacious and the showers are finely tuned so they can be adjusted to exactly the temperature required (luxury indeed, in Greece). The double/triple/quad rates are 4500/5500/6000 dr with private bathrooms. You will find them behind Taverna Vasileia Kali Kardia, overlooking Lendou Beach – the building is white with green shutters. Incidentally, the owners of this domatia are also the owners of the *Rena Express*, so if you travel to Lipsi on this boat, you can enquire about the rooms on board. There are several other domatia in Lipsi town and one at Katsadia Beach.

Places to Eat

Lipsi town has several tavernas. The aforementioned *Taverna Vasileia Kali Kardia* has a terrace overlooking the sea. A huge meal of whitebait, chips, tzatziki and Amstel beer will cost about 1400 dr. The *Dolphin Taverna*, behind Plateia Nikiforias, is also good. A meal here of kalamaria, chips, Greek salad and Amstel beer will set you back about 1500 dr. *Dimitris Seith Kafeneion*, on the central square, is a nice place for breakfast. Yoghurt with honey, and Nescafé are only 350 dr; toast, omelettes and Greek salads are also reasonably priced. The tables are outside, under shady trees – it's a lovely, peaceful traffic-free square. If you go up the street by the side of the post office you will come to another square, where there is a supermarket, fruit and vegetable shop. Also on this square is the *C Mylos Café*, where filter coffee is 200 dr and cakes and cheese pies cost around 300 dr.

BEACHES

All of Lipsi's beaches are signposted from the town. The town beach of **Lendou** is just a few minutes' walk from the waterfront. Walking from Plateia Nikiforeias towards the large quay, turn right at Taverna Vasileia Kali Kardia and you will come to the beach on the left. If you continue for a little further along you will reach a fork in the road; bearing left, you will arrive in a few minutes at **Kambos Beach**. If you take the right fork and keep going along this road which skirts the east coast you will arrive in about 40 minutes at **Plati Gialos**, the island's best beach. Along the way there are views over the sea to the islands of Arki, Marathi and Agathonisi. The beach is a long sandy one with a very gradual slope in the sea. Behind the beach there is a pretty little church with a blue and white belfry and on the beach there's a taverna and a family of friendly ducks. From Plati Gialos a track leads northwest to the **Church of Agias Theologias**, close to a small sheltered beach.

Katsadia, on the south coast, is a sandy beach with a taverna, 25 minutes' walk from Lipsi town. **Kohlakura**, also on the south coast, has a long stony beach. The island's unofficial nudist beach is **Monodendri**, on the east coast, about an hour's walk from town. **Kamaris** is a pleasant shingle beach, to the north of Monodendri.

Minor Dodecanese Islets

The area of the Dodecanese north of Patmos, and south of the North-Eastern Aegean island of Samos is speckled with numerous islets, mostly uninhabited, but with good anchorages and good beaches. If you are going to charter a yacht it is probably the best region of the Aegean to do so, as weather conditions are good. Alternatively, you can visit some of the islets on excursion boats from Patmos and Lipsi. There is also the possibility of 'hitching' a lift on a fishing boat or yacht, though this is not common practice, and shouldn't be taken for granted.

Two of these islets are inhabited – only just. They are **Arki** (Αρκοί) and the tiny islet of **Marathi** (Μάραθος). Arki is just four km long and one km wide, but it has 50 inhabitants, electricity, water and a metered telephone. There are several coves around its coast; one, with its incredibly vivid blue water, is appropriately called the **Blue Lagoon**. It's is a great place for snorkelling. There are two tavernas at the port. The one owned by *Lefterus Katsavidis* is also a domatia, with doubles for 4000 dr.

Up until WW II, tiny Marathi, supported a dozen or so inhabitants, of which only one, a shepherd, remains. However, the island has two seasonal tavernas both of which rent rooms. The two tavernas, owned by *Mr Pandelis* and *Mr Michaelis* respectively, have comfortable doubles for 4000 dr. Mr Michaelis is the son of Marathi's one permanent inhabitant. Mr Pandelis, who was born on Arki, has lived for many years in Australia, but spends the summer months (Greek summer months that is) on Marathi with his family. The island has a superb 500-metre-long sandy beach. There is electricity, but no telephone – there is a two-way radio for emergencies. Needless to say neither Arki or

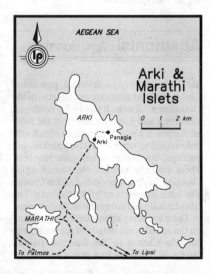

Marathi has a bank or post office – bring some drachma with you.

Getting There & Away
Excursion Boat These islands are not on the F/B *Nissos Kalimnos'* ports of call, but in high season both are visited by excursion boats from Lipsi and Patmos.

Yacht Charter One of the most reliable yacht charter companies operating in the region is Seaways Sailing, Pythagorion, Samos (☎ 0273-61 422; fax 0273-61 695). You'll find them on the waterfront at Pythagorion. They also have an Athens base – Irakleos 23, Glyfada (☎ 01-963 3356; fax 964 9678). They quote their prices in Deutschmark because most of their clients are German, but payment may be made in any major currency. A one-week trip starting and ending in Samos and visiting the islands of Agathonisi, Lipsi, Arki, Marathi, Patmos and Farmako (uninhabited, but with good beaches) costs from DM1000 to DM1170 per person (all inclusive), depending on the season. The price range for bare-boat hire is from US$260 to US$770 per week, depending on the type of craft.

Agathonisi Αγαθονήσι

Tiny Agathonisi (Aga-tho-NI-si, population 120) is the most northerly and isolated of the Dodecanese islands. It lies to the north-east of Patmos and just eight km from the coast of Turkey. It's a little gem of an island, still only visited by adventurous backpackers and yachties, but neither in any great numbers. There are three villages: the port of Agios Giorgios, Megalo Chorio and Mikro Chorio. The latter is home to only 10 inhabitants. The island is hilly and covered with thorn bushes.

There are many opportunities for walking on the island – see details of the walk from Megalo Chorio to the deserted fishing village of Katholika later in this section.

Getting To/From Agathonisi
The F/B *Nissos Kalimnos* is the only passenger ferry which calls at Agathonisi. See the Getting To/From Kalymnos section for its schedule. The twice-weekly supply boat from Samos also takes passengers, but its schedule is subject to change – check with the police officer or locals.

Getting Around Agathonisi
The island's one motorised public transport vehicle is a spluttering, bone-shaking three-wheeler truck. When a boat arrives, the driver emerges from one of the waterfront tavernas to transport people from Agios Giorgios to both Megalo Chorio and Mikro Chorio.

AGIOS GIORGIOS Αγιοσ Γεώργιος
Agios Giorgios is a pleasant little place with just enough waterfront activity to stop you sinking into a state of inertia. It has a nice pebble beach, and, except in July or August, in all probability, your only companions here will be a large number of resident ducks. Ask locals to direct you to Spillia, a sheltered cove just west of Agios Giorgios – you may

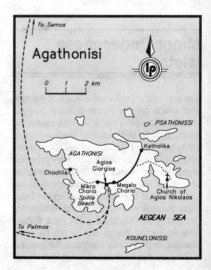

be able to persuade a fisherman to take you there by boat.

Orientation & Information

Boats dock at Agios Giorgios, from where a cement road leads up right (facing inland) to Megalo Chorio and another leads up left to Mikro Chorio. Both villages are less than one km from the port. There is no post office or bank, but the owner of George's Taverna in Agios Giorgios will change major currencies of cash or travellers' cheques. Neither is there an OTE, but Taverna Limanaki, near the quay, has a metered telephone. Agathonisi's telephone code is 0247.

There is no tourist information office or tourist police. The one police officer, who is also the tourist police officer and port police officer, has an office (☎ 23 770) on the right side of the beginning of the road from Agios Giorgios to Megalo Chorio.

Places to Stay

There is no official camp site, but you may be able to camp freelance, except on Agios Giorgios Beach.

There are two pensions in Agios Giorgios. The one on the waterfront, almost hidden behind a garden full of flowers, is *Pension Maria Kamitsa* (☎ 23 650/690). The other pension is behind this one above George's Taverna (☎ 24 385). Both are clean and comfortable and charge 4000 dr for doubles with private bathrooms.

Places to Eat

There are three tavernas in Agios Giorgios. *Taverna Limanaki* is pricey, with a meal of grey mullet, chips, Greek salad and soft drink costing 2200 dr. *George's Taverna* is more moderately priced and the food is excellent. George's kalamaria stifado is superlative; this, with Greek salad, chips and Amstel costs about 1400 dr. The taverna between these two specialises in fish dishes but was temporarily closed when I visited the island. Taverna Limanaki doubles up as a pantopoleion.

AROUND THE ISLAND

Megalo Chorio Μεγάλο Χωριό

Megalo Chorio is where most of the island's inhabitants live. It has one domatia which belongs to *Mrs Katsoulieri* (☎ 24 385). From the central square, walk straight ahead and the accommodation is on the right. Rates are 4000 dr for doubles. The village has one restaurant and one kafeneion, both of which are on the central square. At the *Restaurant I Eireni* a huge helping of fried sardines and chips will cost only about 700 dr. The pantopoleion on the central square stocks a limited amount of foodstuffs.

Walk from Megala Chorio to Katholika

Katholika (Καθολικά) is a deserted fishing hamlet in the north of the island. Its derelict stone dwellings are inhabited by numerous cats and a herd of goats. There is a tiny beach so bring your swimming gear. It can be reached on foot along a cement road in about 30 minutes from Megalo Chorio. However, if you would like to take a more adventurous route, it can be reached in about one hour along goat paths over the hills. Make sure you wear sensible shoes if you plan to do this walk, as if you wear sandals you'll get your feet badly scratched by thorn bushes. This applies to any walk off the cement road on Agathonisi.

From the central square turn right at Restaurant I Eireni. Beyond the basketball field, on the left, you will see a stone-wall enclosure and beyond it a second enclosure. Walk around the back of the first, and the front of the second, and then proceed to the crest of the hill. The terrain is a mixture of rocks and thorn bushes with paths winding between them. At the crest look half-left (north-east) and you will see at the top of the next hill a square stone building, which you walk to next.

The view from the building is tremendous. You will see Samos to the north and the Menderes estuary, and ancient Didyma, both in Turkey, to the north-east. From the hut look half-left and you will see two large olive trees – proceed to these. These trees would make a superb picnic spot, but they offer the only substantial shade in the area, so the goats, cattle and donkeys who graze hereabouts, retreat to them in hot weather and cover the ground with their droppings. Little wonder the trees are so large and robust – they get a lot of nourishment. From here,

walk towards the long narrow island of Psathonisi which you will see ahead and slightly to the left. Soon you will see ahead, and half-right, a large oblong enclosure; walk to this and turn right. Continue down to the cement road, turn left, and in a few minutes you will reach Katholika.

North-Eastern Aegean Islands
Τα Νησιά του Βορειοανατολικού Αιγαίου

The islands of the North-Eastern Aegean are grouped together more for convenience than for any historical, geographical or administrative parity. With the exceptions of Thassos and Samothrace, they are, like the Dodecanese, much closer to Turkey than to the Greek mainland, but unlike the Dodecanese they are not close to one another. This means island hopping is not the easy matter it is within the Dodecanese and Cyclades, although, with the exceptions of Thassos and Samothrace, it is possible.

The islands are less visited than either the Dodecanese or the Cyclades. Scenically, they also differ from these groups. Mountainous, green and mantled with forests, they are ideal choices for walkers but most are also blessed with long stretches of delectable beaches. Although historically diverse, a list of the islands' inhabitants from far-off times reads like a Who's Who of the ancient world. Some can also boast important ancient sites. All of them became part of the Ottoman Empire and were united with Greece after the Balkan Wars in 1912.

There are seven major islands in the group: Samos, Chios, Ikaria, Lesbos, Lemnos, Samothrace and Thassos. Fourni near Ikaria, Psara and Inousses near Chios and Agios Efstratios near Lemnos are small, little-visited islands in the group.

Getting To/From the North-Eastern Aegean Islands

Following is a brief overview of travel options to/from and between the islands of the North-Eastern Aegean. For additional information, see the entries at the beginning of sections on individual islands.

Air Samos, Chios, Lesbos and Lemnos have airports with flights to Athens. In addition, Chios, Lesbos and Lemnos have flights to Thessaloniki. An airport is under construction on Ikaria.

Ferry (Domestic) Chios, Samos, Lesbos and Ikaria have daily connections with Piraeus. Some of the Samos and Ikaria ferries to Piraeus go via Mykonos, Naxos, Paros and Syros. Lemnos has three connections a week with Piraeus, Rafina and Kavala. Chios and Lesbos have two connections a week with Thessaloniki, and Lemnos has one. Thassos and Samothrace have no connections with Piraeus or any other islands. Thassos has daily connections with Kavala and Keramoti, both in Macedonia. Samothrace has daily connections with Alexandroupolis in Thrace and a twice or thrice (depending on demand) summer connection with Kavala. An excursion boat links Samos with Patmos in the Dodecanese daily in summer. The F/B *Nissos Kalimnos* (a Dodecanese-based ferry) links Samos (Pythagorion) twice a week with the Dodecanese islands of Agathonisi, Lipsi, Patmos, Leros, Kalymnos, Kos, Nisyros, Tilos, Symi and Rhodes.

Ferry (International) In summer there are daily boats from Samos to Kusadaşı (for

North-Eastern
Aegean Islands

0   50   100 km

Ephesus), from Chios to Çeşme and from Lesbos to Ayvalik, all in Turkey.

Hydrofoil In summer there are hydrofoils between Samos and the Dodecanese islands of Leros and Kos. Many hydrofoils a day ply between Thassos and Kavala.

Getting Around the North-Eastern Aegean Islands

Air Lesbos and Lemnos are the only islands in the group with air connections between them.

Ferry There are daily ferries between Ikaria and Samos, Chios and Lesbos, three times a week between Lesbos and Lemnos and twice a week between Chios and Samos.

Samos Σάμος

Samos (SA-mos, population 32,000), the most southerly island of the group, is the closest of all the Greek islands to Turkey, from which it is separated by the three-km-wide Mykale Straits. The island is the most visited of all the North-Eastern Aegean group. Charter flights of tourists descend upon the island from many Northern European countries. Try to avoid Samos in July and August when rooms are hard to come by.

Despite the package tourists, Samos is still worth a visit: forays into its hinterland are rewarded with unspoilt villages and mountain vistas. In summer the humid air of Samos is permeated with heavy floral scents, especially jasmine. This, and the prolific greenery of the landscape, lend Samos an exotic and tropical air. Samos has three ports, Samos town and Karlovasi on the north coast and Pythagorion on the south coast.

History

The first inhabitants of Samos, the Pelasgian tribes, worshipped Hera, whose birthplace was Samos. Pythagoras was born on Samos in the 6th century BC. Unfortunately, his life coincided with that of the tyrant Polycrates,

who in 550 BC deposed the Samiot oligarchy. As the two did not see eye to eye, Pythagoras spent much of his time in exile in Italy. Despite this, under Polycrates Samos became a mighty naval power, and the arts and sciences also flourished. 'Big is Beautiful' seems to have been Polycrates' maxim; almost every construction and art work he commissioned appears to have been Ancient Greece's biggest. The historian Herodotus wrote glowingly of the tyrant's achievements, stating that the Samians had accomplished the three greatest projects in Greece at that time: the Temple of Hera – one of the Seven Wonders of the Ancient World – the Eupalinos Tunnel and a huge jetty.

Other celebrated Samians were the astronomers Aristarchus (the first scientist to postulate that the planets of our solar system revolved around the sun, not the earth), Aristides and Aristilos. The philosophers Melissus and Epicurus were also born on Samos.

After the decisive Battle of Plataea (479 BC), in which Athens had been aided by the Samians, Samos allied itself to Athens and returned to democracy. In the Battle of Mykale which took place on the same day as the Battle of Plataea, the Greek navy (with many Samian sailors) defeated the Persian fleet. However, during the Peloponnesian Wars, Samos was taken by Sparta.

Under Roman rule Samos enjoyed many privileges, but after successive occupations by the Venetians and Genoese it was conquered by the Turks in 1453. Samos took a major role in the uprising against the Turks in the early 19th century, much to the detriment of its neighbour, Chios (see Chios' History section).

Getting To/From Samos (Island)

Air There are at least two flights a day from Samos to Athens (11,300 dr). The Olympic Airways office (☎ 27 237) is on the corner of Odos Kanari and Smyrnis in Samos town. There is also an Olympic Airways office (☎ 61 213) on Lykourgou Logotheti in Pythagorion. The airport is four km west of Pythagorion.

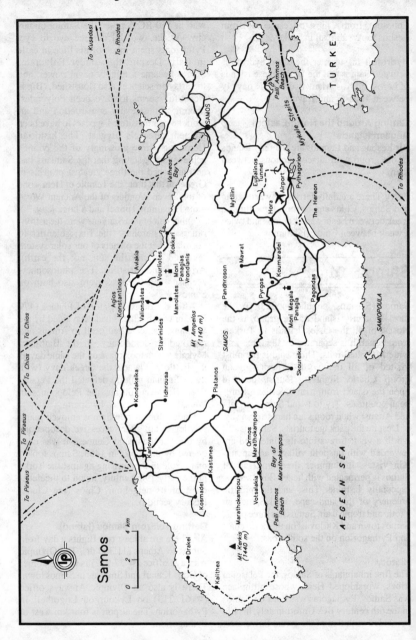

Ferry (Domestic) Samos is the transport hub of the North-Eastern Aegean, with ferries to the Dodecanese and Cyclades as well as the other North-Eastern Aegean islands. The F/B *Dimitra* leaves Samos town on Tuesday at 7 am for Piraeus (12½ hours, 3610 dr) via Karlovasi, Ikaria (Agios Kirikos) (3½ hours, 1300 dr), Mykonos, (2650 dr) and Syros (2650 dr); on Wednesday at 4.30 pm and Sunday at 4 pm via Karlovasi, Fourni (840 dr), Ikaria (Agios Kirikos), Naxos (2650 dr) and Paros (2650 dr).

The F/B *Captain Stamatis* leaves Samos town for Chios (1590 dr) via Karlovasi on Monday at 8 pm and Friday at 4 pm.

The F/B *Golden Vergina* leaves Samos town on Tuesday, Thursday and Sunday at 4 pm and Saturday at 6 am for Piraeus via Karlovasi, Ikaria, Naxos and Paros. The Thursday ferry calls at Agios Kirikos; the others call at Evdilos on Ikaria. In addition the Thursday ferry calls at Fourni.

The F/B *Samena* leaves Samos town on Wednesday at 4.30 pm and Sunday at 7.15 am for Piraeus via Karlovasi and Ikaria (Evdilos); on Friday at 5.30 pm it does the same trip but calls at Agios Kirikos on Ikaria instead of Evdilos.

Once a week ferries leave for Rhodes (12 hours, 4065 dr) via Patmos, Leros, Kalymnos and Kos; and Kavala (18 hours, 5380 dr) via Chios (four hours, 1590 dr), Lesbos (seven hours, 2640 dr) and Lemnos (12 hours).

The F/B *Nissos Kalimnos* links Samos' southern port of Pythagorion twice a week with Rhodes via the Dodecanese islands of Agathonisi, Lipsi, Patmos, Kalymnos, Kos, Nisyros, Tilos and Symi. Tickets for most ferries can be bought at Pythagoras Tours (☎ 27 240), on the waterfront in Samos town.

Ferry (International) In summer there are daily ferries at 8 am and 5 pm from Samos town to Kuşadası (for Ephesus) in Turkey. In spring and autumn there are four ferries a week. Tickets cost 5000/9000 dr one-way/return (plus 1250 dr port tax) and can be purchased from Samos Tours (☎ 27 715/738, 22 382 or 24 852), in Samos town.

As always when travelling by sea from Greece to Turkey you must submit your passport the day before you travel.

Excursion Boat In summer there are daily excursion boats between Pythagorion and Patmos (2500 dr).

Hydrofoil In summer hydrofoils link Pythagorion with Patmos, Leros, Kos and Rhodes. Schedules are subject to frequent change, so contact the EOT in Pythagorion or the port police (☎ 61 225) for up-to-date information.

Getting Around Samos (Island)
To/From the Airport At the time of writing there were no buses to the airport, but this may change. Check at one of the Olympic Airways offices. A taxi from Samos town will cost 1800 dr.

Bus Samos has an adequate bus service although buses stop running quite early in the evening. There are 13 buses a day from Samos town to both Kokkari and Pythagorion; eight to Agios Konstantinos; seven to Karlovasi (via the north coast); six to the Hereon; four to Mytilini, three to Psili Ammos Beach (the one on the east coast) and two buses a day travel to Ormos Marathokampou and Votsalakia.

In addition to frequent buses to Samos town there are six buses to the Hereon from Pythagorion and two to both Mytilini and Karlovasi.

Car & Motorbike Samos has many car-rental outlets. They include Hertz (☎ 61 730), Lykourgou Logotheti 77, and Europcar (☎ 61 522), Lykourgou Logotheti 65, both in Pythagorion. There are also many motorbike-hire outlets on Lykourgou Logotheti. Motorbikes can be rented from the Hotel Graceland in Samos town (see Places to Stay) which also has an office (☎ 22 663 or 27 504) on Plateia Nikolaou, just north of Plateia Pythagora.

Taxi From the taxi rank (☎ 28 404) on Plateia

Pythagora, Samos town, tariffs are: Kokkari 1200 dr; Pythagorion 1500 dr; Avlakia 1600 dr; airport 1800 dr; and the Hereon 2200 dr.

SAMOS TOWN (VATHI)
The island's capital is large and bustling Samos town (also called Vathi) (Βαθύ) , on the north-east coast. The waterfront is crowded with tourists who rarely venture to the older and extremely attractive upper town of Ano Vathi where 19th-century red-tiled houses perch on a hillside.

Orientation
From the quay (facing inland) turn right to reach the waterfront central square of Plateia Pythagora, recognisable by its four palm trees and statue of a lion. A little further along and one block inland are the shady municipal gardens with a pleasant outdoor café.

Information
The Municipal Tourist Office (☎ 28 530) is just north of Plateia Pythagora, but it only operates in July and August; the staff will assist in finding accommodation. The tourist police (☎ 27 333) are in the same building as the regular police on Plateia Iroon. The port police (☎ 27 318) are just north of the quay and one block back from the waterfront.

The post office is on Odos Smyrnis, four blocks from the waterfront. The OTE is on Plateia Iroon, behind the municipal gardens. Samos' postcode is 83100 and the telephone code is 0273. The National Bank of Greece is on the waterfront just south of Plateia Pythagora and the Commercial Bank is on the east side of the square. The bus station is just back from the waterfront on Odos Ioannou Lekati. The taxi rank (☎ 28 404) is on Plateia Pythagora. Samos General Hospital (☎ 27 407) is on the waterfront, north of the ferry quay.

Things to See
Apart from the charming old quarter of Ano Vathi, which is a peaceful place to stroll, and the municipal gardens which are a pleasant place to sit, the main attraction of Samos town is the **Archaeological Museum** (☎ 27 469). Many of the fine exhibits in this well laid out museum are a legacy of Polycrates' time. They include a gargantuan Kouros (4½ metres) which was found in the Hereon (Sanctuary to Hera). In true Polycrates fashion it was the largest standing Kouros ever produced. The collection also includes many more statues, mostly from the Hereon, bronze sculptures, stele and pottery. The museum is east of the municipal gardens. Opening times are Tuesday to Sunday from 8.30 am to 3 pm. Admission is 500 dr.

Places to Stay
Samos does not have a camp site. The cheapest hotel is the *Hotel Ionia* (☎ 28 782), on Manoli Kalomiri (classed as a pension). Its clean and pretty rooms cost 1500/3000/4000 dr for singles/doubles/triples with shared bathrooms and 2000/3500 dr with private bathrooms. From the quay, turn right onto the waterfront, left at Stamatiadou, then left onto Manoli Kalomiri. Close by, the traditional *Pension Avli* (☎ 22 939) is a former Roman Catholic convent, built around a lovely courtyard (*avli* is Greek for courtyard). The rooms are spacious and nicely furnished. Rates are 4400/5300 dr for doubles/triples with private bathrooms. The C class *Hotel Helen* (☎ 22 866), Grammou 2, has cosy rooms with fitted carpets and attractive furniture. Doubles are 4500 dr with private bathrooms. Turn right from the quay, and left at the Roman Catholic church, veer right at the intersection and the hotel is on the right. The similarly priced *Hotel Graceland* (☎ 22 963), further up Grammou, has very pleasant rooms with private bathrooms.

The nearest hotel to the quay is the grand-looking C class *Samos Hotel* (☎ 28 377/378). With 105 rooms it is one of the town's largest hotels. It is well kept with spacious and elegant common areas comprising a cafeteria, bar, snack bar, restaurant, breakfast room, TV room and billiard room. The comfortable rooms have fitted carpets, balconies, telephones and private bathrooms. Rates are 4800/6000 dr for singles/doubles. On leaving the quay turn right and you'll come to the hotel on the left. The B class *Hotel Emily*

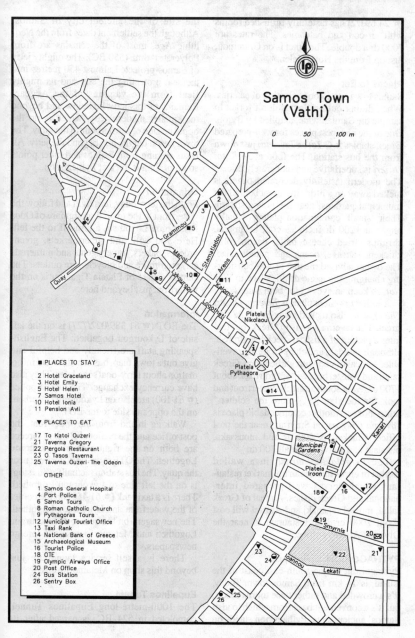

Samos Town
(Vathi)

0   50   100 m

■ PLACES TO STAY

2 Hotel Graceland
3 Hotel Emily
5 Hotel Helen
7 Samos Hotel
10 Hotel Ionia
11 Pension Avli

▼ PLACES TO EAT

17 To Katoi Ouzeri
21 Taverna Gregory
22 Pergola Restaurant
23 O Tasos Taverna
25 Taverna Ouzeri The Odeon

OTHER

1 Samos General Hospital
4 Port Police
6 Samos Tours
8 Roman Catholic Church
9 Pythagoras Tours
12 Municipal Tourist Office
13 Taxi Rank
14 National Bank of Greece
15 Archaeological Museum
16 Tourist Police
18 OTE
19 Olympic Airways Office
20 Post Office
24 Bus Station
26 Sentry Box

(☎ 24 691/2) has tastefully furnished rooms with air-con and balconies. The rates are 7000 dr a double. The hotel is on Grammou, just up from the Hotel Helen.

Places to Eat

Samos town has a good selection of eateries. When dining out on Samos don't forget to sample the Samian wine, extolled by Byron. One of the cheapest places for well-prepared Greek staples is *O Tasos Taverna*, just down from the bus station. The food at *To Katoi Ouzeri* is superlative and moderately priced. The modern tastefully decorated ouzeri is tucked away on a little side street behind the municipal gardens, near the police station. Their 'small' combination platter (actually huge) at 1200 dr includes cod, kalamaria, shrimps, fried cheese balls, bacon rolls, chicken, sausage, beans and potato salad. The owner advised me that he was considering changing the name of this place to *Why Not*, so keep an eye out for both names.

Another excellent place is *Taverna Ouzeri The Odeon*, also tucked away in a little side street. The taverna sign is in Greek, but features a picture of a fish. It specialises in fish, although souvlaki and chicken are also available. A meal of cod with garlic sauce, Greek salad and Amstel beer will set you back about 1700 dr. Walk south along the waterfront and look for the sign just before the soldiers' sentry boxes. Another commendable place is *Taverna Gregory* on Smyrnis, near the post office. Chicken is 500 dr and moussaka, pistatsio and souvlaki are all 700 dr.

The *Pergola Restaurant*, in a walled garden of citrus trees, is an up-market restaurant which serves well-prepared international and Greek dishes. A meal of Greek salad, mussel saganaki and Amstel will cost about 2000 dr. The restaurant is near the Olympic Airways office.

PYTHAGORION Πυθαγόρειο

Pythagorion, on the south-east coast of the island, is 14 km from Samos town. Today, it's a crowded and rather twee tourist resort, but it's a convenient base from which to visit Samos' ancient sites. Pythagorion stands on the site of the ancient city of Samos. Although the settlement dates from the Neolithic Age, most of the remains are from Polycrates' time (550 BC). The mighty jetty of Samos projected almost 450 metres into the sea, protecting the city and its mighty fleet from the vagaries of the Aegean. Remains of this jetty lie below and beyond the smaller modern jetty, which is on the opposite side of the harbour to the quay. The town beach begins just beyond the jetty. All boats coming from Patmos and other points south of Samos dock at Pythagorion.

Orientation

From the ferry quay, turn right and follow the waterfront to the main thoroughfare of Odos Lykourgou Logotheti, a turn-off to the left. Here you will find supermarkets, greengrocers, bakers, travel agents and numerous car, motorbike and bicycle-hire outlets. The central square of Plateia Tiganiou is on the waterfront just beyond here.

Information

The EOT (☎ 61 389/022/727) is on the left side of Lykourgou Logetheti. The English-speaking staff are friendly and helpful and give out a town map, bus schedule and information about ferry-boat schedules. They also have currency exchange. The tourist police (☎ 61 100) are also on Lykourgou Logetheti, on the opposite side to the EOT.

Walking inland from the waterfront, the post office and the National Bank of Greece are both on the right side of Lykourgou Logotheti. The OTE is on the waterfront near the quay. The bus station (actually a bus stop) is on the left side of Lykourgou Logotheti. There is a taxi rank (☎ 61 450) on the corner of the waterfront and Lykourgou Logotheti. The newsagent on the corner of Lykourgou Logotheti and Metamorfoseos sells foreign newspapers.

There is a self-service laundrette just beyond this shop on Metamorfoseos.

Eupalinos Tunnel

The 1000-metre-long Eupalinos Tunnel, completed in 524 BC, is named after its

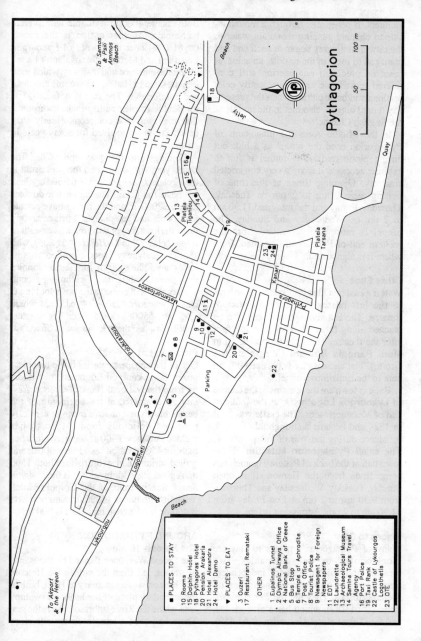

Pythagorion

PLACES TO STAY
10 Rooms
15 Dolphin Hotel
18 Pythagoras Hotel
21 Pension Alexandra
22 Hotel Alexandra
24 Hotel Damo

PLACES TO EAT
3 Ouzeri
17 Restaurant Remataki

OTHER
1 Eupalinos Tunnel
2 Olympic Airways Office
4 National Bank of Greece
5 Bus Stop
6 Temple of Aphrodite
7 Post Office
8 Tourist Police
9 Newsagent for Foreign
   Newspapers
11 EOT
12 Laundrette
13 Archaeological Museum
14 Samina Tours Travel
   Agency
16 Port Police
19 Taxi Rank
22 Castle of Lykourgos
23 OTE

architect. It penetrated through a mountainside to channel gushing mountain water to the city. The diggers began at each end and managed to meet in the middle, an achievement of precision engineering still considered remarkable enough to justify celebrations and back-patting when the present-day tunnel diggers also met in the middle of the English Channel.

In the Middle Ages the inhabitants of Pythagorion used the tunnel as a hide-out during pirate raids. The tunnel is fun to explore; access to it is via a very constricted stairway. Opening times at the time of writing were 9 am to 2 pm on Tuesday, Thursday, Friday and Saturday and 11.30 am to 2 pm on Wednesday and Sunday. The tunnel is most easily reached from the western end of Lykourgou Logotheti, from where it is signposted.

Other Sites

Walking east on Odos Polykratou, a path off to the left passes traces of an **ancient theatre**. The Eupalinos Tunnel can also be reached along this path – take the left fork after the theatre. The right fork leads up to **Moni Panagia Spiliani** (Virgin of the Grotto). The ancient city walls extend from here to the Eupalinos Tunnel.

Back in town are the remains of the **Castle of Lykourgos Logothetis**, at the southern end of Metamorfoseos. The castle was built in 1824 and became a stronghold of Greek resistance during the War of Independence. The small **Pythagorion Museum** in the town hall at the back of Plateia Tiganiou has some finds from the Hereon. It is open Sunday, Tuesday, Wednesday and Thursday from 9.30 am to 2 pm and on Friday from 11.30 am to 2 pm. Admission is free.

Places to Stay

Many of Pythagorion's places to stay are block-booked by tour companies. Two pleasant and quiet places for independent travellers are opposite one another on Metamorfoseos. They are the *Pension Arakaria* (☎ 61 287), which has a nice garden, and the D class *Hotel Alexandra* (☎ 61 429).

Both charge 4000 dr a double with private bathrooms. Another option is the rooms (☎ 61 032) near the corner of Lykourgou Logetheti and Metamorfoseos. Don't be put off by the entrance and stairway which look like the Gate to Hades – the rooms are clean and comfortable. The rate is 4500/5400 dr for doubles/triples with private bathrooms. The manager is a courteous elderly man called Steven, who lived for many years in Australia.

Coming from the quay one of the first hotels you will come to on the waterfront is the C class *Hotel Damo* (☎ 61 303), which is above the OTE. The agreeable doubles here are 7000 dr, and the rooms have private bathrooms and telephones. Further around the waterfront, beyond the main intersection, is the C class *Dolphin Hotel* (☎ 61 205), with spotless and cosy wood-panelled rooms. Rates are 5000/7000 dr for singles/doubles with private bathrooms. Continuing around the bay you will come to the posh-looking C class *Pythagoras Hotel* (☎ 61 373) where rates are 5500/7000/8500 dr for singles/doubles/triples; the price includes breakfast.

Places to Eat

One of the cheapest eateries is the nameless ouzeri on Lykourgou Logotheti, two doors up from the National Bank of Greece. *Restaurant Remataki*, at the beginning of the beach, has an imaginative menu of carefully prepared delicious food. Meze dishes include sausages at 400 dr and fried chickpea balls for 450 dr; rabbit casserole is 900 dr and grilled shrimps and swordfish are both 1500 dr. A good place for breakfast is the *Dolphin Snack Bar* in front of the Dolphin Hotel. Yoghurt with honey is 300 dr, ham omelette is 400 dr and English breakfast is 900 dr.

AROUND PYTHAGORION

The Hereon Ηραίον

The Sacred Way, once flanked by thousands of statues, led from the city to the Hereon. The Hereon was a sanctuary to Hera, built at the legendary place of her birth, on swampy land where the River Imbrasos enters the sea. There had been a temple on the site since

Myceneaen times, but the one built in the time of Polycrates was the most extraordinary; it was four times the size of the Parthenon. As a result of plunderings and earthquakes only one column remains standing, although the extent of the temple can be gleaned from the foundations. Other remains on the site include a stoa, more temples and a 5th-century basilica. The site (☎ 91 577) is on the coast eight km west of Pythagorion. Opening times are Tuesday to Sunday from 8.30 am to 3 pm. Admission is 500 dr.

Mytilini Μυτιλήνη

The fascinating **Paleontology Museum** (☎ 51 205), on the main thoroughfare of the inland village of Mytilini, between Pythagorion and Samos town, houses bones and skeletons of prehistoric animals. Included in the collection are remains of animals which were the antecedents of the giraffe and elephant. The museum is open daily from 8.30 am to 2 pm. Admission is 200 dr.

Beaches

Back on the coast, sandy **Psili Ammos** (not to be confused with a beach of the same name to the west of Pythagorion) is the finest beach in the vicinity of Pythagorion. The beach can be reached by excursion boats from Pythagorion and bus from Samos town. From Pythagorion, excursion boats also go to the islet of **Samiopoula** where there is a beach.

SOUTH-WEST SAMOS

The south-west coast of Samos remained unspoilt for longer than the north coast, but in recent years a series of resorts have sprung up alongside the best beaches. **Ormos Marathokampou**, 55 km from Samos town, has a pebble and stone beach. From here a road leads six km to the inland village of **Marathokampou**, worth a visit for the stunning vistas down to the immense Bay of Marathokampos. **Votsalakia**, four km west of Ormos Marathokampou, and **Psili Ammos** (not to be confused with the Psili Ammos Beach near Pythagorion), two km beyond, have long sandy beaches. There are

many domatia and tavernas on this stretch of coast.

With your own transport you may like to continue on the dirt road from Psili Ammos which skirts Mt Kerkis, above the totally undeveloped and isolated west coast. The road passes through the village of **Kalithea**, and continues to **Drakei** where it terminates.

WEST OF SAMOS TOWN

The road which skirts the north coast to the west of Samos town passes many beaches and resorts. **Kokkari**, 10 km from Samos town, is a fishing village-cum-holiday resort with a pebble beach. Beaches, a mixture of pebble, stone and sand, extend from here to **Avlakia**, but they are too near the road for nude bathing. Continuing west, beyond Avlakia, the road is flanked by trees, a foretaste of the alluring scenery encountered on the roads leading inland from the coast. A turn-off left along this stretch leads to the delightful mountain village of **Vourliotes**, from where you can walk another three km to **Moni Panagias Vrondianis**. Built in the 1550s, it is the island's oldest extant monastery; a sign in the village points the way.

Continuing along the coast, just before the little resort of Agios Konstantinos, a five-km road winds its way up the lower slopes of Mt Ampelos through thick, well-watered woodland of pine and deciduous trees, to the gorgeous village of **Manolates**. The area is rich in bird life, with a proliferation of nightingales, warblers and thrushes. There are no buses to Manolates so you'll have to find alternative means of transport up and walk down. In the village there are many old houses built of stone with projecting balconies. The surface of the narrow streets and idyllic little square ares decorated with whitewashed floral designs.

Back on the coast, the road continues to the quiet resort of **Agios Konstantinos**. Beyond here it continues through rugged coastal and mountain scenery to the town of **Karlovasi**, Samos' second port. The town consists of three contiguous settlements, Paleo (Old), Meson (Middle) and Neo (New). It once boasted a thriving tanning industry, but now it's a lacklustre town with little of interest to visitors. The nearest beach is the sand and pebble **Potami**, two km to the west of town.

Places to Stay

Despite the onset of package tourism, Kokkari still has many accommodation alternatives for independent travellers. In high season an EOT (☎ 0273-92 217) operates in the village and they will assist in finding accommodation. The bus stops on the main road at a large stone church; the EOT is a little way down the street opposite the church. The *Pension Elini* (☎ 92 317) has immaculate tastefully furnished rooms for 6000 dr a double with private bathrooms. Adjoining the pension are some pleasant domatia where rates are 3700 dr a double with shared bathrooms and a communal kitchen. From the large stone church in Kokkari, continue along the main road; at the T-junction veer left and, 50 metres along on the left, next to the Taverna Dionysos, you will see a sign pointing to the pension. There are many more domatia along this stretch of road, which is just one block back from the waterfront.

Further west along the coast road, close to a beach, are the *Calypso Rooms to Rent* (☎ 94 124), named after their friendly and kind owner. The rooms are well kept and surrounded by a gorgeous garden. Rates are 4750 dr for doubles with private bathrooms and use of a communal kitchen. Coming from Kokkari, turn right opposite the turn-off for Manolates (signposted) and you will come to a sign pointing right to the rooms. There are more domatia in this area. The bus stop is just before the Manolates turn-off.

There are as yet no pensions or hotels in Manolates. The construction of a purpose-built domatia was begun some years ago, but at the time of writing it was still unfinished. In the meantime a limited number of beds are available in private homes. Ask about these in the kafeneia and tavernas. If you get stuck in Karlovasi there are several budget hotels and a domatia (☎ 32 133/707) with doubles for 4000 dr. This accommodation is

signposted from the central square where the bus terminates.

Places to Eat

There are many reasonably priced restaurants in Kokkari. *Paradisos Restaurant* at the turn-off to Manolates serves delectable dishes; a full meal with wine or beer will cost around 1700 dr. *Alpha Snack Bar*, on the tiny central square in Manolates, serves low-priced tasty food. Tzatziki is 200 dr, chicken is 400 dr, stuffed tomatoes and meatballs are 460 dr and yoghurt and honey is 300 dr.

Ikaria Ικαρία

Ikaria (Ik-a-REE-a, population 9000), lying west of Samos, is a rocky and mountainous island. Like Samos it is also fertile with an abundance of cypress trees, pine forests, olive and fruit trees – Ikarian apricots are especially luscious. At present the island's tourism is low key, but the impending opening of an airport may change this. Ailing Greeks have visited Ikaria since ancient times for its therapeutic radioactive springs which they believed to be the most efficacious in Europe. One was so highly radioactive it was deemed unsafe and forced to close.

Ikaria has two ports, Agios Kirikos on the south coast, and Evdilos on the north coast. The island's best beaches are on the north coast west of Evdilos.

The name Ikaria originates from the mythical Icarus, who plummeted into the sea close to the island. Whilst escaping from a prison on the island of Crete, Icarus failed to heed the warning of his father, Daedalus, and flew too close to the sun. This caused the wax with which he had secured wings to his body to melt, resulting in his untimely and rapid descent.

Another myth ascribes the island as the birthplace of Dionysos.

Getting To/From Ikaria

Ferry All ferries which call at Ikaria's two

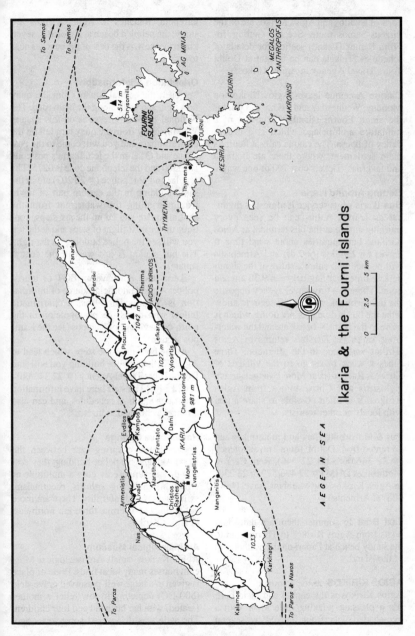

Ikaria & the Fourni Islands

ports of Evdilos and Agios Kirikos are on the Piraeus-Samos route. See the Getting To/From Samos (Island) section for details of schedules. Tickets can be bought at Dolihi Tours Travel Agency in Agios Kirikos.

Caïque A caïque leaves Agios Kirikos on Monday, Wednesday and Friday at 1 pm for the small Fourni island, the largest of a miniature archipelago which is a dependency of Ikaria. The caïque calls at Fourni's main settlement, where there are domatia and tavernas. Tickets cost 700 dr one way.

Getting Around Ikaria
Bus Ikaria's bus service is almost as mythical as Icarus. A bus can be seen every morning sitting at the bus terminal at Agios Kirikos, but enquiries about what time it leaves for Eydilos (600 dr) and Armenistis will be met with either a shrug of the shoulders or times varying between 9.30 am and noon. There is a tiny travel agency opposite the bus terminal, whose staff seem to know what the bus is doing (or not doing, which is more to the point) – or ask around the waterfront kafeneia. The bus returns to Agios Kirikos sometime in the afternoon. Three times a week buses go to the villages of Christos Raches (near Moni Evangelistrias), Xylosirtis and Chrisostomos from Agios Kirikos. It is often possible to share a taxi with locals or other tourists.

Car & Motorbike Cars and motorbikes can be rented from Dolihi Tours Travel Agency (☎ 22 346/068; fax 22 346), Rent Cars & Motorbikes DHM (☎ 22 426/579 or 23 230) in Agios Kirikos, and Marabou Travel (☎ 41 403) at Armenistis.

Taxi Boat In summer there are daily taxi boats from Agios Kirikos to Therma and to the sandy beach at Fanari on the northern tip of the island.

AGIOS KIRIKOS Αγιος Κήρυκος
Agios Kirikos is the capital and main port. It's a pleasant relaxing little town with a tree-shaded waterfront flanked by several

kafeneia. Beaches in Agios Kirikos are stony; the pebbled beach at Xylosirtis, seven km to the west, is the best of the beaches near town.

Orientation & Information
To reach the central square from the quay turn right and walk along the main road. The National Bank of Greece is on this square. Walking away from the quay turn left on the central square and you will come to the post office and OTE on the left. Ikaria's postcode is 83300 and the telephone code is 0275. The regular and port police (☎ 22 207) are in the same building in the eastern part of town. Continue along the waterfront from the central square and go up the six steps, continue up the next flight of steps and at the top you will see the police building on the right. The bus station is just west of the central square.

Ikaria does not have an EOT or tourist police. A good unofficial source of information is Vassilis Dionysos, a charismatic fellow who owns the pantopoleion in the north-coast village of Kampos (see the Kampos section).

At the bottom of the steps which lead to Agios Kirikos' police building you will find Dolihi Tours Travel Agency (☎ 22 346/068; fax 22 346). The staff here have information about bus and boat schedules, and can also arrange accommodation.

Radioactive Springs
The radioactive springs are between the Hotel Akti and the police building; they cost 500 dr and supposedly cure a multitude of afflictions including arthritis, rheumatism, skin diseases and infertility. There are more hot springs at Therma, three km north-east of Agios Kirikos.

Archaeological Museum
Agios Kirikos' small Archaeological Museum houses many local finds. Pride of place is given to a large well-preserved grave stele (500 BC) depicting in low relief a mother (seated) with her husband and four children. The stele was discovered some years ago,

during the building of a school in a nearby village. It took a court case (held recently) to prise the stele from the possessive clutches of the school.

The museum is open mornings, from Tuesday to Sunday. It's west of the quay and is well signposted.

Places to Stay – bottom end

One of the cheapest places in Agios Kirikos is the *Hotel Akti* (☎ 22 694), which is classed as a pension. The tidy rooms cost 3300/4200/4700 dr for singles/doubles/triples with private bathrooms; doubles with shared bathrooms are 3600 dr. The pension has great sea views from its appealing garden. To reach it, make a right turn facing Dolihi Tours, go up the steps to the left and follow the signs.

Pension Maria-Elena (☎ 22 530/835) has impeccable rooms. Rates are 5700/6800 dr for doubles/triples with private bathrooms. From the quay turn left at the main road, take the first right, and then first left onto Odos Artemidos, and the pension is along here on the right. On the waterfront just beyond the central square (coming from the quay), there is a new, as yet nameless domatia (☎ 23 496 or 22 750) above the kafeneion, two doors before the butchers – look for the black wrought-iron balconies. These pleasant rooms have rates of 5500 dr a double with private bathrooms.

Places to Stay – middle

Agios Kirikos' most luxurious hotel is the new C class *Hotel Kastro* (☎ 23 480/770). The rooms are beautifully furnished and have a telephone, three-channel music system, private bathrooms and balconies. Rates are 6500/9000 dr for singles/doubles, including breakfast. The hotel is opposite the police building. From the communal terraces on a clear day you can see the islands of Amorgos, Naxos, Fourni, Patmos, Samos, Arki and Lipsi.

Places to Eat

Agios Kirikos has three restaurants and a number of snack bars, ouzeria and kafeneia.

Taverna Klimataria serves tasty moderately priced Greek staples. Moussaka is 650 dr, meatballs are 700 dr and a pork chop is 900 dr. Turn left at the butchers, the last shop on the waterfront coming from the quay. At the top of the narrow cobbled street, turn left and then first right, and the taverna is on the left. *T'Adelfia Taverna* on the waterfront between the quay and the central square is similarly priced. *Filoti Pizzeria Restaurant* is the town's best restaurant. Pizzas range from 950 to 2600 dr depending on the size and topping. The highly commendable souvlaki dishes (served with salad) include chicken for 900 dr, pork for 1000 dr and swordfish for 1500 dr. The restaurant can be found at the top of the cobbled street which starts from the butchers.

AGIOS KIRIKOS TO THE NORTH COAST

The island's one asphalt road begins a little west of Agios Kirikos and links the capital with the north coast. As the road climbs up to the island's mountainous spine there are dramatic mountain, coastal and sea vistas. The road winds through several hamlets, some with traditional stone houses topped with rough-hewn slate roofs. It then descends to the island's second port of Evdilos, 41 km from Agios Kirikos.

This journey is worth taking for the views, but if you are based in Agios Kirikos and want to do the journey by bus, check that it is going to return the same day, as a taxi costs 4000 dr and it is difficult to hitch as there is not much traffic.

EVDILOS Εύδηλος

Evdilos, the island's second port, is a smallish fishing town. Like Agios Kirikos it's a pleasant and relaxing place, but you may prefer to head further west to the island's best beaches.

Places to Stay & Eat

One of the cheapest places to stay in Evdilos is the E class *Georgios Hotel* (☎ 31 218/523). The nicely furnished single/double/triple rooms cost 2000/3500/4000 dr with private bathrooms. Apartments with kitchens are 5000 dr for four or five people. The hotel overlooks the harbour from the central square. Facing the sea from the middle of the waterfront, the plush-looking building with black wrought-iron balconies on the far right is the domatia belonging to *Spyros Rosos* (☎ 31 518). Rates are 5000 dr a double with private bathrooms. The rooms are above a taverna which serves reasonably priced well-prepared food.

WEST OF EVDILOS
Kampos Κάμπος

Kampos, three km west of Evdilos, is an unspoilt little village with few concessions to tourism. Although it takes some believing, sleepy little Kampos was the island's ancient capital of Oinos (Greek for wines). The name derived from the myth that the Ikarians were the first people to make wine. In ancient times Ikarian wine was considered the best in Greece. Ancient coins found in the vicinity of Kampos have a picture of the wine god, Dionysos, on them.

Ancient coin depicting Dionysos

Information Vassilis Dionysos speaks English and is a fount of information on Ikarian history and walking in the mountains. You will find him in his well-stocked pantopole-ion, which is the shop on the right as you come from Evdilos. The village's post box is outside this shop and inside is the village's metered telephone.

Things to See As you enter Kampos from Evdilos, up on the right are the ruins of a **Byzantine palace**. In the centre of the village there is a small **museum** housing Neolithic tools, geometric vases, fragments of Classical sculpture, small figurines and a very fine 'horse head' knife sheath, carved from ivory.

Next to the museum is the 12th-century **Agia Irini**, the island's oldest church. It is built on the site of a 4th-century basilica, and columns standing in the grounds are from this original church. Agia Irini's supposedly fine frescoes are unfortunately covered with whitewash, because of insufficient funds for its removal. The indispensable Vassilis Dionysos has the keys to both the museum and church.

The village is also a good base for mountain walking. A one-day circular walk along dirt roads can be made, taking in the village of **Dafni**, the remains of the 10th-century Byzantine **Castle of Koskinas**, the villages of **Frantato** and **Maratho** and a cave (which, inevitably, is difficult to find).

Places to Stay & Eat There is one domatia in Kampos which is owned by – you guessed it – *Vassilis Dionysos* (☎ 31 300). The very pleasant rooms are 3500/4200 dr for doubles/triples with private bathrooms. Coming from Evdilos they are on the left beyond the church. Vassilis Dionysos meets all the ferries in Evdilos.

There are three moderately priced tavernas in the village. On the east side of Kampos there is a good sandy beach with a seasonal taverna.

Armenistis Αρμενιστής

Armenistis, 15 km west of Evdilos, is the island's largest resort with two long beaches of pale golden sand, separated by a narrow headland. Although places to stay are springing up quickly here, it's still visited predominantly by independent travellers. Marabou Travel (☎ 41 403), on the road which skirts the sea, organises walking tours on the island. Just east of Armenistis a road leads inland to **Moni Evagelistrias**.

From Armenistis a 3½-km-long dirt road continues west to the small and alluring pebbled beach of **Nas** at the mouth of a stream. This is Ikaria's unofficial nudist beach. Behind the beach are some scant remains of a **Temple of Artemis**.

Places to Stay Ikaria's only camp site is *Armenistis Camping* (☎ 41 349), on the beach at Armenistis.

One of the cheapest places to stay in Armenistis is *Ikarus Rooms* (☎ 41 451) – rates are 2300 dr for a double with shared bathrooms. The elderly couple who own the rooms do not speak English but are kind and friendly. Coming from Evdilos, the road forks at the beginning of Armenistis. Take the right fork which skirts the sea, and 50 metres beyond Marabou Travel Agency you will see a sign pointing left to the rooms.

At the approach to the village, before the road forks, you will see *Rooms Fortinos* (☎ 41 457) on the left. The rooms are light, airy and beautifully furnished. Rates are 5700/6800 dr for doubles/triples with private bathrooms. Next to these rooms is a sign to the *Armena Inn* (☎ 41 415), which is 100 metres along a dirt road. The newly refurbished rooms cost 5500 dr a double with private bathrooms. Family apartments with kitchens are 6500 dr. Back on the right fork of the road, just before the Marabou Tourist Office, are pleasant rooms above the *Pashalia Taverna* (☎ 41 458). Rates are 5700 dr a double for rooms with private bathrooms.

Armenistis' best hotel is the C class *Gavos Bay Hotel* (☎ 41 449), which has a cool and inviting interior. The stucco-walled rooms open out onto a large private terrace overlooking a rocky seascape. The hotel has a large restaurant and bar and a seawater swimming pool built into the rocks. Rates are 5000/6500/7700 dr for singles/doubles/triples, breakfast included. The hotel is at the

extreme western end of Armenistis; take the left fork road to reach it.

Nas has one domatia and taverna.

Places to Eat The previously mentioned *Pashalia Taverna* serves well-prepared food. A large souvlaki costs about 900 dr.

Fourni Islands

The Fourni islands are a miniature archipelago of little-visited islands lying between Ikaria and Samos. Two of the islands are inhabited (population 1600); the larger one is also called Fourni and the other is Thymena. The capital of the group is Fourni town (also called Kampos), which is the port of Fourni island. Fourni has one other village, tiny Chrysomilia, which is 10 km north of the port; the island's only road connects the two. The islands are mountainous with a little vegetation and a good number of beaches dotted around the coast.

The telephone number of Fourni's port police is ☎ 51 207.

Fourni is the only island with accommodation for tourists and is ideal for those seeking a quiet retreat. Most of the islanders make a living from fishing, and they catch enough to send a large amount to the Athens fish market.

There are several domatia and tavernas in Fourni town, but no accommodation in Chrysomilia.

See Getting To/From Ikaria for information about how to get to Fourni.

Chios Χίος

Chios (HEE-os, population 54,000), like its neighbours Samos and Lesbos, is a large island, measuring 859 sq km. It is separated from the Turkish peninsula of Karaburnu by the eight-km-wide Chios Straits. It is a verdant island, although in recent years, like

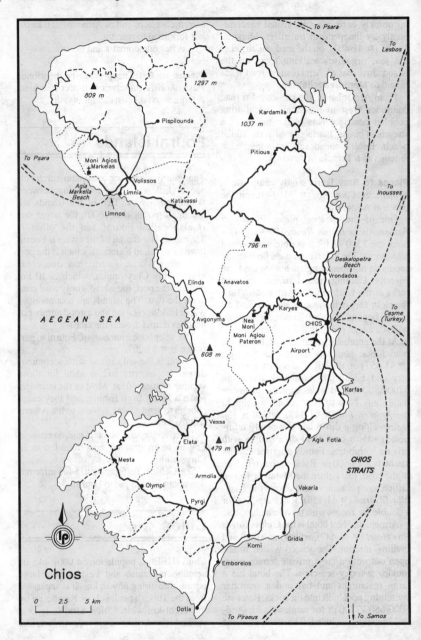

To Psara

To Lesbos

▲ 809 m

▲ 1297 m

● Pispilounda

● Kardamila
1037 m

To Inousses

● Pitious

To Psara

Moni Agios
+ Markelas

Agia
Markella
Beach

● Volissos

● Limnia

● Katavassi

Limnos

▲ 796 m

AEGEAN SEA

● Elinda

● Anavatos

Deskalopetra
Beach

● Vrondados

● Karyes

*To Cesme
(Turkey)*

● Avgonyma

+ Nea
Moni

● CHIOS

Moni Agiou
Pateron

✈ Airport

▲ 608 m

● Karfas

● Vessa

● Elata

▲ 479 m

● Agia Fotia

*CHIOS
STRAITS*

● Mesta

● Armolia

● Olympi

● Vakaria

● Pyrgi

● Gridia

● Komi

● Emboreios

Chios

0   2.5   5 km

● Dotia

To Piraeus

To Samos

many other areas of Greece, fires have destroyed many of its forests.

A large number of highly successful ship owners come from Chios and its dependencies, Inousses and Psara. This, and its mastic production, have meant that Chios has not needed to develop a tourist industry. In recent years, however, package tourism has begun to make inroads, although nothing like on the scale of Samos.

History
In ancient times, Chios, like Samos, excelled in the arts. The island reached its height in the 7th century BC when the Chios School of Sculpture produced some of Greece's most eminent sculptors of the time. The technique of soldering iron was invented in this school. During the Persian Wars Chios was allied to Athens, but after the Battle of Plataea it became independent and so prospered, as it didn't have to pay the annual tribute to Athens.

In Roman times Chios was invaded by Emperor Constantine, who helped himself to its fine sculptures. After the fall of Byzantium the island fell prey to attacks by pirates, Venetians, Catalans and Turks. It revived somewhat under the Genoese who took control in the 14th century. However, it was recaptured by the Turks in 1566 and became part of the Ottoman Empire.

In the 19th century Chios suffered two devastating tragedies. In 1822 the Samians cajoled the people of Chios into assisting them in an uprising against Ottoman rule. The Turks retaliated by sacking Chios, killing 25,000 of its inhabitants and taking almost twice that number into slavery. The massacre was the subject of Victor Hugo's poem *L'Enfant de Chios* and Eugene Delacroix's painting *La Massacre de Chios* (in the Louvre). In 1881 the island suffered a violent earthquake which killed almost 6000 people, destroyed many of the buildings in the capital and caused considerable damage throughout the island.

It is well known that Chios is one of a number of places around the Mediterranean that lays claim to being Homer's birthplace.

What is less well known is that the island is also in the running for birthplace of Christopher Columbus. Ruth G Durlacher-Wolper, director of the New World Museum in San Salvador, has researched the life of the great seafarer, and in a 1982 report she hypothesised that he was born on Chios and the island may have been his port of departure to the New World.

Getting To/From Chios (Island)
Air Chios has five flights a day to Athens (9200 dr) and two a week to Thessaloniki (18,000 dr). The Olympic Airways office (☎ 24 515 or 22 414) is on Leoforos Aegaiu in Chios town. The airport is four km from Chios town.

Ferry (Domestic) There are daily ferries to Piraeus (10 hours, 3142 dr), Lesbos (three hours, 2118 dr) and Inousses (one hour, 500 dr); three a week to Psara (2½ hours, 1200 dr); two a week to Kavala (17 hours, 4312 dr) and Thessaloniki (22 hours, 5310 dr), both via Lemnos (five hours, 3517 dr); and one a week to Rhodes (15 hours, 4748 dr) via Samos, Patmos, Leros, Kalymnos and Kos. Tickets for most lines can be bought from the Boat Ticket Office (☎ 23 971), on Leoforos Aegaiu, in Chios town.

Ferry (International) During April and October there are ferries to Çeşme on Wednesday, Friday and Saturday leaving Chios at 8 am and returning at 6 pm. During May there is an additional sailing on Tuesday. During July, August and September there are daily sailings. The fare is 7000/9500 dr one-way/return (including the 1500 dr port tax). The cost for a car is 12,000 dr, a motorbike is 6000 dr, a moped is 4000 dr and a bicycle is 1500 dr. Further information and tickets can be obtained from Miniotis Tours (☎ 41 073/423; fax 41 468), Neorion 23, Chios town.

Getting Around Chios (Island)
Bus From the long-distance bus station in Chios town there are four buses a day to Pyrgi (350 dr), three buses to Mesta (550 dr),

and four buses to Kardamila (550 dr) via Langadas; take this bus for the camp site. Only one or two buses a week do the journey to Anavatos via Nea Moni and Avgonyma – check the schedule at the bus station.

Car & Motorbike Car-rental outlets in Chios town include Budget (☎ 23 205), Evgenias Handris 3 and Chios Rent A Car (☎ 21 793 or 27 758), Kountouriotou 2. Chios' ELPA representative is K Michalakis (☎ 22 445 or 23 076), Rodokanaki 19. There are many moped and motorbike-hire outlets on and near the waterfront.

CHIOS TOWN

Chios town, on the east coast, is the island's port and capital. It's a large town, home to almost half of the island's inhabitants. Its waterfront, flanked by unattractive modern buildings and trendy coffee shops, is noisy in the extreme with an inordinate amount of cars and motorbikes careering up and down. However, things improve considerably once you begin exploring the back streets. The atmospheric old quarter, with many Turkish houses built around a Genoese castle, and the lively market area, are both worth a stroll. Chios town doesn't have a beach; the nearest

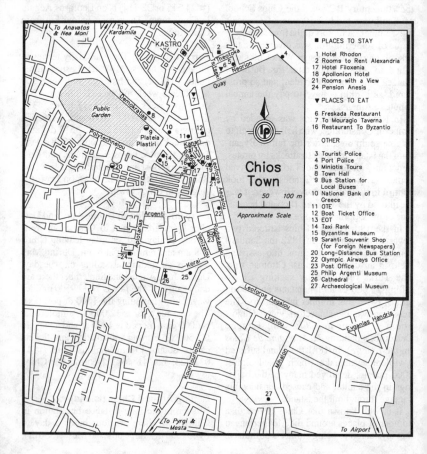

Chios Town

0   50   100 m

Approximate Scale

■ PLACES TO STAY
1 Hotel Rhodon
2 Rooms to Rent Alexandria
17 Hotel Filoxenia
18 Apollonion Hotel
21 Rooms with a View
24 Pension Anesis

▼ PLACES TO EAT
6 Freskada Restaurant
7 To Mouragio Taverna
16 Restaurant To Byzantio

OTHER
3 Tourist Police
4 Port Police
5 Miniotis Tours
8 Town Hall
9 Bus Station for Local Buses
10 National Bank of Greece
11 OTE
12 Boat Ticket Office
13 EOT
14 Taxi Rank
15 Byzantine Museum
19 Saranti Souvenir Shop (for Foreign Newspapers)
20 Long-Distance Bus Station
22 Olympic Airways Office
23 Post Office
25 Philip Argenti Museum
26 Cathedral
27 Archaeological Museum

one is the sandy beach at Karfas, six km south.

Orientation & Information

Most ferries dock at the northern end of the waterfront at the western end of Odos Neorion. The old Turkish quarter (called Kastro) is to the north of here. To reach the town centre from the ferry quay, follow the waterfront round to your left and walk along Leoforos Aegaiu. Turn right onto Kanari to reach the central square of Plateia Plastiri (also called Plateia Vournaki). To the north-west of the square are the public gardens, and to the south-east is the market area. Facing inland, the bus station for local buses (blue) is on the right side of the public gardens and for long-distance buses (green) on the left.

Continuing along the waterfront, the next turn after Kanari is Roidou. Turn right here and then first left onto Rodokanaki. The post office is two blocks along here on the right. Facing inland, take the first right along Kanari and you'll see the OTE on the left. Chios' postcode is 82100 and the telephone code is 0271. Most banks, including the National Bank of Greece, are between Kanari and Plateia Plastiri.

The EOT (☎ 24 217 or 20 488) is at Kanari 11. The helpful staff give information on accommodation, bus and boat schedules, and have the free magazine *Chios Summertime*. The tourist police (☎ 25 914) and the port police (☎ 22 837) are near one another at the eastern end of Neorion.

Museums

Chios town's most interesting museum is the **Philip Argenti Museum** (☎ 23 463), in the same building as the Korais library, one of the country's largest libraries. The museum, which is near the cathedral, contains exquisite embroideries, traditional costumes and portraits of the wealthy Argenti family. It is open from 8 am to 2 pm on Monday, Thursday and Friday and 8 am to noon on Saturday. Admission is free.

The town's other museums are less compelling. The **Archaeological Museum** (☎ 26 664), on Porphrya, contains sculptures, pottery and coins. Opening times are 8.45 am to 3 pm (8.45 am to 2.30 pm on Sunday); it's closed on Tuesday. Admission is 200 dr. The **Byzantine Museum** (☎ 26 866) is housed in a former mosque on Plateia Plastiri. Opening times are Monday to Saturday from 10 am to 1 pm.

Places to Stay – bottom end

Chios has one camp site, *Chios Camping* (☎ 74 111/113/135/157), on the beach at Agios Isidoros, between Sikiada and Langadas, 14 km north of Chios town. The site has good facilities, a bar and restaurant. To reach it take a Kardamila or Langadas bus.

A good choice for backpackers is *Rooms with a View* (☎ 20 364), Rodokanaki 7. It's a friendly place with decent single/double/triple rooms for 2000/3000/4400 dr with shared bathrooms. There are also rooms with four and five beds at 1400 dr per person; there is a communal kitchen. From the quay, walk south along the waterfront, and turn right at Roidou, and first left onto Rodokanaki and the rooms are on the left. If you continue up Roidou you will come to the D class *Hotel Filoxenia* (☎ 26 559) on the left, above the Restaurant To Byzantio. The unadorned but clean rooms cost 2500/3500/4500 dr with shared bathrooms and 3500/4500/5600 dr with private bathrooms.

If you turn right into a little cul-de-sac between Rodokanaki and the Hotel Filoxenia you will come to the *Apollonion Hotel* (☎ 24 842), Roidou 5. Opulent rooms here cost 3800/5000/6700 dr with private bathrooms. If these don't suit you, you'll be ushered into the older part of the building where institutional rooms with hospital beds and linoleum floors await you for 2000/3000/4000 dr with shared bathrooms.

In the old quarter *Rooms to Rent Alexandria* (☎ 20 795 or 25 119), on Theotoka, has agreeable single/double/triple/quad rooms for 2000/3000/4000/4500 dr with shared bathrooms. Walking east along Neorion, turn left onto Tsitseki, and first right onto Theotoka, and the rooms are on the left, behind the periptero. The *Hotel Rhodon* (☎ 24 335 or 23 638), Zahariou 17, has cosy and clean rooms for 3500/4500/5000/6000 dr with shared bathrooms. To reach the hotel walk along Odos Plataion, a northern continuation of the waterfront, and the hotel is on your right.

Pension Anesis (☎ 24 572 or 23 925), on Aplotarias, has rooms with the works for 3000/6000/7000 dr for singles/doubles/triples with private bathrooms. Coming from the quay, Argenti is a turn-off to the right at the southern end of the waterfront.

Places to Stay – middle

The C class *Hotel Kyma* (☎ 25 551/2/3) occupies a turn-of-the-century mansion and has lots of character. Rates are 7200/8600 dr. The B class *Hotel Chandris* (☎ 25 761) is considered by some to be Chios town's best hotel. It has two bars, a restaurant and a swimming pool. Rates are 8700/11,000 dr. Both of these hotels are on Evgenias Handris, off the map in this book.

Places to Eat

Restaurant To Byzantio, on the corner of Rali and Roidou, is a bright, cheerful and unpretentious place, which serves traditional Greek fare at low prices. Greek salad is 500 dr, moussaka and pastitsio are both 650 dr and veal in tomato sauce is 850 dr. *To Mouragio Taverna*, on Leoforos Aegaiu, opposite the ferry quay, is rather gloomy; however, it serves tasty Greek staples at similar prices to

To Byzantio. *Freskada Restaurant*, Neorion 11, is one of the town's best eating establishments. It specialises in fish dishes.

MASTIC VILLAGES

There are some 20 Mastichochoria (mastic villages); the two best preserved are Pyrgi and Mesta. As mastic was such a highly lucrative commodity in the Middle Ages, many an invader cast an acquisitive eye upon the villages, necessitating sturdy fortification. The archways spanning the streets were to prevent the houses from collapsing during earthquakes. Because of the sultan's fondness for mastic chewing gum, the inhabitants of the Mastichochoria were not included in the 1822 massacre.

Pyrgi Πύργοι

Pyrgi (population 1300), 24 km south-west of Chios town, is the largest of the Mastichochoria, and one of the most extraordinary villages in the whole of Greece. The vaulted streets of the fortified village are narrow and labyrinthine. However, what makes Pyrgi unique are the façades of its buildings, which are decorated with intricate grey and white designs. Some of the patterns are geometric and others are based on flowers, leaves and animals. The technique used is called *xysta* and is achieved by coating the walls with a mixture of cement and black volcanic sand, painting over this with white lime, and then

---

Gum Mastic

Gum mastic is a product of the *lentisk* bush and conditions in southern Chios are ideal for its growth. Mastic has been utilised since Classical times. Many Ancient Greeks, including Hippocrates, proclaimed its pharmaceutical benefits. Amongst ailments it was claimed to cure were stomach upsets, chronic coughs and diseases of the liver, intestines and bladder. It was also used as an antidote for snake bites. During Turkish rule Chios received preferential treatment from the sultans who, along with the ladies of the harem, seem to have become hooked on chewing gum made from mastic – try the stuff and you will no doubt wonder why.

Until recently mastic was widely used in the pharmaceutical industry, as well as for the manufacture of chewing gum and certain alcoholic drinks, particularly arrack, a Middle Eastern liqueur. In most cases mastic has now been replaced by other more easily available products. However, mastic production may yet have a future, as some adherents of alternative medicine claim that it stimulates the immune system and reduces blood pressure and cholesterol. Chewing gum made from mastic can be bought on Chios, under the brand name Elma. ∎

scraping off parts of the lime to reveal the matt grey beneath. Nowadays the scraping is done with the bent prong of a fork.

From the main road, a fork to the right (coming from Chios town) leads into the heart of the village and the central square. The little 12th-century **Church of Agios Apostolos**, just off the square, is profusely decorated with well-preserved 17th-century frescoes. Ask at the taverna or kafeneion for the whereabouts of the caretaker, who will open it up for you. The façade of the larger church, on the opposite side of the square, has the most impressive xysta of all the buildings in the village.

Places to Stay & Eat Pyrgi is the headquarters of the *Women's Agricultural Co-operative of Chios*. This organisation rents a number of traditionally furnished rooms in private houses throughout the village. Rates are around 3600/5000/5800 dr for singles/doubles/triples with shared bathrooms and 4800/7300/8700 dr with private bathrooms. The Co-operative's office (☎ 72 496) is near the central square of Pyrgi and is signposted. There are cheaper domatia in the village such as *Rooms to Rent Rita*, which are clean and simply furnished and cost 3000 dr a double. These rooms are signposted from the bus stop.

The little taverna on the central square (on the right as you face the large church) serves a very good stifado for 850 dr.

Emboreios Εμπορειός
Emboreios, six km to the south of Pyrgi, was the port of Pyrgi. In the days when mastic production was big business the product was exported from here. These days Emboreios is a burgeoning holiday resort with a beautiful beach of black stones formed from volcanic lava. On either side of this main beach there are less crowded secluded little bays. Coming from Chios town a signpost points left to Emboreios, just before you arrive at Pyrgi.

Mesta Μεστά
Continuing on the main road from Pyrgi, in

five km you will reach the mastic village of **Olympi**, less immediately attractive than its two neighbours but still worth a brief stop. Mesta, five km further on, has a very different atmosphere from that created by the striking visual impact of Pyrgi. The village is completely enclosed within massive fortifying walls. Its labyrinthine cobbled streets of bare stone houses and arches emanate a mute and melancholy aura. The village has two churches of the Taxiarchs: the older one dates from Byzantine times and has a magnificent 17th-century iconostasis; the second one, built in the 19th century, has very fine frescoes.

Orientation Buses stop on Plateia Nikolaou Poumpaki, on the main road outside Mesta. To reach the central square of Plateia Taxiarchou, with your back to the bus shelter, turn right, and then immediately left, and you will see a sign pointing to the centre of the village.

Places to Stay The small EOT office, Plateia Taxiarchou 51, is staffed by the Greek-Australian Dimitris Pippides (☎ 76 319). Dimitris has a list of many of the rooms to rent in private houses in Mesta and will make a reservation for you. Most of these traditionally furnished rooms are part of the Women's Cooperative and the prices are the same as those in Pyrgi, but Dimitris may be able to find somewhere cheaper for you. One option is the accommodation belonging to *Despina Syrimis* (☎ 76 494). The room, which costs 4200 dr, will sleep up to four people, and has a kitchen and private bathroom. The room is difficult to find but Despina speaks English so you could telephone her. Otherwise you can find her in the central square's Mesaionas Restaurant where she works.

Places to Eat There are two restaurants on the central square; both are good. At *Mesaionas Restaurant* moussaka and pastitsio are both 620 dr, and veal in tomato sauce and stuffed vegetables are both 650 dr. At *Restaurant O Morias Ta Mesta* a very good meal of pork in wine, potatoes, Greek salad and soft drink will cost about 1500 dr.

WEST OF CHIOS TOWN
Nea Moni Νέα Μονή
The 11th-century Nea Moni stands in a beautiful setting in the mountains, 14 km from Chios town. Like so many monasteries in Greece it was built to house an icon which appeared miraculously. The icon in question was of the Virgin Mary and it materialised before the eyes of three shepherds. In its heyday the monastery was one of the wealthiest in Greece and the most pre-eminent artists of Byzantium were commissioned to execute the mosaics in its katholikon.

During the 1822 atrocities the buildings were set on fire and all the resident monks massacred. There is a macabre display of their skulls in the ossuary at the monastery's little chapel. In the earthquake of 1881 the katholikon's dome caved in causing considerable damage to the mosaics. Nonetheless, these mosaics still rank amongst the most outstanding examples of Byzantine art in Greece, esteemed for the striking contrasts of their vivid colours and the fluidity and juxtapositions of the figures. A small number of nuns live at the monastery. Opening times are from 8 am until 1 pm and 4 to 8 pm. Admission is free. Bus service is poor to the monastery, but travel agents in Chios town have excursions to both here and the village of Anavatos.

Avgonyma & Anavatos
From Nea Moni the road continues to the delightful little village of Avgonyma (Αυγώνυμα) and then on to Anavatos (Ανάβατος), 11 km from Nea Moni), a dramatic and almost deserted medieval village of formidable looking stone houses built on a precipitous cliff. Narrow stepped pathways winding between the houses lead to the castle on the summit of the cliff. Nearly all the inhabitants of the village perished in the atrocities of 1822. Today, only a small number of elderly people live in Anavatos, mostly in houses at the base of the village.

Neither Avgonyma or Anavatos have accommodation, but both have cafés.

Inousses Οινούσσες

Off the north-east coast of Chios lie nine tiny islets, called collectively Inousses (In-OU-ses). Only one of these, also called Inousses, is inhabited. Around 400 people live here permanently, making their living from fishing and sheep farming. The island has three fish farms and exports small amounts of fish to Italy and France. Inousses is hilly and covered in scrub and has good beaches.

However, these facts apart, this is no ordinary Greek island. Small, Inousses may be, but it is the ancestral home of around 30% of Greece's ship owners. Most of these exceedingly wealthy maritime barons conduct their businesses from Athens, London and New York, but in summer return with their families to Inousses where they own luxurious mansions.

There is a rumour that these ship owners offer financial incentives to discourage people from opening tavernas or domatia on the island, because they do not want foreign tourists to go there. I can't vouch for the truth of this but certainly tourism is not encouraged on the island; no domatia owners come to meet the boat, there are no domatia signs and wanders around the streets fail to bring offers of accommodation. I was told by several islanders that Inousses had a few

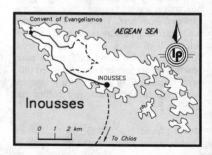

domatia, but they were vague as to their whereabouts and I was unable to find any.

If these quirks have not discouraged you from going to Inousses, on a more positive note the island has a picturesque town of neoclassical mansions, superb beaches, lots of opportunities for walking, stunning vistas and no package tourists; in fact not many tourists at all. In Inousses town there is a large naval boarding school. If you visit during term time you may well encounter the pupils parading around town to bellowing marching orders.

Getting To/From Inousses (Island)

The island is only served by the local ferry boat *Oinoussai II* which plies daily between the island and Chios town. It leaves Chios town at 2 pm and Inousses at 9 am. Tickets cost 500 dr and are purchased on board. In summer there are sometimes excursion boats from Chios town to the island. Enquire about these at one of the travel agencies in Chios town.

Getting Around Inousses (Island)

Inousses has no public transport.

INOUSSES TOWN
Orientation & Information

Inousses has one settlement, the little town which is also called Inousses. From the boat quay, facing inland turn left and follow the waterfront to Plateia Antoniou P Laimou; veer slightly right here, and you will immediately come to Plateia T Nautisynis; veer right once again and you will see ahead the Restaurant and Kafeneion Pateronissa. Facing this establishment turn right and ascend the steps to reach the centre of town.

If you turn left at the Restaurant Pateronissa and then first right onto Odos Konstantinou Antonopolou you will come to the National Bank of Greece, which I imagine is kept very busy. Next door to the bank is a combined post office and OTE. Inousses' telephone code is 0272.

There are no EOT or tourist police on the island. The regular police (☎ 51 222) are at the top of the steps which lead to the town centre.

Maritime Museum

This museum is between the Restaurant Pateronissia and the National Bank of Greece. It opened in 1990 and the benefactors were wealthy ship owners from the island. Many island families donated nautical memorabilia, which includes *objets d'art*, photographs, models of early ships, cannons and nautical instruments. The museum keeps very erratic opening times. If you find it closed (which is highly likely), ask around and someone may open it up for you.

Island Walk

This is a three-hour circular walk. Although most of it is on a narrow cement road, you are unlikely to meet much traffic. Take plenty of water and a snack as there are no refreshments along the way. Also take your swimming gear as you will pass many of the island's beaches. You will also pass the **Convent of Evangelismos** in the west of the island.

Just beyond the Maritime Museum you will see a signpost to the Convent of Evangelismos. This will take you along the cement road which skirts the west coast. Along the way you will pass several inviting beaches and coves. Only **Apiganos Beach** is signposted, but there are others which are easily accessible from the road. After about one hour the road loops inland, and a little further along is the entrance to the very palatial convent which stands in extensive grounds.

Within the convent is the mummified body of Irini Pateras, daughter of the late Panagos Pateras who was a multimillionaire ship owner. Irini became a nun in her late teens and died in the early 1960s when she was 20. Her distraught mother decided to build the convent in memory of her daughter. In the Greek Orthodox religion, three years after burial the body is exhumed and the bones cleaned and reburied in a casket. When Irini's body was exhumed it was found to have mummified rather than decomposed; this phenomenon is regarded in Greece as evidence of sainthood. Irini's mother is now abbess of the convent which houses around 20 nuns. Only women may visit the convent and of course they must be appropriately (modestly) dressed.

Continuing along the cement road, beyond the entrance to the convent, you will come to two stone pillars on the left. The wide path between the pillars leads in 10 minutes to an enormous white cross which is a memorial to St Irini. This is the highest point of the island and commands stunning views over to northern Chios and the Turkish peninsula of Karaburna. About 20 minutes further along, the cement road gives way to a dirt track. Continue straight ahead to reach Inousses town.

Places to Stay
There is no camp site on the island and camping freelance would definitely be frowned upon. For domatia, ask at one of the restaurants or kafeneia. Good luck!

Inousses' one hotel is the very comfortable, but pricey, C class *Hotel Thalassoporos* (☎ 51 475/6), at the top of the steps which lead to the town centre. Rates are 5800/8800 dr for singles/doubles with private bathrooms. These prices drop to 4400/6500 dr in the low season. It's unlikely ever to be full, but just in case phone ahead in July and August.

Places to Eat
Of Inousses' three restaurants, the *Restaurant Pateronissa* has been established the longest. The food is reasonably priced and well prepared. The town has three pantopoleion: one is near the Restaurant Pateronissa and the other two are in the centre of town on the road which leads up to the prominent Agios Nicholaos church.

Psara Ψαρά

Psara (Psar-A), Chios' other dependency, lies off the north-west coast of Chios. The island is nine km long and five km wide and is rocky with little vegetation. During Ottoman times Greeks settled on this remote island to escape Turkish oppression. By the 19th century, many of these inhabitants, like those of Chios and Inousses, had become successful ship owners and admirals. When the rallying cry for self determination reverberated through the country, the Psariots zealously took up arms, and contributed a large number of ships to the Greek cause. In retaliation the Turks stormed the island and killed all but 3000 of the 30,000 inhabitants. The island never regained its former glory and today has only around 500 inhabitants, all of whom live in the island's one settlement, also called Psara.

Ferries leave Chios town for Psara at 7 am on Tuesday, Thursday and Saturday.

Places to Stay & Eat
Like Inousses, the island sees few tourists.

The old parliament building has been converted into an *EOT Guest House* (☎ 0274-61 293). Doubles with shared bathrooms are 4100 dr and with private bathrooms, 4800 dr. Extension and renovation work is currently being carried out on the building. Information may be obtained by either telephoning the guesthouse or ringing ☎ 0251-27 908 in Lesbos. In addition, there are domatia in Psara.

There are a small number of eating places on the island.

Lesbos (Mytilini)
Λέσβος (Μυτιλήνη)

Lesbos (LES-vos, population 88,800) is the third-largest island in Greece, after Crete and Evia. It lies north of Chios and south-east of Lemnos. The island is mountainous with two bottleneck gulfs penetrating its south coast. The south and east of the island are fertile, with numerous olive groves. Lesbos produces the best olive oil in Greece and the island has many olive-oil refineries. In contrast to the south and east the west has rocky and barren mountains creating a dramatic moonscape.

Lesbos is becoming a popular package-holiday destination, but is large enough to be able to absorb tourists without seeming to be overrun. Most Greeks call the island Mytilini, which is also the name of the capital.

History
In the 6th century BC, Lesbos was unified under the rule of the tyrant Pittachos, one of Ancient Greece's Seven Sages. Pittachos succeeded in dispelling the long-standing animosity between the island's two cities of Mytilini and Methymna. This new-found peace generated an atmosphere conducive to creativity, and Lesbos became a centre of artistic and philosophical achievement. Terpander, the musical composer, and Arion the poet, were born on Lesbos in the 7th century BC. Arion's works influenced the tragedians

of the 5th century BC such as Sophocles and Euripides. Sappho, one of the greatest poets of Ancient Greece, was born on Lesbos almost a century later. Unfortunately little of her poetry is extant, but what remains reveals a genius for combining passion with simplicity and detachment, in verses of great beauty and power.

Sappho's works tell us not only about her own experiences, but give us a glimpse of life on Lesbos during her lifetime. Her poetry reveals that the women of Lesbos enjoyed an unusual degree of independence. Sappho gathered around her unmarried young women, and under her guidance they practised music, singing and dancing, wrote poetry and became versed in the social graces. The poet, Alcaeus, another native of the island, was a contemporary of Sappho. In the 4th century BC, Aristotle and Epicurus taught at an exceptional school of philosophy which flourished on Lesbos.

On a more prosaic level Lesbos suffered at the hands of invaders and occupiers to the same extent as all other Greek islands. In 527 BC the Persians conquered the island, but in 479 BC it was captured by Athens and became a member of the Delian League. In the following centuries the island suffered numerous invasions, and in 70 BC it was conquered by Julius Caesar. Byzantines, Venetians, Genoese and Turks followed. However, through all these vicissitudes the arts retained a high degree of importance. The primitive painter Theophilos (1873-1934) and the Nobel prize-winning poet Odysseus Elytis were both born on Lesbos. The island is to this day a spawning ground for innovative ideas in the arts and politics, and is the headquarters of the University of the Aegean.

Getting To/From Lesbos
Air Lesbos has five flights a day to Athens (11,600 dr), one a day to Thessaloniki (16,000 dr) and three a week to Lemnos (8500 dr). Note that Lesbos is always referred to as Mytilini on air schedules. The Olympic Airways office (☎ 28 659/660 or 22 820) in Mytilini is at Kavetsou 44, which is

a southerly continuation of Ermou. The airport is eight km south of Mytilini.

Ferry (Domestic) There is at least one ferry every day to Piraeus (15 hours, 3700 dr) via Chios, three a week to Kavala (11 hours, 3500 dr) via Lemnos, one a week to Thessaloniki (17 hours, 5100 dr) via Lemnos and one a week to Rhodes (6800 dr, 20 hours) via Chios, Samos, Patmos, Leros, Kalymnos and Kos. Ferry ticket offices line the eastern side of Pavlou Koundouriotou, in Mytilini. One of the most reliable for obtaining information is the Maritime Company of Lesbos (☎ 28 480, 25 800 or 22 220), Pavlou Koundouriotou 47. The port police (☎ 28 827/647) are on the same stretch of waterfront.

Ferry (International) From April to October there are ferries every day except Sunday to Ayvalik in Turkey. In winter they drop to about three a week. Ferries leave at 8 am and the journey takes two hours. Tickets cost 6000/8000 dr one-way/return and can be bought at the Maritime Company of Lesbos. As always when you sail from a Greek island to Turkey you must submit your passport a day in advance. Ayvalik is a coastal resort and fishing village, quite near the ruins of Pergamum.

Getting Around Lesbos

Bus Lesbos' transport hub is the capital, Mytilini. From the long-distance bus station there are six buses a day to Skala Eressou (three hours, 1300 dr) via Eressos; the first one leaves at 5.30 am and the last one at 3.30 pm. There are four buses a day to Methymna (two hours, 1000 dr) via Petra and two buses to Sigri (three hours, 1300 dr). There are no direct buses between Eressos, Sigri and Methymna. If you wish to travel from one of these villages to another, change buses in the

town of Kalloni, which is 48 km from Eressos and 22 km from Methymna. There are five buses a day to the south-coast resort of Plomari (1½ hours, 700 dr). The first bus leaves at 7.15 am and the last one at 5 pm.

Car & Motorbike There are many car-hire outlets in Mytilini. They include Kosmos Rent A Car (☎ 27 865), Pavlou Koundouriotou 73 and Lesvos Car (☎ 28 242), Pavlou Koundouriotou 47. Many motorbike-rental firms are along the same stretch of waterfront. There are also car and motorbike-hire outlets in Methymna and Skala Eressos. Bear in mind that Lesbos is large, and a moped is not really a practical mode of transport for exploring the entire island.

MYTILINI Μυτιλήνη

Mytilini, the capital and port of Lesbos, is a large workaday town. If you are enthralled by pretty and sparkling towns like Mykonos and Paros then you will want to get out of Mytilini quickly, for it is a crumbling town, and most of its once grand 19th-century mansions are now decaying amidst tangled overgrown gardens. Many of its old Turkish dwellings, with projecting wooden first floors almost meeting across narrow cobbled streets, look on the point of collapse.

Neither will Mytilini enthral sun, sea and sand lovers, for its town beach is mediocre, crowded and what's more you have to pay to use it (adults 200 dr and children 100 dr). However, you will appreciate Mytilini if you enjoy seeking out traditional kafeneia and little back-street ouzeria, or simply take pleasure in wandering in unfamiliar towns where people get on with their lives oblivious to tourists.

The northern end of Odos Ermou, the town's main commercial thoroughfare, is a wonderful street, full of character, ramshackle and authentic, with old-fashioned zaharoplasteia, grocers, fruit and vegetable stores, bakers, antique, embroidery, ceramic and jewellery shops. The latter four are there for the benefit of discerning locals rather than spendthrift tourists.

Orientation

Mytilini is built around two harbours (the north and south) which occupy both sides of a promontory, and are linked by the main thoroughfare of Odos Ermou. East of the harbours is a large fortress surrounded by a pine forest. All passenger ferries dock at the southern harbour. The waterfront here is called Pavlou Koundouriotou and the ferry quay is at its southern end. The northern harbour's waterfront is called Naumahias Ellis.

Information

The EOT (☎ 28 199) and tourist police (☎ 22 776) share the same office at the entrance to the quay. There is also an EOT at the airport.

The post office is on Vournazon, which is west of the southern harbour. The OTE is on the same street just west of the post office. Mytilini's postcode is 81100; its telephone code is 0251. Banks, including the National Bank of Greece, can be found on Pavlou Koundouriotou.

Mytilini has two bus stations: the one for long-distance buses is just beyond the south-western end of Pavlou Koundouriotou; the bus station for buses to local villages is on the northernmost section of Pavlou Koundouriotou.

Things to See & Do

Mytilini's imposing **castle**, with well-preserved walls, was built in early Byzantine times and renovated in the 14th century by Fragistco Gatelouzo; it was enlarged by the Turks. The surrounding pine forest is a pleasant place for a picnic. The castle is open daily from 8.30 am to 3 pm. Admission is 400 dr.

The **Archaeological Museum** (☎ 22 087), housed in a neoclassical mansion one block north of the quay, has impressive finds from Neolithic to Roman times. Opening times are Tuesday to Sunday from 8.30 am to 3 pm. Admission is 400 dr.

The dome of the **Church of Agios Therapon** can be spotted from almost anywhere on the southern waterfront. The church has a highly ornate interior with a huge chandelier, an intricately carved iconostasis and priest's

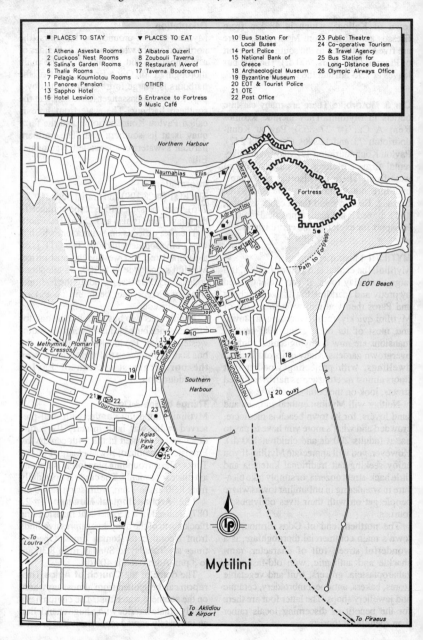

PLACES TO STAY
1 Athena Asvesta Rooms
2 Cuckoos' Nest Rooms
4 Salina's Garden Rooms
6 Thalia Rooms
7 Pelagia Koumiotou Rooms
11 Panorea Pension
13 Sappho Hotel
16 Hotel Lesvion

PLACES TO EAT
3 Albatros Ouzeri
8 Zoubouli Taverna
12 Restaurant Averof
17 Taverna Boudroumi

OTHER
5 Entrance to Fortress
9 Music Café

10 Bus Station For Local Buses
14 Port Police
15 National Bank of Greece
18 Archaeological Museum
19 Byzantine Museum
20 EOT & Tourist Police
21 OTE
22 Post Office

23 Public Theatre
24 Co-operative Tourism & Travel Agency
25 Bus Station for Long-Distance Buses
26 Olympic Airways Office

Mytilini

throne, and a frescoed dome. The **Byzantine Museum** (☎ 28 916) in the church's courtyard houses some fine icons. The museum is open from Monday to Saturday from 9 am to 1 pm. Admission is 100 dr.

Whatever you do don't miss the **Theophilos Museum** (☎ 41 644), which houses the works of the prolific primitive painter Theophilos, who was born on Lesbos in 1868. Several prestigious museums and galleries around the country now proudly display works by Theophilos. However, he lived in abject poverty painting the walls of kafeneia and tavernas in return for sustenance. The museum is open Tuesday to Sunday from 9 am to 1 pm and 4.30 to 8 pm. Admission is 100 dr.

The **Teriade Museum** (☎ 23 372), next door, commemorates the artist and critic Teriade who was born on Lesbos but lived and worked in Paris. It was largely due to the efforts of Teriade that the works of Theophilos gained international renown. On display are reproductions of Teriade's own illustrations and his collection of works by 20th-century artists, which include such greats as Picasso, Chagall and Matisse. The museum is open Tuesday to Sunday from 9 am to 2 pm and 5 to 8 pm and admission is 400 dr.

These museums are four km from Mytilini in the village of **Varia** where Theophilos was born. Take a local bus from the bus station at the northernmost section of Pavlou Koundouriotou (see Information).

Places to Stay – bottom end

The Co-operative Tourism and Travel Agency (☎ 21 329), Konstantinoupoleos 5, can arrange for you to stay with a family in one of 16 small villages on the island. Their office is near the long-distance bus station.

In Mytilini, domatia owners belong to a co-operative called *Sappho Self-catering Rooms in Mytilini*. There are 22 establishments; if any of the ones recommended are full or don't suit, the owner will direct you to another. Most of these domatia are in little side streets off Ermou, near the northern

harbour. The nearest to the quay is *Panorea Pension* (☎ 28 433), Komninaki 21. The clean and simply furnished double/triple rooms cost 4500/5400 dr with shared bathrooms. Komninaki is one block behind the eastern section of Pavlou Koundouriotou. *Salina's Garden Rooms* (☎ 42 073 or 23 860), Fokeas 7, are cosy and clean with a delightful garden. Rates are 3500/4800 dr for doubles/triples with shared bathrooms. The rooms are signposted from the corner of Ermou and Adramytiou.

Coming from Ermou, if you turn right opposite Salina's rooms you will come to *Thalia Rooms* (☎ 24 640), at Kinikion 1. The pleasant double/triple rooms in this large family house are 3500/4800 dr with shared bathrooms.

The *Cuckoos Nest* (☎ 23 901 or 29 419) are delightful rooms with some homely knick-knacks, pictures and ornaments. Rates are 3550 dr for a double room with shared bathrooms. The rooms have a pleasant roof garden. They are on a side street behind Naumahias Ellis and are signposted from the northern end of Ermou. *Athena Asvesta Rooms* (☎ 250 55), Naumahias Ellis 7, are spacious, light and attractively furnished. Rates are 5500 dr a double with private bathrooms. *Pelagia Koumiotou Rooms* (☎ 20 643), Tertseti 6, near the castle, are lovely cosy rooms in an old family house. Rates are 2500/4000/5000 dr for singles/doubles/triples with shared bathrooms. To find the rooms walk along Odos Mikras Asias and turn left onto Tertseti and the rooms are on the right.

Places to Stay – middle

There are several hotels on the southern waterfront, but you will pay more at these than in the domatia. The C class *Sappho Hotel* (☎ 28 888), on the north-west section of Pavlou Koundouriotou, has rates of 5500/8000/9600 dr for singles/doubles/triples with private bathrooms. The more luxurious B class *Hotel Lesvion* (☎ 22 038, 28 177 or 24 343), just two doors away, has doubles for 10,000 dr.

Places to Eat

You will eat well on Lesbos whether you enjoy fish dishes, traditional Greek food, international cuisine or vegetarian meals, and Mytilini is no exception. You might wish to avoid the restaurants on the western section of the southern waterfront where the waiters tout for customers. These restaurants are atypical of Mytilini as they pander to tourists and serve bland overpriced food.

The *Albatros Ouzeri*, on the corner of Ermou and Adramytiou, has to be seen to be believed. It has no pretensions and to say it is ethnic is an understatement. It is at least 100 years old, and everything in it looks grimy. The place is jam-packed with paraphernalia so that it looks far more like a junk shop or disorganised museum than an eating establishment. There are stuffed birds, painted shells, musical instruments, photographs, postcards, paintings, banknotes, bottles, gourds, dried vegetables, gas lights, oil lamps, ornaments (including a fat buddha and an elegant geisha) vases, brass bells and lots more. The tables are covered in oil cloths, despite the ban on these which was imposed by the government. The food, which seems to be something of an afterthought, is limited, but good and cheap. A meal of kalamaria, Greek salad and a small bottle of ouzo will cost around 1200 dr.

The *Restaurant Averof*, in the middle of the southern waterfront, is a no-nonsense traditional restaurant serving hearty Greek staples. Veal with potatoes is 700 dr and moussaka, pistatsio and stuffed tomatoes are all 530 dr.

The *Zoubouli Taverna*, at the southern end of Mitropoleos (next door to the Music Café), serves Greek food at its best. The taverna has a bright and folksy décor and is popular with locals. Another place serving high quality Greek dishes is *Taverna Boudroumi*. Meze dishes range from 250 to 500 dr. The restaurant is set back from the southern end of Komninaki and is a bit difficult to find – look for a stone building with black wrought-iron wall lamps at the entrance.

Entertainment

The *Music Café*, on the corner of Mitropoleos and Vernardaki, is a hip place – arty without being pretentious. Drinks are in the mid-price range rather than cheap, but worth it for the terrific atmosphere. Tapes of jazz, blues and classical music are played, and there is live music on Wednesday evenings – usually jazz. The café is open from 7.30 am to 2 am.

METHYMNA Μήθυμνα

Although this town has officially reverted to its ancient name of Methymna most locals still refer to it as Molyvos. It is 62 km from Mytilini and the principal town of northern Lesbos. The one-time rival to Mytilini, Methymna is nowadays the antithesis of the island capital, being extremely picturesque. Its impeccable stone houses with brightly coloured shutters pour down to the harbour from a castle-crowned hill. Its two main thoroughfares of Odos Kastrou and Odos 17 Novembriou are winding, cobbled and shaded by arbours of vines. In contrast to Mytilini, which gets on with its business oblivious to tourism, Methymna's pretty streets are lined with souvenir shops.

Orientation & Information

From the bus stop walk straight ahead towards the town. Where the road forks, take the right fork onto 17 Novembriou, which is the main street of Methymna. Along here, at the top of the hill, the road forks again; the right fork is Odos Kastrou and the post office is along here on the left. The left fork is a continuation of 17 Novembriou and the OTE is almost at the end, on the left. Methymna's postcode is 81108 and the telephone code is 0253. A little beyond the OTE you will find the National Bank of Greece on the right.

There is a small tourist information office (☎ 71 347/069) on the left, between the bus stop and the fork in the road.

Things to See & Do

One of the nicest things to do in Methymna is simply to stroll along its gorgeous streets. If you have the energy, the ruined 14th-century **Genoese castle** is worth clambering up to for fine views of the coastline and over the sea to Turkey. From this castle in the 15th century, Onetta d'Oria, wife of the Genoese governor, repulsed an onslaught by the Turks by putting on her husband's armour and leading the people of Methymna into battle. In summer the castle is the venue for a drama festival; ask for details at the tourist office.

The beach at Methymna is pebbled and crowded, but in summer excursion boats leave daily at 10 am for the superior beaches of Eftalous, Skala Sikaminias, Petra and Anaxos (see Around Methymna).

Places to Stay

The well-maintained camp site *Camping Methymna* (☎ 71 169/079) is 1½ km from town and signposted from near the tourist office.

There are over 50 official domatia in Methymna; most consist of only one or two rooms. All display domatia signs and most are of a high standard. The best street to start looking is 17 Novembriou. As you walk up here, the first rooms you come to are those of *Elini Vourgoutsi* (☎ 71 065), on the right. The rooms are nicely furnished and there is a terrace overlooking an attractive garden. The cost is 3000 dr a double with shared bathrooms. The beautifully furnished double room that *Kostindena Stavrinou* (☎ 71 011) lets is on the overhanging first floor of her house. It features pine-wood panelling on both the interior and exterior walls. The cost is 3500 dr with private bathroom. From the bus stop walk towards the town and take the second right onto Odos Myrasillou. Ascend the steps, turn right and the rooms are on the left – look for the wood panelling.

Places to Eat

Odos 17 Novembriou and Odos Kastrou have a good selection of restaurants serving typical Greek fare. But for something different try *Melinda's International Restaurant*, 17 Novembriou 52, which serves both meat and vegetarian dishes. A combination platter of salads, including carrots and currants, tabbouleh, lentils and walnuts is 1300 dr. Other dishes include fresh vegetables with rice for 420 dr, Kashmiri curried chicken for 1050 dr and mussels in garlic and dill butter for 1250 dr.

AROUND METHYMNA

At **Eftalous**, five km east along the coast, there are fine beaches, and radioactive springs where a thermal bath costs 200 dr. According to the EOT brochure these are a panacea for everything from gout to gynaecological diseases. Eftalous was the birthplace of the writer Kleanthes Michaelides, who, in honour of his village, wrote under the pseudonym Argyris Eftaliotis. His bust stands in the centre of Methymna town. Further east, the charming little coastal town of **Skala Sikaminias** also has literary connections, being much loved by the writer Stratis Myrivilis.

Petra Πέτρα

Petra (the Rock), five km south of Methymna, is a popular coastal resort with a long sandy beach shaded by tamarisk trees. Despite tourist development it remains an attractive village retaining some traditional houses. Immediately upon arrival, it will be obvious from where Petra derived its name – looming over the village is an enormous almost perpendicular rock which looks as if it's been lifted from Meteora. The rock is crowned by the 18th-century Panagia Glykophiloussa (Church of the Sweet Kissing Virgin). You can reach it by climbing up the rock-hewn steps – worth it for the view. **Anaxos**, three km west of Petra, also has a good sandy beach.

Places to Stay & Eat Domatia and pensions line Petra's waterfront. Greece's first Women's Agricultural Tourism Collective (☎ 0253-41 238) began here 10 years ago and is still going strong. The women run a restaurant and can arrange for you to stay with a family in the village; you will pay around 2500/4500 dr for a single/double. Their restaurant and office are on the central square – signposted from the waterfront.

SKALA ERESSOU & ERESSOS

Eressos (Ερεσός), 90 km from Mytilini, is a traditional inland village. Skala Eressou, four km beyond on the west coast, is a popular resort. An attractive, very straight tree-lined road links the two villages.

Skala Eressou is built over ancient Eressos where Sappho was born (628-568 BC). Although it gets crowded in summer it has a good laid-back atmosphere. If you're a beach freak you should certainly visit as it has the island's best – almost two km of fine silvery-brown sand.

Orientation & Information

From the bus turnaround at Skala Eressou, walk towards the sea to reach the central square of Plateia Anthis & Evristhenous, which abuts the waterfront. The beach stretches to the left and right of this square. Turn right at the square onto Odos Gyrinnis and just under 50 metres along you will come to a sign pointing left to the post office; the OTE is next door. Skala Eressou's postcode is 88105 and the telephone code is 0253. Neither Skala Eressou nor Eressos has a bank.

There is no EOT or tourist police, but Exeresis Travel (☎ 53 044), 200 metres to the right of the bus station (facing the sea), is helpful. The staff here arrange car, motorbike and bicycle hire, treks on foot, and on horses and donkeys. They also have currency exchange.

Archaeological Museum

Eressos' Archaeological Museum houses Archaic, Classical and Roman finds including statues, coins and grave stele. The museum, which is in the centre of Skala Eressou, stands near the remains of the early Christian Basilica of Agios Andreas. Opening times are Tuesday to Sunday from 8.30 am to 3 pm. Admission is free.

Petrified Forest of Sigri

'Petrified Forest' is the EOT's hyperbolic description of the scattering of ancient tree stumps near the village of Sigri, on the west coast, north of Skala Eressou. Experts reckon the petrified wood is at least 500,000 but possibly 20 million years old. If you're intrigued, the forest is easiest reached by excursion from Skala Eressou; enquire at Exeresis Travel. The village of Sigri has one hotel, several domatia and a good beach.

Places to Stay

There is an official *free* camp site at the western end of the beach at Skala Eressou; to reach it turn right at the waterfront. The site has cold showers and toilets, but as the upkeep is minimal the latter get pretty filthy when the site is crowded.

There are a few domatia in Eressou but most people head for Skala Eressou, where there are many domatia, pensions and hotels. Skala Eressou's cheapest hotel is the E class *Hotel Minerva* (☎ 55 202); double/triple rooms are nicely furnished and go for 4500/5000 dr with private bathrooms; the triples have sinks and hot plates. From the bus turnaround face the main road from Eressos, and take Odos Akaiou, which is to the right, and the hotel is a little way along on the right.

The double/triple rooms of *Loukas Kovros* (☎ 53 331/553) are clean, tastefully furnished and excellent value at 4000/6000 dr with private bathrooms. From the bus turnaround, face the sea and turn right onto Odos Koundouriotou; the rooms are almost at the end of here on the right – look for the house with green shutters.

The *Dimitra Frantzi Rooms* (☎ 53 030) are a superior domatia, with immaculate single/double rooms for 3000/6000 dr with private bathrooms. They are on the left of the main road as you come into Skala Eressou from Eressos, about 200 metres from the waterfront. Look for a beige building with white plaster balustrades.

Skala Eressou's best hotel is the C class *Hotel Galini* (☎ 53 137/8 or 53 205). Its light and airy rooms cost 3800/5500/6700 dr for

Coast near Alykes, Zakynthos, Ionian Islands (DH)

Top: Near the fountain Arethusa, Ithaka, Ionian Islands (DH)
Bottom: Mountain path, Ithaka, Ionian Islands (DH)

singles/doubles/triples with private bathrooms. The hotel has a comfortable TV room-cum-bar and an outside terrace under a bamboo shade. Follow the directions for the Hotel Minavra and then continue further up the road to reach the Galini.

Places to Eat

Skala Eressou has a large number of restaurants serving typical Greek fare, but for something different try *Bennet's International & Vegetarian Restaurant*.

Lemnos Λήμνος

Lemnos (LIM-nos, population 16,000) belongs to the nomos (prefecture) of Lesbos. There is a saying on Lemnos that when people come to live for a time on the island they cry twice, once when they arrive and once when they leave. The implication is that Lemnos' appeal is not immediate, but one that slowly but surely captivates. Such is the charm of the island.

The deeply penetrating Moudros Bay almost severs the island in two. The landscape of Lemnos lacks the imposing grandeur of the forested and mountainous islands and the stark beauty of the barren and rocky ones. However, gently undulating Lemnos, with its little farmsteads, has a unique understated appeal all of its own. In spring vibrant wild flowers dot the landscape, and in autumn purple crocuses sprout forth in profusion. The coastline boasts some of the best beaches in the North-Eastern Aegean group. The island is sufficiently off the beaten track to have escaped the adverse effects of mass tourism.

History

Lemnos' position near the Straits of the Dardenelles, midway between the Mt Athos peninsula and Turkey, has given it a traumatic history. To this day it maintains a large garrison.

Lemnos had advanced Neolithic and Bronze-Age civilisations, and during these times had contact with peoples in western Anatolia, including the Trojans. In Classical times the Kabeirou gods were worshipped at a sanctuary on the island, but later the Sanctuary of the Great Gods on Samothrace became the centre of this cult.

Aphrodite's Revenge

Lemnos features prominently in mythology. Zeus, in one of his habitual rages, threw his son Hephaestus (god of iron and fire) from Mt Olympus. Hephaestus, the ugliest of all the gods, landed on Lemnos. Not surprisingly the fall made him lame. Aphrodite's family, anxious to curtail her promiscuous lifestyle, married her off to Hephaestus, but as soon as her husband's back was turned she hopped into bed with Ares. When the women of Lemnos deprecated her for her infidelity, Aphrodite inflicted them with bad breath. Their husbands then refused to make love to them, so the women took their revenge by murdering not only their spouses, but every man on the island. Soon after, the fortuitous arrival of the less fastidious Jason and the Argonauts saved the Lemniots from extinction. ■

Hephaestus, God of Iron & Fire

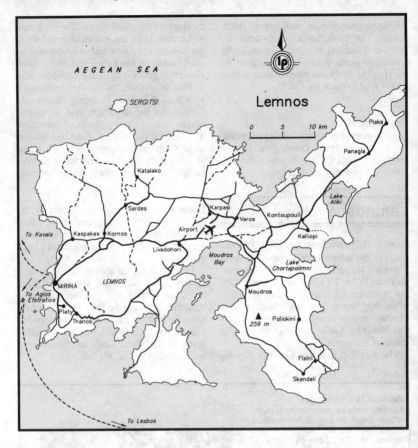

During the Peloponnesian Wars Lemnos sided with Athens and suffered many Persian attacks. After the split of the Roman Empire it became an important outpost of Byzantium. In 1462 it came under the domination of the Genoese Gateluzians who ruled Lesbos. The Turks succeeded in conquering the island in 1478 and it remained under Turkish rule until 1912. Moudros Bay, on Lemnos, was the Allies' base for the disastrous Gallipoli campaign in WW I.

Getting To/From Lemnos

Air In summer there are daily flights to Lemnos from Athens (9900 dr) and Thessaloniki (10,200 dr); and three flights a week from Lesbos (8500 dr). The Olympic Airways office (☎ 22 214/5) is on Odos Nikolaou Garofalidi, opposite the Hotel Paris, in Mirina. The airport is 22 km north-east of Mirina.

Ferry In summer there are five ferries a week to Kavala from Lemnos; four a week to Rafina, all via Agios Efstratios and one via Lesbos and Chios; two to Piraeus via Lesbos and Chios; one a week to Rhodes via Lesbos, Chios, Samos, Patmos, Leros, Kalymnos and Kos; and one a week to Thessaloniki. Tickets can be bought at Mirina Tourist & Travel Agency (☎ 22 460), next door to the Hotel Aktaion, in Mirina.

Excursion Boat In July and August there are daily excursion boats to the small island of Agios Efstratios, which is a dependency of Lemnos. The island is untouristy and has several beaches, tavernas and domatia. For information enquire at Mirina Tourist & Travel Agency.

Getting Around Lemnos

Bus The bus service on Lemnos is poor. In summer there are two buses a day from Mirina to most of the villages. Check the schedule at the bus station on Plateia El Venizelou.

Car & Motorbike In Mirina, cars and jeeps can be rented from Theodoros Retrides Travel Agency (☎ 22 039/998 or 24 787), on the right side of Odos Kyda as you walk away from the harbour. There are several motorbike-hire outlets on Odos Kyda.

MIRINA Μύρινα

Mirina is the capital and port of Lemnos. Surrounded by massive hunks of volcanic rock, it is by no stretch of the imagination a picturesque town, but it is animated, full of character and unfettered by establishments pandering to tourism. The main thoroughfare of Odos Kyda is a charming paved street with shops and eating places of every description, including traditional shops selling nuts and honey and old-fashioned kafeneia. Wandering along the side streets you will see interspersed between modern buildings little whitewashed stone dwellings, decaying neoclassical mansions and 19th-century wattle-and-daub houses with overhanging wooden balconies. A Genoese castle looms dramatically over the town.

Orientation & Information

From the end of the quay turn right onto Plateia Ilia Iliou. Continue along the waterfront passing the Hotel Lemnos and the town hall. A little further along you will see the Hotel Aktaion, set back from the waterfront. Turn left here, then immediately veer half left onto Odos Kyda, the town's main thoroughfare. Proceeding up here you will reach the central square where you will find the National Bank of Greece and the OTE. The taxi rank (☎ 23 033 or 22 348) is also on this square. Continue up Odos Kyda and take the next turn right onto Odos Nikolaou Garofalidi. The post office is here on the right. Back on Odos Kyda, continue for another 100 metres and you will come to Plateia El Venizelou where you will see the bus station.

The Municipal Tourist Office (☎ 24 110) is in the town hall, next to the Hotel Lemnos on the waterfront. It is only open during July and August. The tourist police (☎ 22 200) are at the far end of Nikolaou Garofalidi – on the right coming from Odos Kyda. The port police (☎ 22 225) are on the waterfront near the quay.

Things to See & Do

As with all Greek-island castles the one towering over Mirina is worth climbing up to for the vistas. From its vantage point there are magnificent views over the sea to Mt Athos. Walking from the harbour a sign at the beginning of Odos Kyda points left to the castle.

Mirina has a lovely long sandy beach right in town. It stretches north from the castle and can be reached by walking along Odos Kyda from the harbour, and taking any of the streets off to the left. Mirina's **museum**, housed in a neoclassical mansion, was closed at the time of writing for renovation but should be open again by the time this book hits the shelves. It overlooks the beach, next to the Kastro Hotel.

Organised Tours

In the absence of a decent bus service Theodoros Retrides Travel Agency (see Car & Motorbike under Getting Around Lemnos) organises bus excursions around the island which include a visit to ancient Piolokini.

Places to Stay – bottom end

Lemnos doesn't have any official camp sites.

Rooms to Let Argyro (☎ 23 908 or 24 152) has spacious nicely furnished rooms a telephone, refrigerator and balcony. Rates are 5500/7000 dr for doubles/triples. Walk to the end of Odos Kyda from the waterfront, at the crossroad continue straight ahead and the rooms are on the right just beyond a school and football pitch.

Another option for budget travellers is the lovely *Apollo Pavillion* (☎ 23 712), with friendly English-speaking owners. The Pavillion is a new building in neoclassical style with ornate wrought-iron balconies; inside there is lots of cool grey marble. The rooms are spacious and clean and a variety of accommodation is offered. Cheapest are the four-bed rooms in the basement which are intended for backpackers. They cost 2000 dr per person. Studios with private bathrooms and kitchens cost 6700/8000 dr for doubles/triples. Two-roomed apartments with kitchens are 10,000/11,000 dr for four and five people. The Pavillion has a nice garden with a barbecue for guests' use. Walk along Odos Nikolaou Garofalidi from Odos Kyda and you will see the sign 100 metres along on the right.

The D class *Hotel Aktaion* (☎ 22 258), on the waterfront, is the town's cheapest hotel. The single/double/triple rooms are pleasant and clean and cost 3877/6425/8308 dr. The *Hotel Lemnos* (☎ 22 153) is the nearest hotel to the quay. The rooms are comfortable enough, but it is in a noisy position and the owners seem to dislike backpackers. Rates are 4500/9000 dr for singles/doubles with private bathrooms. The *Hotel Paris* (☎ 23 266) is a more pleasant option, with rates of 5000/8800/10,560/12,000 dr for singles/doubles/triples/quads. Five and six-bed rooms are 15,000 dr. The hotel is on Nikolaou Garofalidi, opposite the post office.

Places to Stay – middle
The new B class *Kastro Hotel* (☎ 22 772/748/725) is built in neoclassical style. The rooms have fitted carpets, balconies, telephone, three-channel music and TV on request. Rates are 7000/10,500/12,980/15,850 dr for singles/doubles/triples/quads

with breakfast. The hotel has a restaurant, bar, snack bar, TV room and sunbathing terrace, and overlooks the beach. It is signposted from the crossroad at the top of Kyda.

The *Hotel Ifestos* (☎ 24 960/962; fax 23 623) is another new B class, with tastefully furnished rooms; doubles cost 10,000 dr. The hotel is 100 metres from the town beach and one km from the quay. Walk to the end of Kyda, and continue straight ahead to the intersection from where the airport and the village of Kaspakas are signposted. Take the Kaspakas road, at the T-junction turn left again and you will see the hotel on the left.

Places to Eat
Eating doesn't present any problems in Lemnos as establishments are of a high standard. There are several fish restaurants around the waterfront. Locals give top marks to *Taverna Glaros*, where an excellent meal of whitebait, potato chips, Greek salad and retsina will cost about 1700 dr. Facing the waterfront the taverna is on the far left beside the small fishing boats. Odos Kyda is packed with kafeneia, fast-food places and snack bars. One of its best restaurants is *O Platanos Taverna*, on the left as you walk from the waterfront.

AROUND THE ISLAND
Beaches
One of Lemnos' best beaches is below the village of Platy, three km south of Mirina. As well as the huge expensive Lemnos Village Resort Hotel, **Plati Beach** has a few budget places to stay. The rooms belonging to *Ioannis Trataris* (☎ 24 127/060) are simply and attractively furnished with a kitchen area and private bathroom. Rates are 5600 dr a double. The rooms are on the left side of the road which leads from Platy village to the beach. If you turn left at the bottom of this road, you will come to *Rooms to Let* (☎ 24 142), behind Jimmy's Fish Tavern; the rates are 4000 dr a double. Both of the tavernas on the beach are reasonably priced.

If you continue along the dirt road which passes the Lemnos Village Resort Hotel, you will come to a sheltered sandy cove with an islet in the bay. The beach here will probably be less crowded than Platy. **Thanos Beach** is the next bay around from Platy; it is also less crowded, and long and sandy. To get to this beach continue on the main road from Platy village to Thanos village, from where a sign points to the beach. If you have your own transport many more beaches can be found around the coast.

Ancient Poliokini

The Italian School of Archaeologists has uncovered four ancient settlements at Poliokini (Πολεοκήνη), on the island's east coast. Each settlement appears to have been one of the most advanced in the Aegean for its time. The first settlement was Neolithic and the third and most interesting one was a sophisticated pre-Mycenaean city, which predated Troy VI (1800-1275 BC).

Samothrace Σαμοθράκη

The egg-shaped island of Samothrace (Sam-o-THRA-ki, population 2800) is 32 km south-west of Alexandroupolis and belongs to the Thracian nomos of Evros. Scenically it is one of the most awe-inspiring of all Greek islands. It is a small island, but a great deal of diverse landscape is packed into its 176 sq km. Its natural attributes are dramatic, big and untamed, and culminate in the mighty peak of Mt Fengari (1611 metres), the highest mountain in the Aegean. Homer related that Poseidon watched the Trojan War from its summit. Poseidon's interest in the progress of this war was inspired by an unfulfilled pledge. Poseidon had helped King Dardanus to build the walls of Troy and in return the king had promised to worship him, but failed to do so. In true god-like fashion Poseidon bore an almighty grudge, causing him to take a vehemently anti-Trojan stance in the war.

The jagged boulder-strewn Mt Fengari looms over valleys of massive gnarled oak and plane trees, thick forests of olive trees,

dense shrubbery and damp dark glades where waterfalls plunge into deep icy pools. On the gentler western slopes of the island there are corn fields studded with wild flowers. Samothrace is also rich in fauna: its springs are the habitat for a large number of frogs, toads and turtles, and in its meadows you will see swarms of butterflies and may come across the odd lumbering tortoise. On the mountain slopes there are an inordinate number of bell-clanking goats. The island's beaches, with one exception, are stony or pebbly.

Samothrace's ancient site, the Sanctuary of the Great Gods, at Paleopolis, is one of the most evocative in Greece. Historians have been unable to ascertain the nature of the rites performed here, and the aura of potent mysticism it emanates prevails over the whole island.

Poseidon

Essentially, Samothrace is a union of two powerful forces – those of nature and the occult. Although tourism is beginning to make its mark – the port now boasts one disco, and three souvenir shops – the island is the antithesis of lying on a beach all day and dancing the night away. This is an island on which to be contemplative, to enjoy the beauty of nature or to be challenged by it.

Samothrace is relatively difficult to reach and does not have any package tourism. It does, however, attract a fair number of Greek holiday-makers in July and August, so you may have some difficulty finding a room during these months. The island is lucky in that the indiscriminate erection of concrete hotels in the 1960s and 70s passed it by. With the exception of the Xenia Hotel, all of Samothrace's hotels were built in the 1980s and were designed to a high standard with sensitive regard to the environment. All are extremely pleasant places to stay but none falls into the budget category. This doesn't mean budget travellers are not welcome or catered for as there are a fair number of domatia and two camp sites.

History
Samothrace was first settled around 1000 BC by Thracians who worshipped the Great Gods, a cult of Anatolian origin. In 700 BC the island was colonised by inhabitants of Lesbos, who assimilated the Thracian cult into the Greek's worship of the Olympian gods.

This marriage of two cults was highly successful, for by the 5th century BC Samothrace had become one of Greece's major religious centres, attracting prospective initiates from far and wide to its Sanctuary of the Great Gods. Among the luminaries initiated into the cult were King Lysander of Sparta, Philip II of Macedonia and Piso, Julius Caesar's father-in-law. One famous visitor who did not come to be initiated was St Paul who dropped in en route to Philipi.

The cult survived until paganism was outlawed in the 4th century AD. After this time the island became insignificant. It fell to the Turks in 1457 and became united with Greece along with the other North-Eastern Aegean islands in 1912. During WW II Samothrace was occupied by the Bulgarians.

Getting To/From Samothrace
Samothrace has ferry connections with Alexandroupolis (two hours, 1200 dr) and Kavala (3¾ hours, 2100 dr). The sailing times in summer to Alexandroupolis are 11.30 am, 4 and 7 pm on Monday; 6 pm on Tuesday; 1 and 7.30 pm on Wednesday; 9 am, 3 and 7 pm on Thursday; 1.30 and 8.30 pm on Friday; 11.30 am and 7 pm on Saturday; and 8.30 am, 2 and 8 pm on Sunday. Tickets can be bought at Saos Travel, in Kamariotisa.

Sailing times to Kavala are 8 am on Wednesday; 11 am on Friday; 9 am on Saturday; and 4 pm on Sunday. Tickets can be bought at Niki Tours, Kamariotisa.

Getting Around Samothrace
Bus In summer there are at least nine buses a day from Kamariotisa to Chora and Loutra (Therma) (via Paleopolis). Some of the Loutra buses continue to the nearby camp sites. There are four buses a day to Profitis Ilias (via Lacoma). A bus schedule is displayed in the window of Saos Travel, Kamariotisa.

Motorbike Motorbikes can be rented from Rent A Motor Bike, opposite the ferry quay. There is no car hire on Samothrace.

Excursion Boat On Tuesday in summer, F/B *Saos* takes a break from its daily grind of carrying passengers to and from Alexandroupolis and does a three-hour jaunt around the island (11 am to 2 pm). This trip is highly commendable, for Samothrace's magnificent beauty can only be appreciated to the full from its rugged southern coast. Tickets cost 1500 dr and can be bought from Saos Travel. Every day in summer the *Samothraki Express Boat* does the same trip for 3500 dr. It leaves Kamariotisa at 11 am from the jetty just east of the bus terminal and picks up passengers in Loutra (Therma) at noon; tickets are sold on board. Depending on demand, caïques do trips from the Kamariotisa jetty to Pahia Ammos and Kipos beaches.

KAMARIOTISA Καμαριώτισσα
Kamariotisa, on the north-west coast, is Samothrace's port. Chora (also called Samothraki), the island's capital, is five km inland from here. Kamariotisa is the transport hub of the island, so you may wish to use it as a base; otherwise it has little to offer.

Orientation & Information
The bus station is on the waterfront just east of the quay (turn left when you disembark). There is a National Bank of Greece on the waterfront, but no post office or OTE; these are in Chora. There is no EOT or tourist police and the regular police are in Chora. Opposite the bus station you will find Saos Travel (☎ 41 505) and Niki Tours (☎ 41 465; fax 41 304), both of whom are reasonably helpful. The port police (☎ 41 305) are on the eastern waterfront at Kamariotisa.

Organised Tours
See under Excursion Boat for details of day trips to sites around the island.

Places to Stay
Domatia owners meet the ferries in Kamariotisa. Otherwise, the *Pension Kyma* (☎ 41 268), at the eastern end of the waterfront, has comfortable singles/doubles for 3500/4500 dr with shared bathrooms and 4000/5000 dr with private bathrooms. Further along the waterfront, the C class *Niki Beach Hotel* (☎ 41 561/461) is modern and spacious. Room rates are 5500/8540/10,000 dr for singles/doubles/triples with private bathrooms; the price includes breakfast. The hotel is at the eastern end of the waterfront.

Behind this is Samothrace's most luxurious hotel, the B class *Aeolis Hotel* (☎ 41 595/895), where room rates are 7800/12,000/14,000 dr with breakfast. The hotel has a swimming pool and a commanding position on a hill, overlooking the sea.

Places to Eat
Eating is nothing to write home about in Kamariotisa, or anywhere else on Samothrace for that matter. Restaurants serve an unimaginative range of standard Greek fare. *The Horizon* is one of Kamariotisa's better restaurants. Main courses include chicken casserole at 600 dr, and meatballs, moussaka and souvlaki are all 700 dr. The restaurant is just back from the waterfront on the left side of the road which leads up to Chora. At the eastern end of the waterfront *Klimitaria Restaurant* serves a very good *gianiotiko* for 800 dr. This is a dish of diced pork, potatoes and egg baked in the oven.

CHORA Χώρα
Chora, concealed in a fold of the mountains above Kamariotisa, is one of the most striking of Greek island villages. The crumbling red-tiled houses, some of grey stone, others whitewashed, are stacked up two steep adjacent mountain sides. The twisting cobbled streets resound with cockerels crowing, dogs barking and donkeys braying, rather than the ubiquitous roar of motorbikes and honking of car horns. The village is totally authentic with no concessions to tourism. The ruined castle at the top of the main thoroughfare is fascinating to explore and from its vantage point there are sweeping vistas down to Kamariotisa. It is an open site with free entrance.

Orientation & Information
To get to Chora's narrow winding main street, follow the signs for the Kastro from the central square where the bus does a turnaround. Here on the main street, which is nameless, as are all of Chora's streets (houses are distinguished by numbers), are the OTE, the Agricultural Bank and the post office. Samothrace's telephone code is 0551 and the postcode is 68002. The police (☎ 41 203) are next to the ruined castle at the top of Chora's main street. A little way up the main street, on the right, a fountain gushes refreshing mountain spring water.

Walk from Chora to Paleopolis (Sanctuary of the Great Gods)

It takes between 45 minutes and one hour to walk along a dirt track from Chora to Paleopolis (Παλαιόπολη). On this walk there are tremendous views of Fengari to the right and rolling hills, corn fields and the sea to the left. To get to the track, walk up to the castle ruins in Chora and take the dirt track which leads down to the right.

At the first T-junction turn right. After about 15 minutes the track forks; take the right fork. Continue straight ahead on the main track ignoring the four turn-offs to the left. Soon you will see the Kastro Hotel ahead and the top of a circular concrete building. Ignore the turn-off to the right opposite this building, and after a few minutes you will come to a smaller path which leads half right off the main path. Take this path and at the crossroads turn right to reach the tiny hamlet of Paleopolis. Keep going along the path to reach the museum and ancient site.

Places to Stay & Eat

There are no hotels in Chora. There are two reasonably priced pensions just off the central square but the nicest places to stay in Chora are rooms in private houses. Almost all of these are unofficial so do not display signs. If you ask in one of the kafeneia you will be put in touch with a room owner. On my last visit here only the taverna on the central square was operating. The menu here is limited but the food is good. The little nameless taverna on the left of the main street as you walk to the kastro serves excellent vegetable dishes – if it's open. There are several kafeneia and grocers along this street.

SANCTUARY OF THE GREAT GODS

Τέμενος των Μεγάλων Θεών

The Sanctuary of the Great Gods, next to the little hamlet of Paleopolis, is six km north-east of Kamariotisa. The extensive site, lying in a valley of luxuriant vegetation between Mt Fengari and the sea, is one of the most magical in the whole of Greece. The Great Gods were of greater antiquity than the Olympian gods worshipped in the official religion of Ancient Greece. The principal deity was the Great Mother (Alceros Cybele), who was worshipped as a goddess of fertility.

When the original Thracian religion became integrated with the state religion the Great Mother was merged with the Olympian female deities Demeter, Aphrodite and Hekate. The last of these was a mysterious goddess associated with darkness, the underworld and witchcraft. Other deities worshipped here were the Great Mother's consort, the virile young Kadmilos (god of the phallus), who was later integrated with the Olympian god Hermes; and the demonic Kabeiroi twins, Dardanos and Aeton, who were integrated with Kastor and Pollux (known as the Dioscuri), the twin sons of Zeus and Leda. These twins were invoked by mariners to protect them against the perils of the sea. The formidable deities of Samothrace were venerated for their immense power and were not to be messed with; in comparison the Olympian gods were a frivolous and fickle lot.

Initiates were sworn on punishment of death not to reveal what went on at the sanctuary. Consequently, there is only very flimsy knowledge of what these initiations involved. All that has been gleaned from archaeological evidence is that there were two initiations, a lower and a higher. In the first initiation, gods were invoked to bring

The Dioscuri

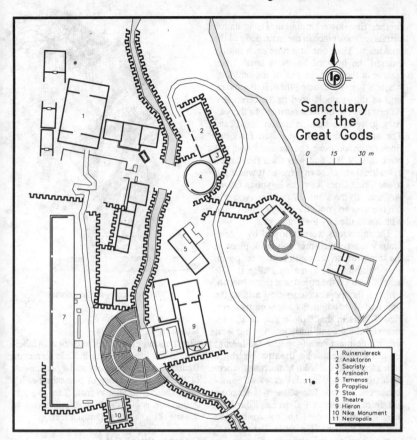

Sanctuary of the Great Gods

0   15   30 m

1 Ruinenviereck
2 Anaktoron
3 Sacristy
4 Arsinoein
5 Temenos
6 Propyliou
7 Stoa
8 Theatre
9 Hieron
10 Nike Monument
11 Necropolis

about a spiritual rebirth within the candidate. In the second initiation the candidate was absolved of transgressions. There was no prerequisite for initiation – it was available to anyone and everyone.

The site's most celebrated relic, the Winged Victory of Samothrace, was found by Champoiseau, the French Consul, at Adrianople (present day Edirne in Turkey) in 1863. Sporadic excavations followed in the late 19th and early 20th centuries, but did not begin in earnest until just before WW II, when the Institute of Fine Arts, New York University, under the direction of Karl Lehmann and Phyllis Williams Lehmann, began digging.

The site is open Tuesday to Saturday from 8.30 am to 3 pm and Sunday and holidays from 11 am to 1 pm. It is closed on Monday. Admission is 400 dr.

Exploring the Site

The site is labelled in both Greek and English. Taking the path which leads south from the entrance you will come to the rectangular **anaktoron** on the left. At its southern end was a **sacristy**, an antechamber where candidates put on white gowns ready for their first (lower) initiation. The initiation ceremony took place in the main body of the anaktoron. Then one at a time each initiate entered the holy of holies, a small inner temple at the northern end of the building, where a priest instructed them in the meanings of the symbols used in the ceremony. Afterwards the initiates returned to the sacristy to receive their initiation certificate. The **arsinoein**, which was used for sacrifices, to the south-west of the anaktoron, was built in 289 BC and was then the largest cylindrical structure in Greece. It was a gift to the Great Gods from the Egyptian Queen Arsinou. To the south-east of here you will see the **sacred rock**, the site's earliest altar, which was used by the Thracians.

The initiations were followed by a celebratory feast which probably took place in the **temenos**, to the south of the Arsinoein. This building was given by Philip II. The next building is the prominent Doric **hieron**, which is the most photographed ruin on the site; five of its columns have been reassembled. It was in this temple that candidates received the second initiation. On the west side of the main path (opposite the hieron) are a few remnants of a **theatre**. Nearby, a path ascends to the **Nike Monument** where the magnificent Winged Victory of Samothrace once stood. The statue was a votive gift from Demetrius Poliorketes (the Besieger of Cities) to the Kabeirou for helping him defeat Ptolemy II in battle. To the north-west of here are the remains of a massive **stoa**, which was a two-aisled portico where pilgrims to the sanctuary sheltered; names of initiates were recorded on its walls. North of the stoa are the ruins of the **ruinenviereck**, a medieval fortress.

Retrace your steps to the Nike Monument and walk along the path leading east; on the left is a good plan of the site. The path continues to the southern **necropolis** which is the most important ancient cemetery so far found on the island. It was used from the Bronze Age to early Roman times. North of the cemetery was the **propyliou**, an elaborate Ionic entrance to the sanctuary; it was a gift from Ptolemy II.

Winged Victory of Samothrace

Museum

The site's museum is well laid out with labelling in English. Exhibits include terracotta figurines, vases, jewellery and a plaster cast of the Winged Victory of Samothrace. It's open Tuesday to Sunday from 9 am to 3 pm. Admission is 400 dr. A good guidebook to the site is on sale at the museum shop.

Places to Stay & Eat

There are several domatia at Paleopolis, all of which are signposted from near the museum. The B class *Xenia Hotel* (☎ 41 230) near the museum was built 40 years ago to provide accommodation for archaeologists. Although clean and comfortable, it lacks the sophistication of Samothrace's new hotels. However, you may prefer to stay here, where most guests are on the island for more meaningful reasons than mere enjoyment. The double/triple room rates are 5600/6600 dr with private bathrooms. Just west of Paleopolis, above the coast road, is the C class *Kastro Hotel* (☎ 41 850), the island's newest hotel. The rooms are simply and tastefully furnished and rates are 6500/9000/11,500/13,800 dr for singles/doubles/triples/quads, including breakfast. The hotel has a swimming pool. There are no tavernas at Paleopolis but both hotels have restaurants.

AROUND THE ISLAND

Loutra (Therma) Λουτρά (Θέρμα)

Loutra, also called Therma, is 13 km east of Kamariotisa and a short walk inland from the coast. It's in an attractive setting with a profusion of plane and horse chestnut trees, dense greenery and gurgling creeks. However, it is not an authentic village, but the nearest Samothrace comes to a holiday resort, as most of its buildings are purpose-built domatia. Whatever, most visitors to the island seem to make for here. The village takes both its names from its therapeutic sulphurous mineral springs. Whether or not you are arthritic you may like to take a thermal bath here. The baths are in the large white building on the right as you walk to the central square from the bus stop. Opening times are 6 to 11 am and 5 to 7 pm. Admission is 300 dr. There is a tiny OTE in the village, which unlike the one in Chora remains open at weekends. It is signposted from Loutra's central square.

You may hear that Mt Fengari can be climbed from Loutra. There is a path but it is badly maintained and the climb is difficult and dangerous, so the police on Samothrace discourage people from attempting it. If you're determined, it may be possible to hire a guide in Loutra. There is also a path from Chora but this is longer than the one from Loutra and no better maintained.

Places to Stay Samothrace has two official camp sites; both are near Loutra, and both are signposted Multilary (sic) Campings. Rest assured, the authorities mean Municipal Campings and not Military Campings. The first *Multilary Camping* (☎ 41 784) is to the left of the main road, two km beyond the turn-off for Loutra, coming from Kamariotisa. It is very spartan, with toilets and cold showers but no other amenities. The charges are 260 dr per person, 200 dr per tent and 150

dr for a car. The second *Multilary Camping* (☎ 41 491) is two km further along the road. It has a minimarket, restaurant and hot showers, and charges are 500 dr per person, 350 dr per tent and 200 dr for a car. Both sites are open only during June, July and August.

Domatia owners meet the buses at Loutra. If you can afford something more expensive, then Loutra has two lovely hotels. The C class *Mariva Hotel* (☎ 41 759/758) is on three levels on a hillside in a secluded part of the island near a waterfall. The spacious rooms cost 5000/6000/7000 dr for singles/doubles/triples with private bathrooms. To reach the hotel take the first turn left along the road which leads from the coast up to Loutra. Follow the signs to the hotel which is 600 metres along this road. The B class *Kaviros Hotel* (☎ 41 577/497) is bang in the middle of Loutra, just beyond the central square. It is a very pleasant family-run hotel with single/double/triple rates of 6000/8600/10,300 dr. The hotel is surrounded by a pretty garden and draped in copious greenery.

Places to Eat In Loutra there is little to choose from between the four or five restaurants. *Restaurant O Thodoros*, just beyond the central square, is the cheapest. Pastitsio, moussaka, stuffed peppers and chicken with potatoes are all 680 dr and souvlaki is 800 dr. *Feggari Restaurant*, next to the OTE, is slightly more expensive, but the food is no better. My best meal in Loutra was at *Paradeisos Taverna* where I had a good beef rissole, Greek salad and Amstel for 1500 dr. Facing inland, take the first turn right after the central square to reach the taverna.

Other Villages

The small villages of **Profitis Ilias**, **Lacoma** and **Xiropotamos** in the south-west, and **Alonia** near Chora, are serene unspoilt villages all worth a visit. The hillside Profitis Ilias, with many trees and springs, is particularly delightful and has several tavernas. Asphalt roads lead to all of these villages.

Beaches

The Great Gods did not overendow Samothrace with good beaches. However, having said this, its one sandy beach, **Pahia Ammos**, on the south coast, is superb. You can reach this 800-metre stretch of fine white sand by walking along a five-km dirt track (just driveable) from Lacoma. In summer there are caïques from Kamariotisa to the beach. A domatia, taverna and camp site were due to open here at the time of writing, but there was a delay in their completion. The staff at Saos Travel should be able to tell you if they are operating.

Samothrace's other decent beach is the pebbled **Kipos Beach** on the south-east coast. This beach can be reached on a non-asphalt but reasonable road, which is an easterly continuation of the road skirting the north coast. The beach can also be reached by caïque from Kamariotisa.

Thassos Θάσσος

Thassos (THA-sos, population 13,300) lies 10 km south-east of Kavala to whose nomos it belongs. It is almost circular in shape and although its scenery is not as awesome as

Thassos

Samothrace it has some pleasing mountain vistas. The EOT brochures tout it as the 'Emerald Isle', but like so many other Greek islands it has suffered bad fires in recent years which have destroyed much of its forest. The main attractions of Thassos are its excellent beaches and the many archaeological remains in and around the capital of Limenas. A good asphalt road goes around the island so all the beaches are easily accessible.

Although Thassos doesn't have an airport, package tourism is on the increase, but as yet this has not spoilt the island. These holiday-makers fly to Kavala's airport (Khristoupolis) and are ferried over to Thassos from Keramoti. As yet, there are still enough rooms for everyone even in high season and Thassos has no less than eight camp sites dotted around the coast. A notice opposite the bus station in Limenas lists the town's hotels, and also, very helpfully, indicates which hotels remain open in the winter – if only all Greek islands did this.

History

Thassos has been continuously inhabited since the Stone Age. Its ancient city was founded by Parians in 700 BC who were led there by a message from the Delphic oracle. The oracle told them to 'Find a city in the Isle of Mists'. From Thassos the Parians established settlements in Thrace where they mined for gold in Mt Pangaeun.

Gold was also mined on Thassos itself. With this highly desirable commodity the islanders were able to develop a lucrative export trade, based on ore, marble, timber and wine, as well as gold. As a result Thassos built a powerful navy and culture also flourished.

Famous ancient Thassiots included the painters Polygnotus, Aglafon, Aristofon and the sculptors Polyklitos and Sosikles. The merchants of Thassos traded with Asia Minor, Egypt and Italy.

After the Battle of Plataea, Thassos became an ally of Athens, but when Athens attempted to curtail Thassos' trade with Egypt and Asia Minor, war broke out between the two. The islanders were defeated and forced into becoming part of the Delian League; the heavy tax this imposed crippled its economy. Decline set in and continued through Macedonian and Roman times. Heavy taxes were imposed by the Turks, many inhabitants left the island and during the 18th century the population dropped from 8000 to 2500.

Thassos revived in the 19th century when Mohammed Ali Pasha of Egypt became governor of Kavala and Thassos. Ali allowed the islanders to govern themselves and exempted them from paying taxes. The revival was, however, short-lived. The Egyptian governors who superseded Ali Pasha usurped the island's natural resources and imposed heavy taxes. In 1912, along with the other islands of the group, Thassos was united with Greece. Like Samothrace, Thassos was occupied by Bulgarians in WW II.

In recent years Thassos has once again struck 'gold'. This time it's 'black gold', in the form of off-shore oil which has been found in the sea around the island.

Getting To/From Thassos

Ferry There are ferries every hour between Kavala, on the mainland, and Skala Prinou (1½ hours, 400 dr). The 2 and 8.30 pm ferries continue to Limenas. Ferries direct to Limenas leave every 45 minutes (45 minutes, 480 dr) from Keramoti, 46 km southeast of Kavala.

Hydrofoil There are six hydrofoils every day bet- ween Limenas and Kavala (30 minutes, 1045 dr).

Getting Around Thassos

Bus Limenas is the transport hub of the island. There are many buses a day to Limenaria (via the west-coast villages) and to Golden Beach via Panagia and Potamia. There are five buses to Theologos and four to Aliki. Two or three buses a day journey in a clockwise direction all the way around the island. The cost to do a complete circuit of the island by bus is 1350 dr.

Excursion Boat The *Eros 2* excursion boat

does daily trips around the island, with stops for swimming and a barbecue. The boat leaves from the small Limenaki harbour at 9.30 am and returns at 5.30 pm. The price is 3500 dr.

Car, Motorbike & Bicycle Cars can be hired from Thassos Rent a Car (☎ 22 535 or 23 081) on the central square in Limenas. They also have offices in Skala Prinou (☎ 71 202) and Potamia (☎ 61 506). Motorbikes and mopeds can be hired from Billy's Bikes; and motorbikes, mopeds and bicycles from Babi's Bikes (☎ 22 129). Both of these outlets are on a side street between 28 Oktovriou and the central square, in Limenas.

LIMENAS Λημενάς

Limenas, on the north-east coast, is the main port and capital of the island. Confusingly, it is also called Thassos town and Limin. The island's other port is Skala Prinou on the west coast. Limenas is built on top of the ancient city, so ruins are scattered all over the place. It is also the island's transport hub with a reasonable bus service to the coastal resorts and villages.

Orientation & Information

The quay for both ferries and hydrofoils is in the centre of the waterfront. The central square is straight ahead from the waterfront. The main thoroughfare is 28 Oktovriou, which is parallel to the waterfront and north of the central square. Turn left onto 28 Oktovriou from the quay to reach the OTE on the right. Take the next turn right onto Theogenous and the second turn right to reach the post office which is on the left. Thassos' telephone code is 0593 and the postcode is 64004.

The National Bank of Greece is on the waterfront opposite the quay. The newsagent on Theogenous sells English-language newspapers. The bus station is on the waterfront; to reach it turn left from the quay. To reach the town's picturesque small harbour turn left from the quay and walk along the waterfront. The crowded town beach begins at the end of the western waterfront.

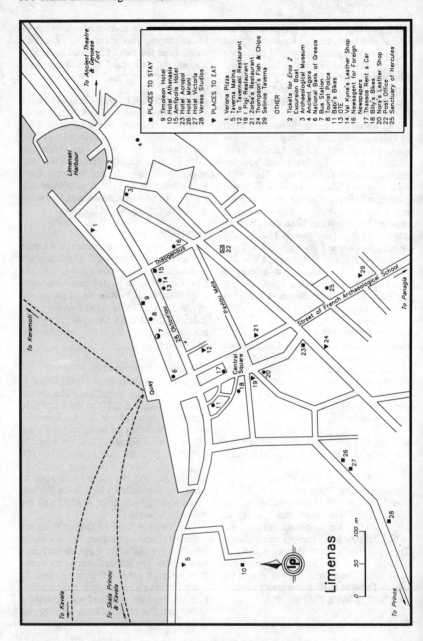

PLACES TO STAY
9 Timoleon Hotel
10 Hotel Athanasia
15 Akropolis Hotel
23 Hotel Akropol
26 Hotel Mironi
27 Hotel Victoria
28 Verssa Studios

PLACES TO EAT
1 Verona Pizza
5 Taverna Marina
19 Taverna Tavernaki Restaurant
21 I Pigi Restaurant
24 Zorba's Restaurant
24 Thompson's Fish & Chips
29 Selinos Taverna

OTHER
2 Tickets for Eros 2
3 Excursion Boat
4 Archaeological Museum
5 Ancient Agora
6 National Bank of Greece
7 Bus Station
8 Tourist Police
11 Babi's Bikes
13 OTE
14 Val Kyne's Leather Shop
16 Newsagent for Foreign
   Newspapers
17 Thassos Rent a Car
18 Billy's Bikes
20 Noa Leather Shop
22 Post Office
25 Sanctuary of Hercules

Limenas

There is no EOT on Thassos. The extremely helpful tourist police (☎ 22 500) are on the waterfront near the bus station. They will assist in finding accommodation.

Museum & Sites

Thassos' **Archaeological Museum** is next to the ancient agora at the small harbour. The most striking exhibit is a very elongated 6th-century kouros which stands in the foyer; it was found on the acropolis of the ancient city of Thassos. Other exhibits include pottery and terracotta figurines and a large well-preserved head of a very effeminate looking Dionysos. The ancient city of Thassos was excavated by the French School of Archaeology, so the museum's labelling is in French and Greek. The museum is open Tuesday to Sunday from 8.30 am to 3 pm. Admission is 400 dr.

The **ancient agora** next to the museum was the bustling market place of ancient and Roman Thassos – the centre of its civic, social and business life. It's a pleasant, verdant site with the foundations of two stoas, shops and dwellings. Entrance is free.

The **ancient theatre**, in a lovely wooded setting, has been fitted with wooden seats (now a bit dilapidated), and performances of ancient drama are staged here annually. See under Festival following this section for details. The theatre is signposted from the small harbour.

From the theatre a path leads up to the **Acropolis of Ancient Thassos** where there are substantial remains of a medieval fortress, built on the foundations of the ancient walls which encompassed the entire city. From the topmost point of the acropolis there are magnificent views. From the far side of the acropolis, steps carved into the rock (with a dodgy looking metal handrail), lead down to the foundations of the ancient wall, from where it's a short walk to the Limenas to Panagia road at the southern edge of town.

Festival

In July and August, performances of ancient drama are held at Limenas' ancient theatre, as part of the Kavala Festival of Drama.

Information and tickets can be obtained from the EOT in Kavala or the tourist police on Thassos.

Walk from Limenas to Panagia

This walk can be done in one go or as three separate walks. It begins at Limenas and ends at Panagia. If you do it in one go it will take four to five hours. It is a strenuous walk and you should only attempt it if you are fit. Along the way there are magnificent vistas of the coast and mountains. In summer begin the walk early in the morning or wait until after 4 pm, as for most of the way there is no shade. Take plenty of water with you as there is none to be had along the way.

Begin at the small harbour in Limenas. Follow the sign to the ancient theatre and take the first turn to the left which has a dead end road sign. Soon the road becomes a track which skirts the coast. After about half an hour you will come to a T-junction; the left turn leads down to a white house. Turn right, and a sudden turn in the path reveals fine views of mountains and a wooded valley. After another 15 to 20 minutes the path comes out onto an asphalt road with Disco Romantica on the left. If you wish you can end the walk here by turning right and then right again at the T-junction. This road will take you back to Limenas.

The next stretch of the walk is a hard slog of two hours along one of the island's fire breaks, and there is no shade along the way. At Disco Romantica turn left and almost immediately right onto a sand track (the fire break). From now on it's steadily uphill for about 1½ hours. After 50 minutes to one hour you will see a path going down to the left; ignore it (sorry!) and continue uphill. After another half-hour the path levels out and you will pass a tall red mast on your left. A few minutes further on you will see Panagia to your right; the path now descends and is shaded by trees. In another 15 minutes you will come to a crossroad; turn right here and walk straight ahead to another crossroad, turn right again and you will come out onto the Limenas to Panagia road. You can wait here for the bus to either Limenas or Panagia or continue the walk.

The last section of the walk is easy and takes about 50 minutes. Ascend the steps to the little white chapel opposite. Walk around the chapel and you will see a track; with your back to the chapel turn left on the track. After about 20 minutes you will come to a fork; take the left fork which leads downhill and soon you will be in the shade of abundant foliage. A couple of minutes further on, the road forks; take the left fork and in six or seven minutes you'll be in Panagia. If you have any energy left you can continue to Golden Beach for a swim.

Places to Stay – bottom end

The nearest camp site to Limenas is *Nysteri Camping*, just west of the town. With the exception of the camp site on Golden Beach all of Thassos' other camp sites are on the west and south-west coasts.

Limenas has many reasonably priced domatia. If you are not offered anything when you arrive then look for signs around the small harbour and the road to Prinos. Limenas' cheapest hotel is the E class *Hotel Athanasia* (☎ 22 545). The pleasant rooms cost 3000/4345/6000 dr for singles/doubles/triples with shared bathrooms. From the quay turn right and walk along the waterfront. Turn left after the Xenia Hotel, at the top of this road turn right and then first left and the hotel is on the right.

The *Hotel Acropol* (☎ 22 488), one block south of the central square, is a well-maintained turn of the century mansion, with a lovely garden. The beautifully furnished rooms cost 5000/6000 dr for singles/doubles with private bathrooms. The *Hotel Mironi* (☎ 23 256) is modern and spacious with lots of cool marble. Rates are 4500/6200/7400 dr for singles/doubles/triples with private bathrooms. From the ferry quay walk to 28 Oktovriou and turn right and then left on the road signposted to Prinos. The hotel is along here on the left.

Just beyond here the *Hotel Victoria* (☎ 22 556) is a lovely traditional place which is similarly priced. Further along this road

(opposite the large and expensive Arethria Hotel) you will find the *Verssa Studios*, where spotless single/double rooms cost 4000/5000 dr. Each room has a private bathroom, cooker, refrigerator and sink.

The B class *Timoleon Hotel* (☎ 22 177/179/163; fax 23 277) has clean spacious rooms with balconies. Rates are a reasonable 4500/9000 dr with private bathrooms; the price includes breakfast. The hotel is on the waterfront just beyond the bus station.

Places to Stay – middle

The A class *Amfipolis Hotel* (☎ 23 101/2/3/4), on the corner of 28 Oktovriou and Theogenous, is an attractive mock castle complete with turrets. Rates are 8900/11,500/14,300 dr including breakfast. The hotel has a swimming pool.

Places to Eat

Limenas has a good selection of restaurants serving well-prepared food. Perhaps the chefs could give their counterparts on Samothrace a few lessons. If you've been in Greece for some time, and particularly if you are English, you may like to have a meal at *Thompson's Fish & Chips*, owned by friendly Craig from Macclesfield, Cheshire. English breakfast is 900 dr, fish & chips are 800 dr and pork curry is 1000 dr. Walk inland from the central square, turn right after the Hotel Acropol, and the restaurant is on the left. *I Pigi Restaurant* (The Spring), on the central square, is a nice unpretentious restaurant which is (surprisingly) next to a spring. The food is good and the service friendly and attentive. Dishes include stifado for 800 dr, mussel saganaki for 850 dr and swordfish for 1380 dr.

To Tavernaki Restaurant is a delightful place with a stylish but simple décor. They have at least one vegetarian dish every day. If you want a blowout to set you up for the day try their buffet breakfast, which costs around 1200 dr. The taverna has bottled sparkling mineral water – a rarity in Greece. It is tucked away in a little side street off 28 Oktovriou – difficult to find but worth the effort.

of pizzas costing around 1500 dr. The restaurant is on the eastern waterfront near the small harbour.

Zorba's Restaurant, despite its tourist-trap name, is popular with Greeks and probably Thassos' best restaurant. It is owned by Ioannis Lousos who, according to a Dutch expat on Thassos, used to run one of the best Greek restaurants in Amsterdam. It's an elegant restaurant (it has oil lamps and a fresh flower on each table), with a variety of delicious meals. The tables are in a roofed-over garden on a side street off the main square.

Things to Buy

Limenas has two excellent leather shops, both of which sell high quality leather bags. They are *Nora's Leather Shop* on the central square and *Val Kyne's Leather Shop* on 28 Oktovriou. The latter also has a used book exchange (mostly English and German).

PANAGIA, POTAMIA & THE EAST COAST

The neighbouring hillside villages of Panagia (Παναγία) and Potamia (Ποταμιά) are quite touristy but picturesque. Both are four km west of **Golden Beach**. The Greek-American artist Polygnotos Vagis was born in Potamia in 1894 and some of his work can be seen in a small museum in the village. It is open daily from 9.30 am to 1 pm. The Municipal Museum in Kavala also has a collection of Vagis' work. The long and mostly sandy Golden Beach is the island's best beach and roads from both Panagia and Potamia lead down to it. These roads are very pleasant to walk along, but if you prefer, the bus from Limenas calls at both villages before going down to the southern end of the beach.

The next beach south is at the village of **Kinira**, and just south of here is the very pleasant **Paradise Beach**. The little islet just off the coast here is also called Kinira. **Aliki**, on the south-east coast, consists of two idyllic beaches back to back on a headland. There is a small ancient archaeological site near the beach and a marble quarry.

The speciality at *Selinos Restaurant* is delicious *htapodhike ftedhes* (octopus rissoles) costing 600 dr. According to the waiter the ability to pronounce this is a good indication of your competence in Greek. Other dishes include octopus in wine for 550 dr and mussel saganaki for 800 dr. Walk inland from the central square and the restaurant is a little way beyond the Sanctuary of Hercules. The taverna is only open in the evenings. *Taverna Marina*, on the western waterfront, serves delicious mussel saganaki and octopus saganaki which both cost 800 dr. A large choice of fish is also available, priced per kg according to season. The speciality at *Verona Pizza* is the tasty spaghetti Verona (850 dr). They also have a wide range

Places to Stay & Eat

Chryssi Ammoudia (☎ 61 207/472/3), on Golden Beach, is the only camp site on this side of the island.

In Panagia *Hotel Elvetia* (☎ 61 231) has pleasant single/double/triple rooms costing 3500/4000/4800 dr with shared bathrooms. With your back to the fountain in the central square of Panagia (where the bus stops), turn left and take the first main road to the left and the hotel is on the left. Just beyond here on the right the *Hotel Chrysafis* (☎ 61 451), which has doubles/triples for 6000/8000 dr with private bathrooms. The owners also have some well-equipped studios on Golden Beach for 6800 dr a double. There are domatia at both Kinira and Aliki.

There are reasonably priced restaurants in Panagia. *Restaurant Vigli*, overlooking the northern end of Golden Beach, has superb views and food to match. There are tavernas on the beach at Kinira and Aliki.

WEST COAST

The west coast consists of a series of seaside villages with Skala (by the sea) before their names. Roads lead from each of these to inland villages with the same name (minus the skala). Travelling north to the south the first village is **Skala Rachonis**. This is Thassos' latest development, having recently been discovered by the package-tour companies. However, it has an excellent camp site and the inland village of Rachoni remains unspoilt. Just before Rachoni there is a turn-off left to Moni Agiou Georgiou.

Skala Prinou, the next coastal village, and Thassos' second port, is crowded and unattractive. **Skala Sotirou** and **Skala Kallirachis** are more pleasant and both have small beaches. Kallirachi, two km inland from Skala Kallirachis, is a peaceful village of steep narrow streets and old stone houses. It has a large population of skinny anxious-looking cats and, judging by the the graffiti, a lot of communists.

Skala Marion is a delightful fishing village and one of the least touristy places around the coast. It was from here, earlier this century, that the German Speidel Metal Company exported ore from Thassos to Europe. There are beaches at both sides of the village, and between here and Limenaria there are stretches of uncrowded beach.

Limenaria (42 km from Limenas) is Thassos' second largest town and a very crowded resort with a narrow sandy beach. The town was built in 1903 by the German Speidel Metal Company who mined ore in the area. There are slightly less crowded beaches around the coast at **Pefkari** and **Potos**. From Potos a scenic 10 km road leads inland to **Theologos** which was the capital of the island in medieval and Turkish times. This is the island's most beautiful village and the only mountain settlement served by public transport. The village houses are of whitewashed stone with slate roofs; it's a serene place, unblemished by tourism.

Places to Stay

Camping Perseus (☎ 81 352), at Skala Rachonis, is an excellent camp site in a pretty setting of flowers, olives and willow trees. The cook at the site's taverna will prepare any Greek dish you wish if you make your order a day in advance. The next camp site along is *Camping Ioannidis* (☎ 71 377), between Skala Rachonis and Skala Prinou. It's another pleasant site with a minimarket, restaurant and bar. The EOT-owned *Camping Prinos* (☎ 71 171/270), at Skala Prinou, is well maintained but like most EOT sites is rather regimented. The next camp site, *Camping Deadalos* (☎ 71 365/766), is just north of Skala Sotirou. It also has a minimarket, restaurant and bar. The next two sites are south of Limenaria. They are *Pefkari Camping* (☎ 51 190/595), at Pefkari Beach and *Paradissos Camping* (☎ 51 950/906), at Potos Beach. All the sites charge around 650 dr per person and 500 dr per tent.

All of the seaside villages have hotels and domatia and the inland villages have rooms in private houses. For information about these enquire at kafeneia. The rooms of *Stelios Kontogeorgudis*, overlooking the harbour at Skala Marion, are clean and attractive and cost 3000/4000/5500 dr for singles/doubles/triples with shared bathrooms and kitchen.

Places to Eat

All of the coastal villages have tavernas. *Taverna Drossia*, in Rachoni, features live bouzouki on Friday and Saturday evenings. *Taverna Orizontes*, in Theologos, features rembetika nights. *Kostas Taverna*, on the main street in Theologos, has an outdoor terrace with wonderful views of the surrounding mountains.

Ionian Islands Τα Ιόνια Νησιά

The Ionian group consists of seven main islands: Corfu, Paxoi, Kefallonia, Zakynthos, Ithaki, Lefkada and Kythera. The last of these, although traditionally part of the group, is now administered from Piraeus and most easily reached from the southern Peloponnese and so is included in the Peloponnese chapter.

Strung along the west coast of Greece, the Ionian islands are the only group not in the Aegean. Their location has caused them to differ in many ways from the other groups and also to be less quintessentially Greek. In many ways they are more reminiscent of their close neighbour Italy, not least in their light, which is mellow compared with the harsh, dazzling light of the Aegean. The islands also have a much heavier rainfall than the Aegean islands, giving them luxuriant vegetation. They do not experience the meltemi wind, which sweeps the east coast of mainland Greece and the islands of the Aegean. This means the Ionian islands can become oppressively hot in summer.

Apart from tiny Meganisi (see Lefkada), none are 'undiscovered', although, as with all Greek islands, forays into their hinterlands will be rewarded with the delights of unspoilt villages.

History & Mythology

The origin of the name Ionian is obscure but is thought to derive from the goddess Io. Yet another one of Zeus' countless paramours, Io, whilst fleeing the wrath of a jealous Hera, happened to pass through the stretch of water which is now known as the Ionian Sea.

If we are to believe Homer, the islands were important during Mycenaean times; however, no magnificent palaces or even modest villages from that time have come to light. Perhaps archaeologists will never get to the bottom of the truth about the Ionian islands in those far-off times, for their ancient history lies buried beneath tonnes of

earthquake rubble. Seismic activity has been a constant feature of all Ionian islands.

According to Homer, Odysseus' kingdom consisted not only of Ithaca (Ithaki) but also encompassed Kefallonia, Zakynthos and Lefkada. However, the location of Ithaca has long been a subject of controversy amongst those who worry their heads about such things. The general consensus arrived at by classicists and archaeologists in the 19th century was that Homer's Ithaca was modern-day Ithaki, his Sami was modern-day Sami on Kefallonia, and his Zakynthos was modern-day Zakynthos, which all sounds credible enough. However, early this century German archaeologist Wilhelm Dorpfeld put a spanner in the works by adducing that Lefkada was ancient Ithaca, modern Ithaki was ancient Sami and Kefallonia was ancient Doulichion. His theories have now fallen out of favour with everyone, except of course the people of Lefkada.

By the 8th century BC the Ionian islands were in the clutches of mighty Corinth, who regarded them as a valuable asset, being stepping stones on the route to Sicily and Italy. A century later Corfu staged a successful revolt against Corinth, which was allied to Sparta, and became an ally of Sparta's archenemy, Athens. This alliance provoked Sparta into challenging Athens, thus precipitating the Peloponnesian Wars. The wars left Corfu depleted as they did all the participants and Corfu became nothing more than a staging post for whoever happened to be holding sway in Greece at the time.

By the end of the 3rd century, Corfu, along with the other Ionian islands, had become Roman. Following the decline of the Roman Empire, the islands saw the usual waves of invaders that Greece as a whole was subject to. After the fall of Constantinople, the islands became Venetian.

Corfu was never part of the Ottoman Empire. Paxoi, Kefallonia, Zakynthos and Ithaki were at various times occupied briefly by the Turks, but the Venetians held them for the longest. The exception was Lefkada, which was Turkish for 200 years. The other islands fared better under the Venetians than their counterparts in the Cyclades. Not only did they benefit culturally through contact with Italy, but the tradition of icon-painting was able to continue. In Turkish-occupied Greece, icon-painting was driven underground as Islamic law prohibited the portrayal of the human form.

Venice fell to Napoleon in 1797, and two years later in the Treaty of Campo Formio the Ionian islands were allotted to France. In 1799 Russian forces wrested the islands from Napoleon, but by 1807 they were back in his hands again. By then the all-powerful British couldn't resist meddling. As a result, in 1815, after Napoleon's downfall, the islands became a British protectorate, under the jurisdiction of a series of Lord High Commissioners, who by all accounts ranged from eccentric to downright nutty.

British rule was oppressive, but on a more positive note they constructed roads, schools and hospitals, established trade links and developed agriculture and industry. However the fervour of nationalism in the rest of Greece soon reached the Ionian islands.

The call for enosis (union with Greece) was realised in 1862 when Britain relinquished the islands to Greece. In WW II the Italians invaded Corfu as part of Mussolini's plan to resurrect the mighty Roman Empire. Italy surrendered to the Allies in September

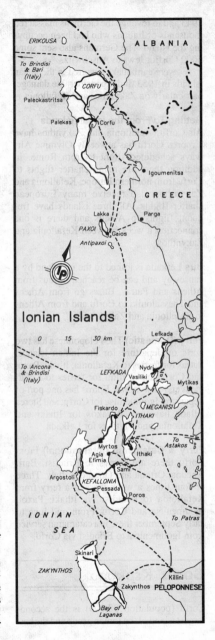

Ionian Islands

1943 and in revenge the Germans massacred thousands of Italians who had been occupying the island. The Germans also sent some 5000 Corfiot Jews to Auschwitz.

A severe earthquake occurred in the Ionian islands in 1953. It did considerable damage, particularly on Zakynthos and Kefallonia.

Getting To/From the Ionian Islands

Air Corfu, Kefallonia and Zakynthos have airports. Corfu has a weekly Olympic Airways scheduled flight to/from Rome. In addition there are many charter flights to Corfu from northern Europe. Kefallonia and Zakynthos also receive many European charter flights. All three islands have frequent flights to Athens and there is one connection a week between Kefallonia and Zakynthos.

Bus Lefkada is joined to the mainland by a causeway and can be reached by bus from Athens and Patras. Buses go from Athens and Thessaloniki to Corfu and from Athens to Kefallonia and Zakynthos.

Ferry (Domestic) The Peloponnese has two ports of departure for the Ionian islands: Patras for ferries to Kefallonia, Ithaki, Paxoi and Corfu; and Killini for ferries to Kefallonia and Zakynthos. Epiros has one port of departure: Igoumenitsa for Corfu; and Sterea Ellada has two: Astakos for Ithaki and Kefallonia; and Mytikas for Lefkada.

Ferry & Catamaran (International) From Corfu there are ferries to Brindisi, Bari, Ancona, Ortona and Otranto in Italy. Three or four times a week there is a ferry from Kefallonia to Brindisi via Ithaki, Paxoi, Igoumenitsa and Corfu. From mid-June to early September there is a catamaran service from Igoumenitsa to Brindisi via Corfu.

Corfu Κέρκυρα

Corfu (population 98,000) is the second-largest island of the Ionian group and the best

known. In Greek the island is called Kerkyra (KER-kee-ra). It was Homer's 'beautiful and rich land', and Odysseus' last stop on his journey home to Ithaca. Shakespeare reputedly used it as the background for *The Tempest* and in this century the Durrell brothers amongst others have extolled its virtues. With its beguiling landscape of vibrant wild flowers and slender cypress trees rising out of shimmering olive groves, Corfu is considered by many to be the most beautiful of all the Greek islands.

Getting To/From Corfu (Island)

Air Corfu has three flights a day to Athens (15,900 dr).

The Olympic Airways office (☎ 38 694/5/6) in Corfu town is at Kapodistriou 20.

Bus There is a daily bus to Athens (11 hours, 6050 dr) at 9 am, and a daily bus to Thessaloniki (5970 dr) at 6.30 am. Tickets must be bought in advance for these two buses.

Ferry (Domestic) From Corfu there are hourly ferries to Igoumenitsa (1½ hours, 620 dr). There is one ferry a day to Paxoi (three hours, 1630 dr). These ferries leave from the old port. For ferries to Ithaki, Kefallonia (Sami) and Patras see the following section.

The telephone number of Corfu's port police is ☎ 32 655.

Ferry (International) Corfu is on the Patras/Igoumenitsa to Italy (Brindisi, Bari, Ancona, Ortona and Otranto) ferry route. Some of the Ancona ferries go direct from Igoumenitsa, but all the others go via Corfu (10 hours; 3500 dr), where some lines allow a free stopover. There are around six ferries a day to Brindisi (9½ hours); at least one a day to Bari and Ancona; five a week to Otranto; and three a week to Ortona.

The Brindisi-bound ferries leave Corfu in the morning between 8.30 and 9.30 am. For prices of tickets see the Igoumenitsa Getting There & Away section in the Northern Greece chapter. These ferries leave from the new port. Agencies selling tickets are mostly on Xenofondos Stratigou, opposite this port. Shop around for the best deal.

You can take one of the frequent international ferries to Patras (10 hours, 3500 dr). One of these, the F/B *Ionis*, goes via Paxoi, Ithaki and Kefallonia (Sami) three or four times a week.

Catamaran (International) At the time of writing a daily catamaran service had commenced between Igoumenitsa and Brindisi via Corfu, from mid-June to early September. It will operate less frequently out of season. A one-way fare to Brindisi from Corfu is 10,000 dr in the low season and 14,500 dr in high season. Children under two travel free and between two and 12 travel at half-price. Return tickets attract a 15% reduction.

Getting Around Corfu (Island)
To/From the Airport There is no Olympic Airways shuttle bus between Corfu town and the airport. City bus Nos 5 or 6 from Plateia San Rocco stop on the main road 500 metres from the airport.

Bus Destinations of buses (green and cream) from Corfu town's long-distance bus station are:

Agios Stefanos (via Sidhari) – 1½ hours, five buses daily, 600 dr

Glyfada (via Vatos) – 45 minutes, four buses daily, 200 dr

Kassiopi (via Loutses) – one hour, four buses daily, 400 dr

Kavos (via Lefkimmi) – 1½ hours, eight buses daily, 600 dr

Messongi – 45 minutes, four buses daily, 280 dr

Paleokastritsa – 45 minutes, six buses daily, 280 dr

Pyrgi (via Ipsos) – 30 minutes, four buses daily, 200 dr

Roda (via Acharavi) – 1½ hours, four buses daily, 600 dr

Sinarades (via Agios Gordios) – 45 minutes, four buses daily, 280 dr

Numbers and destinations of buses (dark blue) from the bus station at Plateia San Rocco, Corfu town, are:

Achillion (via Gastouri) – Bus No 10, 20 minutes, six
 buses daily
Afra – Bus No 8, 30 minutes, eight buses daily
Agios Ioannis (via Pelekas) – Bus No 11, 30 minutes,
 nine buses daily
Kastellani (via Kourmades) – Bus No 5, 25 minutes,
 14 buses daily
Kontokali (via Gouvia & Dassia) – Bus No 7, 30
 minutes, hourly from 7 am to 10 pm
Perama (via Benitses) – Bus No 6, 30 minutes, 12
 buses daily
Potamos (via Evropouli & Tembloni) – Bus No 4, 45
 minutes, 12 buses daily

There is a flat fare of 125 dr on local buses.
Tickets can be bought on board.

Car & Motorbike Car-hire companies in
Corfu town include: Autorent (☎ 44 623/
4/5), Xenofondos Stratigou 34; Avis (☎ 24
042), Ethnikis Antistaseos 42; Budget (☎ 22
062), Donzelot 5; and Europcar (☎ 46 931/2/
3), Xenofondos Stratigou 32. There are
several motorbike-hire outlets on Xenofondos Stratigou.

CORFU TOWN

The capital of the island is Corfu town, built
on a promontory. The town is a harmonious
and gracious medley of the legacies of its
numerous occupiers. The Spianada (Espla-
nade) has a cricket pitch, a legacy of the
British. The Liston, a row of arcaded buildings flanking the north-western side of the
Spianada, was built during the French occupation and modelled on rue de Rivoli. The
buildings now function as up-market cafés.
Georgian mansions and Byzantine churches
complete the picture. However, it is the
Venetian influence which prevails, and no
more so than in the enchanting old town,
wedged between two fortresses. Narrow
alleyways of 18th-century shuttered tene-
ments in mellow ochres and pinks make it
more reminiscent of Venice or Naples than
Greece.

Orientation

The town is separated into a northern and
southern section. The old town is in the
northern section. The Palaion Frourion (Old

Fortress) lies to the east of the northern
section and projects out to sea, cut off from
the town by a moat. The Neo Frourion (New
Fortress) lies to the west. The Spianada, a
huge open area of green, with gardens and a
cricket pitch, separates the Old Fortress from
the town. The old town lies between the
Spianada and the New Fortress. The southern section is the new town.

The old port is north of the old town and
the new port is west of here. Between them
is the hulking New Fortress. The long-distance bus station is on Avrami, inland from
the new port and west of the Neo Frourion.
The bus station for local buses is on Plateia
San Rocco. Local buses serve the town and
nearby villages.

Information

Tourist Offices The EOT (☎ 37 520/638) is
in the former Palace of St Michael & St
George. The office may be moving in the
near future, but will keep the same telephone
number. The tourist police (☎ 30 265) are
next door to the EOT. Pick up a free copy of
the *Corfu News*, Corfu's English-language
newspaper, from the EOT.

Money The National Bank of Greece is in
the old town at the junction of Voulgareos
and G Theotoki. American Express is represented by Greek Skies Tours (☎ 32 469 or 30
883) at Kapodistriou 20a.

Post & Telecommunications The main
post office is on the right side of Alexandras
as you walk from Plateia San Rocco (the site
of the local bus station). It is open Monday
to Friday from 7.30 am to 8 pm; on Saturday
from 7.30 am to 2 pm; and on Sunday from
9 am to 1.30 pm. The postcode for Corfu
town is 49100.

The main OTE office is nearby at Mant-
zarou 9, and opens from 6 am to midnight
daily. The telephone code for Corfu town and
all villages on Corfu island except Paleokastritsa is 0661. Paleokastritsa's code is
0663.

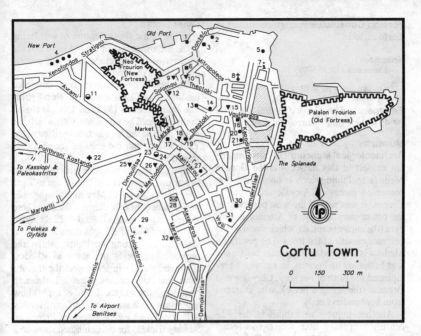

Corfu Town

0   150   300 m

■ **PLACES TO STAY**

3   Hotel Astron
6   Konstantinopoulis Hotel
13   Hotel Cyprus
16   Hotel Arcadian
17   Hotel Hermes
30   Corfu Palace

▼ **PLACES TO EAT**

9   Naftikon Restaurant
10   Restaurant Dionysos
12   Gistakis Restaurant
15   Taverna Krysi Kardia
18   Taverna O Rouvas
25   Taverna Stamatis
26   Restaurant Prokopis Kantas

OTHER

1   Departure Point for Igoumenista Boats
2   Budget Rent-a-Car
4   Agents for Boat Tickets to Italy
5   Palace of St Michael & St George
7   EOT
8   Church of Agios Spiridon
11   Long-Distance Bus Station
14   National Bank of Greece
19   Pallas Indoor Cinema
20   Greek Skies Tours
21   Olympic Airways Office
22   Hospital
23   Plateia San Rocco
24   Local Bus Station
27   OTE
28   Post Office
29   British Cemetery
31   Archaeological Museum
32   Outdoor Cinema

Foreign Consulates Foreign consulates in Corfu include:

Netherlands
   Idromenon 2 (☎ 39 900)
UK
   Menekratous 1 (☎ 30 055)

Emergency The Corfu General Hospital (☎ 45 811) is on Polithroni Kostanda.

Museums

Archaeological Museum The most important exhibit in this museum is the Gorgon Medusa sculpture which is one of the best preserved pieces of Archaic sculptures in Greece. It was part of the west pediment of the 6th-century Temple of Artemis at Corcyra (the ancient capital), which stood on the peninsula south of the town. The petrifying Medusa is depicted at the instant before she was beheaded by Perseus, an act which precipitated the birth of her sons, Chrysaor and Pegasus (the winged horse), who emerged from her headless body.

Another impressive exhibit is the 7th-century crouching lion, which was found near the Tomb of Menekrates. Archaeologists ascertained that the sculpture stood on top of the tomb. The museum (☎ 30 680) is on Odos Vraili. Opening times are Tuesday to Saturday from 8.45 am to 3 pm and Sunday from 9.30 am to 2.30 pm. Admission is 400 dr.

Museum of Asiatic Art This museum houses over 10,000 items, which were bequeathed by the Greek diplomats Gregoris Manos and Nicholas Hajivasiliou. It is an outstanding collection of Chinese and Japanese porcelain, bronzes, screens, sculptures, theatrical masks, armour, books and prints from Nepal, Tibet, India, Thailand, Korea and Japan. The museum (☎ 30 443), open Tuesday to Sunday from 8.45 am to 3 pm, is housed in a section of the splendid Palace of St Michael & St George, which was built in 1819 as the residence for the British Lord High Commissioner; the architect was Sir George Whitmore. Admission is 500 dr.

Other Sights

Apart from the sheer pleasure of wandering in the narrow streets of the old town and the gardens of the Spianada there are several other places of interest.

The two fortresses are the most dominant landmarks of Corfu town. The **Neo Frourion**, built between 1576 and 1588, is closed to the public. The promontory on which the Neo Frourion stands was first fortified in the 12th century, but the existing remains date from 1588.

You can walk around the ruins of **Palaion Frourion**, which is open from 8 am to 7 pm (free entry). From 15 May to 30 September performances of folk dances take place here in conjunction with a Sound & Light show. The Athens Sound & Light show is weak on dialogue but strong on lights, whilst the opposite applies to the show in Rhodes. However, the Corfu show gets the thumbs down on both counts. The folk dancing begins at 9 pm and the Sound & Light show at 9.30 pm. Both are in English from Monday to Friday, Greek on Saturday, and French on Sunday. Tickets for the combined show cost 500 dr (students 300 dr).

After a very short time in Corfu you will realise that a disproportionate number of males have the Christian name Spiros. This is because they are called after the island's miracle-working patron saint St Spyridon. His mummified body is contained in a silver, glass-fronted coffin in the 16th-century **Church of Agios Spyridon**. He's not a pretty sight but what can you expect of someone who's over 1000 years old? He is paraded around on Palm Sunday, Easter Sunday, 11 August and the first Sunday in November.

The well-kept **British cemetery** is as much a garden as a graveyard, and a beautiful one at that. The graves are those of soldiers (and civilians) who lost their lives during the British occupation and during WW II. It has a wonderful display of wild orchids indigenous to the island and fine trees including araucarias, cypresses, Californian sequoias and jacarandas. The cemetery is at the northern end of Kolokotroni.

Festival

The Corfu Festival, which has dance and music performances, is held in August and September.

Places to Stay – bottom end

Out of high season, domatia owners meet the ferries at both ports. I have to say that once or twice in Corfu I've gone along with a domatia owner only to find that what's on offer is diabolical, although this has not always been the case. I'm not advising against this time-honoured means of getting accommodation – it's often the most convenient way for budget travellers – and there are decent domatia in Corfu, but just bear in mind you may be taken to something resembling a prison cell. You don't have to take it, but if you're tired, desperate and/or broke you can always haggle for a lower price.

The nearest camp site to Corfu town is *Camping Kontokali Beach* (☎ 91 170/202), next to the youth hostel. Take bus No 7 from Plateia San Rocco bus station.

Corfu's *YHA Hostel* (☎ 91 292) is at Kontokali Beach, next to the camp site. The large E class *Konstantinopoulis Hotel* (☎ 39 326) stands in dilapidated elegance overlooking the old port. Although it's gloomy, it is clean and well maintained, and offers singles/doubles/triples for 2700/4800/6400 dr with shared bathrooms.

The D class *Hotel Cyprus* (☎ 30 032 or 40 675), Agios Paterou 13, is a super place with spotless rooms full of character. Rates are 5500/6000 dr for doubles/triples with shared bathrooms. To reach it go up Agios Paterou, which is opposite the western end of Voulgareos, turn left at the top of the short, steep hill and you'll see the hotel.

Another pleasant option for budget travellers is the D class *Hotel Europa* (☎ 39 304), at the new port. The clean and prettily furnished singles/doubles are a bargain at 2000/4000 dr with shared bathrooms; doubles with private bathrooms are 5000 dr. To reach the hotel walk to the customs at the new port, and take Odos Venizelou which forks left; a little way along here you will see a sign pointing to the hotel.

The C class *Hotel Arcadian* (☎ 37 6670/1/2), Kapodistriou 44, has small but comfortable rooms for 5000/9000 dr with private bathrooms. Another good value, comfortable C class is the *Hotel Ionian* (☎ 30 628), with singles/doubles for 6000/8000 dr. The hotel is on Xenofondos Stratigou, opposite the new port.

Places to Stay – middle

The C class *Hotel Hermes* (☎ 39 560; fax 58 403), G Markara 14, is in a nice location near the food market and convenient for the old town. The cream, green-shuttered building admittedly looks better from the outside than in, but despite the clashing floral wallpaper and brick-patterned linoleum of the rooms it's not bad value at 6100/7200/8900 dr with private bathrooms; breakfast included.

The *Hotel Atlantis* (☎ 35 560/1/2/3) has pleasant singles/doubles/triples for 7200/8700/10,400 dr. The hotel is on Xenofondos Stratigou, near the Hotel Ionian.

The B class *Hotel Astron* (☎ 39 505/986), Donzelot 15, has a faded neoclassical ambience. Rates are 11,000/14,600/18,200 dr, with breakfast.

Places to Stay – top end

The deluxe *Corfu Palace* (☎ 39 485/6/7; fax 31 749) on Demokratias, is the only deluxe hotel in the town centre. It was built in 1952 but has been renovated several times. It has two bars, two restaurants and two swimming pools. All rooms have air-con and rates are 29,000/38,200 dr for singles/doubles.

The deluxe *Corfu Hilton* (☎ 36 540/1/2/3/4; fax 36 551 or 55 933; telex 33 2148 is at Kanoni, four km from Corfu town. There are two restaurants, two bars and a health club. In the extensive grounds are two pools, tennis courts and a jogging track. Rates are 29,000/35,000.

Places to Eat

Gistakis Restaurant, Solomon 20, is an unpretentious place which serves delicious food. Main meals cost around 900 dr. *Naftikon Restaurant*, 152 N Theotoki, is another good value place with similar prices.

Restaurant Dionysos, on Odos Dona, is also commendable, with main courses from 850 to 1000 dr. These three restaurants are close to one another just back from the old port. *Taverna Kryssi Kardia*, Sevastianou 44, also serves reasonably priced traditional Greek fare. Sevastianou is a narrow street off Voulgareos.

Taverna Stamatis, on Dimoulitsa, is another cheapy, which is popular with locals. Prices start at 550 dr. *Restaurant Prokopis Kantas*, M Methodiou 4, panders a little more to tourists but the food is good. Greek salad is 650 dr and veal with potatoes is 850 dr. *Taverna O Rouvas*, Stamatiou 13, is also good value. These three restaurants are near Plateia San Rocco.

Entertainment

Corfu town has one outdoor cinema; it's halfway down Marasli, on the right as you walk towards the sea. A good indoor cinema is the *Pallas*, just north of Plateia San Rocco. There are lots of bars in the old town but discos (hundreds of them) are at the tourist ghettos. The nearest ones to town are along the coast to the north. Don't forget the Sound & Light show at the Palaion Frourion.

AROUND THE ISLAND
North of Corfu Town

Most of the coast of northern Corfu is 'package-tourist' saturated, and has been thoroughly de-Greeked. There are three camp sites along the north-east coast: *Karda Beach* (☎ 93 595) at Dassia; *Kerkira Camping* (☎ 93 246) at Ipsos; and *Paradise Camping* (☎ 93 558).

At **Pyrgi**, 16 km north of Corfu town, a road continues to skirt the coast around the base of the mighty **Mt Pantokrator** (906 metres), the island's highest peak. At this point, where the island protrudes as if to accommodate the mountain, the 2000-metre-high mountains of Albania are less than two km away. It was in this region that Lawrence and Gerald Durrell spent their idyllic childhood. Back at Pyrgi, another road snakes inland over the western flank of the mountain to the north coast. Along this road a detour can be made to the picturesque village of **Strinila**. A road from here leads through a stark landscape to the summit of Mt Pantokrator, from where there are stupendous views. A monastery and radio mast stand on the summit. The coast road continues to the large resort of Kassiopi, 36 km from Corfu town, above which stands a ruined fortress.

The **Church of Our Lady of Kassiopi** stands on what may have been the site of the Roman Temple of Jupiter, where that showoff the Emperor Nero is supposed to have sung while accompanying himself on the lyre. Beyond Kassiopi there is a turn-off for the remote and half-derelict but delightful village of **Perithia**, high up on Mt Panokrator. Several of the Corfu town-Kassiopi buses continue to Perithia. The coast road continues west passing through the resort of **Roda**, where there is a camp site, *Roda Beach* (☎ 93 120 or 34 761), and on to Sidhari. The resorts along this stretch are now almost as developed as the Corfu town-Pyrgi strip.

South of Corfu Town

The Kanoni peninsula, four km from Corfu town, was the site of the ancient capital, but there is little evidence of this. Its greatest attractions are its two pretty islets. On one stands the **Moni Vlachernas**, which is reached by a causeway. On the other one, known as **Mouse Island**, there is a 13th-century church. Caïques ply back and forth to this islet.

The **Achillion**, near the hillside village of Gastouri, eight km from Corfu town, was built in the 1890s as the summer palace of Empress Elisabeth of Austria. This strange lady perhaps inherited some of the same genes as her unfortunate cousin the 'mad monarch' Ludwig II (King Otho of Greece was her uncle), for she had an Achilles fixation and dedicated the villa to him. The beautifully landscaped garden is watched over by kitsch statues of the empress' other mythological heroes.

The palace is an astonishing farrago of the most excessive elements of styles fashionable in the late 19th century; a few of the rooms are open to the public. After the empress' assassination the palace was bought by Kaiser Wilhelm II. The whole place is bizarre but definitely worth a visit. It is open Monday to Sunday from 8 am to 7 pm. Admission is 400 dr. In the evenings the Achillion functions as a casino (for foreigners only, so take your passport along).

If you thought the development north of Corfu was bad then that of the once tranquil fishing village of **Benitses** will break your heart. This is the playground of the holiday hooligans (ie British lager louts). If you can fight your way through this lot there are the ruins of a 3rd-century AD Roman villa to be seen, just a little way inland. There is also a delightful 30-minute walk to an old waterworks, built during the time of the British protectorate. **Messongi**, 20 km south of Corfu town, is just marginally quieter. The town was founded by Cretan refugees fleeing the Turks. The sea here is shallow for a long way out making it ideal for children.

South of here the development dies down considerably and quiet stretches of good beach can be found.

Western Corfu

Paleokastritsa, 26 km west of Corfu, is the largest resort on the west coast. It has an incredibly beautiful setting built around several sand and pebble coves and a background of mountains draped in greenery. Once upon a time this place must have been like paradise. However, like all of Corfu's beauty spots it has been the victim of rampant development. **Moni Theotokou** perches on the rocky promontory at Paleokastritsa, above the shimmering turquoise sea. The monastery was founded in the 13th century but the present building dates from the 18th century. There is a small **museum** with some 17th-century icons. The monastery is open from 7 am to 1 pm and 3 to 8 pm. Admission is free but a donation is expected.

Paleokastritsa Camping (☎ 0663-41 204) is on the main approach road to the resort; the bus will drop you at the entrance. The resort also has a large number of hotels and domatia.

The mountain villages above Paleokastritsa are worth exploring. **Lakones**, five km inland from Paleokastritsa, is a relatively unspoilt mountain village. From here the Makrades road leads to **Krini**, another delightful village from where you can visit the ruins of the 13th-century Byzantine fortress of **Angelokastro**, where the inhabitants of Paleokastritsa took refuge from attackers. There are superb vistas from the ruins. Relying on public transport, a 'village' bus goes twice a day to Krini from the long-distance bus station in Corfu town.

Glyfada, on the west coast almost opposite Corfu town, has a good sandy beach, so, inevitably, is another place crowded out with package tourists.

Hilltop **Pelekas**, four km away, is no less busy, but more laid back and popular with young, independent travellers. Tourists come in droves to watch the sunset here, supposedly the best place on Corfu to do so. A track leads from the village to a good sandy beach where there is freelance camping. The village has heaps of domatia or there's the well-run *Hotel Nikos* (☎ 94 486) where singles/doubles/triples are 2500/4500/5500 dr with private bathrooms. The hotel is on the main road 200 metres before the village. **Myrtiotissa** is an unofficial nudist beach, north of Glyfada. Take a Glyfada bus and ask to be dropped off at the track which leads down to this beach.

The nearest official camp site in the area is *Vatos Camping* (☎ 94 393) near the village of Vatos.

Paxoi Παξοί

Low-lying, olive-tree-covered Paxoi (population 2600), just 10 km long and four km wide, is the smallest of the main Ionian islands. Olives are the main source of income and tiny Paxoi vies with mighty Lesbos for producing Greece's best olive oil. It's a

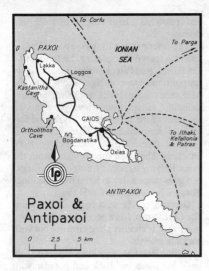

Paxoi & Antipaxoi

0   2.5   5 km

menitsa and Corfu. The telephone number of Paxoi's port police is ☎ 31 259.

Getting Around Paxoi
The island's one bus plies between Gaios and Lakka via Loggos four or five times a day.

GAIOS Γάιος
Gaios, skirting a wide bay on the east coast, is the capital and largest settlement. It's an attractive little place of crumbling 19th-century red-tiled pink, cream and white-washed buildings. Agios Nikolaos islet (also called Kastro), with a 15th-century Venetian fortress and a ruined windmill, almost fills its harbour. The islet at the entrance to the bay is Moni Panagias, named after its monastery. Here, on 15 August there is a very lively **festival** which lasts all day and ends with dancing on the central square in Gaios.

Information
The post office and OTE are near the central square. Paxoi's postcode is 49082 and the telephone code is 0622. There is no tourist office. The tourist police (☎ 31 222) are just back from the waterfront.

Places to Stay & Eat
In high season almost all the accommodation is taken up by package tourists. The tourist police may be able to help you find somewhere or there are several travel agents which advertise room-finding services. You could try: Gaios Travel (☎ 31 823/151; fax 31 975); Paxoi Holiday Agency (☎ 31 269; fax 31 122); or Paxos Sun (☎ 31 201/035; fax 31 010).

For a splurge there's the B class *Paxos Beach* (☎ 31 211/333; fax 31 166), a bungalow complex two km east of Gaios. Doubles cost 12,000 dr (half board). For a good choice of tasty traditional Greek dishes at reasonable prices, try *Taka Taka*.

AROUND THE ISLAND
The west coast of Paxoi has awesome vistas of precipitous cliffs. In the cliffs are several grottos, only accessible by boat. The gentler east coast is speckled with small pebbled

pretty island, although no longer an unspoilt idyll. It was ferreted out long ago by the UK-based Greek Islands Sailing Club who have a windsurfing and sailing centre in Lakka. If you think it's a case of 'if you can't beat them join them' then see the Yacht section in the Getting Around chapter for their UK address.

In addition package tourism has hit Paxoi. Admittedly, it's the small discerning companies who send their clients to Paxoi, but when joined by the day-trippers from Corfu and mainland Parga the island gets pretty crowded.

There are three main settlements: Gaios, Lakka and Loggos, all on the coast, and a number of inland hamlets. For tranquillity drag yourself away from the beaches (which are not that great anyway) and stroll in the centuries-old olive groves of the interior.

Getting To/From Paxoi
There is at least one regular ferry a day between Paxoi and Corfu (three hours, 1630 dr). There are also daily excursion boats from Corfu, and from Parga on the mainland. The F/B *Ionis* goes three or four times a week from Paxoi to Brindisi in Italy via Igou-

beaches, shaded by the ubiquitous olive trees.

Loggos, 10 km north of Gaios on the east coast, is a little fishing village-cum-resort with several pebbled beaches nearby. There are tavernas and accommodation; however, once again the tour companies have the monopoly.

Lakka is in a lovely setting at the end of a deep, narrow bay on the north coast. The place is a favourite location of the Greek Islands Sailing Club who fill the bay with their brightly coloured sailing boats and windsurfers. If you would like to stay in Lakka get in touch with Planos Travel Office (☎ 31 108/821/010; fax 31 010).

The islet of **Mogonissi**, joined by a causeway to the southern tip of Paxoi, has a small sand beach and a taverna.

The diminutive island of **Antipaxoi**, two km south of Paxoi, is covered with grapevines from which a notable wine is produced. The beaches of Antipaxoi are superb. Best of all is the pale sand beach at Voutoumi on the east coast. There is no accommodation on the island, but there are a few tavernas which cater to tourists.

In summer small boats ply frequently between Gaios and Antipaxoi.

Lefkada Λευκάδα

Lefkada (Lef-KAD-ha, population 22,000), between Corfu and Kefallonia, is the fourth-largest of the Ionian group of islands. It was joined to the mainland by a narrow isthmus until the occupying Corinthians dug a canal in the 8th century BC. Nowadays, the 25-metre strait separating it from the mainland is spanned by a causeway. Lefkada has 10 satellite islets: Meganisi, Kastos, Kalamos, Sparti, Madouri, Skorpidi, Skorpios, Thilia, Petalou and Kythros. Lefkada is a mountainous island with a couple of peaks reaching just over 1000 metres, but it is also fertile, being well watered by underground streams. There are cotton fields, acres and acres of dense olive groves, vineyards and fir and pine forests.

An **International Festival of Literature & Art** takes place on the island during the last two weeks in August.

Getting To/From Lefkada (Island)

Air There is no airport on Lefkada, but Preveza airport, on the mainland, is only a 30-minute bus journey away. The airport is two km from Aktion, on the opposite side of the Gulf of Amvrakikos to Preveza. There are daily flights to Athens (9600 dr) in summer. Preveza's Olympic Airways office (☎ 0682-28 674) is at Spiliadou 5.

Bus From Lefkada town there are four buses a day to Patras (2150 dr), Athens (5½ hours, 4100 dr) and Aktion (30 minutes, 250 dr), for Preveza airport and the ferry to the town of Preveza.

Ferry From Vasiliki there are at least two ferries a day to Sami on Kefallonia via Fiskardo (and Ithaki town, in the high season). One ferry a day goes from Nydri to Zakynthos town (high season only) via the islet of Meganisi and Fiskardo on Kefallonia and another ferry goes once a day to Frikes on Ithaki. Ferries also ply between Mytikas, on the mainland, and Nydri, during the high season.

The telephone number of Lefkada's port police is ☎ 22 322.

Getting Around Lefkada (Island)

Bus From Lefkada town there are frequent buses to Karia and Vliho via Nydri; four a day to Vasiliki; and two a day to Poros.

Car & Motorbike Cars can be hired from Europcar (☎ 25 726), Stratigou Mela 7, amongst others. One of several motorbike-hire outlets is Motorbike Rental Santas (☎ 22 371), on Odos Aristotelous Valaoriti. Walk to the top of Dorpfeld from the waterfront, and turn right.

LEFKADA TOWN

Lefkada town, just over the causeway, is the

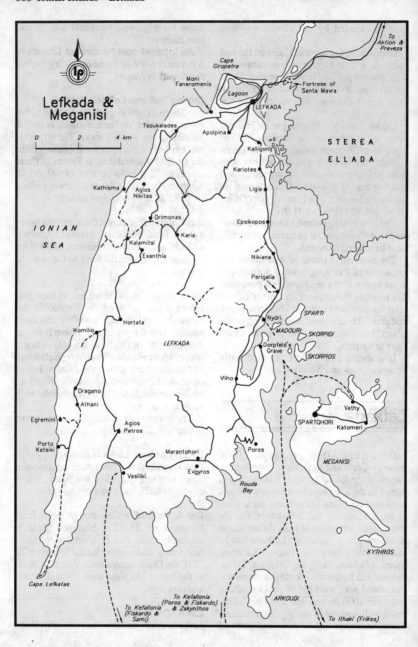

Lefkada & Meganisi

0   2   4 km

To Aktion &
Preveza

Cape
Giropetra

Moni
Faneromenis

Lagoon

Fortress of
Santa Mavra

LEFKADA

Tsoukalades

Apolpina

Kalligoni

STEREA
ELLADA

Kariotes

Kathisma

Agios
Nikitas

Ligia

IONIAN
SEA

Drimonas

Epsikopos

Karia

Kalamitsi

Nikiana

Exanthia

Perigalia

SPARTI

Nydri

MADOURI   SKORPIDI

Hortata

Komilio

LEFKADA

Dorpfeld's
Grave

SKORPIOS

Dragano

Vliho

Athani

Vathy

Egremini

Agios
Petros

SPARTOHORI   Katomeri

Porto
Katsiki

Marantohori

Poros

MEGANISI

Evgyros

Vasiliki

Rouda
Bay

KYTHROS

Cape Lefkatas

To Kefallonia
(Poros & Fiskardo)
& Zakynthos

To Kefallonia
(Fiskardo &
Sami)

To Ithaki (Frikes)

ARKOUDI

Top: Lalaria Beach, Skiathos, Sporades Islands (DH)
Left: Windsurfer, Skiathos, Sporades Islands (DH)
Right: View from old town, Alonissos, Sporades Islands (DH)

Top: View of Poros, Saronic Gulf Islands (GA)
Bottom: View of Spetses, Saronic Gulf Islands (GA)

island's capital and port. It is built on the edge of a salty lagoon which is used as a fish hatchery – it can give off quite a pong in hot weather. The town was devastated by earthquakes in 1867 and 1948, although damage in the 1953 earthquake was minimal. After 1948, many of the houses were rebuilt in a unique style, with upper floors of painted sheet metal or corrugated iron that is strangely attractive in a temporary looking, ramshackle sort of way. They are built like this in the hope they will withstand future earthquakes. The belfries of the churches are constructed from metal girders and look like miniature Eiffel Towers – another earthquake precaution.

Orientation

If you arrive by bus you will probably be dropped off somewhere along the waterfront, or the bus may continue straight on to the bus station. Whatever, walk back to the beginning of the causeway road and turn left at the Nirikos Hotel, onto Odos Dorpfeld. This is the town's animated main thoroughfare, flanked by narrow side streets. In case you hadn't guessed, this street is named after the 19th-century archaeologist Wilhelm Dorpfeld, who, naturally, is held in high esteem here for postulating that Lefkada, not Ithaki, was the home of Odysseus.

Information

There is no tourist office on Lefkada. The tourist police (☎ 22 346) can be found on the right side of Stratigou Mela, on the corner of Mitropolis.

Walking up Dorpfeld you will come to the central square of Plateia Ethnikis Antistasis on the left. After this square the main thoroughfare continues straight ahead, but changes its name to Stratigou Mela. The National Bank of Greece and the post office are up here on the left. To reach the OTE take the second turn right after the bank, onto Odos Mitropolis. At the fork veer right onto Zambelou and you'll come to the OTE on the left. Lefkada's postcode is 31100 and the telephone code is 0645.

Things to See

Lefkada has a **Phonographic Museum** which was temporarily closed when I was there. A notice outside states it has a collection of items from days gone by, which presumably includes gramophones. Walk up Dorpfeld from the waterfront and take the second turn left after the central square to reach the museum.

The 14th-century Venetian **Fortress of Santa Mavra** is just across the bridge on the mainland. **Moni Fanerominis**, three km west of town, was founded in 1634, but destroyed by fire in 1886, and rebuilt. The monastery is no longer inhabited but it's worth a stroll up here for the views, which encompass the lagoon, causeway and town.

The nearest beaches to town are at the northern side of the lagoon, about a two-km walk away.

Places to Stay – bottom end

The nearest camp site to Lefkada town is *Episkopos Beach Camping* (☎ 23 043, 92 410 or 71 388), halfway to Nydri. See the Around the Island section for Lefkada's other camp sites.

The D class *Hotel Byzantio* (☎ 22 629), Dorpfeld 4, is the best choice for budget travellers. The immaculate rooms have wood-beamed ceilings and nice pine furniture. Rates are 3000/4500/5500 dr with shared bathrooms and 3500/5500/6500 dr with private bathrooms. The hotel is just around the corner from the waterfront, on the right side of Dorpfeld.

Another pleasant budget option is *Hotel Patras* (☎ 22 359), on the central square, where tidy singles/doubles are 3400/5600 dr with shared bathrooms.

The C class *Hotel Santa Maura* (☎ 22 342) has very pleasant singles/doubles for 6000/9000 dr. The hotel is on the left side of Dorpfeld, a bit beyond the Hotel Byzantio.

Places to Stay – middle

The plush B class *Hotel Niricos* (☎ 24 132/3), on the corner of the waterfront and Dorpfeld, has singles/doubles/triples for 9200/12,700/17,650 dr (half board). Close by, the positively palatial B class *Hotel Lefkas* (☎ 23 916/7/8), Panagou 2, has rates of 9500/12,700/15,500 dr with breakfast.

Places to Eat
Taverna I Kato Vrisi on the left side of Dorpfeld, opposite the fountain, serves flavoursome traditional Greek fare. Moussaka, pistatsio and chicken are all 700 dr. *Taverna O Recantos* also serves tasty food; main dishes start at around 900 dr. To reach the taverna walk up Dorpfeld, turn right opposite the central square, and it's 60 metres along on the left.

AROUND THE ISLAND
The road south from Lefkada town skirts the coast and in 16 km reaches **Nydri**, the island's biggest resort. Nydri is busy and commercialised, but you may like to take a boat trip around the islets of **Madouri**, **Sparti**, **Skorpidi** and **Skorpios**, which lie a short distance from the shore.

The poet Aristotelous Valaoritis (1824-1879) was born on Lefkada and left to study in France and Italy. He returned to Greece in 1848 and spent the last 10 years of his life on Madouri islet where his villa still stands. The islet is owned by the Valaoritis family and is off limits to visitors. Likewise with Skorpios, which is owned by what's left of the star-crossed Onassis family. Aristotle Onassis' son, and daughter Christina are buried here. It is possible to take trips around the islets for 2500 dr.

The much larger islet of **Meganisi** can also be reached by a daily ferry from Nydri. Meganisi is a delightful island and certainly the least visited of all the inhabited Ionian islands. There are two ports: Vathy and Spartohori. The little capital of Spartohori is one km inland from its port. From here a road leads to the village of Katomeri and continues to Vathy. The island has domatia and tavernas.

Back on Lefkada, the village of **Vliho** is three km south of Nydri, and much quieter. Beyond here a road turns left onto a peninsula, which is the site of the grave of Wilhelm

Dorpfeld. Also here are the Bronze Age ruins which he excavated and which led him to believe that Lefkada was Homer's Ithaca. The pleasant, well-shaded *Desimi Beach* (☎ 95 225/374) camp site is at the southern base of the peninsula.

The main road continues south and then west to Vasiliki. A detour can be made to the village of **Poros** and a pebble beach at **Rouda Bay**. There is another camp site here, *Poros Beach Camping* (☎ 95 452 or 23 303). **Vasiliki**, also with a pebble beach, was once a pretty fishing village, but may soon overtake Nydri as the island's premier resort. It's purported to be one of, if not *the* best place in Europe for windsurfing. The balmy morning breeze is ideal for beginners but the afternoon blast is strictly for virtuoso performances. Unless you're a windsurfing buff you may find Vasiliki too commercial.

A rough but drivable road goes all the way down the island's south-west promontory to **Cape Lefkatas**, where a Sanctuary to Apollo once stood. It was from this cape that Sappho supposedly leapt, distraught over her unrequited love for Phaon. This seems to have set a precedent for further weird goings on. These included more suicides, and the hurling of criminals off the cliff with live birds fastened to them; an act which seems to have been a combination of punishment, religious ritual and an experiment in aerodynamics.

Lefkada's best beaches are on the west coast of this promontory. **Egremini** and **Porto Katsiki** are both gorgeous stretches of fine sand. They are signposted from the road.

Kefallonia Κεφαλλονιά

Kefallonia (population 28,000) is the largest of the Ionian islands. It's an island of rugged, towering mountains, and although it has forests it lacks the sub-tropical lushness of Corfu. It receives a fair number of package tourists, although nothing like on the scale of Corfu or Zakynthos. Like the latter it also receives loggerhead turtles, who lay their

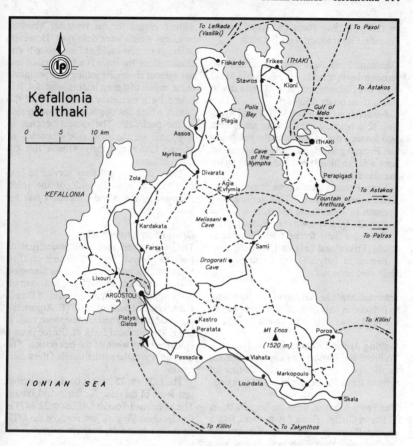

Kefallonia & Ithaki

eggs on the sandy beaches along the south coast. So far the number of turtles coming ashore each year has remained stable, unlike on Zakynthos. (See the Zakynthos section later in this chapter for details.) To ensure this continues, a Marine Turtle Project is currently monitoring the turtles. If you would like more details on this project write to Marine Turtle Project, Care for the Wild, 1 Ashfolds, Horsham Rd, Rusper, West Sussex RH12 4QX.

The capital of Kefallonia is Argostoli, but the main port is Sami. As Kefallonia is so big and mountainous, getting from one resort or town to another takes a long time; bear this in mind when planning your itinerary.

Getting To/From Kefallonia
Air There are daily flights from Kefallonia to Athens (11,600 dr) and one flight a week to Zakynthos (3,300 dr). The Olympic Airways office (☎ 28 808/881) in Argostoli is at Rokou Vergoti 1.

Ferry Kefallonia has six ports (the telephone numbers of the port police are given in brackets): Sami (☎ 0674-22 031), Argostoli

(☎ 0671-22 224), Poros (☎ 0674-72 460), Pessada, Fiskardo and Agia Evfymia.

Domestic From Sami there are at least two ferries a day to Vasiliki on Lefkada via Ithaki town and Fiskardo; and at least one a day to Patras (four hours, 1500 dr).

From Poros (1½ hours, 925 dr) and Argostoli (2¾ hours, 1780 dr) there are at least two ferries a day to Killini in the Peloponnese. From Agia Evfymia there is at least one ferry a day to Ithaki town and Astakos on the mainland.

From Pessada there is one ferry a day to Skinari on Zakynthos. This service only operates in high season and there is no bus to Pessada from elsewhere on Zakynthos.

There are daily ferries from Fiskardo to Ithaki (Frikes) and Lefkada (Nydri).

Ferries to Italy sail via Corfu; see the following section.

International The F/B *Ionis* goes from Sami to Brindisi in Italy three or four times a week via Ithaki, Paxoi, Igoumenitsa and Corfu.

Getting Around Kefallonia
To/From the Airport The airport is nine km to the south of Argostoli. At the time of writing there was no airport shuttle service.

Bus From Argostoli there are frequent buses to Platys Gialios, five a day to Sami, four a day to Poros (via Peratata, Vlahata and Markopoulo), three a day to Skala and two a day to Fiskardo.

Car & Motorbike Car and motorbike-rental firms are almost all on Rokou Vergoti, and Valianou, which is close to the central square in Argostoli.

Ferry Frequent ferries do the 30-minute trip to Lixouri. Tickets cost 190 dr and are bought on board. There are daily ferries to Sami from Fiskardo.

ARGOSTOLI Αργοστόλι
Argostoli was devastated by the 1953 earthquake and unlike Zakynthos it was rebuilt without regard for the beautiful Venetian buildings which were destroyed. However, although its new buildings are modern and characterless, the town is a lively place and not without charm. Its setting on a peninsula at the mouth of a deep inlet is beautiful. It is joined by a causeway to the bulk of the island, which lies opposite the eastern side of the peninsula. The closest beaches to Argostoli are the twin sandy beaches of Makrys Gialos and Platys Gialos, five km south of town.

There is a frequent ferry service to Lixouri, at the opposite side of the inlet. Argostoli is the island's transport hub for buses.

Orientation & Information
The bus station is on the waterfront of Ioannou Metaxa. The post office is on Diad Konstantinou and the OTE is on Georgiou Vergoti, one block inland from, and north of, the post office. The central square of Plateia Kentriki is just north of the OTE. Argostoli's postcode is 28100 and the telephone code is 0671. The National Bank of Greece is on a side street just south of the bus station. The ferry quay is at the northern end of the waterfront.

The EOT (☎ 22 248) is on the waterfront just south of the quay for ferries to Lixouri. The Municipal Tourist Office (☎ 22 847) is on Georgiou Vergoti, just north of the OTE on the opposite side. Both are helpful.

Museums
The **Archaeological Museum** (☎ 28 300) has a small collection from around the island. The most impressive exhibits are Mycenaean, and were found in tombs. To reach the museum walk up Rokou Vergoti from the waterfront. Opening times are Tuesday to Sunday from 8.30 am to 3 pm. Admission is 400 dr.

The **Historical & Cultural Museum** (☎ 28 221), further up Rokou Vergoti, has an interesting collection of traditional costumes, furniture and tools, items which belonged to the British occupiers, and photographs of pre-earthquake-devastated

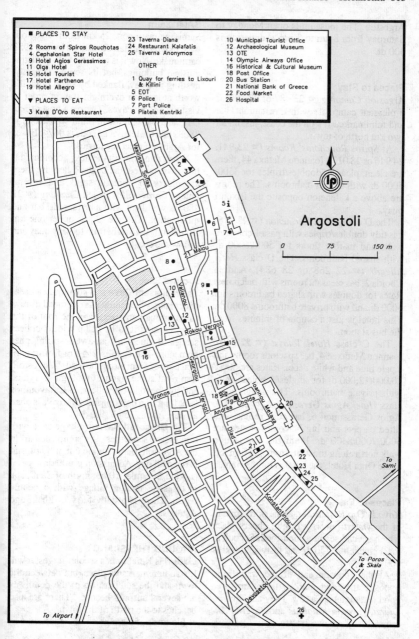

■ PLACES TO STAY
2 Rooms of Spiros Rouchotas
4 Cephalonian Star Hotel
9 Hotel Agios Gerassimos
11 Olga Hotel
15 Hotel Tourist
17 Hotel Parthenon
19 Hotel Allegro

▼ PLACES TO EAT
3 Kava D'Oro Restaurant

23 Taverna Diana
24 Restaurant Kalafatis
25 Taverna Anonymos

OTHER

1 Quay for ferries to Lixouri
& Killini
5 EOT
6 Police
7 Port Police
8 Plateia Kentriki

10 Municipal Tourist Office
12 Archaeological Museum
13 OTE
14 Olympic Airways Office
16 Historical & Cultural Museum
18 Post Office
20 Bus Station
21 National Bank of Greece
22 Food Market
26 Hospital

Argostoli

0   75   150 m

Vassilisis Sofias

21 Maiou

Valianou

Rokou Vergoti

Georgiou

Vironos

Ioannou Metaxa

Andrea Choida

Diad

Vergoti

Konstantinou

Devosetou

To Sami

To Poros
& Skala

To Airport

Argostoli. The museum is open Monday to Saturday from 8 am to 2 pm. Admission is 400 dr.

Places to Stay

Argostoli Camping (☎ 23 487 or 28 100) is a pleasant camp site with a restaurant, bar and minimarket. It's on the coast, just under two km north of town.

At *Spiros Rouchotas' Rooms* (☎ 23 941, 24 946 or 28 017), Ioannou Metaxa 44, there are clean, pleasant doubles/triples for 3500/5000 dr with shared bathrooms. The rooms are above a kafeneion opposite the Lixouri quay.

The D class *Hotel Parthenon* (☎ 22 246) has tidy doubles/triples with pastel-coloured walls and marble floors for 5000/6000 dr with shared bathrooms. The D class *Hotel Allegro* (☎ 22 268 or 28 684), Andrea Choida 2, has pleasant rooms with balconies. Rates for doubles with shared bathrooms are 6000 dr and with private bathrooms 8000 dr. This hotel is just a couple of minutes from the bus station.

The C class *Hotel Tourist* (☎ 22 510), Ioannou Metaxa 94, has spacious rooms and a pale blue and white décor. Rates are 6000/10,000/12,000 dr for singles/doubles/triples with private bathrooms. The delightful C class *Hotel Agios Gerassimos* (☎ 28 697), Agios Gerassimou 6, has cosy rooms with fitted carpets and big balconies. Rates are 6000/7000/8400 dr. From the bus station walk north along the waterfront and turn left at the Olga Hotel; the hotel is on the right.

Places to Eat

Kava D'Oro Restaurant, at the northern end of the waterfront, is a bright, cheery place which specialises in grilled food. Succulent roast chicken is 750 dr and tasty souvlaki is 900 dr.

At the opposite end of the waterfront, opposite the food market, there are three good restaurants in a row. They are *Taverna Diana*, *Taverna Kalafatis* and *Taverna Anonymos* – all are worth a try.

SAMI Σάμη

Sami, the main port, 25 km from Argostoli, was, like the capital, devastated by the 1953 earthquake. Now it is modern, with undistinguished buildings, but its setting is pretty, nestling in a bay, flanked by steep hills. It's worth at least an overnight stay in order to visit the nearby caves. There's a post office, OTE and bank in town; Sami's postcode is 28082 and the telephone code is 0674. Buses for Argostoli meet the ferries.

When things aren't too busy accommodation owners meet the boats; otherwise there are plenty of domatia signs and several hotels. *Caravomilos Beach Camping* (☎ 22 480) is well kept with a restaurant, bar and minimarket. The site is just under one km from Sami. Turn right from the tiny quay and follow the coast.

Around Sami

The **Melissani Cave** is a subterranean sea-water lake. When the sun is overhead its rays shine through an opening in the roof of the cave, causing it to be lit up with countless shades of blue – it's an awe-inspiring phenomenon. The cave is 2½ km from Sami. Walk out of Sami along the road to Argostoli, turn right at the signpost for Agia Evfymia, and just beyond the village of Caravomilos look for a sign pointing left. The cave is open all day. Admission is 400 dr.

The **Drogorati Cave** is a large cave with impressive stalactites. It's signposted from the Argostoli road, four km out of Sami, and is open all day. Admission is 400 dr.

Agia Evfymia, 10 km north of Sami, is a picturesque fishing village with a pebble beach. There is a daily ferry to Ithaki and Astakos.

AROUND THE ISLAND

Lixouri is Kefallonia's second-largest town. It's an unremarkable place, but between the town and the southern tip of the peninsula are several unspoilt beaches. There are also beaches to the north of the town.

Fiskardo, 50 km north of Argostoli, was

the only village not devastated by the 1953 earthquake. It's a delightful, if somewhat twee, fishing village, framed by countless cypress trees, and with some fine Venetian buildings. Fiskardo is extremely popular and it's almost impossible to get accommodation. However, it's worth visiting on a day trip from Argostoli, both for the mountain vistas en route and the village itself. There are two buses every day to Fiskardo from Argostoli.

Assos, between Argostoli and Fiskardo, is a gem of a village. It straddles the isthmus of a peninsula on which stands a Venetian fortress. Assos was damaged in the earthquake but sensitively restored with the help of a donation from the city of Paris. It's a village of whitewashed and pastel houses offset with vibrant flowers. There is a pebble beach and domatia. There is an outstanding beach of white pebbles at **Myrtos**, three km south of Assos.

The south and south-east of the island are also worth exploring. **Kastro**, above the village of Peratata, nine km from Argostoli, was the island's capital in the Middle Ages. The ruined houses stand beneath the 13th-century castle of San Giorgio. The views from up here are magnificent. Peratata has rooms to rent, as has **Vlahata**, a pleasant village further along the road.

Markopoulo is witness to an extraordinary happening on 15 August (the Feast of the Assumption). The village church becomes infested with innoxious snakes with crosses on their heads; these reptiles are regarded as auspicious and are said to have curative powers.

Poros is overdeveloped and only worth a visit to catch a ferry; **Skala**, on the southern tip, is an infinitely preferable resort. There's a large beach of fine gravel which extends quite a way to either side of the village. If you are an independent traveller and your priority is a good beach to rest up on for a few days, then Skala is probably the best place on the island for you – just so long as you don't want a beach entirely to yourself. Rooms in domatia are not too difficult to find. There are three buses a day from Argostoli to Skala.

Ithaki Ιθάκη

Ithaki (ancient Ithaca), as everyone knows, was Odysseus' long lost home, the island where the stoical Penelope sat patiently, knitting one, purling one (or whatever the ancient equivalent of this respectable pastime was), as she awaited his return. What is less well known is that Ithaki, lying amidst the tourist ghettos of the Ionian, remains relatively unspoilt.

Ithaki is separated from Kefallonia by a strait, only two to four km wide. The island is one of contrasts, with a harsh precipitous east coast and a soft green west coast. The interior is mountainous and rocky with pockets of pine forest, clumps of cypresses, olive groves and vineyards. Ithakian wine is reputedly the best in the Ionian islands.

Ithaki is almost bisected by the huge Gulf of Molo, from which a long slender finger penetrates inland, and at the end of which is

---

The Voyage of Odysseus
Odysseus, king of Ithaka, was the hero of Homer's epic, the *Odyssey*. The epic relates the adventures of Odysseus (Ulysses) on his 10-year journey home to his beloved Ithaka, and wife, Penelope, after fighting in the Trojan War. Odysseus invoked the wrath of Poseidon, and it is largely due to the sea god's vindictiveness that it took him so long to return home. Violent storms and mighty waves conjured up by the sea god conspired to prevent Odysseus' reaching Ithaka. But the greatest obstacle was the nymph Calypso, who took such a fancy to the king that she held him prisoner for seven years. Eventually Odysseus managed to escape the nymph's possessive clutches and, after a few more adventures, he arrived home to find Penelope faithfully waiting for him, despite having been constantly pursued by numerous suitors. ■

Ithaki town (called Vathy by the locals), the island's port and capital.

Getting To/From Ithaki (Island)

Ferry From Ithaki there are daily ferries to Sami (one hour), Agia Evfymia and Fiskardo on Kefallonia; Patras (six hours, 2050 dr); Vasiliki on Lefkada; and Astakos (1¾ hours) on the mainland. The F/B *Ionis* goes three or four times a week to Brindisi in Italy via Paxoi, Igoumenitsa and Corfu. In the high season there is a daily ferry between Frikes (Ithaki) and Fiskardo (Kefallonia).

The telephone number of Ithaki's port police is ☎ 32 909.

Getting Around Ithaki (Island)

The island's one bus runs two or three times a day to Kioni (via Stavros and Frikes) from Ithaki town.

ITHAKI TOWN

Ithaki town is a fairly small place by Ionian island standards with just a few twisting streets, a central square and a few tacky tourist shops, grocers and hardware stores.

Orientation & Information

The ferry quay is on the west side of the bay. To reach the central square of Plateia Efstathiou Drakouli turn left and follow the waterfront around. The post office is on the central square and the OTE is further around the waterfront. Ithaki's postcode is 28300 and the telephone code is 0674. The National Bank of Greece is just south-west of the central square.

The main thoroughfare, Odos Kallinikou, is parallel to, and one block inland from, the waterfront.

Ithaki has no tourist office. The tourist police (☎ 32 205) are on the right side of Odos Evmeou, which runs south from the middle of the waterfront.

Things to See

The town's modest **Archaeological Museum** is on Odos Kallinikou. Entrance is free but opening times are erratic.

Festival

A Music & Theatre Festival is held in Ithaki town in the summer.

Places to Stay

When things aren't too busy domatia owners meet the ferries. Otherwise look for signs on Odysseos and Penelopes which (appropriately) lie parallel to one another, to the west of the quay. *Polyctor Tours* (☎ 33 120/130; fax 33 130) on the central square will be able to fix you up with either a room in a private house or a purpose-built apartment.

Ithaki has only two hotels, neither of which is cheap. The *Hotel Odysseus* (☎ 32 381), which is classed as a pension, has pleasant doubles for 8000 dr. The hotel overlooks the bay from its western side. To reach it turn right from the quay.

The posh *Hotel Mentor* (☎ 32 433/293) has a bar, restaurant and roof garden. The attractive rooms have rates of 6500/10,000 dr for singles/doubles with private bathrooms. The hotel is on the waterfront, beyond the central square.

Places to Eat

Taverna Trehantiri is a long-established place which serves the best traditional Greek dishes in Ithaki town. A full meal with retsina will cost about 1700 dr. The taverna is just west of the central square.

There are a comforting number of zaharoplasteia along the waterfront for sweet tooths. A local speciality is ravani, a sweet, gooey pudding.

AROUND THE ISLAND

Ithaki (surprise, surprise) has a few sites associated with Homer's *Odyssey*. Though none are impressive in themselves you may enjoy (or endure) the scenic walks to them. The most renowned is the **Fountain of Arethusa**, where Odysseus' swineherd, Eumaeus, brought his pigs to drink, and where Odysseus on his return to Ithaca went to meet him disguised as a beggar, after receiving directions from the goddess Athena – lesser mortals have to do with inadequate signposting. The walk takes between 1½ to two hours depending on your stamina.

Take Odos Evmeou which leads south out of town and eventually becomes an uphill track. Continue along here and after an hour or so you will come to a sign pointing left to the fountain. The sign indicates a narrow footpath which goes downhill; the path almost disappears at one point and would probably be rejected by any self-respecting mountain goat. Eventually you'll see a big rocky crag above a spring. This is the Koraka (Raven's) Crag (mentioned in the *Odyssey*). Take plenty of water with you on this walk because the spring dries up in summer.

A shorter trek can be made to the **Cave of the Nymphs**, where Odysseus concealed the splendid gifts of gold, copper and fine fabrics that the Phaeacians had given him. Below the cave is the Bay of Dexia, which is thought to be ancient Phorkys where the Phaeacians disembarked and laid the sleeping Odysseus on the sand. The cave is signposted from the town. The location of Odysseus' palace has been much disputed and archaeologists have been unable to find any conclusive evidence. Schliemann erroneously believed it was near Ithaki town whereas present day archaeologists speculate it was on a hill near Stavros.

Beaches

Beaches on Ithaki are mostly pebbled. The village of **Stavros**, 17 km north-west of Ithaki town, is nothing to write home about, but with rooms and tavernas and five roads radiating from it, it makes a good base from which to explore the north of the island. One of the roads leads in around one km to the **Bay of Polis**, which has a stony beach. **Frikes**, 1½ km in the opposite direction, is a delightful fishing village with some low-key development (including a centre of the Greek Islands Sailing Club). Attractive **Kioni**, four km south of Frikes, is similarly low key. There are pebbled coves at, and between, these two villages.

Zakynthos Ζάκινθος

The island of Zakynthos (ZAK-een-thos) has inspired the utterance of many superlatives. The Venetians called it *Fior' di Levante* (Flower of the Orient) and the poet Dionysios Solomos wrote 'Zakynthos could make one forget the Elysian Fields'. Indeed it is an island with exceptional natural beauty and outstanding beaches. This makes it all the more disheartening that its coastline has been the victim of the most unacceptable manifestations of package tourism. Even worse, tourism is endangering the logger-head turtle (*caretta caretta*).

Getting To/From Zakynthos (Island)

Air There are daily flights from Zakynthos to Athens (11,300 dr) and one flight a week to Kefallonia (3,300 dr). The Olympic Airways office (☎ 28 611) in Zakynthos town is at Alexandrou Roma 16.

Bus There are three buses a day from Zakynthos town to Athens (seven hours) via Patras.

Ferry Depending on the season there are between three and seven ferries a day from Zakynthos town to Killini, in the Peloponnese (1½ hours, 780 dr).

From Skinari there is one ferry a day to Pessada on Kefallonia. This service only operates in high season and there is no bus from Pessada to elsewhere on Kefallonia. At the time of writing there was one ferry a day during the high season from Zakynthos town to Nydri, on Lefkada. This service changes from year to year, so check with the port police in advance before planning your journey.

Zakynthos town's port police telephone number is ☎ 22 417.

Getting Around Zakynthos (Island)

To/From the Airport At the time of writing there was an Olympic Airways shuttle bus between Zakynthos town and the airport, six km to the south-west.

Bus There are frequent buses from Zakynthos town to Alykes, Tsilivi and Laganas. The bus service to other villages is poor, with only one or two buses a day. Check the current schedule at the bus station.

Car & Motorbike Car-hire outlets include: Europcar (☎ 23 239 or 25 614) at Lombardou 74 and Hertz (☎ 25 706) at Lombardou 38, in Zakynthos town. A reliable motorbike-hire outlet is Moto Stakis, at Demokratias 3, near Plateia Solomou.

ZAKYNTHOS TOWN

Zakynthos town is the capital and port of Zakynthos. The town was devastated by the 1953 earthquake, but was sensitively reconstructed with its former layout preserved in wide arcaded streets, imposing squares and gracious neoclassical public buildings. Unless you were fortunate enough to have seen the pre-earthquake town, which was by all accounts incredibly beautiful, you will probably be impressed.

Orientation & Information

The central square of Plateia Solomou is on the waterfront of Lombardou, opposite the ferry quay; another large square, Plateia Agiou Markou, is just a short distance away. The bus station is on Filitia, one block back from the waterfront and south of the quay. The main thoroughfare is Odos Alexandrou Roma which runs parallel to the waterfront several blocks inland.

The post office is at Tertseti 27, which is one block west of Alexandrou Roma. The OTE is on the northern side of Plateia Solomou. Zakynthos' postcode is 29100 and the telephone code is 0695. The National Bank of Greece is just west of Plateia

---

The Plight of the Loggerhead Turtle

Female loggerhead turtles return annually to their birthplaces to lay eggs. During the night mature females, measuring around one metre in length and weighing around 100 kg, drag themselves up the beach to above the high-tide line. If the condition of the sand is unsatisfactory they will return to the sea and try another part of the beach. When the ideal conditions are found the turtle digs a nest in which she lays about 100 eggs. She then covers the nest with sand and returns to the sea. About two months later the hatchlings dig their way to the surface and scurry to the sea. Turtles have nested in this way for at least two million years. The temperature and consistency of the sand of southern Zakynthos provide ideal conditions for nests. Unfortunately thousands of tourists find the same sandy beaches ideal for their holidays. The loggerheads' nesting season lasts from May to September which coincides exactly with the tourist season. The tourist industry on Zakynthos and in several other parts of the world is seriously threatening the turtles' survival. The reptiles are deterred from coming ashore by the bright lights of hotels, restaurants, bars and cars on or near beaches. Turtles are being injured by motorboat propellers, and eggs are being

broken by cars and motorbikes driven on beaches, and sun umbrellas dug into the sand. The turtle is now a protected species in Greece, but unconscionable developers (as well as tourists) continue to reduce the turtles' prospects of survival.

If you are concerned about the plight of the loggerhead turtle, you might consider avoiding those beaches where they lay their eggs in large numbers, such as those in the Bay of Laganas. For details and the address of the Marine Turtle Project, see the Kefallonia section earlier in this chapter. ■

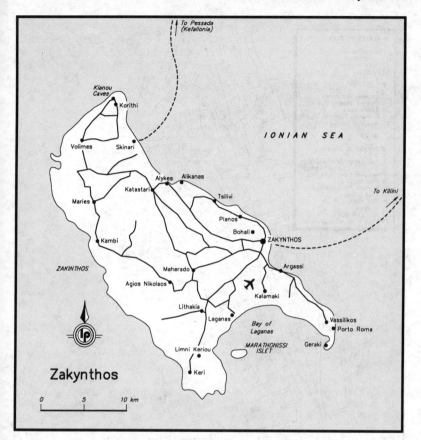

Zakynthos

0   5   10 km

Solomou. Zakynthos' hospital (☎ 22 514) is in the western part of town.

Zakynthos town does not have a tourist office. The helpful tourist police (☎ 22 550) are on the waterfront, south of the quay. They will provide you with information about accommodation.

Museums

The **Museum of Solomos** is dedicated to Dionysios Solomos (1798-1857), who was born on Zakynthos. His work, *Hymn to Liberty*, became the Greek national anthem. Solomos is regarded as the father of modern Greek poetry, because he was the first Greek poet to use demotic Greek, rather than Katharevousa. This museum houses a collection of memorabilia associated with his life, as well as displays pertaining to the poets Andreas Kalvos (1792-1869) and Ugo Foskolo (1778-1827), who were also born on Zakynthos. The museum is on Plateia Agiou Markou. Opening times are 9 am to 2 pm every day, and entrance is free.

The **Neo-Byzantine Museum**, on Plateia Solomou, houses a collection of ecclesiastical art (mostly icons) which was rescued from the churches razed in the earthquake.

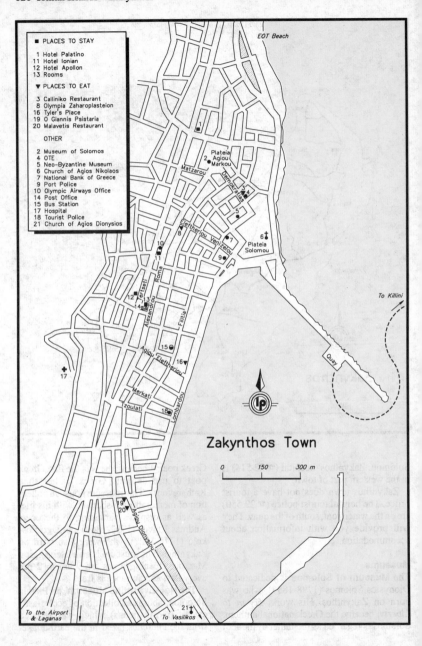

PLACES TO STAY
1 Hotel Palatino
11 Hotel Ionian
12 Hotel Apollon
13 Rooms

PLACES TO EAT
3 Calliniko Restaurant
8 Olympia Zaharoplasteion
16 Tyler's Place
19 O Giannis Psistaria
20 Malavetis Restaurant

OTHER
2 Museum of Solomos
4 OTE
5 Neo-Byzantine Museum
6 Church of Agios Nikolaos
7 National Bank of Greece
9 Port Police
10 Olympic Airways Office
14 Post Office
15 Bus Station
17 Hospital
18 Tourist Police
21 Church of Agios Dionysios

EOT Beach

Plateia Agiou Markou

Matzarou

Dimokratias

Eleftheriou Venizelou

Plateia Solomou

Roma

Tertseti

Alexandrou

Filita

Agiou Eleftheriou

Merkati

Tzoulati

Lombardou

Agiou Dionysiou

To Killini

Quay

Zakynthos Town

0   150   300 m

To the Airport & Laganas

To Vasilikos

Opening times are Tuesday to Sunday from 8.30 am to 3 pm.

Churches

At the southern end of town the **Church of Agios Dionysios** is named after the island's patron saint. The church contains the saint's relics in a silver coffer. This is paraded around the streets during the **festivals** held in his honour on 24 August and 17 December. The church also has some notable frescoes.

The 16th-century **Church of Agios Nikolaos**, on Plateia Solomou, was built in Italian Renaissance style. It was partially destroyed in the earthquake, but has been carefully reconstructed.

Organised Tours

Zante Tours (☎ 23 735), Lombardou 18, is one of the many travel agents offering tours. An island tour (including the Kianou (Blue) Caves) is 2000 dr.

Places to Stay – bottom end

The nearest camp site to Zakynthos town is *Zante Camping* (☎ 24 754 or 61 710) at Tsilivi, five km away.

The clean, nameless rooms (☎ 26 012), at Alexandrou Roma 40, are a bargain at 4000 dr a double with shared bathrooms and 6000 dr with private bathrooms; small apartments are 9000 dr.

The D class *Hotel Ionian* (☎ 22 511), Alexandrou Roma 18, has tidy singles/doubles/triples for 3000/5000/6000 dr.

Places to Stay – middle

The C class *Hotel Apollon* (☎ 22 838), Tertseti 30, has pleasant single/double/triple rooms for 7000/10,000/12,000 dr with private bathrooms. The new B class *Hotel Palatino* is a gorgeous place. It's built in neoclassical style with extremely comfortable modern rooms. Rates are 11,500/13,800/16,500 dr for singles/doubles/triples with private bathrooms. These rates are for high season; in spring and autumn it's possible to get a substantial reduction.

Places to Eat

The *Calliniko Restaurant*, next to the OTE, is a long-established place which serves well-prepared, good value food, in pleasant surroundings. The *Malavetis Restaurant* is rough and ready but serves tasty grub. Next door, the *O Giannis Psistaria* has roast chicken for 650 dr. If you're fed up with Greek food and especially if you're a Brit you may like to try *Tyler's Place*, on the waterfront. Eggs, bacon and beans are 650 dr, shepherd's pie is 950 dr and fish & chips are 1000 dr.

The *Olympia Zaharoplasteion*, on Alexandrou Roma, is a charming, old-fashioned establishment. Breakfast here will cost about 400 dr. A local speciality is a nougat-like confectionery called mandolato. An independent traveller I met said it was the nicest thing about Zakynthos.

AROUND THE ISLAND

The huge **Bay of Laganas** extends across the whole of Zakynthos' south coast. It is fringed with beaches of golden sand, and it is here where the loggerhead turtles come ashore to lay their eggs. **Laganas** is the most developed resort, but **Kalamaki** is not much quieter and even **Geraki**, where the highest number of turtles lay their eggs, has not been spared water sports. The turtles also nest on nearby **Marathonissi islet**. You may decide to avoid these beaches, both for the sake of the turtles, and to avoid the commercialism.

Vasilikos and **Porto Roma**, south of Zakynthos town, have good, albeit crowded, sand beaches and are less developed than those around the Bay of Laganas. The best beach north of Zakynthos town is at **Alykes**, where there is a long swathe of sand.

The **Kianou (Blue) Caves**, on the northern tip of the island, are one of the highlights of Zakynthos and should not be missed; they are second only to their namesake on Kastellorizo. Various travel agencies offer excursions to the caves, which can only be reached by boat.

You can escape from the tourist hype of Zakynthos by going inland to the farming villages. The village of **Maherado** has a 14th-century church, Agia Mavra, which is one of the most impressive on the island. It has an elaborate interior, a valuable icon and a lovely iconostasis. **Agios Nikolaos** is an attractive village, and the drive north from here to **Maries** is through splendid hilly country.

Evia & The Sporades
Εύβοια και οι Σποράδες

Evia (Εύβοια), Greece's second-largest island, is so close to the mainland historically, physically and topographically that one tends not to regard it as an island at all. Athenians regard Evia as a convenient destination for a weekend break or a holiday, so consequently it gets packed, although, except for the resort of Eretria, it is not much visited by foreign tourists.

The Sporades (Σποράδες) lie to the north and east of Evia and to the east and south-east of the Pelion peninsula, to which they were joined in prehistoric times. With their dense vegetation and mountainous terrain, they seem like a continuation of this peninsula. There are 11 islands in the archipelago, four of which are inhabited: Skiathos, Skopelos, Alonissos and Skyros. The first two have a highly developed tourist industry, whereas Alonissos and Skyros, although by no means remote, are far less visited.

Getting To/From Evia

Bus From Athens' Terminal B bus station there are buses every half hour to Halkida from 5.45 am to 9.45 pm (1½ hours, 900 dr), six a day to Kymi from 6 am to 7 pm (3½ hours, 1950 dr) and three a day to Edipsos (for Loutra Edipsou; 3½ hours, 1800 dr). From the Mavromateon terminal in Athens, there are buses every 45 minutes to Rafina (for Karystos; one hour, 300 dr).

Train There are 17 trains a day from Athens' Larissis station to Halkida. The journey takes 1½ hours and costs 500 dr. The Halkida train station is on the mainland side of the bridge. Walk over the bridge, turn left and you will find Leoforos Venizelou, Halkida's main drag, off to the right.

Ferry There are six ferry crossings from the mainland to Evia. They are from north to south: eight a day from Glyfa to Agiokambos (30 minutes, 250 dr); 12 a day from Arkitsa to Loutra Edipsou (one hour, 500 dr); every half hour from Oropou to Eretria (30 minutes, 200 dr); five a day from Agia Marina to Nea Styra (40 minutes, 413 dr); three a day from Rafina to Marmari (1¼ hours, 707 dr); and two a day from Rafina to Karystos (2¼ hours, 1320 dr).

There are two ferries a day from Kymi to Skyros (2½ hours, 1450 dr). To Volos there are two ferries a week (eight hours, 5300 dr) via Alonissos (three hours), Skopelos (3½ hours) and Skiathos (4½ hours).

Getting Around Evia

Bus Halkida is the transport hub for Evia. There are nine buses a day to the port of Kymi (2½ hours, 1000 dr) via Eretria and Kymi town; five to Steni (1¼ hours, 500 dr); and three to Karystos (four hours, 1600 dr) via Eretria.

Hydrofoil There are daily hydrofoils from Halkida to Loutra Edipsou (one hour, 3000 dr) via Limni.

Getting To/From & Around the Sporades

The following is a brief overview of travel options to, from and between the Sporades islands. For more comprehensive informa-

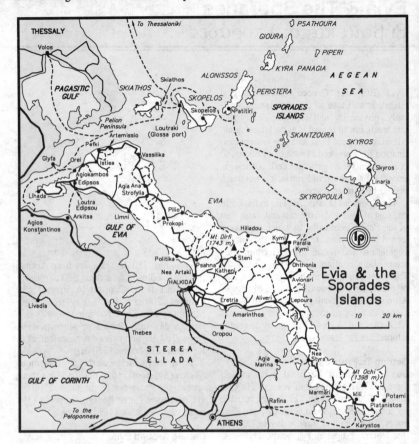

Evia & the Sporades Islands

tion, see the relevant sections under individual island entries.

Air Skiathos has an airport serving charter flights from northern Europe and domestic flights to Athens. Skyros has an airport with flights to Athens only.

Ferry Mainland ports serving Skiathos, Skopelos (Glossa and Skopelos town) and Alonissos are Volos and Agios Konstantinos, in the Thessaly and Sterea Ellada regions respectively. Less frequent ferries go to these three islands from Kymi on Evia. There are hourly buses from Athens' Terminal B bus station to Agios Konstantinos (2½ hours, 2000 dr) and six a day to Kymi (3½ hours 1950 dr).

Note that Skopelos has two ports – Glossa and Skopelos town. All ferries stop at Skopelos town and almost all at Glossa, but check to determine where your ferry's headed. To complicate matters further the port referred to on timetables as Glossa is not Glossa at all but Loutraki; Glossa is a village three km uphill from the port.

Skyros, to the south-east of the other

Sporades islands, is served by at least two ferries a day from Kymi.

Hydrofoil There are hydrofoils every day from Agios Konstantinos and Volos (via Platania on the Pelion peninsula) to Skiathos, Glossa (Skopelos), Skopelos town and Alonissos. Five times a week the hydrofoil from Volos continues from Alonissos to Skyros. There are four hydrofoils a week from Thessaloniki to Skiathos, Skopelos and Alonissos.

Evia Εύβοια

Evia (EV-ia) will probably never be a prime destination for foreign tourists, but if you're based in Athens with a few days to spare, and (preferably) your own transport, a foray into Evia is worthwhile for its scenic mountain roads, pristine inland villages, and a look at some resorts which cater for Greeks (including one for ailing Greeks), rather than foreign tourists.

A mountainous spine runs north-south through the island; the east coast consists of precipitous cliffs, whereas the gentler west coast has a string of beaches and resorts. The island is reached overland by a bridge over the Euripous Channel to the island's capital, Halkida. At the mention of Evia, most Greeks will eagerly tell you that the current of this narrow channel changes direction around seven times a day. The next bit of the story, that Aristotle became so perplexed at not finding an explanation for this mystifying occurrence that he threw himself into the channel and drowned, can almost certainly be taken with a grain of salt.

HALKIDA Χαλκίδα

Halkida (Hal-KEED-a, population 45,000) was an important city-state in ancient times with several colonies dotted around the Mediterranean. The name derives from the bronze which was manufactured here in antiquity (Halkos means 'bronze' in Greek). Today it's a lively industrial and agricultural

town, but with nothing of sufficient note to warrant an overnight stay. However, if you have an hour or two to spare between buses, then the **Archaeological Museum**, Leoforos Venizelou 13, is worth a mosey around. It houses finds from Evia's three ancient cities of Halkida, Eretria and Karystos, including a chunk of the pediment of the Temple of Dafniforos Apollo at Eretria. The museum is open Tuesday to Sunday from 8.30 am to 3 pm. Admission is 400 dr.

The phone number of the Haldiki tourist police is ☎ 0221-83 333.

See Getting To/From Evia and Getting Around Evia at the beginning of this chapter for travel information concerning Halkida.

CENTRAL EVIA
Steni Στενή
From Halkida it's 31 km to the lovely mountain village of Steni, with gurgling springs and plane trees. The village has two hotels, both C class: the *Hotel Direys* (☎ 0228-51 217) has singles with shared bathrooms for 2500 dr and doubles with private bathrooms for 5750 dr; the *Hotel Steni* (☎ 0228-51 221) has singles/doubles for 4000/6000 dr with private bathrooms. Steni is the starting point for the climb up Mt Dirfi (1743 metres), Evia's highest mountain. The EOS-owned Dirfys Refuge (☎ 0228-51 285), at 1120 metres, can be reached along a nine-km dirt road, or a two-hour walk along a forest footpath. From the refuge it's two hours to the summit. For further information contact the EOS (☎ 0221-25 230), Angeli Gyviou 22, Halkida. A rough road continues from Steni to **Hiliadou**, on the east coast, where there is a fine beach. There are five buses a day from Halkida to Steni (1¼ hours, 500 dr).A

Kymi Κύμη
Kymi is a picturesque town built on a cliff 250 metres above the sea. The port of Kymi (called Paralia Kymi), four km downhill, is the only natural harbour on the precipitous east coast, and the departure point for ferries to Skyros. Kymi's postcode is 34003 and the telephone code is 0222.

The **Folklore Museum**, on the road to

Paralia Kymi, has an impressive collection of local costumes and memorabilia, and a display commemorating Dr George Papanikolaou, the inventor of the Pap smear test, who was born in Kymi. Opening times are 10 am to 1 pm and 5 to 7.30 pm every day.

Kymi has two hotels, both D class. The *Hotel Krineion* (☎ 0222-22 287), on the central square, has doubles for 5000 dr. Close by, *Hotel Kimi* (☎ 0222-22 408) has doubles for 4000 dr.

See the Getting To/From Evia and Getting Around Evia sections at the beginning of the chapter for travel information concerning Kymi.

NORTHERN EVIA

From Halkida a road heads north to **Psahna**, the gateway to the highly scenic mountainous interior of northern Evia. The road climbs through pine forests to the beautiful agricultural village of **Prokopi**, 52 km from Halkida. The inhabitants are descended from refugees who came from Prokopion (present day Ürgüp) in Turkey in 1923, bringing with them the relics of St John the Russian. On 27 May (St John's festival), hordes of pilgrims come to worship his relics in the Church of Agios Ioannis Rosses.

At **Strofylia**, 14 km beyond Prokopi, a road heads west to **Limni**, a pretty (but pretty crowded) fishing village with whitewashed houses and a beach. With your own transport or a penchant for walking, you can visit the 16th-century **Convent of Galataki**, eight km south-east of Limni; its katholikon (main church) has fine frescoes. Limni has plenty of places to stay, and there's a camp site – *Rovies Camping* (☎ 0227-71 120), on the coast, 13 km north-west of Limni.

The road continues to the sedate spa resort of **Loutra Edipsou**, 119 km from Halkida, whose therapeutic sulphur waters have been celebrated since antiquity; many luminaries, including Aristotle, Plutarch, Strabo and Plinius, sang their praises. The waters are reputed to cure many ills, mostly of a rheumatic, arthritic or gynaecological nature. Today the town has the most up-to-date hydrotherapy-physiotherapy centre in Greece.

If you're interested contact any EOT or the EOT Hydrotherapy-Physiotherapy Centre (☎ 0226-23 500), Loutra Edipsou. Even if you don't rank amongst the infirm you may enjoy a visit to this resort which has an attractive setting, a beach and many domatia and hotels.

See Getting To/From Evia and Getting Around Evia at the beginning of this chapter for travel information concerning Loutra Edipsou.

SOUTHERN EVIA
Eretria Ερέτρια

Heading south from Halkida, Eretria is the first place of interest. It has metamorphosed from Evia's major archaeological site into a tacky resort patronised by British package tourists. Ancient Eretria was a major maritime power and also had an eminent school of philosophy. The city was destroyed in 87 AD during the Mithridatic War. This war was fought between Mithridates (king of Pontos) and the Roman commander, Sulla. The modern town was founded in the 1820s by islanders from Psara fleeing the Turkish.

Things to See From the top of the ancient acropolis, at the northern end of town, there are splendid views over to the mainland. West of the acropolis are the remains of a palace, temple, and a theatre with a subterranean passage which was used by actors. Close by, the **Museum of Eretria** (☎ 0221-62 206) contains well-displayed finds from ancient Eretria. Opening times are Tuesday to Sunday from 8.30 am to 3 pm. Admission is 400 dr. In the centre of town there are remains of a **Temple of Dafniforos Apollo** and a mosaic from an ancient bath.

Places to Stay Eretria has loads of hotels and domatia, and the *Eva Camping* (☎ 61 081/024) camp site is just north on the coast.

Getting There & Away See Getting To/From Evia and Getting Around Evia at the beginning of the chapter for travel information concerning Eretria.

Karystos Κάρυστος

Continuing south, the road branches at **Lepoura** – left goes to Kymi, and right, to Karystos (KAR-is-tos, population 4500). Set in the wide Karystian Bay, below Mt Ochi (1398 metres), Karystos is the most attractive of south Evia's resorts. The town was designed on a grid system by the Bavarian architect Bierbach, who was commissioned by King Otho. If you turn right from the quay you will come to the **Bourtzi**, the remains of a 14th-century Venetian castle, which has marble from a temple to Apollo incorporated into its walls. Beyond here there is a sandy beach. There is also a beach at the other end of the waterfront.

Karystos' postcode is 34001 and the telephone code is 0224.

Places to Stay Look for domatia signs along the waterfront or there are three C class hotels in town, on streets which run inland from the centre of the waterfront. The *Hotel Als* (☎ 22 202) and *Hotel Karystion* (☎ 22 391/191) are both on Odos Kriezotou and the *Hotel Plaza* (☎ 22 337) is at Ioannou Kotsika 9. All three hotels have rates of around 6000 dr for a double room.

Getting There & Away See the Getting To/From Evia and Getting Around Evia sections at the beginning of the chapter for travel information on Karystos.

Around Karystos

The ruins of the 13th-century Frankish fortress of **Castello Rossa** (Red Castle) is a short walk from **Mili**, a delightful well-watered village, four km inland from Karystos. The aqueduct behind the castle once carried water from the mountain springs and a tunnel once led from this castle to the Bourtzi in Karystos. A little beyond Mili there is an **ancient quarry** scattered with fragments of the once prized Kariston marble.

With your own transport you can explore the sleepy villages nestling in the southern foothills of Mt Ochi. The rough road winds through citrus orchards and pine trees high above the south coast. At **Platanistos**, a charming village named for its plane trees, a five-km dirt road (drivable) leads to the coastal hamlet of **Potami** with its sand and pebble beach. The 'main road' continues to the east coast.

Skiathos Σκίαθος

The good news is that much of the coast of pine-covered Skiathos (SKEE-ath-os, population 4100) consists of exquisite beaches of golden sand. The bad news is that the island's overrun with package tourists, and very expensive.

Skiathos has only one settlement, the port and capital of Skiathos town, on the southeast coast. The rest of the south coast is one long chain of holiday villas and hotels. The north coast is precipitous and less accessible. Most people come to the island for the beaches and nightlife – if you've come for anything else you may depart quickly.

Getting To/From Skiathos (Island)

Air As well as the numerous charter flights from northern Europe to Skiathos there are at least five flights a day to Athens (9500 dr). The Olympic Airways office (☎ 22 229/200) is on the right side of Papadiamanti, Skiathos town, walking inland.

Ferry There are daily ferries from Skiathos to Volos (three hours, 1800 dr), Agios Konstantinos (3½ hours, 2243 dr) and to Alonissos via Glossa (Skopelos) and Skopelos town. There are two or three ferries a week from Skiathos to Kymi (five hours, 3300 dr). There are many agencies on the waterfront selling ferry tickets. The port police telephone no is ☎ 22 017.

Hydrofoil There are daily hydrofoils from Skiathos to Volos (one hour, 3469 dr) via Platania, and to Alonissos via Glossa (Skopelos) and Skopelos town. There are also daily hydrofoils to Agios Konstantinos (1½ hours, 3469 dr). Five times a week there is a

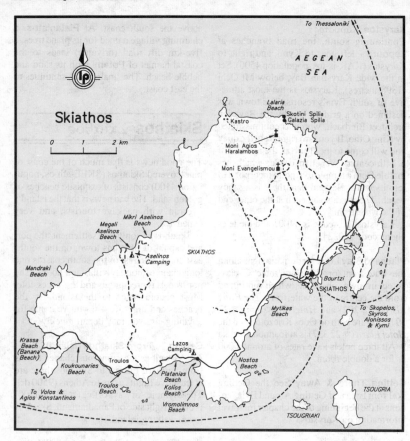

hydrofoil to Skyros. There are four hydrofoils a week from Thessaloniki to Skiathos (3½ hours, 5599 dr). Most travel agents sell hydrofoil tickets.

Getting Around Skiathos (Island)

Bus Crowded buses leave Skiathos town for Koukounaries Beach every half hour between 7.30 am and 10.30 pm. The buses stop at all the access points to the beaches along the south coast. There are three buses a day to Megali Aselinos Beach, on the north coast.

Car & Motorbike There are heaps of motor-bike-hire outlets on the waterfront in Skiathos town. Car-hire outlets include Autorent (☎ 21 797) and Eurocar (☎ 21 124), both on the waterfront.

Excursion Boat As well as the bus, there are excursion boats to most of the south-coast beaches. There are also excursion boats which do around-the-island trips (2500 dr). These include a visit to Kastro, Lalaria Beach, and the three caves of Chalkini Spilia, Skotini Spilia and Galazia Spilia, which are only accessible by boat. Excursion boats leave from the old harbour.

SKIATHOS TOWN

Skiathos town, with red-roofed, white-washed houses, built on two low hills, is picturesque enough, although not as over-whelmingly so as Skopelos or Skyros towns. The pine-forested islet of Bourtzi (reached by a causeway) between the two harbours adds the finishing touch. Inevitably, hotels, souvenir shops, travel agents, bars and such-like dominate the scene on the waterfront and main thoroughfares.

Orientation

The quay is in the middle of the waterfront, just north of Bourtzi islet. To the right (as you face inland) is the straight new harbour; to the left, and with more character, is the curving old harbour used by local fishers and excursion boats. The main thoroughfare of Papadiamanti strikes inland from opposite the quay. The central square of Plateia Trion Ierarkhon is just back from the middle of the old harbour.

Information

There is no tourist office or tourist police; the regular police (☎ 21 111) are at the far end of Papadiamanti on the left.

The post office and OTE are on the right side of Papadiamanti and the National Bank of Greece is on the left. Skiathos' postcode is 37002 and the telephone code is 0427. The bus terminus is at the northern end of the new harbour.

Museum

Skiathos was the birthplace of the Greek short-story writer and poet Alexandros Papadiamantis, and novelist Alexandros Moraitides. Alexandros Papadiamantis' house is now a museum with a small collection documenting the writer's life.

Opening times are 9.30 am to 1 pm and 5 to 7 pm. It is just off the right side of Odos Papadiamanti.

Organised Tours

Various local operators run excursion boat trips around the island. See the relevant section under Getting Around Skiathos (Island) at the beginning of the Skiathos entry.

Places to Stay – bottom end

Skiathos has two camp sites: *Lazos Camping* (no telephone), at Kolios Beach, seven km west of Skiathos town (take the Skiathos-Koukounaries Beach bus); and *Aselinos Camping* (☎ 49 312), on the north coast, at Megali Aselinos Beach.

Most accommodation is booked solid from July to September. Outside these months you may be offered a room when you get off the ferry – if not look up Papadiamanti and around Plateia Trion Ierarkhon for domatia signs. If you're brave enough to arrive during the summer rush then just about any travel agent will endeavour to fix you up with somewhere. Worth trying are Alkyon Travel (☎ 22 029/948), at the bottom of Papadiamanti; Meridian (☎ 21 309/477), Papadiamanti 8; or Mare Nostrum Holidays (☎ 21 463/4), Papadiamanti 21.

The D class *Hotel Karafelas* (☎ 21 235) is one of the town's best-value hotels. The comfortable singles/doubles are 3500/6000 dr with private bathrooms. The hotel is at the far end of Papadiamanti, on the left. Also worth a try is the slightly cheaper D class *Australia Hotel* (☎ 22 488), which has tidy singles/doubles for 3000/4000 dr with private bathrooms. Walk up Papadiamanti to the post office, turn right and take the first left.

Places to Stay – middle

The C class *Hotel Morfo* (☎ 21 737) has nicely furnished single/double rooms for 6500/10,000 dr with private bathrooms. From the waterfront take Ananiniou (parallel, and to the right of, Papadiamanti), and you'll come to the hotel on the left. The B class *Hotel Alkyon* (☎ 22 981/2/3/4/5 or 21 643), on the new harbour waterfront, is a large plush place which may have a spare room. Rates are 7000/12,000 dr for singles/doubles with private bathrooms.

Places to Stay – top end

Most of the island's top-end hotels are on the

coast to the west of Skiathos town. The A class *Hotel Paradise* (☎ 21 939; fax 21 939), three km west of Skiathos town, is one of the newest and smallest of these hotels. It has tastefully furnished air-con rooms and a restaurant and bar. Doubles are 17,000 dr.

The A class *Nostos Bungalows* (☎ 22 420/520) is a well-designed bungalow complex at Nostos Beach, five km west of town. The complex has bars, a restaurant, taverna, swimming pool and tennis court. Rates for the bungalows are 27,000 dr. The *Atrium Hotel* (☎ 49 345/376; fax 49 444) is an attractive place with a bar, restaurant, swimming pool and gymnasium. Singles/doubles are 19,000/23,000 dr. The hotel is seven km west of town.

Places to Eat

Yes well...if you want your Sporades trip to be gastronomically memorable stay on the ferry till it gets to Skopelos or, better still, Alonissos. Otherwise *Stavros Taverna* is one of the few places which serves a semblance of traditional Greek fare and at reasonable prices. Walk up Papadiamanti, turn right at the post office and the taverna's on the right.

Entertainment

Scan Papadiamanti and Politechniou (parallel, and to the left of Papadiamanti) and see which disco or bar takes your fancy. The *Adagio Bar* is one of the most civilised, playing classical music and jazz. Walk up Papadiamanti, turn left at the post office and it's on the left. In contrast, the *Banana Bar*, on Politechniou, is one of the rowdiest and wildest, if that's your scene.

AROUND THE ISLAND
Beaches

Buses ply the south coast stopping at the access points to the beaches. The ones nearest town are extremely crowded; the first one worth getting off the bus for is the pine-fringed long and sandy **Vromolimnos Beach**. **Platanias** and **Troulos**, the next two beaches along, are also good sandy beaches

but both, alas, are popular. The bus continues to **Koukounaries Beach**, backed by pine trees and a lagoon and touted as the best beach in Greece. It's best nowadays viewed from a distance from where the wide sweep of pale gold sand does indeed look beautiful.

Krassa Beach, at the other side of a narrow headland, is better known as **Banana Beach**, though I'm not sure whether this is because everything's peeled (it's nudist) or because of what's revealed when everything's peeled (it's predominantly male). The north coast beaches are less crowded but exposed to the meltemi.

From Troulos a road heads inland to sandy **Megali Aselinos Beach** (with a camp site). A right fork from this road leads to **Mikri Aselinos Beach**. **Lalaria**, on the north-west coast, is a striking beach of pale grey pebbles, easiest reached by excursion boat from Skiathos town.

Kastro Κάστρο

Kastro, perched dramatically on a rocky headland above the north coast, was the fortified pirate-proof capital of the island from 1540 to 1829. It consisted of some 300 houses and 20 churches and the only access was by a drawbridge. Now it's in ruins except for two of its churches, and access is by steps. The views from Kastro are tremendous. Excursion boats do the trip to the beach below Kastro, from where it's an easy clamber up to the ruins.

Moni Evangelismou
Μονή Ευαγγελίστριας

The 18th-century Moni Evangelismou is the most appealing of the island's monasteries. It is in a delightful setting, poised above a gorge, 450 metres above sea level, and surrounded by pine and cypress trees. The monastery, like many in Greece, was a refuge for freedom fighters during the War of Independence, and the islanders claim the first Greek flag was raised here in 1807.

The monastery is an hour's walk from town or you can drive there. Take the road out of town towards the airport and there is a signpost pointing left to the monastery.

Skopelos Σκόπελος

Skopelos (SKO-pel-os, population 5000) is less commercialised than Skiathos, but following hot on its trail. Like Skiathos, the north-west coast is exposed, with high cliffs. The sheltered south-east coast harbours many beaches, though unlike Skiathos, most are pebbled. The island has pine forests, agricultural pockets of vineyards, olive groves and fruit orchards. There are two large settlements, the capital and main port of Skopelos town, on the east coast, and the lovely unspoilt hill village of Glossa, three km from Loutraki, the island's second port, on the west coast.

Skopelos has yielded one exciting archaeological find. In ancient times the island was an important Minoan outpost ruled by Staphylos, who according to mythology was the son of Ariadne and Dionysos. 'Staphylos' means grape in Greek and the Minoan ruler is said to have introduced wine-making to the island. In the 1930s a tomb containing gold treasures, and believed to be that of Staphylos, was unearthed at Staphylos, now a resort.

Getting To/From Skopelos (Island)
Ferry Skopelos' second port is called Glossa. However, boats actually depart from Loutraki, on the coast. Glossa is three km inland. There are daily ferries from Glossa and Skopelos town to Alonissos (720 dr); and to Volos (4½ hours, 2200 dr) and Agios Konstantinos (5½ hours, 2617 dr) both via Skiathos (820 dr). The times given are for Skopelos town; Glossa is one hour less. There are two or three ferries a week to Skopelos (3100 dr) from Kymi, on Evia.

Skopelos' port police telephone number is ☎ 22 189.

Hydrofoil There are daily hydrofoils from Glossa (Skopelos) and Skopelos town to Alonissos; to Volos (two hours, 4231 dr) via Skiathos and Platania; and to Agios Konstantinos (5324 dr) via Skiathos. Five times

a week there is a hydrofoil to Skyros and four times a week to Thessaloniki (4½ hours, 6450 dr).

Getting Around Skopelos (Island)
Bus There are many buses a day from Skopelos town to Staphylos, Agnotas, Panormos and Milia and eight a day to Glossa and Loutraki (one hour, 440 dr).

Car & Motorbike Motor Tours (☎ 22 986), Skopelos town, hires Fiat Pandas for 14,000 dr, Suzuki jeeps for 16,400 dr, and 50/80/200 cc motorbikes for 3000/3800/7000 dr a day. The outlet is on the waterfront near the Hotel Eleni.

SKOPELOS TOWN
Skopelos town is one of the most captivating island towns. It skirts a semicircular bay and clambers in tiers up a hillside, culminating in a ruined fortress. Dozens of churches are interspersed amongst tall dazzling white houses with brightly shuttered windows and flower-adorned balconies. Traditionally, roofs in Skopelos town were tiled with beautiful rough-hewn bluestone, but these are gradually being replaced with mass-produced red tiles.

Orientation
Skopelos town's quay is on the west side of the bay. From the ferry turn left to reach the bustling waterfront lined with cafés, souvenir shops and travel agencies. The bus station is to the left of the quay at the end of the excursion boat moorings.

Information
There is no tourist office or tourist police on Skopelos. To reach the regular police station (☎ 22 235) go up the steps to the right of the National Bank of Greece, turn left and it's on the left.

The post office lurks in an obscure alleyway; walk up the road opposite the bus station, take the first left, the first right and the first left and it's on the right. To reach the OTE turn left at the quay, right at the Apolafsis Music Bar and you'll come to it on the

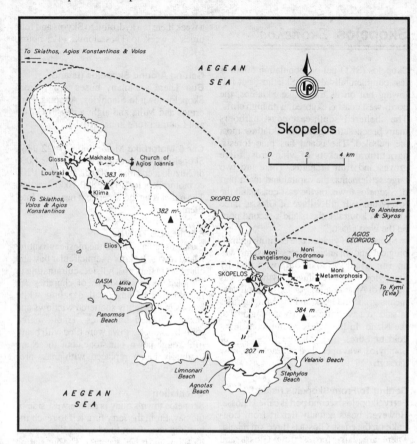

left at the first crossroad. Skopelos' postcode is 37003 and the telephone code is 0424. The National Bank of Greece is on the waterfront near the quay. To reach Skopelos' laundrette go up the street opposite the bus station, turn right at Platanos Taverna and it's on the left.

Museum

Strolling around town and sitting at the waterside cafés will probably be your chief occupations in Skopelos town, but there is also a small **Folk Art Museum** on Odos Hatzistamati. It is open daily from 7 to 10 pm and admission is free. Walk up the steps to the left of the pharmacy on the waterfront, take the first right, the first left, the first right and it's on the right.

Places to Stay – bottom end

Skopelos town is still a place where you have a good chance of renting a room in a family house. People with rooms to offer meet the ferries, but be aware that many of these rooms are in the labyrinthine streets high above the waterfront, so getting to them initially, and finding them again afterwards, tests stamina and powers of orientation to the limit.

One of the cheapest hotels is the E class *Hotel Stella* (☎ 22 081), where tidy doubles/triples are 4400/5200 dr with private bathrooms. Turn left from the quay, and you'll find the hotel on the left, opposite the conspicuous Dolphin Hotel (see under top end). Continue further along to the Hotel Amalias; turn left and you will come to the D class *Hotel Rania* (☎ 22 486) on the left. This clean well-kept hotel has doubles for 6000 dr with private bathrooms.

If you continue along this same road and follow it as it veers right, you will come to the *Pension Soula* (☎ 22 930) on the right. This lovely place is owned by an elderly couple who don't speak English but are very hospitable. The rates are 5800/7200 dr for doubles/triples with private bathrooms; there is a communal kitchen and a tranquil garden. Back on the waterfront the similarly priced *Pension Ulla* (☎ 22 637) has rooms with oak-beamed ceilings, fitted carpets and brass bedsteads. Turn left at the port and the pension is on the right, above a souvenir shop. There are no camp sites on Skopelos.

Places to Stay – middle
The D class *Hotel Eleni* (☎ 22 393/934/176) has lovely traditionally furnished rooms with balconies. The cost is 6200/7400 dr for singles/doubles with private bathrooms. Turn left from the quay and the hotel is on the right, two buildings before the Dolphin Hotel.

Places to Stay – top end
The B class *Dolphin Hotel* is a striking pastel-coloured building with an ultra-modern, luxurious interior and an extensive garden with a swimming pool and an ornamental pond. The rooms have a minibar, telephone, radio and balcony. Rates are 12,000/18,000 dr for singles/doubles; apartments for three or four people are 22,000 dr.

Places to Eat
Probably the best of the rather nondescript waterfront eateries is *Restaurant Molos*, opposite the quay. Away from the waterfront there are a couple of good places which dish up something more than the usual Greek staples, although neither is low-priced. At *Alexander Restaurant & Bar* you eat in a pleasant garden. Tasty entrées are 900 dr and souvlaki is 1900 dr. To reach the restaurant turn left at the quay, right at the Apolafsis Music Bar, left again after the OTE and the restaurant is along here on the right.

The *Selina Restaurant* could well be the island's best. It's a sophisticated place which also has a garden, and a stage. The owner told me the stage was for interesting 'happenings', but nothing happened the evening I was there, except that I was served delicious food. Main meals start at 1300 dr and desserts are 700 dr. The restaurant is opposite the Hotel Rania (see Places to Stay).

Entertainment
The *Platanos Jazz Club*, opposite the quay, is a long-time favourite hang-out with backpackers. New Age music is played at breakfast time, and jazz and blues in the evenings. Yoghurt and honey is 600 dr and cocktails are 800 to 1000 dr. The *Marionette Bar* is bedecked with (surprise, surprise) marionettes. These are large, wonderfully realistic and include a witch, a drunkard and a juggler. Coffee is 300 dr and cocktails are 1200 dr. Turn left opposite the Dolphin Hotel and it's on the right.

GLOSSA Γλώσσα
Glossa, Skopelos' other major settlement, is another whitewashed delight and considerably quieter than the capital. It manages to combine being a pristine Greek village with having most of the amenities that visitors require. The bus stops at a large church at a T-junction. Facing the church, left winds down to Loutraki and right to the main thoroughfare of Agiou Riginou. Along here you'll find a bank and a shop with a metered telephone. There is a disco and a music bar just out of the village, on the road to Skopelos town.

Skopelos' beaches are just as accessible by bus from Glossa as they are from Skopelos town; Milia, the island's best beach, is actually closer to Glossa. There are also places to stay and tavernas at Loutraki, but it's an uninteresting and unattractive place.

Places to Stay & Eat

In summer, at the time this book was researched when Skopelos town was packed to the gills with tourists and some were paying 2000 dr for roof space and 4000 dr for rooms like prison cells, the *Hotel Atlantes* (☎ 33 223), at the T-junction in Glossa, was languishing, almost empty. The clean, attractive single/double/triple rooms are 4000/5700/6800 dr. Glossa also has rooms in private houses – enquire at kafeneia.

Taverna Agnanti serves well-prepared, reasonably priced Greek fare. It's on the left side of Agiou Riginou as you walk from the T-junction.

AROUND THE ISLAND
Monasteries

Skopelos has many monasteries, several of which can be visited on a scenic, although quite strenuous, one-day trek from Skopelos town. Facing inland from the waterfront turn left and follow the road which skirts the bay and then climbs inland (signposted Hotel Aegeon). Continue beyond the hotel and you will come to a fork. Take the left fork for the 18th-century **Moni Evangelismou** (now a convent). From here there are breathtaking views of Skopelos town, four km away. The monastery's prize piece is a beautiful highly ornate carved and gilded iconostasis in which there is an 11th-century icon of the Virgin Mary.

The right fork leads to the uninhabited 16th-century **Moni Metamorphosis**, which is the island's oldest. From here the track continues to the 18th-century **Moni Prodromou** (now a nunnery), eight km from Skopelos town.

Beaches

Skopelos' beaches are almost all on the sheltered south-west coast. All the buses stop at the beginning of paths which lead down to them. First encountered is the crowded sand and pebble **Staphylos Beach** (site of Staphylos' tomb), four km from Skopelos

town. From the eastern end of the beach a path leads over a small headland to quieter **Velanio Beach**, the island's official nudist beach. **Agnotas**, three km west of Staphylos, has a small, pebble beach and from here caïques ply to superior and sandy **Limnonari Beach** (you can also walk here along a path from Agnotas, or a track from the main road). From Agnotas the road cuts inland through pine forests and re-emerges at sheltered **Panormos Beach**. **Milia**, the next beach along, is considered the island's best – a long swathe of minute pebbles.

All of these beaches have tavernas and/or cantinas. There are hotels and/or domatia at Staphylos, Limnonari, Panormos and Milia.

Alonissos Αλόννησος

Alonissos (Al-ON-is-os, population 3000) is still a serene island despite having been ferreted out by 'high- quality' package tourist companies. Package tourism would no doubt have taken off in a bigger way had the airport (erroneously and optimistically shown on island maps) materialised. This project was begun in the mid-1980s, but the rocks of Alonissos proved unyielding, making the construction of a runway impossible.

Alonissos once had a flourishing wine industry, but in 1950 the vines were struck with disease and, robbed of their livelihood, many islanders moved away. Fate struck another cruel blow when in 1965 a violent earthquake destroyed the hilltop capital of Alonissos town (now called Old Alonissos). The then ruling colonels' junta dispossessed the inhabitants of their wrecked homes and rehoused them in hastily assembled concrete dwellings at Patitiri. In recent years many of the derelict houses in the capital have been bought for a song from the government and renovated by northern Europeans.

Alonissos is a green island with pine and oak trees, mastic and arbutus bushes, and fruit trees. The west coast is mostly precipitous cliffs but the east coast is speckled with many pebbled beaches. The water around

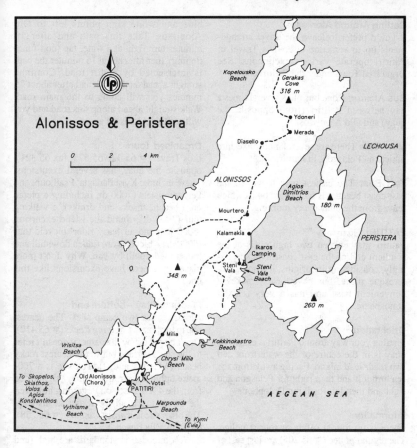

Alonissos & Peristera

0   2   4 km

Kopelousko Beach

Gerakas Cove 316 m

Ydoneri

Merada

Diasello

LECHOUSA

ALONISSOS

Agios Dimitrios Beach

180 m

Mourtero

PERISTERA

Kalamakia

Ikaros Camping

Steni Vala

Steni Vala Beach

348 m

260 m

Milia

Kokkinokastro Beach

Vrisitsa Beach

Chrysi Milia Beach

To Skopelos, Skiathos, Volos & Agios Konstantinos

Old Alonissos (Chora)

Votsi

PATITIRI

Vythisma Beach

Marpounda Beach

To Kymi (Evia)

AEGEAN SEA

Alonissos has been declared a marine park, and consequently is the cleanest in the Aegean. Every house has a cesspit, so no sewage goes into the sea.

Getting To/From Alonissos

Ferry There are daily ferries from Alonissos to Volos (five hours, 2400 dr) via Skopelos town, Glossa (Skopelos) and Skiathos, and also to Agios Konstantinos (six hours, 2886 dr) via Glossa (Skopelos), Skopelos town and Skiathos. There are two or three ferries a week from Alonissos (three hours, 2900 dr)

to Kymi (Evia). The ferry ticket office (☎ 65 220) is opposite the quay in Patitiri. The port police (☎ 65 595) are on the left side of Ikion Dolophon.

Hydrofoil There are daily hydrofoils from Alonissos to Volos (three hours, 4743 dr) and Agios Konstantinos (three hours, 5577 dr), both via Glossa (Skopelos), Skopelos town and Skiathos. Five times a week there is a hydrofoil to Skyros. Buy tickets from Ikos Travel (☎ 65 320/575), opposite the quay. There are four hydrofoils a week from Thessaloniki to Alonissos.

Getting Around Alonissos

If you'd prefer to leave the travel arrangements up to someone else, Ikos Travel in Patitiri operate various excursions. See Organised Tours under the Patitiri entry.

Bus Alonissos' one bus plies several times a day between Patitiri (from opposite the quay) and Old Alonissos.

Motorbike There are several motorbike-hire outlets on Pelagson, in Patitiri.

Taxi Boat The easiest way to get to the east-coast beaches is by the taxi boats which leave from the quay every morning.

PATITIRI Πατητήρι

Patitiri sits between two high cliffs at the southern end of the east coast. Not surprisingly, considering its origins, it's not a picturesque place, but nevertheless makes a convenient base and has a very relaxed atmosphere.

Orientation

Finding your way around Patitiri is easy. The quay is in the centre of the waterfront and two roads lead inland. Facing away from the sea turn left and then right for Pelagson and right and then left for Ikion Dolophon.

Information

There is no tourist office or tourist police. The regular police (☎ 65 205) are just east of the southern end of Ikion Dolophon.

The post office is on the right side of Ikion Dolophon and the OTE is on the waterfront to the right of the quay. The postcode is 37005 and the telephone code is 0424. The bank was due to move at the time of writing, but will probably be somewhere on Ikion Dolophon. There is a laundrette on the left side of Pelagson.

Walk to Old Alonissos

From Patitiri to Old Alonissos there is a delightful path which winds through shrubbery and orchards. Walk up Pelagson and 40 metres beyond Pension Galini a battered

blue and white sign points left to Old Alonissos. Take this path and after 10 minutes turn right at a water tap (non-functioning), then after about 15 minutes the path is intersected by a dirt road. Continue straight ahead on the path and after about 25 minutes you will come to the main road. Walk straight ahead along this road and you will see Old Alonissos ahead.

Organised Tours

Ikos Travel (☎ 65 320/65 575; fax 65 321), opposite the quay, has several excursions. These include: Kyra Panagia, Psathoura and Peristera islets (7000 dr, including a picnic on a beach, snacks and drinks); a walking tour (3000 dr); round the island excursion (6000 dr); and an 'easy rider' bicycle tour (5000 dr) – bicycles are ridden downhill and transported uphill by van. Why don't more places in Greece have excursions like this one?

Places to Stay – bottom end

Alonissos has two camp sites. The nearest one to the port is *Camping Rocks* (☎ 65 410). Don't be put off by the name; it doesn't refer to the site's surface but to the nearest rocky beach (which is nudist). The site is a 700-metre uphill slog from the quay (signposted from the 4 X 4 Disco on Pegason); however, the owner meets all the ferries in his jeep. The other site is *Ikaros Camping* (☎ 65 258), on Steni Vala Beach.

Accommodation standards are high (and cheaper than Skiathos and Skopelos) on Alonissos and except for the first two weeks in August you shouldn't have any difficulty finding a room. The Rooms to Let Service (☎ 65 577) opposite the quay will endeavour to find a room for you on any part of the island.

At *Nikolaos Dimakis Rooms* (☎ 65 294) the accommodation is clean and pleasant with rates of 3500 dr a double with shared bathrooms and 3000/4000 dr for singles/doubles with private bathrooms. The rooms are just 20 metres up Pelagson, on the right. Further up Pelagson, on the left at No 27, are the prettily furnished *Rooms of Magdelina*

Bassini (☎ 65 451). They cost 3500/4200 dr
for doubles/triples with shared bathrooms
and 4500/5400 dr with private bathrooms.
Pension Galini (☎ 65 573/094) is beautifully
furnished and has a flower-festooned terrace.
Doubles/triples are 5000/6000 dr with private bathrooms; well-equipped apartments
for five/six people are 10,000/13,000 dr. The
pension can be found on the left 400 metres
up Pelasgon.

Elini Athanaziou (☎ 65 240) rents lovely
rooms in a sparkling white, blue-shuttered
building high above the harbour. Rates are
4500/5500 dr for doubles/triples with private
bathrooms; five-people apartments are 10,000
dr. The rooms are next to the Balcony Café,
which is signposted from the right side of
Ikion Dolophon. The *Alkyon Guest House*
(☎ 65 450/220), on the waterfront, has comfortable singles/doubles for 5000/8000 dr
with private bathrooms.

The attractive rooms in the C class *Liadro-
mia Hotel* (☎ 65 521) have stucco walls,
stone floors, balconies and traditional carved
wood furniture. Walk inland up Ikion
Dolophon and take the first turn right, follow
the road around and the hotel is on the left.
Doubles are 8000 dr.

Places to Stay – middle

Alonissos' poshest hotel is the C class
Galaxy Hotel (☎ 65 251/2/3/4), where luxurious balconied single/double/triple rooms
cost 6100/8100/10,000 dr. The hotel is built
on a hill to the left of the bay if you're facing
inland. Turn left at the port and beyond the
waterfront tavernas take the steps up to the
right; turn left at the top to reach the hotel.

Places to Eat

If you feel you can't stomach another moussaka, pastitsio or souvlaki, then Alonissos
will come as a revelation, for the island has
some of rural and island Greece's best eating
places. Most specialise in imaginatively prepared fish dishes. At *To Kamaki Ouzeri*, on
the left side of Ikion Dolophon, mussels in
cream sauce are 900 dr and delicious
saganaki dishes are 900 to 1350 dr.

Another superlative little ouzeri is *Ouzeri*

Lefteris, on the right side of Pelasgon, where
stuffed cuttlefish is 900 dr and lobster with
tomatoes and peppers is 2100 dr. Further up
Pelasgon on the left, the *Astakos Fish Tavern*
is also highly commendable. The kalamaria
(800 dr) I ate here was among the best I've
had in Greece – very tender and fresh. The
Argos Restaurant has wonderful views of the
sea from its terrace and the food is good, with
main meals at 1300 dr. Face the sea, walk to
the extreme left of the harbour and the restaurant is signposted. For breakfast try the
Balcony Café (well signposted) with panoramic views down to the harbour.

OLD ALONISSOS

Nowadays, Old Alonissos (Chora) has a
strange appearance. Its narrow streets are
made of mud and stone but it is dominated
by highly renovated stone villas. These
dwellings are owned by wealthy northern
Europeans hankering after the simple life.

Old Alonissos is a tranquil, picturesque
place with lovely views. From the main road
just outside Old Alonissos a path leads down
to Vrisitsa Beach, and paths lead south to
Vythisma and Marpounda beaches.

Places to Stay

There are no hotels in Old Alonissos, but
there are a few domatia. One agreeable place
is the rooms of *John Tsoukanas* (☎ 65
135/469), with rates of 3500/4500/5000 dr
for singles/doubles/triples with private bathrooms. The domatia are on the central square
of Plateia Christos, which is named after its
17th-century church.

Places to Eat

Old Alonissos has three tavernas, all on the
main street. All are good but my favourite
was the *Paraport Taverna*, which has main
meals for around 1300 dr. On Plateia Christos the snack bar below John Tsoukanas'
rooms has tasty small souvlaki sticks for 180
dr and Greek salad for 550 dr. Live Greek
music is performed now and again at the
Rempetiko Bar in Old Alonissos. These
events are widely advertised – look for the
posters.

BEACHES

Most of Alonissos' beaches are on the east coast. Apart from the Patitiri-Old Alonissos road, the only road is one which goes north to the tip of the island. It is drivable all the way but only has tarmac for a few km out of Patitiri. Dirt tracks lead off the road to the beaches. The first beach is the gently shelving **Chrysi Milia Beach**. The next beach up is **Kokkinokastro**. Kokkinokastro is the site of the city of Ikos (the capital in ancient times) and there are remains of city walls and a necropolis under the sea. **Steni Vala** is a small fishing hamlet with a permanent population of 30, three tavernas and 30-odd rooms in domatia as well as the *Ikaros Camping* camp site. **Kalamakia**, further north, also has rooms and tavernas. **Agios Dimitrios**, further up, is an unofficial nudist beach.

ISLETS AROUND ALONISSOS

Alonissos is surrounded by seven uninhabited islets, all of which have a rich flora and fauna. The monk seal (*Monachus monachus*) is a Mediterranean sea mammal threatened with extinction; the largest existing population lives in the waters around the Sporades. These factors were the incentive behind the formation of the marine park in 1983. The park encompasses the sea and the islets around Alonissos. Its research station is on Alonissos, near Gerakas cove. **Piperi**, to the north-east of Alonissos, is a refuge for the monk seal and it is forbidden to set foot there without a licence to carry out research.

Gioura, also north-east of Alonissos, has many rare plants and a rare species of wild goat. **Skantzoura**, to the south-east of Alonissos, is the habitat of falcons and the rare Aegean seagull. **Peristera**, just off Alonissos' east coast, has several sandy beaches and the remains of a castle.

Kyra Panagia also has good beaches and two abandoned monasteries. **Psathoura** has the submerged remains of an ancient city and the brightest lighthouse in the Aegean. Both of these islands are to the north of Alonissos.

The seventh island is tiny **Adelphi**, between Peristera and Skantzoura.

Skyros Σκύρος

Skyros (SKEE-ros, population 2800) is some distance from the rest of the group and differs from them topographically. Almost bisected, its northern half is pine forested, but the south is barren and rocky. There are only two settlements, the small port of Linaria, and Skyros town, the capital, 10 km away on the east coast. Skyros is visited by poseurs rather than package tourists – and as many of these are wealthy young Athenians as foreigners.

Some visitors come to Skyros to attend courses at the Skyros Institute, a centre for holistic health and fitness. See under Skyros town for details.

Skyros' factual history was mundane in comparison to its mythological origins until Byzantine times, when rogues and criminals

---

The Life & Death of Achilles

Skyros figures prominently in Greek mythology. The gods predicted that Achilles, son of King Peleus and the sea-goddess, Thetis, would be killed at Troy, but that his participation was a prerequisite for a Greek victory. His adoring mum, anxious to avoid this fate, took him to Skyros dressed as a girl, and he was brought up as one of King Lykomedes' daughters. Achilles didn't have such a bad time here, managing to father a son, Neoptolemis, to Deidamia, one of his stepsisters. However, when the cunning Odysseus arrived bearing gifts, the king's daughters made a beeline for the trinkets, but Achilles' eyes lit up when he spotted a sword. His disguise unmasked, Achilles was whisked off to Troy, where Paris' arrow got him in the heel and killed him. Odysseus returned to Skyros and hauled Neoptolemis off to the war, where he fought valiantly, contributing to Greece's victory. ■

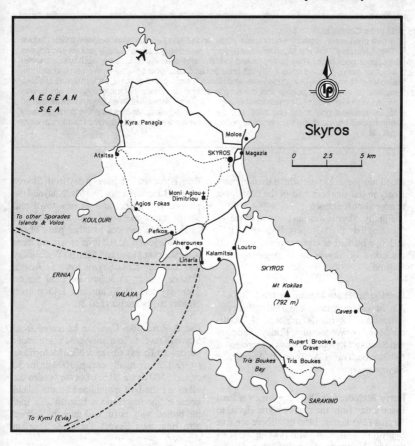

from the mainland were exiled there. When pirates invaded, these opportunist exiles, rather than drive them away, entered into a mutually lucrative collaboration with them. The exiles became the elite of Skyriot society, furnishing and decorating their houses with elaborately hand-carved furniture, and plates and copper ornaments from Europe, the Middle East and Far East. Some were brought by seafarers and some were simply looted by pirates from merchant ships. The peasants soon began to emulate the elite in their choice of décor, so local artisans cashed in by making copies of the

furniture and plates, a tradition which continues to this day. Almost every Skyriot house is festooned with plates, copperware and hand-carved furniture.

Other traditions endure. Many elderly Skyriot males still dress in traditional baggy pantaloons and *trohadia* (multi-thonged footwear unique to the island). The Skyros Carnival is Greece's most weird and wonderful, and the subject of Joy Coulentianou's book *The Goat Dance of Skyros*.

Another feature of Skyros which shouldn't go unmentioned, although it will probably go unseen, is the wild Skyrian pony, a

---

Skyros Carnival
In this pre-Lenten festival, which takes place on the last two Sundays before *Kathari Deftera* (Clean Monday – the first Monday in Lent), young men don goat masks, hairy jackets and dozens of copper goat bells. They then proceed to clank and dance around town, each with a partner (another man), dressed up as a Skyrian bride but also wearing a goat mask. Women and children also wear fancy dress. During these revelries there is singing and dancing, performances of plays, recitations of satirical poems and drinking and feasting. These riotous goings-on are overtly pagan, with elements of Dionysian festivals, goat worship (in ancient times Skyros was renowned for its excellent goat meat and milk), and the cult of Achilles. Achilles was the principal deity worshipped here and the transvestism evident in the carnival probably derives from this ancient cult. ■

---

breed unique to Skyros which used to roam freely in the southern half of the island, but is now almost extinct.

Finally, Skyros was the last port of call of the English poet Rupert Brooke (1887-1915), who died of septicaemia on a ship off the coast of Skyros in 1915, en route to Gallipoli.

Getting To/From Skyros (Island)

Air In summer there are flights between Athens and Skyros (50 minutes, 11,000 dr) on Monday, Wednesday, Friday, Saturday and Sunday. Olympic Airways is represented by Skyros Travel & Tourism Agency, in Skyros town.

Ferry & Hydrofoil There are ferries at least twice a day from the port of Kymi (Evia) to Skyros (2½ hours, 1450 dr). There are five hydrofoils a week to Volos (4¼ hours, 7588 dr) via Alonissos, Skopelos town, Glossa (Skopelos) and Skiathos.

Buy ferry tickets from Lykomides Ticket Office (☎ 91 789/890), opposite Plateia Iroon, in Skyros town. The hydrofoil ticket office is on Agoras, 40 metres north of Skyros Travel & Tourism. There are also ferry and hydrofoil ticket offices at Linaria. The port police telephone no is ☎ 91 475.

Getting Around Skyros (Island)

In addition to the options listed below, it is also possible to join either a boat or bus trip to sites around the island. See Organised Tours under the Skyros town entry.

Bus There are five buses a day from Skyros town to Linaria, Molos (via Magazia) and the airport. Buses for both Skyros town and Molos meet the boats and hydrofoils at Linaria. Bus services to other parts of the island are lousy. At the time of writing there were buses at 11 am and 5 pm on Wednesday and Saturday from Skyros town to Atsitsa (250 dr) and at 11.30 am and 5.30 pm on Thursday and 11.30 am and 1.45 pm on Sunday to Kalamitsa (180 dr).

Car & Motorbike Cars can be rented from Skyros Travel & Tourism Agency (see under Organised Tours). Cheap & Nice Motorbikes (☎ 92 022) are hardly cheap (3000 dr for 50 cc and 3500 dr for 80 cc), but they claim the bikes are the best maintained on the island because 'the mechanic is English'. To find the outlet, walk north and take the second turn right past Skyros Travel & Tourism Agency.

SKYROS TOWN

Skyros' capital is a striking, dazzling white town of flat-roofed Cycladic-style houses draped over a high rocky bluff, topped by a 13th-century fortress and the monastery of Agios Georgios.

Orientation

The bus terminal is at the southern end of town on the main thoroughfare of Agoras, an animated street lined with tavernas, snack bars and grocery shops, flanked by narrow winding alleyways. To reach the central square of Plateia Iroon walk straight ahead.

Walk along Agoras, beyond Plateia Iroon, and eventually you will come to a fork in the road. The right fork leads up to the fortress and Moni Agios Georgios (with fine frescoes), from where there are breathtaking views. The left fork leads to Plateia Rupert Brooke, which is dominated by the somewhat disconcerting bronze statue of a naked Rupert Brooke. This caused an outcry amongst the islanders when it was first installed in the 1930s. From this square a cobbled, stepped path leads in 15 minutes to Magazia Beach.

Information

Skyros does not have a tourist office or tourist police. The regular police (☎ 91 274) are just beyond Cheap & Nice Motorbikes (see the Getting Around Skyros (Island) section).

To get to the post office, take the first turn right after the bus terminal and it's on the left. The OTE is on the main road, a little way back towards Linaria, on the right as you walk from the bus terminal. Skyros' postcode is 34007 and the telephone code is 0222. The National Bank of Greece is on Agoras, a little way up from the bus terminal on the left.

Museums

There are three museums in Skyros town. The **Archaeological Museum** has an impressive collection from Mycenaean to Roman times. It is open Tuesday to Sunday from 8.30 am to 3 pm. Admission is 400 dr.

The **Faltaitz Museum** is a private museum housing the outstanding collection of Manos Faltaitz, a Skyriot ethnologist. The contents include costumes, furniture, ceramics and photographs. Opening times are 10 am to 1 pm and 5.30 to 9.30 pm. Admission is free. Both museums are just off Plateia Rupert Brooke.

The little known **Municipal Traditional Skyrion House** is just what its name implies. It's difficult to find, but worth the effort. Take the steps which lead up to the fortress. When you come to a crossroad with house No 993 straight ahead, turn left and the

museum is a little way along on the left. Opening times are Monday to Saturday from 11 am to noon and 6 to 8 pm. Admission is 200 dr.

Skyros Institute

The Skyros Institute runs courses on a whole range of subjects, from yoga and dancing, to massage and wind surfing. The emphasis is on learning to appreciate and develop an holistic approach to life. The main centre is in Skyros town, and there is a branch at Atsitsa Beach, on the west coast. For information contact The Skyros Centre (☎ 071-267 4424/284 3065; fax 071-284 3063), 92 Prince of Wales Rd, London NW5 3NE, UK.

Organised Tours

Skyros Travel & Tourism Agency (☎ 91 123/600; fax 92 123), on the left, just north of the central square, has bus excursions to Atsitsa (1300 dr), Pefkos (1150 dr) and Kalamitsa (2000 dr) beaches. They also operate two boat excursions: one to the Nyfi spring, Tris Boukes, Rubert Brooke's grave and Kalamitsa Beach; and the other to Sarakino islet and the sea caves of Pendekali and Gerania. Both excursions cost 3000 dr.

Places to Stay

In Skyros town there are many rooms (decorated with traditional plates) to rent in private houses; the owners meet the buses from Linaria.

The cheapest hotel is the E class *Hotel Eleni* (☎ 91 738), next to the post office, with tidy doubles for 4000 dr with bathrooms. The luxurious *Lykomedes House* (☎ 91 697) has spacious rooms with terraces affording fine hill vistas. There is an ultramodern communal kitchen and dining area; doubles are 7000 dr. Walk north along Agoras and turn sharp left at the Flying Dolphin Agency; at the bottom turn right, and the rooms are a little beyond Kabanera Restaurant, on the left. The B class *Hotel Nefeli* (☎ 91 964) is one of the best hotels in Skyros town. The lovely rooms have enlarged black and white photographs depicting traditional Skyrian life. Rates are 5700/9900/11,900 dr for singles/

doubles/triples with private bathrooms. The hotel is on the left just before you enter Skyros town.

Places to Eat
With two exceptions, Skyros town lacks memorable eating establishments. The most exceptional is *Kristina's Restaurant* in a delightful walled garden. Kristina is an Australian who conjures up delectable local and international dishes. *Kaseri* cheese and *sac* cheese (local specialities) are 400 dr, chicken fricassee is 800 dr and cheesecake is 400 dr. The restaurant is open only in the evenings. Walk south along the main street, beyond the OTE where the road forks, continue straight ahead and the restaurant is on the left. The unpretentious *Glaros Restaurant*, on Agoras, near the central square, serves the best Greek food in town.

The Sweets Workshop, on Agoras, has a vast array of mouthwatering traditional cakes, chocolates, nuts and Turkish delight.

Entertainment
The popularity enjoyed by particular bars in Skyros is ephemeral, but flavours of the month when I was there were the stylish *Artistico*, *Kalipso* and the *Renaissance Pub*, all on Agoras. *On the Rocks*, down the cobbled path towards Magazia, and *Borio*, just south of Skyros town, were the 'in' discos.

MAGAZIA & MOLOS
The resort of Magazia (Μαγαζιά) is at the southern end of a splendid long sandy beach, a short distance east of Skyros town; quieter Molos (Μώλος) is at the northern end.

Places to Stay – bottom end & middle
Skyros has one camp site, *Skyros Camping* (☎ 92 458), at Magazia. It's a scruffy run-down place with a few thirsty looking olive trees offering shade. Freelance campers stake out without hassle at Atsitsa amongst the pines, and at nearby Kyra Panagia, both on the west coast (see Beaches).

Efrosini Varsamou Rooms (☎ 91 142), above the family ceramics shop, in Magazia, are spacious and beautifully furnished. Rates are 6280/7360/9000 dr for doubles/triples/quads. If you're walking, go down the cobbled path from Skyros town, turn right at the bottom, and then right at the camp site (signposted Magazia and the Xenia Hotel) and the rooms are on the left. If you get the bus, get off at the camp site.

If you turn left at the Xenia Hotel, in just under 150 metres you will come to the *Alekos Domatia* (☎ 91 828), on the right, overlooking the beach. Pleasant and comfortable doubles/triples are 5600/6700 dr with private bathrooms.

At Molos, the *Motel Hara* (☎ 91 763) has clean, pine-furnished double/triple rooms for 5800/6800 dr. If you arrive by bus look for the motel on the right. *Angela's Bungalows* (☎ 91 764 or 92 030), set in a lovely garden, have large, immaculate single/double/triple rooms with private bathrooms, balconies and telephones for 6000/8500/10,000 dr. The bungalows are signposted from the Molos bus terminal. The C class *Hotel Paradise* (☎ 91 220), next to the bus terminal, is an attractive hotel with cream marble floors and white walls. Rates are 11,300/12,500 dr for doubles/triples.

Places to Stay – top end
The island's most luxurious hotel is the A class *Skyros Palace* (☎ 91 994; fax 92 070), a complex of attractive apartments, which stands in splendid isolation just north of Molos. The apartments have air-con, verandahs and music channels. The complex has a café, bar, restaurant, TV lounge and seawater swimming pool, and is 50 metres from a beach.

Things to Buy
A good selection of ceramics are on sale at Efrosini Varsamou's shop below the domatia of the same name at Magazia (see Places to Stay). It's hard to imagine any non-Skyriot wanting to wear the multi-thonged trohadia, but maybe they'd appeal to someone with a foot fetish who is into bondage. They can be bought at the Skyros Shop, on the street which leads to Plateia Rupert Brooke.

AROUND THE ISLAND
Beaches

At **Atsitsa**, on the west coast, there's a tranquil pebble beach shaded by pines. The beach attracts freelance campers and there's a branch of the Skyros Institute and a taverna/domatia here. Just to the north is the even less crowded beach of **Kyra Panagia** (also with freelance campers). At **Pefkos**, 10 km south of Atsitsa, there is another good beach. If you don't have transport take a Skyros town-Linaria bus and ask to be let off at the turn-off. Further south, the pebble and sand beach at **Kalamitsa** is rated as one of the island's best.

Rupert Brooke's Grave

Rupert Brooke's well-tended grave is in an olive grove on the east side of Tris Boukes bay in the south of the island. The grave stone is inscribed with the apt epitaph:

> If I should die think only this of me:
> That there's some corner of a foreign field
> That is forever England.

No buses go to this corner. You can take an excursion boat, or drive or walk along a rough scenic road from Kalamitsa. If you walk it will take about 1½ hours; take food and water.

The five Saronic Gulf islands are those closest of all to Athens. The closest one, Salamis (also called Salamina), is no more than a suburb of the sprawling capital and can in no way be regarded as a tourist destination. However, it may be of interest to a Greek historian who wants to see at first hand where the great Battle of Salamis took place in 480 BC.

The next island, Aegina, is still close enough to Athens for many of its inhabitants to commute there daily to work. Along with Poros, the next island south, it is also a popular package-holiday destination. Hydra, once the rendezvous of artists, writers and the beautiful people, is now overrun with all sorts of holiday-makers, but manages to retain an air of superiority and grandeur.

Spetses, the most southerly island in the group, receives an inordinate number of British package tourists, but retains a touch of class. All of the islands are heavily visited by Athenians, who come on day trips, for weekends and for annual holidays.

As you've probably guessed, finding accommodation on the spot on these islands is difficult. If you visit any of the group you may get the distinct impression there's a conspiracy against independent travellers. Most hotels are booked months in advance. If you arrive without a reservation the best thing to do is to ask a travel agent to find somewhere for you. There are no official camp sites on any of the islands.

None of the islands are cheap: in the price stakes it's a case of high (Aegina and Poros), higher (Spetses), and highest (Hydra). Having said all this, the islands are still eminently worth a visit and their big advantage (as well as disadvantage) is they can easily be visited on a day trip from Athens, either on a minicruise (see the Organised Tours section in the Athens chapter) or independently.

The islands are surprisingly varied in both architecture and terrain. Aegina is mountainous and forested, with a bustling town with

loads of character. Poros is actually two islands: one small and rocky, and entirely taken up with the pretty whitewashed capital; the other larger and verdant. Hydra is a barren rock with an amazingly beautiful town of grand mansions. Spetses, in contrast, is covered in pines, with a less immediately alluring, but nevertheless attractive, capital. While none of the islands are totally devoid of beaches, none is worth visiting for these alone. With the exception of the Temple of Aphaia, at Aegina, the islands have no significant archaeological remains.

Getting To/From the Saronic Gulf Islands

Ferry There are at least 12 ferries a day from Piraeus' Great Harbour to Aegina town (1½ hours, 715 dr). At least half of these continue to Methana, in the Peloponnese (two hours, 910 dr), and Poros (3½ hours, 1200 dr); two or three continue from Poros to Hydra (4½ hours, 1500 dr), Ermione, in the Peloponnese (five hours, 1750 dr) and Spetses (5½ hours, 1750 dr); and one continues from Spetses to Porto Heli (Peloponnese; 5¾ hours, 1750 dr). There are at least four ferries a day to both Agia Marina and Souvala on Aegina, most of which continue to Aegina town.

It is of course possible to board ferries

from the mainland ports of Methana, Ermione and Porto Heli, in the Peloponnese.

Hydrofoil There are hourly hydrofoils from Piraeus' Great Harbour to Aegina (40 minutes, 1142 dr). From Zea Marina there are at least 10 hydrofoils a day to Poros (one hour, 2200 dr), Hydra (1¾ hours, 2700 dr), and Spetses (two hours, 3000 dr). There are at least two hydrofoils a day from Zea Marina to Aegina, with connections through to ports in the Peloponnese via the other Saronic Gulf islands. See the relevant sections under individual island entries for details.

Getting Around the Saronic Gulf Islands
There is a comprehensive network of ferries and hydrofoils between the Saronic Gulf islands. See individual island entries for details.

Aegina Αίγινα

Unassuming Aegina (E-yee-na, population 11,000) seems an unlikely candidate for one of the most historically important islands in Greece. However, its strategic position between the two mighty city-states of Athens and Corinth, and Asia Minor, made it an important trading and maritime centre from Archaic times. By the 7th century BC it had amassed considerable wealth, and, ahead of any other country in Europe, it minted its own coins. In 456 BC, even though Aegina had aided the Greek side in the Battle of Salamis, green-eyed Athens set about devastating the island, and eventually Aegina capitulated, its fortifications wrecked and its ships taken by the Athenians.

Aegina was never to return to its former glory. The nearest it came to doing so was when it became the capital of the nascent Greek state, in 1827. This glory was, however, short-lived, for a year later it was superseded by Nafplion.

Aegina then slipped into a humbler role as Greece's premier producer of pistachio nuts.

Saronic Gulf Islands

At the beginning of the century a Greek from Alexandria, Nikolaos Peroglou, bought a summer villa on the island and soon discovered that the pistachio trees he planted flourished, faring better than any of the other trees in his garden. Other islanders planted pistachio trees and today cultivation of pistachios is the island's major industry.

The success of the nuts (which are reputedly the best in Greece) is attributed to the island's climate and the limestone soil. However, in 1992 the industry was threatened due to Aegina's chronic water shortage, which is exacerbated by intensive pistachio production. Pistachios require great amounts of water, and the rising costs of importing water from Athens is threatening Aegina's pistachio industry. Greeks claim pistachio nuts, eaten with yoghurt and honey, increase fertility.

Aegina's other claim to fame in modern times is that Nikos Kazantzakis was fond of the island and wrote *Zorba the Greek* while living in a house in Livadi, just north of Aegina town.

Getting To/From Aegina (Island)

Ferry In summer there are at least 12 ferries a day from Aegina town to Piraeus (1½ hours, 715 dr) and at least five from Agia Marina and Souvala; around eight to Methana and Poros and at least two to Hydra, Ermione and Spetses and one to Porto Heli. The port police (☎ 22 328) are on the right side of Aiakou, Aegina town, just round the corner from the waterfront. There is also a port police kiosk at the hydrofoil quay. There is a ferry ticket office at the quay.

Hydrofoil There are hourly hydrofoils from Piraeus' Great Harbour to Aegina (40 minutes, 1142 dr). There are at least two hydrofoils a day from Aegina to Methana (20 minutes, 650 dr), Poros (40 minutes, 1100 dr), Hydra (1¼ hours, 900 dr), Ermione (1¾ hours, 1800 dr), Spetses (2¼ hours, 1800 dr) and Porto Heli (2½ hours, 2300 dr). One of these continues from Porto Heli to Tolo and Nafplion, and one to Leonidio. Twice a week hydrofoils continue to Monemvassia in the Peloponnese and the island of Kythera. Hydrofoil tickets can be bought from a kiosk at the quay in Aegina town.

Getting Around Aegina (Island)

There are frequent buses from Aegina town to Agia Marina (via Paleohora and the Temple of Aphaia), Souvala and Perdika. There are several motorbike and moped-hire outlets along the waterfront in Aegina town.

AEGINA TOWN

Aegina town, on the west coast, is the island's capital and main port (the other ports are Agia Marina, on the east coast, and Souvala, on the north coast). The town, although not beautiful, is a charming, bustling, if slightly ramshackle place. Its harbour is lined with colourful caïques. Opposite the harbour there's a lively fish market. Some crumbling neoclassical buildings in pink and yellow ochres survive from its days as the Greek capital.

Orientation

The ferry quay is just left of the hydrofoil quay as you face inland. The harbour is to the right of the hydrofoil quay. To get to the bus terminal and post office, which are on Plateia Ethnigerious, face inland, cross over the road, turn left and you will come to the square. The post office is on the right side of this square. Plateia Ethnigerious abuts Leoforos Kazantzaki which skirts the northern waterfront and the Hill of Koloni. The town beach is south of the harbour – turn right from the quay to reach it.

Information

Aegina doesn't have a tourist office. To reach the amiable and helpful tourist police (☎ 22 100 or 23 333) take Odos Leonardou Lada, which runs inland from opposite the quay, and they're 50 metres up on the left. The office is open 24 hours and the tourist police will help you find accommodation.

To reach the OTE turn right from either quay, walk a little way along the waterfront, and turn left onto Aiakou. After 100 metres you will come to a crossroad; continue straight ahead along Aiakou, which now narrows to an alleyway, and the OTE is 50 metres up here, on the right. Aegina's postcode is 18010 and the telephone code is 0297. The National Bank of Greece is on the waterfront, just past the turn-off for Aiakou.

Temple of Apollo

Temple is a bit of a misnomer for the one Doric column which stands at this site. This column is all that's left of the 5th-century Temple of Apollo which once stood on the Hill of Koloni. The hill was the site of the ancient acropolis, and there are remains of a Helladic settlement. The site also has a small **museum**. Both are open Tuesday to Sunday from 8.30 am to 3 pm. Admission to the site (including the museum) is 400 dr. Turn left at the quay, walk along Leoforos Kazantzaki, and you'll come to the site on the left.

Places to Stay – bottom end

The *Xenon Pavlou Guest House* (☎ 22 795) has quaint old-fashioned double/triple rooms

which are good value at 6000/7000 dr with private bathrooms. Face inland from the quay and turn right, walk along the waterfront until you come to the large church on the left (beyond the turn-off for Aiakou), turn left here, cross a small square and you will see the guesthouse.

The C class *Hotel Marmarinos* (☎ 22 474 or 23 510), Leonardou Lada 24, had just been renovated at the time of writing. The clean, nicely furnished rooms cost 5000/6000/7500 dr for singles/doubles/triples with private bathrooms. The hotel is a little way beyond the tourist police, on the opposite side.

Places to Stay – middle

The C class *Hotel Brown* (☎ 22 271) has comfortable singles/doubles for 6300/9500 dr with private bathrooms. The hotel is on the waterfront beyond the large church. The *Eginitiko Arkhontiko* (☎ 24 156/968), Thomaidou 1, is an arkhontiko converted into a pension. The rates for the pleasant rooms are 6300/9400 dr. Thomaidou crosses over Aiakou a few blocks inland from the waterfront. Two other C class options are the *Avra Hotel* (☎ 22 303/968), Leoforos Kazantzaki 2, with rates of 6000/7500 dr for singles/doubles with private bathrooms and the *Hotel Areti* (☎ 22 806 or 23 917), Leoforos Kazantzaki 8, where double rooms cost 7000 dr.

The B class *Hotel Danae* (☎ 22 424/5), Leoforos Kazantzaki 43, has a bar, restaurant and pool. Rates are 5500/8500 dr for singles/doubles with private bathrooms.

Places to Eat

The *Restaurant Maridaki*, on the waterfront, between the National Bank of Greece and the large church, serves good traditional Greek fare. A full meal will cost about 1400 dr. *Dionisos Taverna*, Pan Irioti 47, is a good place to try grilled octopus, or a variety of other fish dishes, at reasonable prices. The taverna is behind the fish market.

You can buy pistachio nuts from the Pistachio Producers Association kiosk at the quay, or from numerous street vendors. The nuts cost around 1000 dr for 500 grams.

AROUND THE ISLAND
Temple of Aphaia

The splendid, well-preserved Doric Temple of Aphaia is the major ancient site of the Saronic Gulf islands. It was built in 480 BC when Aegina was at its height. Aphaia was a local deity of pre-Hellenic times.

The temple's pediments were decorated with outstanding Trojan War sculptures, most of which were spirited away in the 19th century, and eventually fell into the hands of Ludwig I (father of Greece's King Otho and grandfather of Ludwig II, the 'mad monarch'). They now have pride of place in Munich's Glyptothek. Even minus these sculptures the temple is impressive, with 24 extant columns, some of which form part of an inner colonnade. It stands on a hill of pine

trees, and commands imposing vistas of the Saronic Gulf and Cape Sounion.

The site (☎ 32 398) is open Monday to Friday from 8 am to 5 pm and Saturday and Sunday from 8.30 am to 3 pm. Admission is 600 dr. Aphaia is 12 km east of Aegina and can be reached by taking an Agia Marina bus.

Paleohora Παλαιοχώρα

Paleohora, on a hillside 6½ km east of Aegina town, was the island's capital from the 9th century to 1826, during which time attacks from pirates caused the inhabitants to flee the coast. The town is now in ruins, but around 20 of its churches remain, some of which have beautiful frescoes, especially the **Church of Agios Theodoros**. The remains of a fortress are on the summit of the hill.

Close by, **Moni Agiou Nektariou** is an important place of pilgrimage for both locals and Athenians. The monastery contains the relics of a hermit monk, Anastasios Kefalas, who died in 1920. When his body was exhumed in 1940 it was found to have mummified – a sure sign of sainthood in Greek Orthodoxy. In addition to defying the laws of nature in death, he reputedly also did so when he was alive, as a number of miraculous cures have been attributed to him. Anastasios Kefalas was canonised in 1961 – the first Orthodox saint of the 20th century. A track leads south from here to the 16th-century **Moni Chrysoleontissas**, in a lovely mountainous setting.

The Aegina town-Agia Marina bus stops at Paleohora or it's a pleasant walk from Aegina town.

Beaches

Agia Marina (Αγία Μαρίνα), on the east

The Pursuit of Aphaia

According to mythology Aphaia was originally called Dyctynna and was a daughter of Leto and Zeus. Like her sister, Artemis, she was fond of hunting. When she herself was hunted relentlessly by the lascivious King Minos of Crete she dived into the sea to escape him, but was caught in the net of a fisherman. The fisherman, like Minos, was captivated by her so into the sea she went again, ending up on Aegina. Artemis now came to her rescue by making her invisible (*aphanes* in Greek). She was renamed Aphaia, and worshipped on Aegina as the protector of women. ■

coast, is Aegina's premier tourist resort. There's a good sandy beach, but also hordes of package tourists. The resort of **Souvala**, a former spa town on the north coast, is more low key, but the beach is mediocre. **Perdika**, at the southern tip of the west coast, is a charming fishing village with a small beach and tavernas and domatia. There are several stretches of beach between Perdika and Aegina town.

Moni & Angistri Islets

Moni Islet (Νήσος Μονή) and Angistri islet (Νήσος Αγκίστρι) lie off the west coast of Aegina, opposite Perdika. Moni, the smaller of the two, is only a 10-minute boat ride from Perdika – frequent boats do the trip in summer. It's small, rocky and uninhabited, but gets some day-trippers from Aegina, and is popular with freelance campers.

Angistri is a much bigger, green island with around 500 inhabitants. There's a sandy beach at the port and other smaller beaches around the coast. Both package-holiday tourists and independent travellers find their way to Angistri. There are tavernas, hotels and domatia on the island. In summer five caïques a day do the 25-minute trip from Aegina town to Angistri.

Poros Πόρος

Poros (POR-ros, population 4000) is just an ouzo bottle's throw from the mainland. A slender passage of water (only 360 metres at the narrowest point) separates the island from the Peloponnesian town of Galatas. This passage was the inspiration behind Henry Miller's oft-quoted observation in which he compares floating through the straits of Poros to the joy of passing through the neck of the womb. If he saw the place today no doubt he'd want to return hastily to the womb, given the number of visitors to the island.

The two islands which comprise Poros, Sferia and Kalavria, are separated by a canal and connected by a bridge. Sferia is rocky

and, like Methana on the mainland, volcanic in origin, whereas Kalavria is fertile and well wooded. Poros can be used as a base for exploring the ancient sites of the prefecture of Argolis in the Peloponnese.

Getting To/From Poros (Island)

Ferry There are eight ferries a day to Piraeus (3½ hours, 1200 dr), Aegina and Methana from Poros, and at least one a day to Hydra, Ermione, Spetses and Porto Heli.

Small ferries ply every 20 minutes to/from Galatas (80 dr) on the mainland. The port police (☎ 22 274) are on the waterfront in Poros town, near the quay.

Hydrofoil There are at least 10 hydrofoils a day from Poros to Piraeus (one hour, 2200 dr), Hydra and Spetses; at least two a day to Ermione and Porto Heli; and one a day to Tolo, Nafplion and Leonidio. Twice a week hydrofoils continue to Monemvassia in the Peloponnese, and the island of Kythera.

Getting Around Poros (Island)

Frequent buses travel east along the coast as far as Moni Zoodochou Pigis, and west as far as Neorion Beach. There are several motorbike-rental outlets on the waterfront.

POROS TOWN

Poros town is the island's only settlement. It's a pretty place of white houses with terracotta tiled roofs, and there are wonderful views over to the mountains of Argolis. However, be warned, Poros is a popular destination with package tourists and daytrippers.

Orientation & Information

The ferry and hydrofoil quay are in the middle of the waterfront. The post office is on Plateia Karamanou, abutting the waterfront, to the right of the quay as you face inland. The OTE is along the waterfront to the left of the quay. Poros' postcode is 18020 and the telephone code is 0298. The National Bank of Greece is also on the waterfront, to the right of the quay, beyond the post office. The bus terminal is opposite the ferry quay.

Poros does not have a tourist office. The tourist police (☎ 22 462/256) are on Agiou Nikolaou, which runs inland from the waterfront – turn right from the ferry quay.

Places to Stay – bottom end

If things aren't too hectic you may be offered a room when you get off the ferry. Otherwise you can start looking around, or seek the assistance of one of the many travel agents which have a room-finding service. These include: Askeli Travel (☎ 24 566/900; fax 24 766); Family Tours (☎ 23 743 or 22 549); and Epsilon Travel (☎ 24 555; fax 24 802). All these agents are on the waterfront near the quay. One place worth trying is *Nicos Douras Rooms* (☎ 22 633), which are well kept and good value. The rates are 5000/6000 dr for doubles/triples with shared bathrooms. Turn right at the quay, walk along the waterfront and turn right onto Mitropoleos, and you will come to the rooms on the right.

The *Hotel Latsi* (☎ 22 392/543), Papadopoulou 74, has comfortable but characterless single/double rooms for 4500/6500 dr with private bathrooms. To reach the hotel turn left from the quay and walk along the waterfront. The C class *Hotel Akteon* (☎ 22 281), overlooking the quay, has reasonable rooms for a similar price.

Places to Stay – middle

Close to the Hotel Akteon, the B class *Hotel Saron* (☎ 22 279 or 23 670) is ageing but still has very pleasant singles/doubles for 5500/8300 dr with private bathrooms. The B Class *Hotel Dionyssos* (☎ 23 511), Papadopoulou 78, has singles/doubles for 9000/11,000 dr. Most of the more expensive places to stay on Poros are on Kalavria. The huge B class *Hotel Poros* (☎ 22 216) has a bar, restaurant and disco. Rates are 7500/11,000 dr for singles/doubles. The smaller *Hotel Pavlou* (☎ 22 734/766) has a bar and restaurant.

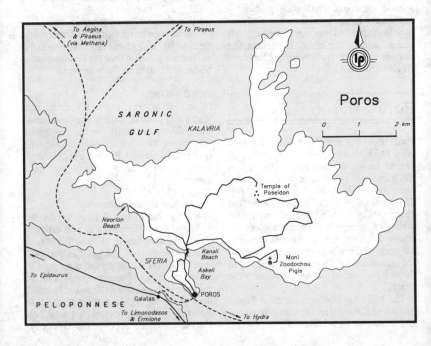

Singles/doubles cost 6000/9400 dr. Both of these hotels are at Neorion Beach.

The large B class *Hotel Sirene* (☎ 22 741/2/3/4/5) has a bar, restaurant and pool. The rates are 7100/11,000 dr. The hotel is just before Moni Zoodochou Pigis, east of Poros town.

Places to Eat

O Pantelis Taverna is a lively unpretentious place which serves hearty Greek fare at low prices; moussaka is 750 dr. The taverna is just back from the waterfront; turn right from the quay and it's to the right of the market. *Seven Brothers Restaurant* (in the pension of the same name), on the central square, is more up-market and has tasty food. A full meal with Amstel will cost about 1800 dr.

AROUND THE ISLAND

Poros has a paucity of places of interest and its beaches are no great shakes. **Kanali Beach**, just east of the bridge, is a mediocre pebble beach. **Neorion Beach**, three km west of the bridge, is marginally better.

The 18th-century **Moni Zoodochou Pigis** is the principal sight. It has a beautiful gilded iconostasis which came from Asia Minor and is decorated with paintings from the gospels. The monastery is in an attractive, verdant setting four km east of Poros town.

From the road below the monastery you can strike inland to the 6th-century **Temple of Poseidon**. The god of the sea and earthquakes was the principal deity worshipped on Poros. There's very little left of this temple, but the walk is worth doing for the lovely scenery on the way. From the site there are superb vistas of the Saronic Gulf and the Argolis.

In 322 BC, the orator Demosthenes committed suicide here, after failing to shake off the Macedonians, who were after his blood. Demosthenes had incited the city-states to rebel against the Macedonians. This rebellion culminated in the War of Lamian (323 BC) in which the city-states were defeated. Archaeological buffs may remember the Head of Demosthenes in the National Archaeological Museum (Room 29) in Athens. The expression on this sculpture does indeed look suicidal.

From the ruins you can continue along the road, which eventually winds back to the bridge. The road is drivable, but it's also a fine walk.

PELOPONNESE MAINLAND

The Peloponnese mainland opposite Poros is easily accessible from the island, and is a fascinating area to explore on a day trip.

From the port of Galatas, a short 20 to 30-minute walk to the south-east will take you to the vast citrus groves of **Limonodasos**, where you can have your senses pleasantly assaulted by thousands of fragrant lemon trees, and sample locally made lemonade.

About nine km to the north-west of Galatas is the ancient site of **Trizine**, which, according to legend, is the birthplace of Theseus. Take a bus to Dhamala, six km from Galatas, and walk to the site from there. Alternatively, a Methana-bound bus will let you off at Agios Georgious, from where it is a three-km walk inland to the site.

A range of accommodation can be found in Galatas. There's a camp site one km north-west of the town.

Getting There & Around There are frequent ferries across the strait for the five-minute trip (80 dr) from Poros town to Galatas. A couple of buses a day depart for Nafplion (two hours, 1050 dr), which will drop you off at the renowned ancient site of Epidaurus (see the Peloponnese chapter for details on this site).

The district around Galatas is ideal for exploring by bicycle; these can be hired in Galatas village.

Hydra Ύδρα

Hydra (EE-dhra, population 3000) is the Saronic Gulf island with the most style – and

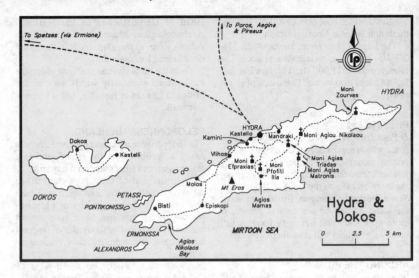

To Spetses (via Ermione)

To Poros, Aegina & Pireaus

HYDRA

Moni Zourvas

HYDRA
Kastello
Kamini
Mandraki
Moni Agiou Nikolaou

Vlihos
Moni Efpraxias
Moni Pfofiti Ilia
Moni Agias Triadas
Moni Agias Matronis

Dokos
Kastelli

Molos
Mt Eros
Agios Mamas

Hydra & Dokos

PETASSI
PONTIKONISSI
Bisti
Episkopi

DOKOS

ERMONISSA
Agios Nikolaos Bay

ALEXANDROS

MIRTOON SEA

0   2.5   5 km

prices to match. When you sail into Hydra you are greeted by gracious stone, and white and pastel mansions stacked up a rocky hillside. The first foreigners to be seduced by the beauty of Hydra were film makers who began arriving in the 1950s; the island was used as a location for the film *Boy on a Dolphin*, amongst others. The artists and writers moved in next, followed by the celebs, and nowadays it seems the whole world is welcomed ashore.

If you've been in Greece for some time you may fall in love with Hydra for one reason alone: its absence of kamikaze motorcyclists who are endemic elsewhere in Greece. Hydra is free of motorised transport except for sanitation and construction vehicles. Donkeys (hundreds of them) are the only means of transport on the island. On one visit I met a northern European guy who was earning some extra cash shovelling the ubiquitous donkey droppings from the streets – worth enquiring about if you're in the area and broke.

The biggest houses you see in Hydra are the arkhontika, stone mansions built in the late 18th and early 19th century for Hydra's wealthy shipping merchants.

History

Like many of the Greek islands, Hydra was ignored by the Turks, so many Greeks from the Peloponnese settled on the island to escape Ottoman suppression and high taxes. The population was further boosted by an influx of Albanians. The infertility of Hydra's soil forced these settlers to turn to the sea for a living, either by bona fide means or dabbling in piracy. They began building boats in the 1700s and by the 19th century the island had become a great maritime power. The canny Hydriots boosted their economy further by running a British blockade during the Napoleonic Wars. During the 19th century the island was a fashionable resort for Greek socialites, and lavish balls were a regular feature.

Hydra made a considerable contribution in the War of Independence, both in its leaders, and the supply of 150 ships. Most famous of the Hydriot leaders were Georgios Koundouriotis and Admiral Andreas Miaoulis. You will find streets and squares all over Greece named after these two. A mock battle is staged during the **Miaoulia Festival** which is held in honour of Admiral Miaoulis in late June.

Getting To/From Hydra (Island)

Ferry In summer ferries leave Hydra at least twice a day for Piraeus (4½ hours, 1500 dr), Poros, Aegina, Ermione, Spetses and Porto Heli. To reach the port police (☎ 52 279) turn left from the quay as you face inland.

Hydrofoil From Hydra there are at least 10 hydrofoils a day to Zea Marina (1¾ hours, 2700 dr), Poros, Ermione and Spetses.

Getting Around Hydra (Island)

Low-priced caïques go from Hydra town to most of the island's beaches. Water taxis go like bats out of hell to most of the beaches, but the fares are astronomical.

HYDRA TOWN

If you find Hydra town chock-a-block all is not lost as most visitors head for the beaches, or hang around the waterfront cafés, leaving the upper reaches of the narrow stepped streets deserted, and a joy to explore.

Orientation & Information

The quay is on the left side of the harbour as you face inland. Step off the ferry or hydrofoil and turn right to reach the centre of the waterfront. From here the main thoroughfare of Odos Miaouli strikes inland, just before the prominent marble clock tower. The National Bank of Greece is on the waterfront before Miaouli. The post office is on a little side street just before the bank. To reach the OTE on Odos Votsi, walking from the quay, turn left after the clock tower, and it's on the left. Hydra's postcode is 18040 and the telephone code is 0298.

There is no tourist office on Hydra. The tourist police (☎ 52 205) are on the right side of Odos Votsi.

Things to See

Several of Hydra town's arkhontika are worth seeking out. George Koundouriotis was a wealthy Hydriot ship owner of Albanian extraction, and a War of Independence leader. His great grandson Pavlos Koundouriotis was regent and president of Greece from 1924-26. The **George Koundouriotis Mansion** is west of the harbour, just back from the waterfront. Another very grand arkhontiko is the **Tombazis Mansion**, which overlooks the harbour from its western side. It is now a branch of the Fine Art faculty of Athens Polytechnic and sometimes holds exhibitions. The **Economou-Merikles Mansion** is just beyond here, right on the waterfront. There are many other arkhontika and fine houses around the town.

Moni Panagias, behind the waterfront clock tower, is now used as offices but it has a peaceful courtyard and quite lavish ecclesiastical decorations inside its church.

Places to Stay – bottom end

You're unlikely to be offered anything on arrival, but there are plenty of travel agents who will try to fix you up with somewhere. They include: Pan Travel (☎ 53 135/260; fax 53 525) and Saronic Tours (☎ 52 184; fax 53 469), both near the quay.

One very reasonably priced place is *Savvas Rooms* (☎ 52 259), on Lihnou. The delightful, old-fashioned rooms cost 5500 dr for a double with shared bathrooms. Take the second turn left after the clock tower and the rooms are on the right.

Amongst the hotels, the dilapidated D class *Hotel Sophia* (☎ 52 313) is the best bet for budget travellers; doubles are 4500 dr with shared bathrooms. The hotel is on the waterfront on the corner of Miaouli.

Places to Stay – middle

The *Hotel Amarylis* (☎ 52 249), Tombazi 15, is classed as a pension and has clean, attractive doubles for 8000 dr with private bathrooms. Walk along the waterfront from the quay, and then inland along Tombazi, and the hotel's on the right. The *Hydra Hotel* (☎ 52 102/597), Voulgari 8, is a converted arkhontiko with tastefully furnished rooms. Rates are 7400/10,400 dr for singles/doubles with private bathrooms. Voulgari is just back from the western side of the harbour.

Places to Stay – top end

Hydra's most expensive hotels are at Mandraki (see Around the Island). Two of them are the A class *Miramare* (☎ 52 300/1) which has singles/doubles for 10,400/15,000 dr and the *Miranda* (☎ 52 230) which has singles/doubles for 10,000/15,600 dr and suites for 19,500 dr.

Places to Eat

One of the nicest eating places in Hydra town is the reasonably priced *Lulu's Taverna*, on Miaouli, which has been going strong for almost 25 years. Another authentic place with scrumptious meals is *O Barba Dimas*, on Tombazi. Expect to pay about 1600 dr for a full meal.

AROUND THE ISLAND

It's a strenuous but worthwhile one-hour walk up to **Moni Profiti Ilia**, starting from Odos Miaouli. Monks still inhabit the monastery, which affords superb views down to the town. From this monastery it's a short walk to **Moni Efpraxias**, which is now a convent.

Beaches on Hydra are a dead loss but the walks to them are enjoyable. **Kamini**, around 30 minutes' walk along a path from town, has rocks and a small pebble beach. **Vlihos**, 20 minutes further on, is an attractive hamlet with another small pebble beach, two tavernas and a ruined 19th-century stone bridge. From here walkaholics can continue either to the small bay at **Molos**, or take a left fork before the bay, to the inland hamlet of **Episkopi**. There are no facilities at Episkopi; a seasonal café may be open at Molos but don't bank on it – take sustenance with you. An even more ambitious walk is the three-hour stint to **Moni Zourvas**, in the north-east of the island. Along the way you will pass **Moni Agias Triadas** and **Moni Agiou Nikolaou**.

A path leads east from Hydra town to the pebble beach at **Mandraki** which, due to its large hotel (the Miramare), is always very crowded.

Spetses Σπέτσες

Pine-covered Spetses (SPET-ses, population 3700), the most distant of the group from Piraeus, withstood the tourist onslaught for longer than its neighbours. However, the 1980s heralded its discovery by British package-tour operators.

Spetses' history is similar to Hydra's. It became wealthy through shipbuilding, ran the British blockade during the Napoleonic Wars, and played a prominent part in the War of Independence. The most unusual feature of this period of the island's history is that one of the leading Spetsiots during the War of Independence was a woman, Admiral Lascarina Bouboulina. Her picture is on the 50 drachma note.

Getting To/From Spetses (Island)

Ferry In summer ferries leave Spetses at least twice a day for Piraeus (5½ hours, 1750 dr), Ermione, Hydra, Poros, Methana, Aegina and Porto Heli. At least four small ferries a day ply to/from Kosta (100 dr) on the mainland. The port police (☎ 72 245) are opposite the quay.

Hydrofoil In summer there are at least 10 hydrofoils a day from Zea Marina to Spetses (1¾ hours, 3000 dr) via Poros and Ermione. Ferries continue from Spetses to Porto Heli, from where one ferry a day departs for Nafplion, and one for Leonidio. Twice a week hydrofoils continue to Monemvassia and the island of Kythera.

Getting Around Spetses (Island)

Buses run three times a day from Spetses town to Anargyri (via Agia Marina). There is no ban on motorised transport as there is on neighbouring Hydra, but there are restrictions on cars. Unfortunately there is no restriction on motorbikes, which are widely available for rent. Horse-drawn carriages are a popular means of transportation around town and to the nearby beaches.

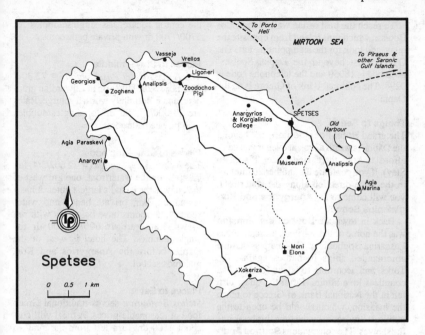

Spetses

0   0.5   1 km

SPETSES TOWN

Spetses town is divided into two parts, the district of Dapia, built around the Dapia harbour, and the old harbour, a 25-minute walk away, at the east end of the long waterfront. Spetses town is not as overtly beautiful as Hydra town, but nonetheless has the requisite maze of streets to invite and reward exploration.

Like Hydra it has some arkhontika, one of which belonged to Sotirios Anargyrios, an extremely generous benefactor. He was born on Spetses in 1849, emigrated to the USA, and returned to Spetses in 1914 an exceedingly rich man. He endowed the town with many grand buildings, including the Hotel Possidonion; founded the Anargyrios and Korgialenios College (a boys' school modelled on English public schools); and reafmforested the island with Aleppo pines, with which it was covered in antiquity.

Pre-war Spetses was a favourite resort for British high society. From 1950-51, John

Fowles taught English at the Anargyrios and Korgialenios College, and used the island as a setting for his novel *The Magus*.

Orientation

The quay at Dapia harbour serves both ferries and hydrofoils. Turn left from here to reach the waterfront. If you continue along the waterfront you will reach the old harbour, which is used for caïques and yachts. The square to the right of the quay, with the row of cannons, is known as the Dapia. The central square (known simply as Clocktower Square) is one block back from the waterfront, just left of the quay. The town beach is along the waterfront to the left of the quay. The bus terminal is on the waterfront at the town beach.

Information

There is no tourist office on Spetses. The tourist police (☎ 73 100) are on the right side of Botassi.

To reach the post office walk along Odos Botassi, which runs inland from opposite the quay, and look for the sign pointing left. The OTE is just beyond the Dapia. Spetses' postcode is 18050 and the telephone code is 0298. The National Bank of Greece is on the Dapia.

Things to See
The grand **Hotel Possidonion**, just beyond the Dapia, is worth a look at even if you can't afford to stay there (see under Places to Stay). If you continue for another 20 minutes in the same direction along the waterfront, you will come to the **Anargyrios and Korgialenios School**.

Back in town the **Bouboulina Mansion** was the home of the spirited and scandalous Lascarina Bouboulina. This fearless heroine commanded ships in battles against the Turks, and according to island folklore had countless love affairs. From the quay, turn left at the National Bank of Greece to reach the mansion, which should be open to the public as a museum by the time this book hits the shelves. The conspicuous **Sotirios Anargyrios Mansion** is between the Bouboulina Mansion and Odos Botassi.

The **Mexis Museum** has a collection of bits and pieces from the War of Independence (including Lascarina Bouboulina's bones) and some folklore items. The museum is the arkhontiko of Hadziyiannis Mexis, who was a ship owner, and Spetses' first governor. It's open Tuesday to Sunday from 8.30 am to 3 pm. Admission is free. A road running inland from the town beach leads to the museum.

Places to Stay – bottom end
Travel agents who can assist in finding accommodation are Takis Travel (☎ 72 888) and Pine Island Tours (☎ 72 464), both near the quay.

The D class *Hotel Saronikos* (☎ 73 741), opposite the quay, has tidy doubles for 5000 dr with shared bathrooms. The slightly smarter C class *Hotel Faros* (☎ 72 613), on

the central square, has singles/doubles for 5700/7700 dr with private bathrooms.

Places to Stay – middle
The A class *Hotel Possidonion* (☎ 72 308/006; fax 72 208) lives on in Edwardian grandeur, and is definitely worth a splurge. Rates are 11,000/17,000 dr for singles/doubles with private bathrooms.

Places to Stay – top end
The A class *Hotel Spetses* (☎ 72 602/3/4; fax 72 494), on the waterfront, one km west of the quay, is the island's largest hotel. It has a restaurant, bar, private beach and water sports. The rooms have balconies with sea views. Rates are 16,600/17,700 dr for singles/doubles. The hotel is west of the Dapia, before the Anargyrios and Korgialenios school.

Places to Eat
Stelios Restaurant serves traditional Greek food at reasonable prices. A meal will cost about 1500 dr. Turn left from the quay to reach the restaurant. *The Bakery Restaurant*, near the tourist police, has a more salubrious ambience and an imaginative range of dishes.

AROUND THE ISLAND
Spetses' coastline is speckled with numerous coves with small pine-shaded beaches. A 24-km road (part tarmac, part dirt) skirts the entire coastline. However, in some places you will have to clamber down steep paths to reach the coves. Of the beaches near Spetses town, **Ligoneri** and **Vrellos**, to the west, are pleasant. **Agia Marina**, to the south of the old harbour, is a small resort with a crowded beach. **Agia Paraskevi** and **Anargyri**, on the south-west coast, have good, albeit crowded, beaches; both have water sports of every description. A large mansion between the two beaches was the inspiration for the Villa Bourani in *The Magus*.

Glossary

Achaean Civilisation – see *Mycenaean Civilisation*.

acropolis – highest point of an ancient city.

agora – commercial area of an ancient city.

amphora – large two-handled vase in which wine or oil was kept.

Archaic Age (800-480 BC) – period in which the *city-states* emerged from the *Dark Age* and traded their way to wealth and power. They were unified by a Greek alphabet and common cultural pursuits, engendering a sense of national identity. Also known as the *Middle Age*.

architrave – part of the *entablature* which rests on the columns of a temple.

arkhontika – 17th and 18th-century AD mansions which belonged to arkhons, the leading citizens of a town.

basilica – early Christian church.

Byzantine Empire – characterised by the merging of Hellenistic culture and Christianity, the Byzantine Empire is named after Byzantium, the city on the Bosporus which became the capital of the Roman Empire in 324 AD. When the Roman Empire was formally divided in 395 AD, Rome declined and the eastern capital, renamed Constantinople after Emperor Constantine I, flourished. The Byzantine Empire dissolved after the fall of Constantinople to the Turks in 1453.

capital – top of a column.

cella – room in a temple where the cult statue stood.

Chora (or **Hora**) – main town (usually on an island).

choregos – wealthy citizen who financed choral and dramatic performances.

chryselephantine statue – ivory and gold statue.

city-states – states comprising a sovereign city and its dependencies. The city-states of Athens and Sparta were famous rivals.

Classical Greece – period of Greek history

in which the *city-states* reached the height of their wealth and power after the defeat of the Persians in the 5th century BC. The period ends with the decline of the city-states as a result of the Peloponnesian Wars, and the expansionist aspirations of Philip II, King of Macedon (ruled 359-336 BC), and his son, Alexander the Great (ruled 336-323 BC).

Corinthian – order of Greek architecture recognisable by columns with bell-shaped *capitals* with sculpted elaborate ornaments based on acanthus leaves.

crypt – lowest part of a church, often a burial chamber.

Cycladic Civilisation (3000-1100 BC) – civilisation which emerged following the settlement of Phoenician colonists on the Cycladic islands of the Aegean. The peoples of this civilisation built and lived in houses, built boats and began mining obsidian.

Cyclopes – Mythical one-eyed giants.

Dark Age Greece – period of Greece under Dorian rule. See *Dorians*.

Dorians – Hellenic warriors who invaded Greece around 1200 BC, demolishing the *city-states* and destroying the *Mycenaean Civilisation*. They heralded Greece's *Dark Age*, when the artistic and cultural advancements of the Mycenaeans and Minoans were abandoned. The Dorians later developed into land-holding aristocrats which encouraged the resurgence of independent city-states led by wealthy aristocrats.

Doric – order of Greek architecture characterised by a column which has no base, a shaft with sharp flutes and a relatively plain *capital*, when compared with the flourishes evident on *Ionic* and *Corinthian* capitals.

entablature – part of a temple between the tops of the columns and the roof.

Epitaphios – picture on cloth of Christ on His bier.

fluted – vertical indentations on the shaft of some columns.

frieze – part of the *entablature* which is above the *architrave*.

galaktopoleion (plural: galaktopoleia) – shop which sells dairy products.

Geometric Age (1200-800 BC) – period characterised by pottery decorated with geometrical designs. Sometimes referred to as Greece's *Dark Age*.

Helots – original inhabitants of Lakonia whom the Spartans used as slaves.

iconostasis – altar screen embellished with icons.

Ionic – order of Greek architecture characterised by a column with truncated flutes and *capitals* with ornaments resembling scrolls.

kafeneion (plural: kafeneia) – traditionally a male-only coffee house where cards and backgammon are played.

kalderimi – cobbled footpath.

kastro – walled-in town.

katholikon – principal church of a monastic complex.

kore – female statue of the *Archaic Age*. See *kouros*.

kouros (plural: kouroi; female: *kore*) – male statue of the *Archaic Age*, characterised by a stiff body posture and enigmatic smile.

libations – in Ancient Greece, wine or food which was offered to the gods.

libation vessel – utensil from which the wine offered to the gods was poured.

Linear A – Minoan script; so far undeciphered.

Linear B – Mycenaean script, which has been deciphered.

megaron – central room of a Mycenaean palace.

meltemi – north-east wind which blows throughout much of Greece during the summer.

metope – sculpted sections of a *Doric frieze*.

Middle Age – see *Archaic Age*.

Minoan Civilisation (3000-1100 BC) – Bronze Age culture of Crete, named after the mythical King Minos. The period was characterised by pottery and metalwork of great beauty and artisanship.

moni – monastery.

Mycenaean Civilisation (1900-1100 BC) – first great civilisation of the Greek mainland, characterised by powerful independent *city-states* ruled by kings. Also known as the *Achaean Civilisation*.

narthex – porch of a church.

nave – aisle of a church.

necropolis – ancient cemetery (literally: city of the dead).

nefos – cloud; usually used to refer to pollution in Athens.

nomos – prefectures into which the regions and island groups of Greece are divided.

nymphaeum – in Ancient Greece, building containing a fountain, and often dedicated to nymphs.

odeion – Ancient Greek indoor theatre.

omphalos – sacred stone at Delphi which the Ancient Greeks believed marked the centre of the world.

ouzeri – traditionally, place which serves ouzo and light snacks.

Panagia – Mother of God; name frequently used for churches.

Pantocrator – painting or mosaic of Christ in the centre of the dome of a Byzantine church.

paralia – waterfront.

pediment – triangular section (often filled with sculpture) above the columns, found at the front and back of a Classical Greek temple.

periptera – streek kiosks.

peristyle – columns surrounding a building (usually a temple) or courtyard.

pithos (plural: pithoi) – large Minoan storage jar.

propylon (plural: propylaia) – elaborately built main entrance to an ancient city or sanctuary. A propylon had one gateway and a propylaia more than one.

rhyton – another name for a *libation vessel*.

spilia – cave.

stele – grave stone which stands upright.

stoa – long colonnaded building, usually in an *agora*, used as a meeting place and shelter in Ancient Greece.

stylobate – top step of a temple, upon which the columns stand.

tholos tomb – Mycenaean tomb shaped like a beehive.

triglyph – sections of a Doric *frieze* between the *metopes*.

trireme – Ancient Greek galley with three rows of oars on each side.

volta – promenade; ie the summer evening walkabout.

volute – spiral decoration on Ionic *capitals*.

zaharoplasteion (plural: zaharoplasteia) – patisserie; shop which sells cakes, chocolates, sweets and, sometimes, alcoholic drinks.

Index

TEXT

LONELY PLANET TV SERIES & VIDEOS

Lonely Planet travel guides have been brought to life on television screens around the world. Like our guides, the programmes are based on the joy of independent travel, and look honestly at some of the most exciting, picturesque and frustrating places in the world. Each show is presented by one of three travellers from Australia, England or the USA and combines an innovative mixture of video, Super-8 film, atmospheric soundscapes and original music.

Videos of each episode – containing additional footage not shown on television – are available from good book and video shops, but the availability of individual videos varies with regional screening schedules.

Video destinations include:
Alaska; the Arctic (Norway & Finland); Australia (Southeast); Baja California; Brazil; Chile & Easter Island; China (Southeast); Costa Rica; East Africa (Tanzania & Zanzibar); Ecuador & the Galapagos Islands; Great Barrier Reef (Australia); Indonesia; Israel & the Sinai Desert; Jamaica; Japan; La Ruta Maya (Yucatan, Guatemala & Belize); Morocco; North India (Varanasi to the Himalaya); Pacific Islands; Papua New Guinea; the Rockies (USA); Syria & Jordan; Turkey; Vietnam; Zimbabwe, Botswana & Namibia.

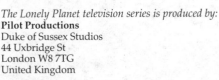

The Lonely Planet television series is produced by:
Pilot Productions
Duke of Sussex Studios
44 Uxbridge St
London W8 7TG
United Kingdom

Lonely Planet videos are distributed by:
IVN Communications Inc
2246 Camino Ramon
California 94583, USA

For further information on both the television series and the availability of individual videos please contact Lonely Planet.

PLANET TALK
Lonely Planet's FREE quarterly newsletter

We love hearing from you and think you'd like to hear from us.

When...*is the right time to see reindeer in Finland?*
Where...*can you hear the best palm-wine music in Ghana?*
How...*do you get from Asunción to Areguá by steam train?*
What...*is the best way to see India?*

For the answer to these and many other questions read PLANET TALK.

Every issue is packed with up-to-date travel news and advice including:

- *a letter from Lonely Planet founders Tony and Maureen Wheeler*
- *travel diary from a Lonely Planet author - find out what it's really like out on the road*
- *feature article on an important and topical travel issue*
- *a selection of recent letters from our readers*
- *the latest travel news from all over the world*
- *details on Lonely Planet's new and forthcoming releases*

To join our mailing list contact any Lonely Planet office.

Also available: Lonely Planet T-shirts. 100% heavyweight cotton (S, M, L, XL)

LONELY PLANET PUBLICATIONS
Australia: PO Box 617, Hawthorn 3122, Victoria
tel: (03) 9819 1877 fax: (03) 9819 6459 e-mail: talk2us@lonelyplanet.com.au

USA: Embarcadero West, 155 Filbert St, Suite 251, Oakland, CA 94607
tel: (510) 893 8555 TOLL FREE: 800 275-8555 fax: (510) 893 8563
e-mail: info@lonelyplanet.com

UK: 10 Barley Mow Passage, Chiswick, London W4 4PH
tel: (0181) 742 3161 fax: (0181) 742 2772 e-mail: 100413.3551@compuserve.com

France: 71 bis rue du Cardinal Lemoine – 75005 Paris
tel: 1 46 34 00 58 fax: 1 46 34 72 55 e-mail: 100560.415@compuserve.com

World Wide Web: http://www.lonelyplanet.com/

Lonely Planet guides to Europe

Central Europe on a shoestring
From the snow-capped peaks of the Austrian Alps, the medieval castles of Hungary and the vast forests of Poland to the festivals of Germany, the arty scene in Prague and picturesque lakes of Switzerland, this guide is packed with practical travel advice to help you make the most of your visit. This new shoestring guide covers travel in Austria, Czech Republic, Germany, Hungary, Liechtenstein, Poland, Slovakia and Switzerland.

Eastern Europe on a shoestring
This guide has opened up a whole new world for travellers – Albania, Bulgaria, Czechoslovakia, eastern Germany, Hungary, Poland, Romania and the former republics of Yugoslavia.
'...a thorough, well-researched book. Only a fool would go East without it.' – *Great Expeditions*

Mediterranean Europe on a shoestring
Details on hundreds of galleries, museums and architectural masterpieces and information on outdoor activities including hiking, sailing and skiing. Information on travelling in Albania, Andorra, Cyprus, France, Greece, Italy, Malta, Morocco, Portugal, Spain, Tunisia, Turkey and the former republics of Yugoslavia.

Scandinavian & Baltic Europe on a shoestring
A comprehensive guide to travelling in this region including details on galleries, festivals and museums, as well as outdoor activities, national parks and wildlife. Countries featured are Denmark, Estonia, the Faroe Islands, Finland, Iceland, Latvia, Lithuania, Norway and Sweden.

Western Europe on a shoestring
This long-awaited guide covers all of Western Europe's well-loved sights and provides routes for cycling and driving tours, plus details on hiking, climbing and skiing. All the travel facts on Andorra, Austria, Belgium, Britain, France, Germany, Greece, Ireland, Italy, Liechtenstein, Luxembourg, Netherlands, Portugal, Spain and Switzerland.

Britain – travel survival kit
Britain remains one of the most beautiful islands in the world. All the words, paintings and pictures that you have read and seen are not just romantic exaggerations. This comprehensive guide will help you to discover and enjoy this ever-popular destination.

Dublin – city guide
Where to enjoy a pint of Guinness and a plate of Irish stew, where to see spectacular Georgian architecture or experience Irish hospitality – Dublin city guide will ensure you won't miss out on anything.

Finland – travel survival kit
Finland is an intriguing blend of Swedish and Russian influences. With its medieval stone castles, picturesque wooden houses, vast forest and lake district, and interesting wildlife, it is a wonderland to delight any traveller.

France – travel survival kit
Stylish, diverse, celebrated by romantics and revolutionaries alike, France is a destination that's always in fashion. A comprehensive guide packed with invaluable advice.

Hungary – travel survival kit
Formerly seen as the gateway to eastern Europe, Hungary is a romantic country of music, wine and folklore. This guide contains detailed background information on Hungary's cultural and historical past as well as practical advice on the many activities available to travellers.

Ireland – travel survival kit
Ireland is one of Europe's least 'spoilt' countries. Green, relaxed and welcoming, it does not take travellers long before they feel at ease. An entertaining and comprehensive guide to this troubled country.

Italy – travel survival kit
Italy is art – not just in the galleries and museums. You'll discover its charm on the streets and in the

markets, in rustic hill-top villages and in the glamorous city boutiques. A thorough guide to the thousands of attractions of this ever-popular destination.

Prague – city guide
Since the 'Velvet Revolution' in 1989, Prague and its residents have grasped their freedom with a youthful exuberance, even frenzy. This thoroughly comprehensive guide will show you the sights and hidden delights of this vivacious city.

Switzerland – travel survival kit
Ski enthusiasts and chocolate addicts know two excellent reasons for heading to Switzerland. This travel survival kit gives travellers many more: jazz, cafés, boating trips...and the Alps of course!

Turkey – a travel survival kit
This acclaimed guide takes you from Istanbul bazaars to Mediterranean beaches, from historic battle-grounds to the stamping grounds of St Paul, Alexander the Great, Emperor Constantine and King Croesus.

Vienna – city guide
There's so much to see and do in Vienna and this guide is the best way to ensure you enjoy it all.

Trekking in Greece
Mountainous landscape, the solitude of ancient pathways and secluded beaches await those who dare to extend their horizons beyond Athens and the antiquities. Covers the main trekking regions and includes contoured maps of trekking routes.

Trekking in Spain
Aimed at both overnight trekkers and day hikers, this guidebook includes useful maps and full details on hikes in some of Spain's most beautiful wilderness areas.

Trekking in Turkey
Few people are aware that Turkey boasts mountains with walks to rival those found in Nepal. This book gives details on treks that are destined to become as popular as those further east.

Also available:
Central Europe phrasebook
Languages in this book cover travel in Austria, the Czech Republic, France, Germany, Hungary, Italy, Liechtenstein, Slovakia and Switzerland.

Eastern Europe phrasebook
Discover the most enjoyable way to get around and make friends in Bulgarian, Czech, Hungarian, Polish, Romanian and Slovak.

Mediterranean Europe phrasebook
Ask for directions to the galleries and museums in Albanian, Greek, Italian, Macedonian, Maltese, Serbian & Croatian and Slovene.

Scandinavian Europe phrasebook
Find your way around the ski trails and enjoy the local festivals in Danish, Finnish, Icelandic, Norwegian and Swedish.

Western Europe phrasebook
Show your appreciation for the great masters in Basque, Catalan, Dutch, French, German, Irish, Portuguese and Spanish (Castilian).

Greek phrasebook
Catch a *ferrybot* to the islands, laze the day away on a golden *baralia*, and say *stin iyia sas!* as you raise your glass to the setting sun... you can explore *tin acropoli* another day.

Turkish phrasebook
Practical words and phrases that will help you to communicate effectively with local people in almost every situation. Includes pronunciation guide.

Lonely Planet Guidebooks

Lonely Planet guidebooks cover every accessible part of Asia as well as Australia, the Pacific, South America, Africa, the Middle East, Europe and parts of North America. There are five series: *travel survival kits*, covering a country for a range of budgets; *shoestring guides* with compact information for low-budget travel in a major region; *walking guides*; *city guides* and *phrasebooks*.

Australia & the Pacific
Australia
Australian phrasebook
Bushwalking in Australia
Islands of Australia's Great Barrier Reef
Outback Australia
Fiji
Fijian phrasebook
Melbourne city guide
Micronesia
New Caledonia
New South Wales
New Zealand
Tramping in New Zealand
Papua New Guinea
Bushwalking in Papua New Guinea
Papua New Guinea phrasebook
Rarotonga & the Cook Islands
Samoa
Solomon Islands
Sydney city guide
Tahiti & French Polynesia
Tonga
Vanuatu
Victoria
Western Australia

North-East Asia
Beijing city guide
China
Cantonese phrasebook
Mandarin Chinese phrasebook
Hong Kong, Macau & Canton
Japan
Japanese phrasebook
Korea
Korean phrasebook
Mongolia
Mongolian phrasebook
North-East Asia on a shoestring
Seoul city guide
Taiwan
Tibet
Tibet phrasebook
Tokyo city guide

South-East Asia
Bali & Lombok
Bangkok city guide
Cambodia
Indonesia
Ho Chi Minh City city guide
Indonesian phrasebook
Jakarta city guide
Java
Laos
Lao phrasebook
Malaysia, Singapore & Brunei
Myanmar (Burma)
Burmese phrasebook
Philippines
Pilipino phrasebook
Singapore city guide
South-East Asia on a shoestring
Thailand
Thailand travel atlas
Thai phrasebook
Thai Hill Tribes phrasebook
Vietnam
Vietnamese phrasebook

Middle East
Arab Gulf States
Egypt & the Sudan
Arabic (Egyptian) phrasebook
Iran
Israel
Jordan & Syria
Middle East
Turkey
Turkish phrasebook
Trekking in Turkey
Yemen

Africa
Africa on a shoestring
Central Africa
East Africa
Trekking in East Africa
Kenya
Swahili phrasebook
Morocco
Arabic (Moroccan) phrasebook
North Africa
South Africa, Lesotho & Swaziland
West Africa
Zimbabwe, Botswana & Namibia